ENGLISH DRAMA OF THE NINETEENTH CENTURY
AN INDEX AND FINDING GUIDE

Compiled and Edited by

James Ellis

Assisted by Joseph Donohue

General Editors
The London Stage 1800-1900:
A Documentary Record and Calendar of Performances

with
Louise Allen Zak, Editorial Associate

Readex Books
A Division of the Readex Microprint Corporation
New Canaan, Connecticut
1985

TABLE OF CONTENTS

INTRODUCTION

Scope of the Collection

This single alphabetical listing by author and title of approximately 9,000 plays constitutes a substantial bibliography of nineteenth-century English drama. Its primary purpose, however, is as an index and finding guide to the English plays issued through 1981 in the Readex Microprint Collection *English and American Drama of the Nineteenth Century*.[1] Its ultimate aim is to present at least one text of every extant English-language play written or published during the century. This compilation, begun in 1965, is now greater than any of its parts, namely the pertinent resources of the fifteen major libraries already drawn upon.[2] The broad scope of the Collection is not fully reflected in its title, as it ranges far beyond the drama proper to include children's plays, pantomime books of words, minstrel dialogues, solo entertainments, opera libretti and vocal scores, and translations of Continental dramatists from Aeschylus to Ibsen. Goethe's *Faust*, for example, is represented in twenty-seven different translations, as well as numerous burlesques and imitative treatments. The earlier English dramatists, most particularly Shakespeare, are also well represented in collected series of the standard repertory and in acting editions citing nineteenth-century casts and reflecting stage productions from the time of Sarah Siddons and John Philip Kemble to that of Henry Irving and Ellen Terry.

Purpose of the Index

This Index should make the remarkable variety of the Collection more accessible to users, who have hitherto had to rely on a search through the boxes of Microprint cards themselves. Several large collections are filed under the publisher's or editor's name, rather than by individual author and title. Collected editions of a single author's works do not always specify on the caption the particular plays included. Co-authored plays are filed after an author's individual works, and may therefore lie undiscovered by the user. Translations of foreign dramas are quite appropriately filed under translators, whose names may be unknown to the user.

This guide will enable users to find any play in the Collection, no matter where it is actually filed, if they know any one of the following:

- —the author's real name
- —the author's pseudonym
- —the arranger's, or adapter's, name
- —the translator's name
- —the foreign author of a work in translation
- —the title of the play
- —a variant title by which the play may also have been known
- —the subtitle of the play

Cross-references from these categories direct the user to the main entry under the primary author (or under the title, if the play is anonymous). Main entries provide full bibliographic information. Main entries of plays indexed differently from their location in the boxes of Microprint cards conclude with a "Filed under" reference. When additional copies of a given work are filed in different places in the Collection, they appear as separate entries in the Index. Although every effort has been made to transcribe accurate title page information verbatim, the entries make no claim to observe all rules of descriptive bibliography. In the interests of clarity, uniformity, and computer processing, a compromise between bibliographic exactitude and categorical regularity seemed warranted.

Authors

Authors' names are given in full, and precede the same word beginning a title (e.g., POWER, TYRONE precedes *Power of Love*). If no first names or initials are known, a question mark appears (e.g., Arbuthnot, ?, Capt.). Variant forms and spellings of an author's name are entered in cross-references as needed (e.g., Bourcicault, D. L. *See* Boucicault, Dionysius Lardner) and are included in the main entry, following the title, if that variant appears on the title page. Fathers and sons with the same name are distinguished as "sr" and "jr," not only in cases such as the elder and younger George Colman but also when some

---

[1] *English and American Drama of the Nineteenth Century*, ed. George Freedley and Allardyce Nicoll, 1965-1975; James Ellis and Joseph Donohue, 1975- (New Canaan, Conn.: Readex Microprint Corporation). The American portion of the Readex Collection issued up to 1977 has already been indexed by Don L. Hixon and Don A. Hennessee, as *Nineteenth-Century American Drama: A Finding Guide* (Metuchen, N.J. & London: Scarecrow Press, 1977).

[2] Archives currently represented in the Collection are: British Library, Columbia University Libraries, Cornell University Library, private collection of James Ellis, Harvard University Library, Henry E. Huntington Library, University of Illinois Library, Library of Congress, University of Michigan Library, Museum of the City of New York, New York Public Library, Charles Patterson Van Pelt Library at the University of Pennsylvania, The Walter Hampden Memorial Library at The Players', Princeton University Library, Yale University Library.

additional names might theoretically distinguish the pair, as with Charles Dibdin and his son Charles Isaac Mungo Dibdin. Ranks and titles are included only if regularly used during the writer's active career. Women are alphabetized under what seems to be the preferred authorial name, maiden or married, with the complete name appearing in the main entry and with appropriate cross-references. An entry under "Barrett, Elizabeth," for instance, directs one to "Browning, Elizabeth Barrett, Mrs. Robert." Appendix A provides a list of all the women authors and translators in the Collection. Comparable treatment is accorded authors who use pseudonyms, with cross-references from the exceptional to the usual form, and with an indication after the title if the atypical form appears on the title page. Appendix B provides a list of all pseudonyms and their real-name equivalents, when known.

All plays by an author, whether written alone or in collaboration, are alphabetized together, the collaborators acknowledged after the title and with cross-references. In cases of collaboration, the primary author is typically the one printed first on the title page. If a second text reverses the order, the actual printed order of the variant is given after the title.

Translators

Whereas an author's single and collaborative efforts are grouped together, translations follow separately. Both Elizabeth Barrett and Robert Browning, for example, have entries first under their names as authors, and then as translators. Given the predilection of many nineteenth-century dramatists to appropriate plots, dialogues, and whole plays from foreign originals, either with or without acknowledgment, translations cited as such in the Index are restricted to those cases where the author's intent seems to have been to render a faithful English version of a work written in another language. In such cases the original author is named after the title, with cross-references under author and title directing the user to the main entry under the translator. Because the present guide is a bibliography of English, not foreign, drama, main entries are under the English translator's name, not the original foreign author's. Anonymous translations, even if the original author is known, have main entries under their titles, with the designation "anon. trans." Preparers of foreign opera libretti are sometimes classified as translators, but no attempt is made to list the names of the original librettists, except in the case of Wagner, who figures both as author and as composer.

Arrangers

Some of the "authors" in the Collection are actually the actor-managers who arranged the texts for stage representation. Half the entries under David Garrick, for example, as well as most of those under John Philip Kemble and all of those under Charles Kean, are arrangements of works by earlier dramatists. Like translations, arrangements are grouped after original compositions (the arranger designated "arr."). Here, too, the original author is named after the title, with a cross-reference from author and title to the main entry under the arranger. Appendix C provides a list of all arrangers in the Collection, together with the works so treated.

Composers

Persons identified in a text as composers—whether of opera, operetta, musical comedy, melodrama, or pantomime—are included in the main entry. Well-known composers are identified by the last name only, but others are granted whatever fullness of name the text provides. Users should bear in mind that the presence of the composer's name does not indicate that the musical score is present, unless the text is described as a "Vocal Score." Appendix D provides a list of all the composers, with full names whenever possible, together with the titles of the works in the Collection with which they are associated.

Titles

Play titles have uniform capitalizations and punctuation, with the link between title and subtitle always consisting of a semicolon, lower-case "or," comma, and capitalized first word of the subtitle. The alphabetization of titles observes the word as the governing unit, so that all titles beginning with the word "In," for instance, precede titles beginning with the word "Ina," "Incarcerated," and so forth. Hyphenated words are treated either as one word or as two, depending upon typical modern practice (e.g., "To-Day" as one word, "Rag-Picker" as two words). The possessive of a singular noun precedes that noun in the plural, so that, for example, *Time's Revenge* precedes *Times*. Numbers in titles are given as the title page dictates, as either numerals or words, but are treated alphabetically as though spelled out in words. The same holds true for the numerical delineation of kings, emperors, and the like, with both Roman and Arabic numbers accepted as found. Any variant titles (whether found in the text, on wrappers, half-title, running head, or alternative on the title page; or known from advertisements, pre-publication proofs, the Lord Chamberlain's file copy, or later popular designation) are included in the main entry following the word "*Also*," and figure as cross-references as well.

Publication Information

Multiple places of publication are recognized only if they are given equal prominence on the title page. If a London borough such as Westminster is given as place of publication, "London" is supplied, with the borough included parenthetically. When place of publication can only be deduced, it is bracketed. The absence of a place of publication is indicated with the abbreviation "N.p." Publishers' names are normally given as found on title pages, without initial articles or final terms such as "Limited." The names of the major publishers of acting editions are regularized as John Cumberland, John Dicks, John Duncombe, Samuel French, and Thomas Hailes Lacy. If only a printer's name can be determined, the designation "printer" is added parenthetically. The absence of any publisher or printer is indicated with the abbreviation "n.pub." Plays privately printed, printed for the author, or printed but not published are identified with the parenthetical abbreviation "priv." Appendix E lists all privately printed plays in the Collection by author and title. Dates of publication are always given in Arabic numbers. If a copyright date has been used, it is preceded by "c." Dates of first performance, or even such descriptions as "Christmas Season 1894-1895" in a pantomime book of words, are not accepted as publication dates. The absence of a date of publication is indicated with the abbreviation "n.d."

Acting Editions

Much of the drama of the nineteenth century was printed in one or more of variously named and often numbered series of so-called "acting editions" issued by a handful of publishers who had the confusing habit of succeeding each other and reissuing titles, often from the same plates, with or without changes.[3] Main entries in the Index incorporate this series information, often available only if wrappers are present. Where wrapper information disagrees with the title page, the difference is noted in brackets. Some series issued early in the century, such as Cumberland's, have volume numbers only. These are indicated with Roman numerals. Later series such as Lacy's, French's, and Dicks' include volume numbers and separate issue numbers for every play (or occasionally for two short plays issued together). The Index ignores volume numbers in these later series, but records issue numbers, always with Arabic numerals. Information about acting editions supplied from a source other than the text itself is bracketed. Appendix E provides a list of all acting editions in the Collection, with the plays arranged in numerical order of issue, or alphabetically by title (if not numbered or if lacking the wrappers that would provide the number).

State and Form of Text

Users should assume that every work in the Collection is the complete text of a printed edition unless it is otherwise described as incomplete, fragment, synopsis, manuscript, typescript, promptbook, vocal score, or libretto (this last term covering pantomime books of words as well as opera libretti). Plays are labeled promptbooks only if they contain such features as manuscript cuts, transpositions, calls, and stage business indicating preparation for actual stage use. The marking of a single part, or a few deletions, or the statement on the title page that the text is taken from the promptbook, does not qualify it for designation as a promptbook in the Index, even though it may be so described on the card caption. Appendices G, H, and I provide lists by author and title of all promptbooks, manuscripts, and typescripts in the Collection.

English Plays in the American Collection

A number of standard English plays can be found in the American portion of the Readex Collection, having been published in large series in the United States that included plays from both countries. Most of these are from four series: Dramatic Leaflets, Massey's Exhibition, Modern Standard Drama, and Silas Sexton Steel's Book of Plays. Appendix J lists the English plays in the American portion of the Collection. Not included in that Appendix are arrangements by American actor-managers of English plays, substantial revisions by Americans of English dramas, and American burlesques and parodies of English plays. Students working in borderline areas will want to consult both parts of the Collection.

---

[3]A fine start at sorting out the various publishers of acting editions, their practices, their dates, and their succession was made by R. Crompton Rhodes in "The Early Nineteenth-Century Drama," *The Library*, 4th series, XVI (1936), 91-112, 210-31.

ACKNOWLEDGMENTS

The Readex Microprint Corporation has given steady support to this project, one of a number of ongoing activities of The London Stage 1800-1900: A Documentary Record and Calendar of Performances. We wish to thank William F. Boni, former president of Readex; Daniel S. Jones, president of Readex; Jessica Milstead, vice president and editorial director; Kestutis K. Miklas, vice president and technical director; and Thomas Bock, director of the Chester, Vermont, plant for their encouragement.

The University Computer Center of the University of Massachusetts at Amherst has been exceedingly cooperative. We acknowledge our indebtedness to its director, Conrad Wogrin; its associate directors, Charles Lyman and Judy Smith; its assistant directors, Kathleen Cowles and Robert Gonter; and their associates, Bud Maziarz, Doris Peterson, and Everard Osbourne. We also thank our resourceful programmer, Ruth Berggren.

The University of Massachusetts at Amherst and its Department of English have been generous in providing facilities and student assistance. We are grateful for the support and encouragement of Charles Moran, former acting chairman of the department; and Vincent DiMarco, chairman. Mount Holyoke College and its Faculty Grants Committee have also contributed funds for student assistance, a computer terminal, and printing expenses.

The student research assistants who have performed so cheerfully and ably in this slogging work are Karen Angeline, Deborah Bell, Jane Donohue, Bronwen Evans, Mary Fitzgerald, Sue Kubica, Paul Manasian, Lisa Maregni, and Laurie Pringle.

The editors of the London Stage 1800-1900 Research Program want to pay special thanks to our editorial associate, Louise Allen Zak, who has seen this endeavor through with the utmost diligence, dedication, and discernment.

James Ellis
Joseph Donohue
Amherst, Massachusetts
1 October 1984

A. S. S.
    See Maddox, John Medex.

AARBERT
    See Marshall, William.

ABANDONDINO, THE BLOODLESS
    See Byron, Henry James.

ABASHED HUSBAND
    See Van Laun, Henri (trans.). George Dandin.

ABBÉ DE L'EPÉE
    See Deaf and Dumb, The.

ABBOT, THE
    See Beverly, Henry Roxby.

ABBOTT, JAMES
    Allaooddeen. London: Smith, Elder, 1880. Pp. [i]-[xii], [1]-230.

ABBOTT, WILLIAM
    Swedish Patriotism; or, The Signal Fire. London: John Miller, 1819. Pp. [i-iv], [1]-41.
    Youthful Days of Frederick the Great, The. London: W. Sams, 1817. Pp. [i-vi], [1]-47. 2nd ed.

ABDALLA
    See Delap, John.
    See Wallace, John, jr.

ABDUCTION
    See Collier, William.

A'BECKETT, ARTHUR WILLIAM
    Faded Flowers. London: Samuel French; New York: T. Henry French, n.d. Pp. [1]-12. [Lacy's Acting Edition].
    £. S. D. By Bertie Vyse (pseud.). London: M'Gowan Steam Printers, 1872. Pp. [1]-54.

A'BECKETT, GILBERT ABBOTT
    Ambassadress, The. London: John Duncombe, n.d. Pp. [1]-54. Duncombe's Edition.
    Angelo; or, The Actress of Padua. New York: Samuel French, n.d. Pp. [7]-42. Text complete. French's Standard Drama, 177.
    Artist's Wife, The. London: Chapman & Hall, n.d. Pp. [1]-24.
    Assignation, The; or, What Will My Wife Say? London: W. Strange, 1837. Pp. [1]-37.
    Black Domino, The. London: John Dicks, n.d. Pp. [1]-15. Dicks' Standard Plays, 443.
    Castle of Otranto, The. London: National Acting Drama Office, n.d. Pp. [1]-31.
    Chimes, The.
        See Lemon, Mark.
    Clear Case, A. London: G. H. Davidson, n.d. Pp. [1]-22. Cumberland's British Theatre, 364.
    Don Caesar de Bazan. Written with Lemon, Mark. New York: William Taylor, n.d. Pp. [1]-47. Modern Standard Drama, 16. Promptbook.
    Don Caesar de Bazan. Written with Lemon, Mark. London: W. Barth, n.d. Pp. [3]-39. Promptbook.
    Figaro in London. London: G. H. Davidson, n.d. Pp. [1]-32.

Jack Brag. London: John Cumberland, n.d. Pp. [1]-32. Cumberland's British Theatre, XXXVII. *Filed under* Cumberland, John. Cumberland's British Theatre, XXXVII.

Jack Brag; or, A Chandler's Chances. London: John Dicks, n.d. Pp. [1]-11. Dicks' Standard Plays, 534.

Joe Miller and His Men. London: William Barth, n.d. Pp. [7]-32.

King Incog., The. London: John Miller, 1834. Pp. [i]-[vi], [1]-25. Promptbook.

King John (with the Benefit of the Act). London: W. Strange, 1837. Pp. [1]-22.

Knight and the Sprite, The; or, The Cold Water Cure! Written with Lemon, Mark. London: William Barth, n.d. Pp. [1]-27.

Liberal Candidate, The. [London: William Barth (printer)], n.d. Pp. [3]-20. Title page lacking.

Love Is Blind. London: John Duncombe, n.d. Pp. [1]-30. Duncombe's Edition.

Magic Mirror, The; or, The Hall of Statues. London: W. S. Johnson, n.d. Pp. [1]-31.

Man with the Carpet Bag, The. London: John Cumberland, n.d. Pp. [1]-31.

Man with the Carpet Bag, The. London: William Strange, n.d. Pp. [1]-24.

Man with the Carpet Bag, The. London: John Cumberland, n.d. Pp. [1]-31. Cumberland's Minor Theatre, XIII. *Filed under* Cumberland, John. Cumberland's Minor Theatre, XIII.

Man-Fred. London: John Cumberland, n.d. Pp. [1]-19. Cumberland's Minor Theatre, IX. *Filed under* Cumberland, John. Cumberland's Minor Theatre, IX.

Man-Fred. London: John Cumberland, n.d. Pp. [1]-19.

Mendicant, The. London: John Cumberland, n.d. Pp. [i-ii], [1]-34. Cumberland's British Theatre, XXXVII. *Filed under* Cumberland, John. Cumberland's British Theatre, XXXVII.

Mendicant, The. London: John Cumberland, n.d. Pp. [1]-34. [Cumberland's British Theatre].

O Gemini!; or, The Brothers of Co(u)rse. Written with Lemon, Mark. London: Webster, n.d. Pp. [1]-22.

Open Sesame; or, A Night with the Forty Thieves. Written with Lemon, Mark. London: W. S. Johnson (printer), n.d. Pp. [1]-24. Title page lacking.

Pascal Bruno. London: W. Strange, 1838. Pp. [1]-29.

Peter Wilkins; or, The Loadstone Rock and the Flying Indians. Written with Lemon, Mark. London: National Acting Drama Office, n.d. Pp. [1]-21.

Postillion of Lonjumeau, The. 22 leaves. Manuscript.

Queen's Ball, The; or, The Black Domino. London: John Duncombe, n.d. Pp. [1]-45. Duncombe's Acting Edition of the British Theatre, 276.

Revolt of the Workhouse. London: John Miller, 1834. Pp. [1]-24. Miller's Modern Acting Drama, [20].

Revolt of the Workhouse, The. London: John Cumberland, n.d. Pp. [1]-28. Cumberland's Minor Theatre, VIII. *Filed under* Cumberland, John. Cumberland's Minor Theatre, VIII.

Roof Scrambler, The. London: John Cumberland, n.d. Pp. [i-ii], [1]-25. Cumberland's Minor Theatre, X. *Filed under* Cumberland, John. Cumberland's Minor Theatre, X.

Roof Scrambler, The. London: John Cumberland, n.d. Pp. [1]-25. Cumberland's Minor Theatre, 83.

Sardanapalus; or, The Fast King of Assyria. Written with Lemon, Mark. London: Webster, n.d. Pp. [1]-24. Webster's Acting National Drama, 193.

Scenes from the Rejected Comedies. London: Punch Office, 1844. Pp. [1]-46.

Siamese Twins, The. New York: Samuel French, n.d. Pp. [1]-17. [French's Minor Drama, 223].

Siamese Twins, The. London: William Strange, n.d. Pp. [1]-23.

Siamese Twins, The. London: John Cumberland, n.d. Pp. [1]-26. Cumberland's Minor Theatre, XIV. *Filed under* Cumberland, John. Cumberland's Minor Theatre, XIV.

Son of the Sun, The; or, The Fate of Phaeton. London: John Miller, 1834. Pp. [1]-24.

St. George and the Dragon. Written with Lemon, Mark. London: National Acting Drama Office, n.d. Pp. [1]-24. Webster's Acting National Drama, [119].

Three Graces, The. London: James Turner, n.d. Pp. [1]-34.

Timour, the Cream of All the Tartars. London: W. S. Johnson, n.d. Pp. [1]-24.

Tradesman's Ball, The. London: John Duncombe, n.d. Pp. [1]-20. Duncombe's Edition.

Turned Head, The. London: John Cumberland, n.d. Pp. [1]-26. Cumberland's Minor Theatre, XIII. *Filed under* Cumberland, John. Cumberland's Minor Theatre, XIII.

Turned Head, The. London: Thomas Hailes Lacy, n.d. Pp. [3]-26. [Lacy's Acting Edition].

Unfortunate Miss Bailey. London: John Cumberland, n.d. Pp. [1]-21. Cumberland's Minor Theatre, XI. *Filed under* Cumberland, John. Cumberland's Minor Theatre, XI.

Unfortunate Miss Bailey. London: John Cumberland, n.d. Pp. [1]-21. [Cumberland's Minor Theatre].

Wanted a Brigand; or, A Visit from Fra-Diavolo. Music by Stansbury, G.; A'Beckett, Mrs. G. A. London: W. Strange, n.d. Pp. [1]-25.

Wonderful Lamp in a New Light, The. London: W. S. Johnson, n.d. Pp. [1]-24.

Yellow Dwarf, The; or, The King of the Gold Mines. London: William Barth, n.d. Pp. [i]-vi, [7]-30. Promptbook.

A'BECKETT, GILBERT ARTHUR

Ali Baba and the Forty Thieves; or, Harlequin and the Genii of the Arabian Nights! London: J. Miles (printer), n.d. Pp. [1]-[26]. Libretto.

Babes in the Wood, The; or, Harlequin Robin Hood and His Merry Men. London: J. Miles (printer), n.d. Pp. [1]-20. Libretto.

Brigand, The.
See Utter Per-version of The Brigand, An.

Canterbury Pilgrims, The. London: Boosey, n.d. Pp. [1-2], [i]-xx, 3-287. Vocal score.

Captain Thérèse.
See Burnand, Francis Cowley.

Cigale, La.
See Burnand, Francis Cowley.

Glitter. London: Thomas Hailes Lacy, n.d. Pp. [1]-26. [Lacy's Acting Edition].

Happy Land, The.
See Gilbert, William Schwenck.

In the Clouds: A Glimpse of Utopia. London & New York: Samuel French, n.d. Pp. [1]-26. [Lacy's Acting Edition].

Last of the Legends, The; or, The Baron, the Bride, and the Battery. London & New York: Samuel French, n.d. Pp. [1]-23. Lacy's Acting Edition, 1478.

Lending a Hand. London: Thomas Hailes Lacy, n.d. Pp. [1]-20. [Lacy's Acting Edition].

Signa. Written with Rudall, H. A.; Weatherly, Frederic Edward. Music by Cowen, Frederic H. London: E. Ascherberg, c.1894. Pp. [i-iv], 1-230. Vocal score.

Three Tenants. Music by Reed, T. German. London: Joseph Williams, c.1897. Pp. [1]-24. German Reed Repertory of Musical Pieces.

Utter Per-version of The Brigand, An; or, New Lines to an Old Ban-ditty. *Also:* The Brigand. London: Phillips, n.d. Pp. [1]-43.

ABEL, WILLIAM HENRY

Dust; or, The Miller of Guibray. 43 leaves. Manuscript.

Hidden Life, The. 40 leaves. Manuscript.

Marked for Life. 12 leaves. Act I only. Manuscript.

Professor, The. 16 leaves. Manuscript.

Self Disinherited; or, The Home Blight. 10 leaves. Act II only. Manuscript.

ABEL DRAKE
See Saunders, John.

ABELARD AND HELOISE
See Buckstone, John Baldwin.

ABON HASSAN
See Dimond, William.
See Talfourd, Francis.

ABOVE AND BELOW!
See Stirling, Edward.

ABRADATAS AND PANTHEA
See Edwards, John.

ABRAHAMS, HENRY

Alderman's Gown, The; or, A Trip to Paris. London: S. G. Fairbrother, n.d. Pp. [1]-20.

ABROAD AND AT HOME
See Holman, Joseph George.

ABSENCE OF MIND
See Poel, William.

ABSENT MAN, THE
See Roberts, George.

ACCEPTED BY PROXY
See Kingsley, Ellis.

ACCOMPLISHED FOOLS
See Steele, Richard. Tender Husband, The.

ACCUSING SPIRIT, THE
See Suter, William E.

ACHARNIANS, THE
See Frere, John Hookham (trans.).

ACHILLES IN SCYROS
See Bridges, Robert Seymour.

ACIS AND GALATAEA
See Burnand, Francis Cowley.

ACIS AND GALATAEA, A VERY NEW EDITION OF
See Plowman, Thomas F.

ACIS AND GALATEA
See Gay, John.

ACIS AND GALATEA PARAPHRASED
See Oxberry, William Henry.

A'COURT, WILLIAM.

Montalto. London: W. Lindsell, 1821. Pp. [i-iv], [1]-91. *Filed under* Montalto (anon.).

ACT OF FOLLY, AN
See Goldman, L. B.

ACT OF PIRACY, AN
See Montague, Leopold.

ACTOR OF ALL WORK, THE
See Colman, George, jr.

ACTOR'S RETREAT, THE
See Brough, William.

ACTORS BY LAMPLIGHT!
See Selby, Charles. Behind the Scenes.

ACTRESS OF ALL WORK, THE
See Oxberry, William Henry.

ACTRESS OF PADUA
See A'Beckett, Gilbert Abbott. Angelo.

ADA THE BETRAYED; OR, THE MURDER AT THE OLD SMITHY (anon.)
[Middlesex County: Henry Frances, 1844]. Pp. [239]-250.

ADAM BUFF
See Blanchard, Edward Litt Leman.

ADAMS, ARTHUR HENRY
Minstrel, The. In *Maoriland and Other Verses*, Sydney: Bulletin Newspaper Co., 1899, pp. [i], [125]-154.

ADAMS, CATHERINE
Feminine Strategy. Music by Hollis, Frank G. London: Joseph Williams, n.d. Pp. [1]-15. Libretto.

ADAMS, FLORENCE DAVENPORT
Home Fairy, A. Chicago: Dramatic Publishing Co., n.d. Pp. [1]-7.

King in Disguise, A. Chicago: Dramatic Publishing Co., n.d. Pp. [1]-7.

Lady Cecil, The. London & New York: Samuel French, n.d. Pp. [1]-8. Children's Plays, 7.

Little Folks' Work, The. London & New York: Samuel French, n.d. Pp. [1]-8.

Magician and the Ring, The. Chicago: Dramatic Publishing Co., n.d. Pp. [1]-8.

Midsummer Frolic, A. Chicago: Dramatic Publishing Co., n.d. Pp. [1]-7.

Prince or Peasant. Chicago: Dramatic Publishing Co., n.d. Pp. [1]-7.

Princess Marguerite's Choice. Chicago: Dramatic Publishing Co., n.d. Pp. [1]-8.

Sleepers Awakened, The. Chicago: Dramatic Publishing Co., n.d. Pp. [1]-8.

Snowwhite. Chicago: Dramatic Publishing Co., n.d. Pp. [1]-8.

ADAMS, FRANCIS WILLIAM LAUDERDALE
Tiberius. London: T. Fisher Unwin, 1894. Pp. [1]-208.

ADAMS, SARAH FULLER FLOWERS, MRS. WILLIAM BRIDGES
Vivia Perpetua. London: Charles Fox, 1841. Pp. [i-viii], [1]-200.

ADAMSON, JOHN (trans.)
Dona Ignez de Castro. By Luiz, Nicola. Newcastle: D. Akenhead & Sons, 1808. Pp. [1]-124.

ADDISON, HENRY ROBERT, CAPT. (later Lieut. Col.)
Blue-faced Baboon!, The; or, The Man-Monkey. London: John Dicks, n.d. Pp. [1]-7. Dicks' Standard Plays, 606. *Filed under* Addison, Henry Robert; Rodwell, G. Herbert.

Jessie, the Flower of Dumblaine; or, Weel May the Keel Row! London: John Duncombe, n.d. Pp. [1]-20. Duncombe's Edition.

King's Word, The. London: John Miller, 1835. Pp. [1]-24.

Locked in with a Lady. London: Thomas Hailes Lacy, n.d. Pp. [1]-12.

Locked in with a Lady. Chicago: Dramatic Publishing Co., n.d. Pp. [1]-12. Sergel's Acting Drama, 85.

Marie: A Tale of the Pont Neuf! London: John Duncombe, n.d. Pp. [3]-20. Duncombe's Edition.

117, Arundel Street, Strand. London: Thomas Hailes Lacy, n.d. Pp. [1]-20. [Lacy's Acting Edition].

Sophia's Supper. Boston: William V. Spencer, 1855. Pp. [1]-16. Boston Theatre, 5.

Tam O'Shanter. London: John Dicks, n.d. Pp. [1]-8. Dicks' Standard Plays, 532.

Zingaro, Lo. London: John Duncombe, n.d. Pp. [1]-26. Duncombe's Edition.

ADDISON, JOHN
Our Court.
See Humphrey, Edward.

ADDISON, JOSEPH
Cato. London: Whittingham & Arliss, 1815. Pp. [1]-56. London Theatre, IX. *Filed under* Dibdin, Thomas John, ed. London Theatre, IX.

Cato. In *New English Drama*, ed. W. Oxberry, 22 vols., London: W. Simpkin & R. Marshall; C. Chapple, 1823, XVII, [i]-[xx], [1]-[52]. *Filed under* Oxberry, William Henry. New English Drama, XVII.

Cato. London: John Cumberland, 1826. Pp. [i]-viii, [9]-[52]. Cumberland's British Theatre, VI. *Filed under* Cumberland, John. Cumberland's British Theatre, VI.

Cato. In *British Drama*, 12 vols., London: John Dicks, 1864, II, [467]-482.

Cato.
See Kemble, John Philip (arr.).

ADELA
See Brown, John Henry.

ADELAIDE
See Ebsworth, Joseph.
See Pye, Henry James.
See Sheil, Richard Lalor.

ADELGITHA
See Lewis, Matthew Gregory.

ADELMORN, THE OUTLAW
See Lewis, Matthew Gregory.

ADELPHI NORMA, THE
See Corri, Montague.

ADMIRABLE CRICHTON, THE
See Galloway, George.

ADMIRAL GUINEA
See Henley, William Ernest.

ADMIRAL'S DAUGHTER
See Trick for Trick.

ADONIS VANQUISHED
See Amcotts, Vincent.

ADOPTED CHILD, THE
See Birch, Samuel.

ADOPTION
See Henry, Richard.

ADRASTUS
See Dallas, Robert Charles.

ADRIAN AND ORRILA
See Dimond, William.

ADRIENNE
See Leslie, Henry.

ADRIENNE LECOUVREUR
See Herman, Henry.

ADRIENNE, THE ACTRESS
See Oxenford, John.

ADVENTURE OF THE LADY URSULA, THE
See Hope, Anthony.

ADVENTURES OF A LOVE LETTER, THE
See Mathews, Charles James.

ADVENTURES OF A SERVANT GIRL
See Mary Price.

ADVENTURES OF A VENTRILOQUIST
See Moncrieff, William Thomas.

ADVENTURES OF AN OPERATIC TROUPE
See Stephenson, Charles H. Tromb-al-ca-zar.

ADVENTURES OF DICK TURPIN AND TOM KING
See Suter, William E.
See Suter, William E. Dick Turpin and Tom King.

ADVENTURES OF ULYSSES, THE
See Mendham, James, jr.

ADVENTURESS
See Roberts, George. Idalia.

ADVERTISEMENT, THE
See Burges, James Bland.

ADVICE GRATIS
See Dance, Charles.

ADVICE TO HUSBANDS
See Lancaster, Charles Sears.

ADVOCATE OF DURANGO, THE
See Wynne, John.

ADZUMA
See Arnold, Edwin, Sir.

AENEAS
See Granville, H. Such.

AESCHYLUS
Agamemnon.
See Browning, Robert (trans.).
See Fitzgerald, Edward (trans.).
See Milman, Henry Hart (trans.).

Prometheus Bound.
See Browning, Elizabeth Barrett (trans.).
See Pember, Edward Henry (trans.).
See Webster, Augusta Davies, Mrs. Thomas (trans.)
AETHIOP, THE
See Dimond, William.
AFFAIR OF HONOUR, AN
See Rede, William Leman.
AFFECTATION
See Becket, Andrew.
AFFECTED YOUNG LADIES, THE
See Mathew, Charles (trans.).
AFFGHANS' CAPTIVE, THE
See Scott, Alfred.
AFFINITIES
See Praed, Rosa Caroline Murray-Prior, Mrs. Campbell.
AFFINITY
See Hilton, B. H. Manager in Love, The.
AFRICAINE, L'
See Arbuthnot, ?, Capt.
See Burnand, Francis Cowley.
See Kenney, Charles Lamb (trans.).
AFRICAN LOVE
See Mérimée, Prosper.
AFRICANS, THE
See Colman, George, jr.
AFTER A STORM COMES A CALM
See Morton, John Maddison.
AFTER DARK
See Boucicault, Dionysius Lardner.
AFTER DINNER
See Gardner, Herbert.
AFTER THE BALL
See Yates, Edmund.
AFTER THE CINDERELLA
See Ridge, William Pett.
AFTER THE PARTY (anon.)
London: Thomas Hailes Lacy, n.d. Pp. [1]-18. Lacy's Acting Edition, 1888.
AFTER THE PLAY
See Ridge, William Pett.
AFTER THE SHOW
See Pleon, Harry.
AGAMEMNON
See Browning, Robert (trans.).
See Fitzgerald, Edward (trans.).
See Galt, John.
See Lloyd, Charles (trans.).
See Milman, Henry Hart (trans.).
AGATHA
See Burnaby, Edwyn Andrew.
See Henderson, Isaac.
AGE, THE
See Bailey, Philip James.
AGE WE LIVE IN!
See Stirling, Edward. Pickwick Club, The.
AGED FORTY
See Courtney, John.
AGES AGO
See Gilbert, William Schwenck.
AGGRAVATING SAM
See Buckingham, Leicester Silk.
AGIS
See Lloyd, Charles (trans.).
AGLAVAINE AND SELYSETTE
See Sutro, Alfred (trans.).
AGNES DE VERE
See Buckstone, John Baldwin.
AGONIES OF MOTHER GOOSE
See Madison Agonistes.
AGREEABLE SURPRISE, THE
See O'Keeffe, John.
AGUILHAR
See Tweddell, H. Maddison.

AÏDÉ, HAMILTON
Doctor Bill. Pp. [i-ii], [1]-22. Typescript.
Nine Days' Wonder, A. London: Samuel French; New York: T. Henry French, n.d. Pp. [1]-40. [Lacy's Acting Edition].
Widows Bewitched. Music by Gabriel, Virginia. London: Metzler, n.d. Pp. [i-ii], 1-78. Vocal score.
AIGLON, L'
See Parker, Louis Napoleon (trans.). Eaglet, The.
AINSLIE, WHITELAW, DR.
Clemenza; or, The Tuscan Orphan. Bath: Richard Cruttwell, 1822. Pp. [i]-[viii], [1]-103.
Pizarro; or, The Peruvian Mother. Edinburgh: Duncan, Stevenson (printer), 1817. Pp. [1]-97.
AIRD, DAVID MITCHELL
Love-Trap, The; or, Hearts Are Trumps. London: H. Bale, 1856. Pp. [1]-24.
Maid of Avenel, The. *Also:* The White Maid of Avenel. London: H. Bale, 1858. Pp. [1]-32.
Stolen Kiss, The. N.p.: n.pub., n.d. Pp. [i]-[vi], [7]-25. Title page lacking.
White Maid of Avenel, The.
See Maid of Avenel, The.
AIRD, THOMAS
Mother's Blessing, A. In *Othuriel and Other Poems,* Edinburgh: William Whyte, 1840, pp. [i], [95]-135.
Murtzoufle. Edinburgh: John Anderson jr, n.d. Pp. [i], [1]-84.
Wold. In *Poetical Works,* new ed., Edinburgh & London: William Blackwood & Sons, 1856, pp. [i], [203]-286.
AIREY ANNIE
See Burnand, Francis Cowley.
AKERMAN, WILLIAM
Cross of Sorrow, The. London: George Bell & Sons, 1894. Pp. [i]-[x], [1]-102.
Rip Van Winkle. Music by Leoni, Franco. London: G. Ricordi, c.1897. Pp. [1]-49. Libretto.
AKHURST, WILLIAM M.
Arthur the King; or, The Knights of the Round Table and Other Funny-ture. London: Thomas Hailes Lacy, n.d. Pp. [1]-38.
Birth of Beauty, The; or, Harlequin William the Conqueror and the Pretty White Horse with the Golden Hoof. London: Phillips Brothers (printer), n.d. Pp. [1]-36. Libretto.
Gulliver on His Travels!; or, Harlequin Old Father Christmas and the Fairy Queen of the Silver Acacias! N.p.: Abbot (printer), n.d. Pp. [i-ii], [1]-23. Libretto.
King Arthur; or, Launcelot the Loose, Gin-ever the Square, and the Knights of the Round Table, and Other Furniture. Melbourne: R. Bell, n.d. Pp. [1-31]. Libretto.
Paris the Prince and Helen the Fair; or, The Giant Horse and the Siege of Troy. Melbourne: R. Bell (printer), 1869. Pp. [1]-34. 3rd ed.
Tom Tom, the Piper's Son, and Mary Mary, Quite Contrary; or, Harlequin Piggy Wiggy and the Good Child's History of England. Melbourne: R. Bell (printer), n.d. Pp. [1]-31. Libretto.
ALABAMA, THE
See Morton, John Maddison.
ALADDIN
See Blanchard, Edward Litt Leman.
See Byron, Henry James.
See Farley, Charles.
See Keating, Eliza H.
See Martin, Theodore, Sir (trans.).
See O'Neill, John Robert.
See Soane, George.
ALADDIN; OR, THE MAGIC LAMP OF HUGO VAMP
See O'Neill, John Robert. Aladdin.
ALADDIN; OR, THE WONDERFUL LAMP (anon.)
London: John Cumberland, n.d. Pp. [1]-36. [Cumberland's British Theatre].
ALADDIN AND HIS WONDERFUL LAMP
See Locke, Fred.

ALADDIN AND THE WONDERFUL LAMP
    See Doyle, Thomas F.
    See Harrison, Samuel M.
    See Millward, Charles.
    See Morton, John Maddison.
    See Smith, Albert Richard.

ALADDIN AND THE WONDERFUL LAMP; OR, HARLE-QUIN AND THE FLYING PALACE (anon.)
    Music by Chapman. Bristol: R. W. Bingham, n.d. Pp. [1]-48. Libretto.

ALADDIN II
    See Thompson, Alfred.

ALADDIN, THE LAD WITH THE WONDERFUL LAMP
    See Conquest, George.

ALAN'S WIFE
    See Bell, Florence Eveleen Eleanore Oliffe, Mrs. Hugh (Lady).

ALARMING SACRIFICE, AN
    See Buckstone, John Baldwin.

ALARMINGLY SUSPICIOUS
    See Simpson, John Palgrave.

ALARMIST, THE
    See Roberdeau, John Peter.

ALASCO
    See Shee, Martin Archer.

ALBERIC, CONSUL OF ROME
    See Dwarris, Fortunatus William Lilley.

ALBERT, ?
    Anneau Magique, L'. *Also:* The Enchanted Ring. Music by Gallenberg, Count. London: King's Theatre, 1832. Pp. [1]-11. Synopsis.
    Enchanted Ring, The.
        See Anneau Magique, L'.

ALBERT AND ROSALIE
    See Warton, Ferdinand Fullarton.

ALBERTO AND ROSABELLA
    See Dibdin, Thomas John. Brazen Mask.

ALBERTO DELLA SCALA
    See Winser, Charles.

ALBERY, JAMES
    Alexander the Great; or, A Pretty Piece of Chiselling. *Also:* Chiselling. By James Allen (pseud.) and Joseph J. Dilley. London: Burgess, n.d. Pp. [i-iv], [1]-24. *Filed under* Allen, James; Dilley, Joseph J.
    Apple Blossoms. In *Dramatic Works,* ed. Wyndham Albery, London: Peter Davies, 1939, I, [223]-303.
    Apple Blossoms. New York: Robert M. DeWitt, n.d. Pp. [1]-39. DeWitt's Acting Plays, 167.
    Chiselling. Written with Dilley, Joseph J. By Joseph J. Dilley and James Allen (pseud.). London & New York: Samuel French, n.d. Pp. [1]-20. [French's Acting Edition]. *Filed under* Dilley, Joseph J.; Allen, James.
    Chiselling. By Joseph J. Dilley and James Allen (pseud.). London: Edward Hastings, n.d. Pp. [1]-20. Hastings's Acting Plays, 5. *Filed under* Dilley, Joseph J.; Allen, James.
    Chiselling. *Also:* Alexander the Great. In *Dramatic Works,* ed. Wyndham Albery, London: Peter Davies, 1939, II, [583]-588. Commentary.
    Coquettes. *Also:* Two Thorns. In *Dramatic Works,* ed. Wyndham Albery, London: Peter Davies, 1939, I, [97]-178.
    Crisis, The. *Also:* The Denhams. In *Dramatic Works,* ed. Wyndham Albery, London: Peter Davies, 1939, II, [285]-361.
    Denhams, The.
        See Crisis, The.
    Doctor Davy. In *Dramatic Works,* ed. Wyndham Albery, London: Peter Davies, 1939, II, [190]-192. Commentary.
    Duty. In *Dramatic Works,* ed. Wyndham Albery, London: Peter Davies, 1939, II, [363]-464.
    Duty. London & New York: Samuel French, n.d. Pp. [1]-75. [Lacy's Acting Edition].
    Fearns.
        See Genevieve.

Featherbrain. In *Dramatic Works,* ed. Wyndham Albery, London: Peter Davies, 1939, II, 575-580. Commentary.
Forgiven. In *Dramatic Works,* ed. Wyndham Albery, London: Peter Davies, 1939, I, [305]-391.
Fortune. In *Dramatic Works,* ed. Wyndham Albery, London: Peter Davies, 1939, I, [531]-623.
Genevieve. *Also:* Fearns. In *Dramatic Works,* ed. Wyndham Albery, London: Peter Davies, 1939, II, [693]-757.
Golden Wreath, The. In *Dramatic Works,* ed. Wyndham Albery, London: Peter Davies, 1939, II, [177]-183. Commentary.
Jacks and Jills. In *Dramatic Works,* ed. Wyndham Albery, London: Peter Davies, 1939, II, [185]-188. Commentary.
Jesuits, The. In *Dramatic Works,* ed. Wyndham Albery, London: Peter Davies, 1939, II, [597]-691.
Jingle. N.p.: n.pub., n.d. Pp. [i-iii], 1-36.
Jingle.
    See Pickwick.
Little Miss Muffet. In *Dramatic Works,* ed. Wyndham Albery, London: Peter Davies, 1939, II, [570]-574. Commentary.
Man in Possession, The. In *Dramatic Works,* ed. Wyndham Albery, London: Peter Davies, 1939, II, [87]-148.
Married. In *Dramatic Works,* ed. Wyndham Albery, London: Peter Davies, 1939, I, [457]-530.
No. 20; or, The Bastille of Calvados. In *Dramatic Works,* ed. Wyndham Albery, London: Peter Davies, 1939, II, 589-593. Commentary.
Old Love and the New, The. In *Dramatic Works,* ed. Wyndham Albery, London: Peter Davies, 1939, II, [465]-470. Commentary.
Oriana. In *Dramatic Works,* ed. Wyndham Albery, London: Peter Davies, 1939, I, [393]-447.
Pickwick. *Also:* Jingle. In *Dramatic Works,* ed. Wyndham Albery, London: Peter Davies, 1939, II, [193]-201. Commentary.
Pink Dominos, The. 94 leaves. Manuscript promptbook.
Pink Dominos. In *Dramatic Works,* ed. Wyndham Albery, London: Peter Davies, 1939, II, [203]-284.
Pride. In *Dramatic Works,* ed. Wyndham Albery, London: Peter Davies, 1939, I, [697]-762.
Spectre Knight, The. In *Dramatic Works,* ed. Wyndham Albery, London: Peter Davies, 1939, II, [150]-176.
Spendthrift, The. In *Dramatic Works,* ed. Wyndham Albery, London: Peter Davies, 1939, II, [i]-[viii], 1-85.
Tweedie's Rights. In *Dramatic Works,* ed. Wyndham Albery, London: Peter Davies, 1939, I, [180]-222.
Tweedie's Rights. New York: Robert M. DeWitt, n.d. Pp. [1]-23. DeWitt's Acting Plays, 168.
Two Roses. London & New York: Samuel French, n.d. Pp. [1]-66. French's Acting Edition (late Lacy's), 1769.
Two Roses. In *Dramatic Works,* ed. Wyndham Albery, London: Peter Davies, 1939, I, [17]-95.
Two Roses. New York: n.pub., n.d. <wrps. Chicago: Dramatic Publishing Co.>. Pp. [1]-39. Sergel's Acting Drama, 288.
Two Thorns.
    See Coquettes.
Two Thorns, The. New York: DeWitt, n.d. Pp. [1]-36. DeWitt's Acting Plays, 292.
Vicar, The. In *Dramatic Works,* ed. Wyndham Albery, London: Peter Davies, 1939, II, 594-596. Commentary.
Welcome, Little Stranger. In *Dramatic Works,* ed. Wyndham Albery, London: Peter Davies, 1939, II, 581-582. Commentary.
Where's the Cat? In *Dramatic Works,* ed. Wyndham Albery, London: Peter Davies, 1939, II, [471]-568.
Wig and Gown. In *Dramatic Works,* ed. Wyndham Albery, London: Peter Davies, 1939, I, [624]-695.
Will of the Wise King Kino, The. In *Dramatic Works,* ed. Wyndham Albery, London: Peter Davies, 1939, I, [450]-455. Commentary.

ALCAID, THE
    See Kenney, James.

ALCANOR
>*See* Cumberland, Richard.

ALCESTIS
>*See* Mason, James.
>*See* Potter, Robert (trans.).
>*See* Spicer, Henry (trans.).
>*See* Todhunter, John.

ALCESTIS; OR, EURIPIDES DESTROYED (anon.)
>Edinburgh: Neill (printer), 1866. Pp. [1]-23.

ALCESTIS, THE ORIGINAL STRONG-MINDED WOMAN
>*See* Talfourd, Francis.
>*See* Talfourd, Francis. Alcestis Travestie.

ALCESTIS TRAVESTIE
>*See* Talfourd, Francis.
>*See* Talfourd, Francis. Alcestis, the Original Strong-Minded Woman.

ALDERMAN'S GOWN, THE
>*See* Abrahams, Henry.

ALDERSON, WILLIAM L.
>**Transgression.** New Brompton: T. E. Hughes, 1883. Pp. [i-iv], [1]-51.

ALEXANDER THE GREAT
>*See* Albery, James.
>*See* Albery, James. Chiselling.
>*See* Boswell, Robert Bruce (trans.).
>*See* de Vere, Aubrey Thomas.
>*See* Lee, Nathaniel.

ALEXANDER THE GREAT, IN LITTLE
>*See* Dibdin, Thomas John.

ALEXINA
>*See* Knowles, James Sheridan.

ALFIERI, VITTORIO
>**Agamemnon.**
>>*See* Lloyd, Charles (trans.).
>**Agis.**
>>*See* Lloyd, Charles (trans.).
>**Antigone.**
>>*See* Lloyd, Charles (trans.).
>**Conspiracy of the Pazzi, The.**
>>*See* Lloyd, Charles (trans.).
>**Don Garcia.**
>>*See* Lloyd, Charles (trans.).
>**First Brutus, The.**
>>*See* Lloyd, Charles (trans.).
>**Mary Stuart.**
>>*See* Lloyd, Charles (trans.).
>**Merope.**
>>*See* Lloyd, Charles (trans.).
>**Myrrha.**
>>*See* Lloyd, Charles (trans.).
>**Octavia.**
>>*See* Lloyd, Charles (trans.).
>**Orestes.**
>>*See* Lloyd, Charles (trans.).
>**Philip.**
>>*See* Lloyd, Charles (trans.).
>**Philip the Second.**
>>*See* Holcroft, Fanny (trans.).
>**Polinices.**
>>*See* Lloyd, Charles (trans.).
>**Rosmunda.**
>>*See* Lloyd, Charles (trans.).
>**Saul.**
>>*See* Lloyd, Charles (trans.).
>**Second Brutus, The.**
>>*See* Lloyd, Charles (trans.).
>**Sophonisba.**
>>*See* Lloyd, Charles (trans.).
>**Timoleon.**
>>*See* Lloyd, Charles (trans.).
>**Virginia.**
>>*See* Lloyd, Charles (trans.).

ALFONSO, KING OF CASTILE
>*See* Lewis, Matthew Gregory.

ALFRED
>*See* Gower, Francis Leveson, Lord.

ALFRED THE GREAT
>*See* Brough, Robert Barnabas.
>*See* Knowles, James Sheridan.
>*See* Pocock, Isaac.

ALFRED THE GREAT IN ATHELNAY
>*See* Canning, Stratford.

ALHAMBRA, THE
>*See* Smith, Albert Richard.

ALI BABA
>*See* Byron, Henry James.
>*See* Keating, Eliza H.
>*See* Kenney, Charles Lamb (trans.).
>*See* O'Neill, John Robert.

ALI BABA; OR, THE FORTY THIEVES (anon.)
>London: Hodgson, n.d. Pp. [1]-24. Hodgson's Juvenile Drama.

ALI BABA AND THE FORTY THIEVES
>*See* A'Beckett, Gilbert Arthur.

ALI BABA AND THE FORTY THIEVES; OR, HARLEQUIN AND THE MAGIC DONKEY (anon.)
>Bristol: R. W. Bingham, n.d. Pp. [1]-40. Libretto.

ALI-BEN-HASSAN
>*See* Wheatley, J. A.

ALI PACHA
>*See* Payne, John Howard.

ALICE
>*See* Mitford, Mary Russell.

ALICE GREY, THE SUSPECTED ONE
>*See* Haines, John Thomas.

ALICE IN WONDERLAND
>*See* Clarke, Henry Saville.

ALICE MAY
>*See* Fitzball, Edward.

ALIENATED MANOR, THE
>*See* Baillie, Joanna.

ALINE, THE ROSE OF KILLARNEY!
>*See* Stirling, Edward.

ALIVE AND MERRY
>*See* Dance, Charles.

ALL A MISTAKE
>*See* Marshall, Francis Albert. Q. E. D.

ALL AT C
>*See* Millett, Sydney Crohan, Maj.

ALL AT COVENTRY
>*See* Moncrieff, William Thomas.

ALL AT SEA
>*See* Law, Arthur.

ALL COMES TO HE WHO WAITS
>*See* Pleon, Harry. Waiter, The.

ALL FOR LOVE
>*See* Coyne, Joseph Stirling.
>*See* Dryden, John.

ALL FOR MONEY
>*See* Towers, Edward.

ALL FOR THE BEST
>*See* Leverson, Mrs. Ernest.

ALL IN A FOG!
>*See* Williams, Thomas John. Who Is Who?

ALL IN A MUDDLE
>*See* Troughton, Adolphus Charles.

ALL IN A MUDDLE; OR, VANDYKE BROWN
>*See* Troughton, Adolphus Charles. Vandyke Brown.

ALL IN THE DARK
>*See* Planché, James Robinson.

ALL IN THE DOWNS
>*See* Jerrold, Douglas William. Black Eyed Susan.
>*See* Jerrold, Douglas William. Black-Ey'd Susan.

ALL IN THE DUMPS
>*See* Cooper, Frederick Fox. Black-eyed Sukey.

ALL IN THE WRONG
>*See* Murphy, Arthur.

ALL IS FAIR IN LOVE AND WAR
>*See* Creyke, Walter P.

ALL MADE UP AGAIN
   See Maclaren, Archibald. Forget and Forgive.
ALL MY EYE AND BETTY MARTYN!
   See Burnand, Francis Cowley. Hit and Miss.
ALL ON THE WING
   See Lunn, Joseph. Three Deep.
ALL PUZZLED!
   See Is He Alive?
ALL THAT GLITTERS IS NOT GOLD
   See Morton, Thomas, jr.
ALL THE TALENTS!
   See Barrett, Eaton Stannard.
ALL THE WORLD'S A STAGE
   See Jackman, Isaac.
ALLADINE AND PALOMIDES
   See Sutro, Alfred (trans.).

ALLAN, A. W.
   Rienzi Reinstated; or, The Last of the Cobbler. London: W. H. & L. Collingridge (printer), 1875. Pp. [1]-36.

ALLAOODDEEN
   See Abbott, James.

ALLEN, JAMES
   See Albery, James.

ALLEN, ROBERT
   Parricide, The. Bath: Wood, Cunningham, & Smith, 1824. Pp. [i-viii], [1]-99.

ALLINGHAM, JOHN TILL
   Fortune's Frolic. London: Whittingham & Arliss, 1814. Pp. [1]-30. London Theatre, III. *Filed under* Dibdin, Thomas John, ed. London Theatre, III.
   Fortune's Frolic. In *New English Drama*, ed. W. Oxberry, 22 vols., London: W. Simpkin & R. Marshall; C. Chapple, 1821, XIII, [1-2], [i]-[iv], [1]-[24]. *Filed under* Oxberry, William Henry. New English Drama, XIII.
   Fortune's Frolic. London: John Cumberland, n.d. Pp. [1]-32. Cumberland's British Theatre, XXX. *Filed under* Cumberland, John. Cumberland's British Theatre, XXX.
   Fortune's Frolic. By J. A. Allingham. In *British Drama*, 12 vols., London: John Dicks, 1871, VIII, [279]-288.
   Hearts of Oak. London: James Ridgway, 1804. Pp. [i-vi], [1]-[72].
   Jack of All Trades. London: Thomas Hailes Lacy, n.d. Pp. [1]-19.
   Marriage Promise, The. London: James Ridgway, 1803. Pp. [i-x], [5]-80. 5th ed.
   Mrs. Wiggins. London: James Ridgway, 1803. Pp. [1]-49.
   Mrs. Wiggins. New York: D. Longworth, 1803. Pp. [1]-36.
   Mrs. Wiggins. London: John Cumberland, n.d. Pp. [1]-24. Cumberland's British Theatre, XXIX. *Filed under* Cumberland, John. Cumberland's British Theatre, XXIX.
   Transformation; or, Love and Law. Baltimore: J. Robinson, 1814. Pp. [1]-30. 1st ed.
   Weathercock, The. London: John Cumberland, 1828. Pp. [1]-32. Cumberland's British Theatre, XVIII. *Filed under* Cumberland, John. Cumberland's British Theatre, XVIII.
   Weathercock, The. Music by King, M. P. London: Lackington, Allen, n.d. Pp. [i-iii], [1]-27.
   Widow, The; or, Who Wins? London: John Cumberland, n.d. Pp. [1]-36. Cumberland's British Theatre, XXXII. *Filed under* Cumberland, John. Cumberland's British Theatre, XXXII.
   Widow, The; or, Who Wins? London: John Cumberland, n.d. Pp. [1]-36.

ALLINGHAM, WILLIAM
   Ashby Manor. In *Thought and Word and Ashby Manor*, London: Reeves & Turner, 1890, pp. [i], [93]-[184].
   News from Pannonia. In *Thought and Word and Ashby Manor*, London: Reeves & Turner, 1890, pp. [i], [43]-58.
   Prince Brightkin. In *Life and Phantasy*, London: Longmans, Green, 1893, pp. 108-122. *Filed under* Stratford-on-Avon.
   Stratford-on-Avon. In *Life and Phantasy*, London: Longmans, Green, 1893, pp. [i], 57-60.

ALLOW ME TO APOLOGIZE
   See Wooler, John Pratt.

ALLOW ME TO EXPLAIN
   See Gilbert, William Schwenck.
ALL'S FAIR IN LOVE
   See Brougham, John.
   See Hersee, Henry.
ALL'S FAIR IN LOVE AND WAR
   See Brougham, John. All's Fair in Love.
ALL'S WELL THAT ENDS WELL
   See Kemble, John Philip (arr.).
   See Shakespeare, William.
ALLURIO AND ADELINA
   See Byron, Henry James.
ALMA MATER
   See Boucicault, Dionysius Lardner.
ALMAHIDE AND HAMET
   See Malkin, Benjamin Heath.

ALMAR, GEORGE
   Battle of Sedgemoor, The; or, The Days of Kirk and Monmouth. London: John Cumberland, n.d. Pp. [i-ii], [1]-48. Cumberland's Minor Theatre, XIII. *Filed under* Cumberland, John. Cumberland's Minor Theatre, XIII.
   Battle of Sedgemoor, The; or, The Days of Kirk and Monmouth. London: John Cumberland, n.d. Pp. [1]-48. [Cumberland's Minor Theatre, 113].
   Bull-Fighter, The; or, The Bridal Ring. London: John Cumberland, n.d. Pp. [1]-39. [Cumberland's Minor Theatre].
   Bull-Fighter, The; or, The Bridal Ring. London: John Cumberland, n.d. Pp. [1]-39. Cumberland's Minor Theatre, XIV. *Filed under* Cumberland, John. Cumberland's Minor Theatre, XIV.
   Cedar Chest, The; or, The Lord Mayor's Daughter. London: John Cumberland, n.d. Pp. [i-ii], [1]-43. Cumberland's Minor Theatre, VIII. *Filed under* Cumberland, John. Cumberland's Minor Theatre, VIII.
   Cedar Chest, The; or, The Lord Mayor's Daughter. London: John Cumberland, n.d. Pp. [1]-43. [Cumberland's Minor Theatre].
   Charcoal Burner, The; or, The Dropping Well of Knaresborough. London: John Cumberland, n.d. Pp. [1]-46. Cumberland's Minor Theatre, IX. *Filed under* Cumberland, John. Cumberland's Minor Theatre, IX.
   Charcoal Burner, The; or, The Dropping Well of Knaresborough. London: John Dicks, n.d. Pp. [1]-16. Dicks' Standard Plays, 767.
   Charcoal-Burner, The; or, The Dropping Well of Knaresborough. Boston: William V. Spencer, n.d. Pp. [1]-32. Spencer's Boston Theatre, 188.
   Clerk of Clerkenwell, The; or, The Three Black Bottles. London: John Cumberland, n.d. Pp. [1]-54. Cumberland's Minor Theatre, VII. *Filed under* Cumberland, John. Cumberland's Minor Theatre, VII.
   Clerk of Clerkenwell, The; or, The Three Black Bottles. London: John Cumberland, n.d. Pp. [1]-54. [Cumberland's Minor Theatre].
   Crossing the Line; or, Crowded Houses! London: John Duncombe, n.d. Pp. [1]-24. Duncombe's Acting Edition of the British Theatre, 87.
   Don Quixote; or, The Knight of the Woeful Countenance. London: Richardson & Clarke, n.d. Pp. [i]-[vi], [9]-30. Pagination irregular.
   Don Quixote; or, The Knight of the Woeful Countenance. London: John Cumberland, n.d. Pp. [1]-30. Cumberland's Minor Theatre, XIV. *Filed under* Cumberland, John. Cumberland's Minor Theatre, XIV.
   Earl of Poverty, The; or, The Old Wooden House of London Wall. London: John Cumberland, n.d. Pp. [3]-54. Promptbook.
   Earl of Poverty, The; or, The Old Wooden House of London Wall. London: John Cumberland, n.d. Pp. [1]-54. Cumberland's Minor Theatre, XIV. *Filed under* Cumberland, John. Cumberland's Minor Theatre, XIV.
   Evil Eye!, The. London: John Duncombe, n.d. Pp. [1]-36. Duncombe's Acting Edition of the British Theatre, 77.

Fire Raiser, The. *Also:* The Haunted Moor. London: Thomas Hailes Lacy, n.d. Pp. [1]-56. [Lacy's Acting Edition].

Fire Raiser, The; or, The Prophet of the Moor. London: John Cumberland, n.d. Pp. [1]-56. Cumberland's Minor Theatre, IX. *Filed under* Cumberland, John. Cumberland's Minor Theatre, IX.

Gaspardo the Gondolier; or, The Three Banished Men of Milan! London: Thomas Hailes Lacy, n.d. Pp. [1]-32. Cumberland's British Theatre. Promptbook.

Good-Looking Fellow, The; or, The Roman Nose. London: John Cumberland, n.d. Pp. [1]-24. Cumberland's Minor Theatre, IX. *Filed under* Cumberland, John. Cumberland's Minor Theatre, IX.

Good-Looking Fellow, The; or, The Roman Nose. London: John Cumberland, n.d. Pp. [1]-24.

Haunted Moor.
> *See* Fire Raiser, The.

Jack Ketch; or, A Leaf from Tyburn Tree. London: John Dicks, n.d. Pp. [1]-18. Dicks' Standard Plays, 508.

Jane of the Hatchet; or, The Siege of Beauvais. London: John Duncombe, n.d. Pp. [1]-34. Duncombe's Acting Edition of the British Theatre, 388.

Knights of St. John!, The; or, The Fire Banner! London: John Duncombe, n.d. <wrps. Thomas Hailes Lacy>. Pp. [1]-38. Duncombe's Edition <wrps. New British Theatre (late Duncombe's), 93>. Promptbook.

Mountain King, The; or, The Castle Burners! London: John Duncombe, n.d. Pp. [1]-40. Duncombe's Edition.

Oliver Twist. New York & London: Samuel French, n.d. Pp. [1]-44. French's Standard Drama, 228.

Oliver Twist. London: John Dicks, n.d. Pp. [1]-26. Dicks' Standard Plays, 293.

Pedlar's Acre; or, The Wife of Seven Husbands. London: John Cumberland, n.d. Pp. [1]-52. Cumberland's Minor Theatre, V. *Filed under* Cumberland, John. Cumberland's Minor Theatre, V.

Pedlar's Acre; or, The Wife of Seven Husbands. London: John Cumberland, n.d. Pp. [1]-52.

Peerless Pool! London: John Duncombe, n.d. Pp. [1]-36. Duncombe's Edition.

Robber of the Rhine, The. London: John Cumberland, n.d. Pp. [1]-40. Cumberland's Minor Theatre, X. *Filed under* Cumberland, John. Cumberland's Minor Theatre, X.

Robber of the Rhine, The. New York: Samuel French, n.d. Pp. [1]-40. French's Standard Drama, 181.

Rover's Bride, The; or, The Bittern's Swamp. London: John Cumberland, n.d. Pp. [1]-47. Cumberland's Minor Theatre, XI. *Filed under* Cumberland, John. Cumberland's Minor Theatre, XI.

Rover's Bride, The; or, The Bittern's Swamp. London: John Cumberland, n.d. Pp. [1]-47.

Seven Sisters, The; or, The Grey Man of Tottenham! London: John Duncombe, n.d. Pp. [1]-40. Duncombe's Acting Edition of the British Theatre, 140.

Shadow!, The: A Mother's Dream. London: John Cumberland, n.d. Pp. [1]-56. [Cumberland's Minor Theatre].

Shadow!, The: A Mother's Dream. London: John Cumberland, n.d. Pp. [1]-56. Cumberland's Minor Theatre, VIII. *Filed under* Cumberland, John. Cumberland's Minor Theatre, VIII.

Silver Palace, The; or, The Golden Poppy. London: John Cumberland, n.d. Pp. 44-48. Text complete. Cumberland's Minor Theatre, VIII. *Filed under* Cumberland, John. Cumberland's Minor Theatre, VIII.

Silver Palace, The; or, The Golden Poppy. London: John Cumberland, n.d. Pp. 44-48. [Cumberland's Minor Theatre]. *Filed under* Cedar Chest.

Tower of Nesle, The; or, The Chamber of Death. London: John Cumberland, n.d. Pp. [1]-51. Cumberland's Minor Theatre, VI. *Filed under* Cumberland, John. Cumberland's Minor Theatre, VI.

Tower of Nesle, The; or, The Chamber of Death. London: G. H. Davidson, n.d. Pp. [1]-51. [Cumberland's Minor Theatre, 50].

Wife of Seven Husbands, The; or, A Legend of Pedlar's Acre. London: Thomas Hailes Lacy, n.d. Pp. [3]-52. [Lacy's Acting Edition].

ALMA-TADEMA, LAURENCE
> **Childe Vyet; or, The Brothers.** In *Four Plays*, London: Green Sheaf, 1905, pp. [31]-65. *Filed under* Four Plays.
> **Merciful Soul, The.** In *Four Plays*, London: Green Sheaf, 1905, pp. [67]-102. *Filed under* Four Plays.
> **New Wrecks upon Old Shoals.** In *Four Plays*, London: Green Sheaf, 1905, pp. [105]-143. *Filed under* Four Plays.
> **One Way of Love.** Edinburgh: R. & R. Clarke (printer) (priv.), 1893. Pp. [i-iv], [1]-32.
> **Unseen Helmsman, The.** In *Four Plays*, London: Green Sheaf, 1905, pp. [i-viii], [1]-28. *Filed under* Four Plays.

ALMOURAH, THE CORSAIR
> *See* Hamilton, R. S.

ALONE
> *See* Simpson, John Palgrave.

ALONE IN LONDON
> *See* Buchanan, Robert Williams.

ALONZO QUIXANO, OTHERWISE DON QUIXOTE
> *See* Morrison, George E.

ALONZO THE BRAVE
> *See* Burnand, Francis Cowley.

ALONZO THE BRAVE AND THE FAIR IMOGINE
> *See* Milner, Henry M.

ALPHONZO ALGARVES
> *See* Wortley, Emmeline Charlotte Elizabeth Manners Stuart, Mrs. Charles (Lady).

ALPHONZUS
> *See* Hyde, George.

ALTAR OF REVENGE!
> *See* Haines, John Thomas. Nick of the Woods.

ALWAYS INTENDED
> *See* Wigan, Horace.

ALWINE AND ADELAIS
> *See* Taylor, Henry.

ALWYN THE SAXON CHIEF
> *See* Atkyns, Samuel. Battle Bridge in Ancient Times.

ALWYNNE
> *See* Scofield, Joseph Alan.

AMADAN, THE
> *See* Boucicault, Dionysius Lardner.

AMALIE
> *See* Amelia, Princess of Saxony.

AMANTS MAGNIFIQUES
> *See* Van Laun, Henri (trans.). Magnificent Lovers, The.

AMARYNTHUS THE NYMPHOLEPT
> *See* Smith, Horatio.

AMATEURS AND ACTORS
> *See* Peake, Richard Brinsley.

AMAZONS, THE
> *See* Pinero, Arthur Wing.

AMBASSADOR, THE
> *See* Hobbes, John Oliver.

AMBASSADOR FROM BELOW
> *See* Brough, Robert Barnabas. Mephistopheles.

AMBASSADOR'S LADY, THE
> *See* Wilks, Thomas Egerton.

AMBASSADRESS, THE
> *See* A'Beckett, Gilbert Abbott.
> *See* Reece, Robert.

AMBER HEART, THE
> *See* Calmour, Alfred Cecil.

AMBER WITCH, THE
> *See* Chorley, Henry Fothergill.

AMBIENT, MARK
> **Oh! Susannah!** New York & London: Samuel French, c.1905. Pp. [1]-74. [French's International Copyrighted Edition of the Works of the Best Authors], 84.

AMBITION
> *See* Mayhew, Thomas Charles Wilson.

AMBROSE GWINETT
> *See* Jerrold, Douglas William.

AMCOTTS, VINCENT
　Adonis Vanquished. London: Thomas Hailes Lacy, n.d. Pp. [1]-56. [Lacy's Acting Edition].
　Fair Helen. Music by Offenbach. N.p.: n.pub., n.d. Pp. [1]-80. Title page lacking.
　Lalla Rookh. Music by Offenbach. London: Thomas Hailes Lacy, n.d. Pp. [1]-40.
　Love Tests, The. Music by Gabriel, Virginia. London: Thomas Hailes Lacy, n.d. Pp. [1]-30. Libretto.
　Lurline. London: Thomas Hailes Lacy, n.d. Pp. [1]-46.
　Pentheus. Written with Anson, William Reynell. Oxford: T. & G. Shrimpton, 1866. Pp. [i-ii], [1]-42. Echoes of the Greek Drama, 1.
　Poisoned. London: Thomas Hailes Lacy, n.d. Pp. [1]-16.

AMELIA, PRINCESS OF SAXONY
　Captain Firnewald.
　　See under title.
　Country Cousin, The.
　　See Jameson, Anna Brownell Murphy, Mrs. Robert (trans.).
　Falsehood and Truth.
　　See Jameson, Anna Brownell Murphy, Mrs. Robert (trans.).
　Heir of Scharfeneck, The.
　　See under title.
　Irresolute Man, The.
　　See under title.
　Princely Bride, The.
　　See Jameson, Anna Brownell Murphy, Mrs. Robert (trans.).
　Son's Return, The.
　　See under title.
　Uncle, The.
　　See Jameson, Anna Brownell Murphy, Mrs. Robert (trans.).
　Uninformed Girl, The.
　　See under title.
　Young Lady from the Country, The.
　　See under title.
　Young Ward, The.
　　See Jameson, Anna Brownell Murphy, Mrs. Robert (trans.).

AMELIA WENTWORTH
　See Cornwall, Barry.

AMERICAN IN ENGLAND, THE
　See Ranger, Edward.

AMERICANS, THE
　See Arnold, Samuel James.

AMERICANS ABROAD
　See Peake, Richard Brinsley.

AMHERST, J. H.
　Battle of Waterloo, The. London: John Duncombe, n.d. Pp. [1]-[36]. Duncombe's Edition.
　Blood Demands Its Victim.
　　See Will Watch!
　Burmese War, The. London: John Duncombe, n.d. Pp. [3]-44. John Duncombe's Edition.
　Fifteen Years of Labour Lost; or, The Youth Who Never Saw a Woman. London: Thomas Hailes Lacy, n.d. Pp. [1]-21. [Lacy's Acting Edition].
　Freischutz, Der; or, The Seven Charmed Bullets. London: John Duncombe, n.d. Pp. [1]-[19]. Duncombe's Edition.
　Ireland As It Is. New York: Samuel French, n.d. Pp. [1]-28. French's American Drama, 113 <wrps. French's Standard Drama>.
　Napoleon Buonaparte's Invasion of Russia; or, The Conflagration of Moscow. London: John Duncombe, n.d. Pp. [1]-46. Duncombe's Edition.
　Who Owns the Hand?; or, The Monk, the Mask, and the Murderer. 34 leaves. Manuscript promptbook.
　Will Watch!; or, The Black Phantom! *Also:* Blood Demands Its Victim. London: John Duncombe, n.d. Pp. [1]-28. Duncombe's Acting Edition of the British Theatre, 18.

AMICO, AMICUS (pseud. of ?)
　Hermesianax. London: Morris (printer), n.d. Pp. [1]-24.

AMILIE
　See Haines, John Thomas.

AMINTA, THE COQUETTE
　See Glover, William Howard.

AMONG THE RELICS
　See Palmer, T. A.

AMOROSO, KING OF LITTLE BRITAIN
　See Planché, James Robinson.

AMOROUS KNIGHT AND THE BELLE WIDOW
　See Valentine's Day.

AMOUR FUGITIF
　See Vestris, Armand. Anacreon.

AMOUR MEDICIN
　See Van Laun, Henri (trans.). Love Is the Best Doctor.

AMPHITRYON
　See Van Laun, Henri (trans.).

AMPLE APOLOGY, AN
　See Roberts, George.

AMY ROBSART
　See Halliday, Andrew.
　See Harris, Augustus Henry Glossop.

ANACREON
　See Vestris, Armand.

ANCESTRESS!, THE
　See Lemon, Mark.

ANCHOR OF HOPE, THE
　See Stirling, Edward.

ANCIENT TIMES
　See Strutt, Joseph.

ANDERDON, WILLIAM HENRY
　Duchess Transformed, The. London: R. Washbourne, 1896. Pp. [1]-24. 3rd ed.

ANDERSON, CHARLES
　Grandmother's Gown. *Also:* Lord Dolly. London & New York: Samuel French, n.d. Pp. [1]-8. [Lacy's Acting Edition].
　Lord Dolly.
　　See Grandmother's Gown.

ANDERSON, DAVID
　Martial Achievements of Sir William Wallace, The. Aberdeen: D. Chalmers (priv.), 1821. Pp. [i]-viii, [9]-200.

ANDERSON, J. F. REYNOLDS
　Spanish Student, The.
　　See Victorian.
　Victorian. *Also:* The Spanish Student. Music by Edwards, Julian. London: Joseph Williams & Son, n.d. Pp. [i-iv], [1]-200. Vocal score.

ANDERSON, JAMES ROBERTSON
　Cloud and Sunshine; or, Love's Revenge. London: Thomas Hailes Lacy, n.d. Pp. [1]-[56]. [Lacy's Acting Edition].

ANDERSON, MARY (later Mrs. Antonio de Navarro) (arr.)
　As You Like It. By Shakespeare, William. London & New York: Samuel French, n.d. Pp. [1]-72. *Filed under* Shakespeare, William.
　Romeo and Juliet. By Shakespeare, William. London: W. S. Johnson, 1884. Pp. [1]-72. *Filed under* Romeo and Juliet (anon.).
　Winter's Tale, The. By Shakespeare, William. London: W. S. Johnson, 1888. Pp. [1]-66. Promptbook. *Filed under* Winter's Tale (anon.).
　Winter's Tale, The. By Shakespeare, William. London: Field & Tuer, c.1888. Pp. 1-56. *Filed under* Winter's Tale (anon.).

ANDERTON, H. ORSMOND
　Baldur. London: T. Fisher Unwin, 1893. Pp. [1]-40.

ANDREA OF HUNGARY
　See Landor, Walter Savage.

ANDREAS
　See Barrett, William John.

ANDREWS, MILES PETER
　Better Late Than Never. In British Drama, 12 vols., London: John Dicks, 1872, XII, [288]-305.

ANDROMACHE
　See Boswell, Robert Bruce (trans.).

ANDY BLAKE
    See Boucicault, Dionysius Lardner.
ANGEL OF MIDNIGHT, THE
    See Suter, William E.
ANGEL OF THE ATTIC, THE
    See Morton, Thomas, jr.
ANGEL OR DEVIL
    See Coyne, Joseph Stirling.
ANGELICA
    See Dubourg, Augustus W.
ANGELINE
    See Haines, John Thomas.
ANGELINE LE LIS
    See Haines, John Thomas. Angeline.
ANGELO
    See A'Beckett, Gilbert Abbott.
    See Reade, Charles.
ANGELO AND THE ACTRESS OF PADUA
    See Davidson, George Henry.
ANGLO–SAXONS
    See Roche, Eugenius. Invasion, The.
ANGUS, J. KEITH
    By This Token. London & New York: Samuel French, n.d.
    Pp. [1]-25. [Lacy's Acting Edition].
    Send Thirty Stamps. London & New York: Samuel French,
    n.d. Pp. [1]-16. [Lacy's Acting Edition].
ANIMAL MAGNETISM
    See Inchbald, Elizabeth Simpson, Mrs. Joseph.
ANNA BOLENA (anon.)
    Music by Donizetti. London: G. Middleton (printer),
    n.d. Pp. [1]-55. Libretto.
ANNA BOLENA
    See Maggioni, Manfredo (trans.).
ANNA RUINA
    See Field, Michael.
ANNE BLAKE
    See Marston, John Westland.
ANNE BOLEYN
    See Edwardes, Conway Theodore Marriott.
    See Grover, Henry Montague.
    See Milman, Henry Hart.
    See Taylor, Tom.
ANNEAU MAGIQUE, L'
    See Albert, ?.
ANNIRA
    See Waterhouse, Benjamin.
ANNUNCIATION, THE
    See Hinkson, Katharine Tynan, Mrs. Henry Albert.
ANONYMOUS PLAY
    See Knowles, James Sheridan.
ANOTHER CAIN, A MYSTERY
    See Battine, William.
ANOTHER GLASS
    See Morton, Thomas, jr.
ANOTHER LESSON TO FATHERS
    See Morton, John Maddison. Going It!
ANOTHER RETREAT FROM MOSCOW
    See Morton, Thomas, jr. Great Russian Bear, The.
ANSON, WILLIAM REYNELL
    Pentheus.
    See Amcotts, Vincent.
ANSTER, JOHN (trans.)
    Faustus. By Goethe. In *Faustus, a Dramatic Mystery* . . . ,
    London: Longman, Rees, Orme, Brown, Green, &
    Longman, 1835, pp. [i]-[xlv], [1]-488.
ANSTEY, F. (pseud. of Guthrie, Thomas Anstey)
    Art in the City. In *Man from Blankley's and Other Sketches,*
    new ed., London: Longmans, Green, 1901, pp. [234]-243.
    Filed under Guthrie, Thomas Anstey. Collected Works.
    At a Hypnotic Seance. In *Man from Blankley's and Other
    Sketches,* new ed., London: Longmans, Green, 1901, pp.
    [136]-145. *Filed under* Guthrie, Thomas Anstey. Collected
    Works.

At a Vegetarian Restaurant. In *Man from Blankley's and Other
    Sketches,* new ed., London: Longmans, Green, 1901, pp.
    [127]-135. *Filed under* Guthrie, Thomas Anstey. Collected
    Works.
At the Confectioner's. In *Man from Blankley's and Other
    Sketches,* new ed., London: Longmans, Green, 1901, pp.
    [244]-254. *Filed under* Guthrie, Thomas Anstey. Collected
    Works.
At the Wild West. In *Man from Blankley's and Other
    Sketches,* new ed., London: Longmans, Green, 1901, pp.
    [217]-224. *Filed under* Guthrie, Thomas Anstey. Collected
    Works.
Automatic Physiognomist, The. In *Man from Blankley's and
    Other Sketches,* new ed., London: Longmans, Green,
    1901, pp. [180]-187. *Filed under* Guthrie, Thomas Anstey.
    Collected Works.
Before the Mechanical Models. In *Man from Blankley's and
    Other Sketches,* new ed., London: Longmans, Green,
    1901, pp. [209]-216. *Filed under* Guthrie, Thomas Anstey.
    Collected Works.
Boat-Race Day. In *Man from Blankley's and Other Sketches,*
    new ed., London: Longmans, Green, 1901, pp. [108]-116.
    Filed under Guthrie, Thomas Anstey. Collected Works.
Choosing Christmas Toys. In *Man from Blankley's and Other
    Sketches,* new ed., London: Longmans, Green, 1901, pp.
    [255]-266. *Filed under* Guthrie, Thomas Anstey. Collected
    Works.
Dilatory Dinners. In *Man from Blankley's and Other Sketches,*
    new ed., London: Longmans, Green, 1901, pp. [154]-161.
    Filed under Guthrie, Thomas Anstey. Collected Works.
Hair-Cutting, Singeing, and Shampooing. In *Man from
    Blankley's and Other Sketches,* new ed., London: Long-
    mans, Green, 1901, pp. [188]-197. *Filed under* Guthrie,
    Thomas Anstey. Collected Works.
Hedda Gabler. In *Mr. Punch's Pocket Ibsen,* New York:
    Macmillan, 1893, pp. [88]-[137]. *Filed under* Guthrie,
    Thomas Anstey. Mr. Punch's Pocket Ibsen.
Lyre and Lancet. New York: Macmillan, 1895. Pp. [i]-viii,
    [1]-256. *Filed under* Guthrie, Thomas Anstey.
Man from Blankley's, The. In *Man from Blankley's and Other
    Sketches,* new ed., London: Longmans, Green, 1901, pp.
    [i]-[xii], [1]-75. *Filed under* Guthrie, Thomas Anstey.
    Collected Works.
Matinee Mania. In *Man from Blankley's and Other Sketches,*
    new ed., London: Longmans, Green, 1901, pp. [162]-171.
    Filed under Guthrie, Thomas Anstey. Collected Works.
Menagerie Race, The. In *Man from Blankley's and Other
    Sketches,* new ed., London: Longmans, Green, 1901, pp.
    [198]-208. *Filed under* Guthrie, Thomas Anstey. Collected
    Works.
More Pot-Pourri from the Park. In *Man from Blankley's and
    Other Sketches,* new ed., London: Longmans, Green,
    1901, pp. [172]-179. *Filed under* Guthrie, Thomas Anstey.
    Collected Works.
Nora; or, The Bird-Cage. In *Mr. Punch's Pocket Ibsen,* New
    York: Macmillan, 1893, pp. [43]-87. *Filed under* Guthrie,
    Thomas Anstey. Mr. Punch's Pocket Ibsen.
On the Threshold of Themis. In *Man from Blankley's and
    Other Sketches,* new ed., London: Longmans, Green,
    1901, pp. [97]-107. *Filed under* Guthrie, Thomas Anstey.
    Collected Works.
One Side of the Canvass. In *Man from Blankley's and Other
    Sketches,* new ed., London: Longmans, Green, 1901, pp.
    [76]-86. *Filed under* Guthrie, Thomas Anstey. Collected
    Works.
Other Side of the Canvass, The. In *Man from Blankley's and
    Other Sketches,* new ed., London: Longmans, Green,
    1901, pp. [87]-96. *Filed under* Guthrie, Thomas Anstey.
    Collected Works.
Pill-Doctor Herdal. In *Mr. Punch's Pocket Ibsen,* New York:
    Macmillan, 1893, pp. [171]-228. *Filed under* Guthrie,
    Thomas Anstey. Mr. Punch's Pocket Ibsen.
Preserved Venice. In *Man from Blankley's and Other Sketches,*
    new ed., London: Longmans, Green, 1901, pp. [117]-126.
    Filed under Guthrie, Thomas Anstey. Collected Works.

Rosmersholm. In *Mr. Punch's Pocket Ibsen,* New York: Macmillan, 1893, pp. [i-x], [11]-42. *Filed under* Guthrie, Thomas Anstey.

Telephonic Theatre-Goers. In *Man from Blankley's and Other Sketches,* new ed., London: Longmans, Green, 1901, pp. [225]-233. *Filed under* Guthrie, Thomas Anstey. Collected Works.

Travelling Companions, The. Leipzig: Heinemann & Balestier, 1892. Pp. [i]-[viii], [1]-221. English Library, 136. *Filed under* Guthrie, Thomas Anstey.

Wild Duck, The. In *Mr. Punch's Pocket Ibsen,* New York: Macmillan, 1893, pp. [138]-170. *Filed under* Guthrie, Thomas Anstey. Mr. Punch's Pocket Ibsen.

Wrestling with Whistlers. In *Man from Blankley's and Other Sketches,* new ed., London: Longmans, Green, 1901, pp. [146]-153. *Filed under* Guthrie, Thomas Anstey. Collected Works.

ANSTRUTHER, RALPH ABERCROMBIE, SIR (trans.)
  Griselda. By Halm, Frederick. London: Black & Armstrong; Dresden & Leipsic: Chr. Arnold, 1840. Pp. [i]-xiv, [1]-141.

ANTHONY BABINGTON
  See Fane, Violet.

ANTHONY'S LEGACY
  See Charleson, Arthur J.

ANTIGONE (anon.)
  London: William Barth, n.d. Pp. [1]-[35].

ANTIGONE
  See Bartholomew, William (trans.).
  See Lloyd, Charles (trans.).
  See Whitelaw, Robert (trans.).

ANTIOCHUS
  See Neele, Henry.

ANTIQUARY, THE (anon.)
  In *Waverley Dramas,* London: George Routledge, 1845, pp. [1]-66. *Filed under* Waverley Dramas (anon.).

ANTIQUARY, THE
  See Pocock, Isaac.
  See Scott, Walter.

ANTIQUITY (anon.)
  London: C. Chapple, 1808. Pp. [i]-[xiv], [15]-45.

ANTONIA
  See Galt, John.

ANTONIO
  See Godwin, William.

ANTONY AND CLEOPATRA
  See Bellew, Kyrle (arr.).
  See Calvert, Charles Alexander (arr.).
  See Halliday, Andrew (arr.).
  See Kemble, John Philip (arr.).
  See Selby, Charles.

ANTONY AND CLEOPATRA MARRIED AND SETTLED
  See Selby, Charles.

ANY THING NEW
  See Pocock, Isaac.

ANYTHING FOR A CHANGE
  See Brooks, Charles William Shirley.

APARTMENTS: VISITORS TO THE EXHIBITION MAY BE ACCOMMODATED, ETC., ETC.
  See Brough, William.

APOLLO'S CHOICE; OR, THE CONTEST OF THE AONIDES (anon.)
  In *New British Theatre,* London: A. J. Valpy (printer), 1815, IV, [i], [199]-219.

APOSTATE, THE
  See Galt, John.
  See Sheil, Richard Lalor.

APPEAL TO THE FEELINGS, AN
  See Palmer, T. A.

APPEARANCE IS AGAINST THEM
  See Inchbald, Elizabeth Simpson, Mrs. Joseph.

APPEARANCES
  See Simpson, John Palgrave.

APPLE BLOSSOMS
  See Albery, James.

APPLES
  See Sturgis, Julian Russell.

APPLEYARD, CHARLES
  Remorse. London: F. Summers (printer), n.d. Pp. [1]-37.

APPRENTICE, THE
  See Murphy, Arthur.

APRIL FOLLY
  See Hurst, James P.

APRIL FOOL
  See Colomb, George Hatton, Col. Davenport Done.
  See Brough, William.

APRIL SHOWER, AN
  See Beerbohm, Constance.

APRIL SHOWERS
  See Bellamy, G. Somers.

AQUATIC HARLEQUIN
  See Dibdin, Charles Isaac Mungo, jr. Fashion's Fools.

ARAB'S FAITH
  See Hamilton, Ralph, Col. Elphi Bey.

ARABELLA STUART
  See Neil, Ross.

ARABIAN NIGHTS, THE
  See Grundy, Sydney.

ARABS OF THE DESERT
  See Irwin, Eyles. Bedouins, The.

ARAJOON
  See Coyne, Joseph Stirling.

ARBUTHNOT, ?, CAPT.
  Africaine, L'; or, The Belle of Madagascar. London: Thomas Hailes Lacy, n.d. Pp. [1]-28.

ARCHER, CHARLES (trans.)
  Lady Inger of Östråt. By Ibsen, Henrik. In *Ibsen's Prose Dramas,* ed. William Archer, 5 vols., London: Walter Scott, 1904, III, [i]-[xviii], [1]-124. *Filed under* Archer, William. Ibsen's Prose Dramas.

  Peer Gynt.
    See Archer, William (trans.).

  Rosmersholm. By Ibsen, Henrik. In *Ibsen's Prose Dramas,* ed. William Archer, 5 vols., London: Walter Scott, 1904, V, [i]-[xiv], [1]-114. *Filed under* Archer, William. Ibsen's Prose Dramas.

ARCHER, FRANCES ELIZABETH, MRS. WILLIAM (trans.)
  Lady from the Sea, The. By Ibsen, Henrik. In *Ibsen's Prose Dramas,* ed. William Archer, 5 vols., London: Walter Scott, 1904, V, [115]-240. *Filed under* Archer, William. Ibsen's Prose Dramas.

  Wild Duck, The. By Ibsen, Henrik. In *Ibsen's Prose Dramas,* ed. William Archer, 5 vols., London: Walter Scott, 1904, II, [239]-381. *Filed under* Archer, William. Ibsen's Prose Dramas.

ARCHER, THOMAS
  Asmodeus; or, The Little Devil's Share. London: Thomas Hailes Lacy, n.d. Pp. [1]-38. New British Theatre (late Duncombe's), 370.

  Cuffs and Kisses. 16 leaves. Manuscript.

  Daughter of the Regiment, The. 19 leaves. Manuscript.

  Dick and His Double. 15 leaves. Manuscript.

  Don Cesar of Bazan. 27 leaves. Manuscript.

  Eligible Situation, An. Written with Brough, John Cargill. New York: Dick & Fitzgerald, n.d. Pp. [1]-15.

  Inundation, The; or, The Miser of the Hill Fort. London: Thomas Hailes Lacy, n.d. Pp. [1]-44. [Lacy's Acting Edition].

  Marguerite's Colours!; or, Passing the Frontier. London: Duncombe & Moon, n.d. Pp. [1]-37. Duncombe's Edition. Promptbook.

  Monseigneur and the Jeweller's Apprentice. Boston: Charles H. Spencer, n.d. Pp. [1]-35. Spencer's Universal Stage, 38.

  Night in the Bastille, A. London: John Duncombe, n.d. <wrps. Thomas Hailes Lacy>. Pp. [1]-38. New British Theatre (late Duncombe's), 310.

  Red Cap, The; or, The Prisoner of Vincennes. 28 leaves. Manuscript.

Strange Intruder, The. London: H. Quelch (printer), n.d. Pp. [106]-143. Stage Plays. Promptbook.

Three Red Men, The; or, The Brothers of Bluthaupt. London: Thomas Hailes Lacy, n.d. Pp. [1]-50. Promptbook.

ARCHER, WILLIAM (trans.)

Doll's House, A. By Ibsen, Henrik. London: T. Fisher Unwin, 1889. Pp. [i-viii], [1]-123.

Doll's House, A. By Ibsen, Henrik. In *Ibsen's Prose Dramas*, ed. William Archer, 3rd ed., 5 vols., London: Walter Scott, 1904, I, [285]-389. *Filed under* Ibsen's Prose Dramas.

Emperor and Galilean. Part 1: Caesar's Apostasy; Part 2: The Emperor Julian. By Ibsen, Henrik. In *Ibsen's Prose Dramas*, ed. William Archer, 5 vols., London: Walter Scott, 1902, IV, [i]-[xii], [1]-353. *Filed under* Ibsen's Prose Dramas.

Enemy of Society, An. By Ibsen, Henrik. In *Pillars of Society and Other Plays*, ed. Havelock Ellis, London: Walter Scott, 1888, pp. [199]-315. *Filed under* Ghosts.

Ghosts. By Ibsen, Henrik. In *Ibsen's Prose Dramas*, ed. William Archer, 5 vols., London: Walter Scott, 1904, II, [i]-[viii], [9]-101. *Filed under* Ibsen's Prose Dramas.

Ghosts. By Ibsen, Henrik. [New York: Brentano's], n.d. Pp. [1]-88. Title page lacking. [Eleanora Duse Series of Plays].

Ghosts. By Ibsen, Henrik. In *Pillars of Society and Other Plays*, ed. Havelock Ellis, London: Walter Scott, 1888, pp. [115]-198.

Hannele. By Hauptmann, Gerhart. London: William Heinemann, 1894. Pp. [i]-[xxiv], [1]-95.

Hedda Gabler. By Ibsen, Henrik. In *Ibsen's Prose Dramas*, ed. William Archer, 5 vols., London: Walter Scott, 1904, V, [241]-364. *Filed under* Ibsen's Prose Dramas.

Interior. By Maeterlinck, Maurice. In *Three Little Dramas for Marionettes*, London: Duckworth, 1899, pp. [63]-87. *Filed under* Sutro, Alfred (trans.).

John Gabriel Borkman. By Ibsen, Henrik. London: William Heinemann, 1897. Pp. [i-vi], [1]-202. Popular ed.

League of Youth, The. By Ibsen, Henrik. In *Ibsen's Prose Dramas*, ed. William Archer, 3rd ed., 5 vols., London: Walter Scott, 1904, I, [i]-[xiv], [1]-154. *Filed under* Ibsen's Prose Dramas.

Little Eyolf. By Ibsen, Henrik. Chicago: Stone & Kimball, 1895. Pp. [1]-[165]. Green Tree Library.

Master Builder, The.
See Gosse, Edmund William (trans.).

Peer Gynt. Written with Archer, Charles . (trans.) By Ibsen, Henrik. London: Walter Scott, 1904. Pp. [i]-[xxiv], [1]-287.

Pillars of Society, The. By Ibsen, Henrik. In *Pillars of Society and Other Plays*, ed. Havelock Ellis, London: Walter Scott, 1888, pp. [i]-[xxxii], [i]-114.

Pillars of Society, The. By Ibsen, Henrik. In *Ibsen's Prose Dramas*, ed. William Archer, 3rd ed., 5 vols., London: Walter Scott, 1904, I, [155]-284. *Filed under* Ibsen's Prose Dramas.

Pretenders, The. By Ibsen, Henrik. In *Ibsen's Prose Dramas*, ed. William Archer, 5 vols., London: Walter Scott, 1904, III, [209]-373. *Filed under* Ibsen's Prose Dramas.

Vikings at Helgeland, The. By Ibsen, Henrik. In *Ibsen's Prose Dramas*, ed. William Archer, 5 vols., London: Walter Scott, 1904, III, [125]-207. *Filed under* Ibsen's Prose Dramas.

ARCHERS OF ISLINGTON AND THE FAYRE MAYDE OF WEST CHEAP
See Wilks, Thomas Egerton. Red Crow, The.

ARCHITECT, THE
See Gypsum, Nicholas.

ARDEN, HENRY T. (pseud. of Arnold, Henry Thomas)

Armourer's Daughter, The. London: Pite & Son (printer), n.d. Pp. [i-ii], [1]-24.

Belle of the Barley-Mow, The; or, The Wooer, the Waitress, and the Willian. London: Thomas Hailes Lacy, n.d. Pp. [1]-20. [Lacy's Acting Edition].

Princess Charming; or, The Bard, the Baron, the Beauty, the Buffer, and the Bogey. London: Thomas Hailes Lacy, n.d. Pp. [1]-24. [Lacy's Acting Edition].

Right-Fall Heir, The; or, The Sea-Rover and the Fall Over. London: Thomas Hailes Lacy, n.d. Pp. [1]-26.

ARDEN OF FEVERSHAM
See Lillo, George.

AREA BELLE, THE
See Brough, William.

AREA SYLPH, THE
See Fry, Betsey.

ARIADNE
See Thurlow, Edward Hovell, Lord.

ARION
See Burnand, Francis Cowley.

ARISTODEMUS
See Burney, Frances.
See Crowe, Catharine Stevens, Mrs. John.

ARISTOPHANES

Acharnians, The.
See Frere, John Hookham (trans.).

Birds, The.
See Frere, John Hookham (trans.).

Birds, The.
See Verrall, Arthur Woolgar (trans.).

Clouds, The.
See under title.

Frogs, The.
See Hogarth, David George (trans.).

Knights, The.
See Frere, John Hookham (trans.).

Peace, The.
See Frere, John Hookham (trans.).

Peace.
See under title.

ARISTOPHANES AT OXFORD
See Y. T. O.

ARIXINA
See Pennie, John Fitzgerald.

ARKWRIGHT'S WIFE
See Taylor, Tom.

ARLINE, THE LOST CHILD
See Bellingham, Henry.

ARMADALE
See Collins, William Wilkie.

ARMED BRITON, THE
See Burke, William.

ARMGART
See Eliot, George.

ARMIDA
See Aveling, Claude.

ARMOURER OF NANTES, THE
See Bridgeman, John Vipon.

ARMOURER'S DAUGHTER, THE
See Arden, Henry T.

ARMS AND THE MAN
See Shaw, George Bernard.

ARMSTRONG, GEORGE FRANCIS

King Solomon. In *Tragedy of Israel*, London: Longmans, Green, Reader, & Dyer, 1876, Part 3, pp. [i-iv], [1]-240. *Filed under* Savage-Armstrong, George Francis.

Ugone. London: Longmans, Green, Reader, & Dyer, 1872. Pp. [iii]-[xii], [1]-251. New ed. *Filed under* Savage-Armstrong, George Francis.

ARMSTRONG, GEORGE P.

Blighted Love. New York: Wheat & Cornett, c.1877. Pp. 23-27. New York Drama, III, 31.

ARMSTRONG, WILLIAM HENRY

Turkish Lovers; or, A Pasha's Revenge. London: Thomas Hailes Lacy, n.d. Pp. [1]-42.

ARMY AND THE NAVY
See Pitt, George Dibdin. My Own Blue Bell.

ARMY WITHOUT RESERVE
See Dibdin, Charles Isaac Mungo, jr. British Amazons.

ARNAULT, A. -V.
    Germanicus.
        See Bernel, George (trans.).
ARNE, THOMAS AUGUSTINE, DR.
    Artaxerxes. Music by Arne. London: John Cumberland,
        1828. Pp. [i], [1]-24. Cumberland's British Theatre, XIX.
        Filed under Cumberland, John. Cumberland's British
        Theatre, XIX.
    Artaxerxes. In *New English Drama,* ed. W. Oxberry, 22 vols.,
        London: W. Simpkin & R. Marshall; C. Chapple, 1828,
        XXII, [i]-[x], [11]-23. *Filed under* Oxberry, William Henry.
        New English Drama, XXII.
ARNOLD, EDWIN, SIR
    Adzuma; or, The Japanese Wife. New York: Charles
        Scribner's Sons, 1893. Pp. [i]-vi, [1]-170.
    Griselda. In *Griselda and Other Poems,* London: David
        Bogue, 1856, pp. [i-iv], [1]-185.
    Passing of Muhammad, The. In *Tenth Muse and Other Poems,*
        London: Longmans, Green, 1895, pp. [i], [17]-41.
ARNOLD, EDWIN, SIR (trans.)
    Secret of Death, The. In *Secret of Death with Some Collected
        Poems,* Boston: Roberts Brothers, 1885, pp. [i], [18]-45.
    With Sa'di in the Garden; or, The Book of Love. Boston:
        Roberts Brothers, 1888. Pp. [i]-viii, [1]-211.
ARNOLD, HENRY THOMAS
    See Arden, Henry T.
ARNOLD, MALCOLM
    Mohawk Minstrels' Ninth Book of Dramas, Stump Speeches,
        Nigger Jokes, and Recitations.
        See Williams, Arthur.
ARNOLD, MATTHEW
    Empedocles on Etna. In *Poems,* London: Macmillan, 1903, II,
        [i], 245-324.
    Merope. London: Longman, Brown, Green, Longmans, &
        Roberts, 1858. Pp. [i], [1]-138.
ARNOLD, SAMUEL JAMES
    Americans, The. *Also:* The War Whoop. Music by King, M.
        P.; Braham, John. London: Lowndes & Hobbs (printer),
        n.d. Pp. [1]-28. Libretto.
    Devil's Bridge, The. New York: D. Longworth, 1817. Pp.
        [3]-57.
    Devil's Bridge, The. London: John Cumberland, n.d. Pp.
        [1]-52. Cumberland's British Theatre, XLII. *Filed under*
        Cumberland, John. Cumberland's British Theatre, XLII.
    Foul Deeds Will Rise. London: Barker & Son, n.d. Pp.
        [i]-[viii], [9]-47.
    Frederick the Great; or, The Heart of a Soldier. Music by
        Cooke, T. London: John Miller, 1815. Pp. [1]-18.
        Libretto.
    Free and Easy. London: John Cumberland, n.d. Pp. [1]-50.
        [Cumberland's British Theatre].
    Free and Easy. London: John Cumberland & Son, n.d. Pp.
        [1]-50. Cumberland's British Theatre, XLII. *Filed under*
        Cumberland, John. Cumberland's British Theatre, XLII.
    Freischutz, Der.
        See Oxenford, John.
    Illusion; or, The Trances of Nourjahad. Music by Kelly,
        Michael. London: J. Barker, 1818. Pp. [i]-[x], [1]-39.
    Jean de Paris. London: Whittingham & Arliss, 1814. Pp.
        [1]-43.
    King's Proxy, The. Music by Cooke, T. London: John
        Miller, 1815. Pp. [1]-18. Libretto.
    Maid and the Magpye, The; or, Which Is the Thief? Music by
        Smart, H. London: John Miller, 1815. Pp. [i-v], [1]-52.
    Man and Wife; or, More Secrets Than One. London:
        Richard Phillips, 1809. Pp. [i-viii], [1]-90.
    Maniac!, The; or, The Swiss Banditti. Music by Bishop,
        Henry. London: Lowndes & Hobbs (printer), n.d. Pp.
        [1]-20. Libretto.
    My Aunt. London: John Miller, 1815. Pp. [1]-16. Libretto.
    My Aunt. Boston: C. Callender, 1820. Pp. [1]-35.
    Plots!; or, The North Tower. Music by King, M. P. London:
        Lowndes & Hobbs (printer), n.d. Pp. [1]-19. Libretto.
    Prior Claim, A.
        See Pye, Henry James.

Sergeant's Wife, The. Boston: William V. Spencer, 1855. Pp.
    [1]-[30]. Spencer's Boston Theatre, 19.
Shipwreck, The. In *New English Drama,* ed. W. Oxberry, 22
    vols., London: W. Simpkin & R. Marshall; C. Chapple,
    1820, IX, [1-2], [i]-[iv], [1]-28. *Filed under* Oxberry,
    William Henry. New English Drama, IX.
Up All Night; or, The Smuggler's Cave. Music by King, M.
    P. London: Lowndes & Hobbs (printer), n.d. Pp. [1]-24.
    Libretto.
Veteran Tar, The. Music by Arnold, Samuel, Dr. London: J.
    Barker, 1801. Pp. [1]-39. Libretto.
War Whoop, The.
    See Americans, The.
Woodman's Hut, The. In *New English Drama,* ed. W.
    Oxberry, 22 vols., London: W. Simpkin & R. Marshall;
    C. Chapple, 1820, IV, [i-vi], [1]-38. *Filed under* Oxberry,
    William Henry. New English Drama, IV.
Woodman's Hut, The. Music by Horn. London: John Miller,
    1814. Pp. [i-vi], [1]-46.
ARNOLD OF WINKELRIED
    See Lemon, Mark.
ARRAH-NA-POGUE
    See Boucicault, Dionysius Lardner.
ART AND ARTIFICE
    See Brougham, John.
ART AND LOVE
    See Dubourg, Augustus W.
ART IN THE CITY
    See Anstey, F.
    See Ridge, William Pett.
ART OF SEEING
    See Gilbert, William Schwenck. Eyes and No Eyes.
ARTAXERXES
    See Arne, Thomas Augustine, Dr.
ARTFUL DODGE, THE
    See Blanchard, Edward Litt Leman.
ARTHUR THE KING
    See Akhurst, William M.
ARTHUR'S BAKERY CO.
    See Silvester, Frank.
ARTIST'S MODEL, AN
    See Hall, Owen.
ARTIST'S WIFE, THE
    See A'Beckett, Gilbert Abbott.
ARTS AND HEARTS
    See Cooper, Herbert B.
ARTS IN AN ATTIC
    See Lunn, Joseph. Lofty Projects.
AS LIKE AS TWO PEAS
    See Lille, Herbert.
AS LONDON LIVES
    See Harvey, Frank.
AS ONCE IN MAY
    See Manners, John Hartley.
AS YOU LIKE IT
    See Anderson, Mary (arr.).
    See Hare, John (arr.).
    See Kemble, John Philip (arr.).
    See Macready, William Charles (arr.).
    See Shakespeare, William.
ASCHER, ISIDORE GORDON
    Circumstances Alter Cases. London & New York: Samuel
        French, n.d. Pp. [1]-20. [French's Acting Edition].
ASHBY MANOR
    See Allingham, William.
ASHBY-STERRY, JOSEPH
    Katharine and Petruchio; or, The Shaming of the True. In
        Drawing-Room Plays and Parlour Pantomimes, ed. Clem-
        ent Scott, London: Stanley Rivers, 1870, pp. [i], [271]-306.
ASHE, NICHOLAS
    Panthea; or, The Susan Captive. Dublin: J. Halpen (printer),
        n.d. Pp. [i-iv], [1]-70.
ASHE, THOMAS
    Sorrows of Hypsipyle, The. London: Bell & Daldy, 1867. Pp.
        [i-iv], [1]-116.

ASHORE AND AFLOAT
   See Hazlewood, Colin Henry.
ASHTAROTH
   See Gordon, Adam Lindsay.
ASHWORTH, JOHN H. E.
   Leonore. Music by Ashworth, John H. E. London: Dunlop, n.d. Pp. [1]-30. Libretto.
ASK NO QUESTIONS
   See Selby, Charles.
ASLOG
   See Winbolt, Frederick I.
ASMODEUS
   See Archer, Thomas.
ASSASSIN OF THE MOUNTAIN
   See Kerr, John. Histerkan.
ASSAULT AND BATTERY
   See Norwood, Eille.
ASSIGNATION, THE
   See A'Beckett, Gilbert Abbott.
ASTON, JOSEPH
   Conscience. New York: D. Longworth, 1816. Pp. [1]-70.
ASTROLOGER, THE
   See Dibdin, Charles Isaac Mungo, jr.
AT A CONCERT
   See Ridge, William Pett.
AT A HYPNOTIC SEANCE
   See Anstey, F.
AT A SMOKER
   See Ridge, William Pett.
AT A VEGETARIAN RESTAURANT
   See Anstey, F.
AT HOME (anon.)
   London: C. Chapple, 1813. Pp. [1]-39.
AT MOLESEY LOCK
   See Ridge, William Pett.
AT SIXES AND SEVENS
   See Morton, John Maddison.
AT THE BOOKING OFFICE
   See Ridge, William Pett.
AT THE BOOKSTALL
   See Ridge, William Pett.
AT THE CONFECTIONER'S
   See Anstey, F.
AT THE CROSS ROADS
   See Dilley, Joseph J.
AT THE GALLERY DOOR
   See Ridge, William Pett.
AT THE NATIONAL GALLERY
   See Ridge, William Pett.
AT THE WILD WEST
   See Anstey, F.
AT THE ZOO
   See Ridge, William Pett.
ATALANTA
   See Talfourd, Francis.
ATALANTA IN CALYDON
   See Swinburne, Algernon Charles.
ATCHI!
   See Morton, John Maddison.
ATHALIAH
   See Boswell, Robert Bruce (trans.).
ATHALIE
   See Bartholomew, William (trans.).
ATHELWOLD
   See Smith, William Henry.
ATHENIAN CAPTIVE, THE
   See Talfourd, Thomas Noon.
ATHERSTONE, EDWIN
   Love, Poetry, Philosophy, and Gout. In *Dramatic Works of Edwin Atherstone,* ed. Mary Elizabeth Atherstone, London: Elliot Stock, 1888, pp. [195]-304. *Filed under* Collected Works.

Pelopidas; or, The Deliverer of Thebes. In *Dramatic Works of Edwin Atherstone,* ed. Mary Elizabeth Atherstone, London: Elliot Stock, 1888, pp. [i]-vi, [1]-118. *Filed under* Collected Works.
   Philip. In *Dramatic Works of Edwin Atherstone,* ed. Mary Elizabeth Atherstone, London: Elliot Stock, 1888, pp. [119]-193. *Filed under* Collected Works.
ATKYNS, SAMUEL
   Battle Bridge in Ancient Times; or, Alwyn the Saxon Chief. Pp. [21]-37. Act II only. Manuscript. *Filed under* Collected Works.
   Bright-Eyed Emma; or, The Son of the Sea. Pp. [1]-[61]. Manuscript. *Filed under* Collected Works.
   Deux Divorces, Les. 9 leaves. Act I only. Manuscript. *Filed under* Collected Works.
   Poacher's Wife, The. Pp. [1]-[14]. Manuscript. *Filed under* Collected Works.
   Rookwood. 25 leaves. Act II only. Manuscript. *Filed under* Collected Works.
   Witch's Stone, The; or, The Warrior of the Lonely Grave! 31 leaves. Acts I and II only. Manuscript. *Filed under* Collected Works.
   Zulor, the Circassian Chief; or, The Robbers of Mount Caucasus! Pp. [i-ii], [1]-[57]. Manuscript. *Filed under* Collected Works.
ATLANTIS DESTROYED
   See Galt, John. Apostate, The.
ATMA BODHA
   See Taylor, J. (trans.).
ATONEMENT
   See Muskerry, William.
   See Poole, John.
ATREUS AND THYESTES
   See Sinnett, Edward.
ATROCIOUS CRIMINAL
   See Simpson, John Palgrave.
   See Simpson, John Palgrave. Awful Criminal, An.
ATTEMPT TO PLEASE
   See Maclaren, Archibald. Touch at the Times, A.
ATTIC STORY, THE
   See Morton, John Maddison.
ATTILA (anon.)
   London: T. & W. Boone, 1832. Pp. [i-vi], [1]-159.
ATTILA, MY ATTILA!
   See Field, Michael.
AUBERGE DES ADRETS!
   See Selby, Charles. Robert Macaire.
AUCHINDRANE
   See Scott, Walter, Sir.
AULD ACQAINTANCE
   See Dilley, Joseph J.
AULD LANG SYNE
   See Pocock, Isaac. Rob Roy MacGregor.
AULD ROBIN GRAY
   See Macfarren, George.
AUNT AND THE ANGEL, THE
   See Bampfylde, Coplestone Richard George Warwick.
AUNT CHARLOTTE'S MAID
   See Morton, John Maddison.
AUNT MADGE
   See Davis, Lillie.
AUNT MINERVA
   See Tudor, Catherine.
AURORA FLOYD
   See Hazlewood, Colin Henry.
   See Webster, Benjamin, jr.
AUSTERLITZ
   See Haines, John Thomas.
AUSTIN, ALFRED
   England's Darling. London: Macmillan, 1896. Pp. [i]-[xx], [1]-94. 2nd ed.
   Fortunatus the Pessimist. London: Macmillan, 1892. Pp. [i-vi], [1]-179.
   Prince Lucifer. London: Macmillan, 1891. Pp. [i-vi], [1]-193. 3rd ed.

Savonarola. London: Macmillan, 1891. Pp. [i]-[x], [1]-306.

Tower of Babel, The. Edinburgh & London: William Blackwood & Sons, 1874. Pp. [i-vi], [1]-256.

Tower of Babel, The. London: Macmillan, 1890. Pp. [i]-[x], [1]-192.

AUTOMATIC PHYSIOGNOMIST, THE
　See Anstey, F.

AVALANCHE, THE
　See Harris, Augustus Glossop.

AVARE
　See Van Laun, Henri (trans.). Miser, The.

AVELING, CLAUDE
　Armida. Music by Gluck. London: Grand Opera Syndicate, n.d. Pp. [1]-23. Libretto.

AVELING, ELEANOR MARX, MRS. EDWARD (trans.)
　Enemy of the People, An. By Ibsen, Henrik. In *Ibsen's Prose Dramas*, ed. William Archer, 5 vols., London: Walter Scott, 1904, II, [103]-237. *Filed under* Archer, William. Ibsen's Prose Dramas.

　Lady from the Sea, The. By Ibsen, Henrik. London: T. Fisher Unwin, 1890. Pp. [1]-184. *Filed under* Marx-Aveling, Eleanor.

AVENGING SPIRIT
　See Wynne, John. Advocate of Durango, The.

AVVENTURA DI SCARAMUCCIA, UN' (anon.)
　Music by Ricci. London: Mitchell's Royal Subscription Library, 1838. Pp. [1]-88. Libretto.

AWAKING
　See Clarke, Campbell.

AWAY WITH MELANCHOLY
　See Morton, John Maddison.

AWFUL CRIMINAL
　See Simpson, John Palgrave. Atrocious Criminal, An.
　See Simpson, John Palgrave.

AWKWARD ARRIVAL, AN
　See Coyne, Joseph Stirling.

AYRES, ARTHUR
　His Own Guest. Written with Blake, Paul. London & New York: Samuel French, n.d. Pp. [1]-40. [Lacy's Acting Edition].

AYRSHIRE TRAGEDY
　See Scott, Walter, Sir. Auchindrane.

AYTON, RICHARD
　Rendezvous, The. London: William Fearman, 1818. Pp. [1]-36.

　Rendezvous, The. London: John Cumberland, 1828. Pp. [1]-28. Cumberland's British Theatre, XVII. *Filed under* Cumberland, John. Cumberland's British Theatre, XVII.

AYTOUN, WILLIAM EDMONDSTONE
　Firmilian. By T. Percy Jones (pseud.). New York: Redfield, 1854. Pp. [i]-[xii], [13]-165.

AZAEL, THE PRODIGAL
　See Fitzball, Edward.
　See Webb, Charles (trans.).

AZAMOGLAN, THE
　See Dixon, William Hepworth.

B., A.
　Girls of the Period, The. In *Drawing Room Plays and Parlour Pantomimes*, ed. Clement Scott, London: Stanley Rivers, 1870, pp. [i], [341]-360.

B. B.
　See Williams, Montagu Stephen.

BABES IN THE WOOD
　See A'Beckett, Gilbert Arthur.
　See Barry, J. L.
　See Buckstone, John Baldwin.
　See McGromagill, Osburn Blackboehm.
　See Taylor, Tom.
　See Thorn, Geoffrey.

BABES IN THE WOOD, THE; OR, HARLEQUIN KING OF THE FAIRIES AND THE CRUEL H'UNCLE (anon.)
　Birmingham: John Tonks (printer), n.d. Pp. [i], [1]-11. Libretto.

BABES IN THE WOOD AND THE BOLD ROBIN HOOD, THE
　See McNeill, A. D.

BABES IN THE WOOD AND THE GOOD LITTLE FAIRY BIRDS!, THE
　See Byron, Henry James.

BABES IN THE WOOD CONTINUED, THE
　See Churchill, Henry George.

BABES IN THE WOOD, ROBIN HOOD AND HIS MERRY MEN, AND HARLEQUIN WHO KILLED COCK ROBIN?
　See Harris, Augustus Henry Glossop.

BABES IN THE WOODS, THE
　See Sturgess, Arthur.

BABIL AND BIJOU
　See Boucicault, Dionysius Lardner.

BABINGTON
　See Doubleday, Thomas.

BABO, JAMES MARCUS
　Otto of Wittelsbach.
　　See Thompson, Benjamin (trans.).

BABYLON
　See Capper, Richard.

BACCHANALS, THE
　See Milman, Henry Hart (trans.).

BACCHUS AND ARIADNE
　See Mereweather, Cavaliere, Rev.

BACHELOR OF ARTS, A
　See Hardwicke, Pelham.

BACHELOR'S BEDROOM, THE
　See Mathews, Charles James.

BACHELOR'S BUTTONS!
　See Stirling, Edward.

BACHELOR'S DIVORCE, A
　See Lease, B. C.

BACHELOR'S FARE
　See Parry, John. Helpless Animals!

BACHELOR'S TORMENTS
　See Rodwell, James Thomas Gooderham.

BACKWARD CHILD, A
　See Childe-Pemberton, Harriet Louisa.

BAD DJINN AND THE GOOD SPIRIT
　See Byron, Henry James. Camaralzaman and the Fair Badoura.

BAD LADY BETTY
　See Scull, W. D.

BAD PENNY, A
　See Lestocq, William.

BADDELEY, G. C.
　End of the Tether, The; or, A Legend of the Patent Office. London: Thomas Hailes Lacy, n.d. Pp. [1]-19. [Lacy's Acting Edition].

BADDELEY, WELBORE ST. CLAIR
　Death of Antar, The. In *Bedoueen Legends and Other Poems*, London: Robson & Kerslake, 1883, pp. [i], [56]-97.

　Drama. In *Dramatic and Narrative Sketches*, London: Robson & Kerslake, 1885, pp. [63]-83.

　Enrico. In *Dramatic and Narrative Sketches*, London: Robson & Kerslake, 1885, pp. [i-iv], [1]-61.

　Legend of the Death of Antar. In *Legend of the Death of Antar . . . and Lyrical Poems, Songs, and Sonnets*, London: David Bogue, 1881, pp. [i-x], [1]-58.

　Return of Tasso to Sorrento, The. In *Bedoueen Legends and Other Poems*, London: Robson & Kerslake, 1883, pp. [i], [98]-107.

BAFFLED SPINSTER, THE
　See Smale, Edith C., Mrs. T. E.

BAGOT, ARTHUR GREVILLE
　Which? London & New York: Samuel French, n.d. Pp. [1]-20. [Lacy's Acting Edition].

BAILDON, ARTHUR
　Giralda; or, The New Psyche. Music by Adam. London: Charles Dickens & Vans, Crystal Palace Press, n.d. Pp. [1]-40. Libretto.

Water Carrier, The. *Also:* Les Deux Journées. *Also:* Der Wassertrager. Music by Cherubini. London & New York: Boosey, n.d. Pp. [i-iv], 1-200. Royal Edition. Vocal score.

Water Carrier, The. Music by Cherubini. London: William C. Bryant, 1871. Pp. [i], [1]-31. Parepa-Rosa Grand English Opera. Libretto.

BAILDON, HENRY BELLYSE

Rosamund. London: Longmans, Green, 1875. Pp. [i]-[viii], [1]-85.

BAILEY, PHILIP JAMES

Age, The. London: Chapman & Hall, 1858. Pp. [i-ii], [1]-204.

Festus. London: William Pickering, 1839. Pp. [i-iv], [1]-[361].

Festus. New York: James Miller, n.d. Pp. [1]-391. 30th ed.

BAILEY, WILLIAM

Grimaldi. London: W. Simpkin & R. Marshall, 1822. Pp. [iii]-[xviii], [1]-101.

BAILIFF, THE

See Broughton, Frederick William.

BAILIFF'S BET

See Peake, Richard Brinsley. Walk for a Wager!

BAILLIE, JOANNA

Alienated Manor, The. In *Dramas,* 3 vols., London: Longman, Rees, Orme, Brown, Green, & Longman, 1836, I, [121]-249. *Filed under* Collected Works.

Beacon, The. In *Series of Plays . . . ,* new ed., London: Longman, Hurst, Rees, Orme, & Brown, 1821, III, [267]-314.

Bride, The. London: Henry Colburn, 1828. Pp. [i]-x, [1]-112.

Bride, The. In *Dramas,* 3 vols., London: Longman, Rees, Orme, Brown, Green, & Longman, 1836, III, [279]-368. *Filed under* Collected Works.

Constantine Paleologus; or, The Last of the Caesars. In *Miscellaneous Plays,* 2nd ed., London: Longman, Hurst, Rees, & Orme, 1805, pp. [279]-438.

Country Inn, The. In *Miscellaneous Plays,* 2nd ed., London: Longman, Hurst, Rees, & Orme, 1805, pp. [137]-278.

Dream, The. In *Series of Plays . . . ,* new ed., London: Longman, Hurst, Rees, Orme, & Brown, 1821, III, [101]-171.

Election, The. In *Series of Plays . . . ,* new ed., London: Longman, Hurst, Rees, Orme, & Brown, 1821, II, [iii]-[xii], [1]-108.

Enthusiasm. In *Dramas,* 3 vols., London: Longman, Rees, Orme, Brown, Green, & Longman, 1836, II, [321]-442. *Filed under* Collected Works.

Ethwald, Part 1. In *Series of Plays . . . ,* new ed., London: Longman, Hurst, Rees, Orme, & Brown, 1821, II, 109-237.

Ethwald, Part 2. In *Series of Plays . . . ,* new ed., London: Longman, Hurst, Rees, Orme, & Brown, 1821, II, [239]-360.

Family Legend, The. Edinburgh: James Ballantyne (printer), 1810. Pp. [i]-[xiv], [i]-iv, [5]-96. 2nd ed.

Family Legend, The. New York: D. Longworth, 1810. Pp. [i]-[viii], [9]-84. Promptbook.

Henriquez. In *Dramas,* 3 vols., London: Longman, Rees, Orme, Brown, Green, & Longman, 1836, I, [251]-370. *Filed under* Collected Works.

Homicide, The. In *Dramas,* 3 vols., London: Longman, Rees, Orme, Brown, Green, & Longman, 1836, III, [165]-278. *Filed under* Collected Works.

Martyr, The. London: Longman, Rees, Orme, Brown, & Green, 1826. Pp. [i]-[xviii], [1]-78.

Martyr, The. In *Dramas,* 3 vols., London: Longman, Rees, Orme, Brown, Green, & Longman, 1836, I, [371]-464. *Filed under* Collected Works.

Match, The. In *Dramas,* 3 vols., London: Longman, Rees, Orme, Brown, Green, & Longman, 1836, III, [369]-495. *Filed under* Collected Works.

Orra. In *Series of Plays . . . ,* new ed., London: Longman, Hurst, Rees, Orme, & Brown, 1821, III, [i]-[xxxii], [1]-100.

Phantom, The. In *Dramas,* 3 vols., London: Longman, Rees, Orme, Brown, Green, & Longman, 1836, II, [215]-319. *Filed under* Collected Works.

Rayner. In *Miscellaneous Plays,* 2nd ed., London: Longman, Hurst, Rees, & Orme, 1805, pp. [i]-[xxiv], [1]-136.

Romiero. In *Dramas,* 3 vols., London: Longman, Rees, Orme, Brown, Green, & Longman, 1836, I, [iii]-[x], [1]-119. *Filed under* Collected Works.

Second Marriage, The. In *Series of Plays . . . ,* new ed., London: Longman, Hurst, Rees, Orme, & Brown, 1821, II, [361]-478.

Separation, The. In *Dramas,* 3 vols., London: Longman, Rees, Orme, Brown, Green, & Longman, 1836, II, [iii]-[xiv], [1]-106. *Filed under* Collected Works.

Siege, The. In *Series of Plays . . . ,* new ed., London: Longman, Hurst, Rees, Orme, & Brown, 1821, III, [173]-265.

Stripling, The. In *Dramas,* 3 vols., London: Longman, Rees, Orme, Brown, Green, & Longman, 1836, II, 107-214. *Filed under* Collected Works.

Witchcraft. In *Dramas,* 3 vols., London: Longman, Rees, Orme, Brown, Green, & Longman, 1836, III, [1]-164. *Filed under* Collected Works.

BAIN, DONALD

Olden Times; or, The Rising of the Session. Edinburgh: John Menzies, 1843. Pp. [1]-108. 2nd ed.

BAJAZET

See Boswell, Robert Bruce (trans.).

BAKER, GEORGE MELVILLE

Under a Veil.

See Roberts, Randal Howland.

BALANCE OF COMFORT, THE

See Bernard, William Bayle.

See Raymond, Richard John.

BALDER, PART 1

See Dobell, Sydney Thompson.

BALDUR

See Anderton, H. Orsmond.

BALFOUR, MARY DEVENS

Kathleen O'Neil. Belfast: Archbold & Dugan (printer), 1814. Pp. [1]-54.

BALL, EDWARD

See Fitzball, Edward.

BALL, WILLIAM

Belshazzar's Feast. London: J. Dickinson, 1834. Pp. [i-vi], [1]-47.

Freemen and Slaves. London: Saunders & Otley, 1838. Pp. [i-iv], [1]-136.

BALL NEXT DOOR, THE

See Rockingham, Charles, Sir.

BALLET GIRL, THE

See Tanner, James Tolman.

BALLO IN MASCHERA, UN

See Kenney, Charles Lamb (trans.).

BALLOON, THE

See Darnley, J. Herbert.

BAMBOOZLING

See Wilks, Thomas Egerton.

BAMPFYLDE, COPLESTONE RICHARD GEORGE WARWICK

Aunt and the Angel, The; or, Funkiboo's Fix. London: Fuller's (printer) (priv.), 1899. Pp. [1]-[40].

BAMPFYLDE MOORE CAREW

See Jerrold, Douglas William.

BANDIT, THE (anon.)

In *New British Theatre,* London: A. J. Valpy (printer), 1814, I, [i], [379]-394, 397-432. Text incomplete.

BANDIT, THE

See Burges, James Bland.

BANDIT MERCHANT

See Farrell, John. Dumb Girl of Genoa, The.

See Farrell, John. Maid of Genoa!, The.

BANDIT OF THE BLIND MINE, THE

See Milner, Henry M.

BANDOS DE VERONA, LOS: MONTESCOS Y CAPULETES

See Cosens, Frederick William (trans.).

BANFIELD, THOMAS C. (trans.)
William Tell. By Schiller. London: Black, Young, & Young, 1831. Pp. [ii]-[vii], [1]-[168].
BANG UP!
See Dibdin, Charles Isaac Mungo, jr.
BANIM, JOHN
Damon and Pythias. Written with Sheil, Richard Lalor. London: John Warren, 1821. Pp. [i]-viii, [1]-70. *Filed under* Sheil, Richard Lalor.
Damon and Pythias. Written with Sheil, Richard Lalor. London: John Warren, 1821. Pp. [i]-viii, [1]-70. 2nd ed. *Filed under* Banim, John.
Damon and Pythias. Written with Sheil, Richard Lalor. In *British Drama*, 12 vols., London: John Dicks, 1865, III, [831]-848. *Filed under* Banim, John.
Sergeant's Wife, The. [Philadelphia: Carey, Hart, Thompson, & W. Marshall, 1835]. Pp. [94]-129. Title page lacking. [Alexander's Modern Acting Drama].
BANK NOTE, THE
See Macready, William.
BANKER'S DAUGHTER
See Webster, Benjamin, jr. Aurora Floyd.
BANKS, BILLY
Mohawk Minstrels' Fifth Book of Dramas, Dialogues, and Drolleries, The. Written with Howard, Walter; Hay, T. J.; Campbell, Thomas. London: Francis, Day & Hunter, n.d. Pp. [i-iv], 1-108.
BANKS OF THE ELBE
See Planché, James Robinson. All in the Dark.
BANKS OF THE HUDSON, THE
See Dibdin, Thomas John.
BANTOCK, GRANVILLE
Rameses II. London: David Stott, 1892. Pp. [iii]-[xvi], [1]-112.
BARARK JOHNSON
See Reeve, William.
BARBARA
See Jerome, Jerome Klapka.
BARBARA ALLEN
See Dibdin, Charles Isaac Mungo, jr.
BARBAROSSA
See Brown, John.
BARBER, JAMES
Comic Opera (untitled). In *Times; or, Views of Society*, London: William Fearman, 1819, pp. [i], [75]-122. *Filed under* Appendix.
Dame de St. Tropez!, La; or, The Poisoner! London: John Duncombe, n.d. Pp. [3]-44. [Duncombe's Edition]. Promptbook.
First Comedy (untitled). In *Times; or, Views of Society*, London: William Fearman, 1819, pp. [123]-144. *Filed under* Appendix.
Jonathan!; or, The Man of Two Masters. London: Duncombe & Moon, n.d. <wrps. Thomas Hailes Lacy>. Pp. [1]-28. Duncombe's Edition <wrps. New British Theatre (late Duncombe's), 490>.
Memoirs of the D*l, The; or, The Mystic Bell of Ronquerolles.** London: John Duncombe, n.d. Pp. [1]-44. Duncombe's Edition.
Second Comedy (untitled). In *Times; or, Views of Society*, London: William Fearman, 1819, pp. [145]-169. *Filed under* Appendix.
Tragedy (untitled). In *Times; or, Views of Society*, London: William Fearman, 1819, pp. [171]-207. *Filed under* Appendix.
Weaver of Lyons!, The; or, The Three Conscripts. London & New York: Samuel French, n.d. Pp. [3]-19. [Lacy's Acting Edition].
BARBER, THE
See Fitzball, Edward.
BARBER AND THE BRAVO, THE
See Vernier, Isabella.
BARBER BARON, THE
See Raymond, Richard John.
See Thackeray, Thomas James.

BARBER OF BAGDAD, THE
See Fitzball, Edward.
BARBER OF BATH, THE
See Farnie, Henry Brougham.
BARBER OF SEVILLE
See Barbiere, Il.
See Fawcett, John.
See Macfarren, Natalia (trans.).
See Maggioni, Manfredo (trans.). Barbiere di Siviglia, Il.
See Mould, Jacob Wrey (trans.).
BARBERS OF BASSORA, THE
See Morton, John Maddison.
BARBIER, P. J.
Jeanne d'Arc.
See Lyster, Frederic (trans.).
BARBIERE, IL (anon.)
Also: The Barber of Seville. Music by Rossini. London & New York: Boosey, n.d. Pp. [i-iv], [1]-233. Royal Edition. Vocal score.
BARBIERE DI SIVIGLIA
See Macfarren, Natalia (trans.). Barber of Seville, The.
See Maggioni, Manfredo (trans.).
See Mould, Jacob Wrey (trans.). Barber of Seville, The.
BARCLAY, JAMES M.
Lesson in Love, A. London: John Duncombe, n.d. Pp. [3]-34. Duncombe's Edition.
My Friend Thompson! London: John Cumberland, n.d. Pp. [1]-30. Cumberland's Minor Theatre, XII. *Filed under* Cumberland, John. Cumberland's Minor Theatre, XII.
My Friend Thompson! London: John Cumberland, n.d. Pp. [1]-30. [Cumberland's Minor Theatre].
BARD, THE BARON, THE BEAUTY, THE BUFFER, AND THE BOGEY
See Arden, Henry T. Princess Charming.
BARDELL V. PICKWICK
See Barrymore, William.
BARDELL VERSUS PICKWICK
See Hollingshead, John.
BARDELL VERSUS PICKWICK, VERSIFIED AND DIVERSIFIED
See Gem, T. H.
BAREFACED IMPOSTERS
See Taylor, Tom.
BARKER, GEORGE
Country Gentleman, The; or, The Force of Gratitude. York: M. W. Carrall (printer) (priv.), 1828. Pp. [1]-72.
BARLOW, GEORGE
Jesus of Nazareth. London (Westminster): Roxburghe Press, n.d. Pp. [1]-[7], 10-188. Text incomplete.
Two Marriages, The. London: Remington, 1878. Pp. [i-iv], [1]-87.
BARMBY, BEATRICE HELEN
Gísli Súrsson. London (Westminster): Archibald Constable, 1900. Pp. [v]-[xxv], 1-206.
BARMBY, JAMES
Beauty and the Beast. Music by Rogers, T. New York: Happy Hours, c.1879. Pp. [7]-25. Text complete. Acting Drama, 138.
BARMECIDE
See Milner, Henry M.
BARNABY RUDGE
See Selby, Charles.
BARNETT, BENJAMIN
Out on the Loose.
See Barnett, Morris.
BARNETT, CHARLES ZACHARY
Bohemians of Paris, The. London: Thomas Hailes Lacy, n.d. Pp. [3]-52. [New British Theatre, 381].
Bravo, The; or, The Bridge of Sighs! London: John Duncombe, n.d. Pp. [1]-34. Duncombe's Edition.
Caesar Borgia, the Scourge of Venice! London: John Duncombe, n.d. Pp. [1]-28. Duncombe's Edition.
Cateran's Son, The; or, The Dread of Military Punishment. N.p.: n.pub., n.d. Pp. [329]-340. Title page lacking.

Christmas Carol, A; or, The Miser's Warning! London: John Duncombe, n.d. Pp. [1]-26. Duncombe's Edition.

Claude Lorraine; or, The Peasant, Libertine, and Brigand. London: J. Pattie, n.d. Pp. [1]-51.

Dominique the Possessed; or, The Devil and the Deserter. London: John Duncombe, n.d. Pp. [1]-24. Duncombe's Edition.

Don Caesar de Bazan!; or, Maritana the Gypsey! London: John Duncombe, n.d. Pp. [1]-48. Duncombe's Acting Edition of the British Theatre, 405.

Dream of Fate, The; or, Sarah the Jewess. London: Thomas Hailes Lacy, n.d. Pp. [1]-38. New British Theatre (late Duncombe's), 239.

Farinelli. Music by Barnett, John. London: John Duncombe, n.d. Pp. [1]-46. Duncombe's Edition. Libretto.

Linda, the Pearl of Savoy. London: Thomas Hailes Lacy, n.d. Pp. [1]-42. New British Theatre (late Duncombe's), 376.

Loss of the Royal George, The; or, The Fatal Land Breeze. London: John Duncombe, n.d. <wrps. Thomas Hailes Lacy>. Pp. [1]-46. Duncombe's Edition <wrps. New British Theatre (late Duncombe's), 582>.

Mariner's Dream, The; or, The Jew of Plymouth. London: J. Pattie, n.d. Pp. [i]-ii, [1]-49.

Midnight: The Thirteenth Chime; or, Old Saint Paul's. London & New York: Samuel French, n.d. Pp. [1]-32. [Lacy's Acting Edition].

Minute Gun at Sea!, The. London: Thomas Hailes Lacy, n.d. Pp. [1]-45.

Oliver Twist; or, The Parish Boy's Progress. London: Thomas Hailes Lacy, n.d. Pp. [1]-48. *Filed under* Oliver Twist (anon.).

Oliver Twist; or, The Parish Boy's Progress. London: John Duncombe, n.d. Pp. [1]-38. Duncombe's Edition.

Phantom Bride, The; or, The Castilian Bandit. London: John Duncombe, n.d. Pp. [3]-32. Duncombe's Edition.

Polka, La; or, Dancing for the Million! London: John Duncombe, n.d. Pp. [1]-21. Duncombe's Acting Edition of the British Theatre, 394.

Rise of the Rotheschildes, The; or, The Honest Jew of Frankfort. London: J. Pattie, n.d. Pp. [1]-46. Pattie's Modern Stage, 66.

Swing! London: John Duncombe, n.d. Pp. [1]-24. Duncombe's Edition.

Victorine; or, The Orphan of Paris! London: John Duncombe, n.d. Pp. [1]-24. Duncombe's Acting Edition of the British Theatre, 68.

Vow of Silence, The; or, The Old Blacksmith's Hovel. N.p.: n.pub., n.d. Pp. [215]-226. Title page lacking.

William the Fourth. *Also:* The Youthful Days of William the Fourth; or, British Tars in 1782. London: John Duncombe, n.d. Pp. [1]-24. [Duncombe's Edition].

Youthful Days of William the Fourth, The; or, British Tars in 1782. *Also:* William the Fourth. London: John Duncombe, n.d. Pp. [i], [1]-24. Duncombe's Acting Edition of the British Theatre, 63.

BARNETT, MORRIS

Bold Dragoons, The. London: Thomas Hailes Lacy, n.d. Pp. [1]-29. [Lacy's Acting Edition].

Bold Dragoons, The. New York: Samuel French, n.d. Pp. [1]-29. French's Standard Drama, 144.

Circumstantial Evidence! London: Thomas Hailes Lacy, n.d. Pp. [1]-15. Lacy's Acting Edition, 65.

Lilian Gervais. London: Thomas Hailes Lacy, n.d. Pp. [1]-39. [Lacy's Acting Edition].

Love by Lantern-Light. Music by Offenbach. London: Thomas Hailes Lacy, n.d. Pp. [1]-20. [Lacy's Acting Edition]. Libretto.

Married Un-Married. London: Thomas Hailes Lacy, n.d. Pp. [1]-23. [Lacy's Acting Edition]. Promptbook.

Married Un-Married. London: Thomas Hailes Lacy, n.d. Pp. [1]-23. [Lacy's Acting Edition].

Monsieur Jacques. London: John Duncombe, n.d. Pp. [3]-23. Duncombe's Edition.

Mrs. G—, of The Golden Pippin! London: John Duncombe, n.d. Pp. [1]-26. Duncombe's Edition.

Out on the Loose. Written with Barnett, Benjamin. London: Thomas Hailes Lacy, n.d. Pp. [1]-22. [Lacy's Acting Edition].

Power and Principle. London: Thomas Hailes Lacy, n.d. Pp. [1]-31.

Sarah Blange.
See Sarah the Creole.

Sarah the Creole; or, A Snake in the Grass. *Also:* Sarah Blange. London: Thomas Hailes Lacy, n.d. Pp. [1]-51. [Lacy's Acting Edition].

Serious Family, The. New York: Samuel French, n.d. Pp. [3]-48. French's Standard Drama, 79. Promptbook.

Serve Him Right! Written with Mathews, Charles James. London: Thomas Hailes Lacy, n.d. Pp. [1]-44. [Lacy's Acting Edition].

Spirit of the Rhine, The. London: John Duncombe, n.d. Pp. [1]-26. Duncombe's Edition.

Tact!; or, The Wrong Box. London: John Duncombe, n.d. Pp. [1]-34. Duncombe's Edition.

Yankee Peddler; or, Old Times in Virginia. New York: Wheat & Cornett, c.1877. Pp. [26]-32. New York Drama, II, 23.

Yankee Peddler; or, Old Times in Virginia. New York: Samuel French, n.d. Pp. [1]-16. Minor Drama, 169.

Yellow Kids, The. London: John Duncombe, n.d. Pp. [1]-22. Duncombe's Edition.

BARNETT, RICHARD WHELDON

White Cockade, The. Written with Harris, Charles. London: n.pub., n.d. Pp. [i]-iv, [5]-32. Libretto.

BARNEY THE BARON
See Lover, Samuel.

BARON, THE
See Holcroft, Fanny (trans.).

BARON FITZARDERN (anon.)
London: William Pickering, 1845. Pp. [i-vi], [1]-65.

BARON, THE BRIDE AND THE BATTERY
See A'Beckett, Gilbert Arthur. Last of the Legends, The.

BARON'S WAGER, THE
See Young, Charles Lawrence, Sir.

BARONESS, THE
See Dick, Cotsford.

BARONET ABROAD AND THE RUSTIC PRIMA DONNA, THE
See Horne, F. Lennox.

BARONET AND THE BANDIT
See Mills, Horace. Pimple, the Pirate.

BARONETS, THE
See Hilton, B. H.

BARONS OF ELBENBERGH, THE
See Weston, Ferdinand Fullerton.

BARON-WILSON, CORNWELL, MRS.
See Wilson, Margaret Harries, Mrs. Cornwell Baron.

BARRACK ROOM, THE
See Bayly, Thomas Haynes.

BARRÉ, ALBERT

Paradise.
See *under title.*

BARRETT, EATON STANNARD

All the Talents! By Polypus (pseud.). London: John Joseph Stockdale, 1807. Pp. [i]-[xvi], [1]-81. 5th ed.

My Wife! What Wife? London: C. Chapple, 1815. Pp. [1]-64.

New Beggar's Opera, The. By Cervantes Hogg (pseud.). In [*Setting Sun; or, Devil Amongst the Placement*, London: T. Hushes, 1809, III], [75]-125. *Filed under* Musical Entertainment.

BARRETT, ELIZABETH
See Browning, Elizabeth Barrett, Mrs. Robert.

BARRETT, WILLIAM ALEXANDER (trans.)

Painter of Antwerp, The. Music by Balfe. London: J. B. Cramer, n.d. Pp. [i]-vi, [7]-36. Libretto.

BARRETT, WILLIAM JOHN

Andreas. London: Thomas Sanderson, 1857. Pp. [i-vi], [1]-106.

BARRETT, WILSON
Black Kitten, The. Written with Parker, Louis Napoleon. N.p.: n.pub., c.1894. Pp. [i], [1]-52.
BARRETT, WILSON (arr.)
Hamlet. By Shakespeare, William. London: J. S. Virtue, n.d. Pp. [i]-xvi, [17]-96.
BARRIE, JAMES MATHEW
Jane Annie; or, The Good Conduct Prize. Written with Doyle, Arthur Conan. Music by Ford, Ernest. London: Chappell, n.d. Pp. [i-iv], [1]-177. Vocal score.
Little Minister, The. Pp. [i-ii], [1]-51. Typescript.
Professor's Love Story, The. Pp. [i-ii], [1]-39, [i], [1]-32, [i], [1]-35. Pagination by act. Typescript.
Walker, London. New York & London: Samuel French, c.1907. Pp. [i-iv], [1]-67.
BARRINGTON'S BUSBY
See Fraser, Julia Agnes.
BARRISTER, THE
See Darnley, J. Herbert.
See Reynoldson, Thomas Herbert. Good for Evil.
BARRY, J. L.
Babes in the Wood. Music by Turner, E. H. N.p.: n.pub., 1895. Pp. [1]-[63]. Libretto.
BARRYMORE, WILLIAM
Bardell v. Pickwick. London: John Dicks, n.d. Pp. [1]-6. Dicks' Standard Plays, 636.
Blood-Red Knight, The; or, The Fatal Bridge. New York: Circulating Library & Dramatic Repository, 1823. Pp. [1]-24. Filed under Blood-Red Knight (anon.).
Blood Red Knight!, The; or, The Fatal Bridge! London: John Duncombe, n.d. Pp. [1]-20. Duncombe's Edition.
Davy Jones; or, Harlequin and Mother Carey's Chickens. Music by Hughes, R. London: W. Kenneth, 1830. Pp. [1]-16. Libretto.
Dog of Montargis, The; or, The Forest of Bondy. Also attrib. to Dibdin, Thomas John. In British Drama, 12 vols., London: John Dicks, 1871, V, [289]-300.
Dog of Montargis, The; or, The Forest of Bondy. London: Thomas Hailes Lacy, n.d. Pp. [1]-31. [Lacy's Acting Edition].
Fatal Snow-Storm, The. London: John Cumberland, n.d. Pp. [1]-34. Cumberland's Minor Theatre, XIII. Filed under Cumberland, John. Cumberland's Minor Theatre, XIII.
Fatal Snow Storm, The; or, Lowina of Tobolski! Also: The Snow Storm; or, Lowina of Tobolskow. London: Thomas Richardson, n.d. Pp. [iii]-[viii], [9]-34.
Gilderoy; or, The Bonnie Boy. London: John Cumberland, n.d. Pp. [1]-54. Cumberland's Minor Theatre, VIII. Filed under Cumberland, John. Cumberland's Minor Theatre, VIII.
Gilderoy; or, The Bonnie Boy. London: Thomas Richardson, n.d. Pp. [i]-[x], [11]-54.
Giovanni in the Country; or, A Gallop to Gretna Green. Music by Reeves, W. London: John Lowndes, 1820. Pp. [1]-8. Libretto.
Hyder, El; or, The Chief of the Ghaut Mountains. London: Thomas Hailes Lacy, n.d. Pp. [1]-25. [Lacy's Acting Edition].
Hyder, El: The Chief of the Ghaut Mountains. In British Drama, 12 vols., London: John Dicks, 1871, VI, [i-iv], [1]-12.
Manfredi the Mysterious Hermit. London: Thomas Hailes Lacy, n.d. Pp. [1]-46. New British Theatre (late Duncombe's), 200.
Meg Murnock, the Hag of the Glen. London: Thomas Hailes Lacy, n.d. Pp. [1]-32. [New British Theatre, 382].
Queen Bee, The; or, Harlequin and the Fairy Hive. Music by Hughes, Richard. London: W. Kenneth, 1828. Pp. [1]-16. Libretto.
Secret, The. London: Thomas Hailes Lacy, n.d. Pp. [iii]-vi, [7]-24. [Lacy's Acting Edition].
Silver Arrow, The; or, Harlequin and the Fairy Pari Banon. London: Rodwell (printer), 1819. Pp. [1]-14. Libretto.

Sisters, The. [Philadelphia: Carey, Hart, Thompson, & W. Marshall, 1835]. Pp. [171]-198. Title page lacking. [Alexander's Modern Acting Drama].
Snow Storm, The; or, Lowina of Toboltskow. Also: The Fatal Snow Storm; or, Lowina of Tobolski!. Baltimore: J. Robinson, 1833. Pp. [1]-36.
Trial by Battle; or, Heaven Defend the Right. London: John Duncombe, n.d. Pp. [1]-24. Duncombe's Edition. Promptbook.
Two Swindlers, The; or, There He Goes! London: John Dicks, n.d. Pp. [i], [7]-14. Dicks' Standard Plays, 636.
Wallace.
See Wallace, the Hero of Scotland.
Wallace, the Hero of Scotland. Also: Wallace. Boston: William V. Spencer, n.d. Pp. [1]-[6], [1]-30. Spencer's Boston Theatre, 48.
BARRYMORE, WILLIAM, JR
See Barrymore, William.
BARTHOLOMEW, ANNE CHARLOTTE FAYERMANN, MRS. VALENTINE (formerly Mrs. Walter Turnbull)
It's Only My Aunt! London: Duncombe & Moon, n.d. <wrps. John Duncombe>. Pp. [1]-22. Duncombe's Acting Edition of the British Theatre, 511.
Ring, The; or, The Farmer's Daughter. By Mrs. Walter Turnbull. N.p.: n.pub., n.d. Pp. [93]-108. Title page lacking.
BARTHOLOMEW, WILLIAM (trans.)
Antigone. By Sophocles. Music by Mendelssohn. London: Novello, n.d. Pp. [i-ii], 1-93. Vocal score.
Antigone. By Sophocles. Music by Mendelssohn. London: Ewer, n.d. Pp. [1]-51. Libretto.
Athalie. By Racine. Music by Mendelssohn. London: Novello, Ewer, n.d. Pp. [1-2], [i]-[ix], [1]-121. Libretto and vocal score.
BASHFUL MAN, THE
See Moncrieff, William Thomas.
BASOCHE, THE
See Harris, Augustus Henry Glossop.
BASTILLE OF CALVADOS
See Albery, James. No. 20.
BATE, FREDERICK
Student, The. London: William Ostell (printer) (priv.), n.d. Pp. [i]-[x], [1]-79.
BATH CHARACTERS
See Warner, Richard.
BATHING
See Bruton, James.
BATTINE, WILLIAM
Another Cain, a Mystery. London: John Cahuac, 1822. Pp. [i]-[viii], [1]-64. 2nd ed.
BATTLE BRIDGE IN ANCIENT TIMES
See Atkyns, Samuel.
BATTLE OF ACTIUM!
See Stirling, Edward. Serpent of the Nile, The.
BATTLE OF BANNOCKBURN
See Kerr, John. King Robert the Bruce.
BATTLE OF BOTHWELL BRIDGE
See Old Mortality.
BATTLE OF BOTHWELL BRIGG, THE
See Farley, Charles.
BATTLE OF BRUNANBURH
See Darley, George. Ethelstan.
BATTLE OF CRECY
See Godmond, Christopher. Campaign of 1346, The.
BATTLE OF HEXHAM, THE
See Colman, George, jr.
BATTLE OF LIFE, THE
See Smith, Albert Richard.
See Stirling, Edward.
BATTLE OF LINCOLN
See Paynter, David William. King Stephen.
BATTLE OF LUNCARTY, THE
See Galloway, George.
BATTLE OF POICTIERS
See Shirley, William. Edward the Black Prince.

BATTLE OF SEDGEMOOR, THE
   See Almar, George.
BATTLE OF THE BORDERS
   See Somerset, Charles A. Chevy Chase.
BATTLE OF THE INCH
   See Milner, Henry M. Fair Maid of Perth, The.
BATTLE OF WATERLOO, THE
   See Amherst, J. H.
BATTLES OF THE WEST
   See Kemp, Joseph. Siege of Isca, The.
BAUBLE SHOP, THE
   See Jones, Henry Arthur.
BAYADERE, THE
   See Horncastle, James Henry.
BAYLEY, PETER
   Orestes in Argos. London: Thomas Dolby, 1825. Pp. [1-4], [i]-[xii], [13]-64. Dolby's British Theatre, XII. *Filed under* Cumberland, John. Cumberland's British Theatre, XII.
   Orestes in Argos. London: Thomas Dolby, 1825. Pp. [i]-[xii], [13]-64. [Cumberland's British Theatre].
   Orestes in Argos. London: Thomas Dolby, 1825. Pp. [i-iv], [1]-61.
BAYLIS, HENRY
   But However--.
   See Mayhew, Henry.
BAYLY, THOMAS HAYNES
   Barrack Room, The. Music by Barnett, John. London: W. Strange, 1837. Pp. [1]-24.
   Barrack Room, The. New York: DeWitt, c.1883. Pp. [1]-22. DeWitt's Acting Plays, 310.
   Barrack Room, The. New York: Samuel French, n.d. Pp. [1]-32. Minor Drama, 12.
   British Legion, The. (Altered, in manuscript, to "Mexican".) London: Chapman & Hall, n.d. Pp. [1]-20. [Webster's Acting National Drama, 47].
   Comfortable Service. London: William Strange, 1836. Pp. [1]-21.
   Comfortable Service. Philadelphia: C. Neal, n.d. Pp. [3]-22.
   Culprit, The. London: Chapman & Hall, 1838. Pp. [1]-21.
   Daughter, The. London: W. Strange, n.d. Pp. [1]-22.
   Fashionable Eclogues. In *Musings and Prosings,* Boulogne: F. Birle (printer), 1833, pp. [i], 158-180.
   Forty and Fifty. London: Chapman & Hall, n.d. Pp. [1]-15. [Acting National Drama].
   Gentleman in Difficulties, A. London: William Strange, 1836. Pp. [1]-24.
   How Do You Manage? London: W. Strange, 1836. Pp. [1]-21.
   Ladder of Love, The. London: W. Strange, n.d. Pp. [1]-27.
   Mr. Greenfinch. London: Chapman & Hall, n.d. Pp. [1]-28.
   My Little Adopted. London: Chapman & Hall, n.d. Pp. [1]-22.
   One Hour; or, The Carnival Ball. London: John Dicks, n.d. Pp. [1]-11. Dicks' Standard Plays, 906.
   Perfection. In *Musings and Prosings,* Boulogne: F. Birle (printer), 1833, pp. [i], [17]-54.
   Perfection; or, The Lady of Munster. N.p.: n.pub., n.d. Pp. [1]-8.
   Perfection; or, The Lady of Munster. [London: John Dicks], n.d. Pp. [1]-8. [Dicks' Standard Plays]. Promptbook.
   Proof of the Pudding, The. In *Musings and Prosings,* Boulogne: F. Birle (printer), 1833, pp. [i], [285]-[326].
   Spitalfields Weaver, The. N.p.: n.pub., n.d. Pp. [5]-19. Title page lacking. Promptbook.
   Swiss Cottage, The; or, Why Don't She Marry? *Also:* Why Don't She Marry?. London & New York: Samuel French, n.d. Pp. [1]-19. French's American Drama, 79. Promptbook.
   Tom Noddy's Secret. Philadelphia & New York: Turner & Fisher; Boston: James Fisher, n.d. Pp. [1]-32. Turner's Dramatic Library. Promptbook.
   Tom Noddy's Secret. New York: Samuel French, n.d. Pp. [1]-22. French's Minor Drama, 280.
   Why Don't She Marry? *Also:* The Swiss Cottage; or, Why Don't She Marry?. London: W. Strange, 1836. Pp. [1]-20.

   You Can't Marry Your Grandmother. London: Webster, n.d. Pp. [1]-28.
BAYNE, PETER
   Days of Jezebel, The. London: Strahan, 1872. Pp. [i]-[xxviii], [1]-212.
BAYNES, E. D.
   Love and Laudanum; or, The Sleeping Dose. London: S. Bagster, 1818. Pp. [i-ii], [1]-56.
BEACON, THE
   See Baillie, Joanna.
BEAR AND THE LADY, THE
   See Kingston, Gertrude.
BEAR AND THE MONKEY!
   See Oxberry, William Henry. Pacha's Pets, The.
BEAR HUNTERS, THE
   See Buckstone, John Baldwin.
BEAR! THE EAGLE! AND THE DOLPHIN!
   See Dance, Charles. Enchanted Forest, The.
BEARDING THE LION
   See Fawcett, Charles S.
BEAR-FACED SWINDLE, A
   See Williams, Arthur.
BÉARNAISE, LA
   See Murray, Alfred.
BEARS NOT BEASTS
   See Milner, Henry M.
BEAST AND THE BEAUTY, THE
   See Burnand, Francis Cowley.
BEATTY-KINGSTON, WILLIAM
   Beggar Student, The. Music by Millocker, Carl. Pp. [1]-79. Typescript promptbook.
BEAU AUSTIN
   See Henley, William Ernest.
BEAU BLANDISH THE RAKE
   See Calmour, Alfred Cecil.
BEAU BRUMMEL, THE KING OF CALAIS
   See Jerrold, William Blanchard.
BEAU NASH, THE KING OF BATH
   See Jerrold, Douglas William.
BEAU NICOLAS, LE
   See Murray, Frank.
BEAU! THE BELLE! AND THE BLACKSMITH!
   See Plowman, Thomas F. Very New Edition of Acis and Galataea, A.
BEAUJOLAIS, THE NECROMANCER
   See Murray, Gaston. Is She His Daughter?
BEAUMONT, FRANCIS
   Chances, The.
   See Garrick, David (arr.).
   Rule a Wife and Have a Wife. Written with Fletcher, John. London: Thomas Dolby, 1825. Pp. [ii]-[viii], [9]-63. Dolby's British Theatre, XII. *Filed under* Cumberland, John. Cumberland's British Theatre, XII.
   Rule a Wife and Have a Wife.
   See Garrick, David (arr.).
   See Kemble, John Philip (arr.).
   Spanish Curate, The.
   See Planché, James Robinson (arr.).
BEAUTIFUL AS A BUTTERFLY
   See Burnand, Francis Cowley. Cupid and Psyche.
BEAUTIFUL FOR EVER
   See Hay, Frederic.
BEAUTIFUL HAIDÉE!
   See Byron, Henry James.
BEAUTY
   See Sims, George Robert.
BEAUTY AND THE BEAST
   See Barmby, James.
   See Bell, Florence Eveleen Eleanore Oliffe, Mrs. Hugh (Lady).
   See Blanchard, Edward Litt Leman.
   See Keating, Eliza H.
   See Planché, James Robinson.
   See White, L.

BEAUTY AND THE BRIGANDS
    See Byron, Henry James. Fra Diavolo.
BEAUTY IN UGLINESS
    See Major, Henry Archibald. Nondescript, The.
BEAUTY OF LYONS, THE
    See Moncrieff, William Thomas.
BEAUTY OR THE BEAST
    See Oxenford, John.
BEAUTY STONE, THE
    See Pinero, Arthur Wing.
BEAUX' STRATAGEM, THE
    See Farquhar, George.
BEAZLEY, SAMUEL, JR
    Boarding House, The; or, Five Hours at Brighton. Music by Horn. London: C. Chapple, 1811. Pp. [i]-[vi], [1]-44. 3rd ed.
    Boarding House, The; or, Five Hours at Brighton. Music by Horn. London: C. Chapple, 1816. Pp. [1]-39. New ed.
    Divorce, The. London: John Dicks, n.d. Pp. [11]-22. Dicks' Standard Plays, 669. *Filed under* Haines, John Thomas. Angeline.
    Fire and Water; or, A Critical Hour. New York: Murden & Thomson, 1821. Pp. [1]-32.
    Hints for Husbands. London: John Cumberland, 1835. Pp. [i-viii], [1]-81.
    Is He Jealous? Music by Welsh, T. London: John Miller, 1816. Pp. [1]-33.
    Is He Jealous? In *New English Drama,* ed. W. Oxberry, 22 vols., London: W. Simpkin & R. Marshall; C. Chapple, 1818, III, [1-2], [i]-[vi], [1]-25. *Filed under* Oxberry, William Henry. New English Drama, III.
    Is He Jealous? London: John Cumberland, n.d. Pp. [1]-28. Cumberland's British Theatre, XXXIV. *Filed under* Cumberland, John. Cumberland's British Theatre, XXXIV.
    Ivanhoe; or, The Knight Templar. London: W. Smith (printer), 1820. Pp. [1]-72.
    Ivanhoe; or, The Knight Templar. Music by Parry, John. London: Goulding, D'Almaine, Potter (printer), n.d. Pp. [1]-52. Title page lacking. Vocal score.
    Jealous on All Sides; or, The Landlord in Jeopardy! Music by Jolly. London: William Fearman, 1818. Pp. [1]-43.
    Knights of the Cross, The; or, The Hermit's Prophecy. London: John Cumberland, n.d. Pp. [1]-43. Cumberland's British Theatre, XXXIV. *Filed under* Cumberland, John. Cumberland's British Theatre, XXXIV.
    Knights of the Cross, The; or, The Hermit's Prophecy. Music by Bishop, H. R. London: John Cumberland, 1826. Pp. [1]-62.
    Lottery Ticket, The; or, The Lawyer's Clerk. London: John Cumberland, n.d. Pp. [1]-35. Cumberland's British Theatre, XXXV. *Filed under* Cumberland, John. Cumberland's British Theatre, XXXV.
    Lottery Ticket, The; or, The Lawyer's Clerk. By J. B. Buckstone. New York: Samuel French, n.d. Pp. [5]-35. Text complete. Minor Drama, 137. *Filed under* Buckstone, John Baldwin.
    Lottery Ticket and the Lawyer's Clerk, The. *Also:* The Lottery Ticket. London: C. Chapple, 1827. Pp. [1]-32.
    Love Among the Roses; or, The Master Key. Music by Kitchener. London: John Lowndes, 1822. Pp. [i-iv], [1]-22.
    Love's Dream. London: John Lowndes, 1821. Pp. [i-viii], [1]-35.
    Love's Dream. London: John Duncombe, n.d. Pp. [1]-24. Duncombe's Acting Edition of the British Theatre, 64.
    My Uncle. Music by Addison. London: John Miller, 1817. Pp. [i-ii], [1]-29.
    Philandering; or, The Rose Queen. Music by Horn, Charles Edward. London: John Miller, 1824. Pp. [i]-[xii], [1]-75.
    Promissory Note, The. Music by Bochsa. London: John Miller, 1820. Pp. [1]-40. *Filed under* Promissory Note (anon.).
    Promissory Note, The. Music by Bochsa. London: John Miller, 1820. Pp. [1]-40.

    Scapegrace, The. London: John Cumberland, n.d. Pp. [1]-28. Cumberland's Minor Theatre, I. *Filed under* Cumberland, John. Cumberland's Minor Theatre, I.
    Scapegrace, The. London: John Cumberland, n.d. Pp. [1]-28. Cumberland's Minor Theatre, 5.
    Sonnambula, La. Music by Bellini. New York: John Perry; London: Thomas Hailes Lacy, n.d. Pp. [1]-34. Lacy's Anglo-American Edition of Standard Plays, 3. Libretto.
    Steward, The; or, Fashion and Feeling. London: John Lowndes, 1819. Pp. [ii]-[xii], [1]-83.
    Steward, The; or, Fashion and Feeling. London: John Cumberland, n.d. Pp. [1]-70. Cumberland's British Theatre, XXXIV. *Filed under* Cumberland, John. Cumberland's British Theatre, XXXIV.
    You Know What. London: John Dicks, n.d. Pp. [1]-13. Dicks' Standard Plays, 653.
BECHER, MARTIN
    Crimeless Criminal, A. London & New York: Samuel French, n.d. Pp. [1]-15. [Lacy's Acting Edition].
    Domestic Hercules, A. London: Edward Hastings, n.d. Pp. [1]-15. Hastings's Acting Plays.
    Hunting the Slippers; or, Painless Dentistry. New York: DeWitt, n.d. Pp. [1]-14.
    In Possession. London: Thomas Hailes Lacy, n.d. Pp. [1]-14. [Lacy's Acting Edition].
    In the Wrong House; or, The Two T. J's. *Also:* The Two T. J's. Chicago: T. S. Denison, n.d. Pp. [1]-12. Star Series.
    My Uncle's Suit. New York: Wheat & Cornett, c.1876. Pp. [29]-32. New York Drama, I, 8.
    No. 6, Duke Street. London & New York: Samuel French, n.d. Pp. [1]-14. [Lacy's Acting Edition].
    Poetic Proposal, A. London: Thomas Hailes Lacy, n.d. Pp. [1]-14. [Lacy's Acting Edition].
    Rule Britannia. London: Thomas Hailes Lacy, n.d. Pp. [1]-14. [Lacy's Acting Edition].
    Two T. J's., The. By Martin Beecher. *Also:* In the Wrong House; or, The Two T. J's. Clyde, Ohio: A. D. Ames, n.d. Pp. [1]-10. Ames' Series of Standard and Minor Drama, 54.
BECK, THOMAS
    Triumphs of the Sons of Belial, The; or, Liberty Vanquished. By Timothy Touch'em (pseud.). London: W. Barrett, 1810. Pp. [i]-[vi], [7]-40.
BECKET, ANDREW
    Affectation. In *Dramatic and Prose Miscellanies,* ed. William Beattie, London: George Virtue, 1838, new ed., I, [i-iv], [1]-141.
    Dialogues Concerning Men, Manners, and Opinions. *See* Lucianus Redivivus.
    Genii, The. In *New British Theatre,* London: A. J. Valpy (printer), 1814, I, [i], [493]-530.
    Genii, The. In *Dramatic and Prose Miscellanies,* ed. William Beattie, London: George Virtue, 1838, new ed., I, [i], [183]-218.
    Lavinia. In *Dramatic and Prose Miscellanies,* ed. William Beattie, London: George Virtue, 1838, new ed., I, [i], [143]-182.
    Lucianus Redivivus. *Also:* Dialogues Concerning Men, Manners, and Opinions. In *Dramatic and Prose Miscellanies,* ed. William Beattie, London: George Virtue, 1838, new ed., II, [1], [i]-iv, [5]-138.
    Socrates. London: Longman, Hurst, Rees, Orme, & Brown, 1811. Pp. [i-xiv], [1]-70. New ed.
BECKET
    See Irving, Henry (arr.).
    See Tennyson, Alfred, Lord.
BECKINGTON, CHARLES
    Hamlet the Dane. Newcastle-upon-Tyne: M. Ross (printer), 1847. Pp. [i-iv], [1]-37.
BED OF ROSES, A
    See Jones, Henry Arthur.
BEDDOES, THOMAS LOVELL
    Brides' Tragedy, The. In *Complete Works,* ed. Edmund Gosse, London: Fanfrolico Press, n.d., pp. [i], [401]-479.

Death's Jest-book; or, The Fool's Tragedy. London: William Pickering, 1850. Pp. [i-vi], [1]-174.

BEDFORD, HERBERT

  Kit Marlowe. Music by Bedford, Herbert. London: Sanders Phillips (printer), n.d. Pp. [1]-20. Libretto. *Filed under* Bedford, Henry.

BEDINGFIELD, RICHARD

  Madeline. London: C. Mitchell, 1847. Pp. [1]-67.

BEDOUINS, THE

  See Irwin, Eyles.

BED-ROOM WINDOW!, THE

  See Stirling, Edward.

BEE AND THE ORANGE TREE, THE

  See Planché, James Robinson.

BEECHER, MARTIN

  See Becher, Martin.

BEEHIVE, THE

  See Millingen, John Gideon.

BEEN HAD

  See Pleon, Harry.

BEER, MICHAEL

  Paria, The.

    See Gower, Francis Leveson, Lord.

BEERBOHM, CONSTANCE

  April Shower, An. In *Little Book of Plays,* London: George Newnes, 1897, pp. [113]-127. *Filed under* Little Book of Plays.

  Charity Begins at Home. In *Little Book of Plays,* London: George Newnes, 1897, pp. [41]-57. *Filed under* Little Book of Plays.

  Chatterbox, The. In *Little Book of Plays,* London: George Newnes, 1897, pp. [93]-111. *Filed under* Little Book of Plays.

  He and She. In *Little Book of Plays,* London: George Newnes, 1897, pp. [1]-[21]. *Filed under* Little Book of Plays.

  Little Surprise, A. In *Little Book of Plays,* London: George Newnes, 1897, pp. [59]-92. *Filed under* Little Book of Plays.

  Secret, A. In *Little Book of Plays,* London: George Newnes, 1897, pp. [23]-40. *Filed under* Little Book of Plays.

BEETHOVEN

  See Hein, Gustav (trans.).

BEFORE AND BEHIND THE CURTAIN

  See Taylor, Tom. Masks and Faces.

BEFORE THE MECHANICAL MODELS

  See Anstey, F.

BEGGAR BOY OF BRUSSELS, THE

  See Buckstone, John Baldwin.

BEGGAR OF BETHNAL GREEN, THE

  See Knowles, James Sheridan.

BEGGAR OF CRIPPLEGATE, THE

  See Moncrieff, William Thomas.

BEGGAR ON HORSEBACK, A

  See Sulivan, Robert.

BEGGAR STUDENT, THE

  See Beatty-Kingston, William.

BEGGAR VENUS, THE

  See Wright, A. L.

BEGGAR'S BUSH

  See Kinnaird, Douglas James William. Merchant of Bruges, The.

BEGGAR'S OPERA, THE

  See Gay, John.

BEGGAR'S PETITION, THE

  See Pitt, George Dibdin.

BEGINNING AND THE END, THE

  See Lovell, Maria Anne Lacy, Mrs.

BEGONE DULL CARE

  See Reynolds, Frederick.

BEHIND A MASK

  See Dixon, Bernard Homer.

BEHIND THE CURTAIN

  See Roberts, George.

BEHIND THE SCENES

  See Selby, Charles.

BEHIND TIME

  See Webster, Benjamin, jr.

BELDAM, JOSEPH

  Pastore Incantato, Il; or, The Enchanted Shepherd. By a Student of the Temple. In *Pastore Incantato and Other Poems,* London: Hurst, Robinson, 1824, pp. [i], [1]-68.

BELFORD CASTLE

  See Lunn, Joseph.

BELFOUR, HUGO JOHN

  Vampire, The.

    See Stephens, George.

BELL, ARCHIBALD

  Caius Toranius. In *Count Clermont . . . Caius Toranius . . . with Other Poems,* Edinburgh & London: William Blackwood & Sons, 1841, pp. [i], [91]-193.

  Count Clermont. In *Count Clermont . . . Caius Toranius . . . with Other Poems,* Edinburgh & London: William Blackwood & Sons, 1841, pp. [i], [1]-89.

BELL, ERNEST (trans.)

  Damon; or, True Friendship. By Lessing, G. E. In *Dramatic Works of G. E. Lessing,* 2 vols., London: George Bell & Sons, 1878, II, [i-vi], [1]-24. *Filed under* Dramatic Works.

  Emilia Galotti. By Lessing, G. E. In *Dramatic Works of G. E. Lessing,* 2 vols., London: George Bell & Sons, 1878, I, [133]-225. *Filed under* Dramatic Works.

  Freethinker, The. By Lessing, G. E. In *Dramatic Works of G. E. Lessing,* 2 vols., London: George Bell & Sons, 1878, II, [219]-287. *Filed under* Dramatic Works.

  Jews, The. By Lessing, G. E. In *Dramatic Works of G. E. Lessing,* 2 vols., London: George Bell & Sons, 1878, II, [185]-217. *Filed under* Dramatic Works.

  Minna von Barnhelm; or, The Soldier's Fortune. By Lessing, G. E. In *Dramatic Works of G. E. Lessing,* 2 vols., London: George Bell & Sons, 1878, II, [331]-413. *Filed under* Dramatic Works.

  Miss Sara Sampson. By Lessing, G. E. In *Dramatic Works of G. E. Lessing,* 2 vols., London: George Bell & Sons, 1878, I, [i]-[xxxii], [1]-101. *Filed under* Dramatic Works.

  Nathan the Wise. By Lessing, G. E. In *Dramatic Works of G. E. Lessing,* 2 vols., London: George Bell & Sons, 1878, I, [227]-382. *Filed under* Dramatic Works.

  Old Maid, The. By Lessing, G. E. In *Dramatic Works of G. E. Lessing,* 2 vols., London: George Bell & Sons, 1878, II, [109]-142. *Filed under* Dramatic Works.

  Philotas. By Lessing, G. E. In *Dramatic Works of G. E. Lessing,* 2 vols., London: George Bell & Sons, 1878, I, [103]-132. *Filed under* Dramatic Works.

  Treasure, The. By Lessing, G. E. In *Dramatic Works of G. E. Lessing,* 2 vols., London: George Bell & Sons, 1878, II, [289]-329. *Filed under* Dramatic Works.

  Woman Hater, The. By Lessing, G. E. In *Dramatic Works of G. E. Lessing,* 2 vols., London: George Bell & Sons, 1878, II, [143]-183. *Filed under* Dramatic Works.

  Young Scholar, The. By Lessing, G. E. In *Dramatic Works of G. E. Lessing,* 2 vols., London: George Bell & Sons, 1878, II, [25]-107. *Filed under* Dramatic Works.

BELL, FLORENCE EVELEEN ELEANORE OLIFFE, MRS. HUGH (Lady)

  Alan's Wife. London: Henry, 1893. Pp. [i]-[lvi], 1-55. [Independent Theatre Series of Plays, 2].

  Beauty and the Beast. In *Chamber Comedies,* London: Longmans, Green, 1901, pp. 302-316. *Filed under* Chamber Comedies.

  Best Children in the World, The. In *Nursery Comedies,* London: Longmans, Green, 1892, pp. [89]-98. *Filed under* Nursery Comedies.

  Between the Posts. London: Samuel French; New York: T. Henry French, n.d. Pp. [1]-16. [Lacy's Acting Edition].

  Cat and Dog. In *Nursery Comedies,* London: Longmans, Green, 1892, pp. [43]-50. *Filed under* Nursery Comedies.

  Chance Interview, A. In *Chamber Comedies,* London: Longmans, Green, 1901, pp. 21-37. *Filed under* Chamber Comedies.

Cinderella. In *Nursery Comedies,* London: Longmans, Green, 1892, pp. [112]-132. *Filed under* Nursery Comedies.

Cross Questions and Crooked Answers.
See Bell, Frances.

Crossing Sweeper, The. In *Chamber Comedies,* London: Longmans, Green, 1901, pp. 276-279. *Filed under* Chamber Comedies.

Foolish Jack. In *Nursery Comedies,* London: Longmans, Green, 1892, pp. [69]-74. *Filed under* Nursery Comedies.

Giving Him Away. In *Dialogues of the Day,* ed. Oswald Crawfurd, London: Chapman & Hall, n.d., pp. [146]-159. *Filed under* Crawfurd, Oswald. Dialogues of the Day.

Golden Goose, The. In *Nursery Comedies,* London: Longmans, Green, 1892, pp. [99]-111. *Filed under* Nursery Comedies.

Hard Day's Work, A. In *Chamber Comedies,* London: Longmans, Green, 1901, pp. 237-247. *Filed under* Chamber Comedies.

In a First-Class Waiting-Room. In *Chamber Comedies,* London: Longmans, Green, 1901, pp. 123-136. *Filed under* Chamber Comedies.

Indecis. In *Chamber Comedies,* London: Longmans, Green, 1901, pp. [i-vi], [1]-20. *Filed under* Chamber Comedies.

Jack and the Beanstalk. In *Chamber Comedies,* London: Longmans, Green, 1901, pp. 287-301. *Filed under* Chamber Comedies.

Joint Household, A. In *Chamber Comedies,* London: Longmans, Green, 1901, pp. 137-153. *Filed under* Chamber Comedies.

Joint Household, A. London & New York: Samuel French, n.d. Pp. [1]-14. [Lacy's Acting Edition].

Last Words. In *Chamber Comedies,* London: Longmans, Green, 1901, pp. 213-226. *Filed under* Chamber Comedies.

Little Petsy. In *Nursery Comedies,* London: Longmans, Green, 1892, pp. [19]-27. *Filed under* Nursery Comedies.

Miss Dobson. In *Nursery Comedies,* London: Longmans, Green, 1892, pp. [51]-57. *Filed under* Nursery Comedies.

Miss Flipper's Holiday.
See Bell, Harrie.

Modern Locusta, A. In *Chamber Comedies,* London: Longmans, Green, 1901, pp. 171-186. *Filed under* Chamber Comedies.

Monster in the Garden, The. In *Nursery Comedies,* London: Longmans, Green, 1892, pp. [36]-42. *Filed under* Nursery Comedies.

Not to Be Forwarded. In *Chamber Comedies,* London: Longmans, Green, 1901, pp. 271-275. *Filed under* Chamber Comedies.

Oh, No! In *Chamber Comedies,* London: Longmans, Green, 1901, pp. 265-270. *Filed under* Chamber Comedies.

Public Prosecutor, The. In *Chamber Comedies,* London: Longmans, Green, 1901, pp. 55-79. *Filed under* Chamber Comedies.

Quite by Ourselves. In *Nursery Comedies,* London: Longmans, Green, 1892, pp. [75]-87. *Filed under* Nursery Comedies.

Rather a Prig. In *Nursery Comedies,* London: Longmans, Green, 1892, pp. [28]-35. *Filed under* Nursery Comedies.

Reliquary, The. In *Chamber Comedies,* London: Longmans, Green, 1901, pp. 248-257. *Filed under* Chamber Comedies.

Sixpenny Telegram, A. London & New York: Samuel French, n.d. Pp. [1]-20. [Lacy's Acting Edition].

Surprise, The. In *Chamber Comedies,* London: Longmans, Green, 1901, pp. 317-321. *Filed under* Chamber Comedies.

Swiss Times, The. In *Chamber Comedies,* London: Longmans, Green, 1901, pp. 187-212. *Filed under* Chamber Comedies.

Time Is Money. Written with Cecil, Arthur (pseud. of Blunt, Arthur Cecil). New York & London: Samuel French, c.1905. Pp. [1]-27. [French's International Copyrighted Edition of the Works of the Best Authors], 95.

Unpublished Ms., An. In *Chamber Comedies,* London: Longmans, Green, 1901, pp. 154-170. *Filed under* Chamber Comedies.

Viceroy's Wedding, The. In *Chamber Comedies,* London: Longmans, Green, 1901, pp. 280-286. *Filed under* Chamber Comedies.

Waterproof, The. In *Chamber Comedies,* London: Longmans, Green, 1901, pp. 258-264. *Filed under* Chamber Comedies.

What Happened to Henny Penny? In *Nursery Comedies,* London: Longmans, Green, 1892, pp. [1]-18. *Filed under* Nursery Comedies.

Wigwam, The; or, The Little Girl from Town. In *Nursery Comedies,* London: Longmans, Green, 1892, pp. [58]-67. *Filed under* Nursery Comedies.

Woman of Courage, A. In *Chamber Comedies,* London: Longmans, Green, 1901, pp. 227-236. *Filed under* Chamber Comedies.

Woman of Culture, A. In *Chamber Comedies,* London: Longmans, Green, 1901, pp. 80-122. *Filed under* Chamber Comedies.

Wrong Poet, The. In *Chamber Comedies,* London: Longmans, Green, 1901, pp. 38-54. *Filed under* Chamber Comedies.

BELL, FRANCES
Cross Questions and Crooked Answers. Written with Bell, Florence Eveleen Eleanore Oliffe, Mrs. Hugh (Lady). London & New York: Samuel French, n.d. Pp. [1]-8. [Lacy's Acting Edition].

BELL, HARRIE
Miss Flipper's Holiday. Written with Bell, Florence Eveleen Eleanore Oliffe, Mrs. Hugh (Lady). London & New York: Samuel French, c.1900. Pp. [1]-8. [Lacy's Acting Edition].

BELL, MRS. HUGH
See Bell, Florence Eveleen Eleanore Oliffe, Mrs. Hugh (Lady).

BELL, LADY
See Bell, Florence Eveleen Eleanore Oliffe, Mrs. Hugh (Lady).

BELL, ROBERT
Marriage. London: Longman, 1842. Pp. [iii]-[xii], [1]-164.
Mothers and Daughters. London: John Mortimer, 1844. Pp. [i]-[xxvi], [1]-128. 2nd ed.
Temper. London: T. H. Brown, 1847. Pp. [i-iv], [1]-73.
Watch-Word, The; or, Quito-Gate (attrib. to Bell). London: Effingham Wilson, 1816. Pp. [i-iv], [1]-28.

BELL RINGER OF ST. PAUL'S, THE
See Hart, James P.
See Townsend, William Thompson.

BELLAMIRA
See Sheil, Richard Lalor.

BELLAMY, CLAXSON
Erminie. Written with Paulton, Harry. Pp. [1-14]. Side for Princess de Gramponeur. Typescript. *Filed under* Paulton, Harry.
Erminie. Written with Paulton, Harry. Music by Jakobowski, Edward. London: Joseph Williams, n.d. Pp. [i-ii], 1-147. Vocal score.

BELLAMY, G. SOMERS
April Showers. Written with Romer, Frederick. London: Samuel French; New York: T. Henry French, n.d. Pp. [1]-57.

BELLE AND THE POMEGRANATE
See Talfourd, Francis. Pluto and Proserpine.

BELLE LAMAR
See Boucicault, Dionysius Lardner.

BELLE OF CAIRO, THE
See Peile, F. Kinsey.

BELLE OF MADAGASCAR
See Arbuthnot, ?, Capt. Africaine, L'.

BELLE OF THE BARLEY-MOW, THE
See Arden, Henry T.

BELLE SAUVAGE
See Brougham, John.
See Dibdin, Charles Isaac Mungo, jr. Ko and Zoa.

BELLE'S STRATAGEM, THE
See Cowley, Hannah Parkhouse, Mrs.
See Stephenson, Charles H. (arr.).

BELLEROPHON
    See Field, Michael.
BELLES OF BELZEBUB
    See Lancaster, Edward Richardson. Devil's Daughters, The.
BELLES OF THE SHANNON
    See Levey, John C. Garryowen.
BELLEW, KYRLE (arr.)
    Antony and Cleopatra. By Shakespeare, William. New York: Charles D. Koppel, n.d. Pp. [1]-52. Promptbook.
BELLINGHAM, HENRY
    Arline, the Lost Child; or, The Pole, the Policeman, and the Polar Bear. Written with Best, William. Music by Isaacson, B. London: E. J. Bath (printer), 1864. Pp. [1]-48.
    Bluebeard Re-Paired; or, A Worn Out Subject Done Up Anew. Music by Offenbach. London: Thomas Hailes Lacy, n.d. Pp. [1]-49. [Lacy's Acting Edition]. Libretto.
    Meddle and Muddle. Written with Best, William. London: Samuel French; New York: T. Henry French, n.d. Pp. [1]-22. [Lacy's Acting Edition].
    Monsieur Laroche. Written with Best, William. London: Arthur J. Farmer (printer), 1878. Pp. [1]-48.
    Prince Camaralzaman; or, The Fairies' Revenge. Written with Best, William. London: Thomas Hailes Lacy, n.d. Pp. [1]-39. [Lacy's Acting Edition].
    Princess Primrose and the Four Pretty Princes. Written with Best, William. London: Thomas Hailes Lacy, n.d. Pp. [1]-43. [Lacy's Acting Edition].
BELLS, THE
    See Lewis, Leopold David.
BELLS OF CORNEVILLE, THE
    See Farnie, Henry Brougham.
BELLS OF HASLEMERE, THE
    See Pettitt, Henry Alfred.
BELPHEGOR
    See Buckingham, Leicester Silk.
    See Courtney, John.
    See Higgie, Thomas Henry.
BELPHEGOR THE BUFFOON
    See Higgie, Thomas Henry.
BELPHEGOR THE MOUNTEBANK
    See Webb, Charles.
    See Webster, Benjamin Nottingham.
BELSHAZZAR
    See Milman, Henry Hart.
BELSHAZZAR'S FEAST
    See Ball, William.
    See MacCarthy, Denis Florence (trans.).
BEN BOLT
    See Johnstone, John Beer.
BEN NAZIR, THE SARACEN
    See Grattan, Thomas Colley.
BEN THE BOATSWAIN
    See Wilks, Thomas Egerton.
BENDING OF THE BOUGH, THE
    See Moore, George.
BENEDIX, JULIUS RODERICH
    Three Bachelors, The.
    See under title.
BENEFICENT BEAR, THE
    See Zimmern, Helen (trans.?).
BENEFIT OF HANGING!
    See Jerrold, Douglas William. Smoked Miser!, The.
BENEFIT OF THE DOUBT, THE
    See Pinero, Arthur Wing.
BENETT, WILLIAM
    Panthea. London: James Carpenter & Son, 1817. Pp. [i-vi], [1]-64.
BENEVOLENT TAR
    See Cross, John C. Purse, The.
BENGAL TIGER, THE
    See Dance, Charles.

BENHAM, ARTHUR
    Theory and Practice. London: Samuel French; New York: T. Henry French, n.d. Pp. [1]-12. [Lacy's Acting Edition].
BENNETT, GEORGE JOHN
    Justiza, The: A Tale of Arragon. London: T. C. Newby, 1848. Pp. [i]-[vi], [7]-94.
    Retribution; or, Love's Trials. London: G. H. Davidson, n.d. Pp. [1]-64. Cumberland's British Theatre, 373.
    Soldier's Orphan, The; or, The Fortune of War! London: John Duncombe, n.d. Pp. [1]-34. Duncombe's Edition.
BENNETT, J. M.
    Thirteen Years' Labour Lost; or, The Force of Nature. London: J. Lowndes, 1822. Pp. [i], [1]-22.
BENNETT, JOHN E.
    Paul Rabaut; or, The Huguenots under Louis XV. Written with Wakely, Charles. London: Relfe Brothers, 1878. Pp. [i-vi], [1]-44, [1]-18. Libretto.
BENNETT, JOSEPH
    Djamileh; or, The Slave in Love. *Also:* L'Esclave Amoureuse. Music by Bizet. London: E. Ascherberg, c.1892. Pp. [1]-146. Vocal score.
    Idyll, An. Music by Herkomer, Hubert. London & New York: Novello, Ewer, n.d. Pp. [i-iv], [1]-[14], 1-152. Libretto and vocal score.
    Jeanie Deans. Music by MacCunn, Hamish. London (Westminster): Phipps & Connor (printer), n.d. Pp. [1]-32. Libretto.
    Thorgrim. Music by Cowen, Frederic Hymen. London & New York: Novello, Ewer, n.d. Pp. [i-vi], [1]-173. Novello's Original Octavo Edition. Vocal score.
BENNETT, JOSEPH (trans.)
    Manon. Music by Massenet. New York: F. Rullman, c.1889. Pp. [1]-30. Libretto.
    Manon. Music by Massenet. London & New York: Novello, Ewer, n.d. Pp. [i-iv], [1]-228. Novello's Original Octavo Edition. Vocal score.
    Philemon et Baucis. Music by Gounod. London: E. Ascherberg, c.1892. Pp. [1]-163. Vocal score.
BENNETT, WILLIAM COX
    Character, A. In *Queen Eleanor's Vengeance and Other Poems,* London: Chapman & Hall, 1857, pp. [i], [30]-49.
    Prometheus the Fire-Giver. London: Chatto & Windus, 1877. Pp. [i-iv], [1]-63.
BENTIVOGLIO
    See Masterton, Charles.
BENTLEY, JOHN
    Royal Penitent, The. London: Button & Son, 1803. Pp. [i-iv], [1]-44.
BENYOWSKY
    See Kenney, James.
BEQUEATHED HEART, THE
    See Peake, Richard Brinsley.
BERARD, PETER
    Uncle's Will, Who Wins?, The; or, The Widow's Choice. London: A. Macpherson (printer) (priv.), 1808. Pp. [i-ii], [1]-30.
BERENICE
    See Boswell, Robert Bruce (trans.).
BERESFORD, A. VON (trans.)
    Faust. By Goethe. Cassel & Göttingen: George H. Wigand, 1862. Pp. [i-vi], [1]-227.
BERINGER, AIMÉE DANIELLE, MRS. OSCAR
    Bit of Old Chelsea, A. New York & London: Samuel French, c.1905. Pp. [i-ii], [1]-25. [Lacy's Acting Edition].
    Holly Tree Inn. New York & London: Samuel French, c.1905. Pp. [i-ii], [1]-[33]. [Lacy's Acting Edition].
BERNARD, BAYLE
    See Bernard, William Bayle.
BERNARD, WILLIAM BAYLE
    Balance of Comfort, The. London: Thomas Hailes Lacy, n.d. Pp. [1]-32. [Lacy's Acting Edition].
    Boarding School, The. London: Webster, n.d. Pp. [1]-27. Promptbook.
    Charlotte Corday. London: John Dicks, n.d. Pp. [1]-11. Dicks' Standard Plays, 1042.

Conquering Game, The. London: John Duncombe, n.d. Pp. [1]-24. Duncombe's Edition.

Dumb Belle, The. London: Thomas Hailes Lacy, n.d. Pp. [1]-22.

Dumb Belle, The. Chicago: Dramatic Publishing Co., n.d. Pp. [1]-20. Sergel's Acting Drama, 242.

Evil Genius, The. London: Thomas Hailes Lacy, n.d. Pp. [1]-68. Last page partly illegible.

Farmer's Story, The. London & New York: Samuel French, n.d. Pp. [1]-45. [Lacy's Acting Edition].

Faust; or, The Fate of Margaret. London & New York: Samuel French, n.d. Pp. [i]-[iv], 5-67. French's Acting Edition (late Lacy's).

Four Sisters, The; or, Woman's Worth and Woman's Ways. New York: John Burrows Wright, 1854. 44 leaves. Manuscript.

Happiest Man Alive, The. London: John Duncombe, n.d. Pp. [1]-20. Duncombe's Acting Edition of the British Theatre, 322.

His Last Legs. New York: Samuel French, n.d. <wrps. H. C. Husted>. Pp. [1]-41. Minor Drama, 6.

Irish Attorney, The; or, Galway Practice in 1770. New York: Berford, 1847. Pp. [1]-38. Minor Drama, 1.

Life's Trial, A. London: Thomas Hailes Lacy, n.d. Pp. [1]-48. Lacy's Acting Edition, 436.

Locomotion. London: Webster, n.d. Pp. [1]-23. Webster's Acting National Drama, 104.

Louison, the Angel of the Attic; or, The Recompense. London: John Dicks, n.d. Pp. [1]-9. Dicks' Standard Plays, 710.

Lucille; or, The Story of the Heart. Philadelphia: Frederick Turner; New York: Turner & Fisher, n.d. Pp. [1]-50. Turner's Dramatic Library of Acting Plays, 20.

Lucille; or, The Story of the Heart. London: Thomas Hailes Lacy, n.d. Pp. [i-iv], [5]-37. [Lacy's Acting Edition].

Maiden's Fame!, A; or, A Legend of Lisbon! London: John Duncombe, n.d. Pp. [1]-40. Duncombe's Edition.

Man About Town, The. London: John Duncombe, n.d. Pp. [1]-24. [Duncombe's Edition].

Man of Two Lives!, The. London: Thomas Hailes Lacy, n.d. Pp. [1]-75. [Lacy's Acting Edition].

Marie Ducange. London: Thomas Hailes Lacy, n.d. Pp. [1]-48.

Middy Ashore, The. [London: Thomas Hailes Lacy], n.d. Pp. [2]-23. Title page lacking. [Lacy's Acting Edition].

Mummy, The. London: Duncombe & Moon, n.d. <wrps. John Duncombe>. Pp. [1]-23. Duncombe's Acting Edition of the British Theatre, 188.

Nervous Man and the Man of Nerve, The. New York: William Taylor, n.d. Pp. [i]-[vi], [7]-45. Modern Standard Drama, 36.

No Name. London: G. Holsworth, 1863. Pp. [i-ii], [1]-59.

Old Regimentals, The. London: John Cumberland, n.d. Pp. [1]-34. Cumberland's British Theatre, XXXIII. Filed under Cumberland, John. Cumberland's British Theatre, XXXIII.

Old Regimentals, The. London: John Cumberland, n.d. Pp. [1]-34.

Passing Cloud, The. New York: William Taylor, n.d. Pp. [1]-59. Modern Standard Drama, 85.

Paulina; or, The Passage of the Beresina. London: John Dicks, n.d. Pp. [i-ii], [1]-19. Dicks' Standard Plays, 516.

Philosophers of Berlin, The. London: John Dicks, n.d. Pp. [1]-14. Dicks' Standard Plays, 779.

Platonic Attachments. London: Hailes Lacy, n.d. Pp. [1]-24.

Practical Man, A. [London: Thomas Hailes Lacy], n.d. Pp. [1]-24. [Lacy's Acting Edition].

Robespierre; or, Two Days of the Revolution! London & New York: Samuel French, n.d. Pp. [1]-52.

Round of Wrong, The; or, A Fireside Story. London: National Acting Drama Office, n.d. <wrps. Webster>. Pp. [1]-46. Webster's Acting National Drama, 139.

Splendid Investment, A. London: Thomas Hailes Lacy, n.d. Pp. [1]-25. [Lacy's Acting Edition].

St. Mary's Eve; or, A Solway Story. London: Thomas Hailes Lacy, n.d. Pp. [1]-39. Promptbook.

Storm in a Tea Cup, A. London: Thomas Hailes Lacy, n.d. Pp. [1]-20. Lacy's Acting Edition, 200.

Tide of Time, The. London: Thomas Hailes Lacy, n.d. Pp. [1]-53. [Lacy's Acting Edition].

Trevanion.
See Marston, John Westland.

Wept of the Wish-ton-Wish, The. New York: Samuel French, n.d. Pp. [1]-26. French's Standard Drama, 154.

Woman Hater!, The. London: Webster, n.d. Pp. [1]-20. Webster's Acting National Drama, 101.

Woman's Faith. London: John Miller, 1835. Pp. [i-iv], [1]-47.

BERNAYS, LEOPOLD JOHN (trans.)
Faust, Part 2. By Goethe. London: Sampson Low, 1839. Pp. [i]-xx, [1]-207.

BERNEL, GEORGE (trans.)
Germanicus. By Arnault, A.-V. London: Samuel Leigh, 1817. Pp. [1]-112.

BERRIE, ERNIE
Capt. Smith. London: Thomas Hailes Lacy, n.d. Pp. [1]-19.
Capt. Smith. [Clyde, Ohio]: Ames & Holgate, n.d. Pp. [1]-14.

BERRY, MARY
Fashionable Friends, The. London: J. Ridgway, 1802. Pp. [1]-85. 3rd ed.

BERTHA
See Fitzball, Edward.

BERTHA'S BRIDAL
See Collier, William. Kiss, The.

BERTRAM
See Maturin, Charles Robert, Rev.

BESANT, WALTER
Charm, The. Written with Pollock, Walter Herries. In Charm and Other Drawing-Room Plays, New York: Frederick A. Stokes, n.d., pp. [i], [1]-64.

Glove, The. Written with Pollock, Walter Herries. In Charm and Other Drawing-Room Plays, New York: Frederick A. Stokes, n.d., pp. [i], [200]-225.

Loved I Not Honour More. Written with Pollock, Walter Herries. In Charm and Other Drawing-Room Plays, New York: Frederick A. Stokes, n.d., pp. [i], [135]-170.

Peer and Heiress. Written with Pollock, Walter Herries. In Charm and Other Drawing-Room Plays, New York: Frederick A. Stokes, n.d., pp. [i], [99]-134.

Shrinking Shoe, The. Written with Pollock, Walter Herries. In Charm and Other Drawing-Room Plays, New York: Frederick A. Stokes, n.d., pp. [i], [171]-199.

Spy, The. Written with Pollock, Walter Herries. In Charm and Other Drawing-Room Plays, New York: Frederick A. Stokes, n.d., pp. [i], 226-251.

Voice of Love, The. Written with Pollock, Walter Herries. In Charm and Other Drawing-Room Plays, New York: Frederick A. Stokes, n.d., pp. [i], [65]-98.

Wife's Confession, The. Written with Pollock, Walter Herries. In Charm and Other Drawing-Room Plays, New York: Frederick A. Stokes, n.d., pp. [i], [252]-275.

BESEMERES, JOHN
See Daly, John.

BESSY BELL AND MARY GRAY
See Hetherington, William Maxwell.

BEST, WILLIAM
Arline, the Lost Child.
See Bellingham, Henry.
Meddle and Muddle.
See Bellingham, Henry.
Monsieur Laroche.
See Bellingham, Henry.
Prince Camaralzaman.
See Bellingham, Henry.
Princess Primrose and the Four Pretty Princes.
See Bellingham, Henry.

BEST CHILDREN IN THE WORLD, THE
See Bell, Florence Eveleen Eleanore Oliffe, Mrs. Hugh (Lady).

BEST MAN, THE
See Playfair, George MacDonald Home.

BEST MAN WINS
  See Melford, Mark.
BEST OF MOTHERS, WITH A BRUTE OF A HUSBAND
  See Brough, Robert Barnabas. Medea.
BEST WAY, THE
  See Wigan, Horace.
BETA (pseud.) (trans.)
  Faust. By Goethe. London: David Nutt, 1895. Pp. [i]-[x], [1]-384. *Filed under* Goethe's Faust.
BETHUNE, GILBERT
  Courtship a-la-Mode. Edinburgh: (priv.), 1831. Pp. [i-iv], [1]-118.
BETHUNE, GILBERT (arr.)
  Gentle Shepherd, The. By Ramsay, Allan. London: John Miller, 1817. Pp. [1]-42.
BETSY
  See Burnand, Francis Cowley.
BETSY BAKER!
  See Morton, John Maddison.
BETTER HALF, THE
  See Williams, Thomas John.
BETTER LATE THAN NEVER
  See Andrews, Miles Peter.
BETTY MARTIN
  See Robertson, Thomas William. Clockmaker's Hat, The.
BETWEEN THE ACTS
  See Ridge, William Pett.
BETWEEN THE POSTS
  See Bell, Florence Eveleen Eleanore Oliffe, Mrs. Hugh (Lady).
BEULAH SPA
  See Dance, Charles.
  See Dance, Charles. Two B'hoys, The.
BEVERLY, HENRY ROXBY
  Abbot, The; or, Mary, Queen of Scots. Music by Kerr, J. London: J. Lowndes, 1820. Pp. [i-iv], [1]-62.
BEWARE A BAD NAME
  See Lamb, Charles. Mr. H.
BEWARE OF SMOOTH WATER
  See Fitzgerald, Edward (trans.).
BIANCA, THE BRAVO'S BRIDE
  See Simpson, John Palgrave.
BICKERSTAFFE, ISAAC
  Hypocrite, The. London: Whittingham & Arliss, 1814. Pp. [1]-64. London Theatre, IX. *Filed under* Dibdin, Thomas John, ed. London Theatre, IX.
  Hypocrite, The. In *New English Drama*, ed. W. Oxberry, 22 vols., London: W. Simpkin & R. Marshall; C. Chapple, 1818, I, [i]-[viii], [1]-63. *Filed under* Oxberry, William Henry. New English Drama, I.
  Hypocrite, The. London: T. Dolby, 1824. Pp. [i]-[vi], [7]-[62]. Dolby's British Theatre, III. *Filed under* Cumberland, John. Cumberland's British Theatre, III.
  Hypocrite, The. In *British Drama*, 12 vols., London: John Dicks, 1865, IV, [1023]-1041.
  Lionel and Clarissa. In *New English Drama*, ed. W. Oxberry, 22 vols., London: W. Simpkin & R. Marshall; C. Chapple, 1818, II, [i]-[viii], [1]-65. *Filed under* Oxberry, William Henry. New English Drama, II.
  Lionel and Clarissa. In *British Drama*, 12 vols., London: John Dicks, 1871, VI, [161]-182.
  Lionel and Clarissa; or, A School for Fathers. London: Whittingham & Arliss, 1815. Pp. [1]-64. London Theatre, VII. *Filed under* Dibdin, Thomas John, ed. London Theatre, VII.
  Love in a Village. London: Whittingham & Arliss, 1814. Pp. [1]-60. London Theatre, III. *Filed under* Dibdin, Thomas John, ed. London Theatre, III.
  Love in a Village. In *New English Drama*, ed. W. Oxberry, 22 vols., London: W. Simpkin & R. Marshall; C. Chapple, 1818, II, [i]-[vi], [1]-55. *Filed under* Oxberry, William Henry. New English Drama, II.
  Love in a Village. London: John Cumberland, 1826. Pp. [i]-[vi], [7]-[54]. Cumberland's British Theatre, V. *Filed*

under Cumberland, John. Cumberland's British Theatre, V.
  Love in a Village. In *British Drama*, 12 vols., London: John Dicks, 1864, I, [48]-64.
  Maid of the Mill, The. London: Whittingham & Arliss, 1815. Pp. [1]-71. London Theatre, V. *Filed under* Dibdin, Thomas John, ed. London Theatre, V.
  Maid of the Mill, The. In *New English Drama*, ed. W. Oxberry, 22 vols., London: W. Simpkin & R. Marshall; C. Chapple, 1818, II, [1-2], [i]-[iv], [1]-62. *Filed under* Oxberry, William Henry. New English Drama, II.
  Maid of the Mill, The. London: T. Dolby, 1825. Pp. [i]-[vi], [7]-59. Dolby's British Theatre, VIII. *Filed under* Cumberland, John. Cumberland's British Theatre, VIII.
  Maid of the Mill, The. In *British Drama*, 12 vols., London: John Dicks, 1871, V, [268]-288.
  Padlock, The. London: Whittingham & Arliss, 1815. Pp. [1]-32. London Theatre, XII. *Filed under* Dibdin, Thomas John, ed. London Theatre, XII.
  Padlock, The. London: T. Dolby, 1823. Pp. [i]-[vi], [7]-[30]. Dolby's British Theatre, III. *Filed under* Cumberland, John. Cumberland's British Theatre, III.
  Padlock, The. In *New English Drama*, ed. W. Oxberry, 22 vols., London: W. Simpkin & R. Marshall; C. Chapple, 1823, XXI, [1], [i]-[vii], [1]-25. *Filed under* Oxberry, William Henry. New English Drama, XXI.
  Padlock, The. In *British Drama*, 12 vols., London: John Dicks, 1871, V, [94]-102.
  Recruiting Sergeant, The. London: Whittingham & Arliss, 1816. Pp. [1]-18. London Theatre, XVIII. *Filed under* Dibdin, Thomas John, ed. London Theatre, XVIII.
  Recruiting Sergeant, The. In *British Drama*, 12 vols., London: John Dicks, 1872, XII, [219]-224.
  Romp, The.
    See Lloyd, ? (arr.).
  Spoiled Child, The. In *New English Drama*, ed. W. Oxberry, 22 vols., London: W. Simpkin & R. Marshall; C. Chapple, 1822, XV, [1-2], [i]-[iv], [1]-22. *Filed under* Oxberry, William Henry. New English Drama, XV.
  Spoiled Child, The. London: John Cumberland, 1826. Pp. [1]-33. Cumberland's British Theatre, XIV. *Filed under* Cumberland, John. Cumberland's British Theatre, XIV.
  Sultan, The; or, A Peep into the Seraglio. London: Sherwood, Neely, & Jones, 1817. Pp. [1]-24. London Theatre, XXV. *Filed under* Dibdin, Thomas John, ed. London Theatre, XXV.
  Sultan, The; or, A Peep into the Seraglio. In *British Drama*, 12 vols., London: John Dicks, 1872, X, [250]-256.
  Thomas and Sally; or, The Sailor's Return. In *British Drama*, 12 vols., London: John Dicks, 1871, V, [343]-348.
BIG O AND SIR GLORY
  See Cobbett, William.
BIGG, JOHN STANYAN
  Night and the Soul. London: Groombridge & Sons, 1854. Pp. [i-iv], [1]-188.
BILBERRY OF TILBURY
  See Dauncey, Silvanus.
BILHAUD, PAUL
  Paradise.
    See under title.
BILIOUS ATTACK, A
  See Wood, Arthur.
BILKINS, TAYLOR (pseud. of Vicars, W. A.)
  Christmas Pantomime, A. London: Thomas Hailes Lacy, n.d. Pp. [1]-14. [Lacy's Acting Edition]. *Filed under* Vicars, W. A.
BILL STEALERS BEWARE
  See Wynne, John. Tricks of the Time.
BILL, THE BELLE, AND THE BULLET!
  See Byron, Henry James. Freischutz, Der.
BILLEE TAYLOR
  See Stephens, Henry Pottinger.
BILLET DOUX
  See Mathews, Charles James. Adventures of a Love Letter, The.

BILLING AND COOING
　　See Oxenford, John.
BILLY
　　See Cooper, G.
BILLY DOO
　　See Rae, Charles Marsham.
　　See Rae, Charles Marsham. Nothing Like Paste.
BILLY DOO, THE BILL-STICKER
　　See Rae, Charles Marsham. Nothing Like Paste.
BILLY TAYLOR
　　See Buckstone, John Baldwin.
BINGHAM, FREDERICK
　　Counsel's Opinion. London & New York: Samuel French,
　　n.d. Pp. [1]-11.
BINKS THE BAGMAN
　　See Coyne, Joseph Stirling.
BINYON, LAURENCE
　　Supper, The. [Edinburgh]: Ballantyne Press, 1897. Pp.
　　[1]-[32].
BIORN
　　See Marshall, Francis Albert.
BIRCH, JONATHAN (trans.)
　　Faust. By Goethe. London: Black & Armstrong; Leipzig: F.
　　A. Brockhaus, 1839. Pp. [i]-[xviii], [1]-276.
BIRCH, SAMUEL
　　Adopted Child, The. In *British Drama,* 12 vols., London: John
　　Dicks, 1864, I, [121]-128.
　　Adopted Child, The. London: John Cumberland, n.d. Pp.
　　[1]-34. Cumberland's British Theatre, XXIX. *Filed under*
　　Cumberland, John. Cumberland's British Theatre,
　　XXIX.
BIRCH, WILLIAM HENRY
　　Eveleen, the Rose of the Vale. Music by Birch, William
　　Henry. Reading: W. H. Birch, n.d. Pp. [1]-16. Libretto.
BIRD, JAMES
　　Cosmo, Duke of Tuscany. London: Rodwell & Martin, 1822.
　　Pp. [i]-[vi], [1]-113.
　　Smuggler's Daughter, The. London: Baldwin & Cradock,
　　1836. Pp. [i-vi], [1]-36.
BIRD IN THE HAND WORTH TWO IN THE BUSH, A
　　See Phillips, Frederick Laurence.
BIRD OF PARADISE, THE
　　See Thompson, Alfred.
BIRD OF PASSAGE, A
　　See Webster, Benjamin Nottingham.
BIRD-CAGE
　　See Anstey, F. Nora.
BIRDS, THE
　　See Frere, John Hookham (trans.).
　　See Verrall, Arthur Woolgar (trans.).
BIRDS IN THEIR LITTLE NESTS AGREE
　　See Rae, Charles Marsham.
BIRDS OF A FEATHER
　　See Hatton, Joseph.
BIRDS OF ARISTOPHANES, THE
　　See Planché, James Robinson.
BIRDS OF PREY
　　See Robertson, Thomas William.
BIRRELL, ANDREW
　　Henry and Almeria. London: W. Blackader (printer), n.d.
　　Pp. [iii]-[viii], [1]-79. Title page lacking.
BIRTH
　　See Robertson, Thomas William.
BIRTH DAY DINNER
　　See Moncrieff, William Thomas. Parson's Nose, The.
BIRTH OF A SOUL, THE
　　See Sharp, William.
BIRTH OF BEAUTY, THE
　　See Akhurst, William M.
BIRTH-DAY OF FREEDOM
　　See Brougham, John. Irish Yankee, The.
BIRTH-PLACE OF PODGERS, THE
　　See Hollingshead, John.

BIRTHRIGHT
　　See Bulwer (later Bulwer-Lytton), Edward George Earle
　　Lytton, Lord Lytton. Sea Captain, The.
BISHOP, HENRY ROWLEY (trans.)
　　Marriage of Figaro, The. Music by Mozart. London: John
　　Miller, 1819. Pp. [i]-[viii], [1]-56. Libretto.
　　Marriage of Figaro, The. Music by Mozart. London:
　　Goulding, D'Almaine, Potter, n.d. Pp. [1]-95. Vocal
　　score.
BISHOP ASTRAY, THE
　　See Sturgis, Julian Russell.
BISSON, ALEXANDRE
　　Captain Thérèse.
　　See Burnand, Francis Cowley.
BIT OF BRUMMAGEM
　　See Craven, Henry Thornton. Bowl'd Out.
BIT OF OLD CHELSEA, A
　　See Beringer, Aimée Danielle, Mrs. Oscar.
BIT OF SCANDAL!
　　See Craven, Henry Thornton. Little Nun, The.
BITER BIT, THE
　　See Livius, Barham.
　　See Livius, Barham. Maid or Wife.
BITS OF BURLESQUE
　　See Byron, Henry James.
BITTER RECKONING, THE
　　See Hazlewood, Colin Henry.
BITTERN'S SWAMP
　　See Almar, George. Rover's Bride, The.
BJØRNSON, BJØRNSTJERNE A.
　　Gauntlet, A.
　　See Edwards, Osman (trans.).
BLACK, JOHN
　　Falls of Clyde, The; or, The Fairies. Edinburgh: William
　　Creech, 1806. Pp. [1]-241.
BLACK AND WHITE
　　See Collins, William Wilkie.
BLACK CAT, THE
　　See Todhunter, John.
BLACK DOCTOR, THE
　　See Bridgeman, John Vipon.
BLACK DOMINO
　　See A'Beckett, Gilbert Abbott.
　　See A'Beckett, Gilbert Abbott. Queen's Ball, The.
　　See Chorley, Henry Fothergill.
　　See Kenney, Charles Lamb (trans.). Domino Noir, Le.
　　See Mathews, Charles James.
　　See Webster, Benjamin Nottingham.
　　See Wilks, Thomas Egerton.
BLACK EYED SUSAN
　　See Jerrold, Douglas William.
BLACK HUGH, THE OUTLAW
　　See Rogers, William.
BLACK KITTEN, THE
　　See Barrett, Wilson.
BLACK MADONNA, THE
　　See Sharp, William.
BLACK PHANTOM!
　　See Amherst, J. H. Will Watch!
BLACK SHEEP
　　See Coyne, Joseph Stirling.
　　See Simpson, John Palgrave.
BLACK TULIP, THE
　　See Grundy, Sydney.
BLACK, WHITE, AND GREY
　　See Robertson, Thomas William. Two Gay Deceivers.
BLACKBURN, VERNON
　　Messalina. Music by De Lara, Isadore. London: J. Miles
　　(printer), n.d. Pp. [1]-36. Libretto.
BLACKET, JOSEPH
　　Dramatic Sketches. In *Specimens of the Poetry of Joseph
　　Blacket,* London: Galabin & Marchant (priv.), 1809, pp.
　　[i], [109]-137.
BLACK-EY'D SUSAN
　　See Jerrold, Douglas William.

BLACK-EYED SUKEY
  See Cooper, Frederick Fox.
BLACK-EYED SUSAN
  See Burnand, Francis Cowley. Latest Edition of Black-Eyed Susan, The.
  See Jerrold, Douglas William.
  See Pleon, Harry.
BLACKIE, JOHN STUART (trans.)
  Faust. By Goethe. Edinburgh: William Blackwood; London: T. Cadell, 1834. Pp. [i]-[lii], [1]-288.
  Faust. By Goethe. In [*Plays by Greek, Spanish, French, German, & English Dramatists,* New York]: Colonial Press, c.1900, II, [i-vi], [1]-150.
BLACKMORE, RICHARD DODDRIDGE
  Eric and Karine. By Melanter (pseud.). In *Poems by Melanter,* London: Saunders & Otley, 1854, pp. [i-iv], [1]-63.
BLACKMORE, W. T.
  Roundhead, The.
    See Bussy, Bernard F.
BLACKSMITH, THE
  See Collier, William.
BLACKWELL, J. A.
  Rudolf of Varosnay. [London: C. & H. Senior, 1841]. Pp. [1]-136. Title page lacking.
BLACKWOOD, HELEN SELINA SHERIDAN
  See Dufferin, Helen Selina Sheridan Blackwood, Lady.
BLAKE, EMILIA
  See Gowing, Emilia Julia Blake, Mrs. William Aylmer.
BLAKE, PAUL
  His Own Guest.
    See Ayres, Arthur.
BLAKE, ROBERT (pseud. of Thompson, Robert Hely)
  Kirk-o-Field. Omagh: Tyrone Constitution Office (printer) (priv.), n.d. Pp. [1]-64.
  Limited. Omagh: Tyrone Constitution Office (printer), n.d. Pp. [1]-46.
  Mary Queen of Scots. London: Simpkin, Marshall, 1894. Pp. [1]-56. 2nd ed.
  Nuns of Minsk, The: A Tale of Russian Atrocities in Poland. London: Remington, 1878. Pp. [i-iv], [1]-63.
BLAKE, THOMAS G.
  Dumb Guide of the Tyrol, The. London: John Dicks, n.d. Pp. [1]-13. Dicks' Standard Plays, 756.
  Life As It Is; or, The Convict's Child. London: James Pattie, 1840. Pp. [1]-40. [Pattie's Universal Stage or Theatrical Prompt Book].
  Lonely Man of the Ocean, The; or, The Night Before the Bridal. London: Thomas Hailes Lacy, n.d. Pp. [1]-40.
  Our Old House at Home. London: J. Pattie, n.d. Pp. [1]-36. Promptbook.
  Spanking Legacy, A; or, The Corsican Vendetta. New York: Dick & Fitzgerald, n.d. Pp. [7]-20. Text complete. Dick's American Edition.
  Wapping Old Stairs. London: James Pattie, n.d. Pp. [1]-[50]. Pattie's Penny Play or Weekly Acting Drama, 39.
BLANCHARD, EDWARD LITT LAMAN
  See Blanchard, Edward Litt Leman.
BLANCHARD, EDWARD LITT LEMAN
  Adam Buff; or, The Man without a —! London: John Duncombe, n.d. Pp. [1]-24. New British Theatre (late Duncombe's), 520.
  Aladdin; or, Harlequin and the Wonderful Lamp. Music by Meyder, Karl. London: Tuck, 1874. Pp. [8]-47. Text complete. Libretto.
  Artful Dodge, The. London: Thomas Hailes Lacy, n.d. Pp. [1]-23. Promptbook.
  Babes in the Wood, Robin Hood and His Merry Men, and Harlequin Who Killed Cock Robin?
    See Harris, Augustus Henry Glossop.
  Beauty and the Beast; or, Harlequin and Old Mother Bunch. Music by Levey, W. C. London: n.pub., 1869. Pp. [1]-32. Libretto.
  Bluebeard. Written with Greenwood, Thomas Longdon. By The Brothers Grinn (pseud.). Music by Wallerstein,

Ferdinand. London: M'Corquodale (printer), n.d. Pp. [1]-[28]. Libretto. *Filed under* Grinn, The Brothers.
Cherry and Fair Star; or, The Singing Apple, the Talking Bird, and the Dancing Waters. London: Music Publishing Co., n.d. Pp. [i-ii], [1]-16. Libretto.
Children in the Wood, The; or, Harlequin Queen Mab and the World of Dreams. Music by Levey, W. C. London: Tuck, n.d. Pp. [1]-39. Libretto.
Cinderella. Music by Barrett, Oscar. London: Alfred Gibbons, n.d. Pp. [1]-46. Libretto.
Cinderella; or, Harlequin and the Fairy Slipper. Music by Meyder, Karl. London: Tuck, 1878. Pp. [i-vii], [1]-[33]. Libretto.
Cinderella; or, Harlequin and the Magic Pumpkin and the Great Fairy of the Little Glass Slipper! Written with Greenwood, Thomas Longdon. By The Brothers Grinn (pseud.). London: J. Miles (printer), n.d. Pp. [1]-20. Libretto. *Filed under* Grinn, The Brothers.
Dragon of Wantley, The; or, Harlequin and Mother Shipton. Music by Levey, W. C. London: Tuck, 1870. Pp. [1]-36. Libretto.
Faith, Hope, and Charity!; or, Chance and Change! London: John Duncombe, n.d. Pp. [1-56]. Cropped at top, with loss of pagination and some text.
Faw! Fee! Fo! Fum!; or, Harlequin Jack the Giant Killer. Music by Tully, J. H. London: Jabez Tuck, 1867. Pp. [1]-[33]. Libretto.
Forty Thieves. Music by Wallerstein, Ferdinand. London: Strand, n.d. Pp. [1]-[76]. Libretto. *Filed under* Blanchard, Edward Litt Laman.
Grimalkin the Great; or, Harlequin Puss in Boots and the Miller's Sons. Music by Levey, W. C. London: Jabez Tuck, 1868. Pp. [1]-31. Libretto.
Harlequin and Friar Bacon; or, Great Grim John of Gaunt and the Enchanted Lance of Robin Goodfellow. By Francesco Frost (pseud.). Music by Tulley, J. H. London: Music Publishing Co., n.d. Pp. [1]-[16]. Libretto.
Harlequin and the Forty Thieves. Music by Meyder, Karl. London: Tuck, 1876. Pp. [9]-53. Text complete. Libretto.
Harlequin and the House That Jack Built; or, Old Mother Hubbard and Her Wonderful Dog. Music by Tully, J. H. London: Music Publishing Co., n.d. Pp. [1]-24. Libretto.
Harlequin and the World of Flowers; or, The Fairy of the Rose and the Sprite of the Silver Star. Music by Isaacson. London: John K. Chapman, n.d. Pp. [1]-16. Libretto.
Harlequin Bluecap and the King of the Golden Waters; or, The Three Kingdoms: Animal, Vegetable, and Mineral. London: John K. Chapman (printer), n.d. Pp. [1]-16. Libretto. *Filed under* Harlequin Bluecap and the King of the Golden Waters (anon.).
Harlequin Hudibras!; or, Old Dame Durden and the Droll Days of the Merry Monarch. Music by Blewitt; Harroway. London: Thomas Hailes Lacy, n.d. Pp. [1]-20. Libretto.
Harlequin Sinbad the Sailor; or, The Great Roc of the Diamond Valley and the Seven Wonders of the World. Music by Barnard, J. London: Music Publishing Co., n.d. Pp. [1]-20. Libretto.
Hey Diddle Diddle; or, Harlequin King Nonsense, and the Seven Ages of Man. Music by Tully, J. H. London: G. H. Davidson, n.d. Pp. [1]-14. Libretto.
Hop o' My Thumb and His Eleven Brothers; or, Harlequin and the Ogre of the Seven League Boots. Music by Barnard, J. London: Thompson & Harrison, 1864. Pp. [1]-24. Libretto.
Induction, An. In *Drawing-Room Plays and Parlour Pantomimes,* ed. Clement Scott, London: Stanley Rivers, 1870, pp. [i], [ix]-xii.
Jack and Jill; or, Old Dame Nature and the Fairy Art. Music by Montgomery, W. H. London (Sydenham): Crystal Palace Co., 1872. Pp. [i-vi], [1]-24. Libretto.
Jack and the Beanstalk; or, Harlequin Leap-year and the Merry Pranks of the Good Little People. Music by Tully, J. H. London: Davidson, n.d. Pp. [1]-20. Libretto.

Jack in the Box; or, Harlequin Little Tom Tucker and the Three Wise Men of Gotham. Music by Levey, W. C. London: Tuck, 1873. Pp. [1]-38. Libretto.

King Humming Top; or, Harlequin and the Land of Toys. London: G. H. Davidson, n.d. Pp. [1]-20. Libretto. *Filed under* Blanchard, Edward Litt Laman.

Little Goody Two-Shoes; or, Harlequin and Cock Robin. Music by Barnard, J. London: Music Publishing Co., n.d. Pp. [1]-21. Libretto.

Little Jack Horner; or, Harlequin A. B. C. and the Enchanted Region of Nursery Rhymes. Music by Tully, J. H. London: Davidson, n.d. Pp. [1]-16. Libretto.

Little King Pippin; or, Harlequin Fortunatus and the Magic Purse and Wishing Cap. Music by Barnard, J. London: Jabez Tuck, 1865. Pp. [1]-36. Libretto.

Number Nip; or, Harlequin and the Gnome King of the Giant Mountain. Music by Tully, J. H. London: Jabez Tuck, 1866. Pp. [1]-34. Libretto.

Peter Wilkins; or, Harlequin and the Flying Women of the Loadstone Rock. Music by Tully, J. H. London: Music Publishing Co., n.d. Pp. [1]-21. Libretto.

Pork Chops; or, A Dream at Home. Music by Caulcott. London: Thomas Hailes Lacy, n.d. Pp. [1]-12. [Lacy's Acting Edition].

Puss in Boots. Music by Slaughter, Walter A. London: Strand, n.d. Pp. [1]-92. Libretto.

Puss in Boots; or, Dame Trot and Her Comical Cat, and the Ogre Fee-Fo-Fum. London: n.pub., n.d. Pp. [3]-24. Title page lacking. *Filed under* Puss in Boots (anon.).

Riquet with the Tuft; or, Harlequin and Old Mother Shipton. London: Music Publishing Co., n.d. Pp. [1]-20. *Filed under* Blanchard, Edward Litt Laman.

Robinson Crusoe. Music by Barrett, Oscar. London: M'Corquodale (printer), n.d. Pp. [1]-32. Libretto.

See, Saw, Margery Daw; or, Harlequin Holiday and the Island of Ups and Downs. Music by Anschuez. London: Davidson, n.d. Pp. [1]-16. Libretto.

Sinbad the Sailor; or, Harlequin and the Fairies of the Diamond Valley. Written with Greenwood, Thomas Longdon. By The Brothers Grinn (pseud.). Music by Barrett, Oscar. London (Sydenham): Crystal Palace Co., 1876. Pp. [1]-26. Libretto.

Sinbad the Sailor; or, Harlequin and the King of the Diamond Valley. Written with Greenwood, Thomas Longdon. Glasgow: William Gilchrist (printer), 1858-9. Pp. [1]-15. Libretto. *Filed under* Grinn, The Brothers.

Tom Thumb the Great; or, Harlequin King Arthur and the Knights of the Round Table. Music by Levey, W. C. London: Tuck, 1871. Pp. [1]-40. Libretto.

White Cat, The. Music by Meyder, Karl. London: Tuck, 1877. Pp. [9]-46. Text complete. Libretto.

Whittington and His Cat; or, Harlequin Lord Mayor of London. Music by Meyder, Karl. London: Tuck, 1875. Pp. [16]-[57]. Text complete. Libretto.

William the Conqueror; or, Harlequin Harold and the Sack of the Saxons. By Francisco Frost (pseud.). Music by Lee, Alexander. London: G. Mansell, n.d. Pp. [1]-16. Libretto.

BLANCHE DE MALETROIT
　　See Mason, Alfred Edward Woodley.
BLANCHE DE NEVERS
　　See Brougham, John.
BLANCHE HERIOT
　　See Smith, Albert Richard.
BLANCHE OF JERSEY
　　See Peake, Richard Brinsley.
BLANCHE OF NAVARRE
　　See James, George Payne Rainsford.
BLANCHE OF NEVERS
　　See Brougham, John. Duke's Daughter, The.
　　See Brougham, John. Duke's Motto, The.
BLANK CARTRIDGE
　　See How to Die for Love.
BLAZING BURGEE, THE
　　See Bowles, Thomas Gibson.

BLEAK HOUSE
　　See Lander, George.
BLECHINGTON HOUSE
　　See Craven, Henry Thornton.
BLEEDING NUN OF LINDENBERG
　　See Grosette, Henry William. Raymond and Agnes!
　　See Lewis, Matthew Gregory. Raymond and Agnes: The Travellers Benighted.
BLIGHTED BEING, A
　　See Taylor, Tom.
BLIGHTED FLOWER
　　See Edwardes, Conway Theodore Marriott. Linda di Chamouni.
BLIGHTED LOVE
　　See Armstrong, George P.
BLIND BARGAIN, THE
　　See Reynolds, Frederick.
BLIND BEGGAR OF BETHNAL GREEN, THE
　　See Milner, Henry M.
BLIND BEGGARS, THE
　　See Farnie, Henry Brougham.
BLIND BOY, THE
　　See Kenney, James.
BLIND GIRL, THE
　　See Morton, Thomas, sr.
BLIND GIRL AND LITTLE GERTY
　　See Seaman, William. Lamplighter, The.
BLIND GIRL OF BONN, THE
　　See Pember, Edward Henry.
BLIND LOVE
　　See Roberts, George.
BLIND WIFE, THE
　　See Powell, Thomas.
BLIND WITNESS!
　　See Reeve, William. Barark Johnson.
BLINK, GEORGE
　　Tiger at Large, The; or, The Cad of the Buss. London: Chapman & Hall, n.d. Pp. [1]-22. [Acting National Drama].
　　Vampire Bride, The; or, Wake Not the Dead. London: Thomas Hailes Lacy, n.d. Pp. [1]-27.
BLISS, HENRY
　　Robespierre. London: B. Kimpton, 1854. Pp. [i]-viii, [1]-272.
　　Thecla. London & Edinburgh: Williams & Norgate, 1866. Pp. [i]-[viii], [1]-211.
BLOCKHEADS INDEED!
　　See Macfarren, George. Latin, Love, and War.
BLODWEN
　　See Rowlands, ?, Prof. (trans.).
BLONDE AND BRUNETTE
　　See O'Shea, J. A.
BLOOD DEMANDS ITS VICTIM
　　See Amherst, J. H. Will Watch!
BLOOD FOR BLOOD
　　See Thompson, C. Pelham. Shade, The.
BLOOD MONEY
　　See Morton, W. E.
BLOOD RED KNIGHT, THE
　　See Amherst, J. H.
　　See Barrymore, William.
BLOOMER COSTUME
　　See Stirling, Edward. Figure of Fun, A.
BLOOMERISM
　　See Nightingale, Joseph Henry.
BLOOMFIELD, ROBERT
　　Hazelwood Hall. London: Baldwin, Cradock, & Joy, 1823. Pp. [i]-[viii], [1]-72.
BLOSSOM OF CHURNINGTON GREEN, THE
　　See Hoskins, Francis Radcliffe.
BLOT IN THE 'SCUTCHEON, A
　　See Browning, Robert.
BLOW FOR BLOW
　　See Byron, Henry James.
BLOW IN THE DARK, THE
　　See Townsend, William Thompson.

BLUE BEAR OF NANGIS!
    See Wynne, John. Napoleon's First Love.
BLUE BEARD
    See also Bluebeard.
    See Burnand, Francis Cowley.
    See Colman, George, jr.
    See Keating, Eliza H.
    See Planché, James Robinson.
    See Tully, James Howard.
BLUE BEARD! FROM A NEW POINT OF HUE
    See Byron, Henry James.
BLUE BIRD OF PARADISE
    See Planché, James Robinson. King Charming.
BLUE DEVILS
    See Colman, George, jr.
BLUEBEARD
    See also Blue Beard.
    See Blanchard, Edward Litt Leman.
    See Bridgeman, John Vipon.
    See Burnand, Francis Cowley.
    See Gower, Francis Leveson, Lord.
    See Millward, Charles.
BLUEBEARD; OR, THE KEY OF THE CELLAR (anon.)
    London: R. Washbourne, 1882. Pp. [1]-31.
BLUEBEARD RE-PAIRED
    See Bellingham, Henry.
BLUE-EYED SUSAN
    See Sims, George Robert.
BLUE-FACED BABOON!, THE
    See Addison, Henry Robert, Capt.
BLUE-JACKETS, THE
    See Stirling, Edward.
BLUES, THE
    See Byron, George Gordon, Lord.
BLUE-STOCKING
    See Moore, Thomas. M. P.
BLUE-STOCKINGS, THE
    See Mathew, Charles (trans.).
BLUM, ERNEST
    Rose Michel.
        See Clarke, Campbell (trans.).
BLUNDERER, THE
    See Mathew, Charles (trans.).
    See Van Laun, Henri (trans.).
BLUNT, ARTHUR CECIL
    Time Is Money.
        See Bell, Florence Eveleen Eleanore Oliffe, Mrs. Hugh (Lady).
BLUNT, WILFRED SCAWEN
    Bride of the Nile, The. In *Poetical Works,* 2 vols., London: Macmillan, 1914, II, [i], [354]-398.
    Little Left Hand, The. In *Poetical Works,* 2 vols., London: Macmillan, 1914, II, [399]-448.
    Satan Absolved: A Victorian Mystery. London & New York: John Lane, 1899. Pp. [i]-viii, [1]-52.
BOADEN, CAROLINE
    Don Pedro the Cruel and Don Manuel the Cobbler!; or, The Corregidor of Seville! London: John Duncombe, n.d. Pp. [1]-33. Duncombe's Edition.
    Fatality. London: John Cumberland, n.d. Pp. [1]-28. [Cumberland's British Theatre].
    Fatality. London: John Cumberland, n.d. Pp. [1]-28. Cumberland's British Theatre, XXIII. *Filed under* Cumberland, John. Cumberland's British Theatre, XXIII.
    First of April, The. London: John Cumberland, n.d. Pp. [1]-36. Cumberland's British Theatre, 185.
    First of April, The. London: John Cumberland, n.d. Pp. [1]-36. Cumberland's British Theatre, XXVI. *Filed under* Cumberland, John. Cumberland's British Theatre, XXVI.
    William Thompson; or, Which Is He? London: John Cumberland, n.d. Pp. [1]-32. [Cumberland's British Theatre].
    William Thompson; or, Which Is He? London: John Cumberland, n.d. Pp. [1]-32. Cumberland's British

Theatre, XXIII. *Filed under* Cumberland, John. Cumberland's British Theatre, XXIII.
BOADEN, JAMES
    Maid of Bristol, The. London: Longman & Rees, 1803. Pp. [i-iv], [1]-48. 2nd ed.
    Maid of Bristol, The. New York: D. Longworth, 1803. Pp. [1]-59.
    Voice of Nature, The. London: James Ridgway, 1803. Pp. [i]-[x], [1]-[44]. Promptbook.
BOADICEA
    See Gowing, Emilia Julia Blake, Mrs. William Aylmer.
BOADICEA THE BEAUTIFUL
    See Burnand, Francis Cowley.
BOARD AND RESIDENCE
    See Edwardes, Conway Theodore Marriott.
BOARDED AND DONE FOR
    See Planché, James Robinson. Jenkinses, The.
BOARDING HOUSE, THE
    See Beazley, Samuel, jr.
BOARDING SCHOOL, THE
    See Bernard, William Bayle.
BOAT-BUILDER'S HOVEL!
    See Fitzball, Edward. Negro of Wapping, The.
BOAT-RACE DAY
    See Anstey, F.
BOBBY A1
    See Hodgson, G. S.
BOHEMIAN, THE
    See Soane, George.
BOHEMIAN GIRL, THE
    See Bunn, Alfred.
BOHEMIAN MOTHER
    See Ebsworth, Joseph. Rosalie.
    See Maddox, John Medex. Infanticide.
BOHEMIANS, THE
    See Stirling, Edward.
BOHEMIANS OF PARIS, THE
    See Barnett, Charles Zachary.
BOLD BUCANIERS
    See Pocock, Isaac. Robinson Crusoe.
BOLD BUCCANIERS
    See Pocock, Isaac. Robinson Crusoe.
BOLD DRAGOONS, THE
    See Barnett, Morris.
BOLD ROBIN HOOD AND HIS FORESTERS GOOD
    See Thorn, Geoffrey. Babes in the Wood.
BOLD STROKE FOR A HUSBAND, A
    See Cowley, Hannah Parkhouse, Mrs.
BOLD STROKE FOR A WIFE, A
    See Centlivre, Susannah Carroll Freeman, Mrs. Joseph.
BOLENO, HENRY (pseud. of Mason, Henry Boleno)
    Harlequin Crusader; or, Richard Coeur de Lion and the Knight Templars. Written with Pearson, H. Liverpool: S. A. Hurton (printer), 1849. Pp. [1]-16. Libretto. *Filed under* Mason, Henry Boleno.
BOLTON, CHARLES
    Caught in a Line; or, The Unrivalled Blondin. London: Thomas Hailes Lacy, n.d. Pp. [1]-14. [Lacy's Acting Edition].
BOMBASTES FURIOSO
    See Rhodes, William Barnes.
BON JUGE, LE (anon.)
    Also: The Good Judge. [London: Mrs. Marshall's Typewriting Office, 1900]. Pp. [i-iii], [1]-63, [i], [1]-40, [i], [1]-48. Pagination by act. Typescript promptbook.
BON TON
    See Garrick, David.
BONA FIDE TRAVELLERS
    See Brough, William.
BONAWITZ, J. H.
    Irma.
        See Dunn, Sinclair (trans.).
BONAWITZ, J. H., JR
    Edgar the Socialist. London: J. W. Kolckmann, n.d. Pp. [1]-63.

BOND, THE
    See Gore, Catherine Grace Frances Moody, Mrs.
    Charles.
BONDMAN, THE
    See Caine, Hall.
BONDOCANI, IL
    See Dibdin, Thomas John.
BONIFACIO AND BRIDGETINA
    See Dibdin, Thomas John.
BONNIE BOY
    See Barrymore, William. Gilderoy.
BONNIE FISH WIFE, THE
    See Selby, Charles.
BONNY BLACK BESS
    See Milner, Henry M. Turpin's Ride to York.
BOOK OF LOVE
    See Arnold, Edwin, Sir (trans.). With Sa'di in the Garden.
BOOK THE THIRD, CHAPTER THE FIRST
    See Webster, Benjamin Nottingham.
BOOTH, GEORGE
    Choice Spirits; or, The Palace of Gin. London: J. Bennett,
    1838. Pp. [1]-51.
BOOTH, JUNIUS BRUTUS
    Ugolino. New York: Samuel French, n.d. Pp. [1]-27.
    French's American Drama, 120 <wrps. French's Stan-
    dard Drama>.
BOOTHBY, BROOKE, SIR (trans.)
    Britannicus. By Racine. London: John Stockdale, 1803. Pp.
    [1]-99.
BOOTS AT THE SWAN
    See Selby, Charles.
BORDER CHIEFTAINS
    See Dibdin, Thomas John. White Plume, The.
BORDER MARRIAGE, A
    See Sorrell, William J.
BORES, THE
    See Van Laun, Henri (trans.).
BORN TO GOOD LUCK
    See Power, Tyrone.
BORO' BENCH, A
    See Breare, William Hammond.
BOROUGH ELECTION
    See Summers, Knight. M.P. for Puddlepool.
BOROUGH POLITICS
    See Marston, John Westland.
BOROUGH REFORM AND CITY DEFORMITY (anon.)
    Edinburgh: R. Gibbons (printer), 1818. Pp. [3]-36.
BORROWED FEATHERS
    See Millingen, John Gideon.
BORROWED PLUMES
    See Maltby, C. Alfred.
BORROWING A HUSBAND
    See Moncrieff, William Thomas.
BORROWING BOOTS
    See Little, Archibald John (trans.).
BOSBACCA, GULIELMERG HENRICUS (pseud. of Hertz,
    Henrick)
    **King Zany's Daughter; or, The Princess Who Was Blind of
    One Eye and Could Not See Out of the Other.** London:
    S. G. Fairbrother, n.d. Pp. [1]-20.
BOSOM FRIENDS
    See Newte, Horace Wykeham Can.
BOSWELL, ROBERT BRUCE (trans.)
    Alexander the Great. By Racine. In *Dramatic Works of Jean
    Racine*, 2 vols., London: George Bell & Sons, 1890, I,
    [63]-119. *Filed under* Dramatic Works.
    Andromache. By Racine. In *Dramatic Works of Jean Racine*,
    2 vols., London: George Bell & Sons, 1890, I, [121]-184.
    Filed under Dramatic Works.
    Athaliah. By Racine. In *Dramatic Works of Jean Racine*, 2
    vols., London: George Bell & Sons, 1890, II, [327]-403.
    Filed under Dramatic Works.
    Bajazet. By Racine. In *Dramatic Works of Jean Racine*, 2
    vols., London: George Bell & Sons, 1890, II, [9]-67. *Filed
    under* Dramatic Works.

Berenice. By Racine. In *Dramatic Works of Jean Racine*, 2
    vols., London: George Bell & Sons, 1890, I, [325]-386.
    Filed under Dramatic Works.
Britannicus. By Racine. In *Dramatic Works of Jean Racine*, 2
    vols., London: George Bell & Sons, 1890, I, [253]-323.
    Filed under Dramatic Works.
Esther. By Racine. In *Dramatic Works of Jean Racine*, 2
    vols., London: George Bell & Sons, 1890, II, [269]-325.
    Filed under Dramatic Works.
Iphigenia. By Racine. In *Dramatic Works of Jean Racine*, 2
    vols., London: George Bell & Sons, 1890, II, [133]-202.
    Filed under Dramatic Works.
Litigants, The. By Racine. In *Dramatic Works of Jean
    Racine*, 2 vols., London: George Bell & Sons, 1890, I,
    [185]-251. *Filed under* Dramatic Works.
Mithridates. By Racine. In *Dramatic Works of Jean Racine*, 2
    vols., London: George Bell & Sons, 1890, II, [69]-132.
    Filed under Dramatic Works.
Phaedra. By Racine. In *Dramatic Works of Jean Racine*, 2
    vols., London: George Bell & Sons, 1890, II, [203]-267.
    Filed under Dramatic Works.
Thebaïd, The. By Racine. In *Dramatic Works of Jean Racine*,
    2 vols., London: George Bell & Sons, 1890, I, [i]-[xviii],
    [1]-61. *Filed under* Dramatic Works.
BOSWORTH, J.
    Gipsy King, The; or, The Perilous Pass of the Cataract.
    London: John Dicks, n.d. Pp. [1]-16. Dicks' Standard
    Plays, 684.
BOTANY BAY
    See Woods, Robert Henry.
BOTHWELL
    See Swinburne, Algernon Charles.
    See Ware, James Redding.
BOTTLE, THE
    See Taylor, Thomas Proclus.
BOTTLE IMP, THE
    See Peake, Richard Brinsley.
BOTTONE, NINO
    Undecided Voter, The. Manchester: John Heywood, 1881.
    Pp. [1]-15.
BOUCICAULT, DION
    See Boucicault, Dionysius Lardner.
BOUCICAULT, DION GEORGE
    My Little Girl. London & New York: Samuel French, n.d.
    Pp. [1]-14. [French's Acting Edition, 129].
BOUCICAULT, DIONYSIUS LARDNER
    After Dark. N.p.: n.pub., n.d. Pp. [1]-39.
    Alma Mater; or, A Cure for Coquettes. By D. Bourcicault.
    London: Webster, n.d. Pp. [1]-48. Webster's Acting
    National Drama, 105.
    Amadan, The. N.p.: n.pub., n.d. Pp. [i-ii], [1]-78. Title page
    lacking.
    Andy Blake; or, The Irish Diamond. New York & London:
    Samuel French, n.d. Pp. [1]-19. Bourcicault's Dramatic
    Works, 2 <wrps. French's Minor Drama, 110>.
    Arrah-na-Pogue; or, The Wicklow Wedding. New York:
    DeWitt, n.d. Pp. [1]-53. DeWitt's Acting Plays, 365.
    Arrah-na-Pogue; or, The Wicklow Wedding. N.p.: n.pub.,
    n.d. Pp. [1]-64. Title page lacking. Promptbook.
    Babil and Bijou; or, The Lost Regalia. Written with Planché,
    James Robinson; Green, Frank W. Music by Jacobi, G.
    London: J. Miles (printer), n.d. Pp. [1]-28. Libretto.
    Belle Lamar. N.p.: n.pub., n.d. 175 leaves, consisting of
    printed and ms. text and nine ms. sides. Promptbook.
    Broken Vow, The. London: Thomas Hailes Lacy, 1851. Pp.
    [i-vi], [1]-52.
    Caesar de Bazan.
    See Webster, Benjamin Nottingham.
    Colleen Bawn, The; or, The Brides of Garryowen. London:
    Thomas Hailes Lacy, n.d. Pp. [1]-52.
    Colleen Bawn, The; or, The Brides of Garryowen. New York:
    T. Henry French; London: Samuel French, n.d. Pp.
    [1]-42. French's Standard Drama, 366. Promptbook.
    Corsican Brothers, The. London: John K. Chapman (printer),
    n.d. Pp. [1]-40.

Curiosities of Literature. London: Webster, n.d. Pp. [1]-20.

Daddy O'Dowd. N.p.: n.pub., n.d. Pp. [1]-17, [1]-29, [1]-31. Title page lacking. Pagination by act. Promptbook.

Dot. N.p.: n.pub., n.d. Pp. [1]-33. Title page lacking. Promptbook.

Dot: A Fairy Tale of Home. In [*America's Lost Plays*, Princeton, N.J.: Princeton University Press, 1940, I], [107]-149.

Elfie; or, The Cherrytree Inn. N.p.: n.pub., n.d. Pp. [1]-34.

Faust and Marguerite.
See Robertson, Thomas William.

Flying Scud; or, A Four-Legged Fortune. In [*America's Lost Plays*, Princeton, N.J.: Princeton University Press, 1940, I], [151]-227.

Flying Scud; or, A Four-Legged Fortune. N.p.: n.pub., n.d. Pp. [1]-55. Title page lacking. Promptbook.

Forbidden Fruit. In *America's Lost Plays*, Princeton, N.J.: Princeton University Press, 1940, I, [iii]-[x], [1]-48.

Formosa (The Most Beautiful); or, The Railroad to Ruin. N.p.: n.pub., n.d. Pp. [1]-44.

Foul Play. N.p.: n.pub., n.d. Pp. [1]-44. Title page lacking. Text incomplete? Promptbook.

Foul Play. Written with Reade, Charles. Chicago: Dramatic Publishing Co., n.d. Pp. [1]-33. [Sergel's Acting Drama].

Fox and the Goose, The.
See Webster, Benjamin Nottingham.

Grimaldi; or, The Life of an Actress. New York: n.pub., 1856. Pp. [1]-36. Promptbook.

Grimaldi; or, The Life of an Actress. New York: n.pub., 1856. Pp. [1]-36.

How She Loves Him! New York & London: Samuel French, n.d. Pp. [1]-48. French's Parlor Comedies, 2.

Hunted Down; or, The Two Lives of Mary Leigh. N.p.: n.pub., n.d. Pp. [1]-36. Title page lacking.

Irish Heiress, The. London: Andrews, 1842. Pp. [i-vi], [1]-99.

Jessie Brown. N.p.: n.pub., n.d. Pp. [1]-32. Title page lacking. Promptbook.

Jessie Brown; or, The Relief of Lucknow. London: John Dicks, n.d. Pp. [1]-16. Dicks' Standard Plays, 473.

Jezebel; or, The Dead Reckoning. N.p.: n.pub., n.d. Pp. [1]-33.

Jilt, The. 154 leaves. Manuscript promptbook.

Kerry; or, Night and Morning. N.p.: n.pub., n.d. Pp. [1]-15.

Knight of Arva, The. New York: Samuel French, n.d. Pp. [1]-28. French's Standard Drama, 231.

Led Astray. New York & London: Samuel French, c.1873. Pp. [1]-57. French's Standard Drama, 372. Promptbook.

Led Astray. New York: Samuel French, c.1873. Pp. [1]-57. French's Standard Drama, 372.

Legend of the Devil's Dyke, A. London: John Dicks, n.d. Pp. [1]-15. Dicks' Standard Plays, 1043.

Lily of Killarney, The. Written with Oxenford, John. Music by Benedict, Julius. London & New York: Boosey, n.d. Pp. [i-viii], 1-272. Royal Edition. Vocal score.

London Assurance. By Dion L. Bourcicault. London: J. Andrews (printer) (priv.), 1841. Pp. [i]-viii, [1]-86. Promptbook.

London Assurance. By Dion L. Bourcicault. New York: Samuel French, n.d. Pp. [i]-[vi], [7]-71. French's Standard Drama, 27. Promptbook.

Long Strike, The. By Dion Baucicault. New York: Samuel French, n.d. Pp. [1]-38. French's Standard Drama, 360.

Long Strike, The. By Dion Baucicault. New York: Samuel French, n.d. Pp. [1]-38. French's Standard Drama, 360. Promptbook.

Louis XI. In [*America's Lost Plays*, Princeton, N.J.: Princeton University Press, 1940, I], [50]-106.

Louis XI. 63 leaves. Manuscript promptbook.

Love in a Maze. London: Hailes Lacy, 1851. Pp. [i-iv], [1]-92.

Lover by Proxy, A. London: Webster, n.d. Pp. [1]-28. Webster's Acting National Drama, 102.

Mercy Dodd; or, Presumptive Evidence. In [*America's Lost Plays*, Princeton, N.J.: Princeton University Press, 1940, I], [230]-259.

Octoroon, The; or, Life in Louisiana. London & New York: Samuel French, n.d. Pp. [1]-43. French's Acting Edition (late Lacy's).

Octoroon, The; or, Life in Louisiana. N.p.: n.pub. (priv.), n.d. Pp. [1]-40. Promptbook.

O'Dowd, The. London & New York: Samuel French, c.1909. Pp. [1]-52.

Old Guard, The. New York: John Douglas, 1848. Pp. [1]-20. Minor Drama, 29. Promptbook.

Old Heads and Young Hearts. By Dion Bourcicault. London: National Acting Drama Office, n.d. Pp. [1]-80. 2nd ed.

Old Heads and Young Hearts. New York: Samuel French, n.d. Pp. [i]-[vi], [7]-73. French's Standard Drama, 62. Promptbook.

Pauvrette. New York: Samuel French, c.1858. Pp. [1]-36. Bourcicault's Dramatic Works, 7.

Pauvrette. N.p.: n.pub., n.d. Pp. [1]-36. Promptbook.

Phantom, The. New York: n.pub., 1856 <wrps. Samuel French, 1857>. Pp. [1]-28. Bourcicault's Dramatic Works, 3 <wrps. French's Standard Drama, 165>.

Poor of New York, The. New York: Samuel French, c.1857. Pp. [1]-45. [Bourcicault's Dramatic Works, 5]. French's Standard Drama, 189.

Poor of New York, The. *Also:* The Streets of New York. New York: Samuel French, c.1857. Pp. [1]-45. French's Standard Drama, 189. Promptbook.

Pope of Rome, The. New York: Samuel French, c.1858. Pp. [1]-40. Bourcicault's Dramatic Works, 8.

Prima Donna, The. London: Thomas Hailes Lacy, n.d. Pp. [1]-20. Text incomplete. [Lacy's Acting Edition].

Queen of Spades, The. London: Thomas Hailes Lacy, n.d. Pp. [1]-30. [Lacy's Acting Edition].

Rapparee, The; or, The Treaty of Limerick. N.p.: n.pub., n.d. Pp. [1]-31.

Rapparee, The; or, The Treaty of Limerick. N.p.: n.pub., n.d. Pp. [1]-44. Title page lacking. Promptbook.

Robert Emmet. In [*America's Lost Plays*, Princeton, N.J.: Princeton University Press, 1940, I], [261]-313.

Schemes and Counter-Schemes. N.p.: n.pub., n.d. Pp. [1]-46. Title page lacking.

School for Scheming, The. By Dion de P. Bourcicault. London: National Acting Drama Office, n.d. Pp. [1]-59. Promptbook.

School for Scheming, The. By Dion de P. Bourcicault. London: National Acting Drama Office, n.d. <wrps. Webster>. Pp. [1]-59. Webster's Acting National Drama, 140.

Seraphine. N.p.: n.pub., n.d. Pp. [1]-38. Title page lacking.

Shaughraun, The. London: John Dicks, n.d. Pp. [1]-26. [Dicks' Standard Plays, 390].

Shaughraun, The. N.p.: n.pub., n.d. Pp. 1-22, [1]-23, [1]-22. Title page lacking. Promptbook.

Streets of New York, The.
See Poor of New York, The.

Used Up.
See Mathews, Charles James.

Wanted—A Widow, with Immediate Possession. Written with Seymour, Charles. New York & London: Samuel French, n.d. Pp. [1]-16. Bourcicault's Dramatic Works, 4 <wrps. French's Minor Drama, 136>.

West End; or, The Irish Heiress. By Dion L. Bourcicault. Boston: William V. Spencer, n.d. Pp. [1]-49. Spencer's Boston Theatre, 210. Promptbook.

Willow Copse, The. Written with Kenney, Charles Lamb. By D. L. Bourcicault. Boston: William V. Spencer, 1855. Pp. [i]-vi, [7]-64. Boston Theatre, 30. Promptbook.

Willow Copse, The. By D. L. Bourcicault. Boston: William V. Spencer, n.d. Pp. [i]-vi, [7]-64. Spencer's Boston Theatre, New Series, 30.

BOUDOUSQUIE, GABRIEL

Poet, The. London & New York: F. Tennyson Neely, c.1899. Pp. [1]-103.

BOUGHT
See Harvey, Frank.

BOUILLY, JEAN NICHOLAS

Deaf and Dumb, The.
See under title.

BOULD SOGER BOY, THE
    See Stirling, Edward.
BOULDING, JAMES WIMSETT
    Mary, Queen of Scots. London & Derby: Bemrose & Sons, n.d. Pp. [i-iv], [5]-67. Promptbook.
    Satan Bound. London & Derby: Bemrose & Sons, 1881. Pp. [i-vi], [1]-272.
BOUND
    See Simpson, John Palgrave.
BOUND 'PRENTICE TO A WATERMAN
    See Campbell, Andrew Leonard Voullaire.
BOUNDING BRIGAND OF THE BAKUMBOILUM
    See Burnand, Francis Cowley. Lord Lovel and Lady Nancy Bell.
BOURCICAULT, DION DE P.
    See Boucicault, Dionysius Lardner.
BOURCICAULT, DION L.
    See Boucicault, Dionysius Lardner.
BOURDILLON, FRANCIS WILLIAM
    Lost God, A. London: Elkin Mathews, 1891. Pp. [1]-[59].
BOURGEOIS GENTILHOMME
    See Van Laun, Henri (trans.). Citizen Who Apes the Nobleman, The.
BOW BELLS
    See Byron, Henry James.
BOWKETT, SIDNEY
    Snowstorm, The. London: Samuel French; New York: T. Henry French, n.d. Pp. [1]-12. [Lacy's Acting Edition].
    What Greater Love? London: Capper & Newton, n.d. Pp. [1]-15. Lynn's Acting Edition, 17.
BOWL'D OUT
    See Craven, Henry Thornton.
BOWLES, EDWARD W.
    Water Babes, The. London: T. Vickers Wood (printer), n.d. Pp. [i-iv], [1]-33.
BOWLES, THOMAS GIBSON
    Blazing Burgee, The; or, The Scarlet Rover. London: Thomas Hailes Lacy, n.d. Pp. [1]-12. Lacy's Sensation Series, 1.
    Port Admiral, The; or, The Mysterious Mariner, the Child of Destiny, and the Rightful Heir. London & New York: Samuel French, n.d. Pp. [1]-12. French's Acting Edition (late Lacy's), 2.
BOWLES, WILLIAM LISLE
    St. John in Patmos. London: J. Murray, 1832. Pp. [i]-[xii], [1]-154.
BOWYER, FREDERICK.
    Two Pro's., The. Music by Jacobi, G. London & New York: Samuel French, n.d. Pp. [1]-8. [Lacy's Acting Edition].
BOX AND COX
    See Morton, John Maddison.
BOX AND COX MARRIED AND SETTLED
    See Coyne, Joseph Stirling.
BOX OF MISCHIEF, A
    See Peake, Richard Brinsley.
BOX-LOBBY CHALLENGE, THE
    See Cumberland, Richard.
BOY
    See Law, Arthur. New Boy, The.
BOY OF CLOGHEEN
    See Power, Tyrone. Paddy Carey.
BOY OF NORMANDY, THE
    See Fitzsimon, Ellen.
BOY OF SANTILLANE
    See Macfarren, George. Gil Blas.
BOYCE, WILLIAM
    Hydropathy. Music by Davies, Alfred Cuthbert. London: W. I. Richardson (printer), 1891. Pp. [i-ii], [1]-30. Libretto.
    Prince of Sauerkrautenberg, The. Music by Davies, Alfred Cuthbert. London: W. I. Richardson (printer), 1895. Pp. [1]-48. Libretto.
BOYD-JONES, ERNEST
    Florodora.
        See Hall, Owen.
BOYNE WATER, THE
    See Buckstone, John Baldwin.

BOYS OF A CERTAIN SCHOOL
    See Eupolis. Sawbones in Trainin'.
BOZ
    See Dickens, Charles.
BRACE OF PARTRIDGES, A
    See Ganthony, Robert.
BRADDON, MARY ELIZABETH (later Mrs. Maxwell)
    Dross; or, The Root of Evil. London: John & Robert Maxwell, n.d. Pp. [1]-56.
    Marjorie Daw. London: John & Robert Maxwell, n.d. Pp. [1]-23.
    Married Beneath Him. London: John & Robert Maxwell, n.d. Pp. [1]-55.
    Missing Witness, The. London: John & Robert Maxwell, n.d. Pp. [1]-53.
BRADLEY, KATHARINE HARRIS
    See Field, Michael (pseud.).
BRADSHAW, CHRISTOPHER BROOKE
    Shakspere and Company. London: Charles Fox (priv.), 1845. Pp. [i-vi], [1]-74.
BRAGANZA
    See Jephson, Robert.
BRAMSEN, JOHN (trans.)
    Sappho. By Grillparzer, Franz. London: Alexander Black, 1820. Pp. [i]-[viii], [1]-86.
BRAND, BARBARINA OGLE WILMOT, MRS. THOMAS
    See Dacre, Barbarina Ogle, Lady.
BRAND, OSWALD
    Mignonette. Music by Parker, Henry. London: J. B. Cramer, n.d. Pp. [i-vi], [7]-30. Libretto.
BRAND
    See Garrett, Fydell Edmund (trans.).
    See Herford, Charles Harold (trans.).
    See Wilson, William (trans.).
BRANDED FOR LIFE
    See Muskerry, William. Atonement.
BRANDON, ISAAC
    Kais; or, Love in the Deserts. London: J. Murray; J. Harding, 1808. Pp. [iii]-[xviii], [1]-68.
BRANSCOMBE, ARTHUR
    I've Seen a Harem.
        See Morocco Bound.
    Morocco Bound. Written with Ross, Adrian (pseud. of Ropes, Arthur Reed). *Also:* I've Seen a Harem. Music by Carr, F. Osmond. London: Joseph Williams, n.d. Pp. [1]-28. Libretto. *Filed under* Branscombe, Arthur.
    Morocco Bound. Written with Ross, Adrian (pseud. of Ropes, Arthur Reed). *Also:* I've Seen a Harem. Music by Carr, F. Osmond. London: Joseph Williams, n.d. Pp. [i-ii], 1-147. Vocal score. *Filed under* Branscombe, Arthur, and Ropes, Arthur Reed.
BRANTINGHAME HALL
    See Gilbert, William Schwenck.
BRASSINGTON, RICHARD, JR
    Tricks upon Travellers. Music by Reeve; Horn, C. London: W. H. Wyatt, 1810. Pp. [1]-15. 2nd ed. Libretto.
BRAVE'S TASK, THE
    See Cobbold, Elizabeth Knipe, Mrs. John.
BRAVO, THE
    See Barnett, Charles Zachary.
BRAVO OF VENICE
    See Lewis, Matthew Gregory. Rugantino.
BRAVO'S HEIR, THE
    See Simpson, John Palgrave.
BRAZEN HEAD
    See Farley, Charles. Harlequin and Friar Bacon.
BRAZEN MASK
    See Dibdin, Thomas John.
BREACH OF PROMISE
    See Buckstone, John Baldwin.
    See Robertson, Thomas William.
BREAKERS AHEAD!
    See Haines, John Thomas.
BREAKING A BUTTERFLY
    See Jones, Henry Arthur.

BREAKING THE ICE
See Thomas, Charles.

BREAKING THE SPELL
See Farnie, Henry Brougham.

BREARE, WILLIAM HAMMOND
Boro' Bench, A. Music by Breare, W. H. Harrogate: R. Ackrill, 1887. Pp. [1]-31. Libretto.

BREEZY MORNING, A
See Phillpotts, Eden.

BRENNUS
See Maclean, William.

BREWER, GEORGE
Martelli. London: Henry Bailey, 1843. Pp. [1]-99.

BREWER OF PRESTON, THE
See Reynoldson, Thomas Herbert.

BRIAN BOROIHME
See Knowles, James Sheridan.

BRIAN BORU
See Stange, Stanislaus.

BRIAN THE PROBATIONER
See Hill, Isabel.

BRIC-A-BRAC WILL, THE
See Fitzgerald, Shafto Justin Adair.

BRIDAL, THE
See Knowles, James Sheridan.

BRIDAL EVE, THE
See Mitford, Mary Russell.

BRIDAL NIGHT
See Haynes, James. Conscience.

BRIDAL OF ARMAGNAC, THE
See Streatfield, T., Rev.

BRIDAL OF NETHERBY
See Moncrieff, William Thomas. Lochinvar.

BRIDAL OF THE BORDERS
See Lynch, Thomas J. Rose of Ettrick Vale, The.

BRIDAL RING
See Almar, George. Bull-Fighter, The.
See Reynolds, Frederick.

BRIDAL THREE CENTURIES BACK!
See Wilks, Thomas Egerton. Ladye of Lambythe, The.

BRIDAL WREATH, THE
See Hazlewood, Colin Henry.

BRIDALS OF MESSINA
See Knowles, James Sheridan. John of Procida.

BRIDE, THE
See Baillie, Joanna.

BRIDE OF ABYDOS, THE
See Byron, Henry James.
See Dimond, William.
See Oxberry, William Henry.

BRIDE OF LAMMERMOOR
See Calcraft, John William.
See Macfarren, Natalia (trans.).

BRIDE OF LUDGATE, THE
See Jerrold, Douglas William.

BRIDE OF MESSINA, THE
See Irvine, George (trans.).
See Lockwood, Percival (trans.).
See Lodge, Adam (trans.).
See Towler, John (trans.).

BRIDE OF PORTUGAL
See Neil, Ross. Inez.

BRIDE OF SONG, THE
See Farnie, Henry Brougham.

BRIDE OF ST. AGNES
See Davies, Blanche. Octavia.

BRIDE OF THE ISLES
See Planché, James Robinson. Vampire, The.

BRIDE OF THE NILE, THE
See Blunt, Wilfred Scawen.

BRIDE OF VENICE
See Stirling, Edward. Queen of Cyprus, The.

BRIDES OF GARRYOWEN
See Boucicault, Dionysius Lardner. Colleen Bawn, The.

BRIDES OF VENICE, THE
See Bunn, Alfred.

BRIDES' TRAGEDY, THE
See Beddoes, Thomas Lovell.

BRIDGE OF NOTRE DAME, THE
See Hudson, E. Neeves.

BRIDGE OF SIGHS!
See Barnett, Charles Zachary. Bravo, The.

BRIDGE OF TRESINO
See Campbell, Andrew Leonard Voullaire. Forest Oracle, The.

BRIDGEMAN, JOHN VIPON
Armourer of Nantes, The. Music by Balfe, M. W. London: Royal English Opera, Covent Garden, n.d. Pp. [1]-69. Libretto.

Black Doctor, The. London: Thomas Hailes Lacy, n.d. Pp. [i-ii], [1]-50. Promptbook.

Bluebeard; or, Harlequin and Freedom in Her Island Home. London: Royal English Opera, Covent Garden, n.d. Pp. [1]-24. Libretto.

Good Run for It, A. London: Thomas Hailes Lacy, n.d. Pp. [1]-18. [Lacy's Acting Edition].

I've Eaten My Friend! London & New York: Samuel French, n.d. Pp. [1]-17. [Lacy's Acting Edition].

Little Red Riding Hood; or, Harlequin and the Wolf in Granny's Clothing. Written with Edwards, Henry Sutherland. London: Royal English Opera, Covent Garden, 1859. Pp. [1]-22. Libretto.

Matrimonial—A Gentleman, &c. for Further Particulars, Apply at——. London: Thomas Hailes Lacy, n.d. Pp. [1]-22. [Lacy's Acting Edition].

Puritan's Daughter, The. Music by Balfe, M. W. London: Royal English Opera, Covent Garden, n.d. Pp. [1]-72. Libretto.

Puss In Boots. London: Royal English Opera, Covent Garden, n.d. Pp. [1]-29. Libretto.

Rifle and How to Use It, The. London: Thomas Hailes Lacy, n.d. Pp. [1]-27. [Lacy's Acting Edition].

Shipmates.
See Bridgman, Cunningham V.

Tam o'Shanter; or, Harlequin and the Witches of Alloway's Auld Haunted Kirk. Edinburgh: A. Reid (printer), n.d. Pp. [1]-24. Libretto.

Where's Your Wife? London: Thomas Hailes Lacy, n.d. Pp. [1]-26. [Lacy's Acting Edition].

BRIDGES, ROBERT SEYMOUR
Achilles in Scyros. In Collected Works, London: George Bell & Sons; J. & E. Bumpus, 1890, [127]-145. Filed under Collected Works.

Christian Captives, The. In Collected Works, London: George Bell & Sons; J. & E. Bumpus, 1890, [101]-126. Filed under Collected Works.

Eden. Music by Stanford, C. V. London: George Bell & Sons, 1891. Pp. [1]-40.

Feast of Bacchus, The. In Collected Works, London: George Bell & Sons; J. & E. Bumpus, 1890, [183]-230. Filed under Collected Works.

Humours of the Court, The. In Collected Works, London: George Bell & Sons; J. & E. Bumpus, 1890, [147]-181. Filed under Collected Works.

Nero, Part 1. In Collected Works, London: George Bell & Sons; J. & E. Bumpus, 1890, [i-vi], [1]-35. Filed under Collected Works.

Nero, Part 2. In Collected Works, London: George Bell & Sons; J. & E. Bumpus, 1890, [231]-264. Filed under Collected Works.

Palicio. In Collected Works, London: George Bell & Sons; J. & E. Bumpus, 1890, [37]-69. Filed under Collected Works.

Return of Ulysses, The. In Collected Works, London: George Bell & Sons; J. & E. Bumpus, 1890, [71]-100. Filed under Collected Works.

BRIDGES, SARAH FULLER FLOWERS, MRS. WILLIAM
See Adams, Sarah Fuller Flowers.

BRIDGET'S BLUNDERS
See Smith, Lita.

BRIDGMAN, CUNNINGHAM V.

He Stoops to Win. Music by Bendall, Wilfred. London: Robert Cocks, n.d. Pp. [1]-20. Libretto.

Shipmates. Also attrib. to Bridgeman, John Vipon. London & New York: Samuel French, n.d. Pp. [1]-44. [Lacy's Acting Edition].

BRIERLEY, BENJAMIN

Cobbler's Stratagem, The. Manchester: John Heywood, n.d. Pp. [1]-31.

Lancashire Weaver Lad, The. Manchester: John Heywood; London: Simpkin, Marshall, n.d. Pp. [1]-63.

BRIGAND

See A'Beckett, Gilbert Arthur. Utter Per-version of The Brigand, An.

See Planché, James Robinson.

BRIGAND AND HIS SON

See Oxberry, William Henry. Matteo Falcone.

BRIGAND'S SACRIFICE

See Kingdom John M. Marcoretti.

BRIGANDS IN THE BUD!

See Mildenhall, Thomas.

BRIGANDS OF CALABRIA, THE

See Suter, William E.

BRIGHT, ADDISON

Bugle Call, The.

See Parker, Louis Napoleon.

BRIGHT, KATE C., MRS. AUGUSTUS

Noblesse Oblige. London & New York: Samuel French, n.d. Pp. [1]-34. [Lacy's Acting Edition].

Not False But Fickle. London & New York: Samuel French, n.d. Pp. [1]-12. [Lacy's Acting Edition].

BRIGHT IDEA, A

See Law, Arthur.

BRIGHT-EYED EMMA

See Atkyns, Samuel.

BRIGSTOCKE, THOMAS

Eustace de St. Pierre. London: Charles Beckett (printer), n.d. Pp. [1]-44. *Filed under* Brigstooke, Thomas.

BRINGING HOME THE BRIDE!

See Moncrieff, William Thomas.

BRISKET FAMILY

See Jerrold, Douglas William. Dolly and the Rat.

BRISTOL DIAMONDS

See Oxenford, John.

BRITANNICUS

See Boothby, Brooke, Sir (trans.).

See Boswell, Robert Bruce (trans.).

BRITISH AMAZONS

See Dibdin, Charles Isaac Mungo, jr.

BRITISH BORN

See Meritt, Paul.

BRITISH BROTHERS, THE

See Buchanan, Robert.

BRITISH CARPENTER, THE

See Maclaren, Archibald.

BRITISH LEGION, THE.

See Bayly, Thomas Haynes.

BRITISH LOYALTY

See Moser, Joseph.

BRITISH TARS IN 1782

See Barnett, Charles Zachary. Youthful Days of William the Fourth, The.

BRITON CHIEF

See Walker, Charles Edward. Caswallon.

BRITONS STRIKE HOME

See Dibdin, Charles, sr.

BRITONS TO ARMS!

See Maclaren, Archibald.

BRIXTON BURGLARY, THE

See Sidney, Frederick W.

BROCKHURST, JOSEPH SUMNER

Wife, The; or, Love and Madness. Cambridge: Deighton, Bell, 1856. Pp. [i]-[xxxii], [1]-213.

BRODIE-INNES, J. W.

Thomas A'Becket. N.p.: (priv.), n.d. Pp. [i-ii], [1]-47.

BROKEN GOLD, THE

See Dibdin, Charles, sr.

BROKEN HEART, THE

See Cornwall, Barry.

BROKEN HEARTS

See Gilbert, William Schwenck.

BROKEN IDYLLS

See Medd, Mabel S.

BROKEN SWORD, THE

See Dimond, William.

BROKEN TIES

See Simpson, John Palgrave.

BROKEN TOYS

See Daly, John.

BROKEN VOW, THE

See Boucicault, Dionysius Lardner.

BROKEN-HEARTED CLUB, THE

See Coyne, Joseph Stirling.

BROMLEY, GEORGE PERCIVAL

Rebellion, The; or, Norwich in 1549. Norwich: Bacon, Kinnebrook (printer), n.d. Pp. [i]-viii, [9]-12, [xiii]-[xvi], [17]-74.

BRONZE HORSE, THE

See Fitzball, Edward.

BROOKE, FRANCES MOORE, MRS. JOHN

Rosina. London: Whittingham & Arliss, 1815. Pp. [1]-[31]. London Theatre, VI. *Filed under* Dibdin, Thomas John, ed. London Theatre, VI.

Rosina. In *New English Drama,* ed. W. Oxberry, 22 vols., London: W. Simpkin & R. Marshall; C. Chapple, 1820, IX, [1-2], [i-viii], [1]-24. *Filed under* Oxberry, William Henry. New English Drama, IX.

Rosina. London: John Cumberland, 1827. Pp. [1]-29. Cumberland's British Theatre, XV. *Filed under* Cumberland, John. Cumberland's British Theatre, XV.

Rosina. In *British Drama,* 12 vols., London: John Dicks, 1872, XII, [152]-160.

BROOKE, HENRY

Gustavus Vasa; or, The Deliverer of His Country. In *British Drama,* 12 vols., London: John Dicks, 1871, VII, [33]-50.

BROOKE, STOPFORD A.

Riquet of the Tuft. London: Macmillan, 1880. Pp. [i-ii], [1]-172.

BROOKES, SHERIDAN

Calypso, Queen of Ogygia. *Also:* Telemachus and Calypso. London: Thomas Hailes Lacy, n.d. Pp. [1]-26. [Lacy's Acting Edition].

Telemachus and Calypso.

See Calypso, Queen of Ogygia.

BROOKFIELD, CHARLES HALLAM ELTON

Burglar and the Judge, The.

See Philips, Francis Charles.

Burnt Ashes. *Also:* Kenyon's Widow. Pp. [i-iii], [1]-35, [i], [1]-31, [i], [1]-27. Typescript. *Filed under* Kenyon's Widow.

By Proxy. *Also:* Done by Deputy. [New York: Z. & L. Rosenfield Stenographic & Typewriting Offices], n.d. Pp. [i-ii], [1]-57, [i-ii], [1]-38, [i-ii], [1]-43, [i-ii], [1]-56. Pagination by act (two variants of Act III). Typescript.

Cuckoo, The. [New York: Z. & L. Rosenfield Stenography & Typewriting], n.d. Pp. [i-ii], [1]-32, [i-ii], [1]-36, [i-ii], [1]-33. Typescript.

Done by Deputy.

See By Proxy.

Kenyon's Widow.

See Burnt Ashes.

Lucky Star, The. Written with Ross, Adrian (pseud. of Ropes, Arthur Reed); Hopwood, Aubrey. Music by Caryll, Ivan. London: Chappell, n.d. Pp. [i-iv], [1]-231. Vocal score.

Nearly Seven. London & New York: Samuel French, n.d. Pp. [1]-10. [Lacy's Acting Edition].

Poet and the Puppets, The. Music by Glover, J. M. London: Mitchell (printer), n.d. Pp. [1]-30. Libretto.

Woman's Reason, A. Written with Philips, Francis Charles. Pp. [i], [1]-37, [i], [1]-29, [i], [1]-25. Typescript.

BROOKFIELD, CHARLES HALLAM ELTON (trans.)

Grand Duchess of Gerolstein, The. Written with Ross, Adrian (pseud. of Ropes, Arthur Reed) (trans.). Music by Offenbach. London: Boosey, c.1897. Pp. [1]-77. New ed. Libretto. *Filed under* Brookfield, Charles Hallam Elton.

BROOKS, CHARLES WILLIAM SHIRLEY

Anything for a Change. London & New York: Samuel French, n.d. Pp. [1]-22.

Creole, The; or, Love's Fetters. London: F. Ledger (printer) (priv.), n.d. Pp. [i]-[vi], [7]-48.

Creole, The; or, Love's Fetters. London: F. Ledger (printer) (priv.), n.d. Pp. [i]-[vi], [7]-48. Promptbook.

Creole, The; or, Love's Fetters. London: Thomas Hailes Lacy, n.d. Pp. [i]-[vi], [7]-48. Promptbook.

Daughter of the Stars, The. London: Thomas Hailes Lacy, n.d. Pp. [1]-36. Lacy's Acting Edition, 22.

Exposition, The. London: Thomas Hailes Lacy, n.d. Pp. [1]-22. [Lacy's Acting Edition].

Guardian Angel, The. London: Thomas Hailes Lacy, n.d. Pp. [1]-19. [Lacy's Acting Edition].

Our New Governess. London: William Barth, n.d. Pp. [3]-42.

Timour the Tartar!
See Oxenford, John.

Wigwam, The. By Shirley Brooks. London: John Dicks, n.d. Pp. [11]-21.

BROOKS, SHIRLEY

See Brooks, Charles William Shirley.

BROTHER AND SISTER, THE

See Dimond, William.

BROTHER BEN

See Morton, John Maddison.

BROTHER BILL AND ME

See Suter, William E.

BROTHER'S LOVE

See Lemon, Mark. Self Accusation.

BROTHER'S VENGEANCE

See Hamilton, R. S. Almourah, the Corsair.

BROTHERS

See Alma-Tadema, Laurence. Childe Vyet.
See Byatt, Henry.
See Coghlan, Charles Francis.
See Cumberland, Richard.
See Forster, William.
See Wilks, Thomas Egerton.

BROTHERS OF BLUTHAUPT

See Archer, Thomas. Three Red Men, The.

BROTHERS OF CO(U)RSE

See A'Beckett, Gilbert Abbott. O Gemini!

BROUGH, JOHN CARGILL

Eligible Situation, An.
See Archer, Thomas.

BROUGH, ROBERT BARNABAS

Alfred the Great; or, The Minstrel King. London: Thomas Hailes Lacy, n.d. Pp. [1]-48.

Camaralzaman and Badoura.
See Brough, William.

Crinoline. London: Thomas Hailes Lacy, n.d. Pp. [1]-20. [Lacy's Acting Edition].

Doge of Duralto, The; or, The Enchanted Eyes. London: Thomas Hailes Lacy, n.d. Pp. [1]-46. [Lacy's Acting Edition].

Enchanted Isle, The.
See Brough, William.

Kensington Gardens; or, Quite a Ladies' Man. London: Thomas Hailes Lacy, n.d. Pp. [1]-35. [Lacy's Acting Edition].

King Alfred and the Cakes. In *Cracker Bon-bon for Christmas Parties,* London: W. Kent, 1861, pp. [i-iv], [1]-17. *Filed under* Cracker Bon-bon.

Last Edition of Ivanhoe, with All the Newest Improvements, The.
See Brough, William.

Lord Bateman.
See Overland Journey to Constantinople.

Masaniello; or, The Fish 'o Man of Naples. London: Thomas Hailes Lacy, n.d. Pp. [1]-[42].

Medea; or, The Best of Mothers, with a Brute of a Husband. London: Thomas Hailes Lacy, n.d. Pp. [1]-35. [Lacy's Acting Edition].

Mephistopheles; or, An Ambassador from Below. Written with Edwards, Henry Sutherland. London: Thomas Hailes Lacy, n.d. Pp. [1]-32. [Lacy's Acting Edition].

Moustache Movement, The. London: Thomas Hailes Lacy, n.d. Pp. [1]-18. [Lacy's Acting Edition].

Orpheus and Eurydice; or, The Wandering Minstrel. In *Cracker Bon-bon for Christmas Parties,* London: W. Kent, 1861, pp. [40]-59. *Filed under* Cracker Bon-bon.

Overland Journey to Constantinople, as Undertaken by Lord Bateman, with Interesting Particulars of the Fair Sophia, The. *Also:* Lord Bateman. London: Thomas Hailes Lacy, n.d. Pp. [1]-36. [Lacy's Acting Edition].

Second Calender, The.
See Brough, William.

Siege of Troy, The. Winchester: Hugh Barclay (printer), n.d. Pp. [1]-47.

Sphinx, The.
See Brough, William.

Twelve Labours of Hercules, The. London: Thomas Hailes Lacy, n.d. <wrps. London & New York: Samuel French>. Pp. [1]-35. [French's Acting Edition (late Lacy's)].

William Tell; or, The Civil War in Switzerland. In *Cracker Bon-bon for Christmas Parties,* London: W. Kent, 1861, pp. [18]-39. *Filed under* Cracker Bon-bon.

BROUGH, WILLIAM

Actor's Retreat, The. Written with Halliday, Andrew. London: Thomas Hailes Lacy, n.d. Pp. [1]-20.

Apartments: Visitors to the Exhibition May Be Accommodated, etc., etc. London: Thomas Hailes Lacy, n.d. Pp. [1]-14.

April Fool, An. Written with Halliday, Andrew. London: Thomas Hailes Lacy, n.d. Pp. [1]-16. [Lacy's Acting Edition].

Area Belle, The. Written with Halliday, Andrew. Chicago: Dramatic Publishing Co., n.d. Pp. [1]-9. Text incomplete. Sergel's Acting Drama, 93.

Area Belle, The. Written with Halliday, Andrew. London: Thomas Hailes Lacy, n.d. Pp. [1]-13.

Bona Fide Travellers (A Point of Law, Arising out of the New Beer Bill). London: Thomas Hailes Lacy, n.d. Pp. [1]-26. [Lacy's Acting Edition].

Caliph of Bagdad, The. London: Thomas Hailes Lacy, n.d. Pp. [1]-[35].

Camaralzaman and Badoura; or, The Peri Who Loved the Prince. Written with Brough, Robert Barnabas. By the Brothers Brough. London: National Acting Drama Office, n.d. Pp. [1]-40.

Census, The. Written with Halliday, Andrew. London & New York: Samuel French, n.d. Pp. [1]-16. [Lacy's Acting Edition].

Ching-Chow-Hi. Written with Reed, Thomas German. Music by Offenbach. London: J. Mallett (printer), n.d. Pp. [13]-20. Title page lacking. Libretto. *Filed under* Ching-Chow-Hi (anon.).

Colleen Bawn Settled at Last, The. Written with Halliday, Andrew. London: Thomas Hailes Lacy, n.d. Pp. [1]-16. [Lacy's Acting Edition].

Comical Countess, A. London: Thomas Hailes Lacy, n.d. <wrps. London & New York: Samuel French>. Pp. [1]-24. French's Acting Edition (late Lacy's).

Conrad and Medora; or, Harlequin Corsair and the Little Fairy at the Bottom of the Sea. *Also:* The Corsair. London: Thomas Hailes Lacy, n.d. Pp. [1]-36.

Corsair, The; or, The Little Fairy at the Bottom of the Sea. *Also:* Conrad and Medora. New York: Samuel French, n.d. Pp. [1]-27. Minor Drama, 131. Promptbook.

Dinorah under Difficulties. London: Thomas Hailes Lacy, n.d. Pp. [1]-22.

Doing Banting. Written with Halliday, Andrew. London: Thomas Hailes Lacy, n.d. Pp. [1]-18. [Lacy's Acting Edition].

Enchanted Isle, The; or, Raising the Wind on the Most Approved Principles. Written with Brough, Robert Barnabas. By the Brothers Brough. London: National Acting Drama Office, n.d. Pp. [1]-[32]. Webster's Acting National Drama, 152.

Endymion; or, The Naughty Boy Who Cried for the Moon. London: Thomas Hailes Lacy, n.d. Pp. [1]-36.

Ernani; or, The Horn of a Dilemma. London & New York: Samuel French, n.d. Pp. [1]-36.

Field of the Cloth of Gold, The. London: Thomas Hailes Lacy, n.d. Pp. [1]-44. Lacy's Acting Edition.

Fox versus Goose.
See Stockton, J. D.

Froggee Would a Wooing Go; or, The Pretty Princess and the Fairy of the Dancing Water. Manchester: n.pub., n.d. Pp. [1]-48.

Gnome King and the Good Fairy of the Silver Mine, The. London: Thomas Hailes Lacy, n.d. Pp. [1]-32. [Lacy's Acting Edition].

Going to the Dogs! Written with Halliday, Andrew. London: Thomas Hailes Lacy, n.d. Pp. [1]-15. [Lacy's Acting Edition].

Great Sensation Trial, The; or, Circumstantial Effie-Deans. London: Dramatic Authors' Society (priv.), n.d. Pp. [1]-32.

Hercules and Omphale; or, The Power of Love. London: Thomas Hailes Lacy, n.d. Pp. [1]-43. [Lacy's Acting Edition].

House out of Windows, A. London: Thomas Hailes Lacy, n.d. Pp. [1]-16. [Lacy's Acting Edition].

How to Make Home Happy. London: Thomas Hailes Lacy, n.d. Pp. [1]-23. Lacy's Acting Edition, 182.

Ivanhoe.
See Last Edition of Ivanhoe, with All the Newest Improvements.

Joan of Arc! London: Thomas Hailes Lacy, n.d. Pp. [1]-38.

Kind to a Fault. New York: Robert M. DeWitt, n.d. Pp. [1]-31. DeWitt's Acting Plays, 17.

King Arthur; or, The Days and Knights of the Round Table. London: Thomas Hailes Lacy, n.d. Pp. [1]-36.

Lalla Rookh; or, The Princess, the Peri, and the Troubadour. London & New York: Samuel French, n.d. <wrps. Thomas Hailes Lacy>. Pp. [1]-40. Lacy's Acting Edition, 501.

Last Edition of Ivanhoe, with All the Newest Improvements, The. Written with Brough, Robert Barnabas. *Also:* Ivanhoe. By the Brothers Brough. London: National Acting Drama Office, n.d. Pp. [1]-43.

Mudborough Election! Written with Halliday, Andrew. London: Thomas Hailes Lacy, n.d. Pp. [1]-18. [Lacy's Acting Edition].

My Heart's in the Highlands. Written with Halliday, Andrew. Clyde, Ohio: A. D. Ames, n.d. Pp. [1]-11.

My Heart's in the Highlands. Written with Halliday, Andrew. London: Thomas Hailes Lacy, n.d. Pp. [1]-14. Lacy's Acting Edition, 838.

My Unfinished Opera. Music by Reed, Thomas German. London: J. Mallett (printer), 1857. Pp. [10]-15. Libretto. *Filed under* Reed, Mr. and Mrs. German. After the Ball.

Number One, Round the Corner. Boston: William V. Spencer, 1856. Pp. [1]-16. Spencer's Boston Theatre, 52.

Papillonetta; or, The Prince, the Butterfly, and the Beetle. London: Thomas Hailes Lacy, n.d. Pp. [1]-44. [Lacy's Acting Edition].

Perdita; or, The Royal Milkmaid. London: Thomas Hailes Lacy, n.d. Pp. [1]-39.

Perseus and Andromeda; or, The Maid and the Monster. London: Thomas Hailes Lacy, n.d. Pp. [1]-36.

Phaeton; or, Pride Must Have a Fall. In *Beeton's Book of Burlesques,* London: S. O. Beeton, 1866, pp. [19]-36. *Filed*

under Brough, William, and Burnand, Francis Cowley. Beeton's Book of Burlesques.

Phenomenon in a Smock Frock, A. New York: Samuel French, n.d. Pp. [1]-20. Minor Drama, 148.

Pretty Horsebreaker, The. Written with Halliday, Andrew. London: Thomas Hailes Lacy, n.d. Pp. [1]-18.

Prince Amabel; or, The Fairy Roses. London: Thomas Hailes Lacy, n.d. Pp. [1]-41. [Lacy's Acting Edition].

Prince Prettypet and the Butterfly. London: F. W. Allcroft, 1854. Pp. [1]-48.

Pygmalion; or, The Statue Fair. London: Thomas Hailes Lacy, n.d. Pp. [1]-36.

Rasselas, Prince of Abyssinia; or, The Happy Valley. London: Thomas Hailes Lacy, n.d. Pp. [1]-34.

Robin Hood. In *Beeton's Book of Burlesques,* London: S. O. Beeton, 1866, pp. [i-iv], [1]-18. *Filed under* Brough, William, and Burnand, Francis Cowley. Beeton's Book of Burlesques.

Second Calender, The; and The Queen of Beauty, Who Had the Fight with the Genie. Written with Brough, Robert Barnabas. By the Brothers Brough. London: National Acting Drama Office, n.d. Pp. [i-ii], [1]-46. Webster's Acting National Drama, 175.

Shilling Day at the Great Exhibition, A. Written with Halliday, Andrew. London: Thomas Hailes Lacy, n.d. Pp. [1]-14. [Lacy's Acting Edition].

Sphinx, The. Written with Brough, Robert Barnabas. By the Brothers Brough. London: National Acting Drama Office, n.d. Pp. [1]-33.

Sylphide, The. London: Thomas Hailes Lacy, n.d. Pp. [1]-32. [Lacy's Acting Edition].

Trying It On. New York: Samuel French, n.d. Pp. [1]-19.

Turko the Terrible; or, The Great Princess Show. London: R. K. Burt, n.d. Pp. [1]-24.

Upstairs and Downstairs; or, The Great Per-centage Question. Written with Halliday, Andrew. London: Thomas Hailes Lacy, n.d. Pp. [1]-18. [Lacy's Acting Edition].

Valentine!, A. Written with Halliday, Andrew. London: Thomas Hailes Lacy, n.d. Pp. [1]-15. [Lacy's Acting Edition].

BROUGHAM, JOHN

All's Fair in Love. *Also:* All's Fair in Love and War. New York: Samuel French, c.1856. Pp. [1]-44. French's Standard Drama, 161.

All's Fair in Love and War.
See All's Fair in Love.

Art and Artifice; or, Woman's Love. New York: Samuel French, c.1859. Pp. [1]-34. Standard Drama, 224.

Belle Sauvage, La. London: n.pub., 1870. Pp. [1]-39. St. James's Theatre Edition.

Blanche de Nevers. Music by Balfe, Michael William. London: Royal English Opera, Covent Garden, n.d. Pp. [1]-55. Libretto.

Blanche of Nevers; or, I Am There.
See Duke's Daughter, The.
See also Duke's Motto, The.

Captain Cuttle. London: John Dicks, n.d. Pp. [9]-16. Dicks' Standard Plays, 572.

Columbus el Filibustero! New York: Samuel French, c.1857. Pp. [1]-24. Minor Drama, 145.

Dark Hour before Dawn, The. Written with Goodrich, Frank B. New York & London: Samuel French, c.1858. Pp. [1]-44. French's Standard Drama, 222.

David Copperfield. London: John Dicks, n.d. Pp. [1]-13. Dicks' Standard Plays, 374.

Decided Case, A. New York & London: Samuel French, n.d. Pp. [1]-18. Minor Drama, 114.

Demon Lover, The; or, My Cousin German. New York: Samuel French, c.1856. Pp. [1]-26. French's Minor Drama, 105.

Dombey and Son. London: John Dicks, n.d. Pp. [1]-16. Dicks' Standard Plays, 375.

Dramas of the Day.
See Revenge.

Dred; or, The Dismal Swamp. New York: Samuel French, c.1856. Pp. [1]-43. French's American Drama, 100.

Duke's Bequest, The.

See Duke's Daughter, The.

See also Duke's Motto, The.

Duke's Daughter, The; or, The Hunchback of Paris. New York: W. C. Wemyss, n.d. Pp. [1]-39. Promptbook.

Duke's Daughter, The; or, The Hunchback of Paris. *Also:* The Duke's Motto. *Also:* The Duke's Bequest. *Also:* Blanche of Nevers; or, I Am There. London: Thomas Hailes Lacy, n.d. Pp. [1]-43. [Lacy's Acting Edition].

Duke's Motto, The; or, I Am Here! *Also:* Duke's Daughter, The; or, The Hunchback of Paris. *Also:* The Duke's Bequest. *Also:* Blanche of Nevers; or, I Am There. In *Metamora and Other Plays,* ed. E. R. Page, Princeton: Princeton University Press, 1941, (America's Lost Plays), XIV, [343]-399.

Evenings at Our Club. In *Basket of Chips,* New York: Bunce & Brother, 1855, pp. 219-244.

Everyday Drama.

See Pigeon and the Hawks, The.

Flies in the Web. London: Thomas Hailes Lacy, n.d. Pp. [1]-50.

Franklin. New York: Samuel French, c.1856. Pp. [1]-26. Text incomplete. French's Standard Drama, 166.

Game of Life, The. New York: Samuel French, c.1856. Pp. [1]-44. French's American Drama, 25.

Game of Love, The. London: John Dicks, n.d. Pp. [1]-24. Dicks' Standard Plays, 628.

Great Tragic Revival, The. New York: Samuel French, c.1856. Pp. [1]-10. Minor Drama, 154.

Gun-maker of Moscow, The. New York: Samuel French, c.1856. Pp. [1]-28. French's Standard Drama, 164.

Irish Emigrant, The. *Also:* Temptation; or, The Irish Emigrant. London: Thomas Hailes Lacy, n.d. Pp. [1]-26. [Lacy's Acting Edition].

Irish Yankee, The; or, The Birth-day of Freedom. New York: T. H. French; London: Samuel French, c.1856. Pp. [1]-28. French's American Drama, 88.

Jane Eyre. New York: Samuel French, c.1856. Pp. [1]-32. French's American Drama, 136 <wrps. French's Standard Drama>.

Life in New York; or, Tom and Jerry on a Visit. New York: Samuel French, c.1856. Pp. [1]-26. French's American Drama, 98.

Life in the Clouds; or, Olympus in an Uproar. London: James Pattie, n.d. Pp. [i]-vi, [7]-26.

Lily of France, The. New York & London: Samuel French, c.1866. Pp. [1]-36. French's Standard Drama, 371.

Lottery of Life, The. London & New York: Samuel French, c.1867. Pp. [1]-[42]. [Lacy's Acting Edition].

Love and Murder. New York: Samuel French, c.1856. Pp. [1]-14. French's American Drama, 34.

Love's Livery. London: James Pattie, n.d. <wrps. W. Barth>. Pp. [1]-20. Barth's Universal Stage or Theatrical Prompt Book, 22.

Message from the Sea, A. Also attrib. to Collins, William Wilkie. London: John Dicks, n.d. Pp. [1]-24. Dicks' Standard Plays, 459. *Filed under* Brougham, John, and Collins, Wilkie.

Metamora; or, The Last of the Pollywogs. New York: Samuel French, n.d. Pp. [1]-18.

Miller of New Jersey, The; or, The Prison-Hulk. New York & London: Samuel French, c.1858. Pp. [1]-28. French's Standard Drama, 221.

Much Ado about a Merchant of Venice. New York: Samuel French, c.1858. Pp. [1]-24. French's Minor Drama, 308.

Musard Ball, The; or, Love at the Academy. New York: Samuel French, c.1858. Pp. [1]-12. Minor Drama, 153.

Neptune's Defeat; or, The Seizure of the Seas. New York: Samuel French, c.1858. Pp. [1]-24. Minor Drama, 165.

Night and Morning. New York: Samuel French, c.1856. Pp. [1]-40. French's American Drama, 48.

O'Flannigan and the Fairies.

See Recollection of O'Flannigan and the Fairies, A.

Pigeon and the Hawks, The. In *Basket of Chips,* New York: Bunce & Brothers, 1855, pp. 143-147. *Filed under* Everyday Drama.

Playing with Fire. London: Thomas Hailes Lacy, n.d. Pp. [1]-58.

Po-ca-hon-tas; or, The Gentle Savage. New York: Samuel French, n.d. Pp. [1]-32. French's American Drama, 69 <wrps. Minor Drama>.

Recollection of O'Flannigan and the Fairies, A. *Also:* O'Flannigan and the Fairies. London: Thomas Hailes Lacy, n.d. Pp. [1]-14. [Lacy's Acting Edition].

Red Mask, The; or, The Wolf of Lithuania. New York: Samuel French, c.1856. Pp. [1]-26. French's Standard Drama, 158.

Revenge; or, The Medium. In *Basket of Chips,* New York: Bunce & Brothers, 1855, pp. 191-199. *Filed under* Dramas of the Day.

Romance and Reality; or, The Young Virginian. New York: Samuel French, c.1856. Pp. [1]-54. French's American Drama, 29.

Shakspeare's Dream. New York: Samuel French, n.d. Pp. [1]-7. Minor Drama, 164.

Take Care of Little Charley. New York: Samuel French, c.1858. Pp. [1]-14. Minor Drama, 167.

Temptation; or, The Irish Emigrant. *Also:* The Irish Emigrant. New York: Samuel French, c.1856. Pp. [1]-22. French's American Drama, 65 <wrps. Minor Drama>. Promptbook.

BROUGHT TO BAY

See Morton, W. E. Blood Money.

BROUGHT UP TO BEG

See Towers, Edward. Chained to Sin.

BROUGHTON, F. C.

Crumpled Rose Leaf, A. New York: Roxbury, n.d. Pp. [1]-15. Wizard Series.

BROUGHTON, FREDERICK WILLIAM

Bailiff, The. London & New York: Samuel French, n.d. Pp. [1]-18. [Lacy's Acting Edition].

Once Again. Written with Browne, Walter. London & New York: Samuel French, n.d. Pp. [1]-12.

Ruth's Romance. London & New York: Samuel French, n.d. Pp. [1]-30.

Simple Sweep, A. Music by Downes, Jason F. London: Joseph Williams, n.d. Pp. [1]-15. Libretto.

Sunshine. London & New York: Samuel French, n.d. Pp. [1]-19.

Why Women Weep. London & New York: Samuel French, n.d. Pp. [1]-22. [Lacy's Acting Edition].

Withered Leaves. London & New York: Samuel French, n.d. Pp. [1]-26. French's Acting Edition (late Lacy's).

Written in Sand. London & New York: Samuel French, n.d. Pp. [1]-22. [French's Acting Edition].

BROWN, CHARLES ARMITAGE

Narensky; or, The Road to Yaroslaf. London: John Cawthorn, 1814. Pp. [i]-iv, [1]-66.

BROWN, JOHN

Barbarossa. London: John Cumberland, 1828. Pp. [1]-46. Cumberland's British Theatre, XVII. *Filed under* Cumberland, John. Cumberland's British Theatre, XVII.

Barbarossa. In *British Drama,* 12 vols., London: John Dicks, 1865, IV, [17]-32.

BROWN, JOHN HENRY

Adela. Music by Selby, Thomas Leeson. Nottingham: A. Johnson (printer), 1887. Pp. [1]-42. Libretto.

BROWN, WILLIAM (pseud. of Cotton, Richard)

Officer and a Gentleman, An. Manchester: John Heywood; London: Thomas Hailes Lacy, n.d. Pp. [1]-55. *Filed under* Cotton, Richard.

BROWN AND THE BRAHMINS

See Reece, Robert.

BROWNBILL, THOMAS ROBSON

See Robson, Frederick.

BROWNE, E. J.

Lucky Sixpence, A. Chicago: T. S. Denison, n.d. Pp. [1]-12. Amateur Series.

BROWNE, FELICIA DOROTHEA
> *See* Hemans, Felicia Dorothea Browne, Mrs. Alfred.

BROWNE, GEORGE WALTER
> **Hearts and Homes.** York: Johnson & Tesseyman (printer), 1875. Pp. [1]-27.

BROWNE, WALTER
> **Love Game, A.** London & New York: Samuel French, n.d. Pp. [1]-12. [Lacy's Acting Edition].
> **Once Again.**
> > *See* Broughton, Frederick William.

BROWNE THE MARTYR
> *See* Lucas, John Templeton.

BROWNE WITH AN E
> *See* Montague, Leopold.

BROWNIE'S BRIG!
> *See* Haines, John Thomas. Wraith of the Lake!, The.

BROWNING, ELIZABETH BARRETT, MRS. ROBERT
> **Psyche Apocalypté.** Written with Horne, Richard Hengist. London & Aylesbury: Hazell, Watson, & Viney (priv.), 1876. Pp. [i], [5]-19. Text complete. Synopsis.

BROWNING, ELIZABETH BARRETT, MRS. ROBERT (trans.)
> **Prometheus Bound.** By Aeschylus. In *Prometheus Bound and Other Poems,* New York: C. S. Francis, 1852, pp. [i-ii], 7-54.

BROWNING, ROBERT
> **Blot in the 'Scutcheon, A.** In *Bells and Pomegranates,* London: Edward Moxon, 1843, pp. [1]-16.
> **Blot in the 'Scutcheon, A.** In *Dramas,* Boston: Houghton, Mifflin, 1883, 2 vols., II, [1]-60.
> **Colombe's Birthday.** In *Dramas,* Boston: Houghton, Mifflin, 1883, 2 vols., I, [303]-384.
> **In a Balcony.** Chicago: Dramatic Publishing Co., n.d. Pp. [1]-35.
> **King Victor and King Charles.** In *Bells and Pomegranates,* London: Edward Moxon, 1842, pp. [1]-20.
> **King Victor and King Charles.** In *Dramas,* Boston: Houghton, Mifflin, 1883, 2 vols., I, [231]-302.
> **Luria.** In *Dramas,* Boston: Houghton, Mifflin, 1883, 2 vols., II, [139]-210.
> **Paracelsus.** In *Dramas,* Boston: Houghton, Mifflin, 1883, 2 vols., I, [i-viii], [1]-161.
> **Pippa Passes.** In *Dramas,* Boston: Houghton, Mifflin, 1883, 2 vols., I, [163]-230.
> **Return of the Druses, The.** In *Dramas,* Boston: Houghton, Mifflin, 1883, 2 vols., II, [61]-137.
> **Soul's Tragedy, A.** In *Dramas,* Boston: Houghton, Mifflin, 1883, 2 vols., II, [211]-251.

BROWNING, ROBERT (trans.)
> **Agamemnon.** By Aeschylus. London: Smith, Elder, 1877. Pp. [iii]-[xii], [1]-148.

BRUCE, JOHN WYNDHAM (trans.)
> **Don Karlos.** By Schiller. Mannheim: Schwan & Goetz, 1837. Pp. [1-6], [i]-xlii, 1-311.

BRUCE
> *See* Davidson, John.

BRUTON, JAMES
> **Bathing.** London & New York: Samuel French, n.d. Pp. [1]-24. [Lacy's Acting Edition].
> **Cut for Partners!** London & New York: Samuel French, n.d. Pp. [1]-22. [Lacy's Acting Edition].
> **Going On Anyhow.** London: R. S. Francis (printer), n.d. Pp. [1]-24.
> **Tale of a Pig, A.** London: W. Brickhill (printer) (priv.), 1858. Pp. [1]-18.
> **Vilikens and His Dinah; or, The Cup of Cold Pisen.** London: John Lofts, n.d. Pp. [1]-24.
> **Wanted an Errand Boy; or, The Maid of All Work.** London: W. Brickhill (printer) (priv.), n.d. Pp. [1]-18.

BRUTUS
> *See* Payne, John Howard.

BRUTUS ULTOR
> *See* Field, Michael.

BRYANT, MICHAEL
> **Florence Macarthy; or, Life in Ireland.** London: George Heaton, 1823. Pp. [i]-[viii], [1]-51.
> **Nine to One; or, He Is Sure to be Done.** London: G. Heaton, 1823. Pp. [1]-35.

BUBBLE AND SQUEAK; OR, THE PLEASURES AND PUNISHMENTS OF CARTHUSIAN REVELS (anon.)
> In *Charterhouse Play and Other Miscellaneous Extracts,* ed. E. Walford, London: Gresham Press, 1885, pp. [1]-29.

BUBBLES
> *See* Fawcett, Charles S.

BUBBLES OF THE DAY
> *See* Jerrold, Douglas William.

BUCCANEER'S BRIDAL
> *See* Williams, William Henry. Wreck, The.

BUCCANEER'S REVENGE
> *See* Thompson, C. Pelham. Rokeby.

BUCHANAN, ROBERT
> **British Brothers, The.** In *Tragic Dramas from History,* 2 vols., Edinburgh: Edmonston & Douglas, 1868, I, [237]-335. *Filed under* Tragic Dramas.
> **Edburga.** In *Tragic Dramas from History,* 2 vols., Edinburgh: Edmonston & Douglas, 1868, II, [115]-212. *Filed under* Tragic Dramas.
> **Gaston Phoebus.** In *Tragic Dramas from History,* 2 vols., Edinburgh: Edmonston & Douglas, 1868, II, [i]-viii, [1]-113. *Filed under* Tragic Dramas.
> **James the First of Scotland.** In *Tragic Dramas from History,* 2 vols., Edinburgh: Edmonston & Douglas, 1868, I, [119]-234. *Filed under* Tragic Dramas.
> **Wallace.** Glasgow: Richard Griffin, 1856. Pp. [i-ii], [1]-96.
> **Wallace.** In *Tragic Dramas from History,* 2 vols., Edinburgh: Edmonston & Douglas, 1868, I, [i-viii], [1]-117. *Filed under* Tragic Dramas.

BUCHANAN, ROBERT WILLIAMS
> **Alone in London.** Written with Marlowe, Charles (pseud. of Jay, Harriet). 148 leaves. Some pagination by acts. Manuscript promptbook.
> **Corinne.** London: n.pub. (priv.), 1876. Pp. [1]-78.
> **Drama of Kings, The (Trilogy: Buonaparte, Napoleon Fallen, The Teuton against Paris).** London: Strahan, 1871. Pp. [i-xviii], [1]-471.
> **Piper of Hamelin, The.** London: William Heinemann, 1893. Pp. [1]-[64]. Libretto.
> **Polypheme's Passion.** In *Undertones,* London: Edward Moxon, 1863, pp. [101]-140.
> **Strange Adventures of Miss Brown, The.** Written with Marlowe, Charles (pseud. of Jay, Harriet). By Robert Buchanan and Charles Marlowe (pseud.). New York & London: Samuel French, c.1909. Pp. [1]-88. French's International Copyrighted Edition of the Works of the Best Authors, 163.
> **Strange Adventures of Miss Brown.** Written with Jay, Harriet. Pp. [i-iv], [1]-36, [i], [1]-48, [i], [1]-25. Paginated by acts. Typescript.

BUCKE, CHARLES
> **Italians, The; or, The Fatal Accusation.** London: G. & W. B. Whittaker, 1819. Pp. [iii]-[xxviii], [29]-112.
> **Julio Romano; or, The Force of the Passions.** London: Whittaker, Treacher, & Arnot, 1830. Pp. [i]-xxvi, [1]-[195].

BUCKINGHAM, LEICESTER SILK
> **Aggravating Sam.** By Mathews and Co. (pseud.). London: Thomas Hailes Lacy, n.d. Pp. [1]-46. Lacy's Acting Edition, 249.
> **Belphegor.** London: Thomas Hailes Lacy, n.d. Pp. [1]-45.
> **Don't Lend Your Umbrella.** London: Thomas Hailes Lacy, n.d. Pp. [1]-43.
> **Faces in the Fire.** London: Thomas Hailes Lacy, n.d. Pp. [1]-57.
> **Harlequin Novelty and the Princess Who Lost Her Heart.** London: Thomas Hailes Lacy, n.d. Pp. [1]-40. Libretto.
> **Jeannette's Wedding.** Written with Harris, Augustus Glossop. London: Thomas Hailes Lacy, n.d. Pp. [1]-30. [Lacy's Acting Edition]. Libretto.

Little Red Riding Hood and the Fairies of the Rose, Shamrock, and Thistle. London: Thomas Hailes Lacy, n.d. Pp. [1]-32. [Lacy's Acting Edition].

Love's Martyr. London: Thomas Hailes Lacy, n.d. Pp. [1]-71. [Lacy's Acting Edition].

Lucrezia Borgia at Home and All Abroad. *Also:* Lucretia Borgia Travestie. London: Thomas Hailes Lacy, n.d. Pp. [1]-32.

Lucretia Borgia Travestie.
  See Lucrezia Borgia at Home and All Abroad.

Merry Widow, The. London: Thomas Hailes Lacy, n.d. Pp. [1]-34. [Lacy's Acting Edition].

Pizarro; or, The Leotard of Peru. London: W. H. Swanborough, 1862. Pp. [1]-36. Strand Acting Edition.

Silken Fetters. London: Thomas Hailes Lacy, n.d. Pp. [1]-52.

Silver Lining, The. London: Thomas Hailes Lacy, n.d. Pp. [1]-54. Lacy's Acting Edition.

Take That Girl Away! London & New York: Samuel French, n.d. Pp. [1]-60.

Virginius; or, The Trials of a Fond Papa! *Also:* Virginius Travestie. London: Thomas Hailes Lacy, n.d. Pp. [1]-36. [Lacy's Acting Edition].

Virginius Travestie.
  See Virginius.

William Tell. London: Thomas Hailes Lacy, n.d. Pp. [1]-33. [Lacy's Acting Edition].

BUCKLE OF BRILLIANTS
  See Wilks, Thomas Egerton. Crown Prince, The.

BUCKMINSTER, ELIZA
  See Lee, Eliza Buckminster, Mrs.

BUCKSTONE, JOHN BALDWIN

Abelard and Heloise. London: William Strange, 1837. Pp. [3]-38.

Agnes de Vere; or, The Wife's Revenge. London: William Strange, n.d. Pp. [1]-32. Promptbook.

Alarming Sacrifice, An. New York & London: Samuel French, n.d. Pp. [1]-18.

Babes in the Wood, The; or, Harlequin and the Cruel Uncle. Written with Dorrington, W. Music by Fitzwilliam, Edward; Spillane. London: W. S. Johnson, 1856. Pp. [1]-20. Libretto.

Bear Hunters, The; or, The Fatal Ravine! London: John Duncombe, n.d. Pp. [1]-36. Duncombe's Edition. Promptbook.

Beggar Boy of Brussels, The. London: John Dicks, n.d. Pp. [1]-14. Dicks' Standard Plays, 833.

Billy Taylor; or, The Gay Young Fellow. London: John Cumberland, n.d. Pp. [1]-33. Cumberland's Minor Theatre, III. *Filed under* Cumberland, John. Cumberland's Minor Theatre, III.

Billy Taylor; or, The Gay Young Fellow. London: John Cumberland, n.d. Pp. [1]-33. [Cumberland's Minor Theatre].

Boyne Water, The; or, The Relief of Londonderry. London: John Dicks, n.d. Pp. [1]-14. Dicks' Standard Plays, 807.

Breach of Promise, The; or, Second Thoughts Are Best. New York: O. A. Roorbach jr, n.d. Pp. [1]-40. Acting Drama, [8].

Christening, The. London: William Strange, 1836. Pp. [1]-17.

Christening, The. Boston: Charles H. Spencer, n.d. Pp. [1]-17.

Damon and Pythias. London: John Cumberland, n.d. Pp. [1]-30. Cumberland's Minor Theatre, VI. *Filed under* Cumberland, John. Cumberland's Minor Theatre, VI.

Damon and Pythias. London: John Cumberland, n.d. Pp. [1]-30.

Dead Shot, The. New York: William Taylor, n.d. Pp. [1]-27. Minor Drama, 5.

Dream at Sea, The. London: William Strange, 1835. Pp. [1]-36. 2nd ed.

Dream at Sea, The. Philadelphia: R. Harris, 1844. Pp. [1]-59. Promptbook.

Duchess de la Vaubalière, The. London: William Strange, n.d. Pp. [1]-32. Strange's Edition of Buckstone's Dramas, 15.

Flowers of the Forest, The: A Gypsy Story. New York & London: Samuel French, n.d. Pp. [1]-53. French's Standard Drama, 297.

Good for Nothing. New York: Samuel French, n.d. Pp. [1]-17. French's Minor Drama, 204.

Green Bushes, The; or, A Hundred Years Ago. London: National Acting Drama Office, n.d. <wrps. Webster>. Pp. [i]-[vi], [7]-63. Webster's Acting National Drama, 116.

Green Bushes, The; or, A Hundred Years Ago. New York: Samuel French, n.d. Pp. [1]-50.

Happiest Day of My Life, The. London: John Cumberland, n.d. Pp. [1]-35. Cumberland's British Theatre, XXIII. *Filed under* Cumberland, John. Cumberland's British Theatre, XXIII.

Happiest Day of My Life, The. London: John Cumberland, n.d. Pp. [1]-35. Cumberland's British Theatre, 156.

Henriette the Forsaken. New York: Samuel French, n.d. Pp. [1]-37. French's Standard Drama, 141.

Husband at Sight, A. London: John Cumberland, n.d. Pp. [1]-35. Cumberland's British Theatre, XXVI. *Filed under* Cumberland, John. Cumberland's British Theatre, XXVI.

Husband at Sight, A. London: John Cumberland, n.d. Pp. [1]-35.

Ice Witch, The; or, The Frozen Hand. London: John Cumberland, n.d. Pp. [1]-36. Cumberland's British Theatre, XXVIII. *Filed under* Cumberland, John. Cumberland's British Theatre, XXVIII.

Ice Witch, The; or, The Frozen Hand. London: Davidson, n.d. Pp. [1]-36.

Irish Lion, The. London: Sherwood, Gilbert, & Piper, n.d. Pp. [1]-20. [Acting National Drama].

Irish Lion, The. Philadelphia & New York: Turner & Fisher, n.d. Pp. [i]-viii, [9]-30. Turner's Dramatic Library.

Isabelle; or, Woman's Life. London: William Strange, 1835. Pp. [3]-64.

Isabelle; or, Woman's Life. New York: Samuel French, n.d. Pp. [1]-45. French's Standard Drama, 175.

Jack Sheppard. London: Webster, n.d. Pp. [i]-vi, [7]-72. Webster's Acting National Drama. Promptbook.

John Jones; or, I'm Haunted by a Fiend! Philadelphia: Frederick Turner, c.1836. Pp. [1]-26. Turner's Dramatic Library.

John Street, Adelphi. *Also:* 23, John Street, Adelphi. London: John Cumberland, n.d. Pp. [1]-27. Cumberland's Minor Theatre, VII. *Filed under* Cumberland, John. Cumberland's Minor Theatre, VII.

John Street, Adelphi. *Also:* 23, John Street, Adelphi. London: John Cumberland, n.d. Pp. [1]-27.

Josephine, the Child of the Regiment; or, The Fortune of War. London: Thomas Hailes Lacy, n.d. Pp. [1]-45. [Lacy's Acting Edition].

King of the Alps, The. London: Thomas Hailes Lacy, n.d. Pp. [1]-60.

Kiss in the Dark, A. New York: Samuel French, n.d. Pp. [i]-iv, [5]-20. Minor Drama, 46.

Kiss in the Dark. 39 leaves. Manuscript promptbook.

Leap Year; or, The Ladies' Privilege. New York: William Taylor, n.d. Pp. [1]-74. Modern Standard Drama, 83. Promptbook.

Lesson for Ladies, A. London: Chapman & Hall, n.d. Pp. [1]-38. Promptbook.

Little Bo-Peep; or, Harlequin and the Girl Who Lost Her Sheep. Music by Spillane. [London: S. G. Fairbrother, 1854]. Pp. [1]-[21]. Libretto.

Little Miss Muffet and Little Boy Blue; or, Harlequin and Old Daddy Long-Legs! Written with Buckstone, ?, jr. London: H. M. Arliss, 1861. Pp. [1]-31. Libretto.

Love in All Corners. Clyde, Ohio: Ames, c.1891. Pp. [1]-11. Ames' Series of Standard and Minor Drama, 288.

Luke the Labourer. London: John Cumberland, n.d. Pp. [1]-47. Cumberland's Minor Theatre, II. *Filed under* Cumberland, John. Cumberland's Minor Theatre, II.

Luke the Labourer; or, The Lost Son. London: William Kenneth, 1828. Pp. [1]-63. 2nd ed.

Maid with the Milking Pail, The. Boston: William V. Spencer, n.d. Pp. [1]-19. Spencer's Boston Theatre, 150.

Married Life. London: William Strange, 1834. Pp. [1]-66. Promptbook.

May Queen, The. London: William Strange, n.d. Pp. [1]-43.

Mischief-Making. London: John Cumberland, n.d. Pp. [1]-26. Cumberland's Minor Theatre, IV. *Filed under* Cumberland, John. Cumberland's Minor Theatre, IV.

Mischief-Making. London: Thomas Hailes Lacy, n.d. Pp. [1]-26. [Lacy's Acting Edition].

New Don Juan!, A. London: T. Richardson, n.d. Pp. [i]-[vi], 7-36. 2nd ed.

Nicholas Flam, Attorney at Law. Boston: George M. Baker, n.d. Pp. [1]-24. Universal Stage, 2.

Open House; or, The Twin Sisters. London: John Cumberland, n.d. Pp. [1]-44. Cumberland's British Theatre, XXXI. *Filed under* Cumberland, John. Cumberland's British Theatre, XXXI.

Open House; or, The Twin Sisters. London: John Cumberland, n.d. Pp. [1]-44. Promptbook.

Our Mary Anne. New York: Elton, 1838. Pp. [1]-24. Elton's Edition of Farces.

Pet of the Petticoats, The. Music by Barnett, John. London: William Strange, 1834. Pp. [1]-59.

Pet of the Petticoats, The. New York: Samuel French, n.d. Pp. [1]-36. French's Minor Drama, 234.

Peter Bell the Waggoner; or, The Murderers of Massiac! London: John Duncombe, n.d. Pp. [1]-[34]. Final page imperfect. Duncombe's Edition.

Popping the Question. London: John Cumberland, n.d. Pp. [1]-25. Cumberland's British Theatre, XXV. *Filed under* Cumberland, John. Cumberland's British Theatre, XXV.

Popping the Question. New York: Samuel French, n.d. <wrps. New York & London>. Pp. [1]-18. French's American Drama, 58 <wrps. Minor Drama>.

Presumptive Evidence; or, Murder Will Out. London: John Cumberland, n.d. Pp. [i-ii], [1]-36. Cumberland's British Theatre, XXXIV. *Filed under* Cumberland, John. Cumberland's British Theatre, XXXIV.

Presumptive Evidence; or, Murder Will Out. London: John Cumberland, n.d. Pp. [1]-36.

Queen of a Day, The. Music by Fitzwilliam, Edward. Boston: J. H. Eastburn's Press, 1855. Pp. [1]-33.

Rake and His Pupil, The; or, Folly, Love, and Marriage. London: William Strange, 1834. Pp. [i]-viii, [9]-[67].

Rough Diamond, A. London: John Dicks, n.d. Pp. [1]-10. Dicks' Standard Plays, 1006.

Rough Diamond, The. New York: Samuel French, n.d. Pp. [1]-26. Minor Drama, 41.

Rural Felicity. London: William Strange, 1834. Pp. [5]-66. Text complete.

Scholar, The. London: William Strange, 1835. Pp. [1]-44.

Scholar, The. New York: O. A. Roorbach jr, n.d. Pp. [1]-30. Acting Drama, 16.

Second Thoughts. London: William Strange, 1835. <wrps. New York: Turner & Fisher>. Pp. [6]-[56]. Text complete. Turner & Fisher's Edition of Buckstone's Dramas.

Shocking Events. London: Chapman & Hall, n.d. Pp. [1]-19.

Single Life. [London: Chapman & Hall, 1839]. Pp. [3]-58. Title page lacking. Promptbook.

Snakes in the Grass. London: John Cumberland, n.d. Pp. [1]-48. Cumberland's British Theatre, XXIV. *Filed under* Cumberland, John. Cumberland's British Theatre, XXIV.

Snakes in the Grass. London: John Cumberland, n.d. Pp. [1]-48.

Snapping Turtles, The; or, Matrimonial Masquerading. New York: Robert M. DeWitt, n.d. Pp. [1]-20.

Theodore the Brigand. London: John Duncombe, n.d. Pp. [1]-36. Duncombe's Edition.

Thimble Rig!, The. London: National Acting Drama Office, n.d. Pp. [1]-20.

23, John Street, Adelphi.
See John Street, Adelphi.

Two Queens, The. London: William Strange, 1837. Pp. [1]-22.

Two Queens, The. New York: Samuel French, n.d. Pp. [1]-20. Minor Drama, 101.

Uncle John. London: John Miller, 1833. Pp. [1]-43.

Uncle John. London: John Dicks, n.d. Pp. [1]-12. Dicks' Standard Plays, 836.

Valentine's Day; or, Harlequin and the Fairy of the True Lover's Knot. London: H. M. Arliss, 1859. Pp. [1]-30. Libretto.

Victorine; or, I'll Sleep on It. London: William Strange, 1836. Pp. [1]-44.

Victorine; or, I'll Sleep on It. New York: Samuel French, n.d. Pp. [1]-45. French's Standard Drama, 210.

Weak Points. London: Chapman & Hall, n.d. Pp. [i]-[vii] (biographical sketch), [1]-36.

Wreck Ashore, The. London: William Strange, n.d. Pp. [1]-58. Strange's Edition of Buckstone's Dramas.

BUCKSTONE, ?, JR
Little Miss Muffet and Little Boy Blue.
See Buckstone, John Baldwin.

BUCKSTONE AT HOME
See Coyne, Joseph Stirling.

BUCKSTONE'S ADVENTURE WITH A POLISH PRINCESS
See Lawrence, Slingsby.

BUDGET OF BLUNDERS, A
See Kemble, Charles.

BUFFALO GIRLS, THE
See Stirling, Edward.

BUGLE CALL, THE
See Parker, Louis Napoleon.

BULL IN A CHINA SHOP, A
See Mathews, Charles James.

BULL-FIGHTER, THE
See Almar, George.

BULLOCK, HENRY
Octavius. London: John Taylor, 1834. Pp. [i]-[vi], [1]-125.

BULWER (later Bulwer-Lytton), **EDWARD GEORGE EARLE LYTTON, LORD LYTTON**
Duchesse de la Vallière, The. London: Saunders & Otley, 1836. Pp. [iii]-[xx], [1]-[180]. 2nd ed. *Filed under* Bulwer-Lytton.

Lady of Lyons, The; or, Love and Pride. London: Saunders & Otley, 1843. Pp. [iii]-[xii], [3]-72.

Lady of Lyons, The; or, Love and Pride. London & New York: George Routledge & Sons, n.d. Pp. [1]-94. Acting Edition of Lord Lytton's Dramas. Promptbook. *Filed under* Bulwer-Lytton.

Lady of Lyons, The; or, Love and Pride. New York: T. Henry French; London: Samuel French, n.d. Pp. [1]-60. Promptbook. *Filed under* Bulwer-Lytton.

Money. London: Saunders & Otley, 1840. Pp. [i-iv], [1]-158. 2nd ed. *Filed under* Bulwer-Lytton.

Money. New York: Robert M. DeWitt, n.d. Pp. [1]-61. DeWitt's Acting Plays, 184. *Filed under* Kingdom, John M.

Not So Bad as We Seem; or, Many Sides to a Character. New York: Harper & Brothers, 1851. Pp. [i]-[viii], 9-166. *Filed under* Bulwer-Lytton.

Richelieu; or, The Conspiracy. N.p.: n.pub., n.d. Pp. [7]-66. Title page lacking. *Filed under* Bulwer-Lytton.

Richelieu; or, The Conspiracy. New York: Douglas, n.d. Pp. [1]-96. Modern Standard Drama, 4. Promptbook. *Filed under* Bulwer-Lytton.

Rightful Heir, The. London: John Murray, 1868. Pp. [1]-62. *Filed under* Bulwer-Lytton.

Rightful Heir, The. New York: Harper & Brothers, 1868. Pp. [1]-61. *Filed under* Bulwer-Lytton.

Sea Captain, The; or, The Birthright. London: Saunders & Otley, 1839. Pp. [i]-[x], [1]-112. *Filed under* Bulwer-Lytton.

Walpole; or, Every Man Has His Price. New York: Robert M. DeWitt, n.d. Pp. [1]-34. DeWitt's Acting Plays, 91.

BULWER, J.

   Slave Sale, The; or, Nature, Bondage, and Liberty. London: J. Pattie, n.d. Pp. [1]-41.

BULWER LYTTON, EDWARD ROBERT, EARL OF LYTTON

   See Meredith, Owen (pseud.).

BUMBLE'S COURTSHIP

   See Emson, Frank E.

BUNCH OF VIOLETS, A

   See Grundy, Sydney.

BUNN, ALFRED

   Bohemian Girl, The. Music by Balfe, Michael William. London & New York: Boosey, n.d. Pp. [i-iv], 1-228. Royal Edition. Vocal score.

   Bohemian Girl, The. Music by Balfe. New York: New York Printing Co., 1870. Pp. [1]-36. Parepa-Rosa Grand English Opera. Libretto.

   Bohemian Girl, The. Music by Balfe. London: W. S. Johnson, n.d. Pp. [1]-32. Libretto.

   Brides of Venice, The. Music by Benedict, Julius. London: W. S. Johnson, n.d. Pp. [i]-iv, [5]-29. Libretto.

   Conrad; or, The Usurper. London: Thomas & George Underwood, 1821. Pp. [i]-[viii], [1]-72.

   Crusaders, The. Music by Benedict, Julius. London: W. S. Johnson, 1846. Pp. [i]-[vi], [7]-45. Libretto.

   Daughter of St. Mark, The. Music by Balfe. London: W. S. Johnson, n.d. Pp. [i]-[vi], [7]-46. Libretto.

   Enchantress, The. Written with Vernoy de Saint-Georges, Jules Henri. By M. D. St. Georges and Mr. Bunn. Music by Balfe. Philadelphia: King & Baird (printer), 1852. Pp. [1]-40. Libretto. *Filed under* Bunn, Alfred.

   Good-looking Fellow, A.

   See Kenney, James.

   Ivanhoe; or, The Jew of York. Birmingham: Beilby & Knotts, 1820. Pp. [i-vi], [1]-76.

   Kinsmen of Naples, The. London: Thomas & George Underwood, 1821. Pp. [73]-146. *Filed under* Conrad; or The Usurper.

   Loretta: A Tale of Seville. Music by Lavenu, L. London: W. S. Johnson, n.d. Pp. [1]-39. Libretto.

   Maid of Artois, The. Music by Balfe. New York: John Douglas, 1847. Pp. [1]-36. Operatic Library, 7. Libretto.

   Matilda of Hungary. Music by Wallace, W. V. London: Cramer, Beale, n.d. Pp. [1]-35. Libretto.

   Minister and the Mercer, The. London: John Miller, 1834. Pp. [i]-[viii], [1]-85.

   My Neighbour's Wife. N.p.: n.pub., n.d. Pp. [77]-105. Title page lacking. Promptbook.

BUNTHORNE'S BRIDE

   See Gilbert, William Schwenck. Patience.

BUONAPARTE

   See Buchanan, Robert Williams. Drama of Kings.
   See Ripon, John Scott.

BUONDELMONTE

   See Woodrooffe, Sophia.

BURGES, JAMES BLAND

   Advertisement, The. In [Collected Works: Dramas, 2 vols., London: E. Kerby, 1817], I, 99-217. Title page lacking. *Filed under* Collected Works.

   Bandit, The. In [Collected Works: Dramas, 2 vols., London: E. Kerby, 1817], I, 219-338. Title page lacking. *Filed under* Collected Works.

   Cortez. In [Collected Works: Dramas, 2 vols., London: E. Kerby, 1817], II, 1-90. Title page lacking. *Filed under* Collected Works.

   Crusaders, The. In [Collected Works: Dramas, 2 vols., London: E. Kerby, 1817], II, [207]-294. Title page lacking. *Filed under* Collected Works.

   Knight of Rhodes, The. In [Collected Works: Dramas, 2 vols., London: E. Kerby, 1817], I, 1-98. Title page lacking. *Filed under* Collected Works.

   Riches; or, The Wife and Brother. London: Samuel Tipper, 1810. Pp. [1]-[8], [1]-[102]. 2nd ed.

   Riches; or, The Wife and Brother. In [Collected Works: Dramas, 2 vols., London: E. Kerby, 1817], II, [295]-422. Title page lacking. *Filed under* Collected Works.

   Riches; or, The Wife and Brother. London: John Cumberland, n.d. Pp. [1]-63. Cumberland's British Theatre, XXIV. *Filed under* Cumberland, John. Cumberland's British Theatre, XXIV.

   Storm, The. In [Collected Works: Dramas, 2 vols., London: E. Kerby, 1817], II, [91]-206. Title page lacking. *Filed under* Collected Works.

   Tricks upon Travellers. London: W. H. Wyatt, 1810. Pp. [1]-15. Libretto.

   Tricks upon Travellers. In [Collected Works: Dramas, 2 vols., London: E. Kerby, 1817], I, 339-439. Title page lacking. *Filed under* Collected Works.

BURGLAR AND THE JUDGE, THE

   See Philips, Francis Charles.

BURGOYNE, JOHN, GEN.

   Heiress, The. In British Drama, 12 vols., London: John Dicks, 1871, VII, [289]-311.

   Lord of the Manor.

   See Dibdin, Charles Isaac Mungo, jr.

   Maid of the Oaks, The. London: Sherwood, Neely, & Jones, 1818. Pp. [1]-32. London Theatre, XXV. *Filed under* Dibdin, Thomas John, ed. London Theatre, XXV.

   Maid of the Oaks, The. In British Drama, 12 vols., London: John Dicks, 1872, XI, [185]-192.

   Richard Coeur de Lion. London: Whittingham & Arliss, 1814. Pp. [1]-32. London Theatre, IV. *Filed under* Dibdin, Thomas John, ed. London Theatre, IV.

   Richard Coeur de Lion. In British Drama, 12 vols., London: John Dicks, 1872, XII, [51]-61.

BURIED TITAN, THE

   See Leifchild, Franklin.

BURKE, WILLIAM

   Armed Briton, The; or, The Invaders Vanquished. London: J. T. Hughes, 1806. Pp. [i], [1]-60.

BURLETTA OF ERRORS

   See Planché, James Robinson.

BURLINGTON ARCADE, THE

   See Dance, Charles.

BURMESE WAR, THE

   See Amherst, J. H.

BURN, DAVID

   De Rullecourt; or, Jersey Invaded. In Plays and Fugitive Pieces in Verse, Hobart Town, Van Diemen's Land: William Pratt (printer), 1842, I, [137]-188.

   Loreda. In Plays and Fugitive Pieces in Verse, Hobart Town, Van Diemen's Land: William Pratt (printer), 1842, I, [189]-233.

   Our First Lieutenant. In Our First Lieutenant and Fugitive Pieces in Prose, Hobart Town, Van Diemen's Land: William Pratt (printer), 1842, II, [i-iii], [275]-310.

   Queen's Love, The. In Plays and Fugitive Pieces in Verse, Hobart Town, Van Diemen's Land: William Pratt (printer), 1842, I, [i], [1]-66.

   Regulus. In Plays and Fugitive Pieces in Verse, Hobart Town, Van Diemen's Land: William Pratt (printer), 1842, I, [i], [67]-136.

BURNABY, EDWYN ANDREW

   Agatha; or, The Convent of St. Bartholomew. London: Longman, Hurst, Rees, Orme, & Brown, 1821. Pp. [3]-75.

BURNAND, FRANCIS COWLEY

   Acis and Galataea; or, The Nimble Nymph and the Terrible Troglodyte! London: Thomas Hailes Lacy, n.d. Pp. [1]-48. Lacy's Acting Edition.

   Africaine, L'; or, The Queen of the Cannibal Islands. Music by Musgrave, Frank. London: Strand, 1865. Pp. [1]-48.

   Airey Annie. London: Bradbury, Agnew (printer), n.d. Pp. [i-ii], [1]-24.

   Alonzo the Brave; or, Faust and the Fair Imogene. *Also:* Faust and Mephistopheles; or, Alonzo the Brave and the Fair Imogene. London: Thomas Hailes Lacy, n.d. Pp. [1]-34. Promptbook.

Arion; or, The Story of a Lyre. London: Restaurant Co., 1872. Pp. [i], [1]-32.

B. B.
> *See* Williams, Montagu Stephen.

Beast and the Beauty, The; or, No Rose Without a Thorn. London: Phillips, n.d. Pp. [1]-39.

Betsy. New York: Dick & Fitzgerald, n.d. Pp. [1]-51. Dick's American Edition.

Black-Eyed Susan.
> *See* Latest Edition of Black-Eyed Susan, The.

Blue Beard; or, The Hazard of the Dye. London: R. Wilson (printer), 1883. Pp. [i-iv], [1]-60.

Boadicea the Beautiful; or, Harlequin Julius Caesar and the Delightful Druid! In *Beeton's Book of Burlesques,* London: S. O. Beeton, 1866, pp. [111]-156. *Filed under* Brough, William, and Burnand, Francis Cowley. Beeton's Book of Burlesques.

Captain Thérèse. Written with A'Beckett, Gilbert Arthur; Bisson, Alexandre. London: Hopwood & Crew, n.d. Pp. [i-iv], 1-230. Vocal score.

Carte de Visite.
> *See* Williams, Montagu Stephen.

Chieftain, The. Music by Sullivan, Arthur. London: Boosey, c.1894. Pp. [i]-[viii], [9]-55. Libretto.

Chieftain, The. Music by Sullivan, Arthur. London: Boosey, c.1895. Pp. [i-iv], [1]-162. Vocal score.

Chieftain, The. Music by Sullivan, Arthur. London: Boosey, c.1895. Pp. [i-iv], [1]-159. Vocal score.

Cigale, La. Written with A'Beckett, Gilbert Arthur. Music by Audran. London: Hopwood & Crew, n.d. Pp. [i-iv], 1-237. Vocal score.

Claude du Val; or, The Highwayman for the Ladies. London: Phillips, n.d. Pp. [1]-47.

Cox and Box. By John Maddison Morton and F. C. Burnand. Music by Sullivan, Arthur. London & New York: Samuel French, n.d. Pp. [1]-28. French's Acting Edition (late Lacy's). *Filed under* Morton, John Maddison; Burnand, Francis Cowley.

Cox and Box; or, The Long-Lost Brothers. Music by Sullivan, Arthur. London & New York: Boosey, n.d. Pp. [1]-72. Vocal score.

Cupid and Psyche; or, Beautiful as a Butterfly. London: Thomas Hailes Lacy, n.d. Pp. [1]-36. [Lacy's Acting Edition].

Deadman's Point; or, The Lighthouse on the Carn Ruth. London: Thomas Hailes Lacy, 1871. Pp. [1]-44. [Lacy's Acting Edition].

Deal Boatmen, The. London: [Thomas Hailes Lacy], n.d. Pp. [3]-34. Title page lacking. [Lacy's Acting Edition, 888]. Promptbook.

Deerfoot. New York: Robert M. DeWitt, n.d. Pp. [1]-15. DeWitt's Acting Plays, 125.

Dido. London: Thomas Hailes Lacy, n.d. Pp. [1]-38.

Easy Shaving. Written with Williams, Montagu Stephen. London: Thomas Hailes Lacy, n.d. Pp. [1]-18.

Fair Rosamond; or, The Maze, the Maid, and the Monarch! London: Thomas Hailes Lacy, n.d. Pp. [1]-43.

Faust and Loose. London: Bradbury, Agnew (printer), n.d. Pp. [i-ii], [1]-29.

Faust and Marguerite. London: Thomas Hailes Lacy, n.d. Pp. [1]-42. [Lacy's Acting Edition].

Faust and Mephistopheles.
> *See* Alonzo the Brave.

Fowl Play; or, A Story of Chikkin Hazard. London: Phillips, n.d. Pp. [1]-44.

Frightful Hair, The; or, Who Shot the Dog? London: Phillips, n.d. Pp. [1]-41.

Guy Fawkes; or, The Ugly Mug and the Couple of Spoons. London: Strand, 1866. Pp. [1]-38. 1st ed. Promptbook.

Helen.
> *See* Latest Edition of Helen, The.

His Majesty; or, The Court of Vingolia. Written with Lehmann, Rudolph Chambers. Music by Mackenzie, Alexander C. London: Joseph Williams, n.d. Pp. [i-iv], 1-228. Vocal score.

Hit and Miss; or, All My Eye and Betty Martyn! London: Phillips, n.d. Pp. [1]-50.

Humbug! London: Thomas Hailes Lacy, n.d. Pp. [1]-38.

In for a Holiday.
> *See* In for a Holyday.

In for a Holyday. *Also:* In for a Holiday. London & New York: Samuel French, n.d. Pp. [1]-17. French's Acting Edition (late Lacy's).

Incognita. Written with Greenbank, Harry Hewetson. Music by Lecocq, Charles. London: Hopwood & Crew, n.d. Pp. [i-iv], 1-312. Vocal score.

Incompleat Angler, The. London: Bradbury, Agnew, 1887. Pp. [i]-[x], [1]-94.

Isle of St. Tropez, The.
> *See* Williams, Montagu Stephen.

Ixion; or, The Man at the Wheel. London & New York: Samuel French, n.d. Pp. [1]-44.

King of the Merrows; or, The Prince and the Piper. Written with Simpson, John Palgrave. London: Thomas Hailes Lacy, n.d. Pp. [1]-48. [Lacy's Acting Edition]. *Filed under* Burnand, Francis Cowley.

Kissi-Kissi. Music by Offenbach. London: Phillips, n.d. Pp. [1]-29. Libretto.

Latest Edition of Black-Eyed Susan, The; or, The Little Bill That Was Taken Up. *Also:* Black-Eyed Susan. London: Thomas Hailes Lacy, n.d. Pp. [1]-44.

Latest Edition of Helen, The; or, Taken from the Greek. *Also:* Helen. London: Thomas Hailes Lacy, n.d. Pp. [1]-40.

Lord Lovel and Lady Nancy Bell; or, The Bounding Brigand of the Bakumboilum. London & New York: Samuel French, n.d. Pp. [1]-22.

Madame Berliot's Ball; or, The Chalet in the Valley. London: Thomas Hailes Lacy, n.d. Pp. [1]-36. [Lacy's Acting Edition].

Mary Turner; or, The Wicious Willin and Wictorious Wirtue! London: Thomas Hailes Lacy, n.d. Pp. [1]-38. [Lacy's Acting Edition].

Military Billy Taylor, The; or, The War in Carriboo. London: Hopwood & Crew, 1869. Pp. [1]-35.

Miller and His Man, The. Music by Sullivan, Arthur. London: Ashdown & Parry, n.d. Pp. [i-iv], [1]-38. Vocal score.

Olympic Games; or, The Major, the Miner, and the Cock-a-doodle-doo. London: Phillips, 1867. Pp. [1]-43.

Orpheus; or, The Magic Lyre. In *Beeton's Book of Burlesques,* London: S. O. Beeton, 1866, pp. [37]-73. *Filed under* Brough, William, and Burnand, Francis Cowley. Beeton's Book of Burlesques.

Paris; or, Vive Lemprière. London: Thomas Hailes Lacy, n.d. Pp. [1]-52. [Lacy's Acting Edition].

Patient Penelope; or, The Return of Ulysses. London: Thomas Hailes Lacy, n.d. Pp. [1]-24.

Penelope Anne. N.p.: n.pub., n.d. Pp. [41]-[58].

Pickwick. Music by Solomon, Edward. London: Boosey, n.d. Pp. [1-2], [i]-[xii], 1-93. Libretto and vocal score.

Pirithous, the Son of Ixion. London: Thomas Hailes Lacy, n.d. Pp. [1]-46.

Poll and Partner Joe; or, The Pride of Putney and the Pressing Pirate. London: Tinsley Brothers, 1871. Pp. [1]-40.

Proof; or, A Celebrated Case. London & New York: Samuel French, n.d. Pp. [1]-52. [Lacy's Acting Edition].

Rise and Fall of Richard III, The; or, A New Front to an Old Dicky. London: Phillips, n.d. Pp. [1]-45.

Robin Hood; or, The Forester's Fate! London: Thomas Hailes Lacy, n.d. Pp. [1]-40.

Romance under Difficulties. London: Thomas Hailes Lacy, n.d. Pp. [1]-16. Lacy's Acting Edition, 388.

Rumplestiltskin; or, The Woman at the Wheel! London: Thomas Hailes Lacy, n.d. Pp. [1]-50.

Sappho; or, Look before You Leap! In *Beeton's Book of Burlesques,* London: S. O. Beeton, 1866, pp. [74]-110. *Filed under* Brough, William, and Burnand, Francis Cowley. Beeton's Book of Burlesques.

Sir Dagobert and the Dragon; or, How to Run through the Scales. In [*Short Plays for Drawing-Room Performance,*

London: Ward, Lock, 1890], pp. [127]-146. Title page lacking.

Snowdrop; or, The Seven Mannikins and the Magic Mirror. London: Thomas Hailes Lacy, n.d. Pp. [1]-44. [Lacy's Acting Edition].

To Let, Furnished. New York: Happy Hours, n.d. Pp. [1]-16. Acting Drama, 73.

Turkish Bath, The.
See Williams, Montagu Stephen.

Turn of the Tide, The. London: n.pub. (priv.), 1869. Pp. [1]-12. Text incomplete.

Ulysses; or, The Iron-Clad Warrior and the Little Tug of War. London: Thomas Hailes Lacy, n.d. Pp. [1]-38. [Lacy's Acting Edition].

Valentine and Orson; or, Harlequin and the Magic Shield. Music by Meyder, Karl. London: J. Miles (printer), n.d. Pp. [9]-48. Text complete. Libretto.

Venus and Adonis; or, The Two Rivals and the Small Boar. London: Thomas Hailes Lacy, n.d. Pp. [1]-50.

Very Little Faust and More Mephistopheles. London: Phillips, n.d. Pp. [1]-40.

Villikins and His Dinah. London: Thomas Hailes Lacy, n.d. Pp. [1]-21. [Lacy's Acting Edition].

White Cat!, The; or, Prince Lardi-Dardi and the Radiant Rosetta. London: Thomas Hailes Lacy, n.d. Pp. [1]-33. [Lacy's Acting Edition].

White Fawn, The; or, The Loves of Prince Buttercup and the Princess Daisy. London: Thomas Hailes Lacy, n.d. Pp. [1]-48. [Lacy's Acting Edition].

Windsor Castle. Music by Musgrave, Frank. London: Thomas Hailes Lacy, n.d. Pp. [1]-48.

BURNEY, ESTELLE

Idyll of the Closing Century, An. London: Samuel French; New York: T. Henry French, n.d. Pp. [1]-10. [Lacy's Acting Edition].

BURNEY, FRANCES (later Mrs. Alexander d'Arblay)

Aristodemus; or, The Spectre. In *Tragic Dramas,* London: Thomas Davison (printer), 1818, pp. [113]-191.

Fitzormond; or, Cherished Resentment. In *Tragic Dramas,* London: Thomas Davison (printer), 1818, pp. [i]-[xviii], [1]-54.

Malek Adhel, the Champion of the Crescent. In *Tragic Dramas,* London: Thomas Davison (printer), 1818, pp. [i-ii], [55]-111.

BURNEYBUSBY, JOHN

Siege of Troy, The. London: James Ridgway, 1819. Pp. [i-iv], [1]-25.

BURNING OF MOSCOW
See Code, H. B. Russian Sacrifice, The.

BURNING OF THE TEMPLE OF DIANA AT EPHESUS
See Mann, J. P. Erostratus.

BURNLEY, JAMES

Fetters. Bradford: William Byles & Son (printer) (priv.), 1876. Pp. [1]-59.

BURNT ASHES
See Brookfield, Charles Hallam Elton.

BURROWS, J. G.

Lurline; or, The Water Nymphs' Revolt. Written with Pitt, George Dibdin. N.p.: n.pub., n.d. Pp. [109]-118. Title page lacking.

BURTON, ?

Paetus and Arria. Also attrib. to Nicholson, John. Cambridge: Francis Hodson, 1809. Pp. [i]-[x], [1]-[76].

Right and Wrong. Also attrib. to Nicholson, John. London: Lackington, Allen, 1812. Pp. [i]-[viii], [1]-79. 2nd ed.

BURTON, WILLIAM EVANS

Court Fool, The; or, A King's Amusement. London: John Dicks, n.d. Pp. [1]-16. Dicks' Standard Plays, 341.

Ellen Wareham. London: John Duncombe, n.d. Pp. [1]-42. Duncombe's Acting Edition of the British Theatre, 90.

Ladies' Man, The. Philadelphia: Carey & Hart; Hogan & Thompson; W. Marshall, 1835. Pp. [81]-122. [Alexander's Modern Acting Drama].

Toodles, The. New York: Samuel French, n.d. Pp. [5]-28. Text complete. Minor Drama, 54.

BUSH ABOON TRAQUAIR, THE
See Hetherington, William Maxwell.

BUSH REVELS
See Stephens, James Brunton. Fayette.

BUSINESS ARRANGEMENT, A
See Hope, Anthony.

BUSSY, BERNARD F.

Roundhead, The. Written with Blackmore, W. T. London & New York: Samuel French, n.d. Pp. [1]-36. [Lacy's Acting Edition].

BUSTLE'S BRIDE
See Capes, Bernard.

BUSY BODY, THE
See Centlivre, Susanna Carroll Freeman, Mrs. Joseph.

BUSY DAY IN MESSINA
See Dufferin, Helen Selina Sheridan Blackwood, Lady. Finesse.

BUT HOWEVER—
See Mayhew, Henry.

BUTLER, ARTHUR GRAY

Charles I. London: Henry Frowde, 1907. Pp. [i]-[xviii], [1]-124. 2nd ed. rev.

Harold. London: Henry Frowde, 1906. Pp. [i-vi], [1]-118. 2nd ed.

BUTLER, MRS. PIERCE
See Kemble, Frances Anne (Fanny).

BUTLER, RICHARD WILLIAM
See Henry, Richard (pseud.).

BUTLER, RICHARD WILLIAM, EARL OF GLENGALL

Follies of Fashion, The. By the Earl of Glengall. London: Henry Colburn & Richard Bentley, 1830. Pp. [iii]-[x], [1]-147.

Irish Tutor, The; or, New Lights. London: John Lowndes, n.d. Pp. [1]-24.

Irish Tutor, The; or, New Lights. London: John Cumberland, n.d. Pp. [1]-24. Cumberland's British Theatre, XXI. *Filed under* Cumberland, John. Cumberland's British Theatre, XXI.

BY, WILLIAM

Richard III Travestie. London: Sherwood, Neely, & Jones, 1816. Pp. [1-4], [i]-[viii], [1]-91.

BY ADVERTISEMENT
See Reeve, John. One, Two, Three, Four, Five.

BY PROXY
See Brookfield, Charles Hallam Elton.

BY ROYAL COMMAND
See Stirling, Edward.

BY SPECIAL REQUEST
See Watson, T. Malcolm.

BY THIS TOKEN
See Angus, J. Keith.

BYAM, MARTIN

Sinbad the Sailor.
See McArdle, John Francis.

BYATT, HENRY

Brothers, The. London & New York: Samuel French, n.d. Pp. [1]-12. [French's Acting Edition].

Golden Age, The; or, Pierrot's Sacrifice. Music by Pascal, Florian. London: Joseph Williams, n.d. Pp. [i-iv], [1]-66. Vocal score.

BYERLEY, JOHN SCOTT
See Ripon, John Scott.

BYRON, GEORGE GORDON, LORD

Blues, The. In *Liberal,* London: John Hunt, 1823, II, [i], [1]-21.

Cain: A Mystery. In [*Collected Works,* 2 vols., London: John Murray, 1837, II], [163]-258. Title page lacking. *Filed under* Collected Works.

Deformed Transformed, The. In [*Collected Works,* 2 vols., London: John Murray, 1837, II], [101]-161. Title page lacking. *Filed under* Collected Works.

Heaven and Earth. In *Liberal,* London: John Hunt, 1822, I, [i], [165]-206.

Heaven and Earth. In [*Collected Works,* 2 vols., London: John Murray, 1837, I], [235]-278. Title page lacking. *Filed under* Collected Works.

Manfred. London: John Murray, 1817. Pp. [1]-80.

Manfred. In [*Collected Works,* 2 vols., London: John Murray, 1837, I], [5]-74. Title page lacking. *Filed under* Collected Works.

Manfred. London: Thomas Hailes Lacy, n.d. Pp. [1]-[42]. *Filed under* Manfred (anon.).

Marino Faliero, Doge of Venice. In [*Collected Works,* 2 vols., London: John Murray, 1837, I], [75]-234. Title page lacking. *Filed under* Collected Works.

Sardanapalus. In [*Collected Works,* 2 vols., London: John Murray, 1837, I], [279]-403. Title page lacking. *Filed under* Collected Works.

Sardanapalus.
See Calvert, Charles Alexander (arr.).
See Kean, Charles John (arr.).

Two Foscari, The. In [*Collected Works,* 2 vols., London: John Murray, 1837, II], [5]-100. Title page lacking. *Filed under* Collected Works.

Werner. London: John Murray, 1823. Pp. [iii]-viii, [1]-188.

Werner. London: John Murray, 1823. Pp. [i]-viii, [1]-188. Promptbook.

Werner. In *British Drama,* 12 vols., London: John Dicks, 1865, III, [767]-789.

Werner; or, The Inheritance. In [*Collected Works,* London: John Murray, 1837, II], 259-391. Title page lacking. *Filed under* Collected Works.

BYRON, HENRY JAMES

Abandondino, the Bloodless. In *Sensation Dramas for the Back Drawing Room,* London: Thomas Hailes Lacy, n.d., pp. 33-36. *Filed under* Sensation Dramas.

Aladdin; or, The Wonderful Scamp! London: Thomas Hailes Lacy, n.d. Pp. [1]-42.

Ali Baba; or, The Thirty-nine Thieves, in Accordance with the Author's Habit of Taking One Off! London: Thomas Hailes Lacy, n.d. Pp. [1]-38.

Allurio and Adelina; or, The Village Inn and the Count Out. In *Sensation Dramas for the Back Drawing Room,* London: Thomas Hailes Lacy, n.d., pp. 70-79. *Filed under* Sensation Dramas.

Babes in the Wood and the Good Little Fairy Birds!, The. London: Thomas Hailes Lacy, n.d. Pp. [1]-30. Lacy's Acting Edition, 612.

Beautiful Haidée!; or, The Sea Nymph and the Sallee Rovers. London: Thomas Hailes Lacy, n.d. Pp. [1]-[31].

Bits of Burlesque. London & New York: Samuel French, n.d. Pp. [1]-46.

Blow for Blow. New York, Chicago, & London: Crest Trading Co., n.d. Pp. [1]-53. French's Acting Edition (late Lacy's), [501].

Blow for Blow. Chicago: Dramatic Publishing Co., n.d. Pp. [1]-41. Sergel's Acting Drama, 160.

Blue Beard! From a New Point of Hue. London & New York: Samuel French, n.d. Pp. [1]-38.

Bow Bells. London & New York: Samuel French, n.d. Pp. [1]-48. [Lacy's Acting Edition].

Bride of Abydos, The; or, The Prince, the Pirate, and the Pearl. London: Thomas Hailes Lacy, n.d. Pp. [1]-24. French's Acting Edition (late Lacy's).

Camaralzaman and the Fair Badoura; or, The Bad Djinn and the Good Spirit. London: Thomas Hailes Lacy, n.d. Pp. [1]-42. [Lacy's Acting Edition].

Cinderella; or, The Lover, the Lackey, and the Little Glass Slipper. London: Thomas Hailes Lacy, n.d. Pp. [1]-45. [Lacy's Acting Edition].

Corsican Bothers, The; or, The Troublesome Twins. London: Thomas Hailes Lacy, n.d. Pp. [1]-44. Lacy's Acting Edition, 1315.

Courtship; or, The Three Caskets. London & New York: Samuel French, n.d. Pp. [1]-48. [Lacy's Acting Edition].

Cyril's Success. Chicago & New York: Dramatic Publishing Co., n.d. Pp. [1]-46. [Sergel's Acting Drama].

Daisy Farm. Chicago: Dramatic Publishing Co., n.d. Pp. [1]-34. Sergel's Acting Drama, 286.

Dearer Than Life. New York: DeWitt, n.d. Pp. [1]-34.

1863; or, The Sensations of the Past Season, with a Shameful Revelation of Lady Somebody's Secret. London: Thomas Hailes Lacy, n.d. Pp. [1]-30. [Lacy's Acting Edition].

Enchanted Wood, The; or, The Three Transformed Princes. London & New York: Samuel French, n.d. Pp. [1]-28. [Lacy's Acting Edition].

English Gentleman, An; or, The Squire's Last Shilling. New York: Robert M. DeWitt, n.d. Pp. [1]-33. DeWitt's Acting Plays, 297.

Esmeralda; or, The Sensation Goat! London: Thomas Hailes Lacy, n.d. Pp. [1]-42. Lacy's Acting Edition, 779.

Eurydice; or, Little Orpheus and His Lute. London: Thomas Hailes Lacy, n.d. Pp. [1]-39. [Lacy's Acting Edition].

Ever-so-Little Bear, The; or, The Pale-Faces and the Put-em-in-the-Cauldron Indians. In *Sensation Dramas for the Back Drawing Room,* London: Thomas Hailes Lacy, n.d., pp. 64-69. *Filed under* Sensation Dramas.

Fine Feathers. London & New York: Samuel French, n.d. Pp. [1]-60. [Lacy's Acting Edition].

Fool and His Money. London & New York: Samuel French, n.d. Pp. [1]-48. French's Acting Edition (late Lacy's), 1670.

Fra Diavolo; or, The Beauty and the Brigands. London & New York: Samuel French, n.d. Pp. [1]-34.

Freischutz, Der; or, The Bill, the Belle, and the Bullet! London: Thomas Hailes Lacy, n.d. Pp. [1]-35.

Full Private Perkins; or, He Wiped Away a Tear. In *Sensation Dramas for the Back Drawing Room,* London: Thomas Hailes Lacy, n.d., pp. 88-94. *Filed under* Sensation Dramas.

Gaiety Gulliver, The. *Also:* Gulliver. *Also:* Gulliver's Travels. [London: Aubert's Steam Printing Works], n.d. Pp. [1]-41. *Filed under* Gulliver.

Garibaldi Excursionists, The. London: Thomas Hailes Lacy, n.d. Pp. [1]-18. [Lacy's Acting Edition].

George de Barnwell. London: Thomas Hailes Lacy, n.d. Pp. [1]-34.

Girls, The. London & New York: Samuel French, n.d. Pp. [1]-52. [Lacy's Acting Edition].

Giselle; or, The Sirens of the Lotus Lake. London: Thomas Hailes Lacy, n.d. Pp. [1]-26. [Lacy's Acting Edition].

Gold and Guilt; or, The True Ring of the Genuine Metal. In *Sensation Dramas for the Back Drawing Room,* London: Thomas Hailes Lacy, n.d., pp. 80-87. *Filed under* Sensation Dramas.

Green Grow the Rushes, Oh!; or, The Squireen, the Informer, and the Illicit Distiller. In *Sensation Dramas for the Back Drawing Room,* London: Thomas Hailes Lacy, n.d., pp. 25-32. *Filed under* Sensation Dramas.

Grin Bushes!, The; or, The Mrs. Brown of the Missis-sippi. London: Thomas Hailes Lacy, n.d. Pp. [1]-36. [Lacy's Acting Edition].

Gulliver.
See Gaiety Gulliver.

Gulliver's Travels.
See Gaiety Gulliver, The.

How to Tame Your Mother-in-law. Clyde, Ohio: A. D. Ames, n.d. Pp. [1]-13. Ames' Series of Standard and Minor Drama, 74.

Ill-treated Il Trovatore; or, The Mother, the Maiden, and the Musicianer. London: Thomas Hailes Lacy, n.d. Pp. [1]-38.

Ivanhoe in Accordance with the Spirit of the Times. London & New York: Samuel French, n.d. Pp. [1]-48.

Jack the Giant Killer; or, Harlequin King Arthur and ye Knights of ye Round Table. London: Thomas Hailes Lacy, n.d. Pp. [1]-31.

La! Sonnambula!; or, The Supper, the Sleeper, and the Merry Swiss Boy. London: Thomas Hailes Lacy, n.d. Pp. [1]-36.

Lady Belle Belle; or, Fortunio and His Seven Magic Men. London: Thomas Hailes Lacy, n.d. Pp. [i-ix], [10]-44. [Lacy's Acting Edition].

Lancashire Lass, The; or, Tempted, Tried, and True. Chicago: Dramatic Publishing Co., n.d. Pp. [1]-45. World Acting Drama.

Lion and the Unicorn, The. London: Her Majesty's Theatre, n.d. Pp. [1]-16. Libretto.

Little Don Giovanni. London: Thomas Hailes Lacy, n.d. Pp. [1]-38.

Lord Bateman; or, The Proud Young Porter and the Fair Sophia. London: Thomas Hailes Lacy, n.d. Pp. [1]-36.

Lucia di Lammermoor; or, The Laird, the Lady, and the Lover. London & New York: Samuel French, n.d. Pp. [1]-35.

Lucretia Borgia, M. D.; or, La Grande Doctresse. London: Thomas Hailes Lacy, n.d. Pp. [1]-32.

Maid and the Magpie, The; or, The Fatal Spoon! London: Thomas Hailes Lacy, n.d. Pp. [1]-36.

Married in Haste. London & New York: Samuel French, n.d. Pp. [1]-52. [Lacy's Acting Edition].

Mazeppa! London: Thomas Hailes Lacy, n.d. Pp. [1]-40. Promptbook.

Mazourka; or, The Stick, the Pole, and the Tartar. London: Thomas Hailes Lacy, n.d. Pp. [1]-36.

McAllister McVitty McNab, The; or, The Laird, the Daftie, and the Highland Maiden. In *Sensation Dramas for the Back Drawing Room*, London: Thomas Hailes Lacy, n.d., pp. 13-18. *Filed under* Sensation Dramas.

Mendacious Mariner, The; or, Pretty Poll of Portsea and the Captain with His Whiskers. In *Sensation Dramas for the Back Drawing Room*, London: Thomas Hailes Lacy, n.d., pp. 44-50. *Filed under* Sensation Dramas.

Miller and His Men, The.
See Talfourd, Francis.

Miss Eily O'Connor. London: Thomas Hailes Lacy, n.d. Pp. [1]-[36].

Miss Eily O'Connor (introductions and alterations). London: Thomas Hailes Lacy, n.d. Pp. [1]-8. [Lacy's Acting Edition]. *Filed under* Introductions and Alterations . . .

Motto, The: I Am All There. London: Thomas Hailes Lacy, n.d. Pp. [1]-43.

Not Such a Fool as He Looks. Chicago: Dramatic Publishing Co., n.d. Pp. [1]-32. Sergel's Acting Drama, 117.

Nymph of the Lurleyburg, The; or, The Knight and the Naiads. London: Thomas Hailes Lacy, n.d. Pp. [1]-36.

Old Sailors. London & New York: Samuel French, n.d. Pp. [1]-42. [Lacy's Acting Edition].

Old Soldier. London & New York: Samuel French, n.d. Pp. [1]-40. [Lacy's Acting Edition].

Old Story!, The. London & New York: Samuel French, n.d. Pp. [1]-32.

One Hundred Thousand Pounds. New York: Robert M. DeWitt, n.d. Pp. [3]-38. DeWitt's Acting Plays, 3.

Orange Tree and the Humble Bee, The; or, The Little Princess Who Was Lost at Sea. London & New York: Samuel French, n.d. Pp. [1]-34. [Lacy's Acting Edition].

Orpheus and Eurydice; or, The Young Gentleman Who Charmed the Rocks. London: Thomas Hailes Lacy, n.d. Pp. [1]-44.

Our Boys. Chicago: Dramatic Publishing Co., n.d. Pp. [1]-59. World Acting Drama.

Pampered Menials.
See £20 a Year—All Found.

Pan. London: Thomas Hailes Lacy, n.d. Pp. [1]-36. [Lacy's Acting Edition].

Pandora's Box; or, The Young Spark and the Old Flame! London: Thomas Hailes Lacy, n.d. Pp. [1]-42. Lacy's Acting Edition.

Partners for Life. London & New York: Samuel French, n.d. Pp. [1]-48. French's Acting Edition (late Lacy's).

Pilgrim of Love!, The. London: Thomas Hailes Lacy, n.d. Pp. [1]-39.

Princess Spring-Time; or, The Envoy Who Stole the King's Daughter. London: Thomas Hailes Lacy, n.d. Pp. [1]-30. [Lacy's Acting Edition].

Prompter's Box, The: A Story of the Footlights and the Fireside. N.p.: n.pub., n.d. Pp. [i], [1]-61. Title page lacking. Promptbook.

Prompter's Box, The: A Story of the Footlights and the Fireside. London & New York: Samuel French, n.d. Pp. [1]-48. [Lacy's Acting Edition].

Punch. London & New York: Samuel French, n.d. Pp. [1]-48. [Lacy's Acting Edition].

Puss in a New Pair of Boots. London: W. H. Swanborough, 1862. Pp. [1]-36.

Rival Rajahs of Ramjam Coodlum, The; or, Sikhs of One and Half-a-dozen of the Other. In *Sensation Dramas for the Back Drawing Room*, London: Thomas Hailes Lacy, n.d., pp. [1]-12. *Filed under* Sensation Dramas.

Robert Macaire; or, The Roadside Inn Turned Inside Out. London: Thomas Hailes Lacy, n.d. Pp. [1]-40. [Lacy's Acting Edition].

Robinson Crusoe; or, Harlequin Friday and the King of the Caribee Islands! Music by Montgomery, W. H. London: Thomas Hailes Lacy, n.d. Pp. 1-30. Libretto.

Rosebud of Stingingnettle Farm, The; or, The Villanous Squire and the Virtuous Villager. London: Nassau Steam Press, 1862. Pp. [1]-12.

Sour Grapes. London & New York: Samuel French, n.d. Pp. [1]-62. French's Acting Edition (late Lacy's), 1890.

Spur of the Moment, The. London & New York: Samuel French, n.d. Pp. [1]-18. [Lacy's Acting Edition].

Taffy Was a Welshman; or, The Child, the Chouse, and the Cheese. In *Sensation Dramas for the Back Drawing Room*, London: Thomas Hailes Lacy, n.d., pp. 19-24. *Filed under* Sensation Dramas.

Timothy to the Rescue. New York: DeWitt, n.d. Pp. [1]-16. DeWitt's Acting Plays, 133.

£20 a Year—All Found; or, Out of a Situation Refusing Twenty. *Also:* Pampered Menials. London & New York: Samuel French, n.d. Pp. [1]-18. [Lacy's Acting Edition].

Uncle. Philadelphia: Penn, 1895. Pp. [1]-47. Keystone Edition of Popular Plays.

Uncle Dick's Darling. New York: DeWitt, n.d. <wrps. Chicago: Dramatic Publishing Co.>. Pp. [1]-29. Sergel's Acting Drama, 294.

Very Latest Edition of the Lady of Lyons, The. London & New York: Samuel French, n.d. Pp. [1]-30.

Village Virtue; or, The Libertine Lord and the Damsel of Daisy Farm. In *Sensation Dramas for the Back Drawing Room*, London: Thomas Hailes Lacy, n.d., pp. 37-43. *Filed under* Sensation Dramas.

War to the Knife. London: Thomas Hailes Lacy, n.d. Pp. [1]-31.

Wayside Wiolets, The; or, The Gipsy Girl and the Guilty Conscience. In *Sensation Dramas for the Back Drawing Room*, London: Thomas Hailes Lacy, n.d., pp. 58-63. *Filed under* Sensation Dramas.

Weak Woman. London & New York: Samuel French, n.d. Pp. [1]-43. [Lacy's Acting Edition].

White Rose of the Plantation, The; or, Lubly Rosa, Sambo Don't Come. In *Sensation Dramas for the Back Drawing Room*, London: Thomas Hailes Lacy, n.d., pp. 95-101. *Filed under* Sensation Dramas.

Whittington and His Cat!; or, Harlequin King Kollywobbol and the Genius of Good Humour! London: A. Harris, 1862. Pp. [1]-27. Libretto.

Wild Wolf of Tartary, The; or, The Empty Khan and the Khurdish Conspirators. In *Sensation Dramas for the Back Drawing Room*, London: Thomas Hailes Lacy, n.d., pp. 51-57. *Filed under* Sensation Dramas.

William Tell, with a Vengeance; or, The Pet, the Patriot, and the Pippin. New York: Robert M. DeWitt, n.d. Pp. [1]-29.

Wrinkles: A Tale of Time. London & New York: Samuel French, n.d. Pp. [1]-53. [Lacy's Acting Edition].

Yellow Dwarf, The; or, Harlequin Cupid and the King of the Gold Mines! Music by Betjemann. London: J. Miles (printer), n.d. Pp. [1]-27. Libretto.

BYRON, HENRY JAMES (trans.)
  Fille de Madame Angot, La. Music by Lecocq, Charles. London & New York: Boosey, n.d. Pp. [i-iv], 1-276. Vocal score.
BYRON, MAY CLARISSA GILLINGTON, MRS. G. F.
  See Gillington, May Clarissa.
BYRON, MEDORA GORDON
  Zameo; or, The White Warrior. Also attrib. to Thompson, C. P. London: John Duncombe, n.d. Pp. [1]-40. Duncombe's Edition.
C., D.
  Vasco de Balboa. London: R. K. Burt (printer) (priv.), 1869. Pp. [1]-[111].
C., T. S.
  Shin Fain; or, Ourselves Alone. By Tom Telephone (pseud.). Dublin: James Duffy & Sons, 1882. Pp. [1]-32.
C., W. M.
  See Cooke, William Major.
C.......LL VOLUNTEER CORPS
  See Coggeshall Volunteer Corps, The.
CABIN BOY, THE
  See Stirling, Edward.
CABINET, THE
  See Dibdin, Thomas John.
CABINET MINISTER, THE
  See Pinero, Arthur Wing.
CABINET QUESTION, A
  See Planché, James Robinson.
CABMAN NO. 93
  See Williams, Thomas John.
  See Williams, Thomas John. Found in a Four-Wheeler!
CAD OF THE BUSS
  See Blink, George. Tiger at Large, The.
CAELINA
  See Wallace, John.
CAESAR AND CLEOPATRA
  See Shaw, George Bernard.
CAESAR BORGIA, THE SCOURGE OF VENICE!
  See Barnett, Charles Zachary.
CAESAR DE BAZAN
  See Webster, Benjamin Nottingham.
CAESAR'S APOSTASY
  See Archer, William (trans.). Emperor and Galilean.
CAGOT, THE
  See Falconer, Edmund.
CAIN: A MYSTERY
  See Byron, George Gordon, Lord.
CAIN THE WANDERER
  See Reade, John Edmund.
CAINE, HALL
  Bondman, The. London: Ballantyne (printer) (priv.), 1906. Pp. [i]-[xviii], [1]-240. Promptbook.
  Christian, The. London: Horace Cox (printer) (priv.), n.d. Pp. [i-iv], [1]-[107].
  Christian, The. Pp. [i-ii], [1]-33, [i], [1]-32, [i], [1]-34, [i], [1]-27, [i], [1]-24. Pagination by act. Typescript.
  Christian, The. Pp. [i-ii], [1]-97. Typescript.
  Manxman, The. Pp. [i-iii], [1]-25, [i], [1]-15, [i], [1]-21, [i], [1]-21, [i], [1]-21. Pagination by act. Typescript. *Filed under* Barrett, Wilson; Caine, Hall.
CAITIFF OF CORSICA, THE; OR, THE UNIVERSAL BANDITTO (anon.)
  London: J. Budd, 1807. Pp. [iii]-vi, [1]-284.
CAIUS GRACCHUS
  See Knowles, James Sheridan.
  See Proby, John Joshua, Earl of Carysfort.
  See Russell, John, Lord (trans.).
CAIUS MARIUS, THE PLEBEIAN CONSUL
  See Doubleday, Thomas.
CAIUS TORANIUS
  See Bell, Archibald.
CALCRAFT, JOHN WILLIAM (pseud. of Cole, John William)
  Bride of Lammermoor, The. Edinburgh: John Anderson, jr, 1823. Pp. [i]-[xii], [1]-62.

Bride of Lammermoor, The. London: Thomas Hailes Lacy, n.d. Pp. [i]-[iii], [4]-48. *Filed under* Cole, John William.
  Ivanhoe; or, The Jewess. Leith: A. Allardice (printer), n.d. Pp. [i-iv], [1]-79. Title page lacking. *Filed under* Cole, John William.
  Waverley. Edinburgh: John Anderson, jr, 1824. Pp. [i-iv], [1]-89. *Filed under* Cole, John William.
CALDERON
  Belshazzar's Feast.
    See MacCarthy, Denis Florence (trans.).
  Beware of Smooth Water.
    See Fitzgerald, Edward (trans.).
  Devotion of the Cross, The.
    See MacCarthy, Denis Florence (trans.).
  Divine Philothea, The.
    See MacCarthy, Denis Florence (trans.).
  Fairy Lady, The.
    See Fox, Henry Richard (trans.).
  Fortune Mends.
    See Holcroft, Fanny (trans.).
  From Bad to Worse.
    See Holcroft, Fanny (trans.).
  Gil Perez, the Gallician.
    See Fitzgerald, Edward (trans.).
  Justina.
    See MacCarthy, Denis Florence (trans.).
  Keep Your Own Secret.
    See Fitzgerald, Edward (trans.).
    See Fox, Henry Richard (trans.).
  Life Is a Dream.
    See MacCarthy, Denis Florence (trans.).
  Love the Greatest Enchantment.
    See MacCarthy, Denis Florence (trans.).
  Mayor of Zalamea, The.
    See Fitzgerald, Edward (trans.).
  Mighty Magician, The.
    See Fitzgerald, Edward (trans.).
  Painter of His Own Dishonour, The.
    See Fitzgerald, Edward (trans.).
  Purgatory of St. Patrick, The.
    See MacCarthy, Denis Florence (trans.).
  Sorceries of Sin, The.
    See MacCarthy, Denis Florence (trans.).
  Such Stuff As Dreams Are Made Of.
    See Fitzgerald, Edward (trans.).
  Three Judgments at a Blow.
    See Fitzgerald, Edward (trans.).
  Two Lovers of Heaven, The: Chrysanthus and Daria.
    See MacCarthy, Denis Florence (trans.).
  Wonder-Working Magician, The.
    See MacCarthy, Denis Florence (trans.).
CALEB QUOTEM AND HIS WIFE!
  See Lee, Henry.
CALEDONIAN FEUDS
  See Manners, George. Edgar.
CALIPH AND THE COBBLER
  See Faucit, John Savill. Justice.
CALIPH OF BAGDAD, THE
  See Brough, William.
CALIPH ROBBER
  See Dibdin, Thomas John. Bondocani, Il.
CALL AGAIN TO-MORROW
  See Trueba y Cosío, Joaquin Telesforo de, Don.
CALLED THERE AND BACK
  See Merivale, Herman Charles.
CALLIRRHOË
  See Field, Michael.
CALMOUR, ALFRED CECIL
  Amber Heart, The. In *Amber Heart and Other Plays*, London: n.pub. (priv.), n.d., pp. [i-viii], [1]-66.
  Beau Blandish the Rake. London: Veale, Chifferiel (printer) (priv.), 1887. Pp. [1]-[56].
  Cromwell. In *Amber Heart and Other Plays*, London: n.pub. (priv.), n.d., pp. [159]-164. *Filed under* Amber Heart and Other Plays.

Cupid's Messenger. In *Amber Heart and Other Plays,* London: n.pub. (priv.), n.d., pp. [129]-157. *Filed under* Amber Heart and Other Plays.

Cupid's Messenger. London: Samuel French; New York: T. Henry French, n.d. Pp. [1]-20.

Elvestine. In *Amber Heart and Other Plays,* London: n.pub. (priv.), n.d., pp. [67]-127. *Filed under* Amber Heart and Other Plays.

Gay Lothario, The. London: Samuel French; New York: T. Henry French, n.d. Pp. [1]-16. [Lacy's Acting Edition].

CALTHORPE CASE, THE
  See Goodrich, Arthur.

CALVERT, CAYLEY
  Have You Got That Ten Pound Note? London & New York: Samuel French, n.d. Pp. [1]-10. [Lacy's Acting Edition].

CALVERT, CHARLES ALEXANDER (arr.)
  Antony and Cleopatra. By Shakespeare, William. Edinburgh: Schenck & McFarlane (printer), n.d. Pp. [1]-64. Promptbook.

  Henry the Eighth. By Shakespeare, William. London: W. S. Johnson, 1878. Pp. [i]-viii, [9]-78.

  Henry the Fifth. By Shakespeare, William. New York: Cushing & Bardua (printer), 1875. Pp. [1]-68.

  Henry the Fourth, Part 2. By Shakespeare, William. Manchester: James F. Wilkinson, 1874. Pp. [1]-64.

  Sardanapalus. By Byron, George Gordon, Lord. Manchester: John Heywood, n.d. Pp. [i]-[viii], [1]-51.

  Twelfth Night. By Shakespeare, William. Manchester: Alex. Ireland (printer), n.d. Pp. [1]-67.

CALYPSO, QUEEN OF OGYGIA
  See Brookes, Sheridan.

CAMARALZAMAN AND BADOURA
  See Brough, William.

CAMARALZAMAN AND THE FAIR BADOURA
  See Byron, Henry James.

CAMBRIAN HERO, THE
  See Sotheby, William.

CAMBRIDGE DIONYSIA, THE
  See Trevelyan, George Otto.

CAMILLA'S HUSBAND
  See Phillips, Watts.

CAMILLE
  See Heron, Matilda.

CAMILLUS AND COLUMNA
  See Powell, Thomas (of Monmouth).

CAMP, THE
  See Sheridan, Richard Brinsley.

CAMP AT CHOBHAM, THE
  See Lemon, Mark.

CAMP AT THE OLYMPIC, THE
  See Planché, James Robinson.

CAMP OF WALLENSTEIN, THE
  See Martin, Theodore, Sir (trans.).

CAMPAIGN OF 1346, THE
  See Godmond, Christopher.

CAMPBELL, ANDREW LEONARD VOULLAIRE
  Bound 'Prentice to a Waterman; or, The Flower of Woolwich. London: John Cumberland, n.d. Pp. [1]-47. Cumberland's Minor Theatre, XII. *Filed under* Cumberland, John. Cumberland's Minor Theatre, XII.

  Bound 'Prentice to a Waterman; or, The Flower of Woolwich. London: John Cumberland, n.d. Pp. [1]-47. [Cumberland's Minor Theatre].

  Demon of the Desert!; or, The Well of Palms. London: John Duncombe, n.d. Pp. [1]-36. Duncombe's Edition. Promptbook.

  Forest Oracle, The; or, The Bridge of Tresino. By M. Campbell. Music by Nicholson. London: John Cumberland, n.d. Pp. [1]-48.

  Forest Oracle, The; or, The Bridge of Tresino. Music by Nicholson. London: John Cumberland, n.d. Pp. [1]-48. Cumberland's Minor Theatre, II. *Filed under* Cumberland, John. Cumberland's Minor Theatre, II.

  Gambler's Life in London, The; or, Views in the Country and Views in Town. London: John Duncombe, n.d. Pp.

[1]-64. Duncombe's Acting Edition of the British Theatre, 21.

  Lyieushee Lovel; or, The Gipsy of Ashburnham Dell! London & New York: Samuel French, n.d. Pp. [1]-51. [Lacy's Acting Edition]. *Filed under* Linishee Lovel.

  Rule Britannia. London: John Cumberland, n.d. Pp. [1]-43.

  Tom Bowling. London: John Cumberland, n.d. Pp. [1]-42. Cumberland's Minor Theatre, III. *Filed under* Cumberland, John. Cumberland's Minor Theatre, III.

  Tom Bowling. London: John Cumberland, n.d. Pp. [1]-42.

  Wreck, The.
    See Williams, William Henry.

CAMPBELL, J. M.
  Through My Heart First! N.p.: n.pub., n.d. Pp. [1]-49.

CAMPBELL, M.
  See Campbell, Andrew Leonard Voullaire.

CAMPBELL, THOMAS
  Mohawk Minstrels' Fifth Book of Dramas, Dialogues, & Drolleries, The.
    See Banks, Billy.

CAMPE, J. H.
  Cortez.
    See Helme, Elizabeth (trans.).
  Pizarro.
    See Helme, Elizabeth (trans.).

CANADIAN WAR, THE
  See Hart, James P.

CANARY, THE
  See Fleming, George.

CANDIDA
  See Shaw, George Bernard.

CANN, R. W.
  Taken for Granted. London & New York: Samuel French, n.d. Pp. [1]-11. [Lacy's Acting Edition].

CANNING, STRATFORD, VISCOUNT STRATFORD DE REDCLIFFE
  Alfred the Great in Athelnay. By Viscount Stratford de Redcliffe. London: Bernard Quaritch, 1876. Pp. [1-2], [i]-[x], [11]-178. *Filed under* Redcliffe, Viscount Stratford de.

CANNINGE, GEORGE
  Dorine. London: Thomas Scott (printer), n.d. Pp. [1]-24.

CANTAB
  See Robertson, Thomas William.
  See Robertson, Thomas William. Young Collegian, The.

CANTATRICI VILLANE
  See Village Singers, The.

CANTERBURY PILGRIMS, THE
  See A'Beckett, Gilbert Arthur.

CANUTE THE GREAT
  See Field, Michael.

CAPE MAIL, THE
  See Scott, Clement William.

CAPERS AND CORONETS
  See Lunn, Joseph.

CAPES, BERNARD
  Bustle's Bride. Music by Cole, J. Parry. London: J. B. Cramer, n.d. Pp. [1]-32. Libretto.

CAPITAL MATCH!, A
  See Morton, John Maddison.

CAPITOLA
  See Hazlewood, Colin Henry.

CAPPER, RICHARD
  Babylon. Melbourne: Clarson, Massina, 1868. Pp. [1]-36.
  Centheres. Melbourne: Clarson, Massina, 1868. Pp. [1]-52.
  Eadburga. Melbourne: Clarson, Massina, 1868. Pp. [1]-55.
  Eurynome, the Greek Maiden. Melbourne: Clarson, Massina, 1868. Pp. [1]-48.
  Judith. Melbourne: Clarson, Massina, 1867. Pp. [1]-46.
  Mummy Makers of Egypt, The. Melbourne: Clarson, Massina, 1868. Pp. [1]-48.
  Nimroud, the Mighty Hunter. Melbourne: Clarson, Massina, 1868. Pp. [1]-51.

CAPT. SMITH
  See Berrie, Ernie.

CAPTAIN BLAND
    See Lawrence, Slingsby.
CAPTAIN BRASSBOUND'S CONVERSION
    See Shaw, George Bernard.
CAPTAIN CHARLOTTE
    See Stirling, Edward.
CAPTAIN CUTTLE
    See Brougham, John.
CAPTAIN FIRNEWALD (anon. trans.)
    By Amalie (Amelia), Princess of Saxony. In *Six Dramas Illustrative of German Life,* London: John W. Parker, pp. [163]-222. *Filed under* Six Dramas (anon.).
CAPTAIN HAWK, THE LAST OF THE HIGHWAYMEN
    See Somerset, Charles A.
CAPTAIN OF THE WATCH, THE
    See Planché, James Robinson.
CAPTAIN STEVENS
    See Selby, Charles.
CAPTAIN SWIFT
    See Chambers, Charles Haddon.
CAPTAIN THÉRÈSE
    See Burnand, Francis Cowley.
CAPTAIN'S NOT A-MISS, THE
    See Wilks, Thomas Egerton.
CAPTIVE, THE
    See Mitford, Mary Russell.
CAPTIVE, THE COFFEE, AND THE COCOATINA
    See Millett, Sydney Crohan, Maj. All at C.
CARACALLA
    See T., H. T.
CARACTACUS
    See D'Egville, ? (arr.).
    See Monney, William.
CARAVAN, THE
    See Reynolds, Frederick.
CARD CASE, THE
    See Craven, Henry Thornton.
CARD FOR LADY ROEDALE, A
    See Sturgis, Julian Russell.
CARD PARTY
    See Planché, James Robinson. High, Low, Jack, and the Game.
CARDINAL BEATON
    See Tennant, William.
CARELESS HUSBAND, THE
    See Cibber, Colley.
CAREY, HENRY
    Chrononhotonthologos. London: John Cumberland & Son, n.d. Pp. [1]-24. Cumberland's British Theatre, XLI. *Filed under* Cumberland, John. Cumberland's British Theatre, XLI.
    Chrononhotonthologos. In *British Drama,* 12 vols., London: John Dicks, 1872, XI, [251]-256.
    Contrivances, The. In *British Drama,* 12 vols., London: John Dicks, 1872, XI, [58]-64.
    Dragon of Wantley, The. In *British Drama,* 12 vols., London: John Dicks, 1871, VII, [312]-316.
CARIB CHIEF, THE
    See Twiss, Horace.
CARLINE, THE FEMALE BRIGAND
    See Stirling, Edward.
CARLISLE, EARL OF
    See Howard, George William Frederick, Earl of Carlisle.
CARLISLE AND BACK FOR TWO BOB
    See Pleon, Harry. North East Lynne.
CARLO
    See Hasbrer, Alfred.
CARLO BROSCHI
    See Horncastle, James Henry. Ma Part.
CARLOS, FRANK
    See Griffith, Frank Carlos.
CARLTON, SIDNEY
    Monte Carlo. Written with Greenbank, Harry Hewetson. Music by Talbot, Howard. London: Hopwood & Crew, n.d. Pp. [1]-32. Libretto.

CARLYON SAHIB
    See Murray, Gilbert.
CARMELITE, THE
    See Cumberland, Richard.
CARMELITE FRIAR, THE
    See Landor, Edward Wilson.
CARMELITES!, THE
    See Fitzball, Edward.
CARMEN
    See Hamilton, Henry.
    See Hersee, Henry (trans.).
CARMEN UP TO DATE
    See Sims, George Robert.
CARMILHAN
    See Fitzball, Edward.
CARMOSINE (anon. trans.)
    By Musset, Alfred de. [New York: Rosenfield], n.d. Pp. [i-iii], [1]-21. Act I only. Typescript. *Filed under* Musset, Alfred de.
CARNAC SAHIB
    See Jones, Henry Arthur.
CARNARVON, EARL OF
    See Herbert, Henry John George.
CARNES, MASON
    Taboo, The. Music by Harraden, Ethel. N.p.: n.pub. (priv.), 1896. Pp. [1]-104. Libretto.
CARNIVAL AT NAPLES, THE
    See Dimond, William.
CARNIVAL BALL
    See Bayly, Thomas Haynes. One Hour.
CAROLINE AND HENRIETTA; OR, INDUSTRY TRIUMPHANT (anon.).
    In *Home Plays for Ladies,* Part 9, London & New York: Samuel French, n.d., pp. [27]-41. *Filed under* Home Plays for Ladies, Part 9.
CARPENTER, EDWARD
    Elfland. In *Narcissus and Other Poems,* London: Henry S. King, 1873, pp. [i], [55]-83.
    Moses. London: E. Moxon & Son, n.d. Pp. [1]-126.
CARPENTER, JOSEPH EDWARDS
    Love and Honour; or, Soldiers at Home—Heroes Abroad. London: G. H. Davidson, n.d. Pp. [1]-[6], [5]-50.
    Sanctuary, The; or, England in 1415. London: G. H. Davidson, n.d. <wrps. Music Publishing Co.>. Pp. [i-ii], [1]-30. Cumberland's Acting Plays.
CARPIO
    See Finnamore, John.
CARR, JOHN
    Sea Side Hero, The. London: J. Johnson, 1804. Pp. [i]-[x], [11]-95.
CARR, JOSEPH WILLIAM COMYNS
    Beauty Stone, The.
        See Pinero, Arthur Wing.
    King Arthur. London: Chiswick Press (printer) (priv.), 1893. Pp. [i-iii], [1]-69.
    King Arthur. London: Macmillan, 1895. Pp. [i-viii], [1]-67.
    Nerves. Pp. [i-iv], [1]-[3], [1]-48, [i-ii], [1]-42, [i-ii], [1]-31. Pagination by act. Typescript promptbook.
CARROLL, SUSANNA
    See Centlivre, Susanna Carroll Freeman, Mrs. Joseph.
CARROTS
    See Sutro, Alfred (trans.).
CARSE, ROLAND
    Yashmak, The.
        See Raleigh, Cecil.
CARSON, MURRAY
    Change Alley.
        See Parker, Louis Napoleon.
    Rosemary, That's for Remembrance.
        See Parker, Louis Napoleon.
    Termagant, The.
        See Parker, Louis Napoleon.
CARTE DE VISITE
    See Williams, Montagu Stephen.

CARTER, BARRINGTON

Maid o' the Mill, The. Music by Forsyth, Robert. Folkestone: D. Sumner (printer), 1896. Pp. [1]-28. Libretto.

CARTON, R. C. (pseud. of Critchett, Richard Claude)

Dinner for Two. New York & London: Samuel French, c.1903. Pp. [1]-13. [Lacy's Acting Edition]. *Filed under* Critchett, Richard Claude.

Great Pink Pearl, The. Written with Raleigh, Cecil. [London: L. Monchablon, typewriter-copyist, 1887.] Pp. [i-vi], 1-20, [i-iii], [1]-[20], [i-iii], [1]-23. Pagination by act. Typescript promptbook. *Filed under* Critchett, Richard Claude.

Home Secretary, The. Pp. [i-iii], [1]-40, [i], [1]-37, [i], [1]-36, [i], [1]-31. Pagination by act. Typescript. *Filed under* Critchett, Richard Claude.

Lady Huntworth's Experiment. New York & London: Samuel French, c.1904. Pp. [i-x], 3-75. *Filed under* Critchett, Richard Claude.

Liberty Hall. London & New York: Samuel French, c.1900. Pp. [1]-76. *Filed under* Critchett, Richard Claude.

Ninth Waltz, The. London & New York: Samuel French, c.1904. Pp. [1]-12. [Lacy's Acting Edition]. *Filed under* Critchett, Richard Claude.

Robin Goodfellow. Pp. [i-ii], [1]-47, [i], [1]-46, [i], [1]-36. Pagination by act. Typescript promptbook. *Filed under* Critchett, Richard Claude.

Squire of Dames, The. Pp. [i], [1]-40, [i], [1]-22, [i], [1]-26, [i], [1]-23. Pagination by act. Typescript promptbook. *Filed under* Critchett, Richard Claude.

Sunlight and Shadow. London & New York: Samuel French, c.1900. Pp. [1]-[57]. *Filed under* Critchett, Richard Claude.

Tree of Knowledge, The. Pp. [i-iv], [1]-2, [i], [1]-33, [1]-24, [1]-27, [1]-25, [1]-[22]. Pagination by act. Typescript promptbook. *Filed under* Critchett, Richard Claude.

Wheels within Wheels. Pp. [i-ii], [1]-2, [i-vi], [1]-50, [i-iv], [1]-59, [i-iv], [1]-36. Pagination by act. Typescript promptbook. *Filed under* Critchett, Richard Claude.

White Elephant, A. London: Mrs. Robinson Type Writing Office, n.d. Pp. [i], [1]-38, [i], 1-34, [i], 1-[29]. Pagination by act. Typescript. *Filed under* Critchett, Richard Claude.

CARTOUCHE, THE FRENCH ROBBER
See Waldron, W. Richard.

CARYSFORT, EARL OF
See Proby, John Joshua, Earl of Carysfort.

CASE FOR EVICTION, A
See Smith, Spencer Theyre.

CASE IS ALTERED
See Dibdin, Thomas John. Gaffer's Mistake.
See Maclaren, Archibald. Good News! Good News!

CASE OF REBELLIOUS SUSAN, THE
See Jones, Henry Arthur.

CASSILIS, INA LEON

Cheerful and Musical. London & New York: Samuel French, n.d. Pp. [1]-11. [Lacy's Acting Edition].

Those Landladies! London: Samuel French; New York: T. Henry French, n.d. Pp. [1]-11. [Lacy's Acting Edition].

Two Misses Ibbetson, The. London & New York: Samuel French, c.1900. Pp. [1]-8. [Lacy's Acting Edition].

CAST KING OF GRANADA, THE
See Colomb, George Hatton, Col.

CASTE
See Robertson, Thomas William.

CASTILIAN BANDIT
See Barnett, Charles Zachary. Phantom Bride, The.

CASTILIAN HONOUR
See Kenney, James. Pledge, The.

CASTLE ADAMANT
See Gilbert, William Schwenck. Princess Ida.

CASTLE BOTHEREM
See Law, Arthur.

CASTLE BURNERS!
See Almar, George. Mountain King, The.

CASTLE IN SPAIN, A
See Montague, Leopold.

CASTLE OF ANDALUSIA, THE
See O'Keeffe, John.

CASTLE OF COMO, THE
See Searle, Charles.

CASTLE OF DUNSTAFFNAGE
See Maclaren, Archibald. Maid of Lorn, The.

CASTLE OF MORSINO, THE
See Loveday, W.

CASTLE OF OLIVAL
See Kerr, John. Wandering Boys, The.

CASTLE OF OTRANTO, THE
See A'Beckett, Gilbert Abbott.

CASTLE OF PALUZZI, THE
See Raymond, Richard John.

CASTLE OF SORRENTO, THE
See Heartwell, Henry.

CASTLE OF ST. ALDOBRAND
See Maturin, Charles Robert, Rev. Bertram.

CASTLE SPECTRE, THE
See Lewis, Matthew Gregory.

CASWALL, EDWARD

Masque of Angels before Our Lady in the Temple, A. In *Masque of Mary and Other Poems*, London: Burns & Lambert, 1858, pp. [i-iv], [1]-55.

CASWALLON
See Walker, Charles Edward.

CASWALLON, KING OF BRITAIN
See Gandy, Edward.

CAT AND DOG
See Bell, Florence Eveleen Eleanore Oliffe, Mrs. Hugh (Lady).

CAT AND THE CHERUB, THE
See Fernald, Chester Bailey.

CAT'S IN THE LARDER, THE
See Horncastle, James Henry.

CATALINE
See Johnston, Andrew (trans.).

CATARACT OF AMAZONIA
See Dibdin, Charles Isaac Mungo, jr. White Witch, The.

CATARACT OF THE GANGES, THE
See Moncrieff, William Thomas.

CATCH A WEAZEL
See Morton, John Maddison.

CATCH HIM WHO CAN!
See Hook, Theodore Edward.

CATCHER CAUGHT
See Simpson, Ella Graham. Demon Spider, The.

CATCHING A GOVERNOR
See Coyne, Joseph Stirling. Pas de Fascination.

CATCHING A MERMAID
See Coyne, Joseph Stirling.

CATCHING AN HEIRESS
See Selby, Charles.

CATERAN'S SON, THE
See Barnett, Charles Zachary.

CATHARINE DE MEDICIS
See Woodley, William.

CATHARINE DOUGLAS
See Helps, Arthur.

CATHEDRAL BELL, THE
See Jones, Jacob.

CATHERINE DE MEDICIS
See Woodley, William.

CATHERINE HOWARD
See Suter, William E.

CATHERINE OF CLEVES
See Gower, Francis Leveson, Lord (trans.).

CATILINE
See Croly, George, Rev.
See Reade, John Edmund.

CATO
See Addison, Joseph.
See Kemble, John Philip (arr.).

CATSPAW, THE
See Jerrold, Douglas William.

CAUGHT BY THE CUFF
    See Hay, Frederic.
CAUGHT BY THE EARS
    See Selby, Charles.
CAUGHT IN A LINE
    See Bolton, Charles.
CAUGHT IN A TRAP
    See Webster, Benjamin Nottingham.
CAUGHT IN HIS OWN TRAP
    See Phillips, Mrs. Alfred.
CAUGHT NOT WON
    See Long, Charles. Chalet, The.
CAUTION TO YOUNG LADIES
    See Maclaren, Archibald. Elopement, The.
CAVALIER!, THE
    See Whitehead, D. Charles.
CAVALLERIA RUSTICANA
    See Lyster, Frederic (trans.). Chivalry in Humble Life.
CAVE OF ILLUSION, THE
    See Sutro, Alfred.
CAVENDISH, CLARA, LADY (pseud.)
    Woman of the World, The. London: Thomas Hailes Lacy, n.d. Pp. [1]-52. [Lacy's Acting Edition].
CAVES OF CARRIG-CLEENA
    See Hood, Basil Charles Willett. Emerald Isle, The.
CECIL, ARTHUR (pseud.)
    Time Is Money.
        See Bell, Florence Eveleen Eleanore Oliffe, Mrs. Hugh (Lady).
CEDAR CHEST, THE
    See Almar, George.
CELEBRATED CASE
    See Burnand, Francis Cowley. Proof.
CELENIO
    Baron, The.
        See Holcroft, Fanny (trans.).
CELLAR SPECTRE!
    See Lawler, Dennis. Earls of Hammersmith, The.
CENCI, THE
    See Shelley, Percy Bysshe.
CENERENTOLA
    See Maggioni, Manfredo (trans.).
CENSUS, THE
    See Brough, William.
CENT. PER CENT
    See Pocock, Isaac.
CENTHERES
    See Capper, Richard.
CENTLIVRE, SUSANNA CARROLL FREEMAN, MRS. JOSEPH
    Bold Stroke for a Wife, A. London: Whittingham & Arliss, 1815. Pp. [1]-[64]. London Theatre, II. *Filed under* Dibdin, Thomas John, ed. London Theatre, II.
    Bold Stroke for a Wife, A. In *New English Drama*, ed. W. Oxberry, 22 vols., London: W. Simpkin & R. Marshall; C. Chapple, 1819, VII, [1-2], [i]-[vi], [9]-65. Text complete. *Filed under* Oxberry, William Henry. New English Drama, VII.
    Bold Stroke for a Wife, A. London: John Cumberland, 1826. Pp. [1], [i]-xii, [13]-[61]. Cumberland's British Theatre, XIII. *Filed under* Cumberland, John. Cumberland's British Theatre, XIII.
    Bold Stroke for a Wife, A. In *British Drama,* 12 vols., London: John Dicks, 1871, VI, [33]-52.
    Busy Body, The. London: Whittingham & Arliss, 1815. Pp. [1]-[76]. London Theatre, VI. *Filed under* Dibdin, Thomas John, ed. London Theatre, VI.
    Busy Body, The. In *New English Drama*, ed. W. Oxberry, 22 vols., London: W. Simpkin & R. Marshall; C. Chapple, 1819, VI, [1-2], [i]-[vi], [1]-[72]. *Filed under* Oxberry, William Henry. New English Drama, VI.
    Busy Body, The. London: T. Dolby, 1825. Pp. [i]-[vi], [7]-[72]. Dolby's British Theatre, VIII. *Filed under* Cumberland, John. Cumberland's British Theatre, VIII.

Busy-Body, The. In *British Drama,* 12 vols., London: John Dicks, 1871, VI, [97]-120.
    Wonder, The; or, A Woman Keeps a Secret. London: Whittingham & Arliss, 1815. Pp. [1]-[76]. London Theatre, XIII. *Filed under* Dibdin, Thomas John, ed. London Theatre, XIII.
    Wonder, The. In *New English Drama*, ed. W. Oxberry, 22 vols., London: W. Simpkin & R. Marshall; C. Chapple, 1820, IV, [i]-[viii], [1]-[74]. *Filed under* Oxberry, William Henry. New English Drama, IV.
    Wonder, The: A Woman Keeps a Secret. London: John Cumberland, 1829. Pp. [1]-[70]. Cumberland's British Theatre, IV. *Filed under* Cumberland, John. Cumberland's British Theatre, IV.
    Wonder, The: A Woman Keeps a Secret. In *British Drama,* 12 vols., London: John Dicks, 1864, II, [543]-562.
CERNY, FREDERICK
    Logroño. London: Marcus Ward, 1877. Pp. [1]-119.
CHAIN OF EVENTS, A
    See Lawrence, Slingsby.
CHAIN OF GOLD, THE
    See Peake, Richard Brinsley.
CHAIN OF GUILT, THE
    See Taylor, Thomas Proclus.
CHAIN OF ROSES
    See Hale, William Palmer. Thetis and Peleus.
CHAINED TO SIN
    See Towers, Edward.
CHAINS FOR THE HEART
    See Hoare, Prince. Chains of the Heart.
CHAINS OF THE HEART
    See Hoare, Prince.
CHALET, THE
    See Long, Charles.
CHALET IN THE VALLEY
    See Burnand, Francis Cowley. Madame Berliot's Ball.
CHALK AND CHEESE
    See Norwood, Eille.
CHALLIS, HENRY W.
    My Wife's Husband. London: John Cumberland, n.d. Pp. [1]-33. Cumberland's Minor Theatre, X. *Filed under* Cumberland, John. Cumberland's Minor Theatre, X.
    My Wife's Husband. London: John Cumberland, n.d. Pp. [1]-33. [Cumberland's Minor Theatre].
    Race for a Wife!, A; or, Win Her and Wear Her. London: John Lowndes, n.d. Pp. [1]-34.
CHAMBER OF DEATH
    See Almar, George. Tower of Nesle, The.
CHAMBER PRACTICE
    See Selby, Charles.
CHAMBERS, CHARLES HADDON
    Captain Swift. New York & London: Samuel French, c.1902. Pp. [1]-69. [French's International Copyrighted Edition of the Works of the Best Authors], 55.
    Fatal Card, The. Pp. [i-ii], [1]-42, D1-D7, E1-E23. Typescript.
    Idler, The. New York & London: Samuel French, c.1902. Pp. [1]-64. [French's International Copyrighted Edition of the Works of the Best Authors, 52].
    Idler, The. [San Francisco: Ayers' Stenographic Institute], n.d. Pp. [i-iii], 1-37, [i], 1-34, [i], 1-31, [i], [1]-22. Pagination by act. Typescript promptbook.
    Open Gate, The. London & New York: Samuel French, n.d. Pp. [1]-18. French's Acting Edition (late Lacy's), 1902.
    Open Gate, The. Chicago: Dramatic Publishing Co., n.d. Pp. [1]-19.
    Tyranny of Tears, The. Boston: Walter H. Baker, 1902. Pp. [1-4], [i]-[vi], [1]-152.
    Upturned Faces of the Roses, The. In [*Souvenir of the Charing Cross Hospital Bazaar,* ed. H. Beerbohm Tree, London: Nassau Press, 1899], pp. [44]-48.
CHAMBERS, MARIANNE
    Ourselves. London: J. Barker, 1811. Pp. [1]-[94].
    School for Friends, The. London: Barker & Son, 1805. Pp. [1]-[95].

School for Friends, The. London: Barker & Son, n.d. Pp. [1]-[87]. 6th ed.

CHAMPAGNE
  See Weatherly, Frederick Edward.

CHANCE AND CHANGE!
  See Blanchard, Edward Litt Leman. Faith, Hope, and Charity!

CHANCE INTERVIEW, A
  See Bell, Florence Eveleen Eleanore Oliffe, Mrs. Hugh (Lady).

CHANCE OF WAR, THE
  See Maclaren, Archibald.

CHANCERY SUIT!, THE
  See Peake, Richard Brinsley.

CHANCES, THE
  See Garrick, David (arr.).

CHANDLER'S CHANCES
  See A'Beckett, Gilbert Abbott. Jack Brag.

CHANG-CHING-FOU! CREAM OF TARTAR
  See Martin, William.

CHANGE ALLEY
  See Parker, Louis Napoleon.

CHANGE OF NAME
  See Hancock, William. Mr. Scroggins.

CHANGE OF SYSTEM, A
  See Paul, Howard.

CHANGE PARTNERS
  See Morton, John Maddison.

CHAOS IS COME AGAIN
  See Morton, John Maddison.

CHAPMAN, JANE FRANCES (trans.)
  King René's Daughter. By Hertz, Henrik. London: Smith, Elder, 1845. Pp. [i]-[vi], [1]-87.

CHAPMAN, MATTHEW JAMES
  Jephtha's Daughter. London: James Fraser, 1834. Pp. [iii]-[xii], [i]-iv, [5]-118.

CHAPMAN, WESTMACOTT
  Deep Red Rover, The.
    See Hay, Frederic.

CHAPTER OF ACCIDENTS
  See Douglass, John T.
  See Lee, Sophia.

CHARACTER, A
  See Bennett, William Cox.

CHARCOAL BURNER, THE
  See Almar, George.

CHARITABLE BEQUEST, A
  See Newnham-Davis, Nathaniel.

CHARITY
  • *See* Gilbert, William Schwenck.

CHARITY BEGINS AT HOME
  See Beerbohm, Constance.
  See Stephenson, Benjamin Charles.

CHARLES I
  See Butler, Arthur Gray.

CHARLES O'MALLEY
  See Sayre, Theodore Burt.

CHARLES O'MALLEY, THE IRISH DRAGOON
  See Macarthy, Eugene.

CHARLES THE FIRST
  See Butler, Arthur Gray.
  See Mitford, Mary Russell.
  See Shelley, Percy Bysshe.
  See Wills, William Gorman.

CHARLES THE SECOND
  See Payne, John Howard.

CHARLES XII
  See Planché, James Robinson.

CHARLESON, ARTHUR J.
  Anthony's Legacy. London & New York: Samuel French, c.1901. Pp. [1]-20.

CHARLOTTE CORDAY
  See Bernard, William Bayle.
  See Mortimer, James.

CHARLTON, FRANK
  On the Dark Road; or, The Trail of the Serpent. 110 leaves. Manuscript.

CHARLTON, WILLIAM HENRY (trans.)
  Gladiator of Ravenna, The. By Halm, Frederick. London: Thomas Hailes Lacy, n.d. Pp. [i-iv], [1]-103.
  Ingomar, the Son of the Wilderness. By Halm, Frederick. *Also:* The Son of the Wilderness. London & New York: Samuel French, n.d. Pp. [1]-59. [Lacy's Acting Edition].
  Son of the Wilderness, The. By Halm, Friedrich. *Also:* Ingomar, the Son of the Wilderness. London: Luke James Hansard, 1847. Pp. [i]-[viii], [1]-136.

CHARM, THE
  See Besant, Walter.

CHARM AND THE CURSE, THE
  See Grant, Charles.

CHARMED HORN
  See Macfarren, George. Oberon.
  See Planché, James Robinson. Oberon.

CHARMING PAIR, A
  See Williams, Thomas John.

CHARMING POLLY, THE
  See Haines, John Thomas.

CHARMING WOMAN, THE
  See Wigan, Horace.

CHARMS
  See Young, Charles Lawrence, Sir.

CHARNOCK, JOHN
  Loyalty; or, Invasion Defeated. London: Sherwood, Neely, & Jones; Cadell & Davies; R. Faulder; Black, Perry, & Kingsbury; J. Asperne, 1810. Pp. [iv]-[xii], [1]-91.

CHASE, THE
  See Darley, George.

CHASTE SALUTE
  See Ebsworth, Mary Emma Fairbrother, Mrs. Joseph. Payable at Sight.

CHASTELARD
  See Swinburne, Algernon Charles.

CHATELARD
  See MacGilchrist, John.

CHATTERBOX, THE
  See Beerbohm, Constance.

CHATTERBOXES
  See Childe-Pemberton, Harriet Louisa.

CHATTERTON, HENRIETTA GEORGIANA MARCIA IREMONGER, MRS. LASCELLES, LADY GEORGIANA
  Oswald of Deira. London: Longmans, Green, 1867. Pp. [i-ii], [1]-155.

CHATTERTON
  See Jones, Henry Arthur.

CHEAP EXCURSION, A
  See Stirling, Edward.

CHEARFUL OPINIONS
  See Roberdeau, John Peter. Alarmist, The.

CHEATS OF SCAPIN, THE
  See Otway, Thomas.

CHECKMATE
  See Halliday, Andrew.

CHECQUE ON MY BANKER
  See Moncrieff, William Thomas. Wanted a Wife.

CHEEK WILL WIN
  See Suter, William E.

CHEER, BOYS, CHEER
  See Harris, Augustus Henry Glossop.

CHEERFUL AND MUSICAL
  See Cassilis, Ina Leon.

CHELSEA PENSIONER, THE
  See Soane, George.

CHELTNAM, CHARLES SMITH
  Christmas Eve in a Watchhouse. London: Thomas Hailes Lacy, n.d. Pp. [1]-16. Lacy's Acting Edition, 1341.
  Deborah; or, The Jewish Maiden's Wrong. London: Thomas Hailes Lacy, n.d. Pp. [1]-38.

Dinner for Nothing. London: Thomas Hailes Lacy, n.d. Pp. [1]-18.

Edendale. London: Thomas Hailes Lacy, n.d. Pp. [1]-42. [Lacy's Acting Edition].

Fairy's Father, A. London: Thomas Hailes Lacy, n.d. Pp. [i]-iv, [5]-14. [Lacy's Acting Edition].

Fireside Diplomacy. New York: Dick & Fitzgerald, n.d. Pp. [1]-14. Dick's American Edition.

Garden Party, A. London & New York: Samuel French, n.d. Pp. [1]-12. French's Acting Edition (late Lacy's), 1866.

Leatherlungos the Great, How He Stormed, Reign'd, and Mizzled. London & New York: Samuel French, n.d. Pp. [1]-32. [Lacy's Acting Edition].

Lesson in Love, A. London: Thomas Hailes Lacy, n.d. Pp. [1]-44. [Lacy's Acting Edition].

Little Madcap, A. London & New York: Samuel French, n.d. Pp. [1]-22. [Lacy's Acting Edition].

Lucky Escape!, A. London: Thomas Hailes Lacy, n.d. Pp. [1]-20. [Lacy's Acting Edition].

Marriage Made Easy. London: Clayton (printer), 1876. Pp. [1]-46.

Matchmaker, The. London: Thomas Hailes Lacy, n.d. Pp. [1]-38. [Lacy's Acting Edition].

May Brierly. *Also:* The Ticket-of-Leave Man's Wife. *Also:* Six Years After; or, The Ticket-of-Leave Man's Wife. N.p.: n.pub., n.d. Pp. [6]-32. Text incomplete. Title page lacking.

More Precious Than Gold! London & New York: Samuel French, n.d. Pp. [1]-24.

Mrs. Green's Snug Little Business. London: Thomas Hailes Lacy, n.d. Pp. [1]-18. [Lacy's Acting Edition].

Procris. London & Edinburgh: Ballantyne, Hanson (printer), n.d. Pp. [i-iv], [1]-69.

Railway Adventure, A. London & New York: Samuel French, n.d. Pp. [1]-12. [Lacy's Acting Edition].

Shadow of a Crime, The. London: Thomas Hailes Lacy, n.d. Pp. [1]-56. [Lacy's Acting Edition].

Six Years After.
   See May Brierly.

Slowtop's Engagements. London: Thomas Hailes Lacy, n.d. Pp. [1]-21. [Lacy's Acting Edition].

Summer Lightning. London: Samuel French, 1899. Pp. [1]-31.

Ticket-of-Leave Man's Wife, The; or, Six Years After. *Also:* May Brierly. London: Thomas Hailes Lacy, n.d. Pp. [1]-72. [Lacy's Acting Edition].

CHENEVIX, RICHARD

Etha and Aidallo. In *Dramatic Poems,* London: J. Bell, 1801, pp. [103]-[164]. *Filed under* Dramatic Poems.

Henry the Seventh. In *Two Plays,* London: J. Johnson, 1812, pp. [147]-319. *Filed under* Two Plays.

Leonora. In *Dramatic Poems,* London: J. Bell, 1801, pp. [i-ii], [1]-102. *Filed under* Dramatic Poems.

Mantuan Revels. In *Two Plays,* London: J. Johnson, 1812, pp. [i-vi], [1]-146. *Filed under* Two Plays.

CHERCHEZ L'HOMME
   See Stainer, A. N.

CHERISHED RESENTMENT
   See Burney, Frances. Fitzormond.

CHERRY, ANDREW

Peter the Great; or, The Wooden Walls. Music by Jouvé. London: Richard Phillips, 1807. Pp. [i-iv], [1]-74. 2nd ed.

Soldier's Daughter, The. London: Richard Phillips, 1804. Pp. [i-viii], [1]-[86]. 3rd ed.

Soldier's Daughter, The. In *New English Drama,* ed. W. Oxberry, 22 vols., London: W. Simpkin & R. Marshall; C. Chapple, 1819, V, [i-ii], [1]-[8], [1]-[72]. *Filed under* Oxberry, William Henry. New English Drama, V.

Soldier's Daughter, The. In *British Drama,* 12 vols., London: John Dicks, 1871, V, [321]-342.

Soldier's Daughter, The. London: John Cumberland, n.d. Pp. [1]-72. Cumberland's British Theatre, XXIII. *Filed under* Cumberland, John. Cumberland's British Theatre, XXIII.

Spanish Dollars!; or, The Priest of the Parish. Music by Davy, J. London: Barker & Son, 1806. Pp. [1]-32. Libretto.

Travellers, The; or, Music's Fascination. Music by Corri. London: Richard Phillips, 1806. Pp. [i-x], [1]-82. 7th ed. Libretto.

Travellers, The; or, Music's Fascination. In *New English Drama,* ed. W. Oxberry, 22 vols., London: W. Simpkin & R. Marshall; C. Chapple, 1823, XVII, [i]-[xii], [1]-59. *Filed under* Oxberry, William Henry. New English Drama, XVII.

Travellers, The; or, Music's Fascination. London: John Cumberland & Son, n.d. Pp. [1]-52. Cumberland's British Theatre, XLI. *Filed under* Cumberland, John. Cumberland's British Theatre, XLI.

CHERRY AND FAIR STAR (anon.)
   New York: R. Hobbs, 1831. Pp. [1]-36.

CHERRY AND FAIR STAR (anon.)
   New York: Samuel French, n.d. Pp. [1]-27. Minor Drama, 90. Promptbook.

CHERRY AND FAIR STAR
   See Blanchard, Edward Litt Leman.
   See Green, Frank William.

CHERRY BOUNCE!
   See Raymond, Richard John.

CHERRY TREE FARM
   See Law, Arthur.

CHERRYTREE INN
   See Boucicault, Dionysius Lardner. Elfie.

CHERTSEY CURFEW
   See Smith, Albert Richard. Blanche Heriot.

CHESTERFIELD THINSKIN
   See Maddox, John Medex.

CHEVALIER DE ST. GEORGE, THE
   See Robertson, Thomas William.

CHEVALIER OF THE MAISON ROUGE, THE
   See Hazlewood, Colin Henry.

CHEVY CHASE
   See Somerset, Charles A.

CHICOT THE JESTER
   See Pollock, Walter Herries.

CHIEF OF THE GHAUT MOUNTAINS
   See Barrymore, William. Hyder, El.

CHIEFTAIN, THE
   See Burnand, Francis Cowley.

CHIEFTAIN'S DAUGHTER
   See Dillon, John. Retribution.

CHILD OF A TAR
   See Fitzball, Edward. Sailor's Legacy, A.

CHILD OF NATURE, THE
   See Inchbald, Elizabeth Simpson, Mrs. Joseph.

CHILD OF THE DESERT
   See Dimond, William. Aethiop, The.

CHILD OF THE WRECK, THE
   See Planché, James Robinson.

CHILD STEALER, THE
   See Suter, William E.

CHILD, THE CHOUSE, AND THE CHEESE
   See Byron, Henry James. Taffy was a Welshman.

CHILDE VYET
   See Alma-Tadema, Laurence.

CHILDE-PEMBERTON, HARRIET LOUISA

Backward Child, A. London: Samuel French; New York: T. Henry French, n.d. Pp. [1]-10. [Lacy's Acting Edition].

Chatterboxes. Chicago & New York: Dramatic Publishing Co., n.d. Pp. [1]-13. Sergel's Acting Drama, 388.

Figure of Speech, A. New York: DeWitt, n.d. Pp. [1]-18. DeWitt's Acting Plays, 362[?].

Nicknames. Chicago: Dramatic Publishing Co., n.d. Pp. [1]-16. Sergel's Acting Drama, 394.

Shattered Nerves. London: Samuel French; New York: T. Henry French, n.d. Pp. [1]-10. [Lacy's Acting Edition].

CHILDHOOD OF CHRIST, THE
   See Chorley, Henry Fothergill.

CHILDHOOD'S DREAMS
   See Young, Charles Lawrence, Sir.

CHILDREN IN THE WOOD, THE
    See Blanchard, Edward Litt Leman.
    See Morton, Thomas, sr.
CHILDREN OF THE CASTLE, THE
    See Fitzball, Edward.
CHILDREN OF THE MIST
    See Montrose (anon.).
    See Pocock, Isaac. Montrose.
CHILDREN OF THE ZINCALI
    See Wilson, John Crawford. Gitanilla, The.
CHIMES, THE
    See Lemon, Mark.
CHIMES OF NORMANDY
    See Farnie, Henry Brougham. Bells of Corneville, The.
CHIMNEY CORNER, THE
    See Craven, Henry Thornton.
CHIMNEY PIECE, THE
    See Rodwell, George Herbert Bonaparte.
CHINESE HONEYMOON, A
    See Dance, George.
CHINESE MOTHER, THE
    See Tanner, ?.
CHINESE SPHINX, THE
    See Novello, Mary Sabilla Hehl, Mrs. Vincent. Turandot.
CHING-CHOW-HI
    See Brough, William.
CHIP OF THE OLD BLOCK, A
    See Knight, Edward P.
CHIP OFF THE OLD BLOCK
    See Jones, Henry Arthur. Hearts of Oak.
CHISELLING
    See Albery, James. Alexander the Great.
    See Albery, James.
CHIVALRY IN HUMBLE LIFE
    See Lyster, Frederic (trans.).
CHOICE, THE
    See Hetherington, William Maxwell.
CHOICE SPIRITS
    See Booth, George.
CHOLERIC COUNT
    See Thompson, Benjamin (trans.). Otto of Wittelsbach.
CHOOSING A BALL DRESS
    See Clarke, Clara Savile.
CHOOSING A BRIDE (anon.)
    In *Home Plays for Ladies*, Part 5, London & New York: Samuel French, n.d., pp. [13]-[51]. *Filed under* Home Plays for Ladies, Part 5.
CHOOSING CHRISTMAS TOYS
    See Anstey, F.
CHOPS OF THE CHANNEL, THE
    See Hay, Frederic.
CHOPSTICK AND SPIKINS
    See Meritt, Paul.
CHORLEY, HENRY FOTHERGILL
    Amber Witch, The. Music by Wallace, William Vincent. New York: William Hall & Son, c.1861. Pp. [1]-361. Vocal score.
    Amber Witch, The. Music by Wallace, William Vincent. London: Cramer, Beale & Chappell, n.d. Pp. [i]-[xiv], [1]-48. Libretto.
    Black Domino, The. Music by Auber. London: Royal English Opera, Covent Garden, n.d. Pp. [1]-60. 1st ed. Libretto.
    Childhood of Christ, The. Music by Berlioz. London: Forsyth Brothers, n.d. Pp. [i]-v, [6]-15. Libretto.
    Dinorah. *Also:* Le Pardon de Ploërmel. Music by Meyerbeer. London: Boosey, n.d. Pp. [i]-iv, 1-280. Royal Edition. Vocal score.
    Dinorah: The Pilgrimage to Ploërmel. Music by Meyerbeer. London: Royal English Opera, Covent Garden, n.d. Pp. [i]-vi, [7]-50. Libretto.
    Duchess Eleanour. London: Thomas Hailes Lacy, n.d. Pp. [1]-74.
    Kenilworth. Music by Sullivan, Arthur. London: Chappell, n.d. Pp. [i-ii], [1]-2, 1-72. New ed., rev. Vocal score.

    May Queen, The. Music by Bennett, W. Sterndale. London & New York: Novello, Ewer, n.d. Pp. [i]-[x], [1]-90. Novello's Original Octavo Edition. Libretto and vocal score.
    Old Love and New Fortune. London: Chapman & Hall, 1850. Pp. [i-viii], [1]-92.
    Son and Stranger. Music by Mendelssohn. Boston: Oliver Ditson, n.d. Pp. [1]-30. Boston Parlor Opera. Libretto.
CHORLEY, HENRY FOTHERGILL (trans.)
    Étoile du Nord, L'. Written with Troutbeck, John (trans.). Music by Meyerbeer. London: Novello, Ewer, n.d. Pp. [i]-iv, [1]-418. Novello's Original Octavo Edition. Vocal score.
    Faust. Music by Gounod. London: Chappell, n.d. Pp. [i-iv], [1]-32. Libretto.
    Faust. Music by Gounod. London: Chappell, n.d. Pp. [1]-[8], [1]-263. Vocal score.
    Mirella. Music by Gounod. London & New York: Boosey, n.d. Pp. [i-iv], 1-176. Royal Edition. Vocal score.
    Orpheus. Music by Gluck. London: Chappell, n.d. Pp. [i-ii], 1-[127]. Vocal score.
CHRISTENING, THE
    See Buckstone, John Baldwin.
CHRISTIAN, THE
    See Caine, Hall.
CHRISTIAN CAPTIVES, THE
    See Bridges, Robert Seymour.
CHRISTMAS BOXES
    See Mayhew, Augustus Septimus.
CHRISTMAS CAROL, A
    See Barnett, Charles Zachary.
CHRISTMAS EVE
    See Fitzball, Edward.
CHRISTMAS EVE IN A WATCHHOUSE
    See Cheltnam, Charles Smith.
CHRISTMAS PANTOMIME, A
    See Bilkins, Taylor.
CHRONONHOTONTHOLOGOS
    See Carey, Henry.
CHRYSANTHUS AND DARIA
    See MacCarthy, Denis Florence (trans.). Two Lovers of Heaven.
CHRYSTABELLE
    See Falconer, Edmund.
CHURCH, FLORENCE MARRYAT, MRS. LEAN
    See Marryat, Florence.
CHURCH IN DANGER!, THE (anon.)
    London: G. Wightman, 1837. Pp. [1]-16.
CHURCHILL, FRANK
    Taking by Storm! London: Thomas Hailes Lacy, n.d. Pp. [1]-20. [Lacy's Acting Edition].
CHURCHILL, HENRY GEORGE
    Babes in the Wood Continued, The. London: M. L. Bennett, 1888. Pp. [1]-36.
CIBBER, COLLEY
    Careless Husband, The. In *British Drama*, 12 vols., London: John Dicks, 1872, XI, [225]-250.
    Double Gallant, The; or, The Sick Lady's Cure. London: Sherwood, Neely, & Jones, 1817. Pp. [1]-[79]. London Theatre, XXIII. *Filed under* Dibdin, Thomas John, ed. London Theatre, XXIII.
    Love Makes a Man; or, The Fop's Fortune. In *British Drama*, 12 vols., London: John Dicks, 1872, XII, [268]-287.
    Provoked Husband, The.
    See Vanbrugh, John.
    Refusal, The; or, The Ladies' Philosophy. London: Sherwood, Neely, & Jones, 1817. Pp. [1]-80. London Theatre, XXII. *Filed under* Dibdin, Thomas John, ed. London Theatre, XXII.
    She Would and She Would Not; or, The Kind Impostor. London: Whittingham & Arliss, 1815. Pp. [1]-84. London Theatre, XVI. *Filed under* Dibdin, Thomas John, ed. London Theatre, XVI.

She Would and She Would Not; or, The Kind Impostor. In *British Drama*, 12 vols., London: John Dicks, 1872, XI, [33]-57.

CIBBER, COLLEY (arr.)
Richard the Third. By Shakespeare, William. In *New English Drama*, ed. W. Oxberry, 22 vols., London: W. Simpkin & R. Marshall; C. Chapple, 1818, III, [i]-[vi], [1]-68. *Filed under* Oxberry, William Henry. New English Drama, III.

CID, THE
See Lyster, Frederic (trans.).
See Neil, Ross.

CIGALE, LA
See Burnand, Francis Cowley.

CINDERELLA
See Bell, Florence Eveleen Eleanore Oliffe, Mrs. Hugh (Lady).
See Blanchard, Edward Litt Leman.
See Byron, Henry James.
See Green, Frank William.
See Jones, John Wilton.
See Keating, Eliza H.
See Lacy, Michael Rophino.
See Leigh, Henry Sambrooke.
See Locke, Fred.
See Smith, Albert Richard.

CINDERELLA; OR, THE LITTLE GLASS SLIPPER (anon.)
Music by Kelly. London: John Fairburn, n.d. Pp. [1]-36.

CINDERELLA AND THE FAIRY GLASS SLIPPER
See Rice, Charles.

CINDERELLA AND THE LITTLE GLASS SLIPPER
See Palmer, T. H.

CINDER-ELLEN UP TOO LATE
See Leslie, Fred.

CINDERS
See Tinsley, Lily.

CIRCASSIAN BRIDE, THE
See Ward, Charles.

CIRCLE OF LODA, THE
See Peacock, Thomas Love.

CIRCUMSTANCES ALTER CASES
See Ascher, Isidore Gordon.

CIRCUMSTANTIAL EFFIE-DEANS
See Brough, William. Great Sensation Trial, The.

CIRCUMSTANTIAL EVIDENCE!
See Barnett, Morris.

CIRCUS GIRL, THE
See Tanner, James Tolman.

CISSY'S ENGAGEMENT
See Lancaster-Wallis, Ellen.

CITIZEN, THE
See Murphy, Arthur.

CITIZEN WHO APES THE NOBLEMAN, THE
See Van Laun, Henri (trans.).

CITY AT FOUR O'CLOCK, THE
See Ridge, William Pett.

CITY FRIENDS
See Collins, Charles James.

CITY OF PLEASURE, THE
See Sims, George Robert.

CITY OF THE PLAGUE, THE
See Wilson, John.

CITY WIVES
See Smith, John Frederick. Lesson for Gentlemen, A.

CIVIL WAR IN SWITZERLAND
See Brough, Robert Barnabas. William Tell.

CIVILIZATION
See Wilkins, John H.

CLAIRVILLE (pseud.)
Jeanne, Jeanette, and Jeanneton.
See Reece, Robert.
Poule aux Oeufs d'Or, La.
See under title.

CLANDESTINE MARRIAGE, THE
See Colman, George, sr.

CLARENCE CLEVEDON, HIS STRUGGLE FOR LIFE OR DEATH!
See Stirling, Edward.

CLARI
See Payne, John Howard.

CLARIBEL; OR, LOVE AND FRIENDSHIP (anon.)
N.p.: n.pub., n.d. Pp. [1]-50.

CLARIDGE, C. J.
Fast Coach, The. Written with Soutar, Robert. London: Thomas Hailes Lacy, n.d. Pp. [1]-17. [Lacy's Acting Edition].

CLARISSA HARLOWE
See Lacy, Thomas Hailes.

CLARISSE
See Robertson, Thomas William. Noémie.
See Stirling, Edward.

CLARK, H. F.
Ruy Blas and the Blasé Roué.
See Torr, A. C.

CLARKE, CAMPBELL
Awaking. London & New York: Samuel French, n.d. Pp. [1]-16. [Lacy's Acting Edition].

CLARKE, CAMPBELL (trans.)
Giroflé-Girofla. Music by Lecocq, Charles. London: Enoch & Sons, n.d. Pp. [i-iv], 1-305. Vocal score.
Rose Michel. By Blum, Ernest. London: Woodfall & Kinder (printer) (priv.), n.d. Pp. [1]-17, [47]-67. Act II missing.

CLARKE, CHARLES ALLEN
Great Catch, A. Manchester & London: John Heywood, n.d. Pp. [1]-16. John Heywood's Series of Plays, Recitations, etc. for School and Popular Entertainments, 14.
Woman's Chance. Manchester & London: John Heywood, n.d. Pp. [1]-16. John Heywood's Series of Plays, Recitations, etc. for School and Popular Entertainments, 15.

CLARKE, CHARLES AUGUSTUS
Crystal-Hunter of Mont Blanc, The; or, The Hut of the Haunted Gorge and the Tourists' Dogs! Pp. [i-ii], [1]-24, [i], [1]-30. Pagination by act. Manuscript promptbook.

CLARKE, CLARA SAVILE
Choosing a Ball Dress. In *Dialogues of the Day*, ed. Oswald Crawfurd, London: Chapman & Hall, n.d., pp. [82]-90. *Filed under* Crawfurd, Oswald. Dialogues of the Day.
Human Sacrifice, A. In *Dialogues of the Day*, ed. Oswald Crawfurd, London: Chapman & Hall, n.d., pp. [254]-262. *Filed under* Crawfurd, Oswald. Dialogues of the Day.
Point of Honour, A. In *Dialogues of the Day*, ed. Oswald Crawfurd, London: Chapman & Hall, n.d., pp. [174]-181. *Filed under* Crawfurd, Oswald. Dialogues of the Day.

CLARKE, ELIZABETH, MRS. WILLIAM
See Cobbold, Elizabeth Knipe, Mrs. John.

CLARKE, HENRY SAVILLE
Alice in Wonderland. Music by Slaughter, Walter. London: Ascherberg, Hopwood, & Crew, c.1906. Pp. [i-iv], 1-99. Vocal score.
Hugger-Mugger. London & New York: Samuel French, n.d. Pp. [1]-16. [Lacy's Acting Edition].
Love Wins. Written with Du Terreau, Louis Henry F. London & New York: Samuel French, n.d. Pp. [1]-40. [Lacy's Acting Edition].
Lyrical Lover, A. London & New York: Samuel French, n.d. Pp. [1]-15. [Lacy's Acting Edition].
Rose and the Ring, The. Music by Slaughter, Walter. London: Court Circular Office, 1890. Pp. [1]-55. Libretto.

CLARKE, JOHN BERTRIDGE
Ravenna; or, Italian Love. London: G. B. Whittaker, 1824. Pp. [i-viii], 1-80.

CLARKE, STEPHEN
Kiss, The. London: Longman, Hurst, Rees, Orme, & Brown, 1811. Pp. [i]-[x], [1]-[62].
Poison Tree, The. In *Dramatic Romances*, London: John Murray, 1809, pp. [i]-[x], [11]-82. *Filed under* Dramatic Romances.

Torrid Zone, The. In *Dramatic Romances,* London: John Murray, 1809, pp. [83]-127. *Filed under* Dramatic Romances.

CLAUDE DU VAL
See Burnand, Francis Cowley.

CLAUDE DUVAL
See Stephens, Henry Pottinger.

CLAUDE DUVAL, THE LADIES' HIGHWAYMAN
See Taylor, Thomas Proclus.

CLAUDE LORRAINE
See Barnett, Charles Zachary.

CLAUDIA'S CHOICE
See Neil, Ross.

CLAVIGO
See Stowell, Thomas Alfred (trans.).

CLAY, CECIL
Pantomime Rehearsal, A. London & New York: Samuel French, n.d. Pp. [1]-56. French's Acting Edition, 2186.

CLAY, THOMAS LINDSAY
Lurline the Nymph of the Rhine.
See Green, Frank William.

CLEANTHES
See Woodrooffe, Sophia.

CLEAR CASE, A
See A'Beckett, Gilbert Abbott.

CLEFT STICK, A
See Oxenford, John.

CLEMENTS, ARTHUR
Cracked Heads. Written with Hay, Frederic. London & New York: Samuel French, n.d. Pp. [1]-12. [Lacy's Acting Edition].
Telephone, The. London & New York: Samuel French, n.d. Pp. [1]-11. [Lacy's Acting Edition].
Two Blinds, The. Music by Offenbach. London & New York: Samuel French, n.d. Pp. [1]-12. [Lacy's Acting Edition]. Libretto.
Two Photographs. London & New York: Samuel French, n.d. Pp. [1]-18. [Lacy's Acting Edition].
Two to One; or, The Irish Footman. London & New York: Samuel French, n.d. Pp. [1]-12. Lacy's Acting Edition.

CLEMENZA
See Ainslie, Whitelaw, Dr.

CLEON
See Thom, Robert W.

CLERICAL ERROR, A
See Jones, Henry Arthur.

CLERK OF CLERKENWELL, THE
See Almar, George.

CLIFFORD, LUCY LANE, MRS. WILLIAM KINGDON
Honeymoon Tragedy, A. London & New York: Samuel French, c.1904. Pp. [1]-14. [Lacy's Acting Edition].
Likeness of the Night, The. London: Adam & Charles Black, 1900. Pp. [i]-[x], [1]-146.

CLIFTON, LEWIS
Marjorie. Written with Dilley, Joseph J. Music by Slaughter, Walter. London: Hopwood & Crew, n.d. Pp. [i-iv], 1-160. Vocal score.
Summoned to Court.
See Dilley, Joseph J.
Tom Pinch.
See Dilley, Joseph J.

CLIMBING BOY, THE
See Peake, Richard Brinsley.

CLINTON, HENRY FYNES
Solyman. London: J. Hatchard, 1807. Pp. [iii]-[x], [1]-99.

CLOCK HAS STRUCK
See Lewis, Matthew Gregory. Wood Daemon, The.

CLOCK ON THE STAIRS, THE
See Hazlewood, Colin Henry.

CLOCKMAKER'S HAT, THE
See Robertson, Thomas William.

CLOSE SIEGE, A
See Dance, Charles.

CLOUD AND SUNSHINE
See Anderson, James Robertson.

CLOUD IN THE HONEYMOON, A
See Simpson, John Palgrave.

CLOUDS, THE (anon. trans.)
By Aristophanes. In *Clouds and Peace of Aristophanes,* Oxford: Henry Slatter, 1840, pp. [i-ii], [1]-60.

CLOUGH, ARTHUR HUGH
Dipsychus. In *Poems,* 11th ed., London: Macmillan, 1885, pp. [i], [65]-128.

CLOWES, WILLIAM LAIRD
Cross Stratagems. 11 leaves. Manuscript.

CLYTEMNESTRA
See Galt, John.
See Meredith, Owen.

CLYTIE
See Hatton, Joseph.

COALS OF FIRE
See Craven, Henry Thornton.

COAPE, HENRY COE
Conspirator in Spite of Himself, A. London: Webster, n.d. Pp. [1]-35. Webster's Acting National Drama, 186.
Our New Lady's Maid. London: Webster, n.d. Pp. [1]-28. Webster's Acting National Drama, 190.
Queen of the Market, The.
See Webster, Benjamin Nottingham.
Samuel in Search of Himself.
See Coyne, Joseph Stirling.

COATES, ALFRED
Honour versus Wealth. Pp. [1]-78. Manuscript promptbook.
Snowdrift, The; or, The Cross on the Boot. London: Samuel French; New York: T. Henry French, n.d. Pp. [1]-32. [Lacy's Acting Edition].

COBB, JAMES
First Floor, The. In *British Drama,* 12 vols., London: John Dicks, 1871, VII, [51]-64.
First Floor, The. London: John Cumberland & Son, n.d. Pp. [1]-36. Cumberland's British Theatre, XLI. *Filed under* Cumberland, John. Cumberland's British Theatre, XLI.
Haunted Tower, The. In *British Drama,* 12 vols., London: John Dicks, 1871, VII, [145]-160.
Haunted Tower, The. London: John Cumberland, n.d. Pp. [1]-49. Cumberland's British Theatre, XXX. *Filed under* Cumberland, John. Cumberland's British Theatre, XXX.
House to Be Sold, A. Music by Kelly, Michael. London: G. & J. Robinson, 1802. Pp. [i-iv], [1]-56. 2nd ed.
Paul and Virginia. London: John Cumberland, 1828. Pp. [1]-34. Cumberland's British Theatre, XX. *Filed under* Cumberland, John. Cumberland's British Theatre, XX.
Paul and Virginia. In *British Drama,* 12 vols., London: John Dicks, 1865, III, [790]-798.
Paul and Virginia. London: John Cumberland, n.d. Pp. [1]-34. [Cumberland's British Theatre]. Libretto.
Ramah Droog. In *Modern Theatre,* ed. Mrs. Inchbald, 10 vols., London: Longman, Hurst, Rees, Orme, & Brown, 1811, VI, [139]-191.
Siege of Belgrade, The. London: John Cumberland, 1828. Pp. [i], [1]-47. Cumberland's British Theatre, XX. *Filed under* Cumberland, John. Cumberland's British Theatre, XX.
Siege of Belgrade, The. In *British Drama,* 12 vols., London: John Dicks, 1864, II, [624]-638.
Wife of Two Husbands, The. In *Modern Theatre,* ed. Mrs. Inchbald, 10 vols., London: Longman, Hurst, Rees, Orme, & Brown, 1811, VI, [75]-138.
Wife of Two Husbands, The. Music by Mazzinghi, J. London: G. & J. Robinson, 1803. Pp. [i-vi], [1]-96. 3rd ed.

COBBETT, WILLIAM
Big O and Sir Glory; or, Leisure to Laugh. London: John Dean, 1825. Pp. [1]-4, [i-ii], [5]-48.
Surplus Population, and Poor-Law Bill. London: Cobbett's Registe. Office, n.d. Pp. [1]-24.

COBBLER OF CRIPPLEGATE!
See Dance, Charles. Lucky Stars.

COBBLER OF PRESTON, THE
See Johnson, Charles.

COBBLER'S STRATAGEM, THE
See Brierley, Benjamin.
COBBOLD, ELIZABETH KNIPE, MRS. JOHN (formerly Mrs. William Clarke)
Brave's Task, The (fragment). In *Poems*, Ipswich: J. Raw, 1825, pp. [i], 158-159. *Filed under* Dramatic Fragments.
Roman Mutiny, The. In *Poems*, Ipswich: J. Raw, 1825, pp. [i], 265-277. *Filed under* Dramatic Fragments.
COCK OF THE WALK
See Poole, John. Year in an Hour, A.
COCK-A-DOODLE-DOO
See Millward, Charles.
COCKNEY SPORTSMEN
See Oxberry, William Henry. First of September, The.
COCKNEYS IN CALIFORNIA
See Coyne, Joseph Stirling.
COCKSHOT YEOMANRY
See Coyne, Joseph Stirling. Our National Defences.
CODANONIA CONQUISTATA
See Sidagero.
CODE, H. B.
Russian Sacrifice, The; or, The Burning of Moscow. Dublin: Graisberry & Campbell (printer) (priv.), 1813. Pp. [1-2], [i]-[lxii], [1]-48, 57-59. Text complete.
Spanish Patriots, a Thousand Years Ago. Music by Stevenson. London: J. Walker, 1812. Pp. [i]-viii, [1]-67.
COFFEY, CHARLES
Devil to Pay, The; or, The Wives Metamorphosed. London: Whittingham & Arliss, 1815. Pp. [1]-28. London Theatre, XV. *Filed under* Dibdin, Thomas John, ed. London Theatre, XV.
Devil to Pay, The. In *New English Drama*, ed. W. Oxberry, 22 vols., London: W. Simpkin & R. Marshall; C. Chapple, 1824, XXI, [i]-[x], [1]-23. *Filed under* Oxberry, William Henry. New English Drama, XXI.
Devil to Pay, The; or, The Wives Metamorphosed. In *British Drama*, 12 vols., London: John Dicks, 1864, I, [113]-120.
Devil to Pay, The; or, The Wives Metamorphosed. London: John Cumberland, n.d. Pp. [1]-33. Cumberland's British Theatre, XXXVIII. *Filed under* Cumberland, John. Cumberland's British Theatre, XXXVIII.
COGGESHALL VOLUNTEER CORPS, THE (anon.)
Colchester: I. Marsden, 1804. Pp. [1]-20. 2nd ed.
COGHILL, JOHN JOCELYN, SIR
Curse of Pontignac, The. London: C. E. Morland's Office, n.d. Pp. [i-ii], 1-19, [i], 1-10, [i], 1-13, [i], 1-15. Pagination by act. Typescript.
COGHLAN, CHARLES FRANCIS
Brothers. London: Woodfall & Kinder (printer), 1881. Pp. [1]-73.
Royal Box, The. [New York: G. W. Kauser Typewriting], n.d. Pp. [i-x], [1]-16, [i], [1]-16, [i], [1]-16, [i], [1]-28, [i], [1]-14, 16-24. Pagination by act. Typescript.
COLD WATER CURE!
See A'Beckett, Gilbert Abbott. Knight and the Sprite, The.
COLE, JOHN WILLIAM
See Calcraft, John William.
COLEMAN, JOHN (arr.)
Henry V (with prologue from Henry IV). By Shakespeare, William. London: Walter Smith (printer), n.d. Pp. [1]-83.
COLERIDGE, ARTHUR DUKE (trans.)
Egmont. By Goethe. London: Chapman & Hall, 1868. Pp. [1]-114, 1-26.
COLERIDGE, SAMUEL TAYLOR
Osorio. London: John Pearson, 1873. Pp. [i]-[xxiv], [1]-204.
Remorse. London: W. Pople, 1813. Pp. [i-xii], [1]-72.
Remorse.
See Thicke, Frank E. (arr.).
Triumph of Loyalty, The. In [*Complete Poetical Works*, 2 vols., Oxford: Clarendon, 1912, II], 1060-1073.
Zapolya: A Christmas Tale. London: Rest Fenner, 1817. Pp. [i-vi], [1]-128.

COLERIDGE, SAMUEL TAYLOR (trans.)
Death of Wallenstein, The. By Schiller. London: T. N. Longman & O. Rees, 1800. Pp. [i-vi], [1]-157.
Piccolomini, The; or, The First Part of Wallenstein. By Schiller. London: T. N. Longman & O. Rees, 1800. Pp. [1-2], [i]-[iv], [1]-214.
COLLEEN BAWN, THE
See Boucicault, Dionysius Lardner.
COLLEEN BAWN SETTLED AT LAST, THE
See Brough, William.
COLLIER, WILLIAM
Abduction; or, The Farmer's Daughter. London: J. Pattie, n.d. Pp. [1]-38. Pattie's Modern Stage or Weekly Acting Drama, 61.
Blacksmith, The. London: John Duncombe, n.d. Pp. [1]-20. Duncombe's Edition.
Is She a Woman? London: John Duncombe, n.d. Pp. [1]-30. Duncombe's Edition.
Kate Kearney; or, The Fairy of the Lakes. London: Thomas Hailes Lacy, n.d. Pp. [1]-30. Libretto.
Kate Kearney; or, The Fairy of the Lakes. London: Thomas Hailes Lacy, n.d. Pp. [1]-30. Lacking pp. 28-29. Promptbook.
Kiss, The; or, Bertha's Bridal. London: S. G. Fairbrother (printer), n.d. Pp. [1]-15. Libretto.
Queen's Jewel, The; or, The Interrupted Ball! London: John Duncombe, n.d. Pp. [1]-20. Duncombe's Edition.
Rival Sergeants, The; or, Love and Lottery! London: Duncombe & Moon, n.d. <wrps. John Duncombe>. Pp. [1]-21. Duncombe's Acting Edition of the British Theatre, 471. Libretto.
COLLINS, ARTHUR PELHAM
Babes in the Woods, The.
See Sturgess, Arthur.
Forty Thieves, The.
See Sturgess, Arthur.
COLLINS, CHARLES JAMES
City Friends. London: Thomas Hailes Lacy, n.d. Pp. [1]-23.
Pizarro: A Spanish Rolla-King Peruvian Drama. London: Thomas Hailes Lacy, 1856. Pp. [i]-viii, [9]-36.
Prince Cherry and Princess Fair Star; or, The Jewelled Children of the Enchanted Isle! London: Thomas Hailes Lacy, 1855. Pp. [1]-32.
COLLINS, MORTIMER
Comedy of Dreams, The. In *Selections from The Poetical Works of Mortimer Collins*, ed. F. Percy Cotton, London: Richard Bentley & Son, 1886, pp. [i], 169-202. Fragments.
COLLINS, WILKIE
See Collins, William Wilkie.
COLLINS, WILLIAM WILKIE
Armadale. London: Smith, Elder (priv.), 1866. Pp. [i-ii], [1]-75.
Black and White. Written with Fechter, Charles Albert. New York: Robert M. DeWitt, n.d. Pp. [1]-34. DeWitt's Acting Plays, 296.
Frozen Deep, The. London: C. Whiting (printer) (priv.), 1866. Pp. [1]-46. Additional ms. notes.
Man and Wife. London: (priv.), 1870. Pp. [1]-77. Promptbook.
Message from the Sea, A.
See Brougham, John.
Miss Gwilt. London: Ranken (printer) (priv.), 1875. Pp. [1]-102.
Moonstone, The. London: Charles Dickens & Evans (printer) (priv.), 1877. Pp. [1]-88.
New Magdalen, The. London: (priv.), 1873. Pp. [1]-81.
No Name. Chicago: Dramatic Publishing Co., n.d. Pp. [1]-39. World Acting Drama.
No Thoroughfare.
See Dickens, Charles.
Woman in White, The. London: (priv.), 1871. Pp. [1]-88.
COLLS, J. H.
Honest Soldier, The. Norwich: Payne (printer), n.d. Pp. [1]-172.

COLMAN, GEORGE, SR

Clandestine Marriage, The. Written with Garrick, David. London: Whittingham & Arliss, 1815. Pp. [1]-95. London Theatre, XII. *Filed under* Dibdin, Thomas John, ed. London Theatre, XII.

Clandestine Marriage, The. Written with Garrick, David. In *New English Drama,* ed. W. Oxberry, 22 vols., London: W. Simpkin & R. Marshall; C. Chapple, 1819, V, [i]-vii, [i]-[v], [1]- 84. *Filed under* Oxberry, William Henry. New English Drama, V.

Clandestine Marriage, The. Written with Garrick, David. London: T. Dolby, 1824. Pp. [i]-[vi], [7]-86. Dolby's British Theatre, VII. *Filed under* Cumberland, John. Cumberland's British Theatre, VII.

Clandestine Marriage, The. Written with Garrick, David. In *British Drama,* 12 vols., London: John Dicks, 1871, V, [52]-77.

Deuce Is in Him, The. In *British Drama,* 12 vols., London: John Dicks, 1871, IX, [215]-224.

English Merchant, The. In *Modern Theatre,* ed. Mrs. Inchbald, 10 vols., London: Longman, Hurst, Rees, Orme, & Brown, 1811, IX, [165]-232. *Filed under* Colman, George, sr; Garrick, David.

Jealous Wife, The. London: Whittingham & Arliss, 1815. Pp. [1]-84. London Theatre, XI. *Filed under* Dibdin, Thomas John, ed. London Theatre, XI.

Jealous Wife, The. In *New English Drama,* ed. W. Oxberry, 22 vols., London: W. Simpkin & R. Marshall; C. Chapple, 1818, I, [iii]-[x], [1]-[80]. *Filed under* Oxberry, William Henry. New English Drama, I.

Jealous Wife, The. London: T. Dolby, 1824. Pp. [i]-[vi], [7]-78. Dolby's British Theatre, VII. *Filed under* Cumberland, John. Cumberland's British Theatre, VII.

Jealous Wife, The. In *British Drama,* 12 vols., London: John Dicks, 1864, I, [207]-228.

Polly Honeycombe. London: Sherwood, Neely, & Jones, 1818. Pp. [1]-32. London Theatre, XXIV. *Filed under* Dibdin, Thomas John, ed. London Theatre, XXIV.

Polly Honeycombe. In *British Drama,* 12 vols., London: John Dicks, 1871, VI, [248]-256.

COLMAN, GEORGE, SR (arr.)

Comus. By Milton, John. London: Whittingham & Arliss, 1815. Pp. [1]-24. London Theatre, X. *Filed under* Dibdin, Thomas John, ed. London Theatre, X.

Comus. By Milton, John. In *British Drama,* 12 vols., London: John Dicks, 1872, XII, [90]-96.

COLMAN, GEORGE, JR

Actor of All Work, The; or, The First and Second Floor. New York: E. M. Murden, 1822. Pp. [1]-24.

Africans, The; or, War, Love, and Duty. Philadelphia: M. Carey, 1811. Pp. [85]-169. Text complete.

Battle of Hexham, The; or, Days of Old. London: John Cumberland, n.d. Pp. [1]-51. Cumberland's British Theatre, XXXVII. *Filed under* Cumberland, John. Cumberland's British Theatre, XXXVII.

Blue Beard. In *New English Drama,* ed. W. Oxberry, 22 vols., London: W. Simpkin & R. Marshall; C. Chapple, 1823, XXI, [i]-[viii], [1]-32. *Filed under* Oxberry, William Henry. New English Drama, XXI.

Blue Beard. London: John Cumberland, n.d. Pp. [1]-39. Cumberland's British Theatre, XXXVI. *Filed under* Cumberland, John. Cumberland's British Theatre, XXXVI.

Blue Devils. In *New English Drama,* ed. W. Oxberry, 22 vols., London: W. Simpkin & R. Marshall; C. Chapple, 1822, XV, [1-2], [i]-[vi], [1]-[20]. *Filed under* Oxberry, William Henry. New English Drama, XV.

Blue Devils. London: John Cumberland, n.d. Pp. [i-ii], [1]-30. Cumberland's British Theatre, XXXIX. *Filed under* Cumberland, John. Cumberland's British Theatre, XXXIX.

Forty Thieves, The (attrib. to Colman). London: J. Scales, n.d. Pp. [3]-30. Scales's Edition. Synopsis. *Filed under* Forty Thieves (anon.).

Forty Thieves, The (attrib. to Colman). London: John Cumberland, n.d. Pp. [1]-39. Promptbook. *Filed under* Forty Thieves (anon.).

Forty Thieves, The (attrib. to Colman). London: John Cumberland, n.d. Pp. [1]-39. Cumberland's British Theatre, XXVII. *Filed under* Cumberland, John. Cumberland's British Theatre, XXVII.

Forty Thieves, The (attrib. to Colman). London: John Cumberland, n.d. Pp. [1]-39. [Cumberland's British Theatre, 192].

Gay Deceivers, The; or, More Laugh Than Love. London: James Cawthorn, 1808. Pp. [1]-46.

Gnome King, The.
See Reynolds, Frederick.

Heir at Law, The. In *British Drama,* 12 vols., London: John Dicks, 1872, XII, [97]-119.

Heir at Law, The. London: John Cumberland, n.d. Pp. [i-ii], [1]-70. Cumberland's British Theatre, XXXVIII. *Filed under* Cumberland, John. Cumberland's British Theatre, XXXVIII.

Inkle and Yarico. London: John Cumberland, 1827. Pp. [1]-54. Cumberland's British Theatre, XVI. *Filed under* Cumberland, John. Cumberland's British Theatre, XVI.

Iron Chest, The. In *British Drama,* 12 vols., London: John Dicks, 1864, II, [411]-432.

Iron Chest, The. London: John Cumberland, n.d. Pp. [1]-69. Cumberland's British Theatre, XXXV. *Filed under* Cumberland, John. Cumberland's British Theatre, XXXV.

Iron Chest, The.
See Irving, Henry (arr.).

John Bull; or, The Englishman's Fireside. London: Longman, Hurst, Rees, & Orme, 1805. Pp. [i-iv], [1]-[102].

John Bull; or, The Englishman's Fireside. New York: Thomas Longworth, 1821. Pp. [1]-82. Text incomplete.

John Bull; or, The Englishman's Fireside. In *British Drama,* 12 vols., London: John Dicks, 1865, III, [735]-756.

John Bull; or, The Englishman's Fireside. London: John Cumberland, n.d. Pp. [1]-76. Cumberland's British Theatre, XXXVI. *Filed under* Cumberland, John. Cumberland's British Theatre, XXXVI.

Law of Java, The. Music by Bishop, Henry R. London: W. Simpkin & R. Marshall, 1822. Pp. [ii]-[vi], [1]-94.

Law of Java, The. Music by Bishop, Henry R. London: Goulding, D'Almaine, Potter, n.d. Pp. [i-iv], 1-87, 1-5. Vocal score.

Love Laughs at Locksmiths. London: James Cawthorn, 1808. Pp. [1]-52.

Love Laughs at Locksmiths. In *New English Drama,* ed. W. Oxberry, 22 vols., London: W. Simpkin & R. Marshall; C. Chapple, 1822, XIII, [1-2], [i]-[vi], [1]-38. *Filed under* Oxberry, William Henry. New English Drama, XIII.

Love Laughs at Locksmiths. London: John Cumberland, n.d. Pp. [1]-41. Cumberland's British Theatre, XXXVII. *Filed under* Cumberland, John. Cumberland's British Theatre, XXXVII.

Love Laughs at Locksmiths. Music by Kelly, Michael. London: T. Woodroof (printer), 1803. Pp. [i-iv], [1]-36.

Mountaineers, The. London: John Cumberland, n.d. Pp. [1]-57. Cumberland's British Theatre, XXXV. *Filed under* Cumberland, John. Cumberland's British Theatre, XXXV.

Poor Gentleman, The. London: T. N. Longman & O. Rees, 1802. Pp. [1]-83.

Poor Gentleman, The. In *British Drama,* 12 vols., London: John Dicks, 1872, XII, [62]-89.

Poor Gentleman, The. London: John Cumberland, n.d. Pp. [1]-70. Cumberland's British Theatre, XXXVII. *Filed under* Cumberland, John. Cumberland's British Theatre, XXXVII.

Review, The; or, The Wags of Windsor. London: James Cawthorn, 1808. Pp. [1]-47.

Review, The; or, The Wags of Windsor. In *New English Drama,* ed. W. Oxberry, 22 vols., London: W. Simpkin & R. Marshall; C. Chapple, 1822, XIII, [1-2], [i]-[vi], [1]-35.

Filed under Oxberry, William Henry. New Engiish Drama, XIII.

Review, The; or, The Wags of Windsor. London: John Cumberland, n.d. Pp. [1]-38. Cumberland's British Theatre, XXXVI. *Filed under* Cumberland, John. Cumberland's British Theatre, XXXVI.

Review, The; or, The Wags of Windsor. London: John Cumberland, n.d. Pp. [3]-38.

Surrender of Calais, The. London: John Cumberland, n.d. Pp. [1]-52. Cumberland's British Theatre, XL. *Filed under* Cumberland, John. Cumberland's British Theatre, XL.

Sylvester Daggerwood; or, New Hay at the Old Market. London: J. Cawthorne, 1808. Pp. [1]-32.

Sylvester Daggerwood. In *New English Drama,* ed. W. Oxberry, 22 vols., London: W. Simpkin & R. Marshall; C. Chapple, 1823, XXI, [i]-[vi], [7]-12. *Filed under* Oxberry, William Henry. New English Drama, XXI.

Sylvester Daggerwood. London: John Cumberland, n.d. Pp. [1]-16. Cumberland's British Theatre, XXXVI. *Filed under* Cumberland, John. Cumberland's British Theatre, XXXVI.

Ways and Means. In *British Drama,* 12 vols., London: John Dicks, 1872, XII, [15]-32.

We Fly by Night; or, Long Stories. Baltimore: George Dobbin & Murphy, n.d. Pp. [1]-46. Promptbook.

Who Wants a Guinea? London: Longman, Hurst, Rees, & Orme, 1805. Pp. [i-vi], [1]-84.

Who Wants a Guinea? In *Modern Theatre,* ed. Mrs. Inchbald, 10 vols., London: Longman, Hurst, Rees, Orme, & Brown, 1811, III, [207]-290.

Who Wants a Guinea? London: John Cumberland, 1828. Pp. [1]-72. Cumberland's British Theatre, XX. *Filed under* Cumberland, John. Cumberland's British Theatre, XX.

X, Y, Z. London: Hunt & Clarke, 1827. Pp. [i-ii], [1]-33. British Theatre.

X. Y. Z. London: John Cumberland, n.d. Pp. [1]-41. Cumberland's British Theatre, XXV. *Filed under* Cumberland, John. Cumberland's British Theatre, XXV.

COLNAGHI, CHARLES PHILIP

Dr. D. Music by Dick, Cotsford. London: Metzler, n.d. Pp. [1]-44. Libretto.

COLOMB, GEORGE HATTON, COL.

Cast King of Granada, The. London & New York: Samuel French, n.d. Pp. [1]-24. [Lacy's Acting Edition].

Davenport Done; or, An April Fool. By Capt. Colomb. London: Thomas Hailes Lacy, n.d. Pp. [1]-23. [Lacy's Acting Edition].

Hamlet Improved; or, Mr. Mendall's Attempt to Ameliorate That Tragedy. London & New York: Samuel French, n.d. Pp. [1]-12. [Lacy's Acting Edition].

COLOMBA

See Hueffer, Francis.

COLOMBE'S BIRTHDAY

See Browning, Robert.

COLOMBINE, DAVID ELWIN

Marcus Manlius. London: Richard Bentley, 1837. Pp. [i]-[xiv], [1]-112.

COLOUR-SERGEANT, THE

See Thomas, Brandon.

COLQUHOUN, W. H. (trans.)

Faust. By Goethe. London: Arthur H. Moxon, 1878. Pp. [i-iv], [1]-327.

COLTON, CHARLES

Richard Savage. In *Richard Savage . . . and Bernicia,* London: Watts, n.d., pp. 1-52.

COLUMBINE BY CANDLELIGHT!

See Dibdin, Thomas John. Harlequin and Humpo.

COLUMBINE RED RIDING-HOOD

See Planché, James Robinson. Rodolph the Wolf.

COLUMBUS

See Rose, Edward.

COLUMBUS EL FILIBUSTERO!

See Brougham, John.

COME TO TOWN

See Rede, William Leman.

COMEDY AND TRAGEDY

See Gilbert, William Schwenck.

See Robson, William.

COMEDY OF DREAMS, THE

See Collins, Mortimer.

COMEDY OF ERRORS, THE

See Kemble, John Philip (arr.).

See Reynolds, Frederick (arr.).

See Shakespeare, William.

COMFORTABLE LODGINGS

See Peake, Richard Brinsley.

COMFORTABLE SERVICE

See Bayly, Thomas Haynes.

COMIC MEDLEY

See Moncrieff, William Thomas.

COMIC OPERA

See Barber, James.

COMIC PASTORAL, A

See Van Laun, Henri (trans.).

COMICAL COUNTESS, A

See Brough, William.

COMING OF PEACE, THE

See Kennedy, Charles Rann.

COMING OF THE PRINCE, THE

See Sharp, William.

COMING WOMAN, THE; OR, THE SPIRIT OF SEVENTY-SIX (anon.)

London & New York: Samuel French, n.d. Pp. [1]-28. [Lacy's Acting Edition].

COMMISSION, A

See Grossmith, Weedon.

COMMITTED FOR TRIAL

See Gilbert, William Schwenck.

COMMODORE, THE

See Farnie, Henry Brougham.

COMPETITORS, THE

See Cubitt, Sydney.

COMPLIMENTS OF THE SEASON, THE

See Planché, James Robinson.

COMPROMISING CASE, A

See Smale, Edith C., Mrs. T. E.

COMTESSE D'ESCARBAGNAS

See Van Laun, Henri (trans.). Countess of Escarbagnas, The.

COMUS

See Colman, George, sr (arr.).

See Milton, John.

CON O'CARROLAN'S DREAM

See Grattan, H. P. Fairy Circle, The.

CONFEDERACY, THE

See Vanbrugh, John.

CONFESSION, THE

See Cumberland, Richard.

See Sotheby, William.

See Sotheby, William. Ellen.

CONFIN'D IN VAIN

See Jones, T.

CONFLAGRATION OF MOSCOW

See Amherst, J. H. Napoleon Buonaparte's Invasion of Russia.

CONFOUNDED FOREIGNERS

See Reynolds, John Hamilton.

CONFUSION

See Derrick, Joseph.

CONFUSION WORSE CONFOUNDED

See Poole, John. Patrician and Parvenu.

CONGRESS TROOPER

See Dibdin, Thomas John. Banks of the Hudson, The.

CONGREVE, WILLIAM

Double Dealer, The. London: Whittingham & Arliss, 1816. Pp. [1]-[80]. London Theatre, XX. *Filed under* Dibdin, Thomas John, ed. London Theatre, XX.

Double-Dealer, The. In *British Drama,* 12 vols., London: John Dicks, 1871, IX, [i-iv], [129]-152.

Double Dealer, The.
See Kemble, John Philip (arr.).
Love for Love. London: Whittingham & Arliss, 1815. Pp. [1]-[80]. London Theatre, XVI. *Filed under* Dibdin, Thomas John, ed. London Theatre, XVI.
Love for Love. London: John Cumberland, 1828. Pp. [7]-75. Cumberland's British Theatre, XIX. *Filed under* Cumberland, John. Cumberland's British Theatre, XIX.
Love for Love. In *British Drama,* 12 vols., London: John Dicks, 1872, X, [225]-249.
Mourning Bride, The. London: Whittingham & Arliss, 1815. Pp. [1]-[60]. London Theatre, XI. *Filed under* Dibdin, Thomas John, ed. London Theatre, XI.
Mourning Bride, The. In *British Drama,* 12 vols., London: John Dicks, 1865, III, [879]-894.
Way of the World, The. London: Sherwood, Neely, & Jones, 1818. Pp. [1]-[92]. London Theatre, XXIV. *Filed under* Dibdin, Thomas John, ed. London Theatre, XXIV.
Way of the World, The. In *British Drama,* 12 vols., London: John Dicks, 1872, XI, [i-iv], [1]-26.
Way of the World, The.
See Kemble, John Philip (arr.).
CONJUGAL LESSON, A
See Danvers, Henry.
CONQUERING GAME, THE
See Bernard, William Bayle.
CONQUEST, GEORGE
Aladdin, the Lad with the Wonderful Lamp; or, The Pretty Princess and the Precious Great Scamp. Written with Spry, Henry. London: Phillips Brothers, 1884. Pp. [1]-32. Libretto.
Hand and Glove; or, Page 13 of the Black Book. Written with Merritt, Paul. London & New York: Samuel French, n.d. Pp. [1]-42. [French's Acting Edition].
Jack and Jill and the Well on the Hill; or, The House That Jack Built. Written with Spry, Henry. London: Phillips Brothers, n.d. Pp. [1]-37. Libretto.
Neck or Nothing.
See Pettitt, Henry Alfred.
Seven Sins; or, Passion's Paradise. Written with Merritt, Paul. London & New York: Samuel French, n.d. Pp. [1]-38. [Lacy's Acting Edition].
Sinbad the Sailor, a Son of the Sea; or, The Old Man of the Ocean and Fair Zoradee. Written with Spry, Henry. London: Phillips Brothers (printer), n.d. Pp. [1]-31. Libretto.
Sole Survivor, The; or, A Tale of the Goodwin Sands. Written with Pettitt, Henry Alfred. London & New York: Samuel French, n.d. Pp. [1]-48. [Lacy's Acting Edition].
Velvet and Rags. Written with Merritt, Paul. London & New York: Samuel French, n.d. Pp. [1]-45. [Lacy's Acting Edition].
CONQUEST OF MEXICO
See Helme, Elizabeth (trans.). Cortez.
See Planché, James Robinson. Cortez.
CONQUEST OF MYSORE
See Coyne, Joseph Stirling. Arajoon.
CONQUEST OF PERU
See Helme, Elizabeth (trans.). Pizarro.
CONQUEST OF TARANTO, THE
See Dimond, William.
CONRAD
See Bunn, Alfred.
CONRAD AND MEDORA
See Brough, William.
See Brough, William. Corsair, The.
CONSCIENCE
See Aston, Joseph.
See Haynes, James.
See Thompson, Benjamin (trans.).
CONSCIOUS LOVERS, THE
See Steele, Richard.
CONSCRIPT, THE
See Oxberry, William Henry.

CONSPIRACY
See Bulwer (later Bulwer-Lytton), Edward George Earle Lytton, Lord Lytton. Richelieu.
CONSPIRACY OF KAMTSCHATKA
See Thompson, Benjamin (trans.). Count Benyowsky.
CONSPIRACY OF THE PAZZI, THE
See Lloyd, Charles (trans.).
CONSPIRATOR IN SPITE OF HIMSELF, A
See Coape, Henry Coe.
CONSPIRATORS OF ST. PETERSBURGH!
See Moncrieff, William Thomas. Lestocq.
CONSTANT COUPLE, THE
See Farquhar, George.
CONSTANTIA
See Neale, Frederick.
CONSTANTINE PALEOLOGUS
See Baillie, Joanna.
CONSUL IN ENGLAND
See Maclaren, Archibald. Britons to Arms!
CONTENTION OF YORK AND LANCASTER
See Richard, Duke of York.
CONTEST OF THE AONIDES
See Apollo's Choice.
CONTESTED ELECTION, THE
See Taylor, Tom.
CONTRADICTIONS
See Leigh, Agnes.
CONTRIVANCES, THE
See Carey, Henry.
CONVENIENT DISTANCE
See Pocock, Isaac. Omnibus, The.
CONVENT MAID
See Parke, Walter. Kitty.
CONVENT OF ST. BARTHOLOMEW
See Burnaby, Edwyn Andrew. Agatha.
CONVICT, THE
See Wilson, John.
CONVICT'S CHILD
See Blake, Thomas G. Life As It Is.
CONVICT'S VENGEANCE
See Selby, Charles. Harold Hawk.
COOK, KENINGALE
King of Kent, The. London: Pickering, 1882. Pp. [i-iv], [1]-75.
Love in a Mist. London: Pickering, 1882. Pp. [i-iv], [1]-118.
COOKE, JOHN
Treasurers, The. Bath: W. Pocock, 1842. Pp. [i-iv], [1]-[83].
COOKE, WILLIAM MAJOR
Hymenaeus. By W. M. C. London: Henry Richards (printer) (priv.), n.d. Pp. [1]-[17].
COOL AS A CUCUMBER
See Jerrold, William Blanchard.
COOPER, EDITH EMMA
See Field, Michael (pseud.).
COOPER, FOX
See Cooper, Frederick Fox.
COOPER, FREDERICK FOX
Black-eyed Sukey; or, All in the Dumps. London: Thomas Richardson, n.d. Pp. [i]-vii, 8-36.
Black-Eyed Sukey; or, All in the Dumps. London: John Cumberland, n.d. Pp. [1]-32. Cumberland's Minor Theatre, XIV. *Filed under* Cumberland, John. Cumberland's Minor Theatre, XIV.
Corsican Brothers, The. London: John Dicks, n.d. Pp. [1]-14. Dicks' Standard Plays, 752.
Deserted Village, The. London: John Duncombe, n.d. Pp. [1]-49. Duncombe's Edition.
Elbow Shakers!, The; or, Thirty Years of a Rattler's Life. London: T. Richardson, n.d. Pp. [1]-35. 2nd ed.
Hard Times. London: C. Harris; Henry Pownceby, 1854. Pp. [1]-48. Pownceby's New Acting Drama, 1.
Hard Times. By Fox Cooper. London: John Dicks, n.d. Pp. [1]-22. Dicks' Standard Plays, 785.
Hercules, King of Clubs! London: John Cumberland, n.d. Pp. [1]-23. Cumberland's Minor Theatre, XIII. *Filed*

under Cumberland, John. Cumberland's Minor Theatre, XIII.

Hercules, King of Clubs! London: Davidson, n.d. Pp. [1-17].

Ion. London: Davidson, n.d. Pp. [3]-31. Cumberland's British Theatre.

Ion. By Fox Cooper. London: John Cumberland, n.d. Pp. [1]-31. Cumberland's Minor Theatre, XII. *Filed under* Cumberland, John. Cumberland's Minor Theatre, XII.

Ivanhoe. London: John Dicks, n.d. Pp. [1]-16. Dicks' Standard Plays, 385.

Jenny Jones. By Fox Cooper. Music by Sloman; Harroway. London: James Pattie, n.d. Pp. [1]-23.

Master Humphrey's Clock. London: John Duncombe, n.d. Pp. [1]-36. Duncombe's Edition.

Ovingdean Grange: A Tale of the South Downs. London: John Dicks, n.d. Pp. [1]-18. Dicks' Standard Plays, 1019.

Queen's Visit, The. London: James Pattie, n.d. Pp. [1]-24. Pattie's Penny Play or Weekly Acting Drama, 3.

Shooting the Moon. London: Thomas Hailes Lacy, n.d. Pp. [1]-25.

Spare Bed, The; or, The Shower Bath. London: John Cumberland, n.d. Pp. [1]-34. Cumberland's Minor Theatre, VII. *Filed under* Cumberland, John. Cumberland's Minor Theatre, VII.

Spare Bed, The; or, The Shower Bath. London: John Cumberland, n.d. Pp. [1]-34.

Tale of Two Cities, The; or, The Incarcerated Victim of the Bastille. London: John Dicks, n.d. Pp. [1]-22. Dicks' Standard Plays, 780.

Who's a Traveller? London: T. H. Lacey; G. Harris; Henry Pounceby, 1855 <wrps. 1854>. Pp. [1]-18. Pownceby's New Acting Drama, 3.

COOPER, G.

Billy. Written with Ross, Adrian (pseud. of Ropes, Arthur Reed). Music by Carr, Osmond. N.p.: n.pub. (priv.), n.d. Pp. [1]-39. Libretto.

COOPER, HERBERT B.

Arts and Hearts. Liverpool: Lee & Nightingale (printer) (priv.), n.d. Pp. [1]-75.

COOPER, JAMES B.

Oor Geordie; or, The Horrid Barbarian. London & New York: Samuel French, n.d. Pp. [1]-23. [Lacy's Acting Edition].

COOTE, ROBERT

Mohawk Minstrels' Fourth Annual of Dramas, Dialogues, & Drolleries The.
See Hunter, Harry.

COQUETTES
See Albery, James.

CORDER, FREDERICK

Sisyphus, King of Ephyra. Written with Corder, Henrietta Louisa Walford, Mrs. Frederick. Music by Orczy, Bodog. London: J. Miles (printer), n.d. Pp. [1]-12. Libretto.

CORDER, FREDERICK (trans.)

Dusk of the Gods, The.
See Corder, Henrietta Louisa Walford, Mrs. Frederick (trans.).

Lohengrin.
See Corder, Henrietta Louisa Walford, Mrs. Frederick (trans.).

Mastersingers of Nuremberg, The.
See Corder, Henrietta Louisa Walford, Mrs. Frederick (trans.).

Parsifal.
See Corder, Henrietta Louisa Walford, Mrs. Frederick (trans.).

Rhine Gold, The.
See Corder, Henrietta Louisa Walford, Mrs. Frederick (trans.).

Siegfried.
See Corder, Henrietta Louisa Walford, Mrs. Frederick (trans.).

Tristan and Isolda.
See Corder, Henrietta Louisa Walford, Mrs. Frederick (trans.).

Valkyrie, The.
See Corder, Henrietta Louisa Walford, Mrs. Frederick (trans.).

CORDER, HENRIETTA LOUISA WALFORD, MRS. FREDERICK

Sisyphus, King of Ephyra.
See Corder, Frederick.

CORDER, HENRIETTA LOUISA WALFORD, MRS. FREDERICK (trans.)

Dusk of the Gods, The. Written with Corder, Frederick (trans.). *Also:* Götterdämmerung. Music by Wagner. London: Schott, n.d. Pp. [i-iv], 1-340. Vocal score. *Filed under* Götterdämmerung.

Lohengrin. Written with Corder, Frederick (trans.). Music by Wagner. Leipzig: Breitkopf & Härtel, n.d. Pp. [i]-viii, [1]-350. Vocal score.

Mastersingers of Nuremberg, The. Written with Corder, Frederick (trans.). *Also:* Die Meistersinger von Nurnberg. Music by Wagner. Mainz: B. Schott's Söhne, n.d. Pp. [i-iv], 1-467. Vocal score.

Parsifal. Written with Corder, Frederick (trans.). Music by Wagner. London: Schott, n.d. Pp. [i-iv], 1-279. Vocal score.

Rhine Gold, The. Written with Corder, Frederick (trans.). Also Das Rheingold. Music by Wagner. London: Schott, n.d. Pp. [i-iv], 1-221. Vocal score. *Filed under* Das Rheingold.

Siegfried. Written with Corder, Frederick (trans.). Music by Wagner. Mainz: B. Schott's Söhne, n.d. <wrps. New York: G. Schirmer>. Pp. [i-iv], 1-337. Vocal score.

Tristan and Isolda. Written with Corder, Frederick (trans.). *Also:* Tristan und Isolde. Music by Wagner. Leipzig: Breitkopf & Härtel, n.d. Pp. [i-iv], [1]-276. Vocal score.

Valkyrie, The. Written with Corder, Frederick (trans.). *Also:* Die Walküre. Music by Wagner. Mainz: B. Schott's Söhne, n.d. Pp. [i-iv], 1-309. Vocal score. *Filed under* Die Walküre.

CORINNE
See Buchanan, Robert Williams.

CORINTH
See Humboldt, Charlotte de.

CORIOLANUS
See Irving, Henry (arr.).
See Kemble, John Philip (arr.).
See Shakespeare, William.

CORNEILLE
Horatius.
See under title.

CORNELIA
See Mason, James.

CORNWALL, BARRY (pseud. of Procter, Bryan Waller)

Amelia Wentworth. In *Marcian Colonna . . . ,* Philadelphia: M. Carey & Sons, 1821, pp. [i], [91]-109. *Filed under* Proctor, Bryan Waller.

Broken Heart, The. In *Dramatic Scenes with Other Poems,* Boston: Ticknor & Fields, 1857, pp. [69]-87. *Filed under* Proctor, Bryan Waller. Collected Works.

Falcon, The. In *Sicilian Story . . . ,* 2nd ed., London: John Warren; C. & J. Ollier, 1820, pp. [i], [29]-47. *Filed under* Proctor, Bryan Waller.

Falcon, The. In *Dramatic Scenes with Other Poems,* Boston: Ticknor & Fields, 1857, pp. [89]-109. *Filed under* Proctor, Bryan Waller. Collected Works.

Florentine Party, The. In *Dramatic Scenes with Other Poems,* Boston: Ticknor & Fields, 1857, pp. [201]-223. *Filed under* Proctor, Bryan Waller. Collected Works.

Juan. In *Dramatic Scenes with Other Poems,* Boston: Ticknor & Fields, 1857, pp. [34]-53. *Filed under* Proctor, Bryan Waller. Collected Works.

Julian the Apostate. In *Marcian Colonna . . . ,* Philadelphia: M. Carey & Sons, 1821, pp. [i], [73]-90. *Filed under* Proctor, Bryan Waller.

Ludovico Sforza. In *Dramatic Scenes with Other Poems*, Boston: Ticknor & Fields, 1857, pp. [i]-viii, [1]-20. *Filed under* Proctor, Bryan Waller. Collected Works.

Lysander and Ione. In *Dramatic Scenes with Other Poems*, Boston: Ticknor & Fields, 1857, pp. [21]-33. *Filed under* Proctor, Bryan Waller. Collected Works.

Michael Angelo. In *Dramatic Scenes with Other Poems*, Boston: Ticknor & Fields, 1857, pp. [163]-180. *Filed under* Proctor, Bryan Waller. Collected Works.

Mirandola. London: John Warren, 1821. Pp. [iii]-[x], [1]-110. *Filed under* Proctor, Bryan Waller.

Pandemonium. In *Dramatic Scenes with Other Poems*, Boston: Ticknor & Fields, 1857, pp. [115]-129. *Filed under* Proctor, Bryan Waller. Collected Works.

Raffaelle and Fornarina. In *Dramatic Scenes with Other Poems*, Boston: Ticknor & Fields, 1857, pp. [181]-199. *Filed under* Proctor, Bryan Waller. Collected Works.

Rape of Proserpine, The. In *Marcian Colonna . . .*, Philadelphia: M. Carey & Sons, 1821, pp. [i], [111]-120. *Filed under* Proctor, Bryan Waller.

Tartarus. In *Flood of Thessaly . . .*, London: Henry Colburn, 1823, pp. [i], [181]-206. *Filed under* Proctor, Bryan Waller.

Temptation, The. In *Dramatic Scenes with Other Poems*, Boston: Ticknor & Fields, 1857, pp. [130]-162. *Filed under* Proctor, Bryan Waller. Collected Works.

Victim, The. In *Dramatic Scenes with Other Poems*, Boston: Ticknor & Fields, 1857, pp. 225-250. *Filed under* Proctor, Bryan Waller. Collected Works.

Way to Conquer, The. In *Dramatic Scenes with Other Poems*, Boston: Ticknor & Fields, 1857, pp. [54]-68. *Filed under* Proctor, Bryan Waller. Collected Works.

CORPORAL'S WEDDING!, THE
    See Morton, John Maddison.
CORREGGIO
    See Lee, Eliza Buckminster, Mrs. (trans.).
    See Martin, Theodore, Sir (trans.).
CORREGIDOR OF SEVILLE!
    See Boaden, Caroline. Don Pedro the Cruel and Don Manuel the Cobbler!

CORRI, MONTAGUE
Adelphi Norma, The. Music by Corri, M. London: Fairbrother & Son (printer), n.d. Pp. [1]-14. *Filed under* Norma.

Georgy Barnwell; or, The Unfortunate London Apprentice. London: John Duncombe, n.d. Pp. [1]-20. Duncombe's Edition.

King Robert the Bruce.
    See Kerr, John.

CORRIE, JESSIE ELIZABETH
Obstinate Woman, An. London & New York: Samuel French, n.d. Pp. [1]-12. [Lacy's Acting Edition].
CORSAIR, THE
    See Brough, William. Conrad and Medora.
    See Brough, William.
    See Farley, Charles.
CORSAIR'S REVENGE, THE
    See Grattan, H. P.
CORSICAN BOTHERS, THE
    See Byron, Henry James.
CORSICAN BROTHERS, THE
    See Boucicault, Dionysius Lardner.
    See Cooper, Frederick Fox.
    See Webb, Charles.
CORSICAN VENDETTA
    See Blake, Thomas G. Spanking Legacy, A.
CORTEZ
    See Burges, James Bland.
    See Helme, Elizabeth (trans.).
    See Planché, James Robinson.

COSENS, FREDERICK WILLIAM (trans.)
Bandos de Verona, Los: Montescos y Capuletes. By Rojas y Zorilla, Francisco de. London: Chiswick Press (priv.), 1874. Pp. [i-viii], [1]-42.
COSMO DE' MEDICI
    See Horne, Richard Hengist.

COSMO, DUKE OF TUSCANY
    See Bird, James.
COSSACK AND NO COSSACK
    See Maclaren, Archibald. Irish Girl, The.
COTTAGE AND THE COURT
    See Wilks, Thomas Egerton. King's Wager, The.
COTTAGE DIALOGUES AMONG THE IRISH PEASANTRY
    See Leadbeater, Mary Shackleton, Mrs. William.
COTTLE, JOSEPH
Killcrop, The. In *Malvern Hills and Other Poems*, 3rd ed., London: T. N. Longman & O. Rees, 1802, pp. [i], 94-107.
COTTON, RICHARD
    See Brown, William.
COTTRELL, CHARLES HERBERT (trans.)
Don Carlos, Infante of Spain. By Schiller. Barnet: J. J. Cowing (printer); London: Longman, Brown, Green, & Longman, 1843. Pp. [1-2], [i]-[viii], [9]-[267].
COUNCIL OF CONSTANCE!
    See Moncrieff, William Thomas. Jewess!, The.
COUNCIL OF TEN
    See Reynoldson, Thomas Herbert. Venetian, The.
COUNSEL'S OPINION
    See Bingham, Frederick.
COUNT AREZZI, THE
    See Landor, Robert Eyres.
COUNT BENYOWSKY
    See Thompson, Benjamin (trans.).
COUNT CLERMONT
    See Bell, Archibald.
COUNT D'ABREU, THE
    See Hilton, B. H. Honour.
COUNT DE DENIA
    See Hoskins, Horatio Huntley.
COUNT JULIAN
    See Landor, Walter Savage.
    See Sturgis, Julian Russell.
COUNT KOENIGSMARK
    See Thompson, Benjamin (trans.).
COUNT OF NARBONNE
    See Jephson, Robert.
COUNT TREMOLIO
    See Wyatt, Edgar.
COUNTER ATTRACTION
    See Tilbury, William Harries.
COUNTERFEIT, THE
    See Franklin, Andrew.
COUNTERPLOTS
    See Van Laun, Henri (trans.). Blunderer, The.
COUNTESS FOR AN HOUR
    See Coyne, Joseph Stirling. Pas de Fascination.
COUNTESS KATHLEEN, THE
    See Yeats, William Butler.
COUNTESS OF ESCARBAGNAS, THE
    See Van Laun, Henri (trans.).
COUNTRY COUSIN, THE
    See Jameson, Anna Brownell Murphy, Mrs. Robert (trans.).
COUNTRY GENTLEMAN, THE
    See Barker, George.
COUNTRY GIRL, THE
    See Garrick, David.
COUNTRY INN, THE
    See Baillie, Joanna.
COUNTRY SQUIRE, THE
    See Dance, Charles.
COUP-DE-MAIN, THE
    See Maclaren, Archibald.
COURIER OF LYONS, THE
    See Reade, Charles.
    See Stirling, Edward.
    See Webster, Benjamin Nottingham.
COURT AND CITY
    See Peake, Richard Brinsley.
COURT AND THE STAGE
    See Taylor, Tom. King's Rival, The.

COURT AT RAVENNA, THE (anon.)
London: G. W. Nickisson, 1844. Pp. [i-iv], [1]-83.

COURT BEAUTIES, THE
See Planché, James Robinson.

COURT CARDS
See Simpson, John Palgrave.

COURT FAVOUR
See Planché, James Robinson.

COURT FOOL, THE
See Burton, William Evans.

COURT LOVERS
See Fraser, Julia Agnes.

COURT OF FLORA, THE
See Woodrooffe, Sophia.

COURT OF JAMES III
See White, James, Rev. Feudal Times.

COURT OF LIONS, THE
See Gilbert, H. P.

COURT OF OBERON, THE
See Yorke, Elizabeth Lindsey, Countess of Hardwicke.

COURT OF OLD FRITZ, THE
See Smith, John Frederick.

COURT OF QUEEN ANNE, THE
See Moncrieff, William Thomas.

COURT OF QUODLIBET
See Walker, Charles Edward. Rumfustian Innamorato.

COURT OF VINGOLIA
See Burnand, Francis Cowley. His Majesty.

COURTHOPE, WILLIAM JOHN
Paradise of Birds, The. Edinburgh & London: William Blackwood & Sons, 1870. Pp. [i]-[x], [1]-147.
Paradise of Birds, The. London: Macmillan, 1896. Pp. [iii]-xii, [1]-136. New ed.

COURTING IN THE NEWSPAPERS
See Jerrold, Douglas William. Wives by Advertisement.

COURTNEY, JOHN
Aged Forty. London: Thomas Hailes Lacy, n.d. Pp. [1]-16. [Lacy's Acting Edition, 879].
Belphegor; or, The Mountebank and His Wife. London: Thomas Hailes Lacy, n.d. Pp. [1]-50. Lacy's Acting Edition, 39.
Clarissa Harlowe.
See Lacy, Thomas Hailes.
Deeds, Not Words. London & New York: Samuel French, n.d. Pp. [1]-34. [Lacy's Acting Edition].
Double Faced People. London: Thomas Hailes Lacy, n.d. Pp. [1]-59. [Lacy's Acting Edition].
Eustache Baudin. New York: Samuel French, n.d. Pp. [1]-45. French's Standard Drama, 142.
Merry Wives of Windsor, The; or, Harlequin and Sir John Falstaff, and the Demon Hunter of the Enchanted Dell. London: Thomas Hailes Lacy, n.d. Pp. [1]-16. Libretto. *Filed under* Merry Wives of Windsor (anon.).
Old Joe and Young Joe. London: Thomas Hailes Lacy, n.d. Pp. [1]-32. [Lacy's Acting Edition, 731].
Soldier's Progress, The; or, The Horrors of War. London: Thomas Hailes Lacy, n.d. Pp. [1]-53.
Time Tries All. Boston: William V. Spencer, n.d. Pp. [1]-26. Spencer's Boston Theatre, 111.
Two Polts, The. London: Thomas Hailes Lacy, n.d. Pp. [1]-20. [Lacy's Acting Edition, 663].
Wicked Wife, A. London: Thomas Hailes Lacy, n.d. Pp. [1]-22. [Lacy's Acting Edition, 445].

COURTNEY, WILLIAM LEONARD
Gaston Bonnier; or, Time's Revenges. In *Anglo-Saxon Review*, VIII (March 1901), 103-124.
Kit Marlowe's Death. In *Dramas and Diversions*, London: Chapman & Hall, 1908, pp. [i], 99-125.

COURTSHIP
See Byron, Henry James.

COURTSHIP A-LA-MODE
See Bethune, Gilbert.

COUSIN CHERRY
See Spicer, Henry.

COUSIN JOE (pseud.)
Harlequin and the Childe of Hale.
See under title.

COUSIN LAMBKIN
See Morton, John Maddison.

COUSIN PETER
See Wilks, Thomas Egerton.

COUSIN TOM
See Roberts, George.

COUSIN ZACHARY
See Gardner, Herbert.

COVENANTERS, THE
See Dibdin, Thomas John.

COWDENKNOWS
See Hetherington, William Maxwell.

COWEN, ?, MISS
Neither of Them. New York & London: Samuel French, c.1899. Pp. [1]-18.

COWLEY, HANNAH PARKHOUSE, MRS.
Belle's Stratagem, The. London: Whittingham & Arliss, 1815. Pp. [1]-[76]. London Theatre, IV. *Filed under* Dibdin, Thomas John, ed. London Theatre, IV.
Belle's Stratagem, The. In *New English Drama*, ed. W. Oxberry, 22 vols., London: W. Simpkin & R. Marshall; C. Chapple, 1819, VI, [1-2], [i]-[viii], [1]-72. *Filed under* Oxberry, William Henry. New English Drama, VI.
Belle's Stratagem, The. London: T. Dolby, 1823. Pp. [i]-[vi], [7]-[75]. Dolby's British Theatre, II. *Filed under* Cumberland, John. Cumberland's British Theatre, II.
Belle's Stratagem, The. In *British Drama*, 12 vols., London: John Dicks, 1871, VII, [i-iv], [1]-23.
Belle's Stratagem, The.
See Stephenson, Charles H. (arr.).
Bold Stroke for a Husband, A. In *British Drama*, 12 vols., London: John Dicks, 1871, VIII, [33]-54.
Bold Stroke for a Husband, A. London: John Cumberland, n.d. Pp. [i-ii], [1]-[64]. Cumberland's British Theatre, XXXVI. *Filed under* Cumberland, John. Cumberland's British Theatre, XXXVI.
Which Is the Man? In [*Modern Theatre*, ed. Mrs. Inchbald, 10 vols., London: Longman, Hurst, Rees, Orme, & Brown, 1811, X], [149]-216.
Which Is the Man? London: Whittingham & Arliss, 1816. Pp. [1]-63. London Theatre, XXIII. *Filed under* Dibdin, Thomas John, ed. London Theatre, XXIII.
Which Is the Man? In *British Drama*, 12 vols., London: John Dicks, 1872, XI, [77]-96.
Who's the Dupe? In *New English Drama*, ed. W. Oxberry, 22 vols., London: W. Simpkin & R. Marshall; C. Chapple, 1821, XI, [i-vi], [1]-24. *Filed under* Oxberry, William Henry. New English Drama, XI.
Who's the Dupe? In *British Drama*, 12 vols., London: John Dicks, 1871, VI, [183]-192.

COX AND BOX
See Burnand, Francis Cowley.

COYNE, J. DENIS
Home Wreck, The.
See Coyne, Joseph Stirling.

COYNE, JOSEPH STIRLING
All for Love; or, The Lost Pleiad. London: Chapman & Hall, n.d. Pp. [1]-36.
Angel or Devil. London: Thomas Hailes Lacy, n.d. Pp. [1]-27. [Lacy's Acting Edition, 434].
Arajoon; or, The Conquest of Mysore. London: John Dicks, n.d. Pp. [1]-16. Dicks' Standard Plays, 700.
Awkward Arrival, An. New York & London: Samuel French, n.d. Pp. [1]-[30]. Minor Drama, 94.
Binks the Bagman. London: Thomas Hailes Lacy, n.d. Pp. [1]-19. Promptbook.
Black Sheep. London: Thomas Hailes Lacy, n.d. Pp. [1]-54. Promptbook.
Box and Cox Married and Settled. New York: Samuel French, n.d. Pp. [1]-20. Minor Drama, [49].
Broken-Hearted Club, The. Chicago: Dramatic Publishing Co., n.d. Pp. [1]-15. Sergel's Acting Drama, 25.

Buckstone at Home; or, The Manager and His Friends. London: Thomas Hailes Lacy, n.d. Pp. [1]-24. [Lacy's Acting Edition, 857].

Catching a Mermaid. London: Thomas Hailes Lacy, n.d. Pp. [1]-26. [Lacy's Acting Edition, 353].

Cockneys in California. New York: M. Douglas, n.d. Pp. [1]-19. Minor Drama, 33.

Dark Doings in the Cupboard. London: Thomas Hailes Lacy, n.d. Pp. [1]-18. [Lacy's Acting Edition].

Did You Ever Send Your Wife to Brooklyn? New York & Philadelphia: Turner & Fisher, n.d. Pp. [1]-18. Turner's Dramatic Library of Acting Plays.

Did You Ever Send Your Wife to Camberwell? London: Nassau Steam Press, n.d. Pp. [1]-16.

Duck Hunting. London: Thomas Hailes Lacy, n.d. Pp. [1]-19. [Lacy's Acting Edition, 833].

Duel in the Dark, A. London: Thomas Hailes Lacy, n.d. Pp. [1]-17. [Lacy's Acting Edition, 76].

Everybody's Friend. London: Thomas Hailes Lacy, n.d. Pp. [1]-54. Lacy's Acting Edition, 586.

Fraud and Its Victims. London: Thomas Hailes Lacy, n.d. Pp. [i-v], [1]-50.

Helen Oakleigh; or, The Wife's Stratagem! London: John Duncombe, n.d. Pp. [1]-32. [Duncombe's Acting Edition of the British Theatre, 334].

Home Wreck, The. Written with Coyne, J. Denis. London: Thomas Hailes Lacy, n.d. Pp. [1]-46. *Filed under* Coyne, Joseph Stirling.

Hope of the Family, The. London: Thomas Hailes Lacy, n.d. Pp. [1]-41. Promptbook.

How to Settle Accounts with Your Laundress. London: John Dicks, n.d. Pp. [11]-19. [Dicks' Standard Plays, 1006].

Leo the Terrible. Written with Talfourd, Francis. London: Thomas Hailes Lacy, n.d. Pp. [1-2], [i]-[iii], [4]-32. [Lacy's Acting Edition, 126]. *Filed under* Coyne, Joseph Stirling.

Little Rebel, The. New York: Robert M. DeWitt, n.d. Pp. [1]-19. DeWitt's Acting Plays, 32.

Lola Montes; or, A Countess for an Hour.
See Pas de Fascination.

Love Knot, The. Boston: William V. Spencer, n.d. Pp. [1]-39. Spencer's Boston Theatre, 163. Promptbook.

Man of Many Friends, The. London: Thomas Hailes Lacy, n.d. Pp. [1]-40.

Merchant and His Clerks, The. London: William Barth, n.d. Pp. [i]-vi, [7]-42.

Mrs. Bunbury's Spoons. London: National Acting Drama Office, n.d. <wrps. Webster>. Pp. [1]-20. Webster's Acting National Drama, 164.

My Friend the Capt. London: William Barth, n.d. Pp. [1]-21.

My Wife's Daughter. London: Hailes Lacy, n.d. Pp. [1]-34. [Lacy's Acting Edition, 29].

Nothing Venture, Nothing Win. London: Thomas Hailes Lacy, n.d. Pp. [1]-39. [Lacy's Acting Edition, 521].

Old Chateau, The; or, A Night of Peril. London: Thomas Hailes Lacy, n.d. Pp. [1]-[40]. [Lacy's Acting Edition, 223].

Ondine; or, The Water Spirit. London: John Dicks, n.d. Pp. [1]-12. Dicks' Standard Plays, 746.

Our National Defences; or, The Cockshot Yeomanry. London: National Acting Drama Office, n.d. Pp. [1]-23. [Acting National Drama].

Pas de Fascination; or, Catching a Governor. *Also:* Lola Montes; or, A Countess for an Hour. New York: Samuel French, n.d. Pp. [1]-19. French's Minor Drama, 270.

Pets of the Parterre, The; or, Love in a Garden. Music by Loder, George. London: Thomas Hailes Lacy, n.d. Pp. [1]-23. Text incomplete. [Lacy's Acting Edition].

Presented at Court. London: National Acting Drama Office, n.d. Pp. [1]-46.

Queen of the Abruzzi, The. London: Thomas Hailes Lacy, n.d. Pp. [3]-30. Cumberland's British Theatre (with Duncombe's).

Queer Subject, The. London: Chapman & Hall, n.d. Pp. [1]-13. [Acting National Drama].

Railway Bubbles. London: William Barth, n.d. Pp. [1]-22.

Richard III. London: William Barth, n.d. Pp. [1]-18.

Samuel in Search of Himself. Written with Coape, Henry Coe. London: Thomas Hailes Lacy, n.d. Pp. 1-21. Lacy's Acting Edition, 529.

Satanas and the Spirit of Beauty. London: Thomas Hailes Lacy, n.d. Pp. [1]-45, [46-51]. Last pages in manuscript. Promptbook.

Scene in the Life of an Unprotected Female, A. *Also:* An Unprotected Female. New York: Samuel French, n.d. Pp. [1]-14. French's Minor Drama, 233.

Secret Agent, The. London: Thomas Hailes Lacy, n.d. Pp. [1]-40. Lacy's Acting Edition, 259.

Separate Maintenance. London: Duncombe & Moon, n.d. <wrps. Thomas Hailes Lacy>. Pp. [1]-23. Duncombe's Edition <wrps. New British Theatre (late Duncombe's), 506>. Promptbook.

Signal, The. London & New York: Samuel French, n.d. Pp. [3]-40. [Lacy's Acting Edition].

Spirit of the Fountain, The. London: William Barth (printer), n.d. Pp. [1]-23. Title page mutilated.

Terrible Secret, A. London: Thomas Hailes Lacy, n.d. Pp. [1]-19. [Lacy's Acting Edition, 782].

That Affair at Finchley. London: Thomas Hailes Lacy, n.d. Pp. [1]-20. [Lacy's Acting Edition, 775].

This House to Be Sold (The Property of the Late William Shakspeare)— Inquire Within. London: National Acting Drama Office, n.d. Pp. [1]-16.

Tipperary Legacy, The. Written with Hamilton, Henry. New York: Harold Roorbach, n.d. Pp. [i]-iv, [5]-18. Acting Drama, 7.

Trumpeter's Daughter, The. New York: Samuel French, n.d. Pp. [1]-17. French's Minor Drama, 276.

Unprotected Female, A.
See Scene in the Life of an Unprotected Female, A.

Urgent Private Affairs. London: Thomas Hailes Lacy, n.d. Pp. [1]-23. [Lacy's Acting Edition, 360].

Valsha; or, The Slave Queen. London: Chapman & Hall, n.d. Pp. [1]-36. Promptbook.

Vicar of Wakefield, The; or, The Pastor's Fireside. London: National Acting Drama Office, n.d. Pp. [1]-36.

Wanted, 1000 Spirited Young Milliners for the Gold Diggings! New York: O. A. Roorbach, jr, n.d. Pp. [1]-22.

Water Witches, The. London: Thomas Hailes Lacy, n.d. Pp. [1]-23. [Lacy's Acting Edition, 613].

What Will They Say at Brompton? London: Thomas Hailes Lacy, n.d. Pp. [1]-28. [Lacy's Acting Edition, 499].

Widow Hunt, A. New York: Robert M. DeWitt, n.d. <wrps. H. L. Hinton>. Pp. [1]-38.

Willikind and Hys Dinah. London: Thomas Hailes Lacy, n.d. Pp. [1]-25. [Lacy's Acting Edition, 197].

Woman in Red, The. Chicago: Dramatic Publishing Co., n.d. Pp. [1]-38. Sergel's Acting Drama, 136.

Woman of the World, The. London: Thomas Hailes Lacy, n.d. Pp. [1]-51.

Women's Club, The. New York: Happy Hours, n.d. Pp. [1]-19.

COZY COUPLE, A
See Lawrence, Slingsby.

CRACKANTHORPE, BLANCHE ALETHEA ELIZABETH HOLT, MRS. HUBERT MONTAGUE
Other People's Shoes. In *Dialogues of the Day*, ed. Oswald Crawfurd, London: Chapman & Hall, n.d., pp. [228]-240. *Filed under* Crawfurd, Oswald. Dialogues of the Day.

CRACKED HEADS
See Clements, Arthur.

CRACKER BON-BON FOR CHRISTMAS PARTIES
See Brough, Robert Barnabas. King Alfred and the Cakes, etc.

CRADOCK, JOSEPH
Czar, The. London: John Nichols & Son (printer) (priv.), 1824. Pp. [i]-xii, [1]-75.

CRAIG, J. H. (pseud.)
See Hogg, James.

CRAIGIE, PEARL MARY TERESA RICHARDS, MRS. REGINALD WALPOLE
    See Hobbes, John Oliver.
CRAMOND BRIG
    See Murray, William Henry Wood.
CRAVEN, HENRY THORNTON
    Blechington House; or, The Surrender! London: John Duncombe, n.d. <wrps. Thomas Hailes Lacy>. Pp. [1]-43. New British Theatre (late Duncombe's), 447.
    Bowl'd Out; or, A Bit of Brummagem. London: Thomas Hailes Lacy, n.d. Pp. [1]-21.
    Card Case, The. 17 leaves. Manuscript.
    Chimney Corner, The. London: Thomas Hailes Lacy, n.d. Pp. [1]-36. Promptbook.
    Coals of Fire. London: Thomas Hailes Lacy, n.d. Pp. [1]-61. [Lacy's Acting Edition].
    Done Brown. London: Thomas Hailes Lacy, n.d. Pp. [1]-20. [Lacy's Acting Edition, 1210].
    Fellow Servants; or, The Tiger Crossed in Love! London: John Duncombe, n.d. <wrps. Thomas Hailes Lacy>. Pp. [1]-33. Duncombe's Edition <wrps. New British Theatre (late Duncombe's), 455>.
    Little Nun, The; or, A Bit of Scandal! London: John Duncombe, n.d. Pp. [1]-26. [Duncombe's Edition]. Promptbook.
    Meg's Diversion. London: Thomas Hailes Lacy, n.d. Pp. [1]-54. Promptbook.
    Milky White. London: Thomas Hailes Lacy, n.d. Pp. [1]-44.
    Miriam's Crime. London: Thomas Hailes Lacy, n.d. Pp. [1]-39. Promptbook.
    My Daughter's Debut. Music by Nelson, S. London & New York: Samuel French, n.d. Pp. [1]-20. [Lacy's Acting Edition].
    My Preserver. London: Thomas Hailes Lacy, n.d. Pp. [1]-26. [Lacy's Acting Edition, 851].
    Not to Be Done. London & New York: Samuel French, n.d. Pp. [3]-26.
    One Tree Hill. London: Thomas Hailes Lacy, n.d. Pp. [1]-47. [Lacy's Acting Edition, 987].
    Our Nelly. London & New York: Samuel French, n.d. Pp. [1]-[40]. [Lacy's Acting Edition].
    Philomel. New York: Robert M. DeWitt, n.d. Pp. [1]-41. DeWitt's Acting Plays, 293.
    Post-Boy, The. London: Thomas Hailes Lacy, n.d. Pp. [1]-32. [Lacy's Acting Edition, 720].
    Tom Smart, the Adventurer! London: Duncombe & Moon, n.d. <wrps. John Duncombe>. Pp. [3]-55. Duncombe's Acting Edition of the British Theatre, 479.
    Unlucky Friday. London: Thomas Hailes Lacy, n.d. Pp. [1]-27. [Lacy's Acting Edition].
    Village Nightingale, The. Music by Nelson, S. London & New York: Samuel French, n.d. Pp. [1]-30. [Lacy's Acting Edition].
CRAVEN, TOM
    Workbox, The. London & New York: Samuel French, c.1904. Pp. [1]-16. [Lacy's Acting Edition].
CRAWFURD, OSWALD
    Election Idyl, An. In *Dialogues of the Day,* ed. Oswald Crawfurd, London: Chapman & Hall, n.d., pp. [56]-65. *Filed under* Dialogues of the Day.
    Modern Lydia, A. In *Dialogues of the Day,* ed. Oswald Crawfurd, London: Chapman & Hall, n.d., pp. [184]-190. *Filed under* Dialogues of the Day.
CRAWLEY, RICHARD
    Younger Brother, The. London: Hardwicke & Bogue, 1878. Pp. [i]-x, [1]-198.
CRAZED
    See Phillips, Alfred R.
CRAZY JANE
    See Somerset, Charles A.
CREATURES OF IMPULSE
    See Gilbert, William Schwenck.
CREOLE, THE
    See Brooks, Charles William Shirley.

CRESSWELL, HENRY
    In Danger.
    See Lestocq, William.
CRESWICK, WILLIAM (arr.)
    Macbeth, King of Scotland. By Shakespeare, William. London (Sydenham): Crystal Palace Co., 1874. Pp. [1]-64.
CREYKE, WALTER P.
    All Is Fair in Love and War (attrib. to Creyke). York: Sampson, 1868. Pp. [i-vi], [1]-58.
    Maxime. Dublin: Hodges, Smith, 1864. Pp. [i-viii], [1]-100.
CRICKET ON THE HEARTH, THE
    See Smith, Albert Richard.
    See Stirling, Edward.
    See Townsend, William Thompson.
CRIME AT THE SYMON'S YAT
    See Lewis, Alexis. Grace Clairville.
CRIMELESS CRIMINAL, A
    See Becher, Martin.
CRIMSON ROCK!
    See Cross, Julian.
    See Cross, Julian. Darkest London.
CRIMSON SCARF, THE
    See Farnie, Henry Brougham.
CRINOLINE
    See Brough, Robert Barnabas.
CRISIS, THE
    See Albery, James.
CRITCHETT, RICHARD CLAUDE
    See Carton, R. C.
CRITIC, THE
    See Sheridan, Richard Brinsley.
CRITICAL HOUR
    See Beazley, Samuel, jr. Fire and Water.
CRITIQUE DE L'ÉCOLE DES FEMMES
    See Van Laun, Henri (trans.). School for Wives Criticised, The.
CROCK OF GOLD!, THE
    See Fitzball, Edward.
CROCKERY'S MISFORTUNES
    See Ebsworth, Joseph.
CROESUS, KING OF LYDIA
    See Richards, Alfred Bate.
CROKER, THOMAS CROFTON
    Daniel O'Rourke; or, Rhymes of a Pantomime. *Also:* Harlequin from Killarney. London: Ainsworth, 1828. Pp. [1]-30. 2nd ed. Libretto. *Filed under* Daniel O'Rourke (anon.).
    Harlequin from Killarney.
    See Daniel O'Rourke.
CROKER, THOMAS FRANCIS DILLON
    Romulus and Remus; or, Rome Was Not Built in a Day. N.p.: n.pub. (priv.), 1859. Pp. [1]-49.
CROLY, GEORGE, REV.
    Catiline. London: Hurst, Robinson, 1822. Pp. [i]-xvi, [1]-177.
    Pride Shall Have a Fall. London: Hurst, Robinson, 1824. Pp. [i-viii], [1]-115.
    Pride Shall Have a Fall. London: Hurst, Robinson, 1824. Pp. [i-x], [1]-115. 2nd ed. *Filed under* Soane, George.
    Pride Shall Have a Fall. London: Hurst, Robinson, 1824. Pp. [i-viii], [1]-115. Promptbook. *Filed under* Soane, George.
CROMPTON, WILLIAM
    Old Woman Who Lived in a Shoe, The; or, Harlequin Child of Childwall and the Choice Spirits of Dingle Dell! Music by Broadhurst. Liverpool: Thomas S. McGhie (printer), 1861. Pp. [1-23]. Libretto.
CROMWELL, THOMAS KITSON
    Druid, The. London: Sherwood, Gilbert, & Piper, 1832. Pp. [i]-[xvi], [1]-142.
CROMWELL
    See Calmour, Alfred Cecil.
    See Duckworth, William.
    See Leigh, James Mathews.
    See Richards, Alfred Bate.

CROSLAND, CAMILLA DUFOUR TOULMIN, MRS. NEWTON (trans.)

Hernani. By Hugo, Victor. In *Dramatic Works of Victor Hugo,* trans. Frederick L. Slous and Mrs. Newton Crosland, New York: P. F. Coller, n.d., V, [i], 15-148.

Ruy Blas. By Hugo, Victor. In *Dramatic Works of Victor Hugo,* trans. Frederick L. Slous and Mrs. Newton Crosland, New York: P. F. Coller, n.d., V, 257-398.

CROSS, JAMES C. (arr.)

Macbeth. By Shakespeare, William. London: Stevens; W. Kemmish, n.d. Pp. [1]-22.

CROSS, JOHN C.

Purse, The; or, The Benevolent Tar. In *British Drama,* 12 vols., London: John Dicks, 1872, XI, [27]-32.

CROSS, JULIAN

Crimson Rock!, The. *Also:* Darkest London. 35 leaves. Manuscript promptbook.

Darkest London. *Also:* The Crimson Rock!. 61 leaves. Manuscript promptbook.

Floating a Company. London: Samuel French; New York: T. Henry French, n.d. Pp. [1]-14. [Lacy's Acting Edition].

Miser, A. London & New York: Samuel French, n.d. Pp. [1]-16. [French's Acting Edition].

CROSS OF SORROW, THE

See Akerman, William.

CROSS OF ST. JOHN, THE

See Lucas, William James.

CROSS ON THE BOOT

See Coates, Alfred. Snowdrift, The.

CROSS PURPOSES

See Farnie, Henry Brougham.

See O'Brien, William.

CROSS QUESTIONS AND CROOKED ANSWERS

See Bell, Frances.

CROSS ROADS OF LIFE!

See Moncrieff, William Thomas. Scamps of London, The.

CROSS STRATAGEMS

See Clowes, William Laird.

CROSS-BOW LETTER

See Wilks, Thomas Egerton. Miller of Whetstone, The.

CROSSED LOVE

See Wolverson, Harry.

CROSSING SWEEPER, THE

See Bell, Florence Eveleen Eleanore Oliffe, Mrs. Hugh (Lady).

CROSSING THE LINE

See Almar, George.

CROWDED HOUSES!

See Almar, George. Crossing the Line.

CROWE, CATHERINE STEVENS, MRS. JOHN

Aristodemus. Edinburgh: William Tait, 1838. Pp. [1]-98.

Cruel Kindness, The. London: George Routledge, 1853. Pp. [i-vi], [1]-64.

CROWLEY, EDWARD ALEISTER

Jephthah. In *Jephthah and Other Mysteries,* London: Kegan Paul, Trench, Trubner, 1899, pp. [i], [1]-71.

Poem, The. In *Jephthah and Other Mysteries,* London: Kegan Paul, Trench, Trubner, 1899, pp. [i], [99]-118.

CROWN BRILLIANTS, THE

See Long, Charles (trans.).

CROWN DIAMONDS, THE

See Fitzball, Edward.

See Reynoldson, Thomas Herbert.

CROWN JEWELS

See Fitzball, Edward.

See Pocock, Isaac. Nigel.

CROWN PRINCE, THE

See Wilks, Thomas Egerton.

CROWQUILL, ALFRED (pseud. of Forrester, Alfred Henry)

Moon Queen and King Night, The; or, Harlequin Twilight. Music by Jolly. London: John K. Chapman, n.d. Pp. [1]-16. Libretto. *Filed under* Forrester, Alfred Henry.

CRUEL KINDNESS, THE

See Crowe, Catherine Stevens, Mrs. John.

CRUEL TO BE KIND

See Williams, Thomas John.

CRUMPLED ROSE LEAF, A

See Broughton, F. C.

CRUSADERS

See Bunn, Alfred.

See Burges, James Bland.

See Hemans, Felicia Dorothea Browne, Mrs. Alfred. De Chatillon.

See Jones, Henry Arthur.

CRYSTAL-GAZER, THE

See Montague, Leopold.

CRYSTAL HUNTER OF MONT BLANC, THE

See Clarke, Charles Augustus.

CUBITT, SYDNEY

Competitors, The; or, The Nymph of Nozenaro. Music by Hackwood, Thomas. Stroud: John White, n.d. Pp. [1]-51. Libretto.

Zanone; or, The Dey and the Knight. Music by Hackwood, Thomas. Stroud: John White (printer), n.d. Pp. [1]-46.

CUCKOO, THE

See Brookfield, Charles Hallam Elton.

CUFFS AND KISSES

See Archer, Thomas.

CULLERNE, EDWARD

Dreadfully Alarming.

See Edwardes, Conway Theodore Marriott.

Only Somebody.

See Edwardes, Conway Theodore Marriott.

CULPRIT, THE

See Bayly, Thomas Haynes.

CUMBERLAND, RICHARD

Alcanor. In *Posthumous Dramatick Works,* 2 vols., London: G. & W. Nicol, 1813, II, [i-iv], [1]-60. *Filed under* Collected Works.

Box-Lobby Challenge, The. In *Modern Theatre,* ed. Mrs. Inchbald, 10 vols., London: Longman, Hurst, Rees, Orme, & Brown, 1811, V, [137]-213.

Brothers, The. London: Whittingham & Arliss, 1814. Pp. [1]-64. London Theatre, IV. *Filed under* Dibdin, Thomas John, ed. London Theatre, IV.

Brothers, The. In *British Drama,* 12 vols., London: John Dicks, 1871, VII, [257]-276.

Carmelite, The. In *Modern Theatre,* ed. Mrs. Inchbald, 10 vols., London: Longman, Hurst, Rees, Orme, & Brown, 1811, V, [283]-336.

Carmelite, The. In *British Drama,* 12 vols., London: John Dicks, 1872, X, [17]-32.

Confession, The. In *Posthumous Dramatick Works,* 2 vols., London: G. & W. Nicol, 1813, I, [155]-225. *Filed under* Collected Works.

Death and Victory of Lord Viscount Nelson, The. Music by King, P.; Braham. London: Lackington, Allen, n.d. Pp. [1]-7.

Don Pedro. In *Posthumous Dramatick Works,* 2 vols., London: G. & W. Nicol, 1813, II, [273]-343. *Filed under* Collected Works.

Eccentric Lover, The. In *Posthumous Dramatick Works,* 2 vols., London: G. & W. Nicol, 1813, II, [61]-129. *Filed under* Collected Works.

False Demetrius, The. In *Posthumous Dramatick Works,* 2 vols., London: G. & W. Nicol, 1813, II, [345]-400. *Filed under* Collected Works.

False Impressions. In *Modern Theatre,* ed. Mrs. Inchbald, 10 vols., London: Longman, Hurst, Rees, Orme, & Brown, 1811, V, [i-ii], [1]-68.

Fashionable Lover, The. London: Whittingham & Arliss, 1814. Pp. [1]-68. London Theatre, VII. *Filed under* Dibdin, Thomas John, ed. London Theatre, VII.

Fashionable Lover, The. In *British Drama,* 12 vols., London: John Dicks, 1871, IX, [193]-214.

First Love. In *British Drama,* 12 vols., London: John Dicks, 1872, XII, [161]-180.

Hint to Husbands, A. London: Lackington, Allen, 1806. Pp. [i]-[x], [1]-99.

Impostors, The. In *Modern Theatre*, ed. Mrs. Inchbald, 10 vols., London: Longman, Hurst, Rees, Orme, & Brown, 1811, VI, [i-ii], [1]-73. *Filed under* Imposter.

Jew, The. In *British Drama*, 12 vols., London: John Dicks, 1871, VIII, [206]-224.

Jew, The. London: John Cumberland, n.d. Pp. [1]-48. Cumberland's British Theatre, XXXVIII. *Filed under* Cumberland, John. Cumberland's British Theatre, XXXVIII.

Jew of Mogadore, The. London: Samuel Tipper, 1808. Pp. [i-iv], [1]-76.

Joanna of Montfaucon. London: Lackington, Allen, 1800. Pp. [i]-[xvi], [1]-88. 2nd ed.

Last of the Family, The. In *Posthumous Dramatick Works*, 2 vols., London: G. & W. Nicol, 1813, II, [195]-271. *Filed under* Collected Works.

Lovers' Resolutions. In *Posthumous Dramatick Works*, 2 vols., London: G. & W. Nicol, 1813, I, [373]-444. *Filed under* Collected Works.

Mysterious Husband, The. In *Modern Theatre*, ed. Mrs. Inchbald, 10 vols., London: Longman, Hurst, Rees, Orme, & Brown, 1811, V, [69]-136.

Mysterious Husband, The. In *British Drama*, 12 vols., London: John Dicks, 1871, VIII, [129]-148.

Natural Son, The. In *Modern Theatre*, ed. Mrs. Inchbald, 10 vols., London: Longman, Hurst, Rees, Orme, & Brown, 1811, V, [215]-281.

Passive Husband, The. In *Posthumous Dramatick Works*, 2 vols., London: G. & W. Nicol, 1813, I, [227]-301. *Filed under* Collected Works.

Sailor's Daughter, The. London: Lackington, Allen, 1804. Pp. [i-viii], [1]-[87]. 2nd ed.

Sybil, The; or, The Elder Brutus. In *Posthumous Dramatick Works*, 2 vols., London: G. & W. Nicol, 1813, I, [1], [i]-viii, [1]-70. *Filed under* Collected Works.

Tiberius in Capreae. In *Posthumous Dramatick Works*, 2 vols., London: G. & W. Nicol, 1813, II, [131]-193. *Filed under* Collected Works.

Torrendal. In *Posthumous Dramatick Works*, 2 vols., London: G. & W. Nicol, 1813, I, [303]-371. *Filed under* Collected Works.

Walloons, The. In *Posthumous Dramatick Works*, 2 vols., London: G. & W. Nicol, 1813, I, [71]-154. *Filed under* Collected Works.

West Indian, The. London: Whittingham & Arliss, 1814. Pp. [1]-80. London Theatre, II. *Filed under* Dibdin, Thomas John, ed. London Theatre, II.

West Indian, The. In *New English Drama*, ed. W. Oxberry, 22 vols., London: W. Simpkin & R. Marshall; C. Chapple, 1818, I, [1-2], [i]-[vi], [1]-[80]. *Filed under* Oxberry, William Henry. New English Drama, I.

West Indian, The. London: T. Dolby, 1823. Pp. [i]-[vi], [1-2], [7]-[79]. Dolby's British Theatre, II. *Filed under* Cumberland, John. Cumberland's British Theatre, II.

West Indian, The. In *British Drama*, 12 vols., London: John Dicks, 1871, VI, [193]-218.

Wheel of Fortune, The. In *New English Drama*, ed. W. Oxberry, 22 vols., London: W. Simpkin & R. Marshall; C. Chapple, 1820, XXII, [1-2], [i]-[x], [1]-60. *Filed under* Oxberry, William Henry. New English Drama, XXII.

Wheel of Fortune, The. London: John Cumberland, 1826. Pp. [1]-66. Cumberland's British Theatre, XIV. *Filed under* Cumberland, John. Cumberland's British Theatre, XIV.

Wheel of Fortune, The. In *British Drama*, 12 vols., London: John Dicks, 1871, V, [167]-186.

CUNIGUNDA'S VOW
  See Mitford, Mary Russell.

CUNNINGHAM, ALLAN
  Sir Marmaduke Maxwell. London: Taylor & Hessey, 1822. Pp. [i]-[x], [1]-135.

CUP, THE
  See Tennyson, Alfred, Lord.

CUP OF COLD PISEN
  See Bruton, James. Vilikens and His Dinah.

CUP OF COLD POISON
  See Halliday, Andrew. Romeo and Juliet.

CUP OF TEA, A (anon. trans.)
  By Nuitter, Charles; Derley, J. New York: Robert M. DeWitt, n.d. Pp. [1]-17. DeWitt's Acting Plays, 52. *Filed under* Nuitter, Charles; Derley, J.

CUP OF TEA, A (anon.)
  New York: Wheat & Cornett, c.1878. Pp. [19]-26. New York Drama, III, 36. *Filed under* Derley, J.

CUP OF TEA, A (anon.)
  London & New York: Samuel French, n.d. Pp. [1]-24.

CUP OF WATER, THE
  See Field, Michael.

CUPBOARD LOVE
  See Hay, Frederic.

CUPID
  See Graves, Joseph.

CUPID AND PSYCHE
  See Burnand, Francis Cowley.

CUPID IN ERMINE
  See Lancaster-Wallis, Ellen.

CUPID IN LONDON
  See Rede, William Leman.

CUPID IN WAITING
  See Jerrold, William Blanchard.

CUPID'S CONSPIRATOR!
  See Marston, John Westland.

CUPID'S MESSENGER
  See Calmour, Alfred Cecil.

CUPS AND SAUCERS
  See Grossmith, George, jr.

CURATE'S DAUGHTER
  See Haines, John Thomas. Life of a Woman, The.

CURE FOR COQUETTES
  See Boucicault, Dionysius Lardner. Alma Mater.

CURE FOR COXCOMBS, A (anon.)
  Music by Watson. London: John Lowndes, 1821. Pp. [i-vi], [1]-28.

CURE FOR LOVE, A
  See Parry, Thomas.

CURE FOR ROMANCE, A
  See Thomson, James.

CURE FOR THE FIDGETS, A
  See Williams, Thomas John.

CURE FOR THE GOUT
  See Maclaren, Archibald. Paddy Bull.

CURE FOR THE HEARTACHE, A
  See Morton, Thomas, sr.

CURFEW, THE
  See Tobin, John.

CURIOSITIES OF LITERATURE
  See Boucicault, Dionysius Lardner.

CURIOSITY
  See Lathom, Francis.

CURIOUS CASE, A
  See Reynoldson, Thomas Herbert.

CURIOUS MISHAP, A
  See Zimmern, Helen (trans.?).

CURLING, HENRY
  Merry Wags of Warwickshire, The; or, The Early Days of Shakspere. *Also:* William Shakspere; or, The Merry Wags of Warwickshire. London: George Wright, 1854. Pp. [i-vi], [1]-81.
  William Shakspere.
    See Merry Wags of Warwickshire.

CURRIE, MARY MONTGOMERIE LAMB, LADY
  See Fane, Violet (pseud.).

CURSE OF MAMMON, THE
  See Reynoldson, Thomas Herbert.

CURSE OF PONTIGNAC, THE
  See Coghill, John Jocelyn, Sir.

CURSE OF ST. VALLIER
  See Slous, Frederick L. (trans.). Francis the First.

CURSED AND THE CAUSE, THE
  See France, C. V. Magician's Daughter, The.

CUSTOM OF DUNMOW
    See Dibdin, Charles Isaac Mungo, jr. Flitch, The.
CUSTOM'S FALLACY
    See Grant, James M.
CUT FOR PARTNERS!
    See Bruton, James.
CUT OFF WITH A SHILLING
    See Smith, Spencer Theyre.
CYMBELINE
    See Irving, Henry (arr.).
    See Kemble, John Philip (arr.).
    See Shakespeare, William.
CYMBIA
    See Paulton, Harry.
CYMON
    See Garrick, David.
CYMON AND IPHIGENIA
    See Planché, James Robinson.
CYRIL'S SUCCESS
    See Byron, Henry James.
CZAR, THE
    See Cradock, Joseph.

DABBS, GEORGE HENRY ROQUE
    Dante. Written with Righton, Edward. London: Macmillan, 1893. Pp. [1]-42.

DACRE, BARBARINA OGLE, LADY (later Mrs. Thomas Wilmot; Baroness Brand)
    Gonsalvo of Cordova. In *Dramas, Translations, and Occasional Poems*, 2 vols., London: John Murray, 1821, I, [i]-[x], [1]-87. *Filed under* Dramas.
    Ina. In *Dramas, Translations, and Occasional Poems*, 2 vols., London: John Murray, 1821, II, [i]-vi, [1]-114. *Filed under* Dramas.
    Ina. By Mrs. Wilmot. London: John Murray, 1815. Pp. [i-viii], [1]-[71]. 2nd ed.
    Pedrarias. In *Dramas, Translations, and Occasional Poems*, 2 vols., London: John Murray, 1821, I, [89]-204. *Filed under* Dramas.
    Xarifa. In *Dramas, Translations, and Occasional Poems*, 2 vols., London: John Murray, 1821, II, [115]-218. *Filed under* Dramas.

DACRE OF THE SOUTH
    See Gore, Catherine Grace Frances Moody, Mrs. Charles.
DADDY GRAY
    See Halliday, Andrew.
DADDY HARDACRE
    See Simpson, John Palgrave.
DADDY O'DOWD
    See Boucicault, Dionysius Lardner.
DAGGER AND THE CROSS, THE
    See Tremayne, W. A.
DAISY
    See Palmer, F. Grove.
DAISY FARM
    See Byron, Henry James.
DALE, FELIX (pseud.)
    See Merivale, Herman Charles.

DALLAS, ROBERT CHARLES
    Adrastus. In *Adrastus, a Tragedy . . . and other Poems*, London: James Cawthorn, 1823, pp. [iii]-[xviii], [1]-94.
    Lucretia. London: R. Ryan; J. Miller; W. & J. Lowndes, 1818. Pp. [1], [i]-viii, [1]-57. *Filed under* Lucretia (anon.).
    Not at Home. London: B. Crosby, 1809. Pp. [i]-[x], [1]-40.

DALRYMPLE, J. S.
    Lurline; or, The Revolt of the Naiades. London: John Cumberland, n.d. Pp. [1]-38. Cumberland's Minor Theatre, IX. *Filed under* Cumberland, John. Cumberland's Minor Theatre, IX.
    Lurline; or, The Revolt of the Naiades. *Also:* The Naiad Queen. London: John Cumberland, n.d. Pp. [1]-38. [Cumberland's Minor Theatre].
    Naiad Queen, The; or, The Revolt of the Naiads. *Also:* Lurline. Boston: William V. Spencer, n.d. Pp. [1]-27. Spencer's Boston Theatre, 140.

DALY, JOHN (pseud. of Besemeres, John)
    Broken Toys. London: Thomas Hailes Lacy, n.d. Pp. [1]-36. [Lacy's Acting Edition]. *Filed under* Besemeres, John.
    Married Daughters and Young Husbands. London: Thomas Hailes Lacy, n.d. Pp. [1]-39. Lacy's Acting Edition. *Filed under* Besemeres, John.
    Times, The. London: Thomas Hailes Lacy, n.d. Pp. [1]-52. [Lacy's Acting Edition]. *Filed under* Besemeres, John.

DAM, HENRY JACKSON WELLS
    Shop Girl, The. Written with Ross, Adrian (pseud. of Ropes, Arthur Reed). Music by Caryll, Ivan; Monckton, Lionel. London: Hopwood Crew, n.d. Pp. [i-iv], 1-106, 111-205. Text complete. Vocal score.
    Shop Girl, The. Written with Ross, Adrian (pseud. of Ropes, Arthur Reed). Music by Caryll, Ivan; Monckton, Lionel. London: Hopwood & Crew, n.d. Pp. [i-iv], 1-196. Vocal score.

DAME DE CHALLANT
    See Lyster, Frederic (trans.). Lady of Challant, The.
DAME DE ST. TROPEZ!, LA
    See Barber, James.
DAME DURDEN AND HER FIVE SERVANT MAIDS
    See Douglass, John T.
DAME TROT AND HER COMICAL CAT
    See Lee, Nelson, sr. Harlequin Blackbeard.
DAME TROT AND HER COMICAL CAT, AND THE OGRE FEE-FO-FUM
    See Blanchard, Edward Litt Leman. Puss in Boots.
DAMON
    See Bell, Ernest (trans.).
DAMON AND PYTHIAS
    See Banim, John.
    See Buckstone, John Baldwin.
DAMON THE DAUNTLESS AND PHILLIS THE FAIR
    See Dryden, Charles.
DAMP BEDS!
    See Parry, Thomas.

DANCE, CHARLES
    Advice Gratis. London: Chapman & Hall, n.d. Pp. [1]-23.
    Alive and Merry. London: John Duncombe, n.d. Pp. [1]-40. Duncombe's Edition.
    Bengal Tiger, The. London: Chapman & Hall, 1838. Pp. [1]-24. Promptbook.
    Beulah Spa, The. London: John Miller, 1833. Pp. [i-iv], [1]-56.
    Burlington Arcade, The. London: Chapman & Hall, n.d. Pp. [1]-24.
    Close Siege, A. By George Dance. London: John Duncombe, n.d. Pp. [1]-24. Duncombe's Edition. *Filed under* Dance, George.
    Close Siege, A. By George Dance. London: John Dicks, n.d. Pp. [1]-10. Dicks' Standard Plays, 709. *Filed under* Dance, George.
    Country Squire, The; or, Two Days at the Hall. London: Chapman & Hall, n.d. Pp. [1]-45.
    Deep Deep Sea, The.
        See Planché, James Robinson.
    Delicate Ground; or, Paris in 1793. London: S. G. Fairbrother, n.d. Pp. [1]-31.
    Dream of the Future, A. London: S. G. Fairbrother, 1853. Pp. [1]-32.
    Dream of the Future, A. London: Thomas Hailes Lacy, n.d. Pp. [1]-35. [Lacy's Acting Edition, 312].
    Dustman's Belle, The. London: S. G. Fairbrother, n.d. Pp. [1]-44.
    Enchanted Forest, The; or, The Bear! the Eagle! and the Dolphin! London: S. G. Fairbrother; W. Strange, 1847. Pp. [1]-44.
    Hasty Conclusions. By George Dance. London: W. Barth, n.d. Pp. [1]-28.
    High, Low, Jack, and the Game.
        See Planché, James Robinson.
    Hush Money. By George Dance. London: John Duncombe, n.d. Pp. [1]-[34]. Duncombe's Edition.

Izaak Walton. London: Chapman & Hall, n.d. Pp. [ii]-vi, [7]-42. Webster's Acting National Drama, 75.

Kill or Cure. New York & London: Samuel French, n.d. Pp. [3]-29. Minor Drama, 48.

Lucky Stars; or, The Cobbler of Cripplegate! By George Dance. London: John Duncombe, n.d. Pp. [1]-20. Duncombe's Edition. *Filed under* Dance, George.

Lucky Stars; or, The Cobbler of Cripplegate! By George Dance. London: Thomas Hailes Lacy, n.d. Pp. [1]-20. [Lacy's Acting Edition].

Magic Horn, The. Music by Lee, Alexander. London: William Grogan, n.d. Pp. [1]-36.

Marriage a Lottery. New York: DeWitt, n.d. Pp. [1]-27. DeWitt's Acting Plays, 249.

Match in the Dark, A. London: John Miller, 1836. Pp. [i-iv], [1]-31.

Morning Call, A. London & New York: Samuel French, n.d. Pp. [1]-24. [Lacy's Acting Edition, 316].

Morning Call, A. London: S. G. Fairbrother, n.d. Pp. [1]-22.

Morning Call, A. London & New York: Samuel French, n.d. Pp. [1]-24. Minor Drama, 57.

My Lord Is Not My Lord. By George Dance. London: John Duncombe, n.d. Pp. [1]-30. Duncombe's Edition. *Filed under* Dance, George.

Naval Engagements. London: Chapman & Hall, n.d. Pp. [1]-35. Promptbook.

Olympic Devils.
    See Planché, James Robinson.

Olympic Revels.
    See Planché, James Robinson.

Paphian Bower, The.
    See Planché, James Robinson.

Petticoat Government. By George Dance. London: John Dicks, n.d. Pp. [1]-10. Dicks' Standard Plays, 750. *Filed under* Dance, George.

Petticoat Government. By George Dance. London & New York: Samuel French, n.d. Pp. [1]-21. Promptbook.

Pleasant Dreams. London: John Miller, 1834. Pp. [1]-43.

Puss in Boots.
    See Planché, James Robinson.

Riquet with the Tuft.
    See Planché, James Robinson.

Sons and Systems. London: Chapman & Hall, n.d. Pp. [1]-36. [Webster's Acting National Drama, 58].

Station House!, The. By George Dance. London: John Duncombe, n.d. Pp. [4]-26. Text complete. Duncombe's Edition.

Stock Exchange, The; or, The Green Business. London: Thomas Hailes Lacy, n.d. Pp. [1]-32.

Telemachus.
    See Planché, James Robinson.

Two B'hoys, The; or, The Beulah Spa. New York: Samuel French, n.d. Pp. [1]-28. French's Minor Drama, 288.

Victor Vanquished, The. New York & London: Samuel French, n.d. Pp. [1]-20.

Water Party, The. London: John Miller, 1836. Pp. [i-vi], [1]-36.

Who Speaks First? London: S. G. Fairbrother; W. Strange, n.d. Pp. [1]-24.

Wonderful Woman, A. London: S. G. Fairbrother, n.d. Pp. [1]-40.

DANCE, GEORGE
    See also Dance, Charles.

Chinese Honeymoon, A. Music by Talbot, Howard. London: Hopwood & Crew, c.1901. Pp. [i-iv], 1-163. Vocal score.

Gay Grizette, The. Music by Kiefert, C. Pp. [i], [1]-74. Act I only. Typescript.

Gay Parisienne, The. Music by Caryll, Ivan. London: Chappell, 1896. Pp. [i-vi], [1]-91, [1-3]. Vocal score.

Girl from Paris, The. Pp. [i-ii], [1]-15. Side for one character. Typescript.

Lord Tom Noddy. Music by Carr, F. Osmond. London: E. Ascherberg, c.1896. Pp. [1]-32. Libretto.

Ma Mie Rosette. Music by Lacome, Paul; Caryll, Ivan. London & New York: Boosey, c.1892. Pp. [i-iv], [1]-187. Vocal score.

Nautch Girl, The; or, The Rajah of Chutneypore. Written with Desprez, Frank. Music by Solomon, Edward. London: Chappell, c.1891. Pp. [1-4], i-vi, [1]-187. Vocal score.

DANCE OF THE SHIRT!, THE
    See Morton, Thomas, jr.

DANCING BARBER, THE
    See Selby, Charles.

DANCING DERVISH
    See Peile, F. Kinsey.

DANCING FOR THE MILLION!
    See Barnett, Charles Zachary. Polka, La.

DANCING GIRL, THE
    See Jones, Henry Arthur.

DANCING MAD
    See Oxberry, William Henry. Grizelle.

DANDELION'S DODGES
    See Williams, Thomas John.

DANDOLO
    See Stirling, Edward.

DANDY DAN, THE LIFEGUARDSMAN
    See Hood, Basil Charles Willett.

DANDY DICK
    See Pinero, Arthur Wing.

DANDY DICK WHITTINGTON
    See Sims, George Robert.

DANDY FIFTH, THE
    See Sims, George Robert.

DANESBURY HOUSE
    See Moulds, Arthur.

DANGEROUS CURIOSITY AND JUSTIFIABLE HOMICIDE
    See Gower, Francis Leveson, Lord. Bluebeard.

DANGEROUS EXPERIMENT, A
    See Paull, Harry Major.

DANGERS OF LONDON
    See Scudamore, F. A.

DANICHEFFS, THE
    See Shirley, Arthur.

DANIEL, GEORGE

Democritus in London. In *Democritus in London . . .*, London: William Pickering, 1852, pp. [i-vii], [1]-297.

Disagreeable Surprise, The; or, Taken Up and Taken In! Music by Reeve. London: J. Lowndes, 1819. Pp. [i-vi], [1]-44.

Disagreeable Surprise, The. London: John Cumberland, 1826. Pp. [i], [1]-46. Cumberland's British Theatre, XIV. *Filed under* Cumberland, John. Cumberland's British Theatre, XIV.

Doctor Bolus. London: W. & J. Lowndes, 1818. Pp. [1]-19. 2nd ed.

Doctor Bolus. London: John Cumberland, 1826. Pp. [1]-30. Cumberland's British Theatre, XIII. *Filed under* Cumberland, John. Cumberland's British Theatre, XIII.

Sworn at Highgate! London: John Cumberland, n.d. Pp. [3]-41.

Sworn at Highgate! London: John Cumberland, n.d. Pp. [1]-41. Cumberland's Minor Theatre, VI. *Filed under* Cumberland, John. Cumberland's Minor Theatre, VI.

DANIEL IN THE LION'S DEN
    See P., Br.

DANIEL O'ROURKE
    See Croker, Thomas Crofton.

DANISCHEFFS, THE
    See Newry, Charles Francis Needham, Earl of Kilmorey, Viscount.

DANISH PIRATES
    See Pennie, John Fitzgerald. Ethelwolf.

DAN'L DRUCE, BLACKSMITH
    See Gilbert, William Schwenck.

DANSEUSE
    See Worrell, James. Violette.

DANTE
    See Dabbs, George Henry Roque.
    See Durant, Héloise.

DANVERS, HENRY
    Conjugal Lesson, A. London: Thomas Hailes Lacy, n.d. Pp. [1]-18. Promptbook.
    Fascinating Individual, A; or, Too Agreeable by Half. London: Thomas Hailes Lacy, n.d. Pp. [1]-26. [Lacy's Acting Edition, 394].

DARA
    See Vetch, ?, Maj.

D'ARBLAY, FRANCES BURNEY, MRS. ALEXANDER
    See Burney, Frances.

DARBYSHIRE, W.
    Mayor's Relations, The. Manchester: Abel Heywood & Son, n.d. Pp. [i], [1]-9.

DARK CLOUD, THE
    See Sketchley, Arthur.

DARK DEED IN THE WOOD
    See Hazlewood, Colin Henry. Aurora Floyd.

DARK DOINGS IN THE CUPBOARD
    See Coyne, Joseph Stirling.

DARK GLEN OF BALLYFOILL, THE
    See Stirling, Edward.

DARK GONDOLA
    See Milner, Henry M. Tower of Nesle, The.

DARK HOUR BEFORE DAWN, THE
    See Brougham, John.

DARK'S THE HOUR BEFORE THE DAWN
    See Falconer, Edmund. Eileen Oge.

DARKEST LONDON
    See Cross, Julian. Crimson Rock!, The.
    See Cross, Julian.

DARKNESS VISIBLE
    See Hook, Theodore Edward.

DARLEY, GEORGE
    Chase, The. In *Complete Poetical Works,* ed. Ramsay Colles, London: George Routledge & Sons, n.d., pp. 527-532. *Filed under* Various Dramatic Works.
    Errors of Ecstasie, The. In *Complete Poetical Works,* ed. Ramsay Colles, London: George Routledge & Sons, n.d., pp. [i], 1-21. *Filed under* Various Dramatic Works.
    Ethelstan; or, The Battle of Brunanburh. London: Edward Moxon, 1841. Pp. [i]-[viii], [1]-95.
    Sylvia; or, The May Queen. London: John Taylor, 1827. Pp. [i]-[viii], [1]-217.
    Thomas à Becket. London: Edward Moxon, 1840. Pp. [i]-[viii], [1]-144.
    Voyage, The. In *Complete Poetical Works,* ed. Ramsay Colles, London: George Routledge & Sons, n.d., pp. 523-527. *Filed under* Various Dramatic Works.

DARLING, ISABELLA FLEMING
    Woman's Rights. In *Whispering Hope,* Edinburgh & Glasgow: John Menzies; London: Simpkin, Marshall, 1893, pp. [i], 154-167.

DARMESTETER, MRS. JAMES
    See Robinson, Agnes Mary Frances.

DARNLEY, J. HERBERT
    Balloon, The. Written with Fenn, George Manville. London & New York: Samuel French, c.1898. Pp. [1]-56. [Lacy's Acting Edition].
    Barrister, The. Written with Fenn, George Manville. London & New York: Samuel French, n.d. Pp. [1]-41. [Lacy's Acting Edition].
    Solicitor, The. New York & London: Samuel French, c.1902. Pp. [1]-71. French's International Copyrighted Edition of the Works of the Best Authors, 53.

DARYL, SIDNEY (pseud. of Straight, Douglas)
    His First Brief. New York: Harold Roorbach, n.d. Pp. [1]-16. Parlor Plays for Home Performance. [Amateur Stage, 31]. *Filed under* Straight, Douglas.

DASH OF THE DAY, THE
    See Lathom, Francis.

DAUB, EMILY JANE
    See Pfeiffer, Emily Jane Daub, Mrs.

DAUGHTER, THE
    See Bayly, Thomas Haynes.
    See Knowles, James Sheridan.

DAUGHTER OF ST. MARK, THE
    See Bunn, Alfred.

DAUGHTER OF THE REGIMENT, THE (anon.)
    Also: La Figlia del Reggimento. Music by Donizetti. London: G. Stuart (printer), n.d. Pp. [i]-iv, [5]-52. Libretto.

DAUGHTER OF THE REGIMENT
    See Archer, Thomas.
    See Fitzball, Edward.
    See Kenney, Charles Lamb (trans.). Figlia del Reggimento, La.

DAUGHTER OF THE STARS, THE
    See Brooks, Charles William Shirley.

DAUGHTER TO MARRY
    See Planché, James Robinson.
    See Planché, James Robinson. My Daughter, Sir!

DAUGHTER'S COURAGE
    See Phillips, R. Heroine, The.

DAUGHTER'S DEVOTION
    See Peake, Richard Brinsley. Chain of Gold, The.

DAUGHTER'S TRIALS
    See Taylor, Tom. Henry Dunbar.

DAUGHTER'S VOW!
    See Dimond, William. Nymph of the Grotto, The.

DAUGHTER-IN-LAW, A
    See Seymour, Mary.

DAUNCEY, SILVANUS
    Bilberry of Tilbury. Written with Day, George D. Music by Jones, Guy. Brighton: Southern Publishing Co., n.d. Pp. [i-ii], [1]-30. Libretto. *Filed under* Day, George D.
    Divided Duty, A.
    See Month After Date, A.
    Matrimonial Catch, A. London (Bloomsbury): Walter Smith (printer), n.d. Pp. [1]-28.
    Month after Date, A. *Also:* A Divided Duty. London & New York: Samuel French, n.d. Pp. [1]-18. [Lacy's Acting Edition].

DAVENPORT BROS. & CO.
    See Pemberton, Thomas Edgar.

DAVENPORT DONE
    See Colomb, George Hatton, Col.

DAVID COPPERFIELD
    See Brougham, John.

DAVID GARRICK
    See Robertson, Thomas William.

DAVID RIZZIO
    See Hamilton, Ralph, Col.
    See Neele, Henry.

DAVIDSON, FRANCES A., MRS.
    Giralda; or, Which Is My Husband? London: G. H. Davidson, n.d. Pp. [7]-45. Text complete. Promptbook.

DAVIDSON, FRANCES A., MRS. (trans.)
    Gustavus III. *Also:* Gustave III. Music by Auber. London: G. H. Davidson, n.d. Pp. [i], [1]-40. Davidson's Illustrated Libretto Books. Libretto.

DAVIDSON, GEORGE HENRY
    Angelo and the Actress of Padua. London: G. H. Davidson, n.d. Pp. [i]-[viii], [9]-42. Cumberland's British Theatre, 392.

DAVIDSON, JOHN
    Bruce. In *Plays,* London: Elkin Mathews & John Lane; Chicago: Stone & Kimball, 1894, pp. [i], [125]-215.
    Diabolus Amans. Glasgow: Wilson & McCormick, 1885. Pp. [1]-143.
    Eclogues. In *Last Ballad and Other Poems,* London & New York: John Lane, 1899, pp. [i], 160-187.
    For the Crown. London: Nassau Press, 1896. Pp. [1]-58.
    Godfrida. New York & London: John Lane, 1898. Pp. [i-iv], [1]-123.
    Knight of the Maypole, The. London: Grant Richards, 1903. Pp. [i-vi], [1]-97.

Romantic Farce, A. In *Plays,* London: Elkin Mathews & John Lane; Chicago: Stone & Kimball, 1894, pp. [i], [83]-124.

Scaramouch in Naxos. In *Plays,* London: Elkin Mathews & John Lane; Chicago: Stone & Kimball, 1894, pp. [i], [249]-294. Libretto.

Smith. In *Plays,* London: Elkin Mathews & John Lane; Chicago: Stone & Kimball, 1894, pp. [i], [217]-248.

Unhistorical Pastoral, An. In *Plays,* London: Elkin Mathews & John Lane; Chicago: Stone & Kimball, 1894, pp. [i-vi], [1]-81.

DAVIES, AUGUSTA
    See Webster, Augusta Davies, Mrs. Thomas.

DAVIES, BLANCHE
    Octavia; or, The Bride of St. Agnes. Doncaster: Brooke; C. White, 1832. Pp. [i-iv], [1]-62.

DAVIES, HILL
    Old Garden, An. London: Samuel French; New York: T. Henry French, n.d. Pp. [1]-23. [Lacy's Acting Edition].

DAVIES, WARBURTON (trans.)
    Faustus. By Goethe. London: Simpkin & Marshall, 1834. Pp. [i]-[x], [1]-231.

DAVIS, HENRY
    Rip Van Winkle.
        See Strachan, John S., jr.

DAVIS, JAMES
    See Hall, Owen.

DAVIS, LILLIE
    Aunt Madge. Manchester: Abel Heywood & Son; London: F. Pitman, n.d. Pp. [i-ii], [1]-15. Abel Heywood & Son's Series of Copyright Plays for the Use of Amateurs, 6.
    Difficult to Please. Manchester: Abel Heywood & Son, n.d. Pp. [i-ii], [1]-[15]. Abel Heywood & Son's Series of Original Dramas, Dialogues, & Readings Adapted for Amateur Entertainments, 162.
    Don't Jump at Conclusions. Manchester: Abel Heywood & Son; London: F. Pitman, n.d. Pp. [i-ii], [1]-11. Abel Heywood & Son's Series of Copyright Plays for the Use of Amateurs, 2.
    Dorothy's Victory. Manchester: Abel Heywood & Son, n.d. Pp. [i-ii], [1]-11. Abel Heywood & Son's Series of Original Dramas, Dialogues, & Readings Adapted for Amateur Entertainments, 159.
    Two Georges, The. Manchester: Abel Heywood & Son; London: F. Pitman, n.d. Pp. [i-ii], [1]-16. Abel Heywood & Son's Series of Copyright Plays for the Use of Amateurs, 3.
    Which Got the Best of It? Manchester: Abel Heywood & Son, n.d. Pp. [i-ii], [1]-12. Abel Heywood & Son's Series of Original Dramas, Dialogues, & Readings Adapted for Amateur Entertainments, 155.

DAVIS, MRS. MAXWELL
    Pamela's Prejudice. London: Samuel French; New York: T. Henry French, n.d. Pp. [1]-9.

DAVIS, NATHANIEL NEWNHAM
    See Newnham-Davis, Nathaniel.

DAVY CROCKETT
    See Dizance, Frank.

DAVY JONES
    See Barrymore, William.

DAWK BUNGALOW, THE
    See Trevelyan, George Otto.

DAWN, THE
    See Symons, Arthur (trans.).

DAWTREY, AUGUSTIN
    Robin Hood and ye Curtall Fryer. In *Record of the Ripon Millenary Festival,* [Ripon: W. Harrison, 1892], pp. [104]-124.

DAY, ERNEST
    Orchard of the King, The. Written with Footman, Maurice H. Lincoln: n.pub., 1889. Pp. [1]-28.

DAY, GEORGE D.
    Bilberry of Tilbury.
        See Dauncey, Silvanus.

DAY AFTER THE FAIR, A
    See Somerset, Charles A.

DAY AFTER THE WEDDING, THE
    See Kemble, Marie Thérèse De Camp, Mrs. Charles.

DAY AND THE NIGHT
    See Farnie, Henry Brougham. Manola.

DAY AT AN INN, A
    See Hook, Theodore Edward.

DAY AT BOULOGNE
    See Peake, Richard Brinsley. Master's Rival.

DAY IN BOULOGNE, A
    See Law, Arthur.

DAY IN PARIS, A
    See Selby, Charles.

DAY OF DUPES
    See Gore, Catherine Grace Frances Moody, Mrs. Charles. Quid Pro Quo.

DAY OF RECKONING, A
    See Hope, Anthony.
    See Planché, James Robinson.

DAY WELL SPENT, A
    See Oxenford, John.

DAY'S FISHING, A
    See Morton, John Maddison.

DAY'S PLEASURE
    See Kenney, James. John Buzzby.

DAYS AND KNIGHTS OF THE ROUND TABLE
    See Brough, William. King Arthur.

DAYS OF JEZEBEL, THE
    See Bayne, Peter.

DAYS OF KING CHARLES II
    See Fitzball, Edward. Peveril of the Peak.

DAYS OF KIRK AND MONMOUTH
    See Almar, George. Battle of Sedgemoor, The.

DAYS OF OLD
    See Colman, George, jr. Battle of Hexham, The.

DAYS OF PRINCE CHARLIE
    See Lyne, S. M. Rose of Sleat, The.

DAYS OF TERROR!
    See Hazlewood, Colin Henry. Chevalier of the Maison Rouge, The.

DAYS WE LIVE IN, THE
    See Maclaren, Archibald.

DEACON, THE
    See Jones, Henry Arthur.

DEACON BRODIE
    See Henley, William Ernest.

DEAD HEART, THE
    See Phillips, Watts.

DEAD HEART, THE: A STORY OF THE FRENCH REVOLUTION
    See Pollock, Walter Herries (arr.).

DEAD RECKONING
    See Boucicault, Dionysius Lardner. Jezebel.

DEAD SHOT, THE
    See Buckstone, John Baldwin.

DEAD WITNESS, THE
    See Reeve, Wybert.

DEADMAN'S POINT
    See Burnand, Francis Cowley.

DEAF AND DUMB
    See Holcroft, Thomas.
    See Thompson, Benjamin (trans.).

DEAF AND DUMB, THE; OR, THE ABBÉ DE L'EPÉE (anon. trans.).
    By Bouilly, Jean Nicholas. London: T. N. Longman & O. Rees, 1801. Pp. [i-viii], [1]-70.

DEAF AS A POST
    See Poole, John.

DEAKIN, H. C.
    Deliverance of Switzerland, The. London: Marsh & Miller, 1830. Pp. [i]-x, [1]-270.

DEAL BOATMEN, THE
    See Burnand, Francis Cowley.

DEARER THAN LIFE
    See Byron, Henry James.

DEAREST MAMMA
See Gordon, Walter.
DEATH
See Driver, Henry Austin.
DEATH AND RACHEL
See Graves, Clotilde Inez Mary.
DEATH AND THE LAWYER
See Maunder, Samuel.
DEATH AND VICTORY OF LORD VISCOUNT NELSON, THE
See Cumberland, Richard.
DEATH-FETCH, THE
See Milner, Henry M.
DEATH GUARD, THE
See Phillips, Morrice.
DEATH IN DISGUISE
See Maclaren, Archibald. Imitation Tea.
DEATH OF ANTAR, THE
See Baddeley, Welbore St. Clair.
DEATH OF CAIN, THE
See Lyndsay, David.
DEATH OF CRICHTON
See Godmond, Christopher. Vincenzo, Prince of Mantua.
DEATH OF DARNLEY, THE
See Sotheby, William.
DEATH OF DEMOSTHENES, THE
See Palaeologus, Gregorios (trans.).
DEATH OF HAMAN!
See Polack, Elizabeth. Esther, the Royal Jewess.
DEATH OF LIFE IN LONDON, THE
See Greenwood, Thomas Longdon.
DEATH OF MARLOWE, THE
See Horne, Richard Hengist.
DEATH OF TINTAGILES, THE
See Sutro, Alfred (trans.).
DEATH OF WALLENSTEIN, THE
See Coleridge, Samuel Taylor (trans.).
See Pearson, Edward Stanhope (trans.).
DEATH OMEN AND THE FATE OF LADY JANE GREY
See Higgie, Thomas Henry. Tower of London, The.
DEATH PLANK, THE
See Lucas, William James.
DEATH-SONG OF THAMYRIS, THE
See Pember, Edward Henry.
DEATH TOKEN!, THE
See Wilks, Thomas Egerton.
DEATH'S JEST-BOOK
See Beddoes, Thomas Lovell.
DEBORAH
See Cheltnam, Charles Smith.
DEBT
See de Pass, E. A.
DEBT OF HONOUR, A
See Grundy, Sydney.
DEBTOR AND CREDITOR
See Kenney, James.
DE CAMP, MARIE THÉRÈSE
See Kemble, Marie Thérèse De Camp, Mrs. Charles.
DE CAUX, JOHN WILLIAM
Silver Ticket, The; or, Love in Bloterland. In *Poetic Fancies,* Great Yarmouth: John Buckle, 1886, pp. [i], 62-95.
DECEIVER DECEIVED
See Livius, Barham. Maid or Wife.
DE CHATILLON
See Hemans, Felicia Dorothea Browne, Mrs. Alfred.
DECIDED CASE, A
See Brougham, John.
DECLINED—WITH THANKS
See Morton, John Maddison.
DEEDS, NOT WORDS
See Courtney, John.
DEEDS OF DREADFUL NOTE
See Dubois, Alfred.
DEEP DEEP SEA, THE
See Planché, James Robinson.

DEEP RED ROVER, THE
See Hay, Frederic.
DEERFOOT
See Burnand, Francis Cowley.
DEFORMED OF NOTRE DAME
See Fitzball, Edward. Esmeralda.
DEFORMED TRANSFORMED, THE
See Byron, George Gordon, Lord.
See Ross, Ronald.
D'EGVILLE, ? (arr.)
Caractacus. London: G. Smeeton, n.d. Pp. [1]-27. Ballet synopsis. *Filed under* Smeeton's Description of Caractacus.
DEIRDRE
See Ferguson, Samuel.
DELAP, JOHN
Abdalla. In *Dramatic Poems,* Lewes: W. & A. Lee (printer), 1803, pp. [225]-295. *Filed under* Dramatic Poems.
Gunilda. In *Dramatic Poems,* Lewes: W. & A. Lee (printer), 1803, pp. [i-xvi], [1]-69. *Filed under* Dramatic Poems.
Matilda. In *Dramatic Poems,* Lewes: W. & A. Lee (printer), 1803, pp. [155]-224. *Filed under* Dramatic Poems.
Usurper, The. In *Dramatic Poems,* Lewes: W. & A. Lee (printer), 1803, pp. [71]-154. *Filed under* Dramatic Poems.
DELAVIGNE, CASIMIR
Maçon, Le.
See Wylde, Mrs. Henry (trans.).
DELAYS AND BLUNDERS
See Reynolds, Frederick.
DELEGATES AND THE CHILDREN OF THE WRECK!
See Phillips, Morrice. Heiress of Glenfillan, The.
DELICATE ATTENTIONS
See Poole, John.
DELICATE GROUND
See Dance, Charles.
DELINQUENT, THE
See Reynolds, Frederick.
DELIVERANCE OF SWITZERLAND, THE
See Deakin, H. C.
DELIVERER OF HIS COUNTRY
See Brooke, Henry. Gustavus Vasa.
DELIVERER OF THEBES
See Atherstone, Edwin. Pelopidas.
DELUGE, THE
See Lyndsay, David.
DELUSION, THE
See Oxberry, William Henry.
DE MATTOS, A. TEIXEIRA (trans.)
Heirs of Rabourdin, The. By Zola, Emile. London: Henry, 1894. Pp. [i]-[xxx], [1]-132. Independent Theatre Series of Plays, 3.
DEMETRIUS
See Martin, Theodore, Sir (trans.).
DEMETRIUS THE IMPOSTOR (anon. trans.).
By Soumarokove, Alexander. London: J. Booth, 1806. Pp. [i]-[viii], 9-76.
DEMOCRITUS IN LONDON
See Daniel, George.
DEMON DOCTOR, THE
See Towers, Edward.
DEMON GAMESTER
See Townsend, William Thompson. Gold Fiend, The.
DEMON GIFT, THE
See Lemon, Mark.
DEMON LOVER, THE
See Brougham, John.
DEMON OF THE DESERT!
See Campbell, Andrew Leonard Voullaire.
DEMON OF THE DRACHENFELS
See Grattan, H. P. Faust.
See Soane, George. Faustus.
DEMON OF THE WOLF'S GLEN AND THE SEVEN CHARMED BULLETS
See Fitzball, Edward. Freischutz, Der.

DEMON SPIDER, THE
    See Simpson, Ella Graham.
DEMONIO, IL
    See Pittman, Josiah (trans.).
DEMONS OF THE CATSKILL MOUNTAINS!
    See Kerr, John. Rip Van Winkle.
D'ENGHIEN
    See Greene, William A.
DENHAMS
    See Albery, James. Crisis, The.
DENNERY, ADOLPHE
    Poule aux Oeufs d'Or, La.
        See under title.
DENOUNCER, THE
    See Wilks, Thomas Egerton.
DENTIST, THE
    See Lindo, Frank.
DE PASS, E. A.
    Debt. London & New York: Samuel French, n.d. Pp. [1]-28.
        [Lacy's Acting Edition].
    Under False Colours. London & New York: Samuel French,
        n.d. Pp. [1]-27.
DÉPIT AMOUREUX
    See Van Laun, Henri (trans.). Love Tiff, The.
DERBY WINNER, THE
    See Harris, Augustus Henry Glossop.
DERLEY, J.
    Cup of Tea, A.
        See under title.
DERRICK, JOSEPH
    Confusion. New York & London: Samuel French, c.1900.
        Pp. [1]-51.
    Confusion. 88 leaves. Manuscript.
    Twins. London & New York: Samuel French, n.d. Pp.
        [1]-48. [Lacy's Acting Edition].
DE RULLECOURT
    See Burn, David.
DESCART, THE FRENCH BUCCANEER
    See Jerrold, Douglas William.
DESCENT OF LIBERTY, THE
    See Hunt, Leigh.
DESCENT OF THE BALLOON
    See Inchbald, Elizabeth Simpson, Mrs. Joseph. Mogul
        Tale, The.
DESERT, LE
    See Fitzball, Edward (trans.).
DESERTED DAUGHTER, THE
    See Holcroft, Thomas.
DESERTED MILL, THE
    See Fitzball, Edward.
DESERTED VILLAGE, THE
    See Cooper, Frederick Fox.
    See Falconer, Edmund.
DESERTER, THE
    See Dibdin, Charles, sr.
DESERTER IN A FIX, A
    See Soane-Roby, Bernard.
DESERTS OF SIBERIA
    See Reynolds, Frederick. Exile, The.
DE SMART, MRS. ALEC
    Purely Platonic. By Mrs. Alec Smart. London & New York:
        Samuel French, n.d. Pp. [1]-12. [Lacy's Acting Edition].
DESOLATE ISLAND
    See Fawcett, John. Perouse.
DE SOLIS, ANTONIO
    One Fool Makes Many.
        See Fox, Henry Richard.
DESPERATE GAME, A
    See Morton, John Maddison.
DESPERATE REMEDY
    See Planché, James Robinson. My Heart's Idol.
DESPREZ, FRANK
    Nautch Girl, The.
        See Dance, George.

DESTINY OF CAIN, THE
    See Lyndsay, David.
DESTROYER OF GENAIZE
    See Young, Charles Michael. Euphernia.
DESTRUCTION OF SODOM, THE
    See Tennant, William.
DEUCE IS IN HER!, THE
    See Raymond, Richard John.
DEUCE IS IN HIM, THE
    See Colman, George, sr.
DEUX DIVORCES, LES
    See Atkyns, Samuel.
DEUX JOURNÉES
    See Baildon, Arthur. Water Carrier, The.
DE VALENCOURT
    See Hoskins, Horatio Huntley.
DE VERE, AUBREY
    Duke of Mercia, The. In *Julian the Apostate and The Duke of
        Mercia,* London: Basil M. Pickering, 1858, pp. [171]-343.
    Julian the Apostate. In *Julian the Apostate and The Duke of
        Mercia,* London: Basil M. Pickering, 1858, pp. [i]-[xxiv],
        [1]-169.
    Mary Tudor. London: George Bell & Sons, 1884. Pp.
        [v]-[xlviii], [1]-330. New ed.
DE VERE, AUBREY THOMAS
    Alexander the Great. London: Henry S. King, n.d. Pp.
        [i]-[xxvi], [1]-231.
    Search after Proserpine, The. In *Poetical Works,* London:
        Kegan Paul, Trench, 1884, I, [i], [1]-37.
    St. Thomas of Canterbury. *Also:* Thomas à Becket. In
        Poetical Works, London: Kegan Paul, Trench, 1884, III,
        [i-ii], [161]-321.
    Thomas à Becket.
        See St. Thomas of Canterbury.
DEVIL AND DOCTOR FAUSTUS, THE
    See Rede, William Leman.
DEVIL AND THE DESERTER
    See Barnett, Charles Zachary. Dominique the Possessed.
DEVIL AND THE LADY, THE
    See Tennyson, Alfred, Lord.
DEVIL OF MARSEILLES, THE
    See Peake, Richard Brinsley.
DEVIL ON TWO STICKS, THE
    See Peake, Richard Brinsley.
DEVIL TO PAY, THE
    See Coffey, Charles.
DEVIL'S BRIDGE, THE
    See Arnold, Samuel James.
DEVIL'S DAUGHTERS, THE
    See Lancaster, Edward Richardson.
    See Stirling, Edward.
DEVIL'S DISCIPLE, THE
    See Shaw, George Bernard.
DEVIL'S DRAUGHT
    See Halford, John. Faust and Marguerite.
DEVIL'S DUCAT, THE
    See Jerrold, Douglas William.
DEVIL'S ELIXIR, THE
    See Fitzball, Edward.
DEVIL'S IN IT, THE
    See Wilks, Thomas Egerton.
DEVIL'S IN THE DICE!
    See Dibdin, Thomas John. Sixes, The.
DEVIL'S MOUNT, THE
    See Higgie, Thomas Henry.
DEVIL'S OPERA, THE
    See Macfarren, George.
DEVIL'S VIOLIN, THE
    See Webster, Benjamin Nottingham.
DEVILISH GOOD JOKE!, A
    See Higgie, Thomas Henry.
DEVOTED ONE, THE
    See Pennie, John Fitzgerald.
DEVOTION OF THE CROSS, THE
    See MacCarthy, Denis Florence (trans.).

DEW, DYER

Harold; or, The English King. London: Effingham Wilson (priv.), 1820. Pp. [i-vi], [1]-72. *Filed under* Dyer, Dew.

DEWDROP AND GLORIO

See Russell, Georgiana Adelaide Peel, Lady.

DEY AND THE KNIGHT

See Cubitt, Sydney. Zanone.

DIABOLUS AMANS

See Davidson, John.

DIADESTE

See Fitzball, Edward.

DIALOGUES

See Morton, Richard.

DIALOGUES CONCERNING MEN, MANNERS, AND OPINIONS.

See Becket, Andrew. Lucianus Redivivus.

DIAMANS DE LA COURONNE

See Fitzball, Edward. Crown Diamonds, The.

See Fitzball, Edward. Crown Jewels, The.

See Williams, Thomas John (trans.).

DIAMANTS DE LA COURONNE, LES (anon.)

Music by Auber. London & New York: Boosey, n.d. Pp. [i-iv], 1-271. Royal Edition. Vocal score.

DIAMANTS DE LA COURONNE

See Long, Charles (trans.). Crown Brilliants, The.

DIAMOND ARROW, THE

See Moncrieff, William Thomas.

DIAMOND CUT DIAMOND

See Maclaren, Archibald. Swindlers, The.

See Murray, William Henry Wood.

DIAMOND RING

See Hook, Theodore Edward. Exchange No Robbery.

See Peake, Richard Brinsley. Three Wives of Madrid, The.

DIBDIN, CHARLES, SR

Britons Strike Home. By Mr. Dibdin. London: Music Warehouse (priv.), n.d. Pp. [i-iv], [1]-53. Libretto.

Broken Gold, The. By Mr. Dibdin. London: T. Woodfall, n.d. Pp. [i-vi], [1]-24. Libretto.

Deserter, The. In *New English Drama*, ed. W. Oxberry, 22 vols., London: W. Simpkin & R. Marshall; C. Chapple, 1820, XI, [1-2], [i]-[iv], [1]-[26]. *Filed under* Oxberry, William Henry. New English Drama, XI.

Deserter, The. In *British Drama*, 12 vols., London: John Dicks, 1871, IX, [119]-128.

Quaker, The. London: Whittingham & Arliss, 1815. Pp. [1]-30. London Theatre, II. *Filed under* Dibdin, Thomas John, ed. London Theatre, II.

Quaker, The. In *New English Drama*, ed. W. Oxberry, 22 vols., London: W. Simpkin & R. Marshall; C. Chapple, 1820, XI, [1-2], [i]-[vi], [1]-23. *Filed under* Oxberry, William Henry. New English Drama, XI.

Quaker, The. In *British Drama*, 12 vols., London: John Dicks, 1865, IV, [1174]-1182. *Filed under* Dibdin, Charles Isaac Mungo, jr.

Quaker, The. London: John Cumberland, n.d. Pp. [1]-28. Cumberland's British Theatre, XXXVII. *Filed under* Cumberland, John. Cumberland's British Theatre, XXXVII.

Waterman, The; or, The First of August. In *British Drama*, 12 vols., London: John Dicks, 1865, IV, [1109]-1118.

Waterman, The; or, The First of August. London: John Cumberland, n.d. Pp. [1]-35. Cumberland's British Theatre, XXIII. *Filed under* Cumberland, John. Cumberland's British Theatre, XXIII.

DIBDIN, CHARLES ISAAC MUNGO, JR

Astrologer, The; or, Harlequin and Moore's Almanack. Music by Reeve. London: W. Glendinning (printer), 1810. Pp. [1]-24. Libretto.

Bang Up!; or, Harlequin Prime. Music by Reeve. London: W. Glendinning (printer), 1810. Pp. [1]-16. Libretto.

Barbara Allen. Music by Reeve, W. London: Glendinning (printer), n.d. Pp. [1]-10. Libretto.

Belle Sauvage, The.

See Ko and Zoa.

British Amazons; or, Army without Reserve. Music by Reeve, W. London: Glendinning (printer), n.d. Pp. [1]-15. Libretto.

Edward and Susan. Music by Reeve, W. London: W. Glendinning (printer), n.d. Pp. [11]-19. Libretto. *Filed under* Fire and Spirit.

Farmer's Wife, The. Music by Bishop; Davy; Reeve; Welsh, T.; Condell. London: G. & S. Robinson, 1814. Pp. [i-iv], [1]-80. Libretto.

Farmer's Wife, The. London: Sherwood, Neely, & Jones, 1817. Pp. [1]-68. London Theatre, XXII. *Filed under* Dibdin, Thomas John, ed. London Theatre, XXII.

Farmer's Wife, The. In *British Drama*, 12 vols., London: John Dicks, 1872, XII, [129]-151.

Fashion's Fools; or, The Aquatic Harlequin. Music by Reeve. London: W. Glendinning (printer), 1809. Pp. [1]-16. Libretto.

Fire and Spirit; or, A Holiday Harlequin. Music by Reeve, W. London: W. Glendinning (printer), n.d. Pp. [21]-26. Libretto.

Flitch, The; or, The Custom of Dunmow. Music by Reeve. [London: W. Glendinning], n.d. Pp. [1]-[4]. Libretto.

Goody Two Shoes; or, Harlequin Alabaster. Music by Reeve, W. London: W. Glendinning, n.d. Pp. [1]-10. Libretto.

Great Devil, The; or, The Robber of Genoa. By Charles Dibdin. London: John Cumberland, n.d. Pp. [1]-22. Cumberland's Minor Theatre, XIV. *Filed under* Cumberland, John. Cumberland's Minor Theatre, XIV.

Great Devil, The; or, The Robber of Genoa. By Charles Dibdin. London: John Cumberland, n.d. Pp. [1]-22. [Cumberland's Minor Theatre].

Jack the Giant Killer. Music by Reeve, W. N.p.: n.pub., n.d. Pp. [7]-9. Libretto of four numbers only.

Ko and Zoa. *Also:* The Belle Sauvage. London: W. Glendinning (printer), 1803. Pp. [1]-4. Libretto.

Law's Two Tails; or, En-tail and Red-tail! By C. Dibdin. Music by Reeve. London: W. Glendinning (printer), 1815. Pp. [1]-16. Libretto.

Life in London; or, The Larks of Logic, Tom, and Jerry. By Charles Dibdin. London: John Lowndes, 1822. Pp. [1]-40. 2nd ed.

London; or, Harlequin and Time. Music by Reeve. London: W. Glendinning (printer), 1814. Pp. [1]-8. Libretto.

Lord of the Manor, The. London: Whittingham & Arliss, 1816. Pp. [1]-60. London Theatre, XXI. *Filed under* Dibdin, Thomas John, ed. London Theatre, XXI.

Lord of the Manor, The. By General Burgoyne. London: John Cumberland, 1826. Pp. [1]-58. Cumberland's British Theatre, XIII. *Filed under* Cumberland, John. Cumberland's British Theatre, XIII.

Lord of the Manor, The. In [*British Drama*, 12 vols., London: John Dicks, 1864, II], [589]-606.

Mermaid, The; or, Harlequin Pearl Diver! By C. Dibdin. Music by Reeve. London: W. Glendinning (printer), 1815. Pp. [1]-8. Libretto.

My Spouse and I. Music by Whitaker. London: Whittingham & Arliss, 1815. Pp. [3]-44. Libretto.

My Spouse and I. London: Whittingham & Arliss, 1816. Pp. [3]-44. 2nd ed. Libretto.

My Spouse and I. London: Sherwood, Neely, & Jones, 1817. Pp. [1]-40. London Theatre, XXVI. *Filed under* Dibdin, Thomas John, ed. London Theatre, XXVI.

My Spouse and I. In *British Drama*, 12 vols., London: John Dicks, 1872, X, [149]-160.

My Spouse and I. By Charles Dibdin. London: John Cumberland, n.d. Pp. [1]-36. Cumberland's British Theatre, XLI. *Filed under* Cumberland, John. Cumberland's British Theatre, XLI.

New Brooms. Music by Reeve, W. N.p.: n.pub., n.d. Pp. [1]-6. Libretto.

Old Man of the Mountains, The; or, A Tale of the Eleventh Century. [London: W.] Glendinning (printer), n.d. Pp. [1]-12. Libretto.

Philip Quarll; or, The English Hermit. Music by Reeve. [London: W.] Glendinning (printer), n.d. Pp. [1]-4. Libretto.

Red Riding Hood; or, The Wolf Robber. Music by Reeve, W. N.p.: n.pub., n.d. Pp. [1]-15. Libretto.

Smuggler's Daughter, The. By Charles Dibdin. London: John Cumberland, n.d. Pp. [1]-31. [Cumberland's Minor Theatre].

Smuggler's Daughter, The. By Charles Dibdin. London: John Cumberland, n.d. Pp. [1]-31. Cumberland's Minor Theatre, VII. *Filed under* Cumberland, John. Cumberland's Minor Theatre, VII.

Spectre Knight, The. Music by Reeve. London: W. Glendinning (printer), 1810. Pp. [1]-32. Libretto.

Thirty Thousand; or, Harlequin's Lottery. Music by Reeve. London: W. Glendinning (printer), 1808. Pp. [1]-16. Libretto.

White Witch, The; or, The Cataract of Amazonia. Music by Reeve. London: W. Glendinning (printer), 1808. Pp. [1]-20. Libretto.

Wild Man, The. By Charles Dibdin. London: John Cumberland, n.d. Pp. [1]-36. Cumberland's Minor Theatre, XI. *Filed under* Cumberland, John. Cumberland's Minor Theatre, XI.

Wild Man, The; or, The Water Pageant. By C. Dibdin. London: Richardson & Clarke, n.d. Pp. [iii]-viii, [9]-36.

Wizard's Wake; or, Harlequin and Merlin. Music by Russell, W. London: W. Glendinning (printer), n.d. Pp. [1]-7. Libretto.

DIBDIN, THOMAS JOHN

Alexander the Great, in Little. London: John Duncombe, n.d. Pp. [1]-28. Duncombe's Edition.

Banks of the Hudson, The; or, The Congress Trooper. London: John Cumberland, n.d. Pp. [1]-44. [Cumberland's Minor Theatre].

Banks of the Hudson, The; or, The Congress Trooper. London: John Cumberland, n.d. Pp. [1]-44. Cumberland's Minor Theatre, IV. *Filed under* Cumberland, John. Cumberland's Minor Theatre, IV.

Bondocani, Il; or, The Caliph Robber. London: T. N. Longman & O. Rees, 1801. Pp. [1]-45.

Bonifacio and Bridgetina; or, The Knight of the Hermitage; or, The Windmill Turrett; or, The Spectre of the North-east Gallery. London: J. Barker, 1808. Pp. [1]-49.

Brazen Mask; or, Alberto and Rosabella. Written with Fawcett, John. Music by Mountain; Davy. London: Barker & Son, 1802. Pp. [1]-23. Synopsis and songs.

Cabinet, The. London: Longman, Hurst, Rees, Orme, & Brown, 1810. Pp. [1]-88.

Cabinet, The. London: John Cumberland, n.d. Pp. [i], [1]-58. Cumberland's British Theatre, XXI. *Filed under* Cumberland, John. Cumberland's British Theatre, XXI.

Covenanters, The. London: John Duncombe, n.d. Pp. [1]-26. Duncombe's Acting Edition of the British Theatre, 143.

Dog of Montargis.
See Barrymore, William.

Don Giovanni; or, A Spectre on Horseback! London: John Miller, 1817. Pp. [i-iv], [1]-30.

Don Giovanni; or, A Spectre on Horseback! London: John Miller, 1818. Pp. [1]-32. 5th ed.

Don Giovanni; or, A Spectre on Horseback. London: John Cumberland, n.d. Pp. [i-iv], [1]-28. Cumberland's Minor Theatre, II. *Filed under* Cumberland, John. Cumberland's Minor Theatre, II.

English Fleet in 1342, The. London: Longman, Hurst, Rees, & Orme, 1805. Pp. [1]-63.

English Fleet in 1342, The. London: John Cumberland, n.d. Pp. [1]-49. Cumberland's British Theatre, XXXII. *Filed under* Cumberland, John. Cumberland's British Theatre, XXXII.

Family Quarrels. London: Longman, Hurst, Rees, & Orme, 1805. Pp. [i-iv], [1]-74.

Fate of Calas, The. London: C. Lowndes, 1820. Pp. [1]-42.

Fate of Calas, The. London: John Cumberland, n.d. Pp. [1]-46. Cumberland's Minor Theatre, VIII. *Filed under* Cumberland, John. Cumberland's Minor Theatre, VIII.

Five Miles Off; or, The Finger Post. London: Barker & Son, 1806. Pp. [1]-[58].

Five Miles Off; or, The Finger Post. London: J. Barker, 1809. Pp. [1]-[54]. New ed.

Five Miles Off; or, The Finger Post. London: John Cumberland & Son, n.d. Pp. [1]-45. Cumberland's British Theatre, XLII. *Filed under* Cumberland, John. Cumberland's British Theatre, XLII.

Gaffer's Mistake; or, The Case Is Altered. N.p.: n.pub., n.d. Pp. [1]-7. Libretto.

Guilty or Not Guilty. London: Lackington, Allen, 1804. Pp. [i-viii], [1]-108. 4th ed.

Harlequin and Humpo; or, Columbine by Candlelight! Music by Kelly. London: Lowndes & Hobbs (printer), n.d. Pp. [3]-17. Synopsis and libretto.

Harlequin and Mother Goose; or, The Golden Egg! Music by Ware. London: Thomas Hailes Lacy, n.d. Pp. [1]-18. Libretto.

Harlequin Harper; or, A Jump from Japan. Music by Whitaker. London: J. Barker, 1813. Pp. [1]-23. Synopsis and libretto.

Harlequin Hoax; or, A Pantomime Proposed. London: Whittingham & Arliss, 1814. Pp. [1]-31.

Harlequin Hoax; or, A Pantomime Proposed. London: Whittingham & Arliss, 1815. Pp. [1]-28. 2nd ed.

Harlequin in His Element; or, Fire, Water, Earth, and Air. London: J. Scales, n.d. Pp. [v]-[x], [11]-28. Scales's Edition. Synopsis. *Filed under* Harlequin in His Element (anon.).

Harlequin in His Element; or, Fire, Water, Earth, and Air. London: Appleyards, n.d. Pp. [i-viii], [1]-21. Libretto.

Harlequin's Habeas; or, The Hall of Spectres. Music by Moorehead; Davy; Ware, W.; Russell; Reeve. London: Barker & Son, 1802. Pp. [1]-19. Libretto.

Harlequin's Magnet; or, The Scandinavian Sorcerer. Music by Davy; Ware. London: Barker & Son, 1806. Pp. [1]-23. Libretto.

Harlequin's Tour; or, The Dominion of Fancy. Music by Moorehead; Attwood. London: J. Barker, 1800. Pp. [1]-15. Libretto.

Haroun Alraschid; or, Wants and Superfluities. London: John Dicks, n.d. Pp. [1]-14. Dicks' Standard Plays, 513.

Harper's Son and the Duke's Daughter, The. London: J. Hartnell (printer), 1810. Pp. [1]-28. Libretto.

Heart of Mid-Lothian, The; or, The Lily of St. Leonard's. London: Robert Stodart, 1819. Pp. [i]-[viii], [1]-66. 2nd ed.

Heart of Mid-Lothian, The. London: John Cumberland, n.d. Pp. [1]-54. Cumberland's Minor Theatre, I. *Filed under* Cumberland, John. Cumberland's Minor Theatre, I.

Humphrey Clinker. London: John Cumberland, n.d. Pp. [1]-36. [Cumberland's Minor Theatre].

Humphrey Clinker. London: John Cumberland, n.d. Pp. [i], [1]-36. Cumberland's Minor Theatre, IV. *Filed under* Cumberland, John. Cumberland's Minor Theatre, IV.

Ivanhoe; or, The Jew's Daughter. London: John Cumberland, n.d. Pp. [1]-64. Cumberland's Minor Theatre, II. *Filed under* Cumberland, John. Cumberland's Minor Theatre, II.

Ivanhoe; or, The Jew's Daughter. Boston: William V. Spencer, n.d. Pp. [1]-44. Spencer's Boston Theatre, 196.

Jew and the Doctor, The. London: John Cumberland, n.d. Pp. [1]-31. Cumberland's British Theatre, XXXIV. *Filed under* Cumberland, John. Cumberland's British Theatre, XXXIV.

Jubilee, The. Music by Reeve. London: J. Barker, 1809. Pp. [1]-23. Libretto.

Kenilworth. Written with Bunn, Alfred. London: John Lowndes, n.d. Pp. [1]-34.

Kenilworth. Written with Bunn, Alfred. London: John Cumberland, n.d. Pp. [1]-35. Cumberland's British

Theatre, XXXIX. *Filed under* Cumberland, John. Cumberland's British Theatre, XXXIX.

Kenilworth. Written with Bunn, Alfred. London: Thomas Hailes Lacy, n.d. Pp. [3]-35. [Lacy's Acting Edition]. *Filed under* Bunn, Alfred.

Lady of the Lake, The. London: John Cumberland, n.d. Pp. [1]-31. Cumberland's Minor Theatre, III. *Filed under* Cumberland, John. Cumberland's Minor Theatre, III.

Lady of the Lake, The. Dublin: W. Figgis, n.d. Pp. [i-ii], [1]-32. Promptbook.

Magpie, The; or, The Maid of Palaiseau. London: J. F. Dove (printer), 1815. Pp. [i-iv], [1]-48.

Magpie, The; or, The Maid of Palaiseau. In *New English Drama*, ed. W. Oxberry, 22 vols., London: W. Simpkin & R. Marshall; C. Chapple, 1820, XI, [1-2], [i]-[iv], [1]-36. *Filed under* Oxberry, William Henry. New English Drama, XI.

Man and the Marquis, The; or, The Three Spectres of the Castle of Saint Valori. London: John Cumberland, n.d. Pp. [1]-33.

Man and the Marquis, The; or, The Three Spectres of the Castle of Saint Valori. London: John Cumberland, n.d. Pp. [1]-33. Cumberland's Minor Theatre, VIII. *Filed under* Cumberland, John. Cumberland's Minor Theatre, VIII.

Melodrame Mad!; or, The Siege of Troy. London: John Miller, 1819. Pp. [i-iv], [1]-42.

Morning, Noon, and Night; or, The Romance of a Day. Music by Perry. London: W. Simpkin & R. Marshall, 1822. Pp. [i-iv], [1]-[61].

Ninth Statue, The; or, The Irishman in Bagdad. London: John Miller, 1814. Pp. [1]-44.

Of Age To-morrow. London: J. Barker, 1805. Pp. [i]-[vi], [7]-39.

Orange Boven; or, More Good News. Music by Whitaker. London: J. Barker, 1813. Pp. [1]-23. Libretto.

Past Ten O'Clock, and a Rainy Night. London: Longman, Hurst, Rees, Orme, & Brown, 1815. Pp. [i-iv], [1]-40.

Past Ten O'Clock and a Rainy Night! London: John Cumberland, n.d. Pp. [1]-39. Cumberland's British Theatre, XXXVIII. *Filed under* Cumberland, John. Cumberland's British Theatre, XXXVIII.

Paul Jones. London: John Cumberland, n.d. Pp. [1]-62. Cumberland's Minor Theatre, 11.

Paul Jones. London: John Cumberland, n.d. Pp. [1]-62. Cumberland's Minor Theatre, II. *Filed under* Cumberland, John. Cumberland's Minor Theatre, II.

Pirate, The. Baltimore: J. Robinson, 1822. Pp. [1]-57.

Ruffian Boy, The. London: John Cumberland, n.d. Pp. [1]-34.

Ruffian Boy, The. London: John Cumberland, n.d. Pp. [1]-34. Cumberland's Minor Theatre, IV. *Filed under* Cumberland, John. Cumberland's Minor Theatre, IV.

School for Prejudice, The. London: T. N. Longman & O. Rees, 1801. Pp. [1]-[85].

School for Prejudice, The. In *Modern Theatre*, ed. Mrs. Inchbald, 10 vols., London: Longman, Hurst, Rees, Orme, & Brown, 1811, IV, [331]-411.

Secret Mine, The.
See Fawcett, John.

Sixes, The; or, The Devil's in the Dice! London: John Cumberland, n.d. Pp. [1]-40. [Cumberland's Minor Theatre].

Sixes, The; or, The Devil's in the Dice! London: John Cumberland, n.d. Pp. [1]-40. Cumberland's Minor Theatre, IX. *Filed under* Cumberland, John. Cumberland's Minor Theatre, IX.

St. David's Day; or, The Honest Welchman. London: T. N. Longman & O. Rees, 1801. Pp. [1]-32.

St. David's Day; or, The Honest Welshman. Music by Attwood, T. London: John Cumberland, n.d. Pp. [1]-28. Cumberland's British Theatre, XXXVII. *Filed under* Cumberland, John. Cumberland's British Theatre, XXXVII.

Suil Dhuv the Coiner. London: John Cumberland, n.d. Pp. [1]-47. Cumberland's Minor Theatre, I. *Filed under* Cumberland, John. Cumberland's Minor Theatre, I.

Suil Dhuv the Coiner. London: G. H. Davidson, n.d. Pp. [1]-47.

Thirty Thousand; or, Who's the Richest? London: Barker & Son, 1804. Pp. [i-viii], [9]-75.

True Friends. Music by Atwood. London: J. Barker, 1800. Pp. [1]-15. Libretto.

Twenty Per Cent.; or, My Father. London: Whittingham & Arliss, 1816. Pp. [1]-32. London Theatre, XXV. *Filed under* Dibdin, Thomas John, ed. London Theatre, XXV.

Two Faces under a Hood. London: Appleyards, n.d. Pp. [i-vi], [1]-80.

Two Gregories, The; or, Where Did the Money Come From? London: Roach's Old Established Library, 1821. Pp. [1]-22.

Two Gregories, The; or, Where Did the Money Come From? London: John Cumberland, n.d. Pp. [1]-28. Cumberland's Minor Theatre, III. *Filed under* Cumberland, John. Cumberland's Minor Theatre, III.

Under the Rose; or, The Great Gentleman in the Little Parlour. London: John Cumberland & Son, n.d. Pp. [1]-24. Cumberland's Minor Theatre, 144.

Up to Town. London: J. Barker, n.d. Pp. [1]-23. Libretto.

Valentine and Orson. London: John Cumberland, n.d. Pp. [1]-28. Cumberland's British Theatre, XXVII. *Filed under* Cumberland, John. Cumberland's British Theatre, XXVII.

Valentine and Orson. Music by Jouvé. London: Barker & Son, 1804. Pp. [1]-50.

Valley of Diamonds, The; or, Harlequin Sindbad. Music by Corri, M. P. London: John Miller, 1814. Pp. [1]-19. Libretto.

Vicar of Wakefield, The. Music by Sanderson. London: John Miller, 1817. Pp. [i-ii], [1]-46.

What Next? London: Whittingham & Arliss, 1816. Pp. [1]-35. London Theatre, XXI. *Filed under* London Theatre, XXI.

What Next? In *British Drama*, 12 vols., London: John Dicks, 1871, IX, [279]-288.

White Plume, The; or, The Border Chieftains. Music by Reeve. London: Barker & Son, 1806. Pp. [1]-23. Libretto.

Who's to Have Her? Music by Reeve; Whitaker. London: J. Barker, 1813. Pp. [3]-40.

Wigwam, The; or, The Red Men of the Wilderness. London: John Dicks, n.d. Pp. [1]-15. Dicks' Standard Plays, 570.

Will for the Deed, The. London: Longman, Hurst, Rees, & Orme, 1805. Pp. [1]-[66].

Zuma; or, The Tree of Health. Music by Bishop; Braham. London: John Miller, 1818. Pp. [i-vi], [1]-46.

DICE OF DEATH!, THE
    See Oxenford, John.

DICK, COTSFORD
    Baroness, The. Music by Dick, Cotsford. London: David Allen & Sons, n.d. Pp. [1]-27. Libretto.

DICK AND HIS DOUBLE
    See Archer, Thomas.

DICK TURPIN AND TOM KING
    See Suter, William E. Adventures of Dick Turpin and Tom King, The.
    See Suter, William E.

DICK TURPIN THE SECOND
    See Wigan, Alfred Sydney. Five Hundred Pounds Reward.

DICK WHITTINGTON
    See Dyall, Clarence G.
    See Harris, Augustus Henry Glossop.
    See Lennard, Horace.

DICKENS, CHARLES
    Is She His Wife?; or, Something Singular. Boston: James R. Osgood, 1877. Pp. [1]-80.
    Is She His Wife?; or, Something Singular. London: John Dicks, n.d. Pp. [1]-9. Dicks' Standard Plays, 470.

Lamplighter, The. London: John Dicks, n.d. Pp. [1]-11. Dicks' Standard Plays, 470.

Mr. Nightingale's Diary. Boston: James R. Osgood, 1877. Pp. [1]-96.

No Thoroughfare. Written with Collins, William Wilkie. [New York: DeWitt], n.d. Pp. [1]-40.

Strange Gentleman, The. By Boz. London: Chapman & Hall, 1837 (undated facsimile). Pp. [i-vi], [1]-46.

Strange Gentleman, The. London: John Dicks, n.d. Pp. [1]-14. Dicks' Standard Plays, 466.

Village Coquettes, The. London: John Dicks, n.d. Pp. [1]-18. Dicks' Standard Plays, 467.

Village Coquettes, The. Music by Hullah, John. London: Richard Bentley, 1836 (undated facsimile). Pp. [1]-71.

DICKINSON, CHARLES H.

Rift within the Lute, The. Written with Griffiths, Arthur. New York & London: Samuel French, c.1899. Pp. [1]-17.

Third Time, The. London & New York: Samuel French, n.d. Pp. [1]-12.

DICKINSON, GOLDSWORTHY LOWES

From King to King. London: George Allen, 1891. Pp. [i]-[vi], [1]-[128].

From King to King. New York: McClure, Phillips, 1907. Fp. [i]-[viii], [1]-129.

DID I DREAM IT?
See Wooler, John Pratt.

DID YOU EVER SEND YOUR WIFE TO BROOKLYN?
See Coyne, Joseph Stirling.

DID YOU EVER SEND YOUR WIFE TO CAMBERWELL?
See Coyne, Joseph Stirling.

DIDO
See Burnand, Francis Cowley.

DIDO DONE!
See Granville, H. Such. Aeneas.

DIFFICULT TO PLEASE
See Davis, Lillie.

DILATORY DINNERS
See Anstey, F.

DILETTANTI, THE
See Peacock, Thomas Love.

DILLEY, JOSEPH J.

Alexander the Great.
See Albery, James.

At the Cross Roads. London: Samuel French; New York: T. Henry French, n.d. Pp. [1]-17. [Lacy's Acting Edition].

Auld Acqaintance. London & New York: Samuel French, n.d. Pp. [1]-28. [Lacy's Acting Edition].

Chiselling.
See Albery, James.

Glimpse of Paradise, A. London & New York: Samuel French, n.d. Pp. [1]-42. [French's Acting Edition].

Highland Fling, A. London & New York: Samuel French, n.d. Pp. [1]-18. French's Acting Edition (late Lacy's), 1710.

Love or Duty—Which Wins? Walworth: P. Burgess, n.d. Pp. [1]-23.

Marjorie.
See Clifton, Lewis.

Summoned to Court. Written with Clifton, Lewis. London & New York: Samuel French, n.d. Pp. [1]-15. French's Acting Edition (late Lacy's), 1776.

Tom Pinch. Written with Clifton, Lewis. London & New York: Samuel French, n.d. Pp. [1]-46. [Lacy's Acting Edition].

DILLON, ARTHUR

Maid of Artemis, The. Music by Baughan, C. Ernest. N. p.: n.pub., n.d. Pp. [1]-47.

DILLON, CHARLES

Mysteries of Paris, The. London: Thomas Hailes Lacy, n.d. Pp. [1]-37. Cumberland's British Theatre, [404].

DILLON, JOHN

Retribution; or, The Chieftain's Daughter. London: Longman, Hurst, Rees, Orme, & Brown, 1818. Pp. [i]-viii, [1]-92. Promptbook.

DIMITY'S DILEMMA
See Salaman, Malcolm Charles.

DIMOND, WILLIAM

Abon Hassan. Music by Weber. London: R. S. Kirby, 1825. Pp. [1]-48.

Adrian and Orrila; or, A Mother's Vengeance. London: T. Cadell & W. Davies, 1806. Pp. [i]-[viii], [9]-[12], [1]-95.

Aethiop, The; or, The Child of the Desert. London: J. Barker, 1812. Pp. [iii]-[viii], [9]-91.

Bride of Abydos, The. London: Richard White, 1818. Pp. [1-2], [i]-ii, [5]-74.

Broken Sword, The. London: J. Barker, 1816. Pp. [1]-43. 2nd ed.

Broken Sword, The. London: John Cumberland & Son, n.d. Pp. [1]-36. Cumberland's British Theatre, XLI. *Filed under* Cumberland, John. Cumberland's British Theatre, XLI.

Brother and Sister, The. New York: E. Murden, 1822. Pp. [1]-36.

Carnival at Naples, The. London: R. S. Kirby, 1831. Pp. [i-vi], [1]-67.

Conquest of Taranto, The; or, St. Clara's Eve. London: J. Barker, 1817. Pp. [1]-67.

Doubtful Son, The; or, Secrets of a Palace. London: W. H. Wyatt, 1810. Pp. [i]-[viii], [1]-82.

England's Golden Days.
See Kenilworth.

Englishmen in India. London: John Duncombe, n.d. Pp. [1]-50. Duncombe's Edition.

Foundling of the Forest, The. London: Longman, Hurst, Rees, & Orme, 1809. Pp. [i-vi], [1]-72.

Foundling of the Forest, The. In *British Drama*, 12 vols., London: John Dicks, 1871, V, [129]-150.

Foundling of the Forest, The. London: John Cumberland, n.d. Pp. [1]-62. Cumberland's British Theatre, XL. *Filed under* Cumberland, John. Cumberland's British Theatre, XL.

Gustavus Vasa, the Hero of the North. *Also:* The Hero of the North. London: J. Barker, 1811. Pp. [5]-83. Text complete. New ed.

Hero of the North, The. *Also:* Gustavus Vasa, the Hero of the North. London: Barker & Son, 1803. Pp. [1]-87. 7th ed.

Hunter of the Alps, The. London: J. Barker, n.d. Pp. [1]-39. 4th ed.

Hunter of the Alps, The. London: John Cumberland, n.d. Pp. [1]-30. Cumberland's British Theatre, XXXIX. *Filed under* Cumberland, John. Cumberland's British Theatre, XXXIX.

Kenilworth (attrib. to Dimond). *Also:* England's Golden Days. Edinburgh: James L. Huie, 1823. Pp. [1]-62.

Lady and the Devil, The. London: R. S. Kirby, n.d. Pp. [1]-44. Promptbook.

Little Jockey, The; or, Youth, Love, and Folly. London: John Dicks, n.d. Pp. [1]-14. Dicks' Standard Plays, 427.

Native Land; or, The Return from Slavery. London: R. S. Kirby, 1824. Pp. [i]-viii, [1]-73.

Native Land; or, The Return from Slavery. London: R. S. Kirby, 1824. Pp. [i]-[viii], [1]-73. 2nd ed.

Nymph of the Grotto, The; or, A Daughter's Vow! Music by Liverati; Lee, Alexander. London: R. S. Kirby, 1829. Pp. [i]-iv, [1]-73.

Peasant Boy, The. London: J. Barker, 1812. Pp. [1]-71. New ed.

Peasant Boy, The. London: John Cumberland, n.d. Pp. [1]-51. Cumberland's British Theatre, XL. *Filed under* Cumberland, John. Cumberland's British Theatre, XL.

Royal Oak, The. London: J. Barker, 1811. Pp. [1]-72. 2nd ed.

Sea-Side Story, The. Music by Attwood. London: Barker & Son, 1801. Pp. [i]-[viii], [9]-59. 2nd ed.

Seraglio, The. Music by Mozart; Kramer. London: R. S. Kirby, 1828. Pp. [i]-[viii], [1]-63.

Stage Struck; or, The Loves of Augustus Portarlington and Celestina Beverley. London & New York: Samuel French, n.d. Pp. [1]-22. Promptbook.

Young Hussar, The. London: John Cumberland, n.d. Pp. [1]-34. Cumberland's British Theatre, XLI. *Filed under* Cumberland, John. Cumberland's British Theatre, XLI.

Young Hussar, The; or, Love and Mercy. London: Barker & Son, 1807. Pp. [1]-40.

Youth, Love, and Folly. Music by Kelly. London: Barker & Son, 1805. Pp. [5]-54. Text complete.

Youth, Love, and Folly; or, The Little Jockey. Music by Kelly, Michael. London: John Cumberland, n.d. Pp. [1]-42. Cumberland's British Theatre, XXXIX. *Filed under* Cumberland, John. Cumberland's British Theatre, XXXIX.

DINNER FOR NOTHING
    See Cheltnam, Charles Smith.

DINNER FOR SIX
    See Morton, John Maddison. Who Stole the Pocket-Book?

DINNER FOR TWO
    See Carton, R. C.

DINORAH
    See Chorley, Henry Fothergill.

DINORAH UNDER DIFFICULTIES
    See Brough, William.

DIOCLESIAN
    See Doubleday, Thomas.

DIOGENES AND HIS LANTERN
    See Taylor, Tom.

DION
    See Rew, Walter.
    See Rhodes, George Ambrose.

DIPLOMACY
    See Scott, Clement William.

DIPSYCHUS
    See Clough, Arthur Hugh.

DIRCKS, RUDOLPH
    Retaliation. London: Samuel French; New York: T. Henry French, n.d. Pp. [1]-17. [Lacy's Acting Edition].

DISAGREEABLE SURPRISE, THE
    See Daniel, George.

DISAPPOINTED MILLER, THE
    See Rhodes, Thomas.

DISCARDED DAUGHTER, THE
    See Raymond, Richard John.

DISCARDED SON, THE
    See Webster, Benjamin Nottingham.

DISCREET PRINCESS, THE
    See Planché, James Robinson.

DISGUISES
    See Haworth, R.

DISHONOURED BILL
    See Peake, Richard Brinsley. House Room.

DISINHERITED SON
    See Lake, John. House of Morville, The.

DISMAL SWAMP
    See Brougham, John. Dred.

DISRAELI, BENJAMIN
    Tragedy of Count Alarcos, The. London: Henry Colburn, 1839. Pp. [1]-108.

DISSOLVING VIEWS
    See Selby, Charles.

DISTRESSED MOTHER, THE
    See Philips, Ambrose.

DISTREST MOTHER, THE
    See Philips, Ambrose.

DIVIDED DUTY
    See Dauncey, Silvanus. Month after Date, A.

DIVINE PHILOTHEA, THE
    See MacCarthy, Denis Florence (trans.).

DIVINE SURRENDER, THE
    See Wallace, William.

DIVORCE, THE
    See Beazley, Samuel James.

DIXON, BERNARD HOMER
    Behind a Mask. Written with Wood, Arthur. London & New York: Samuel French, n.d. Pp. [1]-44. [Lacy's Acting Edition].

DIXON, MARION HEPWORTH
    Truth Will Out. In *Dialogues of the Day,* ed. Oswald Crawfurd, London: Chapman & Hall, n.d., pp. [104]-111. *Filed under* Crawfurd, Oswald. Dialogues of the Day.

DIXON, WILLIAM HEPWORTH
    Azamoglan, The. London: Simpkin, Marshall, 1845. Pp. [1]-79.

DIXON, WILLIAM JOHN
    Sir Walter Ralegh. London: Hatchard, 1897. Pp. [i]-[viii], 1-[91].

DIZANCE, FRANK
    Davy Crockett. Pp. [i-ii], [1]-16, [i], 1-23, [i], 1-18. Pagination by act. Acts III-V only. Manuscript promptbook.

DJAMILEH
    See Bennett, Joseph.

DOBELL, SYDNEY THOMPSON
    Balder, Part 1. London: Smith, Elder, 1854. Pp. [i-iv], [1]-283.
    Roman, The. By Sydney Yendys (pseud.). London: Richard Bentley, 1850. Pp. [i], [1]-166.

DOCTOR BILL
    See Aïdé, Hamilton.

DOCTOR BOLUS
    See Daniel, George.

DOCTOR BY COMPULSION, THE
    See Mathew, Charles (trans.).

DOCTOR DAVY
    See Albery, James.

DOCTOR DILWORTH
    See Oxenford, John.

DOCTOR SYNTAX
    See Planché, James Robinson.

DODGE FOR A DINNER, A
    See Palmer, T. A.

DODSLEY, ROBERT
    Miller of Mansfield, The. In *British Drama,* 12 vols., London: John Dicks, 1872, X, [281]-288.

DOES HE LOVE ME?
    See Falconer, Edmund.

DOG IN THE MANGER
    See Moss, Hugh. P. U. P.

DOG OF MONTARGIS
    See Barrymore, William.
    See Harris, Henry. Forest of Bondy, The.

DOGE OF DURALTO, THE
    See Brough, Robert Barnabas.

DOING BANTING
    See Brough, William.

DOING FOR THE BEST
    See Lacy, Michael Rophino.

DOING MY UNCLE
    See Lacy, Michael Rophino.

DOING THE HANSOM
    See Harris, Augustus Glossop.

DOLL'S HOUSE
    See Archer, William (trans.).
    See Lord, Henrietta Frances (trans.). Nora.

DOLLY (anon.)
    Music by Adam. London: Thomas Hailes Lacy, n.d. Pp. [1]-28. [Lacy's Acting Edition]. Libretto.

DOLLY AND THE RAT
    See Jerrold, Douglas William.

DOLLY'S DELUSION
    See Reece, Robert. May.

DOMBEY AND SON
    See Brougham, John.

DOMESTIC ECONOMY
    See Lemon, Mark.

DOMESTIC EXPERIMENT
    See Smith, Lita. Mr. and Mrs. Muffett.

DOMESTIC HERCULES, A
  See Becher, Martin.
DOMINION OF FANCY
  See Dibdin, Thomas John. Harlequin's Tour.
DOMINIQUE THE DESERTER
  See Murray, William Henry Wood.
DOMINIQUE THE POSSESSED
  See Barnett, Charles Zachary.
DOMINO NERO, IL
  See Kenney, Charles Lamb (trans.). Domino Noir, Le.
DOMINO NOIR, LE
  See Kenney, Charles Lamb (trans.).
DOMINOES! CHESS! AND CARDS!
  See Fitzball, Edward. Zazezizozu.
DON CAESAR DE BAZAN
  See A'Beckett, Gilbert Abbott.
  See Barnett, Charles Zachary.
DON CARLOS
  See Russell, John, Lord (trans.).
DON CARLOS, INFANTE OF SPAIN
  See Cottrell, Charles Herbert (trans.).
  See Towler, John (trans.).
DON CESAR OF BAZAN
  See Archer, Thomas.
DON GARCIA
  See Lloyd, Charles (trans.).
DON GARCIA OF NAVARRE
  See Van Laun, Henri (trans.).
DON GARCIE DE NAVARRE; OU, LE PRINCE JALOUX
  See Van Laun, Henri (trans.). Don Garcia of Navarre.
DON GIOVANNI (anon. trans.)
  Music by Mozart. London & New York: Boosey, n.d.
  Pp. [i-iv], [1]-256. New ed. Vocal score.
DON GIOVANNI (anon. trans.)
  Music by Mozart. London: T. Brettell, n.d. Pp. [1]-88.
  Libretto.
DON GIOVANNI
  See Dibdin, Thomas John.
  See Maggioni, Manfredo (trans.).
DON GIOVANNI IN VENICE
  See Reece, Robert.
DON JOHN
  See Reynolds, Frederick.
DON JUAN
  See Milner, Henry M.
  See Pocock, Isaac.
  See Pocock, Isaac. Libertine, The.
  See Ross, Adrian.
  See Van Laun, Henri (trans.).
DON KARLOS
  See Bruce, John Wyndham (trans.).
DON PASQUALE (anon. trans.)
  Music by Donizetti. London: G. H. Davidson, n.d. Pp.
  [1]-28. Libretto.
DON PASQUALE
  See Kenney, Charles Lamb (trans.).
  See Maggioni, Manfredo (trans.).
  See Reynoldson, Thomas Herbert.
  See Williams, Thomas (trans.).
DON PEDRO
  See Cumberland, Richard.
DON PEDRO, KING OF CASTILE
  See Herbert, Henry John George, Earl of Carnarvon,
  Lord Porchester.
DON PEDRO THE CRUEL AND DON MANUEL THE
  COBBLER!
  See Boaden, Caroline.
DON QUIXOTE
  See Almar, George.
DONA IGNEZ DE CASTRO
  See Adamson, John (trans.).
DONE BROWN
  See Craven, Henry Thornton.
DONE BY DEPUTY.
  See Brookfield, Charles Hallam Elton. By Proxy.

DONE ON BOTH SIDES
  See Morton, John Maddison.
DONNA CHARITEA, QUEEN OF CASTILLE
  See Gower, Francis Leveson, Lord.
DONNA DEL LAGO, LA
  See Maggioni, Manfredo (trans.).
DONNA DIANA
  See Marston, John Westland.
DONNA JUANITA
  See Leigh, Henry Sambrooke.
DONNAY, MAURICE
  Douleureuse, La.
    See under title.
DON'T BE TOO QUICK TO CRY WOLF
  See Pemberton, Thomas Edgar.
DON'T BOOK YOUR MAKE UPS
  See St. George, George.
DON'T JUDGE BY APPEARANCES
  See Morton, John Maddison.
DON'T JUMP AT CONCLUSIONS
  See Davis, Lillie.
DON'T LEND YOUR UMBRELLA
  See Buckingham, Leicester Silk.
DOOM OF BAROSTEIN!
  See Lemon, Mark. Ancestress!, The.
DOOM OF DEVORGOIL, THE
  See Scott, Walter, Sir.
DOOMED TO DIE: A STORY OF OLD PARIS
  See Palmer, T. A. Too Late to Save.
DORA
  See Reade, Charles.
DORA'S DEVICE
  See Reece, Robert.
DORIA
  See Powell, Thomas.
DORINE
  See Canninge, George.
DORIS
  See Stephenson, Benjamin Charles.
DORISI, LISA
  Preciosita. London: Doremi, c.1893. Pp. [1]-16. Libretto.
DOROTHY
  See Stephenson, Benjamin Charles.
DOROTHY'S FORTUNE
  See Jerrold, Douglas William. St. Cupid.
DOROTHY'S VICTORY
  See Davis, Lillie.
DORRINGTON, W.
  Babes in the Wood, The.
    See Buckstone, John Baldwin.
DOT
  See Boucicault, Dionysius Lardner.
DOUBLE-BEDDED ROOM, THE
  See Morton, John Maddison.
DOUBLE DEALER, THE
  See Congreve, William.
  See Kemble, John Philip (arr.).
DOUBLE DEALING
  See Suter, William E.
DOUBLE DUMMY
  See Harrington, Nicholas Herbert.
DOUBLE FACED PEOPLE
  See Courtney, John.
DOUBLE GALLANT, THE
  See Cibber, Colley.
DOUBLE IMPOSTURE
  See Poole, John. Who's Who?
DOUBLE LIFE
  See Henley, William Ernest. Deacon Brodie.
DOUBLE TO DO
  See Jones, T. Confin'd in Vain.
DOUBLEDAY, THOMAS
  Babington. Edinburgh: William Blackwood; London: T.
  Cadell, 1825. Pp. [i-iv], [1]-140.

Caius Marius, the Plebeian Consul. London: John Macrone, 1836. Pp. [iii]-xvi, [1]-93.

Dioclesian. London: Hurst, Chance, 1829. Pp. [i]-[xii], [1]-140.

Italian Wife, The. Edinburgh: William Blackwood; London: T. Cadell, 1823. Pp. [i]-[viii], [1]-122.

DOUBLY SOLD
      See Elliot, Silvia Fogg.

DOUBT AND CONVICTION
      See Wild, James.

DOUBTFUL SON, THE
      See Dimond, William.

DOUBTFUL VICTORY, A
      See Oxenford, John.

DOUGLAS, THOMAS
      Friend at Court, A; or, The King and the Cobler. Burton-upon-Trent: J. Croft (printer) (priv.), 1811. Pp. [1]-54.

DOUGLAS
      See Home, John.

DOUGLAS TRAVESTIE
      See Rede, William Leman.

DOUGLASS, JOHN T.
      Chapter of Accidents. London: Thomas Hailes Lacy, n.d. Pp. [1]-17. Lacy's Acting Edition, 1429.

      Dame Durden and Her Five Servant Maids; or, Robert and Richard Were Two Pretty Men. N.p.: n.pub., n.d. Pp. [1]-16. Title page lacking. Libretto. *Filed under* Dame Durden and Her Servant Maids (anon.).

      Wooing under Difficulties. New York: Harold Roorbach, n.d. Pp. [1]-14. Acting Drama, 184. *Filed under* Douglas, John T.

DOULEUREUSE, LA (anon. trans.)
      By Donnay, Maurice. [New York: Rosenfield Typewriting], n.d. Pp. [i-ii], [1]-22, 25-56, [i], [1]-45, [i], [1]-26, [i], [1]-12. Pagination by act. Typescript.

DOVES IN A CAGE
      See Jerrold, Douglas William.

DOWAGER, THE
      See Mathews, Charles James.

DOWLING, MAURICE G.
      Lady of the Lions, The. London: Purkess, 1838. Pp. [1]-24. Promptbook.

      Othello Travestie. London: John Duncombe, n.d. Pp. [1]-33. Duncombe's Edition.

      Romeo and Juliet: As the Law Directs. London: John Duncombe, n.d. Pp. [1]-24. Duncombe's Edition.

DOWN IN A BALLOON
      See Oxenford, John.

DOWN SUNNY SOUTH
      See Forman, Edmund.

DOWNFALL AND DEATH OF KING OEDIPUS, THE
      See Fitzgerald, Edward (trans.).

DOWNFALL OF TYRANNY
      See Maclean, William. Brennus.

DOWSON, ERNEST CHRISTOPHER
      Pierrot of the Minute, The. London: Leonard Smithers, 1897. Pp. [1]-43.

DOWSON, MRS. H. M.
      See Filippi, Rosina.

DOYLE, ARTHUR CONAN
      In the Days of the Regent (attrib. to Doyle). [Hillhouse Typewriters], n.d. Pp. [i-ii], [1]-22, [i-ii], 1-26, [i-ii], [1]-22, [i-ii], [1]-29, [i-ii], 1-14, [i-ii], [1]-7. Pagination by act. Typescript promptbook.

      Jane Annie.
      See Barrie, James Mathew.

      Waterloo. New York & London: Samuel French, c.1907. Pp. [i-ii], [1]-19. French's International Copyrighted Edition of the Works of the Best Authors, 123. Promptbook.

DOYLE, THOMAS F.
      Aladdin and the Wonderful Lamp. Music by Hermann, Louis. Hull: Critic (printer), n.d. Pp. [1]-40. Libretto.

      Lucre-Land; or, Harlequin Sir Bruno the Brave and the Fairy Casket of Phantom Castle. Music by Lunt, T. Liverpool: Daily Post, n.d. Pp. [1]-41. Libretto.

Sindbad the Sailor. [Birmingham: J. Upton (printer)], n.d. Pp. [1]-24. Libretto.

DR. D.
      See Colnaghi, Charles Philip.

DR. SYNTAX AND HIS ANIMATED ALPHABET
      See Fenton, Frederick. Harlequin Old Aesop.

DRAGON-KING, THE
      See Pennie, John Fitzgerald.

DRAGON KNIGHT, THE
      See Stirling, Edward.

DRAGON OF WANTLEY, THE
      See Blanchard, Edward Litt Leman.
      See Carey, Henry.
      See Hazlewood, Colin Henry.

DRAGOONS, THE
      See Hersee, Henry.

DRAMA
      See Baddeley, Welbore St. Clair.

DRAMA AT HOME, THE
      See Planché, James Robinson.

DRAMA IN DREGS, A: A LIFE STUDY
      See Glyn, Alice Coralie.

DRAMA OF KINGS, THE
      See Buchanan, Robert Williams.

DRAMA'S LEVÉE, THE
      See Planché, James Robinson.

DRAMATIC CHAPTERS
      See Swain, Charles.

DRAMATIC FRAGMENT, A
      See Neele, Henry.

DRAMATIC SCENE, A
      See Wells, Charles Jeremiah.

DRAMATIC SCENES AND FRAGMENTS
      See Marston, John Westland.

DRAMATIC SKETCHES
      See Blacket, Joseph.

DRAMATIST, THE: OR, STOP HIM WHO CAN
      See Reynolds, Frederick.

DRAPER, E.
      Guy Fawkes.
      See Smith, Albert Richard.

DRAPERY QUESTION, THE
      See Selby, Charles.

DRAWING ROOMS, SECOND FLOOR, AND ATTICS
      See Morton, John Maddison.

DRAYTON, HENRI
      Jewess, The. Music by Halevy, F. London: John K. Chapman, n.d. Pp. [1]-35. Libretto.

      Love's Labor Lost. In *Songs, Recitatives...in Mr. & Mrs. Henri Drayton's Parlor Operas,* Providence: Evening Press, n.d., pp. [1]-8. Libretto. *Filed under* Songs, Recitatives...

      Marry in Haste; or, An Hour in the Bastile. Music by Lutz, Meyer. New York: C. A. Alvord (printer) (priv.), 1860. Pp. [1]-12. Libretto. *Filed under* Songs, Recitatives...

      Mephistopheles; or, Faust and Marguerite. Music by Lutz, Meyer. London: John K. Chapman, 1855. Pp. [1]-35. Libretto.

      Never Too Late to Mend. Part 2 of Love Is Blind (by Val Morris). In *Songs, Recitatives...in Mr. & Mrs. Henri Drayton's Parlor Operas,* Providence: Evening Press, n.d., pp. [9]-12. Libretto. *Filed under* Songs, Recitatives...

DREAD OF MILITARY PUNISHMENT
      See Barnett, Charles Zachary. Cateran's Son, The.

DREADFULLY ALARMING
      See Edwardes, Conway Theodore Marriott.
      See Edwardes, Conway Theodore Marriott. Only Somebody.

DREAM, THE
      See Baillie, Joanna.

DREAM AT HOME
      See Blanchard, Edward Litt Leman. Pork Chops.

DREAM AT SEA, THE
      See Buckstone, John Baldwin.

DREAM FACES
    See Miller, Wynn F.
DREAM GIRL OF THE DEVIL-HOLL
    See Fitzball, Edward. Mary Glastonbury.
DREAM OF FATE, THE
    See Barnett, Charles Zachary.
DREAM OF LIFE, A
    See Watts, Walter.
DREAM OF THE FUTURE, A
    See Dance, Charles.
DREAM SPECTRE, THE
    See Wilks, Thomas Egerton.
DREAMS
    See Robertson, Thomas William.
DREAMS OF DELUSION
    See Simpson, John Palgrave.
DRED
    See Brougham, John.
    See Suter, William E.
DRENCHED AND DRIED
    See Kerr, John.
DRESS REHEARSAL, A
    See Sims, George Robert.
DRIFTED APART
    See Young, Charles Lawrence, Sir.
DRINKWATER, ALBERT E.
    Fair Conquest, A. In *Plays and Poems*, London: Griffith, Farran, Okeden, & Welsh, n.d., pp. [95]-114. *Filed under* Plays and Poems.
    Sir Jasper's Vow. In *Plays and Poems*, London: Griffith, Farran, Okeden, & Welsh, n.d., pp. [39]-94. *Filed under* Plays and Poems.
    Trial by Fire. In *Plays and Poems*, London: Griffith, Farran, Okeden, & Welsh, n.d., pp. [i-viii], [1]-38. *Filed under* Plays and Poems.
DRINKWATER (later Bethune), **JOHN ELLIOT** (trans.)
    Maid of Orleans, The. By Schiller. London: W. Wilcockson (printer) (priv.), 1835. Pp. [i-viii], [1]-210.
    Maid of Orleans, The. By Schiller. In *Specimens of Swedish and German Poetry, Part 2*, London: John Murray, 1848, pp. [1]-222. Title page lacking. *Filed under* Bethune, John Elliot Drinkwater.
DRIVER, HENRY AUSTIN
    Death. In *Death's Doings*, ed. R. Dagley, 2nd ed., 2 vols., London: J. Andrews, 1827, I, [i], [215]-224.
DRIVER AND HIS DOG
    See Reynolds, Frederick. Caravan, The.
DROMCOLLOHER, LAWRENCE (pseud. of ?)
    Gretna Green; or, The Elopement. London: Samuel French, n.d.. Pp. [1]-48.
DROPPING WELL OF KNARESBOROUGH
    See Almar, George. Charcoal Burner, The.
DROSS
    See Braddon, Mary Elizabeth.
    See Roberts, George.
DROWNED CREW!
    See Fitzball, Edward. Carmilhan.
DRUGGED AND DROWNED IN DIGBETH
    See Pemberton, Thomas Edgar. Gentle Gertrude of the Infamous Redd Lyon Inn.
DRUID, THE
    See Cromwell, Thomas Kitson.
DRUID, THE; OR, THE VISION OF FINGAL (anon.)
    London: B. McMillan (printer), 1815. Pp. [1]-17.
DRUM HEAD MARRIAGE
    See Long, Charles. Hymen's Muster Roll.
DRUNKARD, THE
    See Lacy, Thomas Hailes.
DRUNKARD'S CHILDREN, THE
    See Johnstone, John Beer.
DRUNKARD'S DOOM
    See Pitt, George Dibdin.
    See Pitt, George Dibdin. Last Nail, The.
DRUNKARD'S FATE, THE
    See Jerrold, Douglas William.

DRUNKARD'S GLASS
    See Morton, Thomas, jr. Another Glass!
DRURY, WILLIAM PRICE
    H.M.S. Missfire; or, The Honest Tar and the Wicked First Luff. Valletta, Malta: L. Critien, n.d. Pp. [i-ii], 1-36.
DRYDEN, CHARLES
    Damon the Dauntless and Phillis the Fair. London: W. H. & L. Collingridge (printer), 1869. Pp. [1]-12.
DRYDEN, JOHN
    All for Love; or, The World Well Lost. London: Sherwood, Neely, & Jones, 1818. Pp. [1]-[68]. London Theatre, XXII. *Filed under* Dibdin, Thomas John, ed. London Theatre, XXII.
    All for Love; or, The World Well Lost. In *British Drama*, 12 vols., London: John Dicks, 1871, VII, [193]-212.
DUBOIS, ALFRED
    Deeds of Dreadful Note. New York: Rathbone Gardner, c.1880. Pp. [21]-26. New York Drama, V, 60.
    Deeds of Dreadful Note. London: National Acting Drama Office, n.d. <wrps. Webster>. Pp. [1]-19. Webster's Acting National Drama, 122. Promptbook.
DUBOURG, AUGUSTUS W.
    Angelica. London: Richard Bentley & Son, 1892. Pp. [i-viii], [1]-112.
    Art and Love. In *Four Original Plays*, London: Richard Bentley & Son, 1883, pp. [i], [218]-239.
    Greencloth: A Story of Monte Carlo. In *Four Original Plays*, London: Richard Bentley & Son, 1883, pp. [i]-xvi, [1]-74.
    Land and Love. In *Four Original Plays*, London: Richard Bentley & Son, 1883, pp. [i], [147]-217.
    New Men and Old Acres.
    See Taylor, Tom.
    Sister's Penance, A.
    See Taylor, Tom.
    Sympathy. London & New York: Samuel French, n.d. Pp. [1]-12. [Lacy's Acting Edition].
    Twenty Minutes under an Umbrella. London & New York: Samuel French, n.d. Pp. [1]-12.
    Vittoria Contarini: A Story of Venice. In *Four Original Plays*, London: Richard Bentley & Son, 1883, pp. [i], [75]-146.
DUCHESS DE LA VAUBALIÈRE, THE
    See Buckstone, John Baldwin.
DUCHESS ELEANOUR
    See Chorley, Henry Fothergill.
DUCHESS OF BAYSWATER AND CO., THE
    See Heathcote, Arthur M.
DUCHESS OF MANSFELDT, THE (anon.)
    London & New York: Samuel French, n.d. Pp. [i], [60]-75.
DUCHESS OF PADUA, THE
    See Wilde, Oscar Fingall O'Flahertie Wills.
DUCHESS OR NOTHING
    See Gordon, Walter.
DUCHESS TRANSFORMED, THE
    See Anderdon, William Henry.
DUCHESSE DE LA VALLIÈRE, THE
    See Bulwer (later Bulwer-Lytton), Edward George Earle Lytton, Lord Lytton.
DUCK HUNTING
    See Coyne, Joseph Stirling.
DUCKWORTH, WILLIAM
    Cromwell. London: William Freeman, 1870. Pp. [i]-[viii], [1]-56.
DUCLAUX, MRS.
    See Robinson, Agnes Mary Frances.
DUDLEY, HENRY BATE
    Woodman, The. In *British Drama*, 12 vols., London: John Dicks, 1871, IX, [33]-52.
DUEL, THE
    See Peake, Richard Brinsley.
DUEL EN AMOUR, UN
    See Reade, Charles. Ladies' Battle, The.
DUEL IN THE DARK
    See Coyne, Joseph Stirling.
    See Robertson, Thomas William. Birds of Prey.

DUEL IN THE MIST!
  See Fitzball, Edward. Walter Brand.
DUEL IN THE SNOW
  See Fitzball, Edward. Christmas Eve.
DUELISTS, THE
  See Maclaren, Archibald.
DUENNA, THE
  See Sheridan, Richard Brinsley.
**DUFFERIN, HELEN SELINA SHERIDAN BLACKWOOD,
LADY**
  Finesse; or, A Busy Day in Messina. In *Songs, Poems, &
  Verses*, 4th ed., London: John Murray, 1895, pp. [i],
  [307]-439.
DUKE D'ORMOND, THE
  See Lloyd, Charles.
DUKE FOR A DAY
  See Neil, Ross.
DUKE OF LONDON, THE
  See Knowles, James Sheridan.
DUKE OF MANTUA, THE
  See Roby, John.
DUKE OF MERCIA, THE
  See de Vere, Aubrey.
DUKE OF MILAN, THE
  See Massinger, Philip.
DUKE'S BEQUEST.
  See Brougham, John. Duke's Daughter, The.
  See Brougham, John. Duke's Motto, The.
DUKE'S COAT, THE; OR, THE NIGHT AFTER WATERLOO
(anon.)
  London: John Miller, 1815. Pp. [i-viii], [1]-35.
DUKE'S DAUGHTER, THE
  See Brougham, John.
  See Brougham, John. Duke's Motto, The.
DUKE'S LABORATORY, THE
  See Meredith, Owen.
DUKE'S MOTTO
  See Brougham, John. Duke's Daughter, The.
  See Brougham, John.
DULCAMARA
  See Gilbert, William Schwenck.
DUMAS, ALEXANDRE
  Catherine of Cleves.
    See Gower, Francis Leveson, Lord (trans.).
  Ladies of Saint-Cyr, The.
    See under title.
  Mademoiselle de Belle Isle.
    See Kemble, Frances Anne (Fanny) (trans.).
DUMB BELLE, THE
  See Bernard, William Bayle.
  See Planché, James Robinson.
DUMB CONSCRIPT, THE
  See Grattan, H. P.
DUMB GIRL OF GENOA, THE
  See Farrell, John.
DUMB GIRL OF PORTICI
  See Macfarren, Natalia (trans.).
  See Milner, Henry M. Masaniello.
DUMB GUIDE OF THE TYROL, THE
  See Blake, Thomas G.
DUMB LADY CURED
  See Fielding, Henry. Mock Doctor, The.
  See Wood, George. Irish Doctor, The.
DUMB MAN OF MANCHESTER, THE
  See Rayner, Barnabas F.
DUMB SAILOR BOY!
  See Lucas, William James. Death Plank, The.
DUMB SAVOYARD AND HIS MONKEY, THE
  See Thompson, C. Pelham.
DUNBAR, THE KING'S ADVOCATE
  See Waddie, Charles.
DUNDREARY
  See Taylor, Tom.

DUNN, SINCLAIR (trans.)
  Irma. By Bonawitz, J. H. London: Stanley Lucas, Weber,
  n.d. Pp. [1]-145. Vocal score.
DUPLICATE KEYS
  See Ebsworth, Joseph. Two Prisoners of Lyons, The.
DUPLICITY
  See Holcroft, Thomas.
DURANT, HÉLOÏSE
  Dante. London: Kegan Paul, Trench, 1889. Pp. [iii]-[xvi],
  [1]-136.
DURAZZO
  See Haynes, James.
DUSK OF THE GODS
  See Corder, Henrietta Louisa Walford, Mrs. Frederick
  (trans.).
  See Forman, Alfred (trans.).
DUST
  See Abel, William Henry.
DUSTMAN'S BELLE, THE
  See Dance, Charles.
DUTCH, J. S.
  Grace. By I. S. Dutch. Manchester: Thomas J. Day, 1878.
  Pp. [i]-vi, [7]-70.
  Vanquished! Manchester: Thomas J. Day, 1875. Pp. [1]-59.
DUTCH GOVERNOR, THE
  See Poole, John. 'Twould Puzzle a Conjuror.
DU TERREAU, LOUIS HENRY F.
  Love Wins.
    See Clarke, Henry Saville.
DUTNALL, MARTIN
  **Harlequin Hey Diddle Diddle the Cat and the Fiddle and the
  Cow That Jumped over the Moon; or, Oranges and
  Lemons and the Twelve Dancing Princesses.** N.p.: n.pub.,
  n.d. Pp. [1]-24. Title page lacking. Libretto. *Filed under*
  Harlequin Hey Diddle Diddle . . . (anon.).
  Queen of Hearts and the Wonderful Tarts, The. N.p.: n.pub.,
  n.d. Author and title supplied in ms. Pp. [1]-24.
DUTY
  See Albery, James.
DUX REDUX
  See Rhoades, James.
DWARF OF NAPLES, THE
  See Soane, George.
DWARRIS, FORTUNATUS WILLIAM LILLEY, SIR
  Alberic, Consul of Rome; or, The School for Reformers.
  London: Saunders & Otley, 1832. Pp. []-[xii], [1]-114.
  Railway Results; or, The Gauge Deliverance. London:
  Chapman & Hall, 1845. Pp. [i-iv], [1]-[44].
DWYER, P. W.
  Soldier of Fortune, The. London: Barker & Son (printer),
  n.d. Pp. [1]-87.
DYALL, CHARLES
  Foxglove; or, The Quaker's Will. Music by Rohner, G. W.
  Liverpool: Gilbert G. Walmsley (printer), n.d. Pp. [1]-40.
  Libretto.
DYALL, CLARENCE G.
  Dick Whittington; or, An Old Story Re-told. London & New
  York: Samuel French, n.d. Pp. [1]-34. [Fairy and Home
  Plays for Home Performance, 22].
D'YE KNOW ME NOW?
  See Martin, William.
DYING FOR LOVE
  See Morton, John Maddison.
DYING GIFT
  See Grattan, H. P. Minerali, The.
EACH FOR HIMSELF (anon.)
  London: Effingham Wilson, 1816. Pp. [i]-iv, [1]-36.
EADBURGA
  See Capper, Richard.
EAGLET, THE
  See Parker, Louis Napoleon (trans.).
EARL OF BRECON, THE
  See Landor, Robert Eyres.
EARL OF ESSEX, THE
  See Jones, Henry.

EARL OF GOWRIE, THE
　　See White, James, Rev.
EARL OF POVERTY, THE
　　See Almar, George.
EARL OF WARWICK, THE
　　See Francklin, Thomas, Dr.
EARLS OF HAMMERSMITH, THE
　　See Lawler, Dennis.
EARLY DAYS OF SHAKSPERE
　　See Curling, Henry. Merry Wags of Warwickshire, The.
EARTHQUAKE, THE
　　See Fitzball, Edward.
EAST LYNNE (anon.)
　　Boston: George M. Baker, n.d. Pp. [1]-45. Spencer's Universal Stage, 47. *Filed under* Wood, Ellen Price.
EAST LYNNE (anon.)
　　London: John Dicks, n.d. Pp. [1]-14. Dicks' Standard Plays, 311.
EASTER RECESS, THE
　　See Morgan, Sydney Owenson, Mrs. Thomas Charles (Lady).
EASY SHAVING
　　See Burnand, Francis Cowley.
EBSWORTH, JOSEPH
　　Adelaide; or, The Fatal Seduction. London: John Lowndes, n.d. Pp. [1]-47.
　　Crockery's Misfortunes; or, Transmogrifications. London: John Lowndes, 1821. Pp. [i-iv], [1]-15.
　　Rival Valets, The. London: Thomas Dolby, 1825. Pp. [1]-38. Dolby's British Theatre, XII. *Filed under* Cumberland, John. Cumberland's British Theatre, XII.
　　Rival Valets, The. London: Thomas Dolby, 1825. Pp. [1]-38. [Cumberland's British Theatre].
　　Rosalie; or, The Bohemian Mother. Edinburgh: W. Reid (printer), 1828. Pp. [i-iv], [1]-28.
　　Rouge et Noir; or, Whigs and Widows. London: S. G. Fairbrother, n.d. Pp. [1]-31.
　　Two Prisoners of Lyons, The; or, The Duplicate Keys. T. Woodfall (printer) (priv.), 1824. Pp. [i-vi], [1]-42.
EBSWORTH, MARY EMMA FAIRBROTHER, MRS. JOSEPH
　　Payable at Sight; or, The Chaste Salute. London: John Cumberland, n.d. Pp. [1]-27. Cumberland's Minor Theatre, XIV. *Filed under* Cumberland, John. Cumberland's Minor Theatre, XIV.
ECCENTRIC LOVER, THE
　　See Cumberland, Richard.
ECCENTRICITY
　　See Maclaren, Archibald.
ECHEGARAY, JOSÉ
　　Folly or Saintliness.
　　　　See Lynch, Hannah (trans.).
　　Great Galeoto, The.
　　　　See Lynch, Hannah (trans.).
　　Mariana.
　　　　See Graham, James (trans.).
　　Son of Don Juan, The.
　　　　See Graham, James (trans.).
ECLIPSING THE SON
　　See Hartopp, W. W.
ECLOGUES
　　See Davidson, John.
ÉCOLE DES FEMMES
　　See Van Laun, Henri (trans.). School for Wives, The.
ÉCOLE DES MARIS
　　See Van Laun, Henri (trans.). School for Husbands, The.
EDBURGA
　　See Buchanan, Robert.
EDDA
　　See Fitzball, Edward.
EDDYSTONE ELF, THE
　　See Pitt, George Dibdin.
EDEN, GUY ERNEST MORTON
　　'Prentice Pillar, The. Music by Somerville, Reginald.

London: John Macqueen, 1897. Pp. [i]-[vi], [7]-31. Libretto.
EDEN
　　See Bridges, Robert Seymour.
EDENDALE
　　See Cheltnam, Charles Smith.
EDGAR
　　See Manners, George.
　　See Ross, Ronald.
EDGAR THE SOCIALIST
　　See Bonawitz, J. H., jr.
EDGEWORTH, MARIA
　　Love and Law. In *Comic Dramas in Three Acts,* London: R. Hunter, 1817, pp. [i]-[viii], [1]-136. *Filed under* Comic Dramas in Three Acts.
　　Love and Law. In *Comic Dramas in Three Acts,* 2nd ed., London: R. Hunter, n.d., pp. [iii]-[viii], [1]-136. *Filed under* Collected Works.
　　Old Poz. London: Thomas Hailes Lacy, n.d. Pp. [1]-14.
　　Organ Grinder, The. London: Thomas Hailes Lacy, n.d. Pp. [1]-27.
　　Rose, Thistle, and Shamrock, The. In *Comic Dramas in Three Acts,* London: R. Hunter, 1817, pp. [255]-381. *Filed under* Comic Dramas in Three Acts.
　　Rose, Thistle, and Shamrock, The. In *Comic Dramas in Three Acts,* 2nd ed., London: R. Hunter, n.d., pp. [255]-381. *Filed under* Collected Works.
　　Two Guardians, The. In *Comic Dramas in Three Acts,* London: R. Hunter, 1817, pp. [137]-254. *Filed under* Comic Dramas in Three Acts.
　　Two Guardians, The. In *Comic Dramas in Three Acts,* 2nd ed., London: R. Hunter, n.d., pp. [137]-254. *Filed under* Collected Works.
EDICT OF CHARLEMAGNE
　　See Reynolds, Frederick. Free Knights, The.
EDINA AND THE WHITE HART OF THE LOTHIANS
　　See Lowe, William.
EDISON, JOHN SIBBALD
　　Henry of Richmond. London: Rivingtons, 1857. Pp. [i]-viii, [1]-236.
　　Jephtha. London: Rivingtons, 1863. Pp. [i]-[viii], [5]-194.
　　King Henry the Third, Part 1. London: T. Cadell, 1840. Pp. i-ii, [1]-122.
　　Northumberland. London: Rivingtons, 1866. Pp. [i-iv], [1]-256.
EDMONSTONE, ARCHIBALD
　　Gaston de Foix. In *Tragedies,* Edinburgh: Thomas Constable, 1837, pp. [151]-300.
　　Leonora. In *Tragedies,* Edinburgh: Thomas Constable, 1837, pp. [1]-150.
EDMUND KEAN; OR, THE GENIUS AND THE LIBERTINE (anon.)
　　London: G. Vickers, 1847. Pp. [1]-116.
EDUCATION
　　See Morton, Thomas, sr.
EDWARD AND SUSAN
　　See Dibdin, Charles Isaac Mungo, jr.
EDWARD THE BLACK PRINCE
　　See Shirley, William.
　　See Sladen, Douglas Brooke Wheelton.
EDWARD THE SEVENTH (anon.)
　　London: J. Ogden (printer), 1876. Pp. [i]-[viii], [1]-90.
EDWARDES, CONWAY THEODORE MARRIOTT
　　Anne Boleyn. London & New York: Samuel French, n.d. Pp. [1]-35.
　　Board and Residence. London: Thomas Hailes Lacy, n.d. Pp. [1]-14. [Lacy's Acting Edition].
　　Dreadfully Alarming. Written with Cullerne, Edward. *Also:* Only Somebody. London: Thomas Hailes Lacy, n.d. Pp. [1]-16. [Lacy's Acting Edition].
　　First Love. London: Sherwood; Bath: E. Williams, 1841. Pp. [i-x], [1]-79.
　　Heroes. London & New York: Samuel French, n.d. Pp. [1]-42. Lacy's Acting Edition.

Linda di Chamouni; or, The Blighted Flower. London: Thomas Hailes Lacy, n.d. Pp. [1]-41.

Long Odds. London & New York: Samuel French, n.d. Pp. [1]-54. Lacy's Acting Edition.

Only Somebody. Written with Cullerne, Edward. *Also:* Dreadfully Alarming. New York: Wheat & Cornett, c.1876. Pp. [28]-32. New York Drama, I, 12.

Our Pet. London & New York: Samuel French, n.d. Pp. [1]-36. [Lacy's Acting Edition].

EDWARDS, HENRY SUTHERLAND

Christmas Boxes.
See Mayhew, Augustus Septimus.

Four Cousins, The.
See Mayhew, Augustus Septimus.

Goose with the Golden Eggs, The.
See Mayhew, Augustus Septimus.

Little Red Riding Hood.
See Bridgeman, John Vipon.

Mephistopheles.
See Brough, Robert Barnabas.

Noureddin and the Fair Persian. London: W. S. Johnson, n.d. Pp. [1]-24.

EDWARDS, JOHN

Abradatas and Panthea. London: James Ridgway, 1803. Pp. [i-ii], [1]-87.

EDWARDS, OSMAN (trans.)

Gauntlet, A. By Bjørnson, Bjørnstjerne. London: Longmans, Green, 1894. Pp. [i]-[xvi], [1]-151.

EDWARDS, PIERREPONT

Honour before Wealth; or, The Romance of a Poor Young Man. Written with Wallack, Lester. *Also:* The Romance of a Poor Young Man. London & New York: Samuel French, n.d. Pp. [1]-54. French's Acting Edition (late Lacy's), 96.

Romance of a Poor Young Man, The. Written with Wallack, Lester. *Also:* Honour before Wealth. New York: Samuel French, c.1859. Pp. [1]-53. Standard Drama, 225. Promptbook.

EDWIN AND ELGIVA
See Pennie, John Fitzgerald.

EDWIN AND EMMA
See Long, Charles.

EDWIN, HEIR OF CRESSINGHAM
See Fitzball, Edward.

EDWIN THE FAIR
See Taylor, Henry.

EDWIG AND ELGIVA
See Tilston, Thomas.

EGERTON, FRANCIS
See Gower, Francis Leveson, Lord.

EGLANTINE
See Neil, Ross.

EGMONT (anon. trans.)
By Goethe. London: Saunders & Otley, 1848. Pp. [i]-[vi], [1]-170.

EGMONT
See Coleridge, Arthur Duke.

EGYPTIAN, THE
See Wilkins, John H.

EGYPTIAN FESTIVAL, THE
See Franklin, Andrew.

EIGHT HOURS AT THE SEA-SIDE
See Morton, John Maddison.

8:30 A.M., THE
See Ridge, William Pett.

1863
See Byron, Henry James.

EILEEN OGE
See Falconer, Edmund.

EILY O'CONNOR
See Wilks, Thomas Egerton.

ELBOW SHAKERS!, THE
See Cooper, Frederick Fox.

ELDER BRUTUS
See Cumberland, Richard. Sybil, The.

ELDEST, THE (anon. trans.)
By Lemaître, Jules. London: Mrs. Fabian, Typewriting Office, n.d. Pp. [i-ii], [1]-22, [i], [1]-21, [i], [1]-15, [i], [1]-12. Pagination by act. Typescript.

ELECTION, THE
See Baillie, Joanna.

ELECTION IDYL, AN
See Crawfurd, Oswald.

ELECTRA
See Potter, Robert (trans.).

ELECTRA IN A NEW ELECTR'IC LIGHT
See Talfourd, Francis.

ELENA UBERTI (anon.)
Music by Mercadante. London: S. G. Fairbrother, n.d. Pp. [1]-31. Libretto.

ELEVENTH HOUR, THE
See Raymond, Richard John.

ELFIE
See Boucicault, Dionysius Lardner.

ELFINELLA
See Neil, Ross.

ELFLAND
See Carpenter, Edward.

ELFRIDA
See Wallace, Albany.

ELIDUKE, COUNT OF YVELOC
See Roscoe, William Caldwell.

ELIGIBLE SITUATION, AN
See Archer, Thomas.

ELIOT, ARTHUR

Money Spider, The; or, On the Spot. Music by Lucas, Clarence. London: Edwin D. Lloyds, c.1897. Pp. [1]-24. Libretto.

ELIOT, GEORGE (pseud. of Evans, Mary Ann) (later Mrs. J. W. Cross)

Armgart. In *Spanish Gypsy . . .*, New York: William L. Allison, n.d., pp. 257-292. *Filed under* Agatha.

Spanish Gypsy, The. Edinburgh & London: William Blackwood & Sons, 1868. Pp. [i-iv], [1]-358.

Spanish Gypsy, The. In *Spanish Gypsy . . .*, New York: William L. Allison, n.d., pp. [3]-226.

ELISIR D' AMORE, L' (anon.)
Music by Donizetti. London: S. G. Fairbrother (printer), 1845. Pp. [1]-18. Libretto.

ELISIR D' AMORE, L'
See Kenney, Charles Lamb (trans.).
See Maggioni, Manfredo (trans.).
See Reynoldson, Thomas Herbert.

ELISIRE D' AMORE, L' (anon.)
Music by Donizetti. *Also:* The Elixir of Love. Boston: Oliver Ditson, c.1860. Pp. [1]-27. Ditson Standard Opera Libretto.. Libretto.

ELIXIR OF LOVE
See Elisire d'Amore, L'.
See Reynoldson, Thomas Herbert. Elisir d'Amore, L'.

ELIZA FENNING
See Neale, Frederick.

ELIZABETH, QUEEN OF ENGLAND (anon. trans.)
By Giacometti, Paolo. New York: Metropolitan Print, 1875. Pp. [1]-40.

ELIZABETH, QUEEN OF ENGLAND
See Williams, Thomas (trans.).

ELLA ROSENBERG
See Kenney, James.

ELLEN
See Sotheby, William.

ELLEN WAREHAM
See Burton, William Evans.

ELLESMERE, EARL OF
See Gower, Francis Leveson, Lord.

ELLIOT, SILVIA FOGG

Doubly Sold. In *Dialogues of the Day*, ed. Oswald Crawfurd, London: Chapman & Hall, n.d., pp. [162]-171. *Filed under* Crawfurd, Oswald. Dialogues of the Day.

ELLIS, GEORGE
    Harlequin Billy Taylor; or, The Flying Dutchman and the King of Raritongo. Written with Sala, George Augustus Henry Fairfield; Sala, C. K. By George Ellis and The Brothers Sala. London: Thomas Hailes Lacy, n.d. Pp. [1]-16. Lacy's Acting Edition, 737. Libretto.
    Harlequin Cherry and Fair Star; or, The Green Bird, the Dancing Waters, and the Singing Tree! Music by Hughes, R. London: Thomas Hailes Lacy, n.d. Pp. [1]-24. Libretto.
    Old Bogey. London: Charles Jaques, 1888. Pp. [1]-20.
ELLIS, WALTER
    Major and Miner. London & New York: Samuel French, n.d. Pp. [1]-24. [Lacy's Acting Edition].
    Mem. VII. London: Samuel French; New York: T. Henry French, n.d. Pp. [1]-20.
    Our Relatives. London & New York: Samuel French, n.d. Pp. [1]-14.
    Troubled Waters.
        See Thomas, Charles Inigo.
    Vol. III. London: Samuel French; New York: T. Henry French, n.d. Pp. [1]-19.
ELLISTON, ROBERT WILLIAM
    Venetian Outlaw, The. London: C. & R. Baldwin, 1805. Pp. [i]-[x], [1]-60.
ELLISTON, ROBERT WILLIAM (arr.)
    King Lear. By Shakespeare, William. London: J. Tabby (printer), 1820. Pp. [i]-[xii], [1]-68.
ELOPEMENT
        See Dromcolloher, Lawrence. Gretna Green.
        See Jones, Henry Arthur.
        See Maclaren, Archibald.
ELOPEMENTS IN HIGH LIFE
        See Sulivan, Robert.
ELPHI BEY
        See Hamilton, Ralph, Col.
ELSHIE
        See Gott, Henry.
        See Gott, Henry. Wizard of the Moor, The.
ELSIE'S RIVAL
        See Greet, Dora Victoire, Mrs.
ELSINA
        See Klanert, Charles Moritz.
ELTON, EDWARD WILLIAM
    Paul the Poacher. London: John Cumberland, n.d. Pp. [1]-35. [Cumberland's Minor Theatre].
    Paul the Poacher. London: John Cumberland, n.d. Pp. [1]-35. Cumberland's Minor Theatre, XI. *Filed under* Cumberland, John. Cumberland's Minor Theatre, XI.
ELVES, THE
        See Selby, Charles.
ELVES OF THE FOREST
        See Hazlewood, Colin Henry. Marble Bride, The.
ELVESTINE
        See Calmour, Alfred Cecil.
EMDEN, WILLIAM SAMUEL
    Evil May Day!, The; or, The London 'Prentices of 1517. London: John Duncombe, n.d. Pp. [1]-28. Duncombe's Edition.
    Head of the Family, The. London & New York: Samuel French, n.d. Pp. [1]-22. [Lacy's Acting Edition].
    Love's Labyrinth. London: Thomas Hailes Lacy, n.d. Pp. [1]-18. [Lacy's Acting Edition].
    New Inventions. London: W. Barth, n.d. Pp. [1]-32. Promptbook.
    Rear Admiral, The. London: John Duncombe, n.d. Pp. [1]-21. Duncombe's Edition.
EMERALD HEART, THE
        See Hazlewood, Colin Henry.
EMERALD ISLE, THE
        See Hood, Basil Charles Willett.
EMIGRANT'S DAUGHTER, THE
        See Raymond, Richard John.
EMIGRANTS
        See Sheil, Richard Lalor. Adelaide.

EMILIA GALOTTI
        See Bell, Ernest (trans.).
        See Holcroft, Fanny (trans.).
        See Thompson, Benjamin (trans.).
EMILY
        See Mitford, Mary Russell.
EMPEDOCLES ON ETNA
        See Arnold, Matthew.
EMPEROR AND GALILEAN. PART 1: CAESAR'S APOSTASY; PART 2: THE EMPEROR JULIAN
        See Archer, William (trans.).
EMPEROR AND THE SOLDIER!
        See Walker, John. Napoleon!
EMPEROR JULIAN
        See Archer, William (trans.). Emperor and Galilean.
EMPEROR'S OWN
        See Morton, Edward A. San Toy.
EMPIRE OF PHILANTHROPY, THE
        See Hall, William Seward.
EMPRESS AND NO EMPRESS
        See Maclaren, Archibald.
EMPTY KHAN AND THE KHURDISH CONSPIRATORS
        See Byron, Henry James. Wild Wolf of Tartary, The.
EMSON, FRANK E.
    Bumble's Courtship. London & New York: Samuel French, n.d. Pp. [1]-11. [Lacy's Acting Edition].
    Gunpowder Plot. London: Simpkin, Marshall, 1874. Pp. [1]-26.
    Ivy Hall, Richmond. London: Simpkin, Marshall, 1873. Pp. [1]-23.
    Weller Family, The. Saffron Walden: Arthur Boardman (printer), 1878. Pp. [1]-32.
ENCHANTED EYES
        See Brough, Robert Barnabas. Doge of Duralto, The.
ENCHANTED FOREST, THE
        See Dance, Charles.
ENCHANTED ISLAND, THE
        See Fawcett, John.
ENCHANTED ISLE, THE
        See Brough, William.
ENCHANTED RING.
        See Albert, ?. Anneau Magique, L'.
ENCHANTED SHEPHERD
        See Beldam, Joseph. Pastore Incantato, Il.
ENCHANTED STANDARD
        See Pocock, Isaac. Alfred the Great.
ENCHANTED WOOD, THE
        See Byron, Henry James.
ENCHANTRESS, THE
        See Bunn, Alfred.
END OF THE BEGINNING, THE
        See Hunt, Violet.
END OF THE TETHER, THE
        See Baddeley, G. C.
ENDYMION
        See Brough, William.
ENEMY OF SOCIETY, AN
        See Archer, William (trans.).
ENEMY OF THE PEOPLE, AN
        See Aveling, Eleanor Marx, Mrs. Edward (trans.).
ENEMY'S CAMP, THE
        See Leonard, Herbert.
ENFANT PRODIGUE
        See Webb, Charles (trans.). Azael, the Prodigal.
ENGAGED
        See Gilbert, William Schwenck.
        See Leverson, Mrs. Ernest.
ENGLAND, PAUL (trans.)
    Flying Dutchman, The. By Wagner. Berlin: Adolph Fürstner, n.d. Pp. [i-ii], [1]-664. Vocal score.
ENGLAND IN 1415
        See Carpenter, Joseph Edwards. Sanctuary, The.
ENGLAND PRESERVED
        See Watson, George.

ENGLAND'S DARLING
    See Austin, Alfred.
ENGLAND'S GOLDEN DAYS
    See Dimond, William. Kenilworth.
ENGLISH FLEET IN 1342, THE
    See Dibdin, Thomas John.
ENGLISH GENTLEMAN
    See Byron, Henry James.
    See Smith, John Frederick. Sir Roger de Coverley.
ENGLISH HERMIT
    See Dibdin, Charles Isaac Mungo, jr. Philip Quarll.
ENGLISH KING
    See Dew, Dyer. Harold.
ENGLISH MERCHANT, THE
    See Colman, George, sr.
ENGLISH SLAVE, THE
    See Pennie, John Fitzgerald.
ENGLISH TRAGEDY, AN
    See Kemble, Frances Anne (Fanny).
ENGLISHMAN'S FIRESIDE
    See Colman, George, jr. John Bull.
ENGLISHMAN'S HOUSE IS HIS CASTLE, AN
    See Morton, John Maddison.
ENGLISHMEN IN INDIA
    See Dimond, William.
ENOCH ARDEN
    See Matthison, Arthur.
ENRICO
    See Baddeley, Welbore St. Clair.
ENSIGN, THE
    See Thompson, Benjamin (trans.).
EN-TAIL AND RED-TAIL!
    See Dibdin, Charles Isaac Mungo, jr. Law's Two Tails.
ENTHUSIASM
    See Baillie, Joanna.
ENVOY WHO STOLE THE KING'S DAUGHTER
    See Byron, Henry James. Princess Spring-Time.
EPICHARIS
    See Lister, Thomas Henry.
EQUALS
    See Rose, Edward.
ERCKMANN-CHATRIAN
    Friend Fritz.
        See Lyster, Frederic (trans.).
ERECHTHEUS
    See Swinburne, Algernon Charles.
ERIC AND KARINE
    See Blackmore, Richard Doddridge.
ERMINIE
    See Bellamy, Claxson.
ERNANI
    See Brough, William.
ERNESTINE
    See Robertson, Thomas William.
    See Robertson, Thomas William. Noémie.
ERNESTINE AND GEORGETTE
    See Long, Charles.
EROSTRATUS
    See Mann, J. P.
ERROR
    See Wortley, Emmeline Charlotte Elizabeth Manners Stuart, Mrs. Charles (Lady). Eva.
ERRORS OF ECSTASIE, THE
    See Darley, George.
ESCAPE FROM LOCH LEVEN
    See Murray, William Henry Wood. Mary Queen of Scots.
ESMERALDA (anon.)
    London: George Odell, 1844. Pp. [3]-43.
ESMERALDA
    See Byron, Henry James.
    See Fitzball, Edward.
    See Marzials, Theophilus Julius Henry.
    See Randegger, Alberto.
    See Smith, Albert Richard.

ESMOND, HENRY VERNON
    Grierson's Way. London: William Clowes & Sons (printer), 1899. Pp. [3]-[91].
    In and Out of a Punt. London & New York: Samuel French, c.1902. Pp. [1]-12.
    My Lady's Lord. Pp. [i-iii], [1]-45, [1]-39, [i], [1]-40, [i], [1]-33. Pagination by act. Typescript.
    One Summer's Day. London: International Typewriting Office, n.d. Pp. [i-ii], [1]-38, [i]-31, [i], 1-24. Pagination by act. Typescript.
    Phroso.
        See Rose, Edward.
ESTHER
    See Boswell, Robert Bruce (trans.).
    See Tennant, William.
ESTHER, THE ROYAL JEWESS
    See Polack, Elizabeth.
ETERNAL MASCULINE, THE
    See Newte, Horace Wykeham Can.
ETHA AND AIDALLO
    See Chenevix, Richard.
ETHELRED
    See Richardson, Mrs. Sarah.
ETHELSTAN
    See Darley, George.
ETHELWOLF
    See Pennie, John Fitzgerald.
ETHWALD
    See Baillie, Joanna.
ÉTOILE DU NORD
    See Chorley, Henry Fothergill (trans.).
    See Maggioni, Manfredo (trans.). Stella del Nord, La.
ETON BOY, THE
    See Morton, Edward.
ÉTOURDI; OU, LES CONTRE-TEMPS
    See Van Laun, Henri (trans.). Blunderer, The.
ETTRICK SHEPHERD (pseud.)
    See Hogg, James.
EUDORA
    See Hayley, William.
EUGENE ARAM
    See Moncrieff, William Thomas.
EUPHERNIA
    See Young, Charles Michael.
EUPOLIS (pseud. of ?)
    Sawbones in Trainin'; or, The Boys of a Certain School. London: J. Pattie, 1839. Pp. [1-4], [i]-[xii], [13]-37.
EURIPIDES
    Alcestis.
        See Potter, Robert (trans.).
        See Spicer, Henry (trans.).
    Bacchanals, The.
        See Milman, Henry Hart (trans.).
    Electra.
        See Potter, Robert (trans.).
    Hippolytus the Wreathbearer.
        See Pember, Edward Henry (trans.).
    Iphigenia in Aulis.
        See Potter, Robert (trans.).
    Iphigenia in Tauris.
        See Potter, Robert (trans.).
    Medea.
        See Webster, Augusta Davies, Mrs. Thomas (trans.).
    Orestes.
        See Potter, Robert (trans.).
    Trojan Dames, The.
        See Potter, Robert (trans.).
EURIPIDES DESTROYED
    See Alcestis.
EURYANTHE
    See Thornthwaite, William (trans.).
EURYDICE
    See Byron, Henry James.
EURYNOME, THE GREEK MAIDEN
    See Capper, Richard.

EUSTACE DE ST. PIERRE
See Brigstocke, Thomas.
EUSTACHE BAUDIN
See Courtney, John.
EVA
See Wortley, Emmeline Charlotte Elizabeth Manners Stuart, Mrs. Charles (Lady).
EVADNE
See Sheil, Richard Lalor.
EVANS, MARY ANN
See Eliot, George.
EVANS, WILLIAM
Fair Reward, A. London: C. F. Roworth (priv.), 1883. Pp. [i]-[x], [1]-104.
EVE OF ST. BRICE
See Pennie, John Fitzgerald. English Slave, The.
EVELEEN, THE ROSE OF THE VALE
See Birch, William Henry.
EVENING WITH PUFF
See Planché, James Robinson. Drama at Home, The.
EVENINGS AT OUR CLUB
See Brougham, John.
EVERARD, WALTER
Uncles and Aunts.
See Lestocq, William.
EVER-SO-LITTLE BEAR, THE
See Byron, Henry James.
EVERY INCH A SAILOR
See Haines, John Thomas. Ocean of Life, The.
EVERY MAN HAS HIS PRICE
See Bulwer (later Bulwer-Lytton) Edward George Earle Lytton, Lord Lytton. Walpole.
EVERY MAN IN HIS HUMOUR
See Jonson, Ben.
EVERY ONE HAS A WHIM
See Maclaren, Archibald. Eccentricity.
EVERY ONE HAS HIS FAULT
See Inchbald, Elizabeth Simpson, Mrs. Joseph.
EVERYBODY'S FRIEND
See Coyne, Joseph Stirling.
EVERYBODY'S HUSBAND
See Ryan, Richard.
EVIL EYE
See Almar, George.
See Peake, Richard Brinsley.
EVIL GENIUS, THE
See Bernard, William Bayle.
EVIL MAY DAY!, THE
See Emden, William Samuel.
EWE-BUGHTS, THE
See Hetherington, William Maxwell.
EXCHANGE NO ROBBERY
See Hook, Theodore Edward.
See Houghton, John W. His Highness.
EXECUTIONER, THE
See Thackeray, Thomas James.
EXILE, THE
See Reynolds, Frederick.
EXILES, THE
See Rowe, George Fawcett.
EXILES OF KAMSCHATKA
See Kenney, James. Benyowsky.
EXPLOITS OF A GENTLEMAN AT LARGE
See Selby, Charles. Robert Macaire.
EXPOSITION, THE
See Brooks, Charles William Shirley.
EXPRESS!
See Morton, John Maddison.
EXPULSION OF THE MOORS
See Spaniards, The.
EXTORTED OATH
See Raymond, Richard John. Castle of Paluzzi, The.
EXTREMES
See Falconer, Edmund.

EYES AND NO EYES
See Gilbert, William Schwenck.
EYRE, EDMUND JOHN
High Life in the City! London: W. H. Wyatt, 1810. Pp. [i]-[x], [1]-87.
Lady of the Lake, The. London: W. H. Wyatt, 1811. Pp. [i-vi], [1]-49.
Look at Home. London: C. Chapple, 1812. Pp. [i-iv], [1]-58.
Look at Home. London: C. Chapple, 1814. Pp. [i-iv], [1]-56. 2nd ed.
Vintagers, The. Music by Bishop. London: J. Barker, 1809. Pp. [1]-39.
FACE IN THE MOONLIGHT, THE
See Osborne, Charles.
FACES IN THE FIRE
See Buckingham, Leicester Silk.
FÂCHEUX
See Van Laun, Henri (trans.). Bores, The.
FACTORY BOY, THE
See Haines, John Thomas.
FACTORY GIRL, THE
See Wallace, John, jr.
FACTORY LAD!, THE
See Walker, John.
FACTORY STRIKE, THE
See Taylor, G. F.
FADED FLOWERS
See A'Beckett, Arthur William.
FADETTE
See Vallentine, Benjamin Bennaton.
FAINT HEART NEVER WON FAIR LADY
See Planché, James Robinson.
FAINT HEART WHICH DID WIN A FAIR LADY, A
See Wooler, John Pratt.
FAIR BRIGANDS
See Somerset, Charles A. Female Massaroni, The.
FAIR CONQUEST, A
See Drinkwater, Albert E.
FAIR CRUSADER, THE (anon.)
In *New British Theatre*, London: A. J. Valpy (printer), 1815, IV, [i], [287]-[329].
FAIR ENCOUNTER, A
See Rae, Charles Marsham.
FAIR EQUESTRIENNE, THE
See Russell, Haslingden.
FAIR EXCHANGE, A
See Williams, Montagu Stephen.
FAIR GABRIELLE, THE
See Planché, James Robinson.
FAIR HELEN
See Amcotts, Vincent.
FAIR MAID OF CLIFTON, THE
See Goodyer, F. R.
FAIR MAID OF PERTH, THE
See Milner, Henry M.
FAIR ONE WITH THE GOLDEN LOCKS, THE
See Planché, James Robinson.
FAIR PENITENT, THE
See Kemble, John Philip (arr.).
See Rowe, Nicholas.
FAIR PRETENDER, A
See Simpson, John Palgrave.
FAIR REWARD, A
See Evans, William.
FAIR ROSAMOND
See Burnand, Francis Cowley.
See Mitford, Mary Russell.
FAIR ROSAMOND'S BOWER
See Langbridge, Frederick.
FAIR ROSAMUND
See Field, Michael.
See Godwin, Edward William.
See Taylor, Thomas Proclus.
FAIR STAR
See Smith, Albert Richard.

FAIR TAKE-IN
    See Reece, Robert. Martha.
FAIRBROTHER, MARY EMMA
    See Ebsworth, Mary Emma Fairbrother, Mrs. Joseph.
FAIRIES
    See Black, John. Falls of Clyde, The.
FAIRIES' BANQUET AND LORD MAYOR'S SHOW
    See Henry, A. Whittington and His Cat.
FAIRIES' REVELS, THE
    See Fawcett, John.
FAIRIES' REVENGE
    See Bellingham, Henry. Prince Camaralzaman.
FAIRLY HIT AND FAIRLY MISSED
    See Martin, John.
FAIRLY TAKEN IN
    See Kemble, Marie Thérèse De Camp, Mrs. Charles. Personation.
FAIRY AND LITTLE GLASS SLIPPER
    See Lacy, Michael Rophino. Cinderella.
FAIRY CIRCLE, THE
    See Grattan, H. P.
FAIRY LADY, THE
    See Fox, Henry Richard.
FAIRY LAKE, THE
    See Selby, Charles.
FAIRY MAN
    See Hazlewood, Colin Henry. Poul a Dhoil.
FAIRY OF THE LAKE, THE
    See Thelwall, John.
FAIRY OF THE LAKES
    See Collier, William. Kate Kearney.
FAIRY OF THE ROSE AND THE SPRITE OF THE SILVER STAR
    See Blanchard, Edward Litt Leman. Harlequin and the World of Flowers.
FAIRY ROSES
    See Brough, William. Prince Amabel.
FAIRY TALE OF HOME
    See Smith, Albert Richard. Cricket on the Hearth, The.
FAIRY'S FATHER, A
    See Cheltnam, Charles Smith.
FAITH
    See Wheatley, J. A.
FAITH AND FALSEHOOD
    See Rede, William Leman.
FAITH, HOPE, AND CHARITY!
    See Blanchard, Edward Litt Leman.
FAITH'S FRAUD
    See Landor, Robert Eyres.
FAITHFUL JAMES
    See Stephenson, Benjamin Charles.
FAITHLESS TOMMY
    See Ross, Adrian. Mary and Sairey.
FALCON, THE
    See Cornwall, Barry.
    See Tennyson, Alfred, Lord.
FALCONER, EDMUND (pseud. of O'Rourke, Edmund)
    Cagot, The; or, Heart for Heart. London: John Mitchell, n.d. Pp. [1]-99.
    Chrystabelle; or, The Rose without a Thorn. London: Thomas Hailes Lacy, n.d. Pp. [1]-36. [Lacy's Acting Edition].
    Deserted Village, The. Music by Glover, J. W. London: Duncan Davison, n.d. Pp. [i-vi], [1]-184. Vocal score.
    Does He Love Me? London & New York: Samuel French, n.d. Pp. [1]-48. [Lacy's Acting Edition].
    Eileen Oge; or, Dark's the Hour Before the Dawn. New York: DeWitt, n.d. Pp. [1]-43. DeWitt's Acting Plays, 202.
    Eileen Oge; or, Dark's the Hour Before the Dawn. London & New York: Samuel French, n.d. Pp. [i], [1]-60.
    Extremes; or, Men of the Day. London: Thomas Hailes Lacy, n.d. Pp. [1]-72. Promptbook.
    Family Secret, The. London: Thomas Hailes Lacy, n.d. Pp. [1]-56. [Lacy's Acting Edition].
    Husband of an Hour, The. London: Thomas Hailes Lacy, n.d. Pp. [1]-52. Text imperfect.

Master Passion.
    See Outlaw of the Adriatic, The.
Next of Kin. London: Thomas Hailes Lacy, n.d. Pp. [1]-26.
Outlaw of the Adriatic, The; or, The Female Spy and the Chief of the Ten. *Also:* Master Passion. London: Thomas Hailes Lacy, n.d. Pp. [1]-43. *Filed under* Outlaw of the Adriatic (anon.).
Peep o' Day; or, Savourneen Deelish. New York: Samuel French, n.d. Pp. [1-2], [i-ii], [3]-44. French's Standard Drama, 349.
Rose of Castile, The.
    See Harris, Augustus Glossop.
Ruy Blas. New York: Wheat & Cornett, c.1877. Pp. [1]-15. New York Drama, III, 32.
Ruy Blas. London & New York: Samuel French, n.d. Pp. [1]-42. French's Acting Edition (late Lacy's), 723. *Filed under* Ruy Blas (anon.).
Satanella.
    See Harris, Augustus Glossop.
Victorine. Music by Mellon, Alfred. London: Royal English Opera, Covent Garden, n.d. Pp. [1]-32. Libretto.
FALKA
    See Farnie, Henry Brougham.
FALKLAND
    See Smith, Sidney.
FALL OF ALGIERS, THE
    See Walker, Charles Edward.
FALL OF ALGIERS BY SEA AND LAND, THE
    See Somerset, Charles A.
FALL OF CARTHAGE, THE
    See Proby, John Joshua, Earl of Carysfort.
    See Watkins, William.
FALL OF CONSTANTINOPLE
    See Howard, George William Frederick, Earl of Carlisle. Last of the Greeks, The.
FALL OF HAMAN
    See Tennant, William. Esther.
FALL OF JERUSALEM, THE
    See Milman, Henry Hart.
FALL OF MORTIMER, THE
    See Rokeby, Matthew Robinson-Morris.
FALL OF POLAND IN 1794, THE (anon.)
    London: Longman, Brown, Green, & Longmans, 1855. Pp. [i]-[lxxx], [1]-90.
FALL OF PORTUGAL, THE
    See Wolcot, John.
FALL OF ROSAMOND
    See Hull, Thomas. Henry the Second.
FALL OF TARQUIN
    See Payne, John Howard. Brutus.
FALL OF THE MOGUL, THE
    See Maurice, Thomas.
FALL OF TUNIS
    See Sheil, Richard Lalor. Bellamira.
FALLEN AMONG THIEVES
    See Harvey, Frank.
FALLEN GOD, THE
    See Sharp, William.
FALLS OF CLYDE, THE
    See Black, John.
    See Soane, George.
FALSE ALARM, A
    See Young, Alfred W.
FALSE ALARMS
    See Kenney, James.
FALSE AND CONSTANT
    See Lunn, Joseph.
FALSE COLOURS
    See Fitzball, Edward.
FALSE CONCLUSIONS
    See Long, Charles.
FALSE DELICACY
    See Thompson, Benjamin (trans.).
FALSE DEMETRIUS, THE
    See Cumberland, Richard.

FALSE EVIDENCE
See Miller, Wynn F.
FALSE IMPRESSIONS
See Cumberland, Richard.
FALSE POSITION
See Marston, John Westland. Trevanion.
FALSE SHAME
See Marshall, Francis Albert.
FALSE START, A
See Sturgis, Julian Russell.
FALSE STEP, A
See Matthison, Arthur.
FALSEHOOD AND TRUTH
See Jameson, Anna Brownell Murphy, Mrs. Robert (trans.).
FALSELY ACCUSED
See Hazlewood, Colin Henry. Waiting for the Verdict.
FAME
See Rae, Charles Marsham.
FAMILIAR FRIEND, A
See Lemon, Mark.
FAMILY ARRANGEMENTS
See Long, Charles.
FAMILY FAILING, A
See Oxenford, John.
FAMILY FRAILTIES
See Father and Son (anon.).
FAMILY JARS
See Lunn, Joseph.
FAMILY LEGEND, THE
See Baillie, Joanna.
FAMILY MASQUERADING
See Macfarren, George. March of Intellect, The.
FAMILY OF ANGLADE
See Kenney, James. Portfolio, The.
FAMILY PICTURES
See Stirling, Edward.
FAMILY POLITICS (anon.)
In *New British Theatre*, London: A. J. Valpy (printer), 1814, II, [i], [191]-255.
FAMILY PRIDE
See Sulivan, Robert.
FAMILY QUARRELS
See Dibdin, Thomas John.
FAMILY SECRET, THE
See Falconer, Edmund.
FAN, THE
See Zimmern, Helen (trans.?).
FANCY FAIR, A
See Lumley, Ralph R.
FANE, SYDNEY
   Mixed Addresses. New York & London: Samuel French, n.d. Pp. [1]-12. Minor Drama, 390.
FANE, VIOLET (pseud. of Lamb, Mary Montgomerie) (later Mrs. Singleton; Lady Currie)
   Anthony Babington. London: Chapman & Hall, 1877. Pp. [i]-x, [1]-180. *Filed under* Currie, Mary Montgomerie Lamb, Lady.
FAN-FAN, THE TULIP
See Suter, William E.
FANS AND FANDANGOES
See Selby, Charles. Spanish Dancers, The.
FANTASTICKS, THE
See Fleming, George.
FANTASTICS
See Pinero, Arthur Wing. Princess and the Butterfly, The.
FAR, FAR AT SEA!
See Townsend, William Thompson. Mary's Dream.
FAREWELL AT THE STATION, THE
See Ridge, William Pett.
FARINELLI
See Barnett, Charles Zachary.
FARJEON, ELEANOR
   Floretta. Music by Farjeon, Harry. London: Henderson & Spalding (printer), n.d. Pp. [1]-31. Libretto.

FARLEY, CHARLES
   Aladdin; or, The Wonderful Lamp. London: John Cumberland, n.d. Pp. [1]-36. Cumberland's British Theatre, XXXVI. *Filed under* Cumberland, John. Cumberland's British Theatre, XXXVI.
   Battle of Bothwell Brigg, The. London: John Lowndes, 1820. Pp. [i-iv], [1]-35.
   Corsair, The; or, The Italian Nuptials. Music by Arnold, Samuel. London: Wigley & Bishop, n.d. Pp. [i], [1]-72. Vocal score.
   Harlequin and Friar Bacon; or, The Brazen Head. Music by Ware. London: John Miller, 1820. Pp. [i]-iv, [5]-16. Libretto.
   Harlequin and Mother Shipton; or, Riquet with the Tuft. Music by Watson; Woodarch. London: John Miller, 1826. Pp. [1]-16. Libretto.
   Harlequin Munchausen; or, The Fountain of Love. Music by Ware. London: John Lowndes, 1818. Pp. [1]-16. Libretto.
   Harlequin Whittington; or, Lord Mayor of London. Music by Ware. London: J. Barker, 1814. Pp. [1]-19. Libretto.
   Red Roy; or, Oswyn and Helen. Music by Davy. London: T. Woodfall (printer) (priv.), n.d. Pp. [1]-18.
   Sadak and Kalasrade; or, The Waters of Oblivion. Music by Bishop, Henry; Ware. London: J. Barker, n.d. Pp. [1]-19. Libretto.
FARM HOUSE, THE
See Kemble, John Philip.
FARMER, THE
See O'Keeffe, John.
FARMER'S DAUGHTER
See Bartholomew, Anne Charlotte Fayermann, Mrs. Valentine. Ring, The.
See Collier, William. Abduction.
FARMER'S DAUGHTER OF THE SEVERN SIDE, THE
See Raymond, Richard John.
FARMER'S SON
See Lake, John. Golden Glove, The.
FARMER'S SONS
See Knight, Edward P. Veteran, The.
FARMER'S STORY, THE
See Bernard, William Bayle.
FARMER'S WIFE, THE
See Dibdin, Charles Isaac Mungo, jr.
FARNIE, HENRY BROUGHAM
   Barber of Bath, The. Music by Offenbach. London: J. B. Cramer, n.d. Pp. [1]-32. Cramer's Opera Bouffe Cabinet. Vocal score.
   Bells of Corneville, The. Written with Reece, Robert. *Also:* The Chimes of Normandy. Music by Planquette, Robert. N. p.: n.pub., n.d. Pp. [1]-39. Title page lacking. Promptbook.
   Blind Beggars, The. Music by Offenbach. New York & London: Samuel French, n.d. Pp. [1]-20. French's Amateur Operas. Vocal score.
   Breaking the Spell. Music by Offenbach. London: Metzler, n.d. Pp. [1]-40. Metzler & Co.'s Opera Bouffe Series. Vocal score.
   Bride of Song, The. Music by Benedict, Jules. London: Cramer, Wood, n.d. Pp. [i-iv], 1-88. Vocal score.
   Chimes of Normandy.
      See Bells of Corneville, The.
   Commodore, The. Written with Reece, Robert. Music by Offenbach. New York: Richard A. Saalfield, n.d. Pp. [i-iv], [1]-121. Vocal score.
   Crimson Scarf, The. Music by Legouix, I. E. London: Metzler, n.d. Pp. [1]-43. Vocal score.
   Cross Purposes: A Misunderstanding. New York: Roorbach, n.d. Pp. [35]-45. Acting Drama, 178.
   Falka. Music by Chassaigne, F. Boston: White-Smith Music Publishing Co., n.d. Pp. [1]-200. Vocal score.
   Fille de Madame Angot, La. Music by Lecocq, Charles. London: W. Gee (printer), n.d. Pp. [1]-47. Libretto.
   Fille du Tambour-Major, La. Music by Offenbach. London: J. B. Cramer, n.d. Pp. [i]-vi, [7]-35. Libretto.

Fleur-de-Lys. Music by Delibes. London: W. Gee (printer), n.d. Pp. [1]-33. Vocal score and libretto.

Forty Winks. Music by Offenbach. London: Metzler, n.d. Pp. [1]-47. Metzler & Co.'s Opera Bouffe Series. Vocal score.

Glamour. Written with Murray, Alfred. Music by Hutchison, W. M. London: Marshall, n.d. Pp. [1]-24. Libretto. *Filed under* Murray, Alfred.

Indiana. Music by Audran, Edmond. London: Boosey, n.d. Pp. [1-4], i-x, 1-203. Vocal score.

Irene. *Also:* Reine de Saba. Music by Gounod. London: Metzler, n.d. Pp. [i-viii], 1-281. Vocal score.

Madame Favart. Music by Offenbach. Boston: Oliver Ditson, c.1881. Pp. [1]-207. Vocal score.

Madame Favart. Music by Offenbach. Boston: Oliver Ditson, c.1881. Pp. [1]-70. Libretto.

Manola; or, The Day and the Night. Music by Lecocq, Charles. [Boston: Oliver Ditson, c.1882]. Pp. [3]-272. Title page lacking. Vocal score.

Mariage aux Lanternes.
See Paquerette.

Marriage Noose!, A. London: John Dicks, n.d. Pp. [9]-18. Dicks' Standard Charades and Comedies, 488. *Filed under* Farjeon, Eleanor.

Mousquetaires au Couvent, Les. Written with Smith, Dexter. Music by Varney, Louis. Boston: Oliver Ditson, c.1881. Pp. 3-156. Title page lacking. Promptbook vocal score.

Nell Gwynne. Music by Planquette, Robert. London: Metzler, c.1884. Pp. [i-ii], [1]-176. Vocal score.

Old Guard, The. Music by Planquette, Robert. London: Enoch & Sons, n.d. Pp. [1]-114. Vocal score.

Olivette. Written with Montgomery, Henry William. Music by Audran. New York: William A. Pond, c.1881. Pp. [i-iv], [1]-47. Pond's Acting Edition. Libretto.

Olivette. Written with Montgomery, Henry William. Music by Audran. London: Chappell, n.d. Pp. [i-ii], [1]-173. Vocal score.

Paquerette. *Also:* Le Mariage aux Lanternes. Music by Offenbach. London: Boosey, n.d. Pp. [1]-51. Boosey & Co.'s Operettas for the Drawing-Room. Vocal score.

Paul Jones. Music by Planquette, Robert. London: Hopwood & Crew, n.d. Pp. [i-iv], [1]-142. Vocal score.

Prima Donna, La. Written with Murray, Alfred. Music by Mattei, Tito. London: Hutchings, n.d. Pp. [i-iv], [5]-31. Libretto.

Punchinello. Music by Levey, William Charles. London: Cramer, n.d. Pp. [1]-31. Libretto.

Reine de Saba.
See Irene.

Retained on Both Sides. Music by Lecocq, Charles. London: Metzler, 1875. Pp. [1]-24. Vocal score.

Rip Van Winkle. Music by Planquette, Robert. Philadelphia: J. M. Stoddart, c.1882. Pp. [i-viii], [1]-166. Vocal score.

Romeo and Juliet.
See Romeo e Giulietta.

Romeo e Giulietta. *Also:* Romeo and Juliet. Music by Gounod. London: J. Miles (printer), n.d. Pp. [i-v], [6]-76. Libretto.

Rose of Auvergne, The; or, Spoiling the Broth. Music by Offenbach. New York: William A. Pond, n.d. Pp. [1]-40. Vocal score.

Rothomago; or, The Magic Watch! Music by Solomon, E.; Bucalossi, P.; Serpette, Gaston; Jacobi, G. London: Swift, n.d. Pp. [1]-31. Libretto.

Soul of Honor!, The. London & New York: Samuel French, n.d. Pp. [1]-48. [Lacy's Acting Edition].

Tobias. London: Cramer, n.d. Pp. [11]-23. Vocal score and libretto.

Up the River. Written with Reece, Robert. Music by Hervé. London: J. B. Cramer, n.d. Pp. [1]-21. Vocal score.

Vie, La. Music by Offenbach. London: Boosey, n.d. Pp. [i-iv], 1-171. Vocal score.

Whittington. Music by Offenbach. London: J. B. Cramer, n.d. Pp. [i-iv], 1-410. Vocal score.

FARO TABLE, THE
See Tobin, John.

FARQUHAR, GEORGE

Beaux' Stratagem, The. London: Whittingham & Arliss, 1814. Pp. [1]-76. London Theatre, VIII. *Filed under* Dibdin, Thomas John, ed. London Theatre, VIII.

Beaux' Stratagem, The. In *New English Drama*, ed. W. Oxberry, 22 vols., London: W. Simpkin & R. Marshall; C. Chapple, 1819, VII, [1-2], [i]-[vi], [1]-[75]. Pagination irregular. *Filed under* Oxberry, William Henry. New English Drama, VII.

Beaux' Stratagem, The. In *British Drama*, 12 vols., London: John Dicks, 1871, VII, [97]-119.

Beaux' Stratagem, The. London: John Cumberland, n.d. Pp. [1]-68. Cumberland's British Theatre, XXI. *Filed under* Cumberland, John. Cumberland's British Theatre, XXI.

Constant Couple, The; or, A Trip to the Jubilee. London: Sherwood, Neely, & Jones, 1818. Pp. [1]-71. London Theatre, XXVI. *Filed under* Dibdin, Thomas John, ed. London Theatre, XXVI.

Constant Couple, The; or, A Trip to the Jubilee. In *British Drama*, 12 vols., London: John Dicks, 1872, XI, [205]-224.

Inconstant, The; or, The Way to Win Him. London: Whittingham & Arliss, 1815. Pp. [1]-[64]. London Theatre, XII. *Filed under* Dibdin, Thomas John, ed. London Theatre, XII.

Inconstant, The; or, The Way to Win Him. In *New English Drama*, ed. W. Oxberry, 22 vols., London: W. Simpkin & R. Marshall; C. Chapple, 1820, X, [1-2], [i]-ii, [i]-ii, [i]-[iv], [1]-60. *Filed under* Oxberry, William Henry. New English Drama, X.

Inconstant, The. London: John Cumberland, 1826. Pp. [i]-[vi], [7]-58. Cumberland's British Theatre, V. *Filed under* Cumberland, John. Cumberland's British Theatre, V.

Inconstant, The. In *British Drama*, 12 vols., London: John Dicks, 1864, I, [176]-192.

Recruiting Officer, The. London: Whittingham & Arliss, 1816. Pp. [1]-[71]. London Theatre, XVII. *Filed under* Dibdin, Thomas John, ed. London Theatre, XVII.

Recruiting Officer, The. In *New English Drama*, ed. W. Oxberry, 22 vols., London: W. Simpkin & R. Marshall; C. Chapple, 1819, VI, [1-2], [i]-[iv], [9]-[78]. *Filed under* Oxberry, William Henry. New English Drama, VI.

Recruiting Officer, The. In *British Drama*, 12 vols., London: John Dicks, 1871, VIII, [257]-278.

Recruiting Officer, The. London: John Cumberland, n.d. Pp. [1]-62. Cumberland's British Theatre, XXII. *Filed under* Cumberland, John. Cumberland's British Theatre, XXII.

FARRELL, JOHN

Dumb Girl of Genoa, The; or, The Bandit Merchant. Boston: William V. Spencer, n.d. Pp. [1]-21. Spencer's Boston Theatre, 44.

It's All a Mistake. London: J. Asperne; J. Chapple, 1820. Pp. [1]-43.

Maid of Genoa!, The; or, The Bandit Merchant! London: John Duncombe, n.d. <wrps. Thomas Hailes Lacy>. Pp. [1]-24. Duncombe's Edition <wrps. New British Theatre (late Duncombe's), 34>.

FARREN, PERCY

Field of Forty Footsteps, The. London: Thomas Hailes Lacy, n.d. Pp. [1]-41.

FASCINATING INDIVIDUAL, A
See Danvers, Henry.

FASHION
See Maclaren, Archibald.

FASHION AND FEELING
See Beazley, Samuel, jr. Steward, The.

FASHION'S FOOLS
See Dibdin, Charles Isaac Mungo, jr.

FASHIONABLE ARRIVALS
See Lemon, Mark.

FASHIONABLE ECLOGUES
See Bayly, Thomas Haynes.

FASHIONABLE FRIENDS, THE
    See Berry, Mary.
FASHIONABLE INTELLIGENCE
    See Fendall, Percy.
FASHIONABLE LEVITIES
    See MacNally, Leonard.
FASHIONABLE LOVER, THE
    See Cumberland, Richard.
FAST COACH, THE
    See Claridge, C. J.
FAST FAMILY, THE
    See Webster, Benjamin, jr.
FAST FRIENDS
    See Henry, Reginald.
FAST KING OF ASSYRIA
    See A'Beckett, Gilbert Abbott. Sardanapalus.
FAST TRAIN! HIGH PRESSURE! EXPRESS!, A SHORT TRIP
    See Maddox, John Medex.
FATAL ACCUSATION
    See Bucke, Charles. Italians, The.
FATAL BLOW, THE
    See Fitzball, Edward.
FATAL BRAND
    See Townsend, William Thompson. Temptation.
FATAL BRIDGE
    See Barrymore, William. Blood Red Knight!, The.
FATAL CARD, THE
    See Chambers, Charles Haddon.
FATAL CHEST
    See Somerset, Charles A. Mistletoe Bough, The.
FATAL CURIOSITY
    See Lillo, George.
FATAL DOWRY, THE
    See Massinger, Philip.
FATAL KEEPSAKE
    See Selby, Charles. Military Execution.
FATAL LAND BREEZE
    See Barnett, Charles Zachary. Loss of the Royal George, The.
FATAL MARRIAGE
    See Garrick, David. Isabella.
    See Kemble, John Philip (arr.). Isabella.
FATAL OFFSPRING
    See Milner, Henry M. Barmecide.
FATAL RAFT
    See Moncrieff, William Thomas. Shipwreck of the Medusa.
FATAL RAVINE!
    See Buckstone, John Baldwin. Bear Hunters, The.
FATAL SECRET!
    See Lee, Nelson, jr. Midnight Spectre!, The.
FATAL SEDUCTION
    See Ebsworth, Joseph. Adelaide.
FATAL SNOW-DRIFT
    See Hart, James P. Post-Boy of Cornwall, The.
FATAL SNOW STORM
    See Barrymore, William.
    See Barrymore, William. Snow Storm, The.
FATAL SPOON!
    See Byron, Henry James. Maid and the Magpie, The.
FATAL WARNING
    See Milner, Henry M. Death-Fetch, The.
FATALITY
    See Boaden, Caroline.
FATE OF A BUSHRANGER!
    See Rede, William Leman. Faith and Falsehood.
FATE OF A COQUETTE
    See Heron, Matilda. Camille.
FATE OF CALAS, THE
    See Dibdin, Thomas John.
FATE OF FRANKENSTEIN
    See Kerr, John. Monster and Magician, The.
    See Milner, Henry M. Man and the Monster!, The.

FATE OF IVAN, THE
    See Kitching, H. St. A.
FATE OF MARGARET
    See Bernard, William Bayle. Faust.
FATE OF PHAETON
    See A'Beckett, Gilbert Abbott. Son of the Sun, The.
FATE OF THE LILY OF ST. LEONARD'S
    See Pitt, George Dibdin. Whistler!, The.
FATE OF THE MACDONALDS
    See Talfourd, Thomas Noon. Glencoe.
FATHER AND DAUGHTER
    See Moncrieff, William Thomas. Lear of Private Life!, The.
    See St. Bo', Theodore. Wilfrid and Mary.
    See Ware, James Redding. Juggler, The.
FATHER AND SON; OR, FAMILY FRAILTIES (anon.)
    In *New British Theatre*, London: A. J. Valpy (printer), 1814, III, [349]-410.
FATHER AND SON
    See Fitzball, Edward.
FATHER AVENGED, A
    See Hunt, Leigh.
FATHER BAPTISTE
    See Stirling, Edward.
FATHER'S DREAM
    See Townsend, William Thompson. Old Adam.
FATHER'S LOVE AND A MOTHER'S CARE
    See Pitt, George Dibdin. Beggar's Petition, The.
FATHER'S TRAGEDY, THE
    See Field, Michael.
FATINITZA
    See Leigh, Henry Sambrooke.
FAUCIT, JOHN SAVILL
    Justice; or, The Caliph and the Cobbler. 24 leaves. Manuscript.
    Miller's Maid, The. Music by Jolly. London: Longman, Hurst, Rees, Orme, & Brown (priv.), 1821. Pp. [iii]-[x], [1]-47.
    Oedipus. London: John Duncombe, 1821. Pp. [i-ii], [1]-44.
    Wapping Old Stairs. By John Faucit Savill (pseud.). London: John Cumberland, n.d. Pp. [1]-58. Cumberland's Minor Theatre, XIII. *Filed under* Cumberland, John. Cumberland's Minor Theatre, XIII.
FAUCQUEZ, ADOLPHE
    Forced Marriage, The; or, The Murder in the Marsh. Pp. [1]-[69]. Manuscript.
    Guilty. 62 leaves. Manuscript.
    Seventh Hour, The; or, The Price of Life. 45 leaves. Title page illegible. Manuscript promptbook.
    Spirit of Vengeance, The. 118 leaves. Manuscript.
FAULKENER
    See Godwin, William.
FAUST (anon. trans.)
    By Goethe. In *Goethe's Faust and Heine's Book of Songs*, New York: White, Stokes, & Allen, 1886, pp. [i-vi], [7]-261.
FAUST; OR, AN OLD FRIEND WITH A NEW FACE (anon.)
    London: Henry Richards (printer) (priv.), n.d. Pp. [1]-31.
FAUST
    (See also Faustus.)
    See Beresford, A. von (trans.).
    See Bernard, William Bayle.
    See Beta (pseud.) (trans.).
    See Birch, Jonathan (trans.).
    See Blackie, John Stuart (trans.).
    See Chorley, Henry Fothergill (trans.).
    See Colquhoun, W. H. (trans.).
    See Filmore, Lewis (trans.).
    See Galvan, John (trans.).
    See Gower, Francis Leveson, Lord (trans.).
    See Grant, John Wynniatt (trans.).
    See Grattan, H. P.
    See Hayward, Abraham (trans.).
    See Hills, John (trans.).
    See Knox, Charles H., Capt. (trans.).

See Lefevre, George William, Sir (trans.).
See Martin, Theodore, Sir (trans.).
See Paul, C. Kegan (trans.).
See Pearson, Henry W.
See Scoones, William Dalton (trans.).
See Shelley, Percy Bysshe (trans.). May-Day Night.
See Swanwick, Anna (trans.).
See Syme, David (trans.).
See Talbot, Robert (trans.).
See Wills, William Gorman (arr.).

FAUST, PART 2
See Bernays, Leopold John (trans.).
See Gurney, Archer Thompson (trans.).

FAUST AND GRETCHEN
See Ross, Adrian.

FAUST AND LOOSE
See Burnand, Francis Cowley.

FAUST AND MARGUERITE
See Burnand, Francis Cowley.
See Drayton, Henri. Mephistopheles.
See Halford, John.
See Robertson, Thomas William.

FAUST AND MEPHISTOPHELES
See Burnand, Francis Cowley. Alonzo the Brave.

FAUST AND THE FAIR IMOGENE
See Burnand, Francis Cowley. Alonzo the Brave.

FAUST UP TO DATE
See Sims, George Robert.

FAUSTUS (anon.)
By Goethe. London: Boosey & Sons; Rodwell & Martin, 1821. Pp. [i]-[x], [1]-[88].

FAUSTUS
See Anster, John (trans.).
See Davies, Warburton (trans.).
See Soane, George.

FAUSTUS, PART 1
See Huth, Alfred Henry (trans.).

FAUVETTE
See Rae, Alfred.

FAVORITA, LA (anon. trans.)
Music by Donizetti. New York & London: Samuel French, n.d. Pp. [1]-22. Libretto.

FAVORITA, LA (anon. trans.)
Music by Donizetti. London: Music-Publishing Co., n.d. Pp. [i-ii], [1]-23. Davidson's Musical Opera-Books. Libretto.

FAVORITA
See Fitzball, Edward. Favourite, The.
See Kenney, Charles Lamb (trans.).
See Maggioni, Manfredo (trans.).

FAVOURITE, THE
See Fitzball, Edward.

FAVOURITE OF FORTUNE, THE
See Marston, John Westland.

FAW! FEE! FO! FUM!
See Blanchard, Edward Litt Leman.

FAWCETT, CHARLES S.
Bearding the Lion. London & New York: Samuel French, n.d. Pp. [1]-20. [Lacy's Acting Edition].
Bubbles. London & New York: Samuel French, n.d. Pp. [1]-24. [Lacy's Acting Edition].
For Charity's Sake.
See Our Lottie.
Jolliboy's Woes. London & New York: Samuel French, n.d. Pp. [1]-20. [Lacy's Acting Edition].
Our Lottie. London & New York: Samuel French, n.d. Pp. [1]-24. French's Acting Edition (late Lacy's), 1977.
Our Lottie. *Also:* For Charity's Sake. London & New York: Samuel French, n.d. Pp. [1]-24. [Lacy's Acting Edition]. *Filed under* For Charity's Sake.
Tragedy, A. London & New York: Samuel French, n.d. Pp. [1]-56. [Lacy's Acting Edition].

FAWCETT, JOHN
Barber of Seville, The. Written with Terry, Daniel. Music by Rossini; Bishop, Henry. London: J. Roach, 1818. Pp. [3]-[55]. Libretto.
Barber of Seville, The. Written with Terry, Daniel. Music by Rossini; Bishop, Henry. London: E. Macleish (printer), 1818. Pp. [1]-16. Libretto. *Filed under* Bishop, Henry.
Barber of Seville, The. Written with Terry, Daniel. London: Thomas Dolby, 1825. Pp. [1-2], [i]-[vi], [5]-46. Dolby's British Theatre, IX. *Filed under* Cumberland, John. Cumberland's British Theatre, IX.
Brazen Mask.
See Dibdin, Thomas John.
Enchanted Island, The. London: T. Woodfall (printer) (priv.), n.d. Pp. [1]-[28]. Libretto.
Fairies' Revels, The; or, Love in the Highlands. Music by Arnold. London: Cadell & Davies, 1802. Pp. [1]-16. Libretto.
Obi; or, Three-finger'd Jack. London: T. Woodfall (printer), 1809. Pp. [1]-20. 11th ed. Libretto.
Perouse; or, The Desolate Island. Music by Knight, T. London: J. Barker, 1801. Pp. [1]-15. Libretto.
Secret Mine, The. Written with Dibdin, Thomas John. By J. Fawcett. Music by Bishop; Condell. Dublin: W. H. Tyrrell (printer), 1813. Pp. [1]-27.

FAWN, THE
See Mitford, Mary Russell.

FAWN IN THE FOREST
See Planché, James Robinson. Prince of Happy Land, The.

FAYERMANN, ANNE CHARLOTTE
See Bartholomew, Anne Charlotte Fayermann, Mrs. Valentine.

FAYETTE
See Stephens, James Brunton.

FAYRE LASS OF LICHFIELD!
See Wilks, Thomas Egerton. Michael Erle the Maniac Lover.

FAZIO
See Milman, Henry Hart, Rev.

FEARFUL TRAGEDY IN THE SEVEN DIALS
See Selby, Charles.

FEARNS
See Albery, James. Genevieve.

FEAST OF ADONIS
See Hunt, Leigh. Syracusan Gossips, The.

FEAST OF BACCHUS, THE
See Bridges, Robert Seymour.

FEAST WITH THE STATUE
See Van Laun, Henri (trans.). Don Juan.

FEATHERBRAIN
See Albery, James.

FEATHERSTONE, J. L.
Mademoiselle Squallino. London & New York: Samuel French, n.d. Pp. [1]-16. [Lacy's Acting Edition].

FEATHERSTONE, THOMAS
Juvenile Temperance Discussion for Sixteen Youths, The. Leeds: John Kershaw, 1857. Pp. [1]-48. 2nd ed., rev. & enl.
Missing Temperance Speakers, The. In *Original Temperance Reciter,* new ed., Leeds: John Kershaw, n.d., pp. [1]-36.
Rhyming Temperance Advocate, The; or, Old Truths in a New Dress. Leeds: John Kershaw, n.d. Pp. [i]-iv, [5]-59.
Student, The. London: W. Strange, 1838. Pp. [1]-40.
Temperance Reciters' Festival, The. In *Original Temperance Reciter,* new ed., Leeds: John Kershaw, n.d., pp. [73]-102.
Temperance Volunteers, The. In *Original Temperance Reciter,* new ed., Leeds: John Kershaw, n.d., pp. 37-72.
Trial of Dr. Abstinence, alias Steadfast Teetotalism, Esq., Temperance Advocate; or, The Trial of John Barleycorn Reversed. Leeds: J. Kershaw, n.d. Pp. [1]-46. New ed., rev.
Trial of Sir Timothy Traffic, alias Daniel Deathspirit, for High Crimes and Misdemeanours against the People of These

Realms, The. Leeds: John Kershaw, n.d. Pp. [1]-36. 2nd ed., rev.

Trial of Suits at the Brewster Sessions of Sotville; or, A Laugh on the License Day. Leeds: John Kershaw, n.d. Pp. [1]-36. New ed.

FECHTER, CHARLES ALBERT
Black and White.
See Collins, William Wilkie.

FECHTER, CHARLES ALBERT (arr.)
Othello. By Shakespeare, William. London: W. R. Sams, 1861. Pp. [i]-[vi], [1]-114. Charles Fechter's Acting Edition, 2nd ed.

FEELING, AND WANT OF FEELING, LAMENTATIONS, DISASTERS, AND PROPHECIES
See Pytches, John. Wounds Heal Wounds.

FELIX
See Oxenford, John.

FELLOW SERVANTS
See Craven, Henry Thornton.

FELON'S BOND, THE
See Suter, William E.

FEMALE BLUEBEARD
See Higgie, Thomas Henry. Devil's Mount, The.

FEMALE CURIOSITY! AND MALE ATROCITY!
See Keating, Eliza H. Blue Beard.

FEMALE DETECTIVE, THE
See Hazlewood, Colin Henry.

FEMALE HEROISM
See West, Matthew.

FEMALE MASSARONI, THE
See Somerset, Charles A.

FEMALE PATRIOTS
See Maclaren, Archibald. Spanish Heroine, The.

FEMALE SERENADERS!
See Stirling, Edward. Buffalo Girls, The.

FEMALE SPY AND THE CHIEF OF THE TEN
See Falconer, Edmund. Outlaw of the Adriatic, The.

FEMININE STRATEGY
See Adams, Catherine.

FEMMES SAVANTES
See Van Laun, Henri (trans.). Learned Ladies, The.

FENDALL, PERCY
Fashionable Intelligence. London & New York: Samuel French, c.1898. Pp. [1]-23.

FENN, GEORGE MANVILLE
Balloon, The.
See Darnley, J. Herbert.
Barrister, The.
See Darnley, J. Herbert.
Shamrock. New York: Happy Hours, n.d. Pp. [1]-13. Acting Drama, 91.
Wardrobe. New York: Happy Hours, n.d. Pp. [i]-iv, 5-14. Acting Drama, 82.

FENNEL
See Jerome, Jerome Klapka.

FENTON, FREDERICK
Harlequin Old Aesop; or, Dr. Syntax and His Animated Alphabet. Written with Osman, W. R. London: Nowell's (late Peel's) Steam Machine (printer), n.d. Pp. [1]-16. Libretto.

FERGUSON, SAMUEL
Deirdre. Dublin: Peter Roe (printer) (priv.), 1880. Pp. [1]-56.

FERNALD, CHESTER BAILEY
Cat and the Cherub, The. Frome & London: Butler & Tanner (printer), n.d. Pp. [2]-35. Title page lacking. Promptbook.
Ghetto, The. London: William Heinemann, 1899. Pp. [i]-vi, [1]-144.
Moonlight Blossom, The. [London: Mrs. Marshall's Typewriting Office, 1899]. Pp. [i], [1]-32, [i], [1]-25, [i], [1]-19. Pagination by act. Typescript promptbook.

FERREIRA, ANTONIO
Ignez de Castro.
See Musgrave, Thomas Moore (trans.).

FERRERS, ERNEST
Private View, A. London: Capper & Newton, n.d. Pp. [319]-337. Lynn's Acting Edition, 32.

FERRIS, EDWARD
Nicolete. Written with Stuart, Arthur. New York & London: Samuel French, c.1899. Pp. [i-ii], [1]-17. [French's International Copyrighted Edition of the Works of the Best Authors, 19].
White Stocking, A. Written with Stuart, Arthur. London: Samuel French; New York: T. Henry French, n.d. Pp. [1]-19. [Lacy's Acting Edition].

FERRYMAN, THE
See Landor, Robert Eyres.

FESTIVAL OF ROSES
See Oxenford, John. Felix.

FESTIVAL OF THE ROSIERE
See Moncrieff, William Thomas. Joconde.

FESTUS
See Bailey, Philip James.

FÊTE AT ROSHERVILLE!
See Selby, Charles. Out on the Sly.

FETE AT THE HERMITAGE
See Macfarren, George. Lestocq.

FETTERS
See Burnley, James.

FETTES, JAMES (trans.)
Love and Intrigue. By Schiller. Edinburgh: A. & C. Black, 1844. Pp. [i-iv], [1]-100.

FEUDAL TIMES
See White, James, Rev.

FEW MORE PASSAGES IN THE LIFE OF THE RENOWNED AND ILLUSTRIOUS ROBERT MACAIRE!
See Selby, Charles. Jacques Strop.

FEYDEAU, GEORGES
My Good Friend.
See under title.

FIDELIO (anon.)
Music by Beethoven. London & New York: Boosey, n.d. Pp. [i-iv], 1-223. [Royal Edition]. Vocal score.

FIDELIO (anon.)
Music by Beethoven. London: A. Schloss, n.d. Pp. [1]-59. Libretto.

FIDELIO
See Maggioni, Manfredo (trans.).
See Phillips, Morrice.

FIELD, JAMES
See Field, Julian.

FIELD, JULIAN
Too Happy by Half. By James Field. Pp. [i-ii], [1]-44. Typescript promptbook. *Filed under* Field, James.

FIELD, MICHAEL (pseud. of Bradley, Katharine Harris; Cooper, Edith Emma)
Anna Ruina. London: David Nutt, 1899. Pp. [i-iv], [1]-101.
Attila, My Attila! London: Elkin Mathews, n.d. Pp. [i-viii], [1]-107.
Bellerophôn. By Arran and Isla Leigh. London: C. Kegan Paul, 1881. Pp. [i-iv], [1]-127.
Brutus Ultor. London: George Bell & Sons; Clifton: J. Baker & Son, 1886. Pp. [i]-[viii], [1]-78.
Callirrhoë. In *Callirrhoë; Fair Rosamund,* London: George Bell & Sons; Clifton: J. Baker & Son, n.d., pp. [1-4], [i]-[vi], 7-127.
Callirrhoë. In *Callirrhoë; Fair Rosamund,* London: George Bell & Sons; Clifton: J. Baker & Son, n.d., 2nd ed., pp. [1], [i]-[xv], 16-132.
Canute the Great. In *Canute the Great; The Cup of Water,* London: George Bell & Sons; Clifton: J. Baker & Son, n.d., pp. [1]-113.
Cup of Water, The. In *Canute the Great; The Cup of Water,* London: George Bell & Sons; Clifton: J. Baker & Son, n.d., pp. [115]-170. *Filed under* Canute the Great.
Fair Rosamund. London: Hacon & Ricketts, 1897. Pp. [i]-[lxxvi].

Fair Rosamund. In *Callirrhoë; Fair Rosamund,* London: George Bell & Sons; Clifton: J. Baker & Son, n.d., pp. [129]-204. *Filed under* Callirrhoë.

Father's Tragedy, The. In *Father's Tragedy . . . ,* New York: Henry Holt, 1886, pp. 1-121.

Father's Tragedy, The. In *Father's Tragedy . . . ,* London: George Bell & Sons; Clifton: J. Baker & Son, n.d., pp. [1-2], [i]-iv, [1]-121.

Loyalty or Love? In *Father's Tragedy . . . ,* New York: Henry Holt, 1886, pp. [i], [225]-312.

Loyalty or Love? In *Father's Tragedy . . . ,* London: George Bell & Sons; Clifton: J. Baker & Son, n.d., pp. [225]-312. *Filed under* Father's Tragedy.

Noontide Branches. Oxford: Henry Daniel (printer), 1899. Pp. [i-viii], [1]-[46].

Question of Memory, A. London: Elkin Mathews & John Lane, 1893. Pp. [i-vi], [1]-48.

Stephania. London: Elkin Mathews & John Lane, 1892. Pp. [i-viii], [1]-100.

Tragic Mary, The. London: George Bell & Sons, 1890. Pp. [i-x], 1-261.

William Rufus. In *Father's Tragedy . . . ,* New York: Henry Holt, 1886, pp. [i], [123]-223.

William Rufus. In *Father's Tragedy . . . ,* London: George Bell & Sons; Clifton: J. Baker & Son, n.d., pp. [123]-223. *Filed under* Father's Tragedy.

FIELD OF FORTY FOOTSTEPS, THE
   See Farren, Percy.

FIELD OF STIRLING BRIDGE
   See Waddie, Charles. Wallace.

FIELD OF THE CLOTH OF GOLD, THE
   See Brough, William.

FIELDING, ANNA MARIA
   See Hall, Anna Maria Fielding, Mrs. Samuel Carter.

FIELDING, HENRY

Miser, The. London: Sherwood, Neely, & Jones, 1818. Pp. [1]-[42]. London Theatre, XXIV. *Filed under* Dibdin, Thomas John, ed. London Theatre, XXIV.

Miser, The. In *New English Drama,* ed. W. Oxberry, 22 vols., London: W. Simpkin & R. Marshall; C. Chapple, 1821, XI, [1-2], [i]-[iv], [1]-31. *Filed under* Oxberry, William Henry. New English Drama, XI.

Miser, The. In *British Drama,* 12 vols., London: John Dicks, 1871, VI, [277]-288.

Miser, The. London: John Cumberland, n.d. Pp. [1]-36. Cumberland's British Theatre, XXXV. *Filed under* Cumberland, John. Cumberland's British Theatre, XXXV.

Mock Doctor, The; or, The Dumb Lady Cured. London: Whittingham & Arliss, 1815. Pp. [1]-[28]. London Theatre, XX. *Filed under* Dibdin, Thomas John, ed. London Theatre, XX.

Mock Doctor, The; or, The Dumb Lady Cured. In *British Drama,* 12 vols., London: John Dicks, 1871, IX, [153]-160.

Tom Thumb. London: John Fairburn, n.d. Pp. [1]-38.

Tom Thumb.
   See O'Hara, Kane (arr.).

Virgin Unmasked, The. London: Sherwood, Neely, & Jones, 1817. Pp. [1]-24. London Theatre, XXIII. *Filed under* Dibdin, Thomas John, ed. London Theatre, XXIII.

Virgin Unmasked, The. In *British Drama,* 12 vols., London: John Dicks, 1871, VIII, [122]-128. *Filed under* Virgin Unmatched, The.

FIEND-FATHER
   See Lacy, Michael Rophino. Robert the Devil.

FIERY ORDEAL
   See Kerr, John. Presumptive Guilt.

FIFTEEN YEARS OF A DRUNKARD'S LIFE
   See Jerrold, Douglas William. Drunkard's Fate, The.
   See Jerrold, Douglas William.

FIFTEEN YEARS OF LABOUR LOST
   See Amherst, J. H.

FIFTH CENTURY
   See Hengist (anon.).

FIFTH OF NOVEMBER, THE
   See Rhodes, George Ambrose.

FIGARO IN LONDON
   See A'Beckett, Gilbert Abbott.

FIGHT FOR THE FRANCHISE
   See Harrison, Wilmot. Once a Week.

FIGHT OF SEMPACH!
   See Lemon, Mark. Arnold of Winkelried.

FIGHTING BY PROXY
   See Kenney, James.

FIGLIA DEL REGGIMENTO
   See Daughter of the Regiment, The (anon.).
   See Kenney, Charles Lamb (trans.).
   See Maggioni, Manfredo (trans.).

FIGURE OF FUN, A
   See Stirling, Edward.

FIGURE OF SPEECH, A
   See Childe-Pemberton, Harriet Louisa.

FILIPPI, ROSINA (later Mrs. H. M. Dowson)

Flower Children, The. In *Three Japanese Plays for Children,* Oxford: H. Daniel, 1897, pp. [13]-33. *Filed under* Dowson, Rosina Filippi.

Mirror, The. In *Three Japanese Plays for Children,* Oxford: H. Daniel, 1897, pp. [1]-12. *Filed under* Dowson, Rosina Filippi.

Night of a Hundred Years, The. In *Three Japanese Plays for Children,* Oxford: H. Daniel, 1897, pp. [35]-57. *Filed under* Dowson, Rosina Filippi.

FILLE DE MADAME ANGOT, LA (anon.)
Music by Lecocq, Charles. London & New York: Samuel French, n.d. Pp. [1]-34. Libretto.

FILLE DE MADAME ANGOT, LA
   See Byron, Henry James (trans.).
   See Farnie, Henry Brougham.
   See Nelson, Carry.

FILLE DU TAMBOUR-MAJOR, LA
   See Farnie, Henry Brougham.

FILMORE, LEWIS (trans.)
Faust. By Goethe. London: William Smith, 1847. Pp. [i]-[xx], [1]-223.

FINDING IN THE TEMPLE, THE
   See Hinkson, Katharine Tynan, Mrs. Henry Albert.

FINDING OF PHEIDIPPIDES, THE
   See Pember, Edward Henry.

FINE FEATHERS
   See Byron, Henry James.

FINESSE
   See Dufferin, Helen Selina Sheridan Blackwood, Lady.

FINGER POST
   See Dibdin, Thomas John. Five Miles Off.

FINIS
   See Sharp, William.

FINNAMORE, JOHN
Carpio. Melbourne: George Robertson, 1875. Pp. [i]-[viii], [1]-80.

FIRE AND SPIRIT
   See Dibdin, Charles Isaac Mungo, jr.

FIRE AND WATER
   See Beazley, Samuel, jr.

FIRE BANNER!
   See Almar, George. Knight of St. John!, The.

FIRE-EATER!, THE
   See Selby, Charles.

FIRE-FLIES
   See Sturgis, Julian Russell.

FIRE KING
   See Warton, Ferdinand Fullarton. Albert and Rosalie.

FIRE OF LONDON
   See Fullerton, Georgiana Charlotte Leveson-Gower, Mrs. Alexander George, Lady Georgiana. Which Is Which?

FIRE RAISER, THE
   See Almar, George.

FIRE, WATER, EARTH, AND AIR
   See Dibdin, Thomas John. Harlequin in His Element.

FIREMAN ON DUTY, THE (anon.)
[London: Mrs. Marshall's Typing Office, 1897]. Pp. [i], [1]-18, [i], [1]-20, [i], [1]-10, [i], [1]-8, [i], [1]-11, [i], [1]-12. Pagination by act. Typescript.

FIRESIDE DIPLOMACY
See Cheltnam, Charles Smith.

FIRESIDE STORY
See Bernard, William Bayle. Round of Wrong, The.
See Gordon, Walter.

FIRMILIAN
See Aytoun, William Edmondstone.

FIRST AFFECTIONS
See Simpson, John Palgrave.

FIRST AND SECOND FLOOR
See Colman, George, jr. Actor of All Work, The.

FIRST BORN, THE
See Harness, William, Rev.

FIRST BRUTUS, THE
See Lloyd, Charles (trans.).

FIRST COME, FIRST SERVED
See Morton, John Maddison.

FIRST COMEDY
See Barber, James.

FIRST EXPERIMENT, A
See Jones, John Wilton.

FIRST FLOOR, THE
See Cobb, James.

FIRST IMPRESSIONS
See Smith, Horatio.

FIRST IN THE FIELD
See Rae, Charles Marsham.

FIRST LOVE
See Cumberland, Richard.
See Edwardes, Conway Theodore Marriott.
See Suter, William E.

FIRST MATE
See Henry, Richard.

FIRST NIGHT, THE
See Maddox, John Medex.
See Parry, Thomas.

FIRST OF APRIL, THE
See Boaden, Caroline.
See Maclaren, Archibald.

FIRST OF AUGUST
See Dibdin, Charles, sr. Waterman, The.

FIRST OF MAY, THE
See Hill, Isabel.
See Younge, A.

FIRST OF SEPTEMBER, THE
See Oxberry, William Henry.

FIRST PART OF WALLENSTEIN
See Coleridge, Samuel Taylor (trans.). Piccolomini, The.

FIRST STEP, THE
See Heinemann, William.

FISH 'O MAN OF NAPLES
See Brough, Robert Barnabas. Masaniello.

FISH OUT OF WATER
See Lunn, Joseph.

FISHER, DAVID
Music Hath Charms. London: Thomas Hailes Lacy, n.d. Pp. [1]-17. [Lacy's Acting Edition].

FISHER, W. J.
Lot 49. London & New York: Samuel French, n.d. Pp. [1]-20. [Lacy's Acting Edition].

FISHERMAN, THE
See Tobin, John.

FITZBALL, EDWARD (also Ball, Edward)
Alice May; or, The Last Appeal. London: John Duncombe, n.d. Pp. [1]-32. Duncombe's Edition. Promptbook.
Azael, the Prodigal. London: John Duncombe, n.d. Pp. [1]-26. Duncombe's Edition.
Barber, The; or, The Mill of Bagdad. By Edward Ball. London: John Lowndes, n.d. Pp. [1]-27.
Barber of Bagdad, The. London: John Dicks, n.d. Pp. [1]-12. Dicks' Standard Plays, 973.

Bertha. By Edward Ball. London: R. Edwards; W. Booth (priv.), 1819. Pp. [i-viii], [1]-59.
Bronze Horse, The; or, The Spell of the Cloud King. London: John Duncombe, n.d. Pp. [i-ii], [1]-26. Duncombe's Acting Edition of the British Theatre, 151. Promptbook.
Carmelites!, The. London: John Duncombe, n.d. Pp. [1]-30. Duncombe's Edition.
Carmilhan; or, The Drowned Crew! London: John Duncombe, n.d. <wrps. Thomas Hailes Lacy>. Pp. [1]-30. Duncombe's Edition <wrps. New British Theatre (late Duncombe's), 131>.
Children of the Castle, The. London: Thomas Hailes Lacy, n.d. Pp. [1]-30. [Lacy's Acting Edition].
Christmas Eve; or, The Duel in the Snow. London: Thomas Hailes Lacy, n.d. Pp. [1]-28. Promptbook.
Crock of Gold!, The; or, The Murder at the Hall. London: Duncombe & Moon, n.d. Pp. [1]-29. Duncombe's Edition.
Crown Diamonds, The. *Also:* Les Diamans de la Couronne. Music by Auber. London: Chappell, n.d. Pp. [1]-48. Libretto.
Crown Jewels, The. Pp. [i-ii], [1]-55. Act I only. Manuscript promptbook libretto.
Crown Jewels, The. *Also:* Les Diamans de la Couronne. Music by Auber. London: Chappell; W. S. Johnson, n.d. Pp. [1]-50. Libretto.
Crown Jewels, The. Music by Auber. Boston: J. H. Eastburn's Press, 1855. Pp. [i-iv], [1]-55. Libretto.
Daughter of the Regiment, The. London: John Dicks, n.d. Pp. [1]-14. Dicks' Standard Plays, 761.
Deserted Mill, The; or, The Soldier's Widow. London: Thomas Hailes Lacy, n.d. Pp. [1]-31. Cumberland's British Theatre (with Duncombe's).
Devil's Elixir, The; or, The Shadowless Man. Music by Rodwell, G. H. London: John Cumberland, n.d. Pp. [1]-36. Promptbook.
Devil's Elixir, The; or, The Shadowless Man. Music by Rodwell, G. H. London: John Cumberland, n.d. Pp. [1]-36. Cumberland's British Theatre, XXII. *Filed under* Cumberland, John. Cumberland's British Theatre, XXII.
Diadeste; or, The Veiled Lady. 20 leaves. Manuscript libretto.
Diamans de la Couronne.
See Crown Diamonds.
See also Crown Jewels.
Earthquake, The; or, The Spectre of the Nile. London: John Cumberland, n.d. Pp. [1]-40.
Earthquake, The; or, The Spectre of the Nile. London: John Cumberland, n.d. Pp. [1]-40. Cumberland's Minor Theatre, I. *Filed under* Cumberland, John. Cumberland's Minor Theatre, I.
Edda; or, The Hermit of Warkworth. By Edward Ball. London: C. Chapple, 1820. Pp. [i]-vi, [1]-29.
Edwin, Heir of Cressingham. By Edward Ball. London: Baldwin, Craddock, & Joy, 1817. Pp. [i-vi], [1]-79.
Esmeralda; or, The Deformed of Notre Dame. London: Thomas Hailes Lacy, n.d. Pp. [1]-34. Promptbook.
False Colours; or, The Free Trader! London: John Duncombe, n.d. Pp. [1]-24. Duncombe's Acting Edition of the British Theatre, 201.
Fatal Blow, The. Clyde, Ohio: A. D. Ames, n.d. Pp. [1]-16. Ames' Series of Standard and Minor Drama, 97.
Father and Son; or, The Rock of Charbonniere. By E. Ball. London: John Cumberland, n.d. Pp. [1]-35.
Father and Son; or, The Rock of La Charbonniere. By E. Ball. London: Thomas Dolby, 1825. Pp. [1]-35. Dolby's British Theatre, X. *Filed under* Cumberland, John. Cumberland's British Theatre, X.
Favourite, The. *Also:* La Favorita. Music by Donizetti. London: G. H. Davidson, n.d. Pp. [1]-27. Davidson's Illustrated Libretto Books. Libretto.
Floating Beacon, The. London: John Cumberland, n.d. Pp. [1]-32. Cumberland's Minor Theatre, II. *Filed under* Cumberland, John. Cumberland's Minor Theatre, II.

Floating Beacon, The; or, Norwegian Wreckers. By Edward Ball. New York & Philadelphia: Turner & Fisher, n.d. Pp. [1]-20. Turner's Dramatic Library of Acting Plays.

Floating Beacon, The; or, The Norwegian Wreckers. By Edward Ball. London: John Lowndes, n.d. Pp. [i-iv], [1]-24.

Floating Beacon, The; or, The Wild Woman of the Wreck. London: Thomas Hailes Lacy, n.d. Pp. [1]-32. Lacy's Acting Edition.

Flying Dutchman, The; or, The Phantom Ship. [London: John Cumberland], n.d. Pp. [8]-48. Title page lacking.

Flying Dutchman, The; or, The Phantom Ship. Music by Rodwell, G. H. London: John Cumberland, n.d. Pp. [1]-48. Cumberland's Minor Theatre, II. *Filed under* Cumberland, John. Cumberland's Minor Theatre, II.

Flying Dutchman, The; or, The Phantom Ship. New York: Samuel French, n.d. Pp. [1]-35. French's American Drama, 6.

Flying Dutchman, The; or, The Spectral Ship. London: Thomas Richardson, n.d. Pp. [i]-xiv, [15]-42. *Filed under* Elliston, Robert William.

Fortunes of Nigel, The. London: John Cumberland, n.d. Pp. [1]-56. Cumberland's Minor Theatre, 32.

Fortunes of Nigel, The. London: John Cumberland, n.d. Pp. [1]-56. Cumberland's Minor Theatre, IV. *Filed under* Cumberland, John. Cumberland's Minor Theatre, IV.

Freischutz, Der; or, The Demon of the Wolf's Glen and the Seven Charmed Bullets. By Edward Ball. Music by Weber. London: J. Lowndes, n.d. Pp. [1]-36.

Greek Slave, The; or, The Spectre Gambler. London & New York: Samuel French, n.d. Pp. [1]-25.

Hans of Iceland. Music by Hughes, R. London: S. G. Fairbrother, n.d. Pp. [1]-11. Synopsis.

Hans von Stein; or, The Robber Knight. London & New York: Samuel French, n.d. Pp. [3]-30. [Lacy's Acting Edition].

Harlequin and Humpty Dumpty; or, Robbin de Bobbin and the First Lord Mayor of Lun'on. London: S. G. Fairbrother, n.d. Pp. [1]-23. Libretto.

Haunted Hulk, The. London: John Cumberland, n.d. Pp. [1]-39. Cumberland's Minor Theatre.

Hofer, the Tell of the Tyrol. London: John Cumberland, n.d. Pp. [1]-48. Cumberland's Minor Theatre, 46.

Hofer, the Tell of the Tyrol. London: John Cumberland, n.d. Pp. [i-ii], [1]-48. Cumberland's Minor Theatre, VI. *Filed under* Cumberland, John. Cumberland's Minor Theatre, VI.

Home Again!; or, The Lieutenant's Daughters. London: John Duncombe, n.d. Pp. [1]-34. Duncombe's Edition. Promptbook.

Inchcape Bell, The. London: John Cumberland, n.d. Pp. [1]-38.

Inchcape Bell, The. London: John Cumberland, n.d. Pp. [1]-38. Cumberland's Minor Theatre, I. *Filed under* Cumberland, John. Cumberland's Minor Theatre, I.

Innkeeper of Abbeville, The; or, The Hostler and the Robber. By Edward Ball. London: John Lowndes, 1822. Pp. [1]-[27].

Innkeeper of Abbeville, The; or, The Ostler and the Robber. London: John Cumberland, n.d. Pp. [1]-32. Cumberland's Minor Theatre, III. *Filed under* Cumberland, John. Cumberland's Minor Theatre, III.

Joan of Arc; or, The Maid of Orleans. By Edward Ball. London: John Lowndes, n.d. Pp. [i-vi], [1]-31.

Joan of Arc; or, The Maid of Orleans. Music by Nicholson. London: John Cumberland, n.d. Pp. [1]-39. Cumberland's Minor Theatre, IV. *Filed under* Cumberland, John. Cumberland's Minor Theatre, IV.

Jonathan Bradford!; or, The Murder at the Road-side Inn. London: Thomas Hailes Lacy, n.d. Pp. [1]-37. New British Theatre (late Duncombe's), 84. Promptbook.

King of the Mist, The; or, The Miller of the Hartz Mountains! London: John Duncombe, n.d. Pp. [1]-30. Duncombe's Edition. Promptbook.

Koeuba, The; or, The Pirate Vessel. London: John Cumberland, n.d. Pp. [1]-36. [Cumberland's Minor Theatre].

Koeuba, The; or, The Pirate Vessel. London: John Cumberland, n.d. Pp. [1]-36. Cumberland's Minor Theatre, XII. *Filed under* Cumberland, John. Cumberland's Minor Theatre, XII.

Last of the Fairies, The. London: John Duncombe, n.d. <wrps. Thomas Hailes Lacy>. Pp. [1]-26. Duncombe's Edition <wrps. New British Theatre (late Duncombe's), 537>.

Lurline. Music by Wallace, William Vincent. New York: William Hall & Son, c.1868. Pp. [1]-31. Libretto.

Lurline. Music by Wallace, W. Vincent. London: Covent Garden, n.d. Pp. [i]-[vi], [7]-54. Libretto.

Maid of Honor, The. Music by Balfe, M. W. London: Chappell, n.d. Pp. [1]-38. Libretto.

Maid of Palaiseau!, The. *Also:* Ninetta. Music by Bishop, H. R. London: W. Wright (printer), n.d. Pp. [1]-31. Libretto.

Margaret's Ghost; or, The Libertine's Ship. N. p.: n.pub., n.d. Pp. [31]-44. Title page lacking.

Maritana. London: W. S. Johnson, n.d. Pp. [1]-33. Promptbook libretto.

Maritana. Music by Wallace, W. Vincent. London: Hutchings & Romer, n.d. Pp. [i-ii], [1]-387. Vocal score.

Marmion! A Tale of Flodden Field! London: Duncombe & Moon, n.d. Pp. [1]-30. Duncombe's Edition.

Mary Glastonbury; or, The Dream Girl of the Devil-Holl. Music by Jolly. London: John Cumberland, n.d. Pp. [1]-44. [Cumberland's Minor Theatre].

Mary Glastonbury; or, The Dream Girl of the Devil-Holl. Music by Jolly. London: John Cumberland, n.d. Pp. [1]-44. Cumberland's Minor Theatre, VI. *Filed under* Cumberland, John. Cumberland's Minor Theatre, VI.

Mary Melvyn; or, A Marriage of Interest. London: G. Berger, 1843. Pp. [1]-38.

Miller of Derwent Water, The. Clyde, Ohio: Ames, n.d. Pp. [1]-27. Ames' Series of Standard and Minor Drama, 36.

Momentous Question, The. London: Thomas Hailes Lacy, n.d. Pp. [1]-26. New British Theatre (late Duncombe's), 399.

Negro of Wapping, The; or, The Boat-Builder's Hovel! London: John Duncombe, n.d. Pp. [1]-24. Duncombe's Edition.

Ninetta; or, The Maid of Palaiseau. Music by Rossini. London: J. Ebers, n.d. Pp. [1]-47. Libretto.

Note Forger!, The. London: John Duncombe, n.d. Pp. [1]-38. Duncombe's Acting Edition of the British Theatre, 130.

Omala; or, Settlers in America. By Edward Ball. London: John Lowndes, 1826. Pp. [1]-40.

Paul Clifford. London: Thomas Hailes Lacy, n.d. Pp. [1]-44. Cumberland's British Theatre (with Duncombe's).

Peter the Great. London: John Duncombe, n.d. Pp. [1]-35. Duncombe's Acting Edition of the British Theatre, 541.

Peveril of the Peak; or, The Days of King Charles II. By Edward Ball. London: John Lowndes, n.d. Pp. [3]-48.

Peveril of the Peak; or, The Days of King Charles II. London: John Cumberland, n.d. Pp. [1]-53. Cumberland's Minor Theatre, V. *Filed under* Cumberland, John. Cumberland's Minor Theatre, V.

Pierette; or, The Village Rivals. Music by Montgomery, W. H. London: Thomas Hailes Lacy, n.d. Pp. [1]-13. [Lacy's Acting Edition]. Libretto.

Pilot, The; or, A Storm at Sea. By Edward Ball. London: Simpkin & Marshall, 1825. Pp. [i-vi], [1]-53.

Pilot, The. In *British Drama*, 12 vols., London: John Dicks, 1864, II, [483]-496.

Pilot, The. New York: Samuel French, n.d. Pp. [1]-32. French's American Drama, 41. Promptbook.

Pilot, The. Music by Rodwell, G. H. London: John Cumberland, n.d. Pp. [i-ii], [1]-51. Cumberland's Minor Theatre, I. *Filed under* Cumberland, John. Cumberland's Minor Theatre, I.

Quasimodo. London: John Duncombe, n.d. Pp. [1]-34. Duncombe's Edition.

Quasimodo. London: John Duncombe, n.d. Pp. [1]-34. Promptbook.

Queen of the Thames, The. Music by Hatton. London: G. Berger, 1843. Pp. [1]-24. Libretto.

Quentin Durward. Music by Laurent, Henri. London: John K. Chapman, 1848. Pp. [1]-26. Libretto.

Rauberbraut.
See Robber's Bride, The.

Red Rover, The; or, The Mutiny of the Dolphin. London: John Cumberland, n.d. Pp. [1]-46. Cumberland's Minor Theatre, VI. *Filed under* Cumberland, John. Cumberland's Minor Theatre, VI.

Red Rover, The; or, The Mutiny of the Dolphin. London: John Cumberland, n.d. Pp. [1]-46. Promptbook.

Robber's Bride, The. *Also:* Rauberbraut. Music by Ries, Ferdinand. London: W. Hawes, n.d. Pp. [i-ii], and 192 pages, paginated by song. Vocal score.

Robin Hood; or, The Merry Outlaws of Sherwood. London: Thomas Hailes Lacy, n.d. Pp. [1]-32. [Lacy's Acting Edition].

Sailor's Legacy, A; or, The Child of a Tar. [London: John Dicks], n.d. Pp. [11]-16. [Dicks' Standard Plays, 919].

Scaramuccia; or, The Villagers of San Quintino. Music by Ricci. London: E. H. Turnour, n.d. Pp. [1]-20. Libretto.

Siege of Rochelle, The. Music by Balfe, Michael William. London: Novello, Ewer, n.d. Pp. [1]-32. Libretto.

Siege of Rochelle, The. Music by Balfe, Michael William. London & New York: Boosey, n.d. Pp. [i-iv], 1-280. [Royal Edition]. Vocal score.

Siege of Rochelle, The. Music by Balfe, M. W. New York & Philadelphia: Turner & Fisher, 1838. Pp. [1]-23. 1st American, from 10th London ed. Libretto.

Thalaba the Destroyer. London: John Cumberland, n.d. Pp. [1]-48. Cumberland's Minor Theatre, V. *Filed under* Cumberland, John. Cumberland's Minor Theatre, V.

Thalaba the Destroyer. London: John Cumberland, n.d. Pp. [1]-48.

Three Hunchbacks, The; or, The Sabre Grinders of Damascus. By Edward Ball. London: John Lowndes, n.d. Pp. [1]-40.

Tom Cringle. London: Thomas Hailes Lacy, n.d. Pp. [1]-36. Promptbook.

Traveller's Room!, The. London: Duncombe & Moon, n.d. Pp. [3]-26. Duncombe's Edition.

Tread Mill, The; or, Tom and Jerry at Brixton. London: J. Lowndes, n.d. Pp. [1]-28.

Walter Brand; or, The Duel in the Mist! London: John Duncombe, n.d. Pp. [3]-50. Duncombe's Edition.

Walter Tyrrel. London: Chapman & Hall, n.d. Pp. [1]-36. Promptbook.

Wardock Kennilson; or, The Wild Woman of the Village. London: John Cumberland, n.d. Pp. [1]-44. Cumberland's Minor Theatre, VIII. *Filed under* Cumberland, John. Cumberland's Minor Theatre, VIII.

Wardock Kennilson; or, The Wild Woman of the Village. London: John Cumberland, n.d. Pp. [1]-44. [Cumberland's Minor Theatre].

Waverley; or, Sixty Years Since. London: John Cumberland, n.d. Pp. [1]-48. Cumberland's Minor Theatre, V. *Filed under* Cumberland, John. Cumberland's Minor Theatre, V.

Waverly; or, Sixty Years Since. By Edward Ball. London: John Lowndes, n.d. Pp. [1]-44.

Zazezizozu; or, Dominoes! Chess! and Cards!. London: John Duncombe, n.d. Pp. [1]-30. Duncombe's Edition.

FITZBALL, EDWARD (trans.)

Desert, Le. Music by David, Félicien. London: Cramer, Beale, n.d. Pp. [i-ii], [1]-37, 1-21, 1-22. Pagination by part. Vocal score.

FITZGERALD, EDWARD (trans.)

Agamemnon. By Aeschylus. N.p.: n.pub., n.d. Pp. [1]-63.

Beware of Smooth Water. By Calderon. In *Six Dramas of Calderon*, London: William Pickering, 1853, pp. [229]-[275]. *Filed under* Six Dramas.

Beware of Smooth Water. By Calderon. In *Eight Dramas of Calderon*, London: Macmillan, 1906, pp. 309-368. *Filed under* Eight Dramas of Calderon.

Downfall and Death of King Oedipus, The. By Sophocles. In *Variorum and Definitive Edition of the Poetical and Prose Writings of Edward Fitzgerald*, New York: Doubleday, Page, 1902, VI, [i]-xiv, [1]-136.

Downfall and Death of King Oedipus, The. By Sophocles. Guildford: Billing & Sons (printer), n.d. Pp. [1], [i]-[x], [5]-46, [3]-45.

Gil Perez, the Gallician. By Calderon. In *Six Dramas of Calderon*, London: William Pickering, 1853, pp. [103]-142. *Filed under* Six Dramas.

Gil Perez, the Gallician. By Calderon. In *Eight Dramas of Calderon*, London: Macmillan, 1906, pp. 139-191. *Filed under* Eight Dramas of Calderon.

Keep Your Own Secret. By Calderon. In *Six Dramas of Calderon*, London: William Pickering, 1853, pp. [59]-102. *Filed under* Six Dramas.

Keep Your Own Secret. By Calderon. In *Eight Dramas of Calderon*, London: Macmillan, 1906, pp. 80-138. *Filed under* Eight Dramas of Calderon.

Mayor of Zalamea, The. By Calderon. In *Six Dramas of Calderon*, London: William Pickering, 1853, pp. [191]-228. *Filed under* Six Dramas.

Mayor of Zalamea, The. By Calderon. In *Eight Dramas of Calderon*, London: Macmillan, 1906, pp. [254]-308. *Filed under* Eight Dramas of Calderon.

Mighty Magician, The. By Calderon. In *Eight Dramas of Calderon*, London: Macmillan, 1906, pp. 369-440. *Filed under* Eight Dramas of Calderon.

Mighty Magician, The. By Calderon. [London]: John Childs & Son (printer) (priv.), n.d. Pp. [1]-63.

Painter of His Own Dishonour, The. By Calderon. In *Six Dramas of Calderon*, London: William Pickering, 1853, pp. [i]-viii, [1]-58. *Filed under* Six Dramas.

Painter of His Own Dishonour, The. By Calderon. In *Eight Dramas of Calderon*, London: Macmillan, 1906, pp. [i-iv], [1]-79. *Filed under* Eight Dramas of Calderon.

Such Stuff As Dreams Are Made Of. By Calderon. London: John Childs & Son (printer) (priv.), n.d. Pp. [65]-131. *Filed under* Mighty Magician.

Such Stuff As Dreams Are Made Of. By Calderon. In *Eight Dramas of Calderon*, London: Macmillan, 1906, pp. 441-517. *Filed under* Eight Dramas of Calderon.

Three Judgments at a Blow. By Calderon. In *Six Dramas of Calderon*, London: William Pickering, 1853, pp. [143]-189. *Filed under* Six Dramas.

Three Judgments at a Blow. By Calderon. In *Eight Dramas of Calderon*, London: Macmillan, 1906, pp. [193]-253. *Filed under* Eight Dramas of Calderon.

FITZGERALD, J. D.

Inspector's Visit, The; or, Paddy Byrnes, the Irish Schoolmaster. In *Glimpses of Irish Life*, Dublin: John F. Fowler (printer), 1860, pp. [i]-x, [11]-29. *Filed under* Glimpses of Irish Life.

Irish Election, The. In *Glimpses of Irish Life*, Dublin: John F. Fowler (printer), 1860, pp. [30]-48. *Filed under* Glimpses of Irish Life.

FITZGERALD, PERCY HETHERINGTON

William Simpson, The. London & New York: Samuel French, n.d. Pp. [1]-15. [Lacy's Acting Edition].

FITZGERALD, SHAFTO JUSTIN ADAIR

Bric-a-Brac Will, The. Written with Moss, Hugh. Music by Pizzi, Emilio. London: Robert Cocks, c.1895. Pp. [1]-32. Libretto. *Filed under* Moss, Hugh.

Jealous Mistake, A. In *One Act Plays*, London: Francis Griffiths, n.d., I, [i], [7]-33.

Parting, The. In *Parting, and Waiting for the Train*, Carpet Plays, ed. Lucian Oldershaw, London: R. Brimley Johnson, 1901, pp. [1]-23.

Pretty Princess and the Prickly Pear, The; or, A Trip to Nodland. London: Samuel French; New York: T. Henry French, n.d. Pp. [1]-24. [Fairy and Home Plays for Home Performance, 27].

Two Hearts. In *One Act Plays,* London: Francis Griffiths, n.d, III, [i], [62]-91.

Waiting for the Train. In *Parting, and Waiting for the Train,* Carpet Plays, ed. Lucian Oldershaw, London: R. Brimley Johnson, 1901, pp. [i], [24]-44.

When I'm a Man. London & New York: Samuel French, c.1899. Pp. [1]-8. Children's Plays, 14.

FITZGERALD, WILLIAM, JR

Siege of Carthage, The. London: Sherwood, Neely, & Jones; Simpkin & Marshall (priv.), 1819. Pp. [i-x], [1]-56.

FITZORMOND

See Burney, Frances.

FITZSIMON, ELLEN

Boy of Normandy, The. In *Darrynane in Eighteen Hundred and Thirty-Two and Other Poems,* Dublin: W. B. Kelly, 1863, pp. [i], 149-194.

FITZSMYTHE OF FITZSMYTHE HALL

See Morton, John Maddison.

FIVE GENERATIONS

See Milner, Henry M. Veteran of 102 Years.

FIVE HOURS AT BRIGHTON

See Beazley, Samuel, jr. Boarding House, The.

FIVE HUNDRED POUNDS REWARD

See Wigan, Alfred Sydney.

FIVE IN ONE

See Walpole, Henry.

FIVE MILES OFF

See Dibdin, Thomas John.

FIVE POUNDS REWARD

See Oxenford, John.

FLAG OF FREEDOM

See Stirling, Edward. White Slave, The.

FLAUTO MAGICO, IL (anon. trans.)

Also: The Magic Flute. Music by Mozart. London & New York: Boosey, n.d. Pp. [i-iv], 1-208. [Royal Edition]. Vocal score.

FLAUTO MAGICO, IL; OR, I MISTERI D'ISIDE

See Walter, William Joseph (trans.). Magic Flute, The.

FLEMING, GEORGE (pseud. of Fletcher, Julia Constance)

Canary, The. [New York: Z. & L. Rosenfield, 1900]. Pp. [i-iii], [1]-48, [i], [1]-23, [i], [1]-44. Pagination by act. Typescript.

FLEMING, GEORGE (pseud. of Fletcher, Julia Constance) (trans.)

Fantasticks, The. By Rostand, Edmond. New York: R. H. Russell, 1900. Pp. [i-iv], [1]-146.

FLETCHER, JOHN

Chances, The.

See Garrick, David (arr.).

Merchant of Bruges, The.

See Kinnaird, Douglas James William (arr.).

Rule a Wife and Have a Wife.

See Beaumont, Francis.

Rule a Wife and Have a Wife.

See Garrick, David (arr.).

Rule a Wife and Have a Wife.

See Kemble, John Philip (arr.).

Spanish Curate, The.

See Planché, James Robinson (arr.).

FLETCHER, JULIA CONSTANCE

See Fleming, George (pseud.).

FLEUR-DE-LYS

See Farnie, Henry Brougham.

FLIEGENDE HOLLANDER

See Jackson, John P. (trans.). Flying Dutchman, The.

FLIES IN THE WEB

See Brougham, John.

FLIGHT INTO EGYPT, THE

See Hinkson, Katharine Tynan, Mrs. Henry Albert.

FLIGHT TO AMERICA, THE

See Rede, William Leman.

FLITCH, THE

See Dibdin, Charles Isaac Mungo, jr.

FLOATING A COMPANY

See Cross, Julian.

FLOATING BEACON, THE

See Fitzball, Edward.

FLODDEN FIELD

See Kemble, Stephen.

See Marmion (anon.).

FLORENCE MACARTHY

See Bryant, Michael.

FLORENTINE PARTY, THE

See Cornwall, Barry.

FLORENTINE TRAGEDY, A

See Wilde, Oscar Fingall O'Flahertie Wills.

FLORETTA

See Farjeon, Eleanor.

FLORIO

See Sturgis, Julian Russell.

FLORODORA

See Hall, Owen.

FLOWER CHILDREN, THE

See Filippi, Rosina.

FLOWER MAKERS OF FINSBURY

See Hazlewood, Colin Henry. Lizzie Lyle.

FLOWER OF WOOLWICH

See Campbell, Andrew Leonard Voullaire. Bound 'Prentice to a Waterman.

FLOWER OF YARROW, THE

See Warde, George Ambrose.

FLOWERS, SARAH FULLER

See Adams, Sarah Fuller Flowers, Mrs. William Bridges.

FLOWERS OF PROGRESS

See Gilbert, William Schwenck. Utopia Limited.

FLOWERS OF THE FOREST, THE: A GYPSY STORY

See Buckstone, John Baldwin.

FLY AND THE WEB, THE

See Troughton, Adolphus Charles.

FLYING DOCTOR, THE

See Van Laun, Henri (trans.).

FLYING DUTCHMAN

See England, Paul (trans.).

See Fitzball, Edward.

See Jackson, John P. (trans.).

See Pittman, Josiah (trans.).

See Taylor, Thomas Proclus. Vanderdecken.

See Troutbeck, John, Rev. (trans.).

FLYING DUTCHMAN AND THE KING OF RARITONGO

See Ellis, George. Harlequin Billy Taylor.

FLYING ISLANDERS

See Peter Wilkins (anon.).

FLYING SCUD

See Boucicault, Dionysius Lardner.

FOGGERTY'S FAIRY

See Gilbert, William Schwenck.

FOLLIES OF A DAY, THE

See Holcroft, Thomas.

See Kemble, John Philip (arr.).

FOLLIES OF A NIGHT, THE

See Planché, James Robinson.

FOLLIES OF FASHION, THE

See Butler, Richard, Earl of Glengall.

FOLLIES OF THE DAY

See Nightingale, Joseph Henry. Bloomerism.

FOLLOW THE LEADER

See Rae, Charles Marsham.

FOLLY AS IT FLIES

See Reynolds, Frederick.

FOLLY, LOVE, AND MARRIAGE

See Buckstone, John Baldwin. Rake and His Pupil, The.

FOLLY OR SAINTLINESS

See Lynch, Hannah (trans.).

FONTAINBLEAU

See O'Keeffe, John.

FONTAINE, L.

Fauvette.

See Rae, Alfred.

FONTAINEBLEAU (anon.)

Manchester: Lowes (printer), 1848. Pp. [1]-73.

FOOL AND HIS MONEY
 See Byron, Henry James.
FOOL'S ERRAND
 See Maclaren, Archibald. First of April, The.
FOOL'S PARADISE, A
 See Grundy, Sydney.
FOOL'S REVENGE, THE
 See Taylor, Tom.
FOOL'S TRAGEDY
 See Beddoes, Thomas Lovell. Death's Jest-book.
FOOLISH JACK
 See Bell, Florence Eveleen Eleanore Oliffe, Mrs. Hugh
 ·(Lady).
FOOT-BOY'S DREAM
 See Fry, Betsey. Area Sylph, The.
FOOTE, SAMUEL
 Liar, The. In *New English Drama*, ed. W. Oxberry, 22 vols.,
 London: W. Simpkin & R. Marshall; C. Chapple, 1822,
 XV, [i]-[x], [11]-[48]. *Filed under* Oxberry, William Henry.
 New English Drama, XV.
 Liar, The. In *British Drama*, 12 vols., London: John Dicks,
 1871, VII, [244]-256.
 Liar, The.
 See Mathews, Charles James (arr.).
 Mayor of Garratt, The. London: Whittingham & Arliss,
 1815. Pp. [1]-28. London Theatre, XVII. *Filed under*
 Dibdin, Thomas John, ed. London Theatre, XVII.
 Mayor of Garratt, The. In *New English Drama*, ed. W.
 Oxberry, 22 vols., London: W. Simpkin & R. Marshall;
 C. Chapple, 1820, IX, [1-2], [i]-[vi], [1]-23. *Filed under*
 Oxberry, William Henry. New English Drama, IX.
 Mayor of Garratt, The. London: T. Dolby, 1824. Pp. [1]-28.
 Dolby's British Theatre, VIII. *Filed under* Cumberland,
 John. Cumberland's British Theatre, VIII.
 Mayor of Garratt, The. In *British Drama*, 12 vols., London:
 John Dicks, 1864, I, [147]-153.
FOOTMAN, MAURICE H.
 Orchard of the King, The.
 See Day, Ernest.
FOP'S FORTUNE
 See Cibber, Colley. Love Makes a Man.
FOR BETTER OR WORSE
 See Maltby, C. Alfred.
FOR CHARITY'S SAKE
 See Fawcett, Charles S. Our Lottie.
FOR ENGLAND
 See Vane, Sutton.
FOR ENGLAND, HO!
 See Pocock, Isaac.
FOR HER CHILD'S SAKE
 See Young, Charles Lawrence, Sir.
FOR HONOR'S SAKE
 See Hazlewood, Colin Henry.
FOR LOVE
 See Robertson, Thomas William.
FOR PAPA'S SAKE
 See Spurr, Mel. B.
FOR THE CROWN
 See Davidson, John.
FOR THE OLD LOVE'S SAKE
 See Rogers, T. Stanley.
FORBES-ROBERTSON, JOHNSTON (arr.)
 Hamlet. By Shakespeare, William. London: Nassau Press,
 1897. Pp. [2]-95. *Filed under* Robertson, Forbes.
 Macbeth. By Shakespeare, William. London: Nassau Press,
 1898. Pp. [1]-72. *Filed under* Robertson, Forbes.
 Romeo and Juliet. By Shakespeare, William. London:
 Nassau Press, 1895. Pp. [2]-78. *Filed under* Robertson,
 Forbes.
FORBIDDEN FRUIT
 See Boucicault, Dionysius Lardner.
FORCE OF GRATITUDE
 See Barker, George. Country Gentleman, The.
FORCE OF NATURE
 See Bennett, J. M. Thirteen Years' Labour Lost.

 See Thackeray, Thomas James.
 See Walker, John. Wild Boy of Bohemia, The.
FORCE OF THE PASSIONS
 See Bucke, Charles. Julio Romano.
FORCED MARRIAGE, THE
 See Faucquez, Adolphe.
 See Mathew, Charles (trans.).
 See Van Laun, Henri (trans.).
FOREST KEEPER, THE
 See Holl, Henry.
FOREST OF BONDY
 See Barrymore, William. Dog of Montargis, The.
 See Harris, Henry.
FOREST OF REMIVAL
 See Tilbury, William Harries. German Jew, The.
FOREST OF SENART!
 See Stirling, Edward. Rose of Corbeil, The.
FOREST ORACLE, THE
 See Campbell, Andrew Leonard Voullaire.
FOREST TANGLE
 See Rhoades, James. Dux Redux.
FORESTER'S FATE!
 See Burnand, Francis Cowley. Robin Hood.
FORESTERS, THE
 See Tennyson, Alfred, Lord.
FORGERY, THE (anon.)
 In *New British Theatre*, London: A. J. Valpy (printer),
 1814, I, [i], [433]-491.
FORGERY
 See Stephens, George.
FORGET AND FORGIVE
 See Maclaren, Archibald.
 See Stirling, Edward. Reapers, The.
FORGET-ME-NOT
 See Merivale, Herman Charles.
FORGIVEN
 See Albery, James.
FORGOTTEN FRIEND
 See Griffin, Gerald. Gisippus.
FORMAN, ALFRED (trans.)
 Dusk of the Gods. Music by Wagner. In *Nibelung's Ring*,
 Mayence: B. Schott's Söhne, 1877, pp. [267]-[353].
 Libretto. *Filed under* Nibelung's Ring.
 Parsifal. Music by Wagner. London: (priv.), 1899. Pp.
 [i-xviii], 1-71.
 Rhinegold, The. Music by Wagner. In *Nibelung's Ring*,
 Mayence: B. Schott's Söhne, 1877, pp. [1]-79. Libretto.
 Filed under Nibelung's Ring.
 Siegfried. Music by Wagner. In *Nibelung's Ring*, Mayence:
 B. Schott's Söhne, 1877, pp. [168]-266. Libretto. *Filed
 under* Nibelung's Ring.
 Tristan and Isolde. Music by Wagner. London: David Nutt,
 1897. Pp. [i-vi], [1]-76. Libretto.
 Walkyrie, The. Music by Wagner. In *Nibelung's Ring*,
 Mayence: B. Schott's Söhne, 1877, pp. [80]-167. Libretto.
 Filed under Nibelung's Ring.
FORMAN, EDMUND
 Down Sunny South. In *Mohawk Minstrels' Tenth Book of
 Nigger Dramas and Sketches*, London: Francis, Day, &
 Hunter, n.d, pp. 49-60. *Filed under* Forman, et al.
 Mohawk Minstrels' Tenth Book.
 In a Trance. In *Mohawk Minstrels' Tenth Book of Nigger
 Dramas and Sketches*, London: Francis, Day, & Hunter,
 n.d, pp. 30-37. *Filed under* Forman, et al. Mohawk
 Minstrels' Tenth Book.
 **Mohawk Minstrels' Eighth Book of Dramas, Dialogues, and
 Drolleries, The.** Written with Morton, John W.; Morton,
 Richard. London: Francis, Day & Hunter, n.d. Pp. [i-vi],
 [1]-104.
 **Mohawk Minstrels' Fourth Annual of Dramas, Dialogues, and
 Drolleries, The.**
 See Hunter, Harry.
 **Mohawk Minstrels' Ninth Book of Dramas, Stump Speeches,
 Nigger Jokes, and Recitations, The.**
 See Williams, Arthur.

Mohawk Minstrels' Tenth Book of Nigger Dramas and Sketches, The. Written with Williams, Arthur; Morton, Richard. London: Francis, Day & Hunter, n.d. Pp. [1]-112.

New Man, The. In *Mohawk Minstrels' Tenth Book of Nigger Dramas and Sketches,* London: Francis, Day, & Hunter, n.d, pp. 16-30. *Filed under* Forman, et al. Mohawk Minstrels' Tenth Book.

One Bed to Let. In *Mohawk Minstrels' Tenth Book of Nigger Dramas and Sketches,* London: Francis, Day, & Hunter, n.d, pp. [1]-16. *Filed under* Forman, et al. Mohawk Minstrels' Tenth Book.

FORMOSA
See Boucicault, Dionysius Lardner.

FORRESTER, ALFRED HENRY
See Crowquill, Alfred.

FORSTER, WILLIAM
Brothers, The. London: Gordon & Gotch, 1877. Pp. [i-iv], [1]-222.
Weirwolf, The. London: Williams & Norgate, 1876. Pp. [i-iv], [1]-290.

FORTESCUE, F.
Gonzalo, the Spanish Bandit. Boston [England]: J. Jackson (printer), 1821. Pp. [i]-[xviii], [1]-59.
Robinson Crusoe; or, The Island of Juan Fernandez. Boston [England]: J. Jackson (printer), 1822. Pp. [iii]-[xiv], [1]-77. Pagination irregular. Libretto.

FORTRESS, THE
See Hook, Theodore Edward.

FORTRESS OF ST. JACQUE!
See Phillips, Morrice. Fidelio!

FORTUNATE IRISHMAN
See Maclaren, Archibald. Ups and Downs of Life, The.

FORTUNATUS AND THE WATER OF LIFE, THE THREE BEARS, THE THREE GIFTS, THE THREE WISHES, AND THE LITTLE MAN WHO WOO'D THE LITTLE MAID
See Gilbert, William Schwenck. Harlequin Cock-Robin and Jenny Wren.

FORTUNATUS THE PESSIMIST
See Austin, Alfred.

FORTUNE
See Albery, James.

FORTUNE FAVOURS THE BRAVE
See Ranger, Edward.

FORTUNE HUNTER, THE
See Gilbert, William Schwenck.

FORTUNE MENDS
See Holcroft, Fanny (trans.).

FORTUNE OF WAR
See Bennett, George John. Soldier's Orphan, The.
See Buckstone, John Baldwin. Josephine, the Child of the Regiment.

FORTUNE'S FOOL
See Reynolds, Frederick.

FORTUNE'S FROLIC
See Allingham, John Till.

FORTUNE'S TOY
See Gilbert, William Schwenck. Tom Cobb.

FORTUNES OF NIGEL, THE
See Fitzball, Edward.
See Murray, William Henry Wood.

FORTUNES OF SMIKE, THE
See Sitrling, Edward.

FORTUNIO AND HIS SEVEN GIFTED SERVANTS
See Planché, James Robinson.

FORTUNIO AND HIS SEVEN MAGIC MEN
See Byron, Henry James. Lady Belle Belle.

FORTY AND FIFTY
See Bayly, Thomas Haynes.

FORTY THIEVES (anon.)
Music by Shickle. Manchester: Theatre Royal, 1857. Pp. [1]-12. 14th ed. Libretto.

FORTY THIEVES
See Ali Baba (anon.).

See Blanchard, Edward Litt Leman.
See Colman, George, jr.
See Jones, John Wilton.
See Reece, Robert.
See Strachan, John S., jr.
See Sturgess, Arthur.

FORTY WINKS
See Farnie, Henry Brougham.

FOSCARI
See Mitford, Mary Russell.

FOSTER SISTERS
See Robertson, Thomas William. Noémie.

FOTHERGILL, F.
Haunted House, The; or, Paddy and the Ghost. Manchester: Abel Heywood & Son, n.d. Pp. [1]-16. [Abel Heywood & Son's Series of Original Dramas, Dialogues, & Readings Adapted for Amateur Entertainments, 112].
Race for a Wife. Chicago: Dramatic Publishing Co., c.1898. Pp. [1]-14. Sergel's Acting Drama, 487.
Wedding at the Mill, The. Manchester: Abel Heywood & Son, n.d. Pp. [1]-16. Abel Heywood & Son's Series of Original Dramas, Dialogues, & Readings Adapted for Amateur Entertainments, [82].

FOUL DEEDS WILL RISE
See Arnold, Samuel James.

FOUL PLAY
See Boucicault, Dionysius Lardner.

FOUND IN A FOUR-WHEELER
See Williams, Thomas John. Cabman No. 93.
See Williams, Thomas John.

FOUNDED ON FACTS
See Wooler, John Pratt.

FOUNDLING, THE
See Lestocq, William.
See Moore, Edward.

FOUNDLING OF THE FOREST, THE
See Dimond, William.

FOUNTAIN OF BEAUTY, THE
See Kingdom, John M.

FOUNTAIN OF LOVE
See Farley, Charles. Harlequin Munchausen.

FOUNTAIN OF YOUTH, THE
See Lee-Hamilton, Eugene.
See Sturgis, Julian Russell.

FOUR COUSINS, THE
See Mayhew, Augustus Septimus.

FOUR LEGS BETTER THAN TWO
See Milner, Henry M. Bears Not Beasts.

FOUR SISTERS, THE
See Bernard, William Bayle.

FOUR THIEVES
See Moncrieff, William Thomas. Pestilence of Marseilles, The.

FOUR WISHES
See Planché, James Robinson. Bee and the Orange Tree, The.

FOURBERIES DE SCAPIN
See Van Laun, Henri (trans.). Rogueries of Scapin, The.

FOURCHAMBOULT AND COMPY.
See Lyster, Frederic.

FOUR-LEGGED FORTUNE
See Boucicault, Dionysius Lardner. Flying Scud.

FOWL PLAY
See Burnand, Francis Cowley.

FOX, GEORGE
Nydia, the Blind Girl of Pompeii. Music by Fox, George. London: Hutchings & Romer; New York: Novello, Ewer, c.1892. Pp. [i-iv], [1]-249. Vocal score.

FOX (later Vassall), **HENRY RICHARD, BARON HOLLAND** (trans.)
Fairy Lady, The. By Calderon. In *Three Comedies,* London: J. Hatchard, 1807, pp. [i]-[xvi], [1]-115. *Filed under* Three Comedies.

Keep Your Own Secret. By Calderon. In *Three Comedies,* London: J. Hatchard, 1807, pp. [117]-230. *Filed under* Three Comedies.

One Fool Makes Many. By de Solis, Antonio. In *Three Comedies,* London: J. Hatchard, 1807, pp. [231]-346. *Filed under* Three Comedies.

FOX AND THE GOOSE, THE
    See Webster, Benjamin Nottingham.
FOX VERSUS GOOSE
    See Stockton, J. D.
FOXGLOVE
    See Dyall, Charles.
FRA DIAVOLO (anon. trans.)
    Music by Auber. London & New York: Boosey, n.d. Pp. [i-vi], 1-287. Vocal score.
FRA DIAVOLO (anon. trans.)
    Music by Auber. Boston: Oliver Ditson, n.d. Pp. [1]-30. Libretto.
FRA DIAVOLO
    See Byron, Henry James.
    See Lacy, Michael Rophino.
    See Maggioni, Manfredo (trans.).
FRA RUPERT
    See Landor, Walter Savage.
FRAGMENT, A
    See Hannan, Charles.
FRAGMENT OF A SPANISH PLAY
    See Knowles, James Sheridan.
FRAGMENTS OF AN UNFINISHED DRAMA
    See Shelley, Percy Bysshe.
FRAILTY AND HYPOCRISY
    See Wild, James.
FRANCE, C. V.
    Magician's Daughter, The; or, The Cursed and The Cause. Music by Wadham, Walter. Bradford: Thomas M. Woodhead (printer), n.d. Pp. [1]-45. Libretto.
FRANCIS THE FIRST
    See Kemble, Frances Anne (Fanny).
    See Slous, Frederick L. (trans.).
FRANCISCO, THE AVENGER (anon.)
    N.p.: n.pub. (priv.), n.d. Pp. [1]-54.
FRANCKLIN, THOMAS, DR.
    Earl of Warwick, The. By Dr. Thomas Franklin. London: Sherwood, Neely, & Jones, 1818. Pp. [1]-60. London Theatre, XXIII. *Filed under* Dibdin, Thomas John, ed. London Theatre, XXIII.
    Earl of Warwick, The. By Dr. Thomas Franklin. In *British Drama,* 12 vols., London: John Dicks, 1871, VI, [65]-81.
    Matilda. In *Modern Theatre,* ed. Mrs. Inchbald, 10 vols., London: Longman, Hurst, Rees, Orme, & Brown, 1811, VIII, [i-ii], [1]-66.
FRANCO ARCIERO
    See Freischutz, Der (anon.).
FRANK FOX PHIPPS, ESQ.
    See Selby, Charles.
FRANKENSTEIN
    See Milner, Henry M.
    See Milner, Henry M. Man and the Monster!, The.
FRANKFORT LOTTERY
    See Thackeray, Thomas James. Barber Baron, The.
FRANKLIN, ANDREW
    Counterfeit, The. London: G. & J. Robinson, 1804. Pp. [i-vi], [1]-47.
    Egyptian Festival, The. London: J. Ridgway, n.d. Pp. [i]-[xii], [1]-54.
FRANKLIN, THOMAS, DR.
    See Francklin, Thomas, Dr.
FRANKLIN
    See Brougham, John.
FRASER, JULIA AGNES
    Barrington's Busby; or, Weathering the Admiral. Plymouth: Trend, n.d. Pp. [i-viii], [1]-[27].
    Court Lovers; or, The Sentinel of the King's Guard. Plymouth: Trend (printer), n.d. Pp. [i]-[x], [1]-101. Libretto.

Hubert's Pride. Strathaven: Alexander Morton (printer), 1871. Pp. [i-ii], [1]-17.
Pat of Mullingar; or, An Irish Lothario. Greenock: Greenock Advertiser Office (printer), n.d. Pp. [i-iv], [5]-[67].
Slight Mistake, A. Edinburgh & Glasgow: John Menzies, 1872. Pp. [1]-24.
Star-Spangled Banner, The; or, The Far West. Plymouth: Trend (printer), n.d. Pp. [i]-[xviii], [1]-163.
FRAUD AND ITS VICTIMS
    See Coyne, Joseph Stirling.
FREDERICK OF PRUSSIA
    See Selby, Charles.
FREDERICK THE GREAT
    See Arnold, Samuel James.
    See Maddox, Frederick More.
    See Maddox, John Medex. King and the Deserter, The.
FREDOLFO
    See Maturin, Charles Robert, Rev.
FREE AND EASY
    See Arnold, Samuel James.
FREE KNIGHTS, THE
    See Reynolds, Frederick.
FREE TRADER!
    See Fitzball, Edward. False Colours.
FREE-BOOTER
    See Ripon, John Scott. Buonaparte.
FREEMAN, SUSANNA CARROLL
    See Centlivre, Susanna Carroll Freeman, Mrs. Joseph.
FREEMASON, THE
    See Hart, James P.
FREEMEN AND SLAVES
    See Ball, William.
FREETHINKER, THE
    See Bell, Ernest (trans.).
FREEZING A MOTHER-IN-LAW
    See Pemberton, Thomas Edgar.
FREISCHUTZ, DER (anon.)
    London: B. Skelt, n.d. Pp. [1]-18. Skelt's Juvenile Drama.
FREISCHÜTZ, DER (anon.)
    Also: Il Franco Arciero. Music by Weber. London & New York: Boosey, n.d. Pp. [i-viii], 1-213. [Royal Edition]. Vocal score.
FREISCHUTZ, DER
    See also Freyschutz.
    See Amherst, J. H.
    See Byron, Henry James.
    See Fitzball, Edward.
    See Kerr, John.
    See Oxenford, John.
    See Soane, George.
FRENCH, GEORGE H.
    King Winter and Princess Summer; or, Harlequin Prince Spring and the Good Fay of All the Year Round. Liverpool: W. M'Call, n.d. Pp. [1]-23. Libretto.
FRENCH, SYDNEY
    Friend in Need, A. Written with Sorrell, William J. London: Thomas Hailes Lacy, n.d. Pp. [1]-39. [Lacy's Acting Edition].
FRENCH EXHIBITION, THE
    See Hay, Frederic.
FRENCH MAID, THE
    See Hood, Basil Charles Willett.
FRENCH POLISH
    See Lunn, Joseph.
FRENCH REFUGEE, THE
    See Hall, Anna Maria Fielding, Mrs. Samuel Carter.
FRENCH SPY, THE
    See Haines, John Thomas.
FRENCHMAN IN LONDON, THE
    See Stafford, John Joseph.
FRERE, BENJAMIN
    Hoaxer, The. Hereford: E. G. Wright, 1837. Pp. [1]-116.
    Olympia. London: n.pub. (priv.), 1821. Pp. [1]-88.

FRERE, JOHN HOOKHAM (trans.)

Acharnians, The. By Aristophanes. In *Acharnians and Three Other Plays,* London: J. M. Dent & Sons; New York: E. P. Dutton, 1911, pp. [iv]-[xvi], 1-59.

Birds, The. By Aristophanes. In *Acharnians and Three Other Plays,* London: J. M. Dent & Sons; New York: E. P. Dutton, 1911, pp. [135]-221. *Filed under* Acharnians.

Knights, The. By Aristophanes. In *Acharnians and Three Other Plays,* London: J. M. Dent & Sons; New York: E. P. Dutton, 1911, pp. [60]-134. *Filed under* Acharnians.

Peace, The. By Aristophanes. In *Acharnians and Three Other Plays,* London: J. M. Dent & Sons; New York: E. P. Dutton, 1911, pp. [223]-253. *Filed under* Acharnians.

FREYSCHUTZ
   See Livius, Barham.
   See Logan, W. McGregor.

FRIDAY AND HIS FUNNY FAMILY
   See McArdle, John Francis. Robinson Crusoe.

FRIEND AT COURT, A
   See Douglas, Thomas.

FRIEND FRITZ
   See Lyster, Frederic (trans.).

FRIEND IN NEED, A
   See French, Sydney.

FRIEND INDEED
   See Oxenford, John. Much Too Clever.

FRIEND WAGGLES
   See Morton, John Maddison.

FRIENDS
   See Parker, Alfred D.

FRIENDS OR FOES?
   See Wigan, Horace.

FRIGHTEN'D TO DEATH!
   See Oulton, Walley Chamberlaine.

FRIGHTFUL FROST
   See Pemberton, Thomas Edgar. Freezing a Mother-in-Law.

FRIGHTFUL HAIR, THE
   See Burnand, Francis Cowley.

FRITH, WALTER

Midsummer Day. London & New York: Samuel French, n.d. Pp. [1]-16. [Lacy's Acting Edition].

Verger, The. Music by Hall, King. London: Joseph Williams; New York: Edward Schuberth, c.1894. Pp. [1]-48. German Reed Repertory of Musical Pieces. Libretto.

FROGGEE WOULD A WOOING GO
   See Brough, William.

FROGS, THE
   See Hogarth, David George (trans.).

FROM BAD TO WORSE
   See Holcroft, Fanny (trans.).

FROM INFORMATION I RECEIVED
   See Suter, William E. John Wopps.

FROM INN TO INN
   See Wild, James.

FROM KING TO KING
   See Dickinson, Goldsworthy Lowes.

FROM VILLAGE TO COURT
   See Morton, John Maddison.

FROST, FRANCISCO (or FRANCESCO) (pseud.)
   See Blanchard, Edward Litt Leman.

FROU-FROU (anon. trans.)
   New York: Wheat & Cornett, c.1877. Pp. [1]-27. New York Drama, III, 29.

FROZEN DEEP, THE
   See Collins, William Wilkie.

FROZEN HAND
   See Buckstone, John Baldwin. Ice Witch, The.

FRUITS OF A SINGLE ERROR
   See Lewis, Matthew Gregory. Adelgitha.

FRUITS OF GENEVA
   See Moncrieff, William Thomas. Tereza Tomkins.

FRY, BETSEY

Area Sylph, The; or, A Foot-boy's Dream. London: J. Pattie, n.d. Pp. [i-ii], [1]-16. Pattie's Universal Stage or Theatrical Prompt Book, 25.

FRYE, WILLIAM EDWARD (trans.)

Guilt; or, The Gipsey's Prophecy. By Mullner, Adolphus. London: Boosey & Son (priv.), 1819. Pp. [i-x], [1]-88.

FRYERS, AUSTIN

Human Sport, A. London & New York: Samuel French, c.1904. Pp. [1]-12. [Lacy's Acting Edition].

Rosmer of Rosmersholm. London: Swan Sonnenschein, 1891. Pp. [i]-[xvii], [1]-79.

FUGITIVE, THE
   See Richardson, Joseph.

FULL PRIVATE PERKINS
   See Byron, Henry James.

FULLERTON, GEORGIANA CHARLOTTE LEVESON-GOWER, MRS. ALEXANDER GEORGE, LADY GEORGIANA

Which Is Which?; or, The Fire of London. New York: D. & J. Sadlier, 1873. Pp. [1]-45.

FULVIUS VALENS
   See Serle, Thomas James.

FUNKIBOO'S FIX
   See Bampfylde, Coplestone Richard George Warwick. Aunt and the Angel, The.

FUNNIBONE'S FIX
   See Williams, Arthur.

FURIBOND; OR, HARLEQUIN NEGRO (anon.)
   London: J. Scales, n.d. Pp. [1]-26. Scales's Edition. Synopsis.

FURNESS, J. R.

Massacre of Abergavenny, The. Conway: R. E. Jones & Bros. (printer), 1897. Pp. [i-ii], [1]-60.

FURNISHED APARTMENTS
   See Hay, Frederic.

GABERLUNZIE MAN, THE
   See Rede, William Leman.

GAFFER'S MISTAKE
   See Dibdin, Thomas John.

GAIETY GIRL, A
   See Hall, Owen.

GAIETY GULLIVER, THE
   See Byron, Henry James.

GALE BREEZELY
   See Johnstone, John Beer.

GALLOP TO GRETNA GREEN
   See Barrymore, William. Giovanni in the Country.

GALLOWAY, GEORGE

Admirable Crichton, The. Edinburgh: John Taylor (printer), n.d. Pp. [i], [1]-4, [7]-66. Pagination irregular.

Battle of Luncarty, The; or, The Valiant Hays. Edinburgh: John Taylor (printer) (priv.), 1804. Pp. [i]-[xii], [1]-[45]. Libretto.

GALT, JOHN

Agamemnon. In *Tragedies of Maddalen, Agamemnon, Lady Macbeth, Antonia, & Clytemnestra,* London: Cadell & Davies, 1812, pp. [61]-110. *Filed under* Collected Works.

Antonia. In *Tragedies of Maddalen, Agamemnon, Lady Macbeth, Antonia, & Clytemnestra,* London: Cadell & Davies, 1812, pp. [159]-214. *Filed under* Collected Works.

Apostate, The; or, Atlantis Destroyed. In *New British Theatre,* London: A. J. Valpy (printer), 1814, III, [i], [305]-[348].

Clytemnestra. In *Tragedies of Maddalen, Agamemnon, Lady Macbeth, Antonia, & Clytemnestra,* London: Cadell & Davies, 1812, pp. [215]-262. *Filed under* Collected Works.

Hector. In *New British Theatre,* London: A. J. Valpy (printer), 1814, IV, [i], [331]-[350].

Lady Macbeth. In *Tragedies of Maddalen, Agamemnon, Lady Macbeth, Antonia, & Clytemnestra,* London: Cadell & Davies, 1812, pp. [111]-158. *Filed under* Collected Works.

Love, Honor, and Interest. In *New British Theatre,* London: A. J. Valpy (printer), 1814, III, [i], [257]-288.

Maddalen. In *Tragedies of Maddalen, Agamemnon, Lady Macbeth, Antonia, & Clytemnestra,* London: Cadell &

Davies, 1812, pp. [i]-vi, [1]-59. *Filed under* Collected
Works.

Masquerade, The. In *New British Theatre,* London: A. J.
Valpy (printer), 1814, I, [i], [219]-[275].

Mermaid, The. In *New British Theatre,* London: A. J. Valpy
(printer), 1814, II, [i], [475]-494.

Orpheus. In *New British Theatre,* London: A. J. Valpy
(printer), 1814, III, [i], [289]-304.

Prophetess, The. In *New British Theatre,* London: A. J. Valpy
(printer), 1814, I, [i], [177]-217.

Watch-house, The. In *New British Theatre,* London: A. J.
Valpy (printer), 1814, I, [i], 43-70.

Witness, The. In *New British Theatre,* London: A. J. Valpy
(printer), 1814, I, [i], [15]-46.

GALVAN, JOHN (trans.)
Faust. By Goethe. Dublin: William Robertson, 1860. Pp.
[i]-[x], [1]-252.

GALWAY PRACTICE IN 1770
See Bernard, William Bayle. Irish Attorney, The.

GAMBLER'S FATE, THE
See Thompson, Charles.

GAMBLER'S LIFE IN LONDON, THE
See Campbell, Andrew Leonard Voullaire.

GAMBLERS, THE (anon.)
London: John Lowndes, n.d. Pp. [1]-22.

GAME OF LIFE, THE
See Brougham, John.
See Poole, W. Howell.

GAME OF LOVE, THE
See Brougham, John.

GAME OF ROMPS, A
See Morton, John Maddison.

GAME OF SPECULATION, THE
See Lawrence, Slingsby.

GAMESTER, THE
See Kemble, John Philip (arr.).
See Moore, Edward.

GAMESTER OF MILAN, THE
See Serle, Thomas James.

GANDY, EDWARD
Caswallon, King of Britain. London: Richard Glynn, 1826.
Pp. [iii]-xvi, [1]-98.

Lorenzo, the Outcast Son. London: W. Simpkin & R.
Marshall, 1823. Pp. [iii]-xiv, [15]-[103].

GANEM, THE SLAVE OF LOVE
See Talfourd, Francis.

GANN, J.
Mr. Midshipman Easy!
See Oxberry, William Henry.

GANTHONY, ROBERT
Brace of Partridges, A. New York & London: Samuel
French, c.1901. Pp. [1]-74. French's International
Copyrighted Edition of the Works of the Best Authors,
44.

Like Mistress, Like Maid. Chicago: Dramatic Publishing Co.,
c.1899. Pp. [i-ii], [1]-15. Sergel's Acting Drama, 549.

GARCIA
See Tomlins, Frederick Guest.

GARDEN PARTY, A
See Cheltnam, Charles Smith.

GARDINER, WILLIAM
Sultana, The; or, The Jealous Queen. Glocester: D. Walker
(printer), 1806. Pp. [1]-92.

GARDNER, HERBERT
After Dinner. London & New York: Samuel French, n.d. Pp.
[1]-16. Lacy's Acting Edition.

Cousin Zachary. London & New York: Samuel French, n.d.
Pp. [1]-16. [Lacy's Acting Edition].

He That Will Not When He May. London & New York:
Samuel French, n.d. Pp. [1]-12. [Lacy's Acting Edition].

Night on Snowdon, A. London & New York: Samuel French,
n.d. Pp. [1]-12. [Lacy's Acting Edition].

Time Will Tell. London & New York: Samuel French, n.d.
Pp. [1]-44. [Lacy's Acting Edition].

GARIBALDI EXCURSIONISTS, THE
See Byron, Henry James.

GARNETT, RICHARD
Iphigenia in Delphi. London: T. Fisher Unwin, 1890. Pp.
1-42.

GARRAWAY, AGNES J.
Marble Arch, The.
See Rose, Edward.

GARRETT, FYDELL EDMUND (trans.)
Brand. By Ibsen, Henrik. London: T. Fisher Unwin, 1894.
Pp. [1]-328.

GARRICK, DAVID
Bon Ton; or, High Life Above Stairs. In *New English Drama,*
ed. W. Oxberry, 22 vols., London: W. Simpkin & R.
Marshall; C. Chapple, 1822, XV, [1-2], [i]-[vi], [1]-[28].
Filed under Oxberry, William Henry. New English
Drama, XV.

Bon Ton; or, High Life Above Stairs. In *British Drama,* 12
vols., London: John Dicks, 1871, VIII, [245]-256.

Clandestine Marriage, The.
See Colman, George, sr.

Country Girl, The. London: Whittingham & Arliss, 1816. Pp.
[1]-[68]. London Theatre, XIX. *Filed under* Dibdin,
Thomas John, ed. London Theatre, XIX.

Country Girl, The. In *New English Drama,* ed. W. Oxberry, 22
vols., London: W. Simpkin & R. Marshall; C. Chapple,
1818, VIII, [1-2], [i]-[vi], [1]-63. *Filed under* Oxberry,
William Henry. New English Drama, VIII.

Country Girl, The. In *British Drama,* 12 vols., London: John
Dicks, 1871, VI, [13]-32.

Country Girl, The. London: John Cumberland, n.d. Pp.
[1]-64. Cumberland's British Theatre, XXI. *Filed under*
Cumberland, John. Cumberland's British Theatre, XXI.

Cymon. London: Whittingham & Arliss, 1816. Pp. [1]-40.
London Theatre, XX. *Filed under* Dibdin, Thomas John,
ed. London Theatre, XX.

Cymon. In *British Drama,* 12 vols., London: John Dicks,
1865, III, [757]-766.

Guardian, The. London: Whittingham & Arliss, 1815. Pp.
[1]-30. London Theatre, XI. *Filed under* Dibdin, Thomas
John, ed. London Theatre, XI.

Guardian, The. In *British Drama,* 12 vols., London: John
Dicks, 1872, X, [307]-316.

Irish Widow, The. London: Whittingham & Arliss, 1815. Pp.
[1]-36. London Theatre, I. *Filed under* Dibdin, Thomas
John, ed. London Theatre, I.

Irish Widow, The. In *British Drama,* 12 vols., London: John
Dicks, 1871, VIII, [149]-160.

Isabella; or, The Fatal Marriage. London: Whittingham &
Arliss, 1815. Pp. [1]-[56]. London Theatre, II. *Filed under*
Dibdin, Thomas John, ed. London Theatre, II.

Isabella; or, The Fatal Marriage. London: T. Dolby, 1825.
Pp. [ii]-[vi], [7]-[48]. Dolby's British Theatre, IX. *Filed
under* Cumberland, John. Cumberland's British Theatre,
IX.

Isabella; or, The Fatal Marriage. In *British Drama,* 12 vols.,
London: John Dicks, 1864, II, [575]-588.

Isabella.
See Kemble, John Philip (arr.).

Lying Valet, The. London: C. Whittingham (printer), 1817.
Pp. [1]-36. London Theatre, XXII. *Filed under* Dibdin,
Thomas John, ed. London Theatre, XXII.

Lying Valet, The. In *New English Drama,* ed. W. Oxberry, 22
vols., London: W. Simpkin & R. Marshall; C. Chapple,
1821, XI, [1-2], [i]-[viii], [1]-26. *Filed under* Oxberry,
William Henry. New English Drama, XI.

Lying Valet, The. In *British Drama,* 12 vols., London: John
Dicks, 1871, VI, [150]-160.

Miss in Her Teens; or, The Medley of Lovers. London:
Whittingham & Arliss, 1815. Pp. [1]-[32]. London
Theatre, VIII. *Filed under* Dibdin, Thomas John, ed.
London Theatre, VIII.

Miss in Her Teens; or, The Medley of Lovers. In *British
Drama,* 12 vols., London: John Dicks, 1871, IX, [88]-96.

GARRICK, DAVID (arr.)
 Chances, The. By Beaumont, Francis; Fletcher, John. In *British Drama,* 12 vols., London: John Dicks, 1872, X, [257]-280.
 Every Man in His Humour. By Jonson, Ben. London: Whittingham & Arliss, 1816. Pp. [1]-76. London Theatre, XVII. *Filed under* Dibdin, Thomas John, ed. London Theatre, XVII.
 Every Man in His Humour. By Jonson, Ben. In *New English Drama,* ed. W. Oxberry, 22 vols., London: W. Simpkin & R. Marshall; C. Chapple, 1822, XVI, [1-2], [i]-[x], [1]-82. *Filed under* Oxberry, William Henry. New English Drama, XVI.
 Every Man in His Humour. By Jonson, Ben. In *British Drama,* 12 vols., London: John Dicks, 1865, IV, [1151]-1173.
 Katharine and Petruchio.
  See Kemble, John Philip (arr.).
 Romeo and Juliet. By Shakespeare, William. In *New English Drama,* ed. W. Oxberry, 22 vols., London: W. Simpkin & R. Marshall; C. Chapple, 1819, VI, [1-2], [i]-[iv], [1]-[68]. *Filed under* Oxberry, William Henry. New English Drama, VI.
 Rule a Wife and Have a Wife. By Beaumont, Francis; Fletcher, John. London: Whittingham & Arliss, 1815. Pp. [1]-64. London Theatre, XIII. *Filed under* Dibdin, Thomas John, ed. London Theatre, XIII.
 Rule a Wife and Have a Wife. By Beaumont, Francis; Fletcher, John. In *New English Drama,* ed. W. Oxberry, 22 vols., London: W. Simpkin & R. Marshall; C. Chapple, 1820, X, [1-2], [i]-[viii], [1]-[66]. *Filed under* Oxberry, William Henry. New English Drama, X.
 Rule a Wife and Have a Wife. By Beaumont, Francis; Fletcher, John. In *British Drama,* 12 vols., London: John Dicks, 1871, V, [301]-320.
 Taming of the Shrew.
  See Kemble, John Philip (arr.).
GARRICK
  See Muskerry, William.
GARRICK FEVER, THE
  See Planché, James Robinson.
GARRICK'S JUBILEE (anon.)
  London: John Miller, 1816. Pp. [1]-16. Libretto.
GARRYOWEN
  See Levey, John C.
GARSTON, LEONARD
 Old Love, The. London: Strand Typewriting Office, [1893]. Pp. [i-ii], [1]-28, [i], [1]-25, [i], [1]-19. Pagination by act. Typescript.
 Ye Fair One with ye Golden Locks.
  See Grattan, H. P.
GASPARDO THE GONDOLIER
  See Almar, George.
GASTON BONNIER
  See Courtney, William Leonard.
GASTON DE BLONDEVILLE
  See Mitford, Mary Russell.
GASTON DE FOIX
  See Edmonstone, Archibald.
  See Mitford, Edward Ledwich.
GASTON PHOEBUS
  See Buchanan, Robert.
GATHERING OF THE CLANS
  See Montrose (anon.).
GATTY, CHARLES TINDAL (trans.)
 Parsifal. Music by Wagner. London: Schott, n.d. Pp. [1]-152. Libretto.
GAUGE DELIVERANCE
  See Dwarris, Fortunatus William Lilley, Sir. Railway Results.
GAUL, KING OF RAGAH
  See Hawkes, W. R.
GAUNTLET, A
  See Edwards, Osman (trans.).

GAY, JOHN
 Acis and Galatea. London: Thomas Hailes Lacy, n.d. Pp. [1]-12. Lacy's Acting Edition, 162. Libretto. *Filed under* Cooke, T.
 Beggar's Opera, The. London: Whittingham & Arliss, 1814. Pp. [1]-48. London Theatre, I. *Filed under* Dibdin, Thomas John, ed. London Theatre, I.
 Beggar's Opera, The. In *New English Drama,* ed. W. Oxberry, 22 vols., London: W. Simpkin & R. Marshall; C. Chapple, 1818, II, [i]-[viii], [1]-36, 73-84 (misnumbered). *Filed under* Oxberry, William Henry. New English Drama, II.
 Beggar's Opera, The. London: T. Dolby, 1823. Pp. [i]-[viii], [7]-[48]. Dolby's British Theatre, III. *Filed under* Cumberland, John. Cumberland's British Theatre, III.
 Beggar's Opera, The. In *British Drama,* 12 vols., London: John Dicks, 1865, III, [849]-862.
GAY DECEIVERS, THE
  See Colman, George, jr.
GAY GRIZETTE, THE
  See Dance, George.
GAY LORD QUEX, THE
  See Pinero, Arthur Wing.
GAY LOTHARIO, THE
  See Calmour, Alfred Cecil.
GAY PARISIENNE, THE
  See Dance, George.
GAY YOUNG FELLOW
  See Buckstone, John Baldwin. Billy Taylor.
GAZETTE EXTRAORDINARY, THE
  See Holman, Joseph George.
GAZZA LADRA, LA
  See Maggioni, Manfredo (trans.).
GEISHA, THE: A STORY OF A TEA HOUSE
  See Hall, Owen.
GELLERT, CHRISTIAN FUERCHTEGOTT
 Tender Sisters, The.
  See Gilbert, ? (trans.).
GEM, T. H.
 Bardell versus Pickwick, Versified and Diversified. Music by Spinney, Frank. Birmingham: Josiah Allen (printer), n.d. Pp. [1]-48. Libretto.
GEMINI
  See Peake, Richard Brinsley.
GEMMELL, ROBERT
 Montague. In *Montague . . . and Other Poems,* London: Simpkin, Marshall, 1868, pp. [i]-viii, [9]-35.
GENERAL ELECTIONS, THE
  See Lyulph, Henry R.
GENEVIEVE
  See Albery, James.
GENII, THE
  See Becket, Andrew.
GENII OF THE ELEMENTS
  See Macfarren, George. Talisman, The.
GENIUS AND THE LIBERTINE
  See Edmund Kean.
GENIUS OF THE RIBSTONE PIPPIN
  See Morton, John Maddison. Harlequin and William Tell.
GENT, J. B.
 Meteor, The; or, A Short Blaze, but a Bright One. London: J. B. Bell & J. de Camp (priv.), 1809. Pp. [i]-[x], [1]-41.
GENTLE GERTRUDE OF THE INFAMOUS REDD LYON INN
  See Pemberton, Thomas Edgar.
GENTLE SAVAGE
  See Brougham, John. Po-ca-hon-tas.
GENTLE SHEPHERD, THE
  See Bethune, Gilbert (arr.).
  See Maclaren, Archibald.
GENTLEMAN, FRANCIS
 Tobacconist, The. London: Whittingham & Arliss, 1815. Pp. [1]-32. London Theatre, XIII. *Filed under* Dibdin, Thomas John, ed. London Theatre, XIII.

Tobacconist, The. In *New English Drama,* ed. W. Oxberry, 22
vols., London: W. Simpkin & R. Marshall; C. Chapple,
1821, XIII, [1-2], [i]-[v], [viii]-[x], [1]-23. *Filed under*
Oxberry, William Henry. New English Drama, XIII.
Tobacconist, The. In *British Drama,* 12 vols., London: John
Dicks, 1871, VII, [120]-128.
GENTLEMAN AND THE UPSTART, THE
See Ranger, Edward.
GENTLEMAN IN BLACK
See Gilbert, William Schwenck.
See Lemon, Mark.
See Murray, William Henry Wood. Dominique the
Deserter.
GENTLEMAN IN DIFFICULTIES, A
See Bayly, Thomas Haynes.
GENTLEMAN JIM
See Walkes, W. R.
GENTLEMAN JOE
See Hood, Basil Charles Willett.
GENTLEMAN WHIP, THE
See Paull, Harry Major.
GENTLEMEN, WE CAN DO WITHOUT YOU
See Millingen, John Gideon. Ladies at Home.
GEORGE, G. H.
**Harlequin Aladdin and the Lamp; or, The Wizard, the Ring,
and the Scamp.** London (Lambeth): Williams & Strahan
(printer), n.d. Pp. [1]-23. Abridged ed. Libretto.
**Sleeping Beauty, The; or, Harlequin Peter Wilkins and the
Flying Women of Wonderland.** London (Lambeth):
Williams & Strahan (printer), n.d. Pp. [1]-24. Abridged
ed. Libretto.
GEORGE BARNWELL
See Lillo, George.
GEORGE DANDIN
See Van Laun, Henri (trans.).
GEORGE DE BARNWELL
See Byron, Henry James.
GEORGE GEITH
See Reeve, Wybert.
GEORGE HERIOT
See Murray, William Henry Wood. Fortunes of Nigel,
The.
GEORGY BARNWELL
See Corri, Montague.
GERALD
See Marston, John Westland.
GERMAN JEW, THE
See Tilbury, William Harries.
GERMANICUS
See Bernel, George (trans.).
GERTRUDE
See Richardson, Sarah Watts, Mrs. Joseph.
GERTRUDE AND BEATRICE
See Stephens, George.
GERTRUDE'S CHERRIES
See Jerrold, Douglas William.
GETTING UP IN THE WORLD
See Sketchley, Arthur.
GHETTO, THE
See Fernald, Chester Bailey.
GHOST, THE
See Zingiber, Zachary.
GHOST IN SPITE OF HIMSELF
See Moncrieff, William Thomas. Spectre Bridegroom,
The.
GHOST STORY, A
See Serle, Thomas James.
GHOST'S TOWER
See Rodwell, George Herbert Bonaparte. Seven Maids of
Munich, The.
GHOSTS
See Archer, William (trans.).

GIACOMETTI, PAOLO
Elizabeth, Queen of England.
See under title.
See Williams, Thomas (trans.).
GIACOSA, GIUSEPPE
Lady of Challant, The.
See Lyster, Frederic (trans.).
GIANT HORSE AND THE SIEGE OF TROY
See Akhurst, William M. Paris the Prince and Helen the
Fair.
GIANT MOUNTAINS
See Reynolds, Frederick. Gnome King, The.
GIFFORD, J. WEAR
Supper for Two; or, The Wolf and the Lamb. London & New
York: Samuel French, n.d. Pp. [1]-18. [Lacy's Acting
Edition].
GIFT OF MAMMON
See Jerrold, Douglas William. Devil's Ducat, The.
GIL BLAS
See Macfarren, George.
GIL BLAS AND THE ROBBERS OF ASTURIA
See Macfarren, George. Gil Blas.
GIL PEREZ, THE GALLICIAN
See Fitzgerald, Edward (trans.).
GILBERT, ? (trans.)
Tender Sisters, The. By Gellert. N.p.: n.pub., n.d. Pp. [1]-50.
GILBERT, H. P.
Court of Lions, The; or, Granada Taken and Done For.
London: Thomas Hailes Lacy, n.d. Pp. [1]-42. [Lacy's
Acting Edition].
GILBERT, WILLIAM SCHWENCK
Ages Ago. Music by Clay, Frederic. New York: n.pub.,
1875. Pp. [1]-40. Libretto.
Ages Ago. Music by Clay, Frederic. London: Joseph
Williams; New York: E. Schuberth, c.1893. Pp. [1]-22.
German Reed Repertory of Musical Pieces. Libretto.
Allow Me to Explain. 26 leaves. Typescript.
Brantinghame Hall. In *Original Plays,* Fourth Series, London:
Chatto & Windus, 1911, pp. [i], [267]-308.
Broken Hearts. London & New York: Samuel French, n.d.
Pp. [1]-35. Promptbook.
Charity. New York: Happy Hours, n.d. Pp. [i]-vi, [7]-45.
[Acting Drama, 46].
Comedy and Tragedy. In *Original Plays,* Third Series,
London: Chatto & Windus, 1910, pp. [1]-17.
Committed for Trial. 28 leaves. Typescript.
Creatures of Impulse. In *Original Plays,* Fourth Series,
London: Chatto & Windus, 1911, pp. [i], [309]-327.
Dan'l Druce, Blacksmith. London & New York: Samuel
French, n.d. Pp. [1]-42. Lacy's Acting Edition.
Dulcamara; or, The Little Duck and the Great Quack.
London: Strand, 1866. Pp. [1]-34. Promptbook.
Engaged. In *Original Plays,* Second Series, London: Chatto &
Windus, 1910, pp. [i], [39]-85.
Engaged. London & New York: Samuel French, n.d. Pp.
[1]-48. French's Acting Edition (late Lacy's). Prompt-
book.
Engaged. London & New York: Samuel French, n.d. Pp.
[1]-48.
Eyes and No Eyes; or, The Art of Seeing. Music by Pascal, F.
London: Joseph Williams, c.1896. Pp. [1]-23. Libretto.
Foggerty's Fairy. In *Original Plays,* Third Series, London:
Chatto & Windus, 1910, pp. [i], [19]-73.
Fortune Hunter, The. In *Original Plays,* Fourth Series,
London: Chatto & Windus, 1911, pp. [i], [385]-442.
Gentleman in Black, The. In *Original Plays,* Fourth Series,
London: Chatto & Windus, 1911, pp. [i], [235]-265.
Gentleman in Black, The. Music by Clay, Frederic. London:
Thomas Hailes Lacy, n.d. Pp. [1]-36.
Gondoliers, The; or, The King of Barataria. Music by
Sullivan, Arthur. London: Henderson & Spalding
(printer), n.d. Pp. [3]-47. Title page lacking. Promptbook
libretto.

Gondoliers, The; or, The King of Barataria. Music by Sullivan, Arthur. London: Chappell, n.d. Pp. [1]-49. Rev. ed. Libretto.

Grand Duke, The; or, The Statutory Duel. Music by Sullivan, Arthur. Boston: George H. Ellis (printer), 1896. Pp. [i], [1]-55. Libretto.

Grand Duke, The; or, The Statutory Duel. Music by Sullivan, Arthur. London: Chappell, c.1896. Pp. [i-iv], [1]-54. Libretto.

Great Expectations. 58 leaves. Typescript.

Gretchen. London: Newman, 1879. Pp. [i-vi], [1]-122.

Gretchen. London & New York: Samuel French, n.d. Pp. [1]-50. Promptbook.

Happy Arcadia. Music by Clay, Frederic. London: Joseph Williams; New York: E. Schuberth, c.1896. Pp. [1]-30. German Reed Repertory of Musical Pieces. Libretto.

Happy Land, The. Written with A'Beckett, Gilbert Arthur. By F. Tomline (pseud.) and Gilbert A'Beckett. London: J. W. Last, 1873. Pp. [1]-28.

Harlequin Cock-Robin and Jenny Wren; or, Fortunatus and the Water of Life, the Three Bears, the Three Gifts, the Three Wishes, and the Little Man Who Woo'd the Little Maid. London: Music Publishing Co., 1867. Pp. [1]-23.

Haste to the Wedding. Music by Grossmith, George. In *Original Plays,* Fourth Series, London: Chatto & Windus, 1911, pp. [i], [147]-185. Libretto.

Highly Improbable. 22 leaves. Typescript.

His Excellency. Music by Carr, F. Osmond. London: Joseph Williams, n.d. Pp. [i-iv], [1]-218. Vocal score.

His Excellency. Music by Carr, F. Osmond. New York: T. B. Harms; London: Chappell, c.1894. Pp. [1]-62. Libretto.

H.M.S. Pinafore; or, The Lass That Loved a Sailor. Music by Sullivan, Arthur. In *Original Plays,* Second Series, London: Chatto & Windus, 1910, pp. [i], [271]-301. Libretto.

H.M.S. Pinafore; or, The Lass That Loved a Sailor. Music by Sullivan, Arthur. London: Chappell, n.d. Pp. [1]-32. Libretto.

Iolanthe; or, The Peer and the Peri. Music by Sullivan, Arthur. [Philadelphia]: J. M. Stoddart, c.1882. Pp. [1]-47. Libretto.

Iolanthe; or, The Peer and the Peri. Music by Sullivan, Arthur. [Philadelphia]: J. M. Stoddart, c.1882. Pp. [1]-155. Vocal score.

Medical Man, A. In [*Drawing-Room Plays and Parlour Pantomimes,* ed. Clement Scott, London: S. Rivers, 1870], pp. [15]-36.

Merry Zingara, The; or, The Tipsy Gipsy and the Pipsy Wipsy. London: Phillips, n.d. Pp. [1]-41.

Mikado, The; or, The Town of Titipu. Music by Sullivan, Arthur. Boston: Oliver Ditson, n.d. Pp. [1]-46. Libretto.

Mikado, The; or, The Town of Titipu. Music by Sullivan, Arthur. London: Chappell, n.d. Pp. [1]-47. Libretto.

Mountebanks, The. Music by Cellier, Alfred. London: Chappell, c.1892. Pp. [1]-61. Libretto.

Ne'er-Do-Weel, The. [London: Joseph Williams], n.d. Pp. [1]-75.

No Cards. Music by Elliott, L. London: Joseph Williams, n.d. Pp. [1]-20. German Reed Repertory of Musical Pieces. Libretto.

Old Score, An. London & New York: Samuel French, n.d. Pp. [1]-42.

On Bail. London & New York: Samuel French, n.d. Pp. [1]-40. [Lacy's Acting Edition].

On Guard. London & New York: Samuel French, n.d. Pp. [1]-47. [Lacy's Acting Edition].

Ought We to Visit Her? 46 leaves. Typescript.

Ought We to Visit Her? London & New York: Samuel French, n.d. Pp. [1]-44.

Our Island Home. 23 leaves. Typescript.

Palace of Truth, The. London: Thomas Hailes Lacy, n.d. Pp. [1]-55. [Lacy's Acting Edition].

Patience; or, Bunthorne's Bride. Music by Sullivan, Arthur. [Philadelphia]: J. M. Stoddart, c.1881. Pp. [1]-42. Promptbook libretto.

Patience; or, Bunthorne's Bride! Music by Sullivan, Arthur. London: Chappell, n.d. Pp. [1]-40. Libretto.

Pirates of Penzance, The; or, The Slave of Duty. Music by Sullivan, Arthur. Philadelphia: J. M. Stoddart, c.1880. Pp. [1]-39. Libretto.

Pirates of Penzance, The; or, The Slave of Duty. Music by Sullivan, Arthur. London: Chappell, n.d. Pp. [1]-32. Libretto.

Pretty Druidess, The; or, The Mother, the Maid, and the Mistletoe Bough. London: Phillips n.d. Pp. [1]-34.

Princess, The. London: Thomas Hailes Lacy, n.d. Pp. [1]-44. Lacy's Acting Edition, 231.

Princess Ida; or, Castle Adamant. Music by Sullivan, Arthur. London: Chappell, n.d. Pp. [1]-48. Libretto.

Princess Toto. Music by Clay, Frederic. London: Metzler, n.d. Pp. [1]-48. Libretto.

Pygmalion and Galatea. Chicago: Dramatic Publishing Co., n.d. Pp. [1]-46. World Acting Drama.

Pygmalion and Galatea. London & New York: Samuel French, n.d. Pp. [1]-36. [French's Acting Edition (late Lacy's), 1545]. Promptbook.

Randall's Thumb. London: Thomas Hailes Lacy, n.d. Pp. [1]-64. [Lacy's Acting Edition].

Randall's Thumb. New York: Samuel French & Son, n.d. Pp. [1]-42. French's Standard Drama, 363.

Realm of Joy, The. 22 leaves. Typescript.

Robert the Devil; or, The Nun, the Dun, and the Son of a Gun. London: Phillips, n.d. Pp. [1]-40.

Rosencrantz and Guildenstern. In *Original Plays,* Third Series, London: Chatto & Windus, 1910, pp. [i], [75]-89.

Ruddigore; or, The Witch's Curse! Music by Sullivan, Arthur. London: Chappell, n.d. Pp. [1]-46. Libretto.

Ruy Blas. [London: The Five Alls, Warne's Christmas Annual, 1866]. Pp. 50-56.

Sensation Novel in Three Volumes, A. Music by Pascal, Florian. London: Joseph Williams, c.1912. Pp. [1]-31. Libretto.

Sorcerer, The. In *Original Plays,* Second Series, London: Chatto & Windus, 1910, pp. [i], [239]-270.

Sorcerer, The. Music by Sullivan, Arthur. London: Chappell, n.d. Pp. [1]-28. Libretto.

Sweethearts. London & New York: Samuel French, n.d. Pp. [1]-20. French's Acting Edition (late Lacy's), 655.

Thespis; or, The Gods Grown Old. In *Original Plays,* Fourth Series, London: Chatto & Windus, 1911, pp. [i], [443]-475.

Tom Cobb; or, Fortune's Toy. London & New York: Samuel French, n.d. Pp. [1]-32. Promptbook.

Tom Cobb; or, Fortune's Toy. London & New York: Samuel French, n.d. Pp. [1]-32. French's Acting Edition (late Lacy's).

Topsyturvydom. Oxford: University Press, 1931. Pp. [1]-26.

Trial by Jury. Music by Sullivan, Arthur. London: Chappell, n.d. Pp. [29]-40. Libretto. *Filed under* Sorcerer.

Trial by Jury. Music by Sullivan, Arthur. London: Royal Aquarium, n.d. Pp. [1]-16. Libretto.

Utopia Limited; or, The Flowers of Progress. Music by Sullivan, Arthur. London: Chappell, c.1893. Pp. [1]-50. Libretto.

Vivandière, La; or, True to the Corps! Music by Wallerstein. Liverpool: H. Montague, 1868. Pp. [1]-31.

Wedding March, The. London & New York: Samuel French, n.d. Pp. [1]-34. Promptbook.

Wedding March, The. London & New York: Samuel French, n.d. Pp. [1]-34.

Wicked World, The. In *Original Plays,* First Series, new ed., London: Chatto & Windus, 1884, pp. [i], [1]-44.

Yeomen of the Guard, The; or, The Merryman and His Maid. Music by Sullivan, Arthur. London: G. Bell & Sons, 1912. Pp. [i-vi], [1]-54. Libretto.

Yeomen of the Guard, The; or, The Merryman and His Maid. Music by Sullivan, Arthur. London: Chappell, n.d. Pp. [1]-48. Libretto.

GILDED YOUTH

See Young, Charles Lawrence, Sir.

GILDEROY
    See Barrymore, William.
    See Murray, William Henry Wood.
GILLINGTON, MAY CLARISSA (later Mrs. G. F. Byron)
    Jewel Maiden, The. Music by Pascal, Florian. London:
    Joseph Williams, n.d. Pp. [1]-31. Libretto. *Filed under*
    Byron, May Clarissa.
GIOVANNA OF NAPLES
    See Landor, Walter Savage.
GIOVANNI IN LONDON
    See Moncrieff, William Thomas.
GIOVANNI IN PARIS
    See Milner, Henry M.
GIOVANNI IN THE COUNTRY
    See Barrymore, William.
    See Moncrieff, William Thomas.
GIOVANNI THE VAMPIRE!
    See Planché, James Robinson.
GIPSEY OF DERNCLEUGH, THE
    See Jerrold, Douglas William.
GIPSEY'S PROPHECY
    See Frye, William Edward (trans.). Guilt.
    See Terry, Daniel. Guy Mannering.
GIPSY
    See Hannan, Charles.
    See Knowles, James Sheridan. Leo.
GIPSY FARMER, THE
    See Johnstone, John Beer.
GIPSY GIRL AND THE GUILTY CONSCIENCE
    See Byron, Henry James. Wayside Wiolets, The.
GIPSY GIRL OF PARIS
    See Halliday, Andrew. Notre Dame.
GIPSY JACK
    See Moncrieff, William Thomas.
GIPSY KING, THE
    See Bosworth, J.
GIPSY OF ASHBURNHAM DELL!
    See Campbell, Andrew Leonard Voullaire. Lyieushee
    Lovel.
GIPSY'S PROPHECY
    See Terry, Daniel. Guy Mannering.
GIPSY'S VENGEANCE, THE
    See Jefferys, Charles.
GIPSY'S WARNING, THE
    See Linley, George.
GIRALDA
    See Baildon, Arthur.
    See Davidson, Frances A., Mrs.
    See Webster, Benjamin Nottingham.
GIRL FROM PARIS, THE
    See Dance, George.
GIRL GRADUATE, A
    See Rose, Edward.
GIRL OF THE LIGHT HOUSE, THE
    See Somerset, Charles A.
GIRLS, THE
    See Byron, Henry James.
GIRLS HE LEFT BEHIND HIM, THE
    See Hunt, Margaret Raine, Mrs. Alfred William.
GIRLS OF THE PERIOD, THE
    See B., A.
GIROFLÉ-GIROFLA
    See Clarke, Campbell (trans.).
GISELA
    See Holroyd, John Joseph.
GISELLE
    See Byron, Henry James.
    See Moncrieff, William Thomas.
GISIPPUS
    See Griffin, Gerald.
GÍSLI SÚRSSON
    See Barmby, Beatrice Helen.
GITANILLA, THE
    See Wilson, John Crawford.

GITANILLA DE MADRID
    See Tobin, John (trans.). Gypsey of Madrid, The.
GIULIANO DE' MEDICI
    See Sandbach, Margaret Roscoe, Mrs. Henry R.
GIVE A DOG A BAD NAME
    See Lawrence, Slingsby.
GIVE ME MY WIFE
    See Suter, William E.
GIVING HIM AWAY
    See Bell, Florence Eveleen Eleanore Oliffe, Mrs. Hugh
    (Lady).
GLADIATOR OF RAVENNA, THE
    See Charlton, William Henry (trans.).
    See Martin, Theodore, Sir (trans.).
    See Vericour, Raymond de (trans.).
GLADSTONE AND THE HOUSE OF LORDS (anon.)
    London: Edward Stanford, 1872. Pp. [1]-23.
GLAMOUR
    See Farnie, Henry Brougham.
GLASS OF FASHION, THE
    See Grundy, Sydney.
GLASS OF WATER, A
    See Suter, William E.
GLEANERS OF LIFE
    See Willett, Ernest Noddall. Prodigal Son, A.
GLENCOE
    See Talfourd, Thomas Noon.
GLENGALL, EARL OF
    See Butler, Richard William, Earl of Glengall.
GLIMPSE OF PARADISE, A
    See Dilley, Joseph J.
GLIMPSE OF UTOPIA, A
    See A'Beckett, Gilbert Arthur. In the Clouds.
GLIN GATH
    See Meritt, Paul.
GLITTER
    See A'Beckett, Gilbert Arthur.
GLORIANA
    See Mortimer, James.
GLORIOUS REVOLUTION, 5TH NOVEMBER 1688, THE
    See Lee, Baron.
GLOVE, THE
    See Besant, Walter.
GLOVER, HOWARD
    See Glover, William Howard.
GLOVER, WILLIAM HOWARD
    Aminta, the Coquette; or, A Match for a Magistrate. London:
    Webster, n.d. Pp. [1]-24. Webster's Acting National
    Drama, 182. Libretto.
GLYN, ALICE CORALIE
    Drama in Dregs, A: A Life Study. London: Simpkin,
    Marshall, Hamilton, Kent, 1897. Pp. [i], [1]-[212].
GLYN, CORALIE
    See Glyn, Alice Coralie.
GNOME KING, THE
    See Reynolds, Frederick.
GNOME KING AND THE GOOD FAIRY OF THE SILVER
    MINE, THE
    See Brough, William.
GO BANG
    See Ross, Adrian.
GO TO PUTNEY
    See Lemon, Harry.
GOAL, THE
    See Jones, Henry Arthur.
GOD AND MAMMON IN THE TRANSVAAL
    See Swan, Howard. Paul and Joseph.
GOD-DAUGHTER
    See Poole, John. Atonement.
GOD SAVE THE QUEEN
    See Palgrave, R.
GODDARD, KATE
    Mistaken Identity. London & New York: Samuel French,
    n.d. Pp. [1]-8. [Lacy's Acting Edition].

Who Won? London & New York: Samuel French, n.d. Pp. [1]-11. [Lacy's Acting Edition].

GODEFROI AND YOLANDE
See Irving, Laurence Sydney Brodribb.

GODFREY, GEORGE WILLIAM
Millionaire, The. London: Williams & Strahan (printer) (priv.), n.d. Pp. [1]-73.
My Milliner's Bill. New York & London: Samuel French, c.1903. Pp. [1]-15. [Lacy's Acting Edition].
Parvenu, The. New York & London: Samuel French, c.1903. Pp. [1]-53. French's International Copyrighted Edition of the Works of the Best Authors, 60.

GODFRIDA
See Davidson, John.

GODIVA
See Hale, William Palmer.

GODLEY, ALFRED DENIS (trans.)
Frogs, The.
See Hogarth, David George (trans.).

GODMOND, CHRISTOPHER
Battle of Crecy.
See Campaign of 1346, The.
Campaign of 1346, The. *Also:* The Battle of Crecy. London: Edward Bull, 1836. Pp. [1-2], [i]-[xx], [1]-152, [1]-14.
Campaign of 1346, Ending with the Battle of Crecy, The. London: Edward Bull, 1836. Pp. [1-2], [i]-[xx], [1]-152.
Vincenzo, Prince of Mantua; or, The Death of Crichton. London: J. Dennett (printer) (priv.), 1840. Pp. [i-iv], [1]-135.

GODS GROWN OLD
See Gilbert, William Schwenck. Thespis.

GODWIN, EDWARD WILLIAM
Fair Rosamund. [Albany: C. P. Brate], c.1895. Pp. [1]-68.

GODWIN, GEORGE, JR
Last Day, The. London: Webster, n.d. Pp. [1]-16. Webster's Acting National Drama, 108.

GODWIN, WILLIAM
Antonio. London: G. G. & J. Robinson, 1800. Pp. [i-iv], [1]-73.
Faulkener. London: Richard Phillips, 1807. Pp. [i]-[x], [1]-80.

GOETHE, JOHANN WOLFGANG VON
Clavigo.
See Stowell, Thomas Alfred (trans.).
Egmont.
See under title.
See Coleridge, Arthur Duke (trans.).
Faust.
See under title.
See Beresford, A. von (trans.).
See Beta (pseud.) (trans.).
See Birch, Jonathan (trans.).
See Blackie, John Stuart (trans.).
See Chorley, Henry Fothergill (trans.).
See Colquhoun, W. H. (trans.).
See Filmore, Lewis (trans.).
See Galvan, John (trans.).
See Gower, Francis Leveson, Lord (trans.).
See Grant, John Wynniatt (trans.).
See Hayward, Abraham (trans.).
See Hills, John (trans.).
See Knox, Charles H., Capt. (trans.).
See Lefevre, George William, Sir (trans.).
See Martin, Theodore, Sir (trans.).
See Paul, C. Kegan (trans.).
See Scoones, William Dalton (trans.).
See Shelley, Percy Bysshe (trans.) May-Day Night.
See Swanwick, Anna (trans.).
See Syme, David (trans.).
See Talbot, Robert (trans.).
See Wills, William Gorman (arr.).
Faust, Part 2.
See Bernays, Leopold John (trans.).
See Gurney, Archer Thompson (trans.).
Faustus.
See under title.

See Anster, John (trans.).
See Davies, Warburton (trans.).
Faustus, Part 1.
See Huth, Alfred Henry (trans.).
Goetz of Berlichingen, with the Iron Hand.
See Scott, Walter, Sir (trans.).
Stella.
See Thompson, Benjamin (trans.).
Torquato Tasso.
See Herbert, M. A. (trans.).

GOETZ OF BERLICHINGEN, WITH THE IRON HAND
See Scott, Walter, Sir (trans.).

GOFF, HENRY
Two Drovers, The. London: John Duncombe, n.d. Pp. [1]-24. Duncombe's Acting Edition of the British Theatre, 75.

GOING IT!
See Morton, John Maddison.

GOING ON ANYHOW
See Bruton, James.

GOING TO CHOBHAM
See Hazlewood, Colin Henry.

GOING TO THE BAD
See Taylor, Tom.

GOING TO THE DERBY
See Morton, John Maddison.

GOING TO THE DOGS!
See Brough, William.

GOLD!
See Reade, Charles.

GOLD AND GUILT
See Byron, Henry James.

GOLD FIEND, THE
See Townsend, William Thompson.

GOLD MINE, THE
See Stirling, Edward.

GOLDEN AGE, THE
See Byatt, Henry.

GOLDEN APPLE, THE
See Silvester, Frank.

GOLDEN BRANCH, THE
See Planché, James Robinson.

GOLDEN CALF, THE
See Jerrold, Douglas William.

GOLDEN CROSS, THE
See Jackson, John P. (trans.).

GOLDEN EGG!
See Dibdin, Thomas John. Harlequin and Mother Goose.

GOLDEN FARMER, THE
See Webster, Benjamin Nottingham.

GOLDEN FETTER, A
See Phillips, Watts.

GOLDEN FLEECE, THE
See Planché, James Robinson.

GOLDEN FRUIT
See Pettitt, Henry Alfred.

GOLDEN GLOVE, THE
See Lake, John.

GOLDEN GOOSE, THE
See Bell, Florence Eveleen Eleanore Oliffe, Mrs. Hugh (Lady).

GOLDEN PLOUGH, THE
See Meritt, Paul.

GOLDEN POPPY
See Almar, George. Silver Palace, The.

GOLDEN WEDDING, A
See Phillpotts, Eden.

GOLDEN WREATH, THE
See Albery, James.

GOLDMAN, L. B.
Act of Folly, An. Basingstoke: C. J. Jacob, n.d. Pp. [1]-35.

GOLDONI, CARLO
Beneficent Bear, The.
See Zimmern, Helen (trans.?).

Curious, Mishap, A.
    See Zimmern, Helen (trans.?).
Fan, The.
    See Zimmern, Helen (trans.?).
Spendthrift Miser, The.
    See Zimmern, Helen (trans.?).
GOLDSMITH, OLIVER
    Good-Natured Man, The. London: Whittingham & Arliss, 1816. Pp. [1]-72. London Theatre, XIX. *Filed under* Dibdin, Thomas John, ed. London Theatre, XIX.
    Good-Natured Man, The. London: John Cumberland, 1826. Pp. [ii]-[ix], 10-[67]. Dolby's British Theatre, XIII. *Filed under* Cumberland, John. Cumberland's British Theatre, XIII.
    Good-Natured Man, The. In *British Drama*, 12 vols., London: John Dicks, 1871, VII, [161]-181.
    She Stoops to Conquer; or, The Mistakes of a Night. London: Whittingham & Arliss, 1814. Pp. [1]-[72]. London Theatre, VI. *Filed under* Dibdin, Thomas John, ed. London Theatre, VI.
    She Stoops to Conquer. In *New English Drama*, ed. W. Oxberry, 22 vols., London: W. Simpkin & R. Marshall; C. Chapple, 1820, IV, [i]-[viii], [1]-67. *Filed under* Oxberry, William Henry. New English Drama, IV.
    She Stoops to Conquer. London: John Cumberland, 1826. Pp. [1]-8, [v]-viii, [9]-68. Cumberland's British Theatre, I. *Filed under* Cumberland, John. Cumberland's British Theatre, I.
    She Stoops to Conquer. In *British Drama*, 12 vols., London: John Dicks, 1864, I, [82]-99.
GOLDSWORTHY, ARNOLD
    My Friend Jarlet. Written with Norman, E. B. London & New York: Samuel French, n.d. Pp. [1]-19. [Lacy's Acting Edition].
GONDOLIER, THE; OR, A NIGHT IN VENICE (anon.)
    In *New British Theatre*, London: A. J. Valpy (printer), 1814, III, [i], [165]-199.
GONDOLIERS, THE
    See Gilbert, William Schwenck.
GONSALVO OF CORDOVA
    See Dacre, Barbarina Ogle, Lady.
GONZALO, THE SPANISH BANDIT
    See Fortescue, F.
GONZALO THE TRAITOR
    See Roscoe, Thomas.
GONZANGA (anon.)
    In *New British Theatre*, London: A. J. Valpy (printer), 1814, III, [i], [97]-164.
GOOD CONDUCT PRIZE
    See Barrie, James Mathew. Jane Annie.
GOOD FAIRY TRIUMPHANT OVER THE DEMON OF DISCORD!
    See Morton, John Maddison. Harlequin Blue Beard, the Great Bashaw.
GOOD FOR EVIL
    See Reynoldson, Thomas Herbert.
GOOD FOR NOTHING
    See Buckstone, John Baldwin.
GOOD JUDGE
    See Bon Juge, Le.
GOOD KING STEPHEN
    See Richards, Alfred Bate. Isolda.
GOOD LITTLE WIFE, A
    See Oxenford, John.
GOOD-LOOKING FELLOW
    See Almar, George.
    See Kenney, James.
GOOD-NATURED MAN, THE
    See Goldsmith, Oliver.
GOOD NEWS! GOOD NEWS!
    See Maclaren, Archibald.
GOOD NIGHT'S REST, A
    See Gore, Catherine Grace Frances Moody, Mrs. Charles.

GOOD QUEEN BESS
    See Lewin, Walpole.
GOOD REGENT, THE
    See Stewart, Thomas Grainger, Sir.
GOOD RUN FOR IT, A
    See Bridgeman, John Vipon.
GOOD WOMAN IN THE WOOD, THE
    See Planché, James Robinson.
GOODE, LOUISE
    See Jopling, Louise Goode, Mrs. Joseph Middleton.
GOODNIGHT, SIGNOR PANTALOON (anon.)
    Music by Grisar. London: Thomas Hailes Lacy, n.d. Pp. [1]-27. [Lacy's Acting Edition]. Libretto. *Filed under* Somerset, Charles A.
GOODRICH, ARTHUR
    Calthorpe Case, The. London & New York: Samuel French, n.d. Pp. [1]-54. [Lacy's Acting Edition].
GOODRICH, FRANK B.
    Dark Hour before Dawn, The.
    See Brougham, John.
GOODWIN, JOHN CHEEVER
    Rightful Heir, The.
    See Sturgess, Arthur.
GOODY TWO SHOES
    See Dibdin, Charles Isaac Mungo, jr.
GOODYER, F. R.
    Fair Maid of Clifton, The. Music by Leverton, H. Nottingham: R. B. Earp (printer), 1872. Pp. [1]-28. Libretto.
    Once upon a Time; or, A Midsummer Night's Dream in Merrie Sherwood. Nottingham: R. Allen & Son (printer), 1868. Pp. [1]-34. Libretto.
GOOGAH, THE
    See Murdoch, J. Mortimer.
GOOSE GIRL, THE
    See Scott-Gatty, Alfred Scott.
GOOSE WITH THE GOLDEN EGGS, THE
    See Mayhew, Augustus Septimus.
GORDON, ADAM LINDSAY
    Ashtaroth. Melbourne: Clarson, Massina, 1867. Pp. [3]-96.
GORDON, GEORGE
    See Byron, George Gordon, Lord.
GORDON, LIONEL SMITH
    Keeper of the Seals. London & New York: Samuel French, n.d. Pp. [1]-10. [Lacy's Acting Edition].
GORDON, WALTER
    Dearest Mamma. N.p.: n.pub., n.d. Pp. [3]-24. Title page lacking. [Lacy's Acting Edition, 689]. Promptbook.
    Duchess or Nothing. London: Thomas Hailes Lacy, n.d. Pp. [1]-24. [Lacy's Acting Edition].
    Fireside Story, A. New York: Dramatic Publishing Co., n.d. Pp. [1]-10. DeWitt's Acting Plays, 329.
    Home for a Holiday. London: Thomas Hailes Lacy, n.d. Pp. [1]-23. [Lacy's Acting Edition].
    My Wife's Relations. London: Thomas Hailes Lacy, n.d. Pp. [1]-22. [Lacy's Acting Edition].
    Odd Lot, An. London: Thomas Hailes Lacy, n.d. Pp. [1]-19. Lacy's Acting Edition.
    Old Trusty. London & New York: Samuel French, n.d. Pp. [1]-24. [Lacy's Acting Edition].
    State Prisoner, The. By William Gowing (pseud.). London & New York: Samuel French, n.d. Pp. [1]-14.
    Through Fire and Water. London: Thomas Hailes Lacy, n.d. Pp. [1]-36.
GORE, CATHERINE GRACE FRANCES MOODY, MRS. CHARLES
    Bond, The. London: John Murray, 1824. Pp. [i-ii], [1]-95.
    Dacre of the South; or, The Olden Time. London: Richard Bentley, 1840. Pp. [i-iv], [1]-95.
    Good Night's Rest, A; or, Two in the Morning! London: John Duncombe, n.d. Pp. [1]-17. Duncombe's Acting Edition of the British Theatre, 307.
    King O'Neil; or, The Irish Brigade. London: John Dicks, n.d. Pp. [1]-16. Dicks' Standard Plays, 461.
    King's Seal, The.
    See Kenney, James.

Maid of Croissey, The; or, Theresa's Vow. London: John Dicks, n.d. Pp. [1]-13. Dicks' Standard Plays, 339.

Maid of Croissey, The; or, Theresa's Vow. New York & Philadelphia: Turner & Fisher, n.d. Pp. [1]-32. Turner's Dramatic Library.

Quid Pro Quo; or, The Day of Dupes. London: National Acting Drama Office, n.d. Pp. [i]-[x], [11]-82.

GOSSE, EDMUND WILLIAM

King Erik. London: William Heinemann, 1893. Pp. [i]-xx, [i]-[x], [1]-182.

Unknown Lover, The. London: Chatto & Windus, 1878. Pp. [1-2], [i]-xvi, [3]-31.

GOSSE, EDMUND WILLIAM (trans.)

Hedda Gabler. By Ibsen, Henrik. Boston: Walter H. Baker, n.d. Pp. [1]-272.

Master Builder, The. Written with Archer, William. By Ibsen, Henrik. London: William Heinemann, 1893. Pp. [i-iv], [1]-227.

Master Builder, The. Written with Archer, William. By Ibsen, Henrik. Boston: Walter H. Baker, 1900. Pp. [1]-203.

GOSSIP

See Harris, Augustus Glossop.

GOTOBED TOM!

See Morton, Thomas, jr.

GOTT, HENRY

Elshie, The; or, The Wizard of the Moor. *Also:* The Wizard of the Moor. London: John Lowndes, n.d. Pp. [i-iv], [1]-43.

Wizard of the Moor, The. London: John Cumberland, n.d. Pp. [1]-42. Cumberland's Minor Theatre, IX. *Filed under* Cumberland, John. Cumberland's Minor Theatre, IX.

Wizard of the Moor, The. *Also:* The Elshie; or, The Wizard of the Moor. London: Thomas Hailes Lacy, n.d. Pp. [1]-42. [Lacy's Acting Edition].

GÖTTERDÄMMERUNG

See Corder, Henrietta Louisa Walford, Mrs. Frederick (trans.). Dusk of the Gods, The.

GOVER, F.

God Save the Queen.

See Palgrave, R.

GOVERNOR'S WIFE, THE

See Mildenhall, Thomas.

GOWER, FRANCIS LEVESON, LORD (later Egerton, Francis, Earl of Ellesmere)

Alfred. N.p.: n.pub., n.d. Pp. [1]-16. *Filed under* Ellesmere, Francis Egerton.

Bluebeard; or, Dangerous Curiosity and Justifiable Homicide. London: T. Brettell, 1841. Pp. [1]-32. *Filed under* Ellesmere, Francis Egerton.

Donna Charitea, Queen of Castille. London: James Bain (printer) (priv.), 1843. Pp. [1]-67. *Filed under* Ellesmere, Francis Egerton, Earl of.

GOWER, FRANCIS LEVESON, LORD (later Egerton, Francis, Earl of Ellesmere) (trans.)

Catherine of Cleves. By Dumas. London: J. Andrews, 1831. Pp. [i]-viii, [1]-116. *Filed under* Ellesmere, Francis Egerton.

Faust. By Goethe. London: John Murray, 1823. Pp. [i]-[viii], [1]-266. *Filed under* Ellesmere, Francis Egerton.

Paria, The. By Beer, Michael. London: W. Sams (printer) (priv.), 1836. Pp. [1]-30. *Filed under* Ellesmere, Francis Egerton.

Wallenstein's Camp. By Schiller. In *Wallenstein's Camp and Original Poems,* London: John Murray, 1830, pp. [1]-84. *Filed under* Ellesmere, Francis Egerton.

GOWING, EMILIA JULIA BLAKE, MRS. WILLIAM AYLMER

Boadicea. London: Kegan Paul, Trench, Trubner, 1899. Pp. [i-iv], [1]-84.

GOWING, WILLIAM

See Gordon, Walter.

GRACE

See Dutch, J. S.

GRACE CLAIRVILLE

See Lewis, Alexis.

GRACE DARLING

See Stirling, Edward.

GRACE HUNTLEY

See Holl, Henry.

GRACE MARY

See Jones, Henry Arthur.

GRACIOSA AND PERCINET

See Planché, James Robinson.

GRAHAM, BEATRICE VIOLET

See Greville, Beatrice Violet Graham, Lady.

GRAHAM, DAVID

King James the First. London: MacMillan, 1887. Pp. [i-iv], [1]-206.

GRAHAM, JAMES (trans.)

Mariana. By Echegaray, José. Boston: Roberts Brothers, 1895. Pp. [1]-126.

Son of Don Juan, The. By Echegaray, José. Boston: Roberts Brothers, 1895. Pp. [1]-131.

GRAHAM-SIMPSON, ELLA

See Simpson, Ella Graham.

GRANADA TAKEN AND DONE FOR

See Gilbert, H. P. Court of Lions, The.

GRAND CASIMIR

See Leigh, Henry Sambrooke. Great Casimir, The.

GRAND DUCHESS OF GEROLSTEIN, THE

See Brookfield, Charles Hallam Elton (trans.).

See Ross, Adrian.

GRAND DUKE, THE

See Gilbert, William Schwenck.

GRANDAD'S DARLING

See Gurney, Edmund.

GRANDE DOCTRESSE

See Byron, Henry James. Lucretia Borgia, M.D.

GRANDE DUCHESSE DE GEROLSTEIN, LA

See Kenney, Charles Lamb (trans.).

GRANDFATHER WHITEHEAD

See Lemon, Mark.

GRANDMOTHER'S GOWN

See Anderson, Charles.

GRANT, CHARLES

Charm and the Curse, The. Jena: E. Frommann; London & Edinburgh: Williams & Norgate, 1873. Pp. [i]-[viii], [1]-197.

GRANT, JAMES M.

Custom's Fallacy. London: Barker & Son (priv.), 1805. Pp. [i-iv], [5]-97.

GRANT, JOHN WYNNIATT (trans.)

Faust. By Goethe. London: Hamilton, Adams, 1867. Pp. [1]-162.

GRANVILLE, H. SUCH

Aeneas; or, Dido Done! Cheltenham: T. B. Shenton (printer), n.d. Pp. [1]-16.

Village Belles. N.p.: n.pub., n.d. Pp. [1]-47.

GRASS WIDOWS

See March, George.

GRASSHOPPER, THE

See Hollingshead, John.

GRASSOT TORMENTED BY RAVEL

See Left the Stage (anon.).

GRATEFUL FATHER, A

See Pemberton, Thomas Edgar.

GRATTAN, H. P. (pseud. of Plunkett, Henry Willoughby Grattan)

Corsair's Revenge, The. London: John Dicks, n.d. Pp. [1]-11. Dicks' Standard Plays, 751. *Filed under* Grattan, Henry Plunkett Willoughby.

Dumb Conscript, The. London: John Dicks, n.d. Pp. [1]-11. Dicks' Standard Plays, 429. *Filed under* Grattan, Henry Plunkett Willoughby.

Fairy Circle, The; or, Con O'Carrolan's Dream. London: John Dicks, n.d. Pp. [1]-18. Dicks' Standard Plays, 432. *Filed under* Plunkett, Henry Willoughby Grattan.

Faust; or, The Demon of the Drachenfels. London: John Dicks, n.d. Pp. [1]-13. Dicks' Standard Plays, 573. *Filed under* Plunkett, Henry Willoughby Grattan.

Minerali, The; or, The Dying Gift. By Henry Grattan Plunkett. London: Thomas Hailes Lacy, n.d. Pp. [1]-31. [Lacy's Acting Edition]. *Filed under* Plunkett, Henry Willoughby Grattan.

Minerali!, The; or, The Dying Gift! By Henry Plunkett. London: John Duncombe, n.d. Pp. [1]-34. Duncombe's Acting Edition of the British Theatre, 184. *Filed under* Plunkett, Henry Willoughby Grattan.

My Uncle's Card; or, The First of April. London: John Dicks, n.d. Pp. [1]-11. Dicks' Standard Plays, 419. *Filed under* Grattan, Henry Plunkett Willoughby. Twins.

Packing Up. By Harry Grattan. London & New York: Samuel French, c.1904. Pp. [1]-10. Lacy's Acting Edition. *Filed under* Plunkett, Henry Willoughby Grattan.

Twins, The; or, A Hero in Spite of Himself. London: John Dicks, n.d. Pp. [1]-10. Dicks' Standard Plays, 419. *Filed under* Grattan, Henry Plunkett Willoughby.

White Boys, The. London: John Dicks, n.d. Pp. [1]-20. Dicks' Standard Plays, 422. *Filed under* Plunkett, Henry Willoughby Grattan.

Ye Fair One with ye Golden Locks. Written with Garston, Leonard. London: E. Rascol, n.d. Pp. [1]-26. Libretto. *Filed under* Plunkett, Henry Willoughby Grattan.

GRATTAN, THOMAS COLLEY
Ben Nazir, the Saracen. London: Henry Colburn, 1827. Pp. [i]-[x], [1]-100.

GRAVES, ALFRED PERCIVAL (arr.)
Out of the Frying Pan. Written with Toft, P. (trans.). London & New York: Samuel French, n.d. Pp. [1]-24. [Lacy's Acting Edition].

GRAVES, CLOTILDE INEZ MARY
Death and Rachel. N.p.: n.pub., n.d. Pp. [59]-67. Title page lacking.

GRAVES, JOSEPH
Cupid. London: W. Strange, 1837. Pp. [1]-22.
Tempter, The; or, The Old Mill of St. Denis! London: John Duncombe, n.d. Pp. [1]-38. Duncombe's Edition.
Wife, The; or, A Tale of a Mantua Maker! London: John Duncombe, n.d. Pp. [1]-24. Duncombe's Edition.

GRAY, SIMON
Spaniard, The; or, Relvindez and Elzora. London: Longman, Orme, 1839. Pp. [i]-[xxiv], [1]-149.

GRAY MARE, A
See Webster, Benjamin, jr.

GRAY PARROT, THE
See Jacobs, William Wymark.

GREAT CASIMIR, THE
See Leigh, Henry Sambrooke.

GREAT CATCH, A
See Clarke, Charles Allen.

GREAT DEVIL, THE
See Dibdin, Charles Isaac Mungo, jr.

GREAT EVENTS FROM TRIFLING CAUSES SPRING
See Suter, William E. Glass of Water, A.

GREAT EXPECTATIONS
See Gilbert, William Schwenck.

GREAT GALEOTO, THE
See Lynch, Hannah (trans.).

GREAT GENTLEMAN IN THE LITTLE PARLOUR
See Dibdin, Thomas John. Under the Rose.

GREAT GRIM JOHN OF GAUNT AND THE ENCHANTED LANCE OF ROBIN GOODFELLOW
See Blanchard, Edward Litt Leman. Harlequin and Friar Bacon.

GREAT GUN TRICK, THE
See Sorrell, William J.

GREAT MILLIONAIRE, THE
See Raleigh, Cecil.

GREAT NEWS FROM FRANCE
See Maclaren, Archibald. Whimsicality.

GREAT PER-CENTAGE QUESTION
See Brough, William. Upstairs and Downstairs.

GREAT PINK PEARL, THE
See Carton, R. C.

GREAT PRINCESS SHOW
See Brough, William. Turko the Terrible.

GREAT ROC OF THE DIAMOND VALLEY AND THE SEVEN WONDERS OF THE WORLD
See Blanchard, Edward Litt Leman. Harlequin Sinbad the Sailor.

GREAT RUSSIAN BEAR, THE
See Morton, Thomas, jr.

GREAT SENSATION TRIAL, THE
See Brough, William.

GREAT TRAGIC REVIVAL, THE
See Brougham, John.

GRECIAN DAUGHTER, THE
See Kemble, John Philip (arr.).
See Murphy, Arthur.

GRECIANS, THE
See Vaughan, Mrs.

GREEK BOY, THE
See Lover, Samuel.

GREEK SLAVE
See Fitzball, Edward.
See Hall, Owen.

GREEN, FRANK WILLIAM
Babil and Bijou.
See Boucicault, Dionysius Lardner.
Cherry and Fairstar; or, The Pretty Green Bird and the Fairies of the Dancing Waters. London & New York: Samuel French, n.d. Pp. [1]-24. [Lacy's Acting Edition].
Cinderella; or, Harlequin Prince Paragon, the Little Glass Slipper, and the Demons of the Realm of Discord! Birmingham: J. Upton (printer), n.d. Pp. [i-ii], [1]-24. Libretto.
Harlequin Beauty and the Beast. Stratford: Wilson & Whitworth (printer), n.d. Pp. [1]-[22]. Libretto.
Jack and Jill; or, Harlequin Sing-a-Song of Sixpence, the Demon Blackbirds, and the Good Fairies of the Gold and Silver Ferns. London: Phillips, n.d. Pp. [1]-32. Libretto.
Jack the Giant Killer and Tom Thumb; or, Harlequin King Arthur and the Knights of the Round Table. London: Phillips Brothers (printer), n.d. Pp. [1]-30. Libretto.
Lurline the Nymph of the Rhine; or, Harlequin Sir Rupert the Reckless in Search of the Rhino, the River Monster, and the Demons of the Deep. Written with Clay, Thomas Lindsay. Glasgow: n.pub., n.d. Pp. [1]-14. Libretto.
Robinson Crusoe.
See McArdle, John Francis.

GREEN BIRD, THE DANCING WATERS, AND THE SINGING TREE!
See Ellis, George. Harlequin Cherry and Fair Star.

GREEN BUSHES, THE
See Buckstone, John Baldwin.

GREEN BUSINESS
See Dance, Charles. Stock Exchange, The.

GREEN GROW THE RUSHES, OH!
See Byron, Henry James.

GREEN MAN, THE
See Jones, Richard.

GREEN OLD AGE
See Reece, Robert.

GREENBANK, HARRY HEWETSON
Artist's Model, An.
See Hall, Owen.
Circus Girl, The.
See Tanner, James Tolman.
Gaiety Girl, A.
See Hall, Owen.
Geisha, The: A Story of a Tea House.
See Hall, Owen.
Greek Slave, A.
See Hall, Owen.
Incognita.
See Burnand, Francis Cowley.
Mirette.
See Weatherly, Frederick Edward.

Monte Carlo.
See Carlton, Sidney.
Runaway Girl, A.
See Hicks, Edmund Seymour.
San Toy.
See Morton, Edward.

GREENBANK, PERCY
Messenger Boy, The.
See Tanner, James Tolman.

GREENCLOTH: A STORY OF MONTE CARLO
See Dubourg, Augustus W.

GREENE, A. E.
Lord Darcy; or, True Till Death. Cheltenham: Built-Leonard (printer), n.d. Pp. [1]-40.

GREENE, LOUISA LILIAS PLUNKET, MRS. RICHARD JONAS (Baroness)
Nettle Coats; or, The Silent Princess. Written with S., F. M. In William Gorman Wills & Mrs. Greene, *Drawing Room Dramas,* Edinburgh & London: William Blackwood & Sons, 1873, pp. [133]-172. *Filed under* Wills, William Gorman. Drawing Room Drama.
Prince Croesus in Search of a Wife. In William Gorman Wills & Mrs. Greene, *Drawing Room Dramas,* Edinburgh & London: William Blackwood & Sons, 1873, pp. [59]-131. *Filed under* Wills, William Gorman. Drawing Room Drama.

GREENE, WILLIAM A.
D'Enghien. London: Smith Brothers & Titford (priv.), 1842. Pp. [i], [1]-[vi], [1]-[58].

GREEN-EYED MONSTER, THE
See Planché, James Robinson.

GREENWOOD, THOMAS LONGDON
Bluebeard.
See Blanchard, Edward Litt Leman.
Cinderella.
See Blanchard, Edward Litt Leman.
Death of Life in London, The; or, Tom and Jerry's Funeral. Baltimore: J. Robinson, 1823. Pp. [1]-24.
Harlequin Robin Hood and Little John; or, Merrie England in the Olden Time. Music by Montgomery, W. Pp. [1]-16. Libretto.
Jack Sheppard; or, The House-breaker of the Last Century. London: John Cumberland, n.d. Pp. [1]-68.
Old Izaak Walton; or, Tom Moore of Fleet Street, the Silver Trout, and the Seven Sisters of Tottenham. London: Davidson, n.d. Pp. [1]-13. Libretto.
Paul the Pilot; or, The Wreck of the Raven. London: John Cumberland, n.d. Pp. [i-ii], [1]-44. Cumberland's Minor Theatre, XV.
Sinbad the Sailor.
See Blanchard, Edward Litt Leman.

GREET, DORA VICTOIRE, MRS.
Elsie's Rival. London & New York: Samuel French, n.d. Pp. [1]-11. [Lacy's Acting Edition].
Thrown Together. London & New York: Samuel French, n.d. Pp. [1]-9. [Lacy's Acting Edition].

GREGG, TRESHAM DAMES, REV.
King Edward the Sixth. London: Charles Westerton, 1857. Pp. [i]-[iv], [1]-128.
Mary Tudor, First Queen Regnant of England. London: J. Kendrick, 1858. Pp. [i]-[x], [1]-126.
Queen Elizabeth; or, The Origin of Shakespeare. London: William MacIntosh, 1872. Pp. [i]-viii, [1]-128.

GREGORY VII
See Horne, Richard Hengist.

GREIN, JACK T. (pseud. of Grein, Jacob Thomas)
On the Brink. London & New York: Samuel French, n.d. Pp. [1]-12. [French's Acting Edition]. *Filed under* Grein, Jacob Thomas.

GREIN, JACOB THOMAS
See Grein, Jack T.

GRETCHEN
See Gilbert, William Schwenck.

GRETNA GREEN
See Dromcolloher, Lawrence.

GREVILLE, BEATRICE VIOLET GRAHAM, LADY
Old Friends. London & New York: Samuel French, n.d. Pp. [1]-22. [Lacy's Acting Edition].

GREY DOUBLET, THE
See Lemon, Mark.

GREY MAN OF TOTTENHAM!
See Almar, George. Seven Sisters, The.

GRIERSON'S WAY
See Esmond, Henry Vernon.

GRIEVING'S A FOLLY
See Leigh, Richard.

GRIFFIN, GERALD
Gisippus; or, The Forgotten Friend. London: Maxwell, 1842. Pp. [1-6], [i]-[iv], [1]-77. 2nd ed.
Gisippus; or, The Forgotten Friend. New York: John Douglas, 1848. Pp. [i]-[viii], [9]-71. Modern Standard Drama, 69. Promptbook.

GRIFFITHS, ARTHUR
Rift within the Lute, The.
See Dickinson, Charles H.

GRILLPARZER, FRANZ
Sappho.
See Bramsen, John (trans.).
See Lee, Eliza Buckminster, Mrs. (trans.).

GRIMALDI
See Bailey, William.
See Boucicault, Dionysius Lardner.

GRIMALKIN
See Rodwell, George Herbert Bonaparte.

GRIMALKIN THE GREAT
See Blanchard, Edward Litt Leman.

GRIMSHAW, BAGSHAW, AND BRADSHAW
See Morton, John Maddison.

GRIN BUSHES!, THE
See Byron, Henry James.

GRINDROD, CHARLES
King Edward II. In [*Plays from English History,* London: Kegan Paul, Trench, 1883], pp. [217]-267.
King Edward V. In [*Plays from English History,* London: Kegan Paul, Trench, 1883], pp. [269]-352.
King Henry I. In *Plays from English History,* London: Kegan Paul, Trench, 1883, pp. [i-iv], [1]-58.
King Henry II. In [*Plays from English History,* London: Kegan Paul, Trench, 1883], pp. [59]-130.
King Henry III. In [*Plays from English History,* London: Kegan Paul, Trench, 1883], pp. [131]-215.
King James I. In [*Plays from English History,* London: Kegan Paul, Trench, 1883], pp. [353]-454.

GRINGOIRE THE BALLAD-MONGER
See Shirley, Arthur.

GRINN, THE BROTHERS
See Blanchard, Edward Litt Leman.

GRISELDA
See Anstruther, Ralph Abercrombie, Sir (trans.).
See Arnold, Edwin, Sir.

GRISELDA; OR, LA VIRTU IN CIMENTO (anon.)
London: W. Winchester & Son (printer), 1815. Pp. [i], [1]-37.

GRIST, WILLIAM (trans.)
Secret Marriage, The. *Also:* Il Matrimonio Segreto. Music by Cimarosa, Domenico. London (Sydenham): Crystal Palace Co., 1877. Pp. [i], [1]-32. Libretto.

GRIST TO THE MILL
See Planché, James Robinson.

GRIZELLE
See Oxberry, William Henry.

GROSETTE, HENRY WILLIAM
Raymond and Agnes!; or, The Bleeding Nun of Lindenberg. London: John Duncombe, n.d. Pp. [1]-26. Duncombe's Edition.

GROSSMITH, GEORGE, JR
Cups and Saucers. Music by Grossmith, George, Jr. Boston: Oliver Ditson, n.d. Pp. [1]-14. Vocal score.

GROSSMITH, WEEDON
    Commission, A. London & New York: Samuel French, c.1904. Pp. [1]-25. [Lacy's Acting Edition].
GROTTO ON THE STREAM, THE
    See Stirling, Edward.
GROVE, FLORENCE CRAUFURD
    Forget-Me-Not.
        See Merivale, Herman Charles.
GROVER, HENRY MONTAGUE
    Anne Boleyn. London: Longman, Rees, Orme, Brown, & Green, 1826. Pp. [i]-[viii], [1]-135.
    Socrates. London: Longman, Rees, Orme, Brown, & Green, 1828. Pp. [ii]-[xvi], [1]-197.
GROVER, JOHN HOLMES
    That Rascal Pat. New York & London: Samuel French, n.d. Pp. [1]-16. French's Minor Drama, 303. Promptbook.
GROVES, CHARLES
    Golden Wedding, A.
        See Phillpotts, Eden.
GROVES OF BLARNEY, THE
    See Hall, Anna Maria Fielding, Mrs. Samuel Carter.
GRUBE, MAX
    Wreckage.
        See Hein, Gustav (trans.).
GRUNDY, SYDNEY
    Arabian Nights, The. London: Samuel French; New York: T. Henry French, n.d. Pp. [1]-49. [French's Acting Edition (late Lacy's), 2004].
    Arabian Nights, The. New York: Dick & Fitzgerald, n.d. Pp. [1]-44.
    Beauty.
        See Sims, George Robert.
    Bells of Haslemere, The.
        See Pettitt, Henry Alfred.
    Black Tulip, The. Pp. [i-iii], [1]-18, [i-ii], [1]-15, [i-ii], [1]-15, [i-ii], [1]-13, [i-ii], [1]-16. Pagination by act. Typescript.
    Bunch of Violets, A. New York & London: Samuel French, c.1901. Pp. [3]-57. French's International Copyrighted Edition of the Works of the Best Authors, 47.
    Debt of Honour, A. London: Thomas Scott (priv.), n.d. Pp. [1]-20.
    Fool's Paradise, A. London: Samuel French; New York: T. Henry French, c.1898. Pp. [1]-57. [Lacy's Acting Edition].
    Fool's Paradise, A. London & New York: Samuel French, c.1898. Pp. [1]-[64].
    Glass of Fashion, The. London & New York: Samuel French, c.1898. Pp. [1]-60. [French's International Copyrighted Edition of the Works of the Best Authors].
    Haddon Hall. Music by Sullivan, Arthur. London: Chappell, c.1892. Pp. [1]-51. Libretto.
    Haddon Hall. Music by Sullivan, Arthur. London: Chappell, c.1892. Pp. [i-iv], [1]-169. Vocal score.
    Head of Romulus, The. New York & London: Samuel French, c.1900. Pp. [1]-24. [Lacy's Acting Edition].
    In Honor Bound. New York: Harold Roorbach, n.d. Pp. [1]-19.
    Late Mr. Castello, The. New York & London: Samuel French, c.1901. Pp. [1]-52. [French's International Copyrighted Edition of the Works of the Best Authors], 46.
    Little Change, A. London & New York: Samuel French, n.d. Pp. [1]-23. French's Acting Edition (late Lacy's), 1414.
    Man Proposes. London: Samuel French; New York: Samuel French & Son, n.d. Pp. [1]-16. Promptbook.
    Marriage of Convenience, A. [London: Mrs. Marshall's Typewriting Office, 1897]. Pp. [i], [1]-25, [i], [1]-22, [i], [1]-26, [i], [1]-27. Pagination by act. Typescript promptbook.
    Musketeers, The. [London: Miss Dickens's Typewriting Office]. Pp. [i-iv], [1]-9, [i], [1]-13, [i], [1]-41, [i], [1]-32. Pagination by tableau. Typescript promptbook.
    New Woman, The. London: Chiswick Press (printer), 1894. Pp. [1]-104. Promptbook.

Old Jew, An. New York: American & Foreign Dramatists, 1894. Pp. [1]-130.
    Pair of Spectacles, A. London: Samuel French; New York: T. Henry French, c.1898. Pp. [1]-57. French's Acting Edition (late Lacy's), 2122.
    Silver Shield, The. London: Samuel French; New York: T. Henry French, c.1898. Pp. [1]-56.
    Snowball, The. London: Samuel French; New York: Samuel French & Son, n.d. Pp. [1]-45. Promptbook.
    Sowing the Wind. N.p.: n.pub., 1893. Pp. [1]-68. Promptbook.
    Sympathetic Souls. New York & London: Samuel French, c.1900. Pp. [1]-19. French's International Copyrighted Edition of the Works of the Best Authors, 33.
GUARDIAN, THE
    See Garrick, David.
GUARDIAN ANGEL, THE
    See Brooks, Charles William Shirley.
GUARDIAN SYLPH!, THE
    See Selby, Charles.
GUARDIANS
    See Tobin, John. Faro Table, The.
GUARDIANS, THE; OR, THE MAN OF MY CHOICE (anon.)
    Bath: Wood & Cunningham (printer), 1808. Pp. [i]-[viii], [5]-100.
GUDEMAN O' BALLANGEICH
    See Murray, William Henry Wood. Cramond Brig.
GUGLIELMO TELL
    See Maggioni, Manfredo (trans.).
    See William Tell (anon.).
GUIDO FAWKES
    See Stirling, Edward.
GUILLAUME TELL
    See Macfarren, Natalia (trans.). William Tell.
GUILT
    See Frye, William Edward (trans.).
GUILTY
    See Faucquez, Adolphe.
GUILTY AND NOT GUILTY
    See Somerset, Charles A. Roebuck, The.
GUILTY OR NOT GUILTY
    See Dibdin, Thomas John.
GUINEA STAMP, THE
    See Hallward, Cyril.
GULLIVER
    See Byron, Henry James. Gaiety Gulliver, The.
GULLIVER; OR, HARLEQUIN AND THE DEMON BOW WOW (anon.)
    N.p.: n.pub., n.d. Pp. [1]-23. Title page lacking. Libretto.
GULLIVER ON HIS TRAVELS!
    See Akhurst, William M.
GULLIVER'S TRAVELS
    See Paulton, Harry.
GULLY, JAMES MANBY
    Lady of Belleisle, The; or, A Night in the Bastille. London: Thomas Hailes Lacy, n.d. Pp. [1]-38. [Lacy's Acting Edition].
GUNILDA
    See Delap, John.
GUN-MAKER OF MOSCOW, THE
    See Brougham, John.
GUNNER AND THE FOUNDLING
    See Townsend, William Thompson. Topsail Sheet Blocks.
GUNNING, ELIZABETH (later Mrs. James Plunkett) (trans.)
    Wife with Two Husbands, The. By Pixérécourt. London: H. D. Symonds, 1803. Pp. [i],-[viii], [1]-104. *Filed under* Plunkett, Elizabeth.
GUNPOWDER PLOT
    See Emson, Frank E.
    See Rhodes, George Ambrose. Fifth of November, The.
GUNPOWDER TREASON
    See Macfarren, George. Guy Faux.

GUNTON, R. T.
Lancashire Witches, The; or, King Jamie's Frolic. Music by Stanislaus, Frederick. London & Manchester: Forsyth Brothers, n.d. Pp. [i-iv], 1-277. Vocal score.

GURNEY, ARCHER THOMPSON
Iphigenia at Delphi. London: Longman, Brown, Green, & Longmans, 1855. Pp. [i]-[viii], [1]-125.
King Charles the First. London: William Pickering, 1846. Pp. [i]-[xvii], [1]-276.
King Charles the First. London: William Pickering, 1852. Pp. [i]-[xiv], [1]-254. 2nd ed.
Turandot, Princess of China. Frankfort: Streng & Schneider, n.d. Pp. [i]-vi, [1]-114.

GURNEY, ARCHER THOMPSON (trans.)
Faust, Part 2. By Goethe. London: Senior, Heathcote, & Senior, 1842. Pp. [i]-iv, [1]-[xii], [1]-336.

GURNEY, EDMUND
Grandad's Darling. London: Capper & Newton, n.d. Pp. [1]-21. Lynn's Acting Edition, 16.

GURNEY, RICHARD
Romeo and Juliet Travesty. London: T. Hookham jr & E. T. Hookam; J. M. Richardson, 1812. Pp. [i]-[xii], [1]-71. *Filed under* Romeo and Juliet Travesty (anon.).

GUSTAVE III
See Davidson, Frances A., Mrs. (trans.). Gustavus III.

GUSTAVUS III
See Davidson, Frances A., Mrs. (trans.).

GUSTAVUS OF SWEDEN
See Thackeray, Thomas James.

GUSTAVUS THE THIRD
See Milner, Henry M.
See Planché, James Robinson.

GUSTAVUS VASA
See Brooke, Henry.
See Dimond, William.
See Dimond, William. Hero of the North, The.

GUTHRIE, THOMAS ANSTEY
See Anstey, F.

GUV'NOR, THE
See Reece, Robert.

GUY, EARL OF WARWICK
See Morton, John Maddison.

GUY FAUX
See Macfarren, George.

GUY FAWKES
See Burnand, Francis Cowley.
See Smith, Albert Richard.

GUY MANNERING
See Terry, Daniel.

GWEN
See Morris, Lewis.

GWYNNETH VAUGHAN
See Lemon, Mark.

GYCIA
See Morris, Lewis.

GYPSEY OF MADRID, THE
See Tobin, John (trans.).

GYPSEY OF THE GLEN
See Jerrold, Douglas William. Bampfylde Moore Carew.

GYPSEY'S PROPHECY
See Terry, Daniel. Guy Mannering.

GYPSUM, NICHOLAS
Architect, The. London: Jordan & Maxwell, 1807. Pp. [i]-[xx], [13]-97.

H., A. L.
Lady Elizabeth Poole Gubbins. London & New York: Samuel French, n.d. Pp. [1]-11. [Lacy's Acting Edition].

H., C.
Two Friends, The; or, The Liverpool Merchant. London: Earle & Hamet; W. Gebhart, 1800. Pp. [i]-iv, [1]-88. *Filed under* Two Friends (anon.).

H., E. B. (arr.)
Hamlet, Prince of Denmark, A Study of. By Shakespeare, William. London: Thomas Scott (printer), 1875. Pp. [1]-53.

H., I. J.
See Holroyd, John Joseph.

H., J.
See MacCarthy, Denis Florence.

H.A.Y.
See Hay, Frederic.

H.B.
See Peake, Richard Brinsley.

HADDON HALL
See Grundy, Sydney.

HAGAR
See Hanham, Ernest E.

HAINES, JOHN THOMAS
Alice Grey, the Suspected One; or, The Moral Brand. London: James Pattie, n.d. Pp. [1]-59. Promptbook.
Amilie; or, The Love Test. Music by Rooke, W. M. Baltimore: Joseph Robinson, n.d. Pp. [1]-35. Robinson's Edition.
Angeline. *Also:* Angeline le Lis. London: Chapman & Hall, n.d. Pp. [1]-19. Webster's Acting National Drama, 37.
Angeline. *Also:* Angeline le Lis. London: John Dicks, n.d. Pp. [1]-10. Dicks' Standard Plays, 669.
Angeline le Lis.
See Angeline.
Austerlitz; or, The Soldier's Bride. Music by Glover, G. W. London: John Cumberland, n.d. Pp. [1]-53. Cumberland's Minor Theatre, XIV. *Filed under* Cumberland, John. Cumberland's Minor Theatre, XIV.
Austerlitz; or, The Soldier's Bride. Music by Glover, G. W. London: John Cumberland, n.d. Pp. [1]-53. Cumberland's Minor Theatre, 126. Promptbook.
Breakers Ahead!; or, A Seaman's Log! London: John Duncombe, n.d. Pp. [1]-48. Duncombe's Edition. Promptbook.
Charming Polly, The; or, Lucky or Unlucky Days. London: John Duncombe, n.d. Pp. [1]-46. Duncombe's Acting Edition of the British Theatre, 235.
Factory Boy, The. London: J. Pattie, n.d. Pp. [1]-50.
French Spy, The; or, The Siege of Constantina. New York: Samuel French, n.d. Pp. [1]-24. French's Standard Drama, 153. Promptbook.
Henrique; or, The Love Pilgrim! Music by Rooke, W. M. London: W. Wright (printer), n.d. Pp. [i]-vi, [7]-44. Libretto.
House Divided, A. London: John Dicks, n.d. Pp. [1]-11. Tightly bound; some loss of text. Dicks' Standard Plays, 576.
Idiot Witness, The; or, A Tale of Blood. London: John Duncombe, n.d. Pp. [1]-24. Duncombe's Edition.
Jacob Faithful; or, The Life of a Thames Waterman! London: John Duncombe, n.d. Pp. [1]-50. Duncombe's Edition.
Legend of Walworth, A.
See Richard Plantagenet.
Life of a Woman, The; or, A Curate's Daughter. N.p.: n.pub., n.d. Pp. [1-15], 16-54, [55-59]. Pp. 1-15, 55-59 in ms. Promptbook.
Maidens Beware! London: John Duncombe, n.d. Pp. [1]-22. Duncombe's Edition.
My Poll and My Partner Joe. London: John Cumberland, n.d. Pp. [1]-53. Cumberland's Minor Theatre, IX. *Filed under* Cumberland, John. Cumberland's Minor Theatre, IX.
My Poll and My Partner Joe. Music by Jolly. London: Thomas Hailes Lacy, n.d. Pp. [3]-51. [Lacy's Acting Edition].
Nick of the Woods; or, The Altar of Revenge! London: Thomas Hailes Lacy, n.d. Pp. [1]-49.
North Pole, The; or, A Tale of the Frozen Regions. N.p.: n.pub., n.d. Pp. [65]-76. Title page lacking. Promptbook.
Ocean of Life, The; or, Every Inch a Sailor. London: Thomas Hailes Lacy, n.d. Pp. [3]-57. [Lacy's Acting Edition].
Ocean of Life, The; or, Every Inch a Sailor! Music by Jolly. London: John Cumberland, n.d. Pp. [1]-57. Cumberland's Minor Theatre, XI. *Filed under* Cumberland, John. Cumberland's Minor Theatre, XI.

Queen for a Day, A. Music by Adam, Adolphe. London: S. G. Fairbrother, n.d. Pp. [1]-24. Libretto.

Rattlin the Reefer; or, The Tiger of the Sea! London: John Duncombe, n.d. Pp. [1]-48. Duncombe's Edition.

Richard Plantagenet. London: John Cumberland, n.d. Pp. [1]-57. Cumberland's Minor Theatre, XIV. *Filed under* Cumberland, John. Cumberland's Minor Theatre, XIV.

Richard Plantagenet. *Also:* A Legend of Walworth. London: John Cumberland, n.d. Pp. [1]-57. [Cumberland's Minor Theatre].

Ruth; or, The Lass That Loves a Sailor. London: Thomas Hailes Lacy, n.d. Pp. [1]-49.

Uncle Oliver; or, A House Divided. London: James Pattie, n.d. Pp. [1]-30. Pattie's Universal Stage or Theatrical Prompt Book, 3.

Wizard of the Wave, The; or, The Ship of the Avenger. London: J. Pattie, n.d. Pp. [i]-[vi], [7]-54.

Wraith of the Lake!, The; or, The Brownie's Brig! London: John Duncombe, n.d. Pp. [1]-34. Duncombe's Edition.

Yew Tree Ruins, The; or, The Wreck, the Miser, and the Mines. London: Thomas Hailes Lacy, n.d. Pp. [1]-51.

HAIR-CUTTING, SINGEING, AND SHAMPOOING
    See Anstey, F.

HAKE, THOMAS GORDON

Piromides, The. London: Saunders & Otley, 1839. Pp. [i-viii], [1]-84.

Serpent Play, The. London: Chatto & Windus, 1883. Pp. [i-iv], [1]-110.

HAL, THE HIGHWAYMAN
    See Paull, Harry Major.

HALE, WILLIAM PALMER

Godiva; or, Ye Ladye of Coventrie and Ye Exyle Fayrie. Written with Talfourd, Francis. London: Hailes Lacy, n.d. Pp. [1]-21.

Guy Fawkes.
    See Smith, Albert Richard.

Mandarin's Daughter!, The; or, The Willow-Pattern Plate. Written with Talfourd, Francis. London: Thomas Hailes Lacy, n.d. Pp. [1]-28. [Lacy's Acting Edition].

Thetis and Peleus; or, The Chain of Roses. Written with Talfourd, Francis. London: Thomas Hailes Lacy, n.d. Pp. [1]-21. [Lacy's Acting Edition].

HALF AN HOUR'S COURTSHIP
    See Planché, James Robinson.

HALF CASTE, THE
    See Robertson, Thomas William.

HALF WAY TO ARCADY
    See Sturgis, Julian Russell.

HALFORD, JOHN

Faust and Marguerite; or, The Devil's Draught. London: Thomas Hailes Lacy, n.d. Pp. [1]-46.

HALIDON HILL
    See Scott, Walter, Sir.

HALL, ANNA MARIA FIELDING, MRS. SAMUEL CARTER

French Refugee, The. London: John Macrone, 1837. Pp. [i-iv], [1]-27.

Groves of Blarney, The. London: John Dicks, n.d. Pp. [1]-19. Dicks' Standard Plays, 453.

Mabel's Curse! London: John Duncombe, n.d. Pp. [1]-24. Duncombe's Edition.

St. Pierre, the Refugee. London: John Macrone, 1837. Pp. [i-ii], [1]-27.

HALL, OWEN (pseud. of Davis, James)

Artist's Model, An. Written with Greenbank, Harry Hewetson. Music by Jones, Sidney. London: Hopwood & Crew, n.d. Pp. [i-iv], [1]-139. Vocal score.

Florodora. Written with Boyd-Jones, Ernest; Rubens, Paul. Music by Stuart, Leslie. London: Francis, Day, & Hunter, c.1899. Pp. [i-iv], [1]-224. Vocal score.

Florodora. Written with Boyd-Jones, Ernest; Rubens, Paul. Music by Stuart, Leslie. Pp. [i-ii], [1]-57, [i], [1]-43. Pagination by act. Typescript libretto.

Gaiety Girl, A. Written with Greenbank, Harry Hewetson. Music by Jones, Sidney. London: Hopwood & Crew, n.d. Pp. [i-iv], 1-152. Vocal score.

Geisha, The: A Story of a Tea House. Written with Greenbank, Harry Hewetson. Music by Jones, Sidney. London: Hopwood & Crew, c.1896. Pp. [i-iv], 1-206. Vocal score.

Greek Slave, A. Written with Greenbank, Harry Hewetson; Ross, Adrian (pseud. of Ropes, Arthur Reed). Music by Jones, Sidney. [London: Mrs. Marshall's Type Writing Office, 1898]. Pp. [i], [1]-50, [i], [1]-47, [i], [1]-36. Pagination by act. Act I (two versions) and part of Act II only. Typescript promptbook libretto.

HALL, WILLIAM SEWARD

Empire of Philanthropy, The. London: Hatchard & Son; John Booth (priv.), 1822. Pp. [i-viii], [1]-156.

HALL OF SPECTRES
    See Dibdin, Thomas John. Harlequin's Habeas.

HALL OF STATUES
    See A'Beckett, Gilbert Abbott. Magic Mirror, The.

HALL PORTER, THE
    See Lover, Samuel.

HALLIDAY, ANDREW

Actor's Retreat, The.
    See Brough, William.

Amy Robsart. 270 leaves. Manuscript.

April Fool, An.
    See Brough, William.

Area Belle, The.
    See Brough, William.

Census, The.
    See Brough, William.

Checkmate. London: Samuel French; New York: Samuel French & Son, n.d. Pp. [1]-42. French's Acting Edition (late Lacy's).

Colleen Bawn Settled at Last, The.
    See Brough, William.

Daddy Gray. New York: Robert M. DeWitt, n.d. Pp. [1]-30. DeWitt's Acting Plays, 20.

Doing Banting.
    See Brough, William.

Going to the Dogs!
    See Brough, William.

Kenilworth; or, Ye Queene, Ye Earle, and Ye Maydenne. Written with Lawrance, Frederic. London: Thomas Hailes Lacy, n.d. Pp. [1]-45. [Lacy's Acting Edition].

Kenilworth; or, Ye Queene, Ye Earle, and Ye Maydenne. Written with Lawrance, Frederic. London: Thomas Hailes Lacy, n.d. Pp. [1]-45. Promptbook.

Kenilworth; or, Ye Queene, Ye Earle, and Ye Maydenne. Written with Lawrance, Frederic. London: Samuel French; New York: Samuel French & Son, n.d. Pp. [1]-46. Last ed., rev.

Little Em'ly. New York: DeWitt, n.d. Pp. [1]-44. DeWitt's Acting Plays, 295.

Loving Cup, The. London: Thomas Hailes Lacy, n.d. Pp. [1]-44.

Mountain Dhu!; or, The Knight! the Lady! and the Lake! London: Strand (printer), 1866. Pp. [1]-37.

Mudborough Election!
    See Brough, William.

My Heart's in the Highlands.
    See Brough, William.

Nicholas Nickleby. Pp. [1]-161. Manuscript promptbook.

Notre Dame; or, The Gipsy Girl of Paris. New York: Robert M. DeWitt, n.d. Pp. [1]-33. DeWitt's Acting Plays, 300.

Pretty Horsebreaker, The.
    See Brough, William.

Romeo and Juliet; or, The Cup of Cold Poison. London: Thomas Scott (printer), n.d. Pp. [i], [1]-39. Title page lacking. Promptbook.

Shilling Day at the Great Exhibition, A.
    See Brough, William.

Upstairs and Downstairs.
    See Brough, William.

Valentine!, A.
    See Brough, William.

HALLIDAY, ANDREW (arr.)
    Antony and Cleopatra. By Shakespeare, William. London: Tinsley Brothers, 1873. Pp. [i]-[ix], 10-64.
HALLWARD, CYRIL
    Guinea Stamp, The. London: Samuel French; New York: T. Henry French, n.d. Pp. [1]-21. [Lacy's Acting Edition].
HALM, FREDERICK
    See Halm, Friedrich.
HALM, FRIEDRICH
    Gladiator of Ravenna, The.
        See Charlton, William Henry (trans.).
        See Martin, Theodore, Sir (trans.).
        See Vericour, Raymond de (trans.).
    Griselda.
        See Anstruther, Ralph Abercrombie, Sir (trans.).
    Ingomar, the Son of the Wilderness.
        See Charlton, William Henry (trans.).
    Son of the Wilderness, The.
        See Charlton, William Henry (trans.).
HALVEI THE UNKNOWN
    See Wilks, Thomas Egerton.
HAMILTON, COSMO
    Jerry and a Sunbeam. London & New York: Samuel French, n.d. Pp. [1]-13.
HAMILTON, EUGENE LEE
    See Lee-Hamilton, Eugene.
HAMILTON, HENRY
    Carmen. Pp. [1]-73. Typescript promptbook.
    Cheer, Boys, Cheer.
        See Harris, Augustus Henry Glossop.
    Derby Winner, The.
        See Harris, Augustus Henry Glossop.
    Dick Whittington.
        See Harris, Augustus Henry Glossop.
    Harvest. London & New York: Samuel French, n.d. Pp. [1]-67. French's Acting Edition (late Lacy's). Promptbook.
    Moths. Pp. [i], [1-47], [1-45], [1-46], [1-48]. Pagination by act. Manuscript promptbook.
    Our Regiment. London & New York: Samuel French, n.d. Pp. [1]-55. [Lacy's Acting Edition].
    Shadow Sceptre, A. Somerset: Excelsior Press (printer) (priv.), n.d. Pp. [1]-103.
    Three Musketeers, The. Pp. [i-vi], [1]-40, [i], [1]-42, [i], [1]-34, [i], [1]-31, [i], [1]-29 Pagination by act. Typescript promptbook.
    Tipperary Legacy, The.
        See Coyne, Joseph Stirling.
    White Heather, The.
        See Raleigh, Cecil.
HAMILTON, R. S.
    Almourah, the Corsair; or, A Brother's Vengeance. Music by Hart, Miss A. J. Belfast: Joseph Smyth (printer), 1821. Pp. [i]-vi, [7]-95.
HAMILTON, RALPH, COL.
    David Rizzio. London: John Lowndes, 1820. Pp. [i-viii], [1]-44.
    Elphi Bey; or, The Arab's Faith. London: W. Clowes (printer), 1817. Pp. [i]-[x], [1]-62.
HAMILTON-KNIGHT, F.
    Postscript, The. London & New York: Samuel French, n.d. Pp. [1]-20. [French's Acting Edition].
HAMLET
    See Barrett, Wilson (arr.).
    See Forbes-Robertson, Johnston (arr.).
    See Irving, Henry (arr.).
    See Kean, Charles John (arr.).
    See Kemble, John Philip (arr.).
    See Shakespeare, William.
    See Taylor, Tom (arr.).
HAMLET IMPROVED
    See Colomb, George Hatton, Col.
HAMLET, PRINCE OF DENMARK, A STUDY OF
    See H., E. B. (arr.).

HAMLET THE DANE
    See Beckington, Charles.
HAMLET TRAVESTIE
    See Poole, John.
HAMPSHIRE HOG, A
    See Melford, Mark.
HANCOCK, WILLIAM
    John Smith. Clyde, Ohio: A. D. Ames, n.d. Pp. [1]-10. Ames' Series of Standard and Minor Drama, 11.
    John Smith. London: Thomas Hailes Lacy, n.d. Pp. [1]-14.
    Margate Sands. London: Thomas Hailes Lacy, n.d. Pp. [3]-16. Title page lacking. Lacy's Acting Edition. Promptbook.
    Mr. Scroggins; or, Change of Name. New York: Robert M. DeWitt, n.d. Pp. [1]-14. DeWitt's Acting Plays, 108.
    Stolen—£20 Reward! London: Thomas Hailes Lacy, n.d. Pp. [1]-16. [Lacy's Acting Edition].
HAND AND GLOVE
    See Conquest, George.
HAND OF CARDS, THE
    See Stirling, Edward.
HANDSEL PENNY, THE
    See Selby, Charles.
HANDSOME HUSBAND, A
    See Planché, Elizabeth (Eliza) St. George, Mrs. James Robinson.
HANDSOME IS THAT HANDSOME DOES
    See Turner, Charles James Ribton.
HANDY ANDY
    See Montgomery, Henry William.
HANHAM, ERNEST E.
    Hagar. Southsea: Frampton (printer), n.d. Pp. [i-ii], [1]-15.
HANNAN, CHARLES
    Fragment, A. London: Samuel French; New York: T. Henry French, n.d. Pp. [1]-18. [Lacy's Acting Edition].
    Gipsy, The; or, Shadows from the Past. London: Capper & Newton, n.d. Pp. [1]-26. Lynn's Acting Edition, 10.
    Lily of the Field, The. London: Capper & Newton, n.d. Pp. [1]-18. Lynn's Acting Edition, 18.
    New Groom, The. London & New York: Samuel French, n.d. Pp. [1]-28. [Lacy's Acting Edition].
    Richard Wye. London & New York: Samuel French, n.d. Pp. [1]-18. [Lacy's Acting Edition].
    Setting of the Sun, The. London: Samuel French; New York: Samuel French & Son, n.d. Pp. [1]-14. [Lacy's Acting Edition].
HANNELE
    See Archer, William (trans.).
HANNIBAL
    See Nichol, John.
    See Shore, Louisa Catherine.
HANS OF ICELAND
    See Fitzball, Edward.
HANS VON STEIN
    See Fitzball, Edward.
HANS WALDMAN
    See Ludorff, Franz.
HAPPIEST DAY OF MY LIFE, THE
    See Buckstone, John Baldwin.
HAPPIEST MAN ALIVE, THE
    See Bernard, William Bayle.
HAPPY ARCADIA
    See Gilbert, William Schwenck.
HAPPY DAY, A
    See Henry, Richard.
HAPPY DISPATCH, THE
    See Thompson, Alfred.
HAPPY LAND, THE
    See Gilbert, William Schwenck.
HAPPY MAN, THE
    See Lover, Samuel.
HAPPY MEDIUM, A
    See Pemberton, Thomas Edgar.
HAPPY PAIR, A
    See Smith, Spencer Theyre.

HAPPY RETURN, THE
See Law, Arthur.
HAPPY VALLEY
See Brough, William. Rasselas, Prince of Abyssinia.
HARD DAY'S WORK, A
See Bell, Florence Eveleen Eleanore Oliffe, Mrs. Hugh (Lady).
HARD STRUGGLE, A
See Marston, John Westland.
HARD TIMES
See Cooper, Frederick Fox.
HARDING, C. T.
He Must Be Married; or, The Miser Outwitted. In *New British Theatre*, London: A. J. Valpy (printer), 1815, IV, [221]-286. *Filed under* He Must Be Married (anon.).
He's No Conjuror! London: John Duncombe, n.d. Pp. [1]-32. Duncombe's Acting Edition of the British Theatre, 24.
HARDWICKE, COUNTESS OF
See Yorke, Elizabeth Lindsey, Countess of Hardwicke.
HARDWICKE, PELHAM
Bachelor of Arts, A. New York: Samuel French & Son; London: Samuel French, n.d. Pp. [1]-38. Promptbook.
HARDY, THOMAS
Three Wayfarers, The. New York: Scholars' Facsimiles & Reprints, 1943. Pp. [i]-[xviii], [1]-[55].
HARE, JOHN (arr.)
As You Like It. Written with Kendal, William Hunter (arr.). By Shakespeare, William. London: J. Miles (printer), n.d. Pp. [1]-63. *Filed under* As You Like It (anon.).
HARLEQUIN A. B. C. AND THE ENCHANTED REGION OF NURSERY RHYMES
See Blanchard, Edward Litt Leman. Little Jack Horner.
HARLEQUIN ALABASTER
See Dibdin, Charles Isaac Mungo, jr. Goody Two Shoes.
HARLEQUIN ALADDIN AND THE LAMP
See George, G. H.
HARLEQUIN ALFRED THE GREAT
See Lee, Nelson, sr.
HARLEQUIN ALI BABA AND THE ROBBERS OF THE MAGIC CAVE
See Jones, John Wilton. Forty Thieves, The.
HARLEQUIN AND A HOUSE ON FIRE!
See Queen Ladybird and Her Children (anon.).
HARLEQUIN AND BLUFF KING HAL AND THE FAIR MAID OF LEASOWE
See Millward, Charles. Jolly Miller of the Dee, The.
HARLEQUIN AND COCK ROBIN
See Blanchard, Edward Litt Leman. Little Goody Two-Shoes.
HARLEQUIN AND FREEDOM IN HER ISLAND HOME
See Bridgeman, John Vipon. Bluebeard.
HARLEQUIN AND FRIAR BACON
See Blanchard, Edward Litt Leman.
See Farley, Charles.
HARLEQUIN AND GEORGE BARNWELL
See Younge, Henry.
HARLEQUIN AND GOOD QUEEN BESS
See Lee, Nelson, sr.
HARLEQUIN AND HUMPO
See Dibdin, Thomas John.
HARLEQUIN AND HUMPTY DUMPTY
See Fitzball, Edward.
HARLEQUIN AND MERLIN
See Dibdin, Charles Isaac Mungo, jr. Wizard's Wake.
HARLEQUIN AND MOORE'S ALMANACK
See Dibdin, Charles Isaac Mungo, jr. Astrologer, The.
HARLEQUIN AND MOTHER CAREY'S CHICKENS
See Barrymore, William. Davy Jones.
HARLEQUIN AND MOTHER GOOSE
See Dibdin, Thomas John.
HARLEQUIN AND MOTHER RED CAP
See Lee, Nelson, sr.
HARLEQUIN AND MOTHER SHIPTON
See Blanchard, Edward Litt Leman. Dragon of Wantley, The.
See Farley, Charles.
HARLEQUIN AND O'DONOGHUE
See Lee, Nelson, sr.
HARLEQUIN AND OLD DADDY LONG-LEGS!
See Buckstone, John Baldwin. Little Miss Muffet and Little Boy Blue.
HARLEQUIN AND OLD MOTHER BUNCH
See Blanchard, Edward Litt Leman. Beauty and the Beast.
HARLEQUIN AND OLD MOTHER SHIPTON
See Blanchard, Edward Litt Leman. Riquet with the Tuft.
HARLEQUIN AND SIR JOHN FALSTAFF, AND THE DEMON HUNTER OF THE ENCHANTED DELL
See Courtney, John. Merry Wives of Windsor, The.
HARLEQUIN AND THE BRITISH LION
See Mayhew, Horace. Plum-Pudding Pantomime, The.
HARLEQUIN AND THE CHILDE OF HALE; OR, THE KING OF THE RED NOSES AND THE LIVER QUEEN (anon.)
By Cousin Joe (pseud.). Liverpool: S. A. Hurton, (printer), n.d. Pp. [1]-12. Libretto.
HARLEQUIN AND THE CRUEL UNCLE
See Buckstone, John Baldwin. Babes in the Wood, The.
HARLEQUIN AND THE DEMON BOW WOW
See Gulliver (anon.).
HARLEQUIN AND THE DUN COW
See Morton, John Maddison. Guy, Earl of Warwick.
HARLEQUIN AND THE FAIRIES OF THE DIAMOND VALLEY
See Blanchard, Edward Litt Leman. Sinbad the Sailor.
HARLEQUIN AND THE FAIRY HIVE
See Barrymore, William. Queen Bee, The.
HARLEQUIN AND THE FAIRY OF THE TRUE LOVER'S KNOT
See Buckstone, John Baldwin. Valentine's Day.
HARLEQUIN AND THE FAIRY PARI BANON
See Barrymore, William. Silver Arrow, The.
HARLEQUIN AND THE FAIRY SLIPPER
See Blanchard, Edward Litt Leman. Cinderella.
HARLEQUIN AND THE FLYING CHEST; OR, MALEK AND THE PRINCESS SCHIRINE (anon.)
Music by Cooke, T. London: John Miller, 1823. Pp. [1]-24. 2nd ed. Libretto.
HARLEQUIN AND THE FLYING PALACE
See Aladdin and the Wonderful Lamp (anon.).
HARLEQUIN AND THE FLYING WOMEN OF THE LOADSTONE ROCK
See Blanchard, Edward Litt Leman. Peter Wilkins.
HARLEQUIN AND THE FORTY THIEVES
See Blanchard, Edward Litt Leman.
HARLEQUIN AND THE GENIE OF THE RING
See Morton, John Maddison. Aladdin and the Wonderful Lamp.
HARLEQUIN AND THE GENII OF THE ARABIAN NIGHTS!
See A'Beckett, Gilbert Arthur. Ali Baba and the Forty Thieves.
HARLEQUIN AND THE GIRL WHO LOST HER SHEEP
See Buckstone, John Baldwin. Little Bo-Peep.
HARLEQUIN AND THE GNOME KING OF THE GIANT MOUNTAIN
See Blanchard, Edward Litt Leman. Number Nip.
HARLEQUIN AND THE HOUSE THAT JACK BUILT
See Blanchard, Edward Litt Leman.
HARLEQUIN AND THE KING OF THE DIAMOND VALLEY
See Blanchard, Edward Litt Leman. Sinbad the Sailor.
HARLEQUIN AND THE LAND OF TOYS
See Blanchard, Edward Litt Leman. King Humming Top.
HARLEQUIN AND THE MAGIC DONKEY
See Ali Baba and the Forty Thieves (anon.).
HARLEQUIN AND THE MAGIC FIDDLE
See King Jamie (anon.).

HARLEQUIN AND THE MAGIC PUMPKIN AND THE GREAT FAIRY OF THE LITTLE GLASS SLIPPER!
See Blanchard, Edward Litt Leman. Cinderella.

HARLEQUIN AND THE MAGIC SHIELD
See Burnand, Francis Cowley. Valentine and Orson.

HARLEQUIN AND THE MIDWINTER NIGHT'S DREAM
See Nicholls, Harry. Jack and the Beanstalk.

HARLEQUIN AND THE OGRE OF THE SEVEN LEAGUE BOOTS
See Blanchard, Edward Litt Leman. Hop o' My Thumb and His Eleven Brothers.

HARLEQUIN AND THE WHITE CAT! AND THE MAGIC SAPPHIRE
See Soutar, Richard.

HARLEQUIN AND THE WITCHES OF ALLOWAY'S AULD HAUNTED KIRK
See Bridgeman, John Vipon. Tam o' Shanter.

HARLEQUIN AND THE WOLF IN GRANNY'S CLOTHING
See Bridgeman, John Vipon. Little Red Riding Hood.

HARLEQUIN AND THE WONDERFUL LAMP
See Blanchard, Edward Litt Leman. Aladdin.

HARLEQUIN AND THE WORLD OF FLOWERS
See Blanchard, Edward Litt Leman.

HARLEQUIN AND TIME
See Dibdin, Charles Isaac Mungo, jr. London.

HARLEQUIN AND WILLIAM TELL
See Morton, John Maddison.

HARLEQUIN BEAUTY AND THE BEAST
See Green, Frank William.
See Muskerry, William.

HARLEQUIN BILLY TAYLOR
See Ellis, George.

HARLEQUIN BLACK BIRD (anon.)
[Manchester]: n.pub., n.d. Pp. [4]-45. Title page lacking. Libretto.

HARLEQUIN BLACKBEARD
See Lee, Nelson, sr.

HARLEQUIN BLACKBIRD
See Thompson, Alfred.

HARLEQUIN BLUE BEARD, THE GREAT BASHAW
See Morton, John Maddison.

HARLEQUIN BLUECAP AND THE KING OF THE GOLDEN WATERS
See Blanchard, Edward Litt Leman.

HARLEQUIN CHERRY AND FAIR STAR
See Ellis, George.

HARLEQUIN CHILD OF CHILDWALL AND THE CHOICE SPIRITS OF DINGLE DELL
See Crompton, William. Old Woman Who Lived in a Shoe, The.

HARLEQUIN COCK-ROBIN AND JENNY WREN
See Gilbert, William Schwenck.

HARLEQUIN CORSAIR AND THE LITTLE FAIRY AT THE BOTTOM OF THE SEA
See Brough, William. Conrad and Medora.

HARLEQUIN CRUSADER
See Boleno, Henry.

HARLEQUIN CUPID AND THE KING OF THE GOLD MINES!
See Byron, Henry James. Yellow Dwarf, The.

HARLEQUIN FORTUNATUS AND THE MAGIC PURSE AND WISHING CAP
See Blanchard, Edward Litt Leman. Little King Pippin.

HARLEQUIN FORTUNIO, KING FROG OF FROG ISLAND, AND THE MAGIC TOYS OF LOWTHER ARCADIA!
See Millward, Charles. Hush-a-Bye Baby on the Tree-top.

HARLEQUIN FRIDAY AND THE KING OF THE CARIBEE ISLANDS!
See Byron, Henry James. Robinson Crusoe.

HARLEQUIN FROM KILLARNEY
See Croker, Thomas Crofton. Daniel O'Rourke.

HARLEQUIN GULLIVER AND HIS WIFE; OR, THE THREE KINGS, THE SEVEN CYCLOPS, AND THE FAIRY FAUNS OF THE LIVING WATERS (anon.)

Liverpool: New Adelphi Theatre, n.d. Pp. [1]-31. Libretto.

HARLEQUIN HAROLD AND THE SACK OF THE SAXONS
See Blanchard, Edward Litt Leman. William the Conqueror.

HARLEQUIN HARPER
See Dibdin, Thomas John.

HARLEQUIN HEY DIDDLE DIDDLE THE CAT AND THE FIDDLE AND THE COW THAT JUMPED OVER THE MOON
See Dutnall, M.

HARLEQUIN HOAX
See Dibdin, Thomas John.

HARLEQUIN HOGARTH
See Morton, John Maddison.

HARLEQUIN HOLIDAY AND THE ISLAND OF UPS AND DOWNS
See Blanchard, Edward Litt Leman. See, Saw, Margery Daw.

HARLEQUIN HUDIBRAS!
See Blanchard, Edward Litt Leman.

HARLEQUIN IN HIS ELEMENT
See Dibdin, Thomas John.

HARLEQUIN IN LONDON
See Planché, James Robinson. Doctor Syntax.

HARLEQUIN JACK THE GIANT KILLER
See Blanchard, Edward Litt Leman. Faw! Fee! Fo! Fum!

HARLEQUIN JACK, THE THREE WITCHES, AND THE FAIRY KING
See House that Jack Built, The (anon.).

HARLEQUIN JULIUS CAESAR AND THE DELIGHTFUL DRUID!
See Burnand, Francis Cowley. Boadicea the Beautiful.

HARLEQUIN KING ARTHUR AND THE KNIGHTS OF THE ROUND TABLE
See Blanchard, Edward Litt Leman. Tom Thumb the Great.
See Green, Frank William. Jack the Giant Killer and Tom Thumb.

HARLEQUIN KING ARTHUR AND YE KNIGHTS OF YE ROUND TABLE
See Byron, Henry James. Jack the Giant Killer.

HARLEQUIN KING CRYSTAL
See Saville, Henry Faucitt.

HARLEQUIN KING KOLLYWOBBOL AND THE GENIUS OF GOOD HUMOUR!
See Byron, Henry James. Whittington and His Cat!

HARLEQUIN KING NONSENSE, AND THE SEVEN AGES OF MAN
See Blanchard, Edward Litt Leman. Hey Diddle Diddle.

HARLEQUIN KING OF THE FAIRIES AND THE CRUEL H'UNCLE
See Babes in the Wood, The (anon.).

HARLEQUIN KING PEE-WIT AND HIS MERRY LITTLE MEN!
See Towers, Edward.

HARLEQUIN KING PEPIN; OR, VALENTINE AND ORSON (anon.)
London: S. G. Fairbrother (printer), n.d. Pp. [1]-[15]. Libretto.

HARLEQUIN LEAP-YEAR AND THE MERRY PRANKS OF THE GOOD LITTLE PEOPLE
See Blanchard, Edward Litt Leman. Jack and the Beanstalk.

HARLEQUIN LITTLE RED RIDING-HOOD
See Hood, Tom.

HARLEQUIN LITTLE RED RIDING HOOD AND PRINCE LOVE THE DAY; OR, QUEEN BUSY BEE AND THE FIEND WOLF (anon.)
London: W. Webb, n.d. Pp. [1]-18. Webb's Juvenile Drama. Libretto.

HARLEQUIN LITTLE TOM TUCKER AND THE THREE WISE MEN OF GOTHAM
See Blanchard, Edward Litt Leman. Jack in the Box.

HARLEQUIN LORD MAYOR OF LONDON
See Blanchard, Edward Litt Leman. Whittington and His Cat.
See Whittington and His Cat (anon.).

HARLEQUIN MAN-IN-THE-MOON, THE GIANT GRUMBLE GRIM, AND THE LOVE BIRDS OF FAIRY-LAND!
See Jack and the Bean Stalk and Margery Daw (anon.).

HARLEQUIN MOORE, OF MOORE HALL, AND HIS FAYRE MARGERY
See Hazlewood, Colin Henry. Dragon of Wantley, The.

HARLEQUIN MUNCHAUSEN
See Farley, Charles.

HARLEQUIN NEGRO
See Furibond (anon.).

HARLEQUIN NOVELTY AND THE PRINCESS WHO LOST HER HEART
See Buckingham, Leicester Silk.

HARLEQUIN OLD AESOP
See Fenton, Frederick.

HARLEQUIN OLD FATHER CHRISTMAS AND THE FAIRY QUEEN OF THE SILVER ACACIAS!
See Akhurst, William M. Gulliver on His Travels!

HARLEQUIN OLD KING COUNTERFEIT AND THE WORLD OF COINS!
See Strachan, John S., jr. Little Goody Two-Shoes and Her Queen Anne's Farthing.

HARLEQUIN OUT OF PLACE
See Planché, James Robinson. New Planet, The.

HARLEQUIN PEARL DIVER!
See Dibdin, Charles Isaac Mungo, jr. Mermaid, The.

HARLEQUIN PETER WILKINS AND THE FLYING WOMEN OF WONDERLAND
See George, G. H. Sleeping Beauty, The.

HARLEQUIN PIGGY WIGGY AND THE GOOD CHILD'S HISTORY OF ENGLAND
See Akhurst, William M. Tom Tom, the Piper's Son, and Mary Mary, Quite Contrary.

HARLEQUIN PRIME
See Dibdin, Charles Isaac Mungo, jr. Bang Up!

HARLEQUIN PRINCE CHANTICLEER AND THE PRINCESS OF THE GOLDEN VALLEY
See Millward, Charles. Cock-a-Doodle-Doo.

HARLEQUIN PRINCE PARAGON, THE LITTLE GLASS SLIPPER, AND THE DEMONS OF THE REALM OF DISCORD!
See Green, Frank William. Cinderella.

HARLEQUIN PRINCE PEACOCK AND THE FAIR BRILLIANTA
See Somerset, Charles A. Ladye Bird Bower.

HARLEQUIN PRINCE SPRING AND THE GOOD FAY OF ALL THE YEAR ROUND
See French, George H. King Winter and Princess Summer.

HARLEQUIN PUSS IN BOOTS AND THE MILLER'S SONS
See Blanchard, Edward Litt Leman. Grimalkin the Great.

HARLEQUIN QUEEN MAB AND THE WORLD OF DREAMS
See Blanchard, Edward Litt Leman. Children in the Wood, The.

HARLEQUIN ROBIN HOOD AND HIS MERRY MEN
See A'Beckett, Gilbert Arthur. Babes in the Wood, The.
See McGromagill, Osburn Blackboehm. Babes in the Wood, The.

HARLEQUIN ROBIN HOOD AND LITTLE JOHN
See Greenwood, Thomas Longdon.

HARLEQUIN SINBAD THE SAILOR
See Blanchard, Edward Litt Leman.

HARLEQUIN SINDBAD
See Dibdin, Thomas John. Valley of Diamonds, The.

HARLEQUIN SING-A-SONG OF SIXPENCE, THE DEMON BLACKBIRDS, AND THE GOOD FAIRIES OF THE GOLD AND SILVER FERNS
See Green, Frank William. Jack and Jill.

HARLEQUIN SIR BRUNO THE BRAVE AND THE FAIRY CASKET OF PHANTOM CASTLE
See Doyle, Thomas F. Lucre-Land.

HARLEQUIN SIR HUON OF GUYENNE AND THE FAIRY OF THE MAGIC HORN!
See Oberon! King of the Elves (anon.).

HARLEQUIN SIR RUPERT THE RECKLESS IN SEARCH OF THE RHINO, THE RIVER MONSTER, AND THE DEMONS OF THE DEEP
See Green, Frank William. Lurline the Nymph of the Rhine.

HARLEQUIN, THE CRUEL PRIOR OF CANONBURY, AND THE CHIVALROUS KNIGHTS OF ST. JOHN
See Ye Faire Maide of Islington (anon.).

HARLEQUIN, THE WICKED DEMON, THE GOOD FAIRY, AND THE LITTLE GLASS SLIPPER!
See Jones, John Wilton. Cinderella.

HARLEQUIN THE WRECK, THE ROC, AND THE DIAMOND VALLEY
See Thorn, Geoffrey. Sinbad the Sailor.

HARLEQUIN TOM, THE PIPER'S SON (anon.)
Music by Reeve. London: John Lowndes, 1820. Pp. [1]-16.

HARLEQUIN TWILIGHT
See Crowquill, Alfred. Moon Queen and King Night, The.

HARLEQUIN VALENTINE AND ORSON; OR, HARLEQUIN WILD MAN OF THE WOODS, THE GREEN KNIGHT, AND THE FAIRY OF THE ENCHANTED VALLEY OF SWEET WATERS (anon.)
Music by Chapman. Bristol: I. Arrowsmith, n.d. Pp. [1]-32. Libretto. *Filed under* Harlequin and Orson (anon.).

HARLEQUIN WHITTINGTON
See Farley, Charles.

HARLEQUIN WILD MAN OF THE WOODS, THE GREEN KNIGHT, AND THE FAIRY OF THE ENCHANTED VALLEY OF SWEET WATERS
See Harlequin Valentine and Orson (anon.).

HARLEQUIN WILLIAM THE CONQUEROR AND THE PRETTY WHITE HORSE WITH THE GOLDEN HOOF
See Akhurst, William M. Birth of Beauty, The.

HARLEQUIN'S HABEAS
See Dibdin, Thomas John.

HARLEQUIN'S LOTTERY
See Dibdin, Charles Isaac Mungo, jr. Thirty Thousand.

HARLEQUIN'S MAGNET
See Dibdin, Thomas John.

HARLEQUIN'S TOUR
See Dibdin, Thomas John.

HARLEY, ST. JOHN (pseud. of Pollock, Ellen, Mrs. Julius)
Judael. London: Vinton (printer), 1881. Pp. [1]-60. *Filed under* Pollock, Ellen.
Violent Passion, A. London: Vinton (printer), 1880. Pp. [1]-44. *Filed under* Pollock, Ellen.

HARMONY
See Jones, Henry Arthur.

HARNESS, WILLIAM, REV.
First Born, The. London: Robson, Levey, & Franklyn (printer) (priv.), 1844. Pp. [i-vi], [1]-121.
Welcome and Farewell. London: George Taylor (printer), 1837. Pp. [i-vi], [1]-119.

HAROLD
See Butler, Arthur Gray.
See Dew, Dyer.
See Malet, Edward.
See Tennyson, Alfred, Lord.
See Zglinitzka, Marie von (trans.).

HAROLD HAWK
See Selby, Charles.

HAROUN ALRASCHID
See Dibdin, Thomas John.

HARP OF ALTENBERG, THE
See Jones, Robert St. Clair.

HARPER'S DAUGHTER, THE
See Lewis, Matthew Gregory.
HARPER'S SON AND THE DUKE'S DAUGHTER, THE
See Dibdin, Thomas John.
HARRIES, MARGARET
See Wilson, Margaret Harries, Mrs. Cornwell Baron.
HARRINGTON, NICHOLAS HERBERT
Double Dummy. Written with Yates, Edmund Hodgson. London: Thomas Hailes Lacy, n.d. Pp. [1]-16. [Lacy's Acting Edition].
Hit Him, He Has No Friends.
See Yates, Edmund Hodgson.
If the Cap Fits. Written with Yates, Edmund Hodgson. London: Thomas Hailes Lacy, n.d. Pp. [1]-19. [Lacy's Acting Edition].
My Friend from Leatherhead.
See Yates, Edmund Hodgson.
Night at Notting Hill, A.
See Yates, Edmund Hodgson.
Your Likeness—One Shilling! Written with Yates, Edmund Hodgson. London: Thomas Hailes Lacy, n.d. Pp. [1]-14. [Lacy's Acting Edition].
HARRINGTON, RICHARD
Pedlar Boy, The; or, The Old Mill Ruin. London: Thomas Hailes Lacy, n.d. Pp. [1]-20. [Lacy's Acting Edition].
HARRIS, AUGUSTUS GLOSSOP
Avalanche, The; or, The Trials of the Heart. London: Thomas Hailes Lacy, n.d. Pp. [5]-50. Text complete. [Lacy's Acting Edition].
Cruel to Be Kind.
See Williams, Thomas John.
Doing the Hansom. London: Thomas Hailes Lacy, n.d. Pp. [1]-24.
Gossip. Written with Williams, Thomas John. London: Thomas Hailes Lacy, n.d. Pp. [1]-37. [Lacy's Acting Edition].
Jeannette's Wedding.
See Buckingham, Leicester Silk.
Little Treasure, The. New York: Samuel French, n.d. Pp. [1]-29. French's American Drama, 26.
My Son Diana. London: Thomas Hailes Lacy, n.d. Pp. [1]-19. [Lacy's Acting Edition].
Rose of Castile, The. Written With Falconer, Edmund (pseud. of O'Rourke, Edmund). Music by Balfe, M. W. London: Boosey, n.d. Pp. [i]-[xxvi], 1-275. Libretto and vocal score.
Ruth Oakley.
See Williams, Thomas John.
Ruthven. London: Thomas Hailes Lacy, n.d. Pp. [1]-52. [Lacy's Acting Edition].
Satanella. Written with Falconer, Edmund (pseud. of O'Rourke, Edmund). Music by Balfe, Michael William. London & New York: Boosey, n.d. Pp. [i-iv], 1-268. Vocal score. *Filed under* Falconer, Edmund; Harris, Augustus Glossop.
Satanella; or, The Power of Love. Written with Falconer, Edmund (pseud. of O'Rourke, Edmund). Music by Balfe, M. W. London: Royal English Opera, Covent Garden, n.d. Pp. [1]-39. Libretto.
Tom Thrasher. London: Thomas Hailes Lacy, n.d. Pp. [1]-21. [Lacy's Acting Edition].
Too Much of a Good Thing! London: Thomas Hailes Lacy, n.d. Pp. [1]-20.
Too Much of a Good Thing! London & New York: Samuel French, n.d. Pp. [1]-20. [Lacy's Acting Edition].
Very Serious Affair, A. London: Thomas Hailes Lacy, n.d. Pp. [1]-21. [Lacy's Acting Edition].
HARRIS, AUGUSTUS HENRY GLOSSOP
Amy Robsart. Written with Milliet, Paul. Music by Lara, Isidore. Paris: Choudens Fils, 1894. Pp. [i-ii], [1]-42. French translation of libretto.
Babes in the Wood, Robin Hood and His Merry Men, and Harlequin Who Killed Cock Robin?. Written with Blanchard, Edward Litt Leman; Nicholls, Harry. Music

by Slaughter, Walter A. London: Strand, n.d. Pp. [1]-[78]. Libretto.
Basoche, The; or, King of the Students. Written with Oudin, Eugene. Music by Messager, André. London: Chappell; Boosey, n.d. Pp. [i-iv], 1-273. Vocal score.
Basoche, The; or, King of the Students. Written with Oudin, Eugene. Music by Messager, André. London: Chappel; Boosey, n.d. Pp. [1]-71. Libretto.
Cheer, Boys, Cheer. Written with Raleigh, Cecil; Hamilton, Henry. Pp. [i-vi], [1]-53, 1-84, [1]-[51], [1]-[28]. Pagination by act. Typescript.
Derby Winner, The. Written with Raleigh, Cecil; Hamilton, Henry. London: J. Miles (printer), 1895. Pp. [1]-131.
Dick Whittington. Written with Raleigh, Cecil; Hamilton, Henry. Music by Glover. London: n.pub., n.d. Pp. [1]-104. Libretto.
Jack and the Beanstalk.
See Nicholls, Harry.
Little Genius, The. Written with Sturgess, Arthur. Music by Glover, James M. London: E. Ascherberg, 1896. Pp. [1]-31. Libretto.
Opera Cloak, The.
See Powles, Louis Diston.
Prodigal Daughter, The.
See Pettitt, Henry Alfred.
World, The.
See Meritt, Paul.
HARRIS, CHARLES
White Cockade, The.
See Barnett, Richard Wheldon.
HARRIS, FRANK
Mr. and Mrs. Daventry. London: Richards Press, 1956. Pp. [1]-114.
HARRIS, G. SHIRLEY (trans.)
Nephew as Uncle, The. By Schiller. Leipzig: Voigt & Günther, 1856. Pp. [i-ii], [1]-56.
Nephew as Uncle, The. By Schiller. Newburgh: Gray & Lawson (printer), 1858. Pp. [1]-33. *Filed under* Nephew as Uncle (anon.).
HARRIS, H. G.
Clockmaker's Hat, The.
See Robertson, Thomas William.
HARRIS, HENRY
Forest of Bondy, The; or, The Dog of Montargis! London: Duncombe and Moon, n.d. Pp. [1]-36. Duncombe's Edition.
HARRIS, RICHARD
Young Wives and Old Husbands. London: Samuel Tinsley (priv.), n.d. Pp. [1]-64.
HARRISON, SAMUEL M.
Aladdin and the Wonderful Lamp! Music by Loveday, H. J. N.p.: n.pub., n.d. Pp. [3]-38. Libretto.
Little Jack the Giant Killer. Music by Loveday, H. J. Liverpool: Daily Post (printer), 1871. Pp. [1]-42. Libretto.
Piebald Possum of the Panting Prairie, The. Liverpool: Daily Post Steam Printing Works, 1870. Pp. [1]-8.
HARRISON, WILMOT
Once a Week; or, A Fight for the Franchise. London & New York: Samuel French, n.d. Pp. [1]-16. [Lacy's Acting Edition].
Special Performances. New York: Robert M. DeWitt, n.d. Pp. [1]-16. DeWitt's Acting Plays, 78.
HARSH STEP-FATHER
See Hazlewood, Colin Henry. Taking the Veil.
HART, JAMES P.
Bell Ringer of St. Paul's, The; or, London in 1665. London: [J. Pattie], n.d. Pp. [1]-72.
Canadian War, The. London: J. Pattie, n.d. Pp. [3]-25.
Freemason, The; or, The Secret of the Lodge Room! London: J. Pattie, n.d. Pp. [1]-33.
Mary Le More; or, The Irish Maniac. London: James Pattie, n.d. Pp. [i-iv], [7]-52. Text complete.
Murder of the Glen, The; or, The Old Stone Quarry. London: James Pattie, n.d. Pp. [1]-42.

Post-Boy of Cornwall, The; or, The Fatal Snow-Drift. London: J. Pattie, n.d. Pp. [1]-28. Pattie's Modern Stage, [63].

HARTFORD BRIDGE
See Pearce, William.

HARTOPP, W. W.
Eclipsing the Son. London: Thomas Hailes Lacy, n.d. Pp. [1]-23. [Lacy's Acting Edition].

HARVEST
See Hamilton, Henry.

HARVEST FIELD, THE
See Hetherington, William Maxwell.

HARVEST HOME, THE
See Parry, Thomas.

HARVEST STORM, THE
See Hazlewood, Colin Henry.

HARVEY, FRANK
As London Lives. Pp. [i-ii], [1]-46, [i], [1]-24, [i], 25-38, [i], [1]-54. Pagination by act. Typescript.
Bought. London & New York: Samuel French, n.d. Pp. [1]-48. Promptbook.
Fallen among Thieves. Pp. [i-iii], [1]-25, [i-iii], [1]-30, [i-iii], [1]-28, [i], [1]-27, [i-ii], [1]-11. Pagination by act. Typescript promptbook.
Shall We Forgive Her? Pp. [1]-[51]. Typescript promptbook.
Terrible Revenge, A. Pp. [i], [1]-30, [1]-39, [i], [1]-30, [i], [1]-28, [i], [1]-8. Pagination by act. Text incomplete. Typescript promptbook.
Woman against Woman. *Also:* The Workman; or, The Shadow of the Hearth. Pp. [1-46], [1-48], [1-21], [1-26], [1-26]. Pagination by act. Typescript promptbook.
Workman, The.
See Woman against Woman.

HARVEY, MARGARET
Raymond de Percy; or, The Tenant of the Tomb. Bishopwearmouth: G. Garbutt (printer), 1822. Pp. [i-viii], [1]-47.

HARWOOD, ISABELLA
See Neil, Ross (pseud.).

HASBRER, ALFRED
Carlo. London: John Camden Hotten (priv.), 1870. Pp. [1]-71.

HASTE TO THE WEDDING
See Gilbert, William Schwenck.

HASTY CONCLUSION, A
See Planché, Elizabeth (Eliza) St. George, Mrs. James Robinson.

HASTY CONCLUSIONS
See Dance, Charles.

HATCH, P. H.
Sunshine and Shade. London: Andrew Vickers, 1849. Pp. [1]-44.

HATTON, JOSEPH
Birds of a Feather. London: Grant (priv.), n.d. Pp. [1]-38.
Clytie. London: (priv.), n.d. Pp. [1]-8. Synopsis.
Liz. Written with Matthison, Arthur. London & New York: Samuel French, n.d. Pp. [1]-40. [Lacy's Acting Edition].
Much Too Clever.
See Oxenford, John.
Romantic Caroline. London: Robson & Sons (printer) (priv.), n.d. Pp. [1]-32.
Scarlet Letter, The; or, Hester Prynne. London: Lindley, n.d. Pp. [1]-30.

HAUNTED HOUSE, THE
See Fothergill, F.

HAUNTED HULK, THE
See Fitzball, Edward.

HAUNTED INN, THE
See Peake, Richard Brinsley.

HAUNTED MILL, THE
See Wooler, John Pratt.

HAUNTED MOOR
See Almar, George. Fire Raiser, The.

HAUNTED TOWER, THE
See Cobb, James.

HAUPTMANN, GERHART
Hannele.
See Archer, William (trans.).
Lonely Lives.
See Morison, Mary (trans.).
Weavers, The.
See Morison, Mary (trans.).

HAVARD, PHILIP
Well Matched. London & New York: Samuel French, n.d. Pp. [1]-19. [Lacy's Acting Edition].

HAVE YOU GOT THAT TEN POUND NOTE?
See Calvert, Cayley.

HAWKES, W. R.
Gaul, King of Ragah. London: Clio Rickman; Sherwood, Neely, & Jones, 1813. Pp. [i]-[vi], [1]-55.

HAWKINS, ANTHONY HOPE
See Hope, Anthony.

HAWKWOOD HALL
See Royd, Lynn.

HAWORTH, R.
Disguises; or, Two Stages from Gretna. London: G. Hebert, 1824. Pp. [1]-28.
Quentin Durward. London: G. Hebert, 1823. Pp. [1]-39. Text incomplete.

HAWTREY, CHARLES HENRY
Private Secretary, The. New York & London: Samuel French, c.1907. Pp. [i-ii], [1]-90. Promptbook.

HAWTREY, GEORGE PROCTOR
Pickpocket, The. London & New York: Samuel French, n.d. Pp. [3]-62. [Lacy's Acting Edition].

HAY, FREDERIC
Beautiful for Ever. London: Thomas Hailes Lacy, n.d. Pp. [1]-13.
Caught by the Cuff. London: Thomas Hailes Lacy, n.d. Pp. [1]-18. Promptbook.
Chops of the Channel, The. London: Thomas Hailes Lacy, n.d. Pp. [1]-15. [Lacy's Acting Edition].
Cracked Heads.
See Clements, Arthur.
Cupboard Love. New York: Robert M. DeWitt, n.d. Pp. [1]-7. Text incomplete. DeWitt's Acting Plays, 107.
Deep Red Rover, The. Written with Chapman, Westmacott. London & New York: Samuel French, n.d. Pp. [1]-28. [Lacy's Acting Edition].
French Exhibition, The; or, The Noodles in Paris. London: Thomas Hailes Lacy, n.d. Pp. [1]-16. [Lacy's Acting Edition].
Furnished Apartments. By H. A. Y. (pseud.). New York: Dick & Fitzgerald, n.d. Pp. [1]-15. Dick's American Edition.
Lame Excuse, A. New York: Wheat & Cornett, c.1876. Pp. [26]-32. New York Drama, I, 9.
Lame Excuse, A. London: Thomas Hailes Lacy, n.d. Pp. [1]-[19]. Promptbook.
Lodgers and Dodgers. London: Thomas Hailes Lacy, n.d. Pp. [1]-14. Lacy's Acting Edition, 1370.
Our Domestics. New York: Robert M. DeWitt, n.d. Pp. [1]-25. DeWitt's Acting Plays, 45.
Photographic Fix, A. London: Thomas Hailes Lacy, n.d. Pp. [1]-18. [Lacy's Acting Edition].
Sudden Arrival, A. London: Thomas Hailes Lacy, n.d. Pp. [1]-20.
Suit of Tweeds, A. London: Thomas Hailes Lacy, n.d. Pp. [1]-22. [Lacy's Acting Edition].

HAY, T. J.
Mohawk Minstrels' Fifth Book of Dramas, Dialogues, & Drolleries, The.
See Banks, Billy.

HAYDÉE
See Lavenu, L. (trans.).
See Soane, George (trans.).

HAYES, FREDERICK WILLIAM
Mistaken Identity. London: Bemrose & Sons, n.d. Pp. [1]-27.
Null and Void. London: Bemrose & Sons, 1880. Pp. [1]-53.
Returned to Life. London: Bemrose & Sons, 1880. Pp. [1]-51.

Smoke. London: Bemrose & Sons, 1880. Pp. [1]-41.

State Secret, A; or, The Iron Mask. London: Bemrose & Sons, n.d. Pp. [1]-78.

Tacticians. London: Bemrose & Sons, 1880. Pp. [1]-59.

Victor Dupres. London: Bemrose & Sons, n.d. Pp. [1]-32.

HAYES, MARIA XIMENA (trans.)

Jean Buscaille. By Valnay, E. London: J. McDowell, n.d. Pp. [1]-84.

Paul and Virginia. Music by Massé, Victor. Paris: Theodore Michaelis, n.d. Pp. [i-iv], [1]-322. Popular ed. Vocal score.

HAYLEY, WILLIAM

Eudora. In *Three Plays,* Chichester: William Mason (printer), 1811, pp. [iii]-[xxxviii], [1]-81.

Heroine of Cambria, The. In *Three Plays,* Chichester: William Mason (printer), 1811, pp. [181]-262.

Viceroy, The. In *Three Plays,* Chichester: William Mason (printer), 1811, pp. [83]-179.

HAYNES, JAMES

Conscience; or, The Bridal Night. London: Hurst, Robinson, 1821. Pp. [i]-x, [1]-94.

Conscience; or, The Bridal Night. New York: Murden & Thomson, 1821. Pp. [3]-[74].

Durazzo. London: Hurst, Robinson, 1823. Pp. [i-vi], [1]-148.

Mary Stuart. London: James Ridgway, 1840. Pp. [1]-103.

Mary Stuart. London: James Ridgway, 1840. Pp. [1]-103. 3rd ed. Promptbook.

HAYWARD, ABRAHAM (trans.)

Faust. By Goethe. Lowell: Daniel Bixby, 1840. Pp. [i]-[xxxii], [1]-317. 1st American from 3rd London ed.

HAZARD OF THE DIE, THE

See Jerrold, Douglas William.

HAZARD OF THE DYE

See Burnand, Francis Cowley. Blue Beard.

HAZELTON, FREDERICK

Sweeney Todd, the Barber of Fleet Street; or, The String of Pearls. London & New York: Samuel French, n.d. Pp. [1]-35. Promptbook.

HAZELWOOD HALL

See Bloomfield, Robert.

HAZLEWOOD, ?, MISS

Kevin's Choice. Music by Wallworth, T. A. *Also:* The Maid of Glendalough. London: J. Bale (printer), n.d. Pp. [1]-16. Libretto.

Maid of Glendalough.

See Kevin's Choice.

HAZLEWOOD, COLIN HENRY

Ashore and Afloat. London & New York: Samuel French, n.d. Pp. [1]-42. [French's Acting Edition]. Promptbook.

Aurora Floyd; or, The Dark Deed in the Wood. London: Thomas Hailes Lacy, n.d. Pp. [1]-36. [Lacy's Acting Edition].

Bitter Reckoning, The. London & New York: Samuel French, n.d. Pp. [1]-40. [Lacy's Acting Edition].

Bridal Wreath, The. London & New York: Samuel French, n.d. Pp. [1]-36. [Lacy's Acting Edition].

Capitola; or, The Masked Mother and the Hidden Hand. London: Thomas Hailes Lacy, n.d. Pp. [1]-35.

Chevalier of the Maison Rouge, The; or, The Days of Terror! London: Thomas Hailes Lacy, n.d. Pp. [1]-52. [Lacy's Acting Edition].

Clock on the Stairs, The. London: Thomas Hailes Lacy, n.d. Pp. [1]-17.

Dragon of Wantley, The; or, Harlequin Moore, of Moore Hall, and His Fayre Margery. Written with Reeve, Wybert. Sheffield: J. Pearce jr (printer), 1861. Pp. [1]-16. Libretto.

Emerald Heart, The; or, A Poor Man's Honour. *Also:* Irishman's Home, The; or, The Stolen Sheep. 40 leaves. Incomplete. Manuscript promptbook.

Female Detective, The; or, The Mother's Dying Child. New York: DeWitt, n.d. Pp. [1]-42. DeWitt's Acting Plays, 128.

For Honor's Sake. London & New York: Samuel French, n.d. Pp. [1]-56. [Lacy's Acting Edition].

Going to Chobham; or, The Petticoat Captains. London: Thomas Hailes Lacy, n.d. Pp. [1]-16. [Lacy's Acting Edition].

Harvest Storm, The. London: Thomas Hailes Lacy, n.d. Pp. [1]-16. Promptbook.

Harvest Storm, The. In *Dramas, Serious and Serio-Comic, for College, Camp, and Cabin,* London: Thomas Hailes Lacy, n.d., pp. [1]-20. *Filed under* Lacy, Thomas Hailes. Dramas for College, Camp, and Cabin.

Headless Horseman, The; or, The Ride of Death. London & New York: Samuel French, n.d. Pp. [1]-36. [Lacy's Acting Edition].

Hop Pickers and Gipsies; or, The Lost Daughter. London: Thomas Hailes Lacy, n.d. Pp. [1]-47. [Lacy's Acting Edition].

House on the Bridge of Notre Dame, The. London & New York: Samuel French, n.d. Pp. [1]-40. [Lacy's Acting Edition].

Irishman's Home, The.

See Emerald Heart, The.

Jenny Foster, the Sailor's Child; or, The Winter Robin. London & New York: Samuel French, n.d. Pp. [1]-29.

Jessamy's Courtship. London & New York: Samuel French, n.d. Pp. [1]-16. [Lacy's Acting Edition].

Jessy Vere; or, The Return of the Wanderer. London: Thomas Hailes Lacy, n.d. Pp. [1]-34. Promptbook.

Lady Audley's Secret. London: Samuel French, n.d. Pp. [1]-[30]. [French's Acting Edition (late Lacy's)]. Promptbook.

Leave It to Me. Written with Williams, Arthur. London & New York: Samuel French, n.d. Pp. [1]-19. Text incomplete. [Lacy's Acting Edition].

Lizzie Lyle; or, The Flower Makers of Finsbury. London: Thomas Hailes Lacy, n.d. Pp. [1]-50. [Lacy's Acting Edition].

Lost Wife, The; or, A Husband's Confession. *Also:* The Outcast's Wife. London: Thomas Hailes Lacy, 1871. Pp. [1]-36. [Lacy's Acting Edition].

Marble Bride, The; or, The Elves of the Forest. London: Thomas Hailes Lacy, n.d. Pp. [1]-28. Lacy's Acting Edition, 479.

Mary Edmonstone. London & New York: Samuel French, n.d. Pp. [1]-30. [Lacy's Acting Edition].

Mother's Dying Child, The. London: Thomas Hailes Lacy, n.d. Pp. [1]-53.

Never Too Late to Mend. New York: Samuel French & Son; London: Samuel French, n.d. Pp. [1]-65. French's Standard Drama, 370.

Outcast's Wife, The; or, A Husband's Confession. *Also:* The Lost Wife. Clyde, Ohio: A. D. Ames, n.d. Pp. [1]-25. Ames' Series of Standard and Minor Drama, 85.

Poul a Dhoil; or, The Fairy Man. London: Thomas Hailes Lacy, n.d. Pp. [1]-46. [Lacy's Acting Edition].

Staff of Diamonds, The. [London: Samuel French], n.d. Pp. [1]-37. Promptbook.

Stolen Jewess, The; or, Two Children of Israel. London & New York: Samuel French, n.d. Pp. [1]-36. [Lacy's Acting Edition].

Taking the Veil; or, The Harsh Step-father. London & New York: Samuel French, n.d. Pp. [1]-[47]. [Lacy's Acting Edition].

Waiting for the Verdict; or, Falsely Accused. London & New York: Samuel French, n.d. Pp. [1]-48. Promptbook.

HE AND SHE

See Beerbohm, Constance.

HE IS SURE TO BE DONE

See Bryant, Michael. Nine to One.

HE LIES LIKE TRUTH

See Kimpton, F.

HE MUST BE MARRIED

See Harding, C. T.

HE, SHE, AND IT

See Muskerry, William.

HE STOOPS TO WIN

See Bridgman, Cunningham V.

HE THAT WILL NOT WHEN HE MAY
See Gardner, Herbert.
HE WIPED AWAY A TEAR
See Byron, Henry James. Full Private Perkins.
HE WOULD BE A LORD (anon.)
London: R. Washbourne, 1890. Pp. [1]-63.
HE WOULD BE A SOLDIER
See McK., F.
See Philon, Frederic.
HEAD OF ROMULUS, THE
See Grundy, Sydney.
HEAD OF THE FAMILY, THE
See Emden, William Samuel.
HEAD OF THE POLL, THE
See Law, Arthur.
HEADLESS HORSEMAN, THE
See Hazlewood, Colin Henry.
HEADS OR TAILS?
See Simpson, John Palgrave.
HEADSMAN
See Moncrieff, William Thomas. Mount St. Bernard.
HEADSMAN OF PARIS, THE; OR, THE LIGHT OF LIFE
(anon.)
55 leaves. Manuscript.
HEADSMAN'S DAUGHTER
See Wills, William Gorman. Hinko.
HEAR BOTH SIDES
See Holcroft, Thomas.
HEAR IT OUT
See Reynolds, Frederick. Blind Bargain, The.
HEART AND THE WORLD, THE
See Marston, John Westland.
HEART FOR HEART
See Falconer, Edmund. Cagot, The.
HEART OF A FATHER
See Milner, Henry M. Jew of Lubeck, The.
HEART OF A SOLDIER
See Arnold, Samuel James. Frederick the Great.
HEART OF GOLD, A
See Jerrold, Douglas William.
HEART OF LONDON, THE
See Moncrieff, William Thomas.
HEART OF MID-LOTHIAN, THE
See Dibdin, Thomas John.
See Terry, Daniel.
**HEART OF MIDLOTHIAN, THE; OR, THE SISTERS OF ST.
LEONARD'S** (anon.)
London: Thomas Hailes Lacy, n.d. Pp. [1]-44. [Lacy's
Acting Edition]. *Filed under* Lacy, Thomas Hailes.
HEARTS AND HOMES
See Browne, George Walter.
HEARTS ARE TRUMPS
See Aird, David Mitchell. Love-Trap, The.
See Lemon, Mark.
See Raleigh, Cecil.
HEARTS OF OAK
See Allingham, John Till.
See Jones, Henry Arthur.
HEARTWELL, HENRY
Castle of Sorrento, The. In *British Drama,* 12 vols., London:
John Dicks, 1864, II, [563]-574.
Castle of Sorrento, The; or, The Prisoner of Rochelle. By
Henry Hartwell. London: John Cumberland, n.d. Pp.
[1]-39. Cumberland's British Theatre, XXXIII. *Filed
under* Cumberland, John. Cumberland's British Theatre,
XXXIII.
HEATHCOTE, ARTHUR M.
Duchess of Bayswater and Co., The. London & New York:
Samuel French, n.d. Pp. [1]-22. [Lacy's Acting Edition].
His Toast. London & New York: Samuel French, n.d. Pp.
[1]-17. [Lacy's Acting Edition].
In Two Minds. London: Samuel French; New York: T.
Henry French, n.d. Pp. [1]-12. [Lacy's Acting Edition].
Till the Half-Hour. London: Capper & Newton, n.d. Pp.
[209]-229. Lynn's Acting Edition, 26.

Woman's Wrongs. London & New York: Samuel French,
n.d. Pp. [1]-20. [French's Acting Edition].
HEATHER
See Sturgis, Julian Russell.
HEATHER FIELD, THE
See Martyn, Edward.
HEAVEN AND EARTH
See Byron, George Gordon, Lord.
HEAVEN AND HELL
See Mérimée, Prosper.
HEAVEN DEFEND THE RIGHT
See Barrymore, William. Trial by Battle.
HEAVYSEGE, CHARLES
Saul. Boston: Fields, Osgood, 1869. Pp. [1]-436, [1]-5. New
and rev. ed.
HEBREW HEROINE
See Tennant, William. Jephthah's Daughter.
HEBREW QUEEN
See Wade, Thomas. Jew of Arragon, The.
HECTOR
See Galt, John.
See Mangin, Edward (trans.).
HEDDA GABLER
See Anstey, F.
See Archer, William (trans.).
See Gosse, Edmund William (trans.).
HEHL, MARY SABILLA
See Novello, Mary Sabilla Hehl, Mrs. Vincent.
HEIGEL, CAESAR MAX
Macbeth.
See under title.
HEIGHWAY, WILLIAM
Pills of Wisdom. London & New York: Samuel French, n.d.
Pp. [1]-16.
HEIN, GUSTAV (trans.)
Beethoven. By Muller, Hugo. Aberdeen: A. & R. Milne, n.d.
Pp. [1]-31.
Wreckage. By Grube, Max. London: Capper & Newton,
n.d. Pp. [49]-69. Lynn's Acting Edition, 20.
HEINEMANN, WILLIAM
First Step, The. London: John Lane, 1895. Pp. [i-x], 1-[71].
Summer Moths. New York: DeWitt, 1898. Pp. [i-vi], [1]-117.
HEIR AT LAW, THE
See Colman, George, jr.
HEIR OF LINNE, THE
See Neil, Ross.
HEIR OF SCHARFENECK, THE (anon. trans.)
By Amalie (Amelia), Princess of Saxony. In *Six Dramas
Illustrative of German Life,* London: John W. Parker, pp.
[59]-118. *Filed under* Six Dramas (anon.).
HEIRESS, THE
See Burgoyne, John, Gen.
See Seymour, Mary.
HEIRESS OF BRUGES, THE
See Selby, Charles.
HEIRESS OF GLENFILLAN, THE
See Phillips, Morrice.
HEIRS OF RABOURDIN, THE
See de Mattos, A. Teixeira (trans.).
HELEN
See Burnand, Francis Cowley. Latest Edition of Helen,
The.
HELEN OAKLEIGH
See Coyne, Joseph Stirling.
HELENA IN TROAS
See Todhunter, John.
H--L UPON EARTH!
See Stirling, Edward. Devil's Daughter, The.
HELLAS
See Shelley, Percy Bysshe.
HELME, ELIZABETH (trans.)
Cortez; or, The Conquest of Mexico. By Campe, J. H.
London: C. Cradock & W. Joy, 1811. Pp. [i]-iv, [1]-259.
New ed.

Pizarro; or, The Conquest of Peru. By Campe, J. H. Dublin: P. Wogan, et al., 1800. Pp. [i-ii], [1]-126, [i]-128.

HELPING HANDS
    See Taylor, Tom.

HELPLESS ANIMALS!
    See Parry, John.

HELPLESS COUPLE, A
    See Williams, Maria Josephine.

HELPS, ARTHUR
    Catharine Douglas. London: William Pickering, 1843. Pp. [i-iv], [1]-148.
    King Henry the Second. London: William Pickering, 1843. Pp. [i-iv], [1]-182.
    Oulita the Serf. London: John W. Parker & Son, 1858. Pp. [i-ii], [1]-190.

HELVELLYN
    See Oxenford, John.

HEMANS, FELICIA DOROTHEA BROWNE, MRS. ALFRED
    De Chatillon; or, The Crusaders. In *Dramatic Works,* Edinburgh & London: William Blackwood & Sons, n.d., pp. [i], [221]-270.
    Sebastian of Portugal. In *Dramatic Works,* Edinburgh & London: William Blackwood & Sons, n.d., pp. [i], [199]-220.
    Siege of Valencia, The. In [*Siege of Valencia . . . with other Poems,* London: John Murray, 1823], pp. [91]-247.
    Vespers of Palermo, The. London: John Murray, 1823. Pp. [i-iv], [1]-116.

HEN AND CHICKENS, THE
    See Webster, Benjamin, jr.

HENDERSON, ISAAC
    Agatha. *Also:* The Silent Battle. N.p.: n.pub., n.d. Pp. [i], [1]-99.
    Silent Battle, The
        See Agatha.

HENDRIKS, HERMAN
    Hurly-Burly, The; or, Number Seven-twenty-eight. London & New York: Samuel French, n.d. Pp. [1]-48. [Lacy's Acting Edition].

HENGIST; OR, THE FIFTH CENTURY (anon.)
    London: J. Gillet (printer) (priv.), 1816. Pp. [1]-33.

HENLEY, WILLIAM ERNEST
    Admiral Guinea. Written with Stevenson, Robert Louis. London: William Heinemann, 1897. Pp. [i-vi], [1]-104.
    Beau Austin. Written with Stevenson, Robert Louis. In *Plays,* London: William Heinemann, 1896, pp. [i], [113]-175.
    Deacon Brodie; or, The Double Life. Written with Stevenson, Robert Louis. In *Plays,* London: William Heinemann, 1896, pp. [i-xiv], [i]-109.
    Macaire. Written with Stevenson, Robert Louis. In *Plays,* London: William Heinemann, 1896, pp. [i], [251]-303.

HENNEQUIN, MAURICE
    Paradise.
        See under title.

HENNING, ALBERT
    His Wife's Little Bill. Written with Standish, Julian. Music by Henning, Albert. Pp. [i-ii], [1]-17. Typescript. *Filed under* Henning, Albert.

HENRI QUATRE
    See Morton, Thomas, sr.

HENRIETTE THE FORSAKEN
    See Buckstone, John Baldwin.

HENRIQUE
    See Haines, John Thomas.

HENRIQUEZ
    See Baillie, Joanna.

HENRY, A.
    Whittington and His Cat; or, The Fairies' Banquet and Lord Mayor's Show. Newcastle-upon-Tyne: M. Benson (printer), 1876. Pp. [i], [1]-16.

HENRY, RE.
    See Henry, Reginald.

HENRY, REGINALD
    Fast Friends. By Re Henry. London & New York: Samuel French, n.d. Pp. [1]-8. [Lacy's Acting Edition].

    Narrow Escape, A. By Re Henry. London & New York: Samuel French, n.d. Pp. [1]-8. [Lacy's Acting Edition].
    Norah. By Re Henry. Chicago: Dramatic Publishing Co., n.d. Pp. [1]-12. World Acting Drama.

HENRY, RICHARD (pseud. of Butler, Richard William and Newton, Henry Chance)
    Adoption. London & New York: Samuel French, n.d. Pp. [1]-22. [Lacy's Acting Edition]. *Filed under* Butler, Richard William; Newton, Henry Chance.
    First Mate. London & New York: Samuel French, n.d. Pp. [1]-31. [Lacy's Acting Edition]. *Filed under* Butler, Richard William; Newton, Henry Chance.
    Happy Day, A. London: Capper & Newton, n.d. Pp. [141]-164. Lynn's Acting Edition, 23.
    Queer Street. London & New York: Samuel French, n.d. Pp. [1]-21. [Lacy's Acting Edition]. *Filed under* Butler, Richard William; Newton, Henry Chance.

HENRY AND ALMERIA
    See Birrell, Andrew.

HENRY DUNBAR
    See Taylor, Tom.

HENRY OF RICHMOND
    See Edison, John Sibbald.

HENRY TALBOT
    See Mitford, Mary Russell.

HENRY THE EIGHTH
    See Calvert, Charles Alexander (arr.).

HENRY THE FIFTH
    See Calvert, Charles Alexander (arr.).

HENRY THE FOURTH, PART 2
    See Calvert, Charles Alexander (arr.).

HENRY THE SECOND
    See Hull, Thomas.

HENRY THE SEVENTH
    See Chenevix, Richard.

HENRY V
    See Coleman, John (arr.).

HER FACE WAS HER FORTUNE
    See Robinson, Frederick William.

HER MAJESTY'S SERVICE!
    See Stirling, Edward. Blue-Jackets, The.

HER NEW DRESSMAKER
    See Walkes, W. R.

HERAUD, JOHN ABRAHAM
    Videna; or, The Mother's Tragedy. London: C. Mitchell, 1854. Pp. [i]-[xiv], [1]-82.

HERBERT, G. C.
    Our Bitterest Foe. London & New York: Samuel French, n.d. Pp. [1]-12. [Lacy's Acting Edition].
    Second Thoughts. London & New York: Samuel French, n.d. Pp. [1]-20.
    Second Thoughts. London & New York: Samuel French, n.d. Pp. [1]-20. Promptbook.

HERBERT, HENRY JOHN GEORGE, EARL OF CARNAR-VON, LORD PORCHESTER
    Don Pedro, King of Castile. By Lord Porchester. London: Henry Colburn, 1828. Pp. [iii]-[x], [1]-99.

HERBERT, M. A. (trans.)
    Torquato Tasso. By Goethe. London: Longman, Brown, Green, & Longmans, 1856. Pp. [i]-[viii], [1]-179.

HERBERT, THOMAS
    Hydrophobia; or, Love-Created Madness. Brighton: Hereford House (priv.), 1820. Pp. [1]-[80].
    Too Much the Way of the World. Brighton: W. Fleet (printer), 1817. Pp. [2]-[101].

HERCULES AND OMPHALE
    See Brough, William.

HERCULES, KING OF CLUBS!
    See Cooper, Frederick Fox.

HERFORD, CHARLES HAROLD (trans.)
    Brand. By Ibsen, Henrik. London: William Heinemann, 1904. Pp. [i]-[c], [1]-288. Fifth impression.
    Love's Comedy. By Ibsen, Henrik. In R. Brimley Johnson and N. Erichsen, eds., *Modern Plays,* London: Ducksworth, 1900, pp. [i]-[xx], [1]-[170].

HERMAN, HENRY
    Adrienne Lecouvreur. London & New York: Samuel French, n.d. Pp. [1]-56. Promptbook.
    Breaking a Butterfly.
        See Jones, Henry Arthur.
    Silver King, The.
        See Jones, Henry Arthur.
HERMANN, CHARLES
    Uncle Tom's Cabin. London: Thomas Hailes Lacy, n.d. Pp. [1]-30. [Lacy's Acting Edition, 178].
HERMANN THE FATALIST
    See Wills, William Gorman.
HERMESIANAX
    See Amico, Amicus (pseud.).
HERMIT OF THE TWEED
    See Trotter, Thomas. Noble Foundling, The.
HERMIT OF WARKWORTH
    See Fitzball, Edward. Edda.
HERMIT'S PROPHECY
    See Beazley, Samuel, jr. Knights of the Cross, The.
HERNANI (anon. trans.)
    By Hugo, Victor. N.p.: n.pub., n.d. Pp. [3]-26. Title page lacking.
HERNANI
    See Crosland, Camilla Dufour Toulmin, Mrs. Newton.
    See Kenney, James.
HERNE THE HUNTER
    See Taylor, Thomas Proclus.
HERO AND LEANDER
    See Jackman, Isaac.
HERO IN SPITE OF HIMSELF
    See Grattan, H. P. Twins, The.
    See Number One A (anon.).
HERO OF ROMANCE, A
    See Marston, John Westland.
HERO OF THE NORTH
    See Dimond, William. Gustavus Vasa, the Hero of the North.
    See Dimond, William.
HEROD
    See Phillips, Stephen.
HEROES
    See Edwardes, Conway Theodore Marriott.
HEROINE, THE
    See Phillips, R.
HEROINE OF CAMBRIA, THE
    See Hayley, William.
HERON, MATILDA (later Mrs. Robert Stoepel)
    Camille; or, The Fate of a Coquette. New York: Samuel French, n.d. <wrps. New York & London>. Pp. [1]-42. French's American Drama, 129 <wrps. French's Standard Drama>. Promptbook.
    Phaedra. Cincinnati: Wrightson, 1858. Pp. [1]-32.
HERON, MATILDA (later Mrs. Robert Stoepel) (trans.)
    Medea. By Legouvé, Ernest. London: Thomas Hailes Lacy, n.d. Pp. [1]-27. Promptbook.
HERSEE, HENRY
    All's Fair in Love. London: John Dicks, n.d. Pp. [1]-12. Dicks' Standard Charades and Comedies, 490.
    Dragoons, The. Music by Maillart, Aimé. London: W. S. Johnson, 1879. Pp. [1]-31. Libretto.
    Pauline. Music by Cowen, F. H. London & New York: Boosey, n.d. Pp. [i-iv], [1]-247. Vocal score.
HERSEE, HENRY (trans.)
    Carmen. Music by Bizet. London: Metzler, n.d. Pp. [i-ii], [1]-230. Vocal score.
    Mary of Ghent. *Also:* Maria di Gand. Music by Mattei, Tito. London: Hutchings & Romer, n.d. Pp. [1]-81. Libretto.
HERSILIA
    See Knowles, James Sheridan.
HERTFORDSHIRE TRAGEDY, THE
    See Milner, Henry M.
HERTZ, HENRIK
    See Bosbacca, Gulielmerg Henricus (pseud.).

King René's Daughter.
    See Chapman, Jane Frances (trans.).
    See Martin, Theodore, Sir (trans.).
    See Phipps, Edmund (trans.).
    See Weatherly, Frederick Edward (trans.).
HE'S A LUNATIC
    See Merivale, Herman Charles.
HE'S MUCH TO BLAME
    See Holcroft, Thomas.
HE'S NO CONJUROR!
    See Harding, C. T.
HESTER PRYNNE
    See Hatton, Joseph. Scarlet Letter, The.
HESTER'S MYSTERY
    See Pinero, Arthur Wing.
HETHERINGTON, WILLIAM MAXWELL
    Bessy Bell and Mary Gray. In *Twelve Dramatic Sketches,* Edinburgh: Constable, 1829, pp. [i]-xvi, [1]-43. *Filed under* Twelve Dramatic Sketches.
    Bush Aboon Traquair, The. In *Twelve Dramatic Sketches,* Edinburgh: Constable, 1829, pp. [161]-174. *Filed under* Twelve Dramatic Sketches.
    Choice, The. In *Twelve Dramatic Sketches,* Edinburgh: Constable, 1829, pp. [211]-232. *Filed under* Twelve Dramatic Sketches.
    Cowdenknows. In *Twelve Dramatic Sketches,* Edinburgh: Constable, 1829, pp. [67]-82. *Filed under* Twelve Dramatic Sketches.
    Ewe-Bughts, The. In *Twelve Dramatic Sketches,* Edinburgh: Constable, 1829, pp. [83]-96. *Filed under* Twelve Dramatic Sketches.
    Harvest Field, The. In *Twelve Dramatic Sketches,* Edinburgh: Constable, 1829, pp. [123]-160. *Filed under* Twelve Dramatic Sketches.
    Logan Braes. In *Twelve Dramatic Sketches,* Edinburgh: Constable, 1829, pp. [193]-209. *Filed under* Twelve Dramatic Sketches.
    Lowland Lass and the Highland Lad, The. In *Twelve Dramatic Sketches,* Edinburgh: Constable, 1829, pp. [45]-66. *Filed under* Twelve Dramatic Sketches.
    Old Maid, The. In *Twelve Dramatic Sketches,* Edinburgh: Constable, 1829, pp. [175]-191. *Filed under* Twelve Dramatic Sketches.
    Rocking, The. In *Twelve Dramatic Sketches,* Edinburgh: Constable, 1829, pp. [233]-256. *Filed under* Twelve Dramatic Sketches.
    Snow-Storm, The. In *Twelve Dramatic Sketches,* Edinburgh: Constable, 1829, pp. [257]-275. *Filed under* Twelve Dramatic Sketches.
    Tochered Maiden of the Glen, The. In *Twelve Dramatic Sketches,* Edinburgh: Constable, 1829, pp. [97]-121. *Filed under* Twelve Dramatic Sketches.
HEWLETT, MAURICE HENRY
    Masque of Dead Florentines, A. London: J. M. Dent, 1895. Pp. [i-vi], [1]-51.
    Masque of Dead Florentines, A. Portland, Maine: Thomas B. Mosher, 1911. Pp. [i-viii], [1]-[50].
    Pan and the Young Shepherd. London & New York: John Lane, 1898. Pp. [i-viii], [1]-140.
    Pan and the Young Shepherd. London: William Heinemann, 1906. Pp. [i-vi], [1]-101.
HEWLINGS, A.
    Nondescript, The. London: C. Chapple, 1813. Pp. [i]-[x], [1]-38.
HEWSON, J. JAMES
    My Cousin. London: Samuel French; New York: T. Henry French, n.d. Pp. [1]-18. [Lacy's Acting Edition].
    Recalled to Life. Liverpool: Willmer Brothers (printer), 1886. Pp. [1]-41.
HEY DIDDLE DIDDLE
    See Blanchard, Edward Litt Leman.
HEYTESBURY, WILLIAM
    Catherine de Medicis.
        See Woodley, William.

James the Third, King of Scotland.
See Woodley, William.

HICKS, EDWARD SEYMOUR

New Sub, The. London & New York: Samuel French, n.d. Pp. [1]-18. [Lacy's Acting Edition].

Runaway Girl, A. Written with Nicholls, Harry; Hopwood, Aubrey; Greenbank, Harry Hewetson. Music by Monckton, Lionel; Caryll, Ivan. London: Chappell, c.1898. Pp. [i-iv], 1-196. Vocal score.

Runaway Girl, A. Written with Nicholls, Harry; Hopwood, Aubrey; Greenbank, Harry Hewetson. Music by Caryll, Ivan; Monckton, Lionel. New York: Douglas Taylor (printer), n.d. Pp. [1]-35. Libretto.

Runaway Girl, A. Written with Nicholls, Harry; Hopwood, Aubrey; Greenbank, Harry Hewetson. Music by Caryll, Ivan; Monckton, Lionel. N.p.: n.pub., n.d. Pp. [1]-38. Libretto.

Yashmak, The.
See Raleigh, Cecil.

HICKS, EDWARD SEYMOUR (arr.)

King Richard III. By Shakespeare, William. [London]: Eyre & Spottiswoode, n.d. Pp. [1]-67.

HICKS, SEYMOUR
See Hicks, Edward Seymour.

HIDDEN GEM, THE
See Wiseman, Nicholas Patrick Stephen, Cardinal.

HIDDEN HAND, THE
See Taylor, Tom.

HIDDEN LIFE, THE
See Abel, William Henry.

HIDDEN TREASURE
See Poole, John. Past and Present.

HIDE AND SEEK
See Lunn, Joseph.

HIGGIE, THOMAS HENRY

Belphegor; or, The Mountebank and His Wife. Written with Lacy, Thomas Hailes. *Also:* Belphegor the Buffoon; or, The Robbers of the Revolution. London: Thomas Hailes Lacy, n.d. Pp. [1]-56. [Lacy's Acting Edition, 39].

Belphegor the Buffoon; or, The Robbers of the Revolution. Written with Lacy, Thomas Hailes. *Also:* Belphegor; or, The Mountebank and His Wife. By Thomas Higgie. London: John Duncombe, n.d. Pp. [1]-45. Duncombe's Edition. *Filed under* Higgie, Thomas H.

Devil's Mount, The; or, The Female Bluebeard. London: Thomas Hailes Lacy, n.d. Pp. [1]-39. [Lacy's Acting Edition, 1319].

Devilish Good Joke!, A; or, A Night's Frolic! London & New York: Samuel French, n.d. Pp. [1]-18. [Lacy's Acting Edition].

House Dog!, The. London: John Duncombe, n.d. <wrps. Thomas Hailes Lacy>. Pp. [1]-25. Duncombe's Edition <wrps. New British Theatre (late Duncombe's), 412>.

Laid up in Port!; or, Sharks along the Shore! London & New York: Samuel French, n.d. Pp. [1]-54. [Lacy's Acting Edition].

Martin Chuzzlewit; or, His Wills and His Ways, What He Did and What He Didn't. Written with Lacy, Thomas Hailes. London: Thomas Hailes Lacy, n.d. Pp. [1]-50. [Lacy's Acting Edition].

Tower of London, The; or, The Death Omen and the Fate of Lady Jane Grey. Written with Lacy, Thomas Hailes. London: Thomas Hailes Lacy, n.d. Pp. [1]-47. [Lacy's Acting Edition, 1406].

Watch and Wait. Written with Shepherd, Richard. London & New York: Samuel French, n.d. Pp. [1]-46. [Lacy's Acting Edition].

Wilful Murder! London: Thomas Hailes Lacy, n.d. Pp. [1]-18.

HIGH LIFE ABOVE STAIRS
See Garrick, David. Bon Ton.

HIGH LIFE BELOW STAIRS
See Townley, James, Rev.

HIGH LIFE IN THE CITY!
See Eyre, Edmund John.

HIGH, LOW, JACK, AND THE GAME
See Planché, James Robinson.

HIGH NOTIONS
See Parry, John.

HIGH STREET MYSTERY, THE
See MacHale, Luke.

HIGH WAYS AND BY WAYS
See Webster, Benjamin Nottingham.

HIGHGATE TUNNEL, THE
See Smith, T.

HIGHLAND FLING, A
See Dilley, Joseph J.

HIGHLAND FUNERAL
See Maclaren, Archibald. Private Theatre, The.

HIGHLAND LEGACY, A
See Thomas, Brandon.

HIGHLAND REEL, THE
See O'Keeffe, John.

HIGHLY IMPROBABLE
See Gilbert, William Schwenck.

HIGHWAYMAN, THE
See Morton, John Maddison.

HIGHWAYMAN FOR THE LADIES
See Burnand, Francis Cowley. Claude du Val.

HIGHWAYMAN OF 1770
See Webster, Benjamin Nottingham. Paul Clifford.

HIGHWAYMAN'S HOLIDAY, THE
See Suter, William E.

HIGHWAYS AND BY-WAYS
See Webster, Benjamin Nottingham.

HILL, AARON

Zara. London: Whittingham & Arliss, 1816. Pp. [1]-56. London Theatre, XIX. *Filed under* Dibdin, Thomas John, ed. London Theatre, XIX.

Zara. In *British Drama*, 12 vols., London: John Dicks, 1871, V, [233]-246.

HILL, ISABEL

Brian the Probationer; or, The Red Hand. London: W. R. Sams, 1842. Pp. [i-vi], [1]-100.

First of May, The; or, A Royal Love-Match. London: William Kenneth, 1829. Pp. [i]-[vi], [5]-53.

Poet's Child, The. London: John Warren, 1820. Pp. [i-viii], [1]-64.

HILLS, JOHN (trans.)

Faust. By Goethe. London: Whittaker, 1840. Pp. [i]-[xxiv], [1]-369.

HILTON, B. H.

Affinity.
See Manager in Love, The.

Baronets, The; or, How Will It End? Liverpool: D. Marples (printer), n.d. Pp. [i-iv], [1]-56.

Honour: The Count d'Abreu. N.p.: n.pub., 1870. Pp. [i-iv], [1]-50.

Manager in Love, The: Lady d'Arcy. *Also:* Affinity. N.p.: n.pub., 1870. Pp. [1-iv], [1]-64.

HINKO
See Wills, William Gorman.

HINKSON, KATHARINE TYNAN, MRS. HENRY ALBERT

Annunciation, The. In *Miracle Plays: Our Lord's Coming and Childhood*, London: John Lane; Chicago: Stone & Kimball, 1895, pp. [7]-[25]. *Filed under* Tynan, Katharine. Miracle Plays.

Finding in the Temple, The. In *Miracle Plays: Our Lord's Coming and Childhood*, London: John Lane; Chicago: Stone & Kimball, 1895, pp. [85]-[99]. *Filed under* Tynan, Katharine. Miracle Plays.

Flight into Egypt, The. In *Miracle Plays: Our Lord's Coming and Childhood*, London: John Lane; Chicago: Stone & Kimball, 1895, pp. [71]-[84]. *Filed under* Tynan, Katharine. Miracle Plays.

Nativity, The. In *Miracle Plays: Our Lord's Coming and Childhood*, London: John Lane; Chicago: Stone & Kimball, 1895, pp. [39]-51, 54-[56]. Text incomplete. *Filed under* Tynan, Katharine. Miracle Plays.

Presentation in the Temple, The. In *Miracle Plays: Our Lord's Coming and Childhood,* London: John Lane; Chicago: Stone & Kimball, 1895, pp. [57]-[70]. *Filed under* Tynan, Katharine. Miracle Plays.

Visitation, The. In *Miracle Plays: Our Lord's Coming and Childhood,* London: John Lane; Chicago: Stone & Kimball, 1895, pp. [29]-[38]. *Filed under* Tynan, Katharine. Miracle Plays.

HINT TO HUSBANDS
    See Cumberland, Richard.
    See Parry, John. Two Wives.

HINTS FOR 1851
    See Taylor, Tom. Novelty Fair.

HINTS FOR HUSBANDS
    See Beazley, Samuel, jr.

HINTS ON ETIQUETTE
    See Lemon, Mark. Jack in the Green.

HINTS TO THE CURIOUS
    See Tully, James Howard. Blue Beard.

HIPKINS, HENRY T.
    Is She His Daughter?
        See Murray, Gaston.
    Nice Quiet Day, A. Written with Murray, Gaston. London: Thomas Hailes Lacy, n.d. Pp. [1]-20. [Lacy's Acting Edition].

HIPPOLYTUS THE WREATHBEARER
    See Pember, Edward Henry (trans.).

HIS EXCELLENCY
    See Gilbert, William Schwenck.
    See Mathews, Charles James.

HIS EXCELLENCY THE GOVERNOR
    See Marshall, Robert.

HIS FIRST BRIEF
    See Daryl, Sidney.

HIS FIRST CHAMPAGNE
    See Rede, William Leman.

HIS FIRST PECCADILLO (anon.)
    London: G. H. Davidson, n.d. Pp. [1]-32. Cumberland's British Theatre, 365.

HIS GRACE THE DUKE
    See Stirling, Edward. Out of Luck.

HIS HIGHNESS
    See Houghton, John W.

HIS LAST LEGS
    See Bernard, William Bayle.

HIS LAST VICTORY
    See Phillips, Watts.

HIS MAJESTY
    See Burnand, Francis Cowley.

HIS NOVICE
    See Spicer, Henry.

HIS OWN ENEMY
    See Meadow, A.

HIS OWN GUEST
    See Ayres, Arthur.

HIS TOAST
    See Heathcote, Arthur M.

HIS WIFE'S LITTLE BILL
    See Henning, Albert.

HIS WILLS AND HIS WAYS, WHAT HE DID AND WHAT HE DIDN'T
    See Higgie, Thomas Henry. Martin Chuzzlewit.

HISTERKAN
    See Kerr, John.

HISTORY OF GEORGE BARNWELL
    See Lillo, George. London Merchant, The.

HIT AND MISS
    See Burnand, Francis Cowley.

HIT HIM, HE HAS NO FRIENDS
    See Yates, Edmund Hodgson.

HIT IF YOU LIKE IT
    See Planché, James Robinson. Success.

HIT OR MISS
    See Pocock, Isaac.

HITCHENER, WILLIAM HENRY
    Ivor; or, The Sighs of Ulla. London: Lowndes & Hobbs (printer), 1808. Pp. [1]-66.
    Love in a Desert. London: Shaw & Son (printer), 1802. Pp. [1]-40.

H.M.S. MISSFIRE
    See Drury, William Price.

H.M.S. PINAFORE
    See Gilbert, William Schwenck.

HOADLY, BENJAMIN
    Suspicious Husband, The. London: Whittingham & Arliss, 1815. Pp. [1]-80. London Theatre, XIV. *Filed under* Dibdin, Thomas John, ed. London Theatre, XIV.
    Suspicious Husband, The. In *New English Drama,* ed. W. Oxberry, 22 vols., London: W. Simpkin & R. Marshall; C. Chapple, 1818, VIII, [1-2], [i]-[viii], [1]-76. *Filed under* Oxberry, William Henry. New English Drama, VIII.
    Suspicious Husband, The. London: John Cumberland, 1826. Pp. [1]-69. Cumberland's British Theatre, I. *Filed under* Cumberland, John. Cumberland's British Theatre, I.
    Suspicious Husband, The. In *British Drama,* 12 vols., London: John Dicks, 1872, XI, [129]-153.

HOARE, PRINCE
    Chains for the Heart.
        See Chains of the Heart.
    Chains of the Heart; or, The Slave by Choice. *Also:* Chains for the Heart; or, The Slaves of Centa. Music by Mazzinghi; Reeve. London: T. Rickaby (printer), 1801. Pp. [1]-27. Libretto. *Filed under* Chains of the Heart (anon.).
    Chains of the Heart; or, The Slave by Choice. Music by Mazzinghi; Reeve. London: Barker & Son, 1802. Pp. [i]-[viii], [5]-92.
    Lock and Key. London: John Cumberland, n.d. Pp. [1]-38. Cumberland's British Theatre, XXIV. *Filed under* Cumberland, John. Cumberland's British Theatre, XXIV.
    My Grandmother. London: John Cumberland, n.d. Pp. [1]-27. Cumberland's British Theatre, XXVII. *Filed under* Cumberland, John. Cumberland's British Theatre, XXVII.
    No Song, No Supper. In *British Drama,* 12 vols., London: John Dicks, 1865, IV, [1266]-1274.
    No Song, No Supper. London: John Cumberland, n.d. Pp. [i], [1]-35. Cumberland's British Theatre, XXIV. *Filed under* Cumberland, John. Cumberland's British Theatre, XXIV.
    Paragraph, The. London: Richard Phillips, 1804. Pp. [iii]-[x], [1]-52.
    Prize, The; or, 2, 5, 3, 8. London: John Cumberland, n.d. Pp. [1]-34. Cumberland's British Theatre, XXVI. *Filed under* Cumberland, John. Cumberland's British Theatre, XXVI.
    Spoiled Child, The. New York: Samuel French, n.d. Pp. [1]-24. Minor Drama, 133.
    Spoiled Child, The. London: John Cumberland, n.d. Pp. [1]-33. Cumberland's British Theatre, 96.
    Three and the Deuce, The; or, Which Is Which? London: John Cumberland, n.d. Pp. [1]-43. Cumberland's British Theatre, XXXVIII. *Filed under* Cumberland, John. Cumberland's British Theatre, XXXVIII.

HOAXER, THE
    See Frere, Benjamin.

HOBBES, JOHN OLIVER (pseud. of Craigie, Pearl Mary Teresa Richards, Mrs. Reginald Walpole)
    Ambassador, The. London: T. Fisher Unwin, 1898. Pp. [i]-[xiv], [1]-152. *Filed under* Craigie, Pearl Mary Teresa Richards.
    Osbern and Ursyne. London & New York: John Lane, 1900. Pp. [i-vi], 1-95. *Filed under* Craigie, Pearl Mary Teresa Richards.
    School for Saints, The. New York: Century; London: T. Fisher Unwin, 1896. Pp. [i], [1]-81. Typescript title page.
    Wisdom of the Wise, The. New York: Frederick A. Stokes, c.1900. Pp. [i-vi], [1]-136. *Filed under* Craigie, Pearl Mary Teresa Richards.

HOBBS, DOBBS, AND STUBBS
    See Webster, Benjamin Nottingham.
    See Webster, Benjamin Nottingham. Three Grocers, The.
HOBBY-HORSE, THE
    See Pinero, Arthur Wing.
HODGES, G. S.
    Quarrel of the Flowers, The; or, Who Shall Be Queen? In *Home Plays for Ladies,* Part 5, London & New York: Samuel French, n.d., pp. [1]-12. *Filed under* Home Plays for Ladies, Part 5 (anon.).
HODGSON, G. S.
    Bobby A1; or, A Warm Reception. London & New York: Samuel French, n.d. Pp. [1]-14. [Lacy's Acting Edition].
HOFER, THE TELL OF THE TYROL
    See Fitzball, Edward.
HOGARTH, DAVID GEORGE (trans.)
    Frogs, The. Written with Godley, Alfred Denis (trans.). By Aristophanes. Music by Parry, C. Hubert H. Leipzig: Breitkopf & Härtel, n.d. Pp. [1]-86. Vocal score.
HOGG, CERVANTES (pseud.)
    See Barrett, Eaton Stannard.
HOGG, JAMES
    Hunting of Badlewe, The. By J. H. Craig (pseud.). London: Henry Colburn, 1814. Pp. [i]-viii, [1]-131.
    Royal Jubilee, The. By the Ettrick Shepherd (pseud.). Edinburgh: William Blackwood, 1822. Pp. [1]-42.
HOGMANAY
    See Sidney, Frederick W.
HOLCROFT, FANNY (trans.)
    Baron, The. By Celenio. In *Theatrical Recorder,* ed. Thomas Holcroft, London: C. Mercier (printer), 1806, II, [i], [287]-322.
    Emilia Galotti. By Lessing. In *Theatrical Recorder,* ed. Thomas Holcroft, London: C. Mercier (printer), 1805, I, [i], [363]-413.
    Fortune Mends. By Calderon. In *Theatrical Recorder,* ed. Thomas Holcroft, London: C. Mercier (printer), 1806, II, [i], [75]-111.
    From Bad to Worse. By Calderon. In *Theatrical Recorder,* ed. Thomas Holcroft, London: C. Mercier (printer), 1805, I, [i], [223]-269.
    Minna von Barnhelm. By Lessing. In *Theatrical Recorder,* ed. Thomas Holcroft, London: C. Mercier (printer), 1806, II, [i], [215]-260.
    Philip the Second. By Alfieri. In *Theatrical Recorder,* ed. Thomas Holcroft, London: C. Mercier (printer), 1805, I, [i], [81]-121.
    Rosamond. By Weisse. In *Theatrical Recorder,* ed. Thomas Holcroft, London: C. Mercier (printer), 1806, II, [i], [359]-397.
HOLCROFT, THOMAS
    Deaf and Dumb; or, The Orphan Protected. Dublin: J. Stockdale (printer), 1801. Pp. [ii]-[vi], [7]-[74]. Promptbook.
    Deaf and Dumb; or, The Orphan Protected. London: J. Ridgway, 1801. Pp. [iii]-[x], [1]-[82].
    Deaf and Dumb. In *New English Drama,* ed. W. Oxberry, 22 vols., London: W. Simpkin & R. Marshall; C. Chapple, 1819, VI, [1-2], [i]-[viii], [1]-60. *Filed under* Oxberry, William Henry. New English Drama, VI.
    Deaf and Dumb; or, The Orphan Protected. London: John Cumberland, 1827. Pp. [1]-60. Cumberland's British Theatre, XV. *Filed under* Cumberland, John. Cumberland's British Theatre, XV.
    Deaf and Dumb; or, The Orphan Protected. In *British Drama,* 12 vols., London: John Dicks, 1871, VII, [65]-84.
    Deserted Daughter, The. New York: D. Longworth, 1806. Pp. [1]-[76].
    Deserted Daughter, The. In *British Drama,* 12 vols., London: John Dicks, 1872, XII, [193]-218.
    Duplicity. In *Modern Theatre,* ed. Mrs. Inchbald, 10 vols., London: Longman, Hurst, Rees, Orme, & Brown, 1811, IV, [i-ii], [1]-74.
    Duplicity. In *British Drama,* 12 vols., London: John Dicks, 1872, X, [33]-53.

Follies of a Day, The. In *New English Drama,* ed. W. Oxberry, 22 vols., London: W. Simpkin & R. Marshall; C. Chapple, 1822, XIII, [i]-[viii], [9]-43. *Filed under* Oxberry, William Henry. New English Drama, XIII.
Follies of a Day, The. In *British Drama,* 12 vols., London: John Dicks, 1871, VII, [213]-224.
Follies of a Day, The.
    See Kemble, John Philip (arr.).
Hear Both Sides. London: R. Phillips, 1803. Pp. [i-viii], [5]-90.
Hear Both Sides. London: R. Phillips, 1803. Pp. [i-viii], [5]-[92]. 2nd ed.
He's Much to Blame. In *Modern Theatre,* ed. Mrs. Inchbald, 10 vols., London: Longman, Hurst, Rees, Orme, & Brown, 1811, IV, [163]-252.
He's Much to Blame. In *British Drama,* 12 vols., London: John Dicks, 1872, XII, [225]-247.
Joseph in Egypt. In *Dramas, Serious and Serio-Comic, for College, Camp, and Cabin,* London: Thomas Hailes Lacy, n.d., pp. [1]-20. *Filed under* Lacy, Thomas Hailes. Dramas for College, Camp, and Cabin.
Lady of the Rock, The. London: Longman, Hurst, Rees, & Orme, 1805. Pp. [i]-[viii], [1]-31.
Lady of the Rock, The. London: Longman, Hurst, Rees, & Orme, 1805. Pp. [i]-[x], [1]-31. 2nd ed.
Road to Ruin, The. In *New English Drama,* ed. W. Oxberry, 22 vols., London: W. Simpkin & R. Marshall; C. Chapple, 1819, VII, [1-2], [i]-[vi], [1]-[87]. *Filed under* Oxberry, William Henry. New English Drama, VII.
Road to Ruin, The. London: John Cumberland, 1829. Pp. [1]-78. Cumberland's British Theatre, IV. *Filed under* Cumberland, John. Cumberland's British Theatre, IV.
Road to Ruin, The. In *British Drama,* 12 vols., London: John Dicks, 1864, I, [154]-175.
School for Arrogance, The. In *Modern Theatre,* ed. Mrs. Inchbald, 10 vols., London: Longman, Hurst, Rees, Orme, & Brown, 1811, IV, [75]-162.
School for Arrogance, The. In *British Drama,* 12 vols., London: John Dicks, 1872, XI, [97]-120.
Seduction. In *Modern Theatre,* ed. Mrs. Inchbald, 10 vols., London: Longman, Hurst, Rees, Orme, & Brown, 1811, IV, [253]-330.
Tale of Mystery, A. Music by Busby. London: R. Phillips, 1802. Pp. [i-x], [1]-51. Promptbook.
Tale of Mystery, A. London: T. Dolby, 1825. Pp. [1]-32. Dolby's British Theatre, VIII. *Filed under* Cumberland, John. Cumberland's British Theatre, VIII.
Tale of Mystery, A. In *British Drama,* 12 vols., London: John Dicks, 1864, II, [533]-542.
Vindictive Man, The. London: H. D. Symonds, 1807. Pp. [i]-[viii], [1]-84. 2nd ed.
HOLD YOUR TONGUE
    See Planché, James Robinson.
HOLE IN THE WALL
    See Moncrieff, William Thomas. Secret, The.
    See Poole, John.
HOLFORD, MARGARET, MRS.
    Way to Win Her, The. In *New British Theatre,* London: A. J. Valpy (printer), 1814, II, [i], [401]-[474]. *Filed under* Way to Win Her, The (anon.).
HOLIDAY, A
    See Rockingham, Charles, Sir.
HOLIDAY HARLEQUIN
    See Dibdin, Charles Isaac Mungo, jr. Fire and Spirit.
HOLL, HENRY
    Forest Keeper, The. London: Thomas Hailes Lacy, n.d. Pp. [1]-40. Lacy's Acting Edition, 658.
    Grace Huntley. London: John Cumberland, n.d. Pp. [i-ii], [1]-44. Cumberland's Minor Theatre, VII. *Filed under* Cumberland, John. Cumberland's Minor Theatre, VII.
    Grace Huntley. London: John Cumberland, n.d. Pp. [1]-44.
    Louise; or, The White Scarf. London: W. Strange, n.d. Pp. [1]-45.
    Wapping Old Stairs! London: John Duncombe, n.d. Pp. [1]-32. Duncombe's Edition.

HOLLAND, BARON
   See Fox, Henry Richard.
HOLLINGSHEAD, JOHN
   Bardell versus Pickwick. London & New York: Samuel
      French, n.d. Pp. [1]-19. [Lacy's Acting Edition].
   Birth-place of Podgers, The. New York: Robert M. DeWitt,
      n.d. Pp. [1]-13. DeWitt's Acting Plays, 67.
   Grasshopper, The. London: Woodfall & Kinder (printer)
      (priv.), n.d. Pp. [i-ii], [1]-45.
HOLLY BUSH HALL
   See Suter, William E.
HOLLY TREE INN
   See Beringer, Aimée Danielle, Mrs. Oscar.
   See Webster, Benjamin Nottingham.
HOLMAN, JOSEPH GEORGE
   Abroad and At Home. London: Barker & Son, 1802. Pp.
      [3]-92. New ed.
   Abroad and At Home. In *British Drama*, 12 vols., London:
      John Dicks, 1872, X, [97]-117.
   Gazette Extraordinary, The. London: Longman, Hurst, Rees,
      Orme, & Brown, 1811. Pp. [i-viii], [1]-[84].
   Votary of Wealth, The. In *Modern Theatre*, ed. Mrs. Inchbald,
      10 vols., London: Longman, Hurst, Rees, Orme, &
      Brown, 1811, III, [i-ii], [1]-84.
   Votary of Wealth, The. In *British Drama*, 12 vols., London:
      John Dicks, 1872, XI, [257]-280.
   What a Blunder! London: W. Miller, 1800. Pp. [i-iv], [1]-59.
      2nd ed.
HOLROYD, JOHN JOSEPH
   Gisela. By I. J. H. London: John Lee, 1839. Pp. [i-vi],
      [1]-[92].
HOLT, FRANCIS LUDLOW
   Land We Live In, The. London: John Bell, 1805. Pp.
      [iii]-[xvi], [1]-103.
HOME, JOHN
   Douglas. London: Whittingham & Arliss, 1814. Pp. [1]-[51].
      London Theatre, III. *Filed under* Dibdin, Thomas John,
      ed. London Theatre, III.
   Douglas. In *New English Drama*, ed. W. Oxberry, 22 vols.,
      London: W. Simpkin & R. Marshall; C. Chapple, 1821,
      XII, [1-2], [i]-[viii], [11]-54. *Filed under* Oxberry, William
      Henry. New English Drama, XII.
   Douglas. London: John Cumberland, 1826. Pp. [1]-45.
      Cumberland's British Theatre, I. *Filed under* Cumberland,
      John. Cumberland's British Theatre, I.
   Douglas. In *British Drama*, 12 vols., London: John Dicks,
      1864, I, [100]-112.
HOME
   See Robertson, Thomas William.
HOME AGAIN!
   See Fitzball, Edward.
HOME AND HAPPINESS
   See Selby, Charles. Paris and Pleasure.
HOME BLIGHT
   See Abel, William Henry. Self Disinherited.
HOME FAIRY, A
   See Adams, Florence Davenport.
HOME FOR A HOLIDAY
   See Gordon, Walter.
HOME FOR THE HOLIDAYS
   See Moncrieff, William Thomas.
HOME FROM FAIRYLAND
   See Neil, Ross. Elfinella.
HOME OF ONE'S OWN, A
   See Lucas, William James.
HOME RULE
   See Taylor, J. G.
HOME SECRETARY, THE
   See Carton, R. C.
HOME SWEET HOME!
   See Pocock, Isaac.
   See Somerset, Charles A.
HOME, SWEET HOME, WITH VARIATIONS
   See Swears, Herbert.

HOME TRUTHS
   See Reynoldson, Thomas Herbert.
HOME WRECK, THE
   See Coyne, Joseph Stirling.
HOMICIDE, THE
   See Baillie, Joanna.
HONAN, MICHAEL BURKE
   Queen's Horse, The. Written with Planché, James Robinson.
      London: Chapman & Hall, n.d. Pp. [i-iv], [5]-22.
HONEST JEW OF FRANKFORT
   See Barnett, Charles Zachary. Rise of the Rotheschildes,
      The.
HONEST SOLDIER, THE
   See Colls, J. H.
HONEST TAR AND THE WICKED FIRST LUFF
   See Drury, William Price. H.M.S. Missfire.
HONEST THIEVES, THE
   See Knight, Thomas.
HONEST WELCHMAN
   See Dibdin, Thomas John. St. David's Day.
HONEST WELSHMAN
   See Dibdin, Thomas John. St. David's Day.
HONESTY
   See Puseley, Daniel.
   See Spicer, Henry.
HONESTY THE BEST POLICY
   See Lemon, Mark.
   See Maclaren, Archibald. Ways of London, The.
HONEY MOON, THE
   See Tobin, John.
HONEY, THE MONEY, AND THE DAINTY DISH
   See Thompson, Alfred. Harlequin Blackbird.
HONEYMOON, THE
   See Tobin, John.
HONEYMOON TRAGEDY, A
   See Clifford, Lucy Lane, Mrs. William Kingdon.
HONI SOIT
   See Magnay, William.
HONOUR
   See Hilton, B. H.
HONOUR BEFORE WEALTH
   See Edwards, Pierrepont.
   See Edwards, Pierrepont. Romance of a Poor Young
      Man, The.
HONOUR VERSUS WEALTH
   See Coates, Alfred.
HOOD, BASIL CHARLES WILLETT
   Dandy Dan, the Lifeguardsman. Music by Slaughter, Walter.
      London: Hopwood & Crew, n.d. Pp. [i-vi], 1-115. Vocal
      score.
   Emerald Isle, The. [London: Mrs. Marshall's Typewriting
      Office], n.d. Pp. [i], [1]-46, [i], [1]-41. Pagination by act.
      Typescript promptbook libretto.
   Emerald Isle, The; or, The Caves of Carrig-Cleena. Music by
      Sullivan, Arthur; German, Edward. London: Chappell,
      n.d. Pp. [i-iv], 1-220. Vocal score.
   French Maid, The. Music by Slaughter, Walter. London: E.
      Ascherberg, c.1896. Pp. [i-iv], 1-144. Vocal score.
   Gentleman Joe. Music by Slaughter, Walter. London: E.
      Ascherberg, c.1895. Pp. [i-ii], [1]-112. Vocal score.
   Ib and Little Christina: The Story of a Hearth. Miss
      Lawrence's Typewriting Office. Pp. [i], [1]-19. Typescript
      promptbook.
   Love in a Cottage. London: Mrs. Marshall's Typewriting
      Office, n.d. Pp. [i-iii], [1-2], [i], [1]-23, [i], [1]-20, [i], [1]-8.
      Pagination by act. Typescript promptbook.
   Rose of Persia, The; or, The Story-Teller and the Slave. Music
      by Sullivan, Arthur. London: Mrs. Marshall's Type-
      writing Office, 1899. Pp. [i-v], [2]-46, [i], [1]-39. Pagi-
      nation by act. Typescript promptbook libretto.
   Rose of Persia, The; or, The Story-Teller and the Slave. Music
      by Sullivan, Arthur. London: Chappell; Hopwood &
      Crew, c.1900. Pp. [i-iv], 1-237. Vocal score.

HOOD, THOMAS, SR

Tail (Tale) of a Shark, The; or, The Wailing (Whaling) Experience of Sally Simpkins. Music by Cooke, T.; Sedgwick, Alfred B. New York: Robert M. DeWitt, c.1876 <wrps. Clinton T. DeWitt>. Pp. [1]-6. DeWitt's Acting Plays, 232.

HOOD, THOMAS, JR

See Hood, Tom.

HOOD, TOM

Harlequin Little Red Riding-Hood; or, The Wicked Wolf and the Wirtuous Woodcutter. New York: Happy Hours, n.d. Pp. [1]-12. Parlor Plays for Home Performance, 21. Libretto. *Filed under* Hood, Thomas.

Lost and Found: A Fragment. London: John Dicks, n.d. Pp. [1]-14. Dicks' Standard Plays, 1070.

York and Lancaster; or, A School without Scholars. London: John Dicks, n.d. Pp. [1]-14. Dicks' Standard Plays, 1069.

HOOK, THEODORE EDWARD

Catch Him Who Can! Music by Hook, sr. London: C. & R. Baldwin, 1806. Pp. [3]-53.

Catch Him Who Can! London: John Cumberland, n.d. Pp. [1]-34. Cumberland's British Theatre, XL. *Filed under* Cumberland, John. Cumberland's British Theatre, XL.

Darkness Visible. London: C. Chapple, 1811. Pp. [i]-[x], [1]-45. 2nd ed.

Day at an Inn, A. London: James Pattie, n.d. Pp. [3]-19.

Exchange No Robbery; or, The Diamond Ring. London: W. Wright, 1820. Pp. [i-iv], [1]-67.

Exchange No Robbery; or, The Diamond Ring. London: W. Wright, 1820. Pp. [i-vi], [1]-67. 2nd ed.

Exchange No Robbery. London: John Cumberland, n.d. Pp. [1]-54. Cumberland's British Theatre, XXXVII. *Filed under* Cumberland, John. Cumberland's British Theatre, XXXVII.

Fortress, The. Music by Hook, sr. London: Samuel Tipper, 1807. Pp. [i]-[vi], [7]-68.

Invisible Girl, The. London: C. & R. Baldwin, 1806. Pp. [i]-[viii], [9]-38.

Invisible Girl, The. London: John Cumberland, n.d. Pp. [1]-22. Cumberland's British Theatre, XL. *Filed under* Cumberland, John. Cumberland's British Theatre, XL.

Killing No Murder. Music by Hook, sr. New York: D. Longworth, 1809. Pp. [1]-44.

Killing No Murder. Music by Hook, sr. London: Samuel Tipper, 1809. Pp. [i]-[xiv], [1]-[53].

Killing No Murder. London: John Cumberland, n.d. Pp. [i-ii], [1]-44. Cumberland's British Theatre, XXXI. *Filed under* Cumberland, John. Cumberland's British Theatre, XXXI.

Music Mad. London: C. Chapple, 1808. Pp. [i]-[vi], [1]-33.

Safe and Sound. Music by Hook, sr. London: Samuel Tipper, 1809. Pp. [i-vi], [1]-70.

Soldier's Return, The; or, What Can Beauty Do? Music by Hook, sr. London: Longman, Hurst, Rees, & Orme, 1805. Pp. [1]-41. Libretto.

Tekeli; or, The Siege of Montgatz. Music by Hook, sr. London: C. & R. Baldwin, 1806. Pp. [1]-47.

Tekeli; or, The Siege of Montgatz. London: John Cumberland, n.d. Pp. [1]-36. Cumberland's British Theatre, XXX. *Filed under* Cumberland, John. Cumberland's British Theatre, XXX.

Trial by Jury, The. London: Sherwood, Neely, & Jones, 1811. Pp. [i]-[x], [1]-35.

HOOK AND EYE

See Norwood, Eille.

HOOP OF GOLD

See Murdoch, J. Mortimer.

HOP-O'-MY-THUMB

See Smith, Albert Richard.

HOP O' MY THUMB AND HIS ELEVEN BROTHERS

See Blanchard, Edward Litt Leman.

HOP PICKERS AND GIPSIES

See Hazlewood, Colin Henry.

HOPE, ANTHONY (pseud. of Hawkins, Anthony Hope)

Adventure of the Lady Ursula, The. New York: R. H. Russell, 1898. Pp. [i-viii], [1]-125. Promptbook. *Filed under* Hawkins, Anthony Hope.

Business Arrangement, A. In *Dialogues of the Day,* ed. Oswald Crawfurd, London: Chapman & Hall, n.d., pp. [242]-253. *Filed under* Crawfurd, Oswald. Dialogues of the Day.

Day of Reckoning, A. In *Dialogues of the Day,* ed. Oswald Crawfurd, London: Chapman & Hall, n.d., pp. [2]-13. *Filed under* Crawfurd, Oswald. Dialogues of the Day.

Love in Leap Year. In *Dialogues of the Day,* ed. Oswald Crawfurd, London: Chapman & Hall, n.d., pp. [124]-132. *Filed under* Crawfurd, Oswald. Dialogues of the Day.

Rupert of Hentzau. Pp. [i], [1-59], [1-21], [1-58], [1-17]. Pagination by act. Typescript. *Filed under* Hawkins, Anthony Hope.

HOPE OF THE FAMILY, THE

See Coyne, Joseph Stirling.

HOPELESS PASSION, A

See Morton, John Maddison.

HOPWOOD, AUBREY

Lucky Star, The.

See Brookfield, Charles Hallam Elton.

Runaway Girl, A.

See Hicks, Edmund Seymour.

HORACE

See Horatius (anon.).

HORACE AT THE UNIVERSITY OF ATHENS

See Trevelyan, George Otto.

HORATIUS (anon. trans.)

Also: Horace. By Corneille. Manchester: Lowes (printer), 1847. Pp. [1]-[96].

HORN OF A DILEMMA

See Brough, William. Ernani.

HORNCASTLE, JAMES HENRY

Bayadere, The. By H. Horncastle. 13 leaves. Manuscript. *Filed under* Horncastle, H.

Cat's in the Larder, The; or, The Maid with A Parasol. New York: William Applegate (printer), 1840. Pp. [1]-11.

Infant Phenomenon, The; or, A Rehearsal Rehearsed. By H. Horncastle. London: John Dicks, n.d. Pp. [1]-8. Dicks' Standard Plays, 572. *Filed under* Horncastle, H..

Ma Part; or, Carlo Broschi. Music by Auber. 31 leaves. Manuscript libretto.

HORNCASTLE, H.

See Horncastle, James Henry.

HORNE, F. LENNOX

Baronet Abroad and the Rustic Prima Donna, The. London: Thomas Hailes Lacy, n.d. Pp. [1]-20.

Tale of a Comet, A. London & New York: Samuel French, n.d. Pp. [1]-20. Lacy's Acting Edition.

Two Heads Are Better than One. By Lenox Horne. Boston: Charles H. Spencer, n.d. Pp. [1]-17.

HORNE, LENOX

See Horne, F. Lennox.

HORNE, RICHARD HENGIST (or Henry)

Cosmo de' Medici. London: J. Templeman, 1837. Pp. [iii]-[xii], [1]-118.

Death of Marlowe, The. London: Thomas Hailes Lacy, 1870. Pp. [1]-23. 5th ed. [Lacy's Acting Edition].

Gregory VII. London: Saunders & Otley, 1840. Pp. [i]-[xl], [1]-104.

John the Baptist; or, The Valour of the Soul. In *Bible Tragedies,* London: Newman, n.d., pp. [i-vi], [1]-46. *Filed under* Bible Tragedies.

Judas Iscariot. London: C. Mitchell, 1848. Pp. [1-2], [i]-[viii], [1]-43.

Judas Iscariot. In *Bible Tragedies,* London: Newman, n.d., pp. [107]-191. *Filed under* Bible Tragedies.

Laura Dibalzo; or, The Patriot Martyrs. London: Newman, 1880. Pp. [i]-[viii], [1]-98.

Prometheus the Fire-Bringer. By Richard Henry Horne. Edinburgh: Edmonston & Douglas, 1864. Pp. [1], [i]-[viii], [9]-55.

Prometheus the Fire-Bringer. By Richard Henry Horne. Melbourne: H. T. Dwight, 1866. Pp. [i]-[viii], [9]-60. Australian Ed. *Filed under* Horne, Richard Henry.

Psyche Apocalypté.
    See Browning, Elizabeth Barrett.

HORNER, FRED
    Bungalow, The. N.p.: n.pub. (priv.), 1892. Pp. [i-iv], [1]-[105].
    Isalda. London: n.pub., n.d. Pp. [i-ii], [1]-17.
    Late Lamented, The. N.p.: n.pub., n.d. Pp. [3]-76. Title page lacking.
    Other Man, The. London: Mrs. Marshall's Typewriting Office, 1893. Pp. [i], [1]-41, [i], [1]-63, [i], [1]-25. Pagination by act. Typescript.

HORRID BARBARIAN
    See Cooper, James B. Oor Geordie.

HORRORS OF WAR
    See Courtney, John. Soldier's Progress, The.

HORTENSIA (anon.)
    In *New British Theatre*, ed. John Galt, London: Henry Colburn, 1815, IV, [147]-198.

HOSKINS, FRANCIS RADCLIFFE
    Blossom of Churnington Green, The; or, Love, Rivalry, and Revenge. London: Thomas Hailes Lacy, n.d. Pp. [1]-23. [Lacy's Acting Edition].

HOSKINS, HORATIO HUNTLEY
    Count de Denia; or, The Spaniard's Ransom. London: J. W. Southgate, 1841. Pp. [i]-[ix], [1]-118.
    De Valencourt. London: C. Mitchell, 1842. Pp. [i-vi], [1]-104.

HOSKINS, JOHN
    Life Buoy, The. In *British Drama*, 12 vols., London: John Dicks, 1871, V, [247]-256.

HOSTILE BROTHERS
    See Lockwood, Percival. Bride of Messina, The.

HOSTLER AND THE ROBBER
    See Fitzball, Edward. Innkeeper of Abbeville, The.

HOTEL CHARGES
    See Selby, Charles.

HOUGHTON, JOHN W.
    His Highness; or, Exchange, No Robbery. Music by Tate, Auscal; O'Donovan, Neill. N.p.: n.pub., n.d. Pp. [i-ii], [1]-16. Libretto.

HOUR AND THE MAN, THE
    See Hunt, Violet.

HOUR AT SEVILLE, AN
    See Selby, Charles.

HOUR IN THE BASTILE
    See Drayton, Henri. Marry in Haste.

HOUR OF RETRIBUTION
    See Weston, Ferdinand Fullerton. St. Aubert.

HOUSE-BREAKER OF THE LAST CENTURY
    See Greenwood, Thomas Longdon. Jack Sheppard.

HOUSE DIVIDED
    See Haines, John Thomas.
    See Haines, John Thomas. Uncle Oliver.

HOUSE DOG!, THE
    See Higgie, Thomas Henry.

HOUSE OF ASPEN, THE
    See Scott, Walter, Sir.

HOUSE OF BARDSLEY, THE
    See Leslie, Henry. Trail of Sin, The.

HOUSE OF COLBERG, THE
    See Serle, Thomas James.

HOUSE OF LADIES, THE
    See Lemon, Mark.

HOUSE OF MORVILLE, THE
    See Lake, John.

HOUSE OF USNA, THE
    See Sharp, William.

HOUSE ON THE BRIDGE OF NOTRE DAME, THE
    See Hazlewood, Colin Henry.

HOUSE OR THE HOME?, THE
    See Taylor, Tom.

HOUSE OUT AT WINDOWS, A
    See Kenney, James.

HOUSE OUT OF WINDOWS, A
    See Brough, William.

HOUSE ROOM
    See Peake, Richard Brinsley.

HOUSE THAT JACK BUILT
    See Conquest, George. Jack and Jill and the Well on the Hill.

HOUSE THAT JACK BUILT, THE; OR, HARLEQUIN JACK, THE THREE WITCHES, AND THE FAIRY KING (anon.)
    London (Holborn): Thomas Scott (printer), n.d. Pp. [1]-28. Libretto.

HOUSE TO BE SOLD, A
    See Cobb, James.

HOUSEHOLD FAIRY, A
    See Talfourd, Francis.

HOUSEKEEPER, THE
    See Jerrold, Douglas William.

HOUSTON, THOMAS
    Term Day; or, The Unjust Steward. Newcastle-upon-Tyne: D. Bass (printer), 1803. Pp. [1]-60.

HOVELL, EDWARD
    See Thurlow, Edward Hovell, Lord.

HOW DO YOU MANAGE?
    See Bayly, Thomas Haynes.

HOW DREAMS COME TRUE
    See Todhunter, John.

HOW HE DID IT!
    See Parry, John.

HOW I FOUND CRUSOE
    See Thompson, Alfred.

HOW SHALL WE GET RID OF HIM?
    See Planché, James Robinson. Giovanni the Vampire!

HOW SHE LOVES HIM!
    See Boucicault, Dionysius Lardner.

HOW STOUT YOU'RE GETTING!
    See Morton, John Maddison.

HOW TO COOK A BIFFIN!
    See Selby, Charles. Hotel Charges.

HOW TO DIE FOR LOVE! (anon.)
    Also: The Blank Cartridge. London: C. Chapple, 1812. Pp. [7]-45. Possibly lacking front matter. 3rd ed.

HOW TO DIE FOR LOVE (anon.)
    Also: The Blank Cartridge. London: John Cumberland, n.d. Pp. [1]-34. Cumberland's British Theatre, XL. *Filed under* Cumberland, John. Cumberland's British Theatre, XL.

HOW TO DIE FOR LOVE (anon.)
    Also: The Blank Cartridge. London: John Cumberland, n.d. Pp. [1]-34. [Cumberland's British Theatre].

HOW TO GROW RICH
    See Reynolds, Frederick.

HOW TO MAKE HOME HAPPY
    See Brough, William.

HOW TO PAY THE RENT
    See Power, Tyrone.

HOW TO RULE A HUSBAND
    See Morton, Thomas, sr. School of Reform, The.

HOW TO RUN THROUGH THE SCALES
    See Burnand, Francis Cowley. Sir Dagobert and the Dragon.

HOW TO SETTLE ACCOUNTS WITH YOUR LAUNDRESS
    See Coyne, Joseph Stirling.

HOW TO TAKE UP A BILL
    See Moncrieff, William Thomas.

HOW TO TAME YOUR MOTHER-IN-LAW
    See Byron, Henry James.

HOW WILL IT END?
    See Hilton, B. H. Baronets, The.
    See Reynolds, Frederick. Begone Dull Care.

HOW WILL THEY GET OUT OF IT?
    See Sketchley, Arthur.

HOW'S YOUR UNCLE?
    See Wilks, Thomas Egerton.

HOWARD, BRONSON
    Knave and Queen.
        See Young, Charles Lawrence, Sir.
HOWARD, GEORGE WILLIAM FREDERICK, EARL OF CARLISLE
    Last of the Greeks, The; or, The Fall of Constantinople. By Lord Morpeth. London: James Ridgway, 1828. Pp. [i]-[viii], [1]-79. *Filed under* Carlisle, Howard, G. W. F., Earl of.
    Step-mother, The. London: R. H. Evans, 1800. Pp. [1-2], [i]-[viii], [1]-[90]. *Filed under* Carlisle, Howard, G. W. F., Earl of.
HOWARD, WALTER
    Mohawk Minstrels' Fifth Book of Dramas, Dialogues, & Drolleries, The.
        See Banks, Billy.
HUBERT'S PRIDE
    See Fraser, Julia Agnes.
HUDSON, E. NEEVES
    Bridge of Notre Dame, The; or, The Parricide's Curse. London: Duncombe & Moon, n.d. Pp. [1]-42. Duncombe's Edition.
HUE AND CRY AFTER HONESTY
    See Taylor, Tom. Diogenes and His Lantern.
HUEFFER, FRANCIS
    Colomba. Music by Mackenzie, A. C. London: Novello, Ewer, n.d. Pp. [i]-xviii, [1]-229. Novello's Original Octavo Edition. Libretto and vocal score.
    Troubadour, The. Music by Mackenzie, A. C. London & New York: Novello, Ewer, n.d. Pp. [i]-[xviii], [1]-201. Novello's Original Octavo Edition. Libretto and vocal score.
HUGGER-MUGGER
    See Clarke, Henry Saville.
HUGHES, FRED
    My Wife's Baby. London & New York: Samuel French, n.d. Pp. [1]-14. [Lacy's Acting Edition].
HUGHES, GEORGE CHARLES
    Tiberius. London: T. F. A. Day (printer), 1861. Pp. [1]-52.
HUGHES, JOHN
    Siege of Damascus, The. London: Whittingham & Arliss, 1815. Pp. [1]-[64]. London Theatre, XIV. *Filed under* Dibdin, Thomas John, ed. London Theatre, XIV.
    Siege of Damascus, The. In *British Drama,* 12 vols., London: John Dicks, 1871, VII, [225]-243.
HUGO, VICTOR
    Francis the First.
        See Slous, Frederick L. (trans.).
    Hernani.
        See under title.
        See Crosland, Camilla Dufour Toulmin, Mrs. Newton (trans.).
    Ruy Blas.
        See Crosland, Camilla Dufour Toulmin, Mrs. Newton (trans.).
HUGUENOT CAPTAIN, THE
    See Phillips, Watts.
HUGUENOTS
    See Maggioni, Manfredo (trans.). Ugonotti, Gli.
    See Romer, Frank (trans.). Ugonotti, Gli.
HUGUENOTS UNDER LOUIS XV
    See Bennett, John E. Paul Rabaut.
HUIE, JAMES L.
    Quentin Durward. Edinburgh: James L. Huie; London: Blake, Young, & Young, 1823. Pp. [1]-78.
HULL, THOMAS
    Henry the Second; or, The Fall of Rosamond. In *Modern Theatre,* ed. Mrs. Inchbald, 10 vols., London: Longman, Hurst, Rees, Orme, & Brown, 1811, IX, [337]-396.
HUMAN NATURE
    See Wheatley, J. A.
HUMAN SACRIFICE, A
    See Clarke, Clara Savile.
HUMAN SPORT, A
    See Fryers, Austin.

HUMANITY
    See Vane, Sutton. For England.
HUMBOLDT, CHARLOTTE DE
    Corinth. In *Corinth, a Tragedy; and Other Poems,* London: Longman, Orme, Brown, Green, & Longmans, 1838, pp. [i], [1]-72.
HUMBUG
    See Burnand, Francis Cowley.
    See Jones, Henry Arthur.
HUME, ROBERT WILLIAM
    Meroth; or, The Sacrifice to the Nile. London: R. W. Hume; W. & T. Piper, 1850. Pp. [1]-43.
HUMOURS OF BLUFF KING HAL
    See Moncrieff, William Thomas. Beggar of Cripplegate, The.
HUMOURS OF THE COURT, THE
    See Bridges, Robert Seymour.
HUMPBACKED LOVER, THE
    See Mathews, Charles James.
HUMPHREY, EDWARD
    Our Court. Written with Addison, John. Music by Weaver, James. London: George Kenning, n.d. Pp. [1]-29. Libretto.
HUMPHREY CLINKER
    See Dibdin, Thomas John.
HUNCHBACK, THE
    See Knowles, James Sheridan.
HUNCHBACK OF PARIS
    See Brougham, John. Duke's Daughter, The.
HUNCHBACKS, THE (anon.)
    London: John Cumberland, n.d. Pp. [1]-36. Cumberland's Minor Theatre, VI. *Filed under* Cumberland, John. Cumberland's Minor Theatre, VI.
HUNDRED POUND NOTE, THE
    See Peake, Richard Brinsley.
HUNDRED THOUSAND POUNDS
    See Byron Henry James. One Hundred Thousand Pounds.
HUNDRED YEARS AGO
    See Buckstone, John Baldwin. Green Bushes, The.
HUNT, LEIGH
    Descent of Liberty, The. London: Gale & Fenner, 1816. Pp. [i]-lix, [1]-82. New ed.
    Father Avenged, A. In *Companion,* I (28 May 1828), [289]-303.
    Father Avenged, A (Sequel of). In *Companion,* I (4 June 1828), [i], [305]-320.
    Legend of Florence, A. London: Edward Moxon, 1840. Pp. [iii]-[xii], [1]-82.
    Scenes from an Unfinished Drama. In *Dedicator,* I (1 March 1820), [i], [161]-168.
    Syracusan Gossips, The; or, The Feast of Adonis. In *Foliage; or, Poems Original and Translated,* London: C. & J. Ollier, 1818, pp. [i], 44-57.
HUNT, MARGARET RAINE, MRS. ALFRED WILLIAM
    Girls He Left Behind Him, The. In *Dialogues of the Day,* ed. Oswald Crawfurd, London: Chapman & Hall, n.d., pp. [114]-122. *Filed under* Crawfurd, Oswald. Dialogues of the Day.
HUNT, VIOLET
    End of the Beginning, The. In *Dialogues of the Day,* ed. Oswald Crawfurd, London: Chapman & Hall, n.d., pp. [26]-41. *Filed under* Crawfurd, Oswald. Dialogues of the Day.
    Hour and the Man, The. In *Dialogues of the Day,* ed. Oswald Crawfurd, London: Chapman & Hall, n.d., pp. [192]-202. *Filed under* Crawfurd, Oswald. Dialogues of the Day.
    Way to Keep Her, The. In *Dialogues of the Day,* ed. Oswald Crawfurd, London: Chapman & Hall, n.d., pp. [134]-143. *Filed under* Crawfurd, Oswald. Dialogues of the Day.
HUNT AFTER HAPPINESS
    See Talfourd, Francis. Abon Hassan.
HUNT FOR A HUSBAND, A
    See Wooler, John Pratt.
HUNTED DOWN
    See Boucicault, Dionysius Lardner.

HUNTER, HARRY
    Mohawk Minstrels' Fourth Annual of Dramas, Dialogues, and Drolleries, The. Written with Coote, Robert; Forman, Edmund; Ray, Ben, jr. London: Francis, Day, & Hunter, n.d. Pp. [1]-112.
HUNTER OF THE ALPS, THE
    See Dimond, William.
HUNTING A TURTLE
    See Selby, Charles.
HUNTING OF BADLEWE, THE
    See Hogg, James.
HUNTING THE SLIPPERS
    See Becher, Martin.
HUNTRESS OF ARLINGFORD
    See Planché, James Robinson. Maid Marian.
HUNTSMAN AND THE SPY!
    See Townsend, William Thompson. Bell Ringer of St. Paul's, The.
HURLY-BURLY, THE
    See Hendriks, Herman.
HURST, CYRIL
    Royal Vagrants, The: A Story of Conscientious Objection. Music by Waldo-Warner, H. London: Henry J. Drane, 1901. Pp. [i-ii], [1]-37. Libretto.
HURST, JAMES P.
    April Folly. London & New York: Samuel French, n.d. Pp. [1]-20. [Lacy's Acting Edition].
    Nearly Severed. London & New York: Samuel French, n.d. Pp. [1]-22. [Lacy's Acting Edition].
    Sugar and Cream. London & New York: Samuel French, n.d. Pp. [1]-16. [Lacy's Acting Edition].
    True Colours. London & New York: Samuel French, n.d. Pp. [1]-23. [French's Acting Edition].
HUSBAND AT SIGHT, A
    See Buckstone, John Baldwin.
HUSBAND IN CLOVER, A
    See Merivale, Herman Charles.
HUSBAND OF AN HOUR, THE
    See Falconer, Edmund.
HUSBAND OF MY HEART, THE
    See Selby, Charles.
HUSBAND OF POVERTY, THE
    See Maugham, Harry Neville.
HUSBAND TO ORDER, A
    See Morton, John Maddison.
HUSBAND'S CONFESSION
    See Hazlewood, Colin Henry. Lost Wife, The.
    See Hazlewood, Colin Henry. Outcast's Wife, The.
HUSBAND'S FIRST JOURNEY
    See Moncrieff, William Thomas. Bringing Home the Bride!
HUSBANDS, WIVES, AND LOVERS
    See Rodwell, George Herbert Bonaparte.
HUSH MONEY
    See Dance, Charles.
HUSH-A-BYE BABY ON THE TREE-TOP
    See Millward, Charles.
HUT OF THE HAUNTED GORGE AND THE TOURISTS' DOGS!
    See Clarke, Charles Augustus. Crystal Hunter of Mont Blanc, The.
HUT OF THE RED MOUNTAIN, THE
    See Milner, Henry M.
HUTH, ALFRED HENRY (trans.)
    Faustus, Part 1. By Goethe. London: Sampson Low, Marston, Searle, & Rivington, 1889. Pp. [i]-[viii], [1]-245.
HYDE, GEORGE
    Alphonzus. London: Thomas Davison (printer), n.d. Pp. [1]-92. Title page lacking.
    Love's Victory; or, The School for Pride. London: Hurst, Robinson, 1825. Pp. [i-vi], [1]-75.
HYDE, JOHN WALKER
    Irish Absentee, The. London: James Pattie, n.d. Pp. [1]-32.
HYDER, EL
    See Barrymore, William.

HYDROPATHY
    See Boyce, William.
HYDROPHOBIA
    See Herbert, Thomas.
HYMEN'S MUSTER ROLL
    See Long, Charles.
HYMENAEUS
    See Cooke, William Major.
HYPATIA
    See Ogilvie, G. Stuart.
HYPOCHONDRIAC, THE
    See Mathew, Charles (trans.).
HYPOCRITE
    See Bickerstaffe, Isaac.
    See Van Laun, Henri (trans.). Tartuffe.
I AM ALL THERE
    See Byron, Henry James. Motto, The.
I AM HERE!
    See Brougham, John. Duke's Motto, The.
I AM THERE
    See Brougham, John. Blanche of Nevers.
I AND MY DOUBLE
    See Oxenford, John.
I COULDN'T HELP IT
    See Oxenford, John.
I LOVE YOU!
    See Reeve, Wybert.
IB AND LITTLE CHRISTINA: THE STORY OF A HEARTH
    See Hood, Basil Charles Willett.
IBSEN, HENRIK
    Brand.
        See Garrett, Fydell Edmund (trans.).
        See Herford, Charles Harold (trans.).
        See Wilson, William (trans.).
    Cataline.
        See Johnston, Andrew (trans.).
    Doll's House.
        See Archer, William (trans.).
        See Lord, Henrietta Frances (trans.).
    Emperor and Galilean.Part 1: Caesar's Apostasy; Part 2: The Emperor Julian.
        See Archer, William (trans.).
    Enemy of Society, An.
        See Archer, William (trans.).
    Enemy of the People, An.
        See Aveling, Eleanor Marx, Mrs. Edward (trans.).
    Ghosts.
        See Archer, William (trans.).
    Hedda Gabler.
        See Archer, William (trans.).
        See Gosse, Edmund William (trans.).
    John Gabriel Borkman.
        See Archer, William (trans.).
    Lady from the Sea, The.
        See Archer, Frances Elizabeth, Mrs. William (trans.).
        See Aveling, Eleanor Marx, Mrs. Edward (trans.).
    Lady Inger of Östrât.
        See Archer, Charles (trans.).
    League of Youth, The.
        See Archer, William (trans.).
    Little Eyolf.
        See Archer, William (trans.).
    Love's Comedy.
        See Herford, Charles Harold (trans.).
    Master Builder, The.
        See Gosse, Edmund William (trans.).
    Nora.
        See Lord, Henrietta Frances (trans.).
    Peer Gynt.
        See Archer, William (trans.).
    Pillars of Society, The.
        See Archer, William (trans.).
    Pretenders, The.
        See Archer, William (trans.).

Rosmersholm.
>> *See* Archer, Charles (trans.).

Vikings at Helgeland, The.
>> *See* Archer, William (trans.).

Wild Duck, The.
>> *See* Archer, Frances Elizabeth, Mrs. William (trans.).

ICE WITCH, THE
>> *See* Buckstone, John Baldwin.

ICI ON PARLE FRANCAIS
>> *See* Williams, Thomas John.

IDALIA
>> *See* Roberts, George.

IDEAL HUSBAND, AN
>> *See* Wilde, Oscar Fingal O'Flahertie Wills.

IDENTITY
>> *See* Lequel, Louis.

IDES OF MAY, THE (anon.)
>> Dublin: W. B. Kelly (priv.), 1869. Pp. [1]-32.

IDIOT OF THE MILL, THE
>> *See* Stirling, Edward.

IDIOT OF THE MOUNTAIN, THE
>> *See* Suter, William E.

IDIOT SON
>> *See* Jerrold, Douglas William. Tower of Lochlain, The.

IDIOT WITNESS, THE
>> *See* Haines, John Thomas.

IDLER, THE
>> *See* Chambers, Charles Haddon.

IDYLL, AN
>> *See* Bennett, Joseph.

IDYLL OF THE CLOSING CENTURY, AN
>> *See* Burney, Estelle.

IF I HAD A THOUSAND A YEAR
>> *See* Morton, John Maddison.

IF THE CAP FITS
>> *See* Harrington, Nicholas Herbert.

IFFLAND, AUGUSTUS WILLIAM
>> **Conscience.**
>>> *See* Thompson, Benjamin (trans.).

IGNEZ DE CASTRO
>> *See* Musgrave, Thomas Moore (trans.).

I'LL BE YOUR SECOND
>> *See* Rodwell, George Herbert Bonaparte.

I'LL SLEEP ON IT
>> *See* Buckstone, John Baldwin. Victorine.

I'LL TELL YOU WHAT
>> *See* Inchbald, Elizabeth Simpson, Mrs. Joseph.

I'LL TELL YOUR WIFE
>> *See* Webster, W. S.

I'LL WRITE TO THE TIMES
>> *See* Wooler, John Pratt.

ILLIAM DHÔNE
>> *See* Windus, W. E.

ILL-TREATED IL TROVATORE
>> *See* Byron, Henry James.

ILLUMINÉ
>> *See* Spencer, William Robert. Urania.

ILLUSION
>> *See* Arnold, Samuel James.

ILLUSTRIOUS STRANGER, THE
>> *See* Kenney, James.

I'M HAUNTED BY A FIEND!
>> *See* Buckstone, John Baldwin. John Jones.

I'M NOT MESILF AT ALL
>> *See* Maltby, C. Alfred.

I'M PERFECTION!
>> *See* Planché, James Robinson. Dumb Belle, The.

IMAGINARY INVALID, THE
>> *See* Van Laun, Henri (trans.).

IMITATION TEA
>> *See* Maclaren, Archibald.

IMOGEN'S NEW COOK
>> *See* Medd, Mabel S.

IMOLINE
>> *See* Rettie, T. Leith.

IMPERIAL PIRATE, THE
>> *See* Pennie, John Fitzgerald.

IMPORTANCE OF BEING EARNEST, THE
>> *See* Wilde, Oscar Fingall O'Flahertie Wills.
>> *See* Wilde, Oscar Fingall O'Flahertie Wills. Lady Lancing.

IMPOSTORS, THE
>> *See* Cumberland, Richard.

IMPOSTURES OF SCAPIN, THE
>> *See* Wall, Charles Heron (trans.).

IMPROMPTU DE VERSAILLES
>> *See* Van Laun, Henri (trans.). Impromptu of Versailles, The.

IMPROMPTU OF VERSAILLES, THE
>> *See* Van Laun, Henri (trans.).

IMPUDENT INTRUDER
>> *See* Reeve, Wybert. Supper Gratis, A.

IN A BALCONY
>> *See* Browning, Robert.

IN A DAY
>> *See* Webster, Augusta Davies, Mrs. Thomas.

IN A FIRST-CLASS WAITING-ROOM
>> *See* Bell, Florence Eveleen Eleanore Oliffe, Mrs. Hugh (Lady).

IN A TRANCE
>> *See* Forman, Edmund.

IN AN ATTIC
>> *See* Jones, John Wilton.

IN AND OUT OF A PUNT
>> *See* Esmond, Henry Vernon.

IN CHANCERY
>> *See* Pinero, Arthur Wing.

IN DANGER
>> *See* Lestocq, William.

IN FOR A HOLIDAY
>> *See* Burnand, Francis Cowley. In for a Holyday.

IN FOR A HOLYDAY
>> *See* Burnand, Francis Cowley.

IN HIS POWER
>> *See* Quinton, Mark.

IN HONOR BOUND
>> *See* Grundy, Sydney.

IN NELSON'S DAYS
>> *See* Paull, Harry Major.

IN POSSESSION
>> *See* Becher, Martin.

IN QUARANTINE
>> *See* Ware, James Redding.

IN THE CLOUDS: A GLIMPSE OF UTOPIA
>> *See* A'Beckett, Gilbert Arthur.

IN THE DAYS OF THE REGENT
>> *See* Doyle, Arthur Conan.

IN THE EYES OF THE WORLD
>> *See* Wood, A. C. Fraser.

IN THE LOWTHER
>> *See* Ridge, William Pett.

IN THE PIGSKIN
>> *See* Morton, John Maddison. Steeple-Chase, The.

IN THE RANKS
>> *See* Sims, George Robert.

IN THE WRONG HOUSE
>> *See* Becher, Martin.
>> *See* Becher, Martin. Two T. J's., The.

IN TOWN
>> *See* Ross, Adrian.

IN TWO MINDS
>> *See* Heathcote, Arthur M.

INA
>> *See* Dacre, Barbarina Ogle, Lady.

INCARCERATED VICTIM OF THE BASTILLE
>> *See* Cooper, Frederick Fox. Tale of Two Cities, The.

INCHBALD, ELIZABETH SIMPSON, MRS. JOSEPH
>> **Animal Magnetism.** London: John Cumberland, 1826. Pp. [1]-33. Cumberland's British Theatre, XIV. *Filed under* Cumberland, John. Cumberland's British Theatre, XIV.

Animal Magnetism. In *British Drama,* 12 vols., London: John Dicks, 1872, X, [118]-128.

Appearance Is Against Them. In *British Drama,* 12 vols., London: John Dicks, 1871, IX, [305]-316.

Child of Nature, The. London: Thomas Dolby, 1825. Pp. [1]-36. Dolby's British Theatre, XI. *Filed under* Cumberland, John. Cumberland's British Theatre, XI.

Child of Nature, The. In *British Drama,* 12 vols., London: John Dicks, 1871, VI, [53]-64.

Every One Has His Fault. In *New English Drama,* ed. W. Oxberry, 22 vols., London: W. Simpkin & R. Marshall; C. Chapple, 1822, XVI, [1-2], [i]-[vi], [i]-[iv], [1]-74. *Filed under* Oxberry, William Henry. New English Drama, XVI.

Every One Has His Fault. London: T. Dolby, 1824. Pp. [i]-[vi], [7]-70. Dolby's British Theatre, VII. *Filed under* Cumberland, John. Cumberland's British Theatre, VII.

Every One Has His Fault. In *British Drama,* 12 vols., London: John Dicks, 1871, IX, [65]-87.

I'll Tell You What. In *Modern Theatre,* ed. Mrs. Inchbald, 10 vols., London: Longman, Hurst, Rees, Orme, & Brown, 1811, VII, [i-ii], [1]-68.

Lovers' Vows. London: John Cumberland, 1828. Pp. [1]-58. Cumberland's British Theatre, XVII. *Filed under* Cumberland, John. Cumberland's British Theatre, XVII.

Lovers' Vows. In *British Drama,* 12 vols., London: John Dicks, 1872, X, [129]-148.

Midnight Hour, The. In *New English Drama,* ed. W. Oxberry, 22 vols., London: W. Simpkin & R. Marshall; C. Chapple, 1821, XIII, [1-2], [i]-[x], [1]-33. *Filed under* Oxberry, William Henry. New English Drama, XIII.

Midnight Hour, The. London: John Cumberland, 1827. Pp. [1]-40. Cumberland's British Theatre, XV. *Filed under* Cumberland, John. Cumberland's British Theatre, XV.

Midnight Hour, The. In *British Drama,* 12 vols., London: John Dicks, 1872, XII, [181]-192.

Midnight Hour, The. London and New York: Samuel French, n.d. Pp. [3]-30. French's Acting Edition (late Lacy's).

Mogul Tale, The; or, The Descent of the Balloon. In *British Drama,* 12 vols., London: John Dicks, 1872, XI, [121]-128.

Mogul Tale, The. London: John Cumberland, n.d. Pp. [1]-25. Cumberland's British Theatre, XLII. *Filed under* Cumberland, John. Cumberland's British Theatre, XLII.

Next Door Neighbours. In *Modern Theatre,* ed. Mrs. Inchbald, 10 vols., London: Longman, Hurst, Rees, Orme, & Brown, 1811, VII, [69]-116.

Such Things Are. In *British Drama,* 12 vols., London: John Dicks, 1871, VI, [129]-149.

Wedding Day, The. In *New English Drama,* ed. W. Oxberry, 22 vols., London: W. Simpkin & R. Marshall; C. Chapple, 1823, XXI, [i]-[viii], [1]-20. *Filed under* Oxberry, William Henry. New English Drama, XXI.

Wedding Day, The. In *British Drama,* 12 vols., London: John Dicks, 1871, VI, [121]-128.

Wedding Day, The. London: John Cumberland, n.d. Pp. [1]-26. Cumberland's British Theatre, XXXIX. *Filed under* Cumberland, John. Cumberland's British Theatre, XXXIX.

Wise Man of the East, The. In *Modern Theatre,* ed. Mrs. Inchbald, 10 vols., London: Longman, Hurst, Rees, Orme, & Brown, 1811, VII, [117]-179.

Wives As They Were and Maids As They Are. London: Thomas Dolby, 1825. Pp. [i]-[vi], [7]-63. Dolby's British Theatre, X. *Filed under* Cumberland, John. Cumberland's British Theatre, X.

Wives As They Were, and Maids As They Are. In *British Drama,* 12 vols., London: John Dicks, 1872, XII, [248]-267.

INCHCAPE BELL, THE
See Fitzball, Edward.

INCOG
See Keep, W. A.

INCOGNITA
See Burnand, Francis Cowley.

INCOMPATIBILITY OF TEMPER
See Suter, William E.

INCOMPLEAT ANGLER, THE
See Burnand, Francis Cowley.

INCONSTANT, THE
See Farquhar, George.

INDÉCIS, L'
See Bell, Florence Eveleen Eleanore Oliffe, Mrs. Hugh (Lady).

INDIAN EXILES, THE
See Thompson, Benjamin (trans.).

INDIANA
See Farnie, Henry Brougham.

INDIANS, THE
See Tobin, John.

INDUCTION, AN
See Blanchard, Edward Litt Leman.

INDUSTRY AND INDOLENCE
See Stirling, Edward.

INDUSTRY TRIUMPHANT
See Caroline and Henrietta.

INES DE CASTRO AT CINTRA
See Landor, Walter Savage.

INES MENDO
See Mérimée, Prosper.

INEZ
See Neil, Ross.

INEZ DE CASTRO
See Mitford, Mary Russell.

INFANT PHENOMENON, THE
See Horncastle, James Henry.

INFANTICIDE
See Maddox, John Medex.

INFATUATION
See Young, Charles Lawrence, Sir.

INGOMAR
See Reece, Robert.

INGOMAR, THE BARBARIAN
See Lovell, Maria Anne Lacy, Mrs. George William.

INGOMAR, THE SON OF THE WILDERNESS
See Charlton, William Henry (trans.).
See Charlton, William Henry (trans.). Son of the Wilderness, The.

INHERITANCE
See Byron, George Gordon, Lord. Werner.

INKLE AND YARICO
See Colman, George, jr.

INMAN, JAMES WILLIAM, REV.
Orioma, the Reclaimed. Grantham: S. Ridge & Son; London: Simpkin, Marshall, n.d. Pp. [1-2], [i]-[v], [1]-[49].

INN OF TERRACINA
See Lacy, Michael Rophino. Fra-Diavolo.

INN ON THE HEATH
See Taylor, Thomas Proclus. Chain of Guilt, The.

INNES, J. W. BRODIE
See Brodie-Innes, J. W.

INNKEEPER OF ABBEVILLE, THE
See Fitzball, Edward.

INNKEEPER'S DAUGHTER, THE
See Soane, George.

INNOCENT CULPRIT
See Lunn, Joseph. Shepherd of Derwent Vale, The.

INO
See Spedding, B. J.

INS AND OUTS
See Lemon, Mark.

INSPECTOR'S VISIT, THE
See Fitzgerald, J. D.

INSURED AT LLOYD'S
See Palmer, T. A.

INTERIOR
See Archer, William (trans.).

INTERRUPTED BALL!
    See Collier, William. Queen's Jewel, The.
INTERVIEW, THE
    See Warren, T. Gideon.
INTIMATE FRIEND, THE
    See Kerr, John.
INTRIGUE
    See Poole, John.
    See Puseley, Daniel.
INTRIGUES OF A DAY, THE (anon.)
    In *New British Theatre*, London: A. J. Valpy (printer),
    1814, I, [i], [69]-150.
INTRUDING WIDOW
    See Lamb, Charles. Wife's Trial, The.
INUNDATION, THE
    See Archer, Thomas.
INVADERS VANQUISHED
    See Burke, William. Armed Briton, The.
INVASION, THE
    See Roche, Eugenius.
INVASION DEFEATED
    See Charnock, John. Loyalty.
INVINCIBLES, THE
    See Morton, Thomas, sr.
INVISIBLE GIRL, THE
    See Hook, Theodore Edward.
INVISIBLE PRINCE, THE
    See Planché, James Robinson.
IOLANTHE
    See Gilbert, William Schwenck.
ION
    See Cooper, Frederick Fox.
    See Talfourd, Thomas Noon.
IPHIGENIA
    See Boswell, Robert Bruce (trans.).
IPHIGENIA AT DELPHI
    See Gurney, Archer Thompson.
IPHIGENIA IN AULIS
    See Potter, Robert (trans.).
IPHIGENIA IN DELPHI
    See Garnett, Richard.
IPHIGENIA IN TAURIS
    See Potter, Robert (trans.).
    See Troutbeck, John, Rev. (trans.).
IPPOLITO DI ESTE
    See Landor, Walter Savage.
IRELAND, WILLIAM HENRY
    Mutius Scaevola; or, The Roman Patriot. London: T. Bent,
    1801. Pp. [i]-viii, [1]-90.
IRELAND AS IT IS
    See Amherst, J. H.
IREMONGER, HENRIETTA GEORGIANA MARCIA LASCELLES
    See Chatterton, Henrietta Georgiana Marcia Iremonger,
    Mrs. Lascelles, Lady Georgiana.
IRENE
    See Farnie, Henry Brougham.
IRIS
    See Pinero, Arthur Wing.
IRISH ABSENTEE, THE
    See Hyde, John Walker.
IRISH AMBASSADOR, THE
    See Kenney, James.
IRISH ATTORNEY, THE
    See Bernard, William Bayle.
IRISH BRIGADE
    See Gore, Catherine Grace Frances Moody, Mrs.
    Charles. King O'Neil.
IRISH DIAMOND
    See Boucicault, Dionysius Lardner. Andy Blake.
IRISH DOCTOR, THE
    See Wood, George.
IRISH DRAGOON, THE
    See Selby, Charles.

IRISH ELECTION, THE
    See Fitzgerald, J. D.
IRISH EMIGRANT
    See Brougham, John.
    See Brougham, John. Temptation.
IRISH ENGAGEMENT, AN
    See Watts, Walter.
IRISH FOOTMAN
    See Clements, Arthur. Two to One.
IRISH GIRL, THE
    See Maclaren, Archibald.
IRISH HEIRESS
    See Boucicault, Dionysius Lardner.
    See Boucicault, Dionysius Lardner. West End.
IRISH LION, THE
    See Buckstone, John Baldwin.
IRISH LOTHARIO, AN
    See Fraser, Julia Agnes. Pat of Mullingar.
IRISH MANIAC
    See Hart, James P. Mary Le More.
IRISH PATRIOT
    See Reeve, Wybert. Pike O'Callaghan.
IRISH POST, THE
    See Planché, James Robinson.
IRISH TIGER, THE
    See Morton, John Maddison.
IRISH TUTOR, THE
    See Butler, Richard William, Earl of Glengall.
IRISH VALET
    See Rodwell, James Thomas Gooderham. More Blunders
    Than One.
IRISH WIDOW, THE
    See Garrick, David.
IRISH YANKEE, THE
    See Brougham, John.
IRISHMAN IN BAGDAD
    See Dibdin, Thomas John. Ninth Statue, The.
IRISHMAN IN FRANCE
    See Maclaren, Archibald. British Carpenter, The.
IRISHMAN IN LONDON, THE
    See Macready, William.
IRISHMAN'S FORTUNE
    See Power, Tyrone. Born to Good Luck.
IRISHMAN'S HOME, THE
    See Hazlewood, Colin Henry. Emerald Heart, The.
IRMA
    See Dunn, Sinclair (trans.).
IRON CHEST, THE
    See Colman, George, jr.
    See Irving, Henry (arr.).
IRON-CLAD WARRIOR AND THE LITTLE TUG OF WAR
    See Burnand, Francis Cowley. Ulysses.
IRON LATCH FARM
    See Mackay, William.
IRON MASK
    See Hayes, Frederick William. State Secret, A.
IRON MASTER OF SAMARKAND-BY-OXUS
    See Oxenford, John. Timour the Tartar!
IRONFOUNDER, THE
    See Muskerry, William.
IRRESISTIBLES, THE
    See Moncrieff, William Thomas.
IRRESOLUTE MAN, THE (anon. trans.)
    By Amalie (Amelia), Princess of Saxony. In *Six Dramas
    Illustrative of German Life*, London: John W. Parker, pp.
    [119]-162. *Filed under* Six Dramas (anon.).
IRVINE, GEORGE (trans.)
    Bride of Messina, The. By Schiller. London: John Macrone,
    1837. Pp. [i]-[viii], [1]-172.
IRVING, HENRY (arr.)
    Becket. By Tennyson, Alfred, Lord. [London: Macmillan],
    1893. Pp. [i-viii], [1]-62. 2nd printing.
    Coriolanus. By Shakespeare, William. London: Chiswick
    Press, 1901. Pp. [i-viii], [1]-67.

Cymbeline. By Shakespeare, William. London: Chiswick Press, 1896. Pp. [i-x], [1]-65. 2nd thousand.

Hamlet. By Shakespeare, William. London: Chiswick Press, 1878. Pp. [i]-[xvi], [1]-82.

Iron Chest, The. By Colman, George, jr. London: Chiswick Press, n.d. Pp. [i-viii], [1]-56.

King Henry the Eighth. By Shakespeare, William. London: Nassau Steam Press, 1892. Pp. [1]-69.

King Lear. By Shakespeare, William. London: Nassau Steam Press, 1892. Pp. [1]-77.

King Richard III. By Shakespeare, William. London: E. S. Boot (printer), n.d. Pp. [1]-93.

Macbeth. By Shakespeare, William. Music by Sullivan, Arthur. London: Nassau Steam Press, 1888. Pp. [1]-72.

Merchant of Venice, The. By Shakespeare, William. New York & London: Samuel French, n.d. Pp. [1]-70.

Much Ado about Nothing. By Shakespeare, William. London: Chiswick Press, 1882. Pp. [1]-74.

Romeo and Juliet. By Shakespeare, William. London: Chiswick Press, 1882. Pp. [i]-[x], [11]-79.

Twelfth Night; or, What You Will. By Shakespeare, William. London: Chiswick Press, 1884. Pp. [1]-73.

IRVING, LAURENCE SYDNEY BRODRIBB

Godefroi and Yolande. London: John Lane, 1898. Pp. [i-vi], 1-89.

Godefroi and Yolande. N.p.: n.pub., n.d. Pp. [i-iv], 1-35. Title page lacking.

Peter the Great. [New York: DeVinne Press (priv.), 1897]. Pp. [1]-113.

IRWIN, EDWARD

King O'Toole's Goose; or, The Legends of Glendalough. London: Thomas Hailes Lacy, n.d. Pp. [i]-iv, [5]-28. [Lacy's Acting Edition].

IRWIN, EYLES

Bedouins, The; or, Arabs of the Desert. Dublin: J. Archer, 1802. Pp. [i]-[xii], [1]-60. Libretto.

IS HE ALIVE?; OR, ALL PUZZLED! (anon.)
London: Richard White, 1818. Pp. [i]-[vi], [1]-32.

IS HE JEALOUS?
See Beazley, Samuel, jr.

IS HIS APPOINTMENT PUCKA?
See Trevelyan, George Otto. Dawk Bungalow, The.

IS SHE A WOMAN?
See Collier, William.

IS SHE HIS DAUGHTER?
See Murray, Gaston.

IS SHE HIS WIFE?; OR, SOMETHING SINGULAR
See Dickens, Charles.

IS SHE MAD?
See Oxberry, William Henry. Delusion, The.

ISAAC COMNENUS
See Taylor, Henry.

ISABELLA
See Garrick, David.
See Kemble, John Philip (arr.).

ISABELLA ALDOBRANDI
See Sorelli, Guido.

ISABELLE
See Buckstone, John Baldwin.

ISALDA
See Horner, Fred.

ISAURE
See Webster, Benjamin Nottingham.

ISLAND OF CALYPSO
See Planché, James Robinson. Telemachus.

ISLAND OF JEWELS, THE
See Planché, James Robinson.

ISLAND OF JUAN FERNANDEZ, THE
See Fortescue, F. Robinson Crusoe.

ISLAND OF TRANQUIL DELIGHTS
See Planché, James Robinson. Invisible Prince, The.

ISLE OF PALMS, THE
See Wilson, John.

ISLE OF ST. TROPEZ, THE
See Williams, Montagu Stephen.

ISOLDA
See Richards, Alfred Bate.

ISOLINE OF BAVARIA
See Suter, William E.

IT MIGHT HAVE BEEN WORSE
See Planché, James Robinson. My Lord and My Lady.

ITALIAN IN ALGIERS, THE (anon.)
Music by Rossini. London: S. G. Fairbrother, n.d. Pp. [1]-24. Copyright ed. Libretto.

ITALIAN LOVE
See Clarke, John Bertridge. Ravenna.

ITALIAN NUPTIALS
See Farley, Charles. Corsair, The.

ITALIAN WIFE
See Doubleday, Thomas.
See Milman, Henry Hart, Rev. Fazio.

ITALIANA IN ALGERI, L'
See Maggioni, Manfredo (trans.).

ITALIANS, THE
See Bucke, Charles.

IT'S A LONG LANE THAT HAS NO TURNING
See Suter, William E. Test of Truth, The.

IT'S ALL A MISTAKE
See Farrell, John.

IT'S NEVER TOO LATE TO MEND
See Reade, Charles.

IT'S ONLY MY AUNT!
See Bartholomew, Anne Charlotte Fayermann, Mrs. Valentine.

IVAN
See Sotheby, William.

IVANHOE (anon.)
Edinburgh: James L. Huie, 1823. Pp. [3]-76. In *Waverley Dramas*, London: George Routledge, 1845. *Filed under* Waverley Dramas (anon.).

IVANHOE
See Beazley, Samuel, jr.
See Brough, Willam. Last Edition of Ivanhoe, with All the Newest Improvements, The.
See Bunn, Alfred.
See Calcraft, John William.
See Cooper, Frederick Fox.
See Dibdin, Thomas John.
See Moncrieff, William Thomas.
See Murray, William Henry Wood.
See Sturgis, Julian Russell.

IVANHOE IN ACCORDANCE WITH THE SPIRIT OF THE TIMES
See Byron, Henry James.

I'VE EATEN MY FRIEND!
See Bridgeman, John Vipon.

I'VE SEEN A HAREM.
See Branscombe, Arthur. Morocco Bound.

I'VE WRITTEN TO BROWNE
See Williams, Thomas John.

IVOR
See Hitchener, William Henry.

IVY HALL, RICHMOND
See Emson, Frank E.

IXION
See Burnand, Francis Cowley.

IZAAK WALTON
See Dance, Charles.

J. P.
See Smelt, Thomas.

JACK AND JACK'S BROTHER
See Johnstone, John Beer. Gipsy Farmer, The.

JACK AND JILL
See Blanchard, Edward Litt Leman.
See Green, Frank William.

JACK AND JILL AND THE WELL ON THE HILL
See Conquest, George.

JACK AND THE BEANSTALK (anon.)
Music by Loder. Manchester: Theatre Royal Press, 1855. Pp. [1]-12. 11th ed. Libretto.

JACK AND THE BEANSTALK
  See Bell, Florence Eveleen Eleanore Oliffe, Mrs. Hugh (Lady).
  See Blanchard, Edward Litt Leman.
  See McArdle, John Francis.
  See Nicholls, Harry.
JACK AND THE BEAN STALK AND MARGERY DAW; OR, HARLEQUIN MAN-IN-THE-MOON, THE GIANT GRUMBLE GRIM, AND THE LOVE BIRDS OF FAIRYLAND! (anon.)
  N.p.: n.pub., n.d. Pp. [3]-36. Title page lacking. Authorized ed. Libretto.
JACK BRAG
  See A'Beckett, Gilbert Abbott.
JACK IN A BOX!
  See Simpson, John Palgrave.
JACK IN THE BOX
  See Blanchard, Edward Litt Leman.
JACK IN THE GREEN
  See Lemon, Mark.
JACK IN THE WATER
  See Rede, William Leman.
JACK KETCH
  See Almar, George.
JACK LONG
  See Johnstone, John Beer.
JACK O' THE HEDGE
  See Suter, William E.
JACK OF ALL TRADES
  See Allingham, John Till.
JACK ROBINSON AND HIS MONKEY!
  See Thompson, C. Pelham.
JACK SHEPPARD
  See Buckstone, John Baldwin.
  See Greenwood, Thomas Longdon.
JACK THE GIANT KILLER
  See Byron, Henry James.
  See Dibdin, Charles Isaac Mungo, jr.
JACK THE GIANT KILLER AND TOM THUMB
  See Green, Frank William.
JACK WHITE'S TRIAL
  See Parr, F. C. W.
JACK'S DELIGHT!
  See Williams, Thomas John.
JACK'S THE LAD
  See Rogers, William.
JACKET OF BLUE, THE
  See Wilks, Thomas Egerton.
JACKMAN, ISAAC
  All the World's a Stage. In *British Drama,* 12 vols., London: John Dicks, 1871, V, [151]-160. *Filed under* Jackson, Isaac.
  Hero and Leander. In *British Drama,* 12 vols., London: John Dicks, 1872, XI, [154]-160.
JACKS AND JILLS
  See Albery, James.
JACKSON, JOHN P. (trans.)
  Flying Dutchman, The. *Also:* Der Fliegende Hollander. Music by Wagner. London & New York: Boosey, n.d. Pp. [i-v], 1-276. Royal Edition. Vocal score. *Filed under* Fliegende Hollander.
  Golden Cross, The. Music by Brüll, Ignaz. New York: Metropolitan Opera House, n.d. Pp. [1-4], i-iii, 2-20 (English); 2-20 (German). Text incomplete. Libretto.
  Lohengrin. Music by Wagner. London: Carl Rosa Opera Co., 1880. Pp. [1]-36. Libretto.
  Mastersingers of Nuremberg, The. Music by Wagner. New York: John P. Jackson, 1892. Pp. [1-4], i-iv, [1]-[41]. Libretto.
  Nero. Music by Rubinstein, Anton. New York: Charles D. Koppel, c.1886. Pp. [1-2], i-vi, [3]-68. Libretto.
  Parsifal. Music by Wagner. New York: Edward Schuberth, 1892. Pp. [1-4], [i]-[vi], [1]-20. Libretto.

Rhinegold, Prelude to The Ring of the Niblung. Music by Wagner. New York: Metropolitan Opera House, c.1888. Pp. [1-4], i-iii, 1-29 (English); 1-29 (German). Libretto.
  Tannhäuser and the Tournament of Song at the Wartburg. Music by Wagner. New York: Edward Schuberth, 1891. Pp. [i-iv], [1]-14. Libretto.
  Templar and Jewess. Music by Marschner, Heinrich. New York: Metropolitan Opera House, 1890. Pp. [1-2], i-[iii], 1-23. Libretto.
  Tristan and Ysolde. Music by Wagner. [New York]: n.pub., 1887. Pp. [1-2], i-iii, 1-33 (English); 1-33 (German). Libretto.
  Trumpeter of Sackingen, The. Music by Nessler, Victor E. New York: Metropolitan Opera House, c.1887. Pp. [1-2], [i]-[xiv], 1-25 (English); 1-25 (German). Libretto.
JACOB FAITHFUL
  See Haines, John Thomas.
JACOBITE, THE
  See Planché, James Robinson.
JACOBS, WILLIAM WYMARK
  Gray Parrot, The. Written with Rock, Charles. New York & London: Samuel French, c.1908. Pp. [i-ii], [1]-19. French's International Copyrighted Edition of the Works of the Best Authors, 137.
JACQUES STROP
  See Selby, Charles.
JALOUSIE DU BARBOUILLE
  See Van Laun, Henri (trans.). Jealousy of le Barbouille, The.
JAMES, CHARLES
  Lady Burglar, The.
  See Malyon, E. J.
JAMES, GEORGE PAYNE RAINSFORD
  Blanche of Navarre. New York: Harper & Brothers, 1839. Pp. [3]-74.
JAMES, WALTER
  Return Ticket, A.
  See Spencer, George.
JAMES THE FIRST OF SCOTLAND
  See Buchanan, Robert.
JAMES THE THIRD, KING OF SCOTLAND
  See Heytesbury, William.
  See Woodley, William.
JAMESON, ANNA BROWNELL MURPHY, MRS. ROBERT (trans.)
  Country Cousin, The. By Amalie (Amelia), Princess of Saxony. In *Social Life in Germany,* London: George Routledge, 1847, II, [267]-399. *Filed under* Collected Works.
  Falsehood and Truth. In *Evergreen,* I (1840), 58-71.
  Falsehood and Truth. By Amalie (Amelia), Princess of Saxony. In *Social Life in Germany,* London: George Routledge, 1847, I, [1]-126. *Filed under* Collected Works.
  Princely Bride, The. By Amalie (Amelia), Princess of Saxony. In *Social Life in Germany,* London: George Routledge, 1847, II, [149]-266. *Filed under* Collected Works.
  Social Life in Germany: An Introductory Dialogue. In *Social Life in Germany,* London: George Routledge, 1847, I, [iii]-lxxix. *Filed under* Collected Works.
  Uncle, The. In *Evergreen,* I (1840), 137-151.
  Uncle, The. By Amalie (Amelia), Princess of Saxony. In *Social Life in Germany,* London: George Routledge, 1847, I, [127]-264. *Filed under* Collected Works.
  Young Ward, The. By Amalie (Amelia), Princess of Saxony. In *Social Life in Germany,* London: George Routledge, 1847, II, [1]-147. *Filed under* Collected Works.
JAMESON, FREDERICK (trans.)
  Tristan and Isolde. Music by Wagner. [London]: Crystal Palace Press (priv.), 1886. Pp. [i-vi], [1]-76. Libretto.
JAMESON, H.
  Wild-Goose Chase, A. London: John Miller, 1820. Pp. [1]-36.
JAMESON, ROBERT FRANCIS
  King and the Duke, The; or, Which Is Which? London: John Miller, 1814. Pp. [1]-44.

Living in London. London: John Miller, 1815. Pp. [i-iv], [1]-83.

Students of Salamanca, The. London: C. Chapple, 1813. Pp. [1]-118.

Timoleon. Edinburgh: Forbes & Wilson, 1852. Pp. [1]-64. 2nd ed.

Touch at the Times, A. London: C. Chapple, 1812. Pp. [i]-[x], 1-80.

JANE
 See Nicholls, Harry.

JANE ANNIE
 See Barrie, James Mathew.

JANE EYRE
 See Brougham, John.

JANE LOMAX
 See Stirling, Edward.

JANE OF THE HATCHET
 See Almar, George.

JANE SHORE
 See Kemble, John Philip (arr.).
 See Rowe, Nicholas.

JAPANESE WIFE
 See Arnold, Edwin, Sir. Adzuma.

JASON IN COLCHIS AND MEDEA IN CORINTH
 See Planché, James Robinson. Golden Fleece, The.

JAY, HARRIET
 Alone in London.
  See Buchanan, Robert Williams.
 Strange Adventures of Miss Brown.
  See Buchanan, Robert Williams.

JEALOUS MISTAKE, A
 See Fitzgerald, Shafto Justin Adair.

JEALOUS ON ALL SIDES
 See Beazley, Samuel, jr.

JEALOUS PRINCE
 See Van Laun, Henri (trans.). Don Garcia of Navarre.

JEALOUS QUEEN
 See Gardiner, William. Sultana, The.

JEALOUS WIFE, THE
 See Colman, George, sr.

JEALOUSY
 See Shannon, Mrs. F. S.

JEALOUSY OF LE BARBOUILLE, THE
 See Van Laun, Henri (trans.).

JEAN BUSCAILLE
 See Hayes, Maria Ximena (trans.).

JEAN DE PARIS
 See Arnold, Samuel James.

JEANIE DEANS
 See Bennett, Joseph.

JEANNE D'ARC
 See Lyster, Frederic (trans.).

JEANNE, JEANNETTE, AND JEANNETON
 See Reece, Robert.

JEANNETTE AND JEANNOT
 See Stirling, Edward.

JEANNETTE'S WEDDING
 See Buckingham, Leicester Silk.

JEANNETTE'S WEDDING DAY
 See Lacy, Thomas Hailes.

JEDBURY JUNIOR
 See Ryley, Madeleine Lucette, Mrs. J. H.

JEFFERSON, GEORGE
 Lady's Dream, The. Northallerton: J. Langdale (printer), n.d. In [*Theatrical Eccentricities*, London: n.pub., 1823, [70]-103].

JEFFERYS, CHARLES (trans.)
 Gipsy's Vengeance, The. *Also:* Il Trovatore. Music by Verdi. London: Charles Jefferys, 1856. Pp. [i-vi], [3]-31. Libretto.
 Trovatore, Il. Music by Verdi. London: Charles Jefferys, n.d. Pp. [i-iv], [1]-242. 2nd ed. Vocal score.

JEFFREYS
 See Spicer, Henry.

JEMMY TWITCHER IN ENGLAND
 See Webster, Benjamin Nottingham. Golden Farmer, The.

JENKINSES, THE
 See Planché, James Robinson.

JENNY FOSTER, THE SAILOR'S CHILD
 See Hazlewood, Colin Henry.

JENNY JONES
 See Cooper, Frederick Fox.

JENNY LIND AT LAST
 See Reach, Angus Bethune.

JEPEY MAYFLOWER
 See Neale, Frederick.

JEPHSON, ROBERT
 Braganza. In *Modern Theatre*, ed. Mrs. Inchbald, 10 vols., London: Longman, Hurst, Rees, Orme, & Brown, 1811, VI, [263]-325.
 Braganza. In *British Drama*, 12 vols., London: John Dicks, 1865, III, [910]-926.
 Count of Narbonne, The. London: Whittingham & Arliss, 1815. Pp. [1]-60. London Theatre, XV. *Filed under* Dibdin, Thomas John, ed. London Theatre, XV.
 Count of Narbonne. In *British Drama*, 12 vols., London: John Dicks, 1871, VIII, [80]-96.
 Law of Lombardy, The. In *Modern Theatre*, ed. Mrs. Inchbald, 10 vols., London: Longman, Hurst, Rees, Orme, & Brown, 1811, VI, [193]-261.
 Law of Lombardy, The. In *British Drama*, 12 vols., London: John Dicks, 1871, VIII, [161]-179.
 Two Strings to Your Bow. In *British Drama*, 12 vols., London: John Dicks, 1871, IX, [53]-64.
 Two Strings to Your Bow. London: John Cumberland, n.d. Pp. [1]-34. Cumberland's British Theatre, XXX. *Filed under* Cumberland, John. Cumberland's British Theatre, XXX.

JEPHTHA
 See Edison, John Sibbald.
 See Vartie, John.

JEPHTHA'S DAUGHTER
 See Chapman, Matthew James.

JEPHTHAH
 See Crowley, Edward Aleister.

JEPHTHAH'S DAUGHTER
 See Pember, Edward Henry.
 See Tennant, William.

JEROME, JEROME KLAPKA
 Barbara. New York: Dick & Fitzgerald, n.d. Pp. [1]-22. Dick's American Edition.
 Fennel. New York: T. H. French; London: Samuel French, n.d. Pp. [1]-23. [French's Minor Drama].
 Maister of Wood Barrow, The. Pp. [i-iii], 1-91. Typescript.
 Miss Hobbs. New York & London: Samuel French, c.1902. Pp. [1]-66.
 Prude's Progress, The. Written with Phillpotts, Eden. London: Chatto & Windus, 1895. Pp. [i-viii], [1]-127.
 Sunset. Chicago: Dramatic Publishing Co., n.d. Pp. [1]-32. Sergel's Acting Drama, 448.
 Tommy. [London: Mrs. Marshall's Typewriting Office, 1900]. Pp. [i], [1]-44, [i], [1]-46, [i], [1]-33. Pagination by act. Typescript.
 Woodbarrow Farm. New York & London: Samuel French, c.1904. Pp. [3]-69. [French's Standard Library Edition].

JERROLD, DOUGLAS WILLIAM
 Ambrose Gwinett; or, A Sea-side Story. London: John Cumberland, n.d. Pp. [i-ii], [1]-54. Promptbook.
 Ambrose Gwinett; or, A Sea-Side Story. London: John Cumberland, n.d. Pp. [1]-54. Cumberland's Minor Theatre, VIII. *Filed under* Cumberland, John. Cumberland's Minor Theatre, VIII.
 Bampfylde Moore Carew; or, The Gypsey of the Glen. London: John Duncombe, n.d. Pp. [1]-36. Duncombe's Edition.
 Beau Nash, the King of Bath. London: John Dicks, n.d. Pp. [1]-18. Dicks' Standard Plays, 554.

Black Eyed Susan; or, All in the Downs. New York: R. H. Elton, 1830. Pp. [1]-30.

Black-Ey'd Susan; or, All in the Downs. In *Comedies and Dramas*, London: Bradbury & Evans, 1854, pp. [251]-287. *Filed under* Comedies and Dramas.

Black-Ey'd Susan; or, All in the Downs. London: Thomas Hailes Lacy, n.d. Pp. [11]-50. No apparent lack of text. Promptbook.

Bride of Ludgate, The. London: John Cumberland, n.d. Pp. [i-ii], [1]-47. Cumberland's British Theatre, XXX. *Filed under* Cumberland, John. Cumberland's British Theatre, XXX.

Bride of Ludgate, The. London: John Cumberland, n.d. Pp. [1]-47.

Bubbles of the Day. In *Comedies*, London: Bradbury & Evans, 1853, pp. [i-iv], [1]-69. *Filed under* Comedies.

Catspaw, The. London: Punch Office, 1850. Pp. [i-vi], [1]-63.

Catspaw, The. In *Comedies*, London: Bradbury & Evans, 1853, pp. [145]-204. *Filed under* Comedies.

Descart, the French Buccaneer. London: John Duncombe, n.d. Pp. [1]-22. Duncombe's Edition.

Devil's Ducat, The; or, The Gift of Mammon. London: John Cumberland, n.d. Pp. [i], [1]-40. Cumberland's Minor Theatre, V. *Filed under* Cumberland, John. Cumberland's Minor Theatre, V.

Devil's Ducat, The; or, The Gift of Mammon. London & New York: Samuel French, n.d. Pp. [1]-40. [Lacy's Acting Edition].

Dolly and the Rat; or, The Brisket Family. London: John Duncombe, 1823. Pp. [1]-28.

Doves in a Cage. In *Comedies and Dramas*, London: Bradbury & Evans, 1854, pp. [197]-230. *Filed under* Comedies and Dramas.

Doves in a Cage. London: John Duncombe, n.d. Pp. [1]-37. Jerrold's Original Dramas, 5.

Drunkard's Fate, The; or, Fifteen Years of a Drunkard's Life. New York: E. B. Clayton, 1830. Pp. [1]-52. Clayton's Edition.

Fifteen Years of a Drunkard's Life. New York: Samuel French, n.d. Pp. [1]-32. French's Standard Drama, 347.

Gertrude's Cherries; or, Waterloo in 1835. London: Thomas Hailes Lacy, n.d. Pp. [1]-36. Lacy's Acting Edition, 1316.

Gipsey of Derncleugh, The. London: John Duncombe, n.d. Pp. [1]-36. Duncombe's Edition.

Golden Calf, The. London: John Cumberland, n.d. Pp. [1]-66. Cumberland's Minor Theatre, 76.

Golden Calf, The. London: John Cumberland, n.d. Pp. [1]-66. Cumberland's Minor Theatre, IX. *Filed under* Cumberland, John. Cumberland's Minor Theatre, IX.

Hazard of the Die, The. London: John Dicks, n.d. Pp. [1]-16. Dicks' Standard Plays, 638.

Heart of Gold, A. London: Bradbury & Evans, 1854. Pp. [i-iv], [1]-[55].

Housekeeper, The. In *Comedies and Dramas*, London: Bradbury & Evans, 1854, pp. [79]-116. *Filed under* Comedies and Dramas.

Housekeeper, The. In *Dramatic Entertainments at Windsor Castle*, ed. Benjamin Webster, London: Mitchell, n.d., pp. [279]-321. *Filed under* Webster, Benjamin Nottingham. Dramatic Entertainments.

Housekeeper, The. London: John Duncombe, n.d. Pp. [1]-42.

John Overy; or, The Miser of Southwark Ferry. London: John Cumberland, n.d. Pp. [1]-42. Cumberland's Minor Theatre, VII. *Filed under* Cumberland, John. Cumberland's Minor Theatre, VII.

John Overy; or, The Miser of Southwark Ferry. London: Thomas Hailes Lacy, n.d. Pp. [1]-42. [Lacy's Acting Edition].

Law and Lions. London: John Duncombe, n.d. Pp. [1]-28. Duncombe's Acting Edition of the British Theatre.

Martha Willis, the Servant Maid. London: Thomas Hailes Lacy, n.d. Pp. [1]-36. Promptbook.

More Frightened than Hurt. London: John Duncombe, 1821. Pp. [1]-33. Duncombe's Edition.

Mr. Paul Pry.
See Paul Pry.

Mutiny at the Nore, The. London: John Cumberland, n.d. Pp. [1]-48.

Mutiny at the Nore, The. London: John Cumberland, n.d. Pp. [1]-48. Cumberland's Minor Theatre, V. *Filed under* Cumberland, John. Cumberland's Minor Theatre, V.

Nell Gwynne; or, The Prologue. London: John Miller, 1833. Pp. [i]-[viii], [1]-48. Promptbook.

Nell Gwynne; or, The Prologue. In *Comedies and Dramas*, London: Bradbury & Evans, 1854, pp. [41]-77. *Filed under* Comedies and Dramas.

Painter of Ghent, The. In *Comedies and Dramas*, London: Bradbury & Evans, 1854, pp. [231]-249. *Filed under* Comedies and Dramas.

Painter of Ghent, The. London: John Duncombe, n.d. Pp. [1]-23.

Paul Pry. *Also:* Mr. Paul Pry. London: Thomas Hailes Lacy, n.d. Pp. [1]-30.

Perils of Pippins, The; or, The Man Who Couldn't Help It. London: John Duncombe, n.d. Pp. [1]-45.

Prisoner of War, The. In *Comedies*, London: Bradbury & Evans, 1853, pp. [205]-244. *Filed under* Comedies.

Prisoner of War, The. London: Thomas Hailes Lacy, n.d. Pp. [1]-49. [Lacy's Acting Edition].

Rent Day, The. In *Comedies and Dramas*, London: Bradbury & Evans, 1854, pp. [i-iv], [1]-40. *Filed under* Comedies and Dramas.

Rent Day, The. Philadelphia: R. H. Lenfestey, n.d. Pp. [1]-52. Lenfestey's Edition. Promptbook.

Retired from Business. London: Punch Office, 1851. Pp. [i-iv], [1]-62.

Retired from Business. Leipsic: Hermann Hartung, 1851. Pp. [1]-90. Modern English Comic Theatre, Series IV.

Retired from Business. In *Comedies*, London: Bradbury & Evans, 1853, pp. [245]-303. *Filed under* Comedies.

Sally in Our Alley. London: John Cumberland, n.d. Pp. [1]-40.

Schoolfellows, The. In *Comedies and Dramas*, London: Bradbury & Evans, 1854, pp. [159]-195. *Filed under* Comedies and Dramas.

Schoolfellows, The. London: John Duncombe, n.d. Pp. [i]-[vi], [7]-40.

Smoked Miser!, The; or, The Benefit of Hanging! London: John Duncombe, n.d. Pp. [1]-20. Duncombe's Edition.

St. Cupid; or, Dorothy's Fortune. London: Bradbury & Evans, 1853. Pp. [i-iv], [1]-44. Promptbook.

St. Cupid; or, Dorothy's Fortune. In *Comedies*, London: Bradbury & Evans, 1853, pp. [305]-347. *Filed under* Comedies.

St. Cupid; or, Dorothy's Fortune. New York: William Taylor, n.d. Pp. [1]-53. Minor Drama, 49.

Statue Lover, The; or, Music in Marble. London: John Duncombe, n.d. Pp. [1]-24. Duncombe's Edition.

Thomas à Becket. London: John Cumberland, n.d. Pp. [1]-60.

Thomas à Becket. London: John Cumberland, n.d. Pp. [1]-60. Cumberland's Minor Theatre, XI. *Filed under* Cumberland, John. Cumberland's Minor Theatre, XI.

Time Works Wonders. London: Punch Office, 1845. Pp. [i-iv], [1]-76. 2nd ed.

Time Works Wonders. In *Comedies*, London: Bradbury & Evans, 1853, pp. [71]-143. *Filed under* Comedies.

Tower of Lochlain, The; or, The Idiot Son. London & New York: Samuel French, n.d. Pp. [1]-36. [Lacy's Acting Edition].

Two Eyes between Two. London: John Duncombe, n.d. Pp. [1]-16. Duncombe's Edition.

Vidocq, the French Police Spy. London: John Duncombe, n.d. Pp. [1]-32. Duncombe's Edition.

Wedding Gown, The. In *Comedies and Dramas*, London: Bradbury & Evans, 1854, pp. [117]-158. *Filed under* Comedies and Dramas.

Wedding Gown, The. London: John Duncombe, n.d. Pp.

[1]-43. Duncombe's Acting Edition of the British Theatre.

White Milliner, The. London: John Duncombe, n.d. Pp. [1]-44.

Wives by Advertisement; or, Courting in the Newspapers. London: John Duncombe, n.d. Pp. [1]-22. Duncombe's Edition.

JERROLD, WILLIAM BLANCHARD

Beau Brummel, the King of Calais. London: Thomas Hailes Lacy, n.d. Pp. [1]-36. [Lacy's Acting Edition].

Cool as a Cucumber. New York: Samuel French, n.d. Pp. [1]-18. Promptbook.

Cool as a Cucumber. Boston: William V. Spencer, n.d. Pp. [i-ii], [1]-18. Spencer's Boston Theatre, 142.

Cupid in Waiting. London: Thomas Hailes Lacy, n.d. Pp. [1]-42. [Lacy's Acting Edition].

JERRY AND A SUNBEAM
> See Hamilton, Cosmo.

JERSEY GIRL, THE
> See Pitt, George Dibdin.

JERSEY INVADED
> See Burn, David. De Rullecourt.

JESSAMY'S COURTSHIP
> See Hazlewood, Colin Henry.

JESSE, JOHN HENEAGE

Last War of the Roses, The. [In *Memoirs of King Richard the Third,* London: John Bentley, 1862], pp. [377]-496.

JESSIE BROWN
> See Boucicault, Dionysius Lardner.

JESSIE, THE FLOWER OF DUMBLAINE
> See Addison, Henry Robert, Capt.

JESSY VERE
> See Hazlewood, Colin Henry.

JESUITS, THE
> See Albery, James.

JESUS OF NAZARETH
> See Barlow, George.

JEW, THE
> See Cumberland, Richard.

JEW AND THE DOCTOR, THE
> See Dibdin, Thomas John.

JEW OF ARRAGON, THE
> See Wade, Thomas.

JEW OF LUBECK, THE
> See Milner, Henry M.

JEW OF MOGADORE, THE
> See Cumberland, Richard.

JEW OF PLYMOUTH
> See Barnett, Charles Zachary. Mariner's Dream, The.

JEW OF YORK
> See Bunn, Alfred. Ivanhoe.

JEW'S DAUGHTER
> See Dibdin, Thomas John. Ivanhoe.
> See Stirling, Edward.

JEWEL MAIDEN, THE
> See Gillington, May Clarissa.

JEWELLED CHILDREN OF THE ENCHANTED ISLE!
> See Collins, Charles James. Prince Cherry and Princess Fair Star.

JEWELLER OF ST. JAMES'S, THE
> See Suter, William E.

JEWESS
> See Calcraft, John William. Ivanhoe.
> See Drayton, Henri.
> See Moncrieff, William Thomas. Ivanhoe.
> See Moncrieff, William Thomas.
> See Planché, James Robinson.

JEWISH MAIDEN'S WRONG
> See Cheltnam, Charles Smith. Deborah.

JEWS, THE
> See Bell, Ernest (trans.).

JEZEBEL
> See Boucicault, Dionysius Lardner.

JILT, THE
> See Boucicault, Dionysius Lardner.

JIM THE PENMAN
> See Young, Charles Lawrence, Sir.

JINGLE
> See Albery, James.
> See Albery, James. Pickwick.

JINKS, THE MAN THAT CAN'T HELP IT!
> See Webb, Charles.

JOAN OF ARC
> See Brough, William.
> See Fitzball, Edward.
> See Serle, Thomas James.
> See Shine, John L.
> See Taylor, Tom.

JOAN THE MAID
> See Skrine, John Huntley.

JOANNA OF MONTFAUCON
> See Cumberland, Richard.

JOCONDE
> See Moncrieff, William Thomas.
> See Santley, Charles.

JOCRISSE THE JUGGLER
> See Robertson, Thomas William.

JODRELL, RICHARD PAUL

Persian Heroine, The. London: Samuel & Richard Bentley (printer) (priv.), 1822. Pp. [i]-[viii], [1]-75, [1]-96. 3rd ed.

JOE MILLER AND HIS MEN
> See A'Beckett, Gilbert Abbott.

JOE THE BUITS
> See Wheatley, J. A.

JOHN AND JEANNETTE
> See MacHale, Luke.

JOHN BALIOL
> See Tennant, William.

JOHN BULL
> See Colman, George, jr.

JOHN BULL IN HIS DOTAGE
> See Jubilee, The (anon.).

JOHN BULL TRIUMPHANT
> See Moncrieff, William Thomas. Reform.

JOHN BUZZBY
> See Kenney, James.

JOHN DOBBS
> See Morton, John Maddison.

JOHN FELTON
> See Stirling, Edward.

JOHN GABRIEL BORKMAN
> See Archer, William (trans.).

JOHN JONES
> See Buckstone, John Baldwin.

JOHN OF PARIS
> See Pocock, Isaac.

JOHN OF PROCIDA
> See Knowles, James Sheridan.

JOHN OVERY
> See Jerrold, Douglas William.

JOHN SAVILE OF HAYSTED
> See White, James, Rev.

JOHN SMITH
> See Hancock, William.

JOHN STAFFORD
> See Townsend, William Thompson.

JOHN STREET, ADELPHI
> See Buckstone, John Baldwin.

JOHN THE BAPTIST
> See Horne, Richard Hengist.

JOHN WOODVIL
> See Lamb, Charles.

JOHN WOPPS
> See Suter, William E.

JOHNNIES IN SPAIN
> See Kitching, H. St. A. Miss Betsy Bull.

JOHNSON, CHARLES

Cobbler of Preston, The. London: John Cumberland & Son, n.d. Pp. [1]-33. Cumberland's British Theatre, XLII.

Filed under Cumberland, John. Cumberland's British Theatre, XLII.

JOHNSON, REGINALD BRIMLEY

Judith. In *Verse Essays,* London: Stanesby; Derby & Nottingham: Frank Murray, 1890, pp. [39]-52.

JOHNSON, W. H.

Paying Guest, The. London & New York: Samuel French, c.1904. Pp. [1]-16. [Lacy's Acting Edition].

JOHNSTON, ANDREW (trans.)

Cataline. By Ibsen, Henrik. In *Translations from the Norse,* Gloucester: John Bellows (priv.), n.d., pp. [1]-41. Act I and synopsis. of Acts II and III only.

JOHNSTON, THOMAS PETER

Patrick Hamilton. Edinburgh & London: William Blackwood & Sons, 1882. Pp. [i-ii], [1]-114.

JOHNSTONE, JOHN BEER

Ben Bolt. New York: Samuel French, n.d. Pp. [1]-25. French's Standard Drama, 156.

Drunkard's Children, The. London & New York: Samuel French, n.d. Pp. [1]-27. [Lacy's Acting Edition].

Gale Breezely; or, The Tale of a Tar. New York: Samuel French, n.d. Pp. [1]-23. Minor Drama, 91.

Gipsy Farmer, The; or, Jack and Jack's Brother. London: Andrew Vickers, 1849. Pp. [1]-38. Promptbook.

Gipsy Farmer, The; or, Jack and Jack's Brother. London: Thomas Hailes Lacy, n.d. Pp. [1]-36. Promptbook.

Jack Long; or, The Shot in the Eye. Chicago: Dramatic Publishing Co., n.d. Pp. [1]-28. Sergel's Acting Drama, 100.

Morley Ashton; or, A Sea Voyage. London: W. S. Johnson, n.d. Pp. [1]-46.

Pedrillo; or, A Search for Two Fathers. London: Thomas Hailes Lacy, n.d. Pp. [1]-28. [Lacy's Acting Edition].

Sailor of France, The; or, The Republicans of Brest. London: Thomas Hailes Lacy, n.d. Pp. [1]-22.

JOINT HOUSEHOLD, A

See Bell, Florence Eveleen Eleanore Oliffe, Mrs. Hugh (Lady).

JOLLIBOY'S WOES

See Fawcett, Charles S.

JOLLY DICK THE LAMPLIGHTER

See Rede, William Leman. Life's a Lottery.

JOLLY MILLER OF THE DEE, THE

See Millward, Charles.

JOLLY MUSKETEER, THE

See Stange, Stanislaus.

JONATHAN!

See Barber, James.

JONATHAN BRADFORD!

See Fitzball, Edward.

JONES, HENRY

Earl of Essex, The. London: Sherwood, Neely, & Jones, 1818. Pp. [1]-54. London Theatre, XXV. *Filed under* London Theatre, XXV.

Earl of Essex, The. In *British Drama,* 12 vols., London: John Dicks, 1871, VII, [129]-144. *Filed under* Jones, Henry Arthur.

JONES, HENRY ARTHUR

Bauble Shop, The. Pp. [i-iii], [1]-38, [i], [1]-29, [i], [1]-24, [i], [1]-[15]. Pagination by act. Typescript.

Bed of Roses, A. London & New York: Samuel French, n.d. Pp. [1]-22.

Breaking a Butterfly. Written with Herman, Henry. Oxford: Vincent (printer) (priv.), n.d. Pp. [1]-76.

Carnac Sahib. New York: Macmillan, 1899. Pp. [i]-[viii], [1]-142.

Case of Rebellious Susan, The. London: Macmillan, 1901. Pp. [i]-x, [1]-118. 2nd ed.

Chatterton. In *One-Act Plays for Stage and Study, Seventh Series,* ed. Zona Gale, New York & Los Angeles: Samuel French, 1932, pp. [17]-37.

Chip off the Old Block, A.

See Hearts of Oak.

Clerical Error, A. London & New York: Samuel French, c.1904. Pp. [1]-21. [Lacy's Acting Edition].

Crusaders, The. London: Macmillan, 1893. Pp. [i]-[xvi], [1]-115.

Dancing Girl, The. New York & London: Samuel French, c.1907. Pp. [1]-119.

Deacon, The. London & New York: Samuel French, n.d. Pp. [1]-23. [Lacy's Acting Edition].

Elopement. London & New York: Samuel French, n.d. Pp. [1]-35. [Lacy's Acting Edition].

Goal, The. London: Chiswick Press (printer) (priv.), 1898. Pp. [i-iv], 1-[20].

Grace Mary. In [*Souvenir of the Charing Cross Hospital Bazaar,* ed. H. Beerbohm Tree, London: Nassau Press, 1899], pp. [109]-116.

Grace Mary. In *Theatre of Ideas,* London: Chapman & Hall, 1915, pp. [151]-173.

Harmony. London & New York: Samuel French, n.d. Pp. [1]-18. [Lacy's Acting Edition].

Hearts of Oak. *Also:* A Chip off the Old Block. London & New York: Samuel French, n.d. Pp. [1]-[30].

Humbug. Ilfracombe: John Tait (printer), n.d. Pp. [1]-70.

Judah. New York: Macmillan, 1894. Pp. [i]-[xxiv], [1]-104.

Liars, The. London: Chiswick Press (printer) (priv.), 1897. Pp. [i-viii], 1-91.

Manoeuvres of Jane, The. New York & London: Samuel French, c.1905. Pp. [i-vi], 1-124.

Masqueraders, The. London: Macmillan, 1899. Pp. [1]-[x], [1]-113.

Masqueraders, The. London: Chiswick Press (printer) (priv.), n.d. Pp. [i-x], 1-84.

Michael and His Lost Angel. London: Chiswick Press (printer) (priv.), 1895. Pp. [i-iv], 1-82.

Michael and His Lost Angel. New York: Macmillan, 1896. Pp. [i]-[xxviii], 1-107.

Middle Man, The. Pp. [i], [1]-16. Typescript sequence of speeches.

Mrs. Dane's Defence. New York: Macmillan, 1905. Pp. [i-vi], 1-127.

Old Master, An. London & New York: Samuel French, n.d. Pp. [1]-22.

Physician, The. New York & London: Samuel French, c.1899. Pp. [i-x], [1]-105. Plays of Henry Arthur Jones.

Rogue's Comedy, The. London: Macmillan, 1898. Pp. [i]-[x], [1]-118.

Saints and Sinners. London: Macmillan, 1891. Pp. [i]-[xxx], [1]-142.

Silver King, The. Written with Herman, Henry. Pp. 1-87, 1-75, 1-78, 1-94, 1-69. Pagination by act. Manuscript.

Sweet Will. London: Samuel French; New York: T. Henry French, n.d. Pp. [1]-24.

Tempter, The. New York & London: Samuel French, c.1893. Pp. [i-x], [1]-108.

Triumph of the Philistines, The. London: Chiswick Press (printer) (priv.), 1895. Pp. [i-ii], 1-83. Promptbook.

Triumph of the Philistines, The. London: Chiswick Press (printer) (priv.), 1895. Pp. [i-iv], 1-83.

Wealth. Pp. [i], 1-31, 1-23, 1-22, 1-14. Pagination by act. Typescript.

Wedding Guest, The. Ilfracombe: John Tait (printer), n.d. Pp. [1]-24.

JONES, JACOB

Cathedral Bell, The. London: John Miller, n.d. Pp. [1]-64.

Longinus. London: Hurst, Chance, 1827. Pp. [i]-[vi], [1]-69.

Spartacus; or, The Roman Gladiator. London: James Ridgway & Sons, 1837. Pp. [1]-56. 2nd ed.

JONES, JOHN WILTON

Cinderella; or, Harlequin, the Wicked Demon, the Good Fairy, and the Little Glass Slipper! Manchester: Guardian Letterpress & Lithographic Works (printer), n.d. Pp. [1]-16. Libretto.

First Experiment, A. London & New York: Samuel French, n.d. Pp. [1]-18. [Lacy's Acting Edition].

Forty Thieves, The; or, Harlequin Ali Baba and the Robbers of the Magic Cave. Bristol: C. T. Jefferies & Sons (printer), n.d. Pp. [1]-99. Libretto.

In an Attic. By Wilton Jones. London: Samuel French; New York: T. Henry French, n.d. Pp. [1]-17. [Lacy's Acting Edition].

On an Island. London & New York: Samuel French, n.d. Pp. [1]-19. [Lacy's Acting Edition].

Woman's Proper Place. Written with Warden, Gertrude. London: Samuel French; New York: T. Henry French, n.d. Pp. [1]-14. [Lacy's Acting Edition].

JONES, RICHARD
    Green Man, The. London: William Fearman, 1818. Pp. [i-viii], [1]-78.
    Peter Fin; or, New Road to Brighton. *Also:* Peter Fin's Trip to Brighton. London: Simpkin & Marshall, 1822. Pp. [i], [1]-40.
    Peter Fin's Trip to Brighton.
        See Peter Fin.
    Too Late for Dinner. London: W. Sams, 1820. Pp. [1]-55. 2nd ed.
    Too Late for Dinner. Philadelphia: Thomas H. Palmer, 1822. Pp. [1]-53.

JONES, ROBERT ST. CLAIR
    Harp of Altenberg, The. London: John Duncombe, n.d. Pp. [1]-38. [Duncombe's Edition].
    Harp of Altenberg!, The. By S. Jones. London: John Duncombe, n.d. Pp. [1]-38. Duncombe's Edition. *Filed under* Jones, S. Stephen.

JONES, S. STEPHEN
    See Jones, Robert St. Clair.

JONES, T.
    Confin'd in Vain; or, A Double to Do. London: M. Jones; J. Peck (priv.), 1805. Pp. [1]-47.

JONES, T. PERCY
    See Aytoun, William Edmondstone.

JONES, WILTON
    See Jones, John Wilton.

JONSON, BEN
    Every Man in His Humour. London: Thomas Dolby, 1825. Pp. [i]-[vi], [7]-68. Dolby's British Theatre, X. *Filed under* Cumberland, John. Cumberland's British Theatre, X.
    Every Man in His Humour.
        See Garrick, David (arr.).
    Tobacconist, The.
        See Gentleman, Francis.

JOPLING, LOUISE GOODE, MRS. JOSEPH MIDDLETON
    (later Mrs. Rowe)
    Affinities.
        See Praed, Rosa Caroline Murray-Prior, Mrs. Campbell.

JOSEPH AND HIS BRETHREN
    See P., Br.
    See Wells, Charles Jeremiah.

JOSEPH IN EGYPT
    See Holcroft, Thomas.

JOSEPH SHARK, THE LAWYER'S CLERK
    See Phillips, G.

JOSEPHINE, THE CHILD OF THE REGIMENT
    See Buckstone, John Baldwin.

JOURDAIN, JOHN
    Khartoum!
        See Muskerry, William.

JOURNEY TO LONDON
    See Vanbrugh, John. Provoked Husband, The.

JOURNEY'S END, THE
    See Newte, Horace Wykeham Can.

JOY IS DANGEROUS
    See Mortimer, James.

JUAN
    See Cornwall, Barry.

JUBILEE, THE
    See Dibdin, Thomas John.

JUBILEE, THE; OR, JOHN BULL IN HIS DOTAGE (anon.)
    London: Sherwood, Neely, & Jones, 1809. Pp. [3]-40.

JUDAEL
    See Harley, St. John.

JUDAH
    See Jones, Henry Arthur.

JUDAS
    See Starkey, Digby Pilot.

JUDAS ISCARIOT
    See Horne, Richard Hengist.

JUDGE NOT
    See Stirling, Edward.

JUDGMENT OF TITHONUS, THE
    See Ross, Ronald.

JUDITH
    See Capper, Richard.
    See Johnson, Reginald Brimley.

JUDITH OF GENEVA!
    See Morton, Thomas, jr.

JUGGLER, THE
    See Ware, James Redding.

JULIAN
    See Mitford, Mary Russell.

JULIAN AND AGNES
    See Sotheby, William.

JULIAN THE APOSTATE
    See Cornwall, Barry.
    See de Vere, Aubrey.

JULIO ROMANO
    See Bucke, Charles.

JULIUS CAESAR
    See Kemble, John Philip (arr.).
    See Shakespeare, William.
    See Tree, Herbert Beerbohm (arr.).

JUMP FROM JAPAN
    See Dibdin, Thomas John. Harlequin Harper.

JUPITER AND ALCMENA
    See Planché, James Robinson. Burletta of Errors.

JUST AS WELL
    See Manners, John Hartley.

JUST LIKE ROGER!
    See Webster, Benjamin, jr.

JUST MY LUCK
    See Maltby, C. Alfred.

JUSTICE
    See Faucit, John Savill.

JUSTINA
    See MacCarthy, Denis Florence.

JUSTIZA, THE: A TALE OF ARRAGON
    See Bennett, George John.

JUVENILE TEMPERANCE DISCUSSION FOR SIXTEEN YOUTHS, THE
    See Featherstone, Thomas.

KAIS
    See Brandon, Isaac.

KALIDASA
    Sakoontala.
        See Williams, Monier (trans.).

KATE KEARNEY
    See Collier, William.

KATE WYNSLEY, THE COTTAGE GIRL
    See Wilks, Thomas Egerton. Woman's Love.

KATHARINE AND PETRUCHIO
    See Ashby-Sterry, Joseph.
    See Kemble, John Philip (arr.).
    See Kemble, John Philip (arr.). Taming of the Shrew.

KATHLEEN MAVOURNEEN
    See Travers, William.

KATHLEEN O'NEIL
    See Balfour, Mary.

KAYE, ARTHUR
    Midsummer-Eve: An Idyll of Sherwood Forest. Music by Boyd, William. London: G. J. Parris (printer), 1893. Pp. [1]-30. Libretto.

KEAN, CHARLES JOHN (arr.)
    Hamlet, Prince of Denmark. By Shakespeare, William. London: John K. Chapman (printer), n.d. Pp. [i]-[vi], [7]-110.
    Hamlet. By Shakespeare, William. In *Dramatic Entertainments at Windsor Castle*, ed. Benjamin Webster, London:

Mitchell, n.d., pp. [121]-189. *Filed under* Webster, Benjamin Nottingham. Dramatic Entertainments.

King Henry the Eighth. By Shakespeare, William. London: John K. Chapman (printer), n.d. Pp. [i]-vii, x, [11]-89. Pp. viii-ix lacking.

King Henry the Eighth. By Shakespeare, William. London: John K. Chapman (printer), n.d. Pp. [i]-x, [11]-89. 2nd ed.

King Henry the Fifth. By Shakespeare, William. London: John K. Chapman (printer), n.d. Pp. [i]-viii, [9]-96. 2nd ed.

King John. By Shakespeare, William. New York: William Taylor, 1846. Pp. [iii]-[xii], [i]-xii, [13]-68. Modern Standard Drama, 35.

King John. By Shakespeare, William. London: John K. Chapman (printer), n.d. Pp. [i]-viii, [9]-83.

King John. By Shakespeare, William. London: John K. Chapman (printer), n.d. Pp. [i]-viii, [9]-83. 2nd ed.

King Lear. By Shakespeare, William. London: John K. Chapman (printer), n.d. Pp. [i]-vi, [7]-89.

King Richard II. By Shakespeare, William. London: John K. Chapman (printer), n.d. Pp. [i]-x, [11]-88.

Macbeth. By Shakespeare, William. London: John K. Chapman (printer), n.d. Pp. [i]-[x], [11]-89.

Merchant of Venice, The. By Shakespeare, William. London: John K. Chapman (printer), n.d. Pp. [i]-viii, [9]-85.

Merchant of Venice, The. By Shakespeare, William. In *Dramatic Entertainments at Windsor Castle,* ed. Benjamin Webster, London: Mitchell, n.d., pp. [i]-x, [1]-58. *Filed under* Webster, Benjamin Nottingham. Dramatic Entertainments.

Midsummer Night's Dream, A. By Shakespeare, William. London: John K. Chapman (printer), n.d. Pp. [i]-vi, [7]-60.

Much Ado about Nothing. By Shakespeare, William. London: John K. Chapman (printer), n.d. Pp. [1]-68.

Pauline. By Oxenford, John. London: John K. Chapman (printer), n.d. Pp. [1]-36. *Filed under* Oxenford, John. Pauline.

Pizarro; or, The Spaniards in Peru. By Sheridan, Richard Brinsley. London: John K. Chapman (printer), n.d. Pp. [i]-[x], [11]-67.

Sardanapalus, King of Assyria. By Byron, George Gordon, Lord. New York: Samuel French, n.d. Pp. [1]-6, [vii]-[x], [9]-62. French's Standard Drama, 101.

Tempest, The. By Shakespeare, William. London: John K. Chapman (printer), n.d. Pp. [i]-[x], [11]-74.

Tempest, The. By Shakespeare, William. London: John K. Chapman (printer), n.d. Pp. [i]-[x], [11]-69. 3rd ed.

Winter's Tale, The. By Shakespeare, William. London: John K. Chapman (printer), n.d. Pp. [i]-x, [11]-105.

Winter's Tale, The. By Shakespeare, William. London: John K. Chapman (printer), n.d. Pp. [i]-x, [11]-100. 2nd ed.

KEATING, ELIZA H.

Aladdin; or, The Very Wonderful Lamp! London: Thomas Hailes Lacy, n.d. Pp. [1]-33. Fairy Plays for Home Performance, 6.

Ali Baba; or, A New Duo-(Decimal) Edition of the Forty Thieves! London: Samuel French; New York: T. Henry French, n.d. Pp. [1]-38. Fairy and Home Plays for Home Performance, 10.

Beauty and the Beast. London & New York: Samuel French, n.d. Pp. [1]-32. Fairy and Home Plays for Home Performance, 1.

Blue Beard; or, Female Curiosity! and Male Atrocity! London & New York: Samuel French, n.d. Pp. [1]-28. Fairy and Home Plays for Home Performance, 2.

Cinderella. London & New York: Samuel French, n.d. Pp. [1]-24.

Little Red Riding Hood; or, The Wolf, the Wooer, and the Wizard! London: Thomas Hailes Lacy, n.d. Pp. [1]-37. Fairy Plays for Home Performance, 8.

Puss in Boots; or, The Marquis, the Miller, and the Mouser! London & New York: Samuel French, n.d. Pp. [1]-35. Fairy and Home Plays for Home Performance, 7.

Sleeping Beauty, The; or, One Hundred and Eighteen Years in as Many Minutes. London & New York: Samuel French, n.d. Pp. [1]-30. Fairy and Home Plays for Home Performance, 9.

White Cat, The. London: Thomas Hailes Lacy, n.d. Pp. [1]-16.

Yellow Dwarf, The. London: Thomas Hailes Lacy, n.d. Pp. [1]-32. Fairy Plays for Home Performance, 5.

KEATS, JOHN

Otho the Great. In [*Poetical Works,* London: S. Bill & Sons, 1883], pp. [331]-401. Title page lacking.

KEELEY WORRIED BY BUCKSTONE

See Lemon, Mark.

KEEP, W. A.

Incog; or, Three Days at a Well-Known Hotel. London: W. Simpkin & R. Marshall, 1817. Pp. [iii]-[viii], [1]-67.

KEEP OF CASTLE HILL!

See Wilks, Thomas Egerton. Lord Darnley.

KEEP YOUR EYE ON HER

See Williams, Thomas John.

KEEP YOUR OWN SECRET

See Fitzgerald, Edward (trans.).

See Fox, Henry Richard.

KEEP YOUR TEMPER

See Kitching, H. St. A.

See Wooler, John Pratt.

KEEPER OF THE SEALS

See Gordon, Lionel Smith.

KELLY, HUGH

School for Wives, The. In *Modern Theatre,* ed. Mrs. Inchbald, 10 vols., London: Longman, Hurst, Rees, Orme, & Brown, 1811, IX, [233]-336.

School for Wives, The. In *British Drama,* 12 vols., London: John Dicks, 1872, XI, [289]-316.

KEMBLE, CHARLES

Budget of Blunders, A. Philadelphia: Mathew Carey, 1811. Pp. [1]-34.

Plot and Counterplot; or, The Portrait of Michael Cervantes. London: Appleyards, 1808. Pp. [i-iv], [1]-41.

Plot and Counterplot; or, The Portrait of Michael Cervantes. London: C. Chapple, 1812. Pp. [i-iv], [1]-41. 2nd ed.

Plot and Counterplot; or, The Portrait of Cervantes. London: John Cumberland & Son, n.d. Pp. [1]-39. Cumberland's British Theatre, XLI. *Filed under* Cumberland, John. Cumberland's British Theatre, XLI.

Point of Honor, The. London: T. N. Longman & O. Rees, 1800. Pp. [1]-64.

Point of Honour, The. London: John Cumberland, n.d. Pp. [1]-44. Cumberland's British Theatre, XXVIII. *Filed under* Cumberland, John. Cumberland's British Theatre, XXVIII.

Wanderer, The; or, The Rights of Hospitality. [London: Appleyards, 1808]. Pp. [1]-64. Title page lacking.

KEMBLE, FRANCES ANNE (Fanny) (later Mrs. Pierce Butler)

English Tragedy, An. In *Plays,* London: Longman, Green, Longman, Roberts, & Green, 1863, pp. [1]-192.

Francis the First. London: John Murray, 1832. Pp. [i-viii], [1]-142. 8th ed.

Star of Seville, The. By Mrs. Butler. New York: Saunders & Otley, 1837. Pp. [i-vi], [1]-130.

Star of Seville, The. By Mrs. Butler. London: Saunders & Otley, 1837. Pp. [i-vi], [1]-146.

KEMBLE, FRANCES ANNE (Fanny) (later Mrs. Pierce Butler) (trans.)

Mademoiselle de Belle Isle. By Dumas, Alexandre. In *Plays,* London: Longman, Green, Longman, Roberts, & Green, 1863, pp. [425]-582.

Mary Stuart. By Schiller. In *Plays,* London: Longman, Green, Longman, Roberts, & Green, 1863, pp. [193]-423.

KEMBLE, HENRY STEPHEN

Flodden Field.

See Kemble, Stephen.

KEMBLE, JOHN PHILIP

Farm House, The. In *British Drama,* 12 vols., London: John Dicks, 1871, VII, [24]-32.

See Halliday, Andrew.
See Oxberry, William Henry.

KENNEDY, CHARLES RANN
    Coming of Peace, The; or, The Old Order Changeth. Chatham, 1900. Pp. [1]-9. Typescript.

KENNEDY, WILLIAM
    Siege of Antwerp, The. London: Edward Moxon, 1838. Pp. [i-vi], [1]-[111].

KENNEY, CHARLES LAMB
    Aladdin and the Wonderful Lamp.
        See Smith, Albert Richard.
    Masaniello.
        See Kenney, James.
    Willow Copse, The.
        See Boucicault, Dionysius Lardner.
    Wood Demon, The; or, One O'Clock. Written with Smith, Albert Richard. By Charles Kenny and Albert Smith. London: T. Brettell (printer), 1847. Pp. [1]-28. *Filed under* Kenny, Charles; Smith, Albert Richard.

KENNEY, CHARLES LAMB (trans.)
    Africaine, L'. Music by Meyerbeer. London: Chappell; Boosey, n.d. Pp. [1]-50. Libretto.
    Ali Baba. Music by Bottesini. London: Hutchings & Romer, n.d. Pp. [1]-11, 2-178, [1-6], 179-294. Pagination irregular. Vocal score.
    Ballo in Maschera, Un. *Also:* The Masked Ball. Music by Verdi. London & New York: Boosey, n.d. Pp. [i-iv], 1-264. Vocal score.
    Black Domino, The.
        See Domino Noir, Le.
    Daughter of the Regiment, The.
        See Figlia del Reggimento, La.
    Domino Noir, Le. *Also:* The Black Domino. *Also:* Il Domino Nero. Music by Auber. London & New York: Boosey, n.d. Pp. [i-iv], 1-256. Boosey's Standard Operas. Vocal score.
    Don Pasquale. Music by Donizetti. London & New York: Boosey, n.d. Pp. [i-iv], 1-224. Vocal score.
    Elisir d'Amore, L'. Music by Donizetti. London: Boosey, n.d. Pp. [i-iv], 1-288. Royal Edition of Operas. Vocal score.
    Favorita, La. Music by Donizetti. London: Boosey, n.d. Pp. [i-iv], 1-280. Vocal score.
    Figlia del Reggimento, La. *Also:* The Daughter of the Regiment. Music by Donizetti. London: Boosey, n.d. Pp. [i-iv], 1-243. Royal Edition of Operas. Vocal score.
    Grande Duchesse de Gerolstein, La. Music by Offenbach. London: Boosey, n.d. Pp. [i-iv], 1-296. Boosey's Standard Operas. Extra Volume. Vocal score.
    Lucia di Lammermoor. Music by Donizetti. London & New York: Boosey, n.d. Pp. [i-iv], 1-244. Vocal score.
    Marriage of Figaro, The.
        See Nozze di Figaro, Le.
    Masked Ball, The.
        See Ballo in Maschera, Un.
    Mock Doctor, The. *Also:* Le Médecin Malgré Lui. Music by Gounod. London & New York: Boosey, n.d. Pp. [i-iv], 1-188. Boosey's Standard Operas. Vocal score.
    Nozze di Figaro, Le. *Also:* The Marriage of Figaro. Music by Mozart. [London: Boosey, n.d.]. Pp. [iii-iv], 1-287. Title page lacking. Vocal score.
    Semiramide. Music by Rossini. London: Boosey, n.d. Pp. [i-vi], 1-402. Vocal score.

KENNEY, JAMES
    Alcaid, The; or, The Secrets of Office. London: T. Dolby, 1825. Pp. [1-2], [i]-[viii], [7]-58. Dolby's British Theatre, VIII. *Filed under* Cumberland, John. Cumberland's British Theatre, VIII.
    Alcaid, The; or, The Secrets of Office. London: T. Dolby, n.d. Pp. [i]-[viii], [7]-58. Dolby's British Theatre [Cumberland's British Theatre].
    Benyowsky; or, The Exiles of Kamschatka. London: Longman, Rees, Orme, Brown, & Green, 1826. Pp. [1]-80.
    Blind Boy, The. London: Longman, Hurst, Rees, & Orme, 1808. Pp. [i-iii], [1]-36.

Blind Boy, The. In *Dramas, Serious and Serio-Comic, for College, Camp, and Cabin,* London: Thomas Hailes Lacy, n.d., pp. [1]-24. *Filed under* Lacy, Thomas Hailes. Dramas for College, Camp, and Cabin.

Blind Boy, The. London: John Cumberland, n.d. Pp. [1]-34. Cumberland's British Theatre, XXV. *Filed under* Cumberland, John. Cumberland's British Theatre, XXV.

Blind Boy, The. London: T. & R. Hughes, 1807. Pp. [5]-32. Synopsis.

Debtor and Creditor. London: John Miller, 1814. Pp. [i-iv], [1]-98.

Ella Rosenberg. London: Longman, Hurst, Rees, & Orme, 1807. Pp. [i-iv], [1]-41.

Ella Rosenberg. London: John Cumberland, n.d. Pp. [1]-35. Cumberland's British Theatre, XXVII. *Filed under* Cumberland, John. Cumberland's British Theatre, XXVII.

False Alarms; or, My Cousin. London: Longman, Hurst, Rees, & Orme, 1807. Pp. [i-iv], [1]-86.

False Alarms; or, My Cousin. London: John Cumberland, n.d. Pp. [1]-64. Cumberland's British Theatre, XXXIX. *Filed under* Cumberland, John. Cumberland's British Theatre, XXXIX.

Fighting by Proxy. London: John Miller, 1835. Pp. [i-iii], [1]-20.

Fighting by Proxy. London: Thomas Hailes Lacy, n.d. Pp. [1]-21. [Lacy's Acting Edition].

Good-looking Fellow, A. Written with Bunn, Alfred. London: John Miller, 1834. Pp. [3]-37.

Hernani; or, The Pledge of Honour. London: Thomas Hailes Lacy, n.d. Pp. [1]-[54].

House out at Windows, A. London: C. Chapple, 1817. Pp. [i-ii], [1]-32.

Illustrious Stranger, The; or, Married and Buried. London: John Cumberland, n.d. Pp. [1]-36. Cumberland's British Theatre, XXIII. *Filed under* Cumberland, John. Cumberland's British Theatre, XXIII.

Illustrious Stranger, The; or, Married and Buried. Music by Nathan. London: G. H. Davidson, n.d. Pp. [1]-36. Promptbook.

Irish Ambassador, The. New York: William Taylor, n.d. Pp. [1]-41. Minor Drama, 37.

John Buzzby; or, A Day's Pleasure. London: W. Simpkin & R. Marshall, 1822. Pp. [i-v], [1]-54.

King's Seal, The. Written with Gore, Catherine Grace Frances Moody, Mrs. Charles. London: John Miller, 1835. Pp. [i-iv], [1]-36.

Love, Law, and Physic. Dublin: T. Charles (printer), 1821. Pp. [1]-34.

Love, Law, and Physic. London: John Cumberland, n.d. Pp. [1]-41. Cumberland's British Theatre, XXIV. *Filed under* Cumberland, John. Cumberland's British Theatre, XXIV.

Masaniello. Written with Kenney, Charles Lamb. By James Kenney. London: Edward Moxon, 1831. Pp. [i-ii], [1]-55. Libretto. *Filed under* Kenney, James.

Masaniello. Written with Kenney, Charles Lamb. *Also:* La Muta di Portici. Music by Auber. London & New York: Boosey, n.d. Pp. [i-vi], 1-376. [Royal Edition]. Vocal score.

Match Breaking; or, The Prince's Present. London: W. Simpkin & R. Marshall, 1821. Pp. [i-x], [1]-49.

Matrimony. Music by King, M. P. London: Longman, Hurst, Rees, & Orme, 1804. Pp. [i-iv], [5]-46. 3rd ed.

Matrimony. London: John Cumberland, n.d. Pp. [1]-36. Cumberland's British Theatre, XXVI. *Filed under* Cumberland, John. Cumberland's British Theatre, XXVI.

Pledge, The; or, Castilian Honour. London: C. Chapple, 1831. Pp. [i-x], [1]-83.

Portfolio, The; or, The Family of Anglade. London: Longman, Hurst, Rees, Orme, & Brown, 1816. Pp. [1]-52.

Raising the Wind. London: T. N. Longman & O. Rees, 1803. Pp. [i-vi], [1]-37.

Raising the Wind. London: John Cumberland, 1828. Pp. [1]-35. Cumberland's British Theatre, XIX. *Filed under* Cumberland, John. Cumberland's British Theatre, XIX.

Sicilian Vespers, The. London: John Miller, 1840. Pp. [3]-66.

Spring and Autumn; or, Married for Money. [London: John Dicks], n.d. Pp. [1]-14. Dicks' Standard Plays, 708.

Sweethearts and Wives. In *Dramatic Entertainments at Windsor Castle*, ed. Benjamin Webster, London: Mitchell, n.d., pp. [323]-372. *Filed under* Webster, Benjamin Nottingham. Dramatic Entertainments.

Sweethearts and Wives. Philadelphia: A. R. Poole; Ash & Mason; P. Thompson, n.d. Pp. [1]-66. Acting American Theatre, Lopez and Wemyss Edition. Promptbook.

Too Many Cooks. Music by King, M. P. London: Longman, Hurst, Rees, & Orme, 1805. Pp. [1]-44.

Touchstone, The; or, The World as It Goes. London: C. Chapple, 1817. Pp. [i-x], [1]-[82].

Turn Out! London: Sharpe & Hailes, 1812. Pp. [i-iv], [1]-56.

Turn Out! London: Sharpe & Hailes, 1812. Pp. [1]-47. 2nd ed.

World!, The. London: Longman, Hurst, Rees, & Orme, 1808. Pp. [i-iv], [1]-94.

KENNYNGTON CROSSE
   See Wilks, Thomas Egerton.

KENSINGTON GARDENS
   See Brough, Robert Barnabas.

KENYON'S WIDOW.
   See Brookfield, Charles Hallam Elton. Burnt Ashes.

KERR, FREDERICK
   Leap Year. London: Samuel French; New York: T. Henry French, n.d. Pp. [1]-12. [Lacy's Acting Edition].

KERR, JOHN
   Drenched and Dried; or, Water and Fire. London: J. & H. Kerr, n.d. Pp. [1]-18.

   Freischutz, Der; or, Zamiel, the Spirit of the Forest. [London: John Dicks], n.d. Pp. [1]-14. Dicks' Standard Plays, 329.

   Histerkan; or, The Assassin of the Mountain. London: Henry Osler, 1816. Pp. [i-vi], [1]-74.

   Intimate Friend, The; or, A Queer Guest at a Wedding. London: John Duncombe, n.d. Pp. [2]-26. John Duncombe's Edition.

   King Robert the Bruce; or, The Battle of Bannockburn. Written with Corri, Montague. London: John Duncombe, n.d. Pp. [1]-28. Duncombe's Edition.

   Michael and Christine; or, Love in Humble Life. London: Havell (printer) (priv.), n.d. Pp. [39]-59. *Filed under* Wandering Boys.

   Monster and Magician, The; or, The Fate of Frankenstein. London: J. & H. Kerr, n.d. Pp. [1]-32.

   Presumptive Guilt; or, The Fiery Ordeal. Music by Hughes. London: John Duncombe, 1818. Pp. [1]-20. 3rd ed.

   Rip Van Winkle; or, A Legend of Sleepy Hollow. Written with Lacy, Thomas Hailes. London: Thomas Hailes Lacy, n.d. Pp. [1]-27. [Lacy's Acting Edition]. *Filed under* Kerr, John.

   Rip Van Winkle; or, The Demons of the Catskill Mountains! Philadelphia: R. H. Lenfestey, n.d. Pp. [1]-76. Lenfestey's Edition.

   Therese, the Orphan of Geneva. In *British Drama*, 12 vols., London: John Dicks, 1871, V, [103]-120.

   Therese, the Orphan of Geneva. [London: John Dicks], n.d. Pp. [103]-120.

   Wandering Boys, The. Music by Nicholson. London: John Cumberland, n.d. Pp. [1]-39. Cumberland's Minor Theatre, III. *Filed under* Cumberland, John. Cumberland's Minor Theatre, III.

   Wandering Boys, The; or, Castle of Olival. London: Havell (printer) (priv.), n.d. Pp. [1]-38.

   Wandering Boys, The; or, The Castle of Olival. London: John Duncombe, n.d. Pp. [1]-38. Duncombe's Edition.

KERRY
   See Boucicault, Dionysius Lardner.

KEVIN'S CHOICE
   See Hazlewood, ?, Miss.

KEY OF THE CELLAR
   See Bluebeard (anon.).

KHARTOUM!
   See Muskerry, William.

KILDROSTAN
   See Smith, Walter Chalmers.

KILL OR CURE
   See Dance, Charles.

KILLCROP, THE
   See Cottle, Joseph.

KILLING NO MURDER
   See Hook, Theodore Edward.

KILLING TIME
   See Morton, John Maddison. Love and Rain.

KILMOREY, EARL OF
   See Newry, Charles Francis Needham, Earl of Kilmorey, Viscount.

KIMPTON, F.
   He Lies Like Truth. London: Thomas Hailes Lacy, n.d. Pp. [1]-26. [Lacy's Acting Edition].

KIND IMPOSTOR
   See Cibber, Colley. She Would and She Would Not.

KIND TO A FAULT
   See Brough, William.

KING, THOMAS (arr.)
   Lovers' Quarrels; or, Like Master Like Man. By Vanbrugh, John. In *British Drama*, 12 vols., London: John Dicks, 1872, XI, [281]-288.

KING ALFRED AND THE CAKES
   See Brough, Robert Barnabas.

KING AND ARTIST
   See Moubrey, Lilian.

KING AND I, THE
   See Morton, John Maddison.

KING AND REBEL
   See Vellère, Edward Raphael Weller, Dr.

KING AND THE ANGEL, THE
   See Neil, Ross.

KING AND THE CARPENTER, THE
   See Lawrance, Frederic.

KING AND THE COBLER
   See Douglas, Thomas. Friend at Court, A.

KING AND THE COMMONER, THE
   See Langford, John Alfred.

KING AND THE DESERTER, THE
   See Maddox, John Medex.

KING AND THE DUKE, THE
   See Jameson, Robert Francis.

KING ARTHUR
   See Akhurst, William M.
   See Brough, William.
   See Carr, Joseph William Comyns.

KING ARTHUR AND THE KNIGHTS OF THE ROUND TABLE
   See Pocock, Isaac.

KING CHARLES II
   See Ryan, Desmond Lumley.

KING CHARLES THE FIRST
   See Gurney, Archer Thompson.

KING CHARLES THE SECOND
   See Longland, Joseph.

KING CHARLES THE SECOND'S MERRY DAYS
   See Moncrieff, William Thomas. Rochester.

KING CHARMING
   See Planché, James Robinson.

KING CHRISTMAS
   See Planché, James Robinson.

KING EDWARD II
   See Grindrod, Charles.

KING EDWARD THE SIXTH
   See Gregg, Tresham Dames, Rev.

KING EDWARD V
   See Grindrod, Charles.

KING ERIK
   See Gosse, Edmund William.

KING HELGE
   See Winbolt, Frederick I.

KING HENRY I
   See Grindrod, Charles.

KING HENRY II
    See Grindrod, Charles.
KING HENRY III
    See Grindrod, Charles.
KING HENRY IV, PART 1
    See Shakespeare, William.
KING HENRY IV, PART 2
    See Kemble, John Philip (arr.).
KING HENRY THE EIGHTH
    See Irving, Henry (arr.).
    See Kean, Charles John (arr.).
    See Kemble, John Philip (arr.).
    See Shakespeare, William.
KING HENRY THE FIFTH
    See Kean, Charles John (arr.).
    See Kemble, John Philip (arr.).
    See Shakespeare, William.
KING HENRY THE FOURTH
    See Shakespeare, William.
KING HENRY THE FOURTH, PART 1
    See Kemble, John Philip (arr.).
KING HENRY THE FOURTH, PART 2
    See Kemble, John Philip (arr.).
    See Valpy, Richard (arr.).
KING HENRY THE SECOND
    See Helps, Arthur.
KING HENRY THE THIRD, PART 1
    See Edison, John Sibbald.
KING HENRY V
    See Shakespeare, William.
KING HENRY VIII
    See Shakespeare, William.
KING HUMMING TOP
    See Blanchard, Edward Litt Leman.
KING IN DISGUISE, A
    See Adams, Florence Davenport.
KING INCOG., THE
    See A'Beckett, Gilbert Abbott.
KING JAMES I
    See Grindrod, Charles.
KING JAMES THE FIRST
    See Graham, David.
KING JAMES THE SECOND
    See Whitehead, John Crawford.
KING JAMIE; OR, HARLEQUIN AND THE MAGIC FIDDLE
    (anon.)
    London: J. & D. A. Darling, n.d. Pp. [1]-18. Libretto.
KING JAMIE'S FROLIC
    See Gunton, R. T. Lancashire Witches, The.
KING JOHN
    See Kean, Charles John (arr.).
    See Kemble, John Philip (arr.).
    See Shakespeare, William.
    See Valpy, Richard (arr.).
KING JOHN (WITH THE BENEFIT OF THE ACT)
    See A'Beckett, Gilbert Abbott.
KING LEAR
    See Elliston, Robert William (arr.).
    See Irving, Henry (arr.).
    See Kean, Charles John (arr.).
    See Shakespeare, William.
    See Tate, Nahum (arr.).
KING NEPTUNE AND THE DANCING PRINCESS
    See Marchant, Frederick. Nip Van Winkle and the Demon Slumber of Twenty Years.
KING OF BARATARIA
    See Gilbert, William Schwenck. Gondoliers, The.
KING OF KENT, THE
    See Cook, Keningale.
KING OF THE ALPS, THE
    See Buckstone, John Baldwin.
KING OF THE BEAN, THE
    See Planché, James Robinson.
KING OF THE COMMONS, THE
    See White, James, Rev.

KING OF THE GOLD MINES
    See A'Beckett, Gilbert Abbott. Yellow Dwarf, The.
KING OF THE MERROWS
    See Burnand, Francis Cowley.
KING OF THE MIST, THE
    See Fitzball, Edward.
KING OF THE PEACOCKS, THE
    See Planché, James Robinson.
KING OF THE RED NOSES AND THE LIVER QUEEN
    See Harlequin and the Childe of Hale.
KING OF THE STUDENTS
    See Harris, Augustus Henry Glossop. Basoche, The.
KING O'NEIL
    See Gore, Catherine Grace Frances Moody, Mrs. Charles.
KING O'TOOLE'S GOOSE
    See Irwin, Edward.
KING, QUEEN, AND KNAVE
    See Morton, John Maddison. Muleteer of Toledo, The.
KING RENÉ'S DAUGHTER
    See Chapman, Jane Frances (trans.).
    See Martin, Theodore, Sir (trans.).
    See Phipps, Edmund (trans.).
    See Weatherly, Frederick Edward (trans.).
KING RICHARD II
    See Kean, Charles John (arr.).
    See Shakespeare, William.
KING RICHARD III
    See Hicks, Edward Seymour (arr.).
    See Irving, Henry (arr.).
KING RICHARD THE FIRST
    See Puseley, Daniel.
    See S., L. M.
KING RICHARD THE SECOND
    See Wroughton, Richard (arr.).
KING RICHARD THE THIRD
    See Kemble, John Philip (arr.).
    See Shakespeare, William.
KING ROBERT THE BRUCE
    See Kerr, John.
KING SOLOMON
    See Armstrong, George Francis.
KING STEPHEN
    See Paynter, David William.
KING, THE PRINCESS, AND THE GENI
    See Kingdom, John M. Fountain of Beauty, The.
KING THRUSHBEARD!
    See Talfourd, Francis.
KING VICTOR AND KING CHARLES
    See Browning, Robert.
KING WINTER AND PRINCESS SUMMER
    See French, George H.
KING ZANY'S DAUGHTER
    See Bosbacca, Gulielmerg Henricus.
KING'S AMUSEMENT
    See Burton, William Evans. Court Fool, The.
KING'S COMMAND, THE
    See Thompson, C. Pelham.
KING'S FAVOURITE, THE
    See White, James, Rev.
KING'S FOOL, THE
    See Millingen, John Gideon.
KING'S GARDENER, THE
    See Selby, Charles.
KING'S PROXY, THE
    See Arnold, Samuel James.
KING'S RIVAL, THE
    See Taylor, Tom.
KING'S SEAL, THE
    See Kenney, James.
KING'S WAGER, THE
    See Wilks, Thomas Egerton.
KING'S WORD, THE
    See Addison, Henry Robert, Capt.

KINGDOM, JOHN M.
  Fountain of Beauty, The; or, The King, the Princess, and the Geni. London: Thomas Hailes Lacy, n.d. Pp. [1]-34. [Lacy's Acting Edition].
  Marcoretti; or, The Brigand's Sacrifice. Chicago & New York: Dramatic Publishing Co., c.1874. Pp. [1]-34. Author's ed.
  Three Princes, The. London: John Duncombe, n.d. Pp. [1]-34. Duncombe's Edition.
KINGE RICHARD YE THIRD
  See Selby, Charles.
KINGSLEY, CHARLES
  Saint's Tragedy, The; or, The True Story of Elizabeth of Hungary. London: John W. Parker, 1848. Pp. [1-4], [i]-[xxvi], [27]-271.
  Saint's Tragedy, The. In Poems, London: Macmillan, 1884, I, [1-3], [1]-267.
KINGSLEY, ELLIS
  Accepted by Proxy. London: Samuel French; New York: T. Henry French, n.d. Pp. [1]-10. [Lacy's Acting Edition].
  Other Woman, The. Chicago: Dramatic Publishing Co., n.d. Pp. [1]-14. Sergel's Acting Drama, 393.
KINGSTON, GERTRUDE
  Bear and the Lady, The. In Dialogues of the Day, ed. Oswald Crawfurd, London: Chapman & Hall, n.d., pp. [16]-24. Filed under Crawfurd, Oswald. Dialogues of the Day.
KINNAIRD, DOUGLAS JAMES WILLIAM
  Merchant of Bruges, The; or, Beggar's Bush. London: Whittingham & Arliss, 1815. Pp. [1]-84.
  Merchant of Bruges, The; or, Beggar's Bush. London: Sherwood, Neely, & Jones, 1818. Pp. [1]-60. London Theatre, XXVI. Filed under Dibdin, Thomas John, ed. London Theatre, XXVI.
  Merchant of Bruges, The. In British Drama, 12 vols., London: John Dicks, 1865, IV, [1231]-1246.
KINSMEN OF NAPLES, THE
  See Bunn, Alfred.
KIRK-O-FIELD
  See Blake, Robert.
KISHUN KOOVUR
  See Soobrow.
KISS, THE
  See Clarke, Stephen.
  See Collier, William.
KISS AND BE FRIENDS
  See Morton, John Maddison.
KISS AND THE ROSE, THE
  See Moncrieff, William Thomas.
KISS FROM THE BRIDE
  See Morton, John Maddison. Corporal's Wedding!, The.
KISS IN THE DARK
  See Buckstone, John Baldwin.
KISSI-KISSI
  See Burnand, Francis Cowley.
KISSING GOES BY FAVOUR
  See Stirling, Edward.
KIT MARLOWE
  See Bedford, Herbert.
KIT MARLOWE'S DEATH
  See Courtney, William Leonard.
KITCHING, H. ST. A.
  Fate of Ivan, The. In Moral Plays, London: Calkins & Budd, 1832, pp. [115]-213.
  Keep Your Temper!; or, Know Whom You Marry. In Moral Plays, London: Calkins & Budd, 1832, pp. [iii]-xvi, [1]-114.
  Miss Betsy Bull; or, The Johnnies in Spain. In Moral Plays, London: Calkins & Budd, 1832, pp. [215]-270.
KITTY
  See Parke, Walter.
KITTY CLIVE
  See Moore, Frank Frankfort.
KITTY GREY
  See Ross, Adrian.

KLANERT, CHARLES MORITZ
  Elsina. London: John Miller, 1824. Pp. [iii]-[x], [1]-104.
KLEPTOMANIA
  See Melford, Mark.
KNAVE AND QUEEN
  See Young, Charles Lawrence, Sir.
KNAVE OF HEARTS, THE
  See Yardley, William.
KNAVES OF HEARTS AND THE COMPANIONS OF CRIME
  See Suter, William E. Rocambole.
KNAVES OF KNAVES' ACRE
  See Wilks, Thomas Egerton. Sixteen String Jack.
KNIGHT, ARTHUR FRANCIS
  Well Played; or, The Major's Dilemma. London: Samuel French; New York: T. Henry French, n.d. Pp. [1]-17. [Lacy's Acting Edition].
KNIGHT, EDWARD P.
  Chip of the Old Block, A; or, The Village Festival. Music by Whitaker. London: C. Chapple, 1815. Pp. [i-x], [1]-41.
  Veteran, The; or, The Farmer's Sons. London: Simpkin & Marshall; Chappell; Rodwell & Martin, 1822. Pp. [i]-[viii], [9]-68.
KNIGHT, F. HAMILTON
  See Hamilton-Knight, F.
KNIGHT, THOMAS
  Honest Thieves, The. In New English Drama, ed. W. Oxberry, 22 vols., London: W. Simpkin & R. Marshall; C. Chapple, 1820, IX, [1-2], [i]-[vi], [1]-28. Filed under Oxberry, William Henry. New English Drama, IX.
  Honest Thieves, The. In British Drama, 12 vols., London: John Dicks, 1871, VII, [85]-96.
  Honest Thieves, The. London: John Cumberland, n.d. Pp. [1]-36. Cumberland's British Theatre, XXV. Filed under Cumberland, John. Cumberland's British Theatre, XXV.
  Turnpike Gate, The. London: John Cumberland, 1828. Pp. [1]-36. Cumberland's British Theatre, XX. Filed under Cumberland, John. Cumberland's British Theatre, XX.
  Turnpike Gate, The. In British Drama, 12 vols., London: John Dicks, 1865, IV, [1204]-1214.
KNIGHT AND THE NAIADS
  See Byron, Henry James. Nymph of the Lurleyburg, The.
KNIGHT AND THE SPRITE, THE
  See A'Beckett, Gilbert Abbott.
KNIGHT AND THE WOOD DAEMON
  See Lewis, Matthew Gregory. One O'Clock!
KNIGHT AND THE WOOD DEMON
  See Lewis, Matthew Gregory. One O'Clock.
KNIGHT OF ARVA, THE
  See Boucicault, Dionysius Lardner.
KNIGHT OF RHODES, THE
  See Burges, James Bland.
KNIGHT OF SNOWDOUN, THE
  See Morton, Thomas, sr.
KNIGHT OF ST. JOHN!, THE
  See Almar, George.
KNIGHT OF THE HERMITAGE
  See Dibdin, Thomas John. Bonifacio and Bridgetina.
KNIGHT OF THE MAYPOLE, THE
  See Davidson, John.
KNIGHT OF THE WOEFUL COUNTENANCE
  See Almar, George. Don Quixote.
KNIGHT TEMPLAR
  See Beazley, Samuel, jr. Ivanhoe.
KNIGHT! THE LADY! AND THE LAKE!
  See Halliday, Andrew. Mountain Dhu!
KNIGHTS, THE
  See Frere, John Hookham (trans.).
KNIGHTS OF THE CROSS, THE
  See Beazley, Samuel, jr.
KNIGHTS OF THE ROUND TABLE, THE
  See Planché, James Robinson.
KNIGHTS OF THE ROUND TABLE AND OTHER FUNNY-TURE
  See Akhurst, William M. Arthur the King.

KNIGHTS TEMPLARS
    See Lacy, Michael Rophino. Maid of Judah, The.
KNIPE, ELIZABETH
    See Cobbold, Elizabeth Knipe, Mrs. John.
KNOBSTICK WEDDING, A
    See Pitt, W. H.
KNOW WHOM YOU MARRY
    See Kitching, H. St. A. Keep Your Temper!
KNOW YOUR OWN MIND
    See Murphy, Arthur.
KNOWLEDGE OF SELF
    See Taylor, J. (trans.). Atma Bodha.
KNOWLES, JAMES SHERIDAN
    Alexina. In *Various Dramatic Works of James Sheridan Knowles,* London: James McHenry (priv.), 1874, I, [205]-274. *Filed under* Various Dramatic Works.
    Alfred the Great; or, The Patriot King. London: James Ridgway, 1831. Pp. [1]-85.
    Alfred the Great; or, The Patriot King. In *Dramatic Works,* London: Edward Moxon, 1841-43, I, [243]-314. *Filed under* Collected Works.
    Anonymous Play (fragment). In *Various Dramatic Works of James Sheridan Knowles,* London: James McHenry (priv.), 1874, II, [115]-168. *Filed under* Various Dramatic Works.
    Beggar of Bethnal Green, The. London: Edward Moxon, 1834. Pp. [i-x], [1]-108.
    Beggar of Bethnal Green, The. London: Edward Moxon, 1834. Pp. [i-viii], [1]-108. 2nd ed.
    Beggar of Bethnal Green, The. In *Dramatic Works,* London: Edward Moxon, 1841-43, II, [73]-140. *Filed under* Collected Works.
    Brian Boroihme; or, The Maid of Erin. New York: E. M. Murden, 1828. Pp. [1]-40.
    Brian Boroihme; or, The Maid of Erin. In *Various Dramatic Works of James Sheridan Knowles,* London: James McHenry (priv.), 1874, I, [75]-126. *Filed under* Various Dramatic Works.
    Bridal, The. London: Chapman & Hall, 1837. Pp. [1]-4, [1]-51. Acting National Drama. *Filed under* Macready, William Charles.
    Bridal, The. In *Various Dramatic Works of James Sheridan Knowles,* London: James McHenry (priv.), 1874, I, [137]-203. *Filed under* Various Dramatic Works.
    Bridal, The. New York & Philadelphia: Turner & Fisher, n.d. Pp. [3]-67. Turner's Dramatic Library.
    Bridal, The. London: Chapman & Hall, n.d. Pp. [1]-51. Promptbook.
    Caius Gracchus. Glasgow: J. Ridgway & Hurst, Robinson; Constable; Reid & Henderson; R. Milliken, 1823. Pp. [2]-101.
    Caius Gracchus. London: John Cumberland, 1826. Pp. [ii]-vi, [9]-79. Cumberland's British Theatre, VI. *Filed under* Cumberland, John. Cumberland's British Theatre, VI.
    Caius Gracchus. In *Dramatic Works,* London: Edward Moxon, 1841-43, I, [i-xiv], [1]-82. *Filed under* Collected Works.
    Caius Gracchus (unpub. scene). In *Various Dramatic Works of James Sheridan Knowles,* London: James McHenry (priv.), 1874, II, [170]-173. *Filed under* Various Dramatic Works.
    Daughter, The. London: Edward Moxon, 1837. Pp. [i-x], [1]-108. 2nd ed.
    Daughter, The. New York: George Dearborn, 1837. Pp. [1]-107.
    Daughter, The. In *Dramatic Works,* London: Edward Moxon, 1841-43, II, [141]-208. *Filed under* Collected Works.
    Duke of London, The. In *Various Dramatic Works of James Sheridan Knowles,* London: James McHenry (priv.), 1874, II, [1]-73. *Filed under* Various Dramatic Works.
    Fragment of a Spanish Play. In *Various Dramatic Works of James Sheridan Knowles,* London: James McHenry (priv.), 1874, I, [13]-25. *Filed under* Various Dramatic Works.

Hersilia. In *Various Dramatic Works of James Sheridan Knowles,* London: James McHenry (priv.), 1874, I, [1]-11. *Filed under* Various Dramatic Works.
Hunchback, The. London: Edward Moxon, 1832. Pp. [i]-[ix], [1]-118.
Hunchback, The. In *Dramatic Works,* London: Edward Moxon, 1841-43, I, [315]-395. *Filed under* Collected Works.
Hunchback, The. New York: William Taylor, n.d. Pp. [i]-[viii], [9]-82. Modern Standard Drama, 15.
Hunchback, The. London: John Cumberland & Son, n.d. Pp. [i-ii], [1]-76. Cumberland's British Theatre, XLII. *Filed under* Cumberland, John. Cumberland's British Theatre, XLII.
John of Procida; or, The Bridals of Messina. London: Edward Moxon, 1840. Pp. [i]-[viii], [1]-116. 3rd ed.
John of Procida; or, The Bridals of Messina. In *Dramatic Works,* London: Edward Moxon, 1841-43, III, [155]-232. *Filed under* Collected Works.
Leo; or, The Gipsy. In *Various Dramatic Works of James Sheridan Knowles,* London: James McHenry (priv.), 1874, I, [45]-74. *Filed under* Various Dramatic Works.
Love. London: Edward Moxon, 1839. Pp. [i-viii], [1]-116. 3rd ed.
Love. In *Dramatic Works,* London: Edward Moxon, 1841-43, III, [77]-154. *Filed under* Collected Works.
Love. London: John Cumberland, n.d. Pp. [i-ii], [1]-74. Cumberland's British Theatre, XL. *Filed under* Cumberland, John. Cumberland's British Theatre, XL.
Love-Chase, The. In *Dramatic Works,* London: Edward Moxon, 1841-43, II, [209]-276. *Filed under* Collected Works.
Love Chase, The. London: John Cumberland, n.d. Pp. [i-ii], [1]-64. Cumberland's British Theatre, XLI. *Filed under* Cumberland, John. Cumberland's British Theatre, XLI.
Love-Chase, The. London: Music Publishing Co., n.d. Pp. [1]-64. Promptbook.
Maid of Mariendorpt, The. London: Edward Moxon, 1838. Pp. [i-viii], [1]-111. Promptbook.
Maid of Mariendorpt, The. In *Dramatic Works,* London: Edward Moxon, 1841-43, III, [1]-75. *Filed under* Collected Works.
Masque, A. In *Various Dramatic Works of James Sheridan Knowles,* London: James McHenry (priv.), 1874, I, [127]-134. *Filed under* Various Dramatic Works.
Old Maids. In *Dramatic Works,* London: Edward Moxon, 1841-43, III, [233]-315. *Filed under* Collected Works.
Old Maids. Philadelphia: Turner & Fisher, n.d. Pp. [7]-84. Turner's Dramatic Library.
Rose of Arragon, The. In *Dramatic Works,* London: Edward Moxon, 1841-43, III, [317]-397. *Filed under* Collected Works.
Rose of Arragon, The. London: Edward Moxon, 1842. Pp. [i-viii], [1]-120. Promptbook.
Secretary, The. London: Edward Moxon, 1843. Pp. [i-viii], [1]-68.
Secretary, The. New York: Wilson, n.d. Pp. [1]-16.
Storm, The. In *Various Dramatic Works of James Sheridan Knowles,* London: James McHenry (priv.), 1874, I, [37]-44. Fragment. *Filed under* Various Dramatic Works.
True unto Death. Boston: George M. Baker, n.d. Pp. [1]-37. Spencer's Universal Stage, 35.
Vaccination. In *Various Dramatic Works of James Sheridan Knowles,* London: James McHenry (priv.), 1874, I, [27]-36. *Filed under* Various Dramatic Works.
Virginius. London: James Ridgway, 1820. Pp. [1]-[87].
Virginius. London: John Cumberland, 1826. Pp. [1]-[72]. Cumberland's British Theatre, VI. *Filed under* Cumberland, John. Cumberland's British Theatre, VI.
Virginius. In *Dramatic Works,* London: Edward Moxon, 1841-43, I, [83]-153. *Filed under* Collected Works.
Virginius. New York: W. A. Moore & C. S. Bernard, n.d. Pp. [1]-72. Edwin Forrest Edition of Shaksperian and Other Plays, 8.

Widow, The. In *Various Dramatic Works of James Sheridan Knowles,* London: James McHenry (priv.), 1874, II, [75]-111. Fragment. *Filed under* Various Dramatic Works.

Wife, The: A Tale of Mantua. London: Edward Moxon, 1833. Pp. [i-x], [1]-120. 3rd ed. Promptbook.

Wife, The: A Tale of Mantua. In *Dramatic Works,* London: Edward Moxon, 1841-43, II, [1]-[72]. *Filed under* Collected Works.

William Tell. In *Dramatic Works,* London: Edward Moxon, 1841-43, I, [155]-242. *Filed under* Collected Works.

William Tell. London: Thomas Dolby, n.d. Pp. [i-vi], [1]-83. Promptbook.

William Tell. London: John Cumberland, n.d. Pp. [1]-86. Cumberland's British Theatre, XXII. *Filed under* Cumberland, John. Cumberland's British Theatre, XXII.

William Tell. Trans. as Guillaume Tell by Marc-Monnier. In *Various Dramatic Works of James Sheridan Knowles,* London: James McHenry (priv.), 1874, II, [187]-272. *Filed under* Various Dramatic Works.

William Tell. In *Various Dramatic Works of James Sheridan Knowles,* London: James McHenry (priv.), 1874, II, [175]-181. Unpublished scene. *Filed under* Various Dramatic Works.

Woman's Wit; or, Love's Disguises. London: Edward Moxon, 1838. Pp. [i-viii], [1]-120. Promptbook.

Woman's Wit; or, Love's Disguises. In *Dramatic Works,* London: Edward Moxon, 1841-43, II, [277]-354. *Filed under* Collected Works.

Wrecker's Daughter, The. Philadelphia & New York: Turner & Fisher, n.d. Pp. [2]-63. Turner's Dramatic Library, 26.

KNOWLES, RICHARD BRINSLEY
  Maiden Aunt, The. London: Edward Moxon, 1845. Pp. [i-vi], [1]-62 (imperfect copy).

KNOX, CHARLES H., CAPT. (trans.)
  Faust. By Goethe. London: John Ollivier, 1847. Pp. [i]-[x], [1]-338.

KO AND ZOA
  See Dibdin, Charles Isaac Mungo, jr.

KOEUBA, THE
  See Fitzball, Edward.

KOHLER, W.
  Faust and Gretchen.
    See Ross, Adrian.

KOTZEBUE, AUGUSTUS VON
  Count Benyowsky.
    See Thompson, Benjamin (trans.).
  Deaf and Dumb.
    See Thompson, Benjamin (trans.).
  False Delicacy.
    See Thompson, Benjamin (trans.).
  Indian Exiles, The.
    See Thompson, Benjamin (trans.).
  Patriot Father, The.
    See Shoberl, Frederic (trans.).
  Rolla.
    See Thompson, Benjamin (trans.).
  Stranger, The.
    See Thompson, Benjamin (trans.).

£. S. D.
  See A'Beckett, Arthur William.

LA! SONNAMBULA!
  See Byron, Henry James.

LA CROIX, JULES
  Oedipus the King.
    See Lyster, Frederic (trans.).

LACY, KATHERINE
  My Aunt's Heiress (attrib. to Lacy). New York: Fitzgerald, n.d. Pp. [1]-30.
  My Aunt's Heiress (attrib. to Lacy). Boston: Walter H. Baker, n.d. Pp. [1]-30. Baker's Edition of Plays. *Filed under* My Aunt's Heiress (anon.).
  Wonderful Cure, A (attrib. to Lacy). Boston: Walter H. Baker, n.d. Pp. [1]-21. Baker's Edition of Plays.

LACY, MARIA ANNE
  See Lovell, Maria Anne Lacy, Mrs. George William.

LACY, MICHAEL ROPHINO
  Cinderella; or, The Fairy and Little Glass Slipper. New York: Samuel French, n.d. Pp. [1]-35. French's Standard Drama, 164. Libretto.
  Cinderella; or, The Fairy and Little Glass Slipper. Music by Rossini. London: Goulding & D'Almaine, n.d. Pp. [1]-210. Vocal score.
  Doing for the Best. London: Thomas Hailes Lacy, n.d. Pp. [1]-34.
  Doing My Uncle. London: Thomas Hailes Lacy, n.d. Pp. [1]-28. [Lacy's Acting Edition].
  Fra-Diavolo; or, The Inn of Terracina. London: John Miller, 1833. Pp. [i-iv], [1]-68. Promptbook libretto.
  Love and Reason. London: Hunt & Clarke, 1827. Pp. [1]-54. British Theatre.
  Maid of Judah, The; or, The Knights Templars. Music by Rossini. London: John Cumberland, n.d. Pp. [1]-63. Cumberland's British Theatre, XXV. *Filed under* Cumberland, John. Cumberland's British Theatre, XXV.
  Maid of Judah, The; or, The Knights Templars. Music by Rossini. London: John Cumberland, n.d. Pp. [1]-63. Promptbook libretto.
  Robert the Devil; or, The Fiend-father. Music by Meyerbeer. London: Thomas Hailes Lacy, n.d. Pp. [1]-55. [Lacy's Acting Edition]. Libretto.
  Two Friends, The. London: John Cumberland, n.d. Pp. [1]-49.
  Two Friends, The. London: John Cumberland, n.d. Pp. [1]-49. Cumberland's British Theatre, XXVII. *Filed under* Cumberland, John. Cumberland's British Theatre, XXVII.

LACY, THOMAS HAILES
  Angel of Midnight, The.
    See Suter, William E.
  Belphegor.
    See Higgie, Thomas Henry.
  Clarissa Harlowe. Written with Courtney, John. London: John Dicks, n.d. Pp. [1]-18. Dicks' Standard Plays, 905.
  Jeannette's Wedding Day. Music by Massé. London: Thomas Hailes Lacy, n.d. Pp. [1]-[29]. [Lacy's Acting Edition].
  Martin Chuzzlewit.
    See Higgie, Thomas Henry.
  Rip Van Winkle.
    See Kerr, John.
  School for Daughters, The.
    See Lawler, Dennis.
  Silent Woman, A. New York: Robert M. DeWitt, n.d. Pp. [1]-[8]. DeWitt's Acting Plays, 35.
  Tower of London, The.
    See Higgie, Thomas Henry.
  Winning a Wife. London: Thomas Hailes Lacy, n.d. Pp. [1]-20. [Lacy's Acting Edition].

LACY, THOMAS HAILES (arr.)
  Drunkard, The. London: Thomas Hailes Lacy, n.d. Pp. [1]-38.
  Pickwickians, The; or, The Peregrinations of Sam Weller. By Moncrieff, William Thomas. London & New York: Samuel French, n.d. Pp. [1]-60.

LAD FROM THE COUNTRY, A
  See Morton, John Maddison.

LADDER OF LIFE
  See Rede, William Leman. Jack in the Water.

LADDER OF LOVE, THE
  See Bayly, Thomas Haynes.

LADIES AT HOME
  See Millingen, John Gideon.

LADIES BEWARE! (anon.)
  New York: Berford, 1848. Pp. [1]-32.

LADIES BEWARE! (anon.)
  New York: William Taylor, n.d. Pp. [1]-35.

LADIES IN PARLIAMENT, THE
  See Trevelyan, George Otto.

**LADIES OF SAINT-CYR, THE; OR, THE RUNAWAY HUS-
BANDS** (anon. trans.)
    By Dumas, Alexandre. London: Thomas Hailes Lacy,
    n.d. Pp. [1]-51. [Lacy's Acting Edition].
LADIES OF THE COURT
    See Wilks, Thomas Egerton. How's Your Uncle?
LADIES' BATTLE, THE
    See Reade, Charles.
    See Robertson, Thomas William.
LADIES' CLUB, THE
    See Lemon, Mark.
LADIES' MAN, THE
    See Burton, William Evans.
LADIES' PHILOSOPHY
    See Cibber, Colley. Refusal, The.
LADIES' PRIVILEGE
    See Buckstone, John Baldwin. Leap Year.
LADY AND GENTLEMAN IN A PECULIARLY PERPLEX-
ING PREDICAMENT!, A
    See Selby, Charles.
LADY AND THE DEVIL, THE
    See Dimond, William.
LADY AUDLEY'S SECRET
    See Hazlewood, Colin Henry.
    See Roberts, George.
LADY BELLE BELLE
    See Byron, Henry James.
LADY BOUNTIFUL: A STORY OF YEARS
    See Pinero, Arthur Wing.
LADY BURGLAR, THE
    See Malyon, E. J.
LADY BY BIRTH, A
    See Smythies, William Gordon.
LADY CECIL, THE
    See Adams, Florence Davenport.
LADY CLANCARTY
    See Taylor, Tom.
LADY D'ARCY
    See Hilton, B. H. Manager in Love, The.
LADY DEDLOCK'S SECRET
    See Simpson, John Palgrave.
LADY ELIZABETH
    See Taylor, Tom. 'Twixt Axe and Crown.
LADY ELIZABETH POOLE GUBBINS
    See H., A. L.
LADY FORTUNE
    See Thomas, Charles.
LADY FROM THE SEA, THE
    See Archer, Frances Elizabeth, Mrs. William (trans.).
    See Aveling, Eleanor Marx, Mrs. Edward (trans.).
LADY HUNTWORTH'S EXPERIMENT
    See Carton, R. C.
LADY IN DIFFICULTIES, A
    See Planché, James Robinson.
LADY IN SEARCH OF AN HEIRESS, A
    See Leigh, Agnes.
LADY INGER OF ÖSTRÅT
    See Archer, Charles (trans.).
LADY INTERVIEWER, THE
    See Swears, Herbert.
LADY JANE GREY
    See Neil, Ross.
    See Rowe, Nicholas.
LADY LANCING
    See Wilde, Oscar Fingall O'Flahertie Wills. Importance
    of Being Earnest, The.
    See Wilde, Oscar Fingall O'Flahertie Wills.
LADY MACBETH
    See Galt, John.
LADY OF BELLEISLE, THE
    See Gully, James Manby.
LADY OF CHALLANT, THE
    See Lyster, Frederic (trans.).

LADY OF LYONS, THE
    See Bulwer (later Bulwer-Lytton), Edward George Earle
    Lytton, Lord Lytton.
LADY OF LYONS MARRIED AND SETTLED, THE
    See Merivale, Herman Charles.
LADY OF MUNSTER
    See Bayly, Thomas Haynes. Perfection.
LADY OF THE CAMELLIAS, THE (anon.)
    London: Thomas Hailes Lacy, n.d. Pp. [1]-36.
LADY OF THE LAKE, THE
    See Dibdin, Thomas John.
    See Eyre, Edmund John.
LADY OF THE LAKE, PLAID IN A NEW TARTAN, THE
    See Reece, Robert.
LADY OF THE LIONS, THE
    See Dowling, Maurice G.
LADY OF THE ROCK, THE
    See Holcroft, Thomas.
LADY WINDERMERE'S FAN
    See Wilde, Oscar Fingall O'Flahertie Wills.
LADY'S DREAM, THE
    See Jefferson, George.
LADYE BIRD BOWER
    See Somerset, Charles A.
LADYE OF LAMBYTHE, THE
    See Wilks, Thomas Egerton.
LAID UP IN PORT!
    See Higgie, Thomas Henry.
LAIRD, THE DAFTIE, AND THE HIGHLAND MAIDEN
    See Byron, Henry James. McAllister McVitty McNab,
    The.
LAIRD, THE LADY, AND THE LOVER
    See Byron, Henry James. Lucia di Lammermoor.
LAIRD-CLOWES, W.
    See Clowes, W. Laird.
LAKE, JOHN
    Golden Glove, The; or, The Farmer's Son. London: (priv.),
    1815. Pp. [i]-[xii], [1]-100.
    House of Morville, The; or, Disinherited Son. London: C.
    Chapple, n.d. Pp. [i]-viii, [5]-120. 2nd ed.
LAKE OF LAUSANNE
    See Reynolds, Frederick. Out of Place.
LALLA ROOKH
    See Amcotts, Vincent.
    See Brough, William.
LAMB, CHARLES
    John Woodvil. London: G. & J. Robinson, 1802. Pp. [i-iv],
    [1]-107.
    Mr. H.; or, Beware a Bad Name. Philadelphia: M. Carey,
    1813. Pp. [1]-36.
    Pawnbroker's Daughter, The. In *Blackwood's Edinburgh
    Magazine,* XXVII (January 1830), 97-109.
    Wife's Trial, The; or, The Intruding Widow. In *Works,* new
    ed., London: Edward Moxon, 1842, pp. 46-56.
LAMB, GEORGE
    Whistle for It. London: Longman, Hurst, Rees, & Orme,
    1807. Pp. [1]-43. Libretto.
LAMB, GEORGE (arr.)
    Timon of Athens. By Shakespeare, William. London: C.
    Chapple, 1816. Pp. [i-iv], [1]-53.
LAMB, MARY MONTGOMERIE
    See Fane, Violet (pseud.).
LAME EXCUSE, A
    See Hay, Frederic.
LAMPLIGHTER, THE
    See Dickens, Charles.
    See Seaman, William.
LANCASHIRE LASS, THE
    See Byron, Henry James.
LANCASHIRE SAILOR, THE
    See Thomas, Brandon.
LANCASHIRE WEAVER LAD, THE
    See Brierley, Benjamin.
LANCASHIRE WITCHES, THE
    See Gunton, R. T.

LANCASTER, CHARLES SEARS
Advice to Husbands. London: John Duncombe, n.d. Pp. [1]-19. Duncombe's Edition.

LANCASTER, EDWARD RICHARDSON
Devil's Daughters, The; or, The Belles of Belzebub. N.p.: n.pub., n.d. Pp. [346]-362. Title page lacking.
Manager's Daughter, The. London: J. Pattie, n.d. Pp. [1]-27.

LANCASTER, FLORENCE
Prior Claim, The. London & New York: Samuel French, n.d. Pp. [1]-13. [Lacy's Acting Edition].

LANCASTER-WALLIS, ELLEN
Cissy's Engagement. London & New York: Samuel French, n.d. Pp. [1]-9.
Cupid in Ermine. London & New York: Samuel French, n.d. Pp. [1]-11. [French's Acting Edition, 2166].
Little Miss Muffet. London & New York: Samuel French, n.d. Pp. [1]-8. [Lacy's Acting Edition].
My Son and I. London & New York: Samuel French, n.d. Pp. [1]-11.

LANCERS, THE
See Payne, John Howard.
See Vernon, Leicester Viney, Capt.

LANCIVAL, J. CHARLES J. LUCE DE
Hector.
See Mangin, Edward (trans.).

LAND AND LOVE
See Dubourg, Augustus W.

LAND AND THE PEOPLE, THE
See Moss, Arthur B.

LAND OF HEART'S DESIRE, THE
See Yeats, William Butler.

LAND WE LIVE IN, THE
See Holt, Francis Ludlow.

LANDECK, BENJAMIN
Woman and Wine.
See Shirley, Arthur.

LANDER, GEORGE
Bleak House; or, Poor Jo. London: John Dicks, n.d. Pp. [1]-22. Dicks' Standard Plays, 388.
Old Curiosity Shop, The. London: John Dicks, n.d. Pp. [1]-20. Dicks' Standard Plays, [398].
Wandering Jew, The. London: John Dicks, n.d. Pp. [1]-20.

LANDLORD IN JEOPARDY!
See Beazley, Samuel, jr. Jealous on All Sides.

LANDON, LETITIA ELIZABETH (later Mrs. George Maclean)
Triumph of Lucca, The. In *New World (New York),* 19 June 1841, pp. [401]-405.

LANDOR, EDWARD WILSON
Carmelite Friar, The; or, The Trial of Duty. Perth, Western Australia: F. B. Timewell (printer), 1872. Pp. [i-viii], [1]-63.
Two Earls, The; or, The Trial of Honour. Perth, Western Australia: F. B. Timewell (printer), 1872. Pp. [i-viii], [1]-67.

LANDOR, ROBERT EYRES
Count Arezzi, The. London: John Booth, 1824. Pp. [i-iv], [1]-192.
Earl of Brecon, The. In *Earl of Brecon . . . ,* London: Saunders & Otley, 1841, pp. [i]-iv, [1]-85.
Faith's Fraud. In *Earl of Brecon . . . ,* London: Saunders & Otley, 1841, pp. [87]-224. *Filed under* Earl of Brecon.
Ferryman, The; or, The Translated Escutcheon. In *Earl of Brecon . . . ,* London: Saunders & Otley, 1841, pp. [225]-306. *Filed under* Earl of Brecon.

LANDOR, WALTER SAVAGE
Andrea of Hungary. In *Works,* London: Edward Moxon, 1846, II, [524]-548.
Count Julian. In *Gebir, Count Julian, and Other Poems,* London: Edward Moxon, 1831, pp. [75]-191.
Count Julian. In *Works,* London: Edward Moxon, 1846, II, [505]-524.
Fra Rupert. In *Works,* London: Edward Moxon, 1846, II, 564-581. *Filed under* Andrea of Hungary.
Giovanna of Naples. In *Works,* London: Edward Moxon, 1846, II, 548-564. *Filed under* Andrea of Hungary.

Ines de Castro at Cintra. In *Gabir, Count Julian, and Other Poems,* London: Edward Moxon, 1831, pp. [194]-243, [385]-388. *Filed under* Count Julian.
Ippolito di Este. In *Gabir, Count Julian, and Other Poems,* London: Edward Moxon, 1831, pp. [245]-260. *Filed under* Count Julian.
Siege of Ancona, The. In *Works,* London: Edward Moxon, 1846, II, [581]-597.

LANDSLIP, THE
See Maugham, Harry Neville.

LANE, LUCY
See Clifford, Lucy Lane, Mrs. William Kingdon.

LANE, PYNGLE (pseud. of Turner, John Fox)
Mother Goose; or, Ye Queene of Heartes That Made ye Tartes, and ye Knave of Heartes Who Ate 'Em. Music by Wallerstein, Ferdinand. Manchester: A. Ireland (printer), n.d. Pp. [1-23]. *Filed under* Turner, John Fox.

LANE, W. E.
Robbers of Calabria, The. In *British Drama,* 12 vols., London: John Dicks, 1871, V, [225]-232.

LANGBRIDGE, FREDERICK
Fair Rosamond's Bower; or, The Monarch, the Maiden, the Maze, and the Mixture. London: Thomas Hailes Lacy, n.d. Pp. [1]-18. [Lacy's Acting Edition].
Man Proposes. London & New York: Samuel French, n.d. Pp. [1]-14. [Lacy's Acting Edition].

LANGFORD, J. M.
Like and Unlike. Written with Sorrell, William J. London: Webster, n.d. Pp. [1]-46.

LANGFORD, JOHN ALFRED
King and the Commoner, The. Birmingham: E. C. Osborne (printer) (priv.), 1870. Pp. [1]-87.

LANKESTER, E. G.
See Reece, Robert.

LAPSE OF TWENTY YEARS
See Thompson, Charles. Gambler's Fate, The.

LARBOARD FIN, THE
See Wills, William Henry.

LARKINS' LOVE LETTERS
See Williams, Thomas John.

LARKS OF LOGIC, TOM, AND JERRY
See Dibdin, Charles Isaac Mungo, jr. Life in London.

LART, JOHN
Phantoms! London: Blades, East, & Blades (printer) (priv.), n.d. Pp. [1]-74.

LASCELLES, MRS.
See Chatterton, Henrietta Georgiana Marcia Iremonger, Mrs. Lascelles, Lady Georgiana.

LASS THAT LOVED A SAILOR
See Gilbert, William Schwenck. H.M.S. Pinafore.

LASS THAT LOVES A SAILOR
See Haines, John Thomas. Ruth.

LAST ACT, THE (anon.)
In *New British Theatre,* London: A. J. Valpy (printer), 1814, II, [357]-400.

LAST APPEAL
See Fitzball, Edward. Alice May.

LAST 'BUS, THE
See Ridge, William Pett.

LAST CRIME
See Webster, Benjamin Nottingham. Golden Farmer, The.

LAST DAY, THE
See Godwin, George, jr.

LAST DAY OF NAPOLEON, THE
See Morton, J. Russell.

LAST EDITION OF IVANHOE, WITH ALL THE NEWEST IMPROVEMENTS, THE
See Brough, Willam.

LAST FEAST OF THE FIANNA, THE
See Milligan, Alice L.

LAST KISS!, THE
See Stirling, Edward.

LAST LIFE, THE
See Palmer, T. A.

LAST LILY, THE
　　See Scott, Clement William.
LAST MAN, THE
　　See Pitt, George Dibdin.
LAST NAIL
　　See Pitt, George Dibdin. Drunkard's Doom, The.
　　See Pitt, George Dibdin.
LAST OF THE CAESARS
　　See Baillie, Joanna. Constantine Paleologus.
LAST OF THE COBBLER
　　See Allan, A. W. Rienzi Reinstated.
LAST OF THE DOGES
　　See Stirling, Edward. Dandolo.
LAST OF THE FAIRIES, THE
　　See Fitzball, Edward.
LAST OF THE FAMILY, THE
　　See Cumberland, Richard.
LAST OF THE GREEKS, THE
　　See Howard, George William Frederick, Earl of Carlisle.
LAST OF THE LEGENDS, THE
　　See A'Beckett, Gilbert Arthur.
LAST OF THE MAGICIANS
　　See Scudamore, G. H. Liberta.
LAST OF THE MOORS
　　See Wheatley, J. A. Ali-Ben-Hassan.
LAST OF THE PIGTAILS, THE
　　See Selby, Charles.
LAST OF THE POLLYWOGS
　　See Brougham, John. Metamora.
LAST PLAGUE, THE
　　See Lindsay, David.
LAST WAR OF THE ROSES, THE
　　See Jesse, John Heneage.
LAST WORDS
　　See Bell, Florence Eveleen Eleanore Oliffe, Mrs. Hugh (Lady).
LATE LAMENTED, THE
　　See Horner, Fred.
LATE MR. CASTELLO, THE
　　See Grundy, Sydney.
LATE SIR BENJAMIN, THE
　　See Young, Charles Lawrence, Sir.
LATEST EDITION OF BLACK-EYED SUSAN, THE
　　See Burnand, Francis Cowley.
LATEST EDITION OF HELEN, THE
　　See Burnand, Francis Cowley.
LATHAIR, HENRY
　　My Uncle, the Ghost. Music by Lecocq; Elliott, Lionel. London: Joseph Williams, n.d. Pp. [i-ii], [2]-18. Vocal score.
LATHOM, FRANCIS
　　Curiosity. London: T. Hurst, n.d. Pp. [i-iv], [1]-41.
　　Dash of the Day, The. Norwich: J. Payne (printer) (priv.), 1800. Pp. [i-vi], [1]-102. 2nd ed.
　　Wife of a Million, The. Norwich: J. Payne (printer), n.d. Pp. [1]-93.
LATIN LESSON, THE
　　See Sturgis, Julian Russell.
LATIN, LOVE, AND WAR
　　See Macfarren, George.
LAUGH ON THE LICENSE DAY
　　See Featherstone, Thomas. Trial of Suits at the Brewster Sessions of Sotville.
LAUGH WHEN YOU CAN
　　See Reynolds, Frederick.
LAUGHABLE ACCIDENT
　　See Maclaren, Archibald. Spite and Malice.
LAUGHABLE LOVER, THE
　　See O'Caustic, Carol (pseud.).
LAUGHING HYENA, THE
　　See Webster, Benjamin Nottingham.
LAUNCELOT THE LOOSE, GIN-EVER THE SQUARE, AND THE KNIGHTS OF THE ROUND TABLE, AND OTHER FURNITURE
　　See Akhurst, William M. King Arthur.

LAURA DIBALZO
　　See Horne, Richard Hengist.
LAURENCE'S LOVE SUIT
　　See Wooler, John Pratt.
LAURENT, ?, MME.
　　Truand Chief!, The.
　　　See Oxberry, William Henry.
LAVATER THE PHYSIOGNOMIST
　　See Planché, James Robinson.
LAVENU, L. (trans.)
　　Haydée; or, The Secret. Music by Auber. London: Jullien, n.d. Pp. [1]-41. Libretto.
LAVINIA
　　See Becket, Andrew.
LAW, ARTHUR
　　All at Sea. London: Joseph Williams, c.1904. Pp. [1]-20.
　　Boy, The.
　　　See New Boy, The.
　　Bright Idea, A. Music by Cecil, Arthur. London: A. S. Mallett (printer), n.d. Pp. [11]-16. Libretto. *Filed under* Cherry Tree Farm.
　　Castle Botherem. London: Joseph Williams, c.1904. Pp. [1]-32.
　　Cherry Tree Farm. Music by Clarke, Hamilton. London: A. S. Mallett (printer), n.d. Pp. [1]-9. Libretto.
　　Day in Boulogne, A. London: Joseph Williams, c.1904. Pp. [1]-17.
　　Happy Return, The. London & New York: Samuel French, n.d. Pp. [1]-15. [Lacy's Acting Edition].
　　Head of the Poll, The. London: Joseph Williams, c.1904. Pp. [1]-39.
　　Magic Opal, The. Music by Albeniz. London: Joseph Williams, c.1911. Pp. [1]-50. Libretto.
　　Merry Christmas, A. London: Joseph Williams, c.1904. Pp. [1]-22.
　　Moss-Rose Rent, A. London: Joseph Williams, c.1904. Pp. [i-ii], [1]-23.
　　New Boy, The. *Also:* The Boy. New York & London: Samuel French, c.1904. Pp. [1]-66.
　　Night Surprise, A. London: Joseph Williams, c.1904. Pp. [1]-18.
　　Nobody's Fault. London: Joseph Williams, c.1904. Pp. [1]-27.
　　Nobody's Fault. Music by Clarke, Hamilton. N.p.: n.pub., n.d. Pp. [1]-14. Libretto.
　　Old Knockles. Music by Caldicott, Alfred J. London: Joseph Williams; New York: Edward Schuberth, c.1894. Pp. [1]-26. German Reed Repertory of Musical Pieces. Libretto.
　　Old Knockles. Music by Caldicott, Alfred J. N.p.: n.pub., n.d. Pp. [1]-10. Libretto.
　　One Hundred Pounds Reward. London: Joseph Williams, c.1904. Pp. [1]-24.
　　Peculiar Case, A. Music by Grossmith, George. N.p.: n.pub., n.d. Pp. [12]-16. Libretto. *Filed under* Old Knockles.
LAW AND LIONS
　　See Jerrold, Douglas William.
LAW IN 1656
　　See Rogers, William. Paul the Reprobate.
LAW OF JAVA, THE
　　See Colman, George, jr.
LAW OF LOMBARDY, THE
　　See Jephson, Robert.
LAW OF THE LAND, THE
　　See Pocock, Isaac. Who Wants a Wife?
　　See Wills, William Henry.
LAW VERSUS LOVE
　　See Linley, George.
LAW'S TWO TAILS
　　See Dibdin, Charles Isaac Mungo, jr.
LAWLER, DENNIS
　　Earls of Hammersmith, The; or, The Cellar Spectre! Written with Poole, John. By Dennis Lawler. London: John Duncombe, n.d. Pp. [1]-16. Duncombe's Edition.

School for Daughters, The. Written with Lacy, Thomas Hailes. London & New York: Samuel French, n.d. Pp. [3]-37.

Sharp and Flat. Music by Hook. London: C. Chapple, 1813. Pp. [i]-[x], [1]-32.

LAWRANCE, FREDERIC

Kenilworth.
See Halliday, Andrew.

King and the Carpenter, The. London: James Pattie, n.d. Pp. [1]-35. Pattie's Penny Play or Weekly Acting Drama, 5-7.

Number 49. London: E. Lacey, n.d. Pp. [1]-[25]. Lacy's Dramas for Private Representation.

LAWRENCE, EWERETTA

On 'Change. London & New York: Samuel French, n.d. Pp. [1]-53. French's Acting Edition (late Lacy's), 2055.

LAWRENCE, JAMES W.

Perfect Menagerie, A. Manchester: John Heywood; London: Thomas Hailes Lacy, 1870. Pp. [1]-24.

LAWRENCE, SLINGSBY (pseud. of Lewes, George Henry)

Buckstone's Adventure with a Polish Princess. London: Thomas Hailes Lacy, n.d. Pp. [1]-24. Promptbook. *Filed under* Lewes, George Henry.

Captain Bland. By George Henry Lewes. [New York, 1864]. Pp. [i-ii], [1]-27, 1-35. Pagination by act. Manuscript. *Filed under* Lewes, George Henry.

Chain of Events, A. Written with Mathews, Charles James. London: S. G. Fairbrother, n.d. <wrps. Thomas Hailes Lacy; New York: Perry>. Pp. [1]-84. Lacy's Acting Edition, 313. *Filed under* Lewes, George Henry.

Cozy Couple, A. London: Thomas Hailes Lacy, n.d. Pp. [1]-28. [Lacy's Acting Edition]. *Filed under* Lewes, George Henry.

Game of Speculation, The. London: Thomas Hailes Lacy, n.d. Pp. [1]-44. [Lacy's Acting Edition]. *Filed under* Lewes, George Henry.

Give a Dog a Bad Name. London: Thomas Hailes Lacy, n.d. Pp. [1]-29. Lacy's Acting Edition, 354. Promptbook. *Filed under* Lewes, George Henry.

Lawyers, The. New York: Samuel French, n.d. Pp. [3]-43. Minor Drama, 52. *Filed under* Lewes, George Henry.

Noble Heart, The. By George Henry Lewes. London: Chapman & Hall, 1850. Pp. [i]-iv, [5]-47. *Filed under* Lewes, George Henry.

Noble Heart, The. By George Henry Lewes. Boston: William V. Spencer, n.d. Pp. [1]-39. Spencer's Boston Theatre, 173. *Filed under* Lewes, George Henry.

Strange History, A. Written with Mathews, Charles James. London: Thomas Hailes Lacy, n.d. Pp. [1]-64. [Lacy's Acting Edition]. *Filed under* Lewes, George Henry.

Sunshine through the Clouds. London: Thomas Hailes Lacy, n.d. Pp. [1]-29. [Lacy's Acting Edition]. *Filed under* Lewes, George Henry.

LAWYER'S CLERK
See Beazley, Samuel, jr. Lottery Ticket, The.

LAWYERS, THE
See Lawrence, Slingsby.

LEADBEATER, MARY SHACKLETON, MRS. WILLIAM

Cottage Dialogues among the Irish Peasantry. Philadelphia: Samuel R. Fisher, jr, 1811. Pp. [i]-[x], [1]-270.

LEADER, JAMES

In Town.
See Ross, Adrian.

LEADING STRINGS
See Troughton, Adolphus Charles.

LEAF FROM TYBURN TREE
See Almar, George. Jack Ketch.

LEAGUE OF YOUTH, THE
See Archer, William (trans.).

LEAN, MRS. FRANCIS
See Marryat, Florence.

LEAP YEAR
See Buckstone, John Baldwin.
See Kerr, Frederick.

LEAR OF CRIPPLEGATE
See Lunn, Joseph. Sharp Practice.

LEAR OF PRIVATE LIFE, THE
See Moncrieff, William Thomas.

LEARNED LADIES, THE
See Van Laun, Henri (trans.).

LEASE, B. C.

Bachelor's Divorce, A. Boston: Walter H. Baker, c.1895. Pp. [1]-52.

LEATHAM, WILLIAM HENRY

Strafford. London: Longman, Brown, Green, & Longmans, 1842. Pp. [i]-[viii], [9]-46.

LEATHERLUNGOS THE GREAT, HOW HE STORMED, REIGN'D, AND MIZZLED
See Cheltnam, Charles Smith.

LEAVE IT TO ME
See Hazlewood, Colin Henry.

LED ASTRAY
See Boucicault, Dionysius Lardner.

LEE, BARON (pseud. of Lee, Francis)

Glorious Revolution, 5th November 1688, The. London: John Warren (priv.), n.d. Pp. [1]-68. 2nd ed.

LEE, ELIZA BUCKMINSTER, MRS. (trans.)

Correggio. By Oehlenschlager, Adam. In *Correggio . . .*, Boston: Phillips & Sampson, 1846, pp. [i]-xxxix, [1]-174.

Sappho. By Grillparzer, Franz. In *Correggio . . .*, Boston: Phillips & Sampson, 1846, pp. [175]-303. *Filed under* Correggio.

LEE, FRANCIS
See Lee, Baron.

LEE, HAROLD

On the Indian Ocean. Liverpool: Lee & Nightingale (printer), 1876. Pp. [1]-22.

LEE, HARRIET

Three Strangers, The. London: Longman, Rees, Orme, Brown, & Green, 1826. Pp. [i-v], [1]-76.

LEE, HENRY

Caleb Quotem and His Wife!; or, Paint, Poetry, and Putty! London: J. Roach, n.d. Pp. [i], [1]-66. Libretto.

LEE, NATHANIEL

Alexander the Great; or, The Rival Queens. London: Whittingham & Arliss, 1815. Pp. [1]-[56]. London Theatre, X. *Filed under* Dibdin, Thomas John, ed. London Theatre, X.

Alexander the Great. In *New English Drama*, ed. W. Oxberry, 22 vols., London: W. Simpkin & R. Marshall; C. Chapple, 1818, III, [1-2], [i]-[x], [1]-[48]. *Filed under* Oxberry, William Henry. New English Drama, III.

Alexander the Great. In *British Drama*, 12 vols., London: John Dicks, 1871, V, [78]-93.

LEE, NELSON, SR

Harlequin Alfred the Great; or, The Magic Banjo and the Mystic Raven! London: Thomas Hailes Lacy, n.d. Pp. [1]-24. [Lacy's Acting Edition]. Libretto.

Harlequin Alfred the Great!; or, The Magic Banjo and the Mystic Raven! London: Hailes Lacy, n.d. Pp. [1]-24. Libretto. *Filed under* Harlequin Alfred the Great (anon.).

Harlequin and Good Queen Bess; or, Merrie England in the Olden Time. Also attrib. to Rodwell, George Herbert. London: J. & D. A. Darling, n.d. Pp. [1]-23. Libretto. *Filed under* Harlequin and Good Queen Bess (anon.).

Harlequin and Mother Red Cap; or, Merlin and the Fairy Queen. London: S. G. Fairbrother (printer), n.d. Pp. [1]-15. Libretto and synopsis.

Harlequin and O'Donoghue; or, The White Horse of Killarney. London: Thomas Hailes Lacy, n.d. Pp. [1]-20. [Lacy's Acting Edition]. Libretto.

Harlequin and O'Donoghue; or, The White Horse of Killarney. Music by Phillips, G. London: Hailes Lacy, n.d. Pp. [1]-20. Libretto. *Filed under* Harlequin and O'Donoghue (anon.).

Harlequin Blackbeard; or, Dame Trot and Her Comical Cat. Liverpool: W. M'Call (printer), n.d. Pp. [1]-16. Libretto.

LEE, NELSON, JR

Midnight Spectre!, The; or, The Fatal Secret! London: W. S. Johnson, 1861. Pp. [1]-7.

LEE, SOPHIA

Chapter of Accidents, The. In *Modern Theatre*, ed. Mrs. Inchbald, 10 vols., London: Longman, Hurst, Rees, Orme, & Brown, 1811, IX, [81]-164.

Chapter of Accidents, The. London: Whittingham & Arliss, 1816. Pp. [1]-75. London Theatre, XXI. *Filed under* Dibdin, Thomas John, ed. London Theatre, XXI.

Chapter of Accidents, The. In *New English Drama*, ed. W. Oxberry, 22 vols., London: W. Simpkin & R. Marshall; C. Chapple, 1823, XVIII, [i]-[xiii], [1-3], 2-[67]. *Filed under* Oxberry, William Henry. New English Drama, XVIII.

Chapter of Accidents, The. In *British Drama*, 12 vols., London: John Dicks, 1871, IX, [257]-278.

LEE-HAMILTON, EUGENE

Fountain of Youth, The. London: Elliot Stock, 1891. Pp. [i-viii], [1]-135.

LE FANU, ALICIA SHERIDAN, MRS. JOSEPH

Sons of Erin, The; or, Modern Sentiment. London: J. Ridgway, 1812. Pp. [ii]-[viii], [9]-[101]. 3rd ed.

LEFEVRE, GEORGE WILLIAM, SIR (trans.)

Faust. By Goethe. Frankfort: Charles Jugel, 1843. Pp. [i]-[x], 1-207. Jugel's Pocket Novelists, 21. 2nd ed.

LEFT IN A CAB
See Stirling, Edward.

LEFT THE STAGE; OR, GRASSOT TORMENTED BY RAVEL (anon.)

London: Thomas Hailes Lacy, n.d. Pp. [1]-14. [Lacy's Acting Edition].

LEGACY OF HONOUR
See Stirling, Edward.

LEGAL IMPEDIMENT, A
See Oxenford, John.

LEGEND OF FLORENCE, A
See Hunt, Leigh.

LEGEND OF LISBON!
See Bernard, William Bayle. Maiden's Fame!, A.

LEGEND OF PEDLAR'S ACRE
See Almar, George. Wife of Seven Husbands, The.

LEGEND OF SLEEPY HOLLOW
See Kerr, John. Rip Van Winkle.

LEGEND OF THE DEAD MAN'S FERRY
See Pitt, W. H. Knobstick Wedding, A.

LEGEND OF THE DEATH OF ANTAR
See Baddeley, Welbore St. Clair.

LEGEND OF THE DEVIL'S DYKE, A
See Boucicault, Dionysius Lardner.

LEGEND OF THE PATENT OFFICE
See Baddeley, G. C. End of the Tether, The.

LEGEND OF WALWORTH
See Haines, John Thomas. Richard Plantagenet.

LEGENDS OF GLENDALOUGH
See Irwin, Edward. King O'Toole's Goose.

LEGOUVÉ, ERNEST

Medea.
See Heron, Matilda (trans.).

LEHMANN, RUDOLPH CHAMBERS

His Majesty.
See Burnand, Francis Cowley.

LEIFCHILD, FRANKLIN

Buried Titan, The. London: Robert Hardwicke, 1859. Pp. [i-vi], [1]-252.

LEIGH, AGNES

Contradictions. London & New York: Samuel French, n.d. Pp. [1]-8.

Lady in Search of an Heiress, A. London & New York: Samuel French, n.d. Pp. [1]-12. [Lacy's Acting Edition].

Lunatic, The. London & New York: Samuel French, n.d. Pp. [1]-11. [Lacy's Acting Edition].

Number Seventeen. London & New York: Samuel French, n.d. Pp. [1]-11.

Rainy Day, A. London & New York: Samuel French, n.d. Pp. [1]-11.

LEIGH, ARRAN
See Field, Michael.

LEIGH, HENRY SAMBROOKE

Cinderella. Music by Farmer, John. Harrow: J. C. Wilbee; London: Novello, Ewer, n.d. Pp. [i-iv], [1]-154. Vocal score.

Donna Juanita. Music by Suppé, Franz von. London: Joseph Williams, n.d. Pp. [i-iv], [1]-254. Vocal score.

Fatinitza. Music by Suppé, Franz von. [New York: Richardson & Foss, 1879]. Pp. [1]-39. Libretto.

Great Casimir, The. *Also:* Le Grand Casimir. Music by Lecocq, Charles. London: Joseph Williams, n.d. Pp. [i-iv], 1-114. Vocal score.

Lurette. Music by Offenbach, Jacques. London: Joseph Williams, n.d. Pp. [1]-124, [1]-3. Vocal score.

LEIGH, ISLA
See Field, Michael.

LEIGH, JAMES MATHEWS

Cromwell. London: Leigh & Son (priv.), 1838. Pp. [ii]-[xii], [1]-128.

LEIGH, RICHARD

Grieving's a Folly. London: Longman, Hurst, Rees, & Orme, 1809. Pp. [i-vi], [1]-[73].

Where to Find a Friend. London: Whittingham & Arliss, 1815. Pp. [i-iii], [1-2], [iv], [5]-96.

LEISURE TO LAUGH
See Cobbett, William. Big O and Sir Glory.

LEMAÎTRE, JULES

Eldest, The.
See under title.

LEMON, HARRY

Go to Putney; or, A Story of the Boat Race. New York: Robert M. DeWitt, n.d. Pp. [1]-12. DeWitt's Acting Plays, 131.

Up for the Cattle Show. London: Thomas Hailes Lacy, n.d. Pp. [1]-16. Promptbook.

Wait for an Answer. London: Thomas Hailes Lacy, n.d. Pp. [1]-12. [Lacy's Acting Edition].

LEMON, MARK

Ancestress!, The; or, The Doom of Barostein! London: John Duncombe, n.d. Pp. [1]-30. Duncombe's Edition.

Arnold of Winkelried; or, The Fight of Sempach! London: John Duncombe, n.d. Pp. [1]-49. Duncombe's Edition.

Camp at Chobham, The. London: Webster, n.d. Pp. [1]-16. Webster's Acting National Drama, 192.

Chimes, The; or, Some Bells That Rang an Old Year Out and a New Year In. Written with A'Beckett, Gilbert Abbott. London: John Dicks, n.d. Pp. [1]-18. Dicks' Standard Plays, 819.

Chimes, The: A Goblin Story of Some Bells That Rang an Old Year Out and a New Year In. Written with A'Beckett, Gilbert Abbott. London: National Acting Drama Office, n.d. Pp. [1]-44. Webster's Acting National Drama, 115. *Filed under* A'Beckett, Gilbert Abbott, and Lemon, Mark.

Demon Gift, The; or, Visions of the Future. London: J. Pattie, n.d. Pp. [i]-iv, [5]-24. Pattie's Universal Stage or Theatrical Prompt Book.

Domestic Economy. London: Thomas Hailes Lacy, n.d. Pp. [1]-17.

Don Caesar de Bazan.
See A'Beckett, Gilbert Abbott.

Familiar Friend, A. London: James Pattie, n.d. Pp. [1]-23. Pattie's Universal Stage or Theatrical Prompt Book.

Fashionable Arrivals. London: J. Pattie, n.d. Pp. [i]-iv, [5]-27. Pattie's Universal Stage or Theatrical Prompt Book, 28.

Gentleman in Black, The. London: John Dicks, n.d. Pp. [9]-16. Text complete. Dicks' Standard Plays, 776.

Grandfather Whitehead. London: Webster, n.d. Pp. [1]-32.

Grey Doublet, The. London: John Duncombe, n.d. Pp. [1]-19. Duncombe's Edition.

Gwynneth Vaughan. London: J. Pattie, n.d. Pp. [i]-iv, [5]-31. Pattie's Universal Stage or Theatrical Prompt Book.

Gwynneth Vaughan. London: Thomas Hailes Lacy, n.d. Pp. [1]-32. [Lacy's Acting Edition].

Hearts Are Trumps. London: National Acting Drama Office, n.d. Pp. [1]-36. Webster's Acting National Drama, 162.

Honesty the Best Policy. London: G. H. Davidson, n.d. Pp. [1]-40. Promptbook.

House of Ladies, The. London: J. Pattie, n.d. Pp. [1]-22. Pattie's Universal Stage or Theatrical Prompt Book.

Ins and Outs. London: J. Pattie, n.d. Pp. [1]-30. Barth's (late Pattie's) Universal Stage or Theatrical Prompt Book, 20.

Jack in the Green; or, Hints on Etiquette. London: Thomas Hailes Lacy, n.d. Pp. [1]-19. [Lacy's Acting Edition].

Keeley Worried by Buckstone. Written with Webster, Benjamin Nottingham. London: Webster, n.d. Pp. [1]-16. Webster's Acting National Drama, 188.

Knight and the Sprite, The.
See A'Beckett, Gilbert Abbott.

Ladies' Club, The. London: Thomas Hailes Lacy, n.d. Pp. [1]-32. [Lacy's Acting Edition].

Ladies' Club, The. London: J. Pattie, n.d. Pp. [1]-32. Pattie's Universal Stage or Theatrical Prompt Book, 9.

Lost and Won. London: J. Pattie, n.d. Pp. [1]-28.

Love and Charity. London: Thomas Hailes Lacy, n.d. Pp. [5]-19. Text complete. New British Theatre (late Duncombe's), 234.

Loving Woman, The. London: Webster, n.d. Pp. [1]-36. Title page lacking. Webster's Acting National Drama, 167.

Mind Your Own Business. New York: Samuel French, n.d. Pp. [1]-72. French's Standard Drama, 94. Promptbook.

Moving Tale, A. London: Thomas Hailes Lacy, n.d. Pp. [1]-23. [Lacy's Acting Edition].

My Sister Kate. London: John Duncombe, n.d. Pp. [1]-24.

O Gemini!
See A'Beckett, Gilbert Abbott.

Old Parr. London: William Barth, n.d. Pp. [1]-32.

Open Sesame.
See A'Beckett, Gilbert Abbott.

P. L., The; or, Thirty, Strand! London: John Duncombe, n.d. Pp. [1]-20. Duncombe's Edition.

Pacha's Bridal!, The. London: John Duncombe, n.d. Pp. [1]-24. Duncombe's Edition. Libretto.

Peter Wilkins.
See A'Beckett, Gilbert Abbott.

Petticoat Parliament, The. New York: Robert M. DeWitt, n.d. Pp. [1]-19. [DeWitt's Acting Plays, 23].

Pupil of Da Vinci, The. London: James Pattie, n.d. Pp. [1]-24. Pattie's Universal Stage or Theatrical Prompt Book.

Railway Belle, The. London: Thomas Hailes Lacy, n.d. Pp. [1]-19. Lacy's Acting Edition, 247.

Robert Burns. N.p.: n.pub., n.d. Pp. [37]-45. Title page lacking.

Sardanapalus.
See A'Beckett, Gilbert Abbott.

School for Tigers, The; or, The Shilling Hop! London: National Acting Drama Office, n.d. Pp. [1]-23.

Sea and Land. London: Webster, n.d. Pp. [1]-58.

Self Accusation; or, A Brother's Love. London: Thomas Hailes Lacy, n.d. Pp. [1]-26.

Sempstress, The. [London: W. Barth (printer)], n.d. Pp. [3]-28. Title page lacking.

Sir John Falstaff. London: Bradbury, Evans (printer), 1868. Pp. [i]-iv, [1-42]. Readings.

Slave Life; or, Uncle Tom's Cabin. Written with Taylor, Tom. London: Webster, n.d. Pp. [i]-iv, [1]-63. Promptbook.

Slow Man, The. London: Thomas Hailes Lacy, n.d. Pp. [1]-20. [Lacy's Acting Edition].

St. George and the Dragon.
See A'Beckett, Gilbert Abbott.

Story of Falstaff, The. In [*With a Show in the North*, ed. Joseph Hatton, London: William H. Allen, 1871], pp. [197]-284.

Three Secrets, The. London: J. Pattie, n.d. Pp. [i]-iv, [5]-24. Pattie's Universal Stage or Theatrical Prompt Book, 18.

Turf, The. London: Berger, 1842. Pp. [1]-34.

What Will the World Say? London: R. Bryant, 1841. Pp. [i-viii], [1]-128. Promptbook.

LEND ME FIVE SHILLINGS
See Morton, John Maddison.

LENDING A HAND
See A'Beckett, Gilbert Arthur.

LENNARD, HORACE
Dick Whittington. Music by Barrett, Oscar. London: J. Burgiss-Brown, n.d. Pp. [3]-[69]. Libretto.

LEO
See Knowles, James Sheridan.

LEO THE TERRIBLE
See Coyne, Joseph Stirling.

LEONARD, HERBERT
Enemy's Camp, The. Pp. [i-xi], [1-30], 1-34, [1]-29, 1-19. Pagination by act. Manuscript promptbook.

LEONORA
See Chenevix, Richard.
See Edmonstone, Archibald.

LEONORE
See Ashworth, John H. E.
See Newte, Horace Wykeham Can.

LEOTARD OF PERU
See Buckingham, Leicester Silk. Pizarro.

LEQUEL, LOUIS
Identity; or, No Thoroughfare. New York: Samuel French, c.1867. Pp. [1]-44. French's Standard Drama, 348.

LE ROS, CHRISTIAN
See Sorrell, William J.

LESLIE, FREDERICK
See Torr, A. C. (pseud.)

LESLIE, HENRY
Adrienne; or, The Secret of a Life. London: Thomas Hailes Lacy, n.d. Pp. [1]-44. [Lacy's Acting Edition].

House of Bardsley, The.
See Trail of Sin, The.

Mariner's Compass, The. London: Thomas Hailes Lacy, n.d. Pp. [1]-53.

Orange Girl, The. Written with Rowe, Nicholas. London: Thomas Hailes Lacy, n.d. Pp. [1]-55.

Sin and the Sorrow, The. London: Thomas Hailes Lacy, n.d. Pp. [1]-59.

Sin and the Sorrow, The. London: Thomas Hailes Lacy, n.d. Pp. [1]-59. Promptbook.

Time and Tide: A Tale of the Thames! London: Thomas Hailes Lacy, n.d. Pp. [1]-55. Lacy's Acting Edition, [1207].

Trail of Sin, The. *Also:* House of Bardsley, The; or, The Trail of Sin. London: Henderson, Rait, & Fenton, n.d. Pp. [1]-64. *Filed under* House of Bardsley.

LESSING, GOTTHOLD EPHRAIM
Damon.
See Bell, Ernest (trans.).

Emilia Galotti.
See Bell, Ernest (trans.).
See Holcroft, Fanny (trans.).
See Thompson, Benjamin (trans.).

Freethinker, The.
See Bell, Ernest (trans.).

Jews, The.
See Bell, Ernest (trans.).

Minna von Barnhelm.
See Bell, Ernest (trans.).
See Holcroft, Fanny (trans.).

Miss Sara Sampson.
See Bell, Ernest (trans.).

Nathan the Wise.
See Bell, Ernest (trans.).

Old Maid, The.
See Bell, Ernest (trans.).

Philosopher, The.
See Milner, Henry M. (trans.).

Philotas.
See Bell, Ernest (trans.).

Treasure, The.
See Bell, Ernest (trans.).

Woman Hater, The.
See Bell, Ernest (trans.).

Young Scholar, The.
    See Bell, Ernest (trans.).
LESSON FOR FATHERS, A
    See Rose, Edward. Vice Versa.
LESSON FOR GENTLEMEN, A
    See Smith, John Frederick.
LESSON FOR LADIES, A
    See Buckstone, John Baldwin.
LESSON FOR LOVERS
    See Rodwell, James Thomas Gooderham. Young Widow, The.
LESSON IN LOVE, A
    See Barclay, James M.
    See Cheltnam, Charles Smith.
LESSONS FOR LADIES
    See Macready, William. Bank Note, The.
L'ESTANGE, JOSEPH
    See Mérimée, Prosper (trans.).
LESTELLE
    See Stirling, Edward.
LESTOCQ, WILLIAM
    Bad Penny, A. London & New York: Samuel French, n.d. Pp. [1]-24. [Lacy's Acting Edition].
    Foundling, The. Written with Robson, E. M. [New York: Z. & L. Rosenfield], n.d. Pp. [i-iii], [1]-43, [i-ii], [1]-49, [i-ii], [1]-38. Pagination by act. Typescript.
    In Danger. Written with Cresswell, Henry. London: Samuel French; New York: T. Henry French, n.d. Pp. [1]-62. [Lacy's Acting Edition].
    Jane.
        See Nicholls, Harry.
    Merry Meeting, A. London & New York: Samuel French, n.d. Pp. [1]-20. [Lacy's Acting Edition].
    Through the Fire. Written with Stephens, Yorke. London & New York: Samuel French, n.d. Pp. [1]-24. [French's Acting Edition].
    Uncles and Aunts. Written with Everard, Walter. London & New York: Samuel French, c.1909. Pp. [1]-52.
LESTOCQ
    See Macfarren, George.
    See Moncrieff, William Thomas.
LEVERSON, MRS. ERNEST
    All for the Best. In *Dialogues of the Day,* ed. Oswald Crawfurd, London: Chapman & Hall, n.d., pp. [214]-225. *Filed under* Crawfurd, Oswald. Dialogues of the Day.
    Engaged. In *Dialogues of the Day,* ed. Oswald Crawfurd, London: Chapman & Hall, n.d., pp. [44]-53. *Filed under* Crawfurd, Oswald. Dialogues of the Day.
LEVESON, FRANCIS
    See Gower, Francis Leveson, Lord.
LEVESON-GOWER, GEORGIANA CHARLOTTE
    See Fullerton, Georgiana Charlotte Leveson-Gower, Mrs. Alexander George, Lady Georgiana.
LEVEY, JOHN C.
    Garryowen; or, The Belles of the Shannon. 115 leaves. Manuscript sides for thirteen parts.
LEWES, GEORGE HENRY
    See Lawrence, Slingsby.
LEWIN, WALPOLE
    Good Queen Bess. London: Delaperrelle (printer), n.d. Pp. [1]-44. Promptbook.
LEWIS, ALEXIS
    Grace Clairville; or, The Crime at the Symon's Yat. London: John Dicks, n.d. Pp. [1]-20. Dicks' Standard Plays, [951].
LEWIS, G. P.
    See Lewis, Matthew Gregory.
LEWIS, LEOPOLD DAVID
    Bells, The. London & New York: Samuel French, n.d. Pp. [1]-30. [French's Acting Edition]. Promptbook.
LEWIS, MATTHEW GREGORY
    Adelgitha; or, The Fruits of a Single Error. London: J. F. Hughes, 1806. Pp. [iii]-[xii], [1]-127. 3rd ed.
    Adelgitha; or, The Fruits of a Single Error. London: John Cumberland, n.d. Pp. [1]-54. Cumberland's British

Theatre, XXXIX. *Filed under* Cumberland, John. Cumberland's British Theatre, XXXIX.
    Adelmorn, the Outlaw. London: J. Bell, 1801. Pp. [1-2], [i]-[xii], [1]-101. 2nd ed.
    Alfonso, King of Castile. London: J. Bell, 1801. Pp. [i]-[viii], [1]-111.
    Alfonso, King of Castile. London: J. Bell, 1802. Pp. [i]-[xviii], [1]-122. 2nd ed.
    Castle Spectre, The. In *New English Drama,* ed. W. Oxberry, 22 vols., London: W. Simpkin & R. Marshall; C. Chapple, 1820, IV, [1-2], [i]-[iv], [1]-[68]. *Filed under* Oxberry, William Henry. New English Drama, IV.
    Castle Spectre, The. London: John Cumberland, 1827. Pp. [1]-66. Cumberland's British Theatre, XV. *Filed under* Cumberland, John. Cumberland's British Theatre, XV.
    Castle Spectre, The. In *British Drama,* 12 vols., London: John Dicks, 1864, I, [129]-146.
    Harper's Daughter, The; or, Love and Ambition. Philadelphia: M. Carey, 1813. Pp. [1]-76.
    One O'Clock!; or, The Knight and the Wood Daemon. In *New English Drama,* ed. W. Oxberry, 22 vols., London: W. Simpkin & R. Marshall; C. Chapple, 1824, XIX, [i]-[x], [1]-66. *Filed under* Oxberry, William Henry. New English Drama, XIX.
    One O'Clock!; or, The Knight and the Wood Daemon. Music by King, Matthew Peter; Kelley, Michael. London: Lowndes & Hobbs, n.d. Pp. [1]-79. Libretto.
    One O'Clock; or, The Knight and the Wood Demon. In *British Drama,* 12 vols., London: John Dicks, 1871, V, [207]-224.
    One O'Clock!; or, The Knight and the Wood Demon. London: John Cumberland, n.d. Pp. [1]-54. Cumberland's British Theatre, XXXII. *Filed under* Cumberland, John. Cumberland's British Theatre, XXXII.
    Raymond and Agnes: The Travellers Benighted; or, The Bleeding Nun of Lindenberg. New York: Samuel French, n.d. Pp. [1]-24. French's Standard Drama, 191.
    Raymond and Agnes, the Travellers Benighted; or, The Bleeding Nun of Lindenberg. *Also:* Raymond and Agnes; or, The Bleeding Nun. London: John Cumberland, n.d. Pp. [1]-35. Cumberland's British Theatre, XXXVIII. *Filed under* Cumberland, John. Cumberland's British Theatre, XXXVIII.
    Rich and Poor. In *New English Drama,* ed. W. Oxberry, 22 vols., London: W. Simpkin & R. Marshall; C. Chapple, 1823, XIX, [i]-[x], [1]-65. *Filed under* Oxberry, William Henry. New English Drama, XIX.
    Rich and Poor. Music by Horn, C. London: C. Chapple, 1814. Pp. [i-iv], [1]-80. 2nd ed. Libretto.
    Rugantino; or, The Bravo of Venice. London: J. F. Hughes, 1806. Pp. [iii]-[viii], [1]-55. 2nd ed.
    Rugantino; or, The Bravo of Venice. In *New English Drama,* ed. W. Oxberry, 22 vols., London: W. Simpkin & R. Marshall; C. Chapple, 1820, IX, [1-2], [i]-[iv], [1]- 30. *Filed under* Oxberry, William Henry. New English Drama, IX.
    Rugantino; or, The Bravo of Venice. London: John Cumberland, n.d. Pp. [1]-38. Cumberland's British Theatre, XXXIV. *Filed under* Cumberland, John. Cumberland's British Theatre, XXXIV.
    Timour the Tartar. London: Lowndes & Hobbs, n.d. Pp. [1]-56.
    Timour the Tartar. London: John Cumberland, n.d. Pp. [1]-41. Cumberland's British Theatre, XXIX. *Filed under* Cumberland, John. Cumberland's British Theatre, XXIX.
    Venoni; or, The Novice of St. Mark's. London: Longman, Hurst, Rees, & Orme, 1809. Pp. [i]-[x], [1]-103.
    Venoni; or, The Novice of St. Mark's. London: John Cumberland, n.d. Pp. [1]-43. Cumberland's British Theatre, XXXVIII. *Filed under* Cumberland, John. Cumberland's British Theatre, XXXVIII.
    Wood Daemon, The; or, The Clock Has Struck. By G. P. Lewis. London: J. Scales, n.d. Pp. [1]-26, 31-34. Pages misnumbered. Scales's Edition. Synopsis.
LIAR, THE
    See Foote, Samuel.
    See Mathews, Charles James (arr.).

LIARS, THE
  See Jones, Henry Arthur.
LIBERAL CANDIDATE, THE
  See A'Beckett, Gilbert Abbott.
LIBERTA
  See Scudamore, G. H.
LIBERTINE, THE
  See Pocock, Isaac. Don Juan.
  See Pocock, Isaac.
LIBERTINE LORD AND THE DAMSEL OF DAISY FARM
  See Byron, Henry James. Village Virtue.
LIBERTINE RECLAIMED
  See Moncrieff, William Thomas. Giovanni in London.
LIBERTINE'S SHIP
  See Fitzball, Edward. Margaret's Ghost.
LIBERTY HALL
  See Carton, R. C.
LIBERTY VANQUISHED
  See Beck, Thomas. Triumphs of the Sons of Belial, The.
LIE OF A DAY
  See O'Keeffe, John.
LIEUTENANT'S DAUGHTERS
  See Fitzball, Edward. Home Again!
LIFE
  See Reynolds, Frederick.
LIFE AND DEATH OF JACK SHEPPARD, THE (anon.)
  London: Thomas Hailes Lacy, n.d. Pp. [1]-63.
LIFE AS IT IS
  See Blake, Thomas G.
LIFE BUOY, THE
  See Hoskins, John.
LIFE CHASE, A
  See Oxenford, John.
LIFE FOR LIFE
  See Marston, John Westland.
LIFE IN IRELAND
  See Bryant, Michael. Florence Macarthy.
LIFE IN LONDON
  See Dibdin, Charles Isaac Mungo, jr.
  See Moncrieff, William Thomas. Tom and Jerry.
LIFE IN LOUISIANA
  See Boucicault, Dionysius Lardner. Octoroon, The.
LIFE IN NEW YORK
  See Brougham, John.
LIFE IN THE CLOUDS
  See Brougham, John.
LIFE IN THE TEMPLE
  See Selby, Charles. Chamber Practice.
LIFE IS A DREAM
  See MacCarthy, Denis Florence (trans.).
LIFE OF A THAMES WATERMAN!
  See Haines, John Thomas. Jacob Faithful.
LIFE OF A WOMAN, THE
  See Haines, John Thomas.
LIFE OF AN ACTRESS
  See Boucicault, Dionysius Lardner. Grimaldi.
LIFE'S A LOTTERY
  See Rede, William Leman.
LIFE'S RANSOM, A
  See Marston, John Westland.
LIFE'S REVENGE, A
  See Suter, William E.
LIFE'S TRIAL, A
  See Bernard, William Bayle.
LIGHT OF LIFE
  See Headsman of Paris, The (anon.).
LIGHTHOUSE ON THE CARN RUTH
  See Burnand, Francis Cowley. Deadman's Point.
LIGHTS AND SHADOWS OF LIFE
  See Selby, Charles. Dissolving Views.
LIGHTS O' LONDON
  See Sims, George Robert.
LIKE AND UNLIKE
  See Langford, J. M.

LIKE FATHER, LIKE SON
  See Raymond, Richard John.
LIKE MASTER LIKE MAN
  See King, Thomas (arr.). Lovers' Quarrels.
  See Lovers' Quarrels.
LIKE MISTRESS, LIKE MAID
  See Ganthony, Robert.
LIKENESS OF THE NIGHT, THE
  See Clifford, Lucy Lane, Mrs. William Kingdon.
LILIAN GERVAIS
  See Barnett, Morris.
LILIAN THE SHOW GIRL
  See Soane, George.
LILLE, HERBERT
  As Like as Two Peas. London: Thomas Hailes Lacy, n.d. Pp. [1]-28.
LILLIPUT REVELS
  See Rands, William Brightly.
LILLO, GEORGE
  Arden of Feversham. In *British Drama*, 12 vols., London: John Dicks, 1864, II, [607]-623.
  Fatal Curiosity. In *British Drama*, 12 vols., London: John Dicks, 1864, I, [310]-320.
  George Barnwell. In *New English Drama*, ed. W. Oxberry, 22 vols., London: W. Simpkin & R. Marshall; C. Chapple, 1823, XVII, [i]-[xvi], [1]-44. *Filed under* Oxberry, William Henry. New English Drama, XVII.
  George Barnwell. London: Thomas Dolby, 1825. Pp. [i]-[viii], [9]-[47]. Dolby's British Theatre, IX. *Filed under* Cumberland, John. Cumberland's British Theatre, IX.
  George Barnwell. In *British Drama*, 12 vols., London: John Dicks, 1864, II, [433]-446.
  London Merchant, The; or, The History of George Barnwell. London: Whittingham & Arliss, 1814. Pp. [1]-[48]. London Theatre, IX. *Filed under* Dibdin, Thomas John, ed. London Theatre, IX.
LILLY DAWSON
  See Stirling, Edward.
LILY OF FRANCE, THE
  See Brougham, John.
LILY OF KILLARNEY, THE
  See Boucicault, Dionysius Lardner.
LILY OF LEOVILLE, THE
  See Remo, Felix.
LILY OF ST. LEONARD'S
  See Dibdin, Thomas John. Heart of Mid-Lothian, The.
LILY OF THE DESERT, THE
  See Stirling, Edward.
LILY OF THE FIELD, THE
  See Hannan, Charles.
LIMITED
  See Blake, Robert.
LINDA DI CHAMOUNI
  See Edwardes, Conway Theodore Marriott.
LINDA DI CHAMOUNIX (anon.)
  Music by Donizetti. London: Swift, n.d. Pp. [1]-63. Libretto.
LINDA DI CHAMOUNIX (anon.)
  Music by Donizetti. London: W. S. Davidson, n.d. <wrps. New York: Samuel French>. Pp. [1]-26. French's Opera Libretti. Libretto.
LINDA OF CHAMOUNI
  See Thompson, Alfred.
LINDA, THE PEARL OF SAVOY
  See Barnett, Charles Zachary.
LINDO, FRANK
  Dentist, The. London & New York: Samuel French, n.d. Pp. [1]-10. [Lacy's Acting Edition].
  Minx and Man, The. Written with Lindo, R. H.; Skelton, A. W. Music by Prentis, Thomas. London: Capper & Newton, n.d. Pp. [1]-24. Lynn's On Tour Edition, 1. Libretto.
  My Soldier Boy.
    See Maltby, C. Alfred.

LINDO, R. H.
  Minx and Man, The.
    See Lindo, Frank.
LINDSAY, DAVID
  Last Plague, The. In *Dramas of the Ancient World,* Edinburgh: William Blackwood, 1822, pp. [91]-100. *Filed under* Dramas of the Ancient World.
LINDSEY, ELIZABETH
    See Yorke, Elizabeth Lindsey, Countess of Hardwicke.
LINKED BY LOVE
    See Meritt, Paul.
LINLEY, GEORGE
  Gipsy's Warning, The. Written with Peake, Richard Brinsley. By George Linley. Music by Benedict, Jules. London: W. Wright (printer), n.d. Pp. [1]-24. Libretto. *Filed under* Linley, George; Peake, Robert Brinsley.
  Law versus Love. London: Thomas Hailes Lacy, n.d. Pp. [1]-16. [Lacy's Acting Edition].
  River Sprite, The. Music by Mori, Frank. London: Cramer, n.d. Pp. [i-iv], [1]-123. Vocal score.
LINLEY, WILLIAM
  Ring, The; or, Love Me for Myself. Music by Linley, William. London: C. Lowndes (printer), n.d. Pp. [1]-12. Libretto.
LION AND THE UNICORN, THE
    See Byron, Henry James.
LION AT BAY, A
    See Phillips, Watts.
LION SLAYER, THE
    See Williams, Thomas John.
LIONEL AND CLARISSA
    See Bickerstaffe, Isaac.
LIONESS OF THE NORTH, THE
    See Selby, Charles.
LIQUOR TRAFFIC A CURSE TO THE DEALER AND CONSUMER
    See Seven Nights in a Bar-Room (anon.).
LISLE, WALTER
  Love Test, The. London & New York: Samuel French, n.d. Pp. [1]-14. [Lacy's Acting Edition].
LISTER, THOMAS HENRY
  Epicharis. London: Henry Colburn & Richard Bentley, 1829. Pp. [i-viii], [1]-115.
LITIGANTS, THE
    See Boswell, Robert Bruce (trans.).
LITTLE, ARCHIBALD JOHN (trans.)
  Borrowing Boots. In [*Gleanings from Fifty Years in China,* Philadelphia: J. B. Lippincott, n.d.], pp. 225-250.
LITTLE ANNIE'S BIRTHDAY
    See Suter, William E.
LITTLE BACK PARLOUR, THE
    See Stirling, Edward.
LITTLE BILL THAT WAS TAKEN UP
    See Burnand, Francis Cowley. Latest Edition of Black-Eyed Susan, The.
LITTLE BO-PEEP
    See Buckstone, John Baldwin.
LITTLE BRIDE, THE
    See Lyster, Frederic (trans.).
LITTLE CHANGE, A
    See Grundy, Sydney.
LITTLE CHRISTOPHER COLUMBUS
    See Sims, George Robert.
LITTLE CRICKET
    See Mortimer, James.
LITTLE DAISY
    See Williams, Thomas John.
LITTLE DEVIL'S SHARE
    See Archer, Thomas. Asmodeus.
LITTLE DON GIOVANNI
    See Byron, Henry James.
LITTLE DUCK AND THE GREAT QUACK
    See Gilbert, William Schwenck. Dulcamara.
LITTLE EM'LY
    See Halliday, Andrew.

LITTLE EYOLF
    See Archer, William (trans.).
LITTLE FAIRY AT THE BOTTOM OF THE SEA
    See Brough, William. Corsair, The.
LITTLE FOLKS' WORK, THE
    See Adams, Florence Davenport.
LITTLE GENIUS, THE
    See Harris, Augustus Henry Glossop.
LITTLE GIRL FROM TOWN
    See Bell, Florence Eveleen Eleanore Oliffe, Mrs. Hugh (Lady). Wigwam, The.
LITTLE GLASS SLIPPER
    See Cinderella (anon.).
LITTLE GOODY TWO-SHOES
    See Blanchard, Edward Litt Leman.
LITTLE GOODY TWO-SHOES AND HER QUEEN ANNE'S FARTHING
    See Strachan, John S., jr.
LITTLE JACK HORNER
    See Blanchard, Edward Litt Leman.
LITTLE JACK THE GIANT KILLER
    See Harrison, Samuel M.
LITTLE JOCKEY
    See Dimond, William.
    See Dimond, William. Youth, Love, and Folly.
LITTLE KING PIPPIN
    See Blanchard, Edward Litt Leman.
LITTLE LEFT HAND, THE
    See Blunt, Wilfred Scawen.
LITTLE LUCIFER (anon.)
    London: Mrs. Marshall's Type Writing Office, 1909. Pp. [i-ii], [1]-48, [i], [1]-39, [i], [1]-30. Pagination by act. Typescript.
LITTLE MADCAP, A
    See Cheltnam, Charles Smith.
LITTLE MAN IN GREEN!
    See Williams, Thomas John. Volunteer Review, The.
LITTLE MINISTER, THE
    See Barrie, James Mathew.
LITTLE MISS MUFFET
    See Albery, James.
    See Lancaster-Wallis, Ellen.
LITTLE MISS MUFFET AND LITTLE BOY BLUE
    See Buckstone, John Baldwin.
LITTLE MOTHER
    See Morton, John Maddison.
LITTLE NUN, THE
    See Craven, Henry Thornton.
LITTLE ORPHEUS AND HIS LUTE
    See Byron, Henry James. Eurydice.
LITTLE PET AND THE GREAT PASSION!
    See Talfourd, Francis. King Thrushbeard!
LITTLE PETSY
    See Bell, Florence Eveleen Eleanore Oliffe, Mrs. Hugh (Lady).
LITTLE PRINCESS WHO WAS LOST AT SEA
    See Byron, Henry James. Orange Tree and the Humble Bee, The.
LITTLE REBEL, THE
    See Coyne, Joseph Stirling.
LITTLE RED RIDING HOOD
    See Bridgeman, John Vipon.
    See Keating, Eliza H.
    See Wade, William.
LITTLE RED RIDING HOOD AND THE FAIRIES OF THE ROSE, SHAMROCK, AND THISTLE
    See Buckingham, Leicester Silk.
LITTLE ROBIN HOOD
    See Reece, Robert.
LITTLE SAVAGE, THE
    See Morton, John Maddison.
LITTLE SENTINEL!, THE
    See Williams, Thomas John.
LITTLE SINS AND PRETTY SINNERS
    See Selby, Charles.

LITTLE SURPRISE, A
    See Beerbohm, Constance.
LITTLE TODDLEKINS
    See Mathews, Charles James.
LITTLE TREASURE, THE
    See Harris, Augustus Glossop.
LITTLE VIXENS, THE
    See Neville, George F.
LIVERPOOL MERCHANT
    See H., C. Two Friends, The.
LIVING AT EASE
    See Sketchley, Arthur.
LIVING IN LONDON
    See Jameson, Robert Francis.
LIVING TOO FAST
    See Troughton, Adolphus Charles.
LIVIUS, BARHAM
    Biter Bit, The; or, Maid or Wife. *Also:* Maid or Wife; or, The Deceiver Deceived. Clyde, Ohio: A. D. Ames, n.d. Pp. [1]-19. Ames' Series of Standard and Minor Drama, 87.
    Freyschutz, The; or, The Wild Huntsman of Bohemia. Music by Weber. London: John Miller, 1824. Pp. [i]-[x], [1]-55. Libretto.
    Maid or Wife; or, The Deceiver Deceived. *Also:* The Biter Bit; or, Maid or Wife. London: William Sams, 1821. Pp. [i-vi], [1]-40.
    Maid or Wife; or, The Deceiver Deceived. London: John Cumberland, n.d. Pp. [1]-34.
    Maid or Wife; or, The Deceiver Deceived. Music by Livius, Barham. London: John Cumberland, n.d. Pp. [i-ii], [1]-34. Cumberland's British Theatre, XXXIII. *Filed under* Cumberland, John. Cumberland's British Theatre, XXXIII.
LIZ
    See Hatton, Joseph.
LIZZIE LEIGH
    See Waldron, W. Richard.
LIZZIE LYLE
    See Hazlewood, Colin Henry.
LLEWELYN THE GREAT
    See Sotheby, William. Cambrian Hero, The.
LLOYD, ? (arr.)
    Romp, The. By Bickerstaffe, Isaac. In *British Drama*, 12 vols., London: John Dicks, 1871, IX, [183]-192.
    Romp, The. By Bickerstaffe, Isaac. London: John Cumberland, n.d. Pp. [1]-28. Cumberland's British Theatre, XXXV. *Filed under* Cumberland, John. Cumberland's British Theatre, XXXV.
LLOYD, CHARLES
    Duke D'Ormond, The. In *Duke D'Ormond . . . ,* London: Longman, Hurst, Rees, Orme, & Brown, 1822, pp. [i-x], 82-285.
LLOYD, CHARLES (trans.)
    Agamemnon. By Alfieri, Vittorio. In *Tragedies of Vittorio Alfieri*, 3 vols., London: Longman, Hurst, Rees, Orme, & Brown, 1815, I, [243]-301. *Filed under* Collected Works.
    Agis. By Alfieri, Vittorio. In *Tragedies of Vittorio Alfieri*, 3 vols., London: Longman, Hurst, Rees, Orme, & Brown, 1815, III, [127]-187. *Filed under* Collected Works.
    Antigone. By Alfieri, Vittorio. In *Tragedies of Vittorio Alfieri*, 3 vols., London: Longman, Hurst, Rees, Orme, & Brown, 1815, I, [122]-179. *Filed under* Collected Works.
    Conspiracy of the Pazzi, The. By Alfieri, Vittorio. In *Tragedies of Vittorio Alfieri*, 3 vols., London: Longman, Hurst, Rees, Orme, & Brown, 1815, II, [310]-371. *Filed under* Collected Works.
    Don Garcia. By Alfieri, Vittorio. In *Tragedies of Vittorio Alfieri*, 3 vols., London: Longman, Hurst, Rees, Orme, & Brown, 1815, III, [1]-59. *Filed under* Collected Works.
    First Brutus, The. By Alfieri, Vittorio. In *Tragedies of Vittorio Alfieri*, 3 vols., London: Longman, Hurst, Rees, Orme, & Brown, 1815, III, [234]-289. *Filed under* Collected Works.

Mary Stuart. By Alfieri, Vittorio. In *Tragedies of Vittorio Alfieri*, 3 vols., London: Longman, Hurst, Rees, Orme, & Brown, 1815, II, [247]-309. *Filed under* Collected Works.
Merope. By Alfieri, Vittorio. In *Tragedies of Vittorio Alfieri*, 3 vols., London: Longman, Hurst, Rees, Orme, & Brown, 1815, II, [183]-246. *Filed under* Collected Works.
Myrrha. By Alfieri, Vittorio. In *Tragedies of Vittorio Alfieri*, 3 vols., London: Longman, Hurst, Rees, Orme, & Brown, 1815, III, [290]-353. *Filed under* Collected Works.
Octavia. By Alfieri, Vittorio. In *Tragedies of Vittorio Alfieri*, 3 vols., London: Longman, Hurst, Rees, Orme, & Brown, 1815, II, [65]-125. *Filed under* Collected Works.
Orestes. By Alfieri, Vittorio. In *Tragedies of Vittorio Alfieri*, 3 vols., London: Longman, Hurst, Rees, Orme, & Brown, 1815, I, [302]-365. *Filed under* Collected Works.
Philip. By Alfieri, Vittorio. In *Tragedies of Vittorio Alfieri*, 3 vols., London: Longman Hurst, Rees, Orme, & Brown, 1815, I, [i]-[xxxii], [1]-60. *Filed under* Collected Works.
Polinices. By Alfieri, Vittorio. In *Tragedies of Vittorio Alfieri*, 3 vols., London: Longman, Hurst, Rees, Orme, & Brown, 1815, I, [61]-121. *Filed under* Collected Works.
Rosmunda. By Alfieri, Vittorio. In *Tragedies of Vittorio Alfieri*, 3 vols., London: Longman, Hurst, Rees, Orme, & Brown, 1815, II, [1]-64. *Filed under* Collected Works.
Saul. By Alfieri, Vittorio. In *Tragedies of Vittorio Alfieri*, 3 vols., London: Longman, Hurst, Rees, Orme, & Brown, 1815, III, [60]-126. *Filed under* Collected Works.
Second Brutus, The. By Alfieri, Vittorio. In *Tragedies of Vittorio Alfieri*, 3 vols., London: Longman, Hurst, Rees, Orme, & Brown, 1815, III, [354]-413. *Filed under* Collected Works.
Sophonisba. By Alfieri, Vittorio. In *Tragedies of Vittorio Alfieri*, 3 vols., London: Longman, Hurst, Rees, Orme, & Brown, 1815, III, [188]-233. *Filed under* Collected Works.
Timoleon. By Alfieri, Vittorio. In *Tragedies of Vittorio Alfieri*, 3 vols., London: Longman, Hurst, Rees, Orme, & Brown, 1815, II, [126]-182. *Filed under* Collected Works.
Virginia. By Alfieri, Vittorio. In *Tragedies of Vittorio Alfieri*, 3 vols., London: Longman, Hurst, Rees, Orme, & Brown, 1815, I, [180]-242. *Filed under* Collected Works.
LOADSTONE ROCK AND THE FLYING INDIANS
    See A'Beckett, Gilbert Abbott. Peter Wilkins.
LOAN OF A LOVER, THE
    See Planché, James Robinson.
LOAN OF A WIFE, THE
    See Wigan, Alfred Sydney.
LOCHINVAR
    See Moncrieff, William Thomas.
LOCK AND KEY
    See Hoare, Prince.
LOCKE, FRED
    Aladdin and His Wonderful Lamp. [Edinburgh]: n.pub, n.d. Pp. [1]-50.
    Cinderella. Music by McKenzie, D. C. Greenwich: W. T. Manning, n.d. Pp. [i-iv], 1-63. Libretto.
LOCKED IN
    See Wooler, John Pratt.
LOCKED IN WITH A LADY
    See Addison, Henry Robert, Capt.
LOCKED OUT
    See Paul, Howard.
LOCKWOOD, PERCIVAL (trans.)
    Bride of Messina, The; or, The Hostile Brothers. By Schiller. Munich: Georg Franz, 1839. Pp. [1]-275. *Filed under* Schiller, Johann Christoph Friedrich.
LOCOMOTION
    See Bernard, William Bayle.
LOCRINE
    See Swinburne, Algernon Charles.
LODGE, ADAM (trans.)
    Bride of Messina, The. By Schiller. In *Works of Frederick Schiller*, 3 vols., London: George Bell & Sons, 1881, III, [i-ii], 445-516.
LODGERS AND DODGERS
    See Hay, Frederic.

LODGINGS FOR SINGLE GENTLEMEN
    See Poole, John.
LODOISKA
    See Kemble, John Philip.
LOFTY PROJECTS
    See Lunn, Joseph.
LOGAN, W. MCGREGOR
    Freyschutz, Der. Music by Weber. London: Cramer, Beale, n.d. Pp. [1]-148. Vocal score.
LOGAN BRAES
    See Hetherington, William Maxwell.
LOGROÑO
    See Cerny, Frederick.
LOHENGRIN
    See Corder, Henrietta Louisa Walford, Mrs. Frederick (trans.).
    See Jackson, John P. (trans.).
    See Macfarren, Natalia (trans.).
    See Oxenford, John (trans.).
LOLA MONTES
    See Coyne, Joseph Stirling. Pas de Fascination.
LONDON
    See Dibdin, Charles Isaac Mungo, jr.
LONDON ASSURANCE
    See Boucicault, Dionysius Lardner.
LONDON, BIRMINGHAM, & BRISTOL
    See Morton, Edward. Railroad Trip, The.
LONDON BRIDGE, 150 YEARS AGO
    See McNab, James.
LONDON BY NIGHT
    See Selby, Charles.
LONDON FROLICS IN 1638
    See Planché, James Robinson. Merchant's Wedding, The.
LONDON IN 1665
    See Hart, James P. Bell Ringer of St. Paul's, The.
LONDON IN THE LAST CENTURY
    See Wills, William Henry. Law of the Land, The.
LONDON IN 1370
    See Milner, Henry M. Whittington and His Cat.
LONDON, LIVERPOOL, AND BRISTOL
    See Stirling, Edward. Wanted a Wife.
LONDON MERCHANT, THE
    See Lillo, George.
LONDON 'PRENTICE
    See Younge, Henry. Harlequin and George Barnwell.
LONDON 'PRENTICES OF 1517
    See Emden, William Samuel. Evil May Day!, The.
LONE HOUSE ON THE BRIDGE OF NOTRE DAME, THE
    See Webb, Charles.
LONELY LIVES
    See Morison, Mary (trans.).
LONELY MAN OF THE OCEAN, THE
    See Blake, Thomas G.
LONG, CHARLES
    Chalet, The; or, Caught Not Won. Music by Adam, Adolphe. 19 leaves. Manuscript libretto.
    Crown Brilliants, The. *Also:* Les Diamants de la Couronne. Music by Auber. London: Royal Grecian Saloon, 1846. Pp. [1]-24. 2nd ed. Libretto.
    Crown Brilliants, The. Music by Auber. 37 leaves. Manuscript libretto.
    Edwin and Emma. 14 leaves. Manuscript.
    Ernestine and Georgette; or, A Lover Lent. 18 leaves. Manuscript.
    False Conclusions. 23 leaves. Manuscript.
    Family Arrangements. 21 leaves. Manuscript.
    Hymen's Muster Roll; or, The Drum Head Marriage. 34 leaves. Manuscript.
    My Friend. 18 leaves. Manuscript.
    Pleasant Courtship, A. 15 leaves. Manuscript.
    Wife or Widow. 20 leaves. Manuscript.
LONG LIVE THE KING!
    See Moser, Joseph. British Loyalty.
LONG-LOST BROTHERS
    See Burnand, Francis Cowley. Cox and Box.

LONG ODDS
    See Edwardes, Conway Theodore Marriott.
LONG STORIES
    See Colman, George, jr. We Fly by Night.
LONG STRIKE, THE
    See Boucicault, Dionysius Lardner.
LONGINUS
    See Jones, Jacob.
LONGLAND, JOSEPH
    King Charles the Second. London: Longmans, Green, 1872. Pp. [i]-vi, [1]-116.
LOOK AT HOME
    See Eyre, Edmund John.
LOOK BEFORE YOU LEAP
    See Burnand, Francis Cowley. Sappho.
    See Lovell, George William.
LOOK ON THIS PICTURE, AND ON THAT
    See Smith, William.
LOPEZ, BERNARD
    Martin Luther.
    See Moore, George.
LORD, HENRIETTA FRANCES (trans.)
    Doll's House, The. By Ibsen, Henrik. New York: D. Appleton, 1907. Pp. [1]-148.
    Nora; or, A Doll's House. By Ibsen, Henrik. London: Griffith, Farran, Okeden, & Welsh, 1890. Pp. [i]-[xxxiv], [1]-116. New ed., rev.
LORD AND LADY RUSSELL
    See Neil, Ross.
LORD BATEMAN
    See Byron, Henry James.
    See Stephens, Henry Pottinger.
LORD DARCY
    See Greene, A. E.
LORD DARNLEY
    See Wilks, Thomas Egerton.
LORD DOLLY
    See Anderson, Charles. Grandmother's Gown.
LORD LOVEL AND LADY NANCY BELL
    See Burnand, Francis Cowley.
LORD MAYOR OF LONDON
    See Farley, Charles. Harlequin Whittington.
LORD MAYOR'S DAUGHTER
    See Almar, George. Cedar Chest, The.
LORD OF THE MANOR, THE
    See Burgoyne, John, Gen.
    See Dibdin, Charles Isaac Mungo, jr (arr.).
LORD TOM NODDY
    See Dance, George.
LORDS OF ELLINGHAM, THE
    See Spicer, Henry.
LOREDA
    See Burn, David.
LORENZO, THE OUTCAST SON
    See Gandy, Edward.
LORETTA: A TALE OF SEVILLE
    See Bunn, Alfred.
LOSS OF THE ROYAL GEORGE, THE
    See Barnett, Charles Zachary.
LOST AND FOUND
    See Hood, Tom.
    See March, George.
    See Masters, Martin Kedgwin.
LOST AND WON
    See Lemon, Mark.
LOST CHILD, THE
    See Suter, William E.
LOST DAUGHTER
    See Hazlewood, Colin Henry. Hop Pickers and Gipsies.
LOST DIAMONDS!, THE
    See Stirling, Edward.
LOST GOD, A
    See Bourdillon, Francis William.
LOST HUSBAND, THE
    See Reade, Charles.

LOST IN LONDON
    See Phillips, Watts.
LOST JEWELS
    See Puseley, Daniel. Intrigue.
LOST LOVE
    See Murdoch, J. Mortimer.
LOST PLEIAD
    See Coyne, Joseph Stirling. All for Love.
LOST REGALIA
    See Boucicault, Dionysius Lardner. Babil and Bijou.
LOST RING
    See Williams, Monier (trans.). Sakoontala.
LOST SHIP
    See Rede, William Leman. Our Village.
    See Townsend, William Thompson.
LOST SHIP AND THE WILD FLOWER OF MEXICO
    See Robertson, Thomas William. Sea of Ice.
LOST SON
    See Buckstone, John Baldwin. Luke the Labourer.
LOST, STOLEN, OR STRAYED
    See Goodwin, J. Cheever.
LOST WIFE
    See Hazlewood, Colin Henry.
    See Hazlewood, Colin Henry. Outcast's Wife.
LOT 49
    See Fisher, W. J.
LOTTERY OF LIFE, THE
    See Brougham, John.
LOTTERY TICKET, THE
    See Beazley, Samuel, jr.
LOTTERY TICKET AND THE LAWYER'S CLERK, THE
    See Beazley, Samuel, jr.
LOUIS XI
    See Boucicault, Dionysius Lardner.
    See Markwell, W. R. S.
LOUISE
    See Holl, Henry.
LOUISE DE LIGNEROLLES
    See Pardoe, Julia.
LOUISON, THE ANGEL OF THE ATTIC
    See Bernard, William Bayle.
LOVE (anon.)
    New York: Wheat & Cornett, c.1878. Pp. [28]-32. New York Drama, IV, 37.
LOVE
    See Knowles, James Sheridan.
LOVE À LA MILITAIRE; OR, 21! 22! 23! (anon.)
    Dublin: William Frederick Wakeman, 1834. Pp. [1-2], [i]-ii, [5]-60.
LOVE A LA MODE
    See Macklin, Charles.
LOVE AMONG THE ROSES
    See Beazley, Samuel, jr.
LOVE AND AMBITION
    See Lewis, Matthew Gregory. Harper's Daughter, The.
LOVE AND CHARITY
    See Lemon, Mark.
LOVE AND DENTISTRY
    See Swears, Herbert.
LOVE AND DUTY
    See Marston, John Westland. Strathmore.
LOVE AND FORTUNE
    See Planché, James Robinson.
LOVE AND FRIENDSHIP
    See Claribel.
LOVE AND HATE
    See Mitford, Edward Ledwich.
LOVE AND HONOUR
    See Carpenter, Joseph Edwards.
    See Webster, Benjamin Nottingham. Caesar de Bazan.
LOVE AND HUNGER
    See Morton, John Maddison.
LOVE AND INTRIGUE
    See Fettes, James (trans.).

LOVE AND LARCENY
    See Stephens, Henry Pottinger. Claude Duval.
LOVE AND LAUDANUM
    See Baynes, E. D.
LOVE AND LAUGH
    See Moncrieff, William Thomas. All at Coventry.
LOVE AND LAW
    See Allingham, John Till. Transformation.
    See Edgeworth, Maria.
LOVE AND LOTTERY!
    See Collier, William. Rival Sergeants, The.
LOVE AND LOYALTY
    See Robson, William James.
LOVE AND MADNESS
    See Brockhurst, Joseph Sumner. Wife, The.
    See Somerset, Charles A. Girl of the Light House, The.
LOVE AND MERCY
    See Dimond, William. Young Hussar, The.
LOVE AND MURDER
    See Brougham, John.
LOVE AND PRIDE
    See Bulwer (later Bulwer-Lytton), Edward George Earle Lytton, Lord Lytton. Lady of Lyons, The.
LOVE AND PROJECTION
    See Union, The.
LOVE AND RAIN (anon.)
    London: Thomas Hailes Lacy, n.d. Pp. [1]-12. Lacy's Acting Edition. *Filed under* Lacy, Thomas Hailes.
LOVE AND RAIN (anon.)
    Chicago: T. S. Dennison, n.d. Pp. [1]-10.
LOVE AND RAIN
    See Morton, John Maddison.
LOVE AND REASON
    See Lacy, Michael Rophino.
LOVE AND WAR IN YANKYLAND
    See Maclaren, Archibald. Coup-de-Main, The.
LOVE AT THE ACADEMY
    See Brougham, John. Musard Ball, The.
LOVE BY LANTERN-LIGHT
    See Barnett, Morris.
LOVE CHASE, THE
    See Knowles, James Sheridan.
LOVE-CREATED MADNESS
    See Herbert, Thomas. Hydrophobia.
LOVE FOR LOVE
    See Congreve, William.
LOVE GAME, A
    See Browne, Walter.
LOVE GIFT, THE
    See Stirling, Edward.
LOVE, HONOR, AND INTEREST
    See Galt, John.
LOVE IN A COTTAGE
    See Hood, Basil Charles Willett.
LOVE IN A DESERT
    See Hitchener, William Henry.
LOVE IN A FRAME
    See Reece, Robert. Paquita.
LOVE IN A GARDEN
    See Coyne, Joseph Stirling. Pets of the Parterre, The.
LOVE IN A MAZE
    See Boucicault, Dionysius Lardner.
LOVE IN A MIST
    See Cook, Keningale.
LOVE IN A VILLAGE
    See Bickerstaffe, Isaac.
LOVE IN ALL CORNERS
    See Buckstone, John Baldwin.
LOVE IN BLOTERLAND
    See de Caux, John William. Silver Ticket, The.
LOVE IN HUMBLE LIFE
    See Kerr, John. Michael and Christine.
    See Payne, John Howard.
LOVE IN LEAP YEAR
    See Hope, Anthony.

LOVE IN LIVERY
See Wooler, John Pratt.
LOVE IN THE DESERTS
See Brandon, Isaac. Kais.
LOVE IN THE HIGHLANDS
See Fawcett, John. Fairies' Revels, The.
LOVE IN THE NURSERY GROUNDS
See Moncrieff, William Thomas. Kiss and the Rose, The.
LOVE IN THE TROPICS
See Morton, John Maddison. Mother and Child Are Doing Well, The.
LOVE IS BLIND
See A'Beckett, Gilbert Abbott.
See Morris, Val.
LOVE IS THE BEST DOCTOR
See Van Laun, Henri (trans.).
LOVE KNOT, THE
See Coyne, Joseph Stirling.
LOVE LAUGHS AT LOCK-SMITHS (anon.)
Baltimore: Samuel Butler, 1804. Pp. [1]-68.
LOVE LAUGHS AT LOCKSMITHS
See Colman, George, jr.
LOVE, LAW, AND PHYSIC
See Kenney, James.
LOVE LEVELS ALL
See Taylor, Tom. Serf, The.
LOVE MAKES A MAN
See Cibber, Colley.
LOVE MAKES THE PAINTER
See Van Laun, Henri (trans.). Sicilian, The.
LOVE ME FOR MYSELF
See Linley, William. Ring, The.
LOVE OR DUTY—WHICH WINS?
See Dilley, Joseph J.
LOVE PILGRIM!
See Haines, John Thomas. Henrique.
LOVE, POETRY, PHILOSOPHY, AND GOUT
See Atherstone, Edwin.
LOVE, RIVALRY, AND REVENGE
See Hoskins, Francis Radcliffe. Blossom of Churnington Green, The.
LOVE SUIT, A
See Smythies, William Gordon.
LOVE TEST
See Haines, John Thomas. Amilie.
See Lisle, Walter.
LOVE TESTS, THE
See Amcotts, Vincent.
LOVE THE GREATEST ENCHANTMENT
See MacCarthy, Denis Florence (trans.).
LOVE, THE LUGGER, AND THE LACKEY
See Reece, Robert. Ruy Blas Righted.
LOVE TIFF, THE
See Van Laun, Henri (trans.).
LOVE-TRAP, THE
See Aird, David Mitchell.
LOVE WINS
See Clarke, Henry Saville.
LOVE'S ALARMS
See Rae, Charles Marsham.
LOVE'S COMEDY
See Herford, Charles Harold (trans.).
LOVE'S DISGUISES
See Knowles, James Sheridan. Woman's Wit.
See Paul, Howard. Mob Cap, The.
LOVE'S DREAM
See Beazley, Samuel, jr.
LOVE'S FETTERS
See Brooks, Charles William Shirley. Creole, The.
LOVE'S FRAILTIES
See Stafford, John Joseph.
LOVE'S LABOR LOST
See Drayton, Henri.
LOVE'S LABOUR'S LOST
See Shakespeare, William.

LOVE'S LABYRINTH
See Emden, William Samuel.
LOVE'S LIVERY
See Brougham, John.
LOVE'S MARTYR
See Buckingham, Leicester Silk.
See Reid, Mayne.
LOVE'S MARTYRDOM
See Saunders, John.
LOVE'S REVENGE
See Anderson, James Robertson. Cloud and Sunshine.
LOVE'S SACRIFICE
See Lovell, George William.
LOVE'S TELEGRAPH (anon.)
London: Thomas Hailes Lacy, n.d. Pp. [1]-48. [Lacy's Acting Edition].
LOVE'S TELEGRAPH (anon.)
[London: W. W. Barth (printer)], n.d. Pp. [5]-50. Title page and front matter lacking. Promptbook.
LOVE'S TRIALS
See Bennett, George John. Retribution.
LOVE'S TRIUMPH
See Planché, James Robinson.
LOVE'S VICTORY
See Hyde, George.
LOVED I NOT HONOUR MORE
See Besant, Walter.
LOVEDAY, W.
Castle of Morsino, The. Exeter: Trewman & Son (printer), 1812. Pp. [i]-[x], [1]-78.
LOVELL, GEORGE WILLIAM
Look before You Leap; or, Wooings and Weddings. London: National Acting Drama Office, n.d. Pp. [i]-[vi], [1]-83. Promptbook.
Love's Sacrifice; or, The Rival Merchants. London: Davidson, n.d. Pp. [1]-[10], [9]-72.
Love's Sacrifice; or, The Rival Merchants. London: John Cumberland, n.d. Pp. [1]-72. Cumberland's British Theatre, XLII. Filed under Cumberland, John. Cumberland's British Theatre, XLII.
Provost of Bruges, The. London: John Macrone, 1836. Pp. [i]-[x], [1]-98.
Wife's Secret, The. London & New York: Samuel French, n.d. Pp. [1]-62. Promptbook.
Wife's Secret, The. Pp.[i-iv], [1]-[22], [i], 1-[22], 1-19, 1-14, 1-16. Pagination by act. Manuscript promptbook.
LOVELL, MARIA ANNE LACY, MRS. GEORGE WILLIAM
Beginning and the End, The. London: G. H. Davidson, n.d. Pp. [i]-[viii], [9]-44. Cumberland's British Theatre, 393.
Ingomar, the Barbarian. New York: William Taylor, n.d. Pp. [i]-iv, [5]-65. Modern Standard Drama, 89.
LOVER, SAMUEL
Barney the Baron. London: John Dicks, n.d. Pp. [1]-8. Dicks' Standard Plays, 328.
Greek Boy, The. London: Sherwood, Gilbert, & Piper, n.d. Pp. [i]-vi, [7]-33. Webster's Acting National Drama, 99.
Hall Porter, The. London: Chapman & Hall, n.d. Pp. [i]-iv, [5]-31.
Happy Man, The. London: Chapman & Hall, n.d. Pp. [1]-20. Promptbook.
MacCarthy More; or, Possession Nine Points of the Law. London & New York: Samuel French, n.d. Pp. [1]-38. [French's Acting Edition (late Lacy's)].
Paddy Whack in Italia, Il. London: John Duncombe, n.d. Pp. [1]-30. Duncombe's Acting Edition of the British Theatre, 346.
Rory O'More. London: Chapman & Hall, n.d. Pp. [1]-51.
White Horse of the Peppers, The. New York: Berford, 1847. Pp. [1]-44. Minor Drama, 18.
White Horse of the Peppers, The. London: Chapman & Hall, n.d. Pp. [1]-35. Promptbook.
LOVER BY PROXY, A
See Boucicault, Dionysius Lardner.
LOVER HUSBAND, THE
See Ranger, Edward.

LOVER LENT
See Long, Charles. Ernestine and Georgette.
LOVER, THE LACKEY, AND THE LITTLE GLASS SLIPPER
See Byron, Henry James. Cinderella.
LOVERS' QUARRELS
See King, Thomas (arr.).
LOVERS' QUARRELS; OR, LIKE MASTER LIKE MAN
(anon. arr.).
By Vanbrugh, John. London: John Duncombe, n.d. Pp.
[1]-20. Imperfect copy. Duncombe's Edition.
LOVERS' QUARRELS; OR, LIKE MASTER LIKE MAN
(anon. arr.)
By Vanbrugh, John. London: J. Pattie, n.d. Pp. [1]-21.
LOVERS' RESOLUTIONS
See Cumberland, Richard.
LOVERS' VOWS
See Inchbald, Elizabeth Simpson, Mrs. Joseph.
LOVES OF AUGUSTUS PORTARLINGTON AND
CELESTINA BEVERLEY
See Dimond, William. Stage Struck.
LOVES OF LORD BATEMAN AND THE FAIR SOPHIA!,
THE
See Selby, Charles.
LOVES OF PRINCE BUTTERCUP AND THE PRINCESS
DAISY
See Burnand, Francis Cowley. White Fawn, The.
LOVING CUP, THE
See Halliday, Andrew.
LOVING WOMAN, THE
See Lemon, Mark.
LOWE, WILLIAM
**Edina and the White Hart of the Lothians; or, Prince Edwin
and the Fairies of the Thistle.** Edinburgh: J. Miller
(printer), 1869. Pp. [1]-27. Libretto.
LOWINA OF TOBOLSKI!
See Barrymore, William. Fatal Snow Storm, The.
LOWINA OF TOBOLSKOW
See Barrymore, William. Snow Storm, The.
LOWLAND LASS AND THE HIGHLAND LAD, THE
See Hetherington, William Maxwell.
LOWRY, JAMES M.
Little Red Riding Hood.
See Wade, William.
Peculiar Proposals. London & New York: Samuel French,
n.d. Pp. [1]-14. [Lacy's Acting Edition].
LOYAL PEASANTS, THE
See Straycock, J.
LOYALTY
See Charnock, John.
LOYALTY OR LOVE?
See Field, Michael (pseud.).
LUBLY ROSA, SAMBO DON'T COME
See Byron, Henry James. White Rose of the Plantation,
The.
LUCAS, JOHN TEMPLETON
Browne the Martyr. London: Thomas Hailes Lacy, n.d. Pp.
[1]-13. [Lacy's Acting Edition].
LUCAS, WILLIAM JAMES
Cross of St. John, The. In *Dramas, Serious and Serio-Comic,
for College, Camp, and Cabin,* London: Thomas Hailes
Lacy, n.d., pp. [1]-32, [1-2]. *Filed under* Lacy, Thomas
Hailes. Dramas for College, Camp, and Cabin.
Death Plank, The; or, The Dumb Sailor Boy! London:
Thomas Hailes Lacy, n.d. Pp. [1]-35.
Home of One's Own, A. London: Thomas Hailes Lacy, n.d.
Pp. [1]-20. [Lacy's Acting Edition].
Man with the Iron Mask, The. London: Thomas Hailes Lacy,
n.d. Pp. [1]-47. [Lacy's Acting Edition].
Traitor's Gate; or, The Tower of London in 1553. London:
Thomas Hailes Lacy, n.d. Pp. [1]-37. [Lacy's Acting
Edition].
White Farm, The; or, The Widow's Vision. By W. T. Lucas.
London: Thomas Hailes Lacy, n.d. Pp. [1]-30.

Who Stole the Clock? Music by Grisar, Albert. London &
New York: Samuel French, n.d. Pp. [1]-24. [Lacy's
Acting Edition]. Libretto.
Widow Bewitched!, The. London: John Duncombe, n.d. Pp.
[1]-26. Duncombe's Acting Edition of the British
Theatre.
LUCETTE, MADELEINE
See Ryley, Madeleine Lucette, Mrs. J. H.
LUCIA DI LAMMERMOOR (anon. trans.)
Music by Donizetti. London: Thomas Hailes Lacy, n.d.
Pp. [1]-24. Libretto.
LUCIA DI LAMMERMOOR
See Byron, Henry James.
See Kenney, Charles Lamb (trans.).
See Macfarren, Natalia (trans.). Bride of Lammermoor.
See Maggioni, Manfredo (trans.).
LUCIANUS REDIVIVUS
See Becket, Andrew.
LUCILLE
See Bernard, William Bayle.
LUCIUS CATILINE, THE ROMAN TRAITOR
See Milner, Henry M.
LUCK'S ALL
See Wigan, Alfred Sydney.
LUCKY ESCAPE!, A
See Cheltnam, Charles Smith.
LUCKY HIT, A
See Paul, Howard.
See Stirling, Edward.
LUCKY HORSE SHOE, THE
See Parry, Thomas.
LUCKY OR UNLUCKY DAYS
See Haines, John Thomas. Charming Polly, The.
LUCKY SIXPENCE, A
See Browne, E. J.
LUCKY STAR, THE
See Brookfield, Charles Hallam Elton.
LUCKY STARS
See Dance, Charles.
LUCRE-LAND
See Doyle, Thomas F.
LUCRETIA
See Dallas, Robert Charles.
LUCRETIA BORGIA
See Lucrezia Borgia (anon.).
See Weston, J. M.
LUCRETIA BORGIA, M.D.
See Byron, Henry James.
LUCRETIA BORGIA TRAVESTIE.
See Buckingham, Leicester Silk. Lucrezia Borgia at Home
and All Abroad.
LUCREZIA BORGIA (anon. trans.)
Also: Lucretia Borgia. Music by Donizetti. London: G.
H. Davidson, n.d. Pp. [1]-24. Davidson's Illustrated
Libretto Books. Libretto.
LUCREZIA BORGIA (anon. trans.)
Music by Donizetti. London & New York: Boosey, n.d.
Pp. [i-vi], 1-232. Royal Edition. Vocal score.
LUCREZIA BORGIA
See Maggioni, Manfredo (trans.).
See Young, William.
LUCREZIA BORGIA AT HOME AND ALL ABROAD
See Buckingham, Leicester Silk.
LUCY OF LAMMERMOOR
See Oxberry, William Henry.
LUDORFF, FRANZ
Hans Waldman. Munster, Westphalia: Regensberg'sche
Buchhandlung; London: Williams & Norgate, 1886. Pp.
[i-viii], [1]-239.
LUDOVICO SFORZA
See Cornwall, Barry.
LUGARTO THE MULATTO
See O'Bryan, Charles.
LUIGI (pseud. of ?)
Vamba. Geneva: R. Burkhardt, n.d. Pp. [1]-59.

LUIZ, NICOLA
 Dona Ignez de Castro.
  See Adamson, John (trans.).
LUKE SOMERTON
 See Soane, George.
LUKE THE LABOURER
 See Buckstone, John Baldwin.
LUMLEY, HENRY ROBERT
 See Lyulph, Henry R. (pseud.).
LUMLEY, RALPH R.
 Fancy Fair, A. London & New York: Samuel French, n.d.
  Pp. [1]-14. [Lacy's Acting Edition].
 Palmistry. London & New York: Samuel French, n.d. Pp.
  [1]-16. [Lacy's Acting Edition].
LUNATIC, THE
 See Leigh, Agnes.
LUNN, JOSEPH
 Belford Castle; or, The Scottish Gold Mine. London: William
  Barth, n.d. Pp. [1]-[10], [9]-42. Barth's (late Pattie's)
  Universal Stage or Theatrical Prompt Book, 40.
 Capers and Coronets. London: John Duncombe, n.d. Pp.
  [1]-26. Imperfect copy. Duncombe's Edition [New
  British Theatre, 136].
 False and Constant. London: Thomas Hailes Lacy, n.d. Pp.
  [1]-30. [Lacy's Acting Edition].
 Family Jars. New York: E. M. Murden, 1826. Pp. [1]-36.
 Fish out of Water. New York: Turner & Fisher, n.d. Pp. [i],
  [1]-38. Neal's Edition.
 French Polish. London: William Barth, n.d. Pp. [1]-23.
 Hide and Seek. London: Thomas Dolby, 1825. Pp. [1]-36.
  Dolby's British Theatre.
 Hide and Seek. London: Thomas Dolby, 1825. Pp. [1]-36.
  Dolby's British Theatre, XII. *Filed under* Cumberland,
  John. Cumberland's British Theatre, XII.
 Lofty Projects; or, Arts in an Attic. London: Thomas Dolby,
  1825. Pp. [1]-29. Dolby's British Theatre.
 Lofty Projects; or, Arts in an Attic. London: Thomas Dolby,
  1825. Pp. [1]-29. Dolby's British Theatre, X. *Filed under*
  Cumberland, John. Cumberland's British Theatre, X.
 Management; or, The Prompter Puzzled. London: John
  Cumberland, n.d. Pp. [1]-32. [Cumberland's British
  Theatre].
 Management; or, The Prompter Puzzled. London: John
  Cumberland, n.d. Pp. [1]-32. Cumberland's British
  Theatre, XXXVIII. *Filed under* Cumberland, John.
  Cumberland's British Theatre, XXXVIII.
 Rights of Woman, The; or, The Rose and the Thistle. London:
  William Barth, n.d. Pp. [1]-39. Barth's (late Pattie's)
  Universal Stage or Theatrical Prompt Book, 44.
 Roses and Thorns; or, Two Houses under One Roof. London:
  Thomas Dolby, 1825. Pp. [1]-57. Dolby's British
  Theatre, XII. *Filed under* Cumberland, John. Cumber-
  land's British Theatre, XII.
 Roses and Thorns; or, Two Houses under One Roof. London:
  John Cumberland, n.d. Pp. [1]-57.
 Sharp Practice; or, The Lear of Cripplegate. London: Thomas
  Hailes Lacy, n.d. Pp. [1]-21. [Lacy's Acting Edition].
 Shepherd of Derwent Vale, The; or, The Innocent Culprit.
  London: T. Dolby, 1825. Pp. [i-iv], [5]-39. Dolby's
  British Theatre, X. *Filed under* Cumberland, John.
  Cumberland's British Theatre, X.
 Shepherd of Derwent Vale, The; or, The Innocent Culprit.
  Music by Horn; Blewitt. London: T. Dolby, n.d. Pp.
  [1]-55.
 Three Deep; or, All on the Wing. Music by Watson. London:
  Hunt & Clarke, 1826. Pp. [1]-35. British Theatre.
 White Lies; or, The Major and the Minor. London: John
  Cumberland, 1826. Pp. [1]-50.
LURALIE, THE WATER SPRITE
 See Wills, William Gorman.
LURETTE
 See Leigh, Henry Sambrooke.
LURIA
 See Browning, Robert.

LURLINE
 See Amcotts, Vincent.
 See Burrows, J. G.
 See Dalrymple, J. S.
 See Dalrymple, J. S. Naiad Queen, The.
 See Fitzball, Edward.
LURLINE THE NYMPH OF THE RHINE
 See Green, Frank William.
LYIEUSHEE LOVEL
 See Campbell, Andrew Leonard Voullaire.
LYING IN ORDINARY
 See Peake, Richard Brinsley.
LYING VALET, THE
 See Garrick, David.
LYNCH, HANNAH (trans.)
 Folly or Saintliness. By Echegaray, José. In *Great Galeoto . . .*
  , London: John Lane; Boston: Lamson Wolffe, 1895, pp.
  [99]-[196]. *Filed under* Great Galeoto.
 Great Galeoto, The. By Echegaray, José. In *Great Galeoto . . .*
  , London: John Lane; Boston: Lamson Wolffe, 1895, pp.
  [i]-[xxxviii], [1]-97.
LYNCH, THOMAS J.
 Rose of Ettrick Vale, The; or, The Bridal of the Borders.
  Glasgow: Dugald Moore; James Duncan, 1834. Pp. [i],
  [1]-70.
LYNDSAY, DAVID
 Death of Cain, The. In *Dramas of the Ancient World,*
  Edinburgh: William Blackwood, 1822, pp. [209]-256.
  Filed under Dramas of the Ancient World.
 Deluge, The. In *Dramas of the Ancient World,* Edinburgh:
  William Blackwood, 1822, pp. [i]-[viii], [1]-64. *Filed under*
  Dramas of the Ancient World.
 Destiny of Cain, The. In *Dramas of the Ancient World,*
  Edinburgh: William Blackwood, 1822, pp. [177]-208.
  Filed under Dramas of the Ancient World.
 Nereid's Love, The. In *Dramas of the Ancient World,*
  Edinburgh: William Blackwood, 1822, pp. [257]-278.
  Filed under Dramas of the Ancient World.
 Plague of Darkness, The. In *Dramas of the Ancient World,*
  Edinburgh: William Blackwood, 1822, pp. [65]-90. *Filed
  under* Dramas of the Ancient World.
 Rizpah. In *Dramas of the Ancient World,* Edinburgh: William
  Blackwood, 1822, pp. [101]-[124]. *Filed under* Dramas of
  the Ancient World.
 Sardanapalus. In *Dramas of the Ancient World,* Edinburgh:
  William Blackwood, 1822, pp. [125]-176. *Filed under*
  Dramas of the Ancient World.
LYNE, S. M.
 Rose of Sleat, The; or, The Days of Prince Charlie. London:
  R. & T. Washbourne, 1900. Pp. [1]-31.
LYRE AND LANCET
 See Anstey, F.
LYRICAL LOVER, A
 See Clarke, Henry Saville.
LYSAGHT, SIDNEY ROYSE
 Modern Ideal, A. London: Kegan Paul, Trench, 1886. Pp.
  [i]-[x], [1]-202.
LYSANDER AND IONE
 See Cornwall, Barry.
LYSTE, HENRY P.
 Only a Penny-a-Liner! London & New York: Samuel
  French, n.d. Pp. [1]-24. [Lacy's Acting Edition].
LYSTER, FREDERIC
 Fourchamboult and Compy., (Limited). San Francisco:
  n.pub., 1878. Pp. [i-iv], [1]-35.
 Uncle Celestin. Music by Audran, Edmond. New York:
  William A. Pond, c.1892. Pp. [1]-32. Vocal score.
LYSTER, FREDERIC (trans.)
 Chivalry in Humble Life. *Also: Cavalleria Rusticana.* Music
  by Mascagni. New York: F. Rullman, Theatre Ticket
  Office, n.d. Pp. [1]-20. Vocal score and libretto.
 Cid, The. Music by Massenet. New York: F. Rullman,
  Theatre Ticket Office, c.1895. Pp. [1]-27. Libretto.
 Friend Fritz. By Erckmann-Chatrian. New York: F. Rull-
  man, Theatre Ticket Office, n.d. Pp. [1]-43.

Jeanne d'Arc. By Barbier, P. J. New York: F. Rullman, Theatre Ticket Office, c.1891. Pp. [1]-33. Libretto.

Lady of Challant, The. *Also:* La Dame de Challant. By Giacosa, Giuseppe. New York: F. Rullman, Theatre Ticket Office, c.1891. Pp. [1]-27. Bernhardt Edition. Libretto.

Little Bride, The. *Also:* La Petite Mariée. Music by Lecocq, Charles. Melbourne: Azzoppardi, Hildreth (printer), n.d. Pp. [1]-50. Libretto.

Oedipus the King. By La Croix, Jules. New York: F. Rullman, Theatre Ticket Office, c.1894. Pp. [1]-37. Mounet-Sulley Edition. Promptbook.

Our Boon Companions. *Also:* Nos Intimes. By Sardou, Victorien. New York: F. Rullman, Theatre Ticket Office, n.d. Pp. [1]-77. Coquelin-Hading Edition.

Samson and Dalilah. Music by Saint-Saens, Camille. New York: F. Rullman, Theatre Ticket Office, c.1893. Pp. [1]-21. Libretto.

LYTTON, EDWARD GEORGE EARLE
    See Bulwer (later Bulwer-Lytton), Edward George Earle Lytton, Lord Lytton.

LYTTON, LORD
    See Bulwer (later Bulwer-Lytton), Edward George Earle Lytton, Lord Lytton.

LYTTON, ROBERT
    See Meredith, Owen (pseud.).

LYULPH, HENRY R. (pseud. of Lumley, Henry Robert)
    General Elections, The. London: W. Rayner, n.d. Pp. [1-56].

M.P.
    See Moore, Thomas.
    See Robertson, Thomas William.

M.P. FOR PUDDLEPOOL
    See Summers, Knight.

MA MIE ROSETTE
    See Dance, George.

MA PART
    See Horncastle, James Henry.

MABEL'S CURSE!
    See Hall, Anna Maria Fielding, Mrs. Samuel Carter.

MABEL'S HOLY DAY
    See Sturgis, Julian Russell.

MACAIRE
    See Henley, William Ernest.

MCALLISTER MCVITTY MCNAB, THE
    See Byron, Henry James.

MCARDLE, JOHN FRANCIS
    Jack and the Beanstalk. Liverpool: Daily Post Steam Printing Works, 1874. Pp. [1]-60. Libretto.
    Robinson Crusoe; or, Friday and His Funny Family. Written with Green, Frank William. Liverpool: Alexandra Theatre, n.d. Pp. [3]-42. Title page lacking. Libretto.
    Sinbad the Sailor. Liverpool: Daily Post Steam Printing Works, 1875. Pp. [1]-56. Libretto.
    Sinbad the Sailor. Written with Byam, Martin; Melville, A. Birmingham: J. G. Hammond (printer), n.d. Pp. [i-vi], [1]-38. Libretto.
    Sleeping Beauty. Liverpool: Daily Post Steam Printing Works, 1876. Pp. [3]-56. Libretto.

MACARTHY, EUGENE
    Charles O'Malley, the Irish Dragoon. London: John Dicks, n.d. Pp. [1]-20. Dicks' Standard Plays, 486.

MACAULEY, ELIZABETH WRIGHT
    Marmion. Cork: John Connor (printer), 1811. Pp. [i]-[xii], [1]-45. 2nd ed.

MACBETH (anon. trans.)
    By Heigel, Caesar Max. Music by Chelard, Andr. Hypolite. London: G. Davidson (printer), 1832. Pp. [1]-89. Libretto.

MACBETH
    See Creswick, William (arr.).
    See Cross, James C. (arr.).
    See Forbes-Robertson, Johnston (arr.).
    See Irving, Henry (arr.).
    See Kean, Charles John (arr.).
    See Rayne, Lin (arr.).

    See Salvini, Tommaso (arr.).
    See Shakespeare, William.

MACBETH, SOMEWHAT REMOVED FROM THE TEXT OF SHAKESPEARE
    See Talfourd, Francis.
    See Talfourd, Francis. Macbeth Travestie.

MACBETH TRAVESTIE (anon.)
    N.p.: n.pub., n.d. Pp. [65]-164. Title page lacking.

MACBETH TRAVESTIE
    See Talfourd, Francis.
    See Talfourd, Francis. Macbeth, Somewhat Removed from the Text of Shakespeare.

MACCARTHY, DENIS FLORENCE (trans.)
    Belshazzar's Feast. By Calderon. In *Mysteries of Corpus Christi*, Dublin: James Duffy, 1867, pp. [i]-viii, [1]-208. *Filed under* Mysteries of Corpus Christi.
    Devotion of the Cross, The. By Calderon. In *Love the Greatest Enchantment . . .*, London: Longman, Green, Longman, & Roberts, 1861, pp. [207]-316. *Filed under* Love the Greatest Enchantment.
    Divine Philothea, The. By Calderon. In *Mysteries of Corpus Christi*, Dublin: James Duffy, 1867, pp. [209]-352. *Filed under* Mysteries of Corpus Christi.
    Justina. By J. H. (pseud.). By Calderon. London: James Burns, 1848. Pp. [i]-iv, [1]-138.
    Life Is a Dream. By Calderon. In *Calderon's Dramas*, London: Henry S. King, 1873, pp. [i]-xvi, [1]-116.
    Life Is a Dream. By Calderon. In *Calderon's Dramas*, London: Kegan Paul, Trench, 1887, pp. [i]-xvi, [1]-116. *Filed under* Calderon's Dramas.
    Love the Greatest Enchantment. By Calderon. In *Love the Greatest Enchantment . . .*, London: Longman, Green, Longman, & Roberts, 1861, pp. [i]-xiv, [1]-142.
    Purgatory of St. Patrick, The. By Calderon. In *Calderon's Dramas*, London: Henry S. King, 1873, pp. [235]-377.
    Purgatory of St. Patrick, The. By Calderon. In *Calderon's Dramas*, London: Kegan Paul, Trench, 1887, pp. [235]-377. *Filed under* Calderon's Dramas.
    Sorceries of Sin, The. By Calderon. In *Love the Greatest Enchantment . . .*, London: Longman, Green, Longman, & Roberts, 1861, pp. [143]-205. *Filed under* Love the Greatest Enchantment.
    Two Lovers of Heaven, The: Chrysanthus and Daria. By Calderon. Dublin: John F. Fowler, 1870. Pp. [1-3], [i]-iv, 5-60.
    Wonder-Working Magician, The. By Calderon. In *Calderon's Dramas*, London: Henry S. King, 1873, pp. [117]-234.
    Wonder-Working Magician, The. By Calderon. In *Calderon's Dramas*, London: Kegan Paul, Trench, 1887, pp. [117]-234. *Filed under* Calderon's Dramas.

MACCARTHY MORE
    See Lover, Samuel.

MACDONALD, GEORGE
    Within and Without. London: Longman, Brown, Green, Longmans, & Roberts, 1857. Pp. [i-iv], [1]-193. 2nd ed.
    Within and Without. New York: Scribner, Armstrong, 1872. Pp. [1]-219.

MACFARREN, GEORGE
    Auld Robin Gray. Music by Blewitt. London: S. G. Fairbrother, 1828. Pp. [1]-43.
    Devil's Opera, The. Music by Macfarren, G. Alexander. London: Chapman & Hall, n.d. Pp. [1]-32. [Acting National Drama].
    Family Masquerading.
        See March of Intellect, The.
    Gil Blas; or, The Boy of Santillane. London: John Cumberland, n.d. Pp. [1]-50. Cumberland's British Theatre, XXXVI. *Filed under* Cumberland, John. Cumberland's British Theatre, XXXVI.
    Gil Blas; or, The Boy of Santillane. *Also:* Gil Blas and the Robbers of Asturia. London: John Cumberland, n.d. Pp. [1]-50. [Cumberland's British Theatre].
    Gil Blas and the Robbers of Asturia.
        See Gil Blas.

Guy Faux; or, The Gunpowder Treason. London: John Cumberland & Son, n.d. Pp. [1]-50. Cumberland's Minor Theatre, 36.

Guy Faux; or, The Gunpowder Treason. London: John Cumberland, n.d. Pp. [1]-50. Cumberland's Minor Theatre, IV. *Filed under* Cumberland, John. Cumberland's Minor Theatre, IV.

Latin, Love, and War; or, Blockheads Indeed! London: John Duncombe, n.d. Pp. [1]-25. Duncombe's Acting Edition of the British Theatre, 288.

Lestocq; or, The Fete at the Hermitage. Music by Auber. London: John Cumberland, n.d. Pp. [1]-68. [Cumberland's British Theatre, 253]. Libretto.

Lestocq; or, The Fete at the Hermitage. Music by Auber. London: John Cumberland, n.d. Pp. [1]-68. Cumberland's British Theatre, XXXIII. *Filed under* Cumberland, John. Cumberland's British Theatre, XXXIII.

Malvina. Music by Cooke, Thomas. London: Jackson & Macfarren, n.d. Pp. [i]-[x], [1]-74. Libretto.

Malvina. Music by Cooke, T. London: John Cumberland, n.d. Pp. [1]-52. Cumberland's British Theatre, XXXVI. *Filed under* Cumberland, John. Cumberland's British Theatre, XXXVI.

March of Intellect, The. London: John Cumberland, n.d. Pp. [1]-31. Cumberland's Minor Theatre, XII. *Filed under* Cumberland, John. Cumberland's Minor Theatre, XII.

March of Intellect, The. *Also:* Family Masquerading. London: John Cumberland, n.d. Pp. [1]-31. [Cumberland's Minor Theatre].

My Old Woman. Music by Rodwell, G. H. London: John Cumberland, n.d. Pp. [1]-47. [Cumberland's Minor Theatre, 8].

My Old Woman. Music by Rodwell, G. H. London: John Cumberland, n.d. Pp. [1]-47. Cumberland's Minor Theatre, I. *Filed under* Cumberland, John. Cumberland's Minor Theatre, I.

Oberon; or, The Charmed Horn Music by Cooke, T. London: John Cumberland, 1826. Pp. [1]-36. Cumberland's British Theatre, XIII. *Filed under* Cumberland, John. Cumberland's British Theatre, XIII.

Oberon; or, The Charmed Horn. New York: Edward M. Murden, 1826. Pp. [1]-58.

Talisman, The; or, The Genii of the Elements. Music by Blewitt. London: S. G. Fairbrother, 1828. Pp. [1]-48. Libretto.

Tom and Jerry in France; or, Vive la Bagatelle. *Also:* Tommy and Jerry t'Other Side the Water. London: J. Lowndes, n.d. Pp. [i], [1]-[46].

Tommy and Jerry t'Other Side of the Water. *See* Tom and Jerry in France.

Winning a Husband; or, Seven's the Main. London: John Cumberland, n.d. Pp. [1]-34. Cumberland's Minor Theatre, V. *Filed under* Cumberland, John. Cumberland's Minor Theatre, V.

Winning a Husband; or, Seven's the Main. Music by Hughes, T. London: J. Barker, 1819. Pp. [1]-36.

MACFARREN, NATALIA (trans.)

Barber of Seville, The. *Also:* Il Barbiere di Siviglia. Music by Rossini. New York: G. Schirmer, n.d. Pp. [i]-[xvi], [1]-328. Vocal score.

Bride of Lammermoor. *Also:* Lucia di Lammermoor. Music by Donizetti. New York: G. Schirmer, c.1898. Pp. [i]-[viii], [1]-240. G. Schirmer's Collection of Operas. Vocal score.

Dumb Girl of Portici, The. *Also:* Masaniello. Music by Auber. London: Novello, Ewer; Simpkin, Marshall, n.d. Pp. [i-iv], [1]-333. Novello's Original Octavo Edition. Vocal score.

Lohengrin. Music by Wagner. London: Novello, Ewer, n.d. Pp. [i-iv], [1]-[267]. Novello's Original Octavo Edition. Vocal score.

Tannhäuser and the Tournament of Song at Wartburg. Music by Wagner. London: Novello, Ewer; Simpkin, Marshall, n.d. Pp. [i-iv], [1]-[273]. Novello's Original Octavo Edition. Vocal score.

William Tell. *Also:* Guillaume Tell. Music by Rossini. London: Novello, Ewer, n.d. Pp. [i-iv], [1]-[421]. Novello's Original Octavo Edition. Vocal score.

MACGILCHRIST, JOHN

Chatelard. Edinburgh: Adam & Charles Black, 1852. Pp. [i-vi], [1]-56.

MCGROMAGILL, OSBURN BLACKBOEHM

Babes in the Wood, The; or, Harlequin Robin Hood and His Merry Men. Edinburgh: n.pub., 1894. Pp. [1]-54. Libretto.

MACHALE, LUKE

High Street Mystery, The. Music by Batchelder, J. Manchester: Abel Heywood & Son; London: F. Pitman; Henry Vickers; H. Darbyshire, n.d. Pp. [i-ii], [1]-40. Abel Heywood's Musical Dramas, Farces, and Dialogues for Amateurs. Libretto.

John and Jeannette. Music by Batchelder, J. Manchester: Able Heywood & Son; London: F. Pitman; Henry Vickers, n.d. Pp. [i-ii], [1]-36. Abel Heywood's Musical Dramas, Farces, and Dialogues for Amateurs. Libretto.

MCK., F.

He Would Be a Soldier; or, The Madcap Student. Dublin: M. H. Gill & Son, 1878. Pp. [1]-30. *Filed under* He Would Be a Soldier (anon.).

MACKAY, WILLIAM

Iron Latch Farm. N.p.: n. pub., n.d. Pp. [1]-56. Title page lacking.

MCKENZIE, WILLIAM PATRICK

Yielding of Pilate, The. In *Songs of the Human,* Toronto: Hart, 1892, pp. [i], [113]-132.

MACKERSY, W. A.

Rats. London: Samuel French; New York: T. Henry French, n.d. Pp. [1]-11. [Lacy's Acting Edition].

MACKLIN, ARTHUR

My Lady Help. London & New York: Samuel French, n.d. Pp. [1]-16. [Lacy's Acting Edition].

MACKLIN, CHARLES

Love a la Mode. In *New English Drama,* ed. W. Oxberry, 22 vols., London: W. Simpkin & R. Marshall; C. Chapple, 1825, XXI, [1-2], [i]-[x], [1]-30. *Filed under* Oxberry, William Henry. New English Drama, XXI.

Love a-la-Mode. In *British Drama,* 12 vols., London: John Dicks, 1871, VIII, [180]-192.

Man of the World, The. London: Whittingham & Arliss, 1814. Pp. [1]-68. London Theatre, V. *Filed under* Dibdin, Thomas John, ed. London Theatre, V.

Man of the World, The. In *New English Drama,* ed. W. Oxberry, 22 vols., London: W. Simpkin & R. Marshall; C. Chapple, 1822, XVI, [i]-[xiv], [15]-80. *Filed under* Oxberry, William Henry. New English Drama, XVI.

Man of the World, The. London: John Cumberland, 1826. Pp. [i]-[vi], [7]-[64]. Cumberland's British Theatre, V. *Filed under* Cumberland, John. Cumberland's British Theatre, V.

Man of the World, The. In *British Drama,* 12 vols., London: John Dicks, 1864, I, [30]-47.

MACLAREN, ARCHIBALD

British Carpenter, The; or, The Irishman in France. London: A. Macpherson (printer) (priv.), 1808. Pp. [1]-24.

Britons to Arms!; or, The Consul in England. London: A. Macpherson (printer) (priv.), 1803. Pp. [1]-24.

Chance of War, The; or, The Villain Reclaimed. London: A. Macpherson (printer) (priv.), 1801. Pp. [i-ii], [1]-24.

Coup-de-Main, The; or, Love and War in Yankyland. London: A. Macpherson (printer) (priv.), 1816. Pp. [1]-24.

Days We Live In, The; or, A Tale of Eighteen Hundred and Five. London: A. Macpherson (printer) (priv.), 1805. Pp. [1]-24.

Duelists, The. In *Elopement . . . ,* London: A. Macpherson (printer) (priv.), 1811, pp. [14]-24. *Filed under* Elopement.

Eccentricity; or, Every One Has a Whim. London: A. Macpherson (printer) (priv.), n.d. Pp. [1]-12.

Elopement, The; or, A Caution to Young Ladies. London: A. Macpherson (printer) (priv.), 1811. Pp. [1]-13.

Empress and No Empress; or, Mr. Bonny's Wedding. London: A. Macpherson (printer) (priv.), 1810. Pp. [1]-24.

Fashion; or, The World As It Goes. London: A. Macpherson (printer) (priv.), 1802. Pp. [1]-24.

First of April, The; or, The Fool's Errand. London: A. Macpherson (printer) (priv.), 1802. Pp. [1]-24.

Forget and Forgive; or, All Made Up Again. London: A. Macpherson (printer) (priv.), 1814. Pp. [1]-22.

Gentle Shepherd, The. In *Spite and Malice . . .* , London: A. Macpherson (printer) (priv.), 1811, pp. [6]-24.

Good News! Good News!; or, The Case is Altered. London: A. Macpherson (printer) (priv.), 1814. Pp. [1]-21.

Imitation Tea; or, Death in Disguise. In *Oliver Cromwell . . .* , London: A. Macpherson (printer) (priv.), 1818, pp. 20-24. *Filed under* Oliver Cromwell.

Irish Girl, The; or, Cossack and No Cossack. London: A. Macpherson (printer) (priv.), 1813. Pp. [1]-24.

Maid of Lorn, The; or, The Castle of Dunstaffnage. London: A. Macpherson (printer) (priv.), 1815. Pp. [1]-24.

Man in the Moon, The; or, Tumble Down Nap. London: A. Macpherson (printer) (priv.), 1813. Pp. [1]-24.

Man Trap, The; or, A Scene in Germany. London: A. Macpherson (printer) (priv.), 1816. Pp. [1]-24.

Mr. Boney's Reception in Paris. In *Good News! Good News! . . .* , London: A. Macpherson (printer) (priv.), 1814, pp. 22-24. *Filed under* Good News! Good News!

Nappy's Reception in Elba. In *Forget and Forgive . . .* , London: A. Macpherson (printer) (priv.), 1814, pp. 22-24. *Filed under* Forget and Forgive.

Oliver Cromwell; or, The Scotch Regalia. London: A. Macpherson (printer) (priv.), 1818. Pp. [1]-19.

Paddy Bull; or, A Cure for the Gout. London: A. Macpherson (printer) (priv.), 1811. Pp. [1]-24.

Prisoner of War, The; or, A Most Excellent Story. London: A. Macpherson (printer) (priv.), 1813. Pp. [1]-24.

Private Theatre, The; or, The Highland Funeral. London: A. Macpherson (printer) (priv.), 1809. Pp. [i]-iv, [5]-24.

Slaver, The. In *Wife to Be Sold . . .* , London: A. Macpherson (printer) (priv.), 1807, pp. [18]-24. *Filed under* Wife to be Sold.

Spanish Heroine, The; or, The Female Patriots. London: A. Macpherson (printer) (priv.), 1808. Pp. [1]-24.

Spite and Malice; or, A Laughable Accident. London: A. Macpherson (printer) (priv.), 1811. Pp. [1]-5.

Swindlers, The; or, Diamond Cut Diamond. London: A. Macpherson (printer) (priv.), 1812. Pp. [1]-21.

Touch at the Times, A; or, An Attempt to Please. London: A. Macpherson (printer) (priv.), 1804. Pp. [1]-24.

Ups and Downs of Life, The; or, The Fortunate Irishman. London: A. Macpherson (printer) (priv.), 1824. Pp. [1]-12.

Wallace the Brave; or, The Siege of Perth. London: A. Macpherson (printer) (priv.), 1819. Pp. [1]-24.

Ways of London, The; or, Honesty the Best Policy. London: A. Macpherson (printer) (priv.), 1812. Pp. [1]-23.

Whimsicality; or, Great News from France. London: A. Macpherson (printer) (priv.), 1810. Pp. [1]-24.

Wife to Be Sold, A; or, Who Bids Most? London: A. Macpherson (printer) (priv.), 1807. Pp. [1]-17.

MACLEAN, MRS. GEORGE
 See Landon, Letitia Elizabeth.

MACLEAN, WILLIAM
 Brennus; or, The Downfall of Tyranny. Glasgow: Thomas Murray & Sons, 1871. Pp. [i-ii], [1]-88.

 Brennus. N.p.: n.pub., n.d. Pp. [1]-54. *Filed under* Brennus (anon.).

MACLEOD, FIONA
 See Sharp, William.

MACMILLAN, A.
 Teetotalism Triumphant. Annan: William Cuthbertson (printer), 1839. Pp. [i-vi], [1]-59.

 Teetotalism Triumphant. Leeds: John Kershaw, n.d. Pp. [1]-60. 3rd ed., rev.

MCNAB, JAMES
 London Bridge, 150 Years Ago; or, The Old Mint. London & New York: Samuel French, n.d. Pp. [1]-60.

MACNALLY, LEONARD
 Fashionable Levities. In *Modern Theatre*, ed. Mrs. Inchbald, 10 vols., London: Longman, Hurst, Rees, Orme, & Brown, 1811, X, [i], [1]-80.

MCNEILL, A. D.
 Babes in the Wood and the Bold Robin Hood, The; or, The Naughty Cock Sparrow Who Killed Poor Cock Robin. Edinburgh: James Brydone (printer), 1876. Pp. [i-ii], [1]-64.

MAÇON, LE
 See Wylde, Mrs. Henry (trans.).

MACREADY, WILLIAM
 Bank Note, The; or, Lessons for Ladies. In *Modern Theatre*, ed. Mrs. Inchbald, 10 vols., London: Longman, Hurst, Rees, Orme, & Brown, 1811, IX, [i-ii], [1]-79.

 Irishman in London, The. London: John Cumberland, n.d. Pp. [i], [1]-31. Cumberland's British Theatre, XXII. *Filed under* Cumberland, John. Cumberland's British Theatre, XXII.

 Village Lawyer, The. London: John Cumberland, 1826. Pp. [1]-34. Cumberland's British Theatre, XIV. *Filed under* Cumberland, John. Cumberland's British Theatre, XIV.

 Village Lawyer, The. New York: Samuel French, n.d. Pp. [1]-16. Minor Drama, 158. *Filed under* Village Lawyer (anon.).

MACREADY, WILLIAM CHARLES (arr.)
 As You Like It. By Shakespere, William. London: Thomas Hailes Lacy, n.d. Pp. [i]-vi, [1]-64. [Lacy's Acting Edition].

MAD AS A HATTER
 See Marshall, Francis Albert.

MADAME BERLIOT'S BALL
 See Burnand, Francis Cowley.

MADAME FAVART
 See Farnie, Henry Brougham.

MADCAP STUDENT
 See McK., F. He Would Be a Soldier.

MADDALEN
 See Galt, John.

MADDOX, FREDERICK MORE
 Frederick the Great. London: John Cumberland, n.d. Pp. [1]-36. Cumberland's Minor Theatre, XIII. *Filed under* Cumberland, John. Cumberland's Minor Theatre, XIII.

 Frederick the Great. London: John Cumberland, n.d. Pp. [1]-36. Cumberland's Minor Theatre, 115.

 Violet, The. London: William W. Barth, n.d. Pp. [1]-39. Barth's Universal Stage or Theatrical Prompt Book, 101. Promptbook.

 Violet, The. London: Thomas Hailes Lacy, n.d. Pp. [1]-43. Lacy's Acting Edition.

MADDOX, JOHN MEDEX
 A. S. S. London: Thomas Hailes Lacy, n.d. Pp. [1]-20. Lacy's Acting Edition.

 Chesterfield Thinskin. London: Thomas Hailes Lacy, n.d. Pp. [1]-24. Lacy's Acting Edition.

 Curious Case, A.
  See Reynoldson, Thomas Herbert.

 Fast Train! High Pressure! Express!, A Short Trip. London: Thomas Hailes Lacy, n.d. Pp. [1]-20. Lacy's Acting Edition.

 First Night, The. London: Thomas Hailes Lacy, n.d. Pp. [1]-30. Lacy's Acting Edition.

 First Night, The; or, A Peep Behind the Scenes. New York: O. A. Roorbach, jr, n.d. Pp. [1]-28. Acting Drama, 1.

 Frederick the Great.
  See King and Deserter, The.

 Infanticide; or, The Bohemian Mother. London: John Duncombe, n.d. Pp. [1]-28. [Duncombe's Edition].

 King and Deserter, The. *Also:* Frederick the Great; or, The King and Deserter. New York: Samuel French, n.d. Pp. [1]-22.

MADELEINE (anon.)
[London]: Mrs. Marshall's Typewriting Office, 1895. Pp. [i], [1]-47, [i], [1]-22, [i], [1]-25, [i], [1]-[18]. Pagination by act. Typescript.

MADELINE
See Bedingfield, Richard.

MADEMOISELLE DE BELLE ISLE
See Kemble, Frances Anne (Fanny) (trans.).

MADEMOISELLE SQUALLINO
See Featherstone, J. L.

MADISON AGONISTES; OR, THE AGONIES OF MOTHER GOOSE (anon.)
London: John Cawthorn, 1814. Pp. [1]-103.

MADONNA PIA
See Martin, Theodore, Sir.

MAETERLINCK, MAURICE
Aglavaine and Selysette.
See Sutro, Alfred (trans.).
Alladine and Palomides.
See Sutro, Alfred (trans.).
Death of Tintagiles, The.
See Sutro, Alfred (trans.).
Interior.
See Archer, William (trans.).

MAEVE
See Martyn, Edward.

MAGGIE'S SITUATION
See Morton, John Maddison.

MAGGIONI, MANFREDO (trans.)
Anna Bolena (attrib. to Maggioni). Music by Donizetti. New York: Snowden (printer), 1850. Pp. [1]-75. Libretto.
Barber of Seville.
See Barbieri di Siviglia, Il.
Barbiere di Siviglia, Il. *Also:* The Barber of Seville. Music by Rossini. London: T. Brettell, 1849. Pp. [1]-81. Libretto.
Barbiere di Siviglia, Il. *Also:* The Barber of Seville. Music by Rossini. London: J. Miles (printer), n.d. Pp. [1]-72. Libretto.
Cenerentola. Music by Rossini. [London]: T. Brettell (printer), n.d. Pp. [1]-84. Libretto.
Don Giovanni, Il. Music by Mozart. London: J. Miles (printer), n.d. Pp. [1]-88. Libretto.
Don Pasquale. Music by Donizetti. London: J. Miles (printer), n.d. Pp. [1]-61. Libretto.
Donna del Lago, La. Music by Rossini. London: Covent Garden, n.d. Pp. [1]-59. Libretto.
Elisir d'Amore, L'. Music by Donizetti. London: J. Miles (printer), n.d. Pp. [1]-59. Libretto.
Étoile du Nord, L'.
See Stella del Nord, La.
Favorita, La. Music by Donizetti. London: J. Miles (printer), n.d. Pp. [1]-63. Libretto.
Fidelio. Music by Beethoven. London: T. Brettell, 1851. Pp. [1]-57. Libretto.
Figlia del Reggimento, La. Music by Donizetti. London: J. Miles (printer), n.d. Pp. [i]-v, 6-55. Libretto.
Fra Diavolo. Music by Auber. London: J. Miles (printer), n.d. Pp. [5]-96. Libretto.
Gazza Ladra, La. Music by Rossini. London: Covent Garden, 1847. Pp. [1]-103. Libretto.
Guglielmo Tell. *Also:* William Tell. Music by Rossini. London: T. Brettell, n.d. Pp. [i]-[vii], [4]-81. Libretto.
Guglielmo Tell. *Also:* William Tell. Music by Rossini. London: J. Miles (printer), n.d. Pp. [i]-[v], [6]-64. Libretto.
Huguenots, Les.
See Ugonotti, Gli.
Italiana in Algeri, L'. Music by Rossini. London: Covent Garden, 1847. Pp. [i-iii], [2]-55. Libretto.
Lucia di Lammermoor. Music by Donizetti. London: J. Miles (printer), n.d. Pp. [1]-50. Libretto.
Lucrezia Borgia. Music by Donizetti. London: T. Brettell (printer), 1848. Pp. [i-iii], [2]-63. Libretto.
Maria di Rohan. Music by Donizetti. New York: Snowden (printer), 1849. Pp. [1]-59. Libretto.

Masaniello (attrib. to Maggioni). Music by Auber. London: T. Brettell (printer), n.d. Pp. [i]-[vii], [8]-69. Libretto.
Nozze di Figaro, Le. Music by Mozart. London: T. Brettell (printer), 1848. Pp. [1]-112. Libretto.
Orfeo e Euridice. Music by Gluck. New York: F. Rullman, n.d. Pp. [1]-20. Libretto.
Prophète, Le. Music by Meyerbeer, G. London: T. Brettell (printer), n.d. Pp. [1]-100. Libretto.
Roberto il Diavolo. Music by Meyerbeer. London: T. Brettell (printer), n.d. Pp. [1]-87. Libretto.
Semiramide. Music by Rossini. London: Covent Garden, 1847. Pp. [i-iii], [2]-69. Libretto.
Stella del Nord, La. *Also:* L'Étoile du Nord. Music by Meyerbeer, G. London: T. Brettell (printer), n.d. Pp. [1]-119. Libretto.
Tancredi, Il. Music by Rossini. London: T. Brettell (printer), 1848. Pp. [1]-67. Libretto.
Trovatore, Il. Music by Verdi. London: T. Brettell (printer), n.d. Pp. [1]-71. Libretto.
Ugonotti, Gli. *Also:* Les Huguenots. Music by Meyerbeer, G. London: T. Brettell (printer), n.d. Pp. [i]-[v], [6]-107. Libretto.
William Tell.
See Guglielmo Tell.
Zampa. Music by Herold. London: T. Brettell (printer), n.d. Pp. [1]-76. Libretto.

MAGIC AND MAZOURKAPHOBIA
See Selby, Charles. Taming a Tartar.

MAGIC BANJO AND THE MYSTIC RAVEN!
See Lee, Nelson, jr. Harlequin Alfred the Great.

MAGIC FLUTE
See Flauto Magico, Il (anon.).
See Walter, William Joseph (trans.).

MAGIC HORN, THE
See Dance, Charles.

MAGIC LAMP OF HUGO VAMP
See O'Neill, John Robert. Aladdin.

MAGIC LYRE
See Burnand, Francis Cowley. Orpheus.

MAGIC MIRROR, THE
See A'Beckett, Gilbert Abbott.

MAGIC OPAL, THE
See Law, Arthur.

MAGIC ROSE!
See Selby, Charles. Guardian Sylph!, The.

MAGIC THIMBLE
See Paulton, Harry. Cymbia.

MAGIC TOYS, THE
See Oxenford, John.

MAGIC VEIL!
See Selby, Charles. Fairy Lake, The.

MAGIC WATCH!
See Farnie, Henry Brougham. Rothomago.

MAGICIAN AND THE RING, THE
See Adams, Florence Davenport.

MAGICIAN'S DAUGHTER, THE
See France, C. V.

MAGISTRATE, THE
See Pinero, Arthur Wing.

MAGLOIRE THE PRESTIGIATOR
See Robertson, Thomas William. Jocrisse the Juggler.

MAGNAY, WILLIAM
Honi Soit. [London]: n.pub., n.d. Pp. [1]-44.

MAGNIFICENT LOVERS, THE
See Van Laun, Henri (trans.).

MAGPIE, THE
See Dibdin, Thomas John.

MAGPIE AND THIMBLE, THE
See Smelt, Thomas.

MAGPIE OR THE MAID?, THE
See Pocock, Isaac.

MAHOMET THE IMPOSTOR
See Miller, James, Rev.

MAID AND THE MAGPIE, THE (anon.)
London: W. Webb, n.d. Pp. [1]-18. Webb's Juvenile Drama.

MAID AND THE MAGPIE, THE (anon.)
[London]: B. Skelt (printer), n.d. Pp. [3]-18. Title page lacking.

MAID AND THE MAGPIE, THE
See Byron, Henry James.

MAID AND THE MAGPYE, THE
See Arnold, Samuel James.

MAID AND THE MONSTER
See Brough, William. Perseus and Andromeda.

MAID MARIAN
See Planché, James Robinson.

MAID O' THE MILL, THE
See Carter, Barrington.

MAID OF ALL WORK
See Bruton, James. Wanted an Errand Boy.

MAID OF ARTEMIS, THE
See Dillon, Arthur.

MAID OF ARTOIS, THE
See Bunn, Alfred.

MAID OF AVENEL, THE
See Aird, David Mitchell.

MAID OF BRISTOL, THE
See Boaden, James.

MAID OF CROISSEY, THE
See Gore, Catherine Grace Frances Moody, Mrs. Charles.

MAID OF ERIN
See Knowles, James Sheridan. Brian Boroihme.

MAID OF GENOA!, THE
See Farrell, John.

MAID OF GLENDALOUGH
See Hazlewood, ?, Miss. Kevin's Choice.

MAID OF HONOR, THE
See Fitzball, Edward.

MAID OF HONOUR, THE
See Massinger, Philip.
See Wooler, John Pratt.

MAID OF JUDAH, THE
See Lacy, Michael Rophino.

MAID OF LORN, THE
See Maclaren, Archibald.

MAID OF MARIENDORPT, THE
See Knowles, James Sheridan.

MAID OF MILAN
See Payne, John Howard. Clari.

MAID OF ORLEANS, THE
See Drinkwater, John Elliot (trans.).
See Fitzball, Edward. Joan of Arc.
See Maxwell, Patrick, Maj. Gen. (trans.).
See Peter, William (trans.).
See Salvin, Hugh, Rev. (trans.).
See Swanwick, Anna (trans.).
See Thompson, Henry (trans.).
See Turner, E. S. (trans.).

MAID OF PALAISEAU
See Dibdin, Thomas John. Magpie, The.
See Fitzball, Edward.
See Fitzball, Edward. Ninetta.

MAID OF SWITZERLAND, THE
See Wilson, Margaret Harries, Mrs. Cornwell Baron.

MAID OF THE COTTAGE
See Soane, George. Self-Sacrifice.

MAID OF THE MILL, THE
See Bickerstaffe, Isaac.

MAID OF THE OAKS, THE
See Burgoyne, John, Gen.

MAID OF THE TYROL
See Thomas, William Lewis. Theresa.

MAID OR WIFE
See Livius, Barham. Biter Bit, The.
See Livius, Barham.

MAID, THE WIFE, AND THE WIDOW
See Wilks, Thomas Egerton. 'Tis She!

MAID WITH A PARASOL
See Horncastle, James Henry. Cat's in the Larder, The.

MAID WITH THE MILKING PAIL, THE
See Buckstone, John Baldwin.

MAIDEN AUNT, THE
See Knowles, Richard Brinsley.

MAIDEN'S FAME!, A
See Bernard, William Bayle.

MAIDENS BEWARE!
See Haines, John Thomas.

MAIDS
See Wild, James.

MAISTER OF WOOD BARROW, THE
See Jerome, Jerome Klapka.

MAJOR, HENRY ARCHIBALD
Nondescript, The; or, Beauty in Ugliness. London: Taylor (printer), n.d. Pp. [1]-40.

MAJOR AND MINER
See Ellis, Walter.

MAJOR AND THE MINOR
See Lunn, Joseph. White Lies.

MAJOR, THE MINER, AND THE COCK-A-DOODLE-DOO
See Burnand, Francis Cowley. Olympic Games.

MAJOR'S DILEMMA
See Knight, Arthur Francis. Well Played.

MAKE YOUR WILLS
See Mayhew, Edward.

MAKE YOURSELF AT HOME
See Maltby, C. Alfred.

MAKLIN, CHARLES
See Macklin, Charles.

MALADE IMAGINAIRE
See Van Laun, Henri (trans.). Imaginary Invalid, The.

MALEK ADHEL, THE CHAMPION OF THE CRESCENT
See Burney, Frances.

MALEK AND THE PRINCESS SCHIRINE
See Harlequin and the Flying Chest.

MALET, EDWARD
Harold; or, The Norman Conquest. Music by Cowen, Frederic H. London: Joseph Williams, n.d. Pp. [i-iii], [1]-251. Vocal score.

MALKIN, BENJAMIN HEATH
Almahide and Hamet. London: Longman & Rees, 1804. Pp. [i], [1]-158.

MALT AND HOPS
See Reynoldson, Thomas Herbert. Brewer of Preston, The.

MALTBY, C. ALFRED
Borrowed Plumes. London & New York: Samuel French, n.d. Pp. [1]-16.

For Better or Worse. [New York]: Wheat & Cornett, c.1875. Pp. [29]-32. New York Drama, I, 6.

I'm Not Mesilf at All. New York: DeWitt, n.d. Pp. [1]-11. DeWitt's Acting Plays, 116.

Just My Luck. London & New York: Samuel French, n.d. Pp. [1]-15. [Lacy's Acting Edition].

Make Yourself at Home. London & New York: Samuel French, n.d. Pp. [1]-16.

My Soldier Boy. Written with Lindo, Frank. London & New York: Samuel French, c.1899. Pp. [1]-72.

Sea-Gulls. Written with Stainforth, Frank. London: Thomas Hailes Lacy, n.d. Pp. [1]-16. [Lacy's Acting Edition].

Should This Meet the Eye. London & New York: Samuel French, n.d. Pp. [1]-20. [Lacy's Acting Edition].

Somebody's Nobody. Clyde, Ohio: A. D. Ames, n.d. Pp. [1]-11. Ames' Series of Standard and Minor Drama, 55.

Taken by Storm. London & New York: Samuel French, n.d. Pp. [1]-14.

Two Flats and a Sharp. London & New York: Samuel French, n.d. Pp. [1]-14. [Lacy's Acting Edition].

Your Vote and Interest. London & New York: Samuel French, n.d. Pp. [1]-15. [Lacy's Acting Edition].

MALVINA
    See Macfarren, George.
MALYON, E. J.
    Lady Burglar, The. Written with James, Charles. London &
    New York: Samuel French, n.d. Pp. [1]-12.
MAMMON AND GAMMON
    See Talfourd, Francis.
MAN ABOUT TOWN
    See Bernard, William Bayle.
    See Stange, Stanislaus.
MAN AND THE MARQUIS, THE
    See Dibdin, Thomas John.
MAN AND THE MONSTER!
    See Milner, Henry M. Frankenstein.
    See Milner, Henry M.
MAN AND THE TIGER
    See Parry, Thomas. P. P.
MAN AND WIFE
    See Arnold, Samuel James.
    See Collins, William Wilkie.
MAN AT THE WHEEL
    See Burnand, Francis Cowley. Ixion.
MAN FROM BLANKLEY'S, THE
    See Anstey, F.
MAN IN POSSESSION, THE
    See Albery, James.
MAN IN THE CLEFT
    See Meritt, Paul. Glin Gath.
MAN IN THE IRON MASK, THE
    See Serle, Thomas James.
MAN IN THE MOON, THE
    See Maclaren, Archibald.
    See Phillips, R.
MAN IN THE STREET, THE
    See Parker, Louis Napoleon.
MAN IS NOT PERFECT, NOR WOMAN NEITHER
    See Webster, Benjamin, jr.
MAN-MONKEY
    See Addison, Henry Robert, Capt. Blue-faced Baboon!,
    The.
MAN OF DESTINY, THE
    See Shaw, George Bernard.
MAN OF FORTY, THE
    See Poel, William.
MAN OF LAW, THE
    See Webster, Benjamin Nottingham.
MAN OF MANY FRIENDS, THE
    See Coyne, Joseph Stirling.
MAN OF MY CHOICE
    See Guardians, The.
MAN OF THE WORLD, THE
    See Macklin, Charles.
MAN OF THOUGHT AND THE MAN OF ACTION, THE
    See St. George, George.
MAN OF TWO LIVES!, THE
    See Bernard, William Bayle.
MAN OF TWO MASTERS
    See Barber, James. Jonathan!
MAN OF WAR AND THE MERCHANTMAN, THE
    See Townsend, William Thompson.
MAN OF WAR'S MAN AND THE PRIVATEER
    See Townsend, William Thompson. Lost Ship, The.
MAN ON THE ROCK!
    See Reece, Robert. Prometheus.
MAN PROPOSES
    See Grundy, Sydney.
    See Langbridge, Frederick.
MAN-SERVANT, A
    See Rockingham, Charles, Sir.
MAN TRAP, THE
    See Maclaren, Archibald.
MAN WHO COULDN'T HELP IT
    See Jerrold, Douglas William. Perils of Pippins, The.
MAN WHO FOLLOWS THE LADIES, THE
    See Paul, Howard.

MAN WHO WASN'T, THE
    See Ransom, Harry Alexander Vincent.
MAN WITH THE CARPET BAG, THE
    See A'Beckett, Gilbert Abbott.
MAN WITH THE IRON MASK, THE
    See Lucas, William James.
MAN WITH THREE WIVES, THE
    See Rae, Charles Marsham.
MAN WITHOUT A ——!
    See Blanchard, Edward Litt Leman. Adam Buff.
MAN WITHOUT A HEAD, A
    See Wooler, John Pratt.
MANABOZO
    See Neilson, Francis.
MANAGEMENT
    See Lunn, Joseph.
MANAGER AND HIS FRIENDS
    See Coyne, Joseph Stirling. Buckstone at Home.
MANAGER IN LOVE, THE
    See Hilton, B. H.
MANAGER'S DAUGHTER, THE
    See Lancaster, Edward Richardson.
MANAGERESS IN A FIX
    See Oxenford, John. Please to Remember the Grotto.
MANDARIN'S DAUGHTER!, THE
    See Hale, William Palmer.
MANDRIN
    See Mathews, Charles James.
MANFRED
    See Byron, George Gordon, Lord.
MAN-FRED
    See A'Beckett, Gilbert Abbott.
MANFREDI THE MYSTERIOUS HERMIT
    See Barrymore, William.
MANGIN, EDWARD (trans.)
    Hector. By Lancival, J. Charles J. Luce de. Bath: M. Gye
    (printer), n.d. Pp. [iii]-[xx], [1]-83.
MANIAC!, THE
    See Arnold, Samuel James.
MANIAC OF THE ALPS
    See Webster, Benjamin Nottingham. Isaure.
MANN, J. P.
    **Erostratus; or, The Burning of the Temple of Diana at
    Ephesus.** London: Samuel French, n.d. Pp. [1]-48.
MANNERS, EMMELINE CHARLOTTE ELIZABETH
    See Wortley, Emmeline Charlotte Elizabeth Manners
    Stuart, Mrs. Charles (Lady).
MANNERS, GEORGE
    Edgar; or, Caledonian Feuds. London: Tipper & Richards,
    1806. Pp. [1]-[92].
MANNERS, JOHN HARTLEY
    As Once in May. London & New York: Samuel French,
    c.1902. Pp. [1]-28. [Lacy's Acting Edition].
    Just as Well. London & New York: Samuel French, c.1902.
    Pp. [1]-18. [Lacy's Acting Edition].
    Queen's Messenger, A. New York & London: Samuel
    French, c.1900. Pp. [3]-26. French's International
    Copyrighted Edition of the Works of the Best Authors,
    40.
MANOEUVERING
    See Raymond, Richard John. Two Make a Pair, The.
MANOEUVRES OF JANE, THE
    See Jones, Henry Arthur.
MANOEUVRING (anon.)
    In *New British Theatre,* ed. John Galt, London: A. J.
    Valpy (printer), 1814, II, [75-136].
MANOLA
    See Farnie, Henry Brougham.
MANON
    See Bennett, Joseph (trans.).
MANOR SACKVILLE
    See Morgan, Sydney Owenson, Mrs. Thomas Charles
    (Lady).

MANSEL, HENRY LONGUEVILLE
Phrontisterion; or, Oxford in the 19th Century. Oxford: J. Vincent, 1852. Pp. [1]-24. 4th ed.
MANSELL, ERNEST
Skirt Dancer, The.
See Ridgwell, George.
MANTEAUX NOIRS
See Parke, Walter.
See Parke, Walter. Three Black Cloaks.
MANTUAN REVELS
See Chenevix, Richard.
MANUEL
See Maturin, Charles Robert, Rev.
MANXMAN, THE
See Caine, Hall.
MANY SIDES TO A CHARACTER
See Bulwer (later Bulwer-Lytton), Edward George Earle Lytton, Lord Lytton. Not So Bad as We Seem.
MARBLE ARCH, THE
See Rose, Edward.
MARBLE BRIDE, THE
See Hazlewood, Colin Henry.
MARBLE HEART, THE
See Selby, Charles.
MARCELINE
See Selby, Charles.
MARCH, GEORGE
Grass Widows. Music by Gabriel, Virginia. London: Metzler, 1875. Pp. [1]-30. Vocal score. *Filed under* March, George Edward.
Lost and Found. Music by Gabriel, Virginia. London: Thomas Hailes Lacy, n.d. Pp. [1]-29. [Lacy's Acting Edition]. Libretto. *Filed under* March, M. George.
One in Hand Is Worth Two in the Bush. London & New York: Samuel French, n.d. Pp. [1]-12. [Lacy's Acting Edition]. *Filed under* March, M. George.
Our Friends. London & New York: Samuel French, n.d. Pp. [1]-90. [Lacy's Acting Edition]. *Filed under* March, M. George.
Shepherd of Cournouailles, The. Music by Gabriel, Virginia. London: Thomas Hailes Lacy, n.d. Pp. [1]-26. [Lacy's Acting Edition]. Libretto. *Filed under* March, M. George.
Who's the Heir? Music by Gabriel, Virginia. London: Thomas Hailes Lacy, n.d. Pp. [1]-20. [Lacy's Acting Edition]. Libretto. *Filed under* March, M. George.
MARCH OF INTELLECT, THE
See Macfarren, George.
MARCHANT, FREDERICK
Nip Van Winkle and the Demon Slumber of Twenty Years; or, King Neptune and the Dancing Princess. [London]: n.pub., n.d. Pp. [i-ii], 1-17. Libretto.
Skeleton Horseman, The; or, The Shadow of Death. 23 leaves. Manuscript.
MARCO SPADA
See Simpson, John Palgrave.
MARCORETTI
See Kingdom, John M.
MARCUS MANLIUS
See Colombine, David Elwin.
MARGARET CATCHPOLE, THE HEROINE OF SUFFOLK
See Stirling, Edward.
MARGARET'S GHOST
See Fitzball, Edward.
MARGATE SANDS
See Hancock, William.
MARGERY DAW
See Morton, John Maddison.
MARGUERITE
See Powell, Thomas.
MARGUERITE'S COLOURS!
See Archer, Thomas.
MARIA
See Meighan, John.
MARIA DI GAND
See Hersee, Henry (trans.). Mary of Ghent.

MARIA DI ROHAN
See Maggioni, Manfredo (trans.).
MARIA MARTIN; OR, THE MURDER IN THE RED BARN (anon.)
London & New York: Samuel French, n.d. Pp. [1]-20. [Lacy's Acting Edition].
MARIAGE AUX LANTERNES
See Farnie, Henry Brougham. Paquerette.
MARIAGE FORCÉ
See Van Laun, Henri (trans.). Forced Marriage, The.
MARIANA
See Graham, James (trans.).
MARIANNE DUVAL
See Phillips, Lewis. Marianne, the Vivandiere.
MARIANNE, THE CHILD OF CHARITY
See Pitt, George Dibdin.
MARIANNE, THE VIVANDIERE
See Phillips, Lewis.
MARIE: A TALE OF THE PONT NEUF!
See Addison, Henry Robert, Capt.
MARIE ANTOINETTE (anon.)
Belfast: D. & J. Allen, 1883. Pp. [1]-68. Title page lacking.
MARIE DE MÉRANIE
See Marston, John Westland.
MARIE DUCANGE
See Bernard, William Bayle.
MARIE MIGNOT
See Mayhew, Thomas Charles Wilson. Ambition.
MARIE STUART
See Wills, William Gorman.
MARINER'S COMPASS, THE
See Leslie, Henry.
MARINER'S DREAM, THE
See Barnett, Charles Zachary.
MARINERS, THE
See Park, Andrew.
MARINO FALIERO
See Byron, George Gordon, Lord.
See Swinburne, Algernon Charles.
MARION; OR, THE PAGE (anon.)
London: C. Mitchell, 1844. Pp. [i-vi], [1]-64.
MARITANA
See Fitzball, Edward.
MARITANA THE GYPSEY!
See Barnett, Charles Zachary. Don Caesar de Bazan!
MARJORIE
See Clifton, Lewis.
MARJORIE DAW
See Braddon, Mary Elizabeth.
MARKED FOR LIFE
See Abel, William Henry.
MARKWELL, W. R. S.
Louis XI. London: Thomas Hailes Lacy, n.d. Pp. [1]-45. [Lacy's Acting Edition].
Louis XI. London: Thomas Hailes Lacy, n.d. Pp. [1]-45. Promptbook.
Prophet's Curse, The. London: W. Jeffs, 1862. Pp. [i-iv], [1]-67.
MARLOWE, CHARLES (pseud. of Jay, Harriet)
Strange Adventures of Miss Brown, The.
See Buchanan, Robert Williams.
MARMION
See Fitzball, Edward.
See Macauley, Elizabeth Wright.
MARMION; OR, FLODDEN FIELD (anon.)
London: J. Murray; Edinburgh: W. Blackwood, 1812. Pp. [i]-[x], [1]-128.
MARPESSA
See Platt, Arthur.
MARQUIS, THE MILLER, AND THE MOUSER!
See Keating, Eliza H. Puss in Boots.
MARRIAGE
See Bell, Robert.

MARRIAGE A LOTTERY
    See Dance, Charles.
MARRIAGE AT ANY PRICE
    See Wooler, John Pratt.
MARRIAGE MADE EASY
    See Cheltnam, Charles Smith.
MARRIAGE NOOSE!, A
    See Farnie, Henry Brougham.
MARRIAGE OF BACCHUS
    See Planché, James Robinson. Theseus and Ariadne.
MARRIAGE OF CONVENIENCE, A
    See Grundy, Sydney.
MARRIAGE OF FIGARO
    See Bishop, Henry Rowley (trans.).
    See Kenney, Charles Lamb (trans.). Nozze di Figaro, Le.
    See Soane, George (trans.).
MARRIAGE OF INTEREST
    See Fitzball, Edward. Mary Melvyn.
MARRIAGE PROMISE, THE
    See Allingham, John Till.
MARRIED
    See Albery, James.
MARRIED AND BURIED
    See Kenney, James. Illustrious Stranger, The.
MARRIED AND SINGLE
    See Poole, John.
MARRIED BACHELOR, THE
    See O'Callaghan, P. P.
MARRIED BENEATH HIM
    See Braddon, Mary Elizabeth.
MARRIED BY FORCE
    See Shirley, Arthur. Danicheffs, The.
MARRIED DAUGHTERS AND YOUNG HUSBANDS
    See Daly, John.
MARRIED FOR MONEY
    See Kenney, James. Spring and Autumn.
    See Mathews, Charles James.
MARRIED IN HASTE
    See Byron, Henry James.
MARRIED LIFE
    See Buckstone, John Baldwin.
MARRIED LOVERS
    See Power, Tyrone.
MARRIED MAID
    See Rodwell, George Herbert Bonaparte. Chimney Piece,
    The.
MARRIED RAKE, THE
    See Selby, Charles.
MARRIED UN-MARRIED
    See Barnett, Morris.
MARRY IN HASTE
    See Drayton, Henri.
MARRY IN HASTE AND REPENT AT LEISURE
    See Rowe, George Fawcett.
MARRYAT, FLORENCE (later Mrs. Church; Mrs. Francis
    Lean)
    Miss Chester. Written with Young, Charles Lawrence, Sir.
    London & New York: Samuel French, n.d. Pp. [1]-38.
    [Lacy's Acting Edition]. *Filed under* Young, Charles
    Lawrence, Sir.
    Miss Chester. Written with Young, Charles Lawrence, Sir.
    London & New York: Samuel French, n.d. Pp. [1]-38.
    Promptbook.
    Woman Against Woman. Pp. [i-ii], [1]-10, [1]-12, [1]-7, [1]-8,
    [1]-5. Title page lacking. Pagination by act. Typescript.
MARSHALL, FRANCIS ALBERT
    Biorn. Music by Rossi, Lauro. [London: Walter Smith
    (printer)], n.d. Pp. [i-iii], [1]-35. Libretto.
    False Shame. London & New York: Samuel French, n.d. Pp.
    [1]-56. [Lacy's Acting Edition].
    Mad as a Hatter. London: Thomas Hailes Lacy, n.d. Pp.
    [1]-24. [Lacy's Acting Edition].
    Q. E. D.; or, All a Mistake. London & New York: Samuel
    French, n.d. Pp. [1]-20. [Lacy's Acting Edition].

MARSHALL, ROBERT
    His Excellency the Governor. Boston: Walter H. Baker,
    c.1901. Pp. [i-vi], [1]-152.
    His Excellency the Governor. Pp. [i-xix], [1]-40, [i], [1]-38, [i],
    [1]-32. Pagination by act. Typescript promptbook.
    Royal Family, A. Pp. [i-xv], [1]-[44], [i], [1]-42, [i], [1]-36.
    Pagination by act. Typescript promptbook.
    Shades of Night. London & New York: Samuel French, n.d.
    Pp. [1]-21.
MARSHALL, WILLIAM
    Aarbert. London: Swan Sonnenschein, 1898. Pp. [i]-[viii],
    [1]-359.
MARSTON, JOHN WESTLAND
    Anne Blake. London: C. Mitchell, 1852. Pp. [i]-[viii], [1]-68.
    Anne Blake. In *Dramatic and Poetical Works,* 2 vols.,
    London: Chatto & Windus, 1876, I, [307]-360. *Filed under*
    Collected Works.
    Anne Blake. Boston: William V. Spencer, n.d. Pp. [1]-35.
    Spencer's Boston Theatre, 57.
    Borough Politics. In *Dramatic and Poetical Works,* 2 vols.,
    London: Chatto & Windus, 1876, II, [287]-318. *Filed
    under* Collected Works.
    Borough Politics. London: National Acting Drama Office,
    n.d. Pp. [1]-24. Webster's Acting National Drama, 132.
    Cupid's Conspirator! 45 leaves. Manuscript promptbook.
    Donna Diana. In *Dramatic and Poetical Works,* 2 vols.,
    London: Chatto & Windus, 1876, II, [1]-65. *Filed under*
    Collected Works.
    Dramatic Scenes and Fragments. In *Dramatic and Poetical
    Works,* 2 vols., London: Chatto & Windus, 1876, II,
    [319]-338. *Filed under* Collected Works.
    Favourite of Fortune, The. In *Dramatic and Poetical Works,* 2
    vols., London: Chatto & Windus, 1876, II, [67]-147. *Filed
    under* Collected Works.
    Gerald. London: C. Mitchell, 1842. Pp. [i]-[x], [1]-118.
    Hard Struggle, A. In *Dramatic and Poetical Works,* 2 vols.,
    London: Chatto & Windus, 1876, II, [257]-286. *Filed
    under* Collected Works.
    Hard Struggle, A. Boston: William V. Spencer, n.d. Pp.
    [1]-21. Spencer's Boston Theatre, 161. Promptbook.
    Hard Struggle, A. London: Thomas Hailes Lacy, n.d. Pp.
    [1]-28. Promptbook.
    Heart and the World, The. London: C. Mitchell, 1847. Pp.
    [i-viii], [5]-85.
    Hero of Romance, A. London: J. Miles (printer), n.d. Pp.
    [1]-40. Text incomplete. Promptbook.
    Life for Life. In *Dramatic and Poetical Works,* 2 vols.,
    London: Chatto & Windus, 1876, I, [127]-196. *Filed under*
    Collected Works.
    Life's Ransom, A. London: C. Mitchell, 1857. Pp. [i]-[xviii],
    [1]-50.
    Life's Ransom, A. In *Dramatic and Poetical Works,* 2 vols.,
    London: Chatto & Windus, 1876, I, [197]-251. *Filed under*
    Collected Works.
    Marie de Méranie. In *Dramatic and Poetical Works,* 2 vols.,
    London: Chatto & Windus, 1876, I, [59]-125. *Filed under*
    Collected Works.
    Patrician's Daughter, The. London: C. Mitchell, 1843. Pp.
    [i]-[xii], [3]-86. 4th ed., enl. and adapt. for representation.
    Patrician's Daughter, The. In *Dramatic and Poetical Works,* 2
    vols., London: Chatto & Windus, 1876, I, [253]-305. *Filed
    under* Collected Works.
    Patrician's Daughter, The. London: Thomas Hailes Lacy,
    n.d. Pp. [1]-48. Promptbook.
    Philip of France and Marie de Méranie. London: C. Mitchell,
    1850. Pp. [i]-[xii], [1]-84.
    Philip of France and Marie de Méranie. London: C. Mitchell,
    1850. Pp. [i]-[xii], [1]-84. 2nd ed. Promptbook.
    Pure Gold. In *Dramatic and Poetical Works,* 2 vols., London:
    Chatto & Windus, 1876, II, [149]-221. *Filed under*
    Collected Works.
    Pure Gold. London: Thomas Hailes Lacy, n.d. Pp. [1]-66.
    Promptbook.
    Strathmore. London: C. Mitchell, 1849. Pp. [iv]-[xii], [1]-91.

Strathmore; or, Love and Duty. In *Dramatic and Poetical Works*, 2 vols., London: Chatto & Windus, 1876, I, [i]-[xii], [1]-58. *Filed under* Collected Works.

Trevanion; or, The False Position. Written with Bernard, William Bayle. London: C. Mitchell, n.d. Pp. [1]-36.

Wife's Portrait, The. In *Dramatic and Poetical Works*, 2 vols., London: Chatto & Windus, 1876, II, [221]-255. *Filed under* Collected Works.

MARTA
  See Martha (anon.).

MARTELLI
  See Brewer, George.

MARTHA (anon. trans.)
  Also: Marta. Music by Flotow. London & New York: Boosey, n.d. Pp. [i-iv], 1-248. [Royal Edition]. Vocal score. *Filed under* Marta (anon.).

MARTHA
  See Reece, Robert.

MARTHA WILLIS, THE SERVANT MAID
  See Jerrold, Douglas William.

MARTIAL ACHIEVEMENTS OF SIR WILLIAM WALLACE, THE
  See Anderson, David.

MARTIN, ?, MRS.
  Reparation; or, The Savoyards. London: John Nichols & Son (printer), 1823. Pp. [1]-115.

MARTIN, JOHN
  Fairly Hit and Fairly Missed. London: John Duncombe, n.d. Pp. [1]-24. Duncombe's Acting Edition of the British Theatre, 340.

MARTIN, THEODORE, SIR
  Madonna Pia. In *Madonna Pia and Three Other Dramas*, Edinburgh & London: William Blackwood & Sons, 1894, pp. [i-vi], [1]-92.
  Madonna Pia. London: n.pub. (priv.), n.d. Pp. [iii]-[viii], [1]-87.

MARTIN, THEODORE, SIR (trans.)
  Aladdin; or, The Wonderful Lamp. By Oehlenschlager, Adam. London: John W. Parker & Son, 1857. Pp. [i]-[xi], [1]-298.
  Camp of Wallenstein, The. By Schiller. In *Madonna Pia and Three Other Dramas*, Edinburgh & London: William Blackwood & Sons, 1894, pp. [161]-214. *Filed under* Madonna Pia and Three Other Dramas.
  Correggio. By Oehlenschlager, Adam. Edinburgh & London: William Blackwood & Sons, 1865. Pp. [1-2], [i]-[x], [1]-147.
  Demetrius. By Schiller. In *Works of Frederick Schiller: Early Dramas and Romances*, London: Henry G. Bohn, 1853, pp. [iii]-xii, [333]-376.
  Faust. By Goethe. Edinburgh & London: William Blackwood & Sons, 1865. Pp. [i-iii], [1]-239.
  Gladiator of Ravenna, The. By Halm, Friedrich. In *Madonna Pia and Three Other Dramas*, Edinburgh & London: William Blackwood & Sons, 1894, pp. [215]-315. *Filed under* Madonna Pia and Three Other Dramas.
  Gladiator of Ravenna, The. By Halm, Friedrich. N.p.: William Blackwood & Sons (printer) (priv.), 1885. Pp. [i]-[x], [1]-77.
  King René's Daughter. By Hertz, Henrik. Boston: William Crosby & Henry P. Nichols, 1850. Pp. [i-vi], [1]-75.
  King René's Daughter. By Hertz, Henrik. In *Madonna Pia and Three Other Dramas*, Edinburgh & London: William Blackwood & Sons, 1894, pp. [93]-159. *Filed under* Madonna Pia and Three Other Dramas.
  Wilhelm Tell. By Schiller. In *Works of Frederick Schiller: Historical and Dramatic*, London: Henry G. Bohn, 1854, pp. [i]-iv, [449]-553.

MARTIN, WILLIAM
  Chang-Ching-Fou! Cream of Tartar; or, The Prince, the Princess, and the Mandarin. London: Thomas Hailes Lacy, n.d. Pp. [1]-24.
  D'ye Know Me Now? London & New York: Samuel French, n.d. Pp. [1]-24. [Lacy's Acting Edition].

MARTIN-SEYMOUR, EDWARD
  Two Jolly Bachelors. London: Samuel French; New York: T. Henry French, n.d. Pp. [1]-13.

MARTIN CHUZZLEWIT
  See Higgie, Thomas Henry.
  See Simms, Harry.
  See Webb, Charles.

MARTIN LUTHER
  See Moore, George.

MARTINETTI, PAUL ROBERT
  Robert Macaire. Music by Phendon. Pp. [1]-47. Typescript promptbook libretto.

MARTINUZZI
  See Stephens, George.

MARTYN, EDWARD
  Heather Field, The. In *Heather Field and Maeve*, London: Duckworth, 1899, pp. [i]-[xxx], [1]-83.
  Maeve. In *Heather Field and Maeve*, London: Duckworth, 1899, pp. [85]-129.

MARTYR, THE
  See Baillie, Joanna.

MARTYR OF ANTIOCH, THE
  See Milman, Henry Hart.

MARTYR OF CAESAREA
  See Serle, Thomas James. Fulvius Valens.

MARX-AVELING, ELEANOR
  See Aveling, Eleanor Marx, Mrs. Edward.

MARY AND SAIREY
  See Ross, Adrian.

MARY EDMONSTONE
  See Hazlewood, Colin Henry.

MARY GLASTONBURY
  See Fitzball, Edward.

MARY LE MORE
  See Hart, James P.

MARY MELVYN
  See Fitzball, Edward.

MARY OF GHENT
  See Hersee, Henry (trans.).

MARY PRICE; OR, THE ADVENTURES OF A SERVANT GIRL (anon.)
  London: Thomas Hailes Lacy, n.d. Pp. [1]-33. Lacking pp. 4-5. [Lacy's Acting Edition].

MARY QUEEN OF SCOTS
  See Beverly, Henry Roxby. Abbot, The.
  See Blake, Robert.
  See Boulding, James Wimsett.
  See Murray, William Henry Wood.
  See Quinn, M.
  See St. John, John.

MARY STUART
  See Haynes, James.
  See Kemble, Frances Anne (Fanny) (trans.).
  See Lloyd, Charles (trans.).
  See Mellish, Joseph Charles (trans.).
  See Peter, William (trans.).
  See Salvin, Hugh, Rev. (trans.).
  See Swinburne, Algernon Charles.
  See Williams, Thomas (trans.).
  See Wingfield, Lewis Strange (trans.).

MARY TUDOR
  See de Vere, Aubrey.
  See Gregg, Tresham Dames.

MARY TURNER
  See Burnand, Francis Cowley.

MARY WARNER
  See Taylor, Tom.

MARY'S DREAM
  See Townsend, William Thompson.

MARZIALS, THEOPHILUS JULIUS HENRY
  Esmeralda. Written with Randegger, Alberto. Music by Thomas, A. Goring. London: Charles Dickens & Evans (printer), n.d. Pp. [1]-32. Libretto.

Esmeralda. Written with Randegger, Alberto. Music by Thomas, A. Goring. London: Boosey, n.d. Pp. [i-iv], 1-323. Vocal score.

MARZIALS, THEOPHILUS JULIUS HENRY (trans.)

Mefistofele. Music by Boito, Arrigo. London: Tito di Giorgio Ricordi, n.d. Pp. [i]-[v], [6]-69. Libretto.

MASANIELLO
 See Brough, Robert Barnabas.
 See Kenney, James.
 See Macfarren, Natalia (trans.). Dumb Girl of Portici, The.
 See Maggioni, Manfredo (trans.).
 See Milner, Henry M.

MASANIELLO; OR, LA MUETTE DE PORTICI (anon. trans.)
 Music by Auber. London: G. H. Davidson, n.d. Pp. i-ix, 1-319. Vocal score.

MASANIELLO; OR, LA MUETTE DE PORTICI (anon. trans.)
 Music by Auber. London: G. H. Davidson, n.d. Pp. [1]-28. Davidson's Illustrated Libretto Books. Libretto.

MASANIELLO, THE FISHERMAN OF NAPLES
 See Milner, Henry M.
 See Soane, George.

MASKED BALL
 See Kenney, Charles Lamb (trans.). Ballo in Maschera, Un.
 See Milner, Henry M. Gustavus the Third.
 See Planché, James Robinson. Gustavus the Third.
 See Thackeray, Thomas James. Gustavus of Sweden.
 See Wilks, Thomas Egerton. Black Domino, The.

MASKED MOTHER AND THE HIDDEN HAND
 See Hazlewood, Colin Henry. Capitola.

MASKS AND FACES
 See Taylor, Tom.

MASON, ALFRED EDWARD WOODLEY

Blanche de Maletroit. London: Capper & Newton, n.d. Pp. [109]-137. Lynn's Acting Edition, 22.

MASON, CARL

Master of Ballantrae, The. Pp. [i-v], [1]-36, [1]-59, [1]-22. Pagination by act. Typescript.

MASON, HENRY BOLENO
 See Boleno, Henry.

MASON, JAMES

Alcestis. In *Cornelia and Alcestis,* London: T. Payne, 1810, pp. [105]-188.

Cornelia. In *Cornelia and Alcestis,* London: T. Payne, 1810, pp. [i]-[lxxxvii], [1]-103.

Natural Son, The. Liverpool: J. M'Creery (printer), 1805. Pp. [i-iv], [1]-111.

MASON
 See Wylde, Mrs. Henry (trans.). Maçon, Le.

MASON AND THE LOCKSMITH
 See Wylde, Mrs. Henry (trans.). Maçon, Le.

MASON OF BUDA, THE
 See Planché, James Robinson.

MASONIC HONOUR
 See Pennie, John Fitzgerald. Varangian, The.

MASQUE, A
 See Knowles, James Sheridan.

MASQUE OF ANGELS BEFORE OUR LADY IN THE TEMPLE, A
 See Caswall, Edward.

MASQUE OF DEAD FLORENTINES, A
 See Hewlett, Maurice Henry.

MASQUE OF THE SEASONS, THE
 See Mitford, Mary Russell.

MASQUE OF WAR AND PEACE, THE
 See Parker, Louis Napoleon.

MASQUERADE
 See Galt, John.
 See Pocock, Isaac. Cent. per Cent.

MASQUERADERS, THE
 See Jones, Henry Arthur.

MASSACRE OF ABERGAVENNY, THE
 See Furness, J. R.

MASSINGER, PHILIP

Duke of Milan, The. London: Whittingham & Arliss, 1816. Pp. [1]-64. London Theatre, XVIII. *Filed under* Dibdin, Thomas John, ed. London Theatre, XVIII.

Duke of Milan, The. In *British Drama,* 12 vols., London: John Dicks, 1871, VI, [257]-276.

Fatal Dowry, The. London: Thomas Dolby, 1825. Pp. [1-3], [i]-[iv], [iii]-[ix], [9]-65. Dolby's British Theatre, X. *Filed under* Cumberland, John. Cumberland's British Theatre, X.

Maid of Honour, The. In *British Drama,* 12 vols., London: John Dicks, 1865, IV, [1119]-1134.

Maid of Honour, The. London: John Cumberland, n.d. Pp. [1]-56. Cumberland's British Theatre, XXIX. *Filed under* Cumberland, John. Cumberland's British Theatre, XXIX.

New Way to Pay Old Debts, A. London: Whittingham & Arliss, 1816. Pp. [1]-74. London Theatre, XVIII. *Filed under* Dibdin, Thomas John, ed. London Theatre, XVIII.

New Way to Pay Old Debts, A. In *New English Drama,* ed. W. Oxberry, 22 vols., London: W. Simpkin & R. Marshall; C. Chapple, 1818, I, [iii]-[x], [7]-78. *Filed under* Oxberry, William Henry. New English Drama, I.

New Way to Pay Old Debts, A. London: T. Dolby, 1824. Pp. [1-4], [iii]-vi, [5]-[72]. Dolby's British Theatre, VII. *Filed under* Cumberland, John. Cumberland's British Theatre, VII.

New Way to Pay Old Debts, A. In *British Drama,* 12 vols., London: John Dicks, 1864, II, [i-iv], [321]-341.

New Way to Pay Old Debts, A.
 See Kemble, John Philip (arr.).

MASTER AND MAN
 See O'Callaghan, P. P. Married Bachelor, The.

MASTER AND SCHOLAR
 See Plumptre, Edward Haynes.

MASTER BUILDER, THE
 See Gosse, Edmund William (trans.).

MASTER CLARKE
 See Serle, Thomas James.

MASTER HUMPHREY'S CLOCK
 See Cooper, Frederick Fox.

MASTER JONES'S BIRTHDAY
 See Morton, John Maddison.

MASTER KEY
 See Beazley, Samuel, jr. Love Among the Roses.

MASTER OF BALLANTRAE, THE
 See Mason, Carl.

MASTER PASSION
 See Falconer, Edmund. Outlaw of the Adriatic, The.
 See Phillips, Mrs. Alfred.

MASTER'S RIVAL
 See Peake, Richard Brinsley.

MASTERS, MARTIN KEDGWIN

Lost and Found. London: W. H. Wyatt, 1811. Pp. [i]-[viii], [1]-81.

MASTERSINGERS OF NUREMBERG, THE
 See Corder, Henrietta Louisa Walford, Mrs. Frederick (trans.).
 See Jackson, John P. (trans.).

MASTERTON, CHARLES

Bentivoglio. London: J. Hearne, 1824. Pp. [1]-68.

Seducer, The. London: C. Chapple (priv.), 1811. Pp. [i-x], [1]-73.

Stern Resolve, The. London: J. Hearne, 1823. Pp. [1]-55.

Wreck, The. London: J. Hearne, 1824. Pp. [1]-39.

MASTERY OF MEN, THE
 See Maugham, Harry Neville.

MATCH, THE
 See Baillie, Joanna.

MATCH BREAKING
 See Kenney, James.

MATCH FOR A KING
 See Smith, Albert Richard. Guy Fawkes.

MATCH FOR A MAGISTRATE
 See Glover, William Howard. Aminta, the Coquette.

MATCH FOR A MOTHER-IN-LAW, A
   See Reeve, Wybert.
MATCH FOR LUCIFER!
   See Talfourd, Francis. Princesses in the Tower, The.
MATCH IN THE DARK, A
   See Dance, Charles.
MATCH MAKING
   See Poole, John.
MATCHMAKER, THE
   See Cheltnam, Charles Smith.
MATHEW, CHARLES (trans.)
   Affected Young Ladies, The. By Molière. In *Comedies by Molière*, 2nd ed., London: Ward, Lock, 1890, pp. [59]-77. *Filed under* Collected Works.
   Blue-Stockings, The. By Molière. In *Comedies by Molière*, 2nd ed., London: Ward, Lock, 1890, pp. [483]-528. *Filed under* Collected Works.
   Blunderer, The. By Molière. In *Comedies by Molière*, 2nd ed., London: Ward, Lock, 1890, pp. [163]-214. *Filed under* Collected Works.
   Doctor by Compulsion, The. By Molière. In *Comedies by Molière*, 2nd ed., London: Ward, Lock, 1890, pp. [97]-122. *Filed under* Collected Works.
   Forced Marriage, The. By Molière. In *Comedies by Molière*, 2nd ed., London: Ward, Lock, 1890, pp. [78]-96. *Filed under* Collected Works.
   Hypochondriac, The. By Molière. In *Comedies by Molière*, 2nd ed., London: Ward, Lock, 1890, pp. [343]-390. *Filed under* Collected Works.
   Misanthrope, The. By Molière. In *Comedies by Molière*, 2nd ed., London: Ward, Lock, 1890, pp. [391]-434. *Filed under* Collected Works.
   Miser, The. By Molière. In *Comedies by Molière*, 2nd ed., London: Ward, Lock, 1890, pp. [287]-342. *Filed under* Collected Works.
   Scapin's Rogueries. By Molière. In *Comedies by Molière*, 2nd ed., London: Ward, Lock, 1890, pp. [123]-162. *Filed under* Collected Works.
   School for Husbands, The. By Molière. In *Comedies by Molière*, 2nd ed., London: Ward, Lock, 1890, pp. [215]-[243]. *Filed under* Collected Works.
   School for Wives, The. By Molière. In *Comedies by Molière*, 2nd ed., London: Ward, Lock, 1890, pp. [244]-286. *Filed under* Collected Works.
   Tartuffe. By Molière. In *Comedies by Molière*, 2nd ed., London: Ward, Lock, 1890, pp. [435]-482. *Filed under* Collected Works.
   Would-Be Gentleman, The. By Molière. In *Comedies by Molière*, 2nd ed., London: Ward, Lock, 1890, pp. [1]-58. *Filed under* Collected Works.
MATHEWS, CHARLES JAMES
   Adventures of a Love Letter, The. *Also:* The Billet Doux. London: Thomas Hailes Lacy, n.d. Pp. [1]-56. [Lacy's Acting Edition].
   Bachelor's Bedroom, The; or, Two in the Morning. Boston: William V. Spencer, 1855. Pp. [1]-21. Boston Theatre, 4.
   Bachelor's Bedroom, The; or, Two in the Morning. Boston: William V. Spencer, n.d. Pp. [1]-15. Spencer's Boston Theatre, 4.
   Billet Doux, The.
      See Adventures of a Love Letter, The.
   Black Domino. London: Chapman & Hall, 1838. Pp. [1]-31. Libretto.
   Bull in a China Shop, A. Boston: Walter H. Baker, n.d. Pp. [i-iv], [5]-25.
   Bull in a China Shop, A. Boston: Charles H. Spencer, n.d. Pp. [i-iv], [5]-25. Spencer's Universal Stage, 26.
   Chain of Events, A.
      See Lawrence, Slingsby.
   Dowager, The. London: John Dicks, n.d. Pp. [1]-14. Dicks' Standard Plays, 662.
   His Excellency. London: Thomas Hailes Lacy, n.d. Pp. [1]-28. [Lacy's Acting Edition].
   Humpbacked Lover, The. London: John Cumberland, n.d. Pp. [i-ii], [1]-31. Cumberland's Minor Theatre, XII. *Filed under* Cumberland, John. Cumberland's Minor Theatre, XII.
   Humpbacked Lover, The. London: John Cumberland, n.d. Pp. [1]-31.
   Little Toddlekins. New York: Samuel French, n.d. Pp. [1]-26.
   Mandrin. London: John Dicks, n.d. Pp. [1]-22. Dicks' Standard Plays, 931.
   Married for Money. London & New York: Samuel French, n.d. Pp. [1]-44. [Lacy's Acting Edition].
   My Awful Dad. London & New York: Samuel French, n.d. Pp. [1]-54. [Lacy's Acting Edition].
   My Wife's Mother. London: Thomas Hailes Lacy, n.d. Pp. [1]-36. [Lacy's Acting Edition].
   Patter versus Clatter. London & New York: Samuel French, n.d. Pp. [1]-22. [Lacy's Acting Edition].
   Paul Pry Married and Settled. London: Thomas Hailes Lacy, n.d. Pp. [1]-24. [Lacy's Acting Edition].
   Ringdoves, The. London: National Acting Drama Office, n.d. Pp. [1]-28.
   Serve Him Right!
      See Barnett, Morris.
   Strange History, A.
      See Lawrence, Slingsby.
   Truth. London: Chapman & Hall, n.d. Pp. [i]-[viii], [1]-23. Acting National Drama.
   Two in the Morning. London: S. G. Fairbrother, n.d. Pp. [1]-20.
   Two in the Morning. London: Thomas Hailes Lacy, n.d. Pp. [1]-20. [Lacy's Acting Edition].
   Used Up. Written with Boucicault, Dionysius Lardner. By Charles Mathews. New York & London: Samuel French, n.d. Pp. [1]-38. Minor Drama, [10].
   Used Up. Written with Boucicault, Dionysius Lardner. By Dion Bourcicault. London: National Acting Drama Ofice, n.d. <wrps. Webster>. Pp. [1]-33. Webster's Acting National Drama, 155. *Filed under* Boucicault, Dion.
   Who Killed Cock Robin? New York: Samuel French, n.d. Pp. [1]-34. French's Minor Drama, 298.
   Why Did You Die? London: John Dicks, n.d. Pp. [15]-28. Dicks' Standard Plays, 662. *Filed under* Dowager.
   Why Did You Die? London: Chapman & Hall, n.d. Pp. [1]-28.
   Wolf and the Lamb, The. Philadelphia: Turner & Fisher, n.d. Pp. [3]-28. Title page lacking. Fisher's Edition of Standard Farces.
MATHEWS, CHARLES JAMES (arr.)
   Liar, The. By Foote, Samuel. New York: Robert M. DeWitt, n.d. Pp. [i], [1]-34. DeWitt's Acting Plays, 111.
MATHEWS & CO.
   See Buckingham, Leicester Silk.
MATILDA
   See Delap, John.
   See Francklin, Thomas, Dr.
MATILDA OF HUNGARY
   See Bunn, Alfred.
MATINEE MANIA
   See Anstey, F.
MATRIMONIAL—A GENTLEMAN, &C. FOR FURTHER PARTICULARS, APPLY AT——
   See Bridgeman, John Vipon.
MATRIMONIAL AGENCY, THE
   See Morland, Charlotte E.
MATRIMONIAL CATCH, A
   See Dauncey, Silvanus.
MATRIMONIAL MASQUERADING
   See Buckstone, John Baldwin. Snapping Turtles, The.
MATRIMONIAL PROSPECTUSES!
   See Simpson, John Palgrave.
MATRIMONIO SEGRETO
   See Grist, William (trans.). Secret Marriage, The.
MATRIMONY
   See Kenney, James.
MATTEO FALCONE
   See Oxberry, William Henry.

MATTHISON, ARTHUR

Enoch Arden. London & New York: Samuel French, c.1872. Pp. [1]-35. French's Standard Drama, 377.

False Step, A. London & New York: Samuel French, n.d. Pp. [1]-48.

Liz.
 See Hatton, Joseph.

Talismano, Il. Music by Balfe, Michael William. London: J. H. Mapleson, 1874. Pp. [i]-[iv], [1-2], [5]-23. Libretto.

MATURIN, CHARLES ROBERT, REV.

Bertram; or, The Castle of St. Aldobrand. London: John Murray, 1816. Pp. [i-viii], [1]-83.

Bertram; or, The Castle of St. Aldobrand. London: John Murray, 1816. Pp. [i-x], [1]-[82]. 2nd ed. Promptbook.

Bertram; or, The Castle of St. Aldobrand. In *New English Drama,* ed. W. Oxberry, 22 vols., London: W. Simpkin & R. Marshall; C. Chapple, 1827, XXII, [i]-[viii], [9]-[60]. *Filed under* Oxberry, William Henry. New English Drama, XXII.

Bertram. In *British Drama,* 12 vols., London: John Dicks, 1865, III, [671]-685.

Fredolfo. London: Archibald Constable (Edinburgh); Longman, Hurst, Rees, Orme, & Brown; Hurst, Robinson, 1819. Pp. [i-x], [1]-114.

Manuel. London: John Murray, 1817. Pp. [i]-[x], [1]-[86].

MAUD'S PERIL
 See Phillips, Watts.

MAUDSLAY, A.

Roland. London: Whittaker, 1856. Pp. [1]-243.

MAUGHAM, HARRY NEVILLE

Husband of Poverty, The. In *Sir Paul Pindar and Other Plays,* London: Grant Richards, 1899, pp. [173]-251. *Filed under* Maugham, Henry Neville.

Landslip, The. In *Sir Paul Pindar and Other Plays,* London: Grant Richards, 1899, pp. [151]-171. *Filed under* Maugham, Henry Neville.

Mastery of Men, The. In *Sir Paul Pindar and Other Plays,* London: Grant Richards, 1899, pp. [61]-149. *Filed under* Maugham, Henry Neville.

Old and the New, The. In *Sir Paul Pindar and Other Plays,* London: Grant Richards, 1899, pp. [253]-[309]. *Filed under* Maugham, Henry Neville.

Sir Paul Pindar. In *Sir Paul Pindar and Other Plays,* London: Grant Richards, 1899, pp. [i-vi], [1]-60. *Filed under* Maugham, Henry Neville.

MAUNDER, SAMUEL

Death and the Lawyer. In *Death's Doings,* ed. R. Dagley, 2nd ed., 2 vols., London: J. Andrews, 1827, II, [376]-386.

Waltonian Reminiscences. In *Death's Doings,* ed. R. Dagley, 2nd ed., 2 vols., London: J. Andrews, 1827, II, 401-422.

MAURICE, THOMAS

Fall of the Mogul, The. London: J. White (priv.), 1806. Pp. [1-4], [i]-[xxii], [23]-127.

MAURICE, WALTER

Philanthropy. Written with Rice, James. London & New York: Samuel French, n.d. Pp. [1]-50. [Lacy's Acting Edition].

Ready-Money. Written with Rice, James. London & New York: Samuel French, n.d. Pp. [1]-42. [Lacy's Acting Edition].

MAURICE THE WOODCUTTER
 See Somerset, Charles A.

MAXIME
 See Creyke, Walter P.

MAXWELL, MARY ELIZABETH BRADDON, MRS.
 See Braddon, Mary Elizabeth.

MAXWELL, PATRICK, MAJ. GEN. (trans.)

Maid of Orleans, The. By Schiller. London: Walter Scott, n.d. Pp. [iii]-[xii], [1]-199, [i]-ix.

William Tell. By Schiller. London: Walter Scott, n.d. Pp. [i]-[xxx], [1]-214.

MAY
 See Reece, Robert.

MAY BRIERLY
 See Cheltnam, Charles Smith.

 See Cheltnam, Charles Smith. Ticket-of-Leave Man's Wife, The.

MAY-DAY NIGHT
 See Shelley, Percy Bysshe (trans.).

MAY QUEEN, THE
 See Buckstone, John Baldwin.
 See Chorley, Henry Fothergill.
 See Darley, George. Sylvia.

MAYFLOWER, THE
 See Parker, Louis Napoleon.

MAYHEW, AUGUSTUS SEPTIMUS

Christmas Boxes. Written with Edwards, Henry Sutherland. London: Thomas Hailes Lacy, n.d. Pp. [1]-20. [Lacy's Acting Edition].

Four Cousins, The. Written with Edwards, Henry Sutherland. London: Thomas Hailes Lacy, n.d. Pp. [1]-44. [Lacy's Acting Edition].

Goose with the Golden Eggs, The. Written with Edwards, Henry Sutherland. New York: Robert M. DeWitt, n.d. Pp. [1]-17. DeWitt's Acting Plays, 30.

MAYHEW, EDWARD

Make Your Wills. Written with Smith, G. London: John Cumberland, n.d. Pp. [1]-29. Cumberland's British Theatre, XXXV. *Filed under* Cumberland, John. Cumberland's British Theatre, XXXV.

Make Your Wills! Written with Smith, G. New York: Samuel French, n.d. Pp. [i-v], [9]-29. Text complete. Minor Drama, 124. Promptbook.

MAYHEW, HENRY

But However—. Written with Baylis, Henry. London: Chapman & Hall, n.d. Pp. [1]-24. [Acting National Drama].

Wandering Minstrel, The. London: John Miller, 1834. Pp. [i-viii], 13-35. Text complete.

MAYHEW, HORACE

Plum-Pudding Pantomime, The; or, Harlequin and the British Lion. London: Bradbury & Evans (printer), n.d. Pp. [1]-24.

MAYHEW, THOMAS CHARLES WILSON

Ambition; or, Marie Mignot. London: Thomas Richardson, 1830. Pp. [i]-viii, [9]-60. Promptbook.

Ambition; or, Marie Mignot. London: John Cumberland, n.d. Pp. [1]-60. Cumberland's British Theatre, XXXIV. *Filed under* Cumberland, John. Cumberland's British Theatre, XXXIV.

MAYOR OF GARRATT, THE
 See Foote, Samuel.

MAYOR OF ROCHESTER, THE
 See Moncrieff, William Thomas.

MAYOR OF ZALAMEA, THE
 See Fitzgerald, Edward (trans.).

MAYOR'S RELATIONS, THE
 See Darbyshire, W.

MAZE, THE MAID, AND THE MONARCH!
 See Burnand, Francis Cowley. Fair Rosamond.

MAZEPPA
 See Byron, Henry James.
 See Milner, Henry M.

MAZOURKA
 See Byron, Henry James.

MEADOW, A.

His Own Enemy. London & New York: Samuel French, n.d. Pp. [1]-24.

MEADOWS, THOMAS

Who's to Blame?; or, No Fool Like an Old One. In *Thespian Gleanings,* rev. ed., Ulverstan: n.pub., 1813, pp. [49]-84.

MEADOWS OF ST. GERVAIS, THE
 See Ware, James Redding.

MEADOWSWEET
 See Prevost, Constance M.

MEASURE FOR MEASURE
 See Kemble, John Philip (arr.).
 See Shakespeare, William.

MEDD, MABEL S.
   Broken Idylls. London & New York: Samuel French, n.d. Pp. [1]-12. [Lacy's Acting Edition].
   Imogen's New Cook. London & New York: Samuel French, n.d. Pp. [1]-12. [Lacy's Acting Edition].
MEDDLE AND MUDDLE
   See Bellingham, Henry.
MEDEA
   See Brough, Robert Barnabas.
   See Heron, Matilda (trans.).
   See Webster, Augusta Davies, Mrs. Thomas (trans.).
   See Wheelwright, Charles Apthrop, Rev. (trans.).
MÉDECIN MALGRÉ LUI
   See Kenney, Charles Lamb (trans.). Mock Doctor, The.
   See Van Laun, Henri (trans.). Physician in Spite of Himself, The.
MÉDECIN VOLANT
   See Van Laun, Henri (trans.). Flying Doctor, The.
MEDICAL MAN, A
   See Gilbert, William Schwenck.
MEDIUM
   See Brougham, John. Revenge.
MEDLAR, MOMUS
   See Smith, T.
MEDLEY OF LOVERS
   See Garrick, David. Miss in Her Teens.
MEET ME BY MOONLIGHT
   See Parry, Thomas.
MEFISTOFELE
   See Marzials, Theophilus Julius Henry (trans.).
MEG MURNOCK, THE HAG OF THE GLEN
   See Barrymore, William.
MEG'S DIVERSION
   See Craven, Henry Thornton.
MEIGHAN, JOHN
   Maria. London: Samuel French; New York: T. Henry French, n.d. Pp. [1]-12. [Lacy's Acting Edition].
MEISTERSINGER VON NURNBERG
   See Corder, Henrietta Louisa Walford, Mrs. Frederick (trans.). Mastersingers of Nuremberg, The.
MELANTER
   See Blackmore, Richard Doddridge.
MELFORD, MARK
   Best Man Wins. In *Mark Melford's Music Hall Sketches*, London & New York: Samuel French, c.1910, pp. [i], 42-62.
   Hampshire Hog, A. In *Mark Melford's Music Hall Sketches*, London & New York: Samuel French, c.1910, pp. [i], 22-32.
   Kleptomania. London: Samuel French; New York: T. Henry French, n.d. Pp. [1]-54. [Lacy's Acting Edition].
   Turned Up. Chicago: Dramatic Publishing Co., n.d. Pp. [1]-52. Sergel's Acting Drama, 427.
MÉLICERTE
   See Van Laun, Henri (trans.).
MELLISH, JOSEPH CHARLES (trans.)
   Mary Stuart. By Schiller. London: G. Auld (printer), 1801. Pp. [i]-[xviii], [1]-224.
MELMOTH THE WANDERER
   See West, B.
MELODRAME MAD!
   See Dibdin, Thomas John.
MELTING MOMENTS
   See Pemberton, Thomas Edgar.
MELTONIANS, THE
   See Peake, Richard Brinsley.
MELVILLE, A.
   Sinbad the Sailor.
   See McArdle, John Francis.
MELVILLE, CHARLES
   Barnaby Rudge.
   See Selby, Charles.
MEM. VII
   See Ellis, Walter.

MEMOIRS OF THE D***L, THE
   See Barber, James.
MEN OF THE DAY
   See Falconer, Edmund. Extremes.
MENAGERIE RACE, THE
   See Anstey, F.
MENDACIOUS MARINER, THE
   See Byron, Henry James.
MENDHAM, JAMES, JR
   Adventures of Ulysses, The; or, The Return to Ithaca. London: Sherwood, Neely, & Jones, 1810. Pp. [iii]-[xii], [1]-60.
MENDICANT, THE
   See A'Beckett, Gilbert Abbott.
MENDOZA
   See Rockingham, Charles, Sir.
MEPHISTOPHELES
   See Brough, Robert Barnabas.
   See Drayton, Henri.
MERCHANT AND HIS CLERKS, THE
   See Coyne, Joseph Stirling.
MERCHANT OF BRUGES, THE
   See Kinnaird, Douglas James William.
MERCHANT OF GUADALOUPE, THE
   See Wallace, John.
MERCHANT OF LONDON, THE
   See Serle, Thomas James.
MERCHANT OF VENICE, THE
   See Irving, Henry (arr.).
   See Kean, Charles John (arr.).
   See Kemble, John Philip (arr.).
   See Shakespeare, William.
   See Valpy, Richard (arr.).
MERCHANT OF VENICE PRESERVED
   See Talfourd, Francis. Shylock.
MERCHANT PIRATE, THE
   See Stirling, Edward.
MERCHANT'S DAUGHTER
   See Stirling, Edward. Clarisse.
MERCHANT'S DAUGHTER OF TOULON, THE
   See Thomas, Jane Penhorn, Mrs. Edward.
MERCHANT'S WEDDING, THE
   See Planché, James Robinson.
MERCIFUL SOUL, THE
   See Alma-Tadema, Laurence.
MERCY DODD
   See Boucicault, Dionysius Lardner.
MEREDITH, OWEN (pseud. of Bulwer Lytton, Edward Robert, Earl of Lytton)
   Clytemnestra. In *Clytemnestra . . .*, London: Chapman & Hall, 1855, pp. [1]-122.
   Duke's Laboratory, The. By Robert Lytton. In *Chronicles and Characters*, London: Chapman & Hall, 1868, II, [163]-207.
   Thanatos Athanatou. By Robert Lytton. In *Chronicles and Characters*, London: Chapman & Hall, 1868, I, 69-125.
MEREWEATHER, CAVALIERE, REV.
   Bacchus and Ariadne. London: J. T. Hayes, 1891. Pp. [i-vi], [1]-55.
MÉRIMÉE, PROSPER (trans.)
   African Love. By Joseph L'Estange (pseud.) (trans.). In *Plays of Clara Gazul*, trans. Joseph L'Estange (pseud.), London: George B. Whittaker, 1825, pp. [161]-[182].
   Heaven and Hell. By Joseph L'Estange (pseud.) (trans.). In *Plays of Clara Gazul*, trans. Joseph L'Estange (pseud.), London: George B. Whittaker, 1825, pp. [293]-[327].
   Ines Mendo, Part 1; or, Prejudice Vanquished. By Joseph L'Estange (pseud.) (trans.). In *Plays of Clara Gazul*, trans. Joseph L'Estange (pseud.), London: George B. Whittaker, 1825, pp. [183]-[223].
   Ines Mendo, Part 2; or, The Triumph of Prejudice. By Joseph L'Estange (pseud.) (trans.). In *Plays of Clara Gazul*, trans. Joseph L'Estange (pseud.), London: George B. Whittaker, 1825, pp. [225]-[291].

Spaniards in Denmark, The. By Joseph L'Estange (pseud.) (trans.). In *Plays of Clara Gazul,* trans. Joseph L'Estange (pseud.), London: George B. Whittaker, 1825, pp. [1]-128.

Woman Is a Devil, A. By Joseph L'Estange (pseud.) (trans.). In *Plays of Clara Gazul,* trans. Joseph L'Estange (pseud.), London: George B. Whittaker, 1825, pp. [129]-160.

MERITT, PAUL

British Born. Written with Pettitt, Henry Alfred. London & New York: Samuel French, n.d. Pp.[1]-48. [Lacy's Acting Edition].

Chopstick and Spikins. London & New York: Samuel French, n.d. Pp. [1]-20. [Lacy's Acting Edition].

Glin Gath; or, The Man in the Cleft. London & New York: Samuel French, n.d. Pp. [1]-44. [Lacy's Acting Edition].

Golden Plough, The. London & New York: Samuel French, n.d. Pp. [1]-48. [Lacy's Acting Edition].

Hand and Glove.
See Conquest, George.

Linked by Love. *Also:* Thad; or, Linked by Love. London & New York: Samuel French, n.d. Pp. [1]-32. [Lacy's Acting Edition]. *Filed under* Thad.

Seven Sins.
See Conquest, George.

Stolen Kisses. London & New York: Samuel French, n.d. Pp. [1]-41. [Lacy's Acting Edition].

Thad.
See Linked by Love.

Velvet and Rags.
See Conquest, George.

White Cliffs, The. Written with Pettitt, Henry Alfred. Liverpool: Bernard Conlon (copyist), 1880. 141 leaves. Manuscript promptbook.

Word of Honour, The: A Jersey Love Story. London & New York: Samuel French, n.d. Pp. [1]-28. French's Acting Edition (late Lacy's).

World, The. Written with Pettitt, Henry Alfred; Harris, Augustus Henry Glossop. c.1881. 54 leaves. Side for one part, Sir Clement Huntingford, only. Manuscript.

Worship of Bacchus, The. Written with Pettitt, Henry Alfred. [Liverpool, 1879]. 161 leaves. Manuscript promptbook.

MERIVALE, HERMAN CHARLES

Alone.
See Simpson, John Palgrave.

Called There and Back. London: [H. Blacklock], n.d. Pp. [1]-40.

Forget-Me-Not. Written with Grove, Florence Craufurd. N.p.: n.pub., n.d. Pp. [1]-45. Promptbook.

He's a Lunatic. By Felix Dale (pseud.). Chicago: Dramatic Publishing Co., n.d. Pp. [1]-15. Sergel's Acting Drama, 19. *Filed under* Dale, Felix.

Husband in Clover, A. New York: Wheat & Cornett, c.1876. Pp. [23]-28. New York Drama, I, 8.

Lady of Lyons Married and Settled, The. London & New York: Samuel French, n.d. Pp. [1]-28. [Lacy's Acting Edition].

Our Joan. Written with Merivale, Mrs. Herman Charles. Pp. [i-ii], [1]-36, [1-29], [1-20]. Irregular pagination by act; text incomplete. Typescript.

Peacock's Holiday. London & New York: Samuel French, n.d. Pp. [1]-34. [Lacy's Acting Edition].

Six Months Ago. By Felix Dale (pseud.). New York: Robert M. DeWitt, n.d. Pp. [1]-14. *Filed under* Dale, Felix.

Son of the Soil, A. London & New York: Samuel French, n.d. Pp. [1]-48. [Lacy's Acting Edition].

Time and the Hour.
See Simpson, John Palgrave.

White Pilgrim, The. London & New York: Samuel French, n.d. Pp. [1]-48. [French's Acting Edition (late Lacy's)]. Promptbook.

MERIVALE, MRS. HERMAN CHARLES

Our Joan.
See Merivale, Herman Charles.

MERLIN AND THE FAIRY QUEEN
See Lee, Nelson, jr. Harlequin and Mother Red Cap.

MERMAID, THE
See Dibdin, Charles Isaac Mungo, jr.
See Galt, John.

MEROPE
See Arnold, Matthew.
See Lloyd, Charles (trans.).

MEROTH
See Hume, Robert William.

MERRIE ENGLAND IN THE OLDEN TIME
See Greenwood, Thomas Longdon. Harlequin Robin Hood and Little John.
See Lee, Nelson, jr. Harlequin and Good Queen Bess.

MERRIFIELD'S GHOST
See Paull, Harry Major.

MERRY CHRISTMAS, A
See Law, Arthur.

MERRY DUCHESS, THE
See Sims, George Robert.

MERRY MAID OF ORLEANS
See Shine, John L. Joan of Arc.

MERRY MEETING, A
See Lestocq, William.

MERRY MONARCH
See Payne, John Howard. Charles the Second.

MERRY MOURNERS
See O'Keeffe, John. Modern Antiques.

MERRY OUTLAWS OF SHERWOOD
See Fitzball, Edward. Robin Hood.

MERRY WAGS OF WARWICKSHIRE, THE
See Curling, Henry.

MERRY WIDOW, THE
See Buckingham, Leicester Silk.

MERRY WIVES OF WINDSOR, THE
See Courtney, John.
See Kemble, John Philip (arr.).
See Shakespeare, William.

MERRY ZINGARA, THE
See Gilbert, William Schwenck.

MERRYMAN AND HIS MAID
See Gilbert, William Schwenck. Yeomen of the Guard, The.

MERTON, CLIFFORD

Unmasked. London: n.pub., n.d. Pp. [i], 1-59. Title page lacking.

MESSAGE FROM THE SEA, A
See Brougham, John.

MESSALINA
See Blackburn, Vernon.

MESSENGER BOY, THE
See Tanner, James Tolman.

METAMORA
See Brougham, John.

METEOR, THE
See Gent, J. B.

METHINKS I SEE MY FATHER!
See Morton, Thomas, sr.

MICHAEL AND CHRISTINE
See Kerr, John.

MICHAEL AND HIS LOST ANGEL
See Jones, Henry Arthur.

MICHAEL ANGELO
See Cornwall, Barry.

MICHAEL ERLE THE MANIAC LOVER
See Wilks, Thomas Egerton.

MIDAS
See O'Hara, Kane.

MIDDLE MAN, THE
See Jones, Henry Arthur.

MIDDLE TEMPLE, THE
See Peake, Richard Brinsley.

MIDDY ASHORE, THE
See Bernard, William Bayle.

MIDNIGHT: THE THIRTEENTH CHIME
See Barnett, Charles Zachary.

MIDNIGHT HOUR, THE
    See Inchbald, Elizabeth Simpson, Mrs. Joseph.
MIDNIGHT SPECTRE!, THE
    See Lee, Nelson, jr.
MIDNIGHT WATCH, THE
    See Morton, John Maddison.
MIDSUMMER DAY
    See Frith, Walter.
MIDSUMMER EVE: AN IDYLL OF SHERWOOD FOREST
    See Kaye, Arthur.
MIDSUMMER FROLIC, A
    See Adams, Florence Davenport.
MIDSUMMER NIGHT'S DREAM, A
    See Kean, Charles John (arr.).
    See Reynolds, Frederick (arr.).
    See Shakespeare, William.
    See Simpson, Mercer H. (arr.).
MIDSUMMER NIGHT'S DREAM IN MERRIE SHERWOOD
    See Goodyer, F. R. Once upon a Time.
MIDSUMMER-NIGHT'S NIGHTMARE
    See Pleon, Harry. Vision of Venus, A.
MIGHTY MAGICIAN, THE
    See Fitzgerald, Edward (trans.).
MIGNONETTE
    See Brand, Oswald.
MIKADO, THE
    See Gilbert, William Schwenck.
MILDENHALL, THOMAS
    Brigands in the Bud! London: Duncombe & Moon, n.d. Pp. [1]-28. Duncombe's Edition.
    Governor's Wife, The. London: W. Barth, n.d. Pp. [1]-37. Promptbook.
    Post of Honour, The. London: John Duncombe, n.d. Pp. [1]-26. Duncombe's Edition <wrps. New British Theatre (late Duncombe's), 373>.
    Sister and I! London: John Duncombe, n.d. <wrps. Thomas Hailes Lacy>. Pp. [1]-28. New British Theatre (late Duncombe's), 448.
    Two Heads Better Than One. London: W. Barth, n.d. Pp. [1]-32.
MILITARY BILLY TAYLOR, THE
    See Burnand, Francis Cowley.
MILITARY EXECUTION
    See Selby, Charles.
MILKY WHITE
    See Craven, Henry Thornton.
MILL OF BAGDAD
    See Fitzball, Edward. Barber, The.
MILLAIS, W. H.
    Princess of Parmesan, The. Music by Latham, Morton. Farnham: John Nichols (printer), n.d. Pp. [1]-27. Libretto.
MILLER, JAMES, REV.
    Mahomet, the Impostor. London: Whittingham & Arliss, 1815. Pp. [1]-[52]. London Theatre, XVI. *Filed under* Dibdin, Thomas John, ed. London Theatre, XVI.
    Mahomet the Impostor. In *British Drama*, 12 vols., London: John Dicks, 1871, IX, [242]-256.
    Siege of Berwick, The; or, The Murdered Hostage. In *St. Baldred of the Bass . . .*, Edinburgh: Oliver & Boyd; George B. Whittaker, 1824, pp. [i], [107]-206.
MILLER, LUKE
    Prevention No Cure. In *Dialogues of the Day,* ed. Oswald Crawfurd, London: Chapman & Hall, n.d., pp. [68]-79. *Filed under* Crawfurd, Oswald. Dialogues of the Day.
MILLER, WYNN F.
    Dream Faces. London & New York: Samuel French, n.d. Pp. [1]-24. [Lacy's Acting Edition].
    False Evidence. Pp. [1]-24, [1]-27, [i], [1]-20, [i], [1]-11. Pagination by act. Typescript promptbook.
MILLER AND HIS MAN, THE
    See Burnand, Francis Cowley.
MILLER AND HIS MEN, THE
    See Pocock, Isaac.
    See Talfourd, Francis.

MILLER OF DERWENT WATER, THE
    See Fitzball, Edward.
MILLER OF GRENOBLE
    See Stirling, Edward. Gold Mine, The.
MILLER OF GUIBRAY
    See Abel, William Henry. Dust.
MILLER OF MANSFIELD, THE
    See Dodsley, Robert.
MILLER OF NEW JERSEY, THE
    See Brougham, John.
MILLER OF THE HARTZ MOUNTAINS!
    See Fitzball, Edward. King of the Mist, The.
MILLER OF WHETSTONE, THE
    See Wilks, Thomas Egerton.
MILLER'S MAID, THE
    See Faucit, John Savill.
MILLER'S WIFE
    See Webster, Benjamin Nottingham. Giralda.
MILLETT, SYDNEY CROHAN, MAJ.
    All at C; or, The Captive, the Coffee, and the Cocoatina. Written with Wilcox, Scott J. B., Lieut. London & New York: Samuel French, n.d. Pp. [1]-18. [Lacy's Acting Edition].
MILLIET, PAUL
    Amy Robsart.
    See Harris, Augustus Henry Glossop.
MILLIGAN, ALICE L.
    Last Feast of the Fianna, The. London: David Nutt, 1900. Pp. [1]-29.
MILLINER'S HOLIDAY, THE
    See Morton, John Maddison.
MILLINGEN, JOHN GIDEON
    Beehive, The. Music by Horn. London: W. H. Wyatt, 1811. Pp. [i-iv], [1]-43.
    Bee-Hive, The. By J. V. Millingen. London: John Cumberland, n.d. Pp. [1]-40. Cumberland's British Theatre, XXX. *Filed under* Cumberland, John. Cumberland's British Theatre, XXX.
    Borrowed Feathers. London: John Duncombe, n.d. Pp. [1]-28. Duncombe's Edition.
    King's Fool, The; or, The Old Man's Curse. London: Baylis & Leighton (printer), n.d. Pp. [i], [1]-61. Title page lacking.
    Ladies at Home; or, Gentlemen, We Can Do Without You. London: C. Chapple, 1819. Pp. [i-v], [1]-22.
    Who'll Lend Me a Wife! London: John Duncombe, n.d. Pp. [1]-32. Duncombe's Edition.
MILLIONAIRE, THE
    See Godfrey, George William.
MILLS, HORACE
    Pimple, the Pirate; or, The Baronet and the Bandit. London: Blades, East, & Blades (printer), n.d. Pp. [1]-47.
MILLWARD, CHARLES
    Aladdin and the Wonderful Lamp. Music by Humphreys, F. W. Birmingham: Theatre Royal Printing Office, n.d. Pp. [1]-24. Libretto. *Filed under* Aladdin and the Wonderful Lamp (anon.).
    Bloomerism.
    See Nightingale, Joseph Henry.
    Bluebeard. Birmingham: Theatre Royal Printing Works, n.d. Pp. [1]-24. Libretto.
    Cock-a-Doodle-Doo; or, Harlequin Prince Chanticleer and the Princess of the Golden Valley. London: Merser & Gardner (printer), 1865. Pp. [1]-22.
    Hush-a-Bye Baby on the Tree-top; or, Harlequin Fortunio, King Fro of Frog Island, and the Magic Toys of Lowther Arcadia! London: Astley's Theatre, n.d. Pp. [1]-28.
    Jolly Miller of the Dee, The; or, Harlequin and Bluff King Hal and the Fair Maid of Leasowe. Liverpool: Lee & Nightingale (printer), n.d. Pp. [1]-20.
MILMAN, HENRY HART
    Anne Boleyn. In *Poetical Works,* 3 vols., London: John Murray, 1839, III, [i]-[x], [1]-114.
    Belshazzar. London: John Murray, 1822. Pp. [i]-[vi], [1]-162.
    Fall of Jerusalem, The. London: John Murray, 1820. Pp. [i]-[viii], [1]-167. New ed.

Fazio. Oxford: Samuel Collingwood (printer), 1815. Pp. [1-2], [i]-[vi], [1]-103.

Fazio. Oxford: Samuel Collingwood (printer), 1816. Pp. [i]-[vi], [1]-103. 2nd ed.

Fazio; or, The Italian Wife. In *British Drama*, 12 vols., London: John Dicks, 1865, IV, [991]-1007.

Martyr of Antioch, The. London: John Murray, 1823. Pp. [iii]-[viii], [1]-168. New ed.

MILMAN, HENRY HART (trans.)

Agamemnon, The. By Aeschylus. In *Agamemnon of Aeschylus . . .*, London: John Murray, 1865, pp. [iii]-[x], [1]-92.

Bacchanals, The. By Euripides. In *Agamemnon of Aeschylus . . .*, London: John Murray, 1865, pp. [93]-180. *Filed under* Agamemnon.

MILNER, HENRY M.

Alonzo the Brave and the Fair Imogine; or, The Spectre Bride! London: John Duncombe, n.d. Pp. [1]-28. John Duncombe's Edition. Promptbook.

Bandit of the Blind Mine, The. London: Thomas Hailes Lacy, n.d. Pp. [1]-[30]. New British Theatre (late Duncombe's), 314.

Barmecide; or, The Fatal Offspring. London: Richard White, 1818. Pp. [i]-[x], [5]-52. Promptbook.

Bears Not Beasts; or, Four Legs Better Than Two. London: John Dicks, n.d. Pp. [1]-8. [Dicks' Standard Plays, 387].

Blind Beggar of Bethnal Green, The. London: n.pub., n.d. Pp. [159]-170. Title page lacking.

Death-Fetch, The; or, The Fatal Warning. Music by Hughes, T. London: John Lowndes, n.d. Pp. [1]-40. Promptbook.

Don Juan. Written with Stirling, Edward. London: W. Strange, 1837. Pp. [1]-32. Duncombe's Acting Edition of the British Theatre, 274.

Fair Maid of Perth, The; or, The Battle of the Inch. *Also:* St. Valentine's Eve. London: Thomas Hailes Lacy, n.d. Pp. [i-ii], [1]-48. [Lacy's Acting Edition].

Frankenstein; or, The Man and the Monster! *Also:* Man and the Monster!, The; or, The Fate of Frankenstein. London: John Duncombe, n.d. Pp. [3]-26. Duncombe's Edition.

Giovanni in Paris. London: John Lowndes, n.d. Pp. [1]-16. Libretto.

Gustavus the Third; or, The Masked Ball! London: John Duncombe, n.d. Pp. [1]-30. Duncombe's Acting Edition of the British Theatre, 99.

Hertfordshire Tragedy, The; or, The Victims of Gaming. London: John Lowndes, n.d. Pp. [1]-32.

Hut of the Red Mountain, The; or, Thirty Years of a Gamester's Life. London: John Lowndes, 1827. Pp. [i]-[vi], [1]-59.

Hut of the Red Mountain, The; or, Thirty Years of a Gamester's Life. London: John Cumberland, n.d. Pp. [1]-60. Cumberland's Minor Theatre, VII. *Filed under* Cumberland, John. Cumberland's Minor Theatre, VII.

Jew of Lubeck, The; or, The Heart of a Father. London: John Lowndes, 1819. Pp. [i-viii], [1]-27. 2nd ed. Promptbook.

Lucius Catiline, the Roman Traitor. London: John Lowndes, n.d. Pp. [i]-[viii], [1]-50.

Man and the Monster!, The; or, The Fate of Frankenstein. *Also:* Frankenstein; or, The Man and the Monster!. London: John Duncombe, n.d. Pp. [1]-28. John Duncombe's Edition.

Masaniello; or, The Dumb Girl of Portici. London: John Cumberland, n.d. Pp. [1]-40. Cumberland's Minor Theatre, I. *Filed under* Cumberland, John. Cumberland's Minor Theatre, I.

Masaniello, the Fisherman of Naples. London: John Lowndes, n.d. Pp. [1]-62.

Mazeppa. London: John Cumberland, n.d. Pp. [1]-52. Cumberland's Minor Theatre, V. *Filed under* Cumberland, John. Cumberland's Minor Theatre, V.

Mazeppa. London: Music Publishing Co., n.d. Pp. [1]-52. Promptbook.

102; or, The Veteran and His Progeny! *Also:* Veteran of 102 Years; or, Five Generations. London: John Duncombe, n.d. Pp. [1]-20. [New British Theatre (late Duncombe's), 542].

St. Valentine's Eve.
See Fair Maid of Perth, The.

Temple of Death, The. London: Thomas Hailes Lacy, n.d. Pp. [1]-45.

Temple of Death, The. London: Thomas Hailes Lacy, n.d. Pp. [1]-45. New British Theatre (late Duncombe's), 333.

Tower of Nesle, The; or, The Dark Gondola. London: John Duncombe, n.d. Pp. [1]-52. Duncombe's Edition. Promptbook.

Turpin's Ride to York; or, Bonny Black Bess. London: John Dicks, n.d. Pp. [1]-12. Dicks' Standard Plays, 632.

Twelve Precisely!; or, A Night at Dover. London: John Lowndes, 1821. Pp. i-ii, [1]-22.

Veteran of 102 Years; or, Five Generations. *Also:* 102; or, The Veteran and His Progeny!. London: Thomas Hailes Lacy, n.d. Pp. [1]-18. [Lacy's Acting Edition].

Victorine, the Maid of Paris. N.p.: n.pub., n.d. Pp. [77]-[92]. Title page lacking.

Whittington and His Cat; or, London in 1370. London: John Lowndes, n.d. Pp. [i-iv], [1]-29.

MILNER, HENRY M. (trans.)

Philosopher, The. By Lessing. London: C. Chapple, 1819. Pp. [i-iv], [1]-31, 41-58. Text incomplete.

MILTON, JOHN

Comus.
See Colman, George, sr (arr.).

Comus. Music by Handel; Arne; Bishop; Cherubini. London: John Miller, 1815. Pp. [1]-29. Libretto.

Comus. London: John Cumberland, n.d. Pp. [1]-23. Cumberland's British Theatre, XXXII. *Filed under* Cumberland, John. Cumberland's British Theatre, XXXII.

MILTON AT ROME
See Vetch, ?, Maj.

MIMA AND HER FRIENDS
See Rockingham, Charles, Sir. Holiday, A.

MIND YOUR OWN BUSINESS
See Lemon, Mark.

MINERALI, THE
See Grattan, H. P.

MINISTER AND THE MERCER, THE
See Bunn, Alfred.

MINNA VON BARNHELM
See Bell, Ernest (trans.).
See Holcroft, Fanny (trans.).

MINOR CHRISTY, THE
See Ridge, William Pett.

MINSTREL, THE
See Adams, Arthur Henry.

MINSTREL KING
See Brough, Robert Barnabas. Alfred the Great.

MINSTREL PRINCE
See Vetch, ?, Maj. Dara.

MINTON, ANN

Wife to Be Lett, A; or, The Miser Cured. London: A. Seale (printer), 1802. Pp. [1]-51, 53-66. Text complete.

MINUTE GUN AT SEA!, THE
See Barnett, Charles Zachary.

MINX AND MAN, THE
See Lindo, Frank.

MIRANDOLA
See Cornwall, Barry.

MIRELLA
See Chorley, Henry Fothergill (trans.).

MIRETTE
See Weatherly, Frederick Edward.

MIRIAM'S CRIME
See Craven, Henry Thornton.

MIRROR, THE
See Filippi, Rosina.

MISANTHROPE, THE
See Mathew, Charles (trans.).
See Van Laun, Henri (trans.).
See Wall, Charles Heron (trans.).

MISCHIEF-MAKING
   See Buckstone, John Baldwin.
MISE OF LEWES, THE; OR, THE RESTORATION OF MAGNA CHARTA (anon.)
   London: Simpkin & Marshall, 1823. Pp. [1]-[10], [1]-76.
MISER
   See Cross, Julian.
   See Fielding, Henry.
   See Mathew, Charles (trans.).
   See Van Laun, Henri (trans.).
MISER CURED
   See Minton, Ann. Wife to Be Lett, A.
MISER OF ELTHAM GREEN
   See Pitt, George Dibdin. Last Man, The.
MISER OF SHOREDITCH, THE
   See Prest, Thomas Peckett.
MISER OF SOUTHWARK FERRY
   See Jerrold, Douglas William. John Overy.
MISER OF THE HILL FORT
   See Archer, Thomas. Inundation, The.
MISER OUTWITTED
   See Harding, C. T. He Must Be Married.
MISER'S DAUGHTER, THE
   See Stirling, Edward.
   See Taylor, Thomas Proclus.
MISER'S WARNING!
   See Barnett, Charles Zachary. Christmas Carol, A.
MISERIES OF HUMAN LIFE, THE
   See Webster, Benjamin Nottingham.
MISS BETSY BULL
   See Kitching, H. St. A.
MISS CHESTER
   See Marryat, Florence.
MISS CLEOPATRA
   See Shirley, Arthur.
MISS DOBSON
   See Bell, Florence Eveleen Eleanore Oliffe, Mrs. Hugh (Lady).
MISS EILY O'CONNOR
   See Byron, Henry James.
MISS GWILT
   See Collins, William Wilkie.
MISS HOBBS
   See Jerome, Jerome Klapka.
MISS HONEY'S TREASURE (anon.)
   London & New York: Samuel French, n.d. Pp. [1]-11. [Lacy's Acting Edition].
MISS IMPUDENCE
   See Morton, Edward A.
MISS IN HER TEENS
   See Garrick, David.
MISS SARA SAMPSON
   See Bell, Ernest (trans.).
MISS TIBBETS' BACK HAIR
   See Robinson, Nugent.
MISSING TEMPERANCE SPEAKERS, THE
   See Featherstone, Thomas.
MISSING WITNESS, THE
   See Braddon, Mary Elizabeth.
MISTAKEN IDENTITY
   See Goddard, Kate.
   See Hayes, Frederick William.
MISTAKEN STORY, A
   See Wilks, Thomas Egerton.
MISTAKES OF A NIGHT
   See Goldsmith, Oliver. She Stoops to Conquer.
MISTAKES OF MARRIAGE, THE. (anon.)
   Pp. [i-ii], [1]-47, [i], [1]-61, [1]-61. Pagination by act. Title page lacking. Typescript promptbook.
MISTLETOE BOUGH, THE
   See Somerset, Charles A.
MISTRESS OF THE MILL
   See Moncrieff, William Thomas.

MITCHELL, ROBERT
   William of Normandy, King of England. London: Effingham Wilson, 1879. Pp. [i-iv], [1]-106.
MITFORD, EDWARD LEDWICH
   Gaston de Foix. In [*Poems Dramatic and Lyrical*, London: Provost, 1869], pp. [245]-[334].
   Love and Hate. In [*Poems Dramatic and Lyrical*, London: Provost, 1869], pp. [109]-142.
   Prince Edward. In [*Poems Dramatic and Lyrical*, London: Provost, 1869], pp. [i-vi], [1]-107.
MITFORD, MARY RUSSELL
   Alice. In *Dramatic Scenes . . .* , London: George B. Whittaker, 1827, pp. [162]-183. *Filed under* Dramatic Scenes.
   Bridal Eve, The. In *Dramatic Scenes . . .* , London: George B. Whittaker, 1827, pp. [249]-268. *Filed under* Dramatic Scenes.
   Captive, The. In *Dramatic Scenes . . .* , London: George B. Whittaker, 1827, pp. [269]-282. *Filed under* Dramatic Scenes.
   Charles the First. London: John Duncombe, 1834. Pp. [i]-[x], [1]-80.
   Cunigunda's Vow. In *Dramatic Scenes . . .* , London: George B. Whittaker, 1827, pp. [i-viii], [1]-25. *Filed under* Dramatic Scenes.
   Emily. In *Dramatic Scenes . . .* , London: George B. Whittaker, 1827, pp. [82]-105. *Filed under* Dramatic Scenes.
   Fair Rosamond. In *Dramatic Scenes . . .* , London: George B. Whittaker, 1827, pp. [133]-161. *Filed under·* Dramatic Scenes.
   Fawn, The. In *Dramatic Scenes . . .* , London: George B. Whittaker, 1827, pp. [27]-56. *Filed under* Dramatic Scenes.
   Foscari. London: George B. Whittaker, 1826. Pp. [i]-iv, [1]-78.
   Foscari. London: John Cumberland, n.d. Pp. [1]-59. Cumberland's British Theatre, XXXVIII. *Filed under* Cumberland, John. Cumberland's British Theatre, XXXVIII.
   Gaston de Blondeville. In *Dramatic Works,* 2 vols., London: Hurst & Blackett, 1854, II, [121]-178.
   Henry Talbot. In *Dramatic Scenes . . .* , London: George B. Whittaker, 1827, pp. [184]-218. *Filed under* Dramatic Scenes.
   Inez de Castro. London: John Dicks, n.d. Pp. [1]-[20]. Dicks' Standard Plays, 672.
   Julian. London: George & W. B. Whittaker, 1823. Pp. [v]-[xiv], [1]-83. 2nd ed.
   Julian. London: George & W. B. Whittaker, 1823. Pp. [i]-xii, [1]-[82], [1]-2.
   Julian. London: John Cumberland, n.d. Pp. [1]-58. Cumberland's British Theatre, XXXII. *Filed under* Cumberland, John. Cumberland's British Theatre, XXXII.
   Masque of the Seasons, The. In *Dramatic Scenes . . .* , London: George B. Whittaker, 1827, pp. [283]-290. *Filed under* Dramatic Scenes.
   Otto of Wittelsbach. In *Dramatic Works,* 2 vols., London: Hurst & Blackett, 1854, II, [179]-256.
   Painter's Daughter, The. In *Dramatic Scenes . . .* , London: George B. Whittaker, 1827, pp. [107]-131. *Filed under* Dramatic Scenes.
   Rienzi. London: John Cumberland, 1828. Pp. [iii]-[x], [11]-66.
   Rienzi. London: John Cumberland, n.d. Pp. [1]-66. Cumberland's British Theatre, XXIV. *Filed under* Cumberland, John. Cumberland's British Theatre, XXIV.
   Sadak and Kalasrade; or, The Waters of Oblivion. Music by Packer. London: S. G. Fairbrother (printer), n.d. Pp. [i]-[vi], [7]-31. Libretto.
   Siege, The. In *Dramatic Scenes . . .* , London: George B. Whittaker, 1827, pp. [219]-248. *Filed under* Dramatic Scenes.
   Wedding Ring, The. In *Dramatic Scenes . . .* , London: George B. Whittaker, 1827, pp. [57]-81. *Filed under* Dramatic Scenes.

MITHRIDATES
    See Boswell, Robert Bruce (trans.).
MIXED ADDRESSES
    See Fane, Sydney.
MOB CAP, THE
    See Paul, Howard.
MOCK DOCTOR, THE
    See Fielding, Henry.
    See Kenney, Charles Lamb (trans.).
MODEL HUSBAND, A
    See Wooler, John Pratt.
MODEL OF A WIFE, A
    See Wigan, Alfred Sydney.
MODERATION VERSUS ABSTINENCE
    See Sayers, T. Albert.
MODERN ANTIQUES
    See O'Keeffe, John.
MODERN COLLEGIANS
    See Moncrieff, William Thomas.
MODERN IDEAL, A
    See Lysaght, Sidney Royse.
MODERN LOCUSTA, A
    See Bell, Florence Eveleen Eleanore Oliffe, Mrs. Hugh (Lady).
MODERN LYDIA, A
    See Crawfurd, Oswald.
MODERN ORPHEUS, THE
    See Webster, Benjamin Nottingham.
MODERN SENTIMENT
    See Le Fanu, Alicia Sheridan, Mrs. Joseph. Sons of Erin, The.
MOGUL TALE, THE
    See Inchbald, Elizabeth Simpson, Mrs. Joseph.
MOHAWK MINSTRELS' EIGHTH BOOK OF DRAMAS, DIALOGUES, AND DROLLERIES, THE
    See Forman, Edmund.
MOHAWK MINSTRELS' FIFTH BOOK OF DRAMAS, DIALOGUES, AND DROLLERIES, THE
    See Banks, Billy.
MOHAWK MINSTRELS' FOURTH ANNUAL OF DRAMAS, DIALOGUES, AND DROLLERIES, THE
    See Hunter, Harry.
MOHAWK MINSTRELS' NIGGER DRAMAS, DIALOGUES, AND DROLLERIES
    See Townley, Charles.
MOHAWK MINSTRELS' NINTH BOOK OF DRAMAS, STUMP SPEECHES, NIGGER JOKES, AND REC-ITATIONS, THE
    See Williams, Arthur, et al.
MOHAWK MINSTRELS' TENTH BOOK OF NIGGER DRAMAS AND SKETCHES
    See Forman, Edmund.
MOIR, GEORGE (trans.)
    Wallenstein's Camp. By Schiller. Boston: James Munroe, 1837. Pp. [i]-[vi], [7]-142.
MOLIÈRE
    Affected Young Ladies, The.
        See Mathew, Charles (trans.).
    Amphitryon.
        See Van Laun, Henri (trans.).
    Blue-Stockings, The.
        See Mathew, Charles (trans.).
    Blunderer, The.
        See Mathew, Charles (trans.).
        See Van Laun, Henri (trans.).
    Bores, The.
        See Van Laun, Henri (trans.).
    Citizen Who Apes the Nobleman, The.
        See Van Laun, Henri (trans.).
    Comic Pastoral, A.
        See Van Laun, Henri (trans.).
    Countess of Escarbagnas, The.
        See Van Laun, Henri (trans.).
    Doctor by Compulsion, The.
        See Mathew, Charles (trans.).

Don Garcia of Navarre.
    See Van Laun, Henri (trans.).
Don Juan.
    See Van Laun, Henri (trans.).
Flying Doctor, The.
    See Van Laun, Henri (trans.).
Forced Marriage, The.
    See Mathew, Charles (trans.).
    See Van Laun, Henri (trans.).
George Dandin.
    See Van Laun, Henri (trans.).
Hypochondriac, The.
    See Mathew, Charles (trans.).
Imaginary Invalid, The.
    See Van Laun, Henri (trans.).
Impostures of Scapin, The.
    See Wall, Charles Heron (trans.).
Impromptu of Versailles, The.
    See Van Laun, Henri (trans.).
Jealousy of le Barbouille, The.
    See Van Laun, Henri (trans.).
Learned Ladies, The.
    See Van Laun, Henri (trans.).
Love Is the Best Doctor.
    See Van Laun, Henri (trans.).
Love Tiff, The.
    See Van Laun, Henri (trans.).
Magnificent Lovers, The.
    See Van Laun, Henri (trans.).
Mélicerte.
    See Van Laun, Henri (trans.).
Misanthrope, The.
    See Mathew, Charles (trans.).
    See Van Laun, Henri (trans.).
    See Wall, Charles Heron (trans.).
Miser, The.
    See Mathew, Charles (trans.).
    See Van Laun, Henri (trans.).
Monsieur de Pourceaugnac.
    See Van Laun, Henri (trans.).
Physician in Spite of Himself, The.
    See Van Laun, Henri (trans.).
Pretentious Young Ladies, The.
    See Van Laun, Henri (trans.).
Princess of Elis, The.
    See Van Laun, Henri (trans.).
Psyche.
    See Van Laun, Henri (trans.).
Rogueries of Scapin, The.
    See Van Laun, Henri (trans.).
Scapin's Rogueries.
    See Mathew, Charles (trans.).
School for Husbands, The.
    See Mathew, Charles (trans.).
    See Van Laun, Henri (trans.).
School for Wives, The.
    See Mathew, Charles (trans.).
    See Van Laun, Henri (trans.).
School for Wives Criticised, The.
    See Van Laun, Henri (trans.).
Sganarelle.
    See Van Laun, Henri (trans.).
Sicilian, The.
    See Van Laun, Henri (trans.).
Tartuffe.
    See Mathew, Charles (trans.).
    See Oxenford, John (trans.).
    See Van Laun, Henri (trans.).
Would-Be Gentleman, The.
    See Mathew, Charles (trans.).
MOMENT OF PERIL
    See Wilks, Thomas Egerton. Wren Boys, The.
MOMENTOUS QUESTION, THE
    See Fitzball, Edward.

MONARCH AND THE MIMIC
> *See* Selby, Charles. Frederick of Prussia.

MONARCH, THE MAIDEN, THE MAZE, AND THE MIXTURE
> *See* Langbridge, Frederick. Fair Rosamond's Bower.

MONASTERY OF ST. JUST, THE
> *See* Oxenford, John.

MONCRIEF, WILLIAM G. T.
> *See* Moncrieff, William Thomas.

MONCRIEFF, WILLIAM THOMAS (pseud. of Thomas, William Thomas)

Adventures of a Ventriloquist; or, The Rogueries of Nicholas. London: John Lowndes, 1822. Pp. [i]-[x], [1]-39.

All at Coventry; or, Love and Laugh. London: J. Phillips, 1816. Pp. [1]-57.

All at Coventry; or, Love and Laugh. London: John Cumberland, n.d. Pp. [1]-44. Cumberland's British Theatre, XXXIII. *Filed under* Cumberland, John. Cumberland's British Theatre, XXXIII.

Bashful Man, The. In *British Drama,* 12 vols., London: John Dicks, 1872, X, [1]-16.

Bashful Man!, The. London & New York: Samuel French, n.d. Pp. [3]-45. [Lacy's Acting Edition].

Beauty of Lyons, The. Clyde, Ohio: A. D. Ames, n.d. Pp. [1]-34. Ames' Series of Standard and Minor Drama, 89.

Beggar of Cripplegate, The; or, The Humours of Bluff King Hal! London: Thomas Richardson, n.d. Pp. [5]-46. Text complete.

Beggar of Cripplegate, The; or, The Humours of Bluff King Hal. London: John Cumberland, n.d. Pp. [1]-46. Cumberland's Minor Theatre, XI. *Filed under* Cumberland, John. Cumberland's Minor Theatre, XI.

Borrowing a Husband; or, Sleeping Out. London: Thomas Hailes Lacy, 1851. Pp. [i]-iv, [1]-38.

Bringing Home the Bride!; or, The Husband's First Journey. London: n.pub. (priv.), 1838. Pp. [i]-iv, [1]-48.

Cataract of the Ganges!, The; or, The Rajah's Daughter. London: Simpkin & Marshall, 1823. Pp. [i]-iv, [5]-50.

Cataract of the Ganges, The; or, The Rajah's Daughter. London: John Cumberland, n.d. Pp. [1]-41. Cumberland's British Theatre, XXXIII. *Filed under* Cumberland, John. Cumberland's British Theatre, XXXIII.

Cataract of the Ganges, The; or, The Rajah's Daughter. London: Hodgson, n.d. Pp. [1]-24. Hodgson's Juvenile Drama.

Comic Medley. In *Crockery's Misfortunes,* London: John Lowndes, 1821, pp. [16]-18. Songs. *Filed under* Ebsworth, Joseph. Crockery's Misfortunes.

Court of Queen Anne, The; or, The Prince and the Breeches Maker! N.p.: n.pub., n.d. Pp. [241]-256. Title page lacking.

Diamond Arrow, The; or, The Postmaster's Wife and the Mayor's Daughter. London: J. Phillips, 1816. Pp. [1]-28.

Diamond Arrow, The. Music by Reeve, G. W. London: John Cumberland, n.d. Pp. [1]-27. Cumberland's Minor Theatre, X. *Filed under* Cumberland, John. Cumberland's Minor Theatre, X.

Eugene Aram; or, Saint Robert's Cave! London: Thomas Richardson, n.d. Pp. [iii]-[x], [11]-32. 2nd ed. Richardson's New Minor Drama, 32.

Eugene Aram; or, Saint Robert's Cave. London: John Cumberland, n.d. Pp. [1]-68. Cumberland's Minor Theatre, X. *Filed under* Cumberland, John. Cumberland's Minor Theatre, X.

Giovanni in London; or, The Libertine Reclaimed. London: John Miller, 1818. Pp. [i]-iv, [1]-23. Libretto.

Giovanni in London; or, The Libertine Reclaimed. London: John Cumberland, 1828. Pp. [1]-48. Cumberland's British Theatre, XVII. *Filed under* Cumberland, John. Cumberland's British Theatre, XVII.

Giovanni in London. In *British Drama,* 12 vols., London: John Dicks, 1865, III, [815]-830.

Giovanni in London; or, The Libertine Reclaimed. London: John Cumberland, n.d. Pp. [3]-48. Libretto.

Giovanni in London; or, The Libertine Reclaimed. London: John Lowndes, n.d. Pp. [1]-24. Libretto.

Giovanni in the Country; or, The Rake Husband. London: John Lowndes, n.d. Pp. [1]-20. Libretto.

Gipsy Jack; or, The Napoleon of Humble Life. London: John Cumberland, n.d. Pp. [1]-36. [Cumberland's Minor Theatre].

Gipsy Jack; or, The Napoleon of Humble Life. London: John Cumberland, n.d. Pp. [1]-36. Cumberland's Minor Theatre, IX. *Filed under* Cumberland, John. Cumberland's Minor Theatre, IX.

Giselle; or, The Phantom Night Dancers. N.p.: n.pub., n.d. Pp. [iii]-xvi, [1]-63.

Heart of London, The; or, The Sharper's Progress. London: John Dicks, n.d. Pp. [1]-23. Dicks' Standard Plays, 430.

Home for the Holidays; or, Young Master. London: John Cumberland, 1828. Pp. [i]-vi], [1]-43.

How to Take Up a Bill; or, The Village Vauxhall. London: J. Limbird, 1837. Pp. [i]-vi], [1]-36.

Irresistibles, The. London: John Duncombe, n.d. Pp. [3]-30. Duncombe's Edition.

Ivanhoe!; or, The Jewess. London: John Lowndes, 1820. Pp. [i]-iv], [1]-80.

Jewess!, The; or, The Council of Constance! London: John Duncombe, n.d. Pp. [1]-54. Duncombe's Edition.

Joconde; or, The Festival of the Rosiere. London: John Cumberland, n.d. Pp. [1]-48.

Joconde; or, The Festival of the Rosiere. London: John Cumberland, n.d. Pp. [1]-48. Cumberland's Minor Theatre, XII. *Filed under* Cumberland, John. Cumberland's Minor Theatre, XII.

Kiss and the Rose, The; or, Love in the Nursery Grounds. London: n.pub. (priv.), 1837. Pp. [i]-iv, [1]-31.

Lear of Private Life!, The; or, Father and Daughter. London: Thomas Richardson, n.d. Pp. [6]-52. Promptbook.

Lear of Private Life, The; or, Father and Daughter. London: John Cumberland, n.d. Pp. [1]-53. Cumberland's Minor Theatre, VII. *Filed under* Cumberland, John. Cumberland's Minor Theatre, VII.

Lestocq; or, The Conspirators of St. Petersburgh! London: John Duncombe, n.d. Pp. [1]-50. Duncombe's Edition.

Lochinvar; or, The Bridal of Netherby. London: n.pub., n.d. Pp. [227]-243. Title page lacking.

Mayor of Rochester, The. [London: John Dicks], n.d. Pp. [11]-21.

Mistress of the Mill. London & New York: Samuel French, n.d. Pp. [i]-ix, [10]-30.

Modern Collegians; or, Over the Bridge. London: John Lowndes, 1820. Pp. [3]-23.

Monsieur Mallet; or, My Daughter's Letter. London: Thomas Hailes Lacy, 1851. Pp. [i]-[xiv], [1]-96.

Monsieur Tonson! London: J. Tabby (printer), 1821. Pp. [iv]-[viii], [5]-46.

Monsieur Tonson. London: John Cumberland, 1827. Pp. [i], [1]-40. Cumberland's British Theatre, XVI. *Filed under* Cumberland, John. Cumberland's British Theatre, XVI.

Monsieur Tonson. In *British Drama,* 12 vols., London: John Dicks, 1871, VIII, [20]-32.

Mount St. Bernard; or, The Headsman. [London (Holborn): John Duncombe], n.d. Pp. [45]-64. Title page lacking.

Paris and London; or, A Trip to Both Cities. New York: E. M. Murden, 1828. Pp. [1]-6, 11-12, 9-10, 7-8, 13-54.

Parson's Nose, The; or, The Birth Day Dinner. London: T. Stagg (printer) (priv.), 1837. Pp. [i]-[iv], [1]-30.

Party Wall!, The. London: John Duncombe, n.d. Pp. [5]-26. Text complete. Duncombe's Edition.

Peer and Peasant, The. London: W. T. Moncrieff, 1836. Pp. [i]-[xx], [1]-109.

Perourou, the Bellows Mender, and the Beauty of Lyons. London: John Duncombe, n.d. Pp. [1]-54. Duncombe's Edition.

Pestilence of Marseilles, The; or, The Four Thieves. London: John Cumberland, n.d. Pp. [1]-7, viii, [9]-48.

Pestilence of Marseilles, The; or, The Four Thieves. London: John Cumberland, n.d. Pp. [1]-48. Cumberland's Minor

Theatre, XI. *Filed under* Cumberland, John. Cumberland's Minor Theatre, XI.

Pickwickians, The.
See Lacy, Thomas Hailes (arr.).

Red Farm, The; or, The Well of St. Marie. London: John Dicks, n.d. Pp. [1]-15. Dicks' Standard Plays, 611.

Reform; or, John Bull Triumphant. London: Thomas Richardson, n.d. Pp. [i]-vii, 8-28.

Reform; or, John Bull Triumphant. London: John Cumberland, n.d. Pp. [1]-28. Cumberland's Minor Theatre, XIII. *Filed under* Cumberland, John. Cumberland's Minor Theatre, XIII.

Rochester; or, King Charles the Second's Merry Days. London: John Lowndes, 1819. Pp. [i]-iv], [1]-63.

Rochester; or King Charles the Second's Merry Days. London: John Cumberland, n.d. Pp. [i]-ii], [1]-64. Cumberland's Minor Theatre, XI. *Filed under* Cumberland, John. Cumberland's Minor Theatre, XI.

Sam Weller; or, The Pickwickians. London: John Dicks, n.d. Pp. [1]-39. Dicks' Standard Plays, 541.

Scamps of London, The; or, The Cross Roads of Life! London: Thomas Hailes Lacy, n.d. Pp. [1]-45. Lacy's Acting Edition, 1213.

Secret, The; or, Natural Magic. London: W. T. Moncrieff, 1825. Pp. [1]-26.

Secret, The; or, The Hole in the Wall. London: John Cumberland & Son, n.d. Pp. [1]-24. Cumberland's British Theatre, XLI. *Filed under* Cumberland, John. Cumberland's British Theatre, XLI.

Shakespeare's Festival; or, New Comedy of Errors! London: Thomas Richardson, n.d. Pp. [i]-viii, [9]-36.

Shakspeare's Festival; or, A New Comedy of Errors. London: John Cumberland, n.d. Pp. [1]-36. Cumberland's Minor Theatre, X. *Filed under* Cumberland, John. Cumberland's Minor Theatre, X.

Shipwreck of the Medusa; or, The Fatal Raft! London: Thomas Richardson, n.d. Pp. [v]-viii, [9]-42. Text complete.

Shipwreck of the Medusa; or, The Fatal Raft. London: John Cumberland, n.d. Pp. [1]-42. Cumberland's Minor Theatre, XII. *Filed under* Cumberland, John. Cumberland's Minor Theatre, XII.

Somnambulist, The; or, The Phantom of the Village! London: W. T. Moncrieff, 1828. Pp. [i]-vi], [1]-45.

Somnambulist, The. London: John Cumberland, 1828. Pp. [1]-40. Cumberland's British Theatre, XVIII. *Filed under* Cumberland, John. Cumberland's British Theatre, XVIII.

Somnambulist, The; or, The Phantom of the Village. London: Thomas Hailes Lacy, n.d. Pp. [1]-40. [Lacy's Acting Edition].

Spectre Bridegroom, The; or, A Ghost in Spite of Himself. London: John Cumberland, 1827. Pp. [1]-32. Cumberland's British Theatre, XVI. *Filed under* Cumberland, John. Cumberland's British Theatre, XVI.

Spectre Bridegroom, The; or, A Ghost in Spite of Himself. London: John Cumberland, n.d. Pp. [1]-32.

Tarnation Strange; or, More Jonathans. London: J. Limbird, 1842. Pp. [iii]-vi, [1-2], vii-[x], [1]-88.

Tereza Tomkins; or, The Fruits of Geneva. London: John Lowndes, 1821. Pp. [i]-[viii], [1]-42.

Tobit's Dog!, The. London: n.pub. (priv.), 1838. Pp. [i]-iv, [1]-51.

Tom and Jerry; or, Life in London. London: John Cumberland, n.d. Pp. [1]-72. Cumberland's British Theatre, XXXIII. *Filed under* Cumberland, John. Cumberland's British Theatre, XXXIII.

Tom and Jerry; or, Life in London. New York: Samuel French, n.d. Pp. [i]-vi, [1]-28. Minor Drama, 157.

Vampire, The. London: Thomas Richardson, 1829. Pp. [i]-vii, 10, [9]-40. Richardson's New Minor Drama, 18.

Van Diemen's Land. London: John Cumberland, n.d. Pp. [1]-76. Cumberland's Minor Theatre, X. *Filed under* Cumberland, John. Cumberland's Minor Theatre, X.

Van Diemen's Land. London: John Cumberland, n.d. Pp. [1]-76. [Cumberland's Minor Theatre].

Wanted a Wife; or, A Checque on My Banker. London: John Lowndes, 1819. Pp. [i]-[x], [1]-68.

Williams' Visits; or, Three Hours before Supper. London: J. Duncombe, n.d. Pp. [1]-56. Duncombe's Edition.

Winterbottoms!, The; or, My Aunt, the Dowager. London: n.pub. (priv.), 1837. Pp. [i]-[vi], [1]-[36].

Zoroaster; or, The Spirit of the Star. London: J. Limbird, 1824. Pp. [1]-44.

MONEY
See Bulwer (later Bulwer-Lytton), Edward George Earle Lytton, Lord Lytton.

MONEY MAKES THE MAN
See Sketchley, Arthur.

MONEY SPIDER, THE
See Eliot, Arthur.

MONEY SPINNER, THE
See Pinero, Arthur Wing.

MONIER-WILLIAMS, MONIER
See Williams, Monier.

MONIMIA
See Proby, John Joshua, Earl of Carysfort.

MONK OF ST. NICHOLAS
See Mystery.

MONK, THE MASK, AND THE MURDERER
See Amherst, J. H. Who Owns the Hand?

MONKS OF THE GREAT ST. BERNARD
See Sotheby, William. Julian and Agnes.

MONMOUTH (anon.)
London: C. Kegan Paul, 1880. Pp. [i]-[x], [1]-162.

MONNEY, WILLIAM
Caractacus. London: Sherwood, Neely, & Jones (priv.), 1816. Pp. [i]-[vi], [7]-117.

MONSEIGNEUR AND THE JEWELLER'S APPRENTICE
See Archer, Thomas.

MONSIEUR DE POURCEAUGNAC
See Van Laun, Henri (trans.).

MONSIEUR JACQUES
See Barnett, Morris.

MONSIEUR LAROCHE
See Bellingham, Henry.

MONSIEUR MALLET
See Moncrieff, William Thomas.

MONSIEUR TONSON
See Moncrieff, William Thomas.

MONSTER AND MAGICIAN, THE
See Kerr, John.

MONSTER IN THE GARDEN, THE
See Bell, Florence Eveleen Eleanore Oliffe, Mrs. Hugh (Lady).

MONSTER OF THE EDDYSTONE
See Pitt, George Dibdin. Eddystone Elf, The.

MONTAGUE, HAROLD
Only Amateurs. London & New York: Samuel French, n.d. Pp. [1]-12. [Lacy's Acting Edition].

MONTAGUE, LEOPOLD
Act of Piracy, An. London & New York: Samuel French, n.d. Pp. [25]-34. Text complete.

Browne with an E. London & New York: Samuel French, n.d. Pp. [33]-61. Text complete. [Lacy's Acting Edition].

Castle in Spain, A. London & New York: Samuel French, n.d. Pp. [9]-19. Text complete. French's Acting Edition, 2203.

Crystal-Gazer, The. London & New York: Samuel French, n.d. Pp. [1]-10.

Strange Relation, A. London & New York: Samuel French, n.d. Pp. [19]-26. Text complete.

MONTAGUE
See Gemmell, Robert.

MONTALTO
See A'Court, William.

MONTCALM
See Young, Charles Lawrence, Sir.

MONTE CARLO
: *See* Carlton, Sidney.

MONTE CRISTO (anon.)
: London & New York: Samuel French, n.d. Pp. [1]-79. French's Acting Edition (late Lacy's).

MONTEM, THE
: *See* Rowe, Henry, Rev.

MONTESCOS Y CAPULETES
: *See* Cosens, Frederick William (trans.). Bandos de Verona, Los.

MONTGOMERY, HENRY WILLIAM
: **Handy Andy.** London & New York: Samuel French, n.d. Pp. [1]-34. [French's Acting Edition (late Lacy's)].
: **Olivette.**
: *See* Farnie, Henry Brougham.

MONTH AFTER DATE, A
: *See* Dauncey, Silvanus.

MONTI
: **Caius Gracchus.**
: *See* Russell, John (trans.).

MONTROSE
: *See* Pocock, Isaac.

MONTROSE; OR, THE CHILDREN OF THE MIST (anon.)
: London: J. L. Marks, n.d. Pp. [1]-24.

MONTROSE; OR, THE GATHERING OF THE CLANS (anon.)
: Glasgow: William Gilchrist (printer), 1847. Pp. [1]-32.

MOODY, CATHERINE GRACE FRANCES
: *See* Gore, Catherine Grace Frances Moody, Mrs. Charles

MOON QUEEN AND KING NIGHT, THE
: *See* Crowquill, Alfred.

MOONLIGHT BLOSSOM, THE
: *See* Fernald, Chester Bailey.

MOONSHINE
: *See* Wortley, Emmeline Charlotte Elizabeth Manners Stuart, Mrs. Charles (Lady).

MOONSTONE, THE
: *See* Collins, William Wilkie.

MOORE, EDWARD
: **Foundling, The.** In *British Drama,* 12 vols., London: John Dicks, 1865, III, [686]-702.
: **Gamester, The.** London: Whittingham & Arliss, 1814. Pp. [1]-[64]. London Theatre, IV. *Filed under* Dibdin, Thomas John, ed. London Theatre, IV.
: **Gamester, The.** In *New English Drama,* ed. W. Oxberry, 22 vols., London: W. Simpkin & R. Marshall; C. Chapple, 1823, XVIII, [i]-[xii], [1]-[58]. *Filed under* Oxberry, William Henry. New English Drama, XVIII.
: **Gamester, The.** London: John Cumberland, 1829. Pp. [1]-56. Cumberland's British Theatre, IV. *Filed under* Cumberland, John. Cumberland's British Theatre, IV.
: **Gamester, The.** In *British Drama,* 12 vols., London: John Dicks, 1864, I, [i-iv], [1]-16.
: **Gamester, The.**
: *See* Kemble, John Philip (arr.).

MOORE, FRANCES
: *See* Brooke, Frances Moore, Mrs. John.

MOORE, FRANK FRANKFORT
: **Kitty Clive.** London & New York: Samuel French, n.d. Pp. [1]-[19]. French's Acting Edition (late Lacy's), 2081.
: **Queen's Room, The.** [London: David Allen & Sons (printer) (priv.), 1891]. Pp. [i-iv], [2]-32.

MOORE, GEORGE
: **Bending of the Bough, The.** London: T. Fisher Unwin, 1900. Pp. [i]-xx, [1]-145.
: **Martin Luther.** Written with Lopez, Bernard. London: Remington, 1879. Pp. [i]-x, [1]-179.
: **Strike at Arlingford, The.** London: Walter Scott, 1893. Pp. [1]-175.

MOORE, J. GEORGE
: **That Blessed Baby.** London: Webster, n.d. Pp. [1]-20. Promptbook.

MOORE, THOMAS
: **M.P.; or, The Blue-Stocking.** [London: J. Power, 1811]. Pp. [1]-94. Title page lacking.

MOORE, THOMAS STURGE
: **Florentine Tragedy, A.**
: *See* Wilde, Oscar Fingall O'Flahertie Wills.

MORAL BRAND
: *See* Haines, John Thomas. Alice Grey, the Suspected One.

MORAL PHILOSOPHER, THE
: *See* Selby, Charles.

MORDRED
: *See* Newbolt, John Henry.

MORE, HANNAH
: **Percy.** In *Modern Theatre,* ed. Mrs. Inchbald, 10 vols., London: Longman, Hurst, Rees, Orme, & Brown, 1811, VII, [181]-236.
: **Reflections of King Hezekiah in His Sickness.** In *Works,* 8 vols., London: T. Cadell, jr & W. Davies, 1801, II, [259]-270.
: **Village Politics.** In *Works,* 8 vols., London: T. Cadell, jr & W. Davies, 1801, I, [321]-348.

MORE BLUNDERS THAN ONE
: *See* Rodwell, James Thomas Gooderham.

MORE FREE THAN WELCOME
: *See* Suter, William E.

MORE FRIGHTENED THAN HURT
: *See* Jerrold, Douglas William.

MORE GOOD NEWS
: *See* Dibdin, Thomas John. Orange Boven.

MORE JONATHANS
: *See* Moncrieff, William Thomas. Tarnation Strange.

MORE LAUGH THAN LOVE
: *See* Colman, George, jr. Gay Deceivers, The.

MORE POT-POURRI FROM THE PARK
: *See* Anstey, F.

MORE PRECIOUS THAN GOLD!
: *See* Cheltnam, Charles Smith.

MORE SECRETS THAN ONE
: *See* Arnold, Samuel James. Man and Wife.

MORGAN, SYDNEY OWENSON, MRS. THOMAS CHARLES (Lady)
: **Easter Recess, The; or, The Tapestry Workers.** In *Dramatic Scenes from Real Life,* 2 vols., New York: J. & J. Harper, 1833, II, [19]-102. *Filed under* Collected Works.
: **Manor Sackville.** In *Dramatic Scenes from Real Life,* 2 vols., New York: J. & J. Harper, 1833, I, [i]-[x], [1]-138; II, [1]-16. *Filed under* Collected Works.
: **Temper.** In *Dramatic Scenes from Real Life,* 2 vols., New York: J. & J. Harper, 1833, II, [103]-134. *Filed under* Collected Works.

MORISON, MARY (trans.)
: **Lonely Lives.** By Hauptmann, Gerhart. London: William Heinemann, 1898. Pp. [i-vi], [1]-179.
: **Weavers, The.** By Hauptmann, Gerhart. London: William Heinemann, 1899. Pp. [i]-viii, [1]-148.

MORLAND, CHARLOTTE E.
: **Matrimonial Agency, The.** London & New York: Samuel French, c.1902. Pp. [1]-16.

MORLEY ASHTON
: *See* Johnstone, John Beer.

MORNING AT VERSAILLES
: *See* Planché, James Robinson. Promotion.

MORNING CALL, A
: *See* Dance, Charles.

MORNING, NOON, AND NIGHT
: *See* Dibdin, Thomas John.

MOROCCO BOUND
: *See* Branscombe, Arthur.

MORPETH, LORD
: *See* Howard, George William Frederick, Earl of Carlisle.

MORRIS, LEWIS
: **Gwen.** London: C. Kegan Paul, 1879. Pp. [i-vi], [1]-170.
: **Gycia.** London: Kegan Paul, Trench, 1886. Pp. [i-vi], [1]-197.

MORRIS, VAL
: **Love Is Blind.** In *Songs, Recitatives . . . in Mr. & Mrs. Henri Drayton's Parlor Operas,* Providence: Evening Press, n.d.,

pp. [1]-8. Libretto. *Filed under* Drayton, Henri. Songs, Recitatives . . .

MORRIS, WILLIAM

Rapunzel. In *Defence of Guenevere and Other Poems,* London: Ellis & White, 1883, pp. [111]-134.

Sir Peter Harpdon's End. In *Defence of Guenevere and Other Poems,* London: Ellis & White, 1883, pp. [65]-109.

Tables Turned, The; or, Nupkins Awakened. [London: Commonweal Office, 1887]. Pp. [i-ii], [1]-32. Title page in manuscript.

MORRISON, GEORGE E.

Alonzo Quixano, Otherwise Don Quixote. London: Elkin Mathews, n.d. Pp. [3]-[104].

MORTIMER, JAMES

Charlotte Corday. London: Figaro Office (priv.), 1876. Pp. [i-ii], [1]-83.

Gloriana. London: n.pub., n.d. Pp. [i], [1]-[40], [i], [1]-51, [i], [1]-39. Pagination by act. Typescript.

Joy Is Dangerous. New York: [R. M. DeWitt], n.d. Pp. [1]-32.

Little Cricket. London: Figaro Office (priv.), 1878. Pp. [1]-40.

MORTON, EDWARD

Eton Boy, The. London: Thomas Hailes Lacy, n.d. Pp. [1]-22. [Lacy's Acting Edition].

My Wife's Come! Written with Morton, John Maddison. London: John Duncombe, n.d. <wrps. Thomas Hailes Lacy>. Pp. [1]-22. Duncombe's Edition <wrps. New British Theatre (late Duncombe's), 380>.

Railroad Trip, The; or, London, Birmingham, & Bristol. Written with Morton, John Maddison. London: John Duncombe, n.d. Pp. [3]-26. Duncombe's Edition.

River God, The. London: John Duncombe, n.d. Pp. [1]-22. Duncombe's Acting Edition of the British Theatre, 397.

Windmill, The. London: John Duncombe, n.d. Pp. [1]-24. Duncombe's Acting Edition of the British Theatre, 350.

MORTON, EDWARD A.

Miss Impudence. London & New York: Samuel French, n.d. Pp. [1]-12. [Lacy's Acting Edition].

San Toy; or, The Emperor's Own. Written with Greenbank, Harry; Ross, Adrian (pseud. of Ropes, Arthur Reed). Music by Jones, Sidney. London: Keith, Prowse, c.1899. Pp. [i-iv], [1]-194. Vocal score.

MORTON, J. RUSSELL

Last Day of Napoleon, The. Written with Pleon, Harry. In *Pleon's Peculiar Parodies on Popular Plays and Pieces,* 5th Series, London: Howard, n.d., pp. 32-39. *Filed under* Pleon, Harry. Pleon's Peculiar Parodies on Popular Plays and Pieces.

MORTON, JOHN MADDISON

After a Storm Comes a Calm. Chicago: Dramatic Publishing Company, c.1886. Pp. [1]-14. Sergel's Acting Drama, 340.

After a Storm Comes a Calm. London & New York: Samuel French, n.d. Pp. [47]-68. Text complete. [Lacy's Acting Edition].

Alabama, The. London: Thomas Hailes Lacy, n.d. Pp. [1]-22. [Lacy's Acting Edition].

Aladdin and the Wonderful Lamp; or, Harlequin and the Genie of the Ring. London: Thomas Hailes Lacy, n.d. Pp. [1]-18. Libretto.

All That Glitters Is Not Gold. *See* Morton, Thomas, jr.

At Sixes and Sevens. New York: Harold Roorbach, n.d. Pp. [1]-17.

Atchi! London: Thomas Hailes Lacy, n.d. Pp. [1]-21. Promptbook.

Atchi! London: Thomas Hailes Lacy, n.d. Pp. [1]-21. [Lacy's Acting Edition].

Attic Story, The. London: John Cumberland, n.d. Pp. [1]-28. Cumberland's British Theatre, XLII. *Filed under* Cumberland, John. Cumberland's British Theatre, XLII.

Attic Story, The. London: John Cumberland, n.d. Pp. [1]-28. [Cumberland's British Theatre].

Aunt Charlotte's Maid. London: Thomas Hailes Lacy, n.d. Pp. [1]-30. Promptbook.

Away with Melancholy. London: Thomas Hailes Lacy, n.d. Pp. [1]-19. [Lacy's Acting Edition].

Barbers of Bassora, The. Music by Hullah, John. London: Chapman & Hall, n.d. Pp. [1]-32. Libretto.

Betsy Baker!; or, Too Attentive by Half. London & New York: Samuel French, n.d. Pp. [1]-19. French's Acting Edition, 118.

Box and Cox. London: Thomas Hailes Lacy, n.d. Pp. [1]-24.

Box and Cox. In *Dramatic Entertainments at Windsor Castle,* ed. Benjamin Webster, London: Mitchell, n.d., pp. [97]-120. *Filed under* Webster, Benjamin Nottingham. Dramatic Entertainments.

Brother Ben. London: J. Pattie, n.d. Pp. [i]-[iv], [5]-22. Promptbook.

Capital Match!, A. London & New York: Samuel French, n.d. Pp. [1]-20.

Catch a Weazel. London: Thomas Hailes Lacy, n.d. Pp. [1]-[28]. [Lacy's Acting Edition].

Change Partners. Written with Williams, Thomas John. London & New York: Samuel French, n.d. Pp. [1]-18. [Lacy's Acting Edition].

Chaos Is Come Again; or, The Race-Ball! London: Chapman & Hall, n.d. Pp. [1]-20.

Corporal's Wedding!, The; or, A Kiss from the Bride. London: John Duncombe, n.d. <wrps. Thomas Hailes Lacy>. Pp. [3]-27. Duncombe's Edition <wrps. New British Theatre (late Duncombe's), 411>.

Cousin Lambkin. London: John Duncombe, n.d. <wrps. Thomas Hailes Lacy>. Pp. [3]-20. Duncombe's Edition <wrps. Cumberland's British Theatre (with Duncombe's)>.

Day's Fishing, A. London: Thomas Hailes Lacy, n.d. Pp. [1]-22. [Lacy's Acting Edition].

Declined—with Thanks. London & New York: Samuel French, n.d. Pp. [105]-130. Text complete. [Lacy's Acting Edition].

Desperate Game, A. Clyde, Ohio: A. D. Ames, n.d. Pp. [1]-17. Ames' Series of Standard and Minor Drama, 2.

Done on Both Sides. London & New York: Samuel French, n.d. Pp. [1]-36.

Don't Judge by Appearances. Boston: Walter H. Baker, c.1889. Pp. [1]-18. Spencer's Universal Stage, 51 <wrps. Baker's Edition of Plays>.

Double-Bedded Room, The. New York: Samuel French, n.d. Pp. [1]-16. Minor Drama, 171.

Drawing Rooms, Second Floor, and Attics. London: Thomas Hailes Lacy, n.d. Pp. [1]-30. [Lacy's Acting Edition].

Dying for Love. London & New York: Samuel French, n.d. Pp. [1]-24. French's Acting Edition (late Lacy's).

Eight Hours at the Sea-Side. London & New York: Samuel French, n.d. Pp. [1]-16. [Lacy's Acting Edition].

Englishman's House Is His Castle, An. London: Thomas Hailes Lacy, n.d. Pp. [1]-20. [Lacy's Acting Edition].

Express! London & New York: Samuel French, n.d. Pp. [67]-86. Text complete. [Lacy's Acting Edition].

First Come, First Served. London & New York: Samuel French, n.d. Pp. [i-ii], [1]-24. [Lacy's Acting Edition].

Fitzsmythe of Fitzsmythe Hall. London: Thomas Hailes Lacy, n.d. Pp. [1]-30. [Lacy's Acting Edition].

Friend Waggles. London: John Duncombe, n.d. <wrps. Thomas Hailes Lacy>. Pp. [1]-30. Duncombe's Edition <wrps. New British Theatre (late Duncombe's), 521>.

From Village to Court. London: Thomas Hailes Lacy, n.d. Pp. [1]-28. [Lacy's Acting Edition].

Game of Romps, A. London & New York: Samuel French, n.d. <wrps. London: Thomas Hailes Lacy>. Pp. [1]-18. Lacy's Acting Edition, 260.

Going It!; or, Another Lesson to Fathers. Written with Vicars, W. A. London & New York: Samuel French, n.d. Pp. [1]-55. [Lacy's Acting Edition].

Going to the Derby. London: Thomas Hailes Lacy, n.d. Pp. [1]-30. [Lacy's Acting Edition].

Grimshaw, Bagshaw, and Bradshaw. London: Thomas Hailes Lacy, n.d. Pp. [1]-21. [Lacy's Acting Edition].

Guy, Earl of Warwick; or, Harlequin and the Dun Cow. Music by Hughes, R. London: S. G. Fairbrother, 1842. Pp. [1]-14. Libretto.

Harlequin and William Tell; or, The Genius of the Ribstone Pippin. London: S. G. Fairbrother, n.d. Pp. [1]-[15]. Libretto.

Harlequin Blue Beard, the Great Bashaw; or, The Good Fairy Triumphant over the Demon of Discord! New York: Samuel French, n.d. Pp. [1]-17. Minor Drama, 146. Libretto.

Harlequin Hogarth; or, The Two London 'Prentices. London: Thomas Hailes Lacy, n.d. Pp. [1]-22. Libretto.

Highwayman, The. London: G. Berger, 1843. Pp. [1]-24.

Hopeless Passion, A. London: Thomas Hailes Lacy, n.d. Pp. [1]-24. [Lacy's Acting Edition].

How Stout You're Getting! London: Thomas Hailes Lacy, n.d. Pp. [1]-23. [Lacy's Acting Edition].

Husband to Order, A. London: Thomas Hailes Lacy, n.d. Pp. [1]-43. Title page imperfect. Promptbook.

If I Had a Thousand a Year. Chicago: Dramatic Publishing Company, n.d. Pp. [1]-25.

Irish Tiger, The. London: Thomas Hailes Lacy, n.d. Pp. [1]-24. [Lacy's Acting Edition].

John Dobbs. London & New York: Samuel French, n.d. Pp. [1]-22.

Killing Time.
    See Love and Rain.

King and I, The. London: John Duncombe, n.d. Pp. [1]-24. Duncombe's Edition. Promptbook.

Kiss and Be Friends. London & New York: Samuel French, n.d. Pp. [1]-16. [Lacy's Acting Edition].

Lad from the Country, A. London & New York: Samuel French, n.d. Pp. [1]-20. [Lacy's Acting Edition].

Lend Me Five Shillings. London & New York: Samuel French, n.d. Pp. [1]-29. French's Acting Edition (late Lacy's).

Little Mother. London: Thomas Hailes Lacy, n.d. Pp. [1]-33. [Lacy's Acting Edition].

Little Savage, The. London: Thomas Hailes Lacy, n.d. Pp. [1]-30.

Love and Hunger. London: Thomas Hailes Lacy, n.d. Pp. [1]-30. [Lacy's Acting Edition].

Love and Rain. *Also:* Killing Time. London: Thomas Hailes Lacy, n.d. Pp. [1]-12. [Lacy's Acting Edition].

Love in the Tropics.
    See Mother and Child Are Doing Well, The.

Maggie's Situation. London & New York: Samuel French, n.d. Pp. [1]-19. [Lacy's Acting Edition].

Margery Daw; or, The Two Bumpkins. London: Thomas Hailes Lacy, n.d. Pp. [1]-24. [Lacy's Acting Edition].

Master Jones's Birthday. New York: Robert M. DeWitt, n.d. Pp. [1]-16. DeWitt's Acting Plays, 39.

Midnight Watch, The. London: Thomas Hailes Lacy, n.d. Pp. [1]-31. Promptbook.

Milliner's Holiday, The. London: Thomas Hailes Lacy, n.d. Pp. [1]-26. [Lacy's Acting Edition].

Most Unwarrantable Intrusion, A. Boston: William V. Spencer, n.d. Pp. [1]-14. Spencer's Boston Theatre, 135.

Mother and Child Are Doing Well, The. *Also:* Love in the Tropics; or, The Mother and Child are Doing Well. New York: Dick & Fitzgerald, n.d. Pp. [1]-23.

Muleteer of Toledo, The; or, King, Queen, and Knave. London & New York: Samuel French, n.d. Pp. [1]-28. French's Acting Edition (late Lacy's).

My Bachelor Days. London & New York: Samuel French, n.d. Pp. [1]-16. [Lacy's Acting Edition].

My First Fit of the Gout. London: Thomas Hailes Lacy, n.d. Pp. [1]-16. [Lacy's Acting Edition].

My Husband's Ghost. London: Thomas Hailes Lacy, n.d. Pp. [1]-25. [Lacy's Acting Edition].

My Husband's Ghost! London: John Cumberland, n.d. Pp. [1]-25. Cumberland's British Theatre, XXXV. *Filed under*

Cumberland, John. Cumberland's British Theatre, XXXV.

My Precious Betsy! New York: O. A. Roorbach, n.d. Pp. [1]-18. Promptbook.

My Wife's Bonnet. London: Thomas Hailes Lacy, n.d. Pp. [1]-[28]. Promptbook.

My Wife's Come!
    See Morton, Edward.

My Wife's Second Floor. London & New York: Samuel French, n.d. Pp. [1]-24. [Lacy's Acting Edition].

Narrow Squeak, A. London & New York: Samuel French, n.d. Pp. [1]-15. [Lacy's Acting Edition].

Newington Butts! London: Thomas Hailes Lacy, n.d. Pp. [1]-20. [Lacy's Acting Edition].

Not If I Know It! *Also:* Le Supplice d'un Homme. Chicago: Dramatic Publishing Company, n.d. Pp. [1]-19. [World Acting Drama].

Old Honesty! London: Duncombe & Moon, n.d. Pp. [1]-49. Duncombe's Edition.

On the Sly! Clyde, Ohio: Ames' Publishing Company, n.d. Pp. [1]-20. Ames' Series of Standard and Minor Drama, 33.

Original, The. London: Chapman & Hall, n.d. Pp. [1]-16.

Our Wife; or, The Rose of Amiens. Boston: William V. Spencer, n.d. Pp. [1]-28. Spencer's Boston Theatre, 67.

Pacha of Pimlico, The. London: Thomas Hailes Lacy, n.d. Pp. [1]-22. [Lacy's Acting Edition].

Pepperpot's Little Pets! London & New York: Samuel French, n.d. Pp. [23]-48. Text complete. [Lacy's Acting Edition].

Poor Pillicoddy. New York: O. A. Roorbach, jr, n.d. Pp. [1]-28. Acting Drama.

Pouter's Wedding. London: Thomas Hailes Lacy, n.d. Pp. [1]-24. [Lacy's Acting Edition].

Prince for an Hour, A. London: Thomas Hailes Lacy, n.d. Pp. [1]-26. [Lacy's Acting Edition].

Railroad Trip, The.
    See Morton, Edward.

Regular Fix!, A. New York: Samuel French, n.d. Pp. [1]-20. French's Minor Drama, 282. Promptbook.

Rights and Wrongs of Woman, The. London: Thomas Hailes Lacy, n.d. Pp. [1]-26. [Lacy's Acting Edition].

Sayings and Doings; or, The Rule of Contrary. London: Chapman & Hall, n.d. Pp. [1]-20. Webster's Acting National Drama, 77.

Sea-Bathing at Home. London: John Dicks, n.d. Pp. [1]-8. Dicks' Standard Plays, 433.

Sent to the Tower! London: John Duncombe, n.d. <wrps. Thomas Hailes Lacy>. Pp. [1]-22. Duncombe's Edition <wrps. New British Theatre (late Duncombe's), 526>.

Sentinel, The. Boston, 1852. 35 leaves. Manuscript promptbook.

She Would and He Wouldn't. London: Thomas Hailes Lacy, n.d. Pp. [1]-40. [Lacy's Acting Edition].

Slasher and Crasher! London: Duncombe & Moon, n.d. Pp. [1]-27. Duncombe's Acting Edition of the British Theatre, 497.

Slice of Luck, A. London: Thomas Hailes Lacy, n.d. Pp. [1]-24. [Lacy's Acting Edition].

Slight Mistakes! London & New York: Samuel French, n.d. Pp. [1]-20. Rev. ed. for 1884 production. [Lacy's Acting Edition].

Something to Do. London & New York: Samuel French, n.d. Pp. [1]-15. Rev. ed. for 1884 production. [Lacy's Acting Edition].

Spitfire, The. London: Chapman & Hall, n.d. Pp. [1]-19. Webster's Acting National Drama.

Steeple-Chase, The; or, In the Pigskin. London: Thomas Hailes Lacy, n.d. Pp. [1]-24. [Lacy's Acting Edition].

Supplice d'un Homme, Le.
    See Not If I Know It.

Take Care of Dowb—. London: Thomas Hailes Lacy, n.d. Pp. [1]-26. [Lacy's Acting Edition].

Taken from the French. London & New York: Samuel French, n.d. Pp. [85]-106. Text complete. [Lacy's Acting Edition].

Thirty-Three Next Birthday. Clyde, Ohio: A. D. Ames, n.d. Pp. [1]-15. Ames' Series of Standard and Minor Drama, 28.

Thirty-Three Next Birthday. London: Thomas Hailes Lacy, n.d. Pp. [1]-24.

Three Cuckoos, The; or, Ticklish Times! London: John Duncombe, n.d. <wrps. Thomas Hailes Lacy>. Pp. [1]-28. Duncombe's Edition <wrps. New British Theatre (late Duncombe's), 518>.

Thumping Legacy, A. London: S. G. Fairbrother, n.d. Pp. [1]-24.

Ticklish Times. London: Thomas Hailes Lacy, n.d. Pp. [1]-31. [Lacy's Acting Edition].

To Paris and Back, for Five Pounds. New York: Samuel French, n.d. Pp. [1]-22. French's American Drama, 43.

Trade. Written with Reece, Robert. New York: n.pub. (priv.), 1877. Pp. [1]-39.

Trumpeter's Wedding!, The. London: Thomas Hailes Lacy, n.d. Pp. [1]-28. Cumberland's British Theatre (with Duncombe's).

Two Bonnycastles, The. New York: William Taylor, n.d. Pp. [3]-32. Minor Drama, 44.

Two Buzzards, The; or, Whitebait at Greenwich. Boston: William V. Spencer, n.d. Pp. [1]-24. Spencer's Boston Theatre, 38. Promptbook.

Two Puddifoots, The. London & New York: Samuel French, n.d. Pp. [1]-23. French's Acting Edition (late Lacy's).

Waiting for an Omnibus in the Lowther Arcade on a Rainy Day. London: Thomas Hailes Lacy, n.d. Pp. [1]-18. [Lacy's Acting Edition].

Wedding Breakfast, The. London & New York: Samuel French, n.d. Pp. [3]-24. [Lacy's Acting Edition].

Where There's a Will There's a Way. London: John Duncombe, n.d. Pp. [1]-30. Duncombe's Edition.

Which of the Two? Chicago: Dramatic Publishing Company, n.d. Pp. [1]-20.

Which of the Two? London: Thomas Hailes Lacy, n.d. Pp. [1]-30.

Whitebait at Greenwich. London: Thomas Hailes Lacy, n.d. Pp. [1]-21.

Who Do They Take Me For? London & New York: Samuel French, n.d. Pp. [3]-26. [Lacy's Acting Edition].

Who Stole the Pocket-Book?; or, A Dinner for Six. London: Thomas Hailes Lacy, n.d. Pp. [1]-19.

Who Stole the Pocket-Book?; or, A Dinner for Six. New York: Samuel French, n.d. Pp. [1]-19. Promptbook.

Who's My Husband? London: Thomas Hailes Lacy, n.d. Pp. [1]-26. Lacy's Acting Edition.

Who's the Composer? London & New York: Samuel French, n.d. Pp. [1]-32. [Lacy's Acting Edition].

Woman I Adore!, The. London: Thomas Hailes Lacy, n.d. Pp. [1]-22. [Lacy's Acting Edition].

Woodcock's Little Game. New York: Robert M. DeWitt, n.d. Pp. [1]-26. DeWitt's Acting Plays, 11.

Wooing One's Wife. London: Thomas Hailes Lacy, n.d. Pp. [1]-28. [Lacy's Acting Edition].

Writing on the Wall, The.
See Morton, Thomas, jr.

Wrong Man, The. London: John Dicks, n.d. Pp. [1]-10. Dicks' Standard Plays, 433. *Filed under* Sea-Bathing at Home.

Young England. London: Thomas Hailes Lacy, n.d. Pp. [1]-20. New British Theatre (late Duncombe's), 400.

Your Life's in Danger. London: Thomas Hailes Lacy, n.d. Pp. [1]-19. Promptbook.

MORTON, JOHN W.

Mohawk Minstrels' Eighth Book of Dramas, Dialogues, and Drolleries, The
See Forman, Edmund.

MORTON, RICHARD

Dialogues. In *Mohawk Minstrels' Tenth Book of Nigger Dramas and Sketches,* London: Francis, Day, & Hunter,

n.d, pp. [61]-78. Text incomplete. *Filed under* Forman, Edmund, et al. Mohawk Minstrels' Tenth Book.

Mohawk Minstrels' Eighth Book of Dramas, Dialogues, and Drolleries, The
See Forman, Edmund.

Mohawk Minstrels' Ninth Book of Dramas, Stump Speeches, Nigger Jokes, and Recitations, The.
See Williams, Arthur.

Mohawk Minstrels' Tenth Book of Nigger Dramas and Sketches, The.
See Forman, Edmund.

MORTON, THOMAS, SR

Blind Girl, The; or, A Receipt for Beauty. Boston: Oliver & Munroe, 1808. Pp. [1]-60.

Children in the Wood, The. London: John Cumberland, 1828. Pp. [i], [1]-28. Cumberland's British Theatre, XVII. *Filed under* Cumberland, John. Cumberland's British Theatre, XVII.

Cure for the Heartache, A. London: John Cumberland, 1827. Pp. [1]-68. Cumberland's British Theatre, XVI. *Filed under* Cumberland, John. Cumberland's British Theatre, XVI.

Education. London: Longman, Hurst, Rees, Orme, & Brown, 1813. Pp. [i-vi], [1]-[78].

Education. London: John Cumberland, 1827. Pp. [1]-[66]. Cumberland's British Theatre, XVI. *Filed under* Cumberland, John. Cumberland's British Theatre, XVI.

Henri Quatre; or, Paris in the Olden Time. Music by Bishop. London: Sampson Low, n.d. Pp. [i-vi], [1]-86.

Invincibles, The. New York: William Van Norden (printer), 1829. Pp. [1]-[39].

Invincibles, The. London: John Cumberland, n.d. Pp. [1]-38. Cumberland's British Theatre, XXXVI. *Filed under* Cumberland, John. Cumberland's British Theatre, XXXVI.

Invincibles, The. London: John Cumberland, n.d. Pp. [1]-38.

Knight of Snowdoun, The. London: Sharpe & Hailes, 1811. Pp. [1]-79.

Methinks I See My Father!; or, Who's My Father? London: G. H. Davidson, n.d. Pp. [1]-29. Cumberland's British Theatre, 372.

Roland for an Oliver, A. London: John Miller, 1819. Pp. [i-iv], [1]-35.

Roland for an Oliver, A. In *New English Drama,* ed. W. Oxberry, 22 vols., London: W. Simpkin & R. Marshall; C. Chapple, 1826, XXII, [i]-[x], [11]-48. *Filed under* Oxberry, William Henry. New English Drama, XXII.

School for Grown Children, A. London: Sampson Low, 1827. Pp. [i-vi], [1]-86. Promptbook.

School of Reform, The; or, How to Rule a Husband. London: Longman, Hurst, Rees, & Orme, 1805. Pp. [1]-[88].

School of Reform, The; or, How to Rule a Husband. London: John Cumberland, 1828. Pp. [1]-65. Cumberland's British Theatre, XVII. *Filed under* Cumberland, John. Cumberland's British Theatre, XVII.

Secrets Worth Knowing. In *Modern Theatre,* ed. Mrs. Inchbald, 10 vols., London: Longman, Hurst, Rees, Orme, & Brown, 1811, III, [141]-205.

Secrets Worth Knowing. London: John Cumberland, 1828. Pp. [1]-57. Cumberland's British Theatre, XVIII. *Filed under* Cumberland, John. Cumberland's British Theatre, XVIII.

Slave, The. Music by Bishop, Henry R. London: John Miller, 1816. Pp. [i-iv], [1]-72. Libretto.

Slave, The. London: John Cumberland, n.d. Pp. [1]-60. Cumberland's British Theatre, XXII. *Filed under* Cumberland, John. Cumberland's British Theatre, XXII.

Slave, The. Music by Bishop, Henry R. London: Goulding, D'Almaine, Potter, n.d. Pp. [i-iv], 1-95. Vocal score.

Speed the Plough. London: John Cumberland, 1827. Pp. [1]-69. Cumberland's British Theatre, XV. *Filed under* Cumberland, John. Cumberland's British Theatre, XV.

Speed the Plough. In *British Drama,* 12 vols., London: John Dicks, 1865, IV, [1247]-1265.

Speed the Plough. London: Thomas Hailes Lacy, n.d. Pp. [1]-56. [Lacy's Acting Edition].

Town and Country. London: Longman, Hurst, Rees, & Orme, 1807. Pp. [i-iii], [1]-[96].

Town and Country. London: Longman, Hurst, Rees, Orme, & Brown, 1815. Pp. [i-iv], [1]-[74].

Town and Country. London: John Cumberland, n.d. Pp. [1]-67. Cumberland's British Theatre, XXIII: *Filed under* Cumberland, John. Cumberland's British Theatre, XXIII.

Town and Country. New York: William Taylor; Baltimore: William & Henry Taylor, n.d. Pp. [i-vi], [7]-68. Modern Standard Drama, 70.

Way to Get Married, The. London: John Cumberland, 1828. Pp. [1]-67. Cumberland's British Theatre, XX. *Filed under* Cumberland, John. Cumberland's British Theatre, XX.

Zorinski. In *Modern Theatre*, ed. Mrs. Inchbald, 10 vols., London: Longman, Hurst, Rees, Orme, & Brown, 1811, III, [85]-139.

MORTON, THOMAS, JR

All That Glitters Is Not Gold. Written with Morton, John Maddison. By Thomas & J. M. Morton. New York: William Taylor, n.d. Pp. [1]-52. Minor Drama, 40. Promptbook.

Angel of the Attic, The. By Thomas Morton. New York: Samuel French, n.d. Pp. [1]-16. French's Minor Drama, 293.

Another Glass. By Thomas Morton. Boston: Charles H. Spencer, n.d. Pp. [1]-17. *Filed under* Morton, Thomas, sr.

Another Glass! By Thomas Morton. *Also:* The Drunkard's Glass. London: John Duncombe, n.d. Pp. [1]-20. [Duncombe's Edition]. *Filed under* Morton, Thomas, sr.

Dance of the Shirt!, The; or, The Sempstress's Ball. By Thomas Morton. London: Duncombe & Moon, n.d. Pp. [1]-25. Duncombe's Edition. *Filed under* Morton, Thomas, sr.

Drunkard's Glass, The.
See Another Glass.

Gotobed Tom! By Thomas Morton. London: Thomas Hailes Lacy, n.d. Pp. [1]-18. [Lacy's Acting Edition].

Great Russian Bear, The; or, Another Retreat from Moscow. By Thomas Morton. London: Davidson, n.d. Pp. [1]-32. Davidson's Actable Drama.

Judith of Geneva! By Thomas Morton. London: Thomas Hailes Lacy, n.d. Pp. [3]-42.

Pretty Piece of Business, A. N.p.: n.pub., n.d. Pp. [3]-22. Title page lacking.

Pretty Piece of Business, A. By Thomas Morton. New York & London: Samuel French, n.d. Pp. [1]-23. French's American Drama, 74.

Seeing Warren. By Thomas Morton. Boston: William V. Spencer, n.d. Pp. [1]-16. Spencer's Boston Theatre, 208.

Seeing Wright. By Thomas Morton. London: William Barth, n.d. Pp. [1]-21. Barth's Universal Stage or Theatrical Prompt Book, 98. *Filed under* Morton, Thomas, sr.

Sink or Swim! By Thomas Morton. London & New York: Samuel French, n.d. Pp. [1]-26. [Lacy's Acting Edition].

Sketches in India. By Thomas Morton. New York: William Taylor, n.d. Pp. [i]-[iv], [5]-29. Modern Standard Drama, 90. Promptbook.

Sketches in India. By Thomas Morton. New York: Samuel French, n.d. Pp. [i]-iv, [5]-29. French's Standard Drama, 90. *Filed under* Morton, Thomas, sr.

White Feather, The. By Thomas Morton. London: William Barth, n.d. Pp. [3]-21. Barth's Universal Stage or Theatrical Prompt Book, 76.

Writing on the Wall, The. Written with Morton, John Maddison. By Thomas & J. M. Morton. New York & London: Samuel French, n.d. Pp. [i]-iv, [5]-64. French's Standard Drama, 95. *Filed under* Morton, John Maddison; Morton, Thomas, sr.

Writing on the Wall, The. Written with Morton, John Maddison. By Thomas & J. M. Morton. New York: Samuel French, n.d. Pp. [i]-iv, [5]-64. French's Standard Drama, 95. Promptbook.

MORTON, W. E.

Blood Money; or, Brought to Bay. 60 leaves. Manuscript.

Tinsel Queen, The. 81 leaves. Manuscript promptbook.

MOSER, JOSEPH

British Loyalty; or, Long Live the King! London: James Asperne, 1809. Pp. [1]-32.

MOSES
See Carpenter, Edward.

MOSS, ARTHUR B.

Land and the People, The. London: Watts, n.d. Pp. [1]-63.

Paul the Rebel. London: Watts, n.d. Pp. [1]-14.

Workman's Foe, The. London: Watts, n.d. Pp. [1]-16.

MOSS, HUGH

Bric-a-Brac Will, The.
See Fitzgerald, Shafto Justin Adair.

P.U.P.; or, The Dog in the Manger. London & New York: Samuel French, n.d. Pp. [1]-14. [Lacy's Acting Edition].

MOSS-ROSE RENT, A
See Law, Arthur.

MOST EXCELLENT STORY
See Maclaren, Archibald. Prisoner of War, The.

MOST UNWARRANTABLE INTRUSION, A
See Morton, John Maddison.

MOTHER AND CHILD ARE DOING WELL, THE
See Morton, John Maddison.

MOTHER GOOSE
See Lane, Pyngle.

MOTHER, THE MAID, AND THE MISTLETOE BOUGH
See Gilbert, William Schwenck. Pretty Druidess, The.

MOTHER, THE MAIDEN, AND THE MUSICIANER
See Byron, Henry James. Ill-treated Il Trovatore.

MOTHER'S BEQUEST, THE
See Stirling, Edward.

MOTHER'S BLESSING, A
See Aird, Thomas.

MOTHER'S CRIME
See Stirling, Edward. Jane Lomax.

MOTHER'S DREAM
See Almar, George. Shadow!, The.

MOTHER'S DYING CHILD
See Hazlewood, Colin Henry. Female Detective, The.
See Hazlewood, Colin Henry.

MOTHER'S TRAGEDY
See Heraud, John Abraham. Videna.

MOTHER'S VENGEANCE
See Dimond, William. Adrian and Orrila.

MOTHERS AND DAUGHTERS
See Bell, Robert.

MOTHS
See Hamilton, Henry.

MOTTO, THE: I AM ALL THERE.
See Byron, Henry James.

MOUBREY, LILIAN

King and Artist. Written with Pollock, Walter Herries. London: William Heinemann, 1897. Pp. [i-iv], [1]-88. *Filed under* Pollock, Walter Herries.

Were-Wolf, The. Written with Pollock, Walter Herries. London: William Heinemann, 1898. Pp. [1]-44. *Filed under* Pollock, Walter Herries.

MOULD, JACOB WREY (trans.)

Barber of Seville, The. *Also:* Il Barbiere di Siviglia. Music by Rossini. London: T. Boosey, n.d. Pp. [i]-viii, [1]-16, [i-iv], 1-370. Standard Lyric Drama, III. Vocal score and libretto.

MOULDS, ARTHUR

Danesbury House. Leicester: E. T. Lawrence, 1862. Pp. [1]-34.

Village Bane, The; or, Two High Roads of Life. Leicester: E. T. Lawrence; London: W. Tweedie, n.d. Pp. [1]-31.

MOUNT ST. BERNARD
See Moncrieff, William Thomas.

MOUNTAIN DHU!
See Halliday, Andrew.

MOUNTAIN KING, THE
See Almar, George.

MOUNTAIN SYLPH, THE
    See Thackeray, Thomas James.
MOUNTAINEERS, THE
    See Colman, George, jr.
MOUNTEBANK AND HIS WIFE
    See Courtney, John. Belphegor.
    See Higgie, Thomas Henry. Belphegor.
MOUNTEBANKS, THE
    See Gilbert, William Schwenck.
MOURNING BRIDE, THE
    See Congreve, William.
MOUSQUETAIRES AU COUVENT, LES
    See Farnie, Henry Brougham.
MOUSTACHE MOVEMENT, THE
    See Brough, Robert Barnabas.
MOVING TALE, A
    See Lemon, Mark.
MOYSE, CHARLES EBENEZER
    See Titmarsh, Belgrave.
MR. AND MRS. DAVENTRY
    See Harris, Frank.
MR. AND MRS. MUFFETT
    See Smith, Lita.
MR. AND MRS. PETER WHITE
    See Raymond, Richard John.
    See Raymond, Richard John. Mrs. White.
MR. AND MRS. PRINGLE
    See Trueba y Cosío, Joaquin Telesforo de, Don.
MR. AND MRS. TOODLES
    See Raymond, Richard John. Farmer's Daughter of the Severn Side, The.
MR. BONEY'S RECEPTION IN PARIS
    See Maclaren, Archibald.
MR. BONNY'S WEDDING
    See Maclaren, Archibald. Empress and No Empress.
MR. BUCKSTONE'S ASCENT OF MOUNT PARNASSUS
    See Planché, James Robinson.
MR. BUCKSTONE'S VOYAGE ROUND THE GLOBE
    See Planché, James Robinson.
MR. FITZ-W—?
    See Newte, Horace Wykeham Can.
MR. GREENFINCH
    See Bayly, Thomas Haynes.
MR. H.
    See Lamb, Charles.
MR. MENDALL'S ATTEMPT TO AMELIORATE THAT TRAGEDY
    See Colomb, George Hatton, Col. Hamlet Improved.
MR. MIDSHIPMAN EASY!
    See Oxberry, William Henry.
MR. NIGHTINGALE'S DIARY
    See Dickens, Charles.
MR. PAUL PRY
    See Jerrold, Douglas William. Paul Pry.
MR. SCROGGINS
    See Hancock, William.
MR. TIBBS
    See Thomson, James.
MRS. BROWN OF THE MISSIS-SIPPI
    See Byron, Henry James. Grin Bushes!, The.
MRS. BUNBURY'S SPOONS
    See Coyne, Joseph Stirling.
MRS. CAUDLE'S CURTAIN LECTURE!
    See Stirling, Edward.
MRS. DANE'S DEFENCE
    See Jones, Henry Arthur.
MRS. FLIPPER'S HOLIDAY
    See Bell, Harrie.
MRS. G—, OF THE GOLDEN PIPPIN!
    See Barnett, Morris.
MRS. GREEN'S SNUG LITTLE BUSINESS
    See Cheltnam, Charles Smith.
MRS. HILARY REGRETS
    See Smith, Spencer Theyre.

MRS. SARAH GAMP'S TEA AND TURN OUT
    See Webster, Benjamin Nottingham.
MRS. WARREN'S PROFESSION
    See Shaw, George Bernard.
MRS. WHITE
    See Raymond, Richard John. Mr. and Mrs. Peter White.
    See Raymond, Richard John.
MRS. WIGGINS
    See Allingham, John Till.
MRS. WILLIS'S WILL (anon.)
    London & New York: Samuel French, n.d. Pp. [39]-57. Text complete.
MUCH ADO ABOUT A MERCHANT OF VENICE
    See Brougham, John.
MUCH ADO ABOUT NOTHING
    See Irving, Henry (arr.).
    See Kean, Charles John (arr.).
    See Kemble, John Philip (arr.).
    See Shakespeare, William.
MUCH TOO CLEVER
    See Oxenford, John.
MUDBOROUGH ELECTION!
    See Brough, William.
MUETTE DE PORTICI
    See Masaniello.
MULDOON'S PICNIC
    See Pleon, Harry.
MULETEER OF TOLEDO, THE
    See Morton, John Maddison.
MULLER, HUGO
    Beethoven.
        See Hein, Gustav (trans.).
MULLNER, ADOLPHUS
    Guilt.
        See Frye, William Edward (trans.).
MUMMY, THE
    See Bernard, William Bayle.
MUMMY MAKERS OF EGYPT, THE
    See Capper, Richard.
MURDER AT SADLER'S WELLS!
    See Wilks, Thomas Egerton. Ruby Ring, The.
MURDER AT THE BLACK FARM
    See Townsend, William Thompson. John Stafford.
MURDER AT THE HALL
    See Fitzball, Edward. Crock of Gold!, The.
MURDER AT THE MOUND
    See Rede, William Leman. Skeleton Witness, The.
MURDER AT THE OLD SMITHY
    See Ada the Betrayed.
MURDER AT THE ROAD-SIDE INN
    See Fitzball, Edward. Jonathan Bradford!
MURDER IN THE MARSH
    See Faucquez, Adolphe. Forced Marriage, The.
MURDER IN THE RED BARN
    See Maria Martin.
MURDER NEAR THE OLD MILL
    See Waldron, W. Richard. Lizzie Leigh.
MURDER OF THE FIVE FIELDS COPSE
    See Pitt, George Dibdin. Poacher's Doom, The.
    See Pitt, George Dibdin. Simon Lee.
MURDER OF THE GLEN, THE
    See Hart, James P.
MURDER WILL OUT
    See Buckstone, John Baldwin. Presumptive Evidence.
MURDERED HOSTAGE
    See Miller, James. Siege of Berwick, The.
MURDERERS OF MASSIAC!
    See Buckstone, John Baldwin. Peter Bell the Waggoner.
MURDOCH, J. MORTIMER
    Googah, The. 150 leaves. Manuscript.
    Hoop of Gold. 154 leaves. Manuscript.
    Lost Love. London: William & Strahan (printers), 1879. Pp. [1]-56.
MURPHY, ANNA BROWNELL
    See Jameson, Anna Brownell Murphy, Mrs. Robert.

MURPHY, ARTHUR

All in the Wrong. London: Whittingham & Arliss, 1815. Pp. [1]-84. London Theatre, X. *Filed under* Dibdin, Thomas John, ed. London Theatre, X.

All in the Wrong. In *New English Drama,* ed. W. Oxberry, 22 vols., London: W. Simpkin & R. Marshall; C. Chapple, 1824, XX, [i]-[xii], [1]-[80]. *Filed under* Oxberry, William Henry. New English Drama, XX.

All in the Wrong. London: John Cumberland, 1826. Pp. [i]-[vi], [9]-75, [i-ii], 76. Cumberland's British Theatre, VI. *Filed under* Cumberland, John. Cumberland's British Theatre, VI.

All in the Wrong. In *British Drama,* 12 vols., London: John Dicks, 1871, VIII, [97]-121.

Apprentice, The. London: Whittingham & Arliss, 1815. Pp. [1]-[28]. London Theatre, XIV. *Filed under* Dibdin, Thomas John, ed. London Theatre, XIV.

Apprentice, The. In *British Drama,* 12 vols., London: John Dicks, 1872, X, [185]-192.

Citizen, The. London: Whittingham & Arliss, 1815. Pp. [1]-[36]. London Theatre, XVI. *Filed under* Dibdin, Thomas John, ed. London Theatre, XVI.

Citizen, The. In *New English Drama,* ed. W. Oxberry, 22 vols., London: W. Simpkin & R. Marshall; C. Chapple, 1820, XI, [1-2], [i]-ii, [i]-[iv], [1]-28. *Filed under* Oxberry, William Henry. New English Drama, XI.

Citizen, The. In *British Drama,* 12 vols., London: John Dicks, 1871, VII, [182]-192.

Citizen, The. London: John Cumberland, n.d. Pp. [1]-34. Cumberland's British Theatre, XXIV. *Filed under* Cumberland, John. Cumberland's British Theatre, XXIV.

Grecian Daughter, The. London: Whittingham & Arliss, 1815. Pp. [1]-56. London Theatre, V. *Filed under* Dibdin, Thomas John, ed. London Theatre, V.

Grecian Daughter, The. In *New English Drama,* ed. W. Oxberry, 22 vols., London: W. Simpkin & R. Marshall; C. Chapple, 1821, XIV, [1-2], [i]-iv, [i]-iv, [1]-[50], [i]-ii. *Filed under* Oxberry, William Henry. New English Drama, XIV.

Grecian Daughter, The. In *British Drama,* 12 vols., London: John Dicks, 1864, II, [342]-355.

Grecian Daughter, The. London: John Cumberland, n.d. Pp. [i], [1]-48. Cumberland's British Theatre, XXV. *Filed under* Cumberland, John. Cumberland's British Theatre, XXV.

Grecian Daughter, The.
See Kemble, John Philip (arr.).

Know Your Own Mind. In *New English Drama,* ed. W. Oxberry, 22 vols., London: W. Simpkin & R. Marshall; C. Chapple, 1821, XIV, [1-2], [i]-[vi], [1]-[76]. *Filed under* Oxberry, William Henry. New English Drama, XIV.

Know Your Own Mind. London: T. Dolby, 1825. Pp. [i]-viii, [9]-72. Dolby's British Theatre, VIII. *Filed under* Cumberland, John. Cumberland's British Theatre, VIII.

Know Your Own Mind. In *British Drama,* 12 vols., London: John Dicks, 1872, X, [161]-184.

Orphan of China, The. London: Whittingham & Arliss, 1816. Pp. [1]-[64]. London Theatre, XVII. *Filed under* Dibdin, Thomas John, ed. London Theatre, XVII.

Orphan of China, The. In *British Drama,* 12 vols., London: John Dicks, 1871, IX, [97]-118.

Three Weeks after Marriage. London: Whittingham & Arliss, 1815. Pp. [1]-32. London Theatre, VII. *Filed under* Dibdin, Thomas John, ed. London Theatre, VII.

Three Weeks after Marriage. In *New English Drama,* ed. W. Oxberry, 22 vols., London: W. Simpkin & R. Marshall; C. Chapple, 1820, IX, [1-2], [i]-[vi], [1]-27. *Filed under* Oxberry, William Henry. New English Drama, IX.

Three Weeks after Marriage. In *British Drama,* 12 vols., London: John Dicks, 1872, X, [54]-64.

Way to Keep Him, The. London: Whittingham & Arliss, 1815. Pp. [1]-[88]. London Theatre, X. *Filed under* Dibdin, Thomas John, ed. London Theatre, X.

Way to Keep Him, The. In *New English Drama,* ed. W. Oxberry, 22 vols., London: W. Simpkin & R. Marshall;

C. Chapple, 1818, III, [i]-[viii], [1]-84. *Filed under* Oxberry, William Henry. New English Drama, III.

Way to Keep Him, The. London: T. Dolby, 1823. Pp. [1-2], [i]-[vi], [7]-[82]. Dolby's British Theatre, III. *Filed under* Cumberland, John. Cumberland's British Theatre, III.

Way to Keep Him, The. In *British Drama,* 12 vols., London: John Dicks, 1871, VIII, [289]-316.

MURPHY'S WEATHER ALMANAC
See Rogers, William.

MURRAY, ALFRED

Béarnaise, La. Music by Messager, André. London: Alfred Hays, 1886. Pp. [i]-vi, [7]-45. Libretto.

Glamour.
See Farnie, Henry Brougham.

Lily of Leoville, The.
See Remo, Felix.

Messenger Boy, The.
See Tanner, James Tolman.

Périchole, La. Music by Offenbach. [London: Mrs. Marshall's Typewriting Office, 1897]. Pp. [i], [1]-45, [i], [1]-24, [i], [1]-34. Pagination by act. Typescript promptbook libretto.

Prima Donna, La.
See Farnie, Henry Brougham.

MURRAY, FRANK

Beau Nicolas, Le. In *Lyrical Poems, Together with Two Operettas,* London: J. R. Lynn (printer), 1876, pp. [47]-71. Libretto.

Under the Thumb. In *Lyrical Poems, Together with Two Operettas,* London: J. R. Lynn (printer), 1876, pp. [i], [29]-46. Libretto.

MURRAY, GASTON

Is She His Daughter?; or, Beaujolais, the Necromancer. Written with Hipkins, Henry T. London: Music Publishing Company, n.d. Pp. [i]-[viii], [9]-65. Cumberland's Acting Plays, 554.

Nice Quiet Day, A.
See Hipkins, Henry T.

MURRAY, GILBERT

Carlyon Sahib. London: William Heinemann, 1900. Pp. [i]-[viii], [1]-156.

MURRAY, ROSA CAROLINE
See Praed, Rosa Caroline Murray-Prior, Mrs. Campbell.

MURRAY, WILLIAM HENRY WOOD

Cramond Brig; or, The Gudeman o' Ballangeich. London: Thomas Hailes Lacy, n.d. Pp. [1]-18. Promptbook.

Diamond Cut Diamond. London & New York: Samuel French, n.d. Pp. [1]-15.

Dominique the Deserter; or, The Gentleman in Black. London: Thomas Hailes Lacy, n.d. Pp. [1]-24. Promptbook.

Fortunes of Nigel, The; or, George Heriot. [Edinburgh: J. L. Huie, 1823]. Pp. [1]-70. [Dramas from . . . Author of Waverley, 5].

Fortunes of Nigel, The; or, George Heriot. In *Waverley Dramas,* London: George Routledge, 1845, pp. [1]-70. *Filed under* Waverley Dramas (anon.).

Gilderoy. London: Thomas Hailes Lacy, n.d. Pp. [1]-24.

Ivanhoe. Edinburgh: James L. Huie, 1823. Pp. [1]-76. [Dramas from . . . Author of Waverley, 7].

Mary Queen of Scots; or, The Escape from Loch Leven. London: Thomas Hailes Lacy, n.d. Pp. [1]-26. Promptbook.

No! Edinburgh: John Anderson, jr, 1829. Pp. [1]-24.

Philippe; or, The Secret Marriage. London: Thomas Hailes Lacy, n.d. Pp. [1]-30. [Lacy's Acting Edition].

MURTZOUFLE
See Aird, Thomas.

MUSARD BALL, THE
See Brougham, John.

MUSGRAVE, THOMAS MOORE (trans.)

Ignez de Castro. By Ferreira, Antonio. London: John Murray, 1825. Pp. [i]-iv, [1]-179.

MUSIC-HALL GODS, THE
See Ridge, William Pett.

MUSIC HATH CHARMS
See Fisher, David.

MUSIC IN MARBLE
See Jerrold, Douglas William. Statue Lover, The.

MUSIC MAD
See Hook, Theodore Edward.

MUSIC THE FOOD OF LOVE
See Webster, Benjamin Nottingham. Modern Orpheus, The.

MUSIC'S FASCINATION
See Cherry, Andrew. Travellers, The.

MUSKERRY, WILLIAM
Atonement; or, Branded for Life. London: John Dicks, 1871. Pp. [289]-316. Dicks' British Drama, 61. Promptbook.
Atonement; or, Branded for Life. In *British Drama*, 12 vols., London: John Dicks, 1871, VI, [289]-316.
Garrick; or, Only an Actor. London & New York: Samuel French, n.d. Pp. [1]-39. [French's Acting Edition].
Harlequin Beauty and the Beast. Bristol: Charles T. Jefferies, n.d. Pp. [1]-56. Libretto.
He, She, and It. New York & London: Samuel French, n.d. Pp. [1]-8. Minor Drama, 361.
Ironfounder, The. London: Samuel French; New York: T. Henry French, n.d. Pp. [1]-54. [Lacy's Acting Edition].
Khartoum!; or, The Star of the Desert. Written with Jourdain, John. London & New York: Samuel French, n.d. Pp. [1]-58. [Lacy's Acting Edition].
Odd Trick, An. London: Samuel French; New York: T. Henry French, n.d. Pp. [1]-19. [Lacy's Acting Edition].
Three Blind Mice. London & New York: Samuel French, n.d. Pp. [1]-15. [Lacy's Acting Edition].
Thrillby. Music by Carr, F. Osmond. London: Samuel French; New York: T. Henry French, n.d. Pp. [i-ii], [1]-16. [Lacy's Acting Edition]. Libretto.

MUSKETEERS, THE
See Grundy, Sydney.

MUSSET, ALFRED DE
Carmosine.
See under title.

MUTA DI PORTICI
See Kenney, James. Masaniello.

MUTINEER'S WIDOW, THE
See Townsend, William Thompson.

MUTINY AT THE NORE, THE
See Jerrold, Douglas William.

MUTINY OF THE DOLPHIN
See Fitzball, Edward. Red Rover, The.

MUTIUS SCAEVOLA
See Ireland, William Henry.

MY AUNT
See Arnold, Samuel James.

MY AUNT, THE DOWAGER
See Moncrieff, William Thomas. Winterbottoms!, The.

MY AUNT'S HEIRESS
See Lacy, Katherine.

MY AUNT'S HUSBAND
See Selby, Charles.

MY AWFUL DAD
See Mathews, Charles James.

MY BACHELOR DAYS
See Morton, John Maddison.

MY COUNTRY COUSIN
See Oxberry, William Henry. Actress of All Work, The.

MY COUSIN
See Hewson, J. James.
See Kenney, James. False Alarms.

MY COUSIN GERMAN
See Brougham, John. Demon Lover, The.

MY DAUGHTER, SIR!
See Planché, James Robinson.

MY DAUGHTER'S DAUGHTER (anon.)
In *Home Plays for Ladies*, Part 5, London & New York: Samuel French, n.d., pp. [53]-80. *Filed under* Home Plays for Ladies, Part 5.

MY DAUGHTER'S DEBUT
See Craven, Henry Thornton.

MY DAUGHTER'S LETTER
See Moncrieff, William Thomas. Monsieur Mallet.

MY DRESS BOOTS
See Williams, Thomas John.

MY FATHER
See Dibdin, Thomas John. Twenty Per Cent.

MY FELLOW CLERK
See Oxenford, John.

MY FIRST CLIENT
See Openshaw, Mary.

MY FIRST FIT OF THE GOUT
See Morton, John Maddison.

MY FRIEND
See Long, Charles.

MY FRIEND FROM LEATHERHEAD
See Yates, Edmund Hodgson.

MY FRIEND IN THE STRAPS
See Selby, Charles.

MY FRIEND JARLET
See Goldsworthy, Arnold.

MY FRIEND THE CAPT.
See Coyne, Joseph Stirling.

MY FRIEND, THE GOVERNOR
See Planché, James Robinson.

MY FRIEND THE MAJOR
See Selby, Charles.

MY FRIEND THOMPSON!
See Barclay, James M.

MY GIRL
See Ross, Adrian.

MY GOOD FRIEND (anon. trans.)
By Feydeau, Georges. [London: Mrs. Marshall's Typewriting Office, 1897]. Pp. [i], [1]-29, [i], [1]-37, [i], [1]-32. Pagination by act. Typescript.

MY GRANDMOTHER
See Hoare, Prince.

MY GRANDMOTHER'S PET!
See Stirling, Edward. Young Scamp, The.

MY HEART'S IDOL
See Planché, James Robinson.

MY HEART'S IN THE HIGHLANDS
See Brough, William.

MY HUSBAND'S GHOST
See Morton, John Maddison.

MY HUSBAND'S SECRET
See Whitty, Walter Devereux.

MY LADY CLARE
See Robertson, Thomas William. Dreams.

MY LADY HELP
See Macklin, Arthur.

MY LADY'S LORD
See Esmond, Henry Vernon.

MY LANDLADY'S GOWN
See Oulton, Walley Chamberlaine.

MY LITTLE ADOPTED
See Bayly, Thomas Haynes.

MY LITTLE GIRL
See Boucicault, Dion George.

MY LORD AND MY LADY
See Planché, James Robinson.

MY LORD IN LIVERY
See Smith, Spencer Theyre.

MY LORD IS NOT MY LORD
See Dance, Charles.

MY MILLINER'S BILL
See Godfrey, George William.

MY MYSTERIOUS RIVAL
See Simpson, John Palgrave.

MY NEIGHBOUR'S WIFE
See Bunn, Alfred.

MY OLD WOMAN
See Macfarren, George.

MY OWN BLUE BELL
 See Pitt, George Dibdin.
MY OWN GHOST!
 See Parry, Thomas. First Night, The.
MY OWN LOVER
 See Rodwell, George Herbert Bonaparte.
MY POLL AND MY PARTNER JOE
 See Haines, John Thomas.
MY PRECIOUS BETSY!
 See Morton, John Maddison.
MY PRESERVER
 See Craven, Henry Thornton.
MY SISTER FROM INDIA
 See Selby, Charles.
MY SISTER KATE
 See Lemon, Mark.
MY SOLDIER BOY
 See Maltby, C. Alfred.
MY SON AND I
 See Lancaster-Wallis, Ellen.
MY SON DIANA
 See Harris, Augustus Glossop.
MY SON'S A DAUGHTER
 See Parselle, J.
MY SPOUSE AND I
 See Dibdin, Charles Isaac Mungo, jr.
MY TURN NEXT
 See Williams, Thomas John.
MY TWO NEPHEWS
 See Peake, Richard Brinsley. Duel, The.
MY UNCLE
 See Beazley, Samuel, jr.
MY UNCLE GABRIEL
 See Parry, John.
MY UNCLE, THE GHOST
 See Lathair, Henry.
MY UNCLE TOBY
 See Stafford, John Joseph.
MY UNCLE'S CARD
 See Grattan, H. P.
MY UNCLE'S SUIT
 See Becher, Martin.
MY UNFINISHED OPERA
 See Brough, William.
MY UNKNOWN FRIEND
 See Scott, Shafto.
MY VALET AND I
 See Wilks, Thomas Egerton.
MY VERY LAST PROPOSAL
 See Phipps, A. J.
MY WIFE, OR MY PLACE
 See Shannon, Charles.
MY WIFE! WHAT WIFE?
 See Barrett, Eaton Stannard.
 See Poole, John.
MY WIFE'S BABY
 See Hughes, Fred.
MY WIFE'S BONNET
 See Morton, John Maddison.
MY WIFE'S COME!
 See Morton, Edward.
MY WIFE'S DAUGHTER
 See Coyne, Joseph Stirling.
MY WIFE'S DENTIST
 See Wilks, Thomas Egerton.
MY WIFE'S DIARY
 See Robertson, Thomas William.
MY WIFE'S FATHER'S SISTER
 See Pemberton, Thomas Edgar.
MY WIFE'S HUSBAND
 See Challis, Henry W.
MY WIFE'S MAID!
 See Williams, Thomas John.
MY WIFE'S MOTHER
 See Mathews, Charles James.

MY WIFE'S OUT
 See Rodwell, George Herbert Bonaparte.
MY WIFE'S RELATIONS
 See Gordon, Walter.
MY WIFE'S SECOND FLOOR
 See Morton, John Maddison.
MY YOUNG WIFE AND MY OLD UMBRELLA
 See Webster, Benjamin Nottingham.
MYNHEER JAN
 See Paulton, Harry.
MYNYDDOG
 Blodwen.
 See Rowlands, ?, Prof. (trans.).
MYRA
 See Thompson, Helen.
MYRRHA
 See Lloyd, Charles (trans.).
MYSTERIES OF CARROW ABBEY
 See Waldron, W. Richard. Will and the Way, The.
MYSTERIES OF ISIS
 See Walter, William Joseph (trans.). Magic Flute, The.
MYSTERIES OF PARIS, THE
 See Dillon, Charles.
MYSTERIOUS FAMILY, THE
 See Rodwell, George Herbert Bonaparte.
MYSTERIOUS HUSBAND, THE
 See Cumberland, Richard.
MYSTERIOUS LADY, THE
 See Planché, James Robinson.
MYSTERIOUS MARINER, THE CHILD OF DESTINY, AND
 THE RIGHTFUL HEIR
 See Bowles, Thomas Gibson. Port Admiral, The.
MYSTERIOUS STRANGER, THE
 See Selby, Charles.
MYSTERY; OR, THE MONK OF ST. NICHOLAS (anon.)
 Oxford: Munday & Slatter, 1819. Pp. [i-iv], [1]-88.
MYSTERY OF TWENTY YEARS
 See Phillips, Lewis. Marianne, the Vivandiere.
MYSTIC BELL OF RONQUEROLLES
 See Barber, James. Memoirs of the D***l, The.
MYSTIFICATION
 See Smythies, William Gordon.
NABOB FOR AN HOUR, A
 See Poole, John.
 See Poole, John. Uncle Sam.
NADESHDA
 See Sturgis, Julian Russell.
NAIAD QUEEN
 See Dalrymple, J. S. Lurline.
 See Dalrymple, J. S.
NAOMI
 See Rouse, Miss T.
NAOMIE
 See Osbaldiston, David Webster.
NAPOLEON (anon.)
 London: Charles Fox (priv.), 1842. Pp. [i]-[xvi], [1]-159.
NAPOLEON!
 See Walker, John.
NAPOLEON BUONAPARTE'S INVASION OF RUSSIA
 See Amherst, J. H.
NAPOLEON FALLEN
 See Buchanan, Robert Williams. Drama of Kings.
NAPOLEON OF HUMBLE LIFE
 See Moncrieff, William Thomas. Gipsy Jack.
NAPOLEON'S BARBER
 See Tweddell, Edward Washington.
NAPOLEON'S FIRST LOVE
 See Wynne, John.
NAPPY'S RECEPTION IN ELBA
 See Maclaren, Archibald.
NARENSKY
 See Brown, Charles Armitage.
NARROW ESCAPE, A
 See Henry, Reginald.

NARROW SQUEAK, A
    See Morton, John Maddison.
NATHAN THE WISE
    See Bell, Ernest (trans.).
NATION, WILLIAM HAMILTON CODRINGTON
    Under the Earth; or, The Sons of Toil. London: John Dicks,
    n.d. Pp. [225]-247. Dicks' British Drama, 59.
NATIVE LAND
    See Dimond, William.
NATIVITY, THE
    See Hinkson, Katharine Tynan, Mrs. Henry Albert.
NATURAL MAGIC
    See Moncrieff, William Thomas. Secret, The.
NATURAL SON, THE
    See Cumberland, Richard.
    See Mason, James.
**NATURE AND PHILOSOPHY; OR, THE YOUTH WHO
NEVER SAW A WOMAN** (anon.)
    New York: Samuel French, n.d. Pp. [1]-16. French's
    Minor Drama, 185. Promptbook.
NATURE, BONDAGE, AND LIBERTY
    See Bulwer, J. Slave Sale, The.
NAUGHTY BOY WHO CRIED FOR THE MOON
    See Brough, William. Endymion.
NAUGHTY COCK SPARROW WHO KILLED POOR COCK
ROBIN
    See McNeill, A. D. Babes in the Wood and the Bold
    Robin Hood, The.
NAUTCH GIRL, THE
    See Dance, George.
NAVAL ENGAGEMENTS
    See Dance, Charles.
NAVARRAISE, LA
    See Weatherly, Frederick Edward (trans.).
NAVARRO, MRS. ANTONIO DE
    See Anderson, Mary.
NEALE, FREDERICK
    Constantia. 91 leaves. Acts II-III lacking. Manuscript
    promptbook.
    Eliza Fenning. 35 leaves. Manuscript.
    Jepey Mayflower; or, The Wild Horde of the Wolf's Lair. 104
    leaves. Act III lacking. Manuscript promptbook.
NEAR THE BAND-STAND
    See Ridge, William Pett.
NEARLY SEVEN
    See Brookfield, Charles Hallam Elton.
NEARLY SEVERED
    See Hurst, James P.
NECK OR NOTHING
    See Pettitt, Henry Alfred.
NEEDHAM, CHARLES FRANCIS, EARL OF KILMOREY
    See Newry, Charles Francis Needham, Earl of Kilmorey,
    Viscount.
NEEDLESS STRATAGEM
    See Williams, Thomas John. I've Written to Browne.
NEELE, HENRY
    Antiochus. In *Poems*, 2 vols., London: Smith, Elder, 1827, II,
    [i], [86]-123.
    David Rizzio. In *Poems*, 2 vols., London: Smith, Elder, 1827,
    II, [i], [45]-85.
    Dramatic Fragment, A. In *Poems*, 2 vols., London: Smith,
    Elder, 1827. I, [i], [199]-209.
    Secret Bridal, The. In *Poems*, 2 vols., London: Smith, Elder,
    1827, II, [i]-xii, [1]-44.
NE'ER-DO-WEEL, THE
    See Gilbert, William Schwenck.
NEGRO OF WAPPING, THE
    See Fitzball, Edward.
NEIGHBOURS
    See Oxenford, John.
NEIL, ROSS (pseud. of Harwood, Isabella)
    Arabella Stuart. In *Plays*, London: Ellis & White, 1879, [i-vi],
    [1]-89.
    Cid, The. In *Plays*, London: Ellis & White, 1874, [i-viii],
    [1]-102.

    Claudia's Choice. N.p.: n.pub., n.d. Pp. [97]-180. Title page
    lacking. *Filed under* Harwood, Isabella.
    Duke for a Day; or, The Tailor of Brussels. In *Plays*, London:
    Ellis & White, 1874, [213]-307. *Filed under* Cid.
    Eglantine. London: Ellis & White (printer), n.d. Pp. [1]-97.
    Filed under Harwood, Isabella.
    Elfinella; or, Home from Fairyland. In *Elfinella . . .*, London:
    Ellis & White, 1876, [i-viii], [1]-100.
    Heir of Linne, The. In *Plays*, London: Ellis & White, 1879,
    [93]-198. *Filed under* Arabella Stuart.
    Inez; or, The Bride of Portugal. In *Lady Jane Grey . . .*,
    London: Ellis & Green, 1871, [138]-291 *Filed under* Lady
    Jane Grey.
    King and the Angel, The. In *Plays*, London: Ellis & White,
    1874, [103]-212. *Filed under* Cid.
    Lady Jane Grey. In *Lady Jane Grey . . .*, London: Ellis &
    Green, 1871, [i-viii], [1]-137.
    Lord and Lady Russell. In *Elfinella . . .*, London: Ellis &
    White, 1876, [101]-260. *Filed under* Elfinella.
    Tasso. In *Plays*, London: Ellis & White, 1879, [199]-307. *Filed
    under* Arabella Stuart.
NEILSON, FRANCIS
    Manabozo. London: John Macqueen, 1899. Pp. [i]-[x],
    [1]-90. Libretto.
    Prince Ananias. Music by Herbert, Victor. New York:
    Edward Schuberth, c.1895. Pp. [i-ii], [1]-199. Vocal score.
    Prince Ananias. Music by Herbert, Victor. New York:
    Edward Schuberth; London: E. Ascherberg; Leipzig: C.
    Dieckmann, n.d. Pp. [1]-72. Libretto.
NEITHER OF THEM
    See Cowen, ?, Miss.
NELL GWYNNE
    See Farnie, Henry Brougham.
    See Jerrold, Douglas William.
    See Walker, John.
NELSON, CARRY
    Fille de Madame Angot, La. Music by Lecocq, Charles.
    London & New York: Samuel French, n.d. Pp. [1]-34.
    [Lacy's Acting Edition]. Libretto.
NEPHEW AS UNCLE, THE
    See Harris, G. Shirley (trans.).
NEPTUNE'S DEFEAT
    See Brougham, John.
NEREID'S LOVE, THE
    See Lyndsay, David.
NERO
    See Jackson, John P. (trans.).
    See Stephens, George.
NERO, PART 1
    See Bridges, Robert Seymour.
NERO, PART 2
    See Bridges, Robert Seymour.
NERVES
    See Carr, Joseph William Comyns.
NERVOUS MAN AND THE MAN OF NERVE, THE
    See Bernard, William Bayle.
NET-MAKER AND HIS WIFE
    See Pocock, Isaac. Zembuca.
NETLEY ABBEY
    See Pearce, William.
NETTLE, THE
    See Warren, Ernest.
NETTLE COATS
    See Greene, Louisa Lilias Plunket, Mrs. Richard Jonas
    (Baroness).
NETTLEWIG HALL
    See Westmacott, Charles Malloy.
NEVER RECKON YOUR CHICKENS &C.
    See Reeve, Wybert.
NEVER TOO LATE TO MEND
    See Drayton, Henri.
    See Hazlewood, Colin Henry.
NEVILLE, GEORGE F.
    Little Vixens, The. London & New York: Samuel French,
    n.d. Pp. [1]-[22]. [Lacy's Acting Edition].

NEW APPLE OF DISCORD
  See Not for Me!
NEW BEGGAR'S OPERA, THE
  See Barrett, Eaton Stannard.
NEW BOY, THE
  See Law, Arthur.
NEW BROOMS
  See Dibdin, Charles Isaac Mungo, jr.
NEW COMEDY OF ERRORS
  See Moncrieff, William Thomas. Shakspeare's Festival.
NEW CORSICAN BROTHERS, THE
  See Raleigh, Cecil.
NEW DON JUAN!, A
  See Buckstone, John Baldwin.
NEW DUO-(DECIMAL) EDITION OF THE FORTY THIEVES!
  See Keating, Eliza H. Ali Baba.
NEW ERA, THE
  See Vaughan, Virginia.
NEW FOOTMAN, THE
  See Selby, Charles.
NEW FRONT TO AN OLD DICKY
  See Burnand, Francis Cowley. Rise and Fall of Richard III, The.
NEW GROOM, THE
  See Hannan, Charles.
NEW HAY AT THE OLD MARKET
  See Colman, George, jr. Sylvester Daggerwood.
NEW HAYMARKET SPRING MEETING, THE
  See Planché, James Robinson.
NEW INVENTIONS
  See Emden, William Samuel.
NEW LAMPS FOR OLD ONES
  See Smith, Albert Richard. Aladdin and the Wonderful Lamp.
NEW LIGHTS
  See Butler, Richard William, Earl of Glengall. Irish Tutor, The.
NEW LINES TO AN OLD BAN-DITTY
  See A'Beckett, Gilbert Arthur. Utter Per-version of The Brigand, An.
NEW MAGDALEN, THE
  See Collins, William Wilkie.
NEW MAN, THE
  See Forman, Edmund.
NEW MEN AND OLD ACRES
  See Taylor, Tom.
NEW PLANET, THE
  See Planché, James Robinson.
NEW PSYCHE
  See Baildon, Arthur. Giralda.
NEW PYGMALION
  See Ross, Ronald. Edgar.
NEW ROAD TO BRIGHTON
  See Jones, Richard. Peter Fin.
NEW SUB, THE
  See Hicks, Edward Seymour.
NEW WAY TO PAY OLD DEBTS, A
  See Kemble, John Philip (arr.).
  See Massinger, Philip.
NEW WOMAN, THE
  See Grundy, Sydney.
NEW WRECKS UPON OLD SHOALS
  See Alma-Tadema, Laurence.
NEW YEAR'S EVE
  See Sidney, Frederick W. Hogmanay.
NEWBIGGING, THOMAS
  Old Gamul. London: T. Fisher Unwin, 1892. Pp. [1]-100.
NEWBOLT, JOHN HENRY
  Mordred. London: T. Fisher Unwin, 1895. Pp. [i-x], [1]-126.
NEWINGTON BUTTS!
  See Morton, John Maddison.

NEWNHAM, FRANCIS, REV.
  Pleasures of Anarchy, The. London: G. Taylor (printer) (priv.), 1829-1859 (4th supplement). Pp. [iii]-xxiv, [1]-314, [i-iv], [1]-99.
NEWNHAM-DAVIS, NATHANIEL
  Charitable Bequest, A. London & New York: Samuel French, c.1901. Pp. [1]-12. [Lacy's Acting Edition].
NEWRY, CHARLES FRANCIS NEEDHAM, EARL OF KILMOREY, VISCOUNT
  Danischeffs, The. London: Stevens & Richardson (printer), n.d. Pp. [1]-60. *Filed under* Kilmorey, Charles Francis Needham.
NEWS FROM PANNONIA
  See Allingham, William.
NEWSPAPER NUPTIALS
  See Norwood, Eille.
NEWTE, HORACE WYKEHAM CAN
  Bosom Friends. London: Samuel French; New York: T. Henry French, n.d. Pp. [1]-9. [Lacy's Acting Edition].
  Eternal Masculine, The. London & New York: Samuel French, n.d. Pp. [1]-12. [Lacy's Acting Edition].
  Journey's End, The. London: Samuel French; New York: T. Henry French, n.d. Pp. [1]-21. [Lacy's Acting Edition].
  Leonore. London: Capper & Newton, n.d. Pp. [1]-20. Lynn's Acting Edition, 14.
  Mr. Fitz-W—?; or, Taking the Bull by the Horns. Written with Parke, Walter. Music by Andrews, Bond. London: Joseph Williams, n.d. Pp. [1]-18. Libretto.
NEWTON, HENRY CHANCE
  See Henry, Richard (pseud.).
NEXT DOOR NEIGHBOURS
  See Inchbald, Elizabeth Simpson, Mrs. Joseph.
  See Rede, William Leman. Come to Town.
NEXT OF KIN
  See Falconer, Edmund.
NICE FIRM, A
  See Taylor, Tom.
NICE QUIET DAY, A
  See Hipkins, Henry T.
NICHOL, JOHN
  Hannibal. Glasgow: James Maclehose, 1873. Pp. [i-x], [1]-284.
NICHOLAS FLAM, ATTORNEY AT LAW
  See Buckstone, John Baldwin.
NICHOLAS NICKLEBY
  See Halliday, Andrew.
  See Simms, Harry.
  See Stirling, Edward.
NICHOLLS, HARRY
  Babes in the Wood, Robin Hood and His Merry Men, and Harlequin Who Killed Cock Robin?
    See Harris, Augustus Henry Glossop.
  Jack and the Beanstalk; or, Harlequin and the Midwinter Night's Dream. Written with Harris, Augustus Henry Glossop. London: Strand Publishing Company, n.d. Pp. [5]-[82]. Text complete. Libretto.
  Jane. Written with Lestocq, William. New York & London: Samuel French, c.1900. Pp. [1]-62. French's International Copyrighted Edition of the Works of the Best Authors, 41.
  Our New Butler. London: Samuel French; New York: T. Henry French, n.d. Pp. [1]-12. [Lacy's Acting Edition].
  Runaway Girl, A.
    See Hicks, Edward Seymour.
  Timson's Little Holiday. London & New York: Samuel French, n.d. Pp. [1]-18. [Lacy's Acting Edition].
NICHOLSON, JOHN
  Paetus and Arria.
    See Burton, ?.
  Right and Wrong.
    See Burton, ?.
NICK OF THE WOODS
  See Haines, John Thomas.
NICKNAMES
  See Childe-Pemberton, Harriet Louisa.

NICOLAIE, LOUIS FRANÇOIS
    Mysterious Stranger.
        See Selby, Charles.
NICOLETE
    See Ferris, Edward.
NIGEL
    See Pocock, Isaac.
NIGHT AFTER WATERLOO
    See Duke's Coat, The.
NIGHT AND MORNING
    See Boucicault, Dionysius Lardner. Kerry.
    See Brougham, John.
NIGHT AND THE SOUL
    See Bigg, John Stanyan.
NIGHT AT DOVER
    See Milner, Henry M. Twelve Precisely!
NIGHT AT NOTTING HILL, A
    See Yates, Edmund Hodgson.
NIGHT BEFORE THE BRIDAL
    See Blake, Thomas G. Lonely Man of the Ocean, The.
NIGHT CHARGES, THE
    See Ridge, William Pett.
NIGHT IN THE BASTILLE
    See Archer, Thomas.
    See Gully, James Manby. Lady of Belleisle, The.
NIGHT IN VENICE
    See Gondolier, The.
NIGHT OF A HUNDRED YEARS, THE
    See Filippi, Rosina.
NIGHT OF PERIL
    See Coyne, Joseph Stirling. Old Chateau, The.
NIGHT OF SUSPENSE, A (anon.)
        London: Thomas Hailes Lacy, n.d. Pp. [1]-10. [Lacy's Acting Edition].
NIGHT ON SNOWDON, A
    See Gardner, Herbert.
NIGHT SURPRISE, A
    See Law, Arthur.
NIGHT WITH THE FORTY THIEVES
    See A'Beckett, Gilbert Abbott. Open Sesame.
    See O'Neill, John Robert. Ali Baba.
NIGHT'S ADVENTURE
    See Webster, Benjamin Nottingham. Black Domino, The.
NIGHT'S FROLIC!
    See Higgie, Thomas Henry. Devilish Good Joke!, A.
NIGHTINGALE, JOSEPH HENRY
    Bloomerism; or, The Follies of the Day. Written with Millward, Charles. London: National Acting Drama Office, n.d. Pp. [1]-23.
    Off to the Diggins. Liverpool: Liverpool Mail Office (printer) (priv.), n.d. Pp. [2]-18.
NIGHTINGALE, THE
    See Robertson, Thomas William.
NIHILISTS
    See Wilde, Oscar Fingall O'Flahertie Wills. Vera.
NIMBLE NYMPH AND THE TERRIBLE TROGLODYTE!
    See Burnand, Francis Cowley. Acis and Galataea.
NIMROUD, THE MIGHTY HUNTER
    See Capper, Richard.
NINA SFORZA
    See Troughton, Richard Zouch Sebbon.
NINE DAYS' WONDER, A
    See Aïdé, Hamilton.
NINE POINTS OF THE LAW
    See Taylor, Tom.
NINE TO ONE
    See Bryant, Michael.
NINETTA
    See Fitzball, Edward.
NINTH STATUE, THE
    See Dibdin, Thomas John.
NINTH WALTZ, THE
    See Carton, R. C.
NIOBE, ALL SMILES
    See Paulton, Harry.

NIP VAN WINKLE AND THE DEMON SLUMBER OF TWENTY YEARS
    See Marchant, Frederick.
NIPPED IN THE BUD
    See Selby, Charles. King's Gardener, The.
NITA THE DANCER
    See Weller, Bernard William.
NITA'S FIRST
    See Warren, T. Gideon.
NO!
    See Murray, William Henry Wood.
    See Reynolds, Francis.
NO CARDS
    See Gilbert, William Schwenck.
NO FOLLOWERS
    See Oxenford, John.
NO FOOL LIKE AN OLD ONE
    See Meadows, Thomas. Who's to Blame?
NO NAME
    See Bernard, William Bayle.
    See Collins, William Wilkie.
NO ROSE WITHOUT A THORN
    See Burnand, Francis Cowley. Beast and the Beauty, The.
NO SONG, NO SUPPER
    See Hoare, Prince.
NO. 6, DUKE STREET
    See Becher, Martin.
NO THOROUGHFARE
    See Dickens, Charles.
    See Lequel, Louis. Identity.
NO. 3, FIG TREE COURT, TEMPLE
    See Taylor, Tom. Our Clerks.
NO. 20
    See Albery, James.
NOBBUT A CUMBERLAND LAD
    See Wheatley, J. A. Joe the Buits.
NOBLE, THOMAS
    Persian Hunters, The; or, The Rose of Gurgistan. Music by Horn, Charles Edward. London: Sherwood, Neely, & Jones, 1817. Pp. [iii]-[xvi], [1]-86. Libretto.
NOBLE ERROR
    See Tomlins, Frederick Guest. Garcia.
NOBLE FOUNDLING, THE
    See Trotter, Thomas.
NOBLE HEART, THE
    See Lawrence, Slingsby.
NOBLE OUTLAW, THE (anon.)
        Music by Bishop, Henry. London: J. Barker, 1815. Pp. [1]-23. Libretto.
NOBLE SAVAGE
    See Reece, Robert. Ingomar.
NOBLESSE OBLIGE
    See Bright, Kate C., Mrs. Augustus.
NOBODY'S CHILD
    See Phillips, Watts.
NOBODY'S FAULT
    See Law, Arthur.
NOÉMIE
    See Robertson, Thomas William.
NONDESCRIPT, THE
    See Hewlings, A.
    See Major, Henry Archibald.
NOODLES IN PARIS
    See Hay, Frederic. French Exhibition, The.
NOONTIDE BRANCHES
    See Field, Michael (pseud.).
NORA
    See Anstey, F.
    See Lord, Henrietta Frances (trans.).
NORA CREINA
    See Stirling, Edward.
NORAH
    See Henry, Reginald.

NORMA (anon.)
Music by Bellini. London & New York: Boosey, n.d. Pp. [i-iv], 1-184. [Royal Edition]. Vocal score.

NORMA
See Planché, James Robinson.
See West, W.

NORMA TRAVESTIE
See Oxberry, William Henry.

NORMAN, E. B.
My Friend Jarlet.
See Goldsworthy, Arnold.

NORMAN CONQUEST
See Malet, Edward. Harold.

NORTH EAST LYNNE
See Pleon, Harry.

NORTH POLE
See Haines, John Thomas.

NORTH TOWER
See Arnold, Samuel James. Plots!

NORTHERN NIGHT, A
See Sharp, William.

NORTHUMBERLAND
See Edison, John Sibbald.

NORWEGIAN VENGEANCE
See Pennie, John Fitzgerald. Edwin and Elgiva.

NORWEGIAN WRECKERS
See Fitzball, Edward. Floating Beacon, The.

NORWICH IN 1549
See Bromley, George Percival. Rebellion, The.

NORWOOD, EILLE
Assault and Battery. London: Samuel French; New York: T. Henry French, n.d. Pp. [1]-22. [Lacy's Acting Edition].
Chalk and Cheese. London & New York: Samuel French, n.d. Pp. [1]-18. [French's Acting Edition].
Hook and Eye. London & New York: Samuel French, n.d. Pp. [1]-20. [French's Acting Edition].
Newspaper Nuptials. London & New York: Samuel French, c.1901. Pp. [1]-20. [Lacy's Acting Edition].
Silver Keepsake, The. London: Samuel French; New York: T. Henry French, n.d. Pp. [1]-20. [Lacy's Acting Edition].

NOS INTIMES
See Lyster, Frederic (trans.). Our Boon Companions.

NOT A BAD JUDGE
See Planché, James Robinson. Lavater the Physiognomist.

NOT AT ALL JEALOUS
See Robertson, Thomas William.

NOT AT HOME
See Dallas, Robert Charles.

NOT FALSE BUT FICKLE
See Bright, Kate C., Mrs. Augustus.

NOT FOR ME!; OR, THE NEW APPLE OF DISCORD
(anon.).
Music by Maucer, Louis. London: S. G. Fairbrother (printer), n.d. Pp. [1]-32. Libretto.

NOT FORMOSA
See Thompson, Alfred. Linda of Chamouni.

NOT GUILTY
See Phillips, Watts.

NOT IF I KNOW IT!
See Morton, John Maddison.

NOT SO BAD AFTER ALL
See Reeve, Wybert.

NOT SO BAD AS WE SEEM
See Bulwer (later Bulwer-Lytton), Edward George Earle Lytton, Lord Lytton.

NOT SUCH A FOOL AS HE LOOKS
See Byron, Henry James.

NOT TO BE DONE
See Craven, Henry Thornton.

NOT TO BE FORWARDED
See Bell, Florence Eveleen Eleanore Oliffe, Mrs. Hugh (Lady).

NOTE AT HAND, THE
See Rodwell, George Herbert Bonaparte. I'll Be Your Second.

NOTE FORGER!, THE
See Fitzball, Edward.

NOTES AND NOTIONS
See Peake, Richard Brinsley. Americans Abroad.

NOTHING LIKE PASTE
See Rae, Charles Marsham. Billy Doo.
See Rae, Charles Marsham.

NOTHING SUPERFLUOUS
See Thompson, C. Pelham.

NOTHING VENTURE, NOTHING WIN
See Coyne, Joseph Stirling.

NOTORIETY
See Reynolds, Frederick.

NOTORIOUS MRS. EBBSMITH, THE
See Pinero, Arthur Wing.

NOTRE DAME
See Halliday, Andrew.

NOUREDDIN AND THE FAIR PERSIAN
See Edwards, Henry Sutherland.

NOVEL EXPEDIENT
See Webster, Benjamin Nottingham. Book the Third, Chapter the First.

NOVELLO, MARY SABILLA HEHL, MRS. VINCENT
Turandot: The Chinese Sphinx. London: Samuel French, 1872. Pp. [1]-35.

NOVELTY FAIR
See Taylor, Tom.

NOVICE OF SAN MARTINO
See Parlby, Brooke Bridges, Maj. Revenge.

NOVICE OF ST. MARK'S
See Lewis, Matthew Gregory. Venoni.

NOZZE DI FIGARO
See Kenney, Charles Lamb (trans.).
See Maggioni, Manfredo (trans.).
See Soane, George (trans.). Marriage of Figaro, The.

NUITTER, CHARLES
Cup of Tea, A.
See under title.

NULL AND VOID
See Hayes, Frederick William.

NUMBER
See also No.

NUMBER 49
See Lawrance, Frederic.

NUMBER NIP
See Blanchard, Edward Litt Leman.

NUMBER ONE A; OR, A HERO IN SPITE OF HIMSELF
(anon.)
London: G. Vickers, 1847. Pp. [1]-24.

NUMBER ONE, ROUND THE CORNER
See Brough, William.

NUMBER SEVEN-TWENTY-EIGHT
See Hendriks, Herman. Hurly-Burly, The.

NUMBER SEVENTEEN
See Leigh, Agnes.

NUN, THE DUN, AND THE SON OF A GUN
See Gilbert, William Schwenck. Robert the Devil.

NUNS OF GLOSSENBURY
See Wild, James. Maids.

NUNS OF MINSK, THE: A TALE OF RUSSIAN ATROCITIES IN POLAND
See Blake, Robert.

NUPKINS AWAKENED
See Morris, William. Tables Turned, The.

NURSERYRHYMIA
See Paxton, Alfred.

NYDIA, THE BLIND GIRL OF POMPEII
See Fox, George.

NYMPH OF NOZENARO
See Cubitt, Sydney. Competitors, The.

NYMPH OF THE GROTTO, THE
See Dimond, William.

NYMPH OF THE LURLEYBURG, THE
 See Byron, Henry James.

O., Y. T.
 See Y. T. O.

O GEMINI!
 See A'Beckett, Gilbert Abbott.

O. W.
 See Y. T. O. Aristophanes at Oxford.

OBERON
 See Macfarren, George.
 See Planché, James Robinson.

OBERON! KING OF THE ELVES; OR, HARLEQUIN SIR HUON OF GUYENNE AND THE FAIRY OF THE MAGIC HORN! (anon.)
 Liverpool: William M'Call (printer), n.d. Pp. [1]-30. Libretto.

OBERON'S OATH
 See Thompson, Benjamin.

OBI
 See Fawcett, John.

OBJECT OF INTEREST, AN
 See Stocqueler, Joachim Hayward.

OBLIGING A FRIEND
 See Reeve, Wybert.

O'BRIEN, WILLIAM
 Cross Purposes. In *British Drama,* 12 vols., London: John Dicks, 1871, VIII, [55]-64.

O'BRYAN, CHARLES
 Lugarto the Mulatto. London: Thomas Hailes Lacy, n.d. Pp. [1]-38. [Lacy's Acting Edition].

OBSERVATION AND FLIRTATION
 See Wigan, Horace.

OBSTINATE FAMILY, THE
 See Phelps, Samuel, jr.

OBSTINATE WOMAN, AN
 See Corrie, Jessie Elizabeth.

O'CALLAGHAN, P. P.
 Married Bachelor, The; or, Master and Man. London: John Cumberland, n.d. Pp. [1]-28. Cumberland's Minor Theatre, X. *Filed under* Cumberland, John. Cumberland's Minor Theatre, X.
 Married Bachelor, The; or, Master and Man. London: John Cumberland, n.d. Pp. [1]-28.

O'CAUSTIC, CAROL (pseud.)
 Laughable Lover, The. Tetbury: J. G. Goodwyn (printer), 1806. Pp. [i]-[viii], [1]-103.

OCEAN OF LIFE, THE
 See Haines, John Thomas.

OCTAVIA
 See Davies, Blanche.
 See Lloyd, Charles (trans.).
 See Wheelwright, Charles Apthrop, Rev. (trans.).

OCTAVIUS
 See Bullock, Henry.

OCTOROON, THE
 See Boucicault, Dionysius Lardner.

ODD LOT, AN
 See Gordon, Walter.

ODD PAIR, AN
 See Watson, T. Malcolm.

ODD TRICK, AN
 See Muskerry, William.

O'DOWD, THE
 See Boucicault, Dionysius Lardner.

OEDIPUS
 See Faucit, John Savill.

OEDIPUS AT COLONOS
 See Pember, Edward Henry (trans.).

OEDIPUS THE KING
 See Lyster, Frederic (trans.).

OEDIPUS TYRANNUS
 See Shelley, Percy Bysshe.

OEHLENSCHLAGER, ADAM
 Aladdin.
  See Martin, Theodore, Sir (trans.).

Correggio.
 See Lee, Eliza Buckminster, Mrs. (trans.).
 See Martin, Theodore, Sir (trans.).

OF AGE TO-MORROW
 See Dibdin, Thomas John.

OFF FOR LONDON
 See Wastell, William. West Wind, A.

OFF TO THE DIGGINS
 See Nightingale, Joseph Henry.

OFFICER AND A GENTLEMAN, AN
 See Brown, William.

O'FLANNIGAN AND THE FAIRIES.
 See Brougham, John. Recollection of O'Flannigan and the Fairies, A.

OGILVIE, G. STUART
 Hypatia. London: William Heinemann, 1894. Pp. [1]-69.
 Sin of St. Hulda, The. London: William Heinemann, 1896. Pp. [1]-96.

OGLE, BARBARINA
 See Dacre, Barbarina Ogle, Lady.

OGRE AND LITTLE THUMB, THE; OR, THE SEVEN-LEAGUE BOOTS (anon.)
 London: T. & R. Hughes, 1807. Pp. [5]-32. Synopsis.

OH, NO!
 See Bell, Florence Eveleen Eleanore Oliffe, Mrs. Hugh (Lady).

OH! SUSANNAH!
 See Ambient, Mark.

O'HARA, KANE
 Midas. London: Whittingham & Arliss, 1815. Pp. [1]-30. London Theatre, IX. *Filed under* Dibdin, Thomas John, ed. London Theatre, IX.
 Midas. In *New English Drama,* ed. W. Oxberry, 22 vols., London: W. Simpkin & R. Marshall; C. Chapple, 1822, XV, [i]-[viii], [9]-33. *Filed under* Oxberry, William Henry. New English Drama, XV.
 Midas. London: Thomas Dolby, 1825. Pp. [ii]-[x], [11]-32. Dolby's British Theatre, XII. *Filed under* Cumberland, John. Cumberland's British Theatre, XII.
 Midas. In *British Drama,* 12 vols., London: John Dicks, 1864, I, [250]-256.
 Two Misers, The. London: Whittingham & Arliss, 1816. Pp. [1]-32. London Theatre, XIX. *Filed under* Dibdin, Thomas John, ed. London Theatre, XIX.

O'HARA, KANE (arr.)
 Tom Thumb. By Fielding, Henry. In *British Drama,* 12 vols., London: John Dicks, 1871, VI, [219]-224.
 Tom Thumb. By Fielding, Henry. London: John Cumberland, n.d. Pp. [i], [1]-27. Cumberland's British Theatre, XXIII. *Filed under* Cumberland, John. Cumberland's British Theatre, XXIII.

O'KEEFFE, JOHN
 Agreeable Surprise, The. London: John Cumberland, n.d. Pp. [1]-39. Cumberland's British Theatre, XXXI. *Filed under* Cumberland, John. Cumberland's British Theatre, XXXI.
 Castle of Andalusia, The. By John O'Keefe. In *British Drama,* 12 vols., London: John Dicks, 1865, III, [703]-719.
 Castle of Andalusia, The. London: John Cumberland, n.d. Pp. [i-ii], [1]-60. Cumberland's British Theatre, XXXII. *Filed under* Cumberland, John. Cumberland's British Theatre, XXXII.
 Farmer, The. London: John Cumberland, n.d. Pp. [1]-36. Cumberland's British Theatre, XXVII. *Filed under* Cumberland, John. Cumberland's British Theatre, XXVII.
 Fontainbleau. London: John Cumberland, n.d. Pp. [1]-59. Cumberland's British Theatre, XXXII. *Filed under* Cumberland, John. Cumberland's British Theatre, XXXII.
 Highland Reel, The. London: John Cumberland, 1828. Pp. [i], [1]-35. Cumberland's British Theatre, XVIII. *Filed under* Cumberland, John. Cumberland's British Theatre, XVIII.

Lie of a Day. In [*Modern Theatre*, ed. Mrs. Inchbald, 10 vols., London: Longman, Hurst, Rees, Orme, & Brown, 1811, X], [299]-346.

Modern Antiques; or, The Merry Mourners. London: John Cumberland, n.d. Pp. [1]-43. Cumberland's British Theatre, XXIX. *Filed under* Cumberland, John. Cumberland's British Theatre, XXIX.

Peeping Tom of Coventry. London: John Cumberland, n.d. Pp. [1]-36. Cumberland's British Theatre, XXXI. *Filed under* Cumberland, John. Cumberland's British Theatre, XXXI.

Poor Soldier, The. London: John Cumberland, 1828. Pp. [1]-42. Cumberland's British Theatre, XX. *Filed under* Cumberland, John. Cumberland's British Theatre, XX.

Prisoner at Large, The. London: John Cumberland, n.d. Pp. [1]-31. Cumberland's British Theatre, XXVI. *Filed under* Cumberland, John. Cumberland's British Theatre, XXVI.

Son-in-Law, The. London: John Cumberland, n.d. Pp. [1]-36. Cumberland's British Theatre, XXXI. *Filed under* Cumberland, John. Cumberland's British Theatre, XXXI.

Sprigs of Laurel. London: John Cumberland, n.d. Pp. [1]-34. Cumberland's British Theatre, XXXIX. *Filed under* Cumberland, John. Cumberland's British Theatre, XXXIX.

Wild Oats; or, The Strolling Gentleman. London: John Cumberland, n.d. Pp. [1]-69. Cumberland's British Theatre, XXXIV. *Filed under* Cumberland, John. Cumberland's British Theatre, XXXIV.

Wild Oats; or, The Strolling Gentlemen. In *New English Drama*, ed. W. Oxberry, 22 vols., London: W. Simpkin & R. Marshall; C. Chapple, 1820, XXII, [1-2], [i]-[vi], [i]-[iv], [1]-75, [i]-iii. *Filed under* Oxberry, William Henry. New English Drama, XXII.

Young Quaker, The. London: John Cumberland, n.d. Pp. [1]-59. Cumberland's British Theatre, XXXVII. *Filed under* Cumberland, John. Cumberland's British Theatre, XXXVII.

OLD ADAM
See Townsend, William Thompson.

OLD AND THE NEW, THE
See Maugham, Harry Neville.

OLD AND THE YOUNG STAGER, THE
See Rede, William Leman.

OLD AND YOUNG
See Poole, John.

OLD BLACKSMITH'S HOVEL
See Barnett, Charles Zachary. Vow of Silence, The.

OLD BOGEY
See Ellis, George.

OLD CHATEAU, THE
See Coyne, Joseph Stirling.

OLD CRONIES
See Smith, Spencer Theyre.

OLD CURIOSITY SHOP, THE
See Lander, George.
See Stirling, Edward.

OLD DAME DURDEN AND THE DROLL DAYS OF THE MERRY MONARCH
See Blanchard, Edward Litt Leman. Harlequin Hudibras!

OLD DAME NATURE AND THE FAIRY ART
See Blanchard, Edward Litt Leman. Jack and Jill.

OLD FORGE, THE
See Osborne, Charles.

OLD FRIEND WITH A NEW FACE
See Faust (anon.).

OLD FRIENDS
See Greville, Beatrice Violet Graham, Lady.

OLD GAMUL
See Newbigging, Thomas.

OLD GARDEN, AN
See Davies, Hill.

OLD GENTLEMAN, THE
See Webster, Benjamin Nottingham.

OLD GOOSEBERRY!
See Williams, Thomas John.

OLD GUARD, THE
See Boucicault, Dionysius Lardner.
See Farnie, Henry Brougham.

OLD HEADS AND YOUNG HEARTS
See Boucicault, Dionysius Lardner.

OLD HONESTY!
See Morton, John Maddison.

OLD HOUSE ON THE BRIDGE OF NOTRE DAME, THE
See Suter, William E.

OLD HOUSE ON THE COMMON
See Wilks, Thomas Egerton. Kennyngton Crosse.

OLD IZAAK WALTON
See Greenwood, Thomas Longdon.

OLD JEW, AN
See Grundy, Sydney.

OLD JOE AND YOUNG JOE
See Courtney, John.

OLD KNOCKLES
See Law, Arthur.

OLD LAMP IN A NEW LIGHT
See Thompson, Alfred. Aladdin II.

OLD LOVE, THE
See Garston, Leonard.

OLD LOVE AND NEW FORTUNE
See Chorley, Henry Fothergill.

OLD LOVE AND THE NEW, THE
See Albery, James.
See Sulivan, Robert.

OLD MAID, THE
See Bell, Ernest (trans.).
See Hetherington, William Maxwell.

OLD MAID'S BABY, AN
See Paulton, Edward Antonio.

OLD MAIDS
See Knowles, James Sheridan.

OLD MAN, AN
See Reece, Robert.

OLD MAN OF THE MOUNTAINS, THE
See Dibdin, Charles Isaac Mungo, jr.

OLD MAN OF THE OCEAN AND FAIR ZORADEE
See Conquest, George. Sinbad the Sailor, a Son of the Sea.

OLD MAN'S CURSE
See Millingen, John Gideon. King's Fool, The.

OLD MARTIN'S TRIALS
See Stirling, Edward.

OLD MASTER, AN
See Jones, Henry Arthur.

OLD MILL OF ST. DENIS!
See Graves, Joseph. Tempter, The.

OLD MILL RUIN
See Harrington, Richard. Pedlar Boy, The.

OLD MINT
See McNab, James. London Bridge, 150 Years Ago.

OLD MORTALITY; OR, THE BATTLE OF BOTHWELL BRIDGE (anon.)
In *Waverley Dramas*, Glasgow: Alison & Ross, 1872, pp. [i], [1]-56. *Filed under* Cole, John William.

OLD MOTHER HUBBARD AND HER WONDERFUL DOG
See Blanchard, Edward Litt Leman. Harlequin and the House That Jack Built.

OLD OAK CHEST, THE
See Scott, Jane M.

OLD OAK TREE, THE
See Raymond, Richard John.

OLD OFFENDER, AN
See Planché, James Robinson.

OLD ORDER CHANGETH
See Kennedy, Charles Rann. Coming of Peace, The.

OLD PARR
See Lemon, Mark.

OLD PHIL'S BIRTHDAY
See Wooler, John Pratt.

OLD POZ
See Edgeworth, Maria.
OLD RALPH
See Wheatley, J. A.
OLD REGIMENTALS, THE
See Bernard, William Bayle.
OLD SAILORS
See Byron, Henry James.
OLD SAINT PAUL'S
See Barnett, Charles Zachary. Midnight: The Thirteenth Chime.
OLD SCORE, AN
See Gilbert, William Schwenck.
OLD SOLDIER
See Byron, Henry James.
OLD STONE QUARRY
See Hart, James P. Murder of the Glen, The.
OLD STORY!, THE
See Byron, Henry James.
OLD STORY RE-TOLD
See Dyall, Clarence G. Dick Whittington.
OLD TIMES IN VIRGINIA
See Barnett, Morris. Yankee Peddler.
OLD TRUSTY
See Gordon, Walter.
OLD TRUTHS IN A NEW DRESS
See Featherstone, Thomas. Rhyming Temperance Advocate, The.
OLD WOMAN WHO LIVED IN A SHOE, THE
See Crompton, William.
OLD WOODEN HOUSE OF LONDON WALL
See Almar, George. Earl of Poverty, The.
OLDEN TIME
See Gore, Catherine Grace Frances Moody, Mrs. Charles. Dacre of the South.
OLDEN TIMES
See Bain, Donald.
OLIVER CROMWELL
See Maclaren, Archibald.
OLIVER TWIST
See Almar, George.
See Barnett, Charles Zachary.
OLIVETTE
See Farnie, Henry Brougham.
OLIFFE, FLORENCE EVELEEN ELEANORE, LADY
See Bell, Florence Eveleen Eleanore Oliffe, Mrs. Hugh (Lady).
OLYMPIA
See Frere, Benjamin.
OLYMPIC DEVILS
See Planché, James Robinson.
OLYMPIC GAMES
See Burnand, Francis Cowley.
OLYMPIC REVELS
See Planché, James Robinson.
OLYMPUS IN AN UPROAR
See Brougham, John. Life in the Clouds.
OMALA
See Fitzball, Edward.
OMNIBUS, THE
See Pocock, Isaac.
ON AN ISLAND
See Jones, John Wilton.
ON AND OFF
See Williams, Thomas John.
ON BAIL
See Gilbert, William Schwenck.
ON 'CHANGE
See Lawrence, Eweretta.
ON GUARD
See Gilbert, William Schwenck.
ON THE BRAIN
See Pleon, Harry.
ON THE BRINK
See Grein, Jack T.

ON THE CLYDE
See Scott, W. S.
ON THE DARK ROAD
See Charlton, Frank.
ON THE INDIAN OCEAN
See Lee, Harold.
ON THE RANK
See Ridge, William Pett.
ON THE SLY!
See Morton, John Maddison.
ON THE SPOT
See Eliot, Arthur. Money Spider, The.
ON THE THRESHOLD OF THEMIS
See Anstey, F.
ON THE TILES
See Stirling, Edward.
ON THE UNDERGROUND
See Ridge, William Pett.
ONCE A WEEK
See Harrison, Wilmot.
ONCE AGAIN
See Broughton, Frederick William.
ONCE UPON A TIME
See Goodyer, F. R.
ONCE UPON A TIME THERE WERE TWO KINGS
See Planché, James Robinson.
ONDINE
See Coyne, Joseph Stirling.
See Stirling, Edward.
ONE BED TO LET
See Forman, Edmund.
ONE FAULT
See Selby, Charles.
ONE FOOL MAKES MANY
See Fox, Henry Richard.
ONE HOUR
See Bayly, Thomas Haynes.
ONE HUNDRED AND EIGHTEEN YEARS IN AS MANY MINUTES
See Keating, Eliza H. Sleeping Beauty, The.
102
See Milner, Henry M.
See Milner, Henry M. Veteran of 102 Years.
ONE HUNDRED POUNDS REWARD
See Law, Arthur.
ONE HUNDRED THOUSAND POUNDS
See Byron, Henry James.
ONE IN HAND IS WORTH TWO IN THE BUSH
See March, George.
ONE O'CLOCK
See Kenny, Charles. Wood Demon, The.
See Lewis, Matthew Gregory.
ONE OF YOU MUST MARRY (anon.)
London: Thomas Hailes Lacy, n.d. Pp. [1]-20.
117, ARUNDEL STREET, STRAND
See Addison, Henry Robert, Capt.
ONE SIDE OF THE CANVASS
See Anstey, F.
ONE SNOWY NIGHT
See Ware, James Redding.
ONE SUMMER'S DAY
See Esmond, Henry Vernon.
ONE TOO MANY
See Ryan, Desmond Lumley.
ONE TOO MANY FOR HIM
See Williams, Thomas John.
ONE TOUCH OF NATURE
See Webster, Benjamin Nottingham.
ONE TREE HILL
See Craven, Henry Thornton.
ONE, TWO, THREE, FOUR, FIVE
See Reeve, John.
ONE WAY OF LOVE
See Alma-Tadema, Laurence.

O'NEILL, I. R.
    See O'Neill, John Robert.
O'NEILL, JOHN ROBERT
    Aladdin; or, The Wonderful Lamp. By I. R. O'Neill. *Also:*
    Aladdin; or, The Magic Lamp of Hugo Vamp. London:
    G. H. Davidson, n.d. Pp. [1]-19.
    Ali Baba; or, A Night with the 40 Thieves. London: Thomas
    Hailes Lacy, 1852. Pp. [1]-24.
    Optical Delusion, An. By I. R. O'Neill. London & New
    York: Samuel French, n.d. Pp. [1]-21. [Lacy's Acting
    Edition].
ONLY A CLOD
    See Simpson, John Palgrave.
ONLY A HALFPENNY!
    See Oxenford, John.
ONLY A JEST
    See Seymour, Mary.
ONLY A PENNY-A-LINER!
    See Lyste, Henry P.
ONLY AMATEURS
    See Montague, Harold.
ONLY AN ACTOR
    See Muskerry, William. Garrick.
ONLY SOMEBODY
    See Edwardes, Conway Theodore Marriott. Dreadfully
    Alarming.
    See Edwardes, Conway Theodore Marriott.
OOR GEORDIE
    See Cooper, James B.
OPEN GATE, THE
    See Chambers, Charles Haddon.
OPEN HOUSE
    See Buckstone, John Baldwin.
OPEN SESAME
    See A'Beckett, Gilbert Abbott.
OPENSHAW, MARY
    My First Client. London & New York: Samuel French,
    c.1903. Pp. [1]-8. [Lacy's Acting Edition].
OPERA CLOAK, THE
    See Powles, Louis Diston.
OPPOSITE NEIGHBOURS
    See Paul, Howard.
OPTICAL DELUSION, AN
    See O'Neill, John Robert.
ORANGE BLOSSOMS
    See Wooler, John Pratt.
ORANGE BOVEN
    See Dibdin, Thomas John.
ORANGE GIRL, THE
    See Leslie, Henry.
ORANGE TREE AND THE HUMBLE BEE, THE
    See Byron, Henry James.
ORANGES AND LEMONS AND THE TWELVE DANCING
    PRINCESSES
    See Dutnall, M. Harlequin Hey Diddle Diddle the Cat
    and the Fiddle and the Cow That Jumped over the Moon.
ORATOR OF THE STREET, THE
    See Ridge, William Pett.
ORCHARD OF THE KING, THE
    See Day, Ernest.
ORDER OF KNIGHTHOOD
    See Verral, Charles. Saladin.
ORDER OF THE DAY
    See Power, Tyrone. St. Patrick's Eve.
ORESTES
    See Lloyd, Charles (trans.).
    See Potter, Robert (trans.).
    See Sotheby, William.
ORESTES IN ARGOS
    See Bayley, Peter.
ORFEO E EURIDICE
    See Maggioni, Manfredo (trans.).
ORFRED (anon.)
    Canterbury: S. Prentice, 1834. Pp. [1]-[47].

ORGAN GRINDER, THE
    See Edgeworth, Maria.
ORGANIC AFFECTION, AN
    See Phillips, Mrs. Alfred.
ORIANA
    See Albery, James.
ORIGIN OF SHAKESPEARE
    See Gregg, Tresham Dames, Rev. Queen Elizabeth.
ORIGINAL, THE
    See Morton, John Maddison.
ORIGINAL A. B. C.
    See Silvester, Frank. Arthur's Bakery Co.
ORIOMA, THE RECLAIMED
    See Inman, James William, Rev.
OROONOKO
    See Southern, Thomas.
O'ROURKE, EDMUND
    See Falconer, Edmund (pseud.).
ORPHAN, THE
    See Otway, Thomas.
    See Thompson, Benjamin (trans.). Deaf and Dumb.
ORPHAN OF CHINA, THE
    See Murphy, Arthur.
ORPHAN OF GENEVA
    See Thérèse (anon.).
ORPHAN OF PARIS!
    See Barnett, Charles Zachary. Victorine.
ORPHAN OF THE FROZEN SEA, THE
    See Stirling, Edward.
    See Stirling, Edward. Struggle for Gold, A.
ORPHAN OF THE WRECK, THE
    See Worrell, James.
ORPHAN PROTECTED
    See Holcroft, Thomas. Deaf and Dumb.
ORPHAN'S LEGACY!
    See Stirling, Edward. Industry and Indolence.
ORPHEUS
    See Burnand, Francis Cowley.
    See Chorley, Henry Fothergill (trans.).
    See Galt, John.
    See Troutbeck, John, Rev. (trans.).
ORPHEUS AND EURYDICE
    See Brough, Robert Barnabas.
    See Byron, Henry James.
    See Planché, James Robinson. Olympic Devils.
ORPHEUS IN THE HAYMARKET
    See Planché, James Robinson.
ORRA
    See Baillie, Joanna.
OSBALDISTON, DAVID WEBSTER
    Naomie; or, The Peasant Girl's Dream. London: James
    Pattie, n.d. Pp. [1]-24.
OSBERN AND URSYNE
    See Hobbes, John Oliver.
OSBORNE, CHARLES
    Face in the Moonlight, The. Pp. [i-iv], [1]-81. Typescript.
    Old Forge, The. London: Thomas Scott, n.d. Pp. [1]-44.
    London Acting Drama, [27].
O'SHEA, J. A.
    Blonde and Brunette. London: D. Lane (printer), 1875. Pp.
    [1]-27.
OSMAN, W. R.
    Harlequin Old Aesop.
    See Fenton, Frederick.
OSORIO
    See Coleridge, Samuel Taylor.
OSTLER AND THE ROBBER
    See Fitzball, Edward. Innkeeper of Abbeville, The.
OSWALD OF DEIRA
    See Chatterton, Henrietta Georgiana Marcia Iremonger,
    Mrs. Lascelles, Lady Georgiana.
OSWYN AND HELEN
    See Farley, Charles. Red Roy.
OTHELLO
    See Fechter, Charles Albert (arr.).

See Kemble, John Philip (arr.).

See Shakespeare, William.

OTHELLO TRAVESTIE (anon.)
London: J. J. Stockdale, 1813. Pp. [1]-78.

OTHELLO TRAVESTIE
See Dowling, Maurice G.

OTHER MAN, THE
See Horner, Fred.

OTHER PEOPLE'S SHOES
See Crackanthorpe, Blanche Alethea Elizabeth Holt, Mrs. Hubert Montague.

OTHER SIDE OF THE CANVASS, THE
See Anstey, F.

OTHER WOMAN, THE
See Kingsley, Ellis.

OTHO THE GREAT
See Keats, John.

OTHO'S DEATH-WAGER
See Spicer, Henry.

OTTO OF WITTELSBACH
See Mitford, Mary Russell.

See Thompson, Benjamin (trans.).

OTWAY, THOMAS
Cheats of Scapin, The. In *British Drama*, 12 vols., London: John Dicks, 1872, X, [84]-96.

Orphan, The; or, The Unhappy Marriage. London: Whittingham & Arliss, 1816. Pp. [1]-[60]. London Theatre, XVIII. *Filed under* Dibdin, Thomas John, ed. London Theatre, XVIII.

Orphan, The; or, The Unhappy Marriage. In *British Drama*, 12 vols., London: John Dicks, 1871, VIII, [225]-244.

Venice Preserved; or, A Plot Discovered. London: Whittingham & Arliss, 1814. Pp. [1]-60. London Theatre, I. *Filed under* Dibdin, Thomas John, ed. London Theatre, I.

Venice Preserved. In *New English Drama*, ed. W. Oxberry, 22 vols., London: W. Simpkin & R. Marshall; C. Chapple, 1820, IV, [1-2], [i]-iv, [i]-[iv], [1]-[60]. *Filed under* Oxberry, William Henry. New English Drama, IV.

Venice Preserved. London: T. Dolby, 1824. Pp. [i]-[vi], [7]-54. Dolby's British Theatre, II. *Filed under* Cumberland, John. Cumberland's British Theatre, II.

Venice Preserved. In *British Drama*, 12 vols., London: John Dicks, 1864, I, [275]-291.

Venice Preserved.
See Kemble, John Philip (arr.).

OUDIN, EUGENE
Basoche, The.
See Harris, Augustus Henry Glossop.

OUGHT WE TO VISIT HER?
See Gilbert, William Schwenck.

OULITA THE SERF
See Helps, Arthur.

OULTON, WALLEY CHAMBERLAINE
Frighten'd to Death! Music by Cooke, T. London: W. Simpkin & R. Marshall, 1817. Pp. [1]-46.

My Landlady's Gown. London: W. Simpkin & R. Marshall, 1816. Pp. [1]-47.

Sixty-Third Letter, The. Music by Arnold, Samuel. London: Barker & Son, 1802. Pp. [1]-44.

Sleep-Walker, The; or, Which Is the Lady? London: J. Roach, 1812. Pp. [1]-44.

Sleep-Walker, The; or, Which Is the Lady? London: Thomas Dolby, 1825. Pp. [1]-36. Dolby's British Theatre, XI. *Filed under* Cumberland, John. Cumberland's British Theatre, XI.

OUR AMERICAN COUSIN
See Taylor, Tom. Dundreary.

See Taylor, Tom.

OUR BITTEREST FOE
See Herbert, G. C.

OUR BOON COMPANIONS
See Lyster, Frederic (trans.).

OUR BOYS
See Byron, Henry James.

OUR CLERKS
See Taylor, Tom.

OUR COURT
See Humphrey, Edward.

OUR DOMESTICS
See Hay, Frederic.

OUR FIRST LIEUTENANT
See Burn, David.

OUR FRIENDS
See March, George.

OUR HELEN
See Reece, Robert.

OUR ISLAND HOME
See Gilbert, William Schwenck.

OUR JOAN
See Merivale, Herman Charles.

OUR LADY OF THE BROKEN HEART
See Robinson, Agnes Mary Francis.

OUR LOTTIE
See Fawcett, Charles S.

OUR MARY ANNE
See Buckstone, John Baldwin.

OUR NATIONAL DEFENCES
See Coyne, Joseph Stirling.

OUR NELLY
See Craven, Henry Thornton.

OUR NEW BUTLER
See Nicholls, Harry.

OUR NEW GOVERNESS
See Brooks, Charles William Shirley.

OUR NEW LADY'S MAID
See Coape, Henry Coe.

OUR OLD HOUSE AT HOME
See Blake, Thomas G.

OUR PET
See Edwardes, Conway Theodore Marriott.

OUR REGIMENT
See Hamilton, Henry.

OUR RELATIVES
See Ellis, Walter.

OUR TEMPERANCE DISCUSSION
See Sayers, T. Albert. Moderation versus Abstinence.

OUR TOYS
See Yardley, William.

OUR VILLAGE
See Rede, William Leman.

OUR WIFE
See Morton, John Maddison.

OURANG OUTANG AND HIS DOUBLE, THE
See Rodwell, George Herbert Buonaparte.

OURS
See Robertson, Thomas William.

OURSELVES
See Chambers, Marianne.

OURSELVES ALONE
See C., T. S. Shin Fain.

OUT FOR A PROWL!
See Williams, Thomas John. Lion Slayer, The.

OUT OF A SITUATION REFUSING TWENTY
See Byron, Henry James. Twenty Pounds a Year—All Found.

OUT OF LUCK
See Stirling, Edward.

OUT OF PLACE
See Reynolds, Frederick.

OUT OF THE FRYING PAN
See Graves, Alfred Percival (arr.).

OUT ON THE LOOSE
See Barnett, Morris.

OUT ON THE SLY
See Selby, Charles.

OUT TO NURSE
See Williams, Thomas John.

OUTCAST'S WIFE, THE
> See Hazlewood, Colin Henry. Lost Wife, The.
> See Hazlewood, Colin Henry.

OUTLAW, THE
> See Story, Robert.

OUTLAW OF BARRA
> See Polack, Elizabeth. St. Clair of the Isles.

OUTLAW OF THE ADRIATIC, THE
> See Falconer, Edmund.

OUTWITTED
> See Smythies, William Gordon.

OVER THE BRIDGE
> See Moncrieff, William Thomas. Modern Collegians.

OVERLAND JOURNEY TO CONSTANTINOPLE
> See Brough, Robert Barnabas.

OVERLAND ROUTE, THE
> See Taylor, Tom.

OVINGDEAN GRANGE: A TALE OF THE SOUTH DOWNS
> See Cooper, Frederick Fox.

OWENSON, SYDNEY
> See Morgan, Sydney Owenson, Mrs. Thomas Charles (Lady).

OXBERRY, WILLIAM HENRY

Acis and Galatea Paraphrased. London: Sherwood, 1849. Pp. [1]-15.

Actress of All Work, The; or, My Country Cousin. London: W. Simpkin & R. Marshall, 1819. Pp. [1-2], [i]-[vi], [3]-18.

Bride of Abydos, The. London: James Harper, 1818. Pp. [i]-[viii], [1]-87.

Conscript, The. London: James Pattie, n.d. Pp. [i]-vi, [7]-20.

Delusion, The; or, Is She Mad? London: John Duncombe, n.d. Pp. [1]-38. Duncombe's Edition. Promptbook.

First of September, The; or, Cockney Sportsmen. Written with Phillips, Frederick Laurence. London: W. Barth, n.d. Pp. [1]-35.

Grizelle; or, Dancing Mad. London: William W. Barth, n.d. Pp. [1]-11. Barth's (late Pattie's) Universal Stage or Theatrical Prompt Book, 33.

Kenilworth. In *New English Drama,* ed. W. Oxberry, 22 vols., London: W. Simpkin & R. Marshall; C. Chapple, 1824, XIX, [i]-[vi], [1]-61. *Filed under* New English Drama, XIX.

Lucy of Lammermoor. London: Harris (printer) (priv.), n.d. Pp. [1]-12.

Matteo Falcone; or, The Brigand and His Son. London: Thomas Hailes Lacy, n.d. Pp. [1]-14. Promptbook.

Mr. Midshipman Easy! Written with Gann, J. London: John Duncombe, n.d. Pp. [1]-32. Duncombe's Edition.

Norma Travestie. London: Thomas Hailes Lacy, n.d. Pp. [1]-10. [Lacy's Acting Edition].

Pacha's Pets, The; or, The Bear and the Monkey! London: John Duncombe, n.d. Pp. [1]-20. Duncombe's Edition.

Three Clerks, The. London: James Pattie, n.d. Pp. [1]-35. Pattie's Penny Play or Weekly Acting Drama, 20.

Truand Chief!, The; or, The Provost of Paris. Written with Laurent, ?, Mme. By Madame Laurent and W. H. Oxberry. London: John Duncombe, n.d. Pp. [1]-32. Duncombe's Edition.

OXENFORD, JOHN

Adrienne, the Actress. 132 leaves. Manuscript promptbook.

Beauty or the Beast. London: Thomas Hailes Lacy, n.d. Pp. [1]-26. [Lacy's Acting Edition].

Billing and Cooing. London: Thomas Hailes Lacy, n.d. Pp. [1]-42.

Bristol Diamonds. London: Thomas Hailes Lacy, n.d. Pp. [1]-24. [Lacy's Acting Edition].

Cleft Stick, A. Boston: Walter H. Baker, c.1871. Pp. [1]-40. Spencer's Universal Stage, 65.

Day Well Spent, A. London: John Miller, 1836. Pp. [i-vi], [1]-24.

Dice of Death!, The. London: John Duncombe, n.d. Pp. [1]-38. Duncombe's Edition. Promptbook.

Doctor Dilworth. New York: Samuel French, n.d. Pp. [1]-18. Promptbook.

Doubtful Victory, A. Boston: Charles H. Spencer, 1871. Pp. [1]-21. Spencer's Universal Stage, 60.

Down in a Balloon. London: Thomas Hailes Lacy, n.d. Pp. [1]-17. [Lacy's Acting Edition].

Fair Star.
> See Smith, Albert Richard.

Family Failing, A. Boston: William V. Spencer, n.d. Pp. [1]-22. Spencer's Boston Theatre, 98.

Felix; or, The Festival of Roses. Music by Lutz, W. Meyer. London: Metzler, n.d. Pp. [1]-34. Libretto.

Five Pounds Reward. London: Thomas Hailes Lacy, n.d. Pp. [1]-28. [Lacy's Acting Edition].

Freischutz, Der; or, The Seventh Bullet. Also attrib. to Arnold, Samuel James. Music by Weber. London; Thomas Dolby, 1825. Pp. [i]-[x], [11]-41. Dolby's British Theatre, IX. *Filed under* Cumberland, John. Cumberland's British Theatre, IX.

Freischutz, Der. Music by Weber. London: Thomas Hailes Lacy, n.d. Pp. [1]-33. Libretto.

Good Little Wife, A. London: Thomas Hailes Lacy, n.d. Pp. [1]-22. [Amateur Theatre, IV].

Helvellyn. Music by Macfarren, G. A. London: Cramer, n.d. Pp. [1]-44. Libretto.

I and My Double. London: W. Strange, n.d. Pp. [1]-36.

I Couldn't Help It. London: Thomas Hailes Lacy, n.d. Pp. [1]-16. [Lacy's Acting Edition].

Legal Impediment, A. London: Thomas Hailes Lacy, n.d. Pp. [1]-22. [Lacy's Acting Edition].

Life Chase, A. Written with Wigan, Horace. London: Thomas Hailes Lacy, n.d. Pp. [1]-64. [Lacy's Acting Edition].

Life Chase, A. Written with Wigan, Horace. New York: Robert M. DeWitt, n.d. Pp. [1]-32. DeWitt's Acting Plays, 119.

Lily of Killarney, The.
> See Boucicault, Dionysius Lardner.

Magic Toys, The. London: Thomas Hailes Lacy, n.d. Pp. [i], [1]-12. Title page mutilated. Lacy's Acting Edition, [629]. Promptbook.

Monastery of St. Just, The. London: Thomas Hailes Lacy, n.d. Pp. [1]-53. [Lacy's Acting Edition].

Much Too Clever; or, A Friend Indeed. Written with Hatton, Joseph. London & New York: Samuel French, n.d. Pp. [1]-30.

My Fellow Clerk. London: John Miller, 1835. Pp. [1]-23.

Neighbours. London: Thomas Hailes Lacy, n.d. Pp. [1]-33. [Lacy's Acting Edition].

No Followers. London: W. Strange, 1837. Pp. [1]-27.

Only a Halfpenny! London: Thomas Hailes Lacy, n.d. Pp. [1]-19. [Lacy's Acting Edition].

Papa Martin.
> See Porter of Havre, The.

Pauline. London: Thomas Hailes Lacy, n.d. Pp. [1]-46. Promptbook.

Pauline.
> See Kean, Charles John (arr.).

Please to Remember the Grotto; or, The Manageress in a Fix. London: Thomas Hailes Lacy, n.d. Pp. [1]-21. [Lacy's Acting Edition].

Porter of Havre, The. *Also:* Papa Martin. Music by Cagnoni. London: Boosey, n.d. Pp. [1]-27. Libretto.

Porter of Havre, The. Music by Cagnoni, Antonio. London & New York: Boosey, n.d. Pp. [i-iv], 1-272. [Royal Edition]. Vocal score.

Porter's Knot, The. New York: Robert M. DeWitt, n.d. Pp. [1]-25. [DeWitt's Acting Plays, 50].

Porter's Knot, The. London: Thomas Hailes Lacy, n.d. Pp. [1]-39. Promptbook.

Quiet Day, A. London: W. Strange, 1837. Pp. [3]-19, 22-28. Text incomplete.

Rape of The Lock, The. London: W. Strange, n.d. Pp. [1]-33.

Reigning Favorite, The. London: Thomas Hailes Lacy, n.d. Pp. [1]-27. Lacy's Acting Edition, [3].

Retained for the Defence. London: Thomas Hailes Lacy, n.d. Pp. [1]-22.

Rigoletto. Music by Verdi. London: Boosey, n.d. Pp. [i-iv], 1-235. Royal Edition of Operas. Vocal score.

Roberto il Diavolo. Music by Meyerbeer. London & New York: Boosey, n.d. Pp. [i-iv], 1-480. Royal Edition of Operas. Vocal score.

Robin Hood. Music by Macfarren, G. A. London: Brewer, n.d. Pp. [5]-48. Libretto.

Sam's Arrival. London: Thomas Hailes Lacy, n.d. Pp. [1]-19. [Lacy's Acting Edition].

Sleeper Awakened, The. Music by Macfarren, G. A. London: John K. Chapman, n.d. Pp. [1]-16. Libretto.

Soldier's Legacy, The. Music by Macfarren, G. A. London: Ewer, n.d. Pp. [i-iv], [1]-179. Vocal score.

Timour the Tartar!; or, The Iron Master of Samarkand-by-Oxus. Written with Brooks, Charles William Shirley. London: Thomas Hailes Lacy, n.d. Pp. [1]-36.

Twice Killed. Chicago: Dramatic Publishing Co., n.d. Pp. [1]-16.

Twice Killed. In *Dramatic Entertainments at Windsor Castle,* ed. Benjamin Webster, London: Mitchell, n.d., pp. [253]-275. *Filed under* Webster, Benjamin Nottingham. Dramatic Entertainments.

Two Orphans, The. London & New York: Samuel French, n.d. Pp. [1]-71. French's Standard Drama, 365.

Uncle Zachary. London: Thomas Hailes Lacy, n.d. Pp. [1]-42. [Lacy's Acting Edition].

Waltz by Arditi, A. London & New York: Samuel French, n.d. Pp. [1]-16. [Lacy's Acting Edition].

What Have I Done? London: John Duncombe, n.d. Pp. [1]-22. Duncombe's Edition. Promptbook.

World of Fashion, The. London: Thomas Hailes Lacy, n.d. Pp. [1]-44. [Lacy's Acting Edition].

Wrong Man in the Right Place, A. Chicago: Dramatic Publishing Co., n.d. Pp. [1]-14. Sergel's Acting Drama, 290.

Young Lad from the Country, A. London: Thomas Hailes Lacy, n.d. Pp. [1]-26. [Lacy's Acting Edition].

OXENFORD, JOHN (trans.)

Lohengrin. Music by Wagner. London & New York: Boosey, n.d. Pp. [i]-xvi, 1-383. Vocal score and libretto.

Tartuffe. By Molière. London: National Acting Drama Office, n.d. Pp. [1]-45.

OXFORD IN THE 19TH CENTURY
See Mansel, Henry Longueville. Phrontisterion.

P., BR.

Daniel in the Lion's Den. In *Three Plays, Scriptural and Historical,* London & New York: Samuel French, n.d., pp. [1]-36. *Filed under* Three Plays, Scriptural and Historical (anon.).

Joseph and His Brethren. In *Three Plays, Scriptural and Historical,* London & New York: Samuel French, n.d., pp. [1]-26. *Filed under* Three Plays, Scriptural and Historical (anon.).

Sir Thomas More. In *Three Plays, Scriptural and Historical,* London & New York: Samuel French, n.d., pp. [1]-27. *Filed under* Three Plays, Scriptural and Historical (anon.).

P. L., THE
See Lemon, Mark.

P. P.
See Parry, Thomas.

P.S.—COME TO DINNER!
See Raymond, Richard John.

P.U.P.
See Moss, Hugh.

PACHA OF PIMLICO, THE
See Morton, John Maddison.

PACHA'S BRIDAL!, THE
See Lemon, Mark.

PACHA'S PETS, THE
See Oxberry, William Henry.

PACKET FROM ENGLAND, A
See Tristram, William Outram.

PACKING UP
See Grattan, H. P.

PADDY AND THE GHOST
See Fothergill, F. Haunted House, The.

PADDY BULL
See Maclaren, Archibald.

PADDY BYRNES, THE IRISH SCHOOLMASTER
See Fitzgerald, J. D. Inspector's Visit, The.

PADDY CAREY
See Power, Tyrone.

PADDY WHACK IN ITALIA, IL
See Lover, Samuel.

PADLOCK, THE
See Bickerstaffe, Isaac.

PAETUS AND ARRIA
See Burton, ?.

PAGE, THE
See Marion (anon.).

PAGE 13 OF THE BLACK BOOK
See Conquest, George. Hand and Glove.

PAINLESS DENTISTRY
See Becher, Martin. Hunting the Slippers.

PAINT, POETRY, AND PUTTY!
See Lee, Henry. Caleb Quotem and His Wife!

PAINTER OF ANTWERP, THE
See Barrett, William Alexander (trans.).

PAINTER OF GHENT, THE
See Jerrold, Douglas William.

PAINTER OF HIS OWN DISHONOUR, THE
See Fitzgerald, Edward (trans.).

PAINTER'S DAUGHTER, THE
See Mitford, Mary Russell.

PAIR OF KNICKERBOCKERS, A
See Phillpotts, Eden.

PAIR OF LUNATICS, A
See Walkes, W. R.

PAIR OF PIGEONS, A
See Stirling, Edward.

PAIR OF SPECTACLES, A
See Grundy, Sydney.

PAIR, THE MEDDLER, AND THE APPLE!
See Talfourd, Francis. Tell! and the Strike of the Cantons.

PALACE OF GIN
See Booth, George. Choice Spirits.

PALACE OF TRUTH, THE
See Gilbert, William Schwenck.

PALADIN AND THE PRINCESS
See Thompson, Benjamin. Oberon's Oath.

PALAEOLOGUS, GREGORIOS (trans.)

Death of Demosthenes, The. Cambridge: Richard Newby (priv.), 1824. Pp. [i]-[xii], [1]-60.

PALE-FACES AND THE PUT-EM-IN-THE-CAULDRON INDIANS
See Byron, Henry James. Ever-so-Little Bear, The.

PALEY, GEORGE BARBER

Saul of Tarsus. London: Rivingtons, 1855. Pp. [i-iv], [1]-107.

PALGRAVE, R.

God Save the Queen. Written with Gover, F. 84 leaves. Manuscript.

PALICIO
See Bridges, Robert Seymour.

PALINGS, W.

Circus Girl, The. See Tanner, James Tolman.

PALLETT, PETER PAUL
See Warner, Richard.

PALMER, F. GROVE

Daisy. Music by Wood, Henry J. London: Henry J. Wood, n.d. Pp. [1]-15. Libretto.

PALMER, T. A.

Among the Relics. London & New York: Samuel French, n.d. Pp. [1]-50. [Lacy's Acting Edition].

Appeal to the Feelings, An. London & New York: Samuel French, n.d. Pp. [1]-20. [Lacy's Acting Edition].

Cinderella and the Little Glass Slipper. Music by Romia, Fred. Plymouth: King & Son (printer), n.d. Pp. [1]-32. Libretto.

Dodge for a Dinner, A. London & New York: Samuel French, n.d. Pp. [1]-23. [Lacy's Acting Edition].

Insured at Lloyd's. N.p.: n.pub., n.d. Pp. [1]-55. Promptbook.

Insured at Lloyd's. London & New York: Samuel French, n.d. Pp. [1]-55. French's Acting Edition (late Lacy's), 1642.

Last Life, The. London & New York: Samuel French, n.d. Pp. [1]-38. [Lacy's Acting Edition].

Rely on My Discretion. London & New York: Samuel French, n.d. Pp. [1]-24. [Lacy's Acting Edition].

Too Late to Save; or, Doomed to Die: A Story of Old Paris. London & New York: Samuel French, n.d. Pp. [1]-36. [Lacy's Acting Edition].

Woman's Rights. London & New York: Samuel French, n.d. Pp. [1]-24.

PALMISTRY
    See Lumley, Ralph R.

PAMELA'S PREJUDICE
    See Davis, Mrs. Maxwell.

PAN
    See Byron, Henry James.

PAN AND THE YOUNG SHEPHERD
    See Hewlett, Maurice Henry.

PANDEMONIUM
    See Cornwall, Barry.

PANDORA
    See Warren, John Byrne Leicester, Lord de Tabley.

PANDORA'S BOX
    See Byron, Henry James.

PANEL, THE
    See Kemble, John Philip.

PANTHEA
    See Ashe, Nicholas.
    See Benett, William.

PANTOMIME PROPOSED
    See Dibdin, Thomas John. Harlequin Hoax.

PANTOMIME REHEARSAL, A
    See Clay, Cecil.

PAOLO AND FRANCESCA
    See Phillips, Stephen.

PAPA MARTIN
    See Oxenford, John. Porter of Havre, The.

PAPER CHASE, THE
    See Thomas, Charles.

PAPER WINGS
    See Phillips, Watts.

PAPHIAN BOWER, THE
    See Planché, James Robinson.

PAPILLONETTA
    See Brough, William.

PAQUERETTE
    See Farnie, Henry Brougham.

PAQUITA
    See Reece, Robert.

PARACELSUS
    See Browning, Robert.

PARADISE (anon. trans.)
    By Hennequin, Maurice; Bilhaud, Paul; Barré, Albert. London: Mrs. Marshall's Typewriting Office, 1895. Pp. [i], [1]-37, [ii], [1]-51, [i], [1]-22. Pagination by act. Typescript.

PARADISE OF BIRDS, THE
    See Courthope, William John.

PARAGRAPH, THE
    See Hoare, Prince.

PARDOE, JULIA
    Louise de Lignerolles. London: Thomas Hailes Lacy, n.d. Pp. [1]-33. [Lacy's Acting Edition].

PARDON DE PLOËRMEL
    See Chorley, Henry Fothergill. Dinorah.

PARIA, THE
    See Gower, Francis Leveson, Lord (trans.).

PARIS
    See Burnand, Francis Cowley.

PARIS AND LONDON
    See Moncrieff, William Thomas.
    See Planché, James Robinson.

PARIS AND PLEASURE
    See Selby, Charles.

PARIS IN 1750
    See Peake, Richard Brinsley. Comfortable Lodgings.

PARIS IN 1793
    See Dance, Charles. Delicate Ground.

PARIS IN THE OLDEN TIME
    See Morton, Thomas, sr. Henri Quatre.

PARIS THE PRINCE AND HELEN THE FAIR
    See Akhurst, William M.

PARISH BOY'S PROGRESS
    See Barnett, Charles Zachary. Oliver Twist.

PARK, ANDREW
    Mariners, The. In *Mariners and Songs for All Seasons,* London: Z. T. Purday, 1843, pp. [i]-[xvi], [17]-66. Libretto.
    Squire's Daughter, The. London: Longman, Brown, Green, & Longmans, 1846. Pp. [i]-[vii], [7]-118.

PARKE, WALTER
    Convent Maid, The..
        See Kitty.
    Kitty. *Also:* The Convent Maid. Music by Parker, Henry. London: Alphonse Cary, n.d. Pp. [i-iv], [1]-139. Vocal score.
    Manteaux Noirs. Written with Paulton, Harry. *Also:* Three Black Cloaks. Music by Bucalossi. New York: William A. Pond, 1882. Pp. [1]-21. Libretto.
    Manteaux Noirs. Written with Paulton, Harry. Music by Bucalossi. London: J. B. Cramer, n.d. Pp. [i]-vi, [5]-26. Libretto.
    Mr. Fitz-W—?
        See Newte, Horace Wykeham Can.
    Three Black Cloaks. Written with Paulton, Harry. *Also:* Manteaux Noirs. Music by Bucalossi. Pp. [1]-135. Title page mutilated. Manuscript promptbook libretto.

PARKER, ALFRED D.
    Friends. Lichfield: Thomas George Lomax, 1871. Pp. [1]-52.

PARKER, LOUIS NAPOLEON
    Black Kitten, The.
        See Barrett, Wilson.
    Bugle Call, The. Written with Bright, Addison. Pp. [i-ii], [1]-42. Typescript.
    Change Alley. Written with Carson, Murray. London: Culliford & Haycock (printer) (priv.), 1899. Pp. [i-x], 1-84.
    Change Alley. Written with Carson, Murray. [London]: Miss Dickens's Typewriting Office], n.d. Pp. [i-vi], [1]-22, [i-ii], [1]-27, [i], [i]-28, [i], [1]-25, [i], [1]-12. Pagination by act. Typescript.
    Man in the Street, The. London & New York: Samuel French, n.d. Pp. [247]-262. [Lacy's Acting Edition].
    Masque of War and Peace, The. Music by MacCunn, Hamish. London: Henderson & Spalding, c.1900. Pp. [1]-16, [1]-70. Libretto and vocal score. *Filed under* War and Peace, The Masque of.
    Mayflower, The. [New York]: n.pub. (priv.), n.d. Pp. [1]-78.
    Rosemary, That's for Remembrance. Written with Carson, Murray. Pp. [i-ii], [1]-2, [1]-30, [i-vii], [1]-50, [i], [1]-35, [i-v], [1]-4. Pagination by act. Typescript.
    Termagant, The. Written with Carson, Murray. [London]: (priv.), n.d. Pp. [1]-145.
    War and Peace.
        See Masque of War and Peace, The.

PARKER, LOUIS NAPOLEON (trans.)
    Eaglet, The. *Also:* L'Aiglon. By Rostand, Edmond. Pp. [i-ii], [1]-56, [i], [1]-53, [i], [1]-35, [i-ii], 1-22, [i-ii], 1-15. Pagination by act. Typescript promptbook.
    Sorceress, The. *Also:* A Sorceress of Love. By Sardou, Victorien. Pp. [i-v], [1]-6, [1]-3, [1]-21, [i-ii], [1]-27, [i-ii], [1]-25, [i-ii], [1]-25, [i-ii], [1]-15. Pagination by act. Typescript.

PARKHOUSE, HANNAH
    See Cowley, Hannah Parkhouse, Mrs.
PARLBY, BROOKE BRIDGES, MAJ.
    Revenge; or, The Novice of San Martino. London: Black,
    Kingsbury, Parbury, & Allen, 1818. Pp. [1]-112.
PAROLE OF HONOUR, THE
    See Serle, Thomas James.
PARR, F. C. W.
    Jack White's Trial. London & New York: Samuel French,
    n.d. Pp. [1]-10. [Lacy's Acting Edition].
PARRICIDE, THE
    See Allen, Robert.
PARRICIDE'S CURSE
    See Hudson, E. Neeves. Bridge of Notre Dame, The.
PARRY, JOHN
    Helpless Animals!; or, Bachelor's Fare. London: J. Lowndes,
    1819. Pp. [i-iv], [1]-16. Promptbook.
    High Notions; or, A Trip to Exmouth. London: R. White,
    1819. Pp. [i]-[viii], [5]-39.
    How He Did It! Clyde, Ohio: A. D. Ames, n.d. Pp. [1]-11.
    My Uncle Gabriel. London: John Miller, 1824. Pp. [i]-[viii],
    [9]-37.
    Trip to Wales, A. London: F. Latour, 1826. Pp. [i]-vi, [1]-26.
    Two Wives; or, A Hint to Husbands. New York: E. M.
    Murden, 1822. Pp. [1]-27.
    Two Wives; or, A Hint to Husbands. London: William
    Fearman, n.d. Pp. [i-vi], [1]-27.
PARRY, THOMAS
    Cure for Love, A. London: Thomas Hailes Lacy, n.d. Pp.
    [1]-30. [Lacy's Acting Edition].
    Damp Beds! London: John Duncombe, n.d. Pp. [1]-40.
    Duncombe's Acting Edition of the British Theatre, 116.
    First Night, The; or, My Own Ghost! London: John
    Duncombe, n.d. Pp. [1]-20. Duncombe's Edition.
    Harvest Home, The. London & New York: Samuel French,
    n.d. Pp. [1]-48. [Lacy's Acting Edition].
    Lucky Horse Shoe, The; or, Woman's Trials. London:
    Thomas Hailes Lacy, n.d. Pp. [1]-32.
    Meet Me by Moonlight. London: John Duncombe, n.d. Pp.
    [1]-34. Duncombe's Acting Edition of the British
    Theatre, 354.
    P. P.; or, The Man and the Tiger. London: John Miller,
    1834. Pp. [1]-40.
PARSELLE, J.
    My Son's a Daughter. London: Thomas Hailes Lacy, n.d.
    Pp. [1]-26. [Lacy's Acting Edition].
PARSIFAL
    See Corder, Henrietta Louisa Walford, Mrs. Frederick
    (trans.).
    See Forman, Alfred (trans.).
    See Gatty, Charles Tindal (trans.).
    See Jackson, John P. (trans.).
PARSON'S NOSE, THE
    See Moncrieff, William Thomas.
PARTED
    See Reeve, Wybert.
PARTING, THE
    See Fitzgerald, Shafto Justin Adair.
PARTNERS FOR LIFE
    See Byron, Henry James.
PARTNERSHIP
    See Roberts, George.
PARTY, THE PRINCE, AND THE PIE
    See Paxton, Alfred. Nurseryrhymia.
PARTY WALL!, THE
    See Moncrieff, William Thomas.
PARVENU, THE
    See Godfrey, George William.
PAS DE FASCINATION
    See Coyne, Joseph Stirling.
PASCAL BRUNO
    See A'Beckett, Gilbert Abbott.
PASHA'S REVENGE
    See Armstrong, William Henry. Turkish Lovers.

PASSAGE OF THE BERESINA
    See Bernard, William Bayle. Paulina.
PASSING CLOUD, THE
    See Bernard, William Bayle.
PASSING OF LILITH, THE
    See Sharp, William.
PASSING OF MUHAMMAD, THE
    See Arnold, Edwin, Sir.
PASSING THE FRONTIER
    See Archer, Thomas. Marguerite's Colours!
PASSION AND REPENTANCE
    See Stafford, John Joseph. Love's Frailties.
PASSION FLOWERS
    See Robertson, Thomas William.
PASSION OF PÈRE HILARION, THE
    See Sharp, William.
PASSION'S PARADISE
    See Conquest, George. Seven Sins.
PASSIVE HUSBAND, THE
    See Cumberland, Richard.
PASSPORT, THE
    See Stephenson, Benjamin Charles.
PAST AND PRESENT
    See Poole, John.
PAST TEN O'CLOCK, AND A RAINY NIGHT
    See Dibdin, Thomas John.
PASTOR'S FIRESIDE
    See Coyne, Joseph Stirling. Vicar of Wakefield, The.
    See Taylor, Tom. Vicar of Wakefield, The.
PASTORALE COMIQUE
    See Van Laun, Henri (trans.). Comic Pastoral, A.
PASTORE INCANTATO, IL
    See Beldam, Joseph.
PAT OF MULLINGAR
    See Fraser, Julia Agnes.
PATIENCE
    See Gilbert, William Schwenck.
PATIENT PENELOPE
    See Burnand, Francis Cowley.
PATRICIAN AND PARVENU
    See Poole, John.
PATRICIAN'S DAUGHTER, THE
    See Marston, John Westland.
PATRICK HAMILTON
    See Johnston, Thomas Peter.
PATRIOT, THE
    See Stephens, George.
PATRIOT FATHER, THE
    See Shoberl, Frederic (trans.).
PATRIOT KING
    See Knowles, James Sheridan. Alfred the Great.
PATRIOT MARTYRS
    See Horne, Richard Hengist. Laura Dibalzo.
PATRON SAINT, A
    See Thomas, Charles.
PATTER VERSUS CLATTER
    See Mathews, Charles James.
PAUL, C. KEGAN (trans.)
    Faust. By Goethe. London: Henry S. King, 1873. Pp.
    [i]-[vii], [i]-ii, [3]-229.
PAUL, HOWARD
    Change of System, A. London: Thomas Hailes Lacy, n.d. Pp.
    [1]-23. [Lacy's Acting Edition].
    Locked Out. New York: DeWitt, n.d. Pp. [1]-12. DeWitt's
    Acting Plays, 87.
    Lucky Hit, A. New York & London: Samuel French, n.d.
    Pp. [1]-15.
    Man Who Follows the Ladies, The. London: Thomas Hailes
    Lacy, n.d. Pp. [1]-14. [Lacy's Acting Edition].
    Mob Cap, The; or, Love's Disguises. New York: Samuel
    French, n.d. Pp. [i-ii], [1]-33. Minor Drama, 55.
    Opposite Neighbours. London: Thomas Hailes Lacy, n.d.
    Pp. [1]-15. [Lacy's Acting Edition].
    Queen of Arragon, The. London: Thomas Hailes Lacy, n.d.
    Pp. [1]-16. [Lacy's Acting Edition].

Rappings and Table Movings. London: Thomas Hailes Lacy, n.d. Pp. [1]-17. [Lacy's Acting Edition].

Thrice Married. London: Thomas Hailes Lacy, n.d. Pp. [1]-20. [Lacy's Acting Edition].

PAUL AND JOSEPH
   See Swan, Howard.

PAUL AND VIRGINIA
   See Cobb, James.
   See Hayes, Maria Ximena (trans.).

PAUL CLIFFORD
   See Fitzball, Edward.
   See Webster, Benjamin Nottingham.

PAUL JONES
   See Dibdin, Thomas John.
   See Farnie, Henry Brougham.

PAUL PRY
   See Jerrold, Douglas William.
   See Poole, John.

PAUL PRY MARRIED AND SETTLED
   See Mathews, Charles James.

PAUL RABAUT
   See Bennett, John E.

PAUL THE PILOT
   See Greenwood, Thomas Longdon.

PAUL THE POACHER
   See Elton, Edward William.

PAUL THE REBEL
   See Moss, Arthur B.

PAUL THE REPROBATE
   See Rogers, William.

PAUL'S RETURN
   See Phillips, Watts.

PAULINA
   See Bernard, William Bayle.

PAULINE
   See Hersee, Henry.
   See Kean, Charles John (arr.).
   See Oxenford, John.

PAULL, HARRY MAJOR
   Dangerous Experiment, A. London: Wyman & Sons, 1887. Pp. [1]-70.
   Gentleman Whip, The. London: Samuel French; New York: T. Henry French, n.d. Pp. [1]-20. [Lacy's Acting Edition].
   Hal, the Highwayman. New York & London: Samuel French, c.1904. Pp. [1]-22. [Lacy's Acting Edition].
   In Nelson's Days. London: Samuel French; New York: T. Henry French, n.d. Pp. [1]-22. [Lacy's Acting Edition].
   Merrifield's Ghost. London: Samuel French; New York: T. Henry French, n.d. Pp. [1]-16. [Lacy's Acting Edition].

PAULTON, EDWARD ANTONIO
   Mynheer Jan.
      See Paulton, Harry.
   Niobe, All Smiles.
      See Paulton, Harry.
   Old Maid's Baby, An. Pp. [1]-12. Typescript.

PAULTON, HARRY
   Cymbia; or, The Magic Thimble. Music by Pascal, Florian. London: Joseph Williams, n.d. Pp. [1]-48. Libretto.
   Erminie.
      See Bellamy, Claxson.
   Gulliver's Travels. Birmingham: Anglo American Advertising Co., n.d. Pp. [i-ii], [1]-68. Libretto.
   Manteaux Noirs.
      See Parke, Walter.
   Mynheer Jan. Written with Paulton, Edward Antonio. Music by Jakobowski, Edward. London: Joseph Williams, c.1907. Pp. [1]-63. Libretto.
   Niobe, All Smiles. Written with Paulton, Edward Antonio. New York & London: Samuel French, c.1904. Pp. [1]-74. [French's Standard Library Edition].
   Queen's Mate, The. Written with Tedde, Mostyn. Music by Lecocq, C. [New York]: n.pub., n.d. Pp. [1]-32. Title page lacking. Libretto.

Three Black Cloaks.
   See Parke, Walter.

Three Musket-Dears and a Little One In, The.
   See Paulton, Joseph.

PAULTON, JOSEPH
   Three Musket-Dears and a Little One In, The. Written with Paulton, Harry. London: Thomas Hailes Lacy, n.d. Pp. [1]-41. [Lacy's Acting Edition].

PAUSANIAS AND CLEONICE
   See Pember, Edward Henry.

PAUVRE JACQUES, LE
   See Ryan, Richard.

PAUVRETTE
   See Boucicault, Dionysius Lardner.

PAWNBROKER'S DAUGHTER, THE
   See Lamb, Charles.

PAXTON, ALFRED
   Nurseryrhymia; or, The Party, the Prince, and the Pie. London & New York: Samuel French, n.d. Pp. [1]-20. Fairy and Home Plays for Home Performance, 11.

PAYABLE AT SIGHT
   See Ebsworth, Mary Emma Fairbrother, Mrs. Joseph.

PAYABLE ON DEMAND
   See Taylor, Tom.

PAYING GUEST, THE
   See Johnson, W. H.

PAYNE, JOHN HOWARD
   Ali Pacha; or, The Signet Ring. London: Thomas Dolby, 1825. Pp. [ii]-[viii], [9]-28. Dolby's British Theatre, XI. *Filed under* Cumberland, John. Cumberland's British Theatre, XI.
   Brutus; or, The Fall of Tarquin. London: Thomas Dolby, 1825. Pp. [1-2], [i]-[viii], [vii]-[xii], [9]-54. Dolby's British Theatre, XI. *Filed under* Cumberland, John. Cumberland's British Theatre, XI.
   Brutus; or, The Fall of Tarquin. In *British Drama*, 12 vols., London: John Dicks, 1865, III, [799]-814.
   Charles the Second; or, The Merry Monarch. London: Thomas Dolby, 1825. Pp. [1]-45. Dolby's British Theatre, IX. *Filed under* Cumberland, John. Cumberland's British Theatre, IX.
   Clari; or, The Maid of Milan. London: John Cumberland, n.d. Pp. [1]-40. Cumberland's British Theatre, XXIV. *Filed under* Cumberland, John. Cumberland's British Theatre, XXIV.
   Fall of Algiers, The.
      See Walker, Charles Edward.
   Lancers, The. London: John Cumberland, 1828. Pp. [1]-27. Cumberland's British Theatre, XIX. *Filed under* Cumberland, John. Cumberland's British Theatre, XIX.
   Love in Humble Life. London: Thomas Dolby, 1825. Pp. [1]-31. Dolby's British Theatre, XI. *Filed under* Cumberland, John. Cumberland's British Theatre, XI.
   Therese, the Orphan of Geneva. London: John Cumberland, n.d. Pp. [1]-46. Cumberland's British Theatre, XL. *Filed under* Cumberland, John. Cumberland's British Theatre, XL.
   Two Galley Slaves, The. London: Thomas Dolby, 1825. Pp. [1]-33. Dolby's British Theatre, X. *Filed under* Cumberland, John. Cumberland's British Theatre, X.

PAYNTER, DAVID WILLIAM
   King Stephen; or, The Battle of Lincoln. Manchester: J. Leigh (printer), 1822. Pp. [i]-[xxii], [1]-57.

PEACE (anon. trans.)
   By Aristophanes. In *Clouds and Peace of Aristophanes*, Oxford: Henry Slatter, 1840, pp. [61]-106. *Filed under* Clouds (anon.).

PEACE, THE
   See Frere, John Hookham (trans.).

PEACE AND QUIET!
   See Williams, Thomas John.

PEACE AT ANY PRICE!
   See Robertson, Thomas William.

PEACOCK, THOMAS LOVE

Circle of Loda, The. In *Plays,* ed. A. B. Young, London: David Nutt, 1910, pp. [71]-118. *Filed under* Collected Works.

Dilettanti, The. In *Plays,* ed. A. B. Young, London: David Nutt, 1910, pp. [i-xiv], [1]-69. *Filed under* Collected Works.

Three Doctors, The. In *Plays,* ed. A. B. Young, London: David Nutt, 1910, pp. [119]-157. *Filed under* Collected Works.

PEACOCK'S HOLIDAY

See Merivale, Herman Charles.

PEAKE, RICHARD BRINSLEY

Amateurs and Actors. London: William Fearman, 1818. Pp. [i]-[vi], [7]-46.

Amateurs and Actors. London: John Cumberland, 1827. Pp. [1]-36. Cumberland's British Theatre, XVI. *Filed under* Cumberland, John. Cumberland's British Theatre, XVI.

Americans Abroad; or, Notes and Notions. London: John Dicks, n.d. Pp. [1]-15. Dicks' Standard Plays, 589.

Bequeathed Heart, The. London: John Dicks, n.d. Pp. [1]-16. Dicks' Standard Plays, 584.

Blanche of Jersey. Music by Barnett, John. London: Chapman & Hall, n.d. Pp. [1]-36. Libretto.

Bottle Imp, The. Music by Rodwell, George. London: Sherwood, Gilbert, & Piper, n.d. Pp. [1]-29.

Box of Mischief, A. London: Thomas Hailes Lacy, n.d. Pp. [1]-37.

Chain of Gold, The; or, A Daughter's Devotion. London: John Dicks, n.d. Pp. [1]-18. Dicks' Standard Plays, 694.

Chancery Suit!, The. London: Edward Bull, 1831. Pp. [iii]-[x], [1]-86.

Climbing Boy, The. London: John Miller, 1834. Pp. [i-iv], [1]-68. Promptbook.

Comfortable Lodgings; or, Paris in 1750. London: John Cumberland, n.d. Pp. [3]-36. Promptbook.

Comfortable Lodgings; or, Paris in 1750. London: John Cumberland, n.d. Pp. [1]-36. Cumberland's British Theatre, XXIX. *Filed under* Cumberland, John. Cumberland's British Theatre, XXIX.

Court and City. London: John Cumberland & Son, n.d. Pp. [1]-72. Promptbook.

Court and City. London: John Cumberland & Son, n.d. Pp. [1]-72. Cumberland's British Theatre, XLII. *Filed under* Cumberland, John. Cumberland's British Theatre, XLII.

Devil of Marseilles, The; or, The Spirit of Avarice. London: William W. Barth, n.d. Pp. [1]-48.

Devil on Two Sticks, The. London: John Dicks, n.d. Pp. [1]-15. Dicks' Standard Plays.

Duel, The; or, My Two Nephews. London: John Miller, 1823. Pp. [1]-52.

Duel, The; or, My Two Nephews. London: John Cumberland, n.d. Pp. [1]-43. Cumberland's British Theatre, XXII. *Filed under* Cumberland, John. Cumberland's British Theatre, XXII.

Evil Eye, The: A Legend of the Levant. London: Thomas Hailes Lacy, n.d. Pp. [1]-29. [Lacy's Acting Edition].

Gemini. London: Chapman & Hall, n.d. Pp. [1]-20. [Acting National Drama, V].

Gipsy's Warning, The.
See Linley, George.

H.B. London: Sherwood, Gilbert, & Piper, n.d. Pp. [i]-iv, [5]-24.

Haunted Inn, The. London: G. H. Davidson, n.d. Pp. [3]-40.

Haunted Inn, The. London: John Cumberland, n.d. Pp. [1]-40. Cumberland's British Theatre, XXX. *Filed under* Cumberland, John. Cumberland's British Theatre, XXX.

House Room; or, The Dishonoured Bill. London: John Miller, 1836. Pp. [i-iv], [1]-23.

Hundred Pound Note, The. New York: E. M. Murden, 1828. Pp. [1]-46. Imperfect copy.

Hundred Pound Note, The. London: John Cumberland, n.d. Pp. [1]-43. Cumberland's British Theatre, XXXIV. *Filed under* Cumberland, John. Cumberland's British Theatre, XXXIV.

Lying in Ordinary. London: Chapman & Hall, n.d. Pp. [1]-24. [Acting National Drama, IV].

Master's Rival; or, A Day at Boulogne. London: John Cumberland, n.d. Pp. [1]-46.

Master's Rival; or, A Day at Boulogne. London: John Cumberland, n.d. Pp. [1]-46. Cumberland's British Theatre, XXII. *Filed under* Cumberland, John. Cumberland's British Theatre, XXII.

Meltonians, The. London: Chapman & Hall, n.d. Pp. [1]-28. [Acting National Drama, IV].

Middle Temple, The; or, Which Is My Son? London: Chapman & Hall, n.d. Pp. [1]-19.

Quarter to Nine, A. London: Chapman & Hall, n.d. Pp. [1]-24.

Sheriff of the County, The. London: National Acting Drama Office, n.d. Pp. [1]-55.

Spring Lock, The. Music by Rodwell, George. London: Chapman & Hall, n.d. Pp. [1]-30.

Ten Thousand a Year. London: John Cumberland, n.d. Pp. [1]-48.

Three Wives of Madrid, The; or, The Diamond Ring. London: W. Barth, n.d. Pp. [1]-35.

Title Deeds, The. London: National Acting Drama Office, n.d. <wrps. Webster>. Pp. [1]-60. Webster's Acting National Drama, 142.

Uncle Rip. London: John Cumberland, n.d. Pp. [1]-40. [Cumberland's British Theatre].

Uncle Rip. London: John Cumberland & Son, n.d. Pp. [1]-40. Cumberland's British Theatre, XLII. *Filed under* Cumberland, John. Cumberland's British Theatre, XLII.

Walk for a Wager!; or, A Bailiff's Bet. London: William Fearman, 1819. Pp. [1]-72.

PEARCE, WILLIAM

Hartford Bridge; or, The Skirts of the Camp. London: John Cumberland, n.d. Pp. [1]-36. Cumberland's British Theatre, XXX. *Filed under* Cumberland, John. Cumberland's British Theatre, XXX.

Netley Abbey. London: John Cumberland, n.d. Pp. [1]-31. Cumberland's British Theatre, XXXVIII. *Filed under* Cumberland, John. Cumberland's British Theatre, XXXVIII.

PEARD, FRANCES MARY

Pins and Needles. Torquay: Standard Printing, Publishing, & Newspaper Co., n.d. Pp. [1]-12.

PEARSON, EDWARD STANHOPE (trans.)

Death of Wallenstein, The. By Schiller. Dresden & Leipzig: E. Pierson, 1886. Pp. [1]-157.

Wallenstein. By Schiller. Dresden & Leipzig: E. Pierson, 1886. Pp. [i-ii], [1]-151.

PEARSON, H.

Harlequin Crusader.
See Boleno, Henry.

PEARSON, HENRY W.

Faust. Liverpool: Daily Post Printing Works, 1864. Pp. [1]-28.

PEASANT BOY, THE

See Dimond, William.

PEASANT GIRL'S DREAM

See Osbaldiston, David Webster. Naomie.

PEASANT, LIBERTINE, AND BRIGAND

See Barnett, Charles Zachary. Claude Lorraine.

PEASANT OF LUCERN, THE

See Soane, George.

PECK'S BAD BOY

See Pleon, Harry.

PECULIAR CASE, A

See Law, Arthur.

PECULIAR POSITION, A

See Planché, James Robinson.

PECULIAR PROPOSALS

See Lowry, James M.

PEDLAR BOY, THE

See Harrington, Richard.

PEDLAR'S ACRE

See Almar, George.

PEDRARIAS
See Dacre, Barbarina Ogle, Lady.

PEDRILLO
See Johnstone, John Beer.

PEEL, EDMUND
Salem Redeemed; or, The Year of Jubilee. London: Francis & John Rivington, 1853. Pp. [i-iv], [1]-98.

PEEL, GEORGIANA ADELAIDE
See Russell, Georgiana Adelaide Peel, Lady.

PEEP AT THE FORUM
See School for Orators, The.

PEEP AT THE PAST
See Planché, James Robinson. Drama's Levée, The.

PEEP BEHIND THE SCENES
See Maddox, John Medex. First Night, The.

PEEP INTO THE SERAGLIO
See Bickerstaffe, Isaac. Sultan, The.

PEEP O' DAY
See Falconer, Edmund.

PEEP-SHOW MAN, THE
See Williams, Thomas John.

PEEPING TOM OF COVENTRY
See O'Keeffe, John.

PEER AND HEIRESS
See Besant, Walter.

PEER AND PEASANT, THE
See Moncrieff, William Thomas.

PEER AND THE PERI
See Gilbert, William Schwenck. Iolanthe.

PEER GYNT
See Archer, William (trans.).

PEERLESS POOL!
See Almar, George.

PEGGY GREEN
See Selby, Charles.

PEILE, F. KINSEY
Belle of Cairo, The. Written with Raleigh, Cecil. Music by Peile, F. Kinsey. London: Chappell, c.1896. Pp. [1]-30. Libretto.
Dancing Dervish. London: Samuel French; New York: T. Henry French, n.d. Pp. [1]-10. [Lacy's Acting Edition].

PELOPIDAS
See Atherstone, Edwin.

PEMBER, EDWARD HENRY
Blind Girl of Bonn, The. In *Adrastus of Phrygia and other Poems,* London: Chiswick Press (printer) (priv.), 1897, pp. [i], [70]-106.
Death-Song of Thamyris, The. In *Death-Song of Thamyris and Other Poems,* London: Chiswick Press (printer) (priv.), 1899, pp. [1]-33.
Finding of Pheidippides, The. In *Finding of Pheidippides and Other Poems,* London: Chiswick Press (printer) (priv.), 1901, pp. [1]-37.
Jephthah's Daughter. In *Jephthah's Daughter and Other Poems,* London: Chiswick Press (printer) (priv.), 1904, pp. [1]-103.
Pausanias and Cleonice. In *Finding of Pheidippides and Other Poems,* London: Chiswick Press (printer) (priv.), 1901, pp. [47]-92.

PEMBER, EDWARD HENRY (trans.)
Hippolytus the Wreathbearer. By Euripides. In *Adrastus of Phrygia and Other Poems,* London: Chiswick Press (printer) (priv.), 1897, pp. [131]-215.
Oedipus at Colonos. By Sophocles. In *Death-Song of Thamyris and Other Poems,* London: Chiswick Press (printer) (priv.), 1899, pp. [103]-200.
Prometheus Bound. By Aeschylus. In *Voyage of the Phocaeans and Other Poems,* London: Chiswick Press (printer) (priv.), 1895, pp. [120]-177.

PEMBERTON, HARRIET LOUISA CHILDE
See Childe-Pemberton, Harriet Louisa.

PEMBERTON, THOMAS EDGAR
Davenport Bros. & Co. London & New York: Samuel French, n.d. Pp. [1]-24. [Lacy's Acting Edition].

Don't Be Too Quick to Cry Wolf. New York: DeWitt, c.1884. Pp. [1]-12. DeWitt's Acting Plays, 330.
Freezing a Mother-in-Law; or, A Frightful Frost. London & New York: Samuel French, n.d. Pp. [1]-24.
Gentle Gertrude of the Infamous Redd Lyon Inn; or, Drugged and Drowned in Digbeth. Music by Anderton, T. London & New York: Samuel French, n.d. Pp. [1]-18. [Lacy's Acting Edition]. Libretto.
Grateful Father, A. London & New York: Samuel French, n.d. Pp. [1]-16. [Lacy's Acting Edition].
Happy Medium, A. London & New York: Samuel French, n.d. Pp. [1]-20. [Lacy's Acting Edition].
Melting Moments. [London & New York: Samuel French], n.d. Pp. [3]-18. Title page lacking. [Lacy's Acting Edition].
My Wife's Father's Sister. London & New York: Samuel French, n.d. Pp. [1]-20. [Lacy's Acting Edition].
Steeple-Jack. London & New York: Samuel French, n.d. Pp. [1]-19. [French's Acting Edition].
Thorough Base. Music by Anderton, T. London & New York: Samuel French, n.d. Pp. [1]-16. [Lacy's Acting Edition].
Title. London & New York: Samuel French, n.d. Pp. [1]-34. [Lacy's Acting Edition].
Weeds. London & New York: Samuel French, n.d. Pp. [1]-20.

PENDRUDGE V. PRETTIWON
See Wallace, John, jr.

PENELOPE ANNE
See Burnand, Francis Cowley.

PENHORN, JANE
See Thomas, Jane Penhorn, Mrs. Edward.

PENLEY, SAMSON
Sleeping Draught, The. London: Richard White, 1818. Pp. [1-6], [i]-[iv], [5]-46.
Sleeping Draught, The. London: John Cumberland, n.d. Pp. [1]-38. Cumberland's British Theatre, XXIX. *Filed under* Cumberland, John. Cumberland's British Theatre, XXIX.

PENNIE, JOHN FITZGERALD
Arixina. In *Britain's Historical Drama,* London: Samuel Maunder, 1832, pp. [1-8], [i]-xvi, [1]-139. *Filed under* Collected Works.
Devoted One, The. In *Britain's Historical Drama,* 2nd series, London: Henry Stocking, 1839, pp. [111]-256.
Dragon-King, The. In *Britain's Historical Drama,* London: Samuel Maunder, 1832, pp. [411]-547. *Filed under* Collected Works.
Edwin and Elgiva; or, Norwegian Vengeance. In *Britain's Historical Drama,* London: Samuel Maunder, 1832, pp. [141]-263. *Filed under* Collected Works.
English Slave, The; or, The Eve of St. Brice. In *Britain's Historical Drama,* 2nd series, London: Henry Stocking, 1839, pp. [i-iv], [1]-109.
Ethelwolf; or, The Danish Pirates. London: G. & W. B. Whittaker, 1821. Pp. [i]-[x], [1]-77.
Imperial Pirate, The. In *Britain's Historical Drama,* London: Samuel Maunder, 1832, pp. [265]-409. *Filed under* Collected Works.
Varangian, The; or, Masonic Honour. In *Britain's Historical Drama,* 2nd series, London: Henry Stocking, 1839, pp. [257]-436.

PENTHEUS
See Amcotts, Vincent.

PEPPERPOT'S LITTLE PETS!
See Morton, John Maddison.

PERCY
See More, Hannah.

PERDITA
See Brough, William.

PEREGRINATIONS OF PICKWICK, THE
See Rede, William Leman.

PEREGRINATIONS OF SAM WELLER
See Lacy, Thomas Hailes (arr.). Pickwickians, The.

PEREGRINE PICKLE
See Reade, Charles.
PERFECT CURE, A
See Sapte, William, jr.
PERFECT LOVE!
See Reece, Robert.
PERFECT MENAGERIE, A
See Lawrence, James W.
PERFECTION
See Bayly, Thomas Haynes.
PERI WHO LOVED THE PRINCE
See Brough, William. Camaralzaman and Badoura.
PERICHOLE, LA
See Murray, Alfred (trans).
PERILOUS PASS OF THE CATARACT
See Bosworth, J. Gipsy King, The.
PERILS OF PIPPINS, THE
See Jerrold, Douglas William.
PEROUROU, THE BELLOWS MENDER, AND THE BEAU-
TY OF LYONS
See Moncrieff, William Thomas.
PEROUSE
See Fawcett, John.
PERSECUTION
See Russell, John, Lord (trans.). Don Carlos.
PERSEUS AND ANDROMEDA
See Brough, William.
See Planché, James Robinson. Deep Deep Sea, The.
PERSIAN HEROINE, THE
See Jodrell, Richard Paul.
PERSIAN HUNTERS, THE
See Noble, Thomas.
PERSONATION
See Kemble, Marie Thérèse De Camp, Mrs. Charles.
PERUVIAN MOTHER
See Ainslie, Whitelaw, Dr. Pizarro.
PESTILENCE OF MARSEILLES, THE
See Moncrieff, William Thomas.
PET LAMB, THE
See Selby, Charles.
PET OF THE PETTICOATS, THE
See Buckstone, John Baldwin.
PET OF THE PUBLIC, A
See Stirling, Edward.
PET, THE PATRIOT AND THE PIPPIN
See Byron, Henry James. William Tell, with a Vengeance.
PETER, WILLIAM (trans.)
Maid of Orleans, The. By Schiller. In *Maid of Orleans and Other Poems*, Cambridge: John Owen, 1843, pp. [1]-218.
Mary Stuart. By Schiller. Philadelphia: Henry Perkins, 1840. Pp. [5]-222. New ed.
William Tell. By Schiller. Luzern: A. Gebhardt, 1873. Pp. [i-viii], [1]-200. 3rd ed.
PETER BELL THE WAGGONER
See Buckstone, John Baldwin.
PETER FIN
See Jones, Richard.
PETER FIN'S TRIP TO BRIGHTON
See Jones, Richard. Peter Fin.
PETER THE GREAT
See Cherry, Andrew.
See Fitzball, Edward.
See Irving, Laurence Sydney Brodribb.
PETER WILKINS
See A'Beckett, Gilbert Abbott.
See Blanchard, Edward Litt Leman.
PETER WILKINS; OR, THE FLYING ISLANDERS (anon.)
London: Thomas Hailes Lacy, n.d. Pp. [i]-v, [6]-28. [Lacy's Acting Edition].
PETITE MARIÉE
See Lyster, Frederic (trans.). Little Bride, The.
PETS OF THE PARTERRE, THE
See Coyne, Joseph Stirling.
PETTICOAT CAPTAINS, THE
See Hazlewood, Charles Henry. Going to Chobham.

PETTICOAT COLONEL
See Wilson, Margaret Harries, Mrs. Cornwell Baron. Venus in Arms.
PETTICOAT GOVERNMENT
See Dance, Charles.
PETTICOAT PARLIAMENT, THE
See Lemon, Mark.
PETTICOAT PERFIDY
See Young, Charles Lawrence, Sir.
PETTITT, HENRY
See Pettitt, Henry Alfred.
PETTITT, HENRY ALFRED
Bells of Haslemere, The. Written with Grundy, Sydney. Pp. [i-iv], 1-26, [i], [1]-26, [i], [1]-29, [i-ii], [1]-19. Pagination by act. Typescript promptbook.
Blue-Eyed Susan.
See Sims, George Robert.
British Born.
See Meritt, Paul.
Carmen up to Date.
See Sims, George Robert.
Faust up to Date.
See Sims, George Robert.
Golden Fruit. Pp. [i], [1]-95, [i], 1-60. Manuscript promptbook.
In the Ranks.
See Sims, George Robert.
Neck or Nothing. Written with Conquest, George. London & New York: Samuel French, n.d. Pp. [1]-42. [Lacy's Acting Edition].
Prodigal Daughter, The. Written with Harris, Augustus Henry Glossop. London: J. Miles (printer), 1892. Pp. [1]-112.
Sole Survivor, The.
See Conquest, George.
Taken from Life. London: Aldine, n.d. Pp. [1]-64. Home Library of Powerful Dramatic Tales, 6. Novelization by Henry Llewellyn Williams.
White Cliffs, The.
See Meritt, Paul.
World, The.
See Meritt, Paul.
Worship of Bacchus, The.
See Meritt, Paul.
PEVERIL OF THE PEAK (anon.)
Edinburgh: James L. Huie, 1823. Pp. [1]-55. In *Waverley Dramas*, London: George Routledge, 1845. *Filed under* Waverley Dramas (anon.).
PEVERIL OF THE PEAK
See Fitzball, Edward.
PFEIFFER, EMILY JANE DAUB, MRS.
Wynnes of Wynhavod, The. In *Under the Aspens*, 2nd ed., London: Kegan Paul, Trench, 1882, pp. [i], [133]-311.
PHAEDRA
See Boswell, Robert Bruce (trans.).
See Heron, Matilda.
PHAETON
See Brough, William.
PHANTOM, THE
See Baillie, Joanna.
See Boucicault, Dionysius Lardner.
PHANTOM BREAKFAST!, THE
See Selby, Charles.
PHANTOM BRIDE, THE
See Barnett, Charles Zachary.
PHANTOM NIGHT DANCERS
See Moncrieff, William Thomas. Giselle.
PHANTOM OF THE VILLAGE
See Moncrieff, William Thomas. Somnambulist, The.
PHANTOM SHIP
See Fitzball, Edward. Flying Dutchman, The.
PHANTOMS!
See Lart, John.
PHELPS, SAMUEL, JR
Obstinate Family, The. New York: Clinton T. DeWitt, n.d. Pp. [1]-15. DeWitt's Acting Plays, 268.

Obstinate Family, The. London: Thomas Hailes Lacy, n.d. Pp. [1]-15. [Lacy's Acting Edition].

PHENOMENON IN A SMOCK FROCK, A
See Brough, William.

PHILANDERER, THE
See Shaw, George Bernard.

PHILANDERING
See Beazley, Samuel, jr.

PHILANTHROPY
See Maurice, Walter.

PHILEMON ET BAUCIS
See Bennett, Joseph (trans.).

PHILIP
See Atherstone, Edwin.
See Lloyd, Charles (trans.).

PHILIP BASIL
See Stephens, George.

PHILIP OF FRANCE AND MARIE DE MÉRANIE
See Marston, John Westland.

PHILIP QUARLL
See Dibdin, Charles Isaac Mungo, jr.

PHILIP THE SECOND
See Holcroft, Fanny (trans.).

PHILIP VAN ARTEVELDE
See Taylor, Henry.

PHILIPPE
See Murray, William Henry Wood.

PHILIPS, AMBROSE
Distressed Mother, The. In *British Drama*, 12 vols., London: John Dicks, 1871, IX, [289]-304.
Distrest Mother, The. London: Whittingham & Arliss, 1816. Pp. [1]-[52]. London Theatre, XXI. *Filed under* Dibdin, Thomas John, ed. London Theatre, XXI.
Distrest Mother, The. In *New English Drama*, ed. W. Oxberry, 22 vols., London: W. Simpkin & R. Marshall; C. Chapple, 1819, V, [i]-[viii], [1]-48. *Filed under* Oxberry, William Henry. New English Drama, V.

PHILIPS, FRANCIS CHARLES
Burglar and the Judge, The. Written with Brookfield, Charles Hallam Elton. London & New York: Samuel French, n.d. Pp. [1]-14. [Lacy's Acting Edition].
Woman's Reason, A.
See Brookfield, Charles Hallam Elton.

PHILLIPS, MRS. ALFRED
Caught in His Own Trap. London & New York: Samuel French, n.d. Pp. [1]-18. [Lacy's Acting Edition].
Master Passion, The. London: Thomas Hailes Lacy, n.d. Pp. [1]-30. [Lacy's Acting Edition].
Organic Affection, An. London: Thomas Hailes Lacy, n.d. Pp. [1]-20. [Lacy's Acting Edition].
Uncle Crotchet. London: Thomas Hailes Lacy, n.d. Pp. [1]-22. [Lacy's Acting Edition].

PHILLIPS, ALFRED R.
Crazed. London & New York: Samuel French, n.d. Pp. [1]-17. [Lacy's Acting Edition].

PHILLIPS, DOROTHEA
See Plowden, Dorthea Phillips, Mrs. Francis.

PHILLIPS, FREDERICK LAURENCE
Bird in the Hand Worth Two in the Bush, A. London: Thomas Hailes Lacy, n.d. Pp. [1]-[42]. [Lacy's Acting Edition].
First of September, The.
See Oxberry, William Henry.
Tramp's Adventure; or, True to the Last. London & New York: Samuel French, n.d. Pp. [1]-24. [Lacy's Acting Edition].

PHILLIPS, G.
Joseph Shark, the Lawyer's Clerk. London: J. Pattie, n.d. Pp. [1]-26.

PHILLIPS, LEWIS
Marianne Duval
See Marianne, the Vivandiere.
Marianne, the Vivandiere; or, The Mystery of Twenty Years. *Also:* Marianne Duval. London: Thomas Hailes Lacy. n.d. Pp. [1]-44.

PHILLIPS, MORRICE
Death Guard, The; or, The Rustic Banditti. 44 leaves. Manuscript.
Fidelio!; or, The Fortress of St. Jacque! London: John Duncombe, n.d. Pp. [1]-32. Duncombe's Edition.
Heiress of Glenfillan, The; or, The Delegates and the Children of the Wreck! 98 leaves. Manuscript.

PHILLIPS, R.
Heroine, The; or, A Daughter's Courage. London: John Duncombe, 1819. Pp. [i-ii], [1]-38.
Man in the Moon, The. London: C. Chapple, 1818. Pp. [i-vi], [1]-30.

PHILLIPS, STEPHEN
Herod. London & New York: John Lane, 1901. Pp. [1]-126.
Paolo and Francesca. London & New York: John Lane, 1900. Pp. [1]-120. 2nd ed.

PHILLIPS, WATTS
Camilla's Husband. London: Thomas Hailes Lacy, n.d. Pp. [1]-44.
Dead Heart, The. By Benjamin Webster. New York: Samuel French, c.1864. Pp. [1]-44. French's Standard Drama, 338.
Dead Heart, The: A Story of the French Revolution.
See Pollock, Walter Herries (arr.).
Golden Fetter, A. London: Thomas Hailes Lacy, n.d. Pp. [1]-49. [Lacy's Acting Edition].
His Last Victory. London: Thomas Hailes Lacy, n.d. Pp. [1]-36.
Huguenot Captain, The. London: Thomas Hailes Lacy, n.d. Pp. [1]-52. Lacy's Acting Edition.
Lion at Bay, A. London: Thomas Hailes Lacy, n.d. Pp. [1]-19. [Lacy's Acting Edition].
Lost in London. Boston: Charles H. Spencer, n.d. Pp. [1]-22. Spencer's Universal Stage, 1. Promptbook.
Maud's Peril. Chicago: Dramatic Publishing Co., n.d. Pp. [1]-28. Sergel's Acting Drama, 7.
Maud's Peril. London: Thomas Hailes Lacy, n.d. Pp. [1]-46. Lacy's Acting Edition, [186]. Promptbook.
Nobody's Child. New York: Robert M. DeWitt, n.d. Pp. [1]-38.
Not Guilty. London: Thomas Hailes Lacy, n.d. Pp. [1]-65. Promptbook.
Not Guilty. Chicago: Dramatic Publishing Co., n.d. Pp. [1]-50. [Sergel's Acting Drama].
Paper Wings. London: Thomas Hailes Lacy, n.d. Pp. [1]-59. [Lacy's Acting Edition].
Paul's Return. London: Thomas Hailes Lacy, n.d. Pp. [1]-46. Promptbook.
Theodora, Actress and Empress. London: Thomas Hailes Lacy, n.d. Pp. [1]-64. [Lacy's Acting Edition].
Ticket-of-Leave, A. Clyde, Ohio: Ames & Holgate, n.d. Pp. [1]-12.
White Cockade, The. London: Thomas Hailes Lacy, n.d. Pp. [1]-57.
Woman in Mauve, The. London: Thomas Hailes Lacy, n.d. Pp. [i]-vi, [6]-58.

PHILLPOTTS, EDEN
Breezy Morning, A. London: Samuel French; New York: T. Henry French, n.d. Pp. [1]-16. [Lacy's Acting Edition].
Golden Wedding, A. Written with Groves, Charles. By Edm. Phillpotto & Charles Groves. New York & London: Samuel French, c.1899. Pp. [1]-22.
Pair of Knickerbockers, A. New York & London: Samuel French, c.1900. Pp. [1]-19.
Prude's Progress, The.
See Jerome, Jerome Klapka.

PHILOMEL
See Craven, Henry Thornton.

PHILON, FREDERIC
He Would Be a Soldier. In *Modern Theatre*, ed. Mrs. Inchbald, 10 vols., London: Longman, Hurst, Rees, Orme, & Brown, 1811, VIII, [225]-307.

PHILOSOPHER, THE
See Milner, Henry M. (trans.).

PHILOSOPHER'S STONE, THE
  See Taylor, Tom.
PHILOSOPHERS OF BERLIN, THE
  See Bernard, William Bayle.
PHILOTAS
  See Bell, Ernest (trans.).
PHIPPS, A. J.
  My Very Last Proposal. London & New York: Samuel French, n.d. Pp. [1]-18. [Lacy's Acting Edition].
  Pretty Predicaments. London & New York: Samuel French, n.d. Pp. [1]-16. [Lacy's Acting Edition].
PHIPPS, EDMUND (trans.)
  King René's Daughter. By Hertz, Henrik. New York: Samuel French, n.d. Pp. [1]-28. French's Minor Drama, 266.
PHOTOGRAPHIC FIX, A
  See Hay, Frederic.
PHRENOLOGISTS, THE
  See Wade, Thomas.
PHRONTISTERION
  See Mansel, Henry Longueville.
PHROSO
  See Rose, Edward.
PHYSICIAN, THE
  See Jones, Henry Arthur.
PHYSICIAN IN SPITE OF HIMSELF, THE
  See Van Laun, Henri (trans.).
PICCOLOMINI, THE
  See Coleridge, Samuel Taylor (trans.).
PICKING UP THE PIECES
  See Sturgis, Julian Russell.
PICKPOCKET, THE
  See Hawtrey, George Proctor.
PICKWICK
  See Albery, James.
  See Burnand, Francis Cowley.
PICKWICK CLUB, THE
  See Stirling, Edward.
PICKWICKIANS, THE
  See Lacy, Thomas Hailes (arr.).
  See Moncrieff, William Thomas. Sam Weller.
PICOTEE'S PLEDGE
  See Stephens, Henry Pottinger. Lord Bateman.
PIEBALD POSSUM OF THE PANTING PRAIRIE, THE
  See Harrison, Samuel M.
PIERETTE
  See Fitzball, Edward.
PIERROT OF THE MINUTE, THE
  See Dowson, Ernest Christopher.
PIERROT THE MARRIED MAN, AND POLICHINELLO
  THE GAY SINGLE FELLOW
  See Webster, Benjamin Nottingham.
PIERROT'S SACRIFICE
  See Byatt, Henry. Golden Age, The.
PIETRO IL GRANDE
  See Ryan, Desmond Lumley (trans.).
PIGEON AND THE HAWKS, THE
  See Brougham, John.
PIKE O'CALLAGHAN
  See Reeve, Wybert.
PILGRIM OF LOVE!, THE
  See Byron, Henry James.
PILGRIMAGE TO PLOËRMEL, THE
  See Chorley, Henry Fotherfill. Dinorah.
PILL-DOCTOR HERDAL
  See Anstey, F.
PILLARS OF SOCIETY, THE
  See Archer, William (trans.).
PILLS OF WISDOM
  See Heighway, William.
PILOT, THE
  See Fitzball, Edward.
PIMPLE, THE PIRATE
  See Mills, Horace.

PINERO, ARTHUR WING
  Amazons, The. Boston: Walter H. Baker, 1895. Pp. [1]-189. Promptbook.
  Beauty Stone, The. Written with Carr, Joseph William Comyns. Music by Sullivan, Arthur. London: Chappell, n.d. Pp. [i]-[viii], [9]-72. Libretto.
  Beauty Stone, The. Written with Carr, Joseph William Comyns. Music by Sullivan, Arthur. London: Chappell, n.d. Pp. [1-4], i-vi, 1-211. Vocal score.
  Benefit of the Doubt, The. London: Chiswick Press (printer) (priv.), 1895. Pp. [i-iv], 1-[113].
  Cabinet Minister, The. Boston: Walter H. Baker, c.1892. Pp. [i]-x, [1]-188.
  Dandy Dick. London: J. Miles (printer) (priv.), 1887. Pp. [i]-vi, [1]-93. Promptbook.
  Dandy Dick. London: William Heinemann, 1893. Pp. [i]-[xiv], [1]-163.
  Dandy Dick. Boston: Walter H. Baker, n.d. Pp. [1]-162.
  Gay Lord Quex, The. London: William Heinemann, 1900. Pp. [i-viii], [1]-225.
  Hester's Mystery. London: W. S. Johnson, 1880. Pp. [1]-30.
  Hester's Mystery. London & New York: Samuel French, n.d. Pp. [1]-24. [Lacy's Acting Edition].
  Hobby-Horse, The. London: William Heinemann, 1892. Pp. [iii]-[xii], [1]-168.
  In Chancery. New York & London: Samuel French, c.1905. Pp. [1-2], [i-iv], [5]-72.
  Iris. Boston: Walter H. Baker, c.1900. Pp. [i-iv], [1]-224.
  Lady Bountiful: A Story of Years. London: William Heinemann, 1891. Pp. [iii]-[xii], [1]-185.
  Magistrate, The. London: William Heinemann, 1892. Pp. [i]-[xii], [1]-164.
  Magistrate, The. Boston: Walter H. Baker (priv.), c.1892. Pp. [i]-[xiv], [1]-164.
  Money Spinner, The. New York & London: Samuel French, c.1900. Pp. [3]-43.
  Notorious Mrs. Ebbsmith, The. London: William Heinemann, 1895. Pp. [i-vi], [1]-224.
  Notorious Mrs. Ebbsmith, The. In *Social Plays,* ed. Clayton Hamilton, New York: E. P. Dutton, 1917, I, [197]-362.
  Princess and the Butterfly, The; or, The Fantastics. London: William Heinemann; New York: Samuel French, c.1897. Pp. [i-x], [1]-244.
  Profligate, The. London: William Heinemann, 1891. Pp. [i]-[xxiv], [1]-123.
  Profligate, The. Boston: Walter H. Baker, 1899. Pp. [i]-[xx], [1]-123.
  Rocket, The. London & New York: Samuel French, c.1905. Pp. [1-2], [i-iv], [5]-76. Text incomplete.
  School Mistress, The. London: William Heinemann, 1894. Pp. [i]-[x], [1]-165.
  Second Mrs. Tanqueray, The. Boston: Walter H. Baker, 1894. Pp. [i-ii], [1]-174.
  Second Mrs. Tanqueray, The. London: William Heinemann, 1895. Pp. [i-vi], [1]-195.
  Second Mrs. Tanqueray, The. In *Social Plays,* ed. Clayton Hamilton, New York: E. P. Dutton, 1917, I, [i-vi], [1]-195.
  Squire, The. London: J. Miles (printer), 1881. Pp. [1]-66.
  Sweet Lavender. Boston: Walter H. Baker, c.1893. Pp. [1]-184.
  Times, The. London: William Heinemann, 1891. Pp. [iii]-[xii], [1]-192.
  Times, The. Boston: Walter H. Baker, c.1892. Pp. [i]-x, [1]-192.
  Trelawny of the Wells. London: William Heinemann, 1899. Pp. [i-viii], [1]-215.
  Trelawny of the Wells. London: William Heinemann, 1925. Pp. [i-iv], [1]-215. Promptbook.
  Weaker Sex, The. Boston: Walter H. Baker, 1894. Pp. [1]-133.
PINK DOMINOS
  See Albery, James.
PINK OF POLITENESS, THE
  See Selby, Charles.

PINS AND NEEDLES
  See Peard, Frances Mary.
PIPER OF HAMELIN, THE
  See Buchanan, Robert Williams.
PIPERMAN'S PREDICAMENTS
  See Ware, James Redding.
PIPKIN'S RUSTIC RETREAT!
  See Williams, Thomas John.
PIPPA PASSES
  See Browning, Robert.
PIRATE, THE
  See Dibdin, Thomas John.
  See Planché, James Robinson.
  See Thomas, Leigh.
PIRATE VESSEL
  See Fitzball, Edward. Koeuba, The.
PIRATES OF PENZANCE, THE
  See Gilbert, William Schwenck.
PIRATES OF THE SAVANNAH, THE
  See Suter, William E.
PIRITHOUS, THE SON OF IXION
  See Burnand, Francis Cowley.
PIROMIDES, THE
  See Hake, Thomas Gordon.

PITT, GEORGE DIBDIN
  Beggar's Petition, The. 74 leaves. Manuscript.
  Beggar's Petition, The; or, A Father's Love and a Mother's Care. London & New York: Samuel French, n.d. Pp. [1]-46.
  Drunkard's Doom, The; or, The Last Nail. New York: Samuel French, n.d. Pp. [1]-24. French's Standard Drama, 345.
  Eddystone Elf, The. London: John Cumberland, n.d. Pp. [1]-36. Cumberland's Minor Theatre, X. *Filed under* Cumberland, John. Cumberland's Minor Theatre, X.
  Eddystone Elf, The. *Also:* The Monster of the Eddystone; or, The Lighthouse Keepers. London: Thomas Hailes Lacy, n.d. Pp. [3]-36. [Lacy's Acting Edition].
  Jersey Girl, The; or, Les Rouge Voleurs. London: Thomas Hailes Lacy, n.d. Pp. [1]-28. [Lacy's Acting Edition].
  Last Man, The; or, The Miser of Eltham Green. Boston: William V. Spencer, n.d. Pp. [1]-24. Spencer's Boston Theatre, 94.
  Last Nail, The; or, The Drunkard's Doom. N.p.: n.pub, n.d. Pp. [187]-198. Title page lacking.
  Lurline.
    See Burrows, J. G.
  Marianne, the Child of Charity. London: Music Publishing Co., n.d. Pp. [1]-8, [11]-43. Text incomplete. Promptbook.
  Monster of the Eddystone, The.
    See Eddystone Elf, The.
  My Own Blue Bell; or, The Army and the Navy. London: John Dicks, n.d. Pp. [1]-6. Dicks' Standard Plays, 515.
  Poacher's Doom, The; or, The Murder of the Five Field's Copse. Clyde, Ohio: Ames & Holgate, n.d. Pp. [1]-24.
  Prisoner of Rochelle, The. London: John Duncombe, n.d. Pp. [1]-24. Duncombe's Edition.
  Simon Lee; or, The Murder of the Five Fields Copse. London: Samuel French; New York: T. Henry French, n.d. Pp. [1]-41. French's Acting Edition (late Lacy's), 1164.
  Susan Hopley; or, The Vicissitudes of a Servant Girl. London: Davidson, n.d. Pp. [1]-50.
  Whistler!, The; or, The Fate of the Lily of St. Leonard's. London: John Duncombe, n.d. Pp. [1]-35. Duncombe's Edition.

PITT, W. H.
  Knobstick Wedding, A; or, A Legend of the Dead Man's Ferry. 67 leaves. Manuscript promptbook.

PITTMAN, JOSIAH (trans.)
  Demonio, Il. Music by Rubinstein, Anton. London: John Miles (printer), n.d. Pp. [i-ii], [1]-84. Libretto.
  Flying Dutchman, The. *Also:* Il Vascello Fantasma. Music by Wagner. London: John Miles (printer), n.d. Pp. [1]-63. Libretto.

  Re di Lahore, Il. Music by Massenet. London: J. Miles (printer), n.d. Pp. [i]-v, [6]-71. Libretto.
  Rienzi, the Last of the Tribunes. Music by Wagner. London: Schott; Berlin: Adolph Furstner, n.d. Pp. [1]-339. Vocal score.
  Tannhauser. Music by Wagner. London: J. Miles (printer), n.d. Pp. [1]-61. Libretto.

PITY
  See Shirley, Arthur. Gringoire the Ballad-Monger.
PITY OF IT, THE
  See Robertson, Ian.
PITY OF LOVE, THE
  See Wratislaw, Theodore.

PIXÉRÉCOURT, GUILBERT DE
  Wife with Two Husbands, The.
    See Gunning, Elizabeth (trans.).

PIZARRO
  See Ainslie, Whitelaw, Dr.
  See Buckingham, Leicester Silk.
  See Helme, Elizabeth (trans.).
  See Kean, Charles John (arr.).
  See Sheridan, Richard Brinsley.
  See West, Matthew.
PIZARRO: A SPANISH ROLLA-KING PERUVIAN DRAMA
  See Collins, Charles James.
PLACE HUNTER, THE
  See Webster, Frederick.
PLAGUE OF DARKNESS, THE
  See Lyndsay, David.
PLAIN COOK, A
  See Stirling, Edward.
PLAIN DEALER, THE
  See Kemble, John Philip (arr.).

PLANCHÉ, ELIZABETH (Eliza) **ST. GEORGE, MRS. JAMES ROBINSON**
  Handsome Husband, A. London: John Miller, n.d. Pp. [i-ii], [1]-26.
  Hasty Conclusion, A. London: Chapman & Hall, 1838. Pp. [1]-22. [Acting National Drama, IV].
  Pleasant Neighbour, A. London: John Miller, n.d. Pp. [1]-22.
  Ransom, The: An Anecdote of Montesquieu. London: John Miller, 1836. Pp. [i-v], [1]-[36]. Promptbook.
  Sledge-Driver, The. London: John Miller, 1834. Pp. [i-ii], [1]-40. Promptbook.
  Welsh Girl, The. London: John Miller, 1834. Pp. 1-37. Miller's Modern Acting Drama.

PLANCHÉ, JAMES ROBINSON
  All in the Dark; or, The Banks of the Elbe. New York: E. M. Murden, 1822. Pp. [1]-52.
  Amoroso, King of Little Britain. London: Richard White, 1818. Pp. [i]-[ii], [1]-21.
  Babil and Bijou.
    See Boucicault, Dionysius Lardner.
  Beauty and the Beast. In *Extravaganzas,* eds. T. F. Dillon Croker & Stephen Tucker, 5 vols., London: Samuel French, 1879, II, [105]-142. *Filed under* Collected Works.
  Beauty and the Beast. New York: Samuel French, n.d. Pp. [1]-32. Minor Drama, 14. Promptbook.
  Bee and the Orange Tree, The; or, The Four Wishes. London: S. G. Fairbrother; W. Strange, 1846. Pp. [1]-31.
  Bee and the Orange Tree, The; or, The Four Wishes. In *Extravaganzas,* eds. T. F. Dillon Croker & Stephen Tucker, 5 vols., London: Samuel French, 1879, III, [43]-78. *Filed under* Collected Works.
  Birds of Aristophanes, The. London: S. G. Fairbrother; W. Strange, 1846. Pp. [1]-28.
  Birds of Aristophanes, The. In *Extravaganzas,* eds. T. F. Dillon Croker & Stephen Tucker, 5 vols., London: Samuel French, 1879, III, [80]-108. *Filed under* Collected Works.
  Blue Beard. In *Extravaganzas,* eds. T. F. Dillon Croker & Stephen Tucker, 5 vols., London: Samuel French, 1879, II, [31]-62. *Filed under* Collected Works.

Brigand, The. London: John Cumberland, n.d. Pp. [1]-36. Cumberland's British Theatre, XXIV. *Filed under* Cumberland, John. Cumberland's British Theatre, XXIV.

Brigand, The. London: Thomas Hailes Lacy, n.d. Pp. [1]-36. [Lacy's Acting Edition].

Brigand, The. London: John Cumberland, n.d. Pp. [3]-36. Promptbook.

Burletta of Errors; or, Jupiter and Alcmena. London: John Lowndes, n.d. Pp. [1]-19.

Cabinet Question, A. London: Thomas Hailes Lacy, n.d. Pp. [1]-24. [Lacy's Acting Edition].

Camp at the Olympic, The. In *Extravaganzas,* eds. T. F. Dillon Croker & Stephen Tucker, 5 vols., London: Samuel French, 1879, IV, [293]-321. *Filed under* Collected Works.

Captain of the Watch, The. New York: William Taylor, n.d. Pp. [1]-33. Minor Drama, 16. Promptbook.

Charles XII. London: John Cumberland, n.d. Pp. [2]-52.

Charles XII. London: John Cumberland, n.d. Pp. [1]-52. Cumberland's British Theatre, XXV. *Filed under* Cumberland, John. Cumberland's British Theatre, XXV.

Child of the Wreck, The. London: Thomas Hailes Lacy, n.d. Pp. [1]-30.

Compliments of the Season, The. In *Pieces of Pleasantry for Private Performance,* London & New York: Samuel French, n.d., pp. 19-31. *Filed under* Pieces of Pleasantry.

Cortez; or, The Conquest of Mexico. London: John Lowndes, n.d. Pp. [i]-[vi], [1]-50.

Court Beauties, The. London: S. G. Fairbrother, n.d. Pp. [1]-32. New ed.

Court Favour; or, Private and Confidential. London: [Chapman & Hall], n.d. Pp. [1]-30.

Cymon and Iphigenia. In *Extravaganzas,* eds. T. F. Dillon Croker & Stephen Tucker, 5 vols., London: Samuel French, 1879, IV, [47]-86. *Filed under* Collected Works.

Daughter to Marry, A. London: Thomas Hailes Lacy, n.d. Pp. [1]-28.

Day of Reckoning, A. London: Thomas Hailes Lacy, n.d. Pp. [1]-44. [Lacy's Acting Edition].

Deep Deep Sea, The; or, Perseus and Andromeda. Written with Dance, Charles. In *Extravaganzas,* eds. T. F. Dillon Croker & Stephen Tucker, 5 vols., London: Samuel French, 1879, I, [142]-169. *Filed under* Collected Works.

Deep Deep Sea, The; or, Perseus and Andromeda. Written with Dance, Charles. London: Thomas Hailes Lacy, n.d. Pp. [1]-27.

Discreet Princess, The; or, The Three Glass Distaffs. In *Extravaganzas,* eds. T. F. Dillon Croker & Stephen Tucker, 5 vols., London: Samuel French, 1879, V, [101]-146. *Filed under* Collected Works.

Doctor Syntax; or, Harlequin in London. London: John Lowndes, 1820. Pp. [1]-15. Libretto.

Drama at Home, The; or, An Evening with Puff. London: S. G. Fairbrother; W. Strange, 1844. Pp. [1]-22. [Lacy's Acting Edition].

Drama at Home, The; or, An Evening with Puff. In *Extravaganzas,* eds. T. F. Dillon Croker & Stephen Tucker, 5 vols., London: Samuel French, 1879, II, [267]-296. *Filed under* Collected Works.

Drama's Levée, The; or, A Peep at the Past. In *Extravaganzas,* eds. T. F. Dillon Croker & Stephen Tucker, 5 vols., London: Samuel French, 1879, II, [1]-29. *Filed under* Collected Works.

Dumb Belle, The; or, I'm Perfection! Philadelphia: Frederick Turner, n.d. Pp. [1]-31.

Faint Heart Never Won Fair Lady. New York: William Taylor, n.d. Pp. [i]-[vi], [7]-31. Modern Standard Drama, 68.

Fair Gabrielle, The. London: C. Chapple, 1822. Pp. [i-vi], [1]-31.

Fair One with the Golden Locks, The. London: S. G. Fairbrother; W. Strange, 1844. Pp. [1]-28.

Fair One with the Golden Locks, The. In *Extravaganzas,* eds. T. F. Dillon Croker & Stephen Tucker, 5 vols., London:

Samuel French, 1879, II, [229]-266. *Filed under* Collected Works.

Follies of a Night, The. New York: William Taylor, n.d. Pp. [i]-[vi], [7]-54. Modern Standard Drama, 46.

Fortunio and His Seven Gifted Servants. Boston: G. E. Locke, 1844. Pp. [1]-28. Locke's Museum Edition.

Fortunio and His Seven Gifted Servants. In *Extravaganzas,* eds. T. F. Dillon Croker & Stephen Tucker, 5 vols., London: Samuel French, 1879, II, [179]-228. *Filed under* Collected Works.

Fortunio and His Seven Gifted Servants. London: S. G. Fairbrother, n.d. Pp. [1]-16. Libretto.

Garrick Fever, The. London & New York: Samuel French, n.d. Pp. [1]-26. French's Acting Edition (late Lacy's).

Giovanni the Vampire!; or, How Shall We Get Rid of Him? London: John Lowndes, 1821. Pp. [1]-15. Libretto.

Golden Branch, The. In *Extravaganzas,* eds. T. F. Dillon Croker & Stephen Tucker, 5 vols., London: Samuel French, 1879, III, [181]-222. *Filed under* Collected Works.

Golden Branch, The. London: Thomas Hailes Lacy, n.d. Pp. [1]-31. [Lacy's Acting Edition].

Golden Fleece, The; or, Jason in Colchis and Medea in Corinth. In *Extravaganzas,* eds. T. F. Dillon Croker & Stephen Tucker, 5 vols., London: Samuel French, 1879, III, [1]-42. *Filed under* Collected Works.

Golden Fleece, The; or, Jason in Colchis and Medea in Corinth. London: Thomas Hailes Lacy, n.d. Pp. [1]-33. [Lacy's Acting Edition].

Good Woman in the Wood, The. In *Extravaganzas,* eds. T. F. Dillon Croker & Stephen Tucker, 5 vols., London: Samuel French, 1879, IV, [211]-256. *Filed under* Collected Works.

Graciosa and Percinet. London: S. G. Fairbrother; W. Strange, 1845. Pp. [1]-30.

Graciosa and Percinet. In *Extravaganzas,* eds. T. F. Dillon Croker & Stephen Tucker, 5 vols., London: Samuel French, 1879, II, [297]-[335]. *Filed under* Collected Works.

Green-Eyed Monster, The. London: John Cumberland, n.d. Pp. [1]-45. Cumberland's British Theatre, XXI. *Filed under* Cumberland, John. Cumberland's British Theatre, XXI.

Green-Eyed Monster, The. London & New York: Samuel French, n.d. Pp. [1]-45. Promptbook.

Grist to the Mill. New York: Samuel French, n.d. Pp. [1]-34. Promptbook.

Gustavus the Third; or, The Masked Ball. Music by Auber. London: D'Almaine, n.d. Pp. [i]-viii, [1]-44. Libretto.

Half an Hour's Courtship. 23 leaves. Manuscript.

High, Low, Jack, and the Game; or, The Card Party. Written with Dance, Charles. London: John Miller, 1833. Pp. [i-iv], [1]-20. Miller's Modern Acting Drama, 10.

High, Low, Jack, and the Game; or, The Card Party. Written with Dance, Charles. In *Extravaganzas,* eds. T. F. Dillon Croker & Stephen Tucker, 5 vols., London: Samuel French, 1879, I, [116]-140. *Filed under* Collected Works.

Hold Your Tongue. London: S. G. Fairbrother, n.d. Pp. [1]-27.

Invisible Prince, The; or, The Island of Tranquil Delights. In *Extravaganzas,* eds. T. F. Dillon Croker & Stephen Tucker, 5 vols., London: Samuel French, 1879, III, [110]-148. *Filed under* Collected Works.

Invisible Prince, The; or, The Island of Tranquil Delights. New York: William Taylor; Baltimore: William & Henry Taylor, n.d. Pp. [1]-35. Minor Drama, 7.

Irish Post, The. London: Thomas Hailes Lacy, n.d. Pp. [1]-34. [Lacy's Acting Edition].

Island of Jewels, The. In *Extravaganzas,* eds. T. F. Dillon Croker & Stephen Tucker, 5 vols., London: Samuel French, 1879, IV, [1]-46. *Filed under* Collected Works.

Island of Jewels, The. London: Thomas Hailes Lacy, n.d. Pp. [1]-38.

Jacobite, The. New York: William Taylor, n.d. Pp. [1]-35. Minor Drama, 19.

Jenkinses, The; or, Boarded and Done For. London: John Dicks, n.d. Pp. [1]-11. Dicks' Standard Plays, 899.

Jewess, The. London: Porter & Wright, 1835. Pp. [i]-[viii], [1]-48.

King Charming; or, The Blue Bird of Paradise. In *Extravaganzas*, eds. T. F. Dillon Croker & Stephen Tucker, 5 vols., London: Samuel French, 1879, IV, [87]-128. *Filed under* Collected Works.

King Christmas. In *Extravaganzas*, eds. T. F. Dillon Croker & Stephen Tucker, 5 vols., London: Samuel French, 1879, V, [277]-307, [308]-331. *Filed under* Collected Works.

King of the Bean, The. In *Pieces of Pleasantry for Private Performance*, London & New York: Samuel French, n.d., pp. [33]-45. *Filed under* Pieces of Pleasantry.

King of the Peacocks, The. In *Extravaganzas*, eds. T. F. Dillon Croker & Stephen Tucker, 5 vols., London: Samuel French, 1879, III, [261]-308. *Filed under* Collected Works.

King of the Peacocks, The. London: Thomas Hailes Lacy, n.d. Pp. [1]-47. [Lacy's Acting Edition].

Knights of the Round Table, The. London: Thomas Hailes Lacy, n.d. Pp. [1]-68. [Lacy's Acting Edition].

Lady in Difficulties, A. London: S. G. Fairbrother, n.d. Pp. [3]-40. Promptbook.

Lavater the Physiognomist; or, Not a Bad Judge. *Also:* Not a Bad Judge. Boston: William V. Spencer, n.d. Pp. [1]-35. Spencer's Boston Theatre, 172. *Filed under* Not a Bad Judge.

Loan of a Lover, The. London: John Miller, 1834. Pp. [i-iv], [1]-[32].

Love and Fortune. In *Extravaganzas*, eds. T. F. Dillon Croker & Stephen Tucker, 5 vols., London: Samuel French, 1879, V, [193]-230. *Filed under* Collected Works.

Love's Triumph. Music by Wallace, W. Vincent. New York: William Hall & Son, c.1862. Pp. [1]-283. Vocal score.

Maid Marian; or, The Huntress of Arlingford. Music by Bishop. London: John Lowndes, n.d. Pp. [i-iv], [1]-52.

Mason of Buda, The. London: John Cumberland, n.d. Pp. [1]-36. Cumberland's Minor Theatre, I. *Filed under* Cumberland, John. Cumberland's Minor Theatre, I.

Mason of Buda, The. London: John Cumberland, n.d. Pp. [3]-36.

Merchant's Wedding, The; or, London Frolics in 1638. London: John Cumberland, 1828. Pp. [1]-79. Cumberland's British Theatre, XIX. *Filed under* Cumberland, John. Cumberland's British Theatre, XIX.

Merchant's Wedding, The; or, London Frolics in 1638. London: John Cumberland, n.d. Pp. [1]-79.

Mr. Buckstone's Ascent of Mount Parnassus. In *Extravaganzas*, eds. T. F. Dillon Croker & Stephen Tucker, 5 vols., London: Samuel French, 1879, IV, [257]-292. *Filed under* Collected Works.

Mr. Buckstone's Voyage Round the Globe (in Leicester Square). In *Extravaganzas*, eds. T. F. Dillon Croker & Stephen Tucker, 5 vols., London: Samuel French, 1879, V, [1]-34. *Filed under* Collected Works.

My Daughter, Sir!; or, A Daughter to Marry. London: John Cumberland, n.d. Pp. [1]-28. Cumberland's British Theatre, XXXVII. *Filed under* Cumberland, John. Cumberland's British Theatre, XXXVII.

My Daughter, Sir!; or, A Daughter to Marry. London: John Cumberland, n.d. Pp. [3]-28. Cumberland's British Theatre, 290.

My Friend, the Governor. London: John Dicks, n.d. Pp. [12]-23. Dicks' Standard Plays, 899. *Filed under* Jenkinses.

My Heart's Idol; or, A Desperate Remedy. London: Thomas Hailes Lacy, n.d. Pp. [1]-43. [Lacy's Acting Edition, 294].

My Lord and My Lady; or, It Might Have Been Worse. London: Thomas Hailes Lacy, n.d. Pp. [1]-72. [Lacy's Acting Edition].

Mysterious Lady, The; or, Worth Makes the Man. London: Thomas Hailes Lacy, n.d. Pp. [1]-32. Promptbook.

New Haymarket Spring Meeting, The. In *Extravaganzas*, eds. T. F. Dillon Croker & Stephen Tucker, 5 vols., London: Samuel French, 1879, V, [75]-100. *Filed under* Collected Works.

New Planet, The; or, Harlequin Out of Place. In *Extravaganzas*, eds. T. F. Dillon Croker & Stephen Tucker, 5 vols., London: Samuel French, 1879, III, [150]-180. *Filed under* Collected Works.

New Planet, The; or, Harlequin Out of Place. London: S. G. Fairbrother; W. Strange, n.d. Pp. [2]-28.

Norma. Music by Bellini. New York: Douglas, n.d. Pp. [3-6], [7]-29 (Italian); [7]-29 (English). Operatic Library, 3. Libretto.

Not a Bad Judge.
See Lavater the Physiognomist.

Oberon; or, The Charmed Horn. London: J. Tabby (printer), 1826. Pp. [1]-46.

Old Offender, An. London & New York: Samuel French, n.d. Pp. [1]-40.

Olympic Devils; or, Orpheus and Eurydice. Written with Dance, Charles. London: John Miller, 1836. Pp. [1]-24.

Olympic Devils; or, Orpheus and Eurydice. Written with Dance, Charles. In *Extravaganzas*, eds. T. F. Dillon Croker & Stephen Tucker, 5 vols., London: Samuel French, 1879, I, [61]-88. *Filed under* Collected Works.

Olympic Revels; or, Prometheus and Pandora. Written with Dance, Charles. In *Extravaganzas*, eds. T. F. Dillon Croker & Stephen Tucker, 5 vols., London: Samuel French, 1879, I, [38]-60. *Filed under* Collected Works.

Olympic Revels; or, Prometheus and Pandora. Written with Dance, Charles. London: Thomas Hailes Lacy, n.d. Pp. [1]-23. [Lacy's Acting Edition].

Once Upon a Time There Were Two Kings. In *Extravaganzas*, eds. T. F. Dillon Croker & Stephen Tucker, 5 vols., London: Samuel French, 1879, IV, [323]-372. *Filed under* Collected Works.

Orpheus in the Haymarket. In *Extravaganzas*, eds. T. F. Dillon Croker & Stephen Tucker, 5 vols., London: Samuel French, 1879, V, [231]-276. *Filed under* Collected Works.

Paphian Bower, The; or, Venus and Adonis. Written with Dance, Charles. In *Extravaganzas*, eds. T. F. Dillon Croker & Stephen Tucker, 5 vols., London: Samuel French, 1879, I, [90]-113. *Filed under* Collected Works.

Paphian Bower, The; or, Venus and Adonis. Written with Dance, Charles. London: Thomas Hailes Lacy, n.d. Pp. [1]-24. [Lacy's Acting Edition].

Paris and London. London: John Cumberland, n.d. Pp. [1]-53.

Paris and London. London: John Cumberland, n.d. Pp. [1]-53. Cumberland's Minor Theatre, III. *Filed under* Cumberland, John. Cumberland's Minor Theatre, III.

Peculiar Position, A. [London: Chapman & Hall], n.d. Pp. [1]-23.

Pirate, The. London: John Lowndes, n.d. Pp. [1]-70.

Pride of the Market, The. London: John Dicks, n.d. Pp. [1]-18. Dicks' Standard Plays, 999.

Prince of Happy Land, The; or, The Fawn in the Forest. In *Extravaganzas*, eds. T. F. Dillon Croker & Stephen Tucker, 5 vols., London: Samuel French, 1879, IV, [170]-210. *Filed under* Collected Works.

Printer's Devil, The. London: John Dicks, n.d. Pp. [13]-22. Text complete. [Dicks' Standard Plays].

Promotion; or, A Morning at Versailles. New York: Samuel French, n.d. Pp. [1]-17. Minor Drama.

Puss in Boots. Written with Dance, Charles. In *Extravaganzas*, eds. T. F. Dillon Croker & Stephen Tucker, 5 vols., London: Samuel French, 1879, I, [247]-288. *Filed under* Collected Works.

Puss in Boots. Written with Dance, Charles. London: National Acting Drama Office, n.d. Pp. [1]-24. Webster's Acting National Drama, [26].

Queen Mary's Bower. London: S. G. Fairbrother; W. Strange, n.d. Pp. [1]-39. [Lacy's Acting Edition].

Queen of the Frogs, The. In *Extravaganzas*, eds. T. F. Dillon Croker & Stephen Tucker, 5 vols., London: Samuel French, 1879, IV, [129]-168. *Filed under* Collected Works.

Queen's Horse, The.
See Honan, Michael Burke.

Returned Killed. London: Sherwood, Gilbert, & Piper, 1826. Pp. [1]-40.

Riquet with the Tuft. Written with Dance, Charles. In *Extravaganzas,* eds. T. F. Dillon Croker & Stephen Tucker, 5 vols., London: Samuel French, 1879, I, [206]-246. *Filed under* Collected Works.

Riquet with the Tuft. Written with Dance, Charles. London: Chapman & Hall, n.d. Pp. [1]-28. [Acting National Drama, I].

Rodolph the Wolf; or, Columbine Red Riding-Hood. London: John Lowndes, 1819. Pp. [1-23].

Romantic Idea, A. London: John Dicks, n.d. Pp. [13]-23. Text complete. Dicks' Standard Plays, [1010].

Secret Service. London: John Miller, 1834. Pp. [1]-56.

Seven Champions of Christendom, The. In *Extravaganzas,* eds. T. F. Dillon Croker & Stephen Tucker, 5 vols., London: Samuel French, 1879, III, [310]-360. *Filed under* Collected Works.

Sleeping Beauty in the Wood, The. In *Extravaganzas,* eds. T. F. Dillon Croker & Stephen Tucker, 5 vols., London: Samuel French, 1879, II, [64]-103. *Filed under* Collected Works.

Sleeping Beauty in the Wood, The. London: S. G. Fairbrother (printer), n.d. Pp. [1]-32.

Somebody Else. New York & London: Samuel French, n.d. Pp. [1]-26.

Spring Gardens. London: John Dicks, n.d. Pp. [1]-11. Dicks' Standard Plays, 997.

Stirring the Pudding. In *Pieces of Pleasantry for Private Performance,* London & New York: Samuel French, n.d., pp. [1]-18. *Filed under* Pieces of Pleasantry.

Success; or, A Hit If You Like It. In *Extravaganzas,* eds. T. F. Dillon Croker & Stephen Tucker, 5 vols., London: Samuel French, 1879, I, [1]-36. *Filed under* Collected Works.

Telemachus; or, The Island of Calypso. Written with Dance, Charles. In *Extravaganzas,* eds. T. F. Dillon Croker & Stephen Tucker, 5 vols., London: Samuel French, 1879, I, [171]-204. *Filed under* Collected Works.

Telemachus; or, The Island of Calypso. Written with Dance, Charles. London: Thomas Hailes Lacy, n.d. Pp. [1]-28.

Theseus and Ariadne; or, The Marriage of Bacchus. In *Extravaganzas,* eds. T. F. Dillon Croker & Stephen Tucker, 5 vols., London: Samuel French, 1879, III, [224]-260. *Filed under* Collected Works.

Thierna-Na-Oge; or, The Prince of the Lakes. Music by Cooke, Thomas. London: Harjette & Savill (printer), 1829. Pp. [1]-18. Libretto.

Two Figaros, The. London: Chapman & Hall, n.d. Pp. [i]-iv, [5]-44. [Acting National Drama, I].

Vampire, The; or, The Bride of the Isles. London: John Lowndes, 1820. Pp. [1]-36.

Vampire, The; or, The Bride of the Isles. London: John Cumberland, n.d. Pp. [1]-42. Cumberland's British Theatre, XXVII. *Filed under* Cumberland, John. Cumberland's British Theatre, XXVII.

White Cat, The. In *Extravaganzas,* eds. T. F. Dillon Croker & Stephen Tucker, 5 vols., London: Samuel French, 1879, II, [143]-178. *Filed under* Collected Works.

White Cat, The. London: S. G. Fairbrother (printer), n.d. Pp. [i-vi], [1]-28.

Who's Your Friend?; or, The Queensberry Fete. New York: Harold Roorbach, n.d. Pp. [i-iv], [5]-36. Acting Drama, 45.

Yellow Dwarf and the King of the Gold Mines, The. In *Extravaganzas,* eds. T. F. Dillon Croker & Stephen Tucker, 5 vols., London: Samuel French, 1879, V, [35]-74. *Filed under* Collected Works.

Yellow Dwarf and the King of the Gold Mines, The. London & New York: Samuel French, n.d. Pp. [1]-39.

Young and Handsome. In *Extravaganzas,* eds. T. F. Dillon Croker & Stephen Tucker, 5 vols., London: Samuel French, 1879, V, [147]-192. *Filed under* Collected Works.

PLANCHÉ, JAMES ROBINSON (arr.)

Spanish Curate, The. By Beaumont, Francis; Fletcher, John. London: S. G. Fairbrother (printer), n.d. Pp. [1]-59. 2nd ed.

Woman Never Vext, A; or, The Widow of Cornhill. By Rowley, William. London: T. Dolby, 1825. Pp. [i]-[vi], [7]-72. Dolby's British Theatre, VIII. *Filed under* Cumberland, John. Cumberland's British Theatre, VIII.

Woman Never Vext, A; or, The Widow of Cornhill. By Rowley, William. London: T. Dolby, n.d. Pp. [i]-[x], [1]-64.

PLATONIC ATTACHMENTS
See Bernard, William Bayle.

PLATT, ARTHUR

Marpessa. Cambridge: Deighton, Bell, 1888. Pp. [i-viii], [1]-39.

PLATT, WILLIAM

Youth's Love-Lore. London: A. Bonner (printer) (priv.), 1896. Pp. [iii]-[xvi], 17-34.

PLAY
See Robertson, Thomas William.

PLAY IN LITTLE, A
See Robertson, Ian.

PLAYFAIR, GEORGE MACDONALD HOME

Best Man, The. Shanghai: Kelly & Walsh (printer), 1895. Pp. [i-ii], [1]-37.

PLAYING WITH FIRE
See Brougham, John.

PLAYMATES
See Warburton, H.

PLEASANT COURTSHIP, A
See Long, Charles.

PLEASANT DREAMS
See Dance, Charles.

PLEASANT NEIGHBOUR, A
See Planché, Elizabeth (Eliza) St. George, Mrs. James Robinson

PLEASE TO REMEMBER THE GROTTO
See Oxenford, John.

PLEASURES AND PUNISHMENTS OF CARTHUSIAN REVELS
See Bubble and Squeak (anon.).

PLEASURES OF ANARCHY, THE
See Newham, Francis, Rev.

PLEDGE, THE
See Kenney, James.

PLEDGE OF HONOUR
See Kenney, James. Hernani.

PLEON, HARRY

After the Show. In *Pleon's Peculiar Parodies on Popular Plays and Pieces,* 5th Series, London: Howard, n.d., pp. [1]-12. *Filed under* Pleon's Peculiar Parodies on Popular Plays and Pieces.

Been Had. London: John Dicks, n.d. Pp. [1]-20. Dicks' Standard Plays, 1026.

Black-Eyed Susan; or, 'Twas in Trafalgar Square. In *Pleon's Peculiar Parodies on Popular Plays and Pieces,* 5th Series, London: Howard, n.d., pp. 13-22. *Filed under* Pleon's Peculiar Parodies on Popular Plays and Pieces.

Last Day of Napoleon, The.
See Morton, J. Russell.

Muldoon's Picnic. London: John Dicks, n.d. Pp. [1]-13. Dicks' Standard Plays, 1022.

North East Lynne; or, Carlisle and Back for Two Bob. In *Pleon's Peculiar Parodies on Popular Plays and Pieces,* 5th Series, London: Howard, n.d., pp. 23-31. *Filed under* Pleon's Peculiar Parodies on Popular Plays and Pieces.

On the Brain. London: John Dicks, n.d. Pp. [1]-8. Dicks' Standard Plays, 1024.

Peck's Bad Boy. London: John Dicks, n.d. Pp. [1]-16. Dicks' Standard Plays, 1063.

Recitations, Rhymes, and Ridiculosities. London: Howard, 1892. Pp. [i]-[viii], [9]-38.

Vision of Venus, A; or, A Midsummer-Night's Nightmare. London: John Dicks, n.d. Pp. [1]-11. Dicks' Standard Plays, 1025.

Waiter, The; or, All Comes to He Who Waits. London: John Dicks, n.d. Pp. [9]-16. Dicks' Standard Plays, 1024. *Filed under* On the Brain.

PLOT AND COUNTERPLOT
See Kemble, Charles.

PLOT AND PASSION
See Taylor, Tom.

PLOT DISCOVERED
See Otway, Thomas. Venice Preserved.

PLOT FOR PLOT
See Young, Charles Lawrence, Sir.

PLOTS!
See Arnold, Samuel James.

PLOTS FOR PETTICOATS
See Wooler, John Pratt.

PLOTS IN CALCUTTA
See Rival Uncle, The.

PLOWDEN, DOROTHEA PHILLIPS, MRS. FRANCIS
Virginia. Music by Plowden, Dorothea. London: J. Barker, 1800. Pp. [i]-[xiv], [1]-63. Libretto.

PLOWMAN, THOMAS F.
Very New Edition of Acis and Galatea, A; or, The Beau! the Belle! and the Blacksmith! London: Thomas Hailes Lacy, n.d. Pp. [1]-34.

PLUM-PUDDING PANTOMIME, THE
See Mayhew, Horace.

PLUMPTRE, EDWARD HAYNES
Master and Scholar. London & New York: Alexander Strahan, 1866. Pp. [i-ii], [1]-46.

PLUNKET, LOUISA LELIAS
See Greene, Louisa Lelias Plunket, Mrs. Richard Jonas (Baroness).

PLUNKETT, HENRY WILLOUGHBY GRATTAN
See Grattan, H. P. (pseud.).

PLUNKETT, MRS. JAMES
See Gunning, Elizabeth.

PLUTO AND PROSERPINE
See Talfourd, Francis.

POACHER'S DOOM, THE
See Pitt, George Dibdin.

POACHER'S WIFE, THE
See Atkyns, Samuel.

PO-CA-HON-TAS
See Brougham, John.

POCOCK, ISAAC
Alfred the Great; or, The Enchanted Standard. London: John Miller, 1827. Pp. [i-iv], [1]-45.

Antiquary, The. Written with Terry, Daniel. London: William Stockdale, 1820. Pp. [iii]-[x], [1]-64.

Antiquary, The. Written with Terry, Daniel. London: John Cumberland, n.d. Pp. [1]-77. Cumberland's British Theatre, XXXI. *Filed under* Cumberland, John. Cumberland's British Theatre, XXXI.

Any Thing New. Music by Smith, C. London: J. Barker, 1811. Pp. [1]-47.

Cent. per Cent.; or, The Masquerade. London: J. Lowndes, n.d. Pp. [i], [1]-37.

Cent. per Cent.; or, The Masquerade. London: J. Lowndes, n.d. Pp. [i], [1]-37. 2nd ed.

Don Juan; or, The Libertine. *Also:* The Libertine. Music by Mozart. London: Goulding, D'Almaine, Potter, n.d. Pp. [i], 1-58. Vocal score.

For England, Ho! London: John Miller, 1814. Pp. [i-vi], [1]-42.

For England, Ho! London: John Cumberland, n.d. Pp. [1]-37. Cumberland's British Theatre, XXXIX. *Filed under* Cumberland, John. Cumberland's British Theatre, XXXIX.

Hit or Miss! London: W. H. Wyatt, 1810. Pp. [1]-48. Final page supplied in typescript.

Hit or Miss! London: Sherwood, Neely, & Jones, 1818. Pp. [1]-40. London Theatre, XXIV. *Filed under* Dibdin, Thomas John, ed. London Theatre, XXIV.

Hit or Miss. London: John Cumberland, n.d. Pp. [1]-34. Cumberland's British Theatre, XXXIV. *Filed under* Cumberland, John. Cumberland's British Theatre, XXXIV.

Home, Sweet Home!; or, The Ranz des Vaches. Music by Bishop, Henry. London: S. R. Kirby, 1829. Pp. [i-iv], [1]-37.

John of Paris. London: John Miller, 1814. Pp. [3]-45. Libretto.

John of Paris. London: John Cumberland, n.d. Pp. [1]-39. Cumberland's British Theatre, XXVI. *Filed under* Cumberland, John. Cumberland's British Theatre, XXVI.

King Arthur and the Knights of the Round Table. Music by Cooke, T. London: John Miller, 1834. Pp. [i]-[vi], [7]-16. Libretto.

Libertine, The. *Also:* Don Juan; or, The Libertine. Music by Mozart. London: John Miller, 1817. Pp. [i-ii], [1]-46. 2nd ed. Libretto.

Libertine, The. Music by Mozart. London: John Miller, 1817. Pp. [i-ii], [1]-46. Libretto. *Filed under* Bishop, Henry.

Magpie or the Maid?, The. London: John Cumberland, n.d. Pp. [1]-48. Cumberland's British Theatre, XXVIII. *Filed under* Cumberland, John. Cumberland's British Theatre, XXVIII.

Magpie or the Maid?, The. Music by Bishop, Henry. London: John Miller, 1815. Pp. [i-iv], [1]-52.

Miller and His Men, The. Music by Bishop, Henry. London: C. Chapple, 1813. Pp. [3]-46. 2nd ed. Promptbook.

Miller and His Men, The. In *British Drama*, 12 vols., London: John Dicks, 1864, II, [356]-367.

Miller and His Men, The. London: John Cumberland, n.d. Pp. [1]-48. Cumberland's British Theatre, XXVI. *Filed under* Cumberland, John. Cumberland's British Theatre, XXVI.

Montrose; or, The Children of the Mist. Music by Bishop; Ware; Watson. London: W. Simpkin & R. Marshall, 1822. Pp. [i-ii], [1]-70.

Nigel; or, The Crown Jewels. London: R. Wilks (printer), 1823. Pp. [i]-[viii], [1]-[98].

Omnibus, The; or, A Convenient Distance. London: John Dicks, n.d. Pp. [1]-9. Dicks' Standard Plays, 725.

Rob Roy MacGregor; or, Auld Lang Syne! New York: D. Longworth, 1818. Pp. [1]-66.

Rob Roy MacGregor; or, Auld Lang Syne. In *New English Drama*, ed. W. Oxberry, 22 vols., London: W. Simpkin & R. Marshall; C. Chapple, 1820, X, [1-2], [i]-[vi], [1]-69. *Filed under* Oxberry, William Henry. New English Drama, X.

Rob Roy MacGregor; or, Auld Lang Syne. In *British Drama*, 12 vols., London: John Dicks, 1864, II, [447]-466.

Robber's Wife, The. London: Music Publishing Company, n.d. Pp. [1]-40. Promptbook.

Robber's Wife, The. London: John Cumberland, n.d. Pp. [i], [1]-40. Cumberland's British Theatre, XXVIII. *Filed under* Cumberland, John. Cumberland's British Theatre, XXVIII.

Robinson Crusoe; or, The Bold Bucaniers. Music by Ware. London: John Miller, 1817. Pp. [i-iv], [1]-48.

Robinson Crusoe; or, The Bold Buccaniers. London: John Cumberland, n.d. Pp. [1]-41. Cumberland's British Theatre, XXVIII. *Filed under* Cumberland, John. Cumberland's British Theatre, XXVIII.

Twenty Years Ago! Music by Welsh, T. London: W. H. Wyatt, 1810. Pp. [3]-40.

Who Wants a Wife?; or, The Law of the Land. London: Goulding, D'Almaine, Potter, n.d. Pp. [i], [1]-25. Vocal score selections. *Filed under* Bishop, Henry.

Woodstock. London: John Miller, 1826. Pp. [i]-[x], [1]-86.

Yes or No? Music by Smith, C. London: J. Barker, 1809. Pp. [1]-38.

Zembuca; or, The Net-Maker and His Wife. Music by Ware. London: John Miller, 1815. Pp. [i-vi], [1]-50.

POEL, WILLIAM

    Absence of Mind; or, Wanted: Five Pounds. London & New York: Samuel French, n.d. Pp. [1]-23. [Lacy's Acting Edition].

    Man of Forty, The. London & New York: Samuel French, n.d. Pp. [1]-20.

    Wayside Cottage, The. London & New York: Samuel French, n.d. Pp. [1]-15.

POEM, THE

    See Crowley, Edward Aleister.

POET, THE

    See Boudousquie, Gabriel.

POET AND THE PUPPETS, THE

    See Brookfield, Charles Hallam Elton.

POET'S CHILD, THE

    See Hill, Isabel.

POET'S FATE

    See Stephens, George. Philip Basil.

POETIC PROPOSAL, A

    See Becher, Martin.

POINT OF HONOUR

    See Clarke, Clara Savile.

    See Kemble, Charles.

POISON TREE, THE

    See Clarke, Stephen.

POISONED

    See Amcotts, Vincent.

POISONED CROWN

    See Reynoldson, Thomas Herbert. Rich Man of Frankfort, The.

POISONED PEARL

    See Robertson, Thomas William. Half Caste, The.

POISONER!

    See Barber, James. Dame de St. Tropez!, La.

POLACK, ELIZABETH

    Esther, the Royal Jewess; or, The Death of Haman! London: John Duncombe, n.d. Pp. [1]-30. Duncombe's Edition.

    St. Clair of the Isles; or, The Outlaw of Barra. London: James Pattie, n.d. Pp. [1]-[51].

POLE, THE POLICEMAN, AND THE POLAR BEAR

    See Bellingham, Henry. Arline, the Lost Child.

POLINICES

    See Lloyd, Charles (trans.).

POLISH JEW, THE

    See Ware, James Redding.

POLKA, LA

    See Barnett, Charles Zachary.

POLKAMANIA

    See Stocqueler, Joachim Hayward.

POLL AND PARTNER JOE

    See Burnand, Francis Cowley.

POLLOCK, ELLEN, MRS. JULIUS

    See Harley, St. John (pseud.).

POLLOCK, WALTER HERRIES

    Charm, The.

        See Besant, Walter.

    Chicot the Jester. N.p.: n.pub., n.d. Pp. [2]-33, [1]-32. Title page lacking.

    Glove, The.

        See Besant, Walter.

    King and Artist.

        See Moubrey, Lilian.

    Loved I Not Honour More.

        See Besant, Walter.

    Peer and Heiress.

        See Besant, Walter.

    Shrinking Shoe, The.

        See Besant, Walter.

    Spy, The.

        See Besant, Walter.

    Voice of Love, The.

        See Besant, Walter.

    Were-Wolf, The.

        See Moubrey, Lilian.

    Wife's Confession, The.

        See Besant, Walter.

POLLOCK, WALTER HERRIES (arr.)

    Dead Heart, The: A Story of the French Revolution. By Phillips, Watts. London & New York: Samuel French, 1889. Pp. [1]-57.

POLLY HONEYCOMBE

    See Colman, George, sr.

POLYPHEME'S PASSION

    See Buchanan, Robert Williams.

POLYPUS (pseud.)

    See Barrett, Eaton Stannard.

POLYXENA

    See Proby, John Joshua, Earl of Carysfort.

POOLE, JOHN

    Atonement; or, The God-Daughter. London: John Miller, 1836. Pp [i]-[viii], [1]-44.

    Deaf as a Post. New York: E. B. Clayton, n.d. Pp. [1]-31. Clayton's Edition.

    Delicate Attentions. London: W. Strange, 1837. Pp. [1]-30. Promptbook.

    Delicate Attentions. London: John Duncombe, n.d. Pp. [1]-30. Duncombe's Edition.

    Dutch Governor, The.

        See 'Twould Puzzle a Conjuror.

    Earls of Hammersmith, The.

        See Lawler, Dennis.

    Hamlet Travestie. London: J. M. Richardson, 1810. Pp. [i]-[xvi], [1]-94.

    Hole in the Wall, The. London: J. M. Richardson, 1813. Pp. [i]-[viii], [1]-42.

    Intrigue. London: John Miller, 1814. Pp. [i-iii], [1]-26.

    Lodgings for Single Gentlemen. London: Thomas Hailes Lacy, n.d. Pp. [1]-30.

    Married and Single. London: John Miller, 1824. Pp. [i]-[xvi], [1]-67.

    Match Making. London: John Dicks, n.d. Pp. [1]-10. Dicks' Standard Plays, 522.

    My Wife!—What Wife? London & New York: Samuel French, n.d. Pp. [1]-30. [Lacy's Acting Edition].

    Nabob for an Hour, A. *Also:* Uncle Sam; or, A Nabob for an Hour. London: John Duncombe, n.d. Pp. [7]-30. Text complete. Duncombe's Edition.

    Old and Young. London: John Cumberland, n.d. Pp. [1]-30. [Cumberland's British Theatre].

    Old and Young. London: John Cumberland, n.d. Pp. [1]-30. Cumberland's British Theatre, XXX. *Filed under* Cumberland, John. Cumberland's British Theatre, XXX.

    Past and Present; or, The Hidden Treasure. London: Thomas Hailes Lacy, n.d. Pp. [1]-46. [Lacy's Acting Edition].

    Patrician and Parvenu; or, Confusion Worse Confounded. London: John Miller, 1835. Pp. [iii]-[xii], [1]-83.

    Paul Pry. New York: William Taylor, n.d. Pp. [i]-[vii], [8]-69. Modern Standard Drama, 76. Promptbook.

    Scan. Mag!; or, The Village Gossip. Philadelphia: Turner & Fisher, n.d. Pp. [1]-34. Fisher's Edition of Standard Farces.

    Scapegoat, The. In *British Drama,* 12 vols., London: John Dicks, 1872, XII, [120]-128.

    Scapegoat, The. London: Thomas Hailes Lacy, n.d. Pp. [1]-22. [Lacy's Acting Edition].

    Short Reign, and a Merry One, A. London: John Miller, 1819. Pp. [i-iv], [1]-49.

    Simpson and Co. New York: William Taylor, n.d. Pp. [i]-[vi], [7]-39. Modern Standard Drama, 60.

    Simpson and Co. London: Thomas Hailes Lacy, n.d. Pp. [1]-42.

    Soldier's Courtship, A. London: John Miller, 1833. Pp. [1]-28.

    Tribulation; or, Unwelcome Visitors. London: Thomas Dolby, 1825. Pp. [i]-[viii], [1]-45.

    Tribulation; or, Unwelcome Visitors. London: Thomas Dolby, 1825. Pp. [1]-42. Dolby's British Theatre, XII.

Filed under Cumberland, John. Cumberland's British Theatre, XII.

Turning the Tables. London: John Duncombe, n.d. Pp. [1]-28.

Two Pages of Frederick the Great, The. London: W. Simpkin & R. Marshall, n.d. Pp. [i-iv], [1]-42.

'Twould Puzzle a Conjuror. *Also:* The Dutch Governor. New York: William Taylor, n.d. Pp. [1]-36. Modern Standard Drama, 47. Promptbook.

Uncle Sam; or, A Nabob for an Hour. *Also:* A Nabob for an Hour. Philadelphia: F. Turner, n.d. Pp. [1]-31. Turner's Dramatic Library. Promptbook.

Uncle Sam; or, A Nabob for an Hour. *Also:* A Nabob for an Hour. Philadelphia: F. Turner, n.d. Pp. [1]-31. Turner's Dramatic Library.

Wealthy Widow, The; or, They're Both to Blame. London: John Miller, n.d. Pp. [iii]-[viii], [1]-61. Page numbers trimmed off.

Who's Who?; or, The Double Imposture. London: Whittingham & Arliss, 1815. Pp. [1]-40.

Year in an Hour, A; or, The Cock of the Walk. London: John Miller, 1824. Pp. [i-iv], [1]-28.

POOLE, W. HOWELL

    Game of Life, The. Pp. [i], [1]-51. Typescript.

    Wheel of Fortune, The. Pp. [1]-58. Typescript.

POOR COUSIN WALTER

    See Simpson, John Palgrave.

POOR GENTLEMAN, THE

    See Colman, George, jr.

POOR GIRL'S STORY!

    See Stirling, Edward. Lilly Dawson.

POOR JO

    See Lander, George. Bleak House.

POOR MAN'S HONOUR

    See Hazlewood, Colin Henry. Emerald Heart, The.

POOR NOBLEMAN, THE

    See Selby, Charles.

POOR OF NEW YORK, THE

    See Boucicault, Dionysius Lardner.

POOR OLD PERKINS

    See Sykes, Percival H. T.

POOR PILLICODDY

    See Morton, John Maddison.

POOR SOLDIER, THE

    See O'Keeffe, John.

POPE OF ROME, THE

    See Boucicault, Dionysius Lardner.

POPOCATAPETL

    See Robson, Frederick.

POPPING IN AND OUT

    See Stirling, Edward.

POPPING THE QUESTION

    See Buckstone, John Baldwin.

POPPLETON'S PREDICAMENTS

    See Rae, Charles Marsham.

PORCHESTER, LORD

    See Herbert, Henry John George.

PORK CHOPS

    See Blanchard, Edward Litt Leman.

PORT ADMIRAL, THE

    See Bowles, Thomas Gibson.

PORTER, HELEN TRACY LOWE, MRS. (trans.)

    Three Heron's Feathers, The. By Sudermann, Hermann. In *Poet-Lore,* New Series IV (April-June 1900), [161]-234.

PORTER OF HAVRE, THE

    See Oxenford, John.

PORTER'S KNOT, THE

    See Oxenford, John.

PORTFOLIO, THE

    See Kenney, James.

PORTRAIT OF CERVANTES

    See Kemble, Charles. Plot and Counterplot.

PORTRAIT OF MICHAEL CERVANTES

    See Kemble, Charles. Plot and Counterplot.

POSSESSION NINE POINTS OF THE LAW

    See Lover, Samuel. MacCarthy More.

POST-BOY, THE

    See Craven, Henry Thornton.

POST-BOY OF CORNWALL, THE

    See Hart, James P.

POST CAPTAIN, THE

    See Townsend, William Thompson.

POST OF HONOUR, THE

    See Mildenhall, Thomas.

POSTILLION OF LONJUMEAU, THE

    See A'Beckett, Gilbert Abbott.

POSTMAN'S KNOCK, THE

    See Thornton, L. M.

POSTMASTER'S WIFE AND THE MAYOR'S DAUGHTER

    See Moncrieff, William Thomas. Diamond Arrow, The.

POSTSCRIPT, THE

    See Hamilton-Knight, F.

POT-POURRI

    See Tanner, James Tolman.

POTTER, ROBERT (trans.)

    Alcestis. By Euripides. In *Alcestis and Other Plays,* London: George Routledge & Sons, n.d., pp. [1]-45. Morley's Universal Library, 54.

    Electra. By Euripides. In *Alcestis and Other Plays,* London: George Routledge & Sons, n.d., pp. [47]-91. Morley's Universal Library, 54.

    Iphigenia in Aulis. By Euripides. In *Alcestis and Other Plays,* London: George Routledge & Sons, n.d., pp. [145]-198. Morley's Universal Library, 54.

    Iphigenia in Tauris. By Euripides. In *Alcestis and Other Plays,* London: George Routledge & Sons, n.d., pp. [199]-244. Morley's Universal Library, 54.

    Orestes. By Euripides. In *Alcestis and Other Plays,* London: George Routledge & Sons, n.d., pp. [93]-144. Morley's Universal Library, 54.

    Trojan Dames, The. By Euripides. In *Alcestis and Other Plays,* London: George Routledge & Sons, n.d., pp. [245]-286. Morley's Universal Library, 54.

POUL A DHOIL

    See Hazlewood, Colin Henry.

POULE AUX OEUFS D'OR, LA (anon. trans.)

    By Dennery, Adolphe; Clairville (pseud.). London: London Co-operative Printing & Stationery Co., n.d. Pp. [1]-43. Libretto.

POUPÉE, LA

    See Sturgess, Arthur.

POUTER'S WEDDING

    See Morton, John Maddison.

POWDER AND BALL

    See Selby, Charles.

POWELL, JAMES

    Venetian Outlaw, The: His Country's Friend. London: M. Allen, 1805. Pp. [i]-[vi], [9]-75. Text complete.

POWELL, THOMAS

    Blind Wife, The; or, The Student of Bonn. London: W. E. Painter, 1843. Pp. [i-iv], [1]-151.

    Doria. In *Dramatic Poems,* London: C. Mitchell, 1845, pp. [i-iv], [1]-60.

    Marguerite. London: C. Mitchell, 1844. Pp. [1]-39.

    Shepherd's Well, The. London: Effingham Wilson, 1843. Pp. [i-iv], [1]-58.

    True at Last. London: C. Mitchell, 1844. Pp. [i-iv], [1]-124.

POWELL, THOMAS (of Monmouth)

    Camillus and Columna; or, The Sleeping Beauty. London: C. Roworth (printer), 1806. Pp. [1]-142.

POWER, TYRONE

    Born to Good Luck; or, The Irishman's Fortune. New York: William Taylor, n.d. Pp. [3]-39. Minor Drama, 45.

    How to Pay the Rent. London: Sherwood, Gilbert, & Piper, n.d. Pp. [1]-24. [Webster's Acting National Drama, 97].

    Married Lovers. Baltimore: J. Robinson, 1831. Pp. [1]-42. Promptbook.

Paddy Carey; or, The Boy of Clogheen. New York: Samuel French, n.d. Pp. [1]-15. French's American Drama, 22. Promptbook.

St. Patrick's Eve; or, The Order of the Day. London & New York: Samuel French, n.d. Pp. [1]-50. Minor Drama, 15.

POWER AND PRINCIPLE
See Barnett, Morris.

POWER OF LOVE
See Brough, William. Hercules and Omphale.
See Harris, Augustus Glossop. Santanella.

POWLES, LOUIS DISTON
Opera Cloak, The. Written with Harris, Augustus Henry Glossop. London: J. B. Day, 1877. Pp. [1]-28.

PRABODHA CHANDRODAYA
See Taylor, J. (trans.).

PRACTICAL MAN, A
See Bernard, William Bayle.

PRAED, ROSA CAROLINE MURRAY-PRIOR, MRS. CAMPBELL
Affinities. Written with Jopling, Louise Goode, Mrs. Joseph Middleton (later Mrs. Rowe). London: Richard Bentley & Son, 1885. Pp. [i-ii], [1]-17.

PRAYER OF THE WRECKED AND THE GOLD-SEEKER OF MEXICO
See Robertson, Thomas William. Sea of Ice, The.

PRECIEUSES RIDICULES
See Van Laun, Henri (trans.). Pretentious Young Ladies, The.

PRECIOSA
See Troutbeck, John, Rev. (trans.).

PRECIOSITA
See Dorisi, Lisa.

PREJUDICE VANQUISHED
See Mérimée, Prosper. Ines Mendo, Part 1.

'PRENTICE PILLAR, THE
See Eden, Guy Ernest Morton.

PRESENTATION IN THE TEMPLE, THE
See Hinkson, Katharine Tynan, Mrs. Henry Albert.

PRESENTED AT COURT
See Coyne, Joseph Stirling.

PRESERVED VENICE
See Anstey, F.

PREST, THOMAS PECKETT
Miser of Shoreditch, The. London: Thomas Hailes Lacy, n.d. Pp. [1]-36. Lacy's Acting Edition, 267. Promptbook.

PRESUMPTIVE EVIDENCE
See Boucicault, Dionysius Lardner. Mercy Dodd.
See Buckstone, John Baldwin.

PRESUMPTIVE GUILT
See Kerr, John.

PRETENDER, THE
See Stafford, John Joseph.

PRETENDERS, THE
See Archer, William (trans.).

PRETENTIOUS YOUNG LADIES, THE
See Van Laun, Henri (trans.).

PRETTY DRUIDESS, THE
See Gilbert, William Schwenck.

PRETTY GIRLS OF STILLBERG, THE
See Webster, Benjamin Nottingham.

PRETTY GREEN BIRD AND THE FAIRIES OF THE DANCING WATERS
See Green, Frank William. Cherry and Fairstar.

PRETTY HORSEBREAKER, THE
See Brough, William.

PRETTY JANE!, THE CRUEL SQUIRE!, AND ROBIN THE PLOUGHMAN!, THE
See Smith, John.

PRETTY PIECE OF BUSINESS, A
See Morton, Thomas, jr.

PRETTY PIECE OF CHISELLING
See Albery, James. Alexander the Great.

PRETTY POLL OF PORTSEA AND THE CAPTAIN WITH HIS WHISKERS
See Byron, Henry James. Mendacious Mariner, The.

PRETTY PREDICAMENTS
See Phipps, A. J.

PRETTY PRINCESS AND THE FAIRY OF THE DANCING WATER
See Brough, William. Froggee Would a Wooing Go.

PRETTY PRINCESS AND THE PRECIOUS GREAT SCAMP
See Conquest, George. Aladdin, the Lad with the Wonderful Lamp.

PRETTY PRINCESS AND THE PRICKLY PEAR
See Fitzgerald, Shafto Justin Adair.

PREVENTION NO CURE
See Miller, Luke.

PREVOST, CONSTANCE M.
Meadowsweet. London: Samuel French; New York: T. Henry French, n.d. Pp. [1]-22. [Lacy's Acting Edition].

PRICE OF LIFE
See Faucquez, Adolphe. Seventh Hour, The.

PRIDE (anon.)
London: Vinton & Son, 1878. Pp. [1]-73.

PRIDE
See Albery, James.

PRIDE MUST HAVE A FALL
See Brough, William. Phaeton.

PRIDE OF BIRTH
See Rodwell, George Herbert Bonaparte.
See Webster, Benjamin Nottingham. Belphegor the Mountebank.

PRIDE OF PUTNEY AND THE PRESSING PIRATE
See Burnand, Francis Cowley. Poll and Partner Joe.

PRIDE OF THE MARKET, THE
See Planché, James Robinson.

PRIDE OF THE OCEAN
See Rogers, William. Jack's the Lad.

PRIDE SHALL HAVE A FALL
See Croly, George, Rev.

PRIEST OF THE PARISH
See Cherry, Andrew. Spanish Dollars!

PRIMA DONNA
See Boucicault, Dionysius Lardner.
See Farnie, Henry Brougham.

PRINCE AMABEL
See Brough, William.

PRINCE ANANIAS
See Neilson, Francis.

PRINCE AND THE BREECHES MAKER!
See Moncrieff, William Thomas. Court of Queen Anne, The.

PRINCE AND THE CHIMNEY-SWEEPER
See Tooth-ache.

PRINCE AND THE PIPER
See Burnand, Francis Cowley. King of the Merrows.

PRINCE BRIGHTKIN
See Allingham, William.

PRINCE CAMARALZAMAN
See Bellingham, Henry.

PRINCE CHERRY AND PRINCESS FAIR STAR
See Collins, Charles James.

PRINCE CROESUS IN SEARCH OF A WIFE
See Greene, Louisa Lilias Plunket, Mrs. Richard Jonas (Baroness).

PRINCE DORUS
See Taylor, Tom.

PRINCE EDWARD
See Mitford, Edward Ledwich.

PRINCE EDWIN AND THE FAIRIES OF THE THISTLE
See Lowe, William. Edina and the White Hart of the Lothians.

PRINCE FOR AN HOUR, A
See Morton, John Maddison.

PRINCE LARDI-DARDI AND THE RADIANT ROSETTA
See Burnand, Francis Cowley. White Cat!, The.

PRINCE LUCIFER
See Austin, Alfred.

PRINCE OF HAPPY LAND, THE
See Planché, James Robinson.

PRINCE OF SAUERKRAUTENBERG, THE
See Boyce, William.
PRINCE OF THE LAKES
See Planché, James Robinson. Thierna-Na-Oge.
PRINCE OR PEASANT
See Adams, Florence Davenport.
PRINCE PRETTYPET AND THE BUTTERFLY
See Brough, William.
PRINCE, THE BUTTERFLY, AND THE BEETLE
See Brough, William. Papillonetta.
PRINCE, THE PIRATE, AND THE PEARL
See Byron, Henry James. Bride of Abydos, The.
PRINCE, THE PRINCESS, AND THE MANDARIN
See Martin, William. Chang-Ching-Fou! Cream of Tartar.
PRINCE'S PRESENT
See Kenney, James. Match Breaking.
PRINCELY BRIDE, THE
See Jameson, Anna Brownell Murphy, Mrs. Robert (trans.).
PRINCESS, THE (anon. arr.)
By Tennyson, Alfred, Lord. Boston: Walter H. Baker, c.1881. Pp. [1]-63.
PRINCESS, THE
See Gilbert, William Schwenck.
PRINCESS AND THE BUTTERFLY, THE
See Pinero, Arthur Wing.
PRINCESS CHARMING
See Arden, Henry T.
PRINCESS IDA
See Gilbert, William Schwenck.
PRINCESS MARGUERITE'S CHOICE
See Adams, Florence Davenport.
PRINCESS OF ELIS, THE
See Van Laun, Henri (trans.).
PRINCESS OF PARMESAN, THE
See Millais, W. H.
PRINCESS OF THE SEA! AND THE LITTLE FAIRY AT THE BOTTOM OF THE WELL
See Saville, Henry Faucitt. Harlequin King Crystal.
PRINCESS PRIMROSE AND THE FOUR PRETTY PRINCES
See Bellingham, Henry.
PRINCESS SPRING-TIME
See Byron, Henry James.
PRINCESS, THE PERI, AND THE TROUBADOUR
See Brough, William. Lalla Rookh.
PRINCESS TOTO
See Gilbert, William Schwenck.
PRINCESS WHO WAS BLIND OF ONE EYE AND COULD NOT SEE OUT OF THE OTHER
See Bosbacca, Gulielmerg Henricus. King Zany's Daughter.
PRINCESS WITH THE RAVEN LOCKS
See Vernier, Isabella. Barber and the Bravo, The.
PRINCESSE D'ÉLIDE
See Van Laun, Henri (trans.). Princess of Elis, The.
PRINCESSES IN THE TOWER, THE
See Talfourd, Francis.
PRINTER'S DEVIL, THE
See Planché, James Robinson.
PRINTER'S DEVIL, THE; OR, A TYPE OF THE OLD ONE (anon.)
London: John Duncombe, n.d. Pp. [i-ii], [1]-18. Duncombe's Edition.
PRIOR CLAIM
See Lancaster, Florence.
See Pye, Henry James.
PRISON AND PALACE
See Simpson, John Palgrave.
PRISON-HULK
See Brougham, John. Miller of New Jersey, The.
PRISONER AT LARGE, THE
See O'Keeffe, John.

PRISONER-KING
See Serle, Thomas James. Windsor Castle.
PRISONER OF ROCHELLE
See Hartwell, Henry. Castle of Sorrento, The.
See Pitt, George Dibdin.
PRISONER OF SHLUSSELBOURG
See Selby, Charles. Lioness of the North, The.
PRISONER OF STATE
See Stirling, Edward.
PRISONER OF TOULON, THE
See Richards, Alfred Bate.
PRISONER OF VINCENNES
See Archer, Thomas. Red Cap, The.
PRISONER OF WAR, THE
See Jerrold, Douglas William.
See Maclaren, Archibald.
PRIVATE AND CONFIDENTIAL
See Planché, James Robinson. Court Favour.
PRIVATE INQUIRY, A
See Webster, Benjamin, jr.
PRIVATE SECRETARY, THE
See Hawtrey, Charles Henry.
PRIVATE THEATRE, THE
See Maclaren, Archibald.
PRIVATE VIEW, A
See Ferrers, Ernest.
PRIZE, THE
See Hoare, Prince.
PROBY, JOHN JOSHUA, EARL OF CARYSFORT
Caius Gracchus. In *Dramatic and Narrative Poems,* 2 vols., London: J. Mackinlay, 1810, I, [i-iv], [1]-105. *Filed under* Carysfort, John Joshua Proby, Earl of. Collected Works.
Fall of Carthage, The. In *Dramatic and Narrative Poems,* 2 vols., London: J. Mackinlay, 1810, I, [213]-285. *Filed under* Carysfort, John Joshua Proby, Earl of. Collected Works.
Monimia. In *Dramatic and Narrative Poems,* 2 vols., London: J. Mackinlay, 1810, I, [107]-212. *Filed under* Carysfort, John Joshua Proby, Earl of. Collected Works.
Polyxena. In *Dramatic and Narrative Poems,* 2 vols., London: J. Mackinlay, 1810, I, [287]-393. *Filed under* Carysfort, John Joshua Proby, Earl of. Collected Works.
PROCRIS
See Cheltnam, Charles Smith.
PROCTER, BRYAN WALLER
See Cornwall, Barry.
PRODIGAL DAUGHTER, THE
See Pettitt, Henry Alfred.
PRODIGAL SON
See Webb, Charles (trans.). Azael, the Prodigal.
See Willett, Ernest Noddall.
PRODIGO
See Webb, Charles (trans.). Azael, the Prodigal.
PROFESSOR, THE
See Abel, William Henry.
PROFESSOR'S LOVE STORY, THE
See Barrie, James Mathew.
PROFETA VELATO
See Squire, William Barclay. Veiled Prophet, The.
PROFLIGATE, THE
See Pinero, Arthur Wing.
See Taylor, George Watson.
PROGRESS
See Robertson, Thomas William.
PROLOGUE
See Jerrold, Douglas William. Nell Gwynne.
PROMETHEUS
See Reece, Robert.
PROMETHEUS AND PANDORA
See Planché, James Robinson. Olympic Revels.
PROMETHEUS BOUND
See Browning, Elizabeth Barrett (trans.).
See Pember, Edward Henry (trans.).
See Webster, Augusta Davies, Mrs. Thomas (trans.).

PROMETHEUS THE FIRE-BRINGER
See Horne, Richard Hengist.
PROMETHEUS THE FIRE-GIVER
See Bennett, William Cox.
PROMETHEUS UNBOUND
See Shelley, Percy Bysshe.
PROMISE OF MAY, THE
See Tennyson, Alfred, Lord.
PROMISSORY NOTE, THE
See Beazley, Samuel, jr.
PROMOTION
See Planché, James Robinson.
PROMPTER PUZZLED
See Lunn, Joseph. Management.
PROMPTER'S BOX, THE
See Byron, Henry James.
PROOF
See Burnand, Francis Cowley.
PROOF OF THE PUDDING, THE
See Bayly, Thomas Haynes.
PROPHET OF THE MOOR
See Almar, George. Fire Raiser, The.
PROPHET'S CURSE, THE
See Markwell, W. R. S.
PROPHÈTE, LE
See Maggioni, Manfredo (trans.).
See Tibbert, J. W. (trans.).
PROPHETESS, THE
See Galt, John.
PROPHETESS OF ORDSALL CAVE!
See Stirling, Edward. Guido Fawkes.
PROTECTOR!, THE
See Smith, John Frederick.
PROUD YOUNG PORTER AND THE FAIR SOPHIA
See Byron, Henry James. Lord Bateman.
PROVOKED HUSBAND, THE
See Vanbrugh, John.
PROVOKED WIFE, THE
See Vanbrugh, John.
PROVOST OF BRUGES, THE
See Lovell, George William.
PROVOST OF PARIS
See Oxberry, William Henry. Truand Chief!, The.
PRUDE'S PROGRESS, THE
See Jerome, Jerome Klapka.
PRYING LITTLE GIRL, THE (anon.)
In *Home Plays for Ladies*, Part 7, London & New York: Samuel French, n.d., pp. [29]-43. *Filed under* Home Plays for Ladies, Part 7.
PSYCHÉ
See Van Laun, Henri (trans.).
PSYCHE APOCALYPTÉ
See Browning, Elizabeth Barrett, Mrs. Robert.
PUBLIC MEN IN PRIVATE LIFE
See Snodgrass, Alfred. State Secrets.
PUBLIC PROSECUTOR, THE
See Bell, Florence Eveleen Eleanore Oliffe, Mrs. Hugh (Lady).
PUNCH
See Byron, Henry James.
PUNCH AND JUDY (anon.)
New York: Neal & Mackenzie, 1828. Pp. [1]-24.
PUNCH AND JUDY (anon.)
London: S. Prowett, 1828. Pp. [i-ii], [1]-111. *Filed under* Cruikshank, George.
PUNCHINELLO
See Farnie, Henry Brougham.
PUNCTURED
See Warren, T. Gideon.
PUPIL OF DA VINCI, THE
See Lemon, Mark.
PURE GOLD
See Marston, John Westland.
PURELY PLATONIC
See de Smart, Mrs. Alec.

PURGATORY OF ST. PATRICK, THE
See MacCarthy, Denis Florence (trans.).
PURITAN'S DAUGHTER, THE
See Bridgeman, John Vipon.
PURITANI, I
See Reece, Robert.
PURITANI E I CAVALIERI, I
See Puritans and the Cavaliers, The.
PURITANS AND THE CAVALIERS, THE (anon. trans.)
Also: Puritani e i Cavalieri, I. Music by Bellini. London: H. N. Millar, n.d. Pp. [1]-47. Libretto. *Filed under* Pepoli, S. C.
PURSE, THE
See Cross, John C.
PUSELEY, DANIEL
Honesty. In *New Plays by an Old Author*, London: Warren Hall & James J. Lovitt, 1876, pp. [101]-149. *Filed under* New Plays by an Old Author.
Intrigue; or, The Lost Jewels. In *New Plays by an Old Author*, London: Warren Hall & James J. Lovitt, 1876, pp. 55-99. *Filed under* New Plays by an Old Author.
King Richard the First. In *New Plays by an Old Author*, London: Warren Hall & James J. Lovitt, 1876, pp. [1]-54. *Filed under* New Plays by an Old Author.
PUSS
See Suter, William E. Woman That Was a Cat, The.
PUSS IN A NEW PAIR OF BOOTS
See Byron, Henry James.
PUSS IN BOOTS
See Blanchard, Edward Litt Leman.
See Bridgeman, John Vipon.
See Keating, Eliza H.
See Planché, James Robinson.
See Wood, Jay Hickory.
PYE, HENRY JAMES
Adelaide. London: John Stockdale, 1800. Pp. [i]-[xii], [9]-78.
Prior Claim, A. Written with Arnold, Samuel James. London: James Ridgway, 1805. Pp. [i]-[viii], [1]-[68].
PYGMALION
See Brough, William.
PYGMALION AND GALATEA
See Gilbert, William Schwenck.
PYTCHES, JOHN
Wounds Heal Wounds; or, Feeling, and Want of Feeling, Lamentations Disasters, and Prophecies. London: [John Cumberland], n.d. Pp. [i]-[vi], [1]-147.
Q. E. D.
See Marshall, Francis Albert.
QUADRILLE, THE; OR, A QUARREL, FOR WHAT? (anon.)
London: John Lowndes, 1819. Pp. [i-ii], [1]-29.
QUAKER, THE
See Dibdin, Charles, sr.
QUAKER'S WILL
See Dyall, Charles. Foxglove.
QUARREL, FOR WHAT?
See Quadrille, The (anon.).
QUARREL OF THE FLOWERS, THE
See Hodges, G. S.
QUARTER TO NINE, A
See Peake, Richard Brinsley.
QUASIMODO
See Fitzball, Edward.
QUEEN AND THE MOGUL, THE (anon.)
London: W. Benbow, 1820. Pp. [1]-24.
QUEEN BEE, THE
See Barrymore, William.
QUEEN BUSY BEE AND THE FIEND WOLF
See Harlequin Little Red Riding Hood and Prince Love the Day (anon.).
QUEEN ELIZABETH
See Gregg, Tresham Dames, Rev.
QUEEN FOR A DAY, A
See Haines, John Thomas.

QUEEN LADYBIRD AND HER CHILDREN; OR, HARLE-QUIN AND A HOUSE ON FIRE (anon.)
London: H. M. Arliss, 1860. Pp. [3]-[30]. Libretto.

QUEEN MARY
See Taylor, Thomas Proclus. Tower of London, The.
See Tennyson, Alfred, Lord.

QUEEN MARY'S BOWER
See Planché, James Robinson.

QUEEN-MOTHER, THE
See Swinburne, Algernon Charles.

QUEEN OF A DAY, THE
See Buckstone, John Baldwin.

QUEEN OF ARRAGON, THE
See Paul, Howard.

QUEEN OF BEAUTY!
See Stirling, Edward. Dragon Knight, The.

QUEEN OF BRILLIANTS, THE
See Thomas, Brandon.

QUEEN OF CYPRUS, THE
See Stirling, Edward.

QUEEN OF HEARTS, THE
See Thomas, Charles.

QUEEN OF HEARTS AND THE WONDERFUL TARTS, THE
See Dutnall, Martin.

QUEEN OF HUNGARY
See Stephens, George. Gertrude and Beatrice.

QUEEN OF SPADES, THE
See Boucicault, Dionysius Lardner.

QUEEN OF THE ABRUZZI, THE
See Coyne, Joseph Stirling.

QUEEN OF THE CANNIBAL ISLANDS
See Burnand, Francis Cowley. Africaine, L'.

QUEEN OF THE FROGS, THE
See Planché, James Robinson.

QUEEN OF THE MARKET, THE
See Webster, Benjamin Nottingham.

QUEEN OF THE THAMES, THE
See Fitzball, Edward.

QUEEN, THE CARDINAL, AND THE ADVENTURER
See Rice, Charles. Three Guardsmen, The.
See Rice, Charles. Three Musketeers, The.

QUEEN'S BALL, THE
See A'Beckett, Gilbert Abbott.

QUEEN'S BENCH, THE
See Rede, William Leman.

QUEEN'S HORSE, THE
See Honan, Michael Burke.

QUEEN'S JEWEL, THE
See Collier, William.

QUEEN'S LOVE, THE
See Burn, David.

QUEEN'S MATE, THE
See Paulton, Harry.

QUEEN'S MESSENGER, A
See Manners, John Hartley.

QUEEN'S ROOM, THE
See Moore, Frank Frankfort.

QUEEN'S VISIT, THE
See Cooper, Frederick Fox.

QUEENSBERRY FETE
See Planché, James Robinson. Who's Your Friend?

QUEER GUEST AT A WEDDING
See Kerr, John. Intimate Friend, The.

QUEER STREET
See Henry, Richard.

QUEER SUBJECT, THE
See Coyne, Joseph Stirling.

QUENTIN DURWARD
See Fitzball, Edward.
See Haworth, R.
See Huie, James L.
See Ross, Sheridan.

QUESTION OF MEMORY, A
See Field, Michael.

QUID PRO QUO
See Gore, Catherine Grace Frances Moody, Mrs. Charles.

QUIET DAY, A
See Oxenford, John.

QUIET FAMILY, A
See Suter, William E.

QUINN, M.
Mary Queen of Scots. London: R. Washbourne, 1884. Pp. [1]-47.

QUINTON, MARK
In His Power. Pp. 1-40. Title page lacking. Typescript.

QUITE A LADIES' MAN
See Brough, Robert Barnabas. Kensington Gardens.

QUITE A NEW BEAU!
See Reece, Robert. Little Robin Hood.

QUITE AT HOME
See Ryan, Richard.
See Sketchley, Arthur.

QUITE BY OURSELVES
See Bell, Florence Eveleen Eleanore Oliffe, Mrs. Hugh (Lady).

QUITO-GATE
See Bell, Robert. Watch-Word, The.

RACE-BALL!
See Morton, John Maddison. Chaos Is Come Again.

RACE FOR A DINNER, A
See Rodwell, James Thomas Gooderham.

RACE FOR A WIDOW, A
See Williams, Thomas John.

RACE FOR A WIFE
See Challis, Henry W.
See Fothergill, F.

RACINE
Alexander the Great.
See Boswell, Robert Bruce (trans.).
Andromache.
See Boswell, Robert Bruce (trans.).
Athaliah.
See Boswell, Robert Bruce (trans.).
Athalie.
See Bartholomew, William (trans.).
Bajazet.
See Boswell, Robert Bruce (trans.).
Berenice.
See Boswell, Robert Bruce (trans.).
Britannicus.
See Boothby, Brooke, Sir (trans.).
See Boswell, Robert Bruce (trans.).
Esther.
See Boswell, Robert Bruce (trans.).
Iphigenia.
See Boswell, Robert Bruce (trans.).
Litigants, The.
See Boswell, Robert Bruce (trans.).
Mithridates.
See Boswell, Robert Bruce (trans.).
Phaedra.
See Boswell, Robert Bruce (trans.).
Thebaid, The.
See Boswell, Robert Bruce (trans.).

RAE, ALFRED
Fauvette. Written with Fontaine, L. Music by Messager, André. London: Enoch & Sons; Alfred Hays, n.d. Pp. [i-ii], [1]-193. Vocal score.

RAE, CHARLES MARSHAM
Billy Doo. Also: Nothing Like Paste; or Billy Doo, the Bill-Sticker. London & New York: Samuel French, n.d. Pp. [1]-19. French's Acting Edition, 1510.
Birds in Their Little Nests Agree. London & New York: Samuel French, n.d. Pp. [1]-18. [Lacy's Acting Edition].
Fair Encounter, A. New York & London: Samuel French, n.d. Pp. [i], [1]-[16].
Fame. London & New York: Samuel French, n.d. Pp. [1]-48. Lacy's Acting Edition.

First in the Field. London & New York: Samuel French, n.d. Pp. [1]-24. [Lacy's Acting Edition].

Follow the Leader. London & New York: Samuel French, n.d. Pp. [1]-24. Lacy's Acting Edition, 1479.

Love's Alarms. London & New York: Samuel French, n.d. Pp. [1]-22. [Lacy's Acting Edition].

Man with Three Wives, The. London & New York: Samuel French, n.d. Pp. [1]-57, 60. Text incomplete. French's Acting Edition (late Lacy's).

Nothing Like Paste; or, Billy Doo, the Bill-Sticker. *Also:* Billy Doo. Chicago: Dramatic Publishing Company, n.d. Pp. [1]-15. Sergel's Acting Drama, 171.

Poppleton's Predicaments. London & New York: Samuel French, n.d. Pp. [1]-20. [Lacy's Acting Edition].

Sunny Side, The. London & New York: Samuel French, n.d. Pp. [1]-20.

RAFFAELLE AND FORNARINA
   See Cornwall, Barry.

RAFFAELLE CIMARO
   See Serle, Thomas James.

RAFFAELLE THE REPROBATE
   See Wilks, Thomas Egerton.

RAG-PICKER OF PARIS AND THE DRESS-MAKER OF ST. ANTOINE, THE
   See Stirling, Edward.

RAGE, THE
   See Reynolds, Frederick.

RAGGED SCHOOL, THE
   See Stirling, Edward.

RAILROAD STATION, THE
   See Wilks, Thomas Egerton.

RAILROAD TO RUIN
   See Boucicault, Dionysius Lardner. Formosa.

RAILROAD TRIP, THE
   See Morton, Edward.

RAILWAY ADVENTURE, A
   See Cheltnam, Charles Smith.

RAILWAY BELLE, THE
   See Lemon, Mark.

RAILWAY BUBBLES
   See Coyne, Joseph Stirling.

RAILWAY RESULTS
   See Dwarris, Fortunatus William Lilley, Sir.

RAIN CLOUDS
   See Walkes, W. R.

RAINE, MARGARET
   See Hunt, Margaret Raine, Mrs. Alfred William.

RAINY DAY, A
   See Leigh, Agnes.

RAISING THE WIND
   See Kenney, James.

RAISING THE WIND ON THE MOST APPROVED PRINCIPLES
   See Brough, William. Enchanted Isle, The.

RAJAH, THE
   See Young, William.

RAJAH OF CHUTNEYPORE
   See Dance, George. Nautch Girl, The.

RAJAH'S DAUGHTER
   See Moncrieff, William Thomas. Cataract of the Ganges, The.

RAKE AND HIS PUPIL, THE
   See Buckstone, John Baldwin.

RAKE HUSBAND
   See Moncrieff, William Thomas. Giovanni in the Country.

RAKE'S PROGRESS, THE
   See Rede, William Leman.

RALEIGH, CECIL
   Belle of Cairo, The.
      See Peile, F. Kinsey.
   Cheer, Boys, Cheer.
      See Harris, Augustus Henry Glossop.
   Derby Winner, The.
      See Harris, Augustus Henry Glossop.

   Dick Whittington.
      See Harris, Augustus Henry Glossop.
   Great Millionaire, The. Pp. [i-iii], 1-42, [i], [1]-54, [i], [1]-30, [i], 1-30. Typescript.
   Great Pink Pearl, The.
      See Carton, R. C.
   Hearts Are Trumps. London: J. Miles (printer) (priv.), 1899. Pp. [1]-143.
   Little Christopher Columbus.
      See Sims, George Robert.
   New Corsican Brothers, The. Music by Slaughter, Walter. London: J. B. Cramer, n.d. Pp. [i-iv], [1]-8, 13-30, 35-130. Text incomplete. Vocal score.
   White Heather, The. Written with Hamilton, Henry. Pp. [i], [1]-44, [i], [1]-35, [i], 1-23, [1]-[12], 12, [1]-22, [i], [1]-7, [1]-6, [1]-4, [1]-8. Pagination by act and scene. Typescript.
   Yashmak, The. Written with Hicks, Edward Seymour; Carse, Roland. Music by Lambelet, Napoleon. London: Francis, Day, & Hunter, c.1897. Pp. [i-iv], [1]-164. Vocal score.

RALEIGH, WALTER
   Riddle, The. Liverpool: D. Marples (printer) (priv.), 1895. Pp. [1-2], [i]-[iv], [1]-26.

RAMAH DROOG
   See Cobb, James.

RAMESES II
   See Bantock, Granville.

RAMSAY, ALLAN
   Gentle Shepard, The.
      See Bethune, Gilbert (arr.).

RANDALL'S THUMB
   See Gilbert, William Schwenck.

RAN-DAN CLUB
   See Worrell, James. Young Waterman's Society, The.

RANDEGGER, ALBERTO
   Esmeralda.
      See Marzials, Theophilus Julius Henry.

RANDS, WILLIAM BRIGHTLY
   Lilliput Revels. New York: George Routledge & Sons, 1871. Pp. [i-iv], [1]-147.

RANELAGH
   See Simpson, John Palgrave.

RANGER, EDWARD
   American in England, The. Long Sutton: John Swain (printer), 1855. Pp. [4]-51.
   Fortune Favours the Brave. Long Sutton: John Swain (printer), 1856. Pp. [3]-75.
   Gentleman and the Upstart, The. London: W. & R. Holmes, 1848. Pp. [1]-[54].
   Lover Husband, The. Edinburgh: A. Cannon (printer), 1846. Pp. [1]-[38].

RANKIN, REGINALD (trans.)
   Rhine Gold, The. Music by Wagner. In *Wagner's Nibelungen Ring*, London: Longmans, Green, 1899, I, [1]-42. Libretto. *Filed under* Nibelungen Ring.
   Siegfried. Music by Wagner. In *Wagner's Nibelungen Ring*, London: Longmans, Green, 1901, II, [1]-84. Libretto. *Filed under* Nibelungen Ring.
   Twilight of the Gods, The. Music by Wagner. In *Wagner's Nibelungen Ring*, London: Longmans, Green, 1901, II, [85]-163. Libretto. *Filed under* Nibelungen Ring.
   Valkyrie, The. Music by Wagner. In *Wagner's Nibelungen Ring*, London: Longmans, Green, 1899, I, [43]-140. Libretto. *Filed under* Nibelungen Ring.

RANSOM, HARRY ALEXANDER VINCENT
   Man Who Wasn't, The. London: Samuel French; New York: T. Henry French, n.d. Pp. [1]-22. [Lacy's Acting Edition].

RANSOM, THE: AN ANECDOTE OF MONTESQUIEU
   See Planché, Elizabeth (Eliza) St. George, Mrs. James Robinson

RANTZAU, I
   See Weatherly, Frederick Edward (trans.).

RANZ DES VACHES
   See Pocock, Isaac. Home, Sweet Home!

RAPE OF PROSERPINE, THE
    See Cornwall, Barry.
RAPE OF THE LOCK, THE
    See Oxenford, John.
RAPHAEL, FRANCIS
    Nita the Dancer.
        See Weller, Bernard William.
RAPPAREE, THE
    See Boucicault, Dionysius Lardner.
RAPPINGS AND TABLE MOVINGS
    See Paul, Howard.
RAPUNZEL
    See Morris, William.
RASSELAS, PRINCE OF ABYSSINIA
    See Brough, William.
RATHER A PRIG
    See Bell, Florence Eveleen Eleanore Oliffe, Mrs. Hugh (Lady).
RATS
    See Mackersy, W. A.
RATTLIN THE REEFER
    See Haines, John Thomas.
RAUBERBRAUT
    See Fitzball, Edward. Robber's Bride, The.
RAVENNA
    See Clarke, John Bertridge.
RAVLAN
    See Watson, Samuel James.
RAY, BEN, JR
    Mohawk Minstrels' Fourth Annual of Dramas, Dialogues, and Drolleries, The.
        See Hunter, Harry.
RAYMOND, RICHARD JOHN
    Balance of Comfort, The; or, To Marry or Not to Marry? London: John Duncombe, n.d. Pp. [1]-42. Duncombe's Edition.
    Barber Baron, The. London: G. H. Davidson, n.d. Pp. [1]-37. Cumberland's Minor Theatre, 151.
    Castle of Paluzzi, The; or, The Extorted Oath. London: William Sams, 1818. Pp. [i]-[vi], 7-53. 2nd ed.
    Cherry Bounce! London: John Duncombe, n.d. Pp. [1]-18. Duncombe's Edition.
    Deuce Is in Her!, The. London: John Duncombe, n.d. Pp. [1]-24. Duncombe's Edition.
    Discarded Daughter, The. London: Duncombe & Moon, n.d. <wrps. Duncombe>. Pp. [1]-32. Duncombe's Acting Edition of the British Theatre, 466.
    Eleventh Hour, The; or, Sixteen Years Ago. London: John Lowndes, n.d. Pp. [1]-40.
    Emigrant's Daughter, The. London: John Duncombe, n.d. Pp. [1]-26. [Duncombe's Edition]. Promptbook.
    Farmer's Daughter of the Severn Side, The; or, Mr. and Mrs. Toodles. London: Thomas Hailes Lacy, n.d. Pp. [1]-24. Lacy's Acting Edition, 386.
    Like Father, Like Son. London: John Duncombe, n.d. Pp. [1]-24. Duncombe's Edition.
    Mr. and Mrs. Peter White. *Also:* Mrs. White. Boston: William V. Spencer, n.d. Pp. [1]-19. Spencer's Boston Theatre, 136.
    Mrs. White. *Also:* Mr. and Mrs. Peter White. London: Thomas Hailes Lacy, n.d. Pp. [1]-25.
    Old Oak Tree, The. London: John Duncombe, n.d. Pp. [1]-40. Duncombe's Edition.
    P.S.—Come to Dinner! London: John Duncombe, n.d. Pp. [1]-34. Duncombe's Edition.
    Robert the Devil! Duke of Normandy. London: John Cumberland, n.d. Pp. [1]-35. Cumberland's British Theatre, XXXIII. *Filed under* Cumberland, John. Cumberland's British Theatre, XXXIII.
    Robert the Devil! Duke of Normandy. *Also:* The Wizard's Ring. London: John Cumberland, n.d. Pp. [1]-35. [Cumberland's British Theatre].
    Two Make a Pair, The; or, Manoeuvering. London: John Lowndes, n.d. Pp. [i], [1]-28.

    Which Is My Cousin? London: John Lowndes, n.d. Pp. [i], [1]-25.
    Wizard's Ring, The.
        See Robert the Devil! Duke of Normandy.
RAYMOND AND AGNES
    See Grosette, Henry William.
    See Lewis, Matthew Gregory.
RAYMOND DE PERCY
    See Harvey, Margaret.
RAYNE, LIN (arr.)
    Macbeth. By Shakespeare, William. London: Thomas Bosworth, 1868. Pp. [1]-40.
RAYNER, BARNABAS F.
    Dumb Man of Manchester, The. London: Thomas Hailes Lacy, n.d. Pp. [1]-30. Promptbook.
    Up to Town and Back Again. London: Thomas Hailes Lacy, n.d. Pp. [1]-20. Lacy's Acting Edition.
    Yorkshire Gamester, The. London: Thomas Hailes Lacy, n.d. Pp. 20-24. Lacy's Acting Edition. *Filed under* Up to Town and Back Again.
RAYNER
    See Baillie, Joanna.
RE DI LAHORE, IL
    See Pittman, Josiah (trans.).
REACH, ANGUS BETHUNE
    Jenny Lind at Last; or, The Swedish Nightingale. Boston: William V. Spencer, 1856. Pp. [1]-16. Spencer's Boston Theatre, New Series, 33.
READE, CHARLES
    Angelo. London: Thomas Hailes Lacy, n.d. Pp. [1]-24. [Lacy's Acting Edition].
    Courier of Lyons, The. London: Dramatic Authors' Society (priv.), 1854. Pp. [i]-vi, [1]-53.
    Dora. Boston: Charles H. Spencer, n.d. Pp. [1]-33. Spencer's Universal Stage, 50.
    Foul Play.
        See Boucicault, Dionysius Lardner.
    Gold! London: Thomas Hailes Lacy, n.d. Pp. [1]-48. [Lacy's Acting Edition].
    It's Never Too Late to Mend. London: W. Clowes & Sons (printer), n.d. Pp. [i-ii], [1]-95. Promptbook.
    King's Rival, The.
        See Taylor, Tom.
    Ladies' Battle, The; or, Un Duel en Amour. London: Thomas Hailes Lacy, n.d. Pp. [1]-41. Lacy's Acting Edition.
    Lost Husband, The. Also attrib. to Robertson, Thomas William. London: Thomas Hailes Lacy, n.d. Pp. [1]-36. Lacy's Acting Edition, 86.
    Masks and Faces.
        See Taylor, Tom.
    Peregrine Pickle. Oxford: Henry Slatter (printer), 1851. Pp. [i-iv], [1]-7.
    Scuttled Ship, The. N.p.: n.pub., n.d. Pp. 72 leaves. Title page lacking. Promptbook.
    Two Loves and a Life.
        See Taylor, Tom.
READE, JOHN EDMUND
    Cain the Wanderer. In *Poetical Works,* new ed., 3 vols., London: Longman, Green, Longman, Roberts, & Green, 1865, II, [i], [70]-131.
    Catiline. In *Poetical Works,* new ed., 3 vols., London: Longman, Green, Longman, Roberts, & Green, 1865, III, [1]-97.
    Record of the Pyramids, A. London: Saunders & Otley, 1842. Pp. [i]-[xxx], [1]-128.
READING A POEM
    See Thackeray, William Makepeace.
READY-MONEY
    See Maurice, Walter.
REAL AND IDEAL
    See Wigan, Horace.
REALM OF JOY, THE
    See Gilbert, William Schwenck.
REAPERS, THE
    See Stirling, Edward.

REAR ADMIRAL, THE
    See Emden, William Samuel.
REBECCA AND HER DAUGHTERS
    See Stephens, George.
REBEL'S GAUNTLET!
    See Smith, John Frederick. Protector!, The.
REBELLION, THE
    See Bromley, George Percival.
RECALLED TO LIFE
    See Hewson, J. James.
RECEIPT FOR BEAUTY
    See Morton, Thomas, sr. Blind Girl, The.
RECITATIONS, RHYMES, AND RIDICULOSITIES
    See Pleon, Harry.
RECOLLECTION OF O'FLANNIGAN AND THE FAIRIES, A
    See Brougham, John.
RECOMPENSE
    See Bernard, William Bayle. Louison, the Angel of the Attic.
RECORD OF THE PYRAMIDS, A
    See Reade, John Edmund.
RECRUITING OFFICER, THE
    See Farquhar, George.
RECRUITING SERGEANT, THE
    See Bickerstaffe, Isaac.
RED BEARD THE TERRIBLE AND THE ENCHANTED FAIRIES OF THE CRYSTAL GROTTO
    See Towers, Edward. Harlequin King Pee-Wit and His Merry Little Men!
RED CAP, THE
    See Archer, Thomas.
RED CROW, THE
    See Wilks, Thomas Egerton.
RED FARM, THE
    See Moncrieff, William Thomas.
RED HAND
    See Hill, Isabel. Brian the Probationer.
RED MASK, THE
    See Brougham, John.
RED MEN OF THE WILDERNESS
    See Dibdin, Thomas John. Wigwam, The.
RED REPUBLICAN, A
    See Steele, Anna Caroline Wood, Mrs.
RED RIDING HOOD
    See Dibdin, Charles Isaac Mungo, jr.
    See Yardley, William.
RED-RIDING HOOD AND HER SISTER, LITTLE BO-PEEP
    See Rice, Charles.
RED ROVER, THE
    See Fitzball, Edward.
RED ROY
    See Farley, Charles.
REDCLIFFE, STRATFORD DE, VISCOUNT
    See Canning, Stratford, Viscount Stratford de Redcliffe.
REDE, WILLIAM LEMAN
    Affair of Honour, An. London: John Miller, 1835. Pp. [i-iv], [1]-19.
    Affair of Honour, An. London & New York: Samuel French, n.d. Pp. [1]-28.
    Come to Town; or, Next Door Neighbours! London: John Duncombe, n.d. Pp. [1]-26. Duncombe's Edition.
    Cupid in London; or, Some Passages in the Life of Love. London: John Duncombe, n.d. Pp. [1]-32. Duncombe's Edition.
    Devil and Doctor Faustus, The. London: G. H. Davidson, n.d. Pp. [1]-36. Cumberland's British Theatre, 367.
    Douglas Travestie. London: John Duncombe, n.d. Pp. [1]-18. Duncombe's Edition.
    Faith and Falsehood; or, The Fate of a Bushranger! London: Thomas Hailes Lacy, n.d. Pp. [1]-38. New British Theatre (late Duncombe's), 263. Promptbook.
    Flight to America, The; or, Ten Hours in New York! London: John Duncombe, n.d. Pp. [1]-43. Duncombe's Edition.

    Gaberlunzie Man, The. London: John Duncombe, n.d. Pp. [1]-26. Duncombe's Acting Edition of the British Theatre, 181.
    His First Champagne. London: W. S. Johnson (printer), n.d. Pp. [2]-35. Title page lacking. Promptbook.
    Jack in the Water; or, The Ladder of Life. London: G. H. Davidson, n.d. Pp. [1]-50.
    Life's a Lottery; or, Jolly Dick the Lamplighter. London: G. H. Davidson, n.d. Pp. [1]-48. Cumberland's British Theatre, 389.
    Old and the Young Stager, The. London: John Duncombe, n.d. Pp. [1]-34. Duncombe's Edition.
    Our Village; or, The Lost Ship. London: Thomas Hailes Lacy, n.d. Pp. [1]-48. [Lacy's Acting Edition].
    Peregrinations of Pickwick, The. London: W. Strange, 1837. Pp. [5]-32. Text complete.
    Queen's Bench, The. London: G. H. Davidson, n.d. Pp. [1]-42. Cumberland's British Theatre, 362.
    Rake's Progress, The. London: John Duncombe, n.d. Pp. [1]-[5], 8-50. Text incomplete. Duncombe's Edition. Promptbook.
    Sixteen-String Jack. London: G. H. Davidson, n.d. Pp. [1]-57.
    Skeleton Witness, The; or, The Murder at the Mound. New York: Samuel French, n.d. Pp. [1]-44. French's Standard Drama, 197.
    Two Greens, The. London: James Pattie, n.d. Pp. [1]-20. Pattie's Universal Stage or Theatrical Prompt Book, 8.
REDGAUNTLET (anon.)
    Edinburgh: John Anderson jr, 1824. Pp. [i-iv], [1]-61. Anderson's Edition, Select British Theatre, 13.
REECE, ROBERT
    Ambassadress, The. Written with Reed, Thomas German. Music by Auber. London: J. Mallett, n.d. Pp. [1]-23. Libretto.
    Bells of Corneville, The.
        See Farnie, Henry Brougham.
    Brown and the Brahmins. [London: Thomas Hailes Lacy], n.d. Pp. [5]-35. Title page lacking. [Lacy's Acting Edition].
    Commodore, The.
        See Farnie, Henry Brougham.
    Don Giovanni in Venice. London: E. Rascol, n.d. Pp. [1]-39.
    Dora's Device. London & New York: Samuel French, n.d. Pp. [1]-37. [Lacy's Acting Edition].
    Forty Thieves!, The. London: Williams & Son (printer), n.d. Pp. [i-ii], [1]-32.
    Green Old Age. London & New York: Samuel French, n.d. Pp. [1]-24. French's Acting Edition (late Lacy's), 1535.
    Guv'nor, The. By E. G. Lankester (pseud.). London & New York: Samuel French, c.1900. Pp. [1]-48. [French's International Copyrighted Edition of the Works of the Best Authors, 39].
    Ingomar; or, The Noble Savage. In *Drawing-Room Plays and Parlour Pantomimes,* ed. Clement Scott, London: Stanley Rivers, n.d., pp. [i], [79]-106.
    Jeanne, Jeannette, and Jeanneton. Music by Lacombe, P. London: J. Miles (printer), n.d. Pp. [1]-38. Libretto.
    Jeanne, Jeannette, and Jeanneton. Music by Lacome, P. London: J. Miles, n.d. Pp. [1]-38. Promptbook libretto. *Filed under* Clairville (pseud.).
    Lady of the Lake, Plaid in a New Tartan, The. London: Thomas Hailes Lacy, n.d. Pp. [1]-36.
    Little Robin Hood; or, Quite a New Beau! London: Thomas Hailes Lacy, n.d. Pp. [1]-34. [Lacy's Acting Edition].
    Martha; or, A Fair Take-In. London: E. Rascol, n.d. Pp. [1]-28.
    May; or, Dolly's Delusion. New York & London: Samuel French, n.d. Pp. [1]-44. French's Standard Drama, 375.
    Old Man, An. London & New York: Samuel French, n.d. Pp. [1]-28. [Lacy's Acting Edition].
    Our Helen. London: Woodfall & Kinder (printer), 1884. Pp. [1]-50.
    Paquita; or, Love in a Frame. London: Thomas Hailes Lacy, n.d. Pp. [1]-32. [Lacy's Acting Edition].

Perfect Love! London: Thomas Hailes Lacy, n.d. Pp. [1]-36. [Lacy's Acting Edition].

Prometheus; or, The Man on the Rock! London: Thomas Hailes Lacy, n.d. Pp. [1]-33.

Puritani, I. Music by Bellini. London & New York: Boosey, n.d. Pp. [i-iv], 1-304. [Royal Edition]. Vocal score.

Romulus and Remus. London & New York: Samuel French, n.d. Pp. [1]-22. [Lacy's Acting Edition].

Ruy Blas Righted; or, The Love, the Lugger, and the Lackey. London & New York: Samuel French, n.d. Pp. [1]-31. [Lacy's Acting Edition].

Stranger—Stranger Than Ever!, The. London: Thomas Hailes Lacy, n.d. Pp. [1]-26.

Trade.
See Morton, John Maddison.

Traviata, La. Music by Verdi. London & New York: Boosey, n.d. Pp. [i-iv], 1-247. [Royal Edition]. Vocal score.

Up the River.
See Farnie, Henry Brougham.

Very Last Days of Pompeii!, The. London: Thomas Hailes Lacy, n.d. Pp. [1]-26. [Lacy's Acting Edition].

Warranted! By E. G. Lankester (pseud.). N.p.: n.pub. (priv.), n.d. Pp. [2]-66. Promptbook.

Whittington, Junior, and His Sensation Cat. London: Thomas Hailes Lacy, n.d. Pp. [1]-37.

REED, JOSEPH

Register Office, The. In *British Drama*, 12 vols., London: John Dicks, 1872, X, [214]-224.

REED, THOMAS GERMAN

Ambassadress, The.
See Reece, Robert.

Ching-Chow-Hi.
See Brough, William.

REEVE, JOHN

One, Two, Three, Four, Five; or, By Advertisement. Also attrib. to Reynolds, John Hamilton. London: John Lowndes, 1819. Pp. [i-iv], [1]-19. *Filed under* One, Two, Three, Four, Five (anon.).

One, Two, Three, Four, Five; or, By Advertisement. Also attrib. to Reynolds, John Hamilton. London: John Cumberland, n.d. Pp. [1]-23. Cumberland's British Theatre, XXXI. *Filed under* Cumberland, John. Cumberland's British Theatre, XXXI.

One, Two, Three, Four, Five; or, By Advertisement. Also attrib. to Reynolds, John Hamilton. London: John Cumberland, n.d. Pp. [1]-23. [Cumberland's British Theatre]. *Filed under* Reeve, William.

REEVE, WILLIAM

Barark Johnson; or, The Blind Witness! London: Thomas Hailes Lacy, n.d. Pp. [1]-18. Cumberland's British Theatre <wrps. New British Theatre (late Duncombe's), 392>.

REEVE, WYBERT

Dead Witness, The; or, Sin and Its Shadow. London & New York: Samuel French, n.d. Pp. [1]-35. [Lacy's Acting Edition].

Dragon of Wantley, The.
See Hazlewood, Colin Henry.

George Geith; or, Romance of a City Life. London & New York: Samuel French, n.d. Pp. [1]-44. Promptbook.

I Love You! London & New York: Samuel French, n.d. Pp. [1]-12. [Lacy's Acting Edition].

Match for a Mother-in-Law, A. Clyde, Ohio: A. D. Ames, n.d. Pp. [1]-21. Ames' Series of Standard and Minor Drama, 231.

Never Reckon Your Chickens &c. London: Thomas Hailes Lacy, n.d. Pp. [1]-18. [Lacy's Acting Edition].

Not So Bad After All. London: Thomas Hailes Lacy, n.d. Pp. [1]-40. [Lacy's Acting Edition].

Obliging a Friend. London & New York: Samuel French, n.d. Pp. [1]-15. [Lacy's Acting Edition].

Parted. London & New York: Samuel French, n.d. Pp. [1]-42. [French's Acting Edition]. Promptbook.

Pike O'Callaghan; or, The Irish Patriot. New York & London: Samuel French, n.d. Pp. [1]-32. French's Standard Drama, 414.

Supper Gratis, A; or, An Impudent Intruder. London: Edward Hastings, n.d. <wrps. London & New York: Samuel French>. Pp. [1]-19. Hastings's Acting Plays <wrps. French's Acting Edition (late Lacy's)>.

True as Steel. London: Thomas Hailes Lacy, n.d. Pp. [1]-49. [Lacy's Acting Edition].

Won at Last! London & New York: Samuel French, n.d. Pp. [1]-40. Promptbook.

REFLECTIONS OF KING HEZEKIAH IN HIS SICKNESS
See More, Hannah.

REFORM
See Moncrieff, William Thomas.

REFUSAL, THE
See Cibber, Colley.

REGENT'S DAUGHTER, THE
See Young, William.

REGISTER OFFICE, THE
See Reed, Joseph.

REGULAR FIX!, A
See Morton, John Maddison.

REGULUS
See Burn, David.

REHEARSAL REHEARSED
See Horncastle, James Henry. Infant Phenomenon, The.

REID, MAYNE

Love's Martyr. Philadelphia: United States Job Printing Office (printer) (priv.), n.d. Pp. [1]-45.

REIGNING FAVORITE, THE
See Oxenford, John.

REINE DE SABA
See Farnie, Henry Brougham. Irene.

REITZENSTEIN, CHARLES VON

Count Koenigsmark.
See Thompson, Benjamin (trans.).

RELIEF OF LONDONDERRY
See Buckstone, John Baldwin. Boyne Water, The.

RELIEF OF LUCKNOW
See Boucicault, Dionysius Lardner. Jessie Brown.

RELIQUARY, THE
See Bell, Florence Eveleen Eleanore Oliffe, Mrs. Hugh (Lady).

RELVINDEZ AND ELZORA
See Gray, Simon. Spaniard, The.

RELY ON MY DISCRETION
See Palmer, T. A.

REMO, FELIX

Lily of Leoville, The. Written with Murray, Alfred; Scott, Clement William. Music by Caryll, Ivan. London: C. Jefferys; W. J. Willcocks, n.d. Pp. [1]-30. Libretto. *Filed under* Scott, Clement William.

REMORSE
See Appleyard, Charles.
See Coleridge, Samuel Taylor.
See Thicke, Frank E. (arr.).

RENARD, JULES

Carrots.
See Sutro, Alfred (trans.).

RENCONTRE, THE (anon.)
N.p.: n.pub., n.d. Pp. [57]-98. Title page lacking. Text complete.

RENDEZVOUS, THE
See Ayton, Richard.

RENEGADE, THE
See Reynolds, Frederick.

RENT DAY, THE
See Jerrold, Douglas William.

REPARATION
See Martin, ?, Mrs.

REPUBLICANS OF BREST
See Johnstone, John Beer. Sailor of France, The.

REPULSED INVASION
See Thermopylae.

RESPECTABLE MAN, THE (anon.)
London: Thomas Hailes Lacy, n.d. Pp. [1]-52.

RESTORATION OF MAGNA CHARTA
See Mise of Lewes, The.

RETAINED FOR THE DEFENCE
See Oxenford, John.

RETAINED ON BOTH SIDES
See Farnie, Henry Brougham.

RETALIATION
See Dircks, Rudolph.

RETIRED FROM BUSINESS
See Jerrold, Douglas William.

RETIRING
See Williamson, Henry W.

RETRIBUTION
See Bennett, George John.
See Dillon, John.
See Taylor, Tom.

RETTIE, T. LEITH
Imoline. In *Plays and Poems,* Aberdeen: John Avery, 1884, pp. [i], [81]- 151.
Stratagems and Spoils. In *Plays and Poems,* Aberdeen: John Avery, 1884, pp. [i-iv], [1]-79.

RETURN FROM SLAVERY
See Dimond, William. Native Land.

RETURN OF TASSO TO SORRENTO, THE
See Baddeley, Welbore St. Clair.

RETURN OF THE DRUSES, THE
See Browning, Robert.

RETURN OF THE GENERAL, THE
See Ridge, William Pett.

RETURN OF THE WANDERER
See Hazlewood, Colin Henry. Jessy Vere.

RETURN OF ULYSSES, THE
See Bridges, Robert Seymour.
See Burnand, Francis Cowley. Patient Penelope.

RETURN TICKET, A
See Spencer, George.

RETURN TICKET TO THE INTERNATIONAL EXHIBITION
See Spencer, George. Return Ticket, A.

RETURN TO ITHACA
See Mendham, James, jr. Adventures of Ulysses, The.

RETURNED KILLED
See Planché, James Robinson.

RETURNED TO LIFE
See Hayes, Frederick William.

REVENGE
See Brougham, John.
See Kemble, John Philip (arr.).
See Parlby, Brooke Bridges, Maj.
See Stephens, George.
See Young, Edward.

REVIEW, THE
See Colman, George, jr.

REVOLT OF THE FLOWERS
See Webster, Benjamin Nottingham. Devil's Violin, The.

REVOLT OF THE NAIADES
See Dalrymple, J. S. Lurline.

REVOLT OF THE NAIADS
See Dalrymple, J. S. Naiad Queen, The.

REVOLT OF THE WORKHOUSE
See A'Beckett, Gilbert Abbott.

REVOLUTION OF 1688
See Whitehead, John Crawford. King James the Second.

REW, WALTER
Dion. In *Dion: A Tragedy, and Poems,* London: Trubner, 1877, pp. [i-iv], [1]-160.

REWARD OF VIRTUE
See Stephens, Henry Pottinger. Billee Taylor.

REYNOLDS, FRANCIS
No! London: John Cumberland, n.d. Pp. [1]-24. Cumberland's Minor Theatre, V. *Filed under* Cumberland, John. Cumberland's Minor Theatre, V.

No! London: G. H. Davidson, n.d. Pp. [1]-24. Cumberland's Minor Theatre, 41.

REYNOLDS, FREDERICK
Begone Dull Care; or, How Will It End? London: Longman, Hurst, Rees, & Orme, 1808. Pp. [1-2], [i]-[viii], [1]-65.
Blind Bargain, The; or, Hear It Out. London: Longman, Hurst, Rees, & Orme, 1805. Pp. [1]-75.
Blind Bargain, The; or, Hear It Out. London: John Cumberland, n.d. Pp. [1]-61. Cumberland's British Theatre, XXVIII. *Filed under* Cumberland, John. Cumberland's British Theatre, XXVIII.
Bridal Ring, The. New York: D. Longworth, 1812. Pp. [1]-31.
Caravan, The; or, The Driver and His Dog. Music by Reeve, William. London: G. & J. Robinson, 1803. Pp. [1]-46.
Caravan, The; or, The Driver and His Dog. Dublin: Espy & Cross (printer), 1815. Pp. [1]-55. *Filed under* Caravan, The (anon.).
Delays and Blunders. London: T. N. Longman & O. Rees, 1803. Pp. [1]-[76].
Delays and Blunders. London: Longman, Hurst, Rees, & Orme, 1805. Pp. [1]-[72].
Delinquent, The; or, Seeing Company. London: Longman, Hurst, Rees, & Orme, 1805. Pp. [1]-[76].
Delinquent, The; or, Seeing Company. In *Modern Theatre,* ed. Mrs. Inchbald, 10 vols., London: Longman, Hurst, Rees, Orme, & Brown, 1811, II, [75]-143.
Delinquent, The; or, Seeing Company. London: John Cumberland, n.d. Pp. [1]-58. Cumberland's British Theatre, XL. *Filed under* Cumberland, John. Cumberland's British Theatre, XL.
Don John; or The Two Violettas. Music by Bishop, Henry; Ware, W. H. London: Goulding, D'Almaine, Potter, n.d. Pp. [i-ii], 1-88. Vocal score.
Don John; or, The Two Violettas. Music by Bishop, Henry; Ware, W. H. London: John Miller, 1821. Pp. [1]-67. Libretto.
Dramatist, The; or, Stop Him Who Can. London: John Cumberland, n.d. Pp. [1]-57. Cumberland's British Theatre, XXXIX. *Filed under* Cumberland, John. Cumberland's British Theatre, XXXIX.
Exile, The. Philadelphia: Bradford & Inskeep, 1810. Pp. [1]-16.
Exile, The; or, The Deserts of Siberia. London: John Cumberland, n.d. Pp. [1]-54. Cumberland's British Theatre, XXIX. *Filed under* Cumberland, John. Cumberland's British Theatre, XXIX.
Folly As It Flies. London: T. N. Longman & O. Rees, 1802. Pp. [1]-67. New ed.
Folly As It Flies. In *Modern Theatre,* ed. Mrs. Inchbald, 10 vols., London: Longman, Hurst, Rees, Orme, & Brown, 1811, II, [287]-353.
Folly As It Flies. London: John Cumberland, n.d. Pp. [1]-62. Cumberland's British Theatre, XXVII. *Filed under* Cumberland, John. Cumberland's British Theatre, XXVII.
Fortune's Fool. In *Modern Theatre,* ed. Mrs. Inchbald, 10 vols., London: Longman, Hurst, Rees, Orme, & Brown, 1811, II, [219]-286.
Free Knights, The; or, The Edict of Charlemagne. London: Westley & Parrish, 1810. Pp. [1]-72.
Gnome King, The; or, The Giant Mountains. Also attrib. to Colman, George, jr. Music by Bishop. London: John Miller, 1819. Pp. [i-iv], [1]-53. *Filed under* Colman, George, jr.
Gnome King!, The. Also attrib. to Colman, George, jr. Music by Bishop, Henry. London: Goulding, D'Almaine, Potter (priv.), n.d. Pp. [i-ii], [1]-76. Vocal score.
How to Grow Rich. In *Modern Theatre,* ed. Mrs. Inchbald, 10 vols., London: Longman, Hurst, Rees, Orme, & Brown, 1811, I, [217]-277.
How to Grow Rich. London: John Cumberland, n.d. Pp. [1]-58. Cumberland's British Theatre, XXX. *Filed under* Cumberland, John. Cumberland's British Theatre, XXX.
Laugh When You Can. In *Modern Theatre,* ed. Mrs. Inchbald, 10 vols., London: Longman, Hurst, Rees, Orme, & Brown, 1811, II, [145]-217.

Laugh When You Can. London: John Cumberland, n.d. Pp. [1]-63. Cumberland's British Theatre, XXIII. *Filed under* Cumberland, John. Cumberland's British Theatre, XXIII.

Life. London: T. N. Longman & O. Rees, 1801. Pp. [i-vi], [1]-78. 6th ed.

Life. In *Modern Theatre*, ed. Mrs. Inchbald, 10 vols., London: Longman, Hurst, Rees, Orme, & Brown, 1811, I, [143]-216.

Notoriety. In *Modern Theatre*, ed. Mrs. Inchbald, 10 vols., London: Longman, Hurst, Rees, Orme, & Brown, 1811, I, [279]-347.

Notoriety. London: John Cumberland, n.d. Pp. [i], [1]-[64]. Cumberland's British Theatre, XXVI. *Filed under* Cumberland, John. Cumberland's British Theatre, XXVI.

Out of Place; or, The Lake of Lausanne. New York: W. Turner, 1808. Pp. [1]-41.

Rage, The. In *Modern Theatre*, ed. Mrs. Inchbald, 10 vols., London: Longman, Hurst, Rees, Orme, & Brown, 1811, I, [67]-142.

Renegade, The. Music by Bishop, Henry. London: C. Chapple, 1812. Pp. [1]-62. 2nd ed.

Speculation. In *Modern Theatre*, ed. Mrs. Inchbald, 10 vols., London: Longman, Hurst, Rees, Orme, & Brown, 1811, II, [i-ii], [1]-73.

Virgin of the Sun, The. Music by Bishop, Henry. London: C. Chapple, 1812. Pp. [1]-78. 3rd ed.

Werter. In *Modern Theatre*, ed. Mrs. Inchbald, 10 vols., London: Longman, Hurst, Rees, Orme, & Brown, 1811, III, [291]-319.

What's a Man of Fashion? London: Whittingham & Arliss, 1815. Pp. [1]-50.

Will, The. In *Modern Theatre*, ed. Mrs. Inchbald, 10 vols., London: Longman, Hurst, Rees, Orme, & Brown, 1811, I, [i-ii], [1]-66.

Will, The. London: John Cumberland, n.d. Pp. [1]-58. Cumberland's British Theatre, XXI. *Filed under* Cumberland, John. Cumberland's British Theatre, XXI.

REYNOLDS, FREDERICK (arr.)
Comedy of Errors, The. By Shakespeare, William. Music by Bishop, Henry. London: Sampson Low, 1819. Pp. [i-vi], [1]-86.

Midsummer Night's Dream, A. By Shakespeare, William. London: John Miller, 1816. Pp. [ii]-[v], [5]-57.

REYNOLDS, JOHN HAMILTON
Confounded Foreigners. London: Chapman & Hall, n.d. Pp. [1]-20.

One, Two, Three, Four, Five.
See Reeve, John.

REYNOLDS-ANDERSON, J. F.
See Anderson, J. F. Reynolds.

REYNOLDSON, THOMAS HERBERT
Barrister, The.
See Good for Evil.

Brewer of Preston, The; or, Malt and Hops. London & New York: Samuel French, n.d. Pp. [1]-22. [Lacy's Acting Edition].

Crown Diamonds, The. Music by Auber. London: Thomas Hailes Lacy, n.d. Pp. [1]-60. [Lacy's Acting Edition]. Libretto.

Curious Case, A. Also attrib. to Maddox, John Medex. New York & London: Samuel French, n.d. Pp. [1]-24. French's Minor Drama, 327. *Filed under* Maddox, John Medex.

Curse of Mammon, The. London: John Cumberland, n.d. Pp. [1]-[51].

Don Pasquale. Music by Donizetti. 21 leaves. Manuscript libretto.

Elisir d'Amore, L'; or, The Elixir of Love. Music by Donizetti. London: Thomas Hailes Lacy, n.d. Pp. [1]-38. [Lacy's Acting Edition]. Libretto.

Good for Evil; or, A Wife's Trial. *Also:* The Barrister. *Also:* Home Truths. London: Thomas Hailes Lacy, n.d. Pp. [1]-24. [Lacy's Acting Edition, 640]. Filed also under Good for Evil (anon.).

Home Truths.
See Good for Evil.

Rich Man of Frankfort, The; or, The Poisoned Crown. London: John Cumberland, n.d. Pp. [1]-55. Cumberland's Minor Theatre, XIV. *Filed under* Cumberland, John. Cumberland's Minor Theatre, XIV.

Rich Man of Frankfort, The; or, The Poisoned Crown. London: John Cumberland, n.d. Pp. [1]-55. [Cumberland's Minor Theatre].

Venetian, The; or, The Council of Ten. London: John Cumberland, n.d. Pp. [1]-45. Cumberland's Minor Theatre, 140.

RHEINGOLD
See Corder, Henrietta Louisa Walford, Mrs. Frederick (trans.). Rhine Gold, The.

RHINE GOLD, THE
See Corder, Henrietta Louisa Walford, Mrs. Frederick (trans.).
See Rankin, Reginald (trans.).

RHINEGOLD, THE
See Forman, Alfred (trans.).

RHINEGOLD, PRELUDE TO THE RING OF THE NIBLUNG
See Jackson, John P. (trans.).

RHOADES, JAMES
Dux Redux; or, A Forest Tangle. London: Kegan Paul, Trench, 1887. Pp. [i-iv], [1]-134.

RHODES, GEORGE AMBROSE
Dion. London: William Miller, 1806. Pp. [i-viii], [1]-126.

Fifth of November, The; or, The Gunpowder Plot. London: Baldwin & Cradock; Carpenter, 1830. Pp. [i-iv], [1]-114.

RHODES, THOMAS
Disappointed Miller, The. Coventry: W. Hickling (printer) (priv.), 1824. Pp. [i]-vi, [7]-24.

RHODES, WILLIAM BARNES
Bombastes Furioso. Dublin: W. Tyrrell (printer), 1813. Pp. [i], [1]-14.

RHYMES OF A PANTOMIME
See Croker, Thomas Crofton. Daniel O'Rourke.

RHYMING TEMPERANCE ADVOCATE, THE
See Featherstone, Thomas.

RICE, CHARLES
Cinderella and the Fairy Glass Slipper. London: E. Rimmel, n.d. Pp. [3]-22. Libretto.

Red-Riding Hood and Her Sister, Little Bo-Peep. Bristol: I. Arrowsmith, n.d. Pp. [1]-[35]. Libretto.

Three Guardsmen, The; or, The Queen, the Cardinal, and the Adventurer. *Also:* The Three Musketeers. New York: Samuel French, n.d. Pp. [1]-60. French's American Drama, 46.

Three Musketeers, The; or, The Queen, the Cardinal, and the Adventurer. *Also:* The Three Guardsmen. London: Thomas Hailes Lacy, n.d. Pp. [3]-66.

RICE, JAMES
Philanthropy.
See Maurice, Walter.

Ready-Money.
See Maurice, Walter.

RICH AND POOR
See Lewis, Matthew Gregory.

RICH MAN OF FRANKFORT, THE
See Reynoldson, Thomas Herbert.

RICHARD COEUR DE LION
See Burgoyne, John, Gen.
See Swanwick, Catherine.

RICHARD COEUR DE LION AND THE KNIGHT TEMPLARS
See Boleno, Henry. Harlequin Crusader.

RICHARD, DUKE OF YORK; OR, THE CONTENTION OF YORK AND LANCASTER (anon. arr.)
By Shakespeare, William. London: Richard White, 1817. Pp. [1-2], [i]-xx, [5]-[81]. *Filed under* Kean, Edmund.

RICHARD III
See Coyne, Joseph Stirling.

RICHARD III TRAVESTIE
    See By, William.
RICHARD PLANTAGENET
    See Haines, John Thomas.
RICHARD SAVAGE
    See Colton, Charles.
RICHARD THE THIRD
    See Cibber, Colley (arr.).
RICHARD WYE
    See Hannan, Charles.
RICHARDS, ALFRED BATE
    Croesus, King of Lydia. London: William Pickering, 1845.
        Pp. [iii]-[xxii], [1]-120.
    Croesus, King of Lydia. London: Longman, Green, Long-
        man, & Roberts, 1861. Pp. [i-iv], [1]-113. 2nd ed., rev.
    Cromwell. London: William Pickering, 1847. Pp. [i-vi],
        [1]-129.
    Isolda; or, Good King Stephen. London: C. Mitchell, 1848.
        Pp. [i-iv], [1]-79.
    Prisoner of Toulon, The. London: Thomas Hailes Lacy,
        1868. Pp. [1]-59.
    Vandyck. London: Longman, Brown, Green, & Longmans,
        1850. Pp. [i-vi], [1]-128.
RICHARDS, PEARL MARY TERESA
    See Hobbes, John Oliver.
RICHARDSON, JOSEPH
    Fugitive, The. In *Modern Theatre,* ed. Mrs. Inchbald, 10 vols.,
        London: Longman, Hurst, Rees, Orme, & Brown, 1811,
        VIII, [133]-223.
RICHARDSON, SARAH WATTS, MRS. JOSEPH
    Ethelred. London: Lowndes & Hobbs (printer), n.d. Pp.
        [i]-vi, [9]-[18], [1]-92. Text complete.
    Gertrude. London: C. Lowndes, n.d. Pp. [v]-xiv, [1]-66. Text
        complete.
RICHELIEU
    See Bulwer (later Bulwer-Lytton), Edward George Earle
        Lytton, Lord Lytton.
RICHELIEU IN LOVE
    See Robinson, Emma.
RICHES
    See Burges, James Bland.
RIDDLE, THE
    See Raleigh, Walter.
RIDE OF DEATH
    See Hazlewood, Colin Henry. Headless Horseman, The.
RIDGE, WILLIAM PETT
    After the Cinderella. In *Minor Dialogues,* Bristol: J. W.
        Arrowsmith, n.d., pp. 118-127. *Filed under* Minor Dia-
        logues.
    After the Play. In *Minor Dialogues,* Bristol: J. W. Arrow-
        smith, n.d., pp. 251-259. *Filed under* Minor Dialogues.
    Art in the City. In *Minor Dialogues,* Bristol: J. W. Arrow-
        smith, n.d., pp. 92-100. *Filed under* Minor Dialogues.
    At a Concert. In *Minor Dialogues,* Bristol: J. W. Arrowsmith,
        n.d., pp. 148-157. *Filed under* Minor Dialogues.
    At a Smoker. In *Minor Dialogues,* Bristol: J. W. Arrowsmith,
        n.d., pp. 179-187. *Filed under* Minor Dialogues.
    At Molesey Lock. In *Minor Dialogues,* Bristol: J. W.
        Arrowsmith, n.d., pp. 138-147. *Filed under* Minor Dia-
        logues.
    At the Booking Office. In *Minor Dialogues,* Bristol: J. W.
        Arrowsmith, n.d., pp. 201-209. *Filed under* Minor Dia-
        logues.
    At the Bookstall. In *Minor Dialogues,* Bristol: J. W.
        Arrowsmith, n.d., pp. 240-250. *Filed under* Minor Dia-
        logues.
    At the Gallery Door. In *Minor Dialogues,* Bristol: J. W.
        Arrowsmith, n.d., pp. 67-74. *Filed under* Minor Dialogues.
    At the National Gallery. In *Minor Dialogues,* Bristol: J. W.
        Arrowsmith, n.d., pp. 270-281. *Filed under* Minor Dia-
        logues.
    At the Zoo. In *Minor Dialogues,* Bristol: J. W. Arrowsmith,
        n.d., pp. 210-219. *Filed under* Minor Dialogues.

    Between the Acts. In *Minor Dialogues,* Bristol: J. W.
        Arrowsmith, n.d., pp. [21]-29. *Filed under* Minor Dia-
        logues.
    City at Four O'Clock, The. In *Minor Dialogues,* Bristol: J. W.
        Arrowsmith, n.d., pp. 282-290. *Filed under* Minor Dia-
        logues.
    8:30 a.m., The. In *Minor Dialogues,* Bristol: J. W. Arrow-
        smith, n.d., pp. 57-66. *Filed under* Minor Dialogues.
    Farewell at the Station, The. In *Minor Dialogues,* Bristol: J.
        W. Arrowsmith, n.d., pp. 83-91. *Filed under* Minor
        Dialogues.
    In the Lowther. In *Minor Dialogues,* Bristol: J. W. Arrow-
        smith, n.d., pp. 128-137. *Filed under* Minor Dialogues.
    Last 'Bus, The. In *Minor Dialogues,* Bristol: J. W. Arrow-
        smith, n.d., pp. 220-228. *Filed under* Minor Dialogues.
    Minor Christy, The. In *Minor Dialogues,* Bristol, J. W.
        Arrowsmith, n.d. Pp. 291-300. *Filed under* Minor Dia-
        logues.
    Music-hall Gods, The. In *Minor Dialogues,* Bristol: J. W.
        Arrowsmith, n.d., pp. 109-117. *Filed under* Minor Dia-
        logues.
    Near the Band-stand. In *Minor Dialogues,* Bristol: J. W.
        Arrowsmith, n.d., pp. 101-108. *Filed under* Minor Dia-
        logues.
    Night Charges, The. In *Minor Dialogues,* Bristol: J. W.
        Arrowsmith, n.d., pp. 188-200. *Filed under* Minor Dia-
        logues.
    On the Rank. In *Minor Dialogues,* Bristol: J. W. Arrowsmith,
        n.d., pp. 158-167. *Filed under* Minor Dialogues.
    On the Underground. In *Minor Dialogues,* Bristol: J. W.
        Arrowsmith, n.d., pp. 30-39. *Filed under* Minor Dialogues.
    Orator of the Street, The. In *Minor Dialogues,* Bristol: J. W.
        Arrowsmith, n.d., pp. 40-48. *Filed under* Minor Dialogues.
    Return of the General, The. In *Minor Dialogues,* Bristol: J.
        W. Arrowsmith, n.d., pp. 75-82. *Filed under* Minor Dialogues.
    Suburban Dance, A. In *Minor Dialogues,* Bristol: J. W.
        Arrowsmith, n.d., pp. 229-239. *Filed under* Minor Dia-
        logues.
    Sunday Night at Ralliano's. In *Minor Dialogues,* Bristol: J. W.
        Arrowsmith, n.d., pp. 168-178. *Filed under* Minor Dia-
        logues.
    Sunday Night 'Bus, The. In *Minor Dialogues,* Bristol: J. W.
        Arrowsmith, n.d., pp. [i]-x, [11]-20. *Filed under* Minor
        Dialogues.
    Watching the Game. In *Minor Dialogues,* Bristol: J. W.
        Arrowsmith, n.d., pp. 49-56. *Filed under* Minor Dialogues.
    With Figaro. In *Minor Dialogues,* Bristol: J. W. Arrowsmith,
        n.d., pp. 260-269. *Filed under* Minor Dialogues.
RIDGWELL, GEORGE
    Skirt Dancer, The. Written with Mansell, Ernest. Music by
        Trotere, H. Pp. [i-iii], 1-45. Act II lacking. Typescript
        promptbook.
RIENZI
    See Mitford, Mary Russell.
    See Seymour, Frederick H. A.
RIENZI REINSTATED
    See Allan, A. W.
RIENZI, THE LAST OF THE TRIBUNES
    See Pittman, Josiah (trans.).
RIENZI, TRIBUNE OF ROME
    See Todhunter, John.
RIFLE AND HOW TO USE IT, THE
    See Bridgeman, John Vipon.
RIFLE BRIGADE, THE
    See Selby, Charles.
RIFLE VOLUNTEER
    See Suter, William E. Double Dealing.
RIFLE VOLUNTEERS, THE
    See Stirling, Edward.
RIFT WITHIN THE LUTE, THE
    See Dickinson, Charles H.
RIGHT AND WRONG
    See Burton, ?.
RIGHT-FALL HEIR, THE
    See Arden, Henry T.

RIGHTFUL HEIR, THE
    See Bulwer (later Bulwer-Lytton), Edward George Earle
    Lytton, Lord Lytton.
    See Sturgess, Arthur.
RIGHTON, EDWARD
    Dante.
    See Dabbs, George Henry Roque.
RIGHTS AND WRONGS OF WOMAN, THE
    See Morton, John Maddison.
RIGHTS OF HOSPITALITY
    See Kemble, Charles. Wanderer, The.
RIGHTS OF WOMAN, THE
    See Lunn, Joseph.
RIGOLETTO
    See Oxenford, John.
RINALDO RINALDINI
    See Wilks, Thomas Egerton.
RING, THE
    See Bartholomew, Anne Charlotte Fayermann, Mrs.
    Valentine.
    See Linley, William.
    See Tennyson, Alfred, Lord.
RING AND THE KEEPER, THE
    See Wooler, John Pratt.
RINGDOVES, THE
    See Mathews, Charles James.
RINGING THE CHANGES
    See Stephens, Henry Pottinger. Virginia.
RIP VAN WINKLE
    See Akerman, William.
    See Farnie, Henry Brougham.
    See Kerr, John.
    See Strachan, John S., jr.
RIPON, JOHN SCOTT (pseud. of Byerley, John Scott)
    Buonaparte; or, The Free-Booter. London: S. Highley, 1803.
    Pp. [1-2], [i]-iv, [1]-33.
RIQUET OF THE TUFT
    See Brooke, Stopford A.
RIQUET WITH THE TUFT
    See Blanchard, Edward Litt Leman.
    See Farley, Charles. Harlequin and Mother Shipton.
    See Planché, James Robinson.
RISE AND FALL OF RICHARD III, THE
    See Burnand, Francis Cowley.
RISE OF THE MOON OF INTELLECT
    See Taylor, J. (trans.). Prabodha Chandrodaya.
RISE OF THE ROTHESCHILDES, THE
    See Barnett, Charles Zachary.
RISING OF THE SESSION
    See Bain, Donald. Olden Times.
RISQUE, W. H.
    Pot-Pourri.
    See Tanner, James T.
RIVAL MERCHANTS
    See Lovell, George William. Love's Sacrifice.
RIVAL PAGES, THE
    See Selby, Charles.
RIVAL QUEENS
    See Lee, Nathaniel. Alexander the Great.
    See Somerset, Charles A. Tower of London, The.
RIVAL RAJAHS OF RAMJAM COODLUM, THE
    See Byron, Henry James.
RIVAL SERGEANTS, THE
    See Collier, William.
RIVAL UNCLE, THE; OR, PLOTS IN CALCUTTA (anon.)
    Calcutta: Scott (printer), 1819. Pp. [i-viii], [1]-123.
RIVAL VALETS, THE
    See Ebsworth, Joseph.
RIVALS, THE
    See Sheridan, Richard Brinsley.
RIVER GOD, THE
    See Morton, Edward.
RIVER SPRITE, THE
    See Linley, George.

RIVERS, HENRY J.
    Tale of Two Cities, The. London: Davidson, n.d. Pp. [1]-62.
    Davidson's Actable Drama in Continuation of Cumber-
    land's Plays.
RIZPAH
    See Lyndsay, David.
ROAD TO RUIN, THE
    See Holcroft, Thomas.
ROAD TO YAROSLAF
    See Brown, Charles Armitage. Narensky.
ROADSIDE INN TURNED INSIDE OUT
    See Byron, Henry James. Robert Macaire.
ROB ROY (anon.)
    In *Waverley Dramas*, London: George Routledge, 1845,
    pp. [1]-68. *Filed under* Waverley Dramas (anon.).
ROB ROY
    See Soane, George.
ROB ROY MACGREGOR
    See Pocock, Isaac.
ROB ROY, THE GREGARACH
    See Soane, George.
ROBBER KNIGHT
    See Fitzball, Edward. Hans von Stein.
ROBBER OF GENOA
    See Dibdin, Charles Isaac Mungo, jr. Great Devil, The.
ROBBER OF THE RHINE, THE
    See Almar, George.
ROBBER'S BRIDE, THE
    See Fitzball, Edward.
ROBBER'S WIFE, THE
    See Pocock, Isaac.
ROBBERS OF CALABRIA, THE
    See Lane, W. E.
ROBBERS OF MOUNT CAUCASUS!
    See Atkyns, Samuel. Zulor, the Circassian Chief.
ROBBERS OF THE PYRENEES, THE
    See Suter, William E.
ROBBERS OF THE REVOLUTION
    See Higgie, Thomas Henry. Belphegor the Buffoon.
ROBBERS' HOLD AND THE BANDIT'S BRIDE
    See Wilks, Thomas Egerton. Scarlet Mantle.
ROBBIN DE BOBBIN AND THE FIRST LORD MAYOR OF
    LUN'ON
    See Fitzball, Edward. Harlequin and Humpty Dumpty.
ROBERDEAU, JOHN PETER
    Alarmist, The; or, Chearful Opinions. In *Fugitive Verse and
    Prose*, 2nd ed., London: W. Button & Son, 1804, pp. [i],
    [20]-25.
ROBERT AND RICHARD WERE TWO PRETTY MEN
    See Douglass, John T. Dame Durden and Her Five
    Servant Maids.
ROBERT BURNS
    See Lemon, Mark.
ROBERT EMMET
    See Boucicault, Dionysius Lardner.
ROBERT MACAIRE
    See Byron, Henry James.
    See Martinetti, Paul Robert.
    See Selby, Charles.
ROBERT THE DEVIL (anon.)
    Music by Meyerbeer. London: Chappell, n.d. Pp. [1]-32.
    Libretto.
ROBERT THE DEVIL
    See Gilbert, William Schwenck.
    See Lacy, Michael Rophino.
    See Raymond, Richard John.
ROBERTO IL DIAVOLO
    See Maggioni, Manfredo (trans.).
    See Oxenford, John.
ROBERTS, GEORGE
    Absent Man, The. London & New York: Samuel French,
    n.d. Pp. [1]-[20]. [Lacy's Acting Edition].
    Ample Apology, An. London: Thomas Hailes Lacy, n.d. Pp.
    [1]-16. [Lacy's Acting Edition].

Behind the Curtain. London: Thomas Hailes Lacy, n.d. Pp. [i-iv], [1]-56.

Blind Love. London: T. Scott (printer), n.d. Pp. [1]-20.

Cousin Tom. London: Thomas Hailes Lacy, n.d. Pp. [1]-18. [Lacy's Acting Edition].

Dross; or, The Root of Evil. By M. E. B. (i.e., from the novel by Mary Elizabeth Braddon). New York: DeWitt, n.d. Pp. [1]-62.

Forty Winks. New York: Samuel French, n.d. Pp. [1]-16. French's Minor Drama, [325].

Idalia; or, The Adventuress. London: Thomas Hailes Lacy, n.d. Pp. [1]-44. [Lacy's Acting Edition].

Lady Audley's Secret. N.p.: n.pub. (priv.), n.d. Pp. [1]-40.

Partnership. London: Thomas Scott (printer), n.d. Pp. [1]-40.

Three Furies, The. London: Thomas Hailes Lacy, n.d. Pp. [1]-16. [Lacy's Acting Edition].

Under the Rose. London & New York: Samuel French, n.d. Pp. [1]-17.

ROBERTS, RANDAL HOWLAND

Silver Trout, The. Written with Stephenson, Benjamin Charles. Music by Clarke, Hamilton. London: Metzler, n.d. Pp. [1]-16. Libretto.

Under a Veil. Written with Baker, George Melville. Boston: George M. Baker, 1877. Pp. [i-ii], [1]-20.

ROBERTSON, CHARLES GRANT

Voces Academicae. New York: M. F. Mansfield, 1898. Pp. [i-viii], 1-207.

ROBERTSON, IAN

Pity of It, The. London & New York: Samuel French, c.1901. Pp. [1]-12.

Play in Little, A. Pp. [i-iii], [1]-26. Typescript.

ROBERTSON, JOHNSTON FORBES

See Forbes-Robertson, Johnston.

ROBERTSON, STUART

Wapping Old Stairs. Music by Talbot, Howard. London: Hopwood & Crew, 1894. Pp. [i-ii], [1]-41. Libretto.

ROBERTSON, THOMAS WILLIAM

Betty Martin.
See Clockmaker's Hat, The.

Birds of Prey; or, A Duel in the Dark. London: Thomas Hailes Lacy, n.d. Pp. [1]-42. [Lacy's Acting Edition].

Birth. London & New York: Samuel French, n.d. In *Principal Dramatic Works,* 2 vols., London: Sampson Low, Marston, Searle, & Rivington, 1889, I, [i], [1]-47.

Breach of Promise, A. New York: DeWitt, n.d. Pp. [1]-20. DeWitt's Acting Plays, 179.

Cantab, The. *Also:* The Young Collegian. London & New York: Samuel French, n.d. Pp. [1]-27. [Lacy's Acting Edition].

Caste. New York: T. H. French, n.d. Pp. [1]-54.

Caste. 113 leaves. Manuscript promptbook.

Chevalier de St. George, The. London: Thomas Hailes Lacy, n.d. Pp. [1]-35. [Lacy's Acting Edition].

Clarisse.
See Noémie.

Clockmaker's Hat, The. *Also:* Betty Martin. Also attrib. to Harris, H. G. London: Thomas Hailes Lacy, n.d. Pp. [1]-14. Lacy's Acting Edition, 266.

David Garrick. New York & London: Samuel French, n.d. Pp. [1]-36. [French's Acting Edition, 117]. Promptbook.

Dreams. *Also:* My Lady Clare. London & New York: Samuel French, n.d. Pp. [186]-231. [Lacy's Acting Edition].

Ernestine. *Also:* Noémie. New York: Samuel French, n.d. Pp. [1]-27. French's American Drama, 13.

Faust and Marguerite. By William Robertson. Also attrib. to Boucicault, Dionysius Lardner. London: Thomas Hailes Lacy, n.d. Pp. [1]-28. [Lacy's Acting Edition].

For Love. 85 leaves. Partly paginated. Manuscript.

Foster Sisters, The.
See Noémie.

Half Caste, The; or, The Poisoned Pearl. London & New York: Samuel French, n.d. Pp. [1]-36.

Home. London & New York: Samuel French, n.d. Pp. [233]-274. French's Acting Edition (late Lacy's).

Jocrisse the Juggler. *Also:* Magloire the Prestigitator. London: Samuel French; New York: T. Henry French, n.d. Pp. [1]-44.

Ladies' Battle, The. London: Thomas Hailes Lacy, n.d. Pp. [1]-43. [Lacy's Acting Edition].

Lost Husband, The.
See Reade, Charles.

M.P. In *Principal Dramatic Works,* 2 vols., London: Sampson Low, Marston, Searle, & Rivington, 1889, I, [i], [321]-376.

Magloire the Prestigitator.
See Jocrisse the Juggler.

My Lady Clare.
See Dreams.

My Wife's Diary. *Also:* A Wife's Journal. New York: Robert M. DeWitt, n.d. Pp. [1]-15.

Nightingale, The. London & New York: Samuel French, n.d. In *Principal Dramatic Works,* 2 vols., London: Sampson Low, Marston, Searle, & Rivington, 1889, II, [i], [377]-418.

Noémie. By William Robertson. *Also:* Ernestine. *Also:* Clarisse; or, The Foster Sister. *Also:* The Foster Sisters. London & New York: Samuel French, n.d. Pp. [1]-36.

Not at All Jealous. London: Thomas Hailes Lacy, n.d. Pp. [1]-20.

Ours. New York & London: Samuel French, n.d. Pp. [1]-56. French's Standard Drama, 384.

Ours. London & New York: Samuel French, n.d. Pp. [1]-56. Promptbook.

Passion Flowers. 47 leaves. Manuscript.

Peace at Any Price! New York: DeWitt, n.d. Pp. [1]-10. DeWitt's Acting Plays, 156.

Play. London & New York: Samuel French, n.d. Pp. [489]-542. [Lacy's Acting Edition].

Progress. [London & New York: Samuel French], n.d. Pp. [543]-601. [Lacy's Acting Edition].

Row in the House, A. London & New York: Samuel French, n.d. In *Principal Dramatic Works,* 2 vols., London: Sampson Low, Marston, Searle, & Rivington, 1889, II, [i], [603]-623.

School. New York: Robert M. DeWitt, n.d. Pp. [1]-40.

School. N.p.: n.pub., n.d. Pp. [i-ii], [1]-54. Promptbook.

Sea of Ice, The; or, The Prayer of the Wrecked and the Gold-Seeker of Mexico. London: Thomas Hailes Lacy, n.d. Pp. [1]-43. [Lacy's Acting Edition]. *Filed under* Sea of Ice (anon.).

Sea of Ice, The; or, The Prayer of the Wrecked and the Gold-Seeker of Mexico. *Also:* The Thirst of Gold; or, The Lost Ship and the Wild Flower of Mexico. *Also:* The Struggle for Gold. *Also:* The Struggle for Gold and the Orphan of the Frozen Sea. London & New York: Samuel French, n.d. Pp. [1]-43.

Society. London: Thomas Hailes Lacy, n.d. Pp. [1]-65.

Star of the North, The. London: Thomas Hailes Lacy, n.d. Pp. [1]-36. [Lacy's Acting Edition].

Struggle for Gold, The.
See Sea of Ice.

Thirst of Gold, The.
See Sea of Ice.

Two Gay Deceivers; or, Black, White, and Grey. Chicago: Dramatic Publishing Co., n.d. Pp. [1]-11. Sergel's Acting Drama, 56.

War. London & New York: Samuel French, n.d. Pp. [742]-789. French's Standard Drama, 407.

Wife's Journal, A.
See My Wife's Diary.

Young Collegian, The. *Also:* The Cantab. Chicago: [Dramatic Publishing Co.], n.d. Pp. [1]-19.

ROBERTSON, WILLIAM

See Robertson, Thomas William.

ROBESPIERRE

See Bernard, William Bayle.

See Bliss, Henry.

ROBIN GOODFELLOW

See Carton, R. C.

ROBIN HOOD
  See Brough, William.
  See Burnand, Francis Cowley.
  See Fitzball, Edward.
  See Oxenford, John.
ROBIN HOOD AND MAID MARIAN
  See Tennyson, Alfred, Lord. Foresters, The.
ROBIN HOOD AND YE CURTALL FRYER
  See Dawtrey, Augustin.
ROBINSON, AGNES MARY FRANCIS (later Mrs. James
  Darmesteter; Mrs. Duclaux)
  Our Lady of the Broken Heart. In *Songs, Ballads, and a
  Garden Play,* London: T. Fisher Unwin, 1888, pp. [i],
  [113]-142. *Filed under* Duclaux, Agnes Mary Francis. A
  Garden Play.
ROBINSON, EMMA
  Richelieu in Love; or, The Youth of Charles I. New York:
  Benjamin & Young, 1844. Pp. [i]-[xx], [1]-54.
ROBINSON, FREDERICK WILLIAM
  Her Face Was Her Fortune. London: E. J. Francis (printer),
  1877. Pp. [1]-57.
ROBINSON, NUGENT
  Miss Tibbets' Back Hair. London & New York: Samuel
  French, n.d. Pp. [1]-20. [Lacy's Acting Edition].
ROBINSON, SAMUEL (trans.)
  William Tell. By Schiller. London: Hurst, Robinson, 1825.
  Pp. [i-vi], [1]-189.
ROBINSON CRUSOE
  See Blanchard, Edward Litt Leman.
  See Byron, Henry James.
  See Fortescue, F.
  See McArdle, John Francis.
  See Pocock, Isaac.
  See Wade, William.
ROBSON, E. M.
  Foundling, The.
  See Lestocq, William.
ROBSON, FREDERICK (pseud. of Brownbill, Thomas Robson)
  Popocatapetl. London & New York: Samuel French, n.d. Pp.
  [1]-15. [Lacy's Acting Edition].
ROBSON, WILLIAM
  Comedy and Tragedy. New York & London: Samuel French,
  n.d. Pp. [1]-24. Minor Drama, 149.
ROBSON, WILLIAM JAMES
  Love and Loyalty. Boston: William V. Spencer, n.d. Pp.
  [1]-71. Spencer's Boston Theatre, 41.
  Waltheof.
  See Serle, Thomas James.
ROBY, BERNARD SOANE
  See Soane-Roby, Bernard.
ROBY, JOHN
  Duke of Mantua, The. London: G. & W. B. Whittaker, 1823.
  Pp. [1]-126. 2nd ed.
ROCAMBOLE
  See Suter, William E.
ROCHE, EUGENIUS
  Invasion, The; or, The Anglo-Saxons. London: T. & R.
  Hughes, 1808. Pp. [230]-296.
  William Tell. London: T. & R. Hughes, 1808. Pp. [153]-227.
ROCHESTER
  See Moncrieff, William Thomas.
ROCK, CHARLES
  Gray Parrot, The.
  See Jacobs, William Wymark.
ROCK OF CHARBONNIERE
  See Fitzball, Edward. Father and Son.
ROCK OF LA CHARBONNIERE
  See Fitzball, Edward. Father and Son.
ROCKET, THE
  See Pinero, Arthur Wing.
ROCKING, THE
  See Hetherington, William Maxwell.
ROCKINGHAM, CHARLES, SIR (pseud. of Rohan-Charot,
  Philippe Ferdinand Auguste de, Count de Jarnac)

Ball Next Door, The. In *Dramatic Sketches,* Worksop: Robert
  White (printer) (priv.), 1866, pp. [115]-133.
Holiday, A; or, Mima and Her Friends. In *Dramatic Sketches,*
  Worksop: Robert White (printer) (priv.), 1866, pp.
  [75]-114.
Man-Servant, A. In *Dramatic Sketches,* Worksop: Robert
  White (printer) (priv.), 1866, pp. [43]-74.
Mendoza. In *Dramatic Sketches,* Worksop: Robert White
  (printer) (priv.), 1866, pp. i-[iv], [1]-41.
RODOLPH THE WOLF
  See Planché, James Robinson.
RODWELL, GEORGE HERBERT BONAPARTE
  Chimney Piece, The; or, The Married Maid. Philadelphia:
  Frederick Turner, n.d. Pp. [1]-26. Turner's Dramatic
  Library, 4.
  Grimalkin; or, A Woman Changed into a Cat. London: John
  Dicks, n.d. Pp. [1]-10. Dicks' Standard Plays, 515.
  Harlequin and Good Queen Bess.
  See Lee, Nelson, sr.
  Husbands, Wives, and Lovers. London: William Barth, n.d.
  Pp. [i-vi], [1]-17. Barth's Universal Stage or Theatrical
  Prompt Book, 54.
  I'll Be Your Second. *Also:* The Note at Hand. London:
  Thomas Hailes Lacy, n.d. Pp. [1]-13. [Lacy's Acting
  Edition].
  My Own Lover. Music by Rodwell. London: W. Reynolds
  (printer), 1832. Pp. [1]-22. Libretto.
  My Wife's Out. London: Thomas Hailes Lacy, n.d. Pp.
  [1]-20. [Lacy's Acting Edition].
  Mysterious Family, The. London: Thomas Hailes Lacy, n.d.
  Pp. [5]-31. Title page lacking. Lacy's Acting Edition, 53.
  Note at Hand, The.
  See I'll Be Your Second.
  **Ourang Outang and His Double, The; or, The Runaway
  Monkey.** London: John Dicks, n.d. Pp. [9]-18. Dicks'
  Standard Plays, 606. *Filed under* Addison, Henry Robert;
  Rodwell, G. Herbert. Blue-faced Baboon.
  Pride of Birth. London: John Duncombe, n.d. Pp. [1]-44.
  Duncombe's Edition.
  Seven Maids of Munich, The; or, The Ghost's Tower. N.p.:
  n.pub., n.d. Pp. [1-25].
  Students of Bonn, The. Music by Rodwell. London: W. S.
  Johnson (printer), 1842. Pp. [1]-16. Libretto.
  Teddy the Tiler. New York: E. B. Clayton, 1830. Pp. [1]-22.
  [Clayton's Edition]. Promptbook.
  Teddy the Tiler. London: John Cumberland, n.d. Pp. [1]-27.
  Cumberland's British Theatre, XXV. *Filed under* Cum-
  berland, John. Cumberland's British Theatre, XXV.
  Was I to Blame? London: Thomas Hailes Lacy, n.d. Pp.
  [1]-19. [Lacy's Acting Edition].
  Where Shall I Dine? London: Duncombe & Moon, n.d. Pp.
  [1]-24. Duncombe's Edition.
RODWELL, JAMES THOMAS GOODERHAM
  Bachelor's Torments; or, The Sweets of a Family. London:
  John Duncombe, n.d. Pp. [1]-20. Duncombe's Edition.
  More Blunders Than One; or, The Irish Valet. London: John
  Miller, 1825. Pp. [i]-[viii], [1]-59.
  More Blunders Than One. London & New York: Samuel
  French, n.d. Pp. [1]-28. [Lacy's Acting Edition].
  Race for a Dinner, A. London: John Cumberland, 1828. Pp.
  [1]-28. Cumberland's British Theatre, XIX. *Filed under*
  Cumberland, John. Cumberland's British Theatre, XIX.
  Race for a Dinner, A. Philadelphia: P. G. Weikel; New York:
  Elton & Perkins, n.d. Pp. [1]-24.
  Trifles Light as Air! London: John Lowndes, n.d. Pp. [i-iv],
  [1]-48.
  Young Widow, The; or, A Lesson for Lovers. London: John
  Miller, 1824. Pp. [i-iv], [1]-40.
ROEBUCK, THE
  See Somerset, Charles A.
ROGERS, MAUD M.
  When the Wheels Run Down. New York & London: Samuel
  French, c.1899. Pp. [1]-15.

ROGERS, T. STANLEY
    For the Old Love's Sake. London & New York: Samuel French, n.d. Pp. [1]-39. [Lacy's Acting Edition].
ROGERS, WILLIAM
    Black Hugh, the Outlaw. London: John Duncombe, n.d. Pp. [1]-36. Duncombe's Edition.
    Jack's the Lad; or, The Pride of the Ocean. New York: Samuel French, n.d. Pp. [1]-24. French's Minor Drama, 307.
    Murphy's Weather Almanac. London: W. Strange, 1838. Pp. [1]-24.
    Paul the Reprobate; or, The Law in 1656. N.p.: n.pub., n.d. Pp. [171]-186. Title page lacking.
    Soldier and a Sailor, a Tinker and a Tailor, A. London: James Pattie, n.d. Pp. [1]-23.
    Soldier and a Sailor, a Tinker and a Tailor, A. Boston: Walter H. Baker, n.d. Pp. [1]-16. Spencer's Universal Stage, 66.
    Tom Tiller and Jack Mizen; or, Sprees Along Shore! London: John Duncombe, n.d. Pp. [1]-42. Duncombe's Acting Edition of the British Theatre, 259.
    Virginius the Rum'un. London: W. Strange, 1837. Pp. [1]-20.
ROGUE'S COMEDY, THE
    See Jones, Henry Arthur.
ROGUERIES OF NICHOLAS
    See Moncrieff, William Thomas. Adventures of a Ventriloquist.
ROGUERIES OF SCAPIN, THE
    See Van Laun, Henri (trans.).
ROGUES OF PARIS
    See Stirling, Edward. Bohemians, The.
ROHAN-CHAROT, PHILIPPE FERDINAND AUGUSTE DE, COUNT DE JARNAC
    See Rockingham, Charles, Sir (pseud.).
ROI S'AMUSE
    See Slous, Frederick L. (trans.). Francis the First.
ROJAS Y ZORILLA, FRANCISCO DE
    Bandos de Verona, Los: Montescos y Capuletes.
    See Cosens, Frederick William (trans.).
ROKEBY, MATTHEW ROBINSON-MORRIS
    Fall of Mortimer, The. London: William Bulmer (printer), 1806. Pp. [i-vi], [1]-105.
ROKEBY
    See Thompson, C. Pelham.
ROLAND
    See Maudslay, A.
ROLAND FOR AN OLIVER, A
    See Morton, Thomas, sr.
ROLL OF THE DRUM, THE
    See Wilks, Thomas Egerton.
ROLLA
    See Thompson, Benjamin (trans.).
ROMAN, THE
    See Dobell, Sydney Thompson.
ROMAN FATHER, THE
    See Whitehead, William.
ROMAN GLADIATOR
    See Jones, Jacob. Spartacus.
ROMAN MATRON
    See Kemble, John Philip (arr.). Coriolanus.
    See Shakespeare, William. Coriolanus.
ROMAN MUTINY, THE
    See Cobbold, Elizabeth Knipe, Mrs. John.
ROMAN NOSE
    See Almar, George. Good-Looking Fellow, The.
ROMAN PATRIOT
    See Ireland, William Henry. Mutius Scaevola.
ROMANCE!
    See Simpson, John Palgrave.
ROMANCE AND REALITY
    See Brougham, John.
ROMANCE OF A CITY LIFE
    See Reeve, Wybert. George Geith.
ROMANCE OF A DAY
    See Dibdin, Thomas John. Morning, Noon, and Night.

ROMANCE OF A POOR YOUNG MAN
    See Edwards, Pierrepont. Honour before Wealth.
    See Edwards, Pierrepont.
ROMANCE OF LOVE, A
    See Steven, Alexander.
ROMANCE OF MARRIAGE
    See Serle, Thomas James. Tender Precautions.
ROMANCE OF THE NOSE
    See Taylor, Tom. Prince Dorus.
ROMANCE UNDER DIFFICULTIES
    See Burnand, Francis Cowley.
ROMANTIC ATTACHMENT, A
    See Wood, Arthur.
ROMANTIC CAROLINE
    See Hatton, Joseph.
ROMANTIC FARCE, A
    See Davidson, John.
ROMANTIC IDEA, A
    See Planché, James Robinson.
ROMANY RYE, THE
    See Sims, George Robert.
ROME WAS NOT BUILT IN A DAY
    See Croker, Thomas Francis Dillon. Romulus and Remus.
ROMEO AND JULIET
    See Anderson, Mary (arr.).
    See Farnie, Henry Brougham. Romeo e Giulietta.
    See Forbes-Robertson, Johnston (arr.).
    See Garrick, David (arr.).
    See Halliday, Andrew.
    See Irving, Henry (arr.).
    See Kemble, John Philip (arr.).
    See Shakespeare, William.
ROMEO AND JULIET: AS THE LAW DIRECTS
    See Dowling, Maurice G.
ROMEO AND JULIET TRAVESTY
    See Gurney, Richard.
ROMEO E GIULIETTA
    See Farnie, Henry Brougham.
ROMER, FRANK (trans.)
    Ugonotti, Gli. *Also:* Les Huguenots. Music by Meyerbeer. London & New York: Boosey, n.d. Pp. [i-vi], 1-500. Vocal score. *Filed under* Romer, Francis.
ROMER, FREDERICK
    April Showers.
    See Bellamy, G. Somers.
ROMIERO
    See Baillie, Joanna.
ROMP, THE
    See Lloyd, ? (arr.).
ROMULUS AND REMUS
    See Croker, Thomas Francis Dillon.
    See Reece, Robert.
ROOF SCRAMBLER, THE
    See A'Beckett, Gilbert Abbott.
ROOKWOOD
    See Atkyns, Samuel.
ROOT OF EVIL
    See Braddon, Mary Elizabeth. Dross.
    See Roberts, George. Dross.
ROPES, ARTHUR REED
    See Ross, Adrian (pseud.).
RORY O'MORE
    See Lover, Samuel.
ROSALIE
    See Ebsworth, Joseph.
ROSAMOND
    See Holcroft, Fanny (trans.).
    See Swinburne, Algernon Charles.
ROSAMUND
    See Baildon, Henry Bellyse.
ROSAMUND, QUEEN OF THE LOMBARDS
    See Swinburne, Algernon Charles.
ROSCOE, MARGARET
    See Sandbach, Margaret Roscoe, Mrs. Henry R.

ROSCOE, THOMAS
    Gonzalo the Traitor. London: Hayward & Roscoe, n.d. Pp. [i-ii], [1]-79.

ROSCOE, WILLIAM CALDWELL
    Eliduke, Count of Yveloc. In *Poems and Essays,* London: Chapman & Hall, 1860, I, [i], [103]-213.
    Violenzia. In *Poems and Essays,* London: Chapman & Hall, 1860, I, [215]-356.

ROSE, EDWARD
    Columbus. London: Effingham Wilson, 1873. Pp. [i-vi], [1]-112.
    Equals. London & New York: Samuel French, n.d. Pp. [1]-34. [Lacy's Acting Edition].
    Girl Graduate, A. London & New York: Samuel French, n.d. Pp. [1]-18. [French's Acting Edition].
    Marble Arch, The. Written with Garraway, Agnes J. Chicago: Dramatic Publishing Co., n.d. Pp. [1]-16. Sergel's Acting Drama, 482.
    Phroso. Written with Esmond, Henry V. [New York: Rosenfield Typewriting], n.d. Pp. [i-ii], [1]-40, [i], [1]-38, [i], [1]-36, [i], [1]-21. Pagination by act. Typescript.
    Under the Red Robe. [New York: Rosenfield Typewriting], n.d. Pp. [i-vi], [1]-33, [1]-33, [1]-37, [1]-17. Pagination by act. Typescript.
    Vice Versa: A Lesson for Fathers. London & New York: Samuel French, n.d. Pp. [1]-28. [Lacy's Acting Edition].
    Wild Flowers. London & New York: Samuel French, n.d. Pp. [1]-14.

ROSE, GEORGE
    See Sketchley, Arthur (pseud.).

ROSE AND THE RING, THE
    See Clarke, Henry Saville.
    See Wilks, Thomas Egerton. Ambassador's Lady, The.

ROSE AND THE THISTLE
    See Lunn, Joseph. Rights of Woman, The.

ROSE MICHEL
    See Clarke, Campbell (trans.).

ROSE OF ALVEY
    See Stafford, John Joseph. Pretender, The.

ROSE OF AMIENS
    See Morton, John Maddison. Our Wife.

ROSE OF ARRAGON, THE
    See Knowles, James Sheridan.

ROSE OF AUVERGNE, THE
    See Farnie, Henry Brougham.

ROSE OF CASTILE, THE
    See Harris, Augustus Glossop.

ROSE OF CORBEIL, THE
    See Stirling, Edward.

ROSE OF ETTRICK VALE, THE
    See Lynch, Thomas J.

ROSE OF GURGISTAN
    See Noble, Thomas. Persian Hunters, The.

ROSE OF PERSIA, THE
    See Hood, Basil Charles Willett.

ROSE OF SLEAT, THE
    See Lyne, S. M.

ROSE QUEEN
    See Beazley, Samuel, jr. Philandering.

ROSE, THISTLE, AND SHAMROCK, THE
    See Edgeworth, Maria.

ROSE WITHOUT A THORN
    See Falconer, Edmund. Chrystabelle.

ROSEBUD OF STINGINGNETTLE FARM, THE
    See Byron, Henry James.

ROSEMARY, THAT'S FOR REMEMBRANCE
    See Parker, Louis Napoleon.

ROSENCRANTZ AND GUILDENSTERN
    See Gilbert, William Schwenck.

ROSES AND THORNS
    See Lunn, Joseph.

ROSINA
    See Brooke, Frances Moore, Mrs. John.

ROSMER OF ROSMERSHOLM
    See Fryers, Austin.

ROSMERSHOLM
    See Anstey, F.
    See Archer, Charles (trans.).

ROSMUNDA
    See Lloyd, Charles (trans.).

ROSS, ADRIAN (pseud. of Ropes, Arthur Reed)
    Ballet Girl, The.
        See Tanner, James Tolman.
    Billy.
        See Cooper, G.
    Circus Girl, The.
        See Tanner, James Tolman.
    Don Juan. Written with Tanner, James Tolman. Music by Lutz, Meyer. London: E. Ascherberg, c.1894. Pp. [i-iv], 1-105. Vocal score. *Filed under* Ropes, Arthur Reed.
    Go Bang. Music by Carr, F. Osmond. London: Joseph Williams, n.d. Pp. [1]-31. Libretto.
    Grand Duchess of Gerolstein, The.
        See Brookfield, Charles Hallam Elton (trans.).
    Greek Slave, A.
        See Hall, Owen.
    In Town. Written with Leader, James. Music by Carr, F. Osmond. Pp. [i-ii], [1]-50, [i], [1]-27. Pagination by act. Typescript libretto. *Filed under* Ropes, Arthur Reed.
    In Town. Written with Leader, James. Music by Carr, F. Osmond. London: Joseph Williams, n.d. Pp. [i-ii], 1-117. Vocal score.
    Joan of Arc.
        See Shine, John L.
    Kitty Grey. Music by Barratt, Augustus; Talbot, Howard. London: E. Ascherberg, c.1900. Pp. [i-ii], 1-113. Vocal score. *Filed under* Ropes, Arthur Reed.
    Lucky Star, The.
        See Brookfield, Charles Hallam Elton.
    Mary and Sairey; or, Faithless Tommy. Music by Thiele, Richard. London: Joseph Williams, c.1898. Pp. [i], [1]-19. Vocal score. *Filed under* Ropes, Arthur Reed.
    Messenger Boy, The.
        See Tanner, James Tolman.
    Morocco Bound.
        See Branscombe, Arthur.
    My Girl. Written with Tanner, James Tolman. Music by Carr, F. Osmond. London: Joseph Williams, c.1896. Pp. [i-ii], [1]-104. Vocal score. *Filed under* Ropes, Arthur Reed.
    San Toy.
        See Morton, Edward.
    Shop Girl, The.
        See Dam, Henry Jackson Wells.

ROSS, ADRIAN (pseud. of Ropes, Arthur Reed) (arr.)
    Faust and Gretchen. By Kohler, W. Music by Thiele, Richard. London: Joseph Williams, n.d. Pp. [1]-22. Vocal score. *Filed under* Ropes, Arthur Reed.

ROSS, RONALD
    Deformed Transformed, The. London: Chapman & Hall, 1892. Pp. [i]-viii, [1]-[158].
    Edgar; or, The New Pygmalion. In *Edgar; or, The New Pygmalion, and The Judgment of Tithonus,* Madras: Higginbotham, 1883, pp. 27-151.
    Judgment of Tithonus, The. In *Edgar; or, The New Pygmalion, and The Judgment of Tithonus,* Madras: Higginbotham, 1883, pp. [i-iv], [1]-26. *Filed under* Edgar.

ROSS, SHERIDAN
    Quentin Durward. Music by Maclean, Alick. London: E. Ascherberg, c.1894. Pp. [i-ii], 1-277. Vocal score.

ROSTAND, EDMOND
    Eaglet, The.
        See Parker, Louis Napoleon (trans.).
    Fantasticks, The.
        See Fleming, George (trans.).

ROTHOMAGO
    See Farnie, Henry Brougham.

ROUGE ET NOIR
    See Ebsworth, Joseph.

ROUGE VOLEURS
See Pitt, George Dibdin. Jersey Girl, The.
ROUGH DIAMOND, A
See Buckstone, John Baldwin.
ROUND DELIA'S BASKET
See Sturgis, Julian Russell.
ROUND OF WRONG, THE
See Bernard, William Bayle.
ROUNDHEAD, THE
See Bussy, Bernard F.
ROUSE, MISS T.
Naomi. London: Hamilton, Adams; Norwich: Jarrold & Sons, n.d. Pp. [i]-vi, [7]-24.
ROUSED LION, THE
See Webster, Benjamin Nottingham.
ROVER'S BRIDE, THE
See Almar, George.
ROW IN THE HOUSE, A
See Robertson, Thomas William.
ROWE, BOLTON
See Stephenson, Benjamin Charles.
ROWE, GEORGE FAWCETT
Exiles, The. N.p.: n.pub., n.d. Pp. [1]-41. Title page lacking.
Marry in Haste and Repent at Leisure. New York: Wheat & Cornett, c.1876. Pp. [29]-32. New York Drama, I, 11.
ROWE, HENRY, REV.
Montem, The. London: J. Stratford (printer) (priv.), 1808. Pp. [1-3], [i]-iv, [1]-92.
ROWE, LOUISE, MRS.
See Jopling, Louise Goode, Mrs. Joseph Middleton.
ROWE, NICHOLAS
Fair Penitent, The. London: Whittingham & Arliss, 1815. Pp. [1]-[52]. London Theatre, VIII. *Filed under* Dibdin, Thomas John, ed. London Theatre, VIII.
Fair Penitent, The. London: T. Dolby, 1825. Pp. [1]-46. Dolby's British Theatre, IX. *Filed under* Cumberland, John. Cumberland's British Theatre, IX.
Fair Penitent, The. In *New English Drama,* ed. W. Oxberry, 22 vols., London: W. Simpkin & R. Marshall; C. Chapple, 1831, XXII, [i]-[viii], [9]-[48]. *Filed under* Oxberry, William Henry. New English Drama, XXII.
Fair Penitent, The. In *British Drama,* 12 vols., London: John Dicks, 1864, II, [497]-510.
Fair Penitent, The.
See Kemble, John Philip (arr.).
Jane Shore. London: Whittingham & Arliss, 1815. Pp. [1]-[56]. London Theatre, VII. *Filed under* Dibdin, Thomas John, ed. London Theatre, VII.
Jane Shore. In *New English Drama,* ed. W. Oxberry, 22 vols., London: W. Simpkin & R. Marshall; C. Chapple, 1818, VIII, [1-2], [i]-[viii], [11]-[60]. *Filed under* Oxberry, William Henry. New English Drama, VIII.
Jane Shore. London: John Cumberland, 1826. Pp. [1]-6, [i-iv], [7]-[50], [iii]-[vi], [51]-54. Cumberland's British Theatre, V. *Filed under* Cumberland, John. Cumberland's British Theatre, V.
Jane Shore. In *British Drama,* 12 vols., London: John Dicks, 1864, I, [17]-29.
Jane Shore.
See Kemble, John Philip (arr.).
Lady Jane Grey. London: Sherwood, Neely, & Jones, 1818. Pp. [1]-[56]. London Theatre, XXV. *Filed under* Dibdin, Thomas John, ed. London Theatre, XXV.
Lady Jane Grey. In *British Drama,* 12 vols., London: John Dicks, 1865, IV, [i-iv], [959]-974.
Orange Girl, The.
See Leslie, Henry.
Tamerlane. London: Whittingham & Arliss, 1815. Pp. [1]-64. London Theatre, XIII. *Filed under* Dibdin, Thomas John, ed. London Theatre, XIII.
Tamerlane. In *New English Drama,* ed. W. Oxberry, 22 vols., London: W. Simpkin & R. Marshall; C. Chapple, 1824, XX, [i]-[xviii], [1]-[55]. *Filed under* Oxberry, William Henry. New English Drama, XX.

Tamerlane. In *British Drama,* 12 vols., London: John Dicks, 1871, VIII, [i-iv], [1]-19.
ROWLANDS, ?, PROF. (trans.)
Blodwen (White-Flower). By Mynyddog. Music by Parry, Joseph. Swansea: J. Parry & Son, n.d. Pp. [i-viii], [1]-156. Vocal score.
ROWLEY, WILLIAM
Woman Never Vext, A.
See Planché, James Robinson (arr.).
ROYAL BOX, THE
See Coghlan, Charles Francis.
ROYAL EXILES
See Wolcot, John. Fall of Portugal, The.
ROYAL FAMILY, A
See Marshall, Robert.
ROYAL JUBILEE, THE
See Hogg, James.
ROYAL LOVE-MATCH
See Hill, Isabel. First of May, The.
ROYAL MILKMAID
See Brough, William. Perdita.
ROYAL OAK, THE
See Dimond, William.
ROYAL PENITENT, THE
See Bentley, John.
ROYAL SUFFERERS
See Waterhouse, Benjamin. Annira.
ROYAL VAGRANTS, THE: A STORY OF CONSCIENTIOUS OBJECTION
See Hurst, Cyril.
ROYD, LYNN
Hawkwood Hall. Music by Richardson, George C. Pp. [1-15]. Typescript libretto.
RUBBER OF LIFE, THE
See Stirling, Edward.
RUBENS, PAUL
Florodora.
See Hall, Owen.
RUBY RING, THE
See Wilks, Thomas Egerton.
RUDALL, H. A.
Signa.
See A'Beckett, Gilbert Arthur.
RUDDIGORE
See Gilbert, William Schwenck.
RUDOLF OF VAROSNAY
See Blackwell, J. A.
RUFFIAN BOY, THE
See Dibdin, Thomas John.
RUGANTINO
See Lewis, Matthew Gregory.
RULE A WIFE AND HAVE A WIFE
See Beaumont, Francis.
See Garrick, David (arr.).
See Kemble, John Philip (arr.).
RULE BRITANNIA
See Becher, Martin.
See Campbell, Andrew Leonard Voullaire.
RULE OF CONTRARY
See Morton, John Maddison. Sayings and Doings.
RULE OF THREE, THE
See Talfourd, Francis.
RUMFUSTIAN INNAMORATO
See Walker, Charles Edward.
RUMPLESTILTSKIN
See Burnand, Francis Cowley.
RUNAWAY GIRL, A
See Hicks, Edward Seymour.
RUNAWAY HUSBANDS
See Ladies of Saint-Cyr, The (anon.).
RUNAWAY MONKEY
See Rodwell, George Herbert Bonaparte. Ourang Outang and His Double, The.
RUPERT OF HENTZAU
See Hope, Anthony.

RURAL FELICITY
    See Buckstone, John Baldwin.
RUSE DE GUERRE
    See Wheatley, J. A.
RUSSELL, GEORGIANA ADELAIDE PEEL, LADY
    Dewdrop and Glorio; or, The Sleeping Beauty in the Wood.
    Written with Russell, Victoria, Lady. London: Charles
    Westerton (printer) (priv.), n.d. Pp. [1]-[33].
RUSSELL, HASLINGDEN
    Fair Equestrienne, The. New York & London: Samuel
    French, c.1899. Pp. [1]-13.
RUSSELL, JOHN, LORD (trans.)
    Caius Gracchus. By Monti. London: J. Moyes (printer),
    1830. Pp. [1]-120.
    Don Carlos; or, Persecution. By Schiller. London: Longman,
    Hurst, Rees, Orme, & Brown, 1822. Pp. [i]-[xviii], [1]-119.
RUSSELL, VICTORIA, LADY
    Dewdrop and Glorio.
    See Russell, Georgiana Adelaide Peel, Lady.
RUSSELL; OR, THE RYE-HOUSE PLOT (anon.)
    London: T. Jones, 1839. Pp. [i-iii], [1]-96.
RUSSIAN SACRIFICE, THE
    See Code, H. B.
RUSTIC BANDITTI
    See Phillips, Morrice. Death Guard, The.
RUTH
    See Haines, John Thomas.
RUTH OAKLEY
    See Williams, Thomas John.
RUTH'S ROMANCE
    See Broughton, Frederick William.
RUTHVEN
    See Harris, Augustus Glossop.
RUY BLAS
    See Crosland, Camilla Dufour Toulmin, Mrs. Newton.
    See Falconer, Edmund.
    See Gilbert, William Schwenck.
RUY BLAS AND THE BLASÉ ROUÉ
    See Torr, A. C.
RUY BLAS RIGHTED
    See Reece, Robert.
RYAN, DESMOND LUMLEY
    King Charles II. Music by Macfarren, George Alexander.
    London: Chappell; Cramer, Beale, n.d. Pp. [1]-40.
    Libretto.
    One Too Many. London: Samuel French; New York: T.
    Henry French, n.d. Pp. [1]-14. [Lacy's Acting Edition].
RYAN, DESMOND LUMLEY (trans.)
    Pietro il Grande. Music by Jullien, L. G. London: T. Brettell,
    n.d. Pp. [i]-[vii], [6]-104. Libretto.
RYAN, RICHARD
    Everybody's Husband. London & New York: Samuel French,
    n.d. Pp. [3]-28. French's Acting Edition (late Lacy's).
    Everybody's Husband. London: John Cumberland, n.d. Pp.
    [1]-28. Cumberland's Minor Theatre, IV. *Filed under*
    Cumberland, John. Cumberland's Minor Theatre, IV.
    Pauvre Jacques, Le. London: John Cumberland, n.d. Pp.
    [1]-33.
    Pauvre Jacques, Le. London: John Cumberland, n.d. Pp.
    [1]-33. Cumberland's Minor Theatre, X. *Filed under*
    Cumberland, John. Cumberland's Minor Theatre, X.
    Quite at Home. London: John Cumberland, n.d. Pp. [1]-25.
    Quite at Home. London: John Cumberland, n.d. Pp. [1]-25.
    Cumberland's British Theatre, XXXV. *Filed under* Cum-
    berland, John. Cumberland's British Theatre, XXXV.
RYE-HOUSE PLOT
    See Russell (anon.).
RYLEY, MADELEINE LUCETTE, MRS. J. H.
    Jedbury Junior. London & New York: Samuel French,
    c.1900. Pp. [i-iv], [1]-65.
S., F. M.
    Nettle Coats.
    See Greene, Louisa Lilias Plunket, Mrs. Richard Jonas
    (Baroness).

S., L. M.
    King Richard the First. London: J. Diprose, 1857. Pp. [1]-39.
SABRE GRINDERS OF DAMASCUS
    See Fitzball, Edward. Three Hunchbacks, The.
SACRIFICE TO THE NILE
    See Hume, Robert William. Meroth.
SAD MEMORIES
    See Withers, Frank.
SADAK AND KALASRADE
    See Farley, Charles.
    See Mitford, Mary Russell.
SAFE AND SOUND
    See Hook, Theodore Edward.
SAILOR OF FRANCE, THE
    See Johnstone, John Beer.
SAILOR'S DAUGHTER, THE
    See Cumberland, Richard.
SAILOR'S LEGACY, A
    See Fitzball, Edward.
SAILOR'S RETURN
    See Bickerstaffe, Isaac. Thomas and Sally.
SAILORS' RETURN, THE (anon.)
    In *New British Theatre*, London: A. J. Valpy (printer),
    1814, II, [i], [311]-[355].
SAINT ROBERT'S CAVE
    See Moncrieff, William Thomas. Eugene Aram.
SAINT'S TRAGEDY, THE
    See Kingsley, Charles.
SAINTS AND SINNERS
    See Jones, Henry Arthur.
SAKOONTALA
    See Williams, Monier (trans.).
SALA, BROTHERS
    See Sala, George Augustus Henry Fairfield; Sala, C. K.
SALA, C. K.
    Harlequin Billy Taylor.
    See Ellis, George.
SALA, GEORGE AUGUSTUS HENRY FAIRFIELD
    Harlequin Billy Taylor.
    See Ellis, George.
    Wat Tyler, M.P. London: n.pub., n.d. Pp. [1]-34.
SALADIN
    See Verral, Charles.
SALAMAN, MALCOLM CHARLES
    Dimity's Dilemma. London & New York: Samuel French,
    n.d. Pp. [1]-18. [Lacy's Acting Edition].
SALEM REDEEMED
    See Peel, Edmund.
SALLY IN OUR ALLEY
    See Jerrold, Douglas William.
SALOMÉ
    See Wilde, Oscar Fingall O'Flahertie Wills.
SALVIN, HUGH, REV. (trans.)
    Maid of Orleans, The. By Schiller. In *Mary Stuart; The Maid
    of Orleans,* London: Longman, Hurst, Rees, Orme,
    Brown, & Green, 1824, [199]-382. *Filed under* Mary
    Stuart.
    Mary Stuart. By Schiller. In *Mary Stuart; The Maid of
    Orleans,* London: Longman, Hurst, Rees, Orme, Brown,
    & Green, 1824, [1-4], [i]-xli, [1]-198.
SALVINI, TOMMASO (arr.)
    Macbeth. By Shakespeare, William. Manchester: Emmott's
    Printing Works, 1884. Pp. [1]-51. *Filed under* Macbeth
    (anon.).
SAM WELLER
    See Moncrieff, William Thomas.
SAM'S ARRIVAL
    See Oxenford, John.
SAMPLE VERSUS PATTERN
    See Sapte, William, jr.
SAMSON AND DALILAH
    See Lyster, Frederic (trans.).
SAMUEL IN SEARCH OF HIMSELF
    See Coyne, Joseph Stirling.

SAN TOY
See Morton, Edward A.
SANCTUARY, THE
See Carpenter, Joseph Edwards.
SANDBACH, MARGARET ROSCOE, MRS. HENRY R.
Giuliano de' Medici. In *Giuliano de' Medici . . . with Other Poems,* London: William Pickering, 1842, pp. [i], [1]-128.
SANDS, JOHN SIM
Tory Member's Awl Brought to His Last, A.; or, The Shoemaker's Cut at Corruption. In *Poems,* Arbroath: Stewart; Montrose: Nichol; Dundee: Shaw, 1833, pp. [i], [158]-183.
SANTLEY, CHARLES
Joconde. Music by Isouard, Nicolo. London: [Carl Rosa Opera Co.], n.d. Pp. [1]-32. Libretto.
SAPPHO
See Bramsen, John (trans.).
See Burnand, Francis Cowley.
See Lee, Eliza Buckminster, Mrs. (trans.).
See Serle, Thomas James (trans.).
SAPTE, WILLIAM, JR
Perfect Cure, A. London: Samuel French; New York: T. Henry French, n.d. Pp. [1]-12. [Lacy's Acting Edition].
Sample versus Pattern. London & New York: Samuel French, n.d. Pp. [1]-9. [Lacy's Acting Edition].
Step-Sister, The. London & New York: Samuel French, n.d. Pp. [1]-12. [Lacy's Acting Edition].
SARAH BLANGE.
See Barnett, Morris. Sarah the Creole.
SARAH THE CREOLE
See Barnett, Morris.
SARAH THE JEWESS
See Barnett, Charles Zachary. Dream of Fate, The.
SARAH'S YOUNG MAN
See Suter, William E.
SARDANAPALUS
See A'Beckett, Gilbert Abbott.
See Byron, George Gordon, Lord.
See Calvert, Charles Alexander (arr.).
See Kean, Charles John (arr.).
See Lyndsay, David.
SARDOU, VICTORIEN
Our Boon Companions.
See Lyster, Frederic (trans.).
Sorceress, The.
See Parker, Louis Napoleon (trans.).
SATAN ABSOLVED: A VICTORIAN MYSTERY
See Blunt, Wilfred Scawen.
SATAN BOUND
See Boulding, J. Wimsett.
SATANAS AND THE SPIRIT OF BEAUTY
See Coyne, Joseph Stirling.
SATANELLA
See Harris, Augustus Glossop.
SATURDAY NIGHT AND MONDAY MORNING
See Touch and Take.
SAUL
See Heavysege, Charles.
See Lloyd, Charles (trans.).
SAUL OF TARSUS
See Paley, George Barber.
SAUNDERS, JOHN
Abel Drake. London: [Chapman & Hall] (priv.), 1873. Pp. [1]-53.
Love's Martyrdom. London: Chapman & Hall, 1855. Pp. [i-vi], [1]-154.
SAVAGE-ARMSTRONG, GEORGE FRANCIS
See Armstrong, George Francis.
SAVED
See Shirley, Arthur.
SAVILL, JOHN FAUCIT
See Faucit, John Savill.

SAVILLE, HENRY FAUCITT
Harlequin King Crystal; or, The Princess of the Sea! and the Little Fairy at the Bottom of the Well. Nottingham: Stafford (printer), n.d. Pp. [1]-[31]. Libretto.
SAVONAROLA
See Austin, Alfred.
SAVOURNEEN DEELISH
See Falconer, Edmund. Peep o' Day.
SAVOYARD, THE (anon.)
In *New British Theatre,* London: A. J. Valpy (printer), 1815, IV, [i], [351]-[377]. Libretto.
SAVOYARDS
See Martin, ?, Mrs. Reparation.
SAWBONES IN TRAININ'
See Eupolis (pseud.).
SAYERS, T. ALBERT
Moderation versus Abstinence; or, Our Temperance Discussion. Leeds: John Kershaw, n.d. Pp. [i]-iv, [5]-22.
SAYINGS AND DOINGS
See Morton, John Maddison.
SAYRE, THEODORE BURT
Charles O'Malley. N.p: n.pub., n.d. Pp. [i-ii], [1]-12. Title page lacking. Typescript synopsis.
SCAMPS OF LONDON, THE
See Moncrieff, William Thomas.
SCAN. MAG!
See Poole, John.
SCANDINAVIAN SORCERER
See Dibdin, Thomas John. Harlequin's Magnet.
SCAPEGOAT, THE
See Poole, John.
SCAPEGRACE, THE
See Beazley, Samuel, jr.
SCAPIN'S ROGUERIES
See Mathew, Charles (trans.).
SCARAMOUCH IN NAXOS
See Davidson, John.
SCARAMUCCIA
See Fitzball, Edward.
SCARLET LETTER, THE
See Hatton, Joseph.
SCARLET MANTLE
See Wilks, Thomas Egerton.
SCARLET ROVER
See Bowles, Thomas Gibson. Blazing Burgee, The.
SCENE IN GERMANY
See Maclaren, Archibald. Man Trap, The.
SCENE IN THE LIFE OF AN UNPROTECTED FEMALE, A
See Coyne, Joseph Stirling.
SCENES FROM AN UNFINISHED DRAMA
See Hunt, Leigh.
SCENES FROM THE REJECTED COMEDIES
See A'Beckett, Gilbert Abbott.
SCENES IN BOTH SERVICES
See Townsend, William Thompson. Man of War and the Merchantman, The.
SCHEMES AND COUNTER-SCHEMES
See Boucicault, Dionysius Lardner.
SCHEMING LIEUTENANT
See Sheridan, Richard Brinsley. St. Patrick's Day.
SCHILLER
Bride of Messina, The.
See Irvine, George (trans.).
See Lockwood, Percival (trans.).
See Lodge, Adam (trans.).
See Towler, John (trans.).
Camp of Wallenstein, The.
See Martin, Theodore, Sir (trans.).
Death of Wallenstein, The.
See Coleridge, Samuel Taylor (trans.).
See Pearson, Edward Stanhope (trans.).
Demetrius.
See Martin, Theodore, Sir (trans.).
Don Carlos.
See Cottrell, Charles Herbert (trans.).

See Russell, John, Lord (trans.).
See Towler, John (trans.).

Don Karlos.
    See Bruce, John Wyndham (trans.).

Love and Intrigue.
    See Fettes, James (trans.).

Maid of Orleans, The.
    See Drinkwater, John Elliot (trans.).
    See Maxwell, Patrick, Maj. Gen. (trans.).
    See Peter, William (trans.).
    See Salvin, Hugh, Rev. (trans.).
    See Swanwick, Anna (trans.).
    See Thompson, Henry (trans.).
    See Turner, E. S. (trans.).

Mary Stuart.
    See Kemble, Frances Anne (Fanny) (trans.).
    See Mellish, Joseph Charles (trans.).
    See Peter, William (trans.).
    See Salvin, Hugh, Rev. (trans.).
    See Williams, Thomas (trans.).
    See Wingfield, Lewis Strange (trans.).

Nephew as Uncle, The.
    See Harris, G. Shirley (trans.).

Piccolomini, The.
    See Coleridge, Samuel Taylor (trans.).

Wallenstein.
    See Pearson, Edward Stanhope (trans.).

Wallenstein's Camp.
    See Gower, Francis Leveson, Lord (trans.).
    See Moir, George (trans.).

Wilhelm Tell.
    See Martin, Theodore, Sir (trans.).

William Tell.
    See under title..
    See Banfield, Thomas C. (trans.).
    See Maxwell, Patrick, Maj. Gen. (trans.).
    See Peter, William (trans.).
    See Robinson, Samuel (trans.).
    See Talbot, Robert (trans.).
    See Thompson, Henry (trans.).

SCHOLAR, THE
    See Buckstone, John Baldwin.

SCHOOL
    See Robertson, Thomas William.

SCHOOL FOR ARROGANCE, THE
    See Holcroft, Thomas.

SCHOOL FOR AUTHORS, THE
    See Tobin, John.

SCHOOL FOR COQUETTES, A
    See Simpson, John Palgrave.

SCHOOL FOR DAUGHTERS, THE
    See Lawler, Dennis.

SCHOOL FOR FATHERS
    See Bickerstaffe, Isaac. Lionel and Clarissa.

SCHOOL FOR FRIENDS, THE
    See Chambers, Marianne.

SCHOOL FOR GROWN CHILDREN, A
    See Morton, Thomas, sr.

SCHOOL FOR HUSBANDS, THE
    See Mathew, Charles (trans.).
    See Van Laun, Henri (trans.).

SCHOOL FOR ORATORS, THE; OR, A PEEP AT THE FORUM (anon.)
    New York: David Longworth, 1810. Pp. [1]-[35]. From 1st London ed. of 1809.

SCHOOL FOR PREJUDICE, THE
    See Dibdin, Thomas John.

SCHOOL FOR PRIDE
    See Hyde, George. Love's Victory.

SCHOOL FOR REFORMERS
    See Dwarris, Fortunatus William Lilley. Alberic, Consul of Rome.

SCHOOL FOR SAINTS, THE
    See Hobbes, John Oliver.

SCHOOL FOR SCANDAL, THE
    See Sheridan, Richard Brinsley.

SCHOOL FOR SCHEMING, THE
    See Boucicault, Dionysius Lardner.

SCHOOL FOR TIGERS, THE
    See Lemon, Mark.

SCHOOL FOR WIVES, THE
    See Kelly, Hugh.
    See Mathew, Charles (trans.).
    See Van Laun, Henri (trans.).

SCHOOL FOR WIVES CRITICISED, THE
    See Van Laun, Henri (trans.).

SCHOOL MISTRESS, THE
    See Pinero, Arthur Wing.

SCHOOL OF REFORM, THE
    See Morton, Thomas, sr.

SCHOOL WITHOUT SCHOLARS
    See Hood, Tom. York and Lancaster.

SCHOOLFELLOWS, THE
    See Jerrold, Douglas William.

SCHROEDER, FRIEDRICH LUDWIG
    Ensign, The.
        See Thompson, Benjamin (trans.).

SCOFIELD, JOSEPH ALAN
    Alwynne; or, The Secret of Narboth. London: Wyman & Sons, n.d. Pp. [i-viii], [1]-105.

SCOONES, WILLIAM DALTON (trans.)
    Faust. By Goethe. London: Trubner, 1879. Pp. [i]-vi, [1]-230.

SCOTCH REGALIA
    See Maclaren, Archibald. Oliver Cromwell.

SCOTT, ALFRED
    Affghans' Captive, The; or, Triumph of the British Flag. London: Lee & Haddock (printer) (priv.), 1842. Pp. [1]-[54].

SCOTT, CLEMENT WILLIAM
    Cape Mail, The. London & New York: Samuel French, n.d. Pp. [1]-16. [Lacy's Acting Edition].
    Diplomacy. Written with Stephenson, Benjamin Charles. [New York: Rosenfield Typewriting], n.d. Pp. [i-iii], [1]-53, [i], [1]-41, [i], [1]-31, [i], [1]-26. Pagination by act. Typescript.
    Doris.
        See Stephenson, Benjamin Charles.
    Last Lily, The. [In *Drawing Room Plays*, London: Stanley Rivers, 1879], pp. [203]-237.
    Lily of Leoville, The.
        See Remo, Felix.
    Tears! Idle Tears! London & New York: Samuel French, n.d. Pp. [1]-20. [Lacy's Acting Edition].

SCOTT, JANE M.
    Old Oak Chest, The; or, The Smuggler's Son and Robber's Daughter. London: John Duncombe, n.d. Pp. [3]-36. Duncombe's Acting Edition of the British Theatre, 3.

SCOTT, SHAFTO
    My Unknown Friend. London: John Dicks, n.d. Pp. [1]-19. Dicks' Standard Plays, 412.

SCOTT, W. S.
    On the Clyde. London & New York: Samuel French, n.d. Pp. [1]-26. [Lacy's Acting Edition].

SCOTT, WALTER, SIR
    Antiquary, The.
        See Pocock, Isaac.
    Auchindrane; or, The Ayrshire Tragedy. New York: J. & J. Harper (printer), 1830. Pp. [97]-106, 109-190. Text incomplete. *Filed under* Doom of Devorgoil.
    Doom of Devorgoil, The. New York: J. & J. Harper (printer), 1830. Pp. [i]-[vi], [7]-95.
    Guy Mannering.
        See Terry, Daniel.
    Halidon Hill. Edinburgh: Archibald Constable, 1822. Pp. [3]-109.
    House of Aspen, The. Philadelphia: C. Alexander, 1830. Pp. [1]-69.

SCOTT, WALTER, SIR (trans.)
    Goetz of Berlichingen, with the Iron Hand. By Goethe. Paris: A. & W. Galignani, 1826. Pp. [1-4], [i]-viii, [9]-187.

SCOTT-GATTY, ALFRED SCOTT
    Goose Girl, The. Music by Scott-Gatty. London & New York: Boosey, 1900. Pp. [i]-xii, 1-81. New ed. Vocal score and libretto.

SCOTTISH GOLD MINE
    See Lunn, Joseph. Belford Castle.

SCRAP OF PAPER, A
    See Simpson, John Palgrave.

SCRIBE, EUGÈNE
    Maçon, Le.
        See Wylde, Mrs. Henry (trans.).

SCUDAMORE, F. A.
    Dangers of London. [London: International Typewriting Offices], n.d. Pp. [i], [1]-27, [i], [1]-29, [2]-37, [i], 1-28. Pagination by act. Typescript.

SCUDAMORE, G. H.
    Liberta; or, The Last of the Magicians. Bristol: I. E. Chillcott, 1872. Pp. [1]-52.

SCULL, W. D.
    Bad Lady Betty. London: Elkin Mathews, 1897. Pp. [1]-108.

SCULPTOR'S DREAM
    See Selby, Charles. Marble Heart, The.

SCUTTLED SHIP, THE
    See Reade, Charles.

SEA!, THE
    See Somerset, Charles A.

SEA AND LAND
    See Lemon, Mark.

SEA-BATHING AT HOME
    See Morton, John Maddison.

SEA CAPTAIN, THE
    See Bulwer (later Bulwer-Lytton), Edward George Earle Lytton, Lord Lytton.

SEA-GULLS
    See Maltby, C. Alfred.

SEA KING'S VOW, THE
    See Stirling, Edward.

SEA NYMPH AND THE SALLEE ROVERS
    See Byron, Henry James. Beautiful Haidée!

SEA OF ICE, THE
    See Robertson, Thomas William.

SEA-ROVER AND THE FALL OVER
    See Arden, Henry T. Right-Fall Heir, The.

SEA SIDE HERO, THE
    See Carr, John.

SEA-SIDE STORY
    See Dimond, William.
    See Jerrold, Douglas William. Ambrose Gwinett.

SEA VOYAGE
    See Johnstone, John Beer. Morley Ashton.

SEALED SENTENCE!, THE
    See Stirling, Edward.

SEALS OF JUSTICE
    See Stirling, Edward. Judge Not.

SEAMAN, WILLIAM
    Lamplighter, The; or, The Blind Girl and Little Gerty. London: Thomas Hailes Lacy, n.d. Pp. [1]-72. Cumberland's British Theatre, 61.

SEAMAN'S LOG!
    See Haines, John Thomas. Breakers Ahead!

SEAMAN'S STAR!
    See Stirling, Edward. Anchor of Hope, The.

SEARCH AFTER PERFECTION, A (anon.)
    In *New British Theatre*, London: A. J. Valpy (printer), 1814, III, [33]-94.

SEARCH AFTER PROSERPINE, THE
    See de Vere, Aubrey Thomas.

SEARCH FOR TWO FATHERS
    See Johnstone, John Beer. Pedrillo.

SEARLE, CHARLES
    Castle of Como, The. Music by Cockle, George. London: David Allen & Sons (printer), n.d. Pp. [1]-24. Libretto.

SEBASTIAN OF PORTUGAL
    See Hemans, Felicia Dorothea Browne, Mrs. Alfred.

SECOND BRUTUS, THE
    See Lloyd, Charles (trans.).

SECOND CALENDER, THE
    See Brough, William.

SECOND COMEDY
    See Barber, James.

SECOND LOVE
    See Simpson, John Palgrave.

SECOND MARRIAGE, THE
    See Baillie, Joanna.

SECOND MRS. TANQUERAY, THE
    See Pinero, Arthur Wing.

SECOND THOUGHTS
    See Buckstone, John Baldwin.
    See Herbert, G. C.

SECOND THOUGHTS ARE BEST
    See Buckstone, John Baldwin. Breach of Promise, The.

SECRET
    See Barrymore, William.
    See Beerbohm, Constance.
    See Lavenu, L. (trans.). Haydée.
    See Moncrieff, William Thomas.
    See Soane, George (trans.). Haydée.

SECRET AGENT, THE
    See Coyne, Joseph Stirling.

SECRET ARCH
    See Smith, T. Highgate Tunnel, The.

SECRET BRIDAL, THE
    See Neele, Henry.

SECRET FOE, THE
    See Stirling, Edward.

SECRET MARRIAGE, THE
    See Grist, William (trans.).
    See Murray, William Henry Wood. Philippe.

SECRET MINE, THE
    See Fawcett, John.

SECRET MISSION AND THE SIGNET RING
    See Wilks, Thomas Egerton. Raffaelle the Reprobate.

SECRET OF A LIFE
    See Leslie, Henry. Adrienne.

SECRET OF DEATH, THE
    See Arnold, Edwin, Sir (trans.).

SECRET OF NARBOTH
    See Scofield, Joseph Alan. Alwynne.

SECRET OF THE LODGE ROOM!
    See Hart, James P. Freemason, The.

SECRET SERVICE
    See Planché, James Robinson.

SECRET WITNESS!
    See Smith, John Frederick. Wolsey!

SECRETARY, THE
    See Knowles, James Sheridan.

SECRETS OF A PALACE
    See Dimond, William. Doubtful Son, The.

SECRETS OF OFFICE
    See Kenney, James. Alcaid, The.

SECRETS OF THE PAVILION DISCLOSED, THE (anon.)
    Edinburgh: Peter Brown (printer) (priv.), 1834. Pp. [1]-60.

SECRETS WORTH KNOWING
    See Morton, Thomas, sr.

SEDUCER, THE
    See Masterton, Charles.

SEDUCTION
    See Holcroft, Thomas.

SEE, SAW, MARGERY DAW
    See Blanchard, Edward Litt Leman.

SEEING COMPANY
    See Reynolds, Frederick. Delinquent, The.

SEEING WARREN
    See Morton, Thomas, jr.

SEEING WRIGHT
    See Morton, Thomas, jr.

SEIZURE OF THE SEAS
See Brougham, John. Neptune's Defeat.
SELBY, CHARLES

Antony and Cleopatra. London: John Dicks, n.d. Pp. [1]-8. Dicks' Standard Plays, 602.

Antony and Cleopatra Married and Settled. 34 leaves. Manuscript.

Ask No Questions. London: Chapman & Hall, n.d. Pp. [i]-[viii], [9]-36. [Acting National Drama, V].

Barnaby Rudge. Written with Melville, Charles. London: John Dicks, n.d. Pp. [1]-21. [Dicks' Standard Plays, 393].

Behind the Scenes; or, Actors by Lamplight! London: John Duncombe, n.d. Pp. [1]-28. Duncombe's Acting Edition of the British Theatre, 298.

Bonnie Fish Wife, The. London: Thomas Hailes Lacy, n.d. Pp. [1]-24. [Lacy's Acting Edition].

Boots at the Swan. New York: Samuel French, n.d. Pp. [1]-29. Minor Drama, 2.

Captain Stevens. London: John Duncombe, n.d. Pp. [1]-24. Duncombe's Edition.

Catching an Heiress. London: John Dicks, n.d. Pp. [1]-13. [Dicks' Standard Plays, 402].

Caught by the Ears. London: Thomas Hailes Lacy, n.d. Pp. [1]-21. [Lacy's Acting Edition].

Chamber Practice; or, Life in the Temple. London: Duncombe & Moon, n.d. Pp. [1]-21. Duncombe's Edition <wrps. Cumberland's British Theatre (with Duncombe's), 510>.

Dancing Barber, The. London: Chapman & Hall, 1838. Pp. [1]-23.

Day in Paris, A. Philadelphia: Turner & Fisher, n.d. Pp. [1]-[32]. Fisher's Edition of Standard Farces.

Dissolving Views; or, Lights and Shadows of Life. London: William Barth, n.d. Pp. [i]-iv, [1]-13.

Drapery Question, The; or, Who's for India? London: Thomas Hailes Lacy, n.d. Pp. [1]-24. [Lacy's Acting Edition].

Elves, The; or, The Statue Bride. Pp. [i], [1]-16, 1-7, [1]-20. Title page lacking. Pagination by acts and scenes. Manuscript promptbook.

Fairy Lake, The; or, The Magic Veil! London: John Duncombe, n.d. Pp. [1]-26. Duncombe's Acting Edition of the British Theatre, [2]90.

Fearful Tragedy in the Seven Dials. London & New York: Samuel French, n.d. Pp. [1]-22. [Lacy's Acting Edition].

Fire-Eater!, The. London: Thomas Hailes Lacy, n.d. Pp. [1]-15. [Lacy's Acting Edition].

Frank Fox Phipps, Esq. London: John Duncombe, n.d. Pp. [1]-26. Duncombe's Edition.

Frederick of Prussia; or, The Monarch and the Mimic. London: John Duncombe, n.d. Pp. [1]-29. Duncombe's Edition. Promptbook.

Guardian Sylph!, The; or, The Magic Rose! London: John Duncombe, n.d. Pp. [1]-24. Duncombe's Edition.

Handsel Penny, The. London: J. Pattie, n.d. Pp. [1]-26. Pattie's Universal Stage or Theatrical Prompt Book, 32.

Harold Hawk; or, The Convict's Vengeance. London: Thomas Hailes Lacy, n.d. Pp. [1]-26. Promptbook.

Heiress of Bruges, The. London: John Duncombe, n.d. Pp. [1]-36. Duncombe's Edition. Promptbook.

Hotel Charges; or, How to Cook a Biffin! London: Thomas Hailes Lacy, n.d. Pp. [1]-15.

Hour at Seville, An. London: Thomas Hailes Lacy, n.d. Pp. [1]-30. [Lacy's Acting Edition].

Hunting a Turtle. Philadelphia: Frederick Turner, n.d. Pp. [1]-29. Turner's Dramatic Library.

Husband of My Heart, The. London: Thomas Hailes Lacy, n.d. Pp. [1]-32. Promptbook.

Irish Dragoon, The; or, Wards in Chancery. London: National Acting Drama Office, n.d. <wrps. Webster>. Pp. [i]-iv, [5]-24. Webster's Acting National Drama, 120.

Jacques Strop; or, A Few More Passages in the Life of the Renowned and Illustrious Robert Macaire! London: John Duncombe, n.d. Pp. [1]-50. Duncombe's Acting Edition of the British Theatre. Promptbook.

King's Gardener, The; or, Nipped in the Bud. London: Thomas Hailes Lacy, n.d. Pp. [1]-22. New British Theatre, 286.

Kinge Richard ye Third; or, Ye Battel of Bosworth Field! London: John Duncombe, n.d. Pp. [i]-[viii], [7]-35. [Duncombe's Edition].

Lady and Gentleman in a Peculiarly Perplexing Predicament!, A. London: John Duncombe, n.d. Pp. [1]-27. Duncombe's Edition.

Last of the Pigtails, The. London: Thomas Hailes Lacy, n.d. Pp. [1]-28. [Lacy's Acting Edition].

Lioness of the North, The; or, The Prisoner of Shlusselbourg. London: Nassau Steam Press, n.d. Pp. [i]-iv, [5]-55.

Little Sins and Pretty Sinners. London: John Duncombe, n.d. Pp. [1]-23. Duncombe's Edition.

London by Night. London: John Dicks, n.d. Pp. [1]-12. Dicks' Standard Plays, 721.

Loves of Lord Bateman and the Fair Sophia!, The. London: John Duncombe, n.d. Pp. [1]-[30]. Duncombe's Edition.

Marble Heart, The; or, The Sculptor's Dream. New York & London: Samuel French, n.d. Pp. [1]-53. French's Standard Drama.

Marble Heart, The; or, The Sculptor's Dream. London & New York: Samuel French, n.d. Pp. [1]-53. Promptbook.

Marceline; or, The Soldier's Legacy. London: John Duncombe, n.d. Pp. [1]-27. Duncombe's Edition.

Married Rake, The. New York: Samuel French, n.d. Pp. [1]-18. French's American Drama, 71. Promptbook.

Military Execution; or, The Fatal Keepsake. [London: John Duncombe], n.d. Pp. [257]-268. Title page lacking.

Moral Philosopher, The. London: John Duncombe, n.d. Pp. [1]-24. Duncombe's Edition.

My Aunt's Husband. London: Thomas Hailes Lacy, n.d. Pp. [1]-22. [Lacy's Acting Edition].

My Friend in the Straps. London: National Acting Drama Office, n.d. Pp. [1]-23.

My Friend the Major. London: Thomas Hailes Lacy, n.d. Pp. [1]-22. [Lacy's Acting Edition].

My Sister from India. London & New York: Samuel French, n.d. Pp. [1]-16. [Lacy's Acting Edition].

Mysterious Stranger, The. [London: National Acting Drama Office], n.d. Pp. [iii]-[v], 6-52. Title page lacking. Promptbook. *Filed under* Nicolaie, Louis Francois.

Mysterious Stranger, The. London: National Acting Drama Office, n.d. Pp. [i]-iv, [5]-52. [Acting National Drama, III].

New Footman, The. London: John Duncombe, n.d. <wrps. Thomas Hailes Lacy>. Pp. [1]-29. Duncombe's Edition <wrps. New British Theatre (late Duncombe's), 353>.

One Fault. London: John Dicks, n.d. Pp. [1]-13. Dicks' Standard Plays, 551.

One Fault. London: J. Onwhyn, n.d. Pp. [1]-30.

Out on the Sly; or, A Fête at Rosherville! London: Thomas Hailes Lacy, n.d. Pp. [1]-26. New British Theatre (late Duncombe's), 475.

Paris and Pleasure; or, Home and Happiness. London: Thomas Hailes Lacy, n.d. Pp. [i]-iv, [5]-55. [Lacy's Acting Edition].

Peggy Green. Chicago: Dramatic Publishing Co., n.d. Pp. [1]-22. Sergel's Acting Drama, 127.

Peggy Green. London: Thomas Hailes Lacy, n.d. Pp. [1]-27.

Pet Lamb, The. London: Thomas Hailes Lacy, n.d. Pp. [1]-20. [Lacy's Acting Edition].

Phantom Breakfast!, The. London: John Duncombe, n.d. Pp. [1]-23. [Duncombe's Edition].

Pink of Politeness, The. London: John Duncombe, n.d. Pp. [1]-24. Duncombe's Edition.

Poor Nobleman, The. London: Thomas Hailes Lacy, n.d. Pp. [1]-52. [Lacy's Acting Edition].

Powder and Ball; or, St. Tibb's Eve! London: John Duncombe, n.d. Pp. [1]-27. Duncombe's Edition.

Rifle Brigade, The. London: Webster, n.d. Pp. [1]-23. Webster's Acting National Drama, [36].

Rival Pages, The. London: John Duncombe, n.d. Pp. [1]-22. Duncombe's Acting Edition of the British Theatre, 199.

Rival Pages, The. London: Thomas Hailes Lacy, n.d. Pp. [1]-22. Promptbook.

Robert Macaire; or, Les Auberge des Adrets! *Also:* Robert Macaire; or, The Exploits of a Gentleman at Large. London: John Duncombe, n.d. Pp. [1]-34. Duncombe's Acting Edition of the British Theatre, 123.

Spanish Dancers, The; or, Fans and Fandangoes. London: Thomas Hailes Lacy, n.d. Pp. [1]-16.

Taken In and Done For. London: John K. Chapman, 1849. Pp. [1]-16. Modern Acting Drama, 8.

Taming a Tartar; or, Magic and Mazourkaphobia. London: Nassau Steam Press, n.d. Pp. [i]-vi, [7]-31. Webster's Acting National Drama, [126].

Tutor's Assistant!, The. London: Duncombe & Moon, n.d. Pp. [1]-32. Duncombe's Acting Edition of the British Theatre, 493.

Unfinished Gentleman, The. Philadelphia: Frederick Turner, n.d. Pp. [5]-38. [Turner's Dramatic Library].

Valet de Sham, The. London: Chapman & Hall, n.d. Pp. [1]-24. Promptbook.

White Sergeants, The. London: National Acting Drama Office, n.d. Pp. [1]-36.

Widow's Victim, The. London: John Duncombe, n.d. Pp. [1]-30. Duncombe's Acting Edition of the British Theatre, 153.

Witch of Windermere, The. London: Thomas Hailes Lacy, n.d. Pp. [1]-24. Title page imperfect. Lacy's Acting Edition.

Young Mother, The. London: Thomas Hailes Lacy, n.d. Pp. [1]-27. [Lacy's Acting Edition].

SELF ACCUSATION
    See Lemon, Mark.
SELF-DECEIVED HUSBAND
    See Van Laun, Henri (trans.). Sganarelle.
SELF DISINHERITED
    See Abel, William Henry.
SELF-GLORIFICATION
    See Stephens, George.
SELF-SACRIFICE
    See Soane, George.
SELIM AND ZULEIKA (anon.)
    In *New British Theatre,* London: A. J. Valpy (printer), 1815, IV, [i], [1]-34.
SEMI-DETACHED
    See Swears, Herbert.
SEMIRAMIDE
    See Kenney, Charles Lamb (trans.).
    See Maggioni, Manfredo (trans.).
SEMPSTRESS, THE
    See Lemon, Mark.
SEMPSTRESS'S BALL
    See Morton, Thomas, jr. Dance of the Shirt!, The.
SEND THIRTY STAMPS
    See Angus, J. Keith.
SENECA
  Medea.
    See Wheelwright, Charles Apthrop, Rev. (trans.).
  Octavia.
    See Wheelwright, Charles Apthrop, Rev. (trans.).
SENIOR WRANGLERS
    See Whitmore, E. H.
SENSATION GOAT!
    See Byron, Henry James. Esmeralda.
SENSATION NOVEL IN THREE VOLUMES, A
    See Gilbert, William Schwenck.
SENSATIONS OF THE PAST SEASON, WITH A SHAMEFUL REVELATION OF LADY SOMEBODY'S SECRET
    See Byron, Henry James. 1863.
SENSE AND SENSATION
    See Taylor, Tom.
SENSIBILITY
    See Stephens, George.
SENT TO THE TOWER!
    See Morton, John Maddison.

SENTENCE, THE
    See Webster, Augusta Davies, Mrs. Thomas.
SENTINEL, THE
    See Morton, John Maddison.
SENTINEL OF THE KING'S GUARD, THE
    See Fraser, Julia Agnes. Court Lovers.
SEPARATE MAINTENANCE
    See Coyne, Joseph Stirling.
SEPARATION, THE
    See Baillie, Joanna.
SEQUEL TO NICHOLAS NICKLEBY
    See Stirling, Edward. Fortunes of Smike, The.
SERAGLIO, IL
    See Troutbeck, John, Rev. (trans.).
SERAGLIO, THE
    See Dimond, William.
SERAPHINE
    See Boucicault, Dionysius Lardner.
SERF, THE
    See Talbot, Robert.
    See Taylor, Tom.
SERGEANT'S WEDDING, THE
    See Wilks, Thomas Egerton.
SERGEANT'S WIFE, THE
    See Arnold, Samuel James.
    See Banim, John.
SERIOUS FAMILY, THE
    See Barnett, Morris.
SERLE, THOMAS JAMES

Fulvius Valens; or, The Martyr of Caesarea. London: Charles Baldwyn, n.d. Pp. [i]-[viii], [1]-103.

Gamester of Milan, The. London: John Duncombe, n.d. Pp. [3]-44. Duncombe's Edition.

Ghost Story, A. London: John Miller, 1836. Pp. [i]-vi, [1]-38.

House of Colberg, The. London: T. Richardson, 1833. Pp. [3]-49.

Joan of Arc, the Maid of Orleans. London: W. Strange, 1837. Pp. [1]-38.

Man in the Iron Mask, The. [London: John Dicks, n.d.]. Pp. [305]-328. [Dicks' Standard Plays, 428].

Master Clarke. London: W. S. Johnson (printer), n.d. Pp. [1]-4], [i]-[vi], [7]-88.

Merchant of London, The. London: W. Sams, 1832. Pp. [1-2], [i]-[vi], [1]-115.

Parole of Honour, The. London: W. Strange, 1837. Pp. [1]-40.

Raffaelle Cimaro. London: John Chappell & Son, 1819. Pp. [i-x], [1]-[66].

Shadow on the Wall, The. London: John Miller, n.d. Pp. [i-viii], [1]-38. Promptbook.

Tender Precautions; or, The Romance of Marriage. London: Thomas Hailes Lacy, n.d. Pp. [1]-28. [Lacy's Acting Edition].

Victim of St. Vincent, The. [London: John Dicks], n.d. Pp. [135]-158. Title page lacking. Promptbook.

Victim of St. Vincent, The. [London: John Dicks], n.d. Pp. [135]-158. Title page lacking.

Waltheof. Also attrib. to Robson, William James. London & New York: John Tallis, 1851. Pp. [1]-60. Tallis's Acting Drama. *Filed under* Robson, William James.

Windsor Castle; or, The Prisoner-King. London: W. S. Johnson, 1838. Pp. [1]-16. Libretto.

Yeoman's Daughter, The. London: John Duncombe, n.d. Pp. [i]-[vi], [7]-40. New British Theatre (late Duncombe's), 91.

SERLE, THOMAS JAMES (trans.)

Sappho. Music by Pacini. London: W. S. Johnson, n.d. Pp. [1]-40. Libretto.

SERPENT OF THE NILE, THE
    See Stirling, Edward.
SERPENT ON THE HEARTH, THE
    See Simpson, John Palgrave. Bound.
SERPENT PLAY, THE
    See Hake, Thomas Gordon.
SERVE HIM RIGHT!
    See Barnett, Morris.

SERVIUS TULLIUS
    See Verral, Charles.
SETON, HUGH
    Spice of the Devil, A. Pp. [i], [1]-[25]. Typescript.
SETTING OF THE SUN, THE
    See Hannan, Charles.
SETTLERS IN AMERICA
    See Fitzball, Edward. Omala.
SETTLING DAY
    See Taylor, Tom.
SEVEN CASTLES OF THE PASSIONS, THE
    See Stirling, Edward.
SEVEN CHAMPIONS OF CHRISTENDOM, THE
    See Planché, James Robinson.
SEVEN CHARMED BULLETS
    See Amherst, J. H. Freischutz, Der.
SEVEN CLERKS, THE
    See Wilks, Thomas Egerton.
SEVEN CLERKS AND THE THREE THIEVES
    See Wilks, Thomas Egerton. Denouncer, The.
SEVEN-LEAGUE BOOTS
    See Ogre and Little Thumb, The (anon.).
    See Smith, Albert Richard. Hop-o'-My-Thumb.
SEVEN MAIDS OF MUNICH, THE
    See Rodwell, George Herbert Bonaparte.
SEVEN MANNIKINS AND THE MAGIC MIRROR
    See Burnand, Francis Cowley. Snowdrop.
SEVEN NIGHTS IN A BAR-ROOM; OR, THE LIQUOR TRAFFIC A CURSE TO THE DEALER AND CON-SUMER (anon.)
    Middlesbro'-on-Tees: J. Jordison, n.d. Pp. [1]-44.
SEVEN SINS
    See Conquest, George.
SEVEN SISTERS, THE
    See Almar, George.
SEVEN SISTERS OF THULE
    See Taylor, Tom. Sense and Sensation.
SEVEN SWAN PRINCES AND THE FAIR MELUSINE
    See Taylor, Tom. Wittikind and His Brothers.
SEVEN'S THE MAIN
    See Macfarren, George. Winning a Husband.
SEVENTH BULLET
    See Oxenford, John. Freischutz, Der.
SEVENTH HOUR, THE
    See Faucquez, Adolphe.
SEYMOUR, CHARLES
    Wanted—A Widow, with Immediate Possession.
        See Boucicault, Dionysius Lardner.
SEYMOUR, EDWARD MARTIN
    See Martin-Seymour, Edward.
SEYMOUR, FREDERICK H. A.
    Rienzi. London: Kegan Paul, Trench, 1886. Pp. [i]-[viii], [1]-233.
SEYMOUR, MARY
    Daughter-in-Law, A. Chicago: Dramatic Publishing Co., n.d. Pp. [1]-8.
    Daughter-in-Law, A. In *Home Plays for Ladies,* Part 9, London & New York: Samuel French, n.d., pp. [1]-11. *Filed under* Home Plays for Ladies, Part 9 (anon.).
    Heiress, The. In *Home Plays for Ladies,* Part 7, London & New York: Samuel French, n.d., pp. [1]-18. *Filed under* Home Plays for Ladies, Part 7 (anon.).
    Only a Jest. In *Home Plays for Ladies,* Part 7, London & New York: Samuel French, n.d., pp. [19]-28. *Filed under* Home Plays for Ladies, Part 7 (anon.).
    Ten Years Hence. Chicago: Dramatic Publishing Co., n.d. Pp. [1]-14.
    Ten Years Hence. In *Home Plays for Ladies,* Part 9, London & New York: Samuel French, n.d., pp. [13]-26. *Filed under* Home Plays for Ladies, Part 9 (anon.).
SGANARELLE
    See Van Laun, Henri (trans.).
SGANARELLE; OU, LE COCU IMAGINAIRE
    See Van Laun, Henri (trans.). Sganarelle.

SHADE, THE
    See Thompson, C. Pelham.
SHADES OF NIGHT
    See Marshall, Robert.
SHADOW!, THE: A MOTHER'S DREAM
    See Almar, George.
SHADOW OF A CRIME, THE
    See Cheltnam, Charles Smith.
SHADOW OF DEATH
    See Marchant, Frederick. Skeleton Horseman, The.
    See Somerset, Charles A. Captain Hawk, the Last of the Highwaymen.
SHADOW OF DEATH IN THE COFFIN CELL
    See Somerset, Charles A. Captain Hawk, the Last of the Highwaymen.
SHADOW OF THE HEARTH
    See Harvey, Frank. Woman against Woman.
SHADOW ON THE WALL, THE
    See Serle, Thomas James.
SHADOW SCEPTRE, A
    See Hamilton, Henry.
SHADOWLESS MAN
    See Fitzball, Edward. Devil's Elixir, The.
SHADOWS
    See Young, Charles Lawrence, Sir.
SHADOWS FROM THE PAST
    See Hannan, Charles. Gipsy, The.
SHADOWS OF THE PAST
    See Simpson, John Palgrave.
SHADOWY WATERS, THE
    See Yeats, William Butler.
SHAKESPEARE, WILLIAM
    All's Well That Ends Well. London: John Cumberland, 1828. Pp. [1]-62. Cumberland's British Theatre, XVIII. *Filed under* Cumberland, John. Cumberland's British Theatre, XVIII.
    All's Well That Ends Well.
        See Kemble, John Philip (arr.).
    Antony and Cleopatra.
        See Bellew, Kyrle (arr.).
        See Calvert, Charles Alexander (arr.).
        See Halliday, Andrew (arr.).
        See Kemble, John Philip (arr.).
    As You Like It. In *New English Drama,* ed. W. Oxberry, 22 vols., London: W. Simpkin & R. Marshall; C. Chapple, 1819, VII, [1-2], [i]-[iv], [1]-68. *Filed under* Oxberry, William Henry. New English Drama, VII.
    As You Like It. London: T. Dolby, 1823. Pp. [i]-[vi], [7]-[66]. Dolby's British Theatre, III. *Filed under* Cumberland, John. Cumberland's British Theatre, III.
    As You Like It.
        See Anderson, Mary (arr.).
        See Hare, John (arr.).
        See Kemble, John Philip (arr.).
        See Macready, William Charles (arr.).
    Comedy of Errors, The. London: John Cumberland, 1827. Pp. [1]-52. Cumberland's British Theatre, XVI. *Filed under* Cumberland, John. Cumberland's British Theatre, XVI.
    Comedy of Errors, The.
        See Kemble, John Philip (arr.).
        See Reynolds, Frederick (arr.).
    Coriolanus; or, The Roman Matron. In *New English Drama,* ed. W. Oxberry, 22 vols., London: W. Simpkin & R. Marshall; C. Chapple, 1818, VIII, [1-2], [i]-[vi], [1]-62. *Filed under* Oxberry, William Henry. New English Drama, VIII.
    Coriolanus. London: T. Dolby, 1824. Pp. [i]-[vi], [7]-[58]. Dolby's British Theatre, VII. *Filed under* Cumberland, John. Cumberland's British Theatre, VII.
    Coriolanus. London: J. Tabby (printer), n.d. Pp. [i]-viii, [1]-61.
    Coriolanus.
        See Irving, Henry (arr.).
        See Kemble, John Philip (arr.).

Cymbeline. In *New English Drama,* ed. W. Oxberry, 22 vols., London: W. Simpkin & R. Marshall; C. Chapple, 1821, XII, [1-2], [i]-[vi], [1]-79. *Filed under* Oxberry, William Henry. New English Drama, XII.

Cymbeline. London: T. Dolby, 1823. Pp. [i]-[vi], [7]-[77]. Dolby's British Theatre, II. *Filed under* Cumberland, John. Cumberland's British Theatre, II.

Cymbeline.
See Irving, Henry (arr.).
See Kemble, John Philip (arr.).

Hamlet. In *New English Drama,* ed. W. Oxberry, 22 vols., London: W. Simpkin & R. Marshall; C. Chapple, 1818, III, [1-2], [i]-[xxx], [1]-84. *Filed under* Oxberry, William Henry. New English Drama, III.

Hamlet. London: John Cumberland, 1829. Pp. [1]-[14], [9]-78. Cumberland's British Theatre, IV. *Filed under* Cumberland, John. Cumberland's British Theatre, IV.

Hamlet.
See Barrett, Wilson (arr.).
See Forbes-Robertson, Johnston (arr.).
See Irving, Henry (arr.).
See Kean, Charles John (arr.).
See Kemble, John Philip (arr.).
See Taylor, Tom (arr.).

Hamlet, Prince of Denmark, A Study of.
See H., E. B. (arr.).

Henry the Eighth.
See King Henry VIII.

Henry the Fifth.
See King Henry V.

Henry the Fourth.
See King Henry IV.

Henry IV.
See King Henry IV.

Henry V.
See King Henry V.

Henry VIII.
See King Henry VIII.

Julius Caesar. In *New English Drama,* ed. W. Oxberry, 22 vols., London: W. Simpkin & R. Marshall; C. Chapple, 1822, XVI, [i]-[viii], [9]-80. *Filed under* Oxberry, William Henry. New English Drama, XVI.

Julius Caesar. London: John Cumberland, 1826. Pp. [i]-[vi], [7]-64. Cumberland's British Theatre, V. *Filed under* Cumberland, John. Cumberland's British Theatre, V.

Julius Caesar.
See Kemble, John Philip (arr.).
See Tree, Herbert Beerbohm (arr.).

Katharine and Petrucio.
See Kemble, John Philip (arr.).

King Henry the Fourth. In *New English Drama,* ed. W. Oxberry, 22 vols., London: W. Simpkin & R. Marshall; C. Chapple, 1822, XIV, [1-2], [i]-[vi], [1]-82. *Filed under* Oxberry, William Henry. New English Drama, XIV.

King Henry IV, Part 1. London: John Cumberland, 1829. Pp. [1]-68. Cumberland's British Theatre, IV. *Filed under* Cumberland, John. Cumberland's British Theatre, IV.

King Henry IV, Part 1.
See Kemble, John Philip (arr.). King Henry the Fourth, Part 1.

King Henry IV, Part 2.
See Calvert, Charles Alexander (arr.). Henry the Fourth, Part 2.
See Kemble, John Philip (arr.). King Henry the Fourth, Part 2.
See Kemble, John Philip (arr.).
See Valpy, Richard (arr.). King Henry the Fourth, Part 2.

King Henry the Fifth. In *New English Drama,* ed. W. Oxberry, 22 vols., W. Simpkin & R. Marshall; C. Chapple, 1823, XVIII, [i]-[xii], [1]-68. *Filed under* Oxberrry, William Henry. New English Drama, XVIII.

King Henry V. London: Thomas Dolby, 1825. Pp. [i]-[vi], [7]-[56]. Dolby's British Theatre, XI. *Filed under* Cumberland, John. Cumberland's British Theatre, XI.

King Henry V.
See Calvert, Charles Alexander (arr.). Henry the Fifth.
See Coleman, John (arr.). Henry V.
See Kean, Charles John (arr.). King Henry the Fifth.
See Kemble, John Philip (arr.). King Henry the Fifth.

King Henry the Eighth. In *New English Drama,* ed. W. Oxberry, 22 vols., London: W. Simpkin & R. Marshall; C. Chapple, 1823, XIX, [i]-[xviii], [1]-70. *Filed under* Oxberry, William Henry. New English Drama, XIX.

King Henry VIII. London: John Cumberland, 1826. Pp. [i]-[vi], [7]-60. Cumberland's British Theatre, V. *Filed under* Cumberland, John. Cumberland's British Theatre, V.

King Henry VIII.
See Calvert, Charles Alexander (arr.). King Henry the Eighth.
See Irving, Henry (arr.). King Henry the Eighth.
See Kean, Charles John (arr.). King Henry the Eighth.
See Kemble, John Philip (arr.). King Henry the Eighth.

King John. In *New English Drama,* ed. W. Oxberry, 22 vols., London: W. Simpkin & R. Marshall; C. Chapple, 1819, VII, [1-2], [i]-[iv], [1]-62. *Filed under* Oxberry, William Henry. New English Drama, VII.

King John. London: John Cumberland, 1829. Pp. [1]-8, [i-iv], [9]-59. Cumberland's British Theatre, IV. *Filed under* Cumberland, John. Cumberland's British Theatre, IV.

King John.
See Kean, Charles John (arr.).
See Kemble, John Philip (arr.).
See Valpy, Richard (arr.).

King Lear. London: John Cumberland, 1826. Pp. [1]-8, [vii]-viii, [7]-[66]. Cumberland's British Theatre, VI. *Filed under* Cumberland, John. Cumberland's British Theatre, VI.

King Lear.
See Elliston, Robert William (arr.).
See Irving, Henry (arr.).
See Kean, Charles John (arr.).
See Tate, Nahum (arr.).

King Richard II. London: John Cumberland, n.d. Pp. [1]-54. Cumberland's British Theatre, XXIX. *Filed under* Cumberland, John. Cumberland's British Theatre, XXIX.

King Richard II.
See Kean, Charles John (arr.).
See Wroughton, Richard (arr.). King Richard the Second.

King Richard the Third. London: John Cumberland, 1826. Pp. [1]-66. Cumberland's British Theatre, I. *Filed under* Cumberland, John. Cumberland's British Theatre, I.

King Richard III.
See Cibber, Colley (arr.). King Richard the Third.
See Hicks, Edward Seymour (arr.).
See Irving, Henry (arr.).
See Kemble, John Philip (arr.). King Richard the Third.

Love's Labour's Lost. London: John Cumberland, n.d. Pp. [1]-58. Cumberland's British Theatre, XL. *Filed under* Cumberland, John. Cumberland's British Theatre, XL.

Macbeth. In *New English Drama,* ed. W. Oxberry, 22 vols., London: W. Simpkin & R. Marshall; C. Chapple, 1821, XIV, [1-2], [i]-[vi], [1]-74. *Filed under* Oxberry, William Henry. New English Drama, XIV.

Macbeth. London: John Cumberland, 1826. Pp. [1]-62. Cumberland's British Theatre, I. *Filed under* Cumberland, John. Cumberland's British Theatre, I.

Macbeth.
See Creswick, William (arr.). Macbeth, King of Scotland.
See Cross, James C. (arr.).
See Forbes-Robertson, Johnston (arr.).
See Irving, Henry (arr.).
See Kean, Charles John (arr.).
See Rayne, Lin (arr.).
See Salvini, Tommaso (arr.).

Measure for Measure. In *New English Drama,* ed. W. Oxberry, 22 vols., London: W. Simpkin & R. Marshall; C. Chapple, 1822, XVI, [i]-[xiv], [1]-[70]. *Filed under* Oxberry, William Henry. New English Drama, XVI.

Measure for Measure. London: T. Dolby, 1824. Pp. [i]-[vi], [7]-[63]. Dolby's British Theatre, VII. *Filed under* Cumberland, John. Cumberland's British Theatre, VII.

Measure for Measure.
   See Kemble, John Philip (arr.).

Merchant of Venice, The. London: Barker & Son, 1802. Pp. [1]-60. *Filed under* Merchant of Venice (anon.).

Merchant of Venice, The. In *New English Drama,* ed. W. Oxberry, 22 vols., London: W. Simpkin & R. Marshall; C. Chapple, 1820, X, [1-2], [i]-[iv], [1]-[66]. *Filed under* Oxberry, William Henry. New English Drama, X.

Merchant of Venice, The. London: John Cumberland, 1826. Pp. [i], [1]-62. Cumberland's British Theatre, VI. *Filed under* Cumberland, John. Cumberland's British Theatre, VI.

Merchant of Venice, The.
   See Irving, Henry (arr.).
   See Kean, Charles John (arr.).
   See Kemble, John Philip (arr.).
   See Valpy, Richard (arr.).

Merry Wives of Windsor, The. In *New English Drama,* ed. W. Oxberry, 22 vols., London: W. Simpkin & R. Marshall; C. Chapple, 1818, VIII, [1-2], [i]-[vi], [1]-75. *Filed under* Oxberry, William Henry. New English Drama, VIII.

Merry Wives of Windsor, The. London: John Cumberland, 1826. Pp. [1]-8, [7]-64. Cumberland's British Theatre, VI. *Filed under* Cumberland, John. Cumberland's British Theatre, VI.

Merry Wives of Windsor, The. London: John Cumberland, n.d. Pp. [1]-64. *Filed under* Daniel, George.

Merry Wives of Windsor, The.
   See Kemble, John Philip (arr.).

Midsummer-Night's Dream, A. London: John Cumberland, 1828. Pp. [1]-67. Cumberland's British Theatre, XX. *Filed under* Cumberland, John. Cumberland's British Theatre, XX.

Midsummer Night's Dream, A.
   See Kean, Charles John (arr.).
   See Reynolds, Frederick (arr.).
   See Simpson, Mercer H. (arr.).

Much Ado About Nothing. In *New English Drama,* ed. W. Oxberry, 22 vols., London: W. Simpkin & R. Marshall; C. Chapple, 1823, XVIII, [i]-[x], [1]-72. *Filed under* Oxberry, William Henry. New English Drama, XVIII.

Much Ado about Nothing. London: T. Dolby, 1824. Pp. [1-2], [i]-[x], [9]-[62]. Dolby's British Theatre, III. *Filed under* Cumberland, John. Cumberland's British Theatre, III.

Much Ado about Nothing.
   See Irving, Henry (arr.).
   See Kean, Charles John (arr.).
   See Kemble, John Philip (arr.).

Othello. In *New English Drama,* ed. W. Oxberry, 22 vols., London: W. Simpkin & R. Marshall; C. Chapple, 1819, V, [i]-[viii], [1]-76. *Filed under* Oxberry, William Henry. New English Drama, V.

Othello. London: T. Dolby, 1823. Pp. [1-2], [i]-[x], [9]-70. Dolby's British Theatre, II. *Filed under* Cumberland, John. Cumberland's British Theatre, II.

Othello.
   See Fechter, Charles Albert (arr.).
   See Kemble, John Philip (arr.). Othello, the Moor of Venice.

Richard, Duke of York.
   See under title..

Richard II.
   See King Richard II.

Richard the Second.
   See King Richard II.

Richard III.
   See King Richard III.

Richard the Third.
   See King Richard III.

Romeo and Juliet. London: John Cumberland, 1826. Pp. [i-ii], [1]-69. Cumberland's British Theatre, I. *Filed under* Cumberland, John. Cumberland's British Theatre, I.

Romeo and Juliet.
   See Anderson, Mary (arr.).
   See Forbes-Robertson, Johnston (arr.).
   See Garrick, David (arr.).
   See Irving, Henry (arr.).
   See Kemble, John Philip (arr.).

Taming of the Shrew.
   See Kemble, John Philip (arr.). Katharine and Petruchio.
   See Kemble, John Philip (arr.).

Tempest, The. In *New English Drama,* ed. W. Oxberry, 22 vols., London: W. Simpkin & R. Marshall; C. Chapple, 1823, XVII, [i]-[xx], [1]-56. *Filed under* Oxberry, William Henry. New English Drama, XVII.

Tempest, The. London: T. Dolby, 1824. Pp. [1]-[51]. Dolby's British Theatre, VII. *Filed under* Cumberland, John. Cumberland's British Theatre, VII.

Tempest, The.
   See Kean, Charles John (arr.).

Timon of Athens. London: John Cumberland, n.d. Pp. [1]-72. Cumberland's British Theatre, XXVI. *Filed under* Cumberland, John. Cumberland's British Theatre, XXVI.

Timon of Athens.
   See Lamb, George (arr.).

Twelfth Night; or, What You Will. In *New English Drama,* ed. W. Oxberry, 22 vols., London: W. Simpkin & R. Marshall; C. Chapple, 1821, XII, [1-2], [i]-[iv], [1]-71. *Filed under* Oxberry, William Henry. New English Drama, XII.

Twelfth Night; or, What You Will. London: Thomas Dolby, 1825. Pp. [ii]-[viii], [9]-64. Dolby's British Theatre, XI. *Filed under* Cumberland, John. Cumberland's British Theatre, XI.

Twelfth Night.
   See Calvert, Charles Alexander (arr.).
   See Irving, Henry (arr.).
   See Kemble, John Philip (arr.).

Two Gentlemen of Verona, The. In *New English Drama,* ed. W. Oxberry, 22 vols., London: W. Simpkin & R. Marshall; C. Chapple, 1823, XVII, [i]-[x], [1]-[70]. *Filed under* Oxberry, William Henry. New English Drama, XVII.

Two Gentlemen of Verona, The.
   See Kemble, John Philip (arr.).

Winter's Tale, The. In *New English Drama,* ed. W. Oxberry, 22 vols., London: W. Simpkin & R. Marshall; C. Chapple, 1823, XIX, [i]-[xii], [1]-87. *Filed under* Oxberry, William Henry. New English Drama, XIX.

Winter's Tale, The. London: John Cumberland, 1826. Pp. [1], [i]-[viii], [7]-72. Cumberland's British Theatre, V. *Filed under* Cumberland, John. Cumberland's British Theatre, V.

Winter's Tale, The.
   See Anderson, Mary (arr.).
   See Kean, Charles John (arr.).
   See Kemble, John Philip (arr.).

SHAKESPEARE'S FESTIVAL
   See Moncrieff, William Thomas.

SHAKLETON, MARY
   See Leadbetter, Mary Shakleton, Mrs. William.

SHAKSPEARE'S DREAM
   See Brougham, John.

SHAKSPEARE'S EARLY DAYS
   See Somerset, Charles A.

SHAKSPEARE'S FESTIVAL
   See Moncrieff, William Thomas.

SHAKSPERE AND COMPANY
   See Bradshaw, Christopher Brooke.

SHAKSPERE'S SKULL AND FALSTAFF'S NOSE
   See Titmarsh, Belgrave.

SHALL WE FORGIVE HER?
   See Harvey, Frank.

SHAMEFUL BEHAVIOUR!
   See Troughton, Adolphus Charles.

SHAMING OF THE TRUE
    See Ashby-Sterry, Joseph. Katharine and Petruchio.
SHAMROCK
    See Fenn, George Manville.
SHANNON, CHARLES
    My Wife, or My Place. Written with Thackeray, Thomas James. London: C. Chapple, 1831. Pp. [i-iv], [1]-54.
    Youthful Queen, The. London: John Cumberland, n.d. Pp. [1]-36.
    Youthful Queen, The. London: John Cumberland, n.d. Pp. [1]-36. Cumberland's British Theatre, XXI. *Filed under* Cumberland, John. Cumberland's British Theatre, XXI.
SHANNON, MRS. F. S.
    Jealousy. London: Samuel French; New York: T. Henry French, n.d. Pp. [3]-25. [Lacy's Acting Edition].
SHARKS ALONG THE SHORE!
    See Higgie, Thomas Henry. Laid up in Port!
SHARP, WILLIAM
    Birth of a Soul, The. In *Vistas,* Derby: Frank Murray (printer), n.d., pp. [i], [45]-57.
    Black Madonna, The. In *Vistas,* Derby: Frank Murray (printer), n.d., pp. [i], [89]-115.
    Coming of the Prince, The. In *Vistas,* Derby: Frank Murray (printer), n.d., pp. [i], [135]-149.
    Fallen God, The. In *Vistas,* Derby: Frank Murray (printer), n.d., pp. [i], [127]-134.
    Finis. In *Vistas,* Derby: Frank Murray (printer), n.d., pp. [i], [1]-13.
    House of Usna, The. By Fiona Macleod (pseud.). Portland, Maine: Thomas B. Mosher, 1903. Pp. [i]-xxxii, [1]-[77].
    House of Usna, The. By Fiona Macleod (pseud.). In *Poems and Dramas,* London: William Heinemann, 1912, VII, [391]-443.
    Northern Night, A. In *Vistas,* Derby: Frank Murray (printer), n.d., pp. [i], [59]-88.
    Passing of Lilith, The. In *Vistas,* Derby: Frank Murray (printer), n.d., pp. [i], [151]-170.
    Passion of Père Hilarion, The. In *Vistas,* Derby: Frank Murray (printer), n.d., pp. [i], [15]-43.
SHARP AND FLAT
    See Lawler, Dennis.
SHARP PRACTICE
    See Lunn, Joseph.
SHARPER'S PROGRESS
    See Moncrieff, William Thomas. Heart of London, The.
SHATTERED NERVES
    See Childe-Pemberton, Harriet Louisa.
SHAUGHRAUN, THE
    See Boucicault, Dionysius Lardner.
SHAW, GEORGE BERNARD
    Arms and the Man. In *Plays Pleasant and Unpleasant,* 2 vols., London: Grant Richards, 1900, II, [i]-[xx], [i]-76. *Filed under* Plays Pleasant and Unpleasant.
    Caesar and Cleopatra. In *Three Plays for Puritans,* Chicago & New York: Herbert S. Stone, 1901, pp. [93]-218. *Filed under* Three Plays for Puritans.
    Candida. In *Plays Pleasant and Unpleasant,* 2 vols., London: Grant Richards, 1900, II, [77]-151. *Filed under* Plays Pleasant and Unpleasant.
    Captain Brassbound's Conversion. In *Three Plays for Puritans,* Chicago & New York: Herbert S. Stone, 1901, pp. [219]-315. *Filed under* Three Plays for Puritans.
    Devil's Disciple, The. In *Three Plays for Puritans,* Chicago & New York: Herbert S. Stone, 1901, pp. [i]-xxxviii, [1]-92. *Filed under* Three Plays for Puritans.
    Man of Destiny, The. In *Plays Pleasant and Unpleasant,* 2 vols., London: Grant Richards, 1900, II, [153]-203. *Filed under* Plays Pleasant and Unpleasant.
    Mrs. Warren's Profession. In *Plays Pleasant and Unpleasant,* 2 vols., London: Grant Richards, 1898, I, [156]-235. *Filed under* Plays Pleasant and Unpleasant.
    Philanderer, The. In *Plays Pleasant and Unpleasant,* 2 vols., London: Grant Richards, 1898, I, [71]-155. *Filed under* Plays Pleasant and Unpleasant.

    Widowers' Houses. London: Henry, 1893. Pp. [i]-[xxvi], [1]-126. Independent Theatre Series of Plays, 1.
    Widowers' Houses. In *Plays Pleasant and Unpleasant,* 2 vols., London: Grant Richards, 1898, I, [i]-[xxviii], [1]-70. *Filed under* Plays Pleasant and Unpleasant.
    You Never Can Tell. In *Plays Pleasant and Unpleasant,* 2 vols., London: Grant Richards, 1900, II, [205]-320. *Filed under* Plays Pleasant and Unpleasant.
SHE STOOPS TO CONQUER
    See Goldsmith, Oliver.
SHE WOULD AND HE WOULDN'T
    See Morton, John Maddison.
SHE WOULD AND SHE WOULD NOT
    See Cibber, Colley.
SHEE, MARTIN ARCHER
    Alasco. London: Sherwood, Jones, 1824. Pp. [iii]-[lx], [1]-169.
SHEEP IN WOLF'S CLOTHING, A
    See Taylor, Tom.
SHEIL, RICHARD LALOR
    Adelaide; or, The Emigrants. Dublin: R. Coyne, 1814. Pp. [i]-[x], [1]-74.
    Apostate, The. London: John Murray, 1817. Pp. [i]-[x], [1]-[86].
    Bellamira; or, The Fall of Tunis. London: John Murray, 1818. Pp. [iii]-[xii], [1]-75. 3rd ed.
    Damon and Pythias.
    See Banim, John.
    Evadne; or, The Statue. London: J. Murray, 1819. Pp. [i]-[x], [1]-[88]. 4th ed.
    Evadne; or, The Statue. In *New English Drama,* ed. W. Oxberry, 22 vols., London: W. Simpkin & R. Marshall; C. Chapple, 1821, XIV, [1-2], [i]-[vi], [1]-62, [i]-ii. *Filed under* Oxberry, William Henry. New English Drama, XIV.
    Evadne; or, The Statue. In *British Drama,* 12 vols., London: John Dicks, 1865, IV, [1215]-1230.
SHELLEY, PERCY BYSSHE
    Cenci, The. London: Reeves & Turner, 1886. Pp. [i]-[xvi], [1]-107.
    Cenci, The. In *Dramatic Poems,* New York: Brentano's, n.d., pp. 131-250. *Filed under* Collected Works.
    Charles the First. In *Dramatic Poems,* New York: Brentano's, n.d., pp. 377-412. *Filed under* Collected Works.
    Fragments of an Unfinished Drama. In *Dramatic Poems,* New York: Brentano's, n.d., pp. 363-375. *Filed under* Collected Works.
    Hellas. London: Reeves & Turner, 1886. Pp. [i]-[x], [i]-[xii], [1]-58.
    Hellas. In *Dramatic Poems,* New York: Brentano's, n.d., pp. 291-[361]. *Filed under* Collected Works.
    Oedipus Tyrannus; or, Swellfoot the Tyrant. London: J. Johnston (priv.), 1820. Pp. [1]-[47].
    Oedipus Tyrannus; or, Swellfoot the Tyrant. In *Dramatic Poems,* New York: Brentano's, n.d., pp. 251-[290]. *Filed under* Collected Works.
    Prometheus Unbound. In *Prometheus Unbound ... with Other Poems,* London: C. & J. Ollier, 1820, pp. [iii]-[xviii], [19]-153.
    Prometheus Unbound. In *Dramatic Poems,* New York: Brentano's, n.d., pp. [5]-130. *Filed under* Collected Works.
    Tasso. In *Dramatic Poems,* New York: Brentano's, n.d., pp. [i]-[xii], [1]-3. Fragment. *Filed under* Collected Works.
SHELLEY, PERCY BYSSHE (trans.)
    May-Day Night (from Faust). By Goethe. [In *Liberal,* I (1822)], [121]-137.
SHEPHERD, RICHARD
    Tradesman's Son, The. London & New York: Samuel French, n.d. Pp. [1]-38. [French's Acting Edition (late Lacy's)].
    Watch and Wait.
    See Higgie, Thomas Henry.
SHEPHERD OF COURNOUAILLES, THE
    See March, George.
SHEPHERD OF DERWENT VALE, THE
    See Lunn, Joseph.

SHEPHERD'S WELL, THE
  See Powell, Thomas.
SHERIDAN, ALICIA
  See Le Fanu, Alicia Sheridan, Mrs. Joseph.
SHERIDAN, HELEN SELINA
  See Dufferin, Helen Selina Sheridan Blackwood, Lady.
SHERIDAN, RICHARD BRINSLEY
  Camp, The. London: John Cumberland, n.d. Pp. [1]-32. Cumberland's British Theatre, XXXII. *Filed under* Cumberland, John. Cumberland's British Theatre, XXXII.
  Critic, The. London: Whittingham & Arliss, 1814. Pp. [1]-44. London Theatre, VIII. *Filed under* Dibdin, Thomas John, ed. London Theatre, VIII.
  Critic, The; or, A Tragedy Rehearsed. In *New English Drama,* ed. W. Oxberry, 22 vols., London: W. Simpkin & R. Marshall; C. Chapple, 1820, IX, [1-2], [i]-[vi], [1]-[39]. *Filed under* Oxberry, William Henry. New English Drama, IX.
  Critic, The; or, A Tragedy Rehearsed. London: John Cumberland, 1827. Pp. [i], [1]-42. Cumberland's British Theatre, XV. *Filed under* Cumberland, John. Cumberland's British Theatre, XV.
  Critic, The; or, A Tragedy Rehearsed. In *British Drama,* 12 vols., London: John Dicks, 1865, III, [657]-670.
  Duenna, The. In *New English Drama,* ed. W. Oxberry, 22 vols., London: W. Simpkin & R. Marshall; C. Chapple, 1818, II, [i]-[vi], [1]-61. *Filed under* Oxberry, William Henry. New English Drama, II.
  Duenna, The. London: T. Dolby, 1823. Pp. [i]-[vi], [7]-60. Dolby's British Theatre, II. *Filed under* Cumberland, John. Cumberland's British Theatre, II.
  Duenna, The. In *British Drama,* 12 vols., London: John Dicks, 1865, IV, [1055]-1072.
  Pizarro. In *New English Drama,* ed. W. Oxberry, 22 vols., London: W. Simpkin & R. Marshall; C. Chapple, 1824, XX, [i]-[xiv], [1]-[64]. *Filed under* Oxberry, William Henry. New English Drama, XX.
  Pizarro. London: John Cumberland, 1826. Pp. [1]-60. Cumberland's British Theatre, I. *Filed under* Cumberland, John. Cumberland's British Theatre, I.
  Pizarro. In *British Drama,* 12 vols., London: John Dicks, 1864, I, [65]-81.
  Pizarro.
    See Kean, Charles John (arr.).
  Rivals, The. London: Whittingham & Arliss, 1814. Pp. [1]-79. London Theatre, I. *Filed under* Dibdin, Thomas John, ed. London Theatre, I.
  Rivals, The. In *New English Drama,* ed. W. Oxberry, 22 vols., London: W. Simpkin & R. Marshall; C. Chapple, 1818, I, [i]-[xii], [9]-[88]. *Filed under* Oxberry, William Henry. New English Drama, I.
  Rivals, The. London: T. Dolby, 1823. Pp. [i]-[vi], [7]-69. Dolby's British Theatre, II. *Filed under* Cumberland, John. Cumberland's British Theatre, II.
  Rivals, The. In *British Drama,* 12 vols., London: John Dicks, 1864, I, [229]-249.
  School for Scandal, The. London: John Cumberland, 1826. Pp. [1]-87. Cumberland's British Theatre, XIV. *Filed under* Cumberland, John. Cumberland's British Theatre, XIV.
  School for Scandal, The. In *British Drama,* 12 vols., London: John Dicks, 1864, II, [385]-410.
  St. Patrick's Day; or, The Scheming Lieutenant. London: John Cumberland, n.d. Pp. [1]-32. Cumberland's British Theatre, XXVIII. *Filed under* Cumberland, John. Cumberland's British Theatre, XXVIII.
  Trip to Scarborough, A. In *Modern Theatre,* ed. Mrs. Inchbald, 10 vols., London: Longman, Hurst, Rees, Orme, & Brown, 1811, VII, [237]-309.
  Trip to Scarborough, A. London: Whittingham & Arliss, 1815. Pp. [1]-70. London Theatre, XIV. *Filed under* Dibdin, Thomas John, ed. London Theatre, XIV.
  Trip to Scarborough, A. In *New English Drama,* ed. W. Oxberry, 22 vols., London: W. Simpkin & R. Marshall;

C. Chapple, 1824, XX, [i]-[ii], [1]-53. *Filed under* Oxberry, William Henry. New English Drama, XX.
  Trip to Scarborough, A. London: John Cumberland, 1829. Pp. [1]-56. Cumberland's British Theatre, IV. *Filed under* Cumberland, John. Cumberland's British Theatre, IV.
  Trip to Scarborough, A. In *British Drama,* 12 vols., London: John Dicks, 1865, III, [943]-958.
SHERIFF OF THE COUNTY, THE
  See Peake, Richard Brinsley.
SHILLING DAY AT THE GREAT EXHIBITION, A
  See Brough, William.
SHILLING HOP!
  See Lemon, Mark. School for Tigers, The.
SHIN FAIN
  See C., T. S.
SHINE, JOHN L.
  Joan of Arc; or, The Merry Maid of Orleans. Written with Ross, Adrian (pseud. of Ropes, Arthur Reed). Music by Carr, F. Osmond. London: E. Ascherberg, n.d. Pp. [1]-54. Vocal score.
SHIP OF THE AVENGER
  See Haines, John Thomas. Wizard of the Wave, The.
SHIPMATES
  See Bridgman, Cunningham V.
SHIPWRECK, THE
  See Arnold, Samuel James.
SHIPWRECK OF THE MEDUSA
  See Moncrieff, William Thomas.
SHIRLEY, ARTHUR
  Danicheffs, The; or, Married by Force. London & New York: Samuel French, n.d. Pp. [1]-34. [French's Acting Edition].
  Gringoire the Ballad-Monger. *Also:* Pity. Chicago: Dramatic Publishing Co., n.d. Pp. [1]-21. Sergel's Acting Drama, 510.
  Miss Cleopatra. London & New York: Samuel French, c.1898. Pp. [1]-40.
  Pity.
    See Gringoire the Ballad-Monger.
  Saved; or, A Wife's Peril. Chicago: Dramatic Publishing Co., n.d. Pp. [1]-42.
  Three Hats. New York: Fitzgerald, n.d. Pp. [1]-37.
  Woman and Wine. Written with Landeck, Benjamin. [New York]: Rialto Service Bureau, [1900]. Pp. [i-v], [1]-38, [1]-34, [1]-28, [1]-18. Pagination by act. Typescript. *Filed under* Landeck, Benjamin; Shirley, Arthur.
SHIRLEY, WILLIAM
  Edward the Black Prince; or, The Battle of Poictiers. London: Sherwood, Neely, & Jones, 1818. Pp. [1]-[72]. London Theatre, XXIV. *Filed under* Dibdin, Thomas John, ed. London Theatre, XXIV.
  Edward, the Black Prince; or, The Battle of Poictiers. In *British Drama,* 12 vols., London: John Dicks, 1865, III, [i-iv], [639]-656.
SHOBERL, FREDERIC (trans.)
  Patriot Father, The. By Kotzebue. London: R. S. Kirby, 1830. Pp. [i]-[xii], [1]-60.
SHOCKING EVENTS
  See Buckstone, John Baldwin.
SHOEMAKER'S CUT AT CORRUPTION
  See Sands, John Sim. Tory Member's Awl Brought to His Last, A.
SHOOTING THE MOON
  See Cooper, Frederick Fox.
SHOP GIRL, THE
  See Dam, Henry Jackson Wells.
SHORE, LOUISA CATHERINE
  Hannibal. London: Grant Richards, 1898. Pp. [i]-[x], [1]-225.
SHORT AND SWEET
  See Troughton, Adolphus Charles.
SHORT BLAZE, BUT A BRIGHT ONE
  See Gent, J. B. Meteor, The.
SHORT REIGN, AND A MERRY ONE, A
  See Poole, John.

SHOT IN THE EYE
    See Johnstone, John Beer. Jack Long.
SHOULD THIS MEET THE EYE
    See Maltby, C. Alfred.
SHOW OF HANDS, A
    See Walkes, W. R.
SHOWER BATH
    See Cooper, Frederick Fox. Spare Bed, The.
SHOWMAN ABROAD
    See Williams, Arthur. Bear-Faced Swindle, A.
SHRINKING SHOE, THE
    See Besant, Walter.
SHYLOCK
    See Talfourd, Francis.
SIAMESE TWINS, THE
    See A'Beckett, Gilbert Abbott.
SICILIAN, THE
    See Van Laun, Henri (trans.).
SICILIAN CAPTIVE, THE
    See Symmons, Charles.
SICILIAN IDYLL, A
    See Todhunter, John.
SICILIAN SUMMER
    See Taylor, Henry. Virgin Widow, The.
SICILIAN VESPERS, THE
    See Kenney, James.
SICILIEN; OU, L'AMOUR PEINTRE
    See Van Laun, Henri (trans.). Sicilian, The.
SICK LADY'S CURE
    See Cibber, Colley. Double Gallant, The.
SIDAGERO; OR, CODANONIA CONQUISTATA (anon.)
    Music by Guglielmi, P. C., jr. London: Brettell (printer),
    1809. Pp. [1]-52. Libretto.
SIDDONS, HENRY
    Time's a Tell-Tale. London: Longman, Hurst, Rees, & Orme,
    1807. Pp. [i]-[viii], [1]-67.
    Time's a Tell-Tale. In [*Modern Theatre*, ed. Mrs. Inchbald, 10
    vols., London: Longman, Hurst, Rees, Orme, & Brown,
    1811, X], [81]-147.
SIDNEY, FREDERICK W.
    Brixton Burglary, The. New York & London: Samuel
    French, c.1905. Pp. [1]-70. Pagination irregular.
    French's [International Copyrighted] Edition of the
    Works of the Best Authors, 83.
    Hogmanay (New Year's Eve). London & New York: Samuel
    French, c.1902. Pp. [1]-16. [Lacy's Acting Edition].
SIEGE, THE
    See Baillie, Joanna.
    See Mitford, Mary Russell.
SIEGE OF ANCONA, THE
    See Landor, Walter Savage.
SIEGE OF ANTWERP, THE
    See Kennedy, William.
SIEGE OF BEAUVAIS
    See Almar, George. Jane of the Hatchet.
SIEGE OF BELGRADE, THE
    See Cobb, James.
SIEGE OF BERWICK, THE
    See Miller, James.
SIEGE OF CARTHAGE, THE
    See Fitzgerald, William, jr.
SIEGE OF CONSTANTINA
    See Haines, John Thomas. French Spy, The.
SIEGE OF CUZCO, THE
    See Sotheby, William.
SIEGE OF DAMASCUS, THE
    See Hughes, John.
SIEGE OF ISCA, THE
    See Kemp, Joseph.
SIEGE OF MALTA, THE (anon.)
    London: John Murray, 1823. Pp. [i]-[viii], [1]-115.
SIEGE OF MONTGATZ
    See Hook, Theodore Edward. Tekeli.
SIEGE OF PERTH
    See Maclaren, Archibald. Wallace the Brave.

SIEGE OF ROCHELLE, THE
    See Fitzball, Edward.
SIEGE OF TROY, THE
    See Brough, Robert Barnabas.
    See Burneybusby, John.
    See Dibdin, Thomas John. Melodrame Mad!
SIEGE OF VALENCIA, THE
    See Hemans, Felicia Dorothea Browne, Mrs. Alfred.
SIEGFRIED
    See Corder, Henrietta Louisa Walford, Mrs. Frederick
    (trans.).
    See Forman, Alfred (trans.).
    See Rankin, Reginald (trans.).
SIGESMAR THE SWITZER
    See Walker, Charles Edward.
SIGHS OF ULLA
    See Hitchener, William Henry. Ivor.
SIGN OF AFFECTION
    See Webster, Benjamin, jr. Hen and Chickens, The.
SIGNA
    See A'Beckett, Gilbert Arthur.
SIGNAL, THE
    See Coyne, Joseph Stirling.
SIGNAL FIRE
    See Abbott, William. Swedish Patriotism.
SIGNET RING
    See Payne, John Howard. Ali Pacha.
SIKHS OF ONE AND HALF-A-DOZEN OF THE OTHER
    See Byron, Henry James. Rival Rajahs of Ramjam
    Coodlum, The.
SILENT BATTLE
    See Henderson, Isaac. Agatha.
SILENT PRINCESS
    See Greene, Louisa Lilias Plunket, Mrs. Richard Jonas
    (Baroness). Nettle Coats.
SILENT PROTECTOR, A
    See Williams, Thomas John.
SILENT SYSTEM, THE
    See Williams, Thomas John.
SILENT WOMAN, A
    See Lacy, Thomas Hailes.
SILKEN FETTERS
    See Buckingham, Leicester Silk.
SILVER ARROW, THE
    See Barrymore, William.
SILVER KEEPSAKE, THE
    See Norwood, Eille.
SILVER KING, THE
    See Jones, Henry Arthur.
SILVER LINING, THE
    See Buckingham, Leicester Silk.
SILVER PALACE, THE
    See Almar, George.
SILVER SHIELD, THE
    See Grundy, Sydney.
SILVER TICKET, THE
    See de Caux, John William.
SILVER TROUT, THE
    See Roberts, Randal Howland.
SILVESTER, FRANK
    Arthur's Bakery Co.; or, The Original A. B. C. Music by
    Elwes, E. Gwenydd. [St. Albans: M. A. Richardson,
    n.d.]. Pp. [1]-4. Libretto.
    Golden Apple, The. Music by Willis, Alfred M. N.p.: n.pub.,
    n.d. Pp. [1]-28. Libretto.
    Who Stole the Tarts? St. Albans: Gibbs & Bamforth
    (printer), n.d. Pp. [1]-29. Libretto.
SIMMS, HARRY
    Martin Chuzzlewit. London: John Dicks, n.d. Pp. [1]-31.
    Dicks' Standard Plays, 738.
    Nicholas Nickleby. London: John Dicks, n.d. Pp. [1]-29.
    Dicks' Standard Plays, 469.
SIMON LEE
    See Pitt, George Dibdin.

SIMPLE SIMON
  See Wallace, John.
SIMPLE SWEEP, A
  See Broughton, Frederick William.
SIMPSON, ELIZABETH
  See Inchbald, Elizabeth Simpson, Mrs. Joseph.
SIMPSON, ELLA GRAHAM
  Demon Spider, The; or, The Catcher Caught. Music by Lawson, W. E. London & Newcastle-on-Tyne: Andrew Reid, n.d. Pp. [5]-20. Libretto.
SIMPSON, JOHN PALGRAVE
  Alarmingly Suspicious. Clyde, Ohio: A. D. Ames, n.d. Pp. [1]-16. Ames' Series of Standard and Minor Drama, 80.
  Alone. Written with Merivale, Herman Charles. London & New York: Samuel French, n.d. Pp. [1]-38. [Lacy's Acting Edition].
  Appearances. London: Thomas Hailes Lacy, n.d. Pp. [1]-38. [Lacy's Acting Edition].
  Atrocious Criminal, An. *Also:* An Awful Criminal. London: Thomas Hailes Lacy, n.d. Pp. [1]-22. [Lacy's Acting Edition].
  Awful Criminal, An. *Also:* An Atrocious Criminal. Clyde, Ohio: A. D. Ames, n.d. Pp. [1]-15. Ames' Series of Standard and Minor Drama, 78.
  Bianca, the Bravo's Bride. Music by Balfe, Michael William. London: Royal English Opera, Covent Garden, n.d. Pp. [1]-64. 1st ed. Libretto.
  Black Sheep. Written with Yates, Edmund Hodgson. London: Thomas Hailes Lacy, n.d. Pp. [1]-52. [Lacy's Acting Edition].
  Bound. *Also:* The Serpent on the Hearth. Pp. [i], [1]-38, 40-[124]. Manuscript promptbook.
  Bravo's Heir, The. Music by Simpson, Palgrave. London: Novello, Ewer (printer) (priv.), n.d. Pp. [i-ii], [1]-[8], [1]-138. Vocal score.
  Broken Ties. London & New York: Samuel French, n.d. Pp. [1]-41. [Lacy's Acting Edition].
  Cloud in the Honeymoon, A. Chicago: Dramatic Publishing Co., c.1884. Pp. [1]-12. Sergel's Acting Drama, 326.
  Court Cards. London: Thomas Hailes Lacy, n.d. Pp. [1]-44. [Lacy's Acting Edition].
  Daddy Hardacre. London & New York: Samuel French, n.d. Pp. [1]-40. [Lacy's Acting Edition].
  Dreams of Delusion. Boston: William V. Spencer, n.d. Pp. [1]-28. Spencer's Boston Theatre, 165.
  Fair Pretender, A. London: Thomas Hailes Lacy, n.d. Pp. [1]-39. [Lacy's Acting Edition].
  First Affections. London: Thomas Hailes Lacy, n.d. Pp. [1]-23. [Lacy's Acting Edition].
  Heads or Tails? London: Thomas Hailes Lacy, n.d. Pp. [1]-36. [Lacy's Acting Edition].
  Jack in a Box! London: Thomas Hailes Lacy, n.d. Pp. [1]-24.
  King of the Merrows.
    See Burnand, Francis Cowley.
  Lady Dedlock's Secret. London & New York: Samuel French, n.d. Pp. [1]-52. [Lacy's Acting Edition].
  Marco Spada. New York: William Taylor, n.d. Pp. [i]-[viii], [9]-51. Modern Standard Drama, 99.
  Matrimonial Prospectuses! London: Thomas Hailes Lacy, n.d. Pp. [1]-21. [Lacy's Acting Edition].
  My Mysterious Rival. New York: DeWitt, c.1884. Pp. [1]-13. DeWitt's Acting Plays, 324.
  Only a Clod. Boston: Walter H. Baker, n.d. Pp. [1]-24. Spencer's Universal Stage, 41.
  Poor Cousin Walter. London: Thomas Hailes Lacy, n.d. Pp. [1]-22. [Lacy's Acting Edition].
  Prison and Palace. New York: Harold Roorbach, n.d. Pp. [1]-40.
  Ranelagh. Written with Wray, Charles. London: Thomas Hailes Lacy, n.d. Pp. [1]-48. [Lacy's Acting Edition].
  Romance! Music by Leslie, Henry. London: Royal English Opera, Covent Garden, 1860. Pp. [1]-32. Libretto.
  School for Coquettes, A. London: Thomas Hailes Lacy, n.d. Pp. [1]-36. [Lacy's Acting Edition].

  Scrap of Paper, A. London & New York: Samuel French, n.d. Pp. [1]-51. French's Acting Edition (late Lacy's).
  Second Love. Boston: William V. Spencer, n.d. Pp. [1]-40. Spencer's Boston Theatre, 65.
  Serpent on the Hearth, The.
    See Bound.
  Shadows of the Past. London & New York: Samuel French, n.d. Pp. [1]-36. [Lacy's Acting Edition].
  Sybilla; or, Step by Step. London: Thomas Hailes Lacy, n.d. Pp. [1]-63.
  That Odious Captain Cutter! London: Thomas Hailes Lacy, n.d. Pp. [1]-24. Lacy's Acting Edition, 42.
  Time and the Hour. Written with Merivale, Herman Charles. By J. Palgrave Simpson and Felix Dale (pseud.). New York: Robert M. DeWitt, n.d. Pp. [1]-44. DeWitt's Acting Plays, 42.
  Time and the Hour. Written with Merivale, Herman Charles. By J. Palgrave Simpson and Felix Dale (pseud.). London & New York: Samuel French, n.d. Pp. [1]-58. Promptbook.
  Two Gentlemen at Mivart's. New York: Dick & Fitzgerald, n.d. Pp. [1]-9. Dick's American Edition.
  Very Suspicious! London: Thomas Hailes Lacy, n.d. Pp. [1]-22. Lacy's Acting Edition, 90. Promptbook.
  Watch Dog of the Walsinghams, The. London: Thomas Hailes Lacy, n.d. Pp. [1]-53. Promptbook.
  Without Incumbrances. London: Thomas Hailes Lacy, n.d. Pp. [1]-24. [Lacy's Acting Edition].
  World and Stage. London & New York: Samuel French, n.d. Pp. [1]-76. [Lacy's Acting Edition].
SIMPSON, MERCER H. (arr.)
  Midsummer Night's Dream, A. By Shakespeare, William. Birmingham: Theatre Royal Printing Office, 1873. Pp. [1]-52. *Filed under* Midsummer Night's Dream (anon.).
SIMPSON AND CO.
  See Poole, John.
SIMS, GEORGE ROBERT
  Beauty. Written with Grundy, Sydney. London: Thomas Scott, n.d. Pp. [1]-40.
  Blue-Eyed Susan. Written with Pettitt, Henry Alfred. Music by Carr, F. Osmond. London: E. Ascherberg, c.1892. Pp. [1]-184. Vocal score.
  Carmen up to Data. Written with Pettitt, Henry Alfred. Music by Lutz, Meyer. Pp. [i], [1]-18, 1-21, [i], 1-21, 1-8. Pagination by scene. Typescript libretto.
  City of Pleasure, The. London: Mrs. Marshall's Typewriting Office, 1895. Pp. [i-iii], [1]-17, [i-iii], [1]-17, [i-iii], [1]-24, [i], [1]-19, [i-iii], [1]-36, [i], [1]-36, [i-viii]. Pagination by act. Typescript promptbook.
  Dandy Dick Whittington. Music by Caryll, Ivan. London: Chappell, c.1895. Pp. [1]-40. Libretto.
  Dandy Fifth, The. Music by Corri, Clarence C. London: Hopwood & Crew, n.d. Pp. [1]-31. Libretto.
  Dress Rehearsal, A. Music by Diehl, Louis. London: Boosey, n.d. Pp. [i-ii], [1]-54. Vocal score.
  Faust up to Date. Written with Pettitt, Henry Alfred. Music by Lutz, Meyer. London: W. S. Johnson, 1889. Pp. [3]-60. Libretto.
  In the Ranks; or, A Soldier's Wife. Written with Pettitt, Henry Alfred. London: Aldine, n.d. Pp. [1]-64. Home Library of Powerful Dramatic Tales, 4. Novelization by Henry Llewellyn Williams. *Filed under* Pettitt, Henry Alfred.
  Lights o' London. 65 leaves. Variously paginated by act and scene. Typescript promptbook.
  Little Christopher Columbus. Written with Raleigh, Cecil. Music by Caryll, Ivan. London: Hopwood & Crew, n.d. Pp. [i-iv], [1]-193. Vocal score.
  Merry Duchess, The. Music by Clay, Frederic. New York: J. J. Little, n.d. Pp. [i-ii], [1]-24. Libretto.
  Romany Rye, The. Pp. [i], [1]-22, [i], [1]-22, [i], [1]-22, [i], [1]-32, [i], [1]-10. Typescript.
SIN AND ITS SHADOW
  See Reeve, Wybert. Dead Witness, The.
SIN AND THE SORROW, THE
  See Leslie, Henry.

SIN OF ST. HULDA, THE
See Ogilvie, G. Stuart.
SINBAD THE SAILOR
See Blanchard, Edward Litt Leman.
See Conquest, George.
See McArdle, John Francis.
See Thorn, Geoffrey.
See Younge, Henry.
SINDBAD THE SAILOR
See Doyle, Thomas F.
SINGING APPLE AND THE DANCING WATERS
See Smith, Albert Richard. Fair Star.
SINGING APPLE, THE TALKING BIRD, AND THE DANC-
ING WATERS
See Blanchard, Edward Litt Leman. Cherry and Fair
Star.
SINGLE LIFE
See Buckstone, John Baldwin.
SINGLETON, MRS.
See Fane, Violet (pseud.).
SINK OR SWIM!
See Morton, Thomas, jr.
SINNETT, EDWARD
Atreus and Thyestes. London: C. & H. Baldwyn, 1822. Pp.
[i]-[iv], [5]-61.
SIR DAGOBERT AND THE DRAGON
See Burnand, Francis Cowley.
SIR JASPER'S VOW
See Drinkwater, Albert E.
SIR JOHN FALSTAFF
See Lemon, Mark.
SIR MARMADUKE MAXWELL
See Cunningham, Allan.
SIR PAUL PINDAR
See Maugham, Harry Neville.
SIR PETER HARPDON'S END
See Morris, William.
SIR ROGER DE COVERLEY
See Smith, John Frederick.
See Taylor, Tom.
SIR THOMAS MORE
See P., Br.
SIR WALTER RALEGH
See Dixon, William John.
SIRENS OF THE LOTUS LAKE
See Byron, Henry James. Giselle.
SIRES AND SONS FROM ALBION SPRUNG, THE
See St. George, George.
SISTER AND I!
See Mildenhall, Thomas.
SISTER'S PENANCE, A
See Taylor, Tom.
SISTERLY SERVICE
See Wooler, John Pratt.
SISTERS, THE
See Barrymore, William.
See Swinburne, Algernon Charles.
SISTERS OF SORROW, THE
See Travers, William.
SISTERS OF ST. LEONARD'S
See Heart of Midlothian, The.
SISYPHUS, KING OF EPHYRA
See Corder, Frederick.
SIX AND EIGHTPENCE
See Tree, Herbert Beerbohm.
SIX MONTHS AGO
See Merivale, Herman Charles.
SIX PERSONS
See Zangwill, Israel.
SIX YEARS AFTER
See Cheltnam, Charles Smith. May Brierly.
See Cheltnam, Charles Smith. Ticket-of-Leave Man's
Wife, The.
SIXES, THE
See Dibdin, Thomas John.

SIXES AND SEVENS: A MISUNDERSTANDING
See Whitmore, E. H.
SIXPENNY TELEGRAM, A
See Bell, Florence Eveleen Eleanore Oliffe, Mrs. Hugh
(Lady).
SIXTEEN AND SIXTY (anon.)
In New British Theatre, London: A. J. Valpy (printer),
1815, IV, [379]-410.
SIXTEEN-STRING JACK
See Rede, William Leman.
See Wilks, Thomas Egerton.
SIXTEEN YEARS AGO
See Raymond, Richard John. Eleventh Hour, The.
SIXTY-THIRD LETTER, THE
See Oulton, Walley Chamberlaine.
SIXTY YEARS SINCE
See Fitzball, Edward. Waverly.
SKEFFINGTON, LUMLEY ST. GEORGE
Sleeping Beauty, The. Music by Addison, John. London:
Kelly's Opera Saloon (priv.), n.d. Pp. [i-ii], [1]-52. Vocal
score.
SKELETON HORSEMAN, THE
See Marchant, Frederick.
SKELETON WITNESS, THE
See Rede, William Leman.
SKELTON, A. W.
Minx and Man, The.
See Lindo, Frank.
SKETCHES FROM LIFE
See Warner, Richard. Bath Characters.
SKETCHES IN INDIA
See Morton, Thomas, jr.
SKETCHLEY, ARTHUR (pseud. of Rose, George)
Dark Cloud, The. London: Thomas Hailes Lacy, n.d. Pp.
[1]-30. [Lacy's Acting Edition]. Filed under Rose, George.
Getting Up in the World; or, The Young Pretender. New
York: Happy Hours, n.d. Pp. [1]-16. Acting Drama, 81.
Filed under Rose, George.
How Will They Get Out of It? London & New York: Samuel
French, n.d. Pp. [1]-48. French's Acting Edition (late
Lacy's). Filed under Rose, George.
Living at Ease. London: J. Mallett (printer), n.d. Pp. [1]-[39].
Filed under Rose, George.
Money Makes the Man. New York: Dick & Fitzgerald, n.d.
Pp. [1]-16. Filed under Rose, George.
Quite at Home. New York: Robert M. DeWitt, n.d. Pp.
[1]-10. Filed under Rose, George.
Up in the World. London: James Wade (printer), n.d. Pp.
[1]-56. Filed under Rose, George.
SKIRT DANCER, THE
See Ridgwell, George.
SKIRTS OF THE CAMP
See Pearce, William. Hartford Bridge.
SKRINE, JOHN HUNTLEY
Joan the Maid. London: Macmillan, 1895. Pp. [i-viii],
[1]-206.
SLADEN, DOUGLAS BROOKE WHEELTON
Edward the Black Prince. London: Griffith, Farran, Okeden,
& Welsh, n.d. Pp. [1]-225.
SLANDERER, THE
See Wallace, John.
SLASHER AND CRASHER!
See Morton, John Maddison.
SLAVE, THE
See Morton, Thomas, sr.
SLAVE BY CHOICE
See Hoare, Prince. Chains of the Heart.
SLAVE IN LOVE
See Bennett, Joseph. Djamileh.
SLAVE LIFE
See Lemon, Mark.
SLAVE OF DUTY
See Gilbert, William Schwenck. Pirates of Penzance, The.
SLAVE QUEEN
See Coyne, Joseph Stirling. Valsha.

SLAVE SALE, THE
See Bulwer, J.

SLAVER, THE
See Maclaren, Archibald.

SLEDGE-DRIVER, THE
See Planché, Elizabeth (Eliza) St. George, Mrs. James Robinson.

SLEEP-WALKER, THE
See Oulton, Walley Chamberlaine.

SLEEPER AWAKENED, THE
See Oxenford, John.

SLEEPERS AWAKENED, THE
See Adams, Florence Davenport.

SLEEPING BEAUTY
See George, G. H.
See Keating, Eliza H.
See McArdle, John Francis.
See Powell, Thomas (of Monmouth). Camillus and Columna.
See Skeffington, Lumley St. George.

SLEEPING BEAUTY IN THE WOOD
See Planché, James Robinson.
See Russell, Georgiana Adelaide Peel, Lady.

SLEEPING DOSE
See Baynes, E. D. Love and Laudanum.

SLEEPING DRAUGHT, THE
See Penley, Samson.

SLEEPING OUT
See Moncrieff, William Thomas. Borrowing a Husband.

SLICE OF LUCK, A
See Morton, John Maddison.

SLIGHT MISTAKE, A
See Fraser, Julia Agnes.

SLIGHT MISTAKES!
See Morton, John Maddison.

SLIGHTED TREASURES
See Suter, William E.

SLOUS, ANGIOLO ROBSON
Templar, The. London: Chapman & Hall, 1850. Pp. [i-viii], [1]-86.
True to the Core: A Story of the Armada. [London: Tinsley Brothers, 1866]. Pp. [1]-61.

SLOUS, FREDERICK L. (trans.)
Francis the First; or, The Curse of St. Vallier. *Also:* Le Roi S'Amuse. By Hugo, Victor. London: Stewart & Murray (printer) (priv.), 1843. Pp. [i]-[xii], [1]-110.

SLOW MAN, THE
See Lemon, Mark.

SLOWTOP'S ENGAGEMENTS
See Cheltnam, Charles Smith.

SMALE, EDITH C., MRS. T. E.
Baffled Spinster, The. London & New York: Samuel French, c.1901. Pp. [1]-9. [Lacy's Acting Edition].
Compromising Case, A. London & New York: Samuel French, n.d. Pp. [1]-22. [French's Acting Edition].

SMART, MRS. ALEC
See de Smart, Mrs. Alec. Purely Platonic.

SMELT, THOMAS
J. P. Manchester: Thomas J. Day, 1878. Pp. [1]-74.
Magpie and Thimble, The. Manchester: Thomas J. Day, 1875. Pp. [i-iv], [1]-20.

SMILES AND TEARS
See Kemble, Marie Thérèse De Camp, Mrs. Charles.

SMITH, ALBERT RICHARD
Aladdin and the Wonderful Lamp; or, New Lamps for Old Ones. Written with Kenney, Charles Lamb. London: W. S. Johnson, n.d. Pp. [1]-32.
Alhambra, The; or, The Three Beautiful Princesses. London: Thomas Hailes Lacy, n.d. Pp. [1]-25. [Lacy's Acting Edition].
Battle of Life, The. London: John Dicks, n.d. Pp. [1]-16. Dicks' Standard Plays, 1001.
Blanche Heriot; or, The Chertsey Curfew. London: William Barth, n.d. Pp. [1]-26. Promptbook.

Cinderella. Written with Taylor, Tom. London: R. Hodson (printer) (priv.), n.d. Pp. [1]-34.
Cricket on the Hearth, The; or, A Fairy Tale of Home. New York: Samuel French, n.d. Pp. [1]-31. French's Standard Drama, 342.
Esmeralda. London: Thomas Hailes Lacy, n.d. Pp. [1]-36.
Fair Star; or, The Singing Apple and the Dancing Waters. Written with Oxenford, John. London: W. Barth, n.d. Pp. [1]-28. 2nd ed.
Guy Fawkes; or, A Match for a King. Written with Taylor, Tom; Hale, W. P.; Draper, E.; Smith, Arthur W. W. By Albert Smith. London: W. S. Johnson, n.d. Pp. [1]-32.
Hop-o'-My-Thumb; or, The Seven League Boots. London: T. Brettell, 1846. Pp. [1]-24.
Novelty Fair.
See Taylor, Tom.
Tarantula, La; or, The Spider King. Written with Talfourd, Francis. By Albert Smith. London: Thomas Hailes Lacy, n.d. Pp. [1]-31. Lacy's Acting Edition, 40.
Tarantula, La; or, The Spider King. Written with Talfourd, Francis. London: Thomas Hailes Lacy, n.d. Pp. [1]-31. [Lacy's Acting Edition]. *Filed under* Tarantula (anon.).
Valentine and Orson. Written with Taylor, Tom. London: R. Hodson (printer), n.d. Pp. [1]-35.
Wood Demon, The.
See Kenney, Charles Lamb.

SMITH, ARTHUR W. W.
Guy Fawkes.
See Smith, Albert Richard.

SMITH, CHARLES
Trip to Bengal, A. London: J. Ridgway; Black & Parry, 1802. Pp. [i-vi], [1]-52. Libretto.
What Is She? In [*Modern Theatre*, ed. Mrs. Inchbald, 10 vols., London: Longman, Hurst, Rees, Orme, & Brown, 1811], X, [217]-297.

SMITH, DEXTER
Mousquetaires au Couvent, Les.
See Farnie, Henry Brougham.

SMITH, G.
Make Your Wills.
See Mayhew, Edward.

SMITH, HORATIO
Amarynthus the Nympholept. London: Longman, Hurst, Rees, Orme, & Brown, 1821. Pp. [i]-xii, [1]-172.
First Impressions; or, Trade in the West. London: Thomas Underwood, 1813. Pp. [i-vi], [1]-[80].

SMITH, JOHN
Pretty Jane!, the Cruel Squire!, and Robin the Ploughman!, The. London: Thomas Hailes Lacy, n.d. Pp. [1]-12. Lacy's Sensation Series.

SMITH, JOHN FREDERICK
Court of Old Fritz, The. London: Chapman & Hall, n.d. Pp. [1]-23.
Lesson for Gentlemen, A; or, The City Wives. London: Thomas Hailes Lacy, n.d. Pp. [1]-21.
Protector!, The; or, The Rebel's Gauntlet! London: John Duncombe, n.d. Pp. [1]-36. Duncombe's Acting Edition of the British Theatre, 406.
Sir Roger de Coverley; or, The English Gentleman. London: John Duncombe, n.d. Pp. [1]-35. Duncombe's Acting Edition of the British Theatre, 192.
Wolsey!; or, The Secret Witness! London: John Duncombe, n.d. Pp. [1]-29. Duncombe's Edition.

SMITH, LITA
Bridget's Blunders. London & New York: Samuel French, n.d. Pp. [1]-19. [Lacy's Acting Edition].
Mr. and Mrs. Muffett; or, A Domestic Experiment. London & New York: Samuel French, n.d. Pp. [1]-12. [Lacy's Acting Edition].

SMITH, SIDNEY
Falkland. London: Edward Turner, 1876. Pp. [i-vi], [1]-88.

SMITH, SPENCER THEYRE
Case for Eviction, A. New York: Dick & Fitzgerald, c.1890. Pp. [1]-20.

Cut Off with a Shilling. Chicago: Dramatic Publishing Co., n.d. Pp. [1]-15. Sergel's Acting Drama, [148].

Happy Pair, A. London & New York: Samuel French, n.d. Pp. [1]-22. French's Minor Drama, 335.

Mrs. Hilary Regrets. London: Joseph Williams, n.d. Pp. [1]-24.

My Lord in Livery. New York: Dick & Fitzgerald, c.1889. Pp. [1]-28.

Old Cronies. London & New York: Samuel French, n.d. Pp. [1]-23. [French's Acting Edition].

Uncle's Will. New York: Dick & Fitzgerald, c.1890. Pp. [1]-22.

Which Is Which? New York: Dick & Fitzgerald, c.1889. Pp. [1]-24.

SMITH, T.
Highgate Tunnel, The; or, The Secret Arch. By Momus Medlar (pseud.). London: John Miller, 1812. Pp. [i-vi], [9]-37. Text complete.

SMITH, WALTER CHALMERS
Kildrostan. Glasgow: James Maclehose & Sons, 1884. Pp. [i-vi], [1]-278.

Kildrostan. In *Poetical Works,* London: Andrew Melrose, 1906, pp. [i], 370-477.

SMITH, WILLIAM
Look on This Picture, and on That. London: J. Miles (printer), n.d. Pp. [i-ii], [1]-16.

SMITH, WILLIAM HENRY
Athelwold. London & Edinburgh: William Blackwood & Sons, 1842. Pp. [i-iv], [1]-124.

SMITH
See Davidson, John.

SMITHEREENS, THE (anon.)
Malvern: Stevens (printer) (priv.), 1898. Pp. [1]-31.

SMOKE
See Hayes, Frederick William.
See Webster, Benjamin, jr.

SMOKED MISER!, THE
See Jerrold, Douglas William.

SMUGGLER'S CAVE
See Arnold, Samuel James. Up All Night.

SMUGGLER'S DAUGHTER, THE
See Bird, James.
See Dibdin, Charles Isaac Mungo, jr.

SMUGGLER'S SON AND ROBBER'S DAUGHTER
See Scott, Jane M. Old Oak Chest, The.

SMYTHE, ALFRED
Victoire. Music by Little, Edgar. Dublin: Powderly, 1893. Pp. [1]-47. Libretto.

SMYTHIES, WILLIAM GORDON
Lady by Birth, A. London: Samuel French; New York: T. Henry French, n.d. Pp. [1]-18. [Lacy's Acting Edition].

Love Suit, A. London: Samuel French; New York: T. Henry French, n.d. Pp. [1]-8. [Lacy's Acting Edition].

Mystification. London & New York: Samuel French, n.d. Pp. [1]-9.

Outwitted. London: Samuel French; New York: T. Henry French, n.d. Pp. [1]-12. French's Acting Edition (late Lacy's), 2037.

SNAKE IN THE GRASS
See Barnett, Morris. Sarah the Creole.

SNAKES IN THE GRASS
See Buckstone, John Baldwin.

SNAPPING TURTLES, THE
See Buckstone, John Baldwin.

SNODGRASS, ALFRED
State Secrets; or, Public Men in Private Life. London: W. Wright, 1821. Pp. [i-x], [11]-28.

SNOWBALL, THE
See Grundy, Sydney.

SNOWDRIFT, THE
See Coates, Alfred.

SNOWDROP
See Burnand, Francis Cowley.

SNOW STORM, THE
See Barrymore, William. Fatal Snow Storm, The.

See Barrymore, William.
See Bowkett, Sidney.
See Hetherington, William Maxwell.

SNOWWHITE
See Adams, Florence Davenport.

SOANE, GEORGE
Aladdin. New York: E. M. Murden, 1826. Pp. [1]-75. Libretto.

Bohemian, The. London: C. Chapple, 1817. Pp. [i-viii], [1]-139.

Chelsea Pensioner, The. London: John Duncombe, n.d. Pp. [1]-38. Duncombe's Edition.

Dwarf of Naples, The. London: T. Rodwell, 1819. Pp. [i-viii], [1]-[52].

Falls of Clyde, The. London: T. Rodwell, 1817. Pp. [1-5], [i]-[iv], [5]-56.

Falls of Clyde, The. London: John Cumberland, n.d. Pp. [1]-40. Cumberland's British Theatre, XXXI. *Filed under* Cumberland, John. Cumberland's British Theatre, XXXI.

Faustus. Written with Terry, Daniel. By George Soane. Music by Bishop, Henry; Cooke, Thomas; Horn, Charles. London: John Miller, 1825. Pp. [i-vi], [1]-59. Libretto.

Faustus. Written with Terry, Daniel. London: John Cumberland, n.d. Pp. [1]-58. Cumberland's British Theatre, XXXIII. *Filed under* Cumberland, John. Cumberland's British Theatre, XXXIII.

Faustus. Written with Terry, Daniel. *Also:* Faustus; or, The Demon of the Drachenfels. Music by Bishop, Henry; Cooke, Thomas; Horn, Charles. London: Goulding & D'Almaine (printer), n.d. Pp. [1]-86. Vocal score.

Faustus; or, The Demon of the Drachenfels. Written with Terry, Daniel. Music by Bishop, Henry; Cooke, Thomas; Horn, Charles. London: J. Marshall (printer), n.d. Pp. [i], [1]-59. Title page lacking. Promptbook libretto.

Freischütz, Der. Music by Weber. London: Simpkin & Marshall, 1825. Pp. [1-46]. 3rd ed. Libretto.

Innkeeper's Daughter, The. Music by Cooke, Thomas. London: W. Simpkin & R. Marshall, 1817. Pp. [i-viii], [9]-67.

Lilian the Show Girl. London: Thomas Hailes Lacy, n.d. Pp. [1]-34. New British Theatre (late Duncombe's), 187.

Luke Somerton. London: John Duncombe, n.d. Pp. [1]-35. Duncombe's Edition.

Masaniello, the Fisherman of Naples. London: John Miller, 1825. Pp. [i-viii], [1]-61.

Peasant of Lucern, The. London: C. Chapple, 1815. Pp. [iii]-[x], [1]-88. Libretto.

Rob Roy. London: John Cumberland, n.d. Pp. [1]-45. Cumberland's British Theatre, XXXVI. *Filed under* Cumberland, John. Cumberland's British Theatre, XXXVI.

Rob Roy, the Gregarach. London: Richard White, 1818. Pp. [i]-xii, [1]-[84].

Self-Sacrifice; or, The Maid of the Cottage. Music by Reeve, George. London: John Lowndes, 1819. Pp. [i]-[vi], [1]-35.

Undine; or, The Spirit of the Waters. New York: Circulating Library & Dramatic Repository, 1822. Pp. [1]-40. Promptbook.

Young Reefer, The. London: John Cumberland, n.d. Pp. [1]-38.

Young Reefer, The. London: John Cumberland, n.d. Pp. [1]-38. Cumberland's Minor Theatre, VIII. *Filed under* Cumberland, John. Cumberland's Minor Theatre, VIII.

Zarah. London: John Cumberland, n.d. Pp. [1]-31. Cumberland's British Theatre, [266].

Zarah. London: John Cumberland, n.d. Pp. [i-ii], [1]-31. Cumberland's British Theatre, XXXV. *Filed under* Cumberland, John. Cumberland's British Theatre, XXXV.

SOANE, GEORGE (trans.)
Haydée; or, The Secret. Music by Auber. London: Davidson, 1848. Pp. [1]-38. Davidson's Dramatic Operas. Libretto.

Marriage of Figaro, The. *Also:* Le Nozze di Figaro. Music by Mozart. London: G. H. Davidson, 1848. Pp. [i-vi], [1]-185. Davidson's Lyrical Drama. Vocal score.

SOANE-ROBY, BERNARD
  Deserter in a Fix, A. London & New York: Samuel French, n.d. Pp. [1]-14. [Lacy's Acting Edition].

SOCIAL HIGHWAYMAN, A (anon.)
  Pp. [i], [1]-28, [1]-24, [1]-24, [1]-18, [1]-29. Pagination by act. Typescript.

SOCIAL LIFE IN GERMANY: AN INTRODUCTORY DIALOGUE
  See Jameson, Anna Brownell Murphy, Mrs. Robert (trans.).

SOCIETY
  See Robertson, Thomas William.

SOCRATES
  See Becket, Andrew.
  See Grover, Henry Montague.

SOLD AGAIN
  See Soutar, Robert.

SOLDIER AND A SAILOR, A TINKER AND A TAILOR, A
  See Rogers, William.

SOLDIER OF FORTUNE, THE
  See Dwyer, P. W.

SOLDIER'S BRIDE
  See Haines, John Thomas. Austerlitz.

SOLDIER'S COURTSHIP, A
  See Poole, John.

SOLDIER'S DAUGHTER, THE
  See Cherry, Andrew.

SOLDIER'S FORTUNE
  See Bell, Ernest (trans.). Minna von Barnhelm.
  See Suter, William E. Fan-Fan, the Tulip.

SOLDIER'S GRAVE!
  See Stirling, Edward. Last Kiss!, The.

SOLDIER'S LEGACY, THE
  See Oxenford, John.
  See Selby, Charles. Marceline.

SOLDIER'S ORPHAN, THE
  See Bennett, George John.

SOLDIER'S PROGRESS, THE
  See Courtney, John.

SOLDIER'S RETURN, THE
  See Hook, Theodore Edward.

SOLDIER'S WIDOW
  See Fitzball, Edward. Deserted Mill, The.

SOLDIER'S WIFE
  See Sims, George Robert. In the Ranks.

SOLDIERS AT HOME—HEROES ABROAD
  See Carpenter, Joseph Edwards. Love and Honour.

SOLE SURVIVOR, THE
  See Conquest, George.

SOLICITOR, THE
  See Darnley, J. Herbert.

SOLIS Y RIBADENEYRA, ANTONIO DE
  Gypsey of Madrid, The.
  See Tobin, John (trans.).

SOLWAY STORY
  See Bernard, William Bayle. St. Mary's Eve.

SOLYMAN
  See Clinton, Henry Fynes.

SOME BELLS THAT RANG AN OLD YEAR OUT AND A NEW YEAR IN
  See Lemon, Mark. Chimes, The.

SOME NAMBULISTIC KNICKERBOCKERS
  See Strachan, John S., jr. Rip Van Winkle.

SOME PASSAGES IN THE LIFE OF LOVE
  See Rede, William Leman. Cupid in London.

SOMEBODY ELSE
  See Planché, James Robinson.

SOMEBODY'S NOBODY
  See Maltby, C. Alfred.

SOMERSET, CHARLES A.
  Captain Hawk, the Last of the Highwaymen. *Also:* The Shadow of Death in the Coffin Cell. *Also:* The Shadow of Death; or, Captain Hawk in the Coffin Cell. 91 Leaves. Manuscript.

Chevy Chase; or, The Battle of the Borders. London: Orlando Hodgson, n.d. Pp. [1]-36.

Crazy Jane. London: John Cumberland, n.d. Pp. [1]-57. [Cumberland's Minor Theatre].

Crazy Jane. London: John Cumberland, n.d. Pp. [1]-57. Cumberland's Minor Theatre, II. *Filed under* Cumberland, John. Cumberland's Minor Theatre, II.

Day after the Fair, A. London: H. Davidson, n.d. Pp. [3]-33.

Day after the Fair, A. London: John Cumberland, n.d. Pp. [1]-33. Cumberland's Minor Theatre, III. *Filed under* Cumberland, John. Cumberland's Minor Theatre, III.

Day after the Fair, A. By G. A. Somerset. New York: Samuel French, n.d. Pp. [1]-33. Minor Drama, 123.

Fall of Algiers by Sea and Land, The. London: John Duncombe, n.d. Pp. [1]-36. Duncombe's Edition.

Female Massaroni, The; or, The Fair Brigands. London: John Cumberland, n.d. Pp. [1]-40.

Female Massaroni, The; or, The Fair Brigands. London: John Cumberland, n.d. Pp. [1]-40. Cumberland's Minor Theatre, XIII. *Filed under* Cumberland, John. Cumberland's Minor Theatre, XIII.

Girl of the Light House, The; or, Love and Madness! Pp. [i], [1]-28. Act I and part of Act II. Manuscript promptbook.

Home Sweet Home!; or, The Swiss Family. Music by Weigl, Joseph. London: John Duncombe, n.d. Pp. [1]-24. Duncombe's Edition. Libretto.

Ladye Bird Bower; or, Harlequin Prince Peacock and the Fair Brillianta. Music by Musgrave. Liverpool: St. George's Office (printer), 1858. Pp. [1]-16. Libretto. *Filed under* Somerset, C.

Maurice the Woodcutter. London: Thomas Hailes Lacy, n.d. Pp. [1]-36. [New British Theatre, 45].

Mistletoe Bough, The; or, The Fatal Chest. Clyde, Ohio: A. D. Ames, n.d. Pp. [1]-22. Ames' Series of Standard and Minor Drama, 34.

Mistletoe Bough, The; or, Young Lovel's Bride. London: John Cumberland, n.d. Pp. [1]-36. Cumberland's Minor Theatre, XII. *Filed under* Cumberland, John. Cumberland's Minor Theatre, XII.

Roebuck, The; or, Guilty and Not Guilty. London: John Duncombe, n.d. Pp. [1]-40. Duncombe's Edition.

Sea!, The. London: G. H. Davidson, n.d. Pp. [1]-42. Cumberland's Minor Theatre, 56. Promptbook.

Sea!, The. London: John Cumberland, n.d. Pp. [1]-42. Cumberland's Minor Theatre, VII. *Filed under* Cumberland, John. Cumberland's Minor Theatre, VII.

Shadow of Death, The.
  See Captain Hawk, the Last of the Highwaymen.

Shakspeare's Early Days. London: Thomas Hailes Lacy, n.d. Pp. [1]-48. [Lacy's Acting Edition].

Shakspeare's Early Days. London: John Cumberland, n.d. Pp. [1]-48. Cumberland's British Theatre, XXVIII. *Filed under* Cumberland, John. Cumberland's British Theatre, XXVIII.

Sylvana. Music by Weber. London: John Cumberland, n.d. Pp. [1]-44. [Cumberland's Minor Theatre]. Libretto.

Sylvana. Music by Weber. London: John Cumberland, n.d. Pp. [1]-44. Cumberland's Minor Theatre, III. *Filed under* Cumberland, John. Cumberland's Minor Theatre, III.

Tower of London, The; or, The Rival Queens. London: J. Pattie, n.d. Pp. [1]-38. Pattie's Universal Stage or Theatrical Prompt Book, 14.

Twins of Warsaw, The. London: Thomas Richardson, n.d. Pp. [i]-x, [9]-56. Promptbook.

Yes! London: John Cumberland, n.d. Pp. [1]-24. [Cumberland's Minor Theatre].

Yes! London: John Cumberland, n.d. Pp. [1]-24. Cumberland's Minor Theatre, II. *Filed under* Cumberland, John. Cumberland's Minor Theatre, II.

Zelina; or, The Triumph of the Greeks. New York & London: Samuel French, n.d. Pp. [1]-27. French's Standard Drama, 291.

Zelina; or, The Triumph of the Greeks. Boston: William V. Spencer, n.d. Pp. [1]-27. Spencer's Boston Theatre, 115.

SOMERSET, G. A.
　　See Somerset, Charles A.

SOMETHING TO DO
　　See Morton, John Maddison.

SOMNAMBULIST, THE
　　See Moncrieff, William Thomas.

SON AND STRANGER
　　See Chorley, Henry Fothergill.

SON OF DON JUAN, THE
　　See Graham, James (trans.).

SON OF THE SEA
　　See Atkyns, Samuel. Bright-Eyed Emma.

SON OF THE SOIL, A
　　See Merivale, Herman Charles.

SON OF THE SUN, THE
　　See A'Beckett, Gilbert Abbott.

SON OF THE WILDERNESS, THE
　　See Charlton, William Henry (trans.).

SON'S RETURN, THE (anon. trans.)
　　By Amalie (Amelia), Princess of Saxony. In *Six Dramas Illustrative of German Life*, London: John W. Parker, pp. [223]-276. *Filed under* Six Dramas (anon.).

SON-IN-LAW, THE
　　See O'Keeffe, John.

SONNAMBULA, LA (anon.)
　　Music by Bellini. London & New York: Boosey, n.d. Pp. [i-iv], 1-200. [Royal Edition]. Vocal score.

SONNAMBULA, LA
　　See Beazley, Samuel, jr.
　　See Byron, Henry James. La! Sonnambula!

SONS AND SYSTEMS
　　See Dance, Charles.

SONS OF ERIN, THE
　　See Le Fanu, Alicia Sheridan, Mrs. Joseph.

SONS OF TOIL
　　See Nation, William Hamilton Codrington. Under the Earth.

SOOBROW, ?
　　Kishun Koovur. Trevandrum (India): Government Press, 1840. Pp. [i]-[vi], [1]-82.

SOPHIA'S SUPPER
　　See Addison, Henry Robert, Capt.

SOPHOCLES
　　Antigone.
　　　　See Bartholomew, William (trans.).
　　　　See Whitelaw, Robert (trans.).
　　Downfall and Death of King Oedipus, The.
　　　　See Fitzgerald, Edward (trans.).
　　Oedipus at Colonos.
　　　　See Pember, Edward Henry (trans.).

SOPHONISBA
　　See Lloyd, Charles (trans.).

SORCERER, THE
　　See Gilbert, William Schwenck.

SORCERESS, THE (anon.)
　　In *New British Theatre*, London: A. J. Valpy (printer), 1814, III, [i], [1]-31.

SORCERESS, THE
　　See Parker, Louis Napoleon (trans.).

SORCERESS OF LOVE
　　See Parker, Louis Napoleon (trans.). Sorceress, The.

SORCERIES OF SIN, THE
　　See MacCarthy, Denis Florence (trans.).

SORELLI, GUIDO
　　Isabella Aldobrandi. London: n.pub. (priv.), 1838. Pp. [i]-[xii], [1]-67 (Italian); [i]-[v], [1]-66 (English).

SORRELL, WILLIAM J.
　　Border Marriage, A. London: Thomas Hailes Lacy, n.d. Pp. [1]-23.
　　Friend in Need, A.
　　　　See French, Sydney.

Great Gun Trick, The. By Christian Le Ros (pseud.). London: Thomas Hailes Lacy, n.d. Pp. [1]-20. [Lacy's Acting Edition].
　　Like and Unlike.
　　　　See Langford, J. M.

SORROWS OF HYPSIPYLE, THE
　　See Ashe, Thomas.

SOTHEBY, WILLIAM
　　Cambrian Hero, The; or, Llewelyn the Great. N.p.: n.pub., n.d. Pp. [1]-90.
　　Confession, The. In *Tragedies*, London: John Murray, 1814, pp. [225]-290. *Filed under* Collected Works.
　　Death of Darnley, The. In *Tragedies*, London: John Murray, 1814, pp. [i-iv], [1]-76. *Filed under* Collected Works.
　　Ellen; or, The Confession. London: John Murray, 1816. Pp. [i-vi], [1]-64.
　　Ivan. In *Tragedies*, London: John Murray, 1814, pp. [77]-157. *Filed under* Collected Works.
　　Ivan. London: John Murray, 1816. Pp. [i]-[x], [11]-86.
　　Julian and Agnes; or, The Monks of the Great St. Bernard. London: J. Wright, 1801. Pp. [i]-[iv], [5]-53.
　　Orestes. In *Tragedies*, London: John Murray, 1814, pp. [291]-361. *Filed under* Collected Works.
　　Siege of Cuzco, The. London: J. Wright, 1800. Pp. [i]-[viii], [1]-112.
　　Zamorin and Zama. In *Tragedies*, London: John Murray, 1814, pp. [159]-223. *Filed under* Collected Works.

SOUL OF HONOR!, THE
　　See Farnie, Henry Brougham.

SOUL'S TRAGEDY, A
　　See Browning, Robert.

SOUMAROKOVE, ALEXANDER
　　Demetrius the Impostor.
　　　　See under title.

SOUR GRAPES
　　See Byron, Henry James.

SOUTAR, RICHARD
　　Harlequin and the White Cat! and the Magic Sapphire; or, The Two Pretty Princes and the Three Fairy Gifts. London: G. Stevens (printer), n.d. Pp. [1]-22. Libretto.

SOUTAR, ROBERT
　　Fast Coach, The.
　　　　See Claridge, C. J.
　　Sold Again. London & New York: Samuel French, n.d. Pp. [1]-15. [Lacy's Acting Edition].

SOUTHERN, THOMAS
　　Fatal Marriage.
　　　　See Garrick, David (arr.). Isabella; or, The Fatal Marriage.
　　Oroonoko. London: Whittingham & Arliss, 1815. Pp. [1]-[68]. London Theatre, XV. *Filed under* Dibdin, Thomas John, ed. London Theatre, XV.
　　Oroonoko. In *British Drama*, 12 vols., London: John Dicks, 1871, IX, [161]-182.
　　Oroonoko. London: John Cumberland, n.d. Pp. [1]-55. Cumberland's British Theatre, XXV. *Filed under* Cumberland, John. Cumberland's British Theatre, XXV.

SOUTHERNER—JUST ARRIVED, A
　　See Wigan, Horace.

SOUTHEY, ROBERT
　　Wat Tyler. London: W. Hone, 1817. Pp. [i]-[xxiv], [1]-70. New ed.

SOWING THE WIND
　　See Grundy, Sydney.

SPANIARD, THE
　　See Gray, Simon.

SPANIARD'S RANSOM
　　See Hoskins, Horatio Huntley. Count de Denia.

SPANIARDS, THE; OR, THE EXPULSION OF THE MOORS (anon.)
　　In *New British Theatre*, London: A. J. Valpy (printer), 1814, III, [i], [201]-255.

SPANIARDS IN DENMARK, THE
　　See Mérimée, Prosper.

SPANIARDS IN PERU
    See Kean, Charles John (arr.). Pizarro.
SPANISH CURATE, THE
    See Planché, James Robinson (arr.).
SPANISH DANCERS, THE
    See Selby, Charles.
SPANISH DOLLARS!
    See Cherry, Andrew.
SPANISH GYPSY, THE
    See Eliot, George.
SPANISH HEROINE, THE
    See Maclaren, Archibald.
SPANISH PATRIOTS, A THOUSAND YEARS AGO
    See Code, H. B.
SPANISH STUDENT
    See Anderson, J. F. Reynolds. Victorian.
SPANKING LEGACY, A
    See Blake, Thomas G.
SPARE BED, THE
    See Cooper, Frederick Fox.
SPARE THE ROD AND SPOIL THE CHILD
    See Travers, William.
SPARTACUS
    See Jones, Jacob.
SPEAK OUT BOLDLY
    See Suter, William E.
SPECIAL PERFORMANCES
    See Harrison, Wilmot.
SPECTRAL SHIP
    See Fitzball, Edward. Flying Dutchman, The.
SPECTRE
    See Burney, Frances. Aristodemus.
SPECTRE BRIDE!
    See Milner, Henry M. Alonzo the Brave and the Fair
    Imogine.
SPECTRE BRIDEGROOM, THE
    See Moncrieff, William Thomas.
SPECTRE GAMBLER
    See Fitzball, Edward. Greek Slave, The.
SPECTRE KNIGHT, THE
    See Albery, James.
    See Dibdin, Charles Isaac Mungo, jr.
SPECTRE OF THE NILE
    See Fitzball, Edward. Earthquake, The.
SPECTRE OF THE NORTH-EAST GALLERY
    See Dibdin, Thomas John. Bonifacio and Bridgetina.
SPECTRE ON HORSEBACK
    See Dibdin, Thomas John. Don Giovanni.
SPECULATION
    See Reynolds, Frederick.
SPEDDING, B. J.
    Ino; or, The Theban Twins. N.p.: n.pub., n.d. Pp. [1]-[47].
SPEED THE PLOUGH
    See Morton, Thomas, sr.
SPELL OF THE CLOUD KING
    See Fitzball, Edward. Bronze Horse, The.
SPENCER, GEORGE
    Return Ticket, A. Written with James, Walter. Also: A
    Return Ticket to the International Exhibition. London:
    Thomas Hailes Lacy, n.d. Pp. [1]-18. [Lacy's Acting
    Edition].
    Return Ticket to the International Exhibition, A.
    See Return Ticket, A.
SPENCER, WILLIAM ROBERT
    Urania; or, The Illuminé. London: J. Ridgway, 1802. Pp.
    [i]-[x], [1]-38.
SPENDTHRIFT, THE
    See Albery, James.
SPENDTHRIFT MISER, THE
    See Zimmern, Helen (trans.?).
SPHINX, THE
    See Brough, William.
SPICE OF THE DEVIL, A
    See Seton, Hugh.

SPICER, HENRY
    Cousin Cherry. London: S. G. Fairbrother, n.d. Pp. [1]-24.
    His Novice. London & New York: Samuel French, n.d. Pp.
    [1]-16. [Lacy's Acting Edition].
    Honesty. In Acted Dramas, London: Chapman & Hall, 1875,
    pp. [i-vi], [1]-78.
    Jeffreys; or, The Wife's Vengeance. London: G. W. Nickis-
    son, 1846. Pp. [i]-[x], [1]-96.
    Jeffreys; or, The Wife's Vengeance. In Acted Dramas,
    London: Chapman & Hall, 1875, pp. [165]-252.
    Lords of Ellingham, The. London: Thomas Bosworth, 1848.
    Pp. [i]-[vi], [1]-56.
    Lords of Ellingham, The. In Acted Dramas, London:
    Chapman & Hall, 1875, pp. [79]-164.
    Otho's Death-Wager. London: Henry S. King, 1876. Pp.
    [iii]-[xiv], [1]-115.
    Witch-Wife, The: A Tale of Malkin Tower. London: Thomas
    Bosworth, 1849. Pp. [i]-[viii], [1]-47.
    Witch-Wife, The: A Tale of Malkin Tower. In Acted Dramas,
    London: Chapman & Hall, 1875, pp. [253]-339.
SPICER, HENRY (trans.)
    Alcestis. By Euripides. London: Thomas Bosworth, 1855.
    Pp. [i]-iv, [1]-23.
SPIDER KING
    See Smith, Albert Richard. Tarantula, La.
SPIRIT OF AVARICE
    See Peake, Richard Brinsley. Devil of Marseilles, The.
SPIRIT OF SEVENTY-SIX
    See Coming Woman, The.
SPIRIT OF THE FOUNTAIN, THE
    See Coyne, Joseph Stirling.
SPIRIT OF THE RHINE, THE
    See Barnett, Morris.
SPIRIT OF THE STAR
    See Moncrieff, William Thomas. Zoroaster.
SPIRIT OF THE WATERS
    See Soane, George. Undine.
SPIRIT OF VENGEANCE, THE
    See Faucquez, Adolphe.
SPITALFIELDS WEAVER, THE
    See Bayly, Thomas Haynes.
SPITE AND MALICE
    See Maclaren, Archibald.
SPITFIRE, THE
    See Morton, John Maddison.
SPLENDID INVESTMENT, A
    See Bernard, William Bayle.
SPOILED CHILD, THE
    See Bickerstaffe, Isaac.
    See Hoare, Prince.
SPOILING THE BROTH
    See Farnie, Henry Brougham. Rose of Auvergne, The.
SPREES ALONG SHORE!
    See Rogers, William. Tom Tiller and Jack Mizen.
SPRIGGE, J. SQUIRE
    Unrehearsed Effect, An. In Dialogues of the Day, ed. Oswald
    Crawfurd, London: Chapman & Hall, n.d., pp. [92]-101.
    Filed under Crawfurd, Oswald. Dialogues of the Day.
SPRIGS OF LAUREL
    See O'Keeffe, John.
SPRING AND AUTUMN
    See Kenney, James.
SPRING GARDENS
    See Planché, James Robinson.
SPRING LOCK, THE
    See Peake, Richard Brinsley.
SPRY, HENRY
    Aladdin, the Lad with the Wonderful Lamp.
        See Conquest, George.
    Jack and Jill and the Well on the Hill.
        See Conquest, George.
    Sinbad the Sailor, a Son of the Sea.
        See Conquest, George.
SPUR OF THE MOMENT, THE
    See Byron, Henry James.

SPURR, MEL. B.

    For Papa's Sake. New York & London: Samuel French, c.1899. Pp. [1]-18. [Lacy's Acting Edition].

SPY, THE

    See Besant, Walter.

SQUEEZE TO THE CORONATION, A

    See Thomson, James.

SQUIRE, WILLIAM BARCLAY

    Veiled Prophet, The. *Also:* Il Profeta Velato. Music by Stanford, C. Villiers. London: Boosey, n.d. Pp. [i-iv], 1-219. Vocal score.

SQUIRE, THE

    See Pinero, Arthur Wing.

SQUIRE OF DAMES, THE

    See Carton, R. C.

SQUIRE'S DAUGHTER, THE

    See Park, Andrew.

SQUIRE'S LAST SHILLING

    See Byron, Henry James. English Gentleman, An.

SQUIREEN, THE INFORMER, AND THE ILLICIT DIS-TILLER

    See Byron, Henry James. Green Grow the Rushes, Oh!

ST. AUBERT

    See Weston, Ferdinand Fullerton.

ST. BO', THEODORE

    Wilfrid and Mary; or, Father and Daughter. Edinburgh: Myles Macphail, 1861. Pp. [1-4], [i]-[viii], 1-72. American Ed.

ST. CLAIR OF THE ISLES

    See Polack, Elizabeth.

ST. CLARA'S EVE

    See Dimond, William. Conquest of Taranto, The.

ST. CLEMENT'S EVE

    See Taylor, Henry.

ST. CUPID

    See Jerrold, Douglas William.

ST. DAVID'S DAY

    See Dibdin, Thomas John.

ST. GEORGE, ELIZABETH (Eliza)

    See Planché, Elizabeth (Eliza) St. George, Mrs. James Robinson.

ST. GEORGE, GEORGE

    Don't Book Your Make Ups. In *Sires and Sons from Albion Sprung . . . ,* London: E. Matthews & Sons (priv.), 1876, pp. [73]-109.

    Man of Thought and the Man of Action, The. In *Sires and Sons from Albion Sprung . . . ,* London: E. Matthews & Sons (priv.), 1876, pp. [1]-72.

    Sires and Sons from Albion Sprung, The. In *Sires and Sons from Albion Sprung . . . ,* London: E. Matthews & Sons (priv.), 1876, pp. [111]-131.

ST. GEORGE AND THE DRAGON (anon.)

    Manchester: Theatre Royal Press, 1856. Pp. [1]-12. 8th ed. Libretto.

ST. GEORGE AND THE DRAGON

    See A'Beckett, Gilbert Abbott.

ST. GEORGES, VERNOY DE.

    See Vernoy de Saint-Georges, Jules Henri.

ST. JAMES'S AND ST. GILES'S

    See Stirling, Edward. Rubber of Life, The.

ST. JOHN, DORSET

    See Stephens, George.

ST. JOHN, JOHN

    Mary Queen of Scots. In *Modern Theatre,* ed. Mrs. Inchbald, 10 vols., London: Longman, Hurst, Rees, Orme, & Brown, 1811, VIII, [67]-131.

ST. JOHN IN PATMOS

    See Bowles, William Lisle.

ST. MARY'S EVE

    See Bernard, William Bayle.

ST. PATRICK'S DAY

    See Sheridan, Richard Brinsley.

ST. PATRICK'S EVE

    See Power, Tyrone.

    See Travers, William. Kathleen Mavourneen.

ST. PIERRE, THE REFUGEE

    See Hall, Anna Maria, Mrs. Samuel Carter.

ST. THOMAS OF CANTERBURY

    See de Vere, Aubrey Thomas.

ST. TIBB'S EVE!

    See Selby, Charles. Powder and Ball.

ST. VALENTINE'S EVE

    See Milner, Henry M. Fair Maid of Perth, The.

STAFF OF DIAMONDS, THE

    See Hazlewood, Colin Henry.

STAFFORD, JOHN JOSEPH

    Frenchman in London, The; or, Where's My Daughter? London: W. Kidd, n.d. Pp. [1]-43.

    Love's Frailties; or, Passion and Repentance. London: W. Kidd, n.d. Pp. [1]-40. Promptbook.

    My Uncle Toby. London: W. Kidd, n.d. Pp. [1]-58.

    Pretender, The; or, The Rose of Alvey. London: W. Kidd, n.d. Pp. [1]-51.

STAGE STRUCK

    See Dimond, William.

STAINER, A. N.

    Cherchez l'Homme. In *Dialogues of the Day,* ed. Oswald Crawfurd, London: Chapman & Hall, n.d., pp. [204]-211. *Filed under* Crawfurd, Oswald. Dialogues of the Day.

STAINFORTH, FRANK

    Sea-Gulls.

    See Maltby, C. Alfred.

STANDISH, JULIAN

    His Wife's Little Bill.

    See Henning, Albert.

STANGE, STANISLAUS

    Brian Boru. Music by Edwards, Julian. New York: William Maxwell Music Co., c.1896. Pp. [1]-253. Vocal score.

    Jolly Musketeer, The. Music by Edwards, Julian. New York: M. Witmark & Sons, c.1899. Pp. [i-iv], [1]-228. Vocal score.

    Man about Town, A. New York: M. Witmark & Sons, c.1906. Pp. [1]-18. Charles Dickson's Famous One Act Plays.

    Wedding Day, The. Music by Edwards, Julian. Cincinnati: John Church, c.1897. Pp. [1]-248. Vocal score.

STAR OF SEVILLE, THE

    See Kemble, Frances Anne (Fanny).

STAR OF THE DESERT

    See Muskerry, William. Khartoum!

STAR OF THE NORTH, THE

    See Robertson, Thomas William.

STAR-SPANGLED BANNER, THE

    See Fraser, Julia Agnes.

STARKEY, DIGBY PILOT

    Judas. Dublin: William Curry, jr, 1843. Pp. [i]-[xxxvi], [1]-230.

STATE PRISONER, THE

    See Gordon, Walter.

STATE SECRET, A

    See Hayes, Frederick William.

STATE SECRETS

    See Snodgrass, Alfred.

    See Wilks, Thomas Egerton.

STATION HOUSE!, THE

    See Dance, Charles.

STATUE

    See Sheil, Richard Lalor. Evadne.

STATUE BRIDE

    See Selby, Charles. Elves, The.

STATUE FAIR

    See Brough, William. Pygmalion.

STATUE LOVER, THE

    See Jerrold, Douglas William.

STATUTORY DUEL

    See Gilbert, William Schwenck. Grand Duke, The.

STEELE, ANNA CAROLINE WOOD, MRS.

    Red Republican, A. Witham: W. R. King (printer), 1874. Pp. [1]-67.

STEELE, RICHARD

Conscious Lovers, The. London: Whittingham & Arliss, 1816. Pp. [1]-[72]. London Theatre, XX. *Filed under* Dibdin, Thomas John, ed. London Theatre, XX.

Tender Husband, The; or, The Accomplished Fools. London: Sherwood, Neely, & Jones, 1818. Pp. [1]-[62]. London Theatre, XXVI. *Filed under* Dibdin, Thomas John, ed. London Theatre, XXVI.

Tender Husband, The; or, The Accomplished Fools. In *British Drama*, 12 vols., London: John Dicks, 1872, X, [289]-306.

STEEPLE-CHASE, THE
See Morton, John Maddison.

STEEPLE-JACK
See Pemberton, Thomas Edgar.

STELLA (anon.)
In [*Parodies and Other Burlesque Pieces*, ed. Henry Morley, London: George Routledge & Sons, 1890], pp. [407]-446.

STELLA
See Thompson, Benjamin (trans.).

STELLA DEL NORD, LA
See Maggioni, Manfredo (trans.).

STEP BY STEP
See Simpson, John Palgrave. Sybilla.

STEPHANIA
See Field, Michael.

STEP-MOTHER, THE
See Howard, George William Frederick, Earl of Carlisle.

STEP-SISTER, THE
See Sapte, William, jr.

STEPHENS, GEORGE

Forgery. In *Dramas for the Stage*, 2 vols., London: Stewart & Murray (printer) (priv.), 1846, I, [113]-232. *Filed under* Dramas for the Stage.

Gertrude and Beatrice; or, The Queen of Hungary. London: C. Mitchell, 1839. Pp. [i]-[viii], [1]-104.

Martinuzzi. London: C. Mitchell, 1841. Pp. [i]-[x], [1]-67. 2nd ed.

Nero. In *Dramas for the Stage*, 2 vols., London: Stewart & Murray (printer) (priv.), 1846, I, [i]-[xii], 1-111. *Filed under* Dramas for the Stage.

Patriot, The. London: C. Mitchell, 1849. Pp. [1-2], [i]-xvi, [1]-78.

Philip Basil; or, A Poet's Fate. In *Dramas for the Stage*, 2 vols., London: Stewart & Murray (printer) (priv.), 1846, II, [261]-[408]. *Filed under* Dramas for the Stage.

Rebecca and Her Daughters. In *Dramas for the Stage*, 2 vols., London: Stewart & Murray (printer) (priv.), 1846, II, [135]-259. *Filed under* Dramas for the Stage.

Revenge; or, Woman's Love. Copenhagen: C. G. Iversen; London: John Russell Smith, 1857. Pp. [1]-99.

Self-Glorification. In *Dramas for the Stage*, 2 vols., London: Stewart & Murray (printer) (priv.), 1846, II, [i-iv], [1]-133. *Filed under* Dramas for the Stage.

Sensibility. In *Dramas for the Stage*, 2 vols., London: Stewart & Murray (printer) (priv.), 1846, I, [233]-323. *Filed under* Dramas for the Stage.

Vampire, The. Written with Belfour, Hugo John. By Dorset St. John (pseud.). London: C. & J. Ollier, 1821. Pp. [i-viii], [1]-108. 2nd ed.

STEPHENS, HENRY POTTINGER

Billee Taylor; or, The Reward of Virtue. Music by Solomon, Edward. New York: William A. Pond, n.d. Pp. [1]-22. Libretto. *Filed under* Stephens, Henry Pottinger; Solomon, Edward.

Billee Taylor; or, The Reward of Virtue. Music by Solomon, Edward. New York: S. T. Gordon & Son, n.d. Pp. [1]-133. Vocal score.

Claude Duval; or, Love and Larceny. Music by Solomon, Edward. Philadelphia: J. M. Stoddart, c.1882. Pp. [1]-40. Libretto.

Lord Bateman; or, Picotee's Pledge. Music by Solomon, Edward. Philadelphia: J. M. Stoddart, c.1882. Pp. [1]-139. Vocal score.

Virginia; or, Ringing the Changes. *Also:* Virginia and Paul. Music by Solomon, Edward. New York: William A. Pond, c.1883. Pp. [1-4], i-iv, [5]-170. Vocal score.

Virginia and Paul.
See Virginia.

STEPHENS, JAMES BRUNTON
Fayette; or, Bush Revels. Music by Allen, G. B. Brisbane: Watson, Ferguson, 1892. Pp. [1]-47. Libretto.

STEPHENS, YORKE
Through the Fire.
See Lestocq, William.

STEPHENSON, BENJAMIN CHARLES

Charity Begins at Home. Music by Cellier, Alfred. N.p.: n.pub., n.d. Pp. [1]-14. Libretto.

Diplomacy.
See Scott, Clement William.

Doris. Written with Scott, Clement William. By B. C. Stephenson. Music by Cellier, Alfred. London: Chappell, n.d. Pp. [i-iv], [1]-179. Vocal score.

Dorothy. Music by Cellier, Alfred. London: Chappell, n.d. Pp. [1]-35. Libretto.

Faithful James. New York & London: Samuel French, c.1902. Pp. [1]-22.

Passport, The. Written with Yardley, William. London & New York: Samuel French, c.1906. Pp. [1]-108.

Silver Trout, The.
See Roberts, Randal Howland.

Zoo, The. By Bolton Rowe (pseud.). Music by Sullivan, Arthur. London: (priv.), 1969. Pp. [1], [i]-[v], 1-108. Vocal score.

STEPHENSON, CHARLES H.
Tromb-al-ca-zar; or, The Adventures of an Operatic Troupe. Music by Offenbach. London: Thomas Hailes Lacy, n.d. Pp. [1]-20. [Lacy's Acting Edition]. Libretto.

STEPHENSON, CHARLES H. (arr.)
Belle's Stratagem, The. By Cowley, Hannah Parkhouse, Mrs. London: Thomas Hailes Lacy, n.d. Pp. [1]-65. Promptbook.

STERLING, EDWARD
See Stirling, Edward.

STERLING, JOHN
Strafford. London: Edward Moxon, 1843. Pp. [i-viii], [1]-224.

STERN RESOLVE, THE
See Masterton, Charles.

STEVEN, ALEXANDER
Romance of Love, A. Berwick-on-Tweed: Offices of The Berwick Journal, 1891. Pp. [i-ii], [1]-14.

STEVENS, CATHERINE
See Crowe, Catherine Stevens, Mrs. John.

STEVENSON, ROBERT LOUIS
Admiral Guinea.
See Henley, William Ernest.
Beau Austin.
See Henley, William Ernest.
Deacon Brodie.
See Henley, William Ernest.
Macaire.
See Henley, William Ernest.

STEWARD, THE
See Beazley, Samuel, jr.

STEWART, THOMAS GRAINGER, SIR
Good Regent, The. Edinburgh & London: William Blackwood & Sons, 1898. Pp. [i]-[xiv], 1-207.

STICK, THE POLE, AND THE TARTAR
See Byron, Henry James. Mazourka.

STILL WATERS RUN DEEP
See Taylor, Tom.

STIRLING, EDWARD
Above and Below! London: John Duncombe, n.d. Pp. [1]-47. Duncombe's Acting Edition of the British Theatre, 450.

Aline, the Rose of Killarney! London: Thomas Hailes Lacy, n.d. Pp. [1]-42. Promptbook.

Anchor of Hope, The; or, The Seaman's Star! London & New York: Samuel French, n.d. Pp. [1]-31. [French's Acting Edition].

Bachelor's Buttons! London & New York: Samuel French, n.d. Pp. [3]-18.

Battle of Life, The. London: John Duncombe, n.d. Pp. [3]-35. Duncombe's Edition.

Bed-room Window!, The. London: Duncombe & Moon, n.d. Pp. [1]-22. Duncombe's Edition.

Blue-Jackets, The; or, Her Majesty's Service! London: John Duncombe, n.d. Pp. [1]-23. Duncombe's Edition. Promptbook.

Bohemians, The; or, The Rogues of Paris. London: John Dicks, n.d. Pp. [193]-213. Dicks' British Drama, 98.

Bould Soger Boy, The. London: John Duncombe, n.d. Pp. [1]-19. Duncombe's Acting Edition of the British Theatre, 533.

Buffalo Girls, The; or, The Female Serenaders! London: Duncombe & Moon, n.d. Pp. [1]-15. [Duncombe's Edition].

By Royal Command. In *British Drama*, 12 vols., London: John Dicks, 1872, XI, [193]-204.

By Royal Command. London & New York: Samuel French, n.d. Pp. [1]-28. [Lacy's Acting Edition].

Cabin Boy, The. London: Nassau Steam Press, n.d. Pp. [1]-28.

Captain Charlotte. London: Thomas Hailes Lacy, n.d. Pp. [1]-28. [Lacy's Acting Edition].

Carline, the Female Brigand. London: John Duncombe, n.d. Pp. [1]-30. Duncombe's Edition.

Cheap Excursion, A. London: Thomas Hailes Lacy, n.d. Pp. [1]-14. [Lacy's Acting Edition].

Clarence Clevedon, His Struggle for Life or Death! London: John Duncombe, n.d. Pp. [1]-50. Duncombe's Edition. Promptbook.

Clarisse; or, The Merchant's Daughter. London: National Acting Drama Office, n.d. Pp. [1]-48. Promptbook.

Courier of Lyons, The. London: S. G. Fairbrother, 1854. Pp. [1]-36.

Courier of Lyons, The. In *British Drama*, 12 vols., London: John Dicks, 1865, IV, [1]-16.

Cricket on the Hearth, The. London: National Acting Drama Office, n.d. Pp. [1]-36.

Dandolo; or, The Last of the Doges. London: W. Strange, 1838. Pp. [1]-26.

Dark Glen of Ballyfoill, The. London: John Dicks, 1871. Pp. [i-ii], [1]-18. Dicks' British Drama, 82.

Devil's Daughters, The; or, H--l upon Earth! London: John Duncombe, n.d. <wrps. Thomas Hailes Lacy>. Pp. [1]-37. Duncombe's Edition <wrps. New British Theatre (late Duncombe's), 313>.

Don Juan.
See Milner, Henry M.

Dragon Knight, The; or, The Queen of Beauty! London: John Duncombe, n.d. <wrps. Thomas Hailes Lacy>. Pp. [1]-30. Duncombe's Edition <wrps. New British Theatre (late Duncombe's), 311>.

Family Pictures. London: S. G. Fairbrother, n.d. Pp. [1]-22.

Father Baptiste. London: John Dicks, 1871. Pp. [65]-79. Dicks' British Drama, 74.

Figure of Fun, A; or, The Bloomer Costume. London: S. G. Fairbrother, 1852. Pp. [1]-16.

Fortunes of Smike, The; or, A Sequel to Nicholas Nickleby. London: Sherwood, Gilbert, & Piper, n.d. Pp. [i]-[viii], [9]-41.

Gold Mine, The; or, The Miller of Grenoble. London: John Dicks, n.d. Pp. [975]-990.

Grace Darling; or, The Wreck at Sea. London: Chapman & Hall, n.d. Pp. [1]-32. Promptbook.

Grotto on the Stream, The. London: John Dicks, n.d. Pp. [1]-14. Dicks' British Drama, 112.

Guido Fawkes; or, The Prophetess of Ordsall Cave! London: John Duncombe, n.d. <wrps. Thomas Hailes Lacy>. Pp. [1]-40. Duncombe's Edition <wrps. New British Theatre (late Duncombe's)>.

Hand of Cards, The: Game, Life—Stakes, Death! London: Thomas Hailes Lacy, n.d. Pp. [1]-43. Cumberland's British Theatre.

Idiot of the Mill, The. London & New York: Samuel French, n.d. Pp. [3]-38.

Industry and Indolence; or, The Orphan's Legacy! London: Duncombe & Moon, n.d. Pp. [1]-46. Duncombe's Acting Edition of the British Theatre, 476.

Jane Lomax; or, A Mother's Crime. London: Chapman & Hall, n.d. Pp. [i]-iv, [5]-34.

Jeannette and Jeannot; or, The Village Pride. London & New York: Samuel French, n.d. Pp. [1]-30. [Lacy's Acting Edition].

Jew's Daughter, The. London: Thomas Hailes Lacy, n.d. Pp. [1]-18. [Lacy's Acting Edition].

John Felton. London: John Dicks, n.d. Pp. [1183]-1203. Dicks' British Drama, 38.

Judge Not; or, The Seals of Justice. London: John Dicks, n.d. Pp. [193]-205. Dicks' British Drama, 78.

Kissing Goes by Favour. London: John Duncombe, n.d. Pp. [1]-17. Duncombe's Edition.

Last Kiss!, The; or, The Soldier's Grave! London: John Duncombe, n.d. <wrps. Thomas Hailes Lacy>. Pp. [1]-38. Duncombe's Edition <wrps. New British Theatre (late Duncombe's), 444>.

Left in a Cab. London: Thomas Hailes Lacy, n.d. Pp. [1]-12. [Lacy's Acting Edition].

Legacy of Honour. London: Thomas Hailes Lacy, n.d. Pp. [1]-28. [Lacy's Acting Edition].

Lestelle; or, The Wrecker's Bride. London: Thomas Hailes Lacy, n.d. Pp. [1]-[36]. Cumberland's British Theatre, 427.

Lilly Dawson; or, A Poor Girl's Story! London & New York: Samuel French, n.d. Pp. [3]-42. [Lacy's Acting Edition].

Lily of the Desert, The. [London: John Dicks], n.d. Pp. [927]-942. Dicks' British Drama, 22.

Little Back Parlour, The. London: John Duncombe, n.d. Pp. [1]-18. Duncombe's Edition.

Lost Diamonds!, The. London: Thomas Hailes Lacy, n.d. Pp. [3]-27.

Love Gift, The; or, The Trials of Poverty. London: William Barth, n.d. Pp. [1]-31. Barth's (late Pattie's) Universal Stage or Theatrical Prompt Book, 43.

Lucky Hit, A. London: Thomas Hailes Lacy, n.d. Pp. [1]-19. [Lacy's Acting Edition].

Margaret Catchpole, the Heroine of Suffolk; or, The Vicissitudes of Real Life. London: Thomas Hailes Lacy, n.d. Pp. [1]-50. [Lacy's Acting Edition].

Merchant Pirate, The. London: John Dicks, n.d. Pp. [225]-241. Dicks' British Drama, 89.

Miser's Daughter, The. London: John Duncombe, n.d. <wrps. Thomas Hailes Lacy>. Pp. [1]-47. New British Theatre (late Duncombe's), 361.

Miser's Daughter, The. London & New York: Samuel French, n.d. Pp. [1]-47. [Lacy's Acting Edition].

Mother's Bequest, The. London: Duncombe & Moon, n.d. Pp. [1]-21. Manuscript promptbook.

Mrs. Caudle's Curtain Lecture! London: John Duncombe, n.d. Pp. [1]-11. Duncombe's Acting Edition of the British Theatre, 422.

Nicholas Nickleby. London: Chapman & Hall, n.d. Pp. [1]-36.

Nora Creina. London: Thomas Hailes Lacy, n.d. Pp. [3]-[18]. [New British Theatre, 439]. Promptbook.

Old Curiosity Shop, The. London & New York: Samuel French, n.d. Pp. [1]-39.

Old Martin's Trials. London: John Dicks, n.d. Pp. [65]-83. Dicks' British Drama, 94.

On the Tiles. London: John Duncombe, n.d. Pp. [1]-15. Duncombe's Acting Edition of the British Theatre, 443.

Ondine; or, The Water Spirit and the Fire Fiend. London: John Duncombe, n.d. Pp. [1]-26. Duncombe's Acting Edition of the British Theatre. Promptbook.

Orphan of the Frozen Sea, The. [London: John Dicks], n.d. Pp. [1008]-1022.

Out of Luck; or, His Grace the Duke. London: James Pattie, n.d. Pp. [1]-23. Pattie's Universal Stage or Theatrical Prompt Book, 7.

Pair of Pigeons, A. New York: Dick & Fitzgerald, n.d. Pp. [1]-11. Dick's American Edition.

Pet of the Public, A. London: Thomas Hailes Lacy, n.d. Pp. [1]-13. Lacy's Acting Edition, 180.

Pickwick Club, The; or, The Age We Live In! Philadelphia: Frederick Turner; New York: Turner & Fisher, n.d. Pp. [1]-60. Turner's Dramatic Library, 32.

Plain Cook, A. London: John Duncombe, n.d. <wrps. Thomas Hailes Lacy>. Pp. [1]-16. New British Theatre (late Duncombe's), 540. Promptbook.

Popping In and Out. London: John Duncombe, n.d. Pp. [1]-17. New British Theatre (late Duncombe's), 432.

Prisoner of State. In *British Drama*, 12 vols., London: John Dicks, 1865, IV, [1042]-1054.

Prisoner of State. *Also:* Ulrica; or, The Prisoner of State. [London: John Dicks], n.d. Pp. [1042]-1054. *Filed under* Ulrica.

Queen of Cyprus, The; or, The Bride of Venice. London: John Duncombe, n.d. <wrps. Thomas Hailes Lacy>. Pp. [1]-38. New British Theatre (late Duncombe's), 349.

Rag-Picker of Paris and the Dress-Maker of St. Antoine, The. New York: Samuel French, n.d. Pp. [1]-35. French's American Drama, 108.

Ragged School. The. London: John Duncombe, n.d. Pp. [i-ii], [1]-18. Duncombe's Edition.

Reapers, The; or, Forget and Forgive! London: Thomas Hailes Lacy, n.d. Pp. [1]-28. [Lacy's Acting Edition].

Rifle Volunteers, The. London: Thomas Hailes Lacy, n.d. Pp. [1]-12. Lacy's Acting Edition, 599.

Rose of Corbeil, The; or, The Forest of Senart! London: John Duncombe, n.d. Pp. [1]-24. Duncombe's Edition.

Rubber of Life, The; or, St. James's and St. Giles's. London: John Duncombe, n.d. Pp. [1]-46. Duncombe's Edition.

Sea King's Vow, The; or, A Struggle for Liberty! London: Thomas Hailes Lacy, n.d. Pp. [1]-39. New British Theatre (late Duncombe's), 441.

Sealed Sentence!, The. London: Thomas Hailes Lacy, n.d. Pp. [3]-28. New British Theatre (late Duncombe's), 407. Promptbook.

Secret Foe, The. London: John Duncombe, n.d. Pp. [5]-38. Title page lacking. Promptbook.

Serpent of the Nile, The; or, The Battle of Actium! London: John Duncombe, n.d. Pp. [1]-38.

Seven Castles of the Passions, The. London: Barth (printer), n.d. Pp. [i-iv], [1]-32. Promptbook.

Struggle for Gold, A; or, The Orphan of the Frozen Sea. London: S. G. Fairbrother, 1854. Pp. [1]-42.

Teacher Taught, The. London: John Duncombe, n.d. Pp. [1]-19. [Duncombe's Edition].

Teddy Roe. New York: Samuel French, n.d. Pp. [1]-15. French's Minor Drama, 194.

Thieves of Paris, The. London: John Dicks, n.d. Pp. [895]-909. Dicks' British Drama, 29.

Three Black Seals, The. London: John Dicks, n.d. Pp. [863]-878. Dicks' British Drama, 28.

Trapping a Tartar. London: Thomas Hailes Lacy, n.d. Pp. [1]-12. [Lacy's Acting Edition].

Ulrica.
See Prisoner of State.

Wanted a Wife; or, London, Liverpool, and Bristol. London: William Barth, n.d. Pp. [2]-24.

White Slave, The; or, The Flag of Freedom. London: Thomas Hailes Lacy, n.d. Pp. [1]-[39]. Cumberland's British Theatre.

Who Is She? In *British Drama*, 12 vols., London: John Dicks, 1872, XI, [65]-76.

Who Is She? n.p.: n.pub., n.d. Pp. [1-25].

Wild Ducks. London: S. G. Fairbrother, n.d. <wrps. Thomas Hailes Lacy>. Pp. [1]-18. Lacy's Acting Edition, 311.

Woman's the Devil! London: John Duncombe, n.d. Pp. [1]-18. Duncombe's Acting Edition of the British Theatre, 216.

Woodman's Spell, The. London: Thomas Hailes Lacy, n.d. Pp. [1]-15. [Lacy's Acting Edition].

Yankee Notes for English Circulation. London: John Duncombe, n.d. <wrps. Thomas Hailes Lacy>. Pp. [1]-20. Duncombe's Edition <wrps. New British Theatre (late Duncombe's), 367>.

Young Scamp, The; or, My Grandmother's Pet! London: Thomas Hailes Lacy, n.d. Pp. [1]-21. Page numbers cut off. New British Theatre (late Duncombe's).

STIRRING THE PUDDING
See Planché, James Robinson.

STOCK EXCHANGE, THE
See Dance, Charles.

STOCKTON, J. D.
Fox versus Goose. Written with Brough, William. N.p.: n.pub., n.d. Pp. [1]-[47]. Title page lacking.

STOCQUELER, JOACHIM HAYWARD
Object of Interest, An. New York: Clinton T. DeWitt, n.d. Pp. [1]-18. DeWitt's Acting Plays, 240. *Filed under* Siddons, Joachim Heyward.

Object of Interest, An. London: Thomas Hailes Lacy, n.d. Pp. [1]-23. Lacy's Acting Edition, 238. *Filed under* Siddons, Joachim Heyward.

Polkamania. London: W. Barth, n.d. Pp. [1]-16. Barth's Universal Stage or Theatrical Prompt Book, 10. *Filed under* Siddons, Joachim Heyward.

STOLEN JEWESS, THE
See Hazlewood, Colin Henry.

STOLEN KISS, THE
See Aird, David Mitchell.

STOLEN KISSES
See Meritt, Paul.

STOLEN—£20 REWARD!
See Hancock, William.

STONE JUG, THE (anon.)
[London: John Dicks], n.d. Pp. [1]-21.

STOP HIM WHO CAN
See Reynolds, Frederick. Dramatist, The.

STORM, THE
See Burges, James Bland.
See Knowles, James Sheridan.

STORM AT SEA
See Fitzball, Edward. Pilot, The.

STORM IN A TEA CUP, A
See Bernard, William Bayle.

STORY, ROBERT
Outlaw, The. London: Simpkin, Marshall, 1839. Pp. [i]-[viii], [9]-176.

STORY OF A LYRE
See Burnand, Francis Cowley. Arion.

STORY OF CHIKKIN HAZARD
See Burnand, Francis Cowley. Fowl Play.

STORY OF FALSTAFF, THE
See Lemon, Mark.

STORY OF ORESTES, THE
See Warr, George Charles Winter.

STORY OF THE BOAT RACE
See Lemon, Harry. Go to Putney.

STORY OF THE HEART
See Bernard, William Bayle. Lucille.

STORY-TELLER AND THE SLAVE
See Hood, Basil Charles Willett. Rose of Persia, The.

STOWELL, THOMAS ALFRED (trans.)
Clavigo. By Goethe. London: David Nutt, 1897. Pp. [i-iv], [1]-[137].

STRACHAN, JOHN S., JR
Forty Thieves, The. Manchester: A. Ireland (printer), n.d. Pp. [1]-16.

Little Goody Two-Shoes and Her Queen Anne's Farthing; or, Harlequin Old King Counterfeit and the World of Coins! Birmingham: James Upton (printer), n.d. Pp. [1]-32.

Rip Van Winkle; or, Some Nambulistic Knickerbockers. Written with Davis, Henry. Newcastle-upon-Tyne: R. Ward (priv.), 1866. Pp. [1]-44.

STRAFFORD
See Leatham, William Henry.
See Sterling, John.

STRAIGHT, DOUGLAS
    See Daryl, Sidney.
STRANGE ADVENTURES OF MISS BROWN, THE
    See Buchanan, Robert Williams.
STRANGE GENTLEMAN, THE
    See Dickens, Charles.
STRANGE HISTORY, A
    See Lawrence, Slingsby.
STRANGE INTRUDER, THE
    See Archer, Thomas.
STRANGE RELATION, A
    See Montague, Leopold.
STRANGER, THE
    See Thompson, Benjamin (trans.).
STRANGER—STRANGER THAN EVER!, THE
    See Reece, Robert.
STRATAGEMS AND SPOILS
    See Rettie, T. Leith.
STRATFORD DE REDCLIFFE, VISCOUNT
    See Canning, Stratford.
STRATFORD-ON-AVON
    See Allingham, William.
STRATHMORE
    See Marston, John Westland.
STRAYCOCK, J.
    Loyal Peasants, The. London: J. Hartnell (printer) (priv.), 1804. Pp. [1]-[68].
STREATFIELD, T., REV.
    Bridal of Armagnac, The. London: Harding, Mavor, & Lepard, 1823. Pp. [iii]-xii, [1]-177.
STREETS OF NEW YORK.
    See Boucicault, Dionysius Lardner. Poor of New York, The.
STRIKE AT ARLINGFORD, THE
    See Moore, George.
STRING OF PEARLS
    See Hazelton, Frederick. Sweeney Todd, the Barber of Fleet Street.
STRIPLING, THE
    See Baillie, Joanna.
STROLLING AND STRATEGEM
    See Tilbury, William Harries. Counter Attraction.
STROLLING GENTLEMAN
    See O'Keeffe, John. Wild Oats.
STROLLING GENTLEMEN
    See O'Keeffe, John. Wild Oats.
STRUGGLE FOR GOLD
    See Robertson, Thomas William. Sea of Ice.
    See Stirling, Edward.
STRUGGLE FOR LIBERTY!
    See Stirling, Edward. Sea King's Vow, The.
STRUTT, JOSEPH
    Ancient Times. In *Queenhoo-Hall, a Romance; and Ancient Times, a Drama,* 4 vols., Edinburgh: Archibald Constable; London: John Murray, 1808, IV, [i], 99-195.
    Test of Guilt, The; or, Traits of Antient Superstition. London: Appleyards, 1808. Pp. [iii]-[x], [1]-119.
STUART, ARTHUR
    Nicolete.
        See Ferris, Edward.
    White Stocking, A.
        See Ferris, Edward.
STUART, EMMELINE CHARLOTTE ELIZABETH MANNERS
    See Wortley, Emmeline Charlotte Elizabeth Manners Stuart, Mrs. Charles (Lady).
STUDENT, THE
    See Bate, Frederick.
    See Featherstone, Thomas.
STUDENT OF BONN
    See Powell, Thomas. Blind Wife, The.
STUDENTS OF BONN, THE
    See Rodwell, George Herbert Bonaparte.
STUDENTS OF SALAMANCA, THE
    See Jameson, Robert Francis.

STURGESS, ARTHUR
    Babes in the Woods, The. Written with Collins, Arthur Pelham. London: J. Miles (printer), n.d. Pp. [1]-92. Libretto.
    Forty Thieves, The. Written with Collins, Arthur Pelham. London: Nassau Steam Press (printer), n.d. Pp. [3]-[95]. Libretto.
    Little Genius, The.
        See Harris, Augustus Henry Glossop.
    Poupée, La. Music by Audran, Edmond. London: Hopwood & Crew, n.d. Pp. [1]-24. Libretto.
    Rightful Heir, The. Written with Goodwin, John Cheever. Music by Warren, Richard Henry; Bruguière, Émile A., jr. New York: Winthrop Press (printer), 1899. Pp. [1]-41. Libretto.
    Topsy-Turvy Hotel, The. Music by Roger, Victor; Monckton, Lionel. London: Chapple, c.1898. Pp. [i-iv], [1]-179. Vocal score.
STURGIS, JULIAN RUSSELL
    Apples. In *Little Comedies,* New York: D. Appleton, 1880, pp. [1]-51. *Filed under* Little Comedies.
    Apples. In *Little Comedies Old and New,* Edinburgh & London: William Blackwood & Sons, 1882, pp. [i-iv], [1]-40.
    Bishop Astray, The. In *Little Comedies Old and New,* Edinburgh & London: William Blackwood & Sons, 1882, pp. [41]-66.
    Card for Lady Roedale, A. In *Little Comedies Old and New,* Edinburgh & London: William Blackwood & Sons, 1882, pp. [149]-176.
    Count Julian. Boston: Little, Brown, 1893. Pp. [1]-122.
    False Start, A. In *Little Comedies Old and New,* Edinburgh & London: William Blackwood & Sons, 1882, pp. [89]-115.
    Fire-flies. In *Little Comedies,* New York: D. Appleton, 1880, pp. [53]-79. *Filed under* Little Comedies.
    Fire-flies. In *Little Comedies Old and New,* Edinburgh & London: William Blackwood & Sons, 1882, pp. [67]-88.
    Florio. In *Little Comedies Old and New,* Edinburgh & London: William Blackwood & Sons, 1882, pp. [251]-267.
    Fountain of Youth, The. In *Little Comedies Old and New,* Edinburgh & London: William Blackwood & Sons, 1882, pp. [269]-281.
    Half Way to Arcady. In *Little Comedies,* New York: D. Appleton, 1880, pp. [125]-136. *Filed under* Little Comedies.
    Half Way to Arcady. In *Little Comedies Old and New,* Edinburgh & London: William Blackwood & Sons, 1882, pp. [135]-147.
    Heather. In *Little Comedies,* New York: D. Appleton, 1880, pp. 163-180. *Filed under* Little Comedies.
    Heather. In *Little Comedies Old and New,* Edinburgh & London: William Blackwood & Sons, 1882, pp. [201]-219.
    Ivanhoe. Music by Sullivan, Arthur. London: Chapple, n.d. Pp. [i-iv], [1]-261. Vocal score.
    Latin Lesson. In *Little Comedies Old and New,* Edinburgh & London: William Blackwood & Sons, 1882, pp. [117]-133.
    Mabel's Holy Day. In *Little Comedies,* New York: D. Appleton, 1880, pp. [137]-162. *Filed under* Little Comedies.
    Mabel's Holy Day. In *Little Comedies Old and New,* Edinburgh & London: William Blackwood & Sons, 1882, pp. [177]-199.
    Nadeshda. Music by Thomas, A. Goring. London: Boosey, n.d. Pp. [1-3], i-vi, 1-345. Vocal score.
    Picking up the Pieces. In *Little Comedies,* New York: D. Appleton, 1880, pp. [81]-123. *Filed under* Little Comedies.
    Picking up the Pieces. In *Little Comedies Old and New,* Edinburgh & London: William Blackwood & Sons, 1882, pp. [283]-317.
    Picking up the Pieces. Chicago & New York: Dramatic Publishing Co., n.d. Pp. [1]-13. Sergel's Acting Drama, 354.
    Round Delia's Basket. In *Little Comedies Old and New,* Edinburgh & London: William Blackwood & Sons, 1882, pp. [221]-249.

SUBURBAN DANCE, A
   See Ridge, William Pett.
SUCCESS
   See Planché, James Robinson.
SUCH IS FAME
   See Swears, Herbert.
SUCH STUFF AS DREAMS ARE MADE OF
   See Fitzgerald, Edward (trans.).
SUCH THINGS ARE
   See Inchbald, Elizabeth Simpson, Mrs. Joseph.
SUDDEN ARRIVAL, A
   See Hay, Frederic.
SUDDEN THOUGHTS
   See Wilks, Thomas Egerton.
SUDERMANN, HERMANN
   Three Heron's Feathers, The.
     See Porter, Helen Tracy Lowe, Mrs. (trans.).
SUGAR AND CREAM
   See Hurst, James P.
SUICIDE, THE
   See Verdon, Thomas Kirwan.
SUIL DHUV THE COINER
   See Dibdin, Thomas John.
SUIT OF TWEEDS, A
   See Hay, Frederic.
SULIEMAN (anon.)
   In *New British Theatre,* London: A. J. Valpy (printer), 1814, II, [i], [1-73].
SULIVAN, ROBERT
   Beggar on Horseback, A. London: Nassau Steam Press, n.d. Pp. [1]-60.
   Elopements in High Life. London: Thomas Hailes Lacy, n.d. Pp. [1]-54. [Lacy's Acting Edition].
   Family Pride. London: National Acting Drama Office, n.d. Pp. [1]-57.
   Old Love and the New, The. London: W. S. Johnson, 1851. Pp. [1]-56.
SULTAN, THE
   See Bickerstaffe, Isaac.
SULTANA, THE
   See Gardiner, William.
SUMMER LIGHTNING
   See Cheltnam, Charles Smith.
SUMMER MOTHS
   See Heinemann, William.
SUMMERS, KNIGHT
   M.P. for Puddlepool; or, The Borough Election. London: Thomas Hailes Lacy, n.d. Pp. [1]-17.
SUMMONED TO COURT
   See Dilley, Joseph J.
SUNDAY NIGHT AT RALLIANO'S
   See Ridge, William Pett.
SUNDAY NIGHT 'BUS, THE
   See Ridge, William Pett.
SUNLIGHT AND SHADOW
   See Carton, R. C.
SUNNY SIDE, THE
   See Rae, Charles Marsham.
SUNSET
   See Jerome, Jerome Klapka.
SUNSHINE
   See Broughton, Frederick William.
SUNSHINE AND SHADE
   See Hatch, P. H.
SUNSHINE THROUGH THE CLOUDS
   See Lawrence, Slingsby.
SUPPER, THE
   See Binyon, Laurence.
SUPPER FOR TWO
   See Gifford, J. Wear.
   See Weller, Bernard William. Nita the Dancer.
SUPPER GRATIS, A
   See Reeve, Wybert.
SUPPER, THE SLEEPER, AND THE MERRY SWISS BOY
   See Byron, Henry James. La! Sonnambula!

SUPPLICE D'UN HOMME
   See Morton, John Maddison. Not If I Know It!
SURPLUS POPULATION, AND POOR-LAW BILL
   See Cobbett, William.
SURPRISE, THE
   See Bell, Florence Eveleen Eleanore Oliffe, Mrs. Hugh (Lady).
SURRENDER!
   See Craven, Henry Thornton. Blechington House.
SURRENDER OF CALAIS, THE
   See Colman, George, jr.
SUSAN CAPTIVE
   See Ashe, Nicholas. Panthea.
SUSAN HOPLEY
   See Pitt, George Dibdin.
SUSPICIOUS HUSBAND, THE
   See Hoadly, Benjamin.
SUTER, WILLIAM E.
   Accusing Spirit, The; or, The Three Travellers of the Tyrol. London: Thomas Hailes Lacy, n.d. Pp. [1]-45. French's Acting Edition (late Lacy's), 894.
   Adventures of Dick Turpin and Tom King, The. *Also:* Dick Turpin and Tom King. London: Thomas Hailes Lacy, n.d. Pp. [1]-32. [Lacy's Acting Edition].
   Angel of Midnight, The. Written with Lacy, Thomas Hailes. London: Thomas Hailes Lacy, n.d. Pp. [1]-56.
   Brigands of Calabria, The. Clyde, Ohio: Ames & Holgate, n.d. Pp. [1]-13. Ames & Holgate's Series of Standard and Minor Drama, 14.
   Brother Bill and Me. Boston: Charles H. Spencer, 1867. Pp. [1]-23.
   Catherine Howard. London & New York: Samuel French, n.d. Pp. [1]-48. French's Acting Edition (late Lacy's), 548.
   Cheek Will Win. Clyde, Ohio: A. D. Ames, n.d. Pp. [1]-13. Ames' Series of Standard and Minor Drama, 84.
   Child Stealer, The. London: Thomas Hailes Lacy, n.d. Pp. [1]-49. Promptbook.
   Dick Turpin and Tom King. *Also:* The Adventures of Dick Turpin and Tom King. New York: Samuel French, n.d. Pp. [1]-24. French's Minor Drama, 283.
   Double Dealing; or, The Rifle Volunteer. London: Thomas Hailes Lacy, n.d. Pp. [1]-20. [Lacy's Acting Edition].
   Dred: A Tale of the Dismal Swamp. London: Thomas Hailes Lacy, n.d. Pp. [1]-21. [Lacy's Acting Edition].
   Fan-Fan, the Tulip; or, A Soldier's Fortune. London: Thomas Hailes Lacy, n.d. Pp. [1]-38. [Lacy's Acting Edition].
   Felon's Bond, The. London: Thomas Hailes Lacy, n.d. Pp. [1]-50.
   First Love; or, The Widowed Bride. London: Thomas Hailes Lacy, n.d. Pp. [1]-53.
   Give Me My Wife. Clyde, Ohio: A. D. Ames, n.d. Pp. [1]-17. Ames' Series of Standard and Minor Drama, 13.
   Give Me My Wife. London: Thomas Hailes Lacy, n.d. Pp. [1]-22.
   Glass of Water, A; or, Great Events from Trifling Causes Spring. London: Thomas Hailes Lacy, n.d. Pp. [1]-[55]. Promptbook.
   Highwayman's Holiday, The. London: Thomas Hailes Lacy, n.d. Pp. [1]-22.
   Holly Bush Hall; or, The Track in the Snow. London & New York: Samuel French, n.d. Pp. [1]-43. [Lacy's Acting Edition].
   Idiot of the Mountain, The. London: Thomas Hailes Lacy, n.d. Pp. [1]-54. [Lacy's Acting Edition].
   Incompatibility of Temper. London: Thomas Hailes Lacy, n.d. Pp. [1]-13. [Lacy's Acting Edition].
   Isoline of Bavaria. London: Thomas Hailes Lacy, n.d. Pp. [1]-36. [Lacy's Acting Edition].
   Jack o' the Hedge. London: Thomas Hailes Lacy, n.d. Pp. [1]-46.
   Jeweller of St. James's, The. London: Thomas Hailes Lacy, n.d. Pp. [1]-36. [Lacy's Acting Edition].

John Wopps; or, From Information I Received. Boston: Charles H. Spencer, n.d. Pp. [1]-14. Spencer's Universal Stage, 4.

Life's Revenge, A; or, Two Loves for One Heart. London & New York: Samuel French, n.d. Pp. [1]-51. French's Acting Edition (late Lacy's), 571.

Little Annie's Birthday. London: Thomas Hailes Lacy, n.d. Pp. [1]-20.

Lost Child, The. London: Thomas Hailes Lacy, n.d. Pp. [1]-18. [Lacy's Acting Edition].

More Free than Welcome. London: Thomas Hailes Lacy, n.d. Pp. [1]-18.

Old House on the Bridge of Notre Dame, The. London: Thomas Hailes Lacy, n.d. Pp. [1]-47. Lacy's Acting Edition, 744.

Pirates of the Savannah, The; or, The Tiger Hunter of the Prairies. London: Thomas Hailes Lacy, n.d. Pp. [1]-44. [Lacy's Acting Edition].

Puss.
> *See* Woman That Was a Cat, The.

Quiet Family, A. New York & London: Samuel French, n.d. Pp. [1]-19. French's Minor Drama, 240.

Robbers of the Pyrenees, The. London: Thomas Hailes Lacy, n.d. Pp. [1]-47. [Lacy's Acting Edition]. Promptbook.

Rocambole; or, The Knaves of Hearts and the Companions of Crime. London: Thomas Hailes Lacy, n.d. Pp. [1]-52. [Lacy's Acting Edition].

Sarah's Young Man. Boston: Charles H. Spencer, n.d. Pp. [1]-21.

Slighted Treasures. New York: Dick & Fitzgerald, n.d. Pp. [1]-13. [Dick's American Edition].

Speak Out Boldly. London: Thomas Hailes Lacy, n.d. Pp. [1]-18. [Lacy's Acting Edition].

Syren of Paris, The. London: Thomas Hailes Lacy, n.d. Pp. [1]-42. [Lacy's Acting Edition].

Test of Truth, The; or, It's a Long Lane That Has No Turning. London: Thomas Hailes Lacy, n.d. Pp. [1]-30. [Lacy's Acting Edition].

Troubadour, The.
> *See* Trovatore, Il.

Trovatore, Il. *Also:* The Troubadour. London: Thomas Hailes Lacy, n.d. Pp. [5]-39. Text complete. [Lacy's Acting Edition].

Two Gentlemen in a Fix. Chicago: T. S. Denison, n.d. Pp. [1]-11. Star Series.

Very Pleasant Evening, A. London: Thomas Hailes Lacy, n.d. Pp. [1]-14.

Wanted, a Young Lady—. London: Thomas Hailes Lacy, n.d. Pp. [1]-17. [Lacy's Acting Edition].

We All Have Our Little Faults. London & New York: Samuel French, n.d. Pp. [1]-27. [French's Acting Edition]. Promptbook.

Which Shall I Marry? London: Thomas Hailes Lacy, n.d. Pp. [1]-18. [Lacy's Acting Edition].

Woman That Was a Cat, The. London: Thomas Hailes Lacy, n.d. Pp. [1]-20. Lacy's Acting Edition, 1072.

Woman That Was a Cat, The. *Also:* Puss. London: Thomas Hailes Lacy, n.d. Pp. [1]-20. [Lacy's Acting Edition]. *Filed under* Puss (anon.).

SUTRO, ALFRED
Cave of Illusion, The. London: Grant Richards, 1900. Pp. [i]-[xx], [1]-196.

SUTRO, ALFRED (trans.)
Aglavaine and Selysette. By Maeterlinck, Maurice. London: Grant Richards, 1897. Pp. [i]-[xxviii], [1]-144.

Alladine and Palomides. By Maeterlinck, Maurice. In *Three Little Dramas for Marionettes,* London: Duckworth, 1899, pp. [1]-61.

Carrots. By Renard, Jules. London & New York: Samuel French, c.1904. Pp. [1]-25. French's Acting Edition (late Lacy's), 2269.

Death of Tintagiles, The. By Maeterlinck, Maurice. In *Three Little Dramas for Marionettes,* London: Duckworth, 1899, pp. [89]-[126].

SWAIN, CHARLES
Dramatic Chapters. London: David Bogue, 1842. Pp. [1]-180.

SWAN, HOWARD
Paul and Joseph; or, God and Mammon in the Transvaal. London: Samuel Baxter, n.d. Pp. [1]-23.

SWANWICK, ANNA (trans.)
Faust. By Goethe. [London: Henry G. Bohn & John Mitchell], n.d. Pp. [i-ii], [1-2], [v]-[x], [1]-154. Title page illegible.

Maid of Orleans, The. By Schiller. In [*Works of Frederick Schiller,* London: G. Bell & Sons, 1881, III], 131-240.

SWANWICK, CATHERINE
Richard Coeur de Lion. London: Women's Printing Society, n.d. Pp. [i-iv], [1]-160.

Talisman, The. London: H. K. Lewis, 1864. Pp. [i-iv], [1]-161.

SWEARS, HERBERT
Home, Sweet Home, with Variations. London: Samuel French; New York: T. Henry French, n.d. Pp. [1]-48. [Lacy's Acting Edition].

Lady Interviewer, The. London: Samuel French; New York: T. Henry French, n.d. Pp. [1]-11. [Lacy's Acting Edition].

Love and Dentistry. London: Samuel French; New York: T. Henry French, n.d. Pp. [1]-14. [Lacy's Acting Edition].

Semi-Detached. London & New York: Samuel French, n.d. Pp. [1]-11. [Lacy's Acting Edition].

Such Is Fame. London & New York: Samuel French, n.d. Pp. [1]-18. [Lacy's Acting Edition].

Twilight. London: Samuel French; New York: T. Henry French, n.d. Pp. [1]-18. [Lacy's Acting Edition].

Wayfarers. London & New York: Samuel French, n.d. Pp. [1]-17. [Lacy's Acting Edition].

SWEDISH NIGHTINGALE
> *See* Reach, Angus Bethune. Jenny Lind at Last.

SWEDISH PATRIOTISM
> *See* Abbott, William.

SWEENEY TODD, THE BARBER OF FLEET STREET
> *See* Hazelton, Frederick.

SWEET LAVENDER
> *See* Pinero, Arthur Wing.

SWEET WILL
> *See* Jones, Henry Arthur.

SWEETHEARTS
> *See* Gilbert, William Schwenck.

SWEETHEARTS AND WIVES
> *See* Kenney, James.

SWEETS OF A FAMILY
> *See* Rodwell, James Thomas Gooderham. Bachelor's Torments.

SWELLFOOT THE TYRANT
> *See* Shelley, Percy Bysshe. Oedipus Tyrannus.

SWIFT, EDMUND LEWES LENTHAL
Woman's Will—A Riddle! London: J. J. Stockdale, 1820. Pp. [1]-79.

SWINBURNE, ALGERNON CHARLES
Atalanta in Calydon. Boston: Ticknor & Fields, 1866. Pp. [3]-113.

Bothwell. London: Chatto & Windus, 1874. Pp. [i-ix], [1]-532.

Chastelard. London: Edward Moxon, 1865. Pp. [i-vi], [1]-219.

Erechtheus. London: Chatto & Windus, 1876. Pp. [i-vi], [1]-105.

Locrine. New York: United States Book Co., n.d. Pp. [i]-[x], [1]-138.

Marino Faliero. London: Chatto & Windus, 1885. Pp. [i]-[viii], [1]-151.

Mary Stuart. London: Chatto & Windus, 1881. Pp. [i]-[vi], [1]-203.

Queen-Mother, The. In [*Two Plays,* London: B. M. Pickering, 1860], pp. [1]-160. Title page lacking.

Rosamond. In [*Two Plays,* London: B. M. Pickering, 1860], pp. [159]-217. Title page lacking. *Filed under* Queen-Mother.

Rosamund, Queen of the Lombards. New York: Dodd, Mead, 1899. Pp. [i-iv], [1]-81.

Sisters, The. London: Chatto & Windus, 1892. Pp. [i]-[xii], [1]-107.

SWINDLERS, THE
> *See* Maclaren, Archibald.

SWING!
> *See* Barnett, Charles Zachary.

SWISS BANDITTI
> *See* Arnold, Samuel James. Maniac!, The.

SWISS COTTAGE, THE
> *See* Bayly, Thomas Haynes.
> *See* Bayly, Thomas Haynes. Why Don't She Marry?

SWISS FAMILY
> *See* Somerset, Charles A. Home Sweet Home!

SWISS SWAINS, THE
> *See* Webster, Benjamin Nottingham.

SWISS TIMES, THE
> *See* Bell, Florence Eveleen Eleanore Oliffe, Mrs. Hugh (Lady).

SWORN AT HIGHGATE!
> *See* Daniel, George.

SYBIL, THE
> *See* Cumberland, Richard.

SYBILLA
> *See* Simpson, John Palgrave.

SYKES, PERCIVAL H. T.
> **Poor Old Perkins.** London & New York: Samuel French, n.d. Pp. [1]-55.

SYLPHIDE, THE
> *See* Brough, William.

SYLVANA
> *See* Somerset, Charles A.

SYLVESTER DAGGERWOOD
> *See* Colman, George, jr.

SYLVIA
> *See* Darley, George.

SYME, DAVID (trans.)
> **Faust.** By Goethe. Edinburgh: Adam & Charles Black, 1834. Pp. [i]-[vi], [1]-241.

SYMMONS, CHARLES
> **Sicilian Captive, The.** London: J. Johnson, 1800. Pp. [1]-146.

SYMONS, ARTHUR (trans.)
> **Dawn, The.** By Verhaeren, Émile. Chicago: Charles H. Sergel Co., 1898. Pp. [i-ii], 1-110.

SYMPATHETIC SOULS
> *See* Grundy, Sydney.

SYMPATHY
> *See* Dubourg, Augustus W.

SYRACUSAN GOSSIPS, THE
> *See* Hunt, Leigh.

SYREN OF PARIS, THE
> *See* Suter, William E.

T., H. T.
> **Caracalla.** London: R. Groombridge; J. Andrews, 1832. Pp. [i-iv], [1]-124. *Filed under* Caracalla (anon.).

TABLES TURNED, THE
> *See* Morris, William.

TABLEY, LORD DE
> *See* Warren, John Byrne Leicester, Lord de Tabley.

TABOO, THE
> *See* Carnes, Mason.

TACT!
> *See* Barnett, Morris.

TACTICIANS
> *See* Hayes, Frederick William.

TAFFY WAS A WELSHMAN
> *See* Byron, Henry James.

TAIL (TALE) OF A SHARK
> *See* Hood, Thomas, sr.

TAILOR OF BRUSSELS
> *See* Neil, Ross. Duke for a Day.

TAILOR OF TAMWORTH
> *See* Wilks, Thomas Egerton. State Secrets.

TAILORS, THE; OR, A TRAGEDY FOR WARM WEATHER (anon.)
> In *British Drama*, 12 vols., London: John Dicks, 1871, IX, [19]-32.

TAKE CARE OF DOWB—
> *See* Morton, John Maddison.

TAKE CARE OF LITTLE CHARLEY
> *See* Brougham, John.

TAKE THAT GIRL AWAY!
> *See* Buckingham, Leicester Silk.

TAKEN BY STORM
> *See* Maltby, C. Alfred.

TAKEN FOR GRANTED
> *See* Cann, R. W.

TAKEN FROM LIFE
> *See* Pettitt, Henry Alfred.

TAKEN FROM THE FRENCH
> *See* Morton, John Maddison.

TAKEN FROM THE GREEK
> *See* Burnand, Francis Cowley. Latest Edition of Helen, The.

TAKEN IN AND DONE FOR
> *See* Selby, Charles.

TAKEN UP AND TAKEN IN!
> *See* Daniel, George. Disagreeable Surprise, The.

TAKING BY STORM!
> *See* Churchill, Frank.

TAKING THE BULL BY THE HORNS
> *See* Newte, Horace Wykeham Can. Mr. Fitz-W—?

TAKING THE VEIL
> *See* Hazlewood, Colin Henry.

TALBOT, ROBERT
> **Serf, The.** London: John Cumberland, 1828. Pp. [1]-54. Cumberland's British Theatre, XIX. *Filed under* Cumberland, John. Cumberland's British Theatre, XIX.
> **Serf, The.** London: John Cumberland, n.d. Pp. [1]-54.

TALBOT, ROBERT (trans.)
> **Faust.** By Goethe. London: J. Wacey, 1839. Pp. [i]-xxvi, [1]-569. 2nd ed.
> **William Tell.** By Schiller. London: Plummer & Brewis (printer), 1829. Pp. [iii]-[xii], [1]-180.

TALE OF A COMET, A
> *See* Horne, F. Lennox.

TALE OF A MANTUA MAKER!
> *See* Graves, Joseph. Wife, The.

TALE OF A PIG, A
> *See* Bruton, James.

TALE OF A TAR
> *See* Johnstone, John Beer. Gale Breezely.

TALE OF BLOOD
> *See* Haines, John Thomas. Idiot Witness, The.

TALE OF EIGHTEEN HUNDRED AND FIVE
> *See* Maclaren, Archibald. Days We Live In, The.

TALE OF FLODDEN FIELD
> *See* Fitzball, Edward. Marmion.

TALE OF MYSTERY, A
> *See* Holcroft, Thomas.
> *See* Wallace, John. Caelina.

TALE OF THE ELEVENTH CENTURY
> *See* Dibdin, Charles Isaac Mungo, jr. Old Man of the Mountains, The.

TALE OF THE FROZEN REGIONS
> *See* Haines, John Thomas. North Pole.

TALE OF THE GOODWIN SANDS
> *See* Conquest, George. Sole Survivor, The.

TALE OF TROY, THE
> *See* Warr, George Charles Winter.

TALE OF TWO CITIES
> *See* Cooper, Frederick Fox.
> *See* Rivers, Henry J.
> *See* Taylor, Tom.

TALFOURD, FRANCIS
> **Abon Hassan; or, The Hunt after Happiness.** London: Thomas Hailes Lacy, n.d. Pp. [1]-38. Lacy's Acting Edition, 248.

Alcestis, the Original Strong-Minded Woman. *Also:* Alcestis Travestie. London: Thomas Hailes Lacy, n.d. Pp. [1]-26. 3rd ed.

Alcestis Travestie. *Also:* Alcestis, the Original Strong-Minded Woman. Oxford: E. T. Spiers, 1850. Pp. [1]-24.

Atalanta; or, The Three Golden Apples. London: Thomas Hailes Lacy, n.d. Pp. [i]-v, [6]-44. [Lacy's Acting Edition].

Electra in a New Electr'ic Light. London: Thomas Hailes Lacy, n.d. Pp. [1]-40.

Ganem, the Slave of Love. London: Thomas Hailes Lacy, n.d. Pp. [1]-27.

Godiva.
See Hale, William Palmer.

Household Fairy, A. New York: Crest Trading Co., n.d. Pp. [1]-16.

King Thrushbeard!; or, A Little Pet and the Great Passion! London: Thomas Hailes Lacy, n.d. Pp. [1]-36.

Leo the Terrible.
See Coyne, Joseph Stirling.

Macbeth, Somewhat Removed from the Text of Shakespeare. *Also:* Macbeth Travestie. London: Thomas Hailes Lacy, n.d. Pp. [1]-37. 4th ed. [Lacy's Acting Edition].

Macbeth Travestie. *Also:* Macbeth, Somewhat Removed from the Text of Shakespeare. Oxford: E. T. Spiers, 1850. Pp. [1]-28. 3rd ed.

Mammon and Gammon. London: Thomas Hailes Lacy, n.d. Pp. [1]-16.

Mandarin's Daughter!, The.
See Hale, William Palmer.

Miller and His Men, The. Written with Byron, Henry James. London: Thomas Hailes Lacy, n.d. Pp. [1]-40. [Lacy's Acting Edition, 670].

Pluto and Proserpine; or, The Belle and the Pomegranate. London: Thomas Hailes Lacy, n.d. Pp. [1]-36. *Filed under* Pluto and Proserpine (anon.).

Princesses in the Tower, The; or, A Match for Lucifer! London: Thomas Hailes Lacy, n.d. Pp. [1]-24. [Lacy's Acting Edition].

Rule of Three, The. London: Thomas Hailes Lacy, n.d. Pp. [1]-23. [Lacy's Acting Edition].

Shylock; or, The Merchant of Venice Preserved. London: Thomas Hailes Lacy, n.d. Pp. [1]-30. [Lacy's Acting Edition].

Tarantula, La.
See Smith, Albert Richard.

Tell! and the Strike of the Cantons; or, The Pair, the Meddler, and the Apple! London: Thomas Hailes Lacy, n.d. Pp. [1]-46. [Lacy's Acting Edition].

Thetis and Peleus.
See Hale, William Palmer.

Tit for Tat. Written with Wigan, Alfred Sydney. London: Thomas Hailes Lacy, n.d. Pp. [1]-49. [Lacy's Acting Edition].

TALFOURD, THOMAS NOON

Athenian Captive, The. London: Edward Moxon, 1838. Pp. [i]-[xii], [1]-103.

Glencoe; or, The Fate of the Macdonalds. London: Edward Moxon, 1840. Pp. [i]-[xvi], [1]-98. 2nd ed.

Glencoe; or, The Fate of the Macdonalds. [London: John Dicks], n.d. Pp. [1]-21. [Dicks' Standard Plays, 323].

Ion. London: Edward Moxon, 1836. Pp. [i]-[viii], [1]-120. 2nd ed.

Ion. London: A. J. Valpy (printer) (priv.), n.d. Pp. [i]-[xx], [1]-204.

TALISMAN, THE
See Macfarren, George.
See Swanwick, Catherine.

TALISMANO, IL
See Matthison, Arthur.

TAM O'SHANTER
See Addison, Henry Robert, Capt.
See Bridgeman, John Vipon.

TAMERLANE
See Rowe, Nicholas.

TAMING A TARTAR
See Selby, Charles.

TAMING A TIGER (anon.)
Also: Twenty Minutes with a Tiger. London: Thomas Hailes Lacy (priv.), n.d. Pp. [1]-20. [Lacy's Acting Edition].

TAMING A TIGER
See Twenty Minutes with a Tiger (anon.).

TAMING OF THE SHREW
See Kemble, John Philip (arr.).
See Troutbeck, John, Rev. (trans.).

TAMING THE TRUANT
See Wigan, Horace.

TANCRED AND SIGISMUNDA
See Thomson, James.

TANCREDI, IL
See Maggioni, Manfredo (trans.).

TANNER, ?
Chinese Mother, The. Baltimore: Kelly, Piet, n.d. Pp. [1]-68.

TANNER, JAMES TOLMAN

Ballet Girl, The. Written with Ross, Adrian (pseud. of Ropes, Arthur Reed). Music by Kiefert, Carl. London: Enoch & Sons, c.1897. Pp. [1]-37. Libretto. *Filed under* Ross, Adrian.

Circus Girl, The. Written with Palings, W.; Greenbank, Harry Hewetson; Ross, Adrian (pseud. of Ropes, Arthur Reed). Music by Caryll, Ivan; Monckton, Lionel. London: Chappell, c.1897. Pp. [i-iv], [1]-195. Vocal score.

Circus Girl, The. Written with Palings, W.; Greenbank, Harry Hewetson; Ross, Adrian (pseud. of Ropes, Arthur Reed). Music by Caryll, Ivan; Monckton, Lionel. London: Waterlow & Sons (Printer), n.d. Pp. [1]-38. Libretto.

Don Juan.
See Ross, Adrian.

Messenger Boy, The. Written with Murray, Alfred; Ross, Adrian (pseud. of Ropes, Arthur Reed); Greenbank, Percy. Music by Caryll, Ivan; Monckton, Lionel. London: Chappell, 1900. Pp. [i-iv], 1-242. Vocal score. [i-iv], 1-242. Vocal score.

My Girl.
See Ross, Adrian.

Pot-Pourri. Written with Risque, W. H. Music by Lambelet, Napoleon. London: Boosey, c.1899. Pp. [i-iv], [1]-126. Vocal score.

TANNHÄUSER
See Jackson, John P. (trans.).
See Macfarren, Natalia (trans.).
See Pittman, Josiah (trans.).

TAPESTRY WORKERS
See Morgan, Sydney Owenson, Mrs. Thomas Charles (Lady). Easter Recess, The.

TARANTULA, LA
See Smith, Albert Richard.

TARNATION STRANGE
See Moncrieff, William Thomas.

TARTARUS
See Cornwall, Barry.

TARTUFFE
See Mathew, Charles (trans.).
See Oxenford, John (trans.).
See Van Laun, Henri (trans.).

TASSO
See Neil, Ross.
See Shelley, Percy Bysshe.

TATE, NAHUM (arr.)
King Lear. By Shakespeare, William. In *New English Drama*, ed. W. Oxberry, 22 vols., London: W. Simpkin & R. Marshall; C. Chapple, 1820, X, [i]-[xii], [1]-71. *Filed under* Oxberry, William Henry. New English Drama, X.

TAYLOR, G. F.
Factory Strike, The. London: James Pattie, n.d. Pp. [1]-47.

TAYLOR, GEORGE WATSON

Profligate, The. London: W. Bulmer & W. Nicol (printer), 1820. Pp. [i-vi], [1]-153. *Filed under* Watson-Taylor, George.

TAYLOR, HENRY

Alwine and Adelais. In *Eve of the Conquest and Other Poems,* London: Edward Moxon, 1847, pp. [i], [58]-68.

Edwin the Fair. In *Works,* London: Henry S. King, 1877, II, [i]-[xiv], [1]-193.

Isaac Comnenus. London: John Murray, 1827. Pp. [i-ii], [1]-219.

Isaac Comnenus. In *Works,* London: Henry S. King, 1877, II, [195]-337.

Philip van Artevelde. Cambridge & Boston: James Munroe, 1835. I, [i]-[xxxii], [33]-259; II, [1]-251.

St. Clement's Eve. In *St. Clement's Eve and Other Poems,* London: C. Kegan Paul, 1878, pp. [i], [133]-272.

Virgin Widow, The; or, A Sicilian Summer. London: C. Kegan Paul, 1878. Pp. [i]-[xviii], 1-131.

TAYLOR, J. (trans.)

Atma Bodha; or, The Knowledge of Self. Bombay: Tookaram Tatya, n.d. Pp. [85]-116. 2nd ed. *Filed under* Prabodha Chandrodaya.

Prabodha Chandrodaya; or, Rise of the Moon of Intellect. Bombay: Tookaram Tatya, n.d. Pp. [i]-[xii], [1]-84. 2nd ed.

TAYLOR, J. G.

Home Rule. London & New York: Samuel French, n.d. Pp. [1]-22. [Lacy's Acting Edition].

TAYLOR, THOMAS PROCLUS

Bottle, The. New York: John Douglas, 1847. Pp. [1]-57. Minor Drama, 20.

Bottle, The. London: Cleave, n.d. Pp. [i-vi], [1]-48.

Chain of Guilt, The; or, The Inn on the Heath. London: John Cumberland, n.d. Pp. [1]-35. Cumberland's Minor Theatre, XII. *Filed under* Cumberland, John. Cumberland's Minor Theatre, XII.

Chain of Guilt, The; or, The Inn on the Heath. London: Thomas Hailes Lacy, n.d. Pp. [1]-35. Cumberland's British Theatre.

Claude Duval, the Ladies' Highwayman. London: John Dicks, n.d. Pp. [1]-9. Dicks' Standard Plays, 613.

Fair Rosamund (According to the History of England). London: James Pattie, n.d. Pp. [1]-19.

Herne the Hunter. London: John Dicks, n.d. Pp. [1]-20. Dicks' Standard Plays, 309.

Miser's Daughter, The. [London: John Dicks], n.d. Pp. [1]-15. [Dicks' Standard Plays, 612].

Tower of London, The; or, Queen Mary. London: John Dicks, n.d. Pp. [1]-17. Dicks' Standard Plays, 502.

Vanderdecken; or, The Flying Dutchman. London: John Dicks, n.d. Pp. [1]-21. Dicks' Standard Plays, 436.

Village Outcast, The. London: John Dicks, n.d. Pp. [1]-15. Dicks' Standard Plays, 444.

TAYLOR, TOM

Anne Boleyn. In *Historical Dramas,* London: Chatto & Windus, 1877, pp. [i], [341]-412.

Arkwright's Wife. In *Historical Dramas,* London: Chatto & Windus, 1877, pp. [i], [287]-340.

Babes in the Wood, The. London: Thomas Hailes Lacy, n.d. Pp. [1]-71.

Barefaced Imposters. By John Doe, Richard Roe, and John Noakes. London: Thomas Hailes Lacy, n.d. Pp. [1]-22. [Lacy's Acting Edition].

Blighted Being, A. London: Thomas Hailes Lacy, n.d. Pp. [1]-24.

Cinderella.
See Smith, Albert Richard.

Contested Election, The. Manchester: T. Chambers (printer), 1868. Pp. [3]-60. Promptbook.

Diogenes and His Lantern; or, A Hue and Cry after Honesty. London: Thomas Hailes Lacy, n.d. Pp. [1]-32. Lacy's Acting Edition.

Dundreary. *Also:* Our American Cousin. Pp. [i-iv], [1]-[5], [1]-23, [i], [1]-23, [i], [1]-[32], [i-ii], [1]-[24]. Pagination by act. Typescript.

Fool's Revenge, The. London: Thomas Hailes Lacy, n.d. Pp. [i]-[iv], [5]-58.

Going to the Bad. London: Thomas Hailes Lacy, n.d. Pp. [1]-[72]. [Lacy's Acting Edition].

Guy Fawkes.
See Smith, Albert Richard.

Helping Hands. New York: O. A. Roorbach, jr, 1856. Pp. [1]-48. Acting Drama, 17.

Henry Dunbar; or, A Daughter's Trials. New York: Robert M. DeWitt, n.d. Pp. [1]-38.

Hidden Hand, The. London & New York: Samuel French, n.d. Pp. [1]-60. [French's Acting Edition (late Lacy's)].

House or the Home?, The. London: Thomas Hailes Lacy, n.d. Pp. [1]-46. [Lacy's Acting Edition].

Joan of Arc. Chicago: Dramatic Publishing Co., n.d. Pp. [1]-41. Sergel's Acting Drama, 299.

King's Rival, The. Written with Reade, Charles. London: Richard Bentley, 1854. Pp. [i-vi], [1]-72.

King's Rival, The; or, The Court and the Stage. Written with Reade, Charles. New York: Samuel French, n.d. Pp. [1]-50. French's American Drama, 33.

Lady Clancarty; or, Wedded and Wooed. London & New York: Samuel French, n.d. Pp. [1]-68. French's Standard Drama, [368].

Mary Warner. Chicago: Dramatic Publishing Co., n.d. Pp. [1]-42.

Masks and Faces; or, Before and Behind the Curtain. Written with Reade, Charles. London: Richard Bentley, 1854. Pp. [i-iv], [1]-71. Promptbook.

New Men and Old Acres. Written with Dubourg, Augustus W. London & New York: Samuel French, n.d. Pp. [1]-76. French's Acting Edition (late Lacy's), 1336.

New Men and Old Acres. Written with Dubourg, Augustus W. New York: Robert M. DeWitt, n.d. Pp. [1]-42. DeWitt's Acting Plays, 115.

New Men and Old Acres. Written with Dubourg, Augustus W. London: Thomas Hailes Lacy, n.d. Pp. [1]-76. [Lacy's Acting Edition].

Nice Firm, A. London: Thomas Hailes Lacy, n.d. Pp. [1]-30. [Lacy's Acting Edition].

Nine Points of the Law. London: Thomas Hailes Lacy, n.d. Pp. [1]-36. [Lacy's Acting Edition, 600].

Novelty Fair; or, Hints for 1851. Written with Smith, Albert Richard. London: Thomas Hailes Lacy, n.d. Pp. [1]-26. [Lacy's Acting Edition].

Our American Cousin. N.p.: n.pub. (priv.), 1869. Pp. [1]-46.

Our Clerks; or, No. 3, Fig Tree Court, Temple. London: Thomas Hailes Lacy, n.d. Pp. [1]-[27]. [Lacy's Acting Edition].

Overland Route, The. Manchester: T. Chambers (printer), 1866. Pp. [1]-50.

Overland Route, The. New York: Robert M. DeWitt, n.d. Pp. [1]-51.

Payable on Demand. London: Thomas Hailes Lacy, n.d. Pp. [1]-53.

Philosopher's Stone, The. London: Thomas Hailes Lacy, n.d. Pp. [1]-35. [Lacy's Acting Edition].

Plot and Passion. New York: Robert M. DeWitt, n.d. Pp. [1]-39. DeWitt's Acting Plays, 61.

Prince Dorus; or, The Romance of the Nose. London: Thomas Hailes Lacy, n.d. Pp. [1]-35. [Lacy's Acting Edition].

Retribution. [New York]: Samuel French, n.d. Pp. [1]-30. French's Standard Drama, 151.

Sense and Sensation; or, The Seven Sisters of Thule. London: Thomas Hailes Lacy, n.d. Pp. [1]-63. [Lacy's Acting Edition].

Serf, The; or, Love Levels All. London: Thomas Hailes Lacy, n.d. Pp. [1]-53. [Lacy's Acting Edition].

Settling Day. London: Thomas Hailes Lacy, n.d. Pp. [1]-84. [Lacy's Acting Edition].

Sheep in Wolf's Clothing, A. London & New York: Samuel French, n.d. Pp. [1]-[34]. Promptbook.

Sir Roger de Coverley; or, The Widow and Her Wooers. London: Thomas Hailes Lacy, n.d. Pp. [1]-58. [Lacy's Acting Edition].

Sister's Penance, A. Written with Dubourg, Augustus W. London: Thomas Hailes Lacy, n.d. Pp. [1]-62. Lacy's Acting Edition.

Slave Life.
 See Lemon, Mark.

Still Waters Run Deep. London & New York: Samuel French, n.d. Pp. [1]-58. French's Acting Edition (late Lacy's), [319].

Tale of Two Cities, A. London: Thomas Hailes Lacy, n.d. Pp. [1]-56. Lacy's Acting Edition. Promptbook.

Ticket-of-Leave Man, The. London & New York: Samuel French, n.d. Pp. [1]-56. French's Standard Drama, 329.

To Oblige Benson. New York & London: Samuel French, n.d. Pp. [1]-24. Imperfect copy. Minor Drama, [86].

To Parents and Guardians: At Jubilee House Establishment, Clapham, Young Gentlemen Are, &c. London: John Dicks, n.d. Pp. [13]-24. Dicks' Standard Plays, 997.

To Parents and Guardians!: At Jubilee House Establishment, Clapham, Young Gentlemen Are, &c. &c. New York: Samuel French, n.d. Pp. [1]-24. French's American Drama, 127.

Trip to Kissengen, A. London: William Barth, n.d. Pp. [1]-28.

'Twixt Axe and Crown. New York: Robert M. DeWitt, n.d. Pp. [1]-41. DeWitt's Acting Plays, 284.

'Twixt Axe and Crown; or, The Lady Elizabeth. New York & London: Samuel French, n.d. Pp. [1]-72.

Two Loves and a Life. Written with Reade, Charles. London: Richard Bentley, 1854. Pp. [i-iv], [1]-85.

Two Loves and a Life. Written with Reade, Charles. Boston: William V. Spencer, n.d. Pp. [1]-48. Spencer's Boston Theatre, 56.

Unequal Match, An. London & New York: Samuel French, n.d. Pp. [1]-66. [Lacy's Acting Edition].

Up at the Hills. London: Thomas Hailes Lacy, n.d. Pp. [1]-60. [Lacy's Acting Edition]. Promptbook.

Valentine and Orson.
 See Smith, Albert Richard.

Vicar of Wakefield, The. *Also:* The Vicar of Wakefield; or, The Pastor's Fireside. London: Thomas Hailes Lacy, n.d. Pp. [1]-60.

Victims, The. New York: Samuel French, n.d. Pp. [1]-44. French's Standard Drama, 186.

Wittikind and His Brothers; or, The Seven Swan Princes and the Fair Melusine. London: Thomas Hailes Lacy, n.d. Pp. [1]-28.

TAYLOR, TOM (arr.)
 Hamlet. By Shakespeare, William. London (Sydenham): Crystal Palace Co., 1873. Pp. [1]-80.

TEACHER TAUGHT, THE
 See Stirling, Edward.

TEARS! IDLE TEARS!
 See Scott, Clement William.

TEDDE, MOSTYN
 Queen's Mate, The.
 See Paulton, Harry.

TEDDY ROE
 See Stirling, Edward.

TEDDY THE TILER
 See Rodwell, George Herbert Bonaparte.

TEETOTALISM TRIUMPHANT
 See MacMillan, A.

TEKELI
 See Hook, Theodore Edward.

TELEMACHUS (anon.)
 Music by Bishop, Henry. London: E. Macleish (printer), 1815. Pp. [1]-19. Libretto.

TELEMACHUS
 See Planché, James Robinson.

TELEMACHUS AND CALYPSO.
 See Brookes, Sheridan. Calypso, Queen of Ogygia.

TELEPHONE, TOM
 See C., T. S.

TELEPHONE, THE
 See Clements, Arthur.

TELEPHONIC THEATRE-GOERS
 See Anstey, F.

TELL! AND THE STRIKE OF THE CANTONS
 See Talfourd, Francis.

TEMPER
 See Bell, Robert.
 See Morgan Sydney Owenson, Mrs. Thomas Charles (Lady).

TEMPERANCE RECITERS' FESTIVAL, THE
 See Featherstone, Thomas.

TEMPERANCE VOLUNTEERS, THE
 See Featherstone, Thomas.

TEMPEST, THE
 See Kean, Charles John (arr.).
 See Shakespeare, William.

TEMPLAR, THE
 See Slous, Angiolo Robson.

TEMPLAR AND JEWESS
 See Jackson, John P. (trans.).

TEMPLE OF DEATH, THE
 See Milner, Henry M.

TEMPTATION
 See Brougham, John. Irish Emigrant, The.
 See Brougham, John.
 See Cornwall, Barry.
 See Townsend, William Thompson.

TEMPTED, TRIED, AND TRUE
 See Byron, Henry James. Lancashire Lass, The.

TEMPTER, THE
 See Graves, Joseph.
 See Jones, Henry Arthur.

TEN HOURS IN NEW YORK!
 See Rede, William Leman. Flight to America, The.

TEN THOUSAND A YEAR
 See Peake, Richard Brinsley.

TEN TO ONE
 See Westmacott, Charles Molloy. Nettlewig Hall.

TEN YEARS HENCE
 See Seymour, Mary.

TENANT OF THE TOMB
 See Harvey, Margaret. Raymond de Percy.

TENDER HUSBAND, THE
 See Steele, Richard.

TENDER PRECAUTIONS
 See Serle, Thomas James.

TENDER SISTERS, THE
 See Gilbert, ? (trans.).

TENNANT, WILLIAM
 Cardinal Beaton. Edinburgh: Archibald Constable; London: Hurst & Robinson, 1823. Pp. [i-iv], [1]-179.

 Destruction of Sodom, The. In *Hebrew Dramas,* Edinburgh: John Menzies, 1845, pp. [233]-324. *Filed under* Hebrew Dramas.

 Esther; or, The Fall of Haman. In *Hebrew Dramas,* Edinburgh: John Menzies, 1845, pp. [123]-232. *Filed under* Hebrew Dramas.

 Jephthah's Daughter; or, The Hebrew Heroine. In *Hebrew Dramas,* Edinburgh: John Menzies, 1845, pp. [i-iv], [1]-121. *Filed under* Hebrew Dramas.

 John Baliol. Edinburgh: Archibald Constable; London: Hurst, Robinson, 1825. Pp. [i-iv], [1]-164.

TENNYSON, ALFRED, LORD
 Becket. London: Macmillan, 1885. Pp. [i-vi], [1]-213.
 Becket.
 See Irving, Henry (arr.).

 Cup, The. In *Cup and The Falcon,* London: Macmillan, 1884, pp. [i], [1]-85.

 Devil and the Lady, The. New York: Macmillan, 1930. Pp. [i]-[xii], 1-68.

 Falcon, The. In *Cup and The Falcon,* London: Macmillan, 1884, pp. [i], [87]-146. *Filed under* Cup and The Falcon.

Foresters, The; or, Robin Hood and Maid Marian. N.p.: N.pub. (priv.), 1892. Pp. [1]-58. Augustin Daly Prompt Book.

Foresters, The; or, Robin Hood and Maid Marian. New York: Macmillan, 1892. Pp. [i-vi], [1]-155.

Harold. Boston: James R. Osgood, 1877. Pp. [1]-170.

Princess, The.
See under title.

Promise of May, The. In *Locksley Hall Sixty Years After,* London: Macmillan, 1886, pp. [i], [47]-201.

Queen Mary. London: Henry S. King, 1875. Pp. [iii]-viii, [1]-278.

Ring, The. In *Demeter and Other Poems,* London: Macmillan, 1889, pp. [i], [48]-84.

TEREZA TOMKINS
See Moncrieff, William Thomas.

TERM DAY
See Houston, Thomas.

TERMAGANT, THE
See Parker, Louis Napoleon.

TERRIBLE REVENGE, A
See Harvey, Frank.

TERRIBLE SECRET, A
See Coyne, Joseph Stirling.

TERRIBLE TINKER!, A
See Williams, Thomas John.

TERRY, DANIEL
Antiquary, The.
See Pocock, Isaac.
Barber of Seville, The.
See Fawcett, John.
Faustus.
See Soane, George.
Guy Mannering; or, The Gipsey's Prophecy. London: John Miller, 1816. Pp. [i-iv], [1]-70. 2nd ed.
Guy Mannering; or, The Gipsey's Prophecy! In *New English Drama,* ed. W. Oxberry, 22 vols., London: W. Simpkin & R. Marshall; C. Chapple, 1820, XII, [1-4], [i]-[iv], [1]-[64]. *Filed under* Oxberry, William Henry. New English Drama, XII.
Guy Mannering; or, The Gypsey's Prophecy. In *Waverley Dramas,* London: George Routledge, 1845, pp. [i], [1]-60. *Filed under* Waverley Dramas (anon.).
Guy Mannering; or, The Gipsy's Prophecy. In *British Drama,* 12 vols., London: John Dicks, 1864, I, [292]-309.
Heart of Mid-Lothian, The. Music by Bishop, Henry. London: William Stockdale, 1819. Pp. [i-iv], [1]-66.
Heart of Mid-Lothian, The. In *Waverley Dramas,* London: George Routledge, 1845, pp. [1]-66. *Filed under* Waverley Dramas (anon.).

TEST OF GUILT, THE
See Strutt, Joseph.

TEST OF TRUTH, THE
See Suter, William E.

TEUTON AGAINST PARIS
See Buchanan, Robert Williams. Drama of Kings.

THACKERAY, J. J.
See Thackeray, Thomas James.

THACKERAY, THOMAS JAMES
Barber Baron, The; or, The Frankfort Lottery. London: Thomas Richardson, n.d. Pp. [1]-36.
Executioner, The; or, Vanrick of Voorn. London: Thomas Richardson, n.d. Pp. [i]-vii, 8-44.
Force of Nature, The. London: John Miller, 1834. Pp. [1]-44.
Gustavus of Sweden; or, The Masked Ball. London: R. Wilkes, 1833. Pp. [i-ii], [1]-35. [Acting National Drama, I].
Mountain Sylph, The. By J. J. Thackeray. Music by Barnett, John. London: Boosey, n.d. Pp. [i-iv], 1-219. New ed., rev. Vocal score.
My Wife, or My Place.
See Shannon, Charles.

THACKERAY, WILLIAM MAKEPEACE
Reading a Poem. London: Chiswick Press (printer) (priv.), 1891. Pp. [i]-[xii], [1]-66. Sette of Odd Volumes, 27.

THAD; OR, LINKED BY LOVE
See Meritt, Paul. Linked by Love.

THALABA THE DESTROYER
See Fitzball, Edward.

THANATOS ATHANATOU
See Meredith, Owen.

THAT AFFAIR AT FINCHLEY
See Coyne, Joseph Stirling.

THAT BLESSED BABY
See Moore, J. George.

THAT DREADFUL DOCTOR!
See Young, Charles Lawrence, Sir.

THAT ODIOUS CAPTAIN CUTTER!
See Simpson, John Palgrave.

THAT RASCAL PAT
See Grover, John Holmes.

THEBAID, THE
See Boswell, Robert Bruce (trans.).

THEBAN TWINS
See Spedding, B. J. Ino.

THECLA
See Bliss, Henry.

THELWALL, JOHN
Fairy of the Lake, The. In *Poems,* Hereford: W. H. Parker (printer), 1801, pp. [1-3], [i]-[l], [1]-92, [203]-208.

THEODORA (anon.)
In *New British Theatre,* London: A. J. Valpy (printer), 1814, I, [i], [277]-388.

THEODORA, ACTRESS AND EMPRESS
See Phillips, Watts.

THEODORE THE BRIGAND
See Buckstone, John Baldwin.

THEORY AND PRACTICE
See Benham, Arthur.

THERE HE GOES!
See Barrymore, William. Two Swindlers, The.

THERESA
See Thomas, William Lewis.

THERESA'S VOW
See Gore, Catherine Grace Frances Moody, Mrs. Charles. Maid of Croissey, The.

THÉRÈSE; OR, THE ORPHAN OF GENEVA (anon.).
Music by Reeve, G. London: John Lowndes, n.d. Pp. [i-iv], [1]-32. 10th ed.

THERESE, THE ORPHAN OF GENEVA
See Kerr, John.
See Payne, John Howard.

THERMOPYLAE; OR, REPULSED INVASION (anon.)
In *New British Theatre,* London: A. J. Valpy (printer), 1814, II, [i], [257]-310.

THESEUS AND ARIADNE
See Planché, James Robinson.

THESPIS
See Gilbert, William Schwenck.

THETIS AND PELEUS
See Hale, William Palmer.

THEY'RE BOTH TO BLAME
See Poole, John. Wealthy Widow, The.

THICKE, FRANK E. (arr.)
Remorse. By Coleridge, Samuel Taylor. Fromme: J. Wheeler (printer), 1884. Pp. [1]-55.

THIERNA-NA-OGE
See Planché, James Robinson.

THIEVES OF PARIS, THE
See Stirling, Edward.

THIMBLE RIG!, THE
See Buckstone, John Baldwin.

THIRD TIME, THE
See Dickinson, Charles H.

THIRST OF GOLD
See Robertson, Thomas William. Sea of Ice.

THIRTEEN YEARS' LABOUR LOST
See Bennett, J. M.

THIRTEENTH CHIME, THE
See Barnett, Charles Zachary. Midnight.

THIRTY-NINE THIEVES, IN ACCORDANCE WITH THE
AUTHOR'S HABIT OF TAKING ONE OFF!
    See Byron, Henry James. Ali Baba.
THIRTY, STRAND!
    See Lemon, Mark. P. L., The.
THIRTY THOUSAND
    See Dibdin, Charles Isaac Mungo, jr.
    See Dibdin, Thomas John.
THIRTY-THREE NEXT BIRTHDAY
    See Morton, John Maddison.
THIRTY YEARS OF A GAMESTER'S LIFE
    See Milner, Henry M. Hut of the Red Mountain, The.
THIRTY YEARS OF A RATTLER'S LIFE
    See Cooper, Frederick Fox. Elbow Shakers!, The.
THIS HOUSE TO BE SOLD
    See Coyne, Joseph Stirling.
THOM, ROBERT W.
    Cleon. London: Hamilton, Adams, 1855. Pp. [i-vi], 1-156.
THOMAS, BRANDON
    Colour-Sergeant, The. London & New York: Samuel French, c.1905. Pp. [1]-20. [Lacy's Acting Edition].
    Highland Legacy, A. London & New York: Samuel French, c.1898. Pp. [1]-29.
    Lancashire Sailor, The. New York & London: Samuel French, c.1898. Pp. [i-ii], [1]-26. [Lacy's Acting Edition].
    Queen of Brilliants, The. Music by Jakobowski, Edward. London: J. Miles (printer), n.d. Pp. [i]-iv, [5]-31. Libretto.
THOMAS, CHARLES
    Breaking the Ice. London & New York: Samuel French, n.d. Pp. [1]-14. [Lacy's Acting Edition].
    Lady Fortune. London & New York: Samuel French, n.d. Pp. [1]-27. [Lacy's Acting Edition].
    Paper Chase, The. London: Samuel Lacy; New York: T. Henry French, n.d. Pp. [1]-60. [Lacy's Acting Edition].
    Patron Saint, A. London: Samuel French; New York: T. Henry French, n.d. Pp. [1]-21. [Lacy's Acting Edition].
    Queen of Hearts, The. Music by Young, Harriet. London & New York: Samuel French, n.d. Pp. [1]-19. [Lacy's Acting Edition]. Libretto.
THOMAS, CHARLES INIGO
    Troubled Waters. Written with Ellis, Walter. London: Court Circular Newspaper Co., n.d. Pp. [1]-108.
THOMAS, JANE PENHORN, MRS. EDWARD
    Merchant's Daughter of Toulon, The. London: Thomas Hailes Lacy, n.d. Pp. [i-x], [1]-75.
THOMAS, LEIGH
    Pirate, The; or, The Wicked Father Who Sold His Daughter and the Don Who Bought Her. London: Stuart Haynes (printer) (priv.), 1871. Pp. [1]-36.
THOMAS, WILLIAM LEWIS
    Theresa; or, The Maid of the Tyrol. London: Alexander Watt, 1843. Pp. [i-vi], [1]-119.
THOMAS, WILLIAM THOMAS
    See Moncrieff, William Thomas (pseud.).
THOMAS À BECKET
    See Brodie-Innes, J. W.
    See Darley, George.
    See de Vere, Aubrey Thomas. St. Thomas of Canterbury.
    See Jerrold, Douglas William.
THOMAS AND SALLY
    See Bickerstaffe, Isaac.
THOMPSON, ALFRED
    Aladdin II; or, An Old Lamp in a New Light. Music by Hervé. Pp. [i-ii], [1]-41. Typescript.
    Bird of Paradise, The. London: Thomas Hailes Lacy, n.d. Pp. [1]-12. [Lacy's Acting Edition].
    Happy Dispatch, The. Music by Ducenozoo. New York: Happy Hours, n.d. Pp. [1]-15. Parlor Plays for Home Performance, 25.
    Harlequin Blackbird; or, The Honey, the Money, and the Dainty Dish. Manchester: Guardian Steam-Printing Works, n.d. Pp. [1]-[46]. Libretto.
    How I Found Crusoe. London: E. Rascol (printer), n.d. Pp. [1]-39.

Linda of Chamouni; or, Not Formosa. London: n.pub., n.d. Pp. [1]-40.
Zampa. Music by Herold. London: Gaiety Theatre, 1870. Pp. [1]-36. Libretto.
THOMPSON, BENJAMIN
    Oberon's Oath; or, The Paladin and the Princess. London: John Miller, 1816. Pp. [1]-41.
THOMPSON, BENJAMIN (trans.)
    Conscience. By Iffland, Augustus William. In *German Theatre*, London: Vernor & Hood, 1805, IV, [165]-244.
    Count Benyowsky; or, The Conspiracy of Kamtschatka. By Kotzebue. In *German Theatre*, London: Vernor & Hood, 1805, II, [183]-300.
    Count Koenigsmark. By Reitzenstein, Charles von. In *German Theatre*, London: Vernor & Hood, 1800, VI, [1], [i-iv], [1]-84.
    Deaf and Dumb; or, The Orphan. By Kotzebue. In *German Theatre*, London: Vernor & Hood, 1805, III, [ii-ii], [1]-60.
    Emilia Galotti. By Lessing, Gotthold Ephraim. In *German Theatre*, London: Vernor & Hood, 1800, VI, [i], [i-iv], [1]-75.
    Ensign, The. By Schroeder, Friedrich Ludwig. In *German Theatre*, London: Vernor & Hood, 1800, VI, [1], [i-iv], [1]-67.
    False Delicacy. By Kotzebue. In *German Theatre*, London: Vernor & Hood, 1805, III, [147]-215.
    Indian Exiles, The. By Kotzebue. In *German Theatre*, London: Vernor & Hood, 1805, III, [61]-146.
    Otto of Wittelsbach; or, The Choleric Count. By Babo, James Marcus. In *German Theatre*, London: Vernor & Hood, 1805, IV, [1]-97.
    Rolla; or, The Virgin of the Sun. By Kotzebue. In *German Theatre*, London: Vernor & Hood, 1805, I, [83]-174.
    Stella. By Goethe. In *German Theatre*, London: Vernor & Hood, 1801, VI, [1], [i-iv], [1]-50.
    Stranger, The. By Kotzebue. In *New English Drama*, ed. W. Oxberry, 22 vols., London: W. Simpkin & R. Marshall; C. Chapple, 1820, XXII, [1-2], [i]-[vi], [1]-62, [i]-ii. *Filed under* Oxberry, William Henry. New English Drama, XXII.
    Stranger, The. By Kotzebue. London: John Cumberland, 1826. Pp. [1]-60. Cumberland's British Theatre, XIV. *Filed under* Cumberland, John. Cumberland's British Theatre, XIV.
    Stranger, The. By Kotzebue. In *British Drama*, 12 vols., London: John Dicks, 1864, I, [257]-274.
    Stranger, The. By Kotzebue. In *Dramatic Entertainments at Windsor Castle*, ed. Benjamin Webster, London: Mitchell, n.d., pp. [190]-251. *Filed under* Webster, Benjamin Nottingham. Dramatic Entertainments.
THOMPSON, C. PELHAM
    Dumb Savoyard and His Monkey, The. London & New York: Samuel French, n.d. Pp. [1]-18. [Lacy's Acting Edition].
    Jack Robinson and His Monkey! London: John Duncombe, n.d. Pp. [1]-24. Duncombe's Edition.
    King's Command, The. London: John Duncombe, n.d. Pp. [1]-26. Duncombe's Edition.
    Nothing Superfluous. London: John Duncombe, n.d. Pp. [1]-22. Duncombe's Acting Edition of the British Theatre, 33.
    Rokeby; or, The Buccaneer's Revenge. Dublin: W. H. Tyrell (printer), 1814. Pp. [1]-47.
    Shade, The; or, Blood for Blood. London: John Duncombe, n.d. Pp. [1]-28. Duncombe's Edition.
    Zameo.
    See Byron, Medora Gordon.
THOMPSON, CHARLES
    Gambler's Fate, The; or, A Lapse of Twenty Years. London: John Cumberland, 1828. Pp. [1]-52. Cumberland's British Theatre, XVII. *Filed under* Cumberland, John. Cumberland's British Theatre, XVII.
    Gambler's Fate, The; or, A Lapse of Twenty Years. London: John Cumberland, n.d. Pp. [1]-52.

THREE WIVES OF MADRID, THE
 See Peake, Richard Brinsley.
THRICE MARRIED
 See Paul, Howard.
THRILLBY
 See Muskerry, William.
THROUGH FIRE AND WATER
 See Gordon, Walter.
THROUGH MY HEART FIRST!
 See Campbell, J. M.
THROUGH THE FIRE
 See Lestocq, William.
THROWN TOGETHER
 See Greet, Dora Victoire, Mrs.
THUMPING LEGACY, A
 See Morton, John Maddison.
THURLOW, EDWARD HOVELL, LORD,
 Ariadne. London: Longman, Hurst, Rees, Orme, & Brown, 1814. Pp. [iii]-viii, [1]-58.
TIBBERT, J. W. (trans.)
 Prophète, Le. Music by Meyerbeer. London: T. Brettell, n.d. Pp. [1]-100. Libretto.
TIBERIUS
 See Adams, Francis William Lauderdale.
 See Hughes, George Charles.
TIBERIUS IN CAPREAE
 See Cumberland, Richard.
TICKET-OF-LEAVE, A
 See Phillips, Watts.
TICKET-OF-LEAVE MAN, THE
 See Taylor, Tom.
TICKET-OF-LEAVE MAN'S WIFE, THE
 See Cheltnam, Charles Smith. May Brierly.
 See Cheltnam, Charles Smith.
TICKLISH TIMES
 See Morton, John Maddison. Three Cuckoos, The.
 See Morton, John Maddison.
TIDE OF TIME, THE
 See Bernard, William Bayle.
TIGER AT LARGE, THE
 See Blink, George.
TIGER CROSSED IN LOVE!
 See Craven, Henry Thornton. Fellow Servants.
TIGER HUNTER OF THE PRAIRIES
 See Suter, William E. Pirates of the Savannah, The.
TIGER OF THE SEA!
 See Haines, John Thomas. Rattlin the Reefer.
TILBURY, WILLIAM HARRIES
 Counter Attraction; or, Strolling and Strategem. London: Thomas Hailes Lacy, n.d. Pp. [1]-21. [Lacy's Acting Edition].
 German Jew, The; or, The Forest of Remival. London: John Duncombe, n.d. Pp. [1]-48. Duncombe's Edition.
TILL THE HALF-HOUR
 See Heathcote, Arthur M.
TILSTON, THOMAS
 Edwy and Elgiva. London: Edward Moxon, 1865. Pp. [i]-[viii], [1]-113.
TIME AND THE HOUR
 See Simpson, John Palgrave.
TIME AND TIDE: A TALE OF THE THAMES!
 See Leslie, Henry.
TIME IS MONEY
 See Bell, Florence Eveleen Eleanore Oliffe, Mrs. Hugh (Lady).
TIME TRIES ALL
 See Courtney, John.
TIME WILL TELL
 See Gardner, Herbert.
TIME WORKS WONDERS
 See Jerrold, Douglas William.
TIME'S A TELL-TALE
 See Siddons, Henry.
TIME'S REVENGES
 See Courtney, William Leonard. Gaston Bonnier.

TIMES, THE
 See Daly, John.
 See Pinero, Arthur Wing.
TIMOLEON
 See Jameson, Robert Francis.
 See Lloyd, Charles (trans.).
TIMON OF ATHENS
 See Lamb, George (arr.).
 See Shakspeare, William.
TIMOTHY TO THE RESCUE
 See Byron, Henry James.
TIMOUR, THE CREAM OF ALL THE TARTARS
 See A'Beckett, Gilbert Abbott.
TIMOUR THE TARTAR
 See Lewis, Matthew Gregory.
 See Oxenford, John.
TIMSON'S LITTLE HOLIDAY
 See Nicholls, Harry.
TINSEL QUEEN, THE
 See Morton, W. E.
TINSLEY, LILY
 Cinders. London & New York: Samuel French, c.1899. Pp. [1]-20. [Lacy's Acting Edition].
TIPPERARY LEGACY, THE
 See Coyne, Joseph Stirling.
TIPSY GIPSY AND THE PIPSY WIPSY
 See Gilbert, William Schwenck. Merry Zingara, The.
'TIS SHE!
 See Wilks, Thomas Egerton.
TIT FOR TAT
 See Talfourd, Francis.
TITLE
 See Pemberton, Thomas Edgar.
TITLE DEEDS, THE
 See Peake, Richard Brinsley.
TITMARSH, BELGRAVE (pseud. of Moyse, Charles Ebenezer)
 Shakspere's Skull and Falstaff's Nose. London: Elliot Stock, 1889. Pp. [3]-80.
TITUS AND LYSANDER (anon.)
 London: Elliot Stock, 1900. Pp., [i-iv], [1]-125.
TO LET, FURNISHED
 See Burnand, Francis Cowley.
TO MARRY OR NOT TO MARRY?
 See Raymond, Richard John. Balance of Comfort, The.
TO OBLIGE BENSON
 See Taylor, Tom.
TO PARENTS AND GUARDIANS: AT JUBILEE HOUSE ESTABLISHMENT, CLAPHAM, YOUNG GENTLEMEN ARE, &C
 See Taylor, Tom.
TO PARIS AND BACK, FOR FIVE POUNDS
 See Morton, John Maddison.
TOBACCONIST, THE
 See Gentleman, Francis.
TOBIAS
 See Farnie, Henry Brougham.
TOBIN, JOHN
 Curfew, The. New York: D. Longworth, 1807. Pp. [1]-54.
 Curfew, The. London: Richard Phillips, 1807. Pp. [i]-[x], [1]-[64]. 3rd ed.
 Curfew, The. In *British Drama*, 12 vols., London: John Dicks, 1865, IV, [1135]-1150.
 Faro Table, The; or, The Guardians. London: John Murray, 1816. Pp. [i-vi], [1]-[56].
 Fisherman, The. In *Memoirs of John Tobin*, London: Longman, Hurst Rees, Orme, & Brown, 1820, pp. [365]-444. *Filed under* Collected Works.
 Honey Moon, The. Philadelphia: E. Bronson, 1805. Pp. [2]-[87]. Title page lacking.
 Honey Moon, The. London: Longman, Hurst, Rees, & Orme, 1805. Pp. [5]-[82]. New ed.
 Honey Moon, The. London: John Cumberland, 1826. Pp. [1]-63. Cumberland's British Theatre, XIII. *Filed under* Cumberland, John. Cumberland's British Theatre, XIII.

Honeymoon, The. In *British Drama*, 12 vols., London: John Dicks, 1864, II, [368]-384.

Indians, The. In *Memoirs of John Tobin*, London: Longman, Hurst Rees, Orme & Brown, 1820, pp. [229]-298. *Filed under* Collected Works.

School for Authors, The. London: Longman, Hurst, Rees, & Orme, 1808. Pp. [1]-45.

Tragedy, The (fragment). In *Memoirs of John Tobin*, London: Longman, Hurst, Rees, Orme, & Brown, 1820, pp. [i], [187]-228. *Filed under* Collected Works.

Yours or Mine. In *Memoirs of John Tobin*, London: Longman, Hurst Rees, Orme, & Brown, 1820, pp. [299]-363. *Filed under* Collected Works.

TOBIN, JOHN (trans.)

Gypsey of Madrid, The. *Also:* La Gitanilla de Madrid. By Solis y Ribadeneyra, Antonio de. In *Memoirs of John Tobin*, London: Longman, Hurst, Rees, Orme, & Brown, 1820, pp. [171]-185. Synopsis. *Filed under* Collected Works.

TOBIT'S DOG!, THE
See Moncrieff, William Thomas.

TOCHERED MAIDEN OF THE GLEN, THE
See Hetherington, William Maxwell.

TODHUNTER, JOHN

Alcestis. London: C. Kegan Paul, 1879. Pp. [i-viii], [1]-131.

Black Cat, The. London: Henry, 1895. Pp. [i]-[xvi], [1]-97.

Helena in Troas. London: Kegan Paul, Trench, 1886. Pp. [i-ii], [1]-84.

How Dreams Come True. London: Bemrose & Sons (printer) (priv.), n.d. Pp. [i-vi], [1]-46. Sette of Odd Volumes, 20.

Rienzi, Tribune of Rome. London: Kegan Paul, Trench, 1881. Pp. [i]-[x], [1]-122. *Filed under* True Tragedy of Rienzi.

Sicilian Idyll, A. London: Elkin Mathews, 1890. Pp. [i-vi], [1]-39.

TOFT, P. (trans.)

Out of the Frying Pan.
See Graves, Alfred Percival (arr.).

TOM AND JERRY
See Moncrieff, William Thomas.

TOM AND JERRY AT BRIXTON
See Fitzball, Edward. Tread Mill, The.

TOM AND JERRY IN FRANCE
See Macfarren, George.

TOM AND JERRY ON A VISIT
See Brougham, John. Life in New York.

TOM AND JERRY'S FUNERAL
See Greenwood, Thomas Longdon. Death of Life in London, The.

TOM BOWLING
See Campbell, Andrew Leonard Voullaire.

TOM COBB
See Gilbert, William Schwenck.

TOM CRINGLE
See Fitzball, Edward.

TOM MOORE OF FLEET STREET, THE SILVER TROUT, AND THE SEVEN SISTERS OF TOTTENHAM
See Greenwood, Thomas Longdon. Old Izaak Walton.

TOM NODDY'S SECRET
See Bayly, Thomas Haynes.

TOM PINCH
See Dilley, Joseph J.

TOM SMART, THE ADVENTURER!
See Craven, Henry Thornton.

TOM THRASHER
See Harris, Augustus Glossop.

TOM THUMB
See Fielding, Henry.
See O'Hara, Kane (arr.).

TOM THUMB THE GREAT
See Blanchard, Edward Litt Leman.

TOM TILLER AND JACK MIZEN
See Rogers, William.

TOM TOM, THE PIPER'S SON, AND MARY MARY, QUITE CONTRARY
See Akhurst, William M.

TOMKINS THE TROUBADOUR (anon.)
London: Thomas Hailes Lacy, n.d. Pp. [1]-22. [Lacy's Acting Edition].

TOMLINE, F. LATOUR
See Gilbert, William Schwenck.

TOMLINS, FREDERICK GUEST

Garcia; or, The Noble Error. London: C. Mitchell, 1849. Pp. [1]-54.

TOMMY
See Jerome, Jerome Klapka.

TOMMY AND JERRY T'OTHER SIDE THE WATER
See Macfarren, George. Tom and Jerry in France.

TOO AGREEABLE BY HALF
See Danvers, Henry. Fascinating Individual, A.

TOO ATTENTIVE BY HALF
See Morton, John Maddison. Betsy Baker!

TOO HAPPY BY HALF
See Field, Julian.

TOO LATE FOR DINNER
See Jones, Richard.

TOO LATE TO SAVE
See Palmer, T. A.

TOO MANY COOKS
See Kenney, James.

TOO MUCH OF A GOOD THING!
See Harris, Augustus Glossop.

TOO MUCH THE WAY OF THE WORLD
See Herbert, Thomas.

TOODLES, THE
See Burton, William Evans.

TOOTH-ACHE; OR, THE PRINCE AND THE CHIMNEY-SWEEPER (anon.)
London: Thomas Hailes Lacy, n.d. Pp. [1]-15. Lacy's Acting Edition, 55.

TOPSAIL SHEET BLOCKS
See Townsend, William Thompson.

TOPSY-TURVY HOTEL, THE
See Sturgess, Arthur.

TOPSYTURVYDOM
See Gilbert, William Schwenck.

TORQUATO TASSO
See Herbert, M. A. (trans.).

TORR, A. C. (pseud. of Leslie, Frederick)

Cinder-Ellen Up Too Late. Written with Vincent, William Thomas. Music by Lutz, Meyer. Cape Town: Argus, 1893. Pp. [i-ii], [1]-18. Libretto. *Filed under* Vincent, William Thomas.

Ruy Blas and the Blasé Roué. Written with Clark, H. F. Music by Lutz, Meyer. London: E. Ascherberg, n.d. Pp. [1]-111. 9th ed. Vocal score. *Filed under* Leslie, Frederick.

TORRENDAL
See Cumberland, Richard.

TORRID ZONE, THE
See Clarke, Stephen.

TORY MEMBER'S AWL BROUGHT TO HIS LAST, A
See Sands, John Sim.

TOUCH AND TAKE; OR, SATURDAY NIGHT AND MONDAY MORNING (anon.)
Philadelphia: W. Turner, n.d. Pp. [1]-30. Turner's American Stage.

TOUCH AT THE TIMES, A
See Jameson, Robert Francis.
See Maclaren, Archibald.

TOUCH'EM, TIMOTHY
See Beck, Thomas.

TOUCHSTONE, THE
See Kenney, James.

TOULMIN, CAMILLA DUFOUR
See Crosland, Camilla Dufour Toulmin, Mrs. Newton.

TOURIST'S TICKET, A
See Williams, Thomas John.

TOWER OF BABEL, THE
　　See Austin, Alfred.
TOWER OF LOCHLAIN, THE
　　See Jerrold, Douglas William.
TOWER OF LONDON, THE
　　See Higgie, Thomas Henry.
　　See Somerset, Charles A.
　　See Taylor, Thomas Proclus.
TOWER OF LONDON IN 1553
　　See Lucas, William James. Traitor's Gate.
TOWER OF NESLE, THE
　　See Almar, George.
　　See Milner, Henry M.
TOWERS, EDWARD
　　All for Money. 91 leaves. Partly paginated. Manuscript.
　　Chained to Sin; or, Brought up to Beg. 72 leaves. Partly paginated. Manuscript.
　　Demon Doctor, The. London: International Typewriting Office, n.d. Pp. [i-ii], [1]-10, [i-ii], [1]-19, [i], [1]-9, [1]-8, [1]-6. Pagination by act and scene. Typescript. *Filed under* Towers, Edward J.
　　Harlequin King Pee-Wit and His Merry Little Men!; or, Red Beard the Terrible and the Enchanted Fairies of the Crystal Grotto. London: E. J. Bath (printer), n.d. Pp. [i-ii], [1]-24. Libretto.
TOWLER, JOHN (trans.)
　　Bride of Messina, The. By Schiller. Carlsruhe: A. Bielefeld, 1850. Pp. [i-ii], [1]-119.
　　Don Carlos, Infante of Spain. By Schiller. Carlsruhe: Francis Noldeke, 1843. Pp. [i-iv], [1]-[268].
TOWN AND COUNTRY
　　See Morton, Thomas, sr.
TOWN OF TITIPU
　　See Gilbert, William Schwenck. Mikado, The.
TOWNLEY, CHARLES
　　Mohawk Minstrels' Nigger Dramas, Dialogues, and Drolleries, The. London: Francis, Day, & Hunter, n.d. Pp. [i]-[viii], [9]-101.
TOWNLEY, JAMES, REV.
　　High Life below Stairs. London: Whittingham & Arliss, 1814. Pp. [1]-32. London Theatre, V. *Filed under* Dibdin, Thomas John, ed. London Theatre, V.
　　High Life below Stairs. In *New English Drama*, ed. W. Oxberry, 22 vols., London: W. Simpkin & R. Marshall; C. Chapple, 1822, XV, [i]-[viii], [1]-27. *Filed under* Oxberry, William Henry. New English Drama, XV.
　　High Life below Stairs. London: John Cumberland, 1826. Pp. [1]-36. Cumberland's British Theatre, XIII. *Filed under* Cumberland, John. Cumberland's British Theatre, XIII.
　　High Life below Stairs. In *British Drama*, 12 vols., London: John Dicks, 1871, V, [257]-267.
TOWNSEND, THOMPSON
　　See Townsend, William Thompson.
TOWNSEND, WILLIAM THOMPSON
　　Bell Ringer of St. Paul's, The; or, The Huntsman and the Spy! London: John Duncombe, n.d. Pp. [1]-30. Duncombe's Edition.
　　Blow in the Dark, The. London & New York: Samuel French, n.d. Pp. [1]-14. [Lacy's Acting Edition].
　　Cricket on the Hearth, The. London: Thomas Hailes Lacy, n.d. Pp. [1]-24. [Lacy's Acting Edition, 649]. Promptbook.
　　Gold Fiend, The; or, The Demon Gamester. London & New York: Samuel French, n.d. Pp. [3]-34. French's Acting Edition (late Lacy's).
　　John Stafford; or, The Murder at the Black Farm. London: John Duncombe, 1834. Pp. [1]-52. Duncombe's Acting Edition of the British Theatre, 172.
　　Lost Ship, The; or, The Man of War's Man and the Privateer. London: S. G. Fairbrother, 1852. Pp. [3]-35. Promptbook.
　　Man of War and the Merchantman, The; or, Scenes in Both Services. London: J. Pattie, n.d. Pp. [1]-53.

Mary's Dream; or, Far, Far at Sea! London: John Duncombe, n.d. Pp. [1]-35. Duncombe's Edition.
Mutineer's Widow, The. London: Pattie, n.d. Pp. [2]-43.
Old Adam; or, A Father's Dream. London: Thomas Hailes Lacy, n.d. Pp. [1]-36.
Post Captain, The; or, Wife, Husband, and Friend. London: James Pattie n.d. Pp. [3]-53. Pattie's Penny Play or Weekly Acting Drama, 45.
Temptation; or, The Fatal Brand. London: Thomas Hailes Lacy, n.d. Pp. [3]-37. Title page lacking. Promptbook.
Topsail Sheet Blocks; or, The Gunner and the Foundling. London: J. Pattie, n.d. Pp. [1]-40. [Pattie's Modern Stage, 58].
Whitefriars. London: John Duncombe, n.d. Pp. [3]-44. [New British Theatre (late Duncombe's), 390].
TRACK IN THE SNOW
　　See Suter, William E. Holly Bush Hall.
TRADE
　　See Morton, John Maddison.
TRADE IN THE WEST
　　See Smith, Horatio. First Impressions.
TRADESMAN'S BALL, THE
　　See A'Beckett, Gilbert Abbott.
TRADESMAN'S SON, THE
　　See Shepherd, R.
TRAGEDY
　　See Barber, James.
　　See Fawcett, Charles S.
　　See Tobin, John.
TRAGEDY FOR WARM WEATHER
　　See Tailors, The.
TRAGEDY OF COUNT ALARCOS, THE
　　See Disraeli, Benjamin.
TRAGEDY REHEARSED
　　See Sheridan, Richard Brinsley. Critic, The.
TRAGIC MARY, THE
　　See Field, Michael.
TRAIL OF SIN, THE
　　See Leslie, Henry.
TRAIL OF THE SERPENT
　　See Charlton, Frank. On the Dark Road.
TRAITOR'S GATE
　　See Lucas, William James.
TRAITS OF ANTIENT SUPERSTITION
　　See Strutt, Joseph. Test of Guilt, The.
TRAMP'S ADVENTURE
　　See Phillips, Frederick Laurence.
TRANCES OF NOURJAHAD
　　See Arnold, Samuel James. Illusion.
TRANSFORMATION
　　See Allingham, John Till.
TRANSGRESSION
　　See Alderson, William L.
TRANSLATED ESCUTCHEON
　　See Landor, Robert Eyres. Ferryman, The.
TRANSMOGRIFICATIONS
　　See Ebsworth, Joseph. Crockery's Misfortunes.
TRAPPING A TARTAR
　　See Stirling, Edward.
TRAVELLER'S ROOM!, THE
　　See Fitzball, Edward.
TRAVELLERS, THE
　　See Cherry, Andrew.
TRAVELLERS BENIGHTED
　　See Lewis, Matthew Gregory. Raymond and Agnes.
TRAVELLING COMPANIONS, THE
　　See Anstey, F.
TRAVERS, WILLIAM
　　Kathleen Mavourneen; or, St. Patrick's Eve. New York: T. H. French; London: Samuel French, n.d. Pp. [1]-32. French's Standard Drama.
　　Sisters of Sorrow, The. 21 leaves. Prologue only. Manuscript.
　　Spare the Rod and Spoil the Child. Pp. [1]-48. Act III only. Manuscript.

TRAVIATA, LA
    See Reece, Robert.
TREAD MILL, THE
    See Fitzball, Edward.
TREASURE, THE
    See Bell, Ernest (trans.).
TREASURERS, THE
    See Cooke, John.
TREATY OF LIMERICK
    See Boucicault, Dionysius Lardner. Rapparee, The.
TREE, HERBERT BEERBOHM
    Six and Eightpence. New York & London: Samuel French, c.1900. Pp. [i-ii], [1]-13. [French's Acting Edition].
TREE, HERBERT BEERBOHM (arr.)
    Julius Caesar. By Shakespeare, William. London: Nassau Press, 1898. Pp. [1]-108.
TREE OF HEALTH
    See Dibdin, Thomas John. Zuma.
TREE OF KNOWLEDGE, THE
    See Carton, R. C.
TRELAWNY OF THE WELLS
    See Pinero, Arthur Wing.
TREMAYNE, W. A.
    Dagger and the Cross, The. Pp. [i-iii], 1-26, [i-ii], [1]-28, [i-ii], [1]-23, [i], [1]-15, [i], 1-15. Pagination by act. Typescript promptbook.
TREVANION
    See Marston, John Westland.
TREVELYAN, GEORGE OTTO
    Cambridge Dionysia, The. In *Ladies in Parliament and Other Pieces,* new ed., London: George Bell, 1888, pp. [i], [59]-75.
    Dawk Bungalow, The; or, Is His Appointment Pucka? In *Ladies in Parliament and Other Pieces,* new ed., London: George Bell, 1888, pp. [i], [77]-119.
    Horace at the University of Athens. Cambridge: Jonathan Palmer, 1867. Pp. [1]-68. 3rd ed.
    Ladies in Parliament, The. In *Ladies in Parliament and Other Pieces,* new ed., London: George Bell, 1888, pp. [i], [1]-27.
TRIAL BY BATTLE
    See Barrymore, William.
TRIAL BY FIRE
    See Drinkwater, Albert E.
TRIAL BY JURY
    See Gilbert, William Schwenck.
    See Hook, Theodore Edward.
TRIAL OF DR. ABSTINENCE, ALIAS STEADFAST TEETOTALISM, ESQ., TEMPERANCE ADVOCATE
    See Featherstone, Thomas.
TRIAL OF DUTY
    See Landor, Edward Wilson. Carmelite Friar, The.
TRIAL OF HONOUR
    See Landor, Edward Wilson. Two Earls, The.
TRIAL OF JOHN BARLEYCORN REVERSED
    See Featherstone, Thomas. Trial of Dr. Abstinence, alias Steadfast Teetotalism, Esq.,
TRIAL OF SIR TIMOTHY TRAFFIC, ALIAS DANIEL DEATHSPIRIT, FOR HIGH CRIMES AND MIS-DEMEANOURS AGAINST THE PEOPLE
    See Featherstone, Thomas.
TRIAL OF SUITS AT THE BREWSTER SESSIONS OF SOTVILLE
    See Featherstone, Thomas.
TRIALS AND TROUBLES OF AN ASPIRING PUBLICAN, THE (anon.)
    Leeds: John Kershaw, n.d. Pp. [i-ii], [1]-24.
TRIALS OF A FOND PAPA!
    See Buckingham, Leicester Silk. Virginius.
TRIALS OF POVERTY
    See Stirling, Edward. Love Gift, The.
TRIALS OF THE HEART
    See Harris, Augustus Glossop. Avalanche, The.
TRIALS OF TOMPKINS!, THE
    See Williams, Thomas John.

TRIBULATION
    See Poole, John.
TRICK FOR TRICK; OR, THE ADMIRAL'S DAUGHTER (anon.)
    London: John Miller, 1812. Pp. [1]-40.
TRICKS OF THE TIME
    See Wynne, John.
TRICKS UPON TRAVELLERS
    See Brassington, Richard, jr.
    See Burges, James Bland.
TRIFLES LIGHT AS AIR!
    See Rodwell, James Thomas Gooderham.
TRIP TO BENGAL, A
    See Smith, Charles.
TRIP TO BOTH CITIES
    See Moncrieff, William Thomas. Paris and London.
TRIP TO EXMOUTH
    See Parry, John. High Notions.
TRIP TO KISSENGEN, A
    See Taylor, Tom.
TRIP TO NODLAND
    See Fitzgerald, Shafto Justin Adair. Pretty Princess and the Prickly Pear, The.
TRIP TO PARIS
    See Abrahams, Henry. Alderman's Gown, The.
TRIP TO SCARBOROUGH, A
    See Sheridan, Richard Brinsley.
TRIP TO THE JUBILEE
    See Farquhar, George. Constant Couple, The.
TRIP TO WALES, A
    See Parry, John.
TRISTAN AND ISOLDA
    See Corder, Henrietta Louisa Walford, Mrs. Frederick (trans.).
TRISTAN AND ISOLDE
    See Forman, Alfred (trans.).
    See Jameson, Frederick (trans.).
TRISTAN AND YSOLDE
    See Jackson, John P. (trans.).
TRISTAN UND ISOLDE
    See Corder, Henrietta Louisa Walford, Mrs. Frederick (trans.). Tristan and Isolda.
TRISTRAM, WILLIAM OUTRAM
    Packet from England, A. N.p.: n.pub., n.d. Pp. [1]-32. Title page imperfect.
TRIUMPH OF LOYALTY, THE
    See Coleridge, Samuel Taylor.
TRIUMPH OF LUCCA, THE
    See Landon, Letitia Elizabeth.
TRIUMPH OF PATIENCE
    See Wade, Thomas. Woman's Love.
TRIUMPH OF PREJUDICE
    See Mérimée, Prosper. Ines Mendo, Part 2.
TRIUMPH OF THE BRITISH FLAG
    See Scott, Alfred. Affghans' Captive, The.
TRIUMPH OF THE GREEKS
    See Somerset, Charles A. Zelina.
TRIUMPH OF THE PHILISTINES, THE
    See Jones, Henry Arthur.
TRIUMPHS OF THE SONS OF BELIAL, THE
    See Beck, Thomas.
TROJAN DAMES, THE
    See Potter, Robert (trans.).
TROMB-AL-CA-ZAR
    See Stephenson, Charles H.
TROTT'S TROUBLES
    See Walton, Fred.
TROTTER, THOMAS
    Noble Foundling, The; or, The Hermit of the Tweed. London: Longman, Hurst, Rees, Orme, & Brown, 1812. Pp. [iii]-[viii], [9]-126.
TROUBADOUR, THE
    See Hueffer, Francis.
    See Suter, William E. Trovatore, Il.

TROUBLED WATERS
  See Thomas, Charles Inigo.
TROUBLESOME TWINS
  See Byron, Henry James. Corsican Bothers, The.
TROUGHTON, ADOLPHUS CHARLES
  All in a Muddle; or, Vandyke Brown. *Also:* Vandyke Brown. By Adolphus Charles Thoughton. Clyde, Ohio: Ames, n.d. Pp. [1]-22. Ames' Series of Standard and Minor Drama, 320.
  Fly and the Web, The. London: Thomas Hailes Lacy, n.d. Pp. [1]-42. [Lacy's Acting Edition].
  Leading Strings. London & New York: Samuel French, n.d. Pp. [1]-50. French's Acting Edition (late Lacy's).
  Living Too Fast; or, A Twelvemonth's Honeymoon. London: Thomas Hailes Lacy, n.d. Pp. [1]-34. [Lacy's Acting Edition].
  Shameful Behaviour! London: Thomas Hailes Lacy, n.d. Pp. [1]-31. [Lacy's Acting Edition].
  Short and Sweet. London: Thomas Hailes Lacy, n.d. Pp. [1]-30. [Lacy's Acting Edition].
  Unlimited Confidence. London: Thomas Hailes Lacy, n.d. Pp. [1]-27.
  Vandyke Brown. *Also:* All in a Muddle; or, Vandyke Brown. London: Thomas Hailes Lacy, n.d. Pp. [1]-27.
  Wooing in Jest and Loving in Earnest. London: Thomas Hailes Lacy, n.d. Pp. [1]-27.
TROUGHTON, RICHARD ZOUCH SEBBON
  Nina Sforza. London: Saunders & Otley, 1840. Pp. [i-vi], [1]-144.
  Nina Sforza. London: Saunders & Otley, 1841. Pp. [i]-[viii], [1]-88. 2nd ed.
TROUTBECK, JOHN, REV. (trans.)
  Étoile du Nord, L'. *See* Chorley, Henry Fothergill (trans.).
  Flying Dutchman, The. Music by Wagner. London & New York: Novello, Ewer, n.d. Pp. [i]-iv, [1]-[229]. Novello's Original Octavo Edition. Vocal score.
  Iphigenia in Tauris. Music by Gluck. London: Novello, n.d. Pp. [i-iv], 1-[139]. Novello's Original Octavo Edition. Vocal score.
  Orpheus. Music by Gluck. London & New York: Novello, Ewer, n.d. Pp. [i-vi], [1]-135. Novello's Original Octavo Edition. Vocal score.
  Preciosa. Music by Weber. London: Novello, Ewer, n.d. Pp. [i]-viii, [1]-[67]. Novello's Original Octavo Edition. Vocal score.
  Seraglio, Il. Music by Mozart. London: Novello, Ewer, n.d. Pp. [i-iv], [1]-[166]. Novello's Original Octavo Edition. Vocal score.
  Taming of the Shrew, The. Music by Goetz, Hermann. London: Augener, n.d. Pp. [i-vi], 2-263. Vocal score.
TROVATORE, IL (anon.)
  Music by Verdi. London & New York: Boosey, n.d. Pp. [i-iv], 1-208. [Royal Edition]. Vocal score.
TROVATORE, IL
  See Jefferys, Charles (trans.). Gipsy's Vengeance, The.
  See Jefferys, Charles (trans.).
  See Maggioni, Manfredo (trans.).
  See Suter, William E.
TRUAND CHIEF!, THE
  See Oxberry, William Henry.
TRUE AS STEEL
  See Reeve, Wybert.
TRUE AT LAST
  See Powell, Thomas.
TRUE COLOURS
  See Hurst, James P.
TRUE FRIENDS
  See Dibdin, Thomas John.
TRUE FRIENDSHIP
  See Bell, Ernest (trans.). Damon.
TRUE RING OF THE GENUINE METAL
  See Byron, Henry James. Gold and Guilt.
TRUE STORY OF ELIZABETH OF HUNGARY
  See Kingsley, Charles. Saint's Tragedy, The.

TRUE TILL DEATH
  See Greene, A. E. Lord Darcy.
TRUE TO THE CORE: A STORY OF THE ARMADA
  See Slous, Angiolo Robson.
TRUE TO THE CORPS!
  See Gilbert, William Schwenck. Vivandière, La.
TRUE TO THE LAST
  See Phillips, Frederick Laurence. Tramp's Adventure.
TRUE UNTO DEATH
  See Knowles, James Sheridan.
TRUEBA Y COSÍO, JOAQUIN TELESFORO DE, DON
  Call Again To-morrow. London: John Duncombe, n.d. Pp. [1]-18. Duncombe's Edition.
  Mr. and Mrs. Pringle. London: John Cumberland, n.d. Pp. [1]-27. Cumberland's British Theatre, XXXI. *Filed under* Cumberland, John. Cumberland's British Theatre, XXXI.
  Mr. and Mrs. Pringle. London: John Cumberland, n.d. Pp. [1]-27.
TRUMPETER OF SACKINGEN, THE
  See Jackson, John P. (trans.).
TRUMPETER'S DAUGHTER, THE
  See Coyne, Joseph Stirling.
TRUMPETER'S WEDDING!, THE
  See Morton, John Maddison.
TRUTH
  See Mathews, Charles James.
TRUTH WILL OUT
  See Dixon, Marion Hepworth.
TRYING IT ON
  See Brough, William.
TUDOR, CATHERINE
  Aunt Minerva. London & New York: Samuel French, c.1899. Pp. [1]-20.
TULLY, JAMES HOWARD
  Blue Beard; or, Hints to the Curious. London: W. W. Barth, n.d. Pp. [1]-22.
TUMBLE DOWN NAP
  See Maclaren, Archibald. Man in the Moon, The.
TUPPER, MARTIN FARQUHAR
  Washington. London: W. F. Millard (printer) (priv.), 1876. Pp. [1]-55.
TURANDOT: THE CHINESE SPHINX
  See Novello, Mary Sabilla Hehl, Mrs. Vincent.
TURANDOT, PRINCESS OF CHINA
  See Gurney, Archer Thompson.
TURF, THE
  See Lemon, Mark.
TURKISH BATH, THE
  See Williams, Montagu Stephen.
TURKISH LOVERS
  See Armstrong, William Henry.
TURKO THE TERRIBLE
  See Brough, William.
TURN AND TURN ABOUT
  See What's in a Name? (anon.)
TURN HIM OUT
  See Williams, Thomas John.
TURN OF THE TIDE, THE
  See Burnand, Francis Cowley.
TURN OUT!
  See Kenney, James.
TURNBULL, MRS. WALTER
  See Bartholomew, Anne Charlotte Fayermann, Mrs. Valentine.
TURNED HEAD, THE
  See A'Beckett, Gilbert Abbott.
TURNED UP
  See Melford, Mark.
TURNER, CHARLES JAMES RIBTON
  Handsome Is That Handsome Does. Guildford: Billing & Sons (printer) (priv.), n.d. Pp. [1]-11. Synopsis.

TURNER, E. S. (trans.)
    Maid of Orleans, The. Written with Turner, F. J. (trans.). By Schiller. In *Maid of Orleans and Other Poems,* London: Smith, Elder, 1842, pp. [i-vi], [1]-208.
TURNER, F. J. (trans.)
    Maid of Orleans, The.
      See Turner, E. S. (trans.).
TURNER, JOHN FOX
    See Lane, Pyngle (pseud.).
TURNING THE TABLES
    See Poole, John.
TURNPIKE GATE, THE
    See Knight, Thomas.
TURPIN'S RIDE TO YORK
    See Milner, Henry M.
TUSCAN ORPHAN
    See Ainslie, Whitelaw, Dr. Clemenza.
TUTOR'S ASSISTANT!, THE
    See Selby, Charles.
'TWAS IN TRAFALGAR SQUARE
    See Pleon, Harry. Black-Eyed Susan.
TWEDDELL, EDWARD WASHINGTON
    Napoleon's Barber. London: J. W. Thomas (printer), n.d. Pp. [1]-44.
TWEDDELL, H. MADDISON
    Aguilhar. London: T. & J. Allman (priv.), 1820. Pp. [i]-[viii], [1]-88.
TWEEDIE'S RIGHTS
    See Albery, James.
TWEEDLETON'S TAIL-COAT
    See Williams, Thomas John.
TWELFTH NIGHT
    See Calvert, Charles Alexander (arr.).
    See Irving, Henry (arr.).
    See Kemble, John Philip (arr.).
    See Shakespeare, William.
TWELVE LABOURS OF HERCULES, THE
    See Brough, Robert Barnabas.
TWELVE MONTHS SINCE
    See Wills, William Henry. Larboard Fin, The.
TWELVE PRECISELY!
    See Milner, Henry M.
TWELVEMONTH'S HONEYMOON
    See Troughton, Adolphus Charles. Living Too Fast.
TWENTY AND FORTY (anon.)
    New York: Harold Roorbach, n.d. Pp. [i]-iv, [5]-28.
TWENTY MINUTES UNDER AN UMBRELLA
    See Dubourg, Augustus W.
TWENTY MINUTES WITH A TIGER (anon.)
    Also: Taming a Tiger. London: Thomas Hailes Lacy, n.d. Pp. [1]-24.
TWENTY MINUTES WITH A TIGER
    See Taming a Tiger (anon.).
TWENTY-ONE
    See Wild, James.
21! 22! 23!
    See Love à la Militaire.
TWENTY PER CENT.
    See Dibdin, Thomas John.
£20 A YEAR—ALL FOUND
    See Byron, Henry James.
TWENTY-THREE, JOHN STREET, ADELPHI
    See Buckstone, John Baldwin. John Street, Adelphi.
23, JOHN STREET, ADELPHI
    See Buckstone, John Baldwin. John Stree, Adelphi.
TWENTY YEARS AGO!
    See Pocock, Isaac.
TWICE KILLED
    See Oxenford, John.
TWICE TOLD TALE, A
    See Wooler, John Pratt.
TWILIGHT
    See Swears, Herbert.
TWILIGHT OF THE GODS, THE
    See Rankin, Reginald (trans.).

TWIN SISTERS
    See Buckstone, John Baldwin. Open House.
TWINS
    See Derrick, Joseph.
    See Grattan, H. P.
TWINS OF WARSAW, THE
    See Somerset, Charles A.
TWISS, HORACE
    Carib Chief, The. London: Longman, Hurst, Rees, Orme, & Brown, 1819. Pp. [i-x], [1]-[80].
'TWIXT AXE AND CROWN
    See Taylor, Tom.
TWO B'HOYS, THE
    See Dance, Charles.
TWO BLINDS, THE
    See Clements, Arthur.
TWO BONNYCASTLES, THE
    See Morton, John Maddison.
TWO BUMPKINS
    See Morton, John Maddison. Margery Daw.
TWO BUZZARDS, THE
    See Morton, John Maddison.
TWO CHILDREN OF ISRAEL
    See Hazlewood, Colin Henry. Stolen Jewess, The.
TWO DAYS AT THE HALL
    See Dance, Charles. Country Squire, The.
TWO DAYS OF THE REVOLUTION!
    See Bernard, William Bayle. Robespierre.
TWO DROVERS, THE
    See Goff, Henry.
TWO EARLS, THE
    See Landor, Edward Wilson.
TWO EYES BETWEEN TWO
    See Jerrold, Douglas William.
TWO FACES UNDER A HOOD
    See Dibdin, Thomas John.
TWO FIGAROS, THE
    See Planché, James Robinson.
2, 5, 3, 8
    See Hoare, Prince. Prize, The.
TWO FLATS AND A SHARP
    See Maltby, C. Alfred.
TWO FOSCARI, THE
    See Byron, George Gordon, Lord.
TWO FRIENDS, THE
    See H., C.
    See Lacy, Michael Rophino.
TWO GALLEY SLAVES, THE
    See Payne, John Howard.
TWO GAY DECEIVERS
    See Robertson, Thomas William.
TWO GENTLEMEN AT MIVART'S
    See Simpson, John Palgrave.
TWO GENTLEMEN IN A FIX
    See Suter, William E.
TWO GENTLEMEN OF VERONA, THE
    See Kemble, John Philip (arr.).
    See Shakespeare, William.
TWO GEORGES, THE
    See Davis, Lillie.
TWO GREENS, THE
    See Rede, William Leman.
TWO GREGORIES, THE
    See Dibdin, Thomas John.
TWO GUARDIANS, THE
    See Edgeworth, Maria.
TWO HEADS ARE BETTER THAN ONE
    See Horne, F. Lennox.
TWO HEADS BETTER THAN ONE
    See Mildenhall, Thomas.
TWO HEARTS
    See Fitzgerald, Shafto Justin Adair.
TWO HIGH ROADS OF LIFE
    See Moulds, Arthur. Village Bane, The.

TWO HOUSES UNDER ONE ROOF
See Lunn, Joseph. Roses and Thorns.
TWO IN THE MORNING
See Gore, Catherine Grace Frances Moody, Mrs. Charles. Good Night's Rest, A.
See Mathews, Charles James. Bachelor's Bedroom, The.
See Mathews, Charles James.
TWO JOLLY BACHELORS
See Martin-Seymour, Edward.
TWO LIVES OF MARY LEIGH
See Boucicault, Dionysius Lardner. Hunted Down.
TWO LONDON 'PRENTICES
See Morton, John Maddison. Harlequin Hogarth.
TWO LOVERS OF HEAVEN, THE: CHRYSANTHUS AND DARIA
See MacCarthy, Denis Florence (trans.).
TWO LOVES AND A LIFE
See Taylor, Tom.
TWO LOVES FOR ONE HEART
See Suter, William E. Life's Revenge, A.
TWO MAKE A PAIR, THE
See Raymond, Richard John.
TWO MARRIAGES, THE
See Barlow, George.
TWO MISERS, THE
See O'Hara, Kane.
TWO MISSES IBBETSON, THE
See Cassilis, Ina Leon.
TWO OLD MAIDS OF FLORENCE, THE (anon.)
London: T. & R. Hughes, 1808. Pp. [1]-36.
TWO ORPHANS, THE
See Oxenford, John.
TWO PAGES OF FREDERICK THE GREAT, THE
See Poole, John.
TWO PHOTOGRAPHS
See Clements, Arthur.
TWO POLTS, THE
See Courtney, John.
TWO PRETTY PRINCES AND THE THREE FAIRY GIFTS
See Soutar, Richard. Harlequin and the White Cat! and the Magic Sapphire.
TWO PRISONERS OF LYONS, THE
See Ebsworth, Joseph.
TWO PRO'S., THE
See Bowyer, Frederick.
TWO PUDDIFOOTS, THE
See Morton, John Maddison.
TWO QUEENS, THE
See Buckstone, John Baldwin.
TWO RIVALS AND THE SMALL BOAR
See Burnand, Francis Cowley. Venus and Adonis.
TWO ROSES
See Albery, James.
TWO SISTERS, THE (anon.)
In *Home Plays for Ladies,* Part 9, London & New York: Samuel French, n.d., pp. [43]-67. *Filed under* Home Plays for Ladies, Part 9.
TWO STAGES FROM GRETNA
See Haworth, R. Disguises.
TWO STRINGS TO YOUR BOW
See Jephson, Robert.
TWO SWINDLERS, THE
See Barrymore, William.
TWO T. J'S., THE
See Becher, Martin. In the Wrong House.
See Becher, Martin.
TWO THORNS, THE
See Albery, James. Coquettes.
See Albery, James.
TWO TO ONE
See Clements, Arthur.
TWO VIOLETTAS
See Reynolds, Frederick. Don John.
TWO WIVES
See Parry, John.

'TWOULD PUZZLE A CONJUROR
See Poole, John.
TYNAN, KATHARINE
See Hinkson, Katharine Tynan, Mrs. Henry Albert.
TYPE OF THE OLD ONE
See Printer's Devil, The.
TYRANNY OF TEARS, THE
See Chambers, Charles Haddon.
TYRANT! THE SLAVE! THE VICTIM! AND THE TAR!, THE (anon.)
London: Thomas Hailes Lacy, n.d. Pp. [1]-10.
UGLY CUSTOMER, AN
See Williams, Thomas John.
UGLY MUG AND THE COUPLE OF SPOONS
See Burnand, Francis Cowley. Guy Fawkes.
UGOLINO
See Booth, Junius Brutus.
UGONE
See Armstrong, George Francis.
UGONOTTI, GLI
See Maggioni, Manfredo (trans.).
See Romer, Frank (trans.).
ULRICA
See Stirling, Edward. Prisoner of State.
ULYSSES
See Burnand, Francis Cowley.
UNCLE
See Byron, Henry James.
See Jameson, Anna Brownell Murphy, Mrs. Robert (trans.).
UNCLE CELESTIN
See Lyster, Frederic.
UNCLE CROTCHET
See Phillips, Mrs. Alfred.
UNCLE DICK'S DARLING
See Byron, Henry James.
UNCLE JOHN
See Buckstone, John Baldwin.
UNCLE OLIVER
See Haines, John Thomas.
UNCLE RIP
See Peake, Richard Brinsley.
UNCLE SAM
See Poole, John. Nabob for an Hour, A.
See Poole, John.
UNCLE TOM'S CABIN
See Hermann, Charles.
See Lemon, Mark. Slave Life.
UNCLE TOO MANY, AN
See Thomson, James.
UNCLE ZACHARY
See Oxenford, John.
UNCLE'S WILL
See Berard, Peter.
See Smith, Spencer Theyre.
UNCLES AND AUNTS
See Lestocq, William.
UNDECIDED VOTER, THE
See Bottone, Nino.
UNDER A VEIL
See Roberts, Randal Howland.
UNDER FALSE COLOURS
See de Pass, E. A.
UNDER THE EARTH
See Nation, William Hamilton Codrington.
UNDER THE RED ROBE
See Rose, Edward.
UNDER THE ROSE
See Dibdin, Thomas John.
See Roberts, George.
UNDER THE THUMB
See Murray, Frank.
UNDINE
See Soane, George.

UNEQUAL MATCH, AN
See Taylor, Tom.
UNFINISHED GENTLEMAN, THE
See Selby, Charles.
UNFORTUNATE LONDON APPRENTICE
See Corri, Montague. Georgy Barnwell.
UNFORTUNATE MISS BAILEY
See A'Beckett, Gilbert Abbott.
UNHAPPY MARRIAGE
See Otway, Thomas. Orphan, The.
UNHISTORICAL PASTORAL, AN
See Davidson, John.
UNINFORMED GIRL, THE (anon. trans.)
By Amalie (Amelia), Princess of Saxony. In *Six Dramas Illustrative of German Life,* London: John W. Parker, pp. [i]-viii, [1]-57. *Filed under* Six Dramas (anon.).
UNION, THE; OR, LOVE AND PROJECTION (anon.)
London: J. Lowndes, n.d. Pp. [1]-14.
UNIVERSAL BANDITTO
See Caitiff of Corsica, The.
UNJUST STEWARD
See Houston, Thomas. Term Day.
UNKNOWN LOVER, THE
See Gosse, Edmund William.
UNLIMITED CONFIDENCE
See Troughton, Adolphus Charles.
UNLUCKY FRIDAY
See Craven, Henry Thornton.
UNMASKED
See Merton, Clifford.
UNPROTECTED FEMALE
See Coyne, Joseph Stirling. Scene in the Life of an Unprotected Female, A.
UNPUBLISHED MS., AN
See Bell, Florence Eveleen Eleanore Oliffe, Mrs. Hugh (Lady).
UNREHEARSED EFFECT, AN
See Sprigge, J. Squire.
UNRIVALLED BLONDIN
See Bolton, Charles. Caught in a Line.
UNSEEN HELMSMAN, THE
See Alma-Tadema, Laurence.
UNWELCOME VISITORS
See Poole, John. Tribulation.
UP A TREE!
See Williams, Thomas John.
UP ALL NIGHT
See Arnold, Samuel James.
UP AT THE HILLS
See Taylor, Tom.
UP FOR THE CATTLE SHOW
See Lemon, Harry.
UP IN THE WORLD
See Sketchley, Arthur.
See Worthington, J.
UP THE RIVER
See Farnie, Henry Brougham.
UP TO TOWN
See Dibdin, Thomas John.
UP TO TOWN AND BACK AGAIN
See Rayner, Barnabas F.
UPPER CLASSES, THE
See Willmer, Frederick.
UPS AND DOWNS OF LIFE, THE
See Maclaren, Archibald.
UPSTAIRS AND DOWNSTAIRS
See Brough, William.
UPTURNED FACES OF THE ROSES
See Chambers, Charles Haddon.
URANIA
See Spencer, William Robert.
URGENT PRIVATE AFFAIRS
See Coyne, Joseph Stirling.
USED UP
See Mathews, Charles James.

USURPER, THE
See Bunn, Alfred. Conrad.
See Delap, John.
UTOPIA LIMITED
See Gilbert, William Schwenck.
UTTER PER-VERSION OF THE BRIGAND, AN
See A'Beckett, Gilbert Arthur.
VACCINATION
See Knowles, James Sheridan.
VAGRANT, HIS WIFE AND FAMILY, THE
See Webb, Charles.
VALENTINE!, A
See Brough, William.
VALENTINE AND ORSON
See Burnand, Francis Cowley.
See Dibdin, Thomas John.
See Harlequin King Pepin (anon.).
See Smith, Albert Richard.
VALENTINE AND ORSON, HYS BROTHER (anon.)
Glasgow: City Steam Printing Works (printer), n.d. Pp. [1]-16. Title page lacking. Libretto.
VALENTINE'S DAY; OR, THE AMOROUS KNIGHT AND THE BELLE WIDOW (anon.)
London: Vernor, Hood, & Sharpe; Taylor & Hessey (priv.), n.d. Pp. [i]-[xx], [21]-[125].
VALENTINE'S DAY
See Buckstone, John Baldwin.
VALET DE SHAM, THE
See Selby, Charles.
VALIANT HAYS
See Galloway, George. Battle of Luncarty, The.
VALKYRIE, THE
See Corder, Henrietta Louisa Walford, Mrs. Frederick (trans.).
See Rankin, Reginald (trans.).
VALLENTINE, BENJAMIN BENNATON
Fadette. Music by Maillart; Mattei, Tito. New York: Charles D. Koppel, n.d. Pp. [1]-47. Libretto.
VALLEY OF DIAMONDS, THE
See Dibdin, Thomas John.
See Younge, Henry. Sinbad the Sailor.
VALNAY, E.
Jean Buscaille.
See Hayes, Maria Ximena (trans.).
VALOUR OF THE SOUL
See Horne, Richard Hengist. John the Baptist.
VALPY, RICHARD (arr.)
King Henry the Fourth, Part 2. By Shakespeare, William. Reading: Smart & Cowslade (printer), 1801. Pp. [i-x], [1]-[98].
King John. By Shakespeare, William. Reading: Smart & Cowslade (printer), 1800. Pp. [i-x], [1]-[85].
Merchant of Venice, The. By Shakespeare, William. Reading: Smart & Cowslade (printer), 1802. Pp. [i-viii], [1]-[85].
VALSHA
See Coyne, Joseph Stirling.
VALUE OF TRUTH, THE (anon.)
In *Home Plays for Ladies,* Part 7, London & New York: Samuel French, n.d., pp. [44]-66. *Filed under* Home Plays for Ladies, Part 7.
VAMBA
See Luigi (pseud.).
VAMPIRE, THE
See Moncrieff, William Thomas.
See Planché, James Robinson.
See Stephens, George.
VAMPIRE BRIDE, THE
See Blink, George.
VANBRUGH, JOHN
Confederacy, The. London: Whittingham & Arliss, 1815. Pp. [1]-[84]. London Theatre, XV. *Filed under* Dibdin, Thomas John, ed. London Theatre, XV.
Confederacy, The. In *New English Drama,* ed. W. Oxberry, 22 vols., London: W. Simpkin & R. Marshall; C. Chapple,

1821, XII, [i]-[viii], [9]-[82]. *Filed under* Oxberry, William Henry. New English Drama, XII.

Confederacy, The. In *British Drama,* 12 vols., London: John Dicks, 1872, XI, [161]-184.

Lovers' Quarrels.
See under title.
See King, Thomas (arr.).

Provoked Husband, The; or, A Journey to London. Written with Cibber, Colley. London: Whittingham & Arliss, 1815. Pp. [1]-88. London Theatre, III. *Filed under* Dibdin, Thomas John, ed. London Theatre, III.

Provoked Husband, The; or, A Journey to London. Written with Cibber, Colley. In *New English Drama,* ed. W. Oxberry, 22 vols., London: W. Simpkin & R. Marshall; C. Chapple, 1819, V, [1-2], [i]-[x], [1]-79. *Filed under* Oxberry, William Henry. New English Drama, V.

Provoked Husband, The. Written with Cibber, Colley. London: T. Dolby, 1823. Pp. [i]-viii, [7]-82. Dolby's British Theatre, III. *Filed under* Cumberland, John. Cumberland's British Theatre, III.

Provoked Husband, The. Written with Cibber, Colley. In *British Drama,* 12 vols., London: John Dicks, 1864, II, [511]-532.

Provoked Wife, The. In *British Drama,* 12 vols., London: John Dicks, 1865, IV, [1087]-1108.

VANDERDECKEN
See Taylor, Thomas Proclus.

VAN DIEMEN'S LAND
See Moncrieff, William Thomas.

VANDYCK
See Richards, Alfred Bate.

VANDYKE BROWN
See Troughton, Adolphus Charles. All in a Muddle.
See Troughton, Adolphus Charles.

VANE, SUTTON
For England. *Also:* Humanity. New York: Rosenfeld Stenography & Typewriting, n.d. Pp. [i-iii], [1]-23, [i-ii], [1]-22, [i-ii], [1]-24, [i-ii], [23]-[38]. Pagination by act, with irregularities. Typescript.

Humanity.
See For England.

VAN LAUN, HENRI (trans.)
Amphitryon. By Molière. In *Dramatic Works of Molière,* Edinburgh: William Paterson, 1876, IV, [228]-331. *Filed under* Collected Works.

Blunderer, The; or, The Counterplots. By Molière. *Also:* L'Étourdi; ou, Les Contre-Temps. In *Dramatic Works of Molière,* Edinburgh: William Paterson, 1875, I, [1-6], [i]-[xxxvi], [i]-103. *Filed under* Collected Works.

Bores, The. By Molière. *Also:* Les Fâcheux. In *Dramatic Works of Molière,* Edinburgh: William Paterson, 1875, II, [83]-136. *Filed under* Collected Works.

Citizen Who Apes the Nobleman, The. By Molière. *Also:* Le Bourgeois Gentilhomme. In *Dramatic Works of Molière,* Edinburgh: William Paterson, 1876, V, [253]-357. *Filed under* Collected Works.

Comic Pastoral, A. By Molière. *Also:* Pastorale Comique. In *Dramatic Works of Molière,* Edinburgh: William Paterson, 1876, IV, [31]-43. *Filed under* Collected Works.

Countess of Escarbagnas, The. By Molière. *Also:* La Comtesse d'Escarbagnas. In *Dramatic Works of Molière,* Edinburgh: William Paterson, 1876, VI, [89]-[121]. *Filed under* Collected Works.

Don Garcia of Navarre; or, The Jealous Prince. By Molière. *Also:* Don Garcie de Navarre; ou, Le Prince Jaloux. In *Dramatic Works of Molière,* Edinburgh: William Paterson, 1875, I, [317]-388. *Filed under* Collected Works.

Don Juan; or, The Feast with the Statue. By Molière. *Also:* Don Juan; ou, Le Festin de Pierre. In *Dramatic Works of Molière,* Edinburgh: William Paterson, 1876, III, [89]-188. *Filed under* Collected Works.

Flying Doctor, The. By Molière. *Also:* Le Médecin Volant. In *Dramatic Works of Molière,* Edinburgh: William Paterson, 1876, VI, [381]-402. *Filed under* Collected Works.

Forced Marriage, The. By Molière. *Also:* Le Mariage Forcé. In *Dramatic Works of Molière,* Edinburgh: William Paterson, 1875, II, [325]-389. *Filed under* Collected Works.

George Dandin; or, The Abashed Husband. By Molière. *Also:* George Dandin; ou, Le Mari Confondu. In *Dramatic Works of Molière,* Edinburgh: William Paterson, 1876, IV, [333]-411. *Filed under* Collected Works.

Imaginary Invalid, The. By Molière. *Also:* Le Malade Imaginaire. In *Dramatic Works of Molière,* Edinburgh: William Paterson, 1876, VI, [219]-358. *Filed under* Collected Works.

Impromptu of Versailles, The. By Molière. *Also:* L'Impromptu de Versailles. In *Dramatic Works of Molière,* Edinburgh: William Paterson, 1875, II, [285]-324. *Filed under* Collected Works.

Jealousy of le Barbouillé, The. By Molière. *Also:* La Jalousie du Barbouillé. In *Dramatic Works of Molière,* Edinburgh: William Paterson, 1876, VI, [359]-380. *Filed under* Collected Works.

Learned Ladies, The. By Molière. *Also:* Les Femmes Savantes. In *Dramatic Works of Molière,* Edinburgh: William Paterson, 1876, VI, [122]-217. *Filed under* Collected Works.

Love Is the Best Doctor. By Molière. *Also:* L'Amour Médecin. In *Dramatic Works of Molière,* Edinburgh: William Paterson, 1876, III, [189]-260. *Filed under* Collected Works.

Love Tiff, The. By Molière. *Also:* Le Dépit Amoureux. In *Dramatic Works of Molière,* Edinburgh: William Paterson, 1875, I, [105]-207. *Filed under* Collected Works.

Magnificent Lovers, The. By Molière. *Also:* Les Amants Magnifiques. In *Dramatic Works of Molière,* Edinburgh: William Paterson, 1876, V, [191]-251. *Filed under* Collected Works.

Mélicerte. By Molière. In *Dramatic Works of Molière,* Edinburgh: William Paterson, 1876, IV, [i-vi], [1]-29. *Filed under* Collected Works.

Misanthrope, The. By Molière. *Also:* Le Misanthrope. In *Dramatic Works of Molière,* Edinburgh: William Paterson, 1876, III, [261]-378. *Filed under* Collected Works.

Miser, The. By Molière. *Also:* L'Avare. In *Dramatic Works of Molière,* Edinburgh: William Paterson, 1876, V, [i-vi], [1]-106. *Filed under* Collected Works.

Monsieur de Pourceaugnac. By Molière. In *Dramatic Works of Molière,* Edinburgh: William Paterson, 1876, V, [107]-189. *Filed under* Collected Works.

Physician in Spite of Himself, The. By Molière. *Also:* Le Médecin Malgré Lui. In *Dramatic Works of Molière,* Edinburgh: William Paterson, 1876, III, [379]-474. *Filed under* Collected Works.

Pretentious Young Ladies, The. By Molière. *Also:* Les Précieuses Ridicules. In *Dramatic Works of Molière,* Edinburgh: William Paterson, 1875, I, [209]-266. *Filed under* Collected Works.

Princess of Elis, The. By Molière. *Also:* La Princesse d'Élide. In *Dramatic Works of Molière,* Edinburgh: William Paterson, 1876, III, [i-vi], [1]-88. *Filed under* Collected Works.

Psyche. By Molière. *Also:* Psyché. In *Dramatic Works of Molière,* Edinburgh: William Paterson, 1876, V, [359]-435. *Filed under* Collected Works.

Rogueries of Scapin, The. By Molière. *Also:* Les Fourberies de Scapin. In *Dramatic Works of Molière,* Edinburgh: William Paterson, 1876, VI, [i-vi], [1]-87. *Filed under* Collected Works.

School for Husbands, The. By Molière. *Also:* L'École des Maris. In *Dramatic Works of Molière,* Edinburgh: William Paterson, 1875, II, [i-vi], [1]-81. *Filed under* Collected Works.

School for Wives, The. By Molière. *Also:* L'École des Femmes. In *Dramatic Works of Molière,* Edinburgh: William Paterson, 1875, II, [137]-234. *Filed under* Collected Works.

School for Wives Criticised, The. By Molière. *Also:* La Critique de L'École des Femmes. In *Dramatic Works of Molière*, Edinburgh: William Paterson, 1875, II, [235]-283. *Filed under* Collected Works.

Sganarelle; or, The Self-Deceived Husband. By Molière. *Also:* Sganarelle; ou, Le Cocu Imaginaire. In *Dramatic Works of Molière*, Edinburgh: William Paterson, 1875, I, [267]-316. *Filed under* Collected Works.

Sicilian, The; or, Love Makes the Painter. By Molière. *Also:* Le Sicilien; ou, L'Amour Peintre. In *Dramatic Works of Molière*, Edinburgh: William Paterson, 1876, IV, [44]-94. *Filed under* Collected Works.

Tartuffe; or, The Hypocrite. By Molière. *Also:* Tartuffe; ou, L'Imposteur. In *Dramatic Works of Molière*, Edinburgh: William Paterson, 1876, IV, [95]-227. *Filed under* Collected Works.

VANQUISHED!
See Dutch, J. S.

VANRICK OF VOORN
See Thackeray, Thomas James. Executioner, The.

VARANGIAN, THE
See Pennie, John Fitzgerald.

VARTIE, JOHN
Jephtha. London: Sampson Low; C. & J. Ollier, 1820. Pp. [iii]-[xx], [1]-51.

VASCELLO FANTASMA
See Pittman, Josiah (trans.). Flying Dutchman, The.

VASCO (anon.)
London: Longmans, Green, 1868. Pp. [i]-[x], [1]-[109].

VASCO DE BALBOA
See C., D.

VASHTI
See Zeto.

VASSALL, HENRY RICHARD
See Fox, Henry Richard.

VAUGHAN, ?, MRS.
Grecians, The. London: (priv.), 1824. Pp. [3]-[8], [1]-56.

VAUGHAN, VIRGINIA
New Era, The. London: Chapman & Hall, 1880. Pp. [i]-[xvi], [1]-238.

VEILED LADY
See Fitzball, Edward. Diadeste.

VEILED PROPHET, THE
See Squire, William Barclay.

VELLÈRE, EDWARD RAPHAEL WELLER, DR.
King and Rebel. London & New York: Samuel French, n.d. Pp. [1]-72. [Lacy's Acting Edition].

VELVET AND RAGS
See Conquest, George.

VENETIAN, THE
See Reynoldson, Thomas Herbert.

VENETIAN OUTLAW, THE
See Elliston, Robert William.
See Powell, James.

VENICE PRESERVED
See Kemble, John Philip (arr.).
See Otway, Thomas.

VENONI
See Lewis, Matthew Gregory.

VENUS AND ADONIS
See Burnand, Francis Cowley.
See Planché, James Robinson. Paphian Bower, The.

VENUS IN ARMS
See Wilson, Margaret Harries, Mrs. Cornwell Baron.

VERA
See Wilde, Oscar Fingall O'Flahertie Wills.

VERDON, THOMAS KIRWAN
Suicide, The. Dublin: Shaw (printer), 1824. Pp. [1]-90.

VERGER, THE
See Frith, Walter.

VERHAEREN, ÉMILE
Dawn, The.
See Symons, Arthur (trans.).

VERICOUR, RAYMOND DE (trans.)
Gladiator of Ravenna, The. By Halm, Friedrich. London: James Blackwood, 1859. Pp. [i]-[xii], [9]-145.

VERNIER, ISABELLA
Barber and the Bravo, The; or, The Princess with the Raven Locks. London: John Duncombe, n.d. Pp. [1]-22. Duncombe's Edition.

VERNON, LEICESTER VINEY, CAPT.
Lancers, The. London & New York: Samuel French, n.d. Pp. [1]-47. French's Standard Drama, 361.

VERNOY DE SAINT-GEORGES, JULES HENRI
Enchantress, The.
See Bunn, Alfred.

VERRAL, CHARLES
Saladin; or, The Order of Knighthood. In *Poems . . .*, London: Clio Rickman, n.d., pp. [135]-259.
Servius Tullius. In *Poems . . .*, London: Clio Rickman, n.d., pp. [1-2], [i]-[xiv], [1]-133.

VERRALL, ARTHUR WOOLGAR (trans.)
Birds, The. By Aristophanes. Music by Parry, C. Hubert H. London: Stanley Lucas, Weber, 1885. Pp. [i]-iv, [i]-[v], 1-77. Vocal score. *Filed under* Verral, A. W.

VERY CIVIL CASE
See Wallace, John, jr. Pendrudge v. Prettiwon.

VERY LAST DAYS OF POMPEII!, THE
See Reece, Robert.

VERY LATEST EDITION OF THE LADY OF LYONS, THE
See Byron, Henry James.

VERY LITTLE FAUST AND MORE MEPHISTOPHELES
See Burnand, Francis Cowley.

VERY NEW EDITION OF ACIS AND GALATAEA, A
See Plowman, Thomas F.

VERY PLEASANT EVENING, A
See Suter, William E.

VERY SERIOUS AFFAIR, A
See Harris, Augustus Glossop.

VERY SUSPICIOUS!
See Simpson, John Palgrave.

VERY WONDERFUL LAMP!
See Keating, Eliza H. Aladdin.

VESPERS OF PALERMO, THE
See Hemans, Felicia Dorothea Browne, Mrs. Alfred.

VESTRIS, ARMAND
Anacreon; or, L'Amour Fugitif. Music by Mortellari. London: Brettell (printer), 1810. Pp. [1]-15. Synopsis. *Filed under* Anacreon (anon.).

VETCH, ?, MAJ.
Dara; or, The Minstrel Prince. Edinburgh: James Hogg, 1850. Pp. i-[viii], [9]-[40].
Milton at Rome. Edinburgh: James Hogg, 1851. Pp. [1]-24.

VETERAN, THE
See Knight, Edward P.

VETERAN AND HIS PROGENY!
See Milner, Henry M. 102.

VETERAN OF 102 YEARS
See Milner, Henry M. 102.
See Milner, Henry M.

VETERAN TAR, THE
See Arnold, Samuel James.

VICAR, THE
See Albery, James.

VICAR OF WAKEFIELD, THE
See Coyne, Joseph Stirling.
See Dibdin, Thomas John.
See Taylor, Tom.

VICARS, W. A.
See Bilkins, Taylor (pseud.).
Going It!
See Morton, John Maddison.

VICE VERSA: A LESSON FOR FATHERS
See Rose, Edward.

VICEROY, THE
See Hayley, William.

VICEROY'S WEDDING, THE
 See Bell, Florence Eveleen Eleanore Oliffe, Mrs. Hugh (Lady).
VICISSITUDES OF A SERVANT GIRL
 See Pitt, George Dibdin. Susan Hopley.
VICISSITUDES OF REAL LIFE
 See Stirling, Edward. Margaret Catchpole, the Heroine of Suffolk.
VICTIM, THE
 See Cornwall, Barry.
VICTIM OF ST. VINCENT, THE
 See Serle, Thomas James.
VICTIMS, THE
 See Taylor, Tom.
VICTIMS OF GAMING
 See Milner, Henry M. Hertfordshire Tragedy, The.
VICTOIRE
 See Smythe, Alfred.
VICTOR DUPRES
 See Hayes, Frederick William.
VICTOR VANQUISHED, THE
 See Dance, Charles.
VICTORIAN
 See Anderson, J. F. Reynolds.
VICTORINE
 See Barnett, Charles Zachary.
 See Buckstone, John Baldwin.
 See Falconer, Edmund.
 See Milner, Henry M.
VIDENA
 See Heraud, John Abraham.
VIDOCQ, THE FRENCH POLICE SPY
 See Jerrold, Douglas William.
VIE, LA
 See Farnie, Henry Brougham.
VIEWS IN THE COUNTRY AND VIEWS IN TOWN
 See Campbell, Andrew Leonard Voullaire. Gambler's Life in London, The.
VIKINGS AT HELGELAND, THE
 See Archer, William (trans.).
VILIKENS AND HIS DINAH
 See Bruton, James.
VILLAGE BANE, THE
 See Moulds, Arthur.
VILLAGE BELLES
 See Granville, H. Such.
VILLAGE COQUETTES, THE
 See Dickens, Charles.
VILLAGE DOCTOR, THE
 See Webster, Benjamin Nottingham.
VILLAGE FESTIVAL
 See Knight, Edward P. Chip of the Old Block, A.
VILLAGE FÊTE, THE (anon.)
 London: Lowndes & Hobbs (printer), n.d. Pp. [1]-39. Libretto.
VILLAGE GOSSIP
 See Poole, John. Scan. Mag!
VILLAGE INN AND THE COUNT OUT
 See Byron, Henry James. Allurio and Adelina.
VILLAGE LAWYER, THE
 See Macready, William.
VILLAGE NIGHTINGALE, THE
 See Craven, Henry Thornton.
VILLAGE OUTCAST, THE
 See Taylor, Thomas Proclus.
VILLAGE POLITICS
 See More, Hannah.
VILLAGE PRIDE
 See Stirling, Edward. Jeannette and Jeannot.
VILLAGE RIVALS
 See Fitzball, Edward. Pierette.
VILLAGE SINGERS, THE (anon. trans.)
 Also: Le Cantatrici Villane. Music by Fioravanti, V. London: Her Majesty's Theatre, n.d. Pp. [1]-48. Authorized ed. Libretto. *Filed under* Palomba, Giovanni.

VILLAGE TALE, A
 See Younge, A.
VILLAGE VAUXHALL
 See Moncrieff, William Thomas. How to Take Up a Bill.
VILLAGE VIRTUE
 See Byron, Henry James.
VILLAGERS OF SAN QUINTINO
 See Fitzball, Edward. Scaramuccia.
VILLAIN AND VICTIM
 See Walkes, W. R.
VILLAIN RECLAIMED
 See Maclaren, Archibald. Chance of War, The.
VILLANOUS SQUIRE AND THE VIRTUOUS VILLAGER
 See Byron, Henry James. Rosebud of Stingingnettle Farm, The.
VILLARIO (anon.)
 In *New British Theatre*, London: A. J. Valpy (printer), 1814, II, [i], [137]-[190].
VILLIKINS AND HIS DINAH
 See Burnand, Francis Cowley.
VINCENT, WILLIAM THOMAS
 Cinder-Ellen Up Too Late.
 See Torr, A. C.
VINCENZO, PRINCE OF MANTUA
 See Godmond, Christopher.
VINDICTIVE MAN, THE
 See Holcroft, Thomas.
VINEYARD OF NABOTH, THE (anon. trans.)
 London: S. & R. Bentley (printer) (priv.), 1825. Pp. [1]-36.
VINTAGERS, THE
 See Eyre, Edmund John.
VIOLENT PASSION, A
 See Harley, St. John.
VIOLENZIA
 See Roscoe, William Caldwell.
VIOLET, THE
 See Maddox, Frederick More.
VIOLETTE
 See Worrell, James.
VIRGIN OF THE SUN, THE
 See Reynolds, Frederick.
 See Thompson, Benjamin (trans.). Rolla.
VIRGIN UNMASKED, THE
 See Fielding, Henry.
VIRGIN WIDOW, THE
 See Taylor, Henry.
VIRGINIA
 See Lloyd, Charles (trans.).
 See Plowden, Dorothea Phillips, Mrs. Francis.
 See Stephens, Henry Pottinger.
VIRGINIA AND PAUL
 See Stephens, Henry Pottinger. Virginia.
VIRGINIUS
 See Buckingham, Leicester Silk.
 See Knowles, James Sheridan.
VIRGINIUS THE RUM'UN
 See Rogers, William.
VIRGINIUS TRAVESTIE.
 See Buckingham, Leicester Silk. Virginius.
VIRTU IN CIMENTO
 See Griselda.
VISION OF FINGAL
 See Druid, The.
VISION OF VENUS, A
 See Pleon, Harry.
VISIONS OF THE FUTURE
 See Lemon, Mark. Demon Gift, The.
VISIT FROM FRA-DIAVOLO
 See A'Beckett, Gilbert Abbott. Wanted a Brigand.
VISITATION, THE
 See Hinkson, Katharine Tynan, Mrs. Henry Albert.
VITTORIA CONTARINI: A STORY OF VENICE
 See Dubourg, Augustus W.

VIVANDIÈRE, LA
 See Gilbert, William Schwenck.
VIVANDIÈRE, THE
 See Whyte, George (trans.).
VIVE LA BAGATELLE
 See Macfarren, George. Tom and Jerry in France.
VIVE LEMPRIÈRE
 See Burnand, Francis Cowley. Paris.
VIVIA PERPETUA
 See Adams, Sarah Fuller Flower, Mrs. William Bridges.
VOCES ACADEMICAE
 See Robertson, Charles Grant.
VOICE OF LOVE, THE
 See Besant, Walter.
VOICE OF NATURE, THE
 See Boaden, James.
VOL. III
 See Ellis, Walter.
VOLUNTEER REVIEW, THE
 See Williams, Thomas John.
VOTARY OF WEALTH, THE
 See Holman, Joseph George.
VOTE BY BALLOT (anon.)
 London & New York: Samuel French, n.d. Pp. [1]-59.
VOW OF SILENCE, THE
 See Barnett, Charles Zachary.
VOYAGE, THE
 See Darley, George.
VYSE, BERTIE
 See A'Beckett, Arthur William.
WADDIE, CHARLES
 Dunbar, the King's Advocate. Edinburgh: Waddie, 1893. Pp. [1]-126. 2nd ed.
 Wallace; or, The Field of Stirling Bridge. Edinburgh: William P. Nimmo; London: W. Kent, 1859. Pp. [i-iv], [1]-95.
WADE, THOMAS
 Jew of Arragon, The; or, The Hebrew Queen. London: Smith, Elder, 1830. Pp. [ii]-[xii], [1]-[83].
 Phrenologists, The. London: J. Onwhyn, 1830. Pp. [i-viii], [1]-56.
 Woman's Love; or, The Triumph of Patience. London: Smith, Elder, 1829. Pp. [i]-[xii], [1]-79.
WADE, WILLIAM
 Little Red Riding Hood. Written with Lowry, James M. Music by Chapman, George R. N.p.: n.pub., n.d. Pp. [1-32]. Promptbook libretto.
 Robinson Crusoe. Music by Byng, G. W. Manchester: Emmott (printer), n.d. Pp. [1]-43. Libretto.
WAGER, THE (anon.)
 In [*Dramatic Appellant*], London: T. & R. Hughes, 1808, pp. [105]-151.
WAGNER, RICHARD
 Dusk of the Gods, The.
  See Corder, Henrietta Louisa Walford, Mrs. Frederick (trans.).
  See Forman, Alfred (trans.).
 Flying Dutchman, The.
  See England, Paul (trans.).
  See Jackson, John P. (trans.).
  See Troutbeck, John, Rev. (trans.).
 Gotterdammerung.
  See Dusk of the Gods, The. *See also* Twilight of the Gods, The.
 Lohengrin.
  See Corder, Henrietta Louisa Walford, Mrs. Frederick (trans.).
  See Jackson, John P. (trans.).
  See Macfarren, Natalia (trans.).
  See Oxenford, John (trans.).
 Mastersingers of Nuremberg, The.
  See Corder, Henrietta Louisa Walford, Mrs. Frederick (trans.).
  See Jackson, John P. (trans.).

 Parsifal.
  See Corder, Henrietta Louisa Walford, Mrs. Frederick (trans.).
  See Forman, Alfred (trans.).
  See Gatty, Charles Tindal (trans.).
  See Jackson, John P. (trans.).
 Rhine Gold, The.
  See Corder, Henrietta Louisa Walford, Mrs. Frederick (trans.).
  See Forman, Alfred (trans.).
  See Jackson, John P. (trans.).
  See Rankin, Reginald (trans.).
 Rienzi, the Last of the Tribunes.
  See Pittman, Josiah (trans.).
 Siegfried.
  See Corder, Henrietta Louisa Walford, Mrs. Frederick (trans.).
  See Forman, Alfred (trans.).
  See Rankin, Reginald (trans.).
 Tannhäuser.
  See Jackson, John P. (trans.).
  See Macfarren, Natalia (trans.).
  See Pittman, Josiah (trans.).
 Tristan and Isolde.
  See Corder, Henrietta Louisa Walford, Mrs. Frederick (trans.). Tristan and Isolda.
  See Forman, Alfred (trans.).
  See Jackson, John P. (trans.). Tristan and Ysolde.
  See Jameson, Frederick (trans.).
 Twilight of the Gods, The.
  See Rankin, Reginald (trans.).
 Valkyrie, The.
  See Corder, Henrietta Louisa Walford, Mrs. Frederick (trans.).
  See Forman, Alfred (trans.).
  See Rankin, Reginald (trans.).
WAGS OF WINDSOR
 See Colman, George, jr. Review, The.
WAILING (WHALING) EXPERIENCE OF SALLY SIMPKINS
 See Hood, Thomas, sr. Tail (Tale) of a Shark, The.
WAIT FOR AN ANSWER
 See Lemon, Harry.
WAITER, THE
 See Pleon, Harry.
WAITING FOR AN OMNIBUS IN THE LOWTHER ARCADE ON A RAINY DAY
 See Morton, John Maddison.
WAITING FOR THE TRAIN
 See Fitzgerald, Shafto Justin Adair.
WAITING FOR THE VERDICT
 See Hazlewood, Colin Henry.
WAKE NOT THE DEAD
 See Blink, George. Vampire Bride, The.
WAKELY, CHARLES
 Paul Rabaut.
  See Bennett, John E.
WALDRON, W. RICHARD
 Cartouche, the French Robber. London: Thomas Hailes Lacy, n.d. Pp. [1]-46. [Lacy's Acting Edition].
 Lizzie Leigh; or, The Murder near the Old Mill. London: Thomas Hailes Lacy, n.d. Pp. [1]-42. Promptbook.
 Will and the Way, The; or, The Mysteries of Carrow Abbey. London: Thomas Hailes Lacy, n.d. Pp. [1]-48. [Lacy's Acting Edition].
 Worth a Struggle. London & New York: Samuel French, n.d. Pp. [3]-36. [Lacy's Acting Edition].
WALFORD, HENRIETTA LOUISA
 See Corder, Henrietta Louisa Walford, Mrs. Frederick.
WALK FOR A WAGER!
 See Peake, Richard Brinsley.
WALKER, CHARLES EDWARD
 Caswallon; or, The Briton Chief. Baltimore: J. Robinson, 1829. Pp. [1]-68.

Caswallon; or, The Briton Chief. London: John Miller, n.d. Pp. [i]-[viii], [1]-83.

Fall of Algiers, The. Also attrib. to Payne, John Howard. London: T. Dolby, 1825. Pp. [1]-[48]. Dolby's British Theatre, IX. *Filed under* Cumberland, John. Cumberland's British Theatre, IX.

Fall of Algiers, The. Music by Bishop, Henry R. London: Goulding, D'Almaine, n.d. Pp. [i-ii], 1-130. Vocal score.

Fall of Algiers, The. Music by Bishop, Henry. London: T. Dolby, n.d. Pp. [i-iv], [9]-50. Text complete. Libretto.

Rumfustian Innamorato; or, The Court of Quodlibet. London: John Miller, 1824. Pp. [1]-16.

Sigesmar the Switzer. London: William Ginger, 1818. Pp. [i]-[x], [1]-[43].

Wallace. London: John Miller, 1820. Pp. [1]-74.

Wallace. In *New English Drama*, ed. W. Oxberry, 22 vols., London: W. Simpkin & R. Marshall; C. Chapple, 1823, XVIII, [i-iv], [1]-58, [i]-[iv]. *Filed under* Oxberry, William Henry. New English Drama, XVIII.

Warlock of the Glen, The. London: John Lowndes, 1820. Pp. [i-iv], [1]-23.

WALKER, JOHN

Factory Lad!, The. London: John Duncombe, n.d. Pp. [1]-24. Duncombe's Edition.

Napoleon!; or, The Emperor and the Soldier! [London: John Duncombe], n.d. Pp. [1]-24. Cumberland's British Theatre (with Duncombe's).

Nell Gwynne. London: John Duncombe, n.d. <wrps. Thomas Hailes Lacy>. Pp. [1]-34. Duncombe's Edition <wrps. New British Theatre (late Duncombe's)>.

Wild Boy of Bohemia, The; or, The Force of Nature. London & New York: Samuel French, n.d. Pp. [1]-30. [Lacy's Acting Edition].

Wild Boy of Bohemia, The; or, The Force of Nature. London: W. West, n.d. <wrps. Thomas Hailes Lacy>. Pp. [1]-35. West's Original Juvenile Drama <wrps. Lacy's Acting Edition>.

WALKER, LONDON

See Barrie, James Mathew.

WALKES, W. R.

Gentleman Jim. New York & London: Samuel French, c.1899. Pp. [1]-12. [Lacy's Acting Edition].

Her New Dressmaker. London: Samuel French; New York: T. Henry French, n.d. Pp. [1]-12. [Lacy's Acting Edition].

Pair of Lunatics, A. New York: Dick & Fitzgerald, n.d. Pp. [1]-7.

Rain Clouds. London: Samuel French; New York: T. Henry French, n.d. Pp. [1]-12. [Lacy's Acting Edition].

Show of Hands, A. London & New York: Samuel French, n.d. Pp. [1]-12. [Lacy's Acting Edition].

Villain and Victim. London: Samuel French; New York: T. Henry French, n.d. Pp. [1]-11. [Lacy's Acting Edition].

WALKÜRE

See Corder, Henrietta Louisa Walford, Mrs. Frederick (trans.). Valkyrie, The.

WALKYRIE, THE

See Forman, Alfred (trans.).

WALL, CHARLES HERON (trans.)

Impostures of Scapin, The. By Molière. London: George Bell & Sons, 1898. Pp. [i]-[viii], [279]-326. Bell's Modern Translations.

Misanthrope, The. By Molière. London: George Bell & Sons, 1897. Pp. [i]-viii, [1]-53. Bell's Modern Translations.

WALLACE, ALBANY

Elfrida. Worthing: n.pub. (priv.), 1850. Pp. [i-iv], [1]-102.

WALLACE, JOHN

Caelina; or, A Tale of Mystery. London: J. & T. Carpenter (priv.), 1802. Pp. [i-iv], [1]-25.

Merchant of Guadaloupe, The. London: J. & T. Carpenter, 1802. Pp. [i]-[x], [1]-34.

Simple Simon. Madras, India: n.pub. (priv.), 1805. Pp. [i-ii], [1]-22.

Slanderer, The. London: John Miller, 1823. Pp. [i-x], [1]-35.

WALLACE, JOHN, JR

Abdalla. London: John Miller, 1845. Pp. [1]-20.

Factory Girl, The. Manchester: Abel Heywood & Son, n.d. Pp. [1]-16.

Pendrudge v. Prettiwon; or, A Very Civil Case. London & New York: Samuel French, n.d. Pp. [1]-30. [Lacy's Acting Edition].

WALLACE, WILLIAM

Divine Surrender, The. London: Elliot Stock, 1895. Pp. [i-iv], [1]-77.

WALLACE

See Barrymore, William.

See Buchanan, Robert.

See Waddie, Charles.

See Walker, Charles Edward.

WALLACE THE BRAVE

See Maclaren, Archibald.

WALLACE, THE HERO OF SCOTLAND

See Barrymore, William.

WALLACK, LESTER

Honour before Wealth.

See Edwards, Pierrepont.

Romance of a Poor Young Man, The.

See Edwards, Pierrepont.

WALLENSTEIN

See Coleridge, Samuel Taylor (trans.). Piccolomini.

See Pearson, Edward Stanhope (trans.).

WALLENSTEIN'S CAMP

See Gower, Francis Leveson, Lord (trans.).

See Moir, George (trans.).

WALLIS, ELLEN LANCASTER

See Lancaster-Wallis, Ellen.

WALLOONS, THE

See Cumberland, Richard.

WALPOLE, HENRY

Five in One. London: John Duncombe, n.d. Pp. [1]-20. Duncombe's Edition.

WALPOLE, MRS. REGINALD

See Hobbes, John Oliver.

WALPOLE

See Bulwer (later Bulwer-Lytton), Edward George Earle Lytton, Lord Lytton.

WALTER, WILLIAM JOSEPH (trans.)

Magic Flute, The; or, The Mysteries of Isis. Music by Mozart. *Also:* Il Flauto Magico; or, I Misteri d'Iside. London: W. Glindon (printer), 1819. Pp. [i]-[vi], [1]-111.

WALTER BRAND

See Fitzball, Edward.

WALTER TYRREL

See Fitzball, Edward.

WALTHEOF

See Serle, Thomas James.

WALTON, FRED

Trott's Troubles. New York: Wheat & Cornett, c.1878. Pp. [27]-32. New York Drama, III, 36.

WALTONIAN REMINISCENCES

See Maunder, Samuel.

WALTZ BY ARDITI, A

See Oxenford, John.

WANDERER, THE

See Kemble, Charles.

WANDERING BOYS, THE

See Kerr, John.

WANDERING JEW, THE

See Lander, George.

WANDERING MINSTREL, THE

See Brough, Robert Barnabas. Orpheus and Eurydice.

See Mayhew, Henry.

WANTED A BRIGAND

See A'Beckett, Gilbert Abbott.

WANTED—A WIDOW, WITH IMMEDIATE POSSESSION

See Boucicault, Dionysius Lardner.

WANTED A WIFE

See Moncrieff, William Thomas.

See Stirling, Edward.

WANTED, A YOUNG LADY—
    See Suter, William E.

WANTED AN ERRAND BOY
    See Bruton, James.

WANTED: FIVE POUNDS
    See Poel, William. Absence of Mind.

WANTED, 1000 SPIRITED YOUNG MILLINERS FOR THE GOLD DIGGINGS!
    See Coyne, Joseph Stirling.

WANTS AND SUPERFLUITIES
    See Dibdin, Thomas John. Haroun Alraschid.

WAPPING OLD STAIRS
    See Blake, Thomas G.
    See Faucit, John Savill.
    See Holl, Henry.
    See Robertson, Stuart.

WAR
    See Robertson, Thomas William.

WAR IN CARRIBOO
    See Burnand, Francis Cowley. Military Billy Taylor, The.

WAR, LOVE, AND DUTY
    See Colman, George, jr. Africans, The.

WAR TO THE KNIFE
    See Byron, Henry James.

WAR WHOOP
    See Arnold, Samuel James. Americans, The.

WARBURTON, H.
    Playmates. London & New York: Samuel French, n.d. Pp. [1]-12. [Lacy's Acting Edition].

WARD, CHARLES
    Circassian Bride, The. Music by Bishop, Henry. London: Lowndes & Hobbs, n.d. Pp. [1]-24. Libretto.

WARDE, GEORGE AMBROSE
    Flower of Yarrow, The. London: W. S. Johnson; Maidstone: Hall & Son, 1846. Pp. [1]-107.

WARDEN, GERTRUDE
    Woman's Proper Place.
    See Jones, John Wilton.

WARDOCK KENNILSON
    See Fitzball, Edward.

WARDROBE
    See Fenn, George Manville.

WARDS IN CHANCERY
    See Selby, Charles. Irish Dragoon, The.

WARE, JAMES REDDING
    Bothwell. London: John Dicks, n.d. Pp. [33]-51. Dicks' British Drama, 42.
    In Quarantine. [London: John Dicks], n.d. Pp. [121]-128. [Dicks' British Drama].
    Juggler, The; or, Father and Daughter. London: John Dicks, n.d. Pp. [33]-50. Dicks' British Drama, 113.
    Meadows of St. Gervais, The. London: John Dicks, n.d. Pp. [193]-206. Dicks' British Drama, 47.
    One Snowy Night. London: John Dicks, n.d. Pp. [161]-166. Dicks' British Drama, 46.
    Piperman's Predicaments. [London: John Dicks], n.d. Pp. [187]-192. [Dicks' British Drama].
    Polish Jew, The. [London: John Dicks], n.d. Pp. [306]-316. [Dicks' British Drama].
    Woman Will Be a Woman, A. London: John Dicks, n.d. Pp. [13]-20. Dicks' Standard Charades and Comedies, 490.

WARLOCK OF THE GLEN, THE
    See Walker, Charles Edward.

WARM RECEPTION
    See Hodgson, G. S. Bobby A1.

WARNER, RICHARD
    Bath Characters; or, Sketches from Life. By Peter Paul Pallett (pseud.). London: G. Wilkie & J. Robinson, 1807. Pp. [iii]-[viii], [1]-80.

WARR, GEORGE CHARLES WINTER
    Story of Orestes, The. In *Echoes of Hellas*, London: Marcus Ward, 1887, pp. [1]-63]. Libretto.
    Story of Orestes, The. Music by Goldschmidt, Otto; Lawson, Malcolm; Parratt, Walter; Monk, W. H. In *Echoes of Hellas*, London: Marcus Ward, 1888, pp. [i-iii], 38-66. Text complete. Vocal score.

    Tale of Troy, The. In *Echoes of Hellas*, London: Marcus Ward, 1887, pp. [1-58]. Libretto.
    Tale of Troy, The. Music by Goldschmidt, Otto; Lawson, Malcolm; Parratt, Walter; Monk, W. H. In *Echoes of Hellas*, London: Marcus Ward, 1888, pp. [i-ii], [1]-37. Vocal score.

WARRANTED!
    See Reece, Robert.

WARREN, ERNEST
    Nettle, The. London & New York: Samuel French, n.d. Pp. [1]-15. [Lacy's Acting Edition].

WARREN, JOHN BYRNE LEICESTER, LORD DE TABLEY
    Pandora. In [*Poems, Dramatic and Lyrical*, London: Elkin Mathews & John Lane, 1893], pp. 99-122.

WARREN, T. GIDEON
    Interview, The. London: Samuel French; New York: T. Henry French, n.d. Pp. [1]-16. [Lacy's Acting Edition].
    Nita's First. London: Samuel French; New York: T. Henry French, n.d. Pp. [1]-40. [Lacy's Acting Edition].
    Punctured. London & New York: Samuel French, c.1904. Pp. [1]-12. [Lacy's Acting Edition].

WARRIOR OF THE LONELY GRAVE!
    See Atkyns, Samuel. Witch's Stone, The.

WARTON, FERDINAND FULLARTON
    Albert and Rosalie; or, The Fire King. London: T. & R. Hughes, 1808. Pp. [63]-102.

WAS I TO BLAME?
    See Rodwell, George Herbert Bonaparte.

WASHINGTON
    See Tupper, Martin Farquhar.

WASSERTRAGER
    See Baildon, Arthur. Water Carrier, The.

WASTELL, WILLIAM
    West Wind, A; or, Off for London. London: C. Chappell, 1812. Pp. [1]-48.

WAT TYLER
    See Southey, Robert.

WAT TYLER, M.P.
    See Sala, George Augustus.

WATCH AND WAIT
    See Higgie, Thomas Henry.

WATCH AND WARD
    See Wigan, Alfred Sydney.

WATCH DOG OF THE WALSINGHAMS, THE
    See Simpson, John Palgrave.

WATCH-HOUSE, THE
    See Galt, John.

WATCH-WORD, THE
    See Bell, Robert.

WATCHING THE GAME
    See Ridge, William Pett.

WATER AND FIRE
    See Kerr, John. Drenched and Dried.

WATER BABES, THE
    See Bowles, Edward W.

WATER CARRIER, THE
    See Baildon, Arthur.

WATER NYMPHS' REVOLT
    See Burrows, J. G. Lurline.

WATER PAGEANT
    See Dibdin, Charles Isaac Mungo, jr. Wild Man, The.

WATER PARTY, THE
    See Dance, Charles.

WATER SPIRIT
    See Coyne, Joseph Stirling. Ondine.

WATER SPIRIT AND THE FIRE FIEND
    See Stirling, Edward. Ondine.

WATER WITCHES, THE
    See Coyne, Joseph Stirling.

WATERHOUSE, BENJAMIN
    Annira; or, The Royal Sufferers. Sheffield: H. A. Bacon, 1822. Pp. [i-ii], [1]-[4], [1]-44.

WATERLOO
>   *See* Doyle, Arthur Conan.

WATERLOO IN 1835
>   *See* Jerrold, Douglas William. Gertrude's Cherries.

WATERMAN, THE
>   *See* Dibdin, Charles, sr.

WATERPROOF, THE
>   *See* Bell, Florence Eveleen Eleanore Oliffe, Mrs. Hugh (Lady).

WATERS OF OBLIVION
>   *See* Farley, Charles. Sadak and Kalasrade.
>   *See* Mitford, Mary Russell. Sadak and Kalasrade.

WATKINS, WILLIAM
>   **Fall of Carthage, The.** Whitby: Thomas Webster (printer), 1802. Pp. [i]-viii, [9]-[72].

WATSON, GEORGE
>   **England Preserved.** In *Modern Theatre,* ed. Mrs. Inchbald, 10 vols., London: Longman, Hurst, Rees, Orme, & Brown, 1811, VIII, [309]-362.

WATSON, MALCOLM
>   *See* Watson, T. Malcolm.

WATSON, SAMUEL JAMES
>   **Ravlan.** In [*Legend of the Roses and Ravlan,* Toronto: Hunter & Rose, 1876], pp. [61]-228.

WATSON, T. MALCOLM
>   **By Special Request.** London: Samuel French; New York: T. Henry French, n.d. Pp. [1]-12.
>   **Odd Pair, An.** By Malcolm Watson. Music by Caldicott, Alfred J. N.p.: n.pub., n.d. Pp. [1]-13. Libretto.

WATSON-TAYLOR, GEORGE
>   *See* Taylor, George Watson.

WATTS, SARAH
>   *See* Richardson, Sarah Watts, Mrs. Joseph.

WATTS, WALTER
>   **Dream of Life, A.** London: S. G. Fairbrother; W. Strange, n.d. Pp. [1]-36.
>   **Irish Engagement, An.** London: S. G. Fairbrother; W. Strange, n.d. Pp. [1]-20.
>   **Which Is the King?** London: S. G. Fairbrother; W. Strange, n.d. Pp. [1]-19.

WAVERLEY
>   *See* Calcraft, John William.
>   *See* Fitzball, Edward.

WAVERLY
>   *See* Fitzball, Edward.

WAY OF THE WORLD, THE
>   *See* Congreve, William.
>   *See* Kemble, John Philip (arr.).

WAY TO CONQUER, THE
>   *See* Cornwall, Barry.

WAY TO GET MARRIED, THE
>   *See* Morton, Thomas, sr.

WAY TO KEEP HER, THE
>   *See* Hunt, Violet.

WAY TO KEEP HIM, THE
>   *See* Murphy, Arthur.

WAY TO WIN HER, THE
>   *See* Holford, Margaret, Mrs.

WAY TO WIN HIM
>   *See* Farquhar, George. Inconstant, The.

WAYFARERS
>   *See* Swears, Herbert.

WAYS AND MEANS
>   *See* Colman, George, jr.

WAYS OF LONDON, THE
>   *See* Maclaren, Archibald.

WAYSIDE COTTAGE, THE
>   *See* Poel, William.

WAYSIDE WIOLETS, THE
>   *See* Byron, Henry James.

WE ALL HAVE OUR LITTLE FAULTS
>   *See* Suter, William E.

WE FLY BY NIGHT
>   *See* Colman, George, jr.

WEAK POINTS
>   *See* Buckstone, John Baldwin.

WEAK WOMAN
>   *See* Byron, Henry James.

WEAKER SEX, THE
>   *See* Pinero, Arthur Wing.

WEALTH
>   *See* Jones, Henry Arthur.

WEALTHY WIDOW, THE
>   *See* Poole, John.

WEATHERCOCK, THE
>   *See* Allingham, John Till.

WEATHERING THE ADMIRAL
>   *See* Fraser, Julia Agnes. Barrington's Busby.

WEATHERLY, ALFRED W. MOORE
>   **Champagne.**
>   *See* Weatherly, Frederick Edward.

WEATHERLY, FREDERICK EDWARD
>   **Champagne.** Written with Weatherly, Alfred W. Moore. London & New York: Samuel French, n.d. Pp. [1]-35. [Lacy's Acting Edition].
>   **Mirette.** Written with Greenbank, Harry Hewetson. Music by Messager, André. London: Chappell, c.1894. Pp. [1]-54. Libretto.
>   **Signa.**
>   *See* A'Beckett, Gilbert Arthur.

WEATHERLY, FREDERICK EDWARD (trans.)
>   **King René's Daughter.** By Hertz, Henrik. Bristol: Taylor Bros. (printer) (priv.), 1872. Pp. [1]-74.
>   **Navarraise, La.** Music by Massenet. New York: Fred Rullman, Theatre Ticket Office, c.1895. Pp. [1]-20. Libretto.
>   **Rantzau, I.** Music by Mascagni. London: E. Ascherberg, n.d. Pp. [i-vi], 1-249. Vocal score.

WEAVER OF LYONS!, THE
>   *See* Barber, James.

WEAVERS, THE
>   *See* Morison, Mary (trans.).

WEBB, CHARLES
>   **Belphegor the Mountebank; or, Woman's Constancy.** London & New York: Samuel French, n.d. Pp. [i-ii], [1-6], [5]-54. [Lacy's Acting Edition].
>   **Corsican Brothers, The.** London: Music Publishing Co., n.d. Pp. [1]-41.
>   **Jinks, the Man That Can't Help It!** London: G. S. Cattermole, n.d. Pp. [1]-20.
>   **Lone House on the Bridge of Notre Dame, The.** London: Music Publishing Co., n.d. Pp. [i]-[viii], [9]-54.
>   **Martin Chuzzlewit.** London: W. Barth, n.d. Pp. [i-viii], [5]-60. Barth's Universal Stage or Theatrical Prompt Book, 78.
>   **Vagrant, His Wife and Family, The.** London: James Pattie, n.d. Pp. [1]-29. Pattie's Penny Play or Weekly Acting Drama.

WEBB, CHARLES (trans.)
>   **Azael, the Prodigal.** *Also:* Il Prodigo. *Also:* L'Enfant Prodigue. *Also:* The Prodigal Son. London: G. H. Davidson, n.d. Pp. [1]-36. Libretto.
>   **Prodigal Son, The.**
>   *See* Azael, the Prodigal.

WEBSTER, AUGUSTA DAVIES, MRS. THOMAS
>   **In a Day.** London: Kegan Paul, Trench, 1882. Pp. [i-ii], [1]-[95].
>   **Sentence, The.** London: T. Fisher Unwin, 1887. Pp. [1]-138.

WEBSTER, AUGUSTA DAVIES, MRS. THOMAS (trans.)
>   **Medea.** By Euripides. London & Cambridge: Macmillan, 1868. Pp. [1]-90.
>   **Prometheus Bound.** By Aeschylus. London & Cambridge: Macmillan, 1866. Pp. [1]-77.

WEBSTER, BENJAMIN, JR
>   **Aurora Floyd; or, The Banker's Daughter.** London: Webster, n.d. Pp. [1]-64.
>   **Behind Time.** London: Thomas Hailes Lacy, n.d. Pp. [1]-24.
>   **Fast Family, The.** London: Webster, n.d. Pp. [1]-69. Webster's Acting National Drama, 207.

Gray Mare, A. London: Webster, n.d. Pp. [1]-24. Webster's Acting National Drama, 203.

Hen and Chickens, The; or, A Sign of Affection. London & New York: Samuel French, n.d. Pp. [1]-39. Promptbook.

Just Like Roger! London: Thomas Hailes Lacy, n.d. Pp. [1]-27. Lacks final leaf. [Lacy's Acting Edition].

Man Is Not Perfect, Nor Woman Neither. London & New York: Samuel French, n.d. Pp. [1]-24. French's Acting Edition (late Lacy's).

Private Inquiry, A. London: Webster, n.d. Pp. [1]-23. [Webster's Acting National Drama, 202].

Smoke. London & New York: Samuel French, n.d. Pp. [1]-36. [Lacy's Acting Edition].

Yule Log, A. London & New York: Samuel French, n.d. Pp. [1]-24. [Lacy's Acting Edition].

WEBSTER, BENJAMIN NOTTINGHAM

Belphegor the Mountebank; or, The Pride of Birth. London: National Acting Drama Office, n.d. Pp. [1]-67. Promptbook.

Bird of Passage, A. London: National Acting Drama Office, n.d. Pp. [1]-24.

Black Domino, The; or, A Night's Adventure. Music by Auber. London: National Acting Drama Office, n.d. <wrps. Webster>. Pp. [1]-60. Promptbook libretto.

Book the Third, Chapter the First. *Also:* A Novel Expedient. London: Thomas Hailes Lacy, n.d. Pp. [1]-21. [Lacy's Acting Edition]. *Filed under* Novel Expedient.

Caesar de Bazan; or, Love and Honour! Written with Boucicault, Dionysius Lardner. London: Webster, n.d. Pp. [1]-40. Webster's Acting National Drama, 113.

Caught in a Trap. London: Webster, n.d. Pp. [1]-44. Webster's Acting National Drama, 110.

Courier of Lyons, The. London: John Dicks, n.d. Pp. [1]-16. Dicks' Standard Plays, 1035.

Devil's Violin, The; or, The Revolt of the Flowers. London: National Acting Drama Office, n.d. Pp. [1]-43.

Discarded Son, The. London: Webster, n.d. Pp. [1]-63. Webster's Acting National Drama, 194.

Fox and the Goose, The; or, The Widow's Husband. Written with Boucicault, Dionysius Lardner. By Benjamin Webster and Dion Bourcicault. Music by Thomas, Ambroise. London: National Acting Drama Office, n.d. Pp. [1]-20. Webster's Acting National Drama, 112. *Also filed under* Boucicault, Dionysius Lardner; Webster, Benjamin Nottingham.

Giralda; or, The Miller's Wife. Boston: William V. Spencer, n.d. Pp. [1]-36. Spencer's Boston Theatre, 101.

Golden Farmer, The; or, Jemmy Twitcher in England. *Also:* The Last Crime. New York: Berford, 1847. Pp. [1]-38. Minor Drama, 8. Promptbook.

Golden Farmer, The; or, The Last Crime. London: John Cumberland, n.d. Pp. [1]-50. Cumberland's Minor Theatre, VI. *Filed under* Cumberland, John. Cumberland's Minor Theatre, VI.

High Ways and By Ways. London: John Cumberland, n.d. Pp. [1]-35. Cumberland's British Theatre, XXVIII. *Filed under* Cumberland, John. Cumberland's British Theatre, XXVIII.

Highways and By-ways. New York: E. B. Clayton, n.d. Pp. [i]-iv, [5]-36. Clayton's Edition.

Hobbs, Dobbs, and Stubbs; or, The Three Grocers. *Also:* The Three Grocers: or Hobbs, Dobbs, and Stubbs. London: Sherwood, Gilbert, & Piper, n.d. Pp. [1]-30.

Holly Tree Inn. London: John Dicks, n.d. Pp. [1]-11. Dicks' Standard Plays, 1068.

Isaure; or, The Maniac of the Alps. [London: John Dicks], n.d. Pp. [199]-214. [Dicks' Standard Plays].

Keeley Worried by Buckstone.
See Lemon, Mark.

Last Crime, The.
See Golden Farmer, The.

Laughing Hyena, The. London: National Acting Drama Office, n.d. <wrps. Webster>. Pp. [1]-28. Webster's Acting National Drama, 165.

Laughing Hyena, The. New York & London: Samuel French, n.d. Pp. [1]-23. French's Minor Drama, 198.

Man of Law, The. London: National Acting Drama Office, n.d. <wrps. Webster>. Pp. [1]-56. Webster's Acting National Drama, 181.

Miseries of Human Life, The. London: National Acting Drama Office, n.d. Pp. [1]-24.

Modern Orpheus, The; or, Music the Food of Love. London: Chapman & Hall, n.d. Pp. [1]-23. [Acting National Drama].

Mrs. Sarah Gamp's Tea and Turn Out. London: National Acting Drama Office, n.d. Pp. [1]-20.

My Young Wife and My Old Umbrella. London: Chapman & Hall, n.d. Pp. [1]-23. [Acting National Drama].

Novel Expedient, A.
See Book the Third, Chapter the First.

Old Gentleman, The. London: John Duncombe, n.d. Pp. [1]-24. Duncombe's Edition.

One Touch of Nature. London: Webster, n.d. Pp. [1]-24. Webster's Acting National Drama, 199.

Paul Clifford; or, The Highwayman of 1770. London: John Cumberland, n.d. Pp. [1]-76. Cumberland's Minor Theatre, VI. *Filed under* Cumberland, John. Cumberland's Minor Theatre, VI.

Paul Clifford, the Highwayman of 1770. London: G. H. Davidson, n.d. Pp. [1]-76. [Cumberland's Minor Theatre, 47].

Pierrot the Married Man, and Polichinello the Gay Single Fellow. London: National Acting Drama Office, n.d. Pp. [1]-12.

Pretty Girls of Stillberg, The. New York: Samuel French, n.d. Pp. [1]-24. French's Minor Drama, 292. *Filed under* Pretty Girls of Stillberg (anon.).

Queen of the Market, The. Written with Coape, Henry Coe. London: Webster, n.d. Pp. [i]-iv, [5]-60. Webster's Acting National Drama, 184.

Roused Lion, The. London: National Acting Drama Office, n.d. Pp. [1]-46. [Acting National Drama, 14].

Swiss Swains, The. Music by Lee, Alexander. London: Chapman & Hall, n.d. Pp. [1]-23.

Three Grocers, The; or, Hobbs, Dobbs, and Stubbs. *Also:* Hobbs, Dobbs, and Stubbs; or, The Three Grocers. New York: Happy Hours, n.d. Pp. [i]-iv, [5]-28. Acting Drama, 40.

Village Doctor, The. London: Chapman & Hall, n.d. Pp. [1]-42. Promptbook.

Wonderful Water Cure, The. London: National Acting Drama Office, n.d. Pp. [1]-20. Libretto.

WEBSTER, FREDERICK

Place Hunter, The. London: Sherwood, Gilbert, & Piper, n.d. Pp. [1]-24.

WEBSTER, W. S.

I'll Tell Your Wife. New York: Wheat & Cornett, c.1876. Pp. [28]-32. New York Drama, I, 7.

WEDDED AND WOOED
See Taylor, Tom. Lady Clancarty.

WEDDING AT THE MILL, THE
See Fothergill, F.

WEDDING BREAKFAST, THE
See Morton, John Maddison.

WEDDING DAY, THE
See Inchbald, Elizabeth Simpson, Mrs. Joseph.
See Stange, Stanislaus.

WEDDING EVE, THE
See Yardley, William.

WEDDING GOWN, THE
See Jerrold, Douglas William.

WEDDING GUEST, THE
See Jones, Henry Arthur.

WEDDING MARCH, THE
See Gilbert, William Schwenck.

WEDDING RING, THE
See Mitford, Mary Russell.

WEEDS
See Pemberton, Thomas Edgar.

WEEL MAY THE KEEL ROW!
    See Addison, Henry Robert, Capt. Jessie, the Flower of
    Dumblaine.
WEIRWOLF, THE
    See Forster, William.
WEISSE, CHRISTIAN FELIX
    Rosamond.
        See Holcroft, Fanny (trans.).
WELCOME AND FAREWELL
    See Harness, William.
WELCOME, LITTLE STRANGER
    See Albery, James.
WELL MATCHED
    See Havard, Philip.
WELL OF PALMS
    See Campbell, Andrew Leonard Voullaire. Demon of the
    Desert!
WELL OF ST. MARIE
    See Moncrieff, William Thomas. Red Farm, The.
WELL PLAYED
    See Knight, Arthur Francis.
WELLER, BERNARD WILLIAM
    Nita the Dancer; or, Supper for Two. Written with Raphael,
    Francis. Music by Eaton, W. G. London & New York:
    Samuel French, n.d. Pp. [1]-11.
WELLER FAMILY, THE
    See Emson, Frank E.
WELLS, CHARLES JEREMIAH
    Dramatic Scene, A. [London: Hodder & Stoughton, 1895].
    Pp. [289]-318. Title page lacking.
    Joseph and His Brethren. London: Chatto & Windus, 1876.
    Pp. [i]-[xx], [1]-252.
WELSH GIRL, THE
    See Planché, Elizabeth (Eliza) St. George, Mrs. James
    Robinson
WENLOCK OF WENLOCK
    See Wilks, Thomas Egerton.
WEPT OF THE WISH-TON-WISH, THE
    See Bernard, William Bayle.
WERE-WOLF, THE
    See Moubrey, Lilian.
WERNER
    See Byron, George Gordon, Lord.
WERTER
    See Reynolds, Frederick.
WEST, B.
    Melmoth the Wanderer. London: John Lowndes, n.d. Pp.
    [i-vi], [1]-36.
WEST, MATTHEW
    Female Heroism. Dublin: William Porter (printer), 1803. Pp.
    [i]-[x], [1]-[56].
    Pizarro. London: T. Hurst, n.d. Pp. [i-iv], [1]-63.
WEST, W.
    Norma. Music by Bellini. London: John Duncombe, n.d.
    Pp. [1]-24. Duncombe's Acting Edition of the British
    Theatre, 353.
WEST END
    See Boucicault, Dionysius Lardner.
WEST INDIAN, THE
    See Cumberland, Richard.
WEST WIND, A
    See Wastell, William.
WESTLAND, R. L.
    Whittington and His Cat. Edinburgh: Thomas Gray (printer),
    n.d. Pp. [1]-40. Libretto.
WESTMACOTT, CHARLES MOLLOY
    Nettlewig Hall; or, Ten to One. Music by Lee, Alexander.
    London: John Cumberland, n.d. Pp. [1]-38. Cumber-
    land's British Theatre, XXXV. *Filed under* Cumberland,
    John. Cumberland's British Theatre, XXXV.
    Nettlewig Hall; or, Ten to One. Music by Lee, Alexander.
    London: John Cumberland, n.d. Pp. [1]-38.
WESTON, FERDINAND FULLERTON
    Barons of Elbenbergh, The. London: T. & R. Hughes, 1808.
    Pp. [i-vi], [1]-61.

    St. Aubert; or, The Hour of Retribution. London: T. & R.
    Hughes, 1808. Pp. [1]-[63].
WESTON, J. M.
    Lucretia Borgia. Boston: William V. Spencer, n.d. Pp. [1]-60.
    Spencer's Boston Theatre, New Series, 35. Promptbook.
WHAT A BLUNDER!
    See Holman, Joseph George.
WHAT CAN BEAUTY DO?
    See Hook, Theodore Edward. Soldier's Return, The.
WHAT GREATER LOVE?
    See Bowkett, Sidney.
WHAT HAPPENED TO HENNY PENNY?
    See Bell, Florence Eveleen Eleanore Oliffe, Mrs. Hugh
    (Lady).
WHAT HAVE I DONE?
    See Oxenford, John.
WHAT IS SHE?
    See Smith, Charles.
WHAT NEXT?
    See Dibdin, Thomas John.
WHAT WILL MY WIFE SAY?
    See A'Beckett, Gilbert Abbott. Assignation, The.
WHAT WILL THE WORLD SAY?
    See Lemon, Mark.
WHAT WILL THEY SAY AT BROMPTON?
    See Coyne, Joseph Stirling.
WHAT WON'T A WOMAN DO?
    See Wilson, Margaret Harries, Mrs. Cornwell Baron.
    Venus in Arms.
WHAT YOU WILL
    See Irving, Henry (arr.). Twelfth Night.
    See Kemble, John Philip (arr.). Twelfth Night.
    See Shakespeare, William. Twelfth Night.
WHAT'S A MAN OF FASHION?
    See Reynolds, Frederick.
WHAT'S IN A NAME?; OR, TURN AND TURN ABOUT
    (anon.)
    London: H. Francis, 1843. Pp. [159]-162. Title page
    lacking.
WHEATLEY, J. A.
    Ali-Ben-Hassan; or, The Last of the Moors. In *Dramatic
    Sketches,* London & Calcutta: W. H. Allen, 1891, pp.
    [207]-327. *Filed under* Dramatic Sketches.
    Faith. In *Dramatic Sketches,* London & Calcutta: W. H.
    Allen, 1891, pp. [133]-206. *Filed under* Dramatic Sketches.
    Human Nature. In *Dramatic Sketches,* London & Calcutta:
    W. H. Allen, 1891, pp. [65]-94. *Filed under* Dramatic
    Sketches.
    Joe the Buits; or, Nobbut a Cumberland Lad. In *Dramatic
    Sketches,* London & Calcutta: W. H. Allen, 1891, pp.
    [i-vi], [1]-28. *Filed under* Dramatic Sketches.
    Old Ralph. In *Dramatic Sketches,* London & Calcutta: W. H.
    Allen, 1891, pp. [29]-64. *Filed under* Dramatic Sketches.
    Ruse de Guerre. In *Dramatic Sketches,* London & Calcutta:
    W. H. Allen, 1891, pp. [95]-132. *Filed under* Dramatic
    Sketches.
WHEEL OF FORTUNE, THE
    See Cumberland, Richard.
    See Poole, W. Howell.
WHEELS WITHIN WHEELS
    See Carton, R. C.
WHEELWRIGHT, CHARLES APTHROP, REV. (trans.)
    Medea. By Seneca. In *Poems,* 2nd ed., 2 vols., London:
    Longman, Hurst, Rees, Orme, & Brown; Cambridge: J.
    Deighton, 1811, I, [i], 1-88, [167]-[193].
    Octavia. By Seneca. In *Poems,* 2nd ed., 2 vols., London:
    Longman, Hurst, Rees, Orme, & Brown; Cambridge: J.
    Deighton, 1811, I, [i], [89]-166, [197]-207.
WHEN I'M A MAN
    See Fitzgerald, Shafto Justin Adair.
WHEN THE WHEELS RUN DOWN
    See Rogers, Maud M.
WHERE DID THE MONEY COME FROM?
    See Dibdin, Thomas John. Two Gregories, The.

WHERE SHALL I DINE?
    See Rodwell, George Herbert Bonaparte.
WHERE THERE'S A WILL THERE'S A WAY
    See Morton, John Maddison.
WHERE TO FIND A FRIEND
    See Leigh, Richard.
WHERE'S MY DAUGHTER?
    See Stafford, John Joseph. Frenchman in London, The.
WHERE'S THE CAT?
    See Albery, James.
WHERE'S YOUR WIFE?
    See Bridgeman, John Vipon.
WHICH?
    See Bagot, Arthur Greville.
WHICH GOT THE BEST OF IT?
    See Davis, Lillie.
WHICH IS HE?
    See Boaden, Caroline. William Thompson.
WHICH IS MY COUSIN?
    See Raymond, Richard John.
WHICH IS MY HUSBAND?
    See Davidson, Frances A., Mrs. Giralda.
WHICH IS MY SON?
    See Peake, Richard Brinsley. Middle Temple, The.
WHICH IS THE KING?
    See Watts, Walter.
WHICH IS THE LADY?
    See Oulton, Walley Chamberlaine. Sleep-Walker, The.
WHICH IS THE MAN?
    See Cowley, Hannah Parkhouse, Mrs.
WHICH IS THE THIEF?
    See Arnold, Samuel James. Maid and the Magpye, The.
WHICH IS WHICH?
    See Fullerton, Georgiana Charlotte Leveson-Gower, Mrs. Alexander George, Lady Georgiana.
    See Hoare, Prince. Three and the Deuce, The.
    See Jameson, Robert Francis. King and the Duke, The.
    See Smith, Spencer Theyre.
WHICH OF THE TWO?
    See Morton, John Maddison.
WHICH SHALL I MARRY?
    See Suter, William E.
WHICH WILL HE MARRY?
    See Wilks, Thomas Egerton.
WHIGS AND WIDOWS
    See Ebsworth, Joseph. Rouge et Noir.
WHIMSICALITY
    See Maclaren, Archibald.
WHISTLE FOR IT
    See Lamb, George.
WHISTLER!, THE
    See Pitt, George Dibdin.
WHITE, JAMES, REV.
    Earl of Gowrie, The. London: T. C. Newby, 1845. Pp. [i]-[x], [1]-196. Pages 197-198 lacking.
    Feudal Times; or, The Court of James III. New York: Samuel French, n.d. Pp. [i]-[vi], [7]-63. French's Standard Drama, 43.
    John Savile of Haysted. London: T. C. Newby, 1847. Pp. [i]-[vi], [1]-108.
    King of the Commons, The. [New York & Philadelphia: W. Taylor; Boston: Redding, 1846]. Pp. [iii]-vi, 7-77. Title page lacking. [Modern Standard Drama]. Promptbook.
    King's Favourite, The. 43 leaves. Manuscript.
WHITE, L.
    Beauty and the Beast. Written with White, L. W. Music by White, Mary Louisa. London: Joseph Williams, n.d. Pp. [1], 1-57. Vocal score.
WHITE, L. W.
    Beauty and the Beast.
    See White, L.
WHITE BOYS, THE
    See Grattan, H. P.
WHITE CAT, THE
    See Blanchard, Edward Litt Leman.

    See Burnand, Francis Cowley.
    See Keating, Eliza H.
    See Planché, James Robinson.
WHITE CLIFFS, THE
    See Meritt, Paul.
WHITE COCKADE, THE
    See Barnett, Richard Wheldon.
    See Phillips, Watts.
WHITE ELEPHANT, A
    See Carton, R. C.
WHITE FARM, THE
    See Lucas, William James.
WHITE FAWN, THE
    See Burnand, Francis Cowley.
WHITE FEATHER, THE
    See Morton, Thomas, jr.
WHITE FLOWER
    See Rowlands, ?, Prof. Blodwen.
WHITE HEATHER, THE
    See Raleigh, Cecil.
WHITE HORSE OF KILLARNEY
    See Lee, Nelson, jr. Harlequin and O'Donoghue.
WHITE HORSE OF THE PEPPERS, THE
    See Lover, Samuel.
WHITE LIES
    See Lunn, Joseph.
WHITE MAID OF AVENEL.
    See Aird, David Mitchell. Maid of Avenel, The.
WHITE MILLINER, THE
    See Jerrold, Douglas William.
WHITE PILGRIM, THE
    See Merivale, Herman Charles.
WHITE PLUME, THE
    See Dibdin, Thomas John.
WHITE ROSE OF THE PLANTATION, THE
    See Byron, Henry James.
WHITE SCARF
    See Holl, Henry. Louise.
WHITE SERGEANTS, THE
    See Selby, Charles.
WHITE SLAVE, THE
    See Stirling, Edward.
WHITE STOCKING, A
    See Ferris, Edward.
WHITE WARRIOR
    See Byron, Medora Gordon. Zameo.
WHITE WITCH, THE
    See Dibdin, Charles Isaac Mungo, jr.
WHITEBAIT AT GREENWICH
    See Morton, John Maddison. Two Buzzards, The.
    See Morton, John Maddison.
WHITEFRIARS
    See Townsend, William Thompson.
WHITEHEAD, D. CHARLES
    Cavalier!, The. London: John Duncombe, n.d. Pp. [5]-42. Text complete. [Duncombe's Edition].
WHITEHEAD, JOHN CRAWFORD
    King James the Second; or, The Revolution of 1688. London: Smith, Elder, 1828. Pp. [i]-[x], [1]-151.
WHITEHEAD, WILLIAM
    Roman Father, The. London: Whittingham & Arliss, 1815. Pp. [1]-48. London Theatre, XII. *Filed under* Dibdin, Thomas John, ed. London Theatre, XII.
    Roman Father, The. In *British Drama*, 12 vols., London: John Dicks, 1865, IV, [1073]-1086.
WHITELAW, ROBERT (trans.)
    Antigone. By Sophocles. In *Ten Greek Plays*, New York: Oxford University Press, 1929, pp. [i-iv], [51]-88.
WHITMORE, E. H.
    Senior Wranglers. London & New York: Samuel French, n.d. Pp. [1]-10. [Lacy's Acting Edition].
    Sixes and Sevens: A Misunderstanding. London: Samuel French; New York: T. Henry French, n.d. Pp. [1]-12. [Lacy's Acting Edition].

WHITTINGTON
See Farnie, Henry Brougham.
WHITTINGTON AND HIS CAT (anon.)
Music by Chapman. Bristol: I. Arrowsmith, n.d. Pp. [1]-32. Libretto.
WHITTINGTON AND HIS CAT (anon.)
Music by Loder. Manchester: Theatre Royal Press (printer), 1853. Pp. [1]-15. 13th ed.
WHITTINGTON AND HIS CAT
See Blanchard, Edward Litt Leman.
See Byron, Henry James.
See Henry, A.
See Milner, Henry M.
See Westland, R. L.
WHITTINGTON AND HIS CAT; OR, HARLEQUIN LORD MAYOR OF LONDON (anon.)
[London]: B. Pollock, n.d. Pp. [1]-16. Pollock's Juvenile Drama.
WHITTINGTON, JUNIOR, AND HIS SENSATION CAT
See Reece, Robert.
WHITTY, WALTER DEVEREUX
My Husband's Secret. New York: George W. Wheat, c.1875. Pp. i, [23]-27. New York Drama, I, 2.
WHO BIDS MOST?
See Maclaren, Archibald. Wife to Be Sold, A.
WHO DO THEY TAKE ME FOR?
See Morton, John Maddison.
WHO IS SHE?
See Stirling, Edward.
WHO IS WHO?
See Williams, Thomas John.
WHO KILLED COCK ROBIN?
See Mathews, Charles James.
WHO OWNS THE HAND?
See Amherst, J. H.
WHO SHALL BE QUEEN?
See Hodges, G. S. Quarrel of the Flowers, The.
WHO SHOT THE DOG?
See Burnand, Francis Cowley. Frightful Hair, The.
WHO SPEAKS FIRST?
See Dance, Charles.
WHO STOLE THE CLOCK?
See Lucas, William James.
WHO STOLE THE POCKET-BOOK?
See Morton, John Maddison.
WHO STOLE THE TARTS?
See Silvester, Frank.
WHO WANTS A GUINEA?
See Colman, George, jr.
WHO WANTS A WIFE?
See Pocock, Isaac.
WHO WINS?
See Allingham, John Till. Widow, The.
WHO WON?
See Goddard, Kate.
WHO'LL LEND ME A WIFE!
See Millingen, John Gideon.
WHO'S A TRAVELLER?
See Cooper, Frederick Fox.
WHO'S FOR INDIA?
See Selby, Charles. Drapery Question, The.
WHO'S MY FATHER?
See Morton, Thomas, sr. Methinks I See My Father!
WHO'S MY HUSBAND?
See Morton, John Maddison.
WHO'S THE COMPOSER?
See Morton, John Maddison.
WHO'S THE DUPE?
See Cowley, Hannah Parkhouse, Mrs.
WHO'S THE HEIR?
See March, George.
WHO'S THE RICHEST?
See Dibdin, Thomas John. Thirty Thousand.
WHO'S TO BLAME?
See Meadows, Thomas.

WHO'S TO HAVE HER?
See Dibdin, Thomas John.
WHO'S TO WIN HIM?
See Williams, Thomas John.
WHO'S WHO?
See Poole, John.
WHO'S YOUR FRIEND?
See Planché, James Robinson.
WHY DID YOU DIE?
See Mathews, Charles James.
WHY DON'T SHE MARRY?
See Bayly, Thomas Haynes. Swiss Cottage, The.
See Bayly, Thomas Haynes.
WHY WOMEN WEEP
See Broughton, Frederick William.
WHYTE, GEORGE (trans.)
Vivandière, The. Music by Godard, Benjamin. London: E. Ascherberg, c.1896. Pp. [i-iv], 1-293. Vocal score.
WICIOUS WILLIN AND WICTORIOUS WIRTUE!
See Burnand, Francis Cowley. Mary Turner.
WICKED FATHER WHO SOLD HIS DAUGHTER AND THE DON WHO BOUGHT HER
See Thomas, Leigh. Pirate, The.
WICKED WIFE, A
See Courtney, John.
WICKED WOLF AND THE WIRTUOUS WOODCUTTER
See Hood, Tom. Harlequin Little Red Riding-Hood.
WICKED WORLD, THE
See Gilbert, William Schwenck.
WICKLOW WEDDING
See Boucicault, Dionysius Lardner. Arrah-na-Pogue.
WIDOW, THE
See Allingham, John Till.
See Knowles, James Sheridan.
WIDOW AND HER WOOERS
See Taylor, Tom. Sir Roger de Coverley.
WIDOW BEWITCHED!, THE
See Lucas, William James.
WIDOW HUNT, A
See Coyne, Joseph Stirling.
WIDOW OF CORNHILL
See Planché, James Robinson. Woman Never Vext, A.
WIDOW'S CHOICE
See Berard, Peter. Uncle's Will, Who Wins?, The.
WIDOW'S HUSBAND
See Webster, Benjamin Nottingham. Fox and the Goose, The.
WIDOW'S STRATAGEM
See Kemble, Marie Thérèse De Camp, Mrs. Charles. Smiles and Tears.
WIDOW'S VICTIM, THE
See Selby, Charles.
WIDOW'S VISION
See Lucas, William James. White Farm, The.
WIDOWED BRIDE
See Suter, William E. First Love.
WIDOWERS' HOUSES
See Shaw, George Bernard.
WIDOWS BEWITCHED
See Aïdé, Hamilton.
WIFE, THE
See Brockhurst, Joseph Sumner.
See Graves, Joseph.
See Knowles, James Sheridan.
WIFE AND BROTHER
See Burges, James Bland. Riches.
WIFE, HUSBAND, AND FRIEND
See Townsend, William Thompson. Post Captain, The.
WIFE OF A MILLION, THE
See Lathom, Francis.
WIFE OF SEVEN HUSBANDS, THE
See Almar, George. Pedlar's Acre.
See Almar, George.
WIFE OF TWO HUSBANDS, THE
See Cobb, James.

WIFE OR WIDOW
    See Long, Charles.
WIFE TO BE LETT, A
    See Minton, Ann.
WIFE TO BE SOLD, A
    See Maclaren, Archibald.
WIFE WITH TWO HUSBANDS, THE
    See Gunning, Elizabeth (trans.).
WIFE'S CONFESSION, THE
    See Besant, Walter.
WIFE'S FIRST LESSON
    See Kemble, Marie Thérèse De Camp, Mrs. Charles. Day after the Wedding, The.
WIFE'S JOURNAL
    See Robertson, Thomas William. My Wife's Diary.
WIFE'S PERIL
    See Shirley, Arthur. Saved.
WIFE'S PORTRAIT, THE
    See Marston, John Westland.
WIFE'S REVENGE
    See Buckstone, John Baldwin. Agnes de Vere.
WIFE'S SECRET, THE
    See Lovell, George William.
WIFE'S STRATAGEM!
    See Coyne, Joseph Stirling. Helen Oakleigh.
WIFE'S TRIAL, THE
    See Lamb, Charles.
    See Reynoldson, Thomas Herbert. Good for Evil.
WIFE'S VENGEANCE
    See Spicer, Henry. Jeffreys.
WIG AND GOWN
    See Albery, James.
WIGAN, ALFRED SYDNEY
    Five Hundred Pounds Reward; or, Dick Turpin the Second. London: John Dicks, n.d. Pp. [1]-15. Dicks' Standard Plays, 1003.
    Loan of a Wife, The. London: John Duncombe, n.d. Pp. [1]-25. Duncombe's Edition.
    Luck's All. London: William W. Barth, n.d. Pp. [1]-31.
    Model of a Wife, A. London: Thomas Hailes Lacy, n.d. Pp. [1]-16.
    Tit for Tat.
    See Talfourd, Francis.
    Watch and Ward. London: William W. Barth, n.d. Pp. [1]-27.
WIGAN, HORACE
    Always Intended. Boston: Walter H. Baker, n.d. Pp. [1]-25.
    Best Way, The. London: Thomas Hailes Lacy, n.d. Pp. [1]-25. [Lacy's Acting Edition].
    Charming Woman, The. London: Thomas Hailes Lacy, n.d. Pp. [1]-45. [Lacy's Acting Edition].
    Friends or Foes? London: Thomas Hailes Lacy, n.d. Pp. [1]-68. Promptbook.
    Life Chase, A.
    See Oxenford, John.
    Observation and Flirtation. London: Thomas Hailes Lacy, n.d. Pp. [1]-34. [Lacy's Acting Edition].
    Real and Ideal. London: Thomas Hailes Lacy, n.d. Pp. [1]-28. [Lacy's Acting Edition].
    Southerner—Just Arrived, A. London: Thomas Hailes Lacy, n.d. Pp. [1]-19. [Lacy's Acting Edition].
    Taming the Truant. London: Thomas Hailes Lacy, n.d. Pp. [1]-44. [Lacy's Acting Edition].
WIGWAM, THE
    See Bell, Florence Eveleen Eleanore Oliffe, Mrs. Hugh (Lady).
    See Brooks, Charles William Shirley.
    See Dibdin, Thomas John.
WILCOX, SCOTT J. B., LIEUT.
    All at C.
    See Millett, Sydney Crohan, Maj.
WILD, JAMES
    Doubt and Conviction. London: John Hayes (priv.), 1804. Pp. [i-ii], [1]-[32]. In *Dramas Adapted to the English Stage,* London: J. Cawthorn; Richardson, 1805. *Filed under* Dramas.

    Frailty and Hypocrisy. London: John Hayes (priv.), 1804. Pp. [i-ii], [1]-[80]. In *Dramas Adapted to the English Stage,* London: J. Cawthorn; Richardson, 1805. *Filed under* Dramas.
    From Inn to Inn. London: John Hayes (priv.), 1804. Pp. [i-ii], [1]-[66]. In *Dramas Adapted to the English Stage,* London: J. Cawthorn; Richardson, 1805. *Filed under* Dramas.
    Maids; or, The Nuns of Glossenbury. London: C. Rickaby (priv.), 1804. Pp. [i-ii], [1]-[40]. In *Dramas Adapted to the English Stage,* London: J. Cawthorn; Richardson, 1805. *Filed under* Dramas.
    Twenty-One. London: John Hayes (priv.), 1804. Pp. [i-ii], [1]-[40]. In *Dramas Adapted to the English Stage,* London: J. Cawthorn; Richardson, 1805. *Filed under* Dramas.
    Wives. London: C. Rickaby (priv.), 1804. Pp. [i-ii], [1]-[40]. In *Dramas Adapted to the English Stage,* London: J. Cawthorn; Richardson, 1805. *Filed under* Dramas.
WILD BOY OF BOHEMIA, THE
    See Walker, John.
WILD DUCK, THE
    See Anstey, F.
    See Archer, Frances Elizabeth, Mrs. William (trans.).
WILD DUCKS
    See Stirling, Edward.
WILD FLOWERS
    See Rose, Edward.
WILD-GOOSE CHASE, A
    See Jameson, H.
WILD HORDE OF THE WOLF'S LAIR
    See Neale, Frederick. Jepey Mayflower.
WILD HUNTSMAN OF BOHEMIA
    See Livius, Barham. Freyschutz, The.
WILD MAN, THE
    See Dibdin, Charles Isaac Mungo, jr.
WILD OATS
    See O'Keeffe, John.
WILD WOLF OF TARTARY, THE
    See Byron, Henry James.
WILD WOMAN OF THE VILLAGE
    See Fitzball, Edward. Wardock Kennilson.
WILD WOMAN OF THE WRECK
    See Fitzball, Edward. Floating Beacon, The.
WILDE, OSCAR FINGALL O'FLAHERTIE WILLS
    Duchess of Padua, The. New York: F. M. Buckles, 1906. Pp. [1]-120.
    Duchess of Padua, The. In *Plays of Oscar Wilde,* Boston & London: John W. Luce, 1907, III, [i-viii], 1-92. *Filed under* Collected Works.
    Duchess of Padua, The. New York: n.pub. (priv.), n.d. Pp. [1]-187. Title page incomplete.
    Florentine Tragedy, A. Written with Moore, Thomas Sturge. In *Plays of Oscar Wilde,* Boston & London: John W. Luce, 1908, IV, [iii]-[xii], [1]-66. *Filed under* Collected Works.
    Ideal Husband, An. London: Leonard Smithers, 1899. Pp. i-xiv, [1]-213.
    Ideal Husband, An. In *Plays of Oscar Wilde,* Boston & London: John W. Luce, 1905, II, [i-vi], 1-128. *Filed under* Collected Works.
    Importance of Being Earnest, The. London: Leonard Smithers, 1899. Pp. [i-xiv], [1]-[152].
    Importance of Being Earnest, The. In *Plays of Oscar Wilde,* Boston & London: John W. Luce, 1905, II, [i-viii], 1-84. *Filed under* Collected Works.
    Importance of Being Earnest, The. *Also:* Lady Lancing. Pp. [i-ii], [1]-34, [i], [1]-43, [i], [1]-24. Pagination by act. Typescript.
    Lady Lancing. *Also:* The Importance of Being Earnest. London: Mrs. Marshall's Typewriting Office, 1894. Pp. [i-ii], [1]-28, [i-ii], [1]-27, [i-ii], [1]-25, [i], [1]-22. Pagination by act. Typescript.
    Lady Windermere's Fan. Paris: n.pub., 1903. Pp. [i-xiv], 1-132.

Lady Windermere's Fan. In *Plays of Oscar Wilde*, Boston & London: John W. Luce, 1905, I, [i-viii], 1-78. *Filed under* Collected Works.

Salomé. San Francisco: J. A. Ephraim (printer), 1896. Pp. [1]-71. Title page lacking.

Salomé. New York: F. M. Buckles, 1906. Pp. [3]-60.

Salomé. In *Plays of Oscar Wilde*, Boston & London: John W. Luce, 1907, III, [i-iv], 1-36. *Filed under* Collected Works.

Vera; or, The Nihilists. N.p.: n.pub. (priv.), 1902. Pp. [1]-75.

Vera; or, The Nihilists. In *Plays of Oscar Wilde*, Boston & London: John W. Luce, 1907, III, [i-iv], [1]-79. *Filed under* Collected Works.

Woman of No Importance, A. London: John Lane, 1894. Pp. [i-xiv], 1-154.

Woman of No Importance, A. In *Plays of Oscar Wilde*, Boston & London: John W. Luce, 1905, I, [i-ii], 1-94. *Filed under* Collected Works.

Woman of No Importance, A. Boston & London: John W. Luce, 1906. Pp. [i-iv], [1]-94.

WILDENBRUCH, ERNST VON

Harold.
   See Zglinitzka, Marie von (trans.).

WILFRID AND MARY
   See St. Bo', Theodore.

WILFUL MURDER!
   See Higgie, Thomas Henry.

WILFUL WARD, THE
   See Wooler, John Pratt.

WILHELM TELL
   See Martin, Theodore, Sir (trans.).

WILKINS, JOHN H.

Civilization. London: Thomas Hailes Lacy, n.d. Pp. [1]-64. Promptbook.

Egyptian, The. London: Thomas Hailes Lacy, n.d. Pp. [3]-54.

WILKS, THOMAS EGERTON

Ambassador's Lady, The; or, The Rose and the Ring! London: John Duncombe, n.d. <wrps. Thomas Hailes Lacy>. Pp. [1]-38. New British Theatre (late Duncombe's), 374.

Bamboozling. London: John Dicks, n.d. Pp. 1-10. Dicks' Standard Plays, 627.

Ben the Boatswain. London: Thomas Hailes Lacy, n.d. Pp. [1]-38.

Black Domino, The; or, The Masked Ball. London: John Duncombe, n.d. Pp. [1]-36. Title page lacking. Promptbook.

Brothers, The; or, The Wolf and the Lamb. London: W. Strange, n.d. Pp. [1]-26. London Acting Drama, 31.

Captain's Not A-miss, The. New York: Samuel French, n.d. Pp. [1]-16. Minor Drama, 159.

Cousin Peter. London & New York: Samuel French, n.d. Pp. [1]-22. [Lacy's Acting Edition].

Crown Prince, The; or, The Buckle of Brilliants. New York: Samuel French, n.d. Pp. [3]-26. Title page lacking. Minor Drama, 100. Promptbook.

Death Token!, The. London: John Duncombe, n.d. Pp. [1]-38. Duncombe's Edition.

Denouncer, The; or, The Seven Clerks and the Three Thieves. Philadelphia & New York: Turner & Fisher, n.d. Pp. [4]-40. Turner's Dramatic Library.

Devil's in It, The. London: John Dicks, n.d. Pp. [1]-16. Dicks' Standard Plays, 649.

Dream Spectre, The. London: Thomas Hailes Lacy, n.d. Pp. [1]-48. [Lacy's Acting Edition].

Eily O'Connor. London: Thomas Hailes Lacy, n.d. Pp. [1]-34.

Halvei the Unknown. London: Thomas Hailes Lacy, n.d. Pp. [1]-44. Promptbook.

How's Your Uncle?; or, The Ladies of the Court. London: Thomas Hailes Lacy, n.d. Pp. [1]-13. [Lacy's Acting Edition].

Jacket of Blue, The. London: John Duncombe, n.d. Pp. [1]-20. Duncombe's Edition.

Kennyngton Crosse; or, The Old House on the Common. London: Thomas Hailes Lacy, n.d. Pp. [1]-48. [Lacy's Acting Edition].

King's Wager, The; or, The Cottage and the Court. London: Thomas Hailes Lacy, n.d. Pp. [1]-71.

Ladye of Lambythe, The; or, A Bridal Three Centuries Back! London: John Duncombe, n.d. Pp. [1]-44. Duncombe's Edition.

Lord Darnley; or, The Keep of Castle Hill! London: John Duncombe, n.d. Pp. [1]-39. Duncombe's Edition. Promptbook.

Michael Erle the Maniac Lover; or, The Fayre Lass of Lichfield! London: John Duncombe, n.d. Pp. [1]-30. Duncombe's Edition. Promptbook.

Miller of Whetstone, The; or, The Cross-Bow Letter. London: Thomas Hailes Lacy, n.d. Pp. [1]-16. [Lacy's Acting Edition].

Mistaken Story, A. London: John Duncombe, n.d. <wrps. Thomas Hailes Lacy>. Pp. [1]-22. New British Theatre (late Duncombe's), 389.

My Valet and I. London: John Duncombe, n.d. Pp. [1]-22. Duncombe's Edition.

My Wife's Dentist. London: John Duncombe, n.d. Pp. [1]-[25]. Duncombe's Edition. Promptbook.

Raffaelle the Reprobate; or, The Secret Mission and the Signet Ring. London: Thomas Hailes Lacy, n.d. Pp. [1]-31. Promptbook.

Railroad Station, The. London: John Duncombe, n.d. Pp. [1]-20. Duncombe's Edition. Promptbook.

Red Crow, The; or, The Archers of Islington and the Fayre Mayde of West Cheap. London: John Duncombe, n.d. Pp. [1]-42. Duncombe's Edition.

Rinaldo Rinaldini. London: John Duncombe, n.d. Pp. [1]-36. Duncombe's Edition.

Roll of the Drum, The. London: Thomas Hailes Lacy, n.d. Pp. [1]-33. Promptbook.

Ruby Ring, The; or, The Murder at Sadler's Wells! London: John Duncombe, n.d. Pp. [1]-42. Duncombe's Acting Edition of the British Theatre, 327.

Scarlet Mantle; or, The Robbers' Hold and the Bandit's Bride. London: Thomas Hailes Lacy, n.d. Pp. [1]-36. New British Theatre (late Duncombe's), 538.

Sergeant's Wedding, The. London: John Dicks, n.d. Pp. [11]-19. Dicks' Standard Plays, 627. *Filed under* Bamboozling.

Seven Clerks, The; or, The Three Thieves and the Denouncer. New York: Samuel French, n.d. Pp. [1]-27. French's American Drama, 115.

Sixteen String Jack; or, The Knaves of Knaves' Acre. London: Thomas Hailes Lacy, n.d. Pp. [1]-40. New British Theatre (late Duncombe's), 505.

State Secrets; or, The Tailor of Tamworth. London: Thomas Hailes Lacy, n.d. Pp. [1]-18. [Lacy's Acting Edition].

Sudden Thoughts. London: W. Strange, 1837 <wrps. Thomas Hailes Lacy>. Pp. [1]-28. New British Theatre (late Duncombe's), 271.

'Tis She!; or, The Maid, the Wife, and the Widow. London: W. Strange, 1838. Pp. [1]-32.

'Tis She!; or, The Maid, the Wife, and the Widow. London: John Dicks, n.d. Pp. [11]-21. Dicks' Standard Plays, 750. *Filed under* Dance, George. Petticoat Government.

Wenlock of Wenlock. London: John Duncombe, n.d. <wrps. Thomas Hailes Lacy>. Pp. [1]-38. Duncombe's Edition <wrps. New British Theatre (late Duncombe's), 132>.

Which Will He Marry? Chicago: [T. S. Denison], n.d. Pp. [1]-10.

Woman's Love; or, Kate Wynsley, the Cottage Girl. London: Thomas Hailes Lacy, n.d. Pp. [1]-40.

Wren Boys, The; or, The Moment of Peril. London: John Dicks, n.d. Pp. [1]-18. Dicks' Standard Plays, 404.

WILL, THE
   See Reynolds, Frederick.

WILL AND THE WAY, THE
   See Waldron, W. Richard.

WILL FOR THE DEED, THE
   See Dibdin, Thomas John.

WILL OF THE WISE KING KINO, THE
   See Albery, James.

WILL THE FISHERMAN
See Thompson, Helen. Myra.
WILL WATCH!
See Amherst, J. H.
WILLETT, ERNEST NODDALL
Prodigal Son, A; or, Gleaners of Life. Music by Nicholls, Frederick C. [Liverpool: Lee & Nightingale, 1896]. Pp. [1]-49. Libretto.
WILLIAM, WILLIAM THOMAS
See Moncrieff, William Thomas (pseud.).
WILLIAM OF NORMANDY, KING OF ENGLAND
See Mitchell, Robert.
WILLIAM RUFUS
See Field, Michael.
WILLIAM SHAKSPERE
See Curling, Henry. Merry Wags of Warwickshire, The.
WILLIAM SIMPSON, THE
See Fitzgerald, Percy Hetherington.
WILLIAM TELL (anon. trans.)
By Schiller. London: James Burns, 1845. Pp. [i]-iv, [1]-135.
WILLIAM TELL (anon.)
Also: Guglielmo Tell. Music by Rossini. London & New York: Boosey, n.d. Pp. [i-vi], 1-538. [Royal Edition]. Vocal score. *Filed under* Guglielmo Tell (anon.).
WILLIAM TELL
See Banfield, Thomas C. (trans.).
See Brough, Robert Barnabas.
See Buckingham, Leicester Silk.
See Knowles, James Sheridan.
See Macfarren, Natalia (trans.).
See Maggioni, Manfredo (trans.). Guglielmo Tell.
See Maxwell, Patrick, Maj. Gen. (trans.).
See Peter, William (trans.).
See Robinson, Samuel (trans.).
See Roche, Eugenius.
See Talbot, Robert (trans.).
See Thompson, Henry (trans.).
WILLIAM TELL, WITH A VENGEANCE
See Byron, Henry James.
WILLIAM THE CONQUEROR
See Blanchard, Edward Litt Leman.
WILLIAM THE FOURTH
See Barnett, Charles Zachary.
See Barnett, Charles Zachary. Youthful Days of William the Fourth, The.
WILLIAM THOMPSON
See Boaden, Caroline.
WILLIAMS, ARTHUR
Bear-Faced Swindle, A; or, The Showman Abroad. In *Mohawk Minstrels' Tenth Book of Nigger Dramas and Sketches,* London: Francis, Day, & Hunter, n.d, pp. 38-48. *Filed under* Forman, Edmund, et al. Mohawk Minstrels' Tenth Book.
Funnibone's Fix. New York: Dick & Fitzgerald, n.d. Pp. [1]-13.
Leave It to Me.
See Hazlewood, Colin Henry.
Mohawk Minstrels' Ninth Book of Dramas, Stump Speeches, Nigger Jokes, and Recitations. Written with Forman, Edmund; Morton, Richard; Arnold, Malcolm. London: Francis, Day, & Hunter, n.d. Pp. [1]-112.
Mohawk Minstrels' Tenth Book of Nigger Dramas and Sketches, The.
See Forman, Edmund.
WILLIAMS, MARIA JOSEPHINE
Helpless Couple, A. London & New York: Samuel French, c.1905. Pp. [1]-8. [Lacy's Acting Edition].
WILLIAMS, MONIER (trans.)
Sakoontala; or, The Lost Ring. By Kalidasa. New York: Dodd, Mead, 1885. Pp. [i]-xxii, [1]-236. *Filed under* Monier-Williams, Monier.

WILLIAMS, MONTAGU STEPHEN
B. B. Written with Burnand, Francis Cowley. London & New York: Samuel French, n.d. Pp. [1]-18. *Filed under* Burnand, Francis Cowley; Williams, Montagu Stephen.
Carte de Visite. Written with Burnand, Francis Cowley. London: Thomas Hailes Lacy, n.d. Pp. [1]-18. [Lacy's Acting Edition].
Easy Shaving.
See Burnand, Francis Cowley.
Fair Exchange, A. London: Thomas Hailes Lacy, n.d. Pp. [1]-19. [Lacy's Acting Edition].
Isle of St. Tropez, The. Written with Burnand, Francis Cowley. London: Thomas Hailes Lacy, n.d. Pp. [1]-32. [Lacy's Acting Edition].
Turkish Bath, The. Written with Burnand, Francis Cowley. Boston: Walter H. Baker, n.d. Pp. [1]-17. Spencer's Universal Stage, 5.
WILLIAMS, THOMAS (trans.)
Don Pasquale. Music by Donizetti. New York: M. Douglas, 1848. Pp. [3]-71. Operatic Library, 29. Libretto.
Elizabeth, Queen of England. By Giacometti, Paolo. Belfast: D. & J. Allen (printer), 1884. Pp. [i-iv], [1]-49. Promptbook.
Mary Stuart. By Schiller. Paris: Morris (printer), 1873. Pp. [1]-43.
WILLIAMS, THOMAS JOHN
Better Half, The. London: Thomas Hailes Lacy, n.d. Pp. [1]-24. [Lacy's Acting Edition].
Cabman No. 93; or, Found in a Four-Wheeler. *Also:* Found in a Four-Wheeler. New York: Robert M. DeWitt, n.d. Pp. [1]-17. DeWitt's Acting Plays, 24.
Change Partners.
See Morton, John Maddison.
Charming Pair, A. Chicago & New York: Dramatic Publishing Co., n.d. Pp. [1]-20. Sergel's Acting Drama, 80.
Cruel to Be Kind. Written with Harris, Augustus Glossop. London: Thomas Hailes Lacy, n.d. Pp. [1]-24. [Lacy's Acting Edition].
Cure for the Fidgets, A. New York: Samuel French, n.d. Pp. [1]-20. French's Minor Drama, 306.
Dandelion's Dodges. New York: Robert M. DeWitt, n.d. Pp. [1]-19. DeWitt's Acting Plays, 4.
Found in a Four-Wheeler! *Also:* Cabman No. 93. London: Thomas Hailes Lacy, n.d. Pp. [1]-22.
Gossip.
See Harris, Augustus Glossop.
Ici On Parle Français. London: Thomas Hailes Lacy, n.d. Pp. [1]-22.
I've Written to Browne; or, A Needless Stratagem. London: Thomas Hailes Lacy, n.d. Pp. [1]-24. [Lacy's Acting Edition].
Jack's Delight! London: Thomas Hailes Lacy, n.d. Pp. [1]-21. [Lacy's Acting Edition].
Keep Your Eye on Her. London & New York: Samuel French, n.d. Pp. [1]-24. [Lacy's Acting Edition].
Larkins' Love Letters. London: Thomas Hailes Lacy, n.d. Pp. [1]-21. [Lacy's Acting Edition].
Lion Slayer, The; or, Out for a Prowl! London: Thomas Hailes Lacy, n.d. Pp. [1]-20.
Little Daisy. London: Thomas Hailes Lacy, n.d. Pp. [1]-22. [Lacy's Acting Edition].
Little Sentinel!, The. London: Thomas Hailes Lacy, n.d. Pp. [1]-22. [Lacy's Acting Edition].
My Dress Boots. London: Thomas Hailes Lacy, n.d. Pp. [1]-20. [Lacy's Acting Edition].
My Turn Next. Boston: Charles H. Spencer, n.d. Pp. [1]-21. Spencer's Universal Stage, 20.
My Wife's Maid! London: Thomas Hailes Lacy, n.d. Pp. [1]-24.
Old Gooseberry! Boston: Charles H. Spencer, 1870. Pp. [1]-23. Spencer's Universal Stage, 52.
On and Off. London & New York: Samuel French, n.d. Pp. [1]-20. French's Acting Edition (late Lacy's), [762].
One Too Many for Him. New York: DeWitt, n.d. Pp. [1]-19. DeWitt's Acting Plays, 33.

Out to Nurse. Boston: William V. Spencer, n.d. Pp. [1]-21. Spencer's Boston Theatre, 155.

Peace and Quiet! London & New York: Samuel French, n.d. Pp. [1]-18.

Peep-Show Man, The. London: Thomas Hailes Lacy, n.d. Pp. [1]-45. Promptbook.

Pipkin's Rustic Retreat! London: Thomas Hailes Lacy, n.d. Pp. [1]-24.

Race for a Widow, A. London: Thomas Hailes Lacy, n.d. Pp. [1]-24.

Ruth Oakley. Written with Harris, Augustus Glossop. N.p.: n.pub., n.d. Pp. [3]-38. Title page lacking. Promptbook.

Ruth Oakley. Written with Harris, Augustus Glossop. London: Thomas Hailes Lacy, n.d. Pp. [1]-43. *Filed under* Harris, Augustus Glossop; Williams, Thomas John.

Silent Protector, A. New York: Robert M. DeWitt, n.d. Pp. [1]-18. DeWitt's Acting Plays, 37.

Silent System, The. London: Thomas Hailes Lacy, n.d. Pp. [1]-20. [Lacy's Acting Edition].

Terrible Tinker!, A. London: Thomas Hailes Lacy, n.d. Pp. [1]-26. [Lacy's Acting Edition].

Tourist's Ticket, A. London: Thomas Hailes Lacy, n.d. Pp. [1]-[28]. [Lacy's Acting Edition].

Trials of Tompkins!, The. London: Thomas Hailes Lacy, n.d. Pp. [1]-21.

Turn Him Out. New York: Samuel French, n.d. <wrps. New York & London>. Pp. [1]-18. French's Minor Drama, 291.

Tweedleton's Tail-Coat. London: Thomas Hailes Lacy, n.d. Pp. [1]-20.

Ugly Customer, An. Boston: Charles H. Spencer, n.d. Pp. [1]-21. Spencer's Universal Stage, 58.

Ugly Customer, An. London & New York: Samuel French, n.d. Pp. [1]-22. French's Acting Edition (late Lacy's), 726.

Up a Tree! London & New York: Samuel French, n.d. Pp. [1]-24. [Lacy's Acting Edition].

Volunteer Review, The; or, The Little Man in Green! New York: DeWitt, n.d. Pp. [1]-20. DeWitt's Acting Plays, 124.

Who Is Who?; or, All in a Fog! London & New York: Samuel French, n.d. Pp. [1]-24. Promptbook.

Who's to Win Him? London & New York: Samuel French, n.d. Pp. [1]-26.

WILLIAMS, THOMAS JOHN (trans.)
Diamans de la Couronne, Les. Music by Auber. London: J. Miles, n.d. Pp. [1]-111. Libretto.

WILLIAMS, WILLIAM HENRY
Wreck, The; or, The Buccaneer's Bridal. London: G. H. Davidson, n.d. Pp. [1]-52.

Wreck, The; or, The Buccaneer's Bridal. Also attrib. to Campbell, Andrew Leonard Voullaire. London: John Cumberland, n.d. Pp. [1]-52. Cumberland's Minor Theatre, IV. *Filed under* Cumberland, John. Cumberland's Minor Theatre, IV.

WILLIAMS' VISITS
See Moncrieff, William Thomas.

WILLIAMSON, HENRY W.
Retiring. London & New York: Samuel French, n.d. Pp. [1]-44. [Lacy's Acting Edition].

WILLIKIND AND HYS DINAH
See Coyne, Joseph Stirling.

WILLMER, FREDERICK
Upper Classes, The. Liverpool: Charles Willmer & Sons, 1876. Pp. [1]-58.

WILLOW COPSE, THE
See Boucicault, Dionysius Lardner.

WILLOW-PATTERN PLATE
See Hale, William Palmer. Mandarin's Daughter!, The.

WILLS, WILLIAM GORMAN
Charles the First. Edinburgh & London: William Blackwood & Sons, 1873. Pp. [i]-[xii], [1]-83.

Hermann the Fatalist. London & New York: Samuel French, n.d. Pp. [1]-56.

Hinko; or, The Headsman's Daughter. New York: Robert M. DeWitt, n.d. Pp. [1]-40. DeWitt's Acting Plays, 301.

Luralie, the Water Sprite. In *Drawing Room Dramas*, William Gorman Wills & Mrs. Greene, Edinburgh & London: William Blackwood & Sons, 1873, pp. [i-iv], [1]-58. *Filed under* Drawing Room Drama.

Marie Stuart. London & New York: Samuel French, n.d. Pp. [1]-52.

WILLS, WILLIAM GORMAN (arr.)
Faust. By Goethe. [London]: n.pub., n.d. Pp. [i-iv], [1]-57.

WILLS, WILLIAM HENRY
Larboard Fin, The; or, Twelve Months Since. London: John Cumberland, n.d. Pp. [1]-37. [Cumberland's Minor Theatre].

Larboard Fin, The; or, Twelve Months Since. London: John Cumberland, n.d. Pp. [1]-37. Cumberland's Minor Theatre, XIII. *Filed under* Cumberland, John. Cumberland's Minor Theatre, XIII.

Law of the Land, The; or, London in the Last Century. London: W. Kenneth, 1837. Pp. [iii]-[x], [1]-[46].

WILMOT, MRS. THOMAS
See Dacre, Barbarina Ogle, Lady.

WILSON, CHARLES W.
Botany Bay.
See Woods, Robert Henry.

WILSON, JOHN
City of the Plague, The. In [*City of the Plague and Other Poems*, Edinburgh: A. Constable, 1816], pp. 1-167. Title page lacking.

Convict, The. In [*City of the Plague and Other Poems*, Edinburgh: A. Constable, 1816], pp. [241]-291. Title page lacking.

Isle of Palms, The. In *Isle of Palms and Other Poems*, Edinburgh: Longman, Hurst, Rees, Orme, & Brown, 1812, pp. [i-iv], [1]-[179].

WILSON, JOHN CRAWFORD
Gitanilla, The; or, The Children of the Zincali. London: Thomas Hailes Lacy, n.d. Pp. [1]-50. Promptbook.

WILSON, MARGARET HARRIES, MRS. CORNWELL BARON
Maid of Switzerland, The. N.p.: n.pub., n.d. Pp. [269]-280. Title page lacking. Promptbook. *Filed under* Baron-Wilson, Mrs. Cornwell.

Venus in Arms. By Mrs. C. B. Wilson. London: John Duncombe, n.d. Pp. [1]-26. Duncombe's Edition. *Filed under* Baron-Wilson, Mrs. Cornwell.

Venus in Arms; or, The Petticoat Colonel. London: John Cumberland, n.d. Pp. [i-ii], [1]-34. Cumberland's Minor Theatre, XIV. *Filed under* Cumberland, John. Cumberland's Minor Theatre, XIV.

Venus in Arms; or, The Petticoat Colonel. *Also:* What Won't a Woman Do?. London: John Cumberland, n.d. Pp. [1]-34. [Cumberland's Minor Theatre].

What Won't a Woman Do?
See Venus in Arms.

WILSON, WILLIAM (trans.)
Brand. By Ibsen, Henrik. London: Methuen, 1899. Pp. [iii]-[xvi], [1]-[303]. 3rd ed.

WIN HER AND WEAR HER
See Challis, Henry W. Race for a Wife!, A.

WINBOLT, FREDERICK I.
Aslog. London: Swan Sonnenschein, 1900. Pp. [68]-106.

King Helge. London: Swan Sonnenschein, 1900. Pp. [5]-67.

WINDMILL, THE
See Morton, Edward.

WINDMILL TURRETT
See Dibdin, Thomas John. Bonifacio and Bridgetina.

WINDSOR CASTLE
See Burnand, Francis Cowley.
See Serle, Thomas James.

WINDUS, W. E.
Illiam Dhône. London: Alfred Boot & Sons (printer), 1886. Pp. [1]-48.

WINE DOES WONDERS (anon.)
London: John Lowndes, 1820. Pp. [i-iv], [1]-36.

WINGFIELD, LEWIS STRANGE (trans.)
    Mary Stuart. By Schiller. Indianapolis: Hasselman-Journal (printer), 1883. Pp. [1]-57. Promptbook.
WINNING A HUSBAND
    See Macfarren, George.
WINNING A WIFE
    See Lacy, Thomas Hailes.
WINNING HAZARD, A
    See Wooler, John Pratt.
WINSER, CHARLES
    Alberto della Scala. [London: J. Rodwell, 1839]. Pp. [iii]-[viii], [9]-169. Title page lacking.
WINTER ROBIN
    See Hazlewood, Colin Henry. Jenny Foster, the Sailor's Child.
WINTER'S TALE, THE
    See Anderson, Mary (arr.).
    See Kean, Charles John (arr.).
    See Kemble, John Philip (arr.).
    See Shakespeare, William.
WINTERBOTTOMS!, THE
    See Moncrieff, William Thomas.
WISDOM OF THE WISE, THE
    See Hobbes, John Oliver.
WISE MAN OF THE EAST, THE
    See Inchbald, Elizabeth Simpson, Mrs. Joseph.
WISEMAN, NICHOLAS PATRICK STEPHEN, CARDINAL
    Hidden Gem, The. London: Burns & Oates, 1858. Pp. [i-ii], [1]-130. 5th ed.
    Witch of Rosenburg, The. New York: P. O'Shea, n.d. Pp. [1]-76.
WITCH OF ROSENBURG, THE
    See Wiseman, Nicholas Patrick Stephen, Cardinal.
WITCH OF WINDERMERE, THE
    See Selby, Charles.
WITCH-WIFE, THE: A TALE OF MALKIN TOWER
    See Spicer, Henry.
WITCH'S CURSE!
    See Gilbert, William Schwenck. Ruddigore.
WITCH'S STONE, THE
    See Atkyns, Samuel.
WITCHCRAFT
    See Baillie, Joanna.
WITH FIGARO
    See Ridge, William Pett.
WITH SA'DI IN THE GARDEN
    See Arnold, Edwin, Sir (trans.).
WITHERED LEAVES
    See Broughton, Frederick William.
WITHERS, FRANK
    Sad Memories. London: Samuel French; New York: T. Henry French, n.d. Pp. [1]-12. [Lacy's Acting Edition].
WITHIN AND WITHOUT
    See MacDonald, George.
WITHOUT INCUMBRANCES
    See Simpson, John Palgrave.
WITNESS, THE
    See Galt, John.
WITTIKIND AND HIS BROTHERS
    See Taylor, Tom.
WIVES
    See Wild, James.
WIVES AS THEY WERE AND MAIDS AS THEY ARE
    See Inchbald, Elizabeth Simpson, Mrs. Joseph.
WIVES BY ADVERTISEMENT
    See Jerrold, Douglas William.
WIVES METAMORPHOSED
    See Coffey, Charles. Devil to Pay, The.
WIZARD OF THE MOOR, THE
    See Gott, Henry. Elshie, The.
    See Gott, Henry.
WIZARD OF THE WAVE, THE
    See Haines, John Thomas.
WIZARD, THE RING, AND THE SCAMP, THE
    See George, G. H. Harlequin Aladdin and the Lamp.

WIZARD'S RING
    See Raymond, Richard John. Robert the Devil! Duke of Normandy.
WIZARD'S WAKE
    See Dibdin, Charles Isaac Mungo, jr.
WOLCOT, JOHN
    Fall of Portugal, The; or, The Royal Exiles. London: Longman, Hurst, Rees, & Orme; J. Walker (priv.), 1808. Pp. [3]-[69].
WOLD
    See Aird, Thomas.
WOLF AND THE LAMB, THE
    See Gifford, J. Wear. Supper for Two.
    See Mathews, Charles James.
    See Wilks, Thomas Egerton. Brothers, The.
WOLF OF LITHUANIA
    See Brougham, John. Red Mask, The.
WOLF ROBBER
    See Dibdin, Charles Isaac Mungo, jr. Red Riding Hood.
WOLF, THE WOOER, AND THE WIZARD!, THE
    See Keating, Eliza H. Little Red Riding Hood.
WOLSEY!
    See Smith, John Frederick.
WOLVERSON, HARRY
    Crossed Love. London & New York: Samuel French, n.d. Pp. [1]-28. [Lacy's Acting Edition].
WOMAN AGAINST WOMAN
    See Harvey, Frank.
    See Marryat, Florence.
WOMAN AND WINE
    See Shirley, Arthur.
WOMAN AT THE WHEEL!
    See Burnand, Francis Cowley. Rumplestiltskin.
WOMAN CHANGED INTO A CAT
    See Rodwell, George Herbert Bonaparte. Grimalkin.
WOMAN HATER, THE
    See Bell, Ernest (trans.).
    See Bernard, William Bayle.
WOMAN I ADORE!, THE
    See Morton, John Maddison.
WOMAN IN MAUVE, THE
    See Phillips, Watts.
WOMAN IN RED, THE
    See Coyne, Joseph Stirling.
WOMAN IN WHITE, THE
    See Collins, William Wilkie.
WOMAN IS A DEVIL, A
    See Mérimée, Prosper.
WOMAN KEEPS A SECRET
    See Centlivre, Susanna Carroll Freeman, Mrs. Joseph. Wonder, The.
WOMAN NEVER VEXT, A
    See Planché, James Robinson.
WOMAN OF COURAGE, A
    See Bell, Florence Eveleen Eleanore Oliffe, Mrs. Hugh (Lady).
WOMAN OF CULTURE, A
    See Bell, Florence Eveleen Eleanore Oliffe, Mrs. Hugh (Lady).
WOMAN OF NO IMPORTANCE, A
    See Wilde, Oscar Fingall O'Flahertie Wills.
WOMAN OF THE WORLD, THE
    See Cavendish, Clara, Lady.
    See Coyne, Joseph Stirling.
WOMAN THAT WAS A CAT, THE
    See Suter, William E.
WOMAN WILL BE A WOMAN, A
    See Ware, James Redding.
WOMAN'S CHANCE
    See Clarke, Charles Allen.
WOMAN'S CONSTANCY
    See Webb, Charles. Belphegor the Mountebank.
WOMAN'S FAITH
    See Bernard, William Bayle.

WOMAN'S LIFE
 See Buckstone, John Baldwin. Isabelle.
WOMAN'S LOVE
 See Brougham, John. Art and Artifice.
 See Stephens, George. Revenge.
 See Wade, Thomas.
 See Wilks, Thomas Egerton.
WOMAN'S PROPER PLACE
 See Jones, John Wilton.
WOMAN'S REASON, A
 See Brookfield, Charles Hallam Elton.
WOMAN'S RIGHTS
 See Darling, Isabella Fleming.
 See Palmer, T. A.
WOMAN'S THE DEVIL!
 See Stirling, Edward.
WOMAN'S TRIALS
 See Parry, Thomas. Lucky Horse Shoe, The.
WOMAN'S WILES
 See Young, William.
WOMAN'S WILL (anon.)
 In New British Theatre, London: A. J. Valpy (printer),
 1815, IV, [i], [35]-[145].
WOMAN'S WILL—A RIDDLE!
 See Swift, Edmund Lewes Lenthal.
WOMAN'S WIT
 See Knowles, James Sheridan.
WOMAN'S WORTH AND WOMAN'S WAYS
 See Bernard, William Bayle. Four Sisters, The.
WOMAN'S WRONGS
 See Heathcote, Arthur M.
WOMEN'S CLUB, THE
 See Coyne, Joseph Stirling.
WON AT LAST!
 See Reeve, Wybert.
WONDER, THE
 See Centlivre, Susanna Carroll Freeman, Mrs. Joseph.
WONDER-WORKING MAGICIAN, THE
 See MacCarthy, Denis Florence (trans.).
WONDERFUL CURE, A
 See Lacy, Katherine.
WONDERFUL LAMP
 See Aladdin (anon.).
 See Farley, Charles. Aladdin.
 See Martin, Theodore, Sir (trans.). Aladdin.
 See O'Neill, John Robert. Aladdin.
WONDERFUL LAMP IN A NEW LIGHT, THE
 See A'Beckett, Gilbert Abbott.
WONDERFUL SCAMP!
 See Byron, Henry James. Aladdin.
WONDERFUL WATER CURE, THE
 See Webster, Benjamin Nottingham.
WONDERFUL WOMAN, A
 See Dance, Charles.
WOOD, A. C. FRASER
 In the Eyes of the World. London: Samuel French; New
 York: T. Henry French, n.d. Pp. [1]-20. [Lacy's Acting
 Edition].
WOOD, ANNA CAROLINE
 See Steele, Anna Caroline Wood, Mrs.
WOOD, ARTHUR
 Behind a Mask.
  See Dixon, Bernard Homer.
 Bilious Attack, A. London & New York: Samuel French,
 n.d. Pp. [1]-15. [Lacy's Acting Edition].
 Romantic Attachment, A. London: Thomas Hailes Lacy, n.d.
 Pp. [1]-19.
WOOD, GEORGE
 Irish Doctor, The; or, The Dumb Lady Cured. London:
 Samuel French; New York: T. Henry French, n.d. Pp.
 [1]-22. French's Acting Edition (late Lacy's).
WOOD, JAY HICKORY
 Puss in Boots. Music by Locknane, Clement; Haines, Alfred;
 Carpenter, Alfred. London: n.pub., n.d. Pp. [1]-48.
 Libretto.

WOOD DAEMON, THE
 See Lewis, Matthew Gregory.
WOOD DEMON, THE
 See Kenny, Charles.
WOODBARROW FARM
 See Jerome, Jerome Klapka.
WOODCOCK'S LITTLE GAME
 See Morton, John Maddison.
WOODEN WALLS
 See Cherry, Andrew. Peter the Great.
WOODLEY, WILLIAM
 Catharine de Medicis. Also attrib. to Heytesbury, William. In
 Catharine de Medicis . . . , London: J. Hatchard & Son,
 1825, pp. [i]-viii, [1]-91.
 Catherine de Medicis. Also attrib. to Heytesbury, William.
 London: W. Sams, 1820. Pp. [i-x], [1]-56. Filed under
 Catherine de Medicis (anon.).
 James the Third, King of Scotland. Also attrib. to Heytesbury,
 William. London: W. Sams, [1820]. Pp. [i-x], [1]-53. Filed
 under James the Third (anon.).
 James the Third, King of Scotland. Also attrib. to Heytesbury,
 William. In Catharine de Medicis . . . , London: J.
 Hatchard & Son, 1825, pp. [i], [121]-215.
WOODMAN, THE
 See Dudley, Henry Bate.
WOODMAN'S HUT, THE
 See Arnold, Samuel James.
WOODMAN'S SPELL, THE
 See Stirling, Edward.
WOODROOFFE, SOPHIA
 Buondelmonte. In Four Dramatic Poems, ed. G. S. Faber,
 London: Seeley, Burnside, & Seeley, 1846, pp. [1],
 [i]-[xxxvi], [1]-85.
 Cleanthes. In Four Dramatic Poems, ed. G. S. Faber, London:
 Seeley, Burnside, & Seeley, 1824, pp. [123]-132. Filed
 under Buondelmonte.
 Court of Flora, The. In Four Dramatic Poems, ed. G. S. Faber,
 London: Seeley, Burnside, & Seeley, 1824, pp. [133]-150.
 Filed under Buondelmonte.
 Zingari, The. In Four Dramatic Poems, ed. G. S. Faber,
 London: Seeley, Burnside, & Seeley, 1824, pp. [87]-121.
 Filed under Buondelmonte.
WOODS, ROBERT HENRY
 Botany Bay. Written with Wilson, Charles W. Dublin:
 Hodges, Figgis, 1892. Pp. [1]-24.
WOODSTOCK
 See Pocock, Isaac.
WOOER, THE WAITRESS, AND THE WILLIAN
 See Arden, Henry T. Belle of The Barley-Mow, The.
WOOING IN JEST AND LOVING IN EARNEST
 See Troughton, Adolphus Charles.
WOOING ONE'S WIFE
 See Morton, John Maddison.
WOOING UNDER DIFFICULTIES
 See Douglass, John T.
WOOINGS AND WEDDINGS
 See Lovell, George William. Look before You Leap.
WOOLER, I. P.
 See Wooler, John Pratt.
WOOLER, JOHN PRATT
 Allow Me to Apologize. London: John Duncombe, n.d. Pp.
 [1]-24. Duncombe's Acting Edition of the British
 Theatre, 527.
 Did I Dream It? [Clyde, Ohio: Ames & Holgate], n.d. Pp.
 [1]-20.
 Faint Heart Which Did Win a Fair Lady, A. London: Thomas
 Hailes Lacy, n.d. Pp. [1]-20. [Lacy's Acting Edition].
 Founded on Facts. London: Thomas Hailes Lacy, n.d. Pp.
 [1]-18. [Lacy's Acting Edition].
 Haunted Mill, The. Music by Mallandaine. London:
 Thomas Hailes Lacy, n.d. Pp. [1]-15. Libretto.
 Hunt for a Husband, A. London: Thomas Hailes Lacy, n.d.
 Pp. [1]-26.
 I'll Write to the Times. London: Thomas Hailes Lacy, n.d.
 Pp. [1]-22. [Lacy's Acting Edition].

Keep Your Temper. London: Thomas Hailes Lacy, n.d. Pp. [1]-23. [Lacy's Acting Edition].

Laurence's Love Suit. London: Thomas Hailes Lacy, n.d. Pp. [1]-34. [Lacy's Acting Edition].

Locked In. New York: DeWitt, n.d. Pp. [1]-14. DeWitt's Acting Plays, 109.

Love in Livery. Boston: William V. Spencer, n.d. Pp. [1]-24. Spencer's Boston Theatre, 86.

Maid of Honour, The. London: Thomas Hailes Lacy, n.d. Pp. [1]-23. [Lacy's Acting Edition].

Man Without a Head, A. New York: Samuel French, n.d. Pp. [1]-16. French's Minor Drama, 272.

Marriage at Any Price. London: Thomas Hailes Lacy, n.d. Pp. [1]-24. [Lacy's Acting Edition].

Model Husband, A. London: Thomas Hailes Lacy, n.d. Pp. [1]-17. [Lacy's Acting Edition].

Old Phil's Birthday. Clyde, Ohio: A. D. Ames, n.d. Pp. [1]-26. Ames' Series of Standard and Minor Drama, 81.

Orange Blossoms. New York: Robert M. DeWitt, n.d. Pp. [1]-21. Promptbook.

Plots for Petticoats. London & New York: Samuel French, n.d. Pp. [1]-18. [Lacy's Acting Edition].

Ring and the Keeper, The. London: Thomas Hailes Lacy, n.d. Pp. [1]-18.

Sisterly Service. By I. P. Wooler. New York: Robert M. DeWitt, n.d. Pp. [1]-18. DeWitt's Acting Plays, 43.

Twice Told Tale, A. Boston: William V. Spencer, n.d. Pp. [1]-20. Spencer's Boston Theatre, 191.

Wilful Ward, The. London: Thomas Hailes Lacy, n.d. Pp. [1]-20.

Winning Hazard, A. London: Thomas Hailes Lacy, n.d. Pp. [1]-20. [Lacy's Acting Edition].

WORD OF HONOR, THE (anon.)
In *New British Theatre,* London: A. J. Valpy (printer), 1814, I, [i], [339]-377.

WORD OF HONOUR, THE: A JERSEY LOVE STORY
See Meritt, Paul.

WORKBOX, THE
See Craven, Tom.

WORKMAN, THE
See Harvey, Frank. Woman against Woman.

WORKMEN'S FOE, THE
See Moss, Arthur B.

WORLD, THE
See Kenney, James.
See Meritt, Paul.

WORLD AND STAGE
See Simpson, John Palgrave.

WORLD AS IT GOES
See Kenney, James. Touchstone, The.
See Maclaren, Archibald. Fashion.

WORLD OF FASHION, THE
See Oxenford, John.

WORLD WELL LOST
See Dryden, John. All for Love.

WORN OUT SUBJECT DONE UP ANEW
See Bellingham, Henry. Bluebeard Re-Paired.

WORRELL, JAMES
Orphan of the Wreck, The. London: Thomas Hailes Lacy, n.d. Pp. [1]-30. Cumberland's British Theatre (with Duncombe's).

Violette; or, The Danseuse. London: John Duncombe, n.d. Pp. [3]-29. Duncombe's Edition.

Young Waterman's Society, The; or, The Ran-Dan Club. London: J. Pattie, n.d. Pp. [1]-19.

WORSHIP OF BACCHUS, THE
See Meritt, Paul.

WORTH A STRUGGLE
See Waldron, W. Richard.

WORTH MAKES THE MAN
See Planché, James Robinson. Mysterious Lady, The.

WORTHINGTON, J.
Up in the World. London & New York: Samuel French, n.d. Pp. [1]-14. [Lacy's Acting Edition].

WORTLEY, EMMELINE CHARLOTTE ELIZABETH MANNERS STUART, MRS. CHARLES (Lady)
Alphonzo Algarves. London: Joseph Rickerby, 1841. Pp. [i-iv], [1]-164.

Eva; or, The Error. London: Joseph Rickerby, 1840. Pp. [i-viii], [1]-153.

Moonshine. London: John Dicks, n.d. Pp. [1]-28. Dicks' Standard Plays, 668.

WOULD-BE GENTLEMAN, THE
See Mathew, Charles (trans.).

WOUNDS HEAL WOUNDS
See Pytches, John.

WRAITH OF THE LAKE!, THE
See Haines, John Thomas.

WRATISLAW, THEODORE
Pity of Love, The. London: Swan Sonnenschein, 1895. Pp. [3]-[44].

WRAY, CHARLES
Ranelagh.
See Simpson, John Palgrave.

WRECK, THE
See Masterton, Charles.
See Williams, William Henry.

WRECK ASHORE, THE
See Buckstone, John Baldwin.

WRECK AT SEA
See Stirling, Edward. Grace Darling.

WRECK OF THE RAVEN
See Greenwood, Thomas Longdon. Paul the Pilot.

WRECK, THE MISER, AND THE MINES
See Haines, John Thomas. Yew Tree Ruins, The.

WRECKAGE
See Hein, Gustav (trans.).

WRECKER'S BRIDE
See Stirling, Edward. Lestelle.

WRECKER'S DAUGHTER, THE
See Knowles, James Sheridan.

WREN BOYS, THE
See Wilks, Thomas Egerton.

WRESTLING WITH WHISTLERS
See Anstey, F.

WRIGHT, A. L.
Beggar Venus, The. Chicago: T. S. Denison, c.1888. Pp. [1]-54. Alta Series.

WRINKLES: A TALE OF TIME
See Byron, Henry James.

WRITING ON THE WALL, THE
See Morton, Thomas, jr.

WRITTEN IN SAND
See Broughton, Frederick William.

WRONG BOX
See Barnett, Morris. Tact!

WRONG MAN, THE
See Morton, John Maddison.

WRONG MAN IN THE RIGHT PLACE, A
See Oxenford, John.

WRONG POET, THE
See Bell, Florence Eveleen Eleanore Oliffe, Mrs. Hugh (Lady).

WROUGHTON, RICHARD (arr.)
King Richard the Second. By Shakespeare, William. London: John Miller, 1815. Pp. [1]-71.

WYATT, EDGAR
Count Tremolio. Music by Watson, Alfred R. Nottingham: J. Derry (printer), 1887. Pp. [1]-56. Libretto.

WYCHERLEY, WILLIAM
Country Girl, The.
See Garrick, David (arr.).

Plain Dealer, The.
See Kemble, John Philip (arr.).

WYLDE, MRS. HENRY (trans.)
Maçon, Le. *Also:* The Mason and the Locksmith. *Also:* The Mason. By Scribe, Eugène; Delavigne, Casimir. Music by Auber. London: A. S. Mallett (printer), 1879. Pp. [1]-38. Libretto.

WYNNE, JOHN

Advocate of Durango, The; or, The Avenging Spirit. In *Three Original Plays,* London: Thomas Bosworth, 1853, pp. [175]-229. *Filed under* Three Original Plays.

Napoleon's First Love; or, The Blue Bear of Nangis! In *Three Original Plays,* London: Thomas Bosworth, 1853, pp. [107]-174. *Filed under* Three Original Plays.

Tricks of the Time; or, Bill Stealers Beware. In *Three Original Plays,* London: Thomas Bosworth, 1853, pp. [i]-[xii], [1]-106. *Filed under* Three Original Plays.

WYNNES OF WYNHAVOD, THE
    See Pfeiffer, Emily Jane Daub, Mrs.

X, Y, Z
    See Colman, George, jr.

XARIFA
    See Dacre, Barbarina Ogle, Lady.

Y., H. A.
    See Hay, Frederic.

Y. T. O.

Aristophanes at Oxford; or, O. W. Oxford: J. Vincent, n.d. Pp. [i]-[viii], [1]-85.

YANKEE NOTES FOR ENGLISH CIRCULATION
    See Stirling, Edward.

YANKEE PEDDLER
    See Barnett, Morris.

YARDLEY, WILLIAM

Knave of Hearts, The. London: n.pub., n.d. Pp. [42]-67. Title page lacking. *Filed under* Our Toys.

Our Toys. London: n.pub., n.d. Pp. [13]-41. Title page lacking.

Passport, The.
    See Stephenson, Benjamin Charles.

Red-Riding-Hood. London: n.pub., n.d. Pp. [68]-91. Title page lacking. *Filed under* Our Toys.

Wedding Eve, The. Music by Toulmouche, Frederic. London: Hopwood & Crew, n.d. Pp. [i-iv], [1]-203. Vocal score.

YASHMAK, THE
    See Raleigh, Cecil.

YATES, EDMUND HODGSON

After the Ball. Music by Reed, Thomas German. London: J. Mallett (printer), 1857. Pp. [1]-8. Libretto. *Filed under* Reed, Mr. and Mrs. German.

Black Sheep.
    See Simpson, John Palgrave.

Double Dummy.
    See Harrington, Nicholas Herbert.

Hit Him, He Has No Friends. Written with Harrington, Nicholas Herbert. Boston: Walter H. Baker, n.d. Pp. [1]-16. Baker's Edition of Plays.

If the Cap Fits.
    See Harrington, Nicholas Herbert.

My Friend from Leatherhead. Written with Harrington, Nicholas Herbert. London: Thomas Hailes Lacy, n.d. Pp. [1]-16. [Lacy's Acting Edition].

Night at Notting Hill, A. Written with Harrington, Nicholas Herbert. London: Thomas Hailes Lacy, n.d. Pp. [1]-14. Lacy's Acting Edition, 428.

Your Likeness—One Shilling!
    See Harrington, Nicholas Herbert.

YE BATTEL OF BOSWORTH FIELD!
    See Selby, Charles. Kinge Richard ye Third.

YE FAIR ONE WITH YE GOLDEN LOCKS
    See Grattan, H. P.

YE FAIRE MAIDE OF ISLINGTON; OR, HARLEQUIN, THE CRUEL PRIOR OF CANONBURY, AND THE CHIVALROUS KNIGHTS OF ST. JOHN (anon.) London: W. F. Bulgin (printer), n.d. Pp. [1]-24.

YE LADYE OF COVENTRIE AND YE EXYLE FAYRIE
    See Hale, William Palmer. Godiva.

YE QUEENE OF HEARTES THAT MADE YE TARTES, AND YE KNAVE OF HEARTES WHO ATE 'EM
    See Lane, Pyngle. Mother Goose.

YE QUEENE, YE EARLE, AND YE MAYDENNE
    See Halliday, Andrew. Kenilworth.

YEAR IN AN HOUR, A
    See Poole, John.

YEAR OF JUBILEE
    See Peel, Edmund. Salem Redeemed.

YEATS, WILLIAM BUTLER

Countess Kathleen, The. In *Countess Kathleen and Various Legends and Lyrics,* London: T. Fisher Unwin, 1892, pp. [1]-89.

Land of Heart's Desire, The. Chicago: Stone & Kimball, 1894. Pp. [1]-43.

Land of Heart's Desire, The. London: T. Fisher Unwin, 1894. Pp. [1]-43.

Shadowy Waters, The. London: Hodder & Stoughton, 1900. Pp. [1]-57.

YELLOW DWARF, THE
    See A'Beckett, Gilbert Abbott.
    See Byron, Henry James.
    See Keating, Eliza H.

YELLOW DWARF AND THE KING OF THE GOLD MINES, THE
    See Planché, James Robinson.

YELLOW KIDS, THE
    See Barnett, Morris.

YELLOW ROSES
    See Young, Charles Lawrence, Sir.

YENDYS, SYDNEY
    See Dobell, Sydney Thompson.

YEOMAN'S DAUGHTER, THE
    See Serle, Thomas James.

YEOMEN OF THE GUARD, THE
    See Gilbert, William Schwenck.

YES!
    See Somerset, Charles A.

YES OR NO?
    See Pocock, Isaac.

YEW TREE RUINS, THE
    See Haines, John Thomas.

YIELDING OF PILATE, THE
    See McKenzie, William Patrick.

YORK AND LANCASTER
    See Hood, Tom.

YORKE, ELIZABETH LINDSEY, COUNTESS OF HARDWICKE

Court of Oberon, The; or, The Three Wishes. By the Countess of Hardwicke. London: Thomas Hailes Lacy, n.d. Pp. [1]-30. [Lacy's Acting Edition].

YORKSHIRE GAMESTER, THE
    See Rayner, Barnabas F.

YOU CAN'T MARRY YOUR GRANDMOTHER
    See Bayly, Thomas Haynes.

YOU KNOW WHAT
    See Beazley, Samuel, jr.

YOU NEVER CAN TELL
    See Shaw, George Bernard.

YOUNG, ALFRED W.

False Alarm, A. London & New York: Samuel French, n.d. Pp. [1]-28. [Lacy's Acting Edition].

YOUNG, CHARLES LAWRENCE, SIR

Baron's Wager, The. London & New York: Samuel French, n.d. Pp. [1]-14.

Charms. London & New York: Samuel French, n.d. Pp. [1]-48. [Lacy's Acting Edition].

Childhood's Dreams. London & New York: Samuel French, n.d. Pp. [1]-24. [Lacy's Acting Edition].

Drifted Apart. London & New York: Samuel French, n.d. Pp. [1]-14. [Lacy's Acting Edition].

For Her Child's Sake. London & New York: Samuel French, n.d. Pp. [1]-27.

Gilded Youth. London & New York: Samuel French, n.d. Pp. [1]-51. [Lacy's Acting Edition].

Infatuation. London & New York; Samuel French, n.d. Pp. [1]-40. [Lacy's Acting Edition].

Jim the Penman. London & New York: Samuel French, n.d. Pp. [1]-65. Promptbook.

Knave and Queen. Written with Howard, Bronson. In *Banker's Daughter & Other Plays by Bronson Howard,* ed. Allan G. Halline, Princeton, N.J.: Princeton University Press, 1941, America's Lost Plays, X, [193]-238.

Late Sir Benjamin, The. London & New York: Samuel French, n.d. Pp. [1]-19. [Lacy's Acting Edition].

Miss Chester.
    See Marryat, Florence.

Montcalm. London & New York: Samuel French, n.d. Pp. [1]-48. [Lacy's Acting Edition].

Petticoat Perfidy. London & New York: Samuel French, n.d. Pp. [1]-19. Final page lacking. [French's Acting Edition].

Plot for Plot. London & New York: Samuel French, n.d. Pp. [1]-15. [Lacy's Acting Edition].

Shadows. London & New York: Samuel French, n.d. Pp. [1]-48. French's Acting Edition (late Lacy's), 1497.

That Dreadful Doctor! London & New York: Samuel French, n.d. Pp. [1]-20.

Yellow Roses. London: Samuel French; New York: T. Henry French, n.d. Pp. [1]-16.

YOUNG, CHARLES MICHAEL
    Euphernia; or, The Destroyer of Genaize. Sheffield: E. M. Charles, 1837. Pp. [1]-63.

YOUNG, EDWARD
    Revenge, The. London: Whittingham & Arliss, 1814. Pp. [1]-[56]. London Theatre, VI. *Filed under* Dibdin, Thomas John, ed. London Theatre, VI.
    Revenge, The. London: John Cumberland, 1827. Pp. [1]-54. Cumberland's British Theatre, XV. *Filed under* Cumberland, John. Cumberland's British Theatre, XV.
    Revenge, The. In *British Drama,* 12 vols., London: John Dicks, 1864, I, [193]-206.
    Revenge, The.
        See Kemble, John Philip (arr.).

YOUNG, WILLIAM
    Lucrezia Borgia. London: n.pub. (priv.), 1847. Pp. [i-iv], [1]-102.
    Rajah, The. New York & London: Samuel French, c.1882. Pp. [1]-96.
    Regent's Daughter, The. New York: D. Appleton, 1854. Pp. [1]-40.
    Woman's Wiles. London & New York: Samuel French, c.1909. Pp. [1]-16. French's International Copyrighted Edition of the Works of the Best Authors, 173.

YOUNG AND HANDSOME
    See Planché, James Robinson.

YOUNG COLLEGIAN, THE
    See Robertson, Thomas William. Cantab, The.
    See Robertson, Thomas William.

YOUNG ENGLAND
    See Morton, John Maddison.

YOUNG GENTLEMAN WHO CHARMED THE ROCKS
    See Byron, Henry James. Orpheus and Eurydice.

YOUNG HUSSAR, THE
    See Dimond, William.

YOUNG LAD FROM THE COUNTRY, A
    See Oxenford, John.

YOUNG LADY FROM THE COUNTRY, THE (anon. trans.)
    By Amalie (Amelia), Princess of Saxony. In *Six Dramas Illustrative of German Life,* London: John W. Parker, pp. [277]-350. *Filed under* Six Dramas (anon.).

YOUNG LOVEL'S BRIDE
    See Somerset, Charles A. Mistletoe Bough, The.

YOUNG MASTER
    See Moncrieff, William Thomas. Home for the Holidays.

YOUNG MOTHER, THE
    See Selby, Charles.

YOUNG PRETENDER
    See Sketchley, Arthur. Getting Up in the World.

YOUNG QUAKER, THE
    See O'Keeffe, John.

YOUNG REEFER, THE
    See Soane, George.

YOUNG SCAMP, THE
    See Stirling, Edward.

YOUNG SCHOLAR, THE
    See Bell, Ernest (trans.).

YOUNG SPARK AND THE OLD FLAME!
    See Byron, Henry James. Pandora's Box.

YOUNG VIRGINIAN
    See Brougham, John. Romance and Reality.

YOUNG WARD, THE
    See Jameson, Anna Brownell Murphy, Mrs. Robert (trans.).

YOUNG WATERMAN'S SOCIETY, THE
    See Worrell, James.

YOUNG WIDOW, THE
    See Rodwell, James Thomas Gooderham.

YOUNG WIVES AND OLD HUSBANDS
    See Harris, Richard.

YOUNGE, A.
    First of May, The. London: S. G. Fairbrother, n.d. Pp. [1]-21.
    Village Tale, A. London: S. G. Fairbrother, n.d. Pp. [1]-18.

YOUNGE, HENRY
    Harlequin and George Barnwell; or, The London 'Prentice. Music by Blewitt. London: W. Kenneth, n.d. Pp. [1]-20. Libretto.
    Sinbad the Sailor; or, The Valley of Diamonds. London: W. Kenneth, 1838. Pp. [1]-47. *Filed under* Serle, Thomas James.

YOUNGER BROTHER, THE
    See Crawley, Richard.

YOUR LIFE'S IN DANGER
    See Morton, John Maddison.

YOUR LIKENESS—ONE SHILLING!
    See Harrington, Nicholas Herbert.

YOUR VOTE AND INTEREST
    See Maltby, C. Alfred.

YOURS OR MINE
    See Tobin, John.

YOUTH, LOVE, AND FOLLY
    See Dimond, William. Little Jockey, The.
    See Dimond, William.

YOUTH OF CHARLES I
    See Robinson, Emma. Richelieu in Love.

YOUTH WHO NEVER SAW A WOMAN
    See Amherst, J. H. Fifteen Years of Labour Lost.
    See Nature and Philosophy (anon.).

YOUTH'S LOVE-LORE
    See Platt, William.

YOUTHFUL DAYS OF FREDERICK THE GREAT, THE
    See Abbott, William.

YOUTHFUL DAYS OF WILLIAM THE FOURTH, THE
    See Barnett, Charles Zachary. William the Fourth.
    See Barnett, Charles Zachary.

YOUTHFUL QUEEN, THE
    See Shannon, Charles.

YULE LOG, A
    See Webster, Benjamin, jr.

ZAMEO
    See Byron, Medora Gordon.

ZAMIEL, THE SPIRIT OF THE FOREST
    See Kerr, John. Freischutz, Der.

ZAMORIN AND ZAMA
    See Sotheby, William.

ZAMPA
    See Maggioni, Manfredo (trans.).
    See Thompson, Alfred.

ZANGWILL, ISRAEL
    Six Persons. [London & New York: Samuel French], n.d. Pp. [3]-14. Title page lacking. [Lacy's Acting Edition].

ZANONE
    See Cubitt, Sydney.

ZAPOLYA: A CHRISTMAS TALE
    See Coleridge, Samuel Taylor.

ZARA
    See Hill, Aaron.

ZARAH
    See Soane, George.

ZAZEZIZOZU
> *See* Fitzball, Edward.

ZELINA
> *See* Somerset, Charles A.

ZEMBUCA
> *See* Pocock, Isaac.

ZETO
> **Vashti.** In *Vashti and Other Poems,* London: Kegan Paul, Trench, Trubner, 1897, pp. [i], [1]-91.

ZGLINITZKA, MARIE VON (trans.)
> **Harold.** By Wildenbruch, Ernst von. Hanover: Carl Schussler, 1884. Pp. [i-iv], 1-174.

ZIMMERN, HELEN (trans.?)
> **Beneficent Bear, The.** By Goldoni, Carlo. In *Comedies of Carlo Goldoni,* ed. Helen Zimmern, London: David Stott, 1892, pp. [95]-145. *Filed under* Comedies of Carlo Goldoni.
> **Curious Mishap, A.** By Goldoni, Carlo. In *Comedies of Carlo Goldoni,* ed. Helen Zimmern, London: David Stott, 1892, pp. [1]-94. *Filed under* Comedies of Carlo Goldoni.
> **Fan, The.** By Goldoni, Carlo. In *Comedies of Carlo Goldoni,* ed. Helen Zimmern, London: David Stott, 1892, pp. [147]-227. *Filed under* Comedies of Carlo Goldoni.

Spendthrift Miser, The. By Goldoni, Carlo. In *Comedies of Carlo Goldoni,* ed. Helen Zimmern, London: David Stott, 1892, pp. [229]-287. *Filed under* Comedies of Carlo Goldoni.

ZINGARI, THE
> *See* Woodrooffe, Sophia.

ZINGARO, LO
> *See* Addison, Henry Robert, Capt.

ZINGIBER, ZACHARY (pseud.)
> **Ghost, The.** Weymouth: G. Kay (printer), 1814. Pp. [i]-[x], [1]-83.

ZOLA, ÉMILE
> **Heirs of Rabourdin, The.**
> *See* de Mattos, A. Teixeira (trans.).

ZOO, THE
> *See* Stephenson, Benjamin Charles.

ZORINSKI
> *See* Morton, Thomas, sr.

ZOROASTER
> *See* Moncrieff, William Thomas.

ZULOR, THE CIRCASSIAN CHIEF
> *See* Atkyns, Samuel.

ZUMA
> *See* Dibdin, Thomas John.

APPENDIX A WOMEN DRAMATISTS

Adams, Catherine
Adams, Florence Davenport
Adams, Sarah Fuller Flowers, Mrs. William Bridges
Anderson, Mary (later Mrs. Antonio de Navarro)
Archer, Frances Elizabeth, Mrs. William
Aveling, Eleanor Marx, Mrs. Edward
Baillie, Joanna
Balfour, Mary Devens
Barmby, Beatrice Helen
Bartholomew, Anne Charlotte Fayermann, Mrs. Valentine
 (formerly Mrs. Walter Turnbull)
Beerbohm, Constance
Bell, Florence Eveleen Eleanore Oliffe, Mrs. Hugh (Lady)
Bell, Frances
Bell, Harrie
Beringer, Aimée Danielle, Mrs. Oscar
Berry, Mary
Boaden, Caroline
Braddon, Mary Elizabeth (later Mrs. Maxwell)
Bradley, Katherine Harris. See Field, Michael (pseud.).
Bright, Kate C., Mrs. Augustus
Brooke, Frances Moore, Mrs. John
Browning, Elizabeth Barrett, Mrs. Robert
Burney, Estelle
Burney, Frances (later Mrs. Alexander D'Arblay)
Byron, Medora Gordon
Cassilis, Ina Leon
Cavendish, Clara, Lady (pseud.)
Centlivre, Susanna Carroll Freeman, Mrs. Joseph
Chambers, Marianne
Chapman, Jane Frances
Chatterton, Henrietta Georgiana Marcia Iremonger, Mrs.
 Lascelles, Lady Georgiana
Childe-Pemberton, Harriet Louisa
Clarke, Clara Savile
Clifford, Lucy Lane, Mrs. William Kingdon
Cobbold, Elizabeth Knipe, Mrs. John (formerly Mrs. William
 Clarke)
Cooper, Edith Emma. See Field, Michael (pseud.).
Corder, Henrietta Louisa Walford, Mrs. Frederick
Corrie, Jessie Elizabeth
Cowen, ?, Miss
Cowley, Hannah Parkhouse, Mrs.
Crackanthorpe, Blanche Alethea Elizabeth Holt, Mrs. Hubert
 Montague
Craigie, Pearl Mary Teresa Richards, Mrs. Reginald Walpole. See
 Hobbes, John Oliver (pseud.).
Crosland, Camilla Dufour Toulmin, Mrs. Newton
Crowe, Catherine Stevens, Mrs. John
Dacre, Barbarina Ogle, Lady (later Mrs. Thomas Wilmot;
 Baroness Brand)
Darling, Isabella Fleming
Davidson, Frances A., Mrs.

Davies, Blanche
Davis, Lillie
Davis, Mrs. Maxwell
de Smart, Mrs. Alec
Dixon, Marion Hepworth
Dorisi, Lisa
Dufferin, Helen Selina Sheridan Blackwood, Lady
Durant, Héloise
Ebsworth, Mary Emma Fairbrother, Mrs. Joseph
Edgeworth, Maria
Eliot, George (pseud. of Mary Ann Evans) (later Mrs. J. W.
 Cross)
Elliot, Silvia Fogg
Evans, Mary Ann. See Eliot, George (pseud.).
Fane, Violet (pseud. of Lamb, Mary Montgomerie) (later Mrs.
 Singleton; Lady Currie)
Farjeon, Eleanor
Field, Michael (pseud. of Katherine Harris Bradley and Edith
 Emma Cooper)
Filippi, Rosina (later Mrs. H. M. Dowson)
Fitzsimon, Ellen
Fleming, George (pseud. of Fletcher, Julia Constance)
Fletcher, Julia Constance. See Fleming, George (pseud.).
Fraser, Julia Agnes
Fullerton, Georgiana Charlotte Leveson-Gower, Mrs. Alexander
 George, Lady Georgiana
Fry, Betsey
Garraway, Agnes J.
Gillington, May Clarissa (later Mrs. G. F. Byron)
Glyn, Alice Coralie
Goddard, Kate
Gore, Catherine Grace Frances Moody, Mrs. Charles
Gowing, Emilia Julia Blake, Mrs. William Aylmer
Graves, Clotilde Inez Mary
Greene, Louisa Lilias Plunket, Mrs. Richard Jonas (Baroness)
Greet, Dora Victoire, Mrs.
Greville, Beatrice Violet Graham, Lady
Grove, Florence Craufurd
Gunning, Elizabeth (later Mrs. James Plunkett)
Hall, Anna Maria Fielding, Mrs. Samuel Carter
Harley, St. John (pseud. of Pollock, Ellen, Mrs. Julius)
Harvey, Margaret
Harwood, Isabella. See Neil, Ross (pseud.).
Hayes, Maria Ximena
Hazlewood, ?, Miss
Helme, Elizabeth
Hemans, Felicia Dorothea Browne, Mrs. Alfred
Heron, Matilda (later Mrs. Robert Stoepel)
Hill, Isabel
Hinkson, Katharine Tynan, Mrs. Henry Albert
Hobbes, John Oliver (pseud. of Craigie, Pearl Mary Teresa
 Richards, Mrs. Reginald Walpole)
Holcroft, Fanny

Holford, Margaret, Mrs.
Humboldt, Charlotte de
Hunt, Margaret Raine, Mrs. Alfred William
Hunt, Violet
Inchbald, Elizabeth Simpson, Mrs. Joseph
Jameson, Anna Brownell Murphy, Mrs. Robert
Jay, Harriet. *See* Marlowe, Charles (pseud.).
Jopling, Louise Goode, Mrs. Joseph Middleton (later Mrs. Rowe)
Keating, Eliza H.
Kemble, Frances Anne (Fanny) (later Mrs. Pierce Butler)
Kemble, Marie Thérèse de Camp, Mrs. Charles
Kingston, Gertrude
Lacy, Katherine
Lamb, Mary Montgomerie. *See* Fane, Violet (pseud.).
Lancaster, Florence
Lancaster-Wallis, Ellen
Landon, Letitia Elizabeth (later Mrs. George Maclean)
Lawrence, Eweretta
Leadbeater, Mary Shakleton, Mrs. William
Lee, Eliza Buckminster, Mrs.
Lee, Harriet
Lee, Sophia
Le Fanu, Alicia Sheridan, Mrs. Joseph
Leigh, Agnes
Leverson, Mrs. Ernest
Lord, Henrietta Frances
Lovell, Maria Anne Lacy, Mrs. George William
Lynch, Hannah
Macauley, Elizabeth Wright
Macfarren, Natalia
Marlowe, Charles (pseud. of Jay, Harriet)
Marryat, Florence (later Mrs. Church; Mrs. Francis Lean)
Martin, ?, Mrs.
Medd, Mabel S.
Merivale, Mrs. Herman Charles
Milligan, Alice L.
Minton, Ann
Mitford, Mary Russell
More, Hannah
Morgan, Sydney Owenson, Mrs. Thomas Charles (Lady)
Morison, Mary
Morland, Charlotte E.
Moubrey, Lilian
Neil, Ross (pseud. of Isabella Harwood)
Norwood, Eille
Novello, Mary Sabilla Hehl, Mrs. Vincent
Openshaw, Mary
Pardoe, Julia

Peard, Frances Mary
Pfeiffer, Emily Jane Daub, Mrs.
Phillips, Mrs. Alfred
Planché, Elizabeth (Eliza) St. George, Mrs. James Robinson
Plowden, Dorothea Phillips, Mrs. Francis
Polack, Elizabeth
Pollock, Ellen, Mrs. Julius. *See* Harley, St. John (pseud.).
Porter, Helen Tracy Lowe, Mrs.
Praed, Rosa Caroline Murray-Prior, Mrs. Campbell
Prevost, Constance M.
Richardson, Sarah Watts, Mrs. Joseph
Robinson, Agnes Mary Francis (later Mrs. James Darmesteter; Mrs. Duclaux)
Robinson, Emma
Rogers, Maud M.
Rouse, Miss T.
Russell, Georgiana Adelaide Peel, Lady
Russell, Victoria, Lady
Ryley, Madeleine Lucette, Mrs. J. H.
Sandbach, Margaret Roscoe, Mrs. Henry R.
Scott, Jane M.
Seymour, Mary
Shannon, Mrs. F. S.
Shore, Louisa Catherine
Simpson, Ella Graham
Smale, Edith C., Mrs. T. E.
Smith, Lita
Steele, Anna Caroline Wood, Mrs.
Swanwick, Anna
Swanwick, Catherine
Thomas, Jane Penhorn, Mrs. Edward
Thompson, Helen
Tinsley, Lily
Tudor, Catherine
Vaughan, ?, Mrs.
Vaughan, Virginia
Vernier, Isabella
Warden, Gertrude
Webster, Augusta Davies, Mrs. Thomas
Williams, Maria Josephine
Wilson, Margaret Harries, Mrs. Cornwell Baron
Woodrooffe, Sophia
Wortley, Emmeline Charlotte Elizabeth Manners Stuart, Mrs. Charles (Lady)
Wylde, Mrs. Henry
Yorke, Elizabeth Lindsey, Countess of Hardwicke
Zglinitzka, Marie von
Zimmern, Helen

APPENDIX B PSEUDONYMS

A'Beckett, Arthur William = Vyse, Bertie (pseud.)
Albery, James = Allen, James (pseud.)
Allen, James (pseud.) = Albery, James
Amico, Amicus (pseud.)
Anstey, F. (pseud.) = Guthrie, Thomas Anstey
Arden, Henry T. (pseud.) = Arnold, Henry Thomas
Arnold, Henry Thomas = Arden, Henry T. (pseud.)
Aytoun, William Edmondstone = Jones, T. Percy (pseud.)
Barrett, Eaton Stannard = Hogg, Cervantes (pseud.) = Polypus (pseud.)
Beck, Thomas = Touch'em, Timothy (pseud.)
Besemeres, John = Daly, John (pseud.)
Beta (pseud.)
Bilkins, Taylor (pseud.) = Vicars, W. A.
Blackmore, Richard Doddridge = Melanter (pseud.)
Blake, Robert (pseud.) = Thompson, Robert Hely
Blanchard, Edward Litt Leman = Frost, Francisco (pseud.) = Grinn, Brothers (pseud.)
Blunt, Arthur Cecil = Cecil, Arthur (pseud.)
Boleno, Henry (pseud.) = Mason, Henry Boleno
Bosbacca, Gulielmerg Henricus (pseud.) = Hertz, Henrick
Boz (pseud.) = Dickens, Charles

Bradley, Katharine Harris = Field, Michael (pseud.)
Brown, William (pseud.) = Cotton, Richard
Brownbill, Thomas Robson = Robson, Frederick (pseud.)
Buckingham, Leicester Silk = Mathews & Co. (pseud.)
Bulwer Lytton, Edward Robert, Earl of Lytton = Meredith, Owen (pseud.)
Butler, Richard William = Henry, Richard (pseud.)
Byerley, John Scott = Ripon, John Scott (pseud.)
C., T. S. = Telephone, Tom (pseud.)
Calcraft, John William (pseud.) = Cole, John William
Carton, R. C. (pseud.) = Critchett, Richard Claude
Cavendish, Clara, Lady (pseud.)
Cecil, Arthur (pseud.) = Blunt, Arthur Cecil
Cole, John William = Calcraft, John William (pseud.)
Cooper, Edith Emma = Field, Michael (pseud.)
Cornwall, Barry (pseud.) = Proctor, Bryan Waller
Cotton, Richard = Brown, William (pseud.)
Cousin Joe (pseud.)
Craig, J. H. (pseud.) = Hogg, James
Craigie, Pearl Mary Teresa Richards, Mrs. Reginald Walpole = Hobbes, John Oliver (pseud.)
Critchett, Richard Claude = Carton, R. C. (pseud.)

Crowquill, Alfred (pseud.) = Forrester, Alfred Henry
Dale, Felix (pseud.) = Merivale, Herman Charles
Daly, John (pseud.) = Besemeres, John
Daryl, Sidney (pseud.) = Straight, Douglas
Davis, James = Hall, Owen (pseud.)
Dickens, Charles = Boz (pseud.)
Dobell, Sydney Thompson = Yendys, Sydney (pseud.)
Dromcolloher, Lawrence (pseud.)
Eliot, George (pseud.) = Evans, Mary Ann
Ettrick Shepherd, The (pseud.) = Hogg, James
Eupolis (pseud.)
Evans, Mary Ann = Eliot, George (pseud.)
Falconer, Edmund (pseud.) = O'Rourke, Edmund
Faucit, John Savill = Savill, John Faucit (pseud.)
Field, Michael (pseud.) = Bradley, Katharine Harris; Cooper, Edith Emma
Fleming, George (pseud.) = Fletcher, Julia Constance
Fletcher, Julia Constance = Fleming, George (pseud.)
Forrester, Alfred Henry = Crowquill, Alfred (pseud.)
Frost, Francisco (pseud.) = Blanchard, Edward Litt Leman
Gilbert, William Schwenck = Tomline, F. Latour (pseud.)
Gordon, Walter = Gowing, William (pseud.)
Gowing, William (pseud.) = Gordon, Walter
Grattan, H. P. (pseud.) = Plunkett, Henry Willoughby Grattan
Greenwood, Thomas Longdon = Grinn, Brothers (pseud.)
Grein, Jack T. (pseud.) = Grein, Jacob Thomas
Grein, Jacob Thomas = Grein, Jack T. (pseud.)
Grinn, Brothers (pseud.) = Blanchard, Edward Litt Leman; Greenwood, Thomas Longdon
Guthrie, Thomas Anstey = Anstey, F. (pseud.)
H., J. (pseud.) = MacCarthy, Denis Florence
Hall, Owen (pseud.) = Davis, James
Harley, St. John (pseud.) = Pollock, Ellen, Mrs. Julius
Harwood, Isabella = Neil, Ross (pseud.)
Hawkins, Anthony Hope = Hope, Anthony (pseud.)
Henry, Richard (pseud.) = Butler, Richard William; Newton, Henry Chance
Hertz, Henrick = Bosbacca, Gulielmerg Henricus (pseud.)
Hobbes, John Oliver (pseud.) = Craigie, Pearl Mary Teresa Richards, Mrs.
Hogg, Cervantes (pseud.) = Barrett, Eaton Stannard
Hogg, James = Craig, J. H. (pseud.) = Ettrick Shepherd (pseud.)
Hope, Anthony (pseud.) = Hawkins, Anthony Hope
Jay, Harriet = Marlowe, Charles (pseud.)
Jones, T. Percy (pseud.) = Aytoun, William Edmondstone
Lane, Pyngle (pseud.) = Turner, John Fox
Lankester, E. G. (pseud.) = Reece, Robert
Lawrence, Slingsby (pseud.) = Lewes, George Henry
Lee, Baron (pseud.) = Lee, Francis
Lee, Francis = Lee, Baron (pseud.)
Le Ros, Christian (pseud.) = Sorrell, William J.
Leslie, Frederick = Torr, A. C. (pseud.)
L'Estange, Joseph (pseud.) = Mérimée, Prosper
Lewes, George Henry = Lawrence, Slingsby (pseud.)
Luigi (pseud.)
Lumley, Henry Robert = Lyulph, Henry R. (pseud.)
Lyulph, Henry R. (pseud.) = Lumley, Henry Robert
MacCarthy, Denis Florence = H., J. (pseud.)

Macleod, Fiona (pseud.) = Sharp, William
Marlowe, Charles (pseud.) = Jay, Harriet
Mason, Henry Bolena = Boleno, Henry (pseud.)
Mathews & Co. (pseud.) = Buckingham, Leicester Silk
Medlar, Momus (pseud.) = Smith, T.
Melanter (pseud.) = Blackmore, Richard Doddridge
Meredith, Owen (pseud.) = Bulwer Lytton, Edward Robert, Earl of Lytton
Mérimée, Prosper = L'Estange, Joseph (pseud.)
Merivale, Herman Charles = Dale, Felix (pseud.)
Moncrieff, William Thomas (pseud.) = Thomas, William Thomas
Moyse, Charles Ebenezer = Titmarsh, Belgrave (pseud.)
Neil, Ross (pseud.) = Harwood, Isabella
Newton, Henry Chance = Henry, Richard (pseud.)
O'Caustic, Carol (pseud.)
O'Rourke, Edmund = Falconer, Edmund (pseud.)
Pallett, Peter Paul (pseud.) = Warner, Richard
Plunkett, Henry Willoughby Grattan = Grattan, H. P. (pseud.)
Pollock, Ellen, Mrs. Julius = Harley, St. John (pseud.)
Polypus (pseud.) = Barrett, Eaton Stannard
Proctor, Bryan Waller = Cornwall, Barry (pseud.)
Reece, Robert = Lankester, E. G. (pseud.)
Ripon, John Scott (pseud.) = Byerley, John Scott
Robson, Frederick (pseud.) = Brownbill, Thomas Robson
Rockingham, Charles, Sir (pseud.) = Rohan-Charot, Philippe Ferdinand Auguste de, Count de Jarnac
Rohan-Charot, Philippe Ferdinand Auguste de, Count de Jarnac = Rockingham, Charles, Sir (pseud.)
Ropes, Arthur Reed = Ross, Adrian (pseud.)
Rose, George = Sketchley, Arthur (pseud.)
Ross, Adrian (pseud.) = Ropes, Arthur Reed
Rowe, Bolton (pseud.) = Stephenson, Bemjamin Charles
Savill, John Faucit (pseud.) = Faucit, John Savill
Sharp, William = Macleod, Fiona (pseud.)
Sketchley, Arthur (pseud.) = Rose, George
Smith, T. = Medlar, Momus (pseud.)
Sorrell, William J. = Le Ros, Christian (pseud.)
St. John, Dorset (pseud.) = Stephens, George
Stephens, George = St. John, Dorset (pseud.)
Stephenson, Benjamin Charles = Rowe, Bolton (pseud.)
Straight, Douglas = Daryl, Sidney (pseud.)
Telephone, Tom (pseud.) = C., T. S.
Thomas, William Thomas = Moncrieff, William Thomas (pseud.)
Thompson, Robert Hely = Blake, Robert (pseud.)
Titmarsh, Belgrave (pseud.) = Moyse, Charles Ebenezer
Tomline, F. Latour (pseud.) = Gilbert, William Schwenck
Torr, A. C. (pseud.) = Leslie, Frederick
Touch'em, Timothy (pseud.) = Beck, Thomas
Turner, John Fox = Lane, Pyngle (pseud.)
Vicars, W. A. = Bilkins, Taylor (pseud.)
Vyse, Bertie (pseud.) = A'Beckett, Arthur William
Warner, Richard = Pallett, Peter Paul (pseud.)
Y., H. A. (pseud.) = Hay, Frederic
Yendys, Sydney (pseud.) = Dobell, Sydney Thompson
Zingiber, Zachary (pseud.)

Anderson, Mary
   As You Like It
   Romeo and Juliet
   Winter's Tale
Barrett, Wilson
   Hamlet
Bellew, Kyrle
   Antony and Cleopatra
Bethune, Gilbert
   Gentle Shepherd
Calvert, Charles Alexander
   Antony and Cleopatra
   Henry the Eighth
   Henry the Fifth
   Henry the Fourth
   Sardanapalus
   Twelfth Night
Cibber, Colley
   Richard the Third
Coleman, John
   Henry V (with prologue from Henry IV)
Colman, George, sr
   Comus
Creswick, William
   Macbeth, King of Scotland
Cross, James C.
   Macbeth
D'Egville, ?
   Caractacus
Elliston, Robert William
   King Lear
Fechter, Charles Albert
   Othello
Forbes-Robertson, Johnston
   Hamlet
   Macbeth
   Romeo and Juliet
Garrick, David
   Chances
   Country Girl
   Every Man in His Humour
   Isabella
   Katharine and Petruchio
   Romeo and Juliet
   Rule a Wife and Have a Wife
   Taming of the Shrew
Graves, Alfred Percival
   Out of the Frying Pan
H., E. B.
   Hamlet, Prince of Denmark
Halliday, Andrew
   Antony and Cleopatra
Hare, John
   As You Like It
Hicks, Edward Seymour
   King Richard III
Irving, Henry
   Becket
   Coriolanus
   Cymbeline
   Hamlet
   Iron Chest
   King Henry the Eighth
   King Lear
   King Richard III
   Macbeth
   Merchant of Venice
   Much Ado about Nothing
   Romeo and Juliet
   Twelfth Night
Kean, Charles John
   Hamlet
   Hamlet, Prince of Denmark
   King Henry the Eighth
   King Henry the Fifth
   King John
   King Lear
   King Richard II
   Macbeth

   Merchant of Venice
   Midsummer Night's Dream
   Much Ado about Nothing
   Pauline
   Pizarro
   Sardanapalus, King of Assyria
   Tempest
   Winter's Tale
Kemble, John Philip
   All's Well That Ends Well
   Antony and Cleopatra
   As You Like It
   Cato
   Comedy of Errors
   Coriolanus
   Cymbeline
   Double Dealer
   Fair Penitent
   Follies of a Day
   Gamester
   Grecian Daughter
   Hamlet
   Isabella
   Jane Shore
   Julius Caesar
   Katharine and Petruchio
   King Henry IV, Part 2
   King Henry the Eighth
   King Henry the Fifth
   King Henry the Fourth, Part 1
   King Henry the Fourth, Part 2
   King John
   King Richard the Third
   Measure for Measure
   Merchant of Venice
   Merry Wives of Windsor
   Much Ado about Nothing
   New Way to Pay Old Debts
   Othello
   Plain Dealer
   Revenge
   Romeo and Juliet
   Rule a Wife and Have a Wife
   Taming of the Shrew
   Twelfth Night
   Two Gentlemen of Verona
   Venice Preserved
   Way of the World
   Winter's Tale
Kendal, William Hunter
   As You Like It
King, Thomas
   Lovers' Quarrels
Lacy, Thomas Hailes
   Pickwickians
Lamb, George
   Timon of Athens
Lloyd, ?
   Romp
Macready, William Charles
   As You Like It
Mathews, Charles James
   Liar
O'Hara, Kane
   Tom Thumb
Planché, James Robinson
   Spanish Curate
   Woman Never Vext
Pollock, Walter Herries
   Dead Heart
Rayne, Lin
   Macbeth
Reynolds, Frederick
   Comedy of Errors
   Midsummer Night's Dream
Ross, Adrian
   Faust and Gretchen
Salvini, Tommaso
   Macbeth

Simpson, Mercer H.
  Midsummer Night's Dream
Stephenson, Charles H.
  Belle's Stratagem
Tate, Nahum
  King Lear
Taylor, Tom
  Hamlet
Thicke, Frank E.
  Remorse

Tree, Herbert Beerbohm
  Julius Caesar
Valpy, Richard
  King Henry the Fourth, Part 2
  King John
  Merchant of Venice
Wills, William Gorman
  Faust
Wroughton, Richard
  King Richard the Second

APPENDIX D COMPOSERS

A'Beckett, Mrs. Gilbert Abbott
  Wanted a Brigand
Adam, Adolphe Charles
  Chalet
  Dolly
  Giralda
  Queen for a Day
Addison, John
  My Uncle
  Sleeping Beauty
Albeniz, Isaac
  Magic Opal
Allen, George Benjamin
  Fayette
Anderton, T.
  Gentle Gertrude of the Infamous Redd Lyon Inn
  Thorough Base
Andrews, Bond
  Mr. Fitz-W—?
Anschutz, Karl
  See, Saw, Margery Daw
Arne, Thomas Augustine
  Artaxerxes
  Comus
Arnold, Samuel, Dr.
  Corsair
  Fairies' Revels
  Sixty-Third Letter
  Veteran Tar
Ashworth, John H. E.
  Leonore
Attwood, Thomas
  Harlequin's Tour
  Sea-Side Story
  St. David's Day
  True Friends
Auber, Daniel François Esprit
  Ambassadress
  Black Domino
  Crown Brilliants
  Crown Diamonds
  Crown Jewels
  Diamants de la Couronne
  Domino Noir
  Dumb Girl of Portici
  Fra Diavolo
  Gustavus III
  Haydée
  Lestocq
  Ma Part
  Maçon
  Masaniello
Audran, Edmond
  Cigale
  Indiana
  Olivette
  Poupée
  Uncle Celestin
Balfe, Michael William
  Armourer of Nantes
  Bianca, the Bravo's Daughter
  Blanche de Nevers
  Bohemian Girl
  Daughter of St. Mark

  Enchantress
  Maid of Artois
  Maid of Honour
  Painter of Antwerp
  Puritan's Daughter
  Rose of Castile
  Satanella
  Siege of Rochelle
  Talismano, Il
Barnard, J.
  Harlequin Sinbad the Sailor
  Hop O' My Thumb and His Eleven Brothers
  Little Goody Two-Shoes
  Little King Pippin
Barnett, John
  Barrack Room
  Blanche of Jersey
  Farinelli
  Mountain Sylph
  Pet of the Petticoats
Barratt, Augustus
  Kitty Grey
Barrett, Oscar
  Cinderella
  Dick Whittington
  Robinson Crusoe
  Sinbad the Sailor
Batchelder, J.
  High Street Mystery
  John and Jeannette
Baughan, C. Ernest
  Maid of Artemis
Bedford, Herbert
  Kit Marlowe
Beethoven, Ludwig van
  Fidelio
Bellini, Vincenzo
  Norma
  Puritani
  Puritans and the Cavaliers
  Sonnambula
Bendall, Wilfred
  He Stoops to Win
Benedict, Julius
  Bride of Song
  Brides of Venice
  Crusaders
  Gipsy's Warning
  Lily of Killarney
Bennett, William Sterndale
  May Queen
Berlioz, Hector
  Childhood of Christ
Betjemann, George Henry
  Yellow Dwarf
Birch, William Henry
  Eveleen, the Rose of the Vale
Bishop, Henry Rowley
  Barber of Seville
  Circassian Bride
  Comedy of Errors
  Comus
  Don John
  Fall of Algiers
  Farmer's Wife

Faustus
Gnome King
Heart of Mid-Lothian
Henri Quatre
Home, Sweet Home
Knights of the Cross
Law of Java
Magpie or the Maid
Maid Marian
Maid of Palaiseau
Maniac
Miller and His Men
Montrose
Noble Outlaw
Renegade
Sadak and Kalasrade
Secret Mine
Slave
Telemachus
Vintagers
Virgin of the Sun
Zuma
Bizet, Georges
Carmen
Djamileh
Blewitt, Jonathan
Auld Robin Gray
Harlequin and George Barnwell
Harlequin Hudibras
Talisman
Blum, Ernest
Rose Michel
Bochsa, Robert
Promissory Note
Boito, Arrigo
Mefistofele
Bottesini, Giovanni
Ali Baba
Boyd, William
Midsummer-Eve: An Idyll of Sherwood Forest
Braham, John.
Americans
Death and Victory of Lord Viscount Nelson
Zuma
Breare, W. H.
Boro' Bench
Brinkworth, W. H.
Babes in the Wood
Broadhurst, ?
Old Woman Who Lived in a Shoe
Bruguière, Emile A., jr.
Rightful Heir
Brüll, Ignaz
Golden Cross
Bucalossi, Procida
Manteaux Noirs
Rothomago
Three Black Cloaks
Busby, Thomas
Tale of Mystery
Byng, G. W.
Robinson Crusoe
Cagnoni, Antonio
Porter of Havre
Caldicott, Alfred J.
Odd Pair
Old Knockles
Carpenter, Alfred
Puss in Boots
Carr, Frank Osmond
Billy
Blue-Eyed Susan
Go Bang
His Excellency
In Town
Joan of Arc
Lord Tom Noddy
Morocco Bound
My Girl
Thrillby

Caryll, Ivan
Circus Girl
Dandy Dick Whittington
Gay Parisienne
Lily of Leoville
Little Christopher Columbus
Lucky Star
Ma Mie Rosette
Messenger Boy
Runaway Girl
Shop Girl
Caulcott, ?
Pork Chops
Cecil, Arthur
Bright Idea
Cellier, Alfred
Charity Begins at Home
Doris
Dorothy
Mountebanks
Chapman, George R.
Aladdin and the Wonderful Lamp
Harlequin Valentine and Orson
Little Red Riding Hood
Whittington and His Cat
Chassaigne, Francis
Falka
Chelard, Hippolyte André
Macbeth
Cherubini, Luigi
Comus
Water Carrier
Cimarosa, Domenico
Secret Marriage
Clarke, Hamilton
Cherry Tree Farm
Nobody's Fault
Silver Trout
Clay, Frederic
Ages Ago
Gentleman in Black
Happy Arcadia
Merry Duchess
Princess Toto
Cockle, George
Castle of Como
Cole, J. Parry
Bustle's Bride
Condell, Henry.
Farmer's Wife
Cooke, Thomas
Faustus
Frederick the Great
Frighten'd to Death
Harlequin and the Flying Chest
Innkeeper's Daughter
King Arthur and the Knights of the Round Table
King's Proxy
Malvina
Oberon
Tail (Tale) of a Shark
Thierna-Na-Oge
Corri, Clarence C.
Dandy Fifth
Corri, Domenico
Travellers
Corri, Montague P.
Adelphi Norma
Valley of Diamonds
Cowen, Frederic Hymen
Harold
Pauline
Signa
Thorgrim
David, Félicien
Desert
Davies, Alfred Cuthbert
Hydropathy
Prince of Sauerkrautenberg

Davy, John
  Brazen Mask
  Farmer's Wife
  Harlequin's Habeas
  Harlequin's Magnet
  Red Roy
  Spanish Dollars
De Lara, Isidore
  Amy Robsart
  Messalina
Delibes, Leo
  Fleur-de-Lys
Dick, Cotsford
  Baroness
  Dr. D.
Diehl, Louis
  Dress Rehearsal
Donizetti, Gaetano
  Anna Bolena
  Bride of Lammermoor
  Daughter of the Regiment
  Don Pasquale
  Elisir d'Amore
  Favorita
  Favourite
  Figlia del Reggimento
  Linda di Chamounix
  Lucia di Lammermoor
  Lucrezia Borgia
  Maria di Rohan
Downes, Jason F.
  Simple Sweep
Ducenozoo, ?
  Happy Dispatch
Eaton, W. G.
  Nita the Dancer
Edwards, Julian
  Brian Boru
  Jolly Musketeer
  Victorian
  Wedding Day
Elliott, Lionel
  My Uncle, the Ghost
  No Cards
Elwes, Ellen Gwenydd
  Arthur's Bakery Co.
Farjeon, Harry
  Floretta
Farmer, John
  Cinderella
Fioravanti, Valentino
  Village Singers
Fitzwilliam, Edward
  Babes in the Wood
  Queen of a Day
Flotow, Friedrich von
  Martha
Ford, Ernest
  Jane Annie
Forsyth, Robert
  Maid o' the Mill
Fox, George
  Nydia, the Blind Girl of Pompeii
Gabriel, Virginia
  Grass Widows
  Lost and Found
  Love Tests
  Shepherd of Cournouailles
  Who's the Heir?
  Widows Bewitched
Gallenberg, Count von
  Anneau Magique
German, Edward.
  Emerald Isle
Glover, Charles W.
  Dick Whittington
Glover, G. W.
  Austerlitz
Glover, James M.
  Little Genius
  Poet and the Puppets

Glover, John William
  Deserted Village
Gluck, Christoph Willibald
  Armida
  Iphigenia in Tauris
  Orfeo e Euridice
  Orpheus
Godard, Benjamin
  Vivandière
Goetz, Hermann
  Taming of the Shrew
Goldschmidt, Otto
  Story of Orestes
  Tale of Troy
Gounod, Charles
  Faust
  Irene
  Mirella
  Mock Doctor
  Philemon et Baucis
  Romeo e Giulietta
Grisar, Albert
  Goodnight, Signor Pantaloon
  Who Stole the Clock?
Grossmith, George
  Haste to the Wedding
  Peculiar Case
Guglielmi, Pietro Carlo, Jr.
  Sidagero
Hackwood, Thomas
  Competitors
  Zanone
Haines, Alfred.
  Puss in Boots
Halevy, Jacques François Fromental
  Jewess
Hall, King
  Verger
Handel, George Frederick
  Comus
Harraden, Ethel
  Taboo
Harroway, John
  Harlequin Hudibras
  Jenny Jones
Hart, Miss A. J.
  Almourah, the Corsair
Hatton, John Liptrot
  Queen of the Thames
Henning, Albert
  His Wife's Little Bill
Herbert, Victor
  Prince Ananias
Herkomer, Hubert
  Idyll
Hermann, Louis
  Aladdin and the Wonderful Lamp
Herold, Louis Joseph Ferdinand
  Zampa
Hervé, Florimond Ronger
  Aladdin II
  Up the River
Hollis, Frank G.
  Feminine Strategy
Hook, James
  Catch Him Who Can
  Fortress
  Killing No Murder
  Safe and Sound
  Sharp and Flat
  Soldier's Return
  Tekeli
Horn, Charles Edward
  Beehive
  Boarding House
  Faustus
  Persian Hunters
  Philandering
  Rich and Poor
  Shepherd of Derwent Vale

Tricks Upon Travellers
Woodman's Hut
Hughes, Richard
Davy Jones
Guy, Earl of Warwick
Hans of Iceland
Queen Bee
Hughes, T.
Death-Fetch
Winning a Husband
Hullah, John
Barbers of Bassora
Village Coquettes
Humphreys, F. W.
Aladdin and the Wonderful Lamp
Sinbad the Sailor
Hutchison, William Marshall
Glamour
Isaacson, B.
Arline, the Lost Child
Harlequin and the World of Flowers
Isouard, Nicolo
Joconde
Jacobi, Georges
Babil and Bijou
Rothomago
Two Pro's
Jacobowski, Edward
Erminie
Mynheer Jan
Queen of Brilliants
Jolly, John
Cure for Romance
Jealous on All Sides
Mary Glastonbury
Miller's Maid
Moon Queen and King Night
My Poll and My Partner Joe
Ocean of Life
Jones, Guy
Bilberry of Tilbury
Jones, Sidney
Artist's Model
Gaiety Girl
Geisha
Greek Slave
San Toy
Jouvé, E. G.
Peter the Great
Valentine and Orson
Jullien, Louis Antoine
Pietro il Grande
Kelly, Michael
Cinderella
Harlequin and Humpo
House to Be Sold
Illusion
Love Laughs at Locksmiths
One O'Clock
Youth, Love, and Folly
Kemp, Joseph
Siege of Isca
Kerr, John
Abbot
Kiefert, Carl
Ballet Girl
Gay Grizette
King, Matthew Peter
Americans
Death and Victory of Lord Viscount Nelson
Matrimony
One O'Clock
Plots
Too Many Cooks
Up All Night
Weathercock
Kitchiner, William
Love Among the Roses
Knight, Thomas
Perouse

Kramer, Christian.
Seraglio
Lacome, Paul
Jeanne, Jeannette, and Jeanneton
Ma Mie Rosette
Lambelet, Napoleon
Pot-Pourri
Yashmak
Lara, Isidore
Amy Robsart
Latham, Morton
Princess of Parmesan
Laurent, Henri
Quentin Durward
Lavenu, Louis Henry
Loretta: A Tale of Seville
Lawson, Malcolm.
Tale of Troy
Lawson, W. E.
Demon Spider
Lecocq, Alexandre Charles
Fille de Madame Angot
Giroflé-Girofla
Great Casimir
Incognita
Little Bride
Manola
My Uncle, the Ghost
Queen's Mate
Retained on Both Sides
Lee, Alexander
Magic Horn
Nettlewig Hall
Nymph of the Grotto
Swiss Swains
William the Conqueror
Legouix, Isidore Edouard
Crimson Scarf
Leoni, Franco
Rip Van Winkle
Leslie, Henry
Romance
Leverton, Henry
Fair Maid of Clifton
Levey, William Charles
Beauty and the Beast
Children in the Wood
Dragon of Wantley
Grimalkin the Great
Jack in the Box
Punchinello
Tom Thumb the Great
Linley, William
Ring
Little, Edgar
Victoire
Liverati, Giovanni
Nymph of the Grotto
Livius, Barham
Maid or Wife
Locknane, Clement
Puss in Boots
Loder, Edward James
Jack and the Beanstalk
Whittington and His Cat
Loder, George
Pets of the Parterre
Loveday, H. J.
Aladdin and the Wonderful Lamp
Little Jack the Giant Killer
Lucas, Clarence
Money Spider
Lunt, T.
Lucre-Land
Lutz, Wilhelm Meyer
Carmen Up to Date
Cinder-Ellen Up Too Late
Don Juan
Faust Up to Date
Felix
Marry in Haste

Mephistopheles
Ruy Blas and the Blasé Roué

MacCunn, Hamish
    Jeanie Deans
    Masque of War and Peace

Macfarren, George Alexander
    Devil's Opera
    Helvellyn
    King Charles II
    Robin Hood
    Sleeper Awakened
    Soldier's Legacy

Mackenzie, Alexander Campbell
    Colomba
    His Majesty
    Troubadour

McKenzie, D. C.
    Cinderella

Maclean, Alick
    Quentin Durward

Maillart, Louis Aimé
    Dragoons
    Fadette

Mallandaine, John E.
    Haunted Mill

Marschner, Heinrich
    Templar and Jewess

Mascagni, Pietro
    Chivalry in Humble Life
    Rantzau

Massé, Victor
    Jeannette's Wedding Day
    Paul and Virginia

Massenet, Jules
    Cid
    Manon
    Navarraise
    Re di Lahore

Mattei, Tito
    Fadette
    Mary of Ghent
    Prima Donna

Maucer, Louis
    Not for Me

Mazzinghi, Joseph
    Chains of the Heart
    Wife of Two Husbands

Mellon, Alfred
    Victorine

Mendelssohn, Felix
    Antigone
    Athalie
    Son and Stranger

Mercadante, Saverio
    Elena Uberti

Messager, André
    Basoche
    Béarnaise
    Fauvette
    Mirette

Meyder, Karl
    Aladdin
    Cinderella
    Harlequin and the Forty Thieves
    Valentine and Orson
    White Cat
    Whittington and His Cat

Meyerbeer, Giacomo
    Africaine
    Dinorah
    Étoile du Nord
    Prophète
    Robert the Devil
    Roberto il Diavolo
    Stella del Nord
    Ugonotti

Millocker, Carl
    Beggar Student

Monckton, Lionel
    Circus Girl
    Messenger Boy
    Runaway Girl
    Shop Girl
    Topsy-Turvy Hotel

Monk, William Henry.
    Tale of Troy

Montgomery, William Henry
    Jack and Jill
    Pierette
    Robinson Crusoe

Moorehead, John
    Harlequin's Habeas
    Harlequin's Tour

Mori, Frank
    River Sprite

Mortellari, M.
    Anacreon

Mountain, Henry
    Brazen Mask

Mozart, Wolfgang Amadeus
    Don Giovanni
    Don Juan
    Flauto Magico
    Libertine
    Magic Flute
    Marriage of Figaro
    Nozze de Figaro
    Seraglio

Musgrave, Frank
    Africaine
    Ladye Bird Bower
    Windsor Castle

Nathan, Isaac
    Illustrious Stranger

Nelson, Sydney
    My Daughter's Debut
    Village Nightingale

Nessler, Viktor Ernst
    Trumpeter of Sackingen

Nicholls, F. C.
    Prodigal Son

Nicholson, John
    Forest Oracle
    Joan of Arc
    Wandering Boys

O'Donovan, Neill
    His Highness

Offenbach, Jacques
    Barber of Bath
    Blind Beggars
    Bluebeard Re-Paired
    Breaking the Spell
    Ching-Chow-Hi
    Commodore
    Fair Helen
    Fille du Tambour-Major
    Forty Winks
    Grand Duchess of Gerolstein
    Grande Duchesse de Gerolstein
    Kissi-Kissi
    Lalla Rookh
    Love by Lantern-Light
    Lurette
    Madame Favart
    Paquerette
    Perichole
    Rose of Auvergne
    Two Blinds
    Vie
    Whittington

Orczy, Bodog
    Sisyphus, King of Ephyra

Pacini, Giovanni
    Sappho

Packer, Charles Sandys
    Sadak and Kalasrade

Parker, Henry
    Kitty
    Mignonette

Parratt, Walter.
    Tale of Troy

Parry, Charles Hubert Hastings
    Birds
    Frogs
Parry, John
    Ivanhoe
Parry, Joseph
    Blodwen (White-Flower)
Pascal, Florian
    Cymbia
    Eyes and No Eyes
    Golden Age
    Jewel Maiden
    Sensation Novel in Three Volumes
Peile, F. Kinsey
    Belle of Cairo
Perry, George Frederick
    Morning, Noon, and Night
Phendon, ?
    Robert Macaire
Phillips, G.
    Harlequin and O'Donoghue
Pizzi, Emilio
    Bric-a-Brac Will
Planquette, Robert
    Bells of Corneville
    Nell Gwynne
    Old Guard
    Paul Jones
    Rip Van Winkle
Plowden, Frances
    Virginia
Prentis, Thomas
    Minx and Man
Reed, Thomas German
    After the Ball
    My Unfinished Opera
    Three Tenants
Reeve, George William
    Astrologer
    Bang Up
    Barbara Allen
    British Amazons
    Caravan
    Chains of the Heart
    Diamond Arrow
    Disagreeable Surprise
    Edward and Susan
    Farmer's Wife
    Fashion's Fools
    Fire and Spirit
    Flitch
    Giovanni in the Country
    Goody Two Shoes
    Harlequin Tom, the Piper's Son
    Harlequin's Habeas
    Jack the Giant Killer
    Jubilee
    Law's Two Tails
    London
    Mermaid
    New Brooms
    Philip Quarll
    Red Riding Hood
    Self-Sacrifice
    Spectre Knight
    Thérèse
    Thirty Thousand
    Tricks upon Travellers
    White Plume
    White Witch
    Who's to Have Her?
Reis, Ferdinand
    Robber's Bride
Ricci, Luigi
    Avventura di Scaramuccia
    Scaramuccia
Richardson, George C.
    Hawkwood Hall
Rodwell, George Herbert Bonaparte
    Bottle Imp
    Devil's Elixir

    Flying Dutchman
    My Old Woman
    Pilot
    Spring Lock
    Students of Bonn
Roger, Victor
    Topsy-Turvy Hotel
Rogers, Thomas
    Beauty and the Beast
Rohner, G. W.
    Foxglove
Romia, Fred
    Cinderella and the Little Glass Slipper
Rooke, William Michael
    Amilie
    Henrique
Rossi, Lauro
    Biorn
Rossini, Gioacchino
    Barber of Seville
    Barbiere
    Barbiere di Siviglia
    Cenerentola
    Cinderella
    Donna del Lago
    Gazza Ladra
    Guglielmo Tell
    Italian in Algiers
    Italiana in Algeri
    Maid of Judah
    Ninetta
    Semiramide
    Tancredi
    William Tell
Rubinstein, Anton
    Demonio
    Nero
Russell, William
    Harlequin's Habeas
    Wizard's Wake
Saint-Saens, Camille
    Samson and Dalilah
Sanderson, James
    Vicar of Wakefield
Scott-Gatty, Alfred
    Goose Girl
Sedgwick, Alfred B.
    Tail (Tale) of a Shark
Selby, Thomas Leeson
    Adela
Serpette, Gaston
    Rothomago
Shickle, ?
    Forty Thives
Simpson, John Palgrave
    Bravo's Heir
Slaughter, Walter
    Alice in Wonderland
    Babes in the Wood
    Dandy Dan, the Lifeguardsman
    French Maid
    Gentleman Joe
    Marjorie
    New Corsican Brothers
    Puss in Boots
    Rose and the Ring
Sloman, Robert
    Jenny Jones
Smart, Henry
    Maid and the Magpye
Smith, Charles
    Any Thing New
    Yes or No?
Solomon, Edward
    Billee Taylor
    Claude Duval
    Lord Bateman
    Nautch Girl
    Pickwick
    Rothomago
    Virginia

Somerville, Reginald
  'Prentice Pillar
Spillane, ?
  Babes in the Wood
  Little Bo-Peep
Spinney, Frank
  Bardell versus Pickwick
Stanford, Charles Villiers
  Eden
  Veiled Prophet
Stanislaus, Frederick
  Lancashire Witches
Stansbury, George Frederick
  Wanted a Brigand
Stevenson, John
  Spanish Patriots, a Thousand Years Ago
Stuart, Leslie
  Florodora
Sullivan, Arthur Seymour
  Beauty Stone
  Chieftain
  Cox and Box
  Emerald Isle
  Gondoliers
  Grand Duke
  H.M.S. Pinafore
  Haddon Hall
  Iolanthe
  Ivanhoe
  Kenilworth
  Macbeth
  Mikado
  Miller and His Man
  Patience
  Pirates of Penzance
  Princess Ida
  Ruddigore
  Sorcerer
  Trial by Jury
  Utopia Limited
  Zoo
Suppé, Franz von
  Donna Juanita
  Fatinitza
Talbot, Howard
  Chinese Honeymoon
  Kitty Grey
  Monte Carlo
  Wapping Old Stairs
Tate, Auscal
  His Highness
Thiele, Richard
  Faust and Gretchen
  Mary and Sairey
Thomas, Ambroise
  Fox and the Goose
Thomas, Arthur Goring
  Esmeralda
  Nadeshda
Toulmouche, Frederic
  Wedding Eve
Trotere, Henry
  Skirt Dancer
Tully, John Howard
  Faw! Fee! Fo! Fum!
  Harlequin and Friar Bacon
  Harlequin and the House That Jack Built
  Hey Diddle Diddle
  Jack and the Beanstalk
  Little Jack Horner
  Number Nip
  Peter Wilkins
Turner, E. H.
  Babes in the Wood
Varney, Louis
  Mousquetaires au Couvent
Verdi, Giuseppe
  Ballo in Maschera
  Gipsy's Vengeance
  Rigoletto
  Traviata
  Trovatore

Wadham, Walter
  Magician's Daughter
Wagner, Richard
  Dusk of the Gods
  Flying Dutchman
  Lohengrin
  Mastersingers of Nuremberg
  Parsifal
  Rhine Gold
  Rhinegold
  Rienzi
  Siegfried
  Tannhäuser
  Tristan and Isolda
  Tristan and Isolde
  Tristan and Ysolde
  Twilight of the Gods
  Valkyrie
  Walkyrie
Wallace, William Vincent
  Amber Witch
  Love's Triumph
  Lurline
  Maritana
  Matilda of Hungary
Wallerstein, Ferdinand
  Bluebeard
  Forty Thieves
  Mother Goose
  Vivandière
Wallworth, Thomas Adlington
  Kevin's Choice
Ware, William Henry
  Don John
  Harlequin and Friar Bacon
  Harlequin and Mother Goose
  Harlequin Munchausen
  Harlequin Whittington
  Harlequin's Habeas
  Harlequin's Magnet
  Montrose
  Robinson Crusoe
  Zembuca
Warren, Richard Henry
  Rightful Heir
Watson, John
  Cure for Coxcombs
  Harlequin and Mother Shipton
  Three Deep
Watson, Alfred R.
  Count Tremolio
  Montrose
Weaver, James
  Our Court
Weber, Carl Maria von
  Abon Hassan
  Euryanthe
  Freischütz
  Freyschutz
  Preciosa
  Sylvana
Weigl, Joseph
  Home Sweet Home
Welsh, Thomas
  Farmer's Wife
  Is He Jealous?
  Twenty Years Ago
Whitaker, John
  Harlequin Harper
  My Spouse and I
  Orange Boven
  Who's to Have Her
White, Mary Louisa
  Beauty and the Beast
Willis, Alfred M.
  Golden Apple
Wood, Henry J.
  Daisy
Woodarch, ?
  Harlequin and Mother Shipton
Young, Harriet
  Queen of Hearts

Alma-Tadema, Laurence
    One Way of Love (1893)
Anderson, David
    Martial Achievements of Sir William Wallace (1821)
Bampfylde, Coplestone
    Aunt and the Angel (1899)
Barker, George
    Country Gentleman (1828)
Bate, Frederick
    Student (n.d.)
Berard, Peter
    Uncle's Will, Who Wins? (1808)
Bethune, Gilbert
    Courtship a-la-Mode (1831)
Blacket, Joseph
    Dramatic Sketches (1809)
Blake, Robert
    Kirk-o-Field (n.d.)
Boucicault, Dionysius Lardner
    London Assurance (1841)
    Octoroon (n.d.)
Bradshaw, Christopher Brooke
    Shakspere and Company (1845)
Brodie-Innes, J. W.
    Thomas A'Becket (n.d.)
Brooks, Charles William Shirley
    Creole (n.d.)
Brough, William
    Great Sensation Trial (n.d.)
Browning, Elizabeth Barrett, Mrs. Robert
    Psyche Apocalypté (1876)
Bruton, James
    Tale of a Pig (1858)
    Wanted, an Errand Boy (n.d.)
Buchanan, Robert Williams
    Corinne (1876)
Burnand, Francis Cowley
    Turn of the Tide (1869)
Burnley, James
    Fetters (1876)
C., D.
    Vasco de Balboa (1869)
Caine, Hall
    Bondman (1906)
    Christian (n.d.)
Calmour, Alfred Cecil
    Amber Heart (n.d.)
    Beau Blandish the Rake (1887)
    Cromwell (n.d.)
    Cupid's Messenger (n.d.)
    Elvestine (n.d.)
Carnes, Mason
    Taboo (1896)
Carr, Joseph William Comyns
    King Arthur (1893)
Clarke, Campbell
    Rose Michel (n.d.)
Code, H. B.
    Russian Sacrifice (1813)
Collins, William Wilkie
    Armadale (1866)
    Frozen Deep (1866)
    Man and Wife (1870)
    Miss Gwilt (1875)
    Moonstone (1877)
    New Magdalen (1873)
    Woman in White (1871)
Cooke, William Major
    Hymenaeus (n.d.)
Cooper, G.
    Billy (n.d.)
Cooper, Herbert B.
    Arts and Hearts (n.d.)
Cosens, Frederick William
    Bandos de Verona (1874)
Cradock, Joseph
    Czar (1824)

Croker, Thomas Francis Dillon
    Romulus and Remus (1859)
Dew, Dyer
    Harold (1820)
Dibdin, Charles, sr
    Britons Strike Home (n.d.)
Douglas, Thomas
    Friend at Court (1811)
Drayton, Henri
    Marry in Haste (1860)
Drinkwater, John Elliot
    Maid of Orleans (1835)
Ebsworth, Joseph
    Two Prisoners of Lyons (1824)
Evans, William
    Fair Reward (1883)
Farley, Charles
    Red Roy (n.d.)
Faucit, John Savill
    Miller's Maid (1821)
Faust (anon.) (n.d.)
Fawcett, John
    Enchanted Island (n.d.)
Ferguson, Samuel
    Deirdre (1880)
Fitzball, Edward
    Bertha (1819)
Fitzgerald, Edward
    Mighty Magician (n.d.)
    Such Stuff As Dreams Are Made Of (n.d.)
Fitzgerald, William, jr
    Siege of Carthage (1819)
Forman, Alfred
    Parsifal (1899)
Francisco, the Avenger (anon.) (n.d.)
Frere, Benjamin
    Olympia (1821)
Frye, William Edward
    Guilt (1819)
Galloway, George
    Battle of Luncarty (1804)
Gent, J. B.
    Meteor (1809)
Godfrey, George William
    Millionaire (n.d.)
Godmond, Christopher
    Vincenzo, Prince of Mantua (1840)
Gower, Francis Leveson, Lord
    Donna Charitea, Queen of Castile (1843)
    Paria (1836)
Grant, James M.
    Custom's Fallacy (1805)
Greene, William A.
    D'Enghien (1842)
Grundy, Sydney
    Debt of Honour (n.d.)
Hall, William Seward
    Empire of Philanthropy (1822)
Hamilton, Henry
    Shadow Sceptre (n.d.)
Harness, William, Rev.
    First Born (1844)
Harris, Richard
    Young Wives and Old Husbands (n.d.)
Hasbrer, Alfred
    Carlo (1870)
Hatton, Joseph
    Birds of a Feather (n.d.)
    Clytie (n.d.)
    Romantic Caroline (n.d.)
Hengist (anon.) (1816)
Herbert, Thomas
    Hydrophopbia (1820)
Hollingshead, John
    Grasshopper (n.d.)
Ides of May (anon.) (1869)

Irving, Laurence Sydney Brodribb
  Peter the Great (1897)
Jameson, Frederick
  Tristan and Isolde (1886)
Jodrell, Richard Paul
  Persian Heroine (1822)
Johnston, Andrew
  Cataline (n.d.)
Jones, Henry Arthur
  Breaking a Butterfly (n.d.)
  Goal (1898)
  Liars (1897)
  Masqueraders (n.d.)
  Michael and His Lost Angel (1895)
  Triumph of the Philistines (1895)
Jones, T.
  Confin'd in Vain (1805)
Kerr, John
  Michael and Christine (n.d.)
  Wandering Boys (n.d.)
Knowles, James Sheridan
  Alexina (1874)
  Brian Boroihme (1874)
  Bridal (1874)
  Caius Gracchus (1874)
  Duke of London (1874)
  Hersilia (1874)
  Leo (1874)
  Masque (1874)
  Storm (1874)
  Vaccination (1874)
  Widow (1874)
  William Tell (1874)
Lake, John
  Golden Glove (1815)
Langford, John Alfred
  King and the Commoner (1870)
Lart, John
  Phantoms (n.d.)
Lathom, Francis
  Dash of the Day (1800)
Lee, Baron
  Glorious Revolution, 5th November 1688 (n.d.)
Leigh, James Mathews
  Cromwell (1838)
Maclaren, Archibald
  British Carpenter (1808)
  Britons to Arms (1803)
  Chance of War (1801)
  Coup-de-Main (1816)
  Days We Live In (1805)
  Duellists (1811)
  Eccentricity (n.d.)
  Elopement (1811)
  Empress and No Empress (1810)
  Fashion (1802)
  First of April (1802)
  Forget and Forgive (1814)
  Gentle Shepherd (1811)
  Good News! Good News! (1814)
  Imitation Tea (1818)
  Irish Girl (1813)
  Maid of Lorn (1815)
  Man in the Moon (1813)
  Man Trap (1816)
  Mr. Boney's Reception in Paris (1814)
  Nappy's Reception in Elba (1814)
  Oliver Cromwell (1818)
  Paddy Bull (1811)
  Prisoner of War (1813)
  Private Theatre (1809)
  Slaver (1807)
  Spanish Heroine (1808)
  Spite and Malice (1811)
  Swindlers (1812)
  Touch at the Times (1804)
  Ups and Downs of Life (1824)
  Wallace the Brave (1819)
  Ways of London (1812)
  Whimsicality (1810)
  Wife to be Sold (1807)

Martin, Theodore, Sir
  Gladiator of Ravenna (1885)
  Madonna Pia (n.d.)
Masterton, Charles
  Seducer (1811)
Maurice, Thomas
  Fall of the Mogul (1806)
Moncrieff, William Thomas
  Bringing Home the Bride (1838)
  Kiss and the Rose (1837)
  Parson's Nose (1837)
  Tobit's Dog (1838)
  Winterbottoms (1837)
Monney, William
  Caractacus (1816)
Moore, Frank Frankfort
  Queen's Room (1891)
Mortimer, James
  Charlotte Corday (1876)
  Little Cricket (1878)
Morton, John Maddison
  Trade (1877)
Napoleon (anon.) (1842)
Newnham, Francis, Rev.
  Pleasures of Anarchy (1829)
Nightingale, Joseph H.
  Off to the Diggins (n.d.)
Oxberry, William Henry
  Lucy of Lammermoor (n.d.)
Palaeologus, Gregorios
  Death of Demosthenes (1824)
Parker, Louis Napoleon
  Change Alley (1899)
  Mayflower (n.d.)
  Termagant (n.d.)
Pember, Edward Henry
  Blind Girl of Bonn (1897)
  Death-Song of Thamyris (1899)
  Finding of Pheidippides (1901)
  Hippolytus the Wreathbearer (1897)
  Jephthah's Daughter (1904)
  Oedipus at Colonos (1899)
  Pausanias and Cleonice (1901)
  Prometheus Bound (1895)
Pinero, Arthur Wing
  Benefit of the Doubt (1895)
  Dandy Dick (1887)
  Magistrate (1892)
Platt, William
  Youth's Love-Lore (1896)
Raleigh, Cecil
  Hearts Are Trumps (1899)
Raleigh, Walter
  Riddle (1895)
Reade, Charles
  Courier of Lyons (1854)
Reece, Robert
  Warranted (n.d.)
Reid, Mayne
  Love's Martyr (n.d.)
Reynolds, Frederick
  Gnome King (n.d.)
Rhodes, Thomas
  Disappointed Miller (1824)
Roberts, George
  Lady Audley's Secret (n.d.)
Rockingham, Charles, Sir
  Ball Next Door (1866)
  Holiday (1866)
  Man-Servant (1866)
  Mendoza (1866)
Rowe, Henry, Rev.
  Montem (1808)
Russell, Georgiana Adelaide Peel, Lady
  Dewdrop and Glorio (n.d.)
Saunders, John
  Abel Drake (1873)
Scott, Alfred
  Affghans' Captive (1842)
Secrets of the Pavilion Disclosed (anon.) (1834)

Shelley, Percy Bysshe
  Oedipus Tyrannus (1820)
Simpson, John Palgrave
  Bravo's Heir (n.d.)
Skeffington, Lumley St. George
  Sleeping Beauty (n.d.)
Slous, Frederick L.
  Francis the First (1843)
Smith, Albert Richard
  Cinderella (n.d.)
Smithereens (anon.) (1898)
Sorelli, Guido
  Isabella Aldobrandi (1838)
St. George, George
  Don't Book Your Make Ups (1876)
  Man of Thought and the Man of Action (1876)
  Sires and Sons from Albion Sprung (1876)
Stephens, George
  Forgery (1846)
  Nero (1846)
  Philip Basil (1846)
  Rebecca and Her Daughters (1846)
  Self-Glorification (1846)
  Sensibility (1846)
Stephenson, Benjamin Charles
  Zoo (1869)
Strachan, John S., jr
  Rip Van Winkle (1866)
Straycock, J.
  Loyal Peasants (1804)
Talfourd, Thomas Noon
  Ion (n.d.)
Taming a Tiger (anon.) (n.d.)
Taylor, Tom
  Our American Cousin (1869)
Tennyson, Alfred Lord
  Foresters (1892)

Thackeray, William Makepeace
  Reading a Poem (1891)
Thomas, Leigh
  Pirate (1871)
Todhunter, John
  How Dreams Come True (n.d.)
Tupper, Martin Farquhar
  Washington (1876)
Turner, Charles James Ribton
  Handsome Is That Handsome Does (n.d.)
Tweddell, H. Maddison
  Aguilhar (1820)
Valentine's Day (anon.) (n.d.)
Vaughan, Mrs.
  Grecians (1824)
Vineyard of Naboth (anon.) (1825)
Wallace, Albany
  Elfrida (1850)
Wallace, John
  Caelina (1802)
  Simple Simon (1805)
Weatherly, Frederick Edward
  King René's Daughter (1872)
Wild, James
  Doubt and Conviction (1804)
  Frailty and Hypocrisy (1804)
  From Inn to Inn (1804)
  Maids (1804)
  Twenty-One (1804)
  Wives (1804)
Wilde, Oscar Fingall O'Flahertie Wills
  Duchess of Padua (n.d.)
  Vera (1902)
Wolcot, John
  Fall of Portugal (1808)
Young, William
  Lucrezia Borgia (1847)

APPENDIX F ACTING EDITIONS AND OTHER SERIES

Abel Heywood & Son's Series of Copyright Plays for the Use of Amateurs
  2, Don't Jump at Conclusions
  3, Two Georges
  6, Aunt Madge
Abel Heywood & Son's Series of Original Dramas, Dialogues, & Readings Adapted for Amateur Entertainments
  82, Wedding at the Mill
  112, Haunted House
  155, Which Got the Best of It?
  159, Dorothy's Victory
  162, Difficult to Please
Abel Heywood's Musical Dramas, Farces, and Dialogues for Amateurs
  High Street Mystery
  John and Jeannette
Acting American Theatre, Lopez and Wemyss Edition
  Sweathearts and Wives
Acting Drama
  1, First Night
  7, Tipperary Legacy
  8, Breach of Promise
  16, Scholar
  17, Helping Hands
  40, Three Grocers
  45, Who's Your Friend?
  46, Charity
  73, To Let, Furnished
  81, Getting Up in the World
  82, Wardrobe
  91, Shamrock
  138, Beauty and the Beast
  178, Cross Purposes
  184, Wooing under Difficulties
  Poor Pillicoddy
Acting Edition of Lord Lytton's Dramas
  Lady of Lyons

Acting National Drama
  I, Bridal
  I, Gustavus of Sweden
  I, Riquet with the Tuft
  I, Two Figaros
  III, Mysterious Stranger
  IV, Hasty Conclusion
  IV, Lying in Ordinary
  IV, Meltonians
  V, Ask No Questions
  V, Gemini
  14, Roused Lion
  But However—
  Devil's Opera
  Forty and Fifty
  Irish Lion
  Modern Orpheus
  My Young Wife and My Old Umbrella
  Our National Defences
  Queer Subject
  Tiger at Large
  Truth
Alexander's Modern Acting Drama
  Ladies' Man
  Sergeant's Wife
  Sisters
Alta Series
  Beggar Venus
Amateur Series
  Lucky Sixpence
Amateur Theatre
  Good Little Wife
Ames' [& Holgate's] Series of Standard and Minor Drama
  2, Desperate Game
  11, John Smith
  13, Give Me My Wife
  14, Brigands of Calabria
  28, Thirty-Three Next Birthday

33, On the Sly
34, Mistletoe Bough
36, Miller of Derwent Water
54, Two T. J's.
55, Somebody's Nobody
74, How to Tame Your Mother-in-Law
78, Awful Criminal
80, Alarmingly Suspicious
81, Old Phil's Birthday
84, Cheek Will Win
85, Outcast's Wife
87, Biter Bit
89, Beauty of Lyons
97, Fatal Blow
231, Match for a Mother-in-Law
288, Love in All Corners
320, All in a Muddle

Anderson's Edition, Select British Theatre
13, Redgauntlet

Augustin Daly Prompt Book
Foresters

Baker's Edition of Plays
Don't Judge by Appearances
Hit Him, He Has No Friends
My Aunt's Heiress
Wonderful Cure

Barth's [late Pattie's] Universal Stage or Theatrical Prompt Book
10, Polkamania
20, Ins and Outs
22, Love's Livery
33, Grizelle
40, Belford Castle
43, Love Gift
44, Rights of Woman
54, Husbands, Wives, and Lovers
76, White Feather
78, Martin Chuzzlewit
98, Seeing Wright
101, Violet

Bell's Modern Translations
Impostures of Scapin
Misanthrope

Bernhardt Edition
Lady of Challant

Boosey & Co.'s Operettas for the Drawing-Room
Paquerette

Boosey's Standard Operas
Domino Noir
Grande Duchesse de Gerolstein
Mock Doctor

Boston Parlor Opera
Son and Stranger

Boston Theatre [Spencer's]
4, Bachelor's Bedroom
5, Sophia's Supper
30, Willow Copse

Bourcicault's Dramatic Works
2, Andy Blake
3, Phantom
4, Wanted—a Widow, with Immediate Possession
5, Poor of New York
7, Pauvrette
8, Pope of Rome

Britain's Historical Drama
Arixina
Devoted One
Dragon-King
Edwin and Elgiva
English Slave
Varangian

British Theatre
Love and Reason
Three Deep
X, Y, Z

Charles Dickson's Famous One Act Plays
Man about Town

Charles Fechter's Acting Edition
Othello

Children's Plays
7, Lady Cecil
14, When I'm a Man

Clayton's Edition
Deaf as a Post
Drunkard's Fate
Highways and By-ways
Teddy the Tiler

Coquelin-Hading Edition
Our Boon Companions

Cramer's Opera Bouffe Cabinet
Barber of Bath

Cumberland's Acting Plays
554, Is She His Daughter?
Sanctuary

Cumberland's British Theatre [with Duncombe's]
I, Romeo and Juliet
I, She Stoops to Conquer
I, Pizarro
I, Douglas
I, Macbeth
I, King Richard the Third
I, Suspicious Husband
IV, Hamlet
IV, Gamester
IV, King Henry IV, Part 1
IV, King John
IV, Wonder
IV, Trip to Scarborough
IV, Road to Ruin
V, Inconstant
V, Jane Shore
V, Love in a Village
V, Man of the World
V, Julius Caesar
V, King Henry VIII
V, Winter's Tale
VI, Cato
VI, King Lear
VI, All in the Wrong
VI, Caius Gracchus
VI, Virginius
VI, Merry Wives of Windsor
VI, Merchant of Venice
XIII, Bold Stroke for a Wife
XIII, High Life Below Stairs
XIII, Oberon
XIII, Doctor Bolus
XIII, Lord of the Manor
XIII, Honey Moon
XIV, School for Scandal
XIV, Animal Magnetism
XIV, Village Lawyer
XIV, Spoiled Child
XIV, Wheel of Fortune
XIV, Stranger
XIV, Disagreeable Surprise
XV, Deaf and Dumb
XV, Rosina
XV, Midnight Hour
XV, Revenge
XV, Castle Spectre
XV, Critic
XV, Speed the Plow
XVI, Cure for the Heartache
XVI, Spectre Bridegroom
XVI, Himself
XVI, Comedy of Errors
XVI, Monsieur Tonson
XVI, Education
XVI, Inkle and Yarico
XVI, Amateurs and Actors
XVII, Barbarossa
XVII, School of Reform
XVII, Rendezvous
XVII, Giovanni in London
XVII, Gambler's Fate
XVII, Children in the Wood
XVII, Lovers' Vows
XVIII, All's Well That Ends Well
XVIII, Taming of the Shrew
XVIII, Weathercock
XVIII, Somnambulist
XVIII, Two Gentlemen of Verona
XVIII, Secrets Worth Knowing
XVIII, Highland Reel

XIX, Love for Love
XIX, Raising the Wind
XIX, Lancers
XIX, Artaxerxes
XIX, Serf
XIX, Merchant's Wedding
XIX, Race for a Dinner
XX, Paul and Virginia
XX, Turnpike Gate
XX, Way to Get Married
XX, Midsummer-Night's Dream
XX, Poor Soldier
XX, Who Wants a Guinea?
XX, Seige of Belgrade
XXI, Will
XXI, Country Girl
XXI, Beaux' Stratagem
XXI, Irish Tutor
XXI, Green-Eyed Monster
XXI, Youthful Queen
XXI, Cabinet
XXII, Irishman in London
XXII, William Tell
XXII, Duel
XXII, Devil's Elixir
XXII, Slave
XXII, Recruiting Officer
XXII, Master's Rival
XXIII, Waterman
XXIII, Happiest Day of My Life
XXIII, Fatality
XXIII, Tom Thumb
XXIII, William Thompson
XXIII, Town and Country
XXIII, Illustrious Stranger
XXIII, Laugh When You Can
XXIII, Soldier's Daughter
XXIV, Citizen
XXIV, Brigand
XXIV, Rienzi
XXIV, Love, Law, and Physic
XXIV, Riches
XXIV, Clari
XXIV, Lock and Key
XXIV, No Song, No Supper
XXIV, Snakes in the Grass
XXV, Blind Boy
XXV, Honest Thieves
XXV, Oroonoko
XXV, X. Y. Z.
XXV, Maid of Judah
XXV, Popping the Question
XXV, Teddy the Tiler
XXV, Charles XII
XXV, Grecian Daughter
XXVI, John of Paris
XXVI, Prisoner at Large
XXVI, Timon of Athens
XXVI, Miller and His Men
XXVI, Prize
XXVI, First of April
XXVI, Husband at Sight
XXVI, Matrimony
XXVI, Notoriety
XXVII, Folly As It Flies
XXVII, Valentine and Orson
XXVII, Farmer
XXVII, Two Friends
XXVII, Ella Rosenberg
XXVII, Vampire
XXVII, My Grandmother
XXVII, King Henry IV, Part 2
XXVII, Forty Thieves
XXVIII, St. Patrick's Day
XXVIII, Ice Witch
XXVIII, High Ways and By Ways
XXVIII, Point of Honour
XXVIII, Blind Bargain
XXVIII, Shakspeare's Early Days
XXVIII, Magpie or the Maid?
XXVIII, Robinson Crusoe
XXVIII, Robber's Wife
XXIX, Adopted Child
XXIX, King Richard II

XXIX, Maid of Honour
XXIX, Sleeping Draught
XXIX, Day after the Wedding
XXIX, Modern Antiques
XXIX, Mrs. Wiggins
XXIX, Comfortable Lodgings
XXIX, Timour the Tartar
XXIX, Exile
XXX, Two Strings to Your Bow
XXX, Hartford Bridge
XXX, Tekeli
XXX, Haunted Tower
XXX, Fortune's Frolic
XXX, Bee-Hive
XXX, How to Grow Rich
XXX, Haunted Inn
XXX, Old and Young
XXX, Bride of Ludgate
XXXI, Antiquary
XXXI, Killing No Murder
XXXI, One, Two, Three, Four, Five
XXXI, Peeping Tom of Coventry
XXXI, Falls of Clyde
XXXI, Mr. and Mrs. Pringle
XXXI, Open House
XXXI, Agreeable Surprise
XXXI, Son-in-Law
XXXII, English Fleet in 1342
XXXII, Camp
XXXII, Personation
XXXII, Widow
XXXII, Julian
XXXII, Fontainbleau
XXXII, Comus
XXXII, Castle of Andalusia
XXXII, One O'Clock
XXXIII, Old Regimentals
XXXIII, Cataract of the Ganges
XXXIII, Faustus
XXXIII, Tom and Jerry
XXXIII, All at Coventry
XXXIII, Castle of Sorrento
XXXIII, Maid or Wife
XXXIII, Lestocq
XXXIII, Robert the Devil! Duke of Normandy
XXXIV, Wild Cats
XXXIV, Presumptive Evidence
XXXIV, Rugantino
XXXIV, Hundred Pound Note
XXXIV, Is He Jealous?
XXXIV, Knights of the Cross
XXXIV, Jew and the Doctor
XXXIV, Ambition
XXXIV, Steward
XXXIV, Hit or Miss
XXXV, Make Your Wills
XXXV, Quite at Home
XXXV, Mountaineers
XXXV, Nettlewig Hall
XXXV, My Husband's Ghost
XXXV, Lottery Ticket
XXXV, Romp
XXXV, Iron Chest
XXXV, Miser
XXXV, Zarah
XXXVI, John Bull
XXXVI, Blue Beard
XXXVI, Aladdin
XXXVI, Gil Blas
XXXVI, Sylvester Daggerwood
XXXVI, Bold Stroke for a Husband
XXXVI, Malvina
XXXVI, Review
XXXVI, Invincibles
XXXVI, Rob Roy
XXXVII, Love Laughs at Locksmiths
XXXVII, St. David's Day
XXXVII, Exchange No Robbery
XXXVII, Quaker
XXXVII, Young Quaker
XXXVII, Battle of Hexham
XXXVII, Mendicant
XXXVII, Poor Gentleman
XXXVII, My Daughter, Sir

XXXVII, Jack Brag
XXXVIII, Devil to Pay
XXXVIII, Foscari
XXXVIII, Jew
XXXVIII, Past Ten O'Clock and a Rainy Night
XXXVIII, Raymond and Agnes, the Travellers Benighted
XXXVIII, Three and the Deuce
XXXVIII, Venoni
XXXVIII, Netley Abbey
XXXVIII, Management
XXXVIII, Heir at Law
XXXIX, Youth, Love, and Folly
XXXIX, Kenilworth
XXXIX, Wedding Day
XXXIX, Blue Devils
XXXIX, Hunter of the Alps
XXXIX, Dramatist
XXXIX, For England, Ho
XXXIX, Sprigs of Laurel
XXXIX, False Alarms
XXXIX, Adelgitha
XL, Love
XL, Invisible Girl
XL, Delinquent
XL, Foundling of the Forest
XL, How to Die for Love
XL, Catch Him Who Can
XL, Peasant Boy
XL, Love's Labour's Lost
XL, Therese, the Orphan of Geneva
XL, Surrender of Callais
XLI, Chrononhotonthologos
XLI, First Floor
XLI, Secret
XLI, Young Hussar
XLI, Love Chase
XLI, My Spouse and I
XLI, Broken Sword
XLI, Travellers
XLI, Lodoiska
XLI, Plot and Counterplot
XLII, Devil's Bridge
XLII, Attic Story
XLII, Mogul Tale
XLII, Five Miles Off
XLII, Court and City
XLII, Uncle Rip
XLII, Hunchback
XLII, Free and Easy
XLII, Cobbler of Preston
XLII, Love's Sacrifice
61, Lamplighter
96, Spoiled Child
156, Happiest Day of My Life
185, First of April
192, Forty Thieves
253, Lestocq
266, Zarah
290, My Daughter, Sir
362, Queen's Bench
364, Clear Case
365, His First Peccadillo
367, Devil and Doctor Faustus
372, Methinks I See My Father
373, Retribution
389, Life's a Lottery
392, Angelo and the Actress of Padua
393, Beginning and the End
404, Mysteries of Paris
427, Lestelle
510, Chamber Practice
Aladdin
Attic Story
Barark Johnson
Chain of Guilt
Deserted Mill
Fatality
Free and Easy
Gaspardo the Gondolier
Gil Blas
Hand of Cards
How to Die for Love
Ion
Management

Mendicant
Napoleon
Old and Young
One, Two, Three, Four, Five
Orestes in Argos
Orphan of the Wreck
Paul and Virginia
Paul Clifford
Queen of the Abruzzi
Revenge
Rival Valets
Robert the Devil
Two Gentlmen of Verona
Uncle Rip
White Slave
William Thompson

Cumberland's Minor Theatre

I, Mason of Buda
I, Masaniello
I, Scapegrace
I, Pilot
I, Earthquake
I, Heart of Mid-Lothian
I, Inchcape Bell
I, Suil Dhuv the Coiner
I, My Old Woman
II, Crazy Jane
II, Luke the Labourer
II, Paul Jones
II, Floating Beacon
II, Ivanhoe
II, Forest Oracle
II, Yes
II, Flying Dutchman
II, Don Giovanni
III, Paris and London
III, Wandering Boys
III, Two Gregories
III, Day after the Fair
III, Billy Taylor
III, Lady of the Lake
III, Tom Bowling
III, Sylvana
III, Innkeeper of Abbeville
IV, Joan of Arc
IV, Guy Faux
IV, Mischief-Making
IV, Banks of the Hudson
IV, Wreck
IV, Ruffian Boy
IV, Fortunes of Nigel
IV, Humphrey Clinker
IV, Everybody's Husband
V, Pedlar's Acre
V, Waverley
V, Devil's Ducat
V, No
V, Mazeppa
V, Mutiny at the Nore
V, Winning a Husband
V, Peveril of the Peak
V, Thalaba the Destroyer
VI, Golden Farmer
VI, Sworn at Highgate
VI, Red Rover
VI, Mary Glastonbury
VI, Devil-Holl
VI, Tower of Nesle
VI, Hunchbacks
VI, Damon and Pythias
VI, Paul Clifford
VI, Hofer, the Tell of the Tyrol
VII, Spare Bed
VII, Grace Huntley
VII, John Overy
VII, Lear of Private Life
VII, John Street, Adelphi
VII, Hut of the Red Mountain
VII, Gamester's Life
VII, Clerk of Clerkenwell
VII, Sea
VII, Smuggler's Daughter
VIII, Fate of Calas
VIII, Silver Palace

VIII, Shadow
VIII, Young Reefer
VIII, Cedar Chest
VIII, Gilderoy
VIII, Revolt of the Workhouse
VIII, Man and the Marquis
VIII, Ambrose Gwinett
VIII, Wardock Kennilson
IX, Gipsy Jack
IX, Sixes
IX, Golden Calf
IX, My Poll and My Partner Joe
IX, Charcoal Burner
IX, Fire Raiser
IX, Wizard of the Moor
IX, Good-Looking Fellow
IX, Man-Fred
IX, Lurline
X, Eddystone Elf
X, Diamond Arrow
X, Van Diemen's Land
X, My Wife's Husband
X, Robber of the Rhine
X, Eugene Aram
X, Roof Scrambler
X, Pauvre Jacques
X, Shakspeare's Festival
X, Married Bachelor
XI, Pestilence of Marseilles
XI, Unfortunate Miss Bailey
XI, Thomas A'Beckett
XI, Paul the Poacher
XI, Beggar of Cripplegate
XI, Rover's Bride
XI, Wild Man
XI, Uncle Too Many
XI, Ocean of Life
XI, Rochester
XII, My Friend Thompson
XII, Joconde
XII, Koeuba
XII, March of Intellect
XII, Mistletoe Bough
XII, Chain of Guilt
XII, Ion
XII, Shipwreck of the Medusa
XII, Bound 'Prentice to a Waterman
XII, Humpbacked Lover
XIII, Battle of Sedgemoor
XIII, Fatal Snow-Storm
XIII, Reform
XIII, Female Massaroni
XIII, Hercules, King of Clubs
XIII, Man with the Carpet Bag
XIII, Wapping Old Stairs
XIII, Turned Head
XIII, Frederick the Great
XIII, Larboard Fin
XIV, Earl of Poverty
XIV, Payable at Sight
XIV, Bull-Fighter
XIV, Don Quixote
XIV, Austerlitz
XIV, Siamese Twins
XIV, Rich Man of Frankfort
XIV, Great Devil
XIV, Black-Eyed Sukey
XIV, Richard Plantagenet
XIV, Venus in Arms
XV, Paul the Pilot
5, Scapegrace
8, My Old Woman
11, Paul Jones
32, Fortunes of Nigel
36, Guy Faux
41, No
46, Hofer, the Tell of the Tyrol
47, Paul Clifford
50, Tower of Nesle
56, Sea
76, Golden Calf
83, Roof Scrambler
113, Battle of Sedgemoor
115, Frederick the Great

126, Austerlitz
140, Venetian
144, Under the Rose
151, Barber Baron
Banks of the Hudson
Billy Taylor
Bound 'Prentice to a Waterman
Bull-Fighter
Cedar Chest
Clerk of Clerkenwell
Crazy Jane
Devil-Holl
Gipsy Jack
Great Devil
Haunted Hulk
Humphrey Clinker
Koeuba
Larboard Fin
Lurline
March of Intellect
Mary Glastonbury
My Friend Thompson
My Wife's Husband
Paul the Poacher
Rich Man of Frankfort
Richard Plantagenet
Shadow
Silver Palace
Sixes
Smuggler's Daughter
Sylvana
Unfortunate Miss Bailey
Van Diemen's Land
Venus in Arms
Wardock Kennilson
Yes

Davidson's Actable Drama [in continuation of Cumberland's]
Great Russian Bear
Tale of Two Cities

Davidson's Dramatic Operas
Haydée

Davidson's Illustrated Libretto Books
Favourite
Gustavus III
Lucrezia Borgia
Masaniello

Davidson's Lyrical Drama
Marriage of Figaro

Davidson's Musical Opera-Books
Favorita

DeWitt's Acting Plays
3, One Hundred Thousand Pounds
4, Dandelion's Dodges
11, Woodcock's Little Game
17, Kind to a Fault
20, Daddy Gray
23, Petticoat Parliament
24, Cabman No. 93
30, Goose with the Golden Eggs
32, Little Rebel
33, One Too Many for Him
35, Silent Woman
37, Silent Protector
39, Master Jones's Birthday
42, Time and the Hour
43, Sisterly Service
45, Our Domestics
50, Porter's Knot
52, Cup of Tea
61, Plot and Passion
67, Birth-place of Podgers
78, Special Performances
87, Locked Out
91, Walpole
124, Volunteer Review
125, Deerfoot
128, Female Detective
131, Go to Putney
133, Timothy to the Rescue
156, Peace at Any Price
167, Apple Blossoms
168, Tweedie's Rights
179, Breach of Promise

184, Money
202, Eileen Oge
232, Tail (Tale) of a Shark
240, Object of Interest
249, Marriage a Lottery
268, Obstinate Family
284, 'Twixt Axe and Crown
292, Two Thorns
293, Philomel
295, Little Em'ly
296, Black and White
297, English Gentleman
300, Notre Dame
301, Hinko
310, Barrack Room
324, My Mysterious Rival
329, Fireside Story
330, Don't Be Too Quick to Cry Wolf
362, Figure of Speech
365, Arrah-na-Pogue

Dick's American Edition

Barbara
Betsy
Fireside Diplomacy
Furnished Apartments
Pair of Pigeons
Slighted Treasures
Spanking Legacy
Two Gentlemen at Mivart's

Dicks' British Drama

I, Adopted Child
I, Castle Spectre
I, Devil to Pay
I, Douglas
I, Fatal Curiosity
I, Gamester
I, Guy Mannering
I, Inconstant
I, Jane Shore
I, Jealous Wife
I, Love in a Village
I, Man of the World
I, Mayor of Garratt
I, Midas
I, Pizarro
I, Revenge
I, Rivals
I, Road to Ruin
I, She Stoops to Conquer
I, Stranger
I, Venice Preserved
II, Arden of Feversham
II, Castle of Sorrento
II, Cato
II, Fair Penitent
II, George Barnwell
II, Grecian Daughter
II, Honeymoon
II, Iron Chest
II, Isabella
II, Lord of the Manor
II, Miller and His Men
II, New Way to Pay Old Debts
II, Pilot
II, Provoked Husband
II, Rob Roy MacGregor
II, School for Scandal
II, Siege of Belgrade
II, Tale of Mystery
II, Wonder, The: A Woman Keeps a Secret
III, Beggar's Opera
III, Bertram
III, Braganza
III, Brutus
III, Castle of Andalusia
III, Critic
III, Cymon
III, Damon and Pythias
III, Edward, the Black Prince
III, Foundling
III, Giovanni in London
III, John Bull
III, Mourning Bride
III, Paul and Virginia

III, Tancred and Sigismunda
III, Trip to Scarborough
III, Werner
IV, Barbarossa
IV, Courier of Lyons
IV, Curfew
IV, Duenna
IV, Evadne
IV, Every Man in His Humour
IV, Fazio
IV, Hypocrite
IV, Lady Jane Grey
IV, Maid of Honour
IV, Merchant of Bruges
IV, No Song, No Super
IV, Prisoner of State
IV, Provoked Wife
IV, Quaker
IV, Roman Father
IV, Speed the Plough
IV, Turnpike Gate
IV, Waterman
V, Alexander the Great
V, All the World's a Stage
V, Clandestine Marriage
V, Dog of Montargis
V, Foundling of the Forest
V, High Life Below Stairs
V, Life Buoy
V, Maid of the Mill
V, One O'Clock
V, Padlock
V, Robbers of Calabria
V, Rule a Wife and Have a Wife
V, Soldier's Daughter
V, Therese
V, Thomas and Sally
V, Wheel of Fortune
V, Zara
VI, Atonement
VI, Bold Stroke for a Wife
VI, Busy-Body
VI, Child of Nature
VI, Country Girl
VI, Duke of Milan
VI, Earl of Warwick
VI, Hyder
VI, Lionel and Clarissa
VI, Lying Valet
VI, Miser
VI, Panel
VI, Polly Honeycombe
VI, Such Things Are
VI, Tom Thumb
VI, Wedding Day
VI, West Indian
VI, Who's the Dupe
VII, All for Love
VII, Beaux' Stratagem
VII, Belle's Stratagem
VII, Brothers
VII, Citizen
VII, Deaf and Dumb
VII, Dragon of Wantley
VII, Earl of Essex
VII, Farm House
VII, First Floor
VII, Follies of a Day
VII, Good-Natured Man
VII, Gustavus Vasa
VII, Haunted Tower
VII, Heiress
VII, Honest Thieves
VII, Liar
VII, Lodoiska
VII, Siege of Damascus
VII, Tobacconist
VIII, All in the Wrong
VIII, Bold Stroke for a Husband
VIII, Bon Ton
VIII, Count of Narbonne
VIII, Cross Purposes
VIII, Fortune's Frolic
VIII, Irish Widow

VIII, Jew
VIII, Law of Lombardy
VIII, Love a-la-Mode
VIII, Monsieur Tonson
VIII, Mysterious Husband
VIII, Orphan
VIII, Recruiting Officer
VIII, Tamerlane
VIII, Virgin Unmasked
VIII, Way to Keep Him
IX, Appearance Is Against Them
IX, Chapter of Accidents
IX, Deserter
IX, Deuce Is in Him
IX, Distressed Mother
IX, Double Dealer
IX, Every One Has His Fault
IX, Fashionable Lover
IX, Mahomet the Imposter
IX, Miss in Her Teens
IX, Mock Doctor
IX, Oroonoko
IX, Orphan of China
IX, Romp
IX, Tailors
IX, Two Strings to Your Bow
IX, What Next
IX, Woodman
X, Abroad and At Home
X, Animal Magnetism
X, Apprentice
X, Bashful Man
X, Carmelite
X, Chances
X, Cheats of Scapin
X, Duplicity
X, Guardian
X, Know Your Own Mind
X, Love for Love
X, Lovers' Vows
X, Miller of Mansfield
X, My Spouse and I
X, Register Office
X, Sultan
X, Tender Husband
X, Three Weeks after Marriage
XI, By Royal Command
XI, Chrononhothologos
XI, Confederacy
XI, Constant Couple
XI, Contrivances
XI, Hero and Leander
XI, Lovers' Quarrels
XI, Maid of the Oaks
XI, Mogul Tale
XI, Purse
XI, School for Arrogance
XI, She Would and She Would Not
XI, Suspicious Husband
XI, Votary of Wealth
XI, Way of the World
XI, Which Is the Man?
XI, Who Is She?
XII, Better Late Than Never
XII, Careless Husband
XII, Comus
XII, Deserted Daughter
XII, Farmer's Wife
XII, First Love
XII, He's Much to Blame
XII, Heir at Law
XII, Love Makes a Man
XII, Midnight Hour
XII, Poor Gentleman
XII, Recruiting Sergeant
XII, Richard Coeur de Lion
XII, Rosina
XII, Scapegoat
XII, School for Wives
XII, Ways and Means
XII, Wives As They Were and Maids As They Are
22, Lily of the Desert
28, Three Black Seals
29, Thieves of Paris

38, John Felton
42, Bothwell
46, One Snowy Night
47, Meadows of St. Gervais
59, Under the Earth
61, Atonement
74, Father Baptiste
78, Judge Not
82, Dark Glen of Ballyfoill
89, Merchant Pirate
94, Old Martin's Trials
98, Bohemians
112, Grotto on the Stream
113, Juggler
Fortune's Frolic
In Quarantine
Piperman's Predicaments
Polish Jew

Dicks' Standard Charades and Comedies
488, Marriage Noose
490, All's Fair in Love
490, Woman Will Be a Woman

Dicks' Standard Plays
293, Oliver Twist
309, Herne the Hunter
311, East Lynne
323, Glencoe
328, Barney the Baron
329, Freischutz
339, Maid of Croissey
341, Court Fool
374, David Copperfield
375, Dombey and Son
385, Ivanhoe
387, Bears Not Beasts
388, Bleak House
390, Shaughraun
393, Barnaby Rudge
398, Old Curiosity Shop
402, Catching an Heiress
404, Wren Boys
412, My Unknown Friend
419, My Uncle's Card
419, Twins
422, White Boys
427, Little Jockey
428, Man in the Iron Mask
429, Dumb Conscript
430, Heart of London
432, Fairy Circle
433, Sea-Bathing at Home
433, Wrong Man
436, Vanderdecken
443, Black Domino
444, Village Outcast
453, Groves of Blarney
459, Message from the Sea
461, King O'Neil
466, Strange Gentleman
467, Village Coquettes
469, Nicholas Nickleby
470, Lamplighter
470, Is She His Wife?
473, Jessie Brown
486, Charles O'Malley
502, Tower of London
508, Jack Ketch
513, Haroun Alraschid
515, Grimalkin
515, My Own Blue Bell
516, Paulina
522, Match Making
532, Tam O'Shanter
534, Jack Brag
541, Sam Weller
551, One Fault
554, Beau Nash, the King of Bath
570, Wigwam
572, Infant Phenomenon
572, Captain Cuttle
573, Faust
576, House Divided
584, Bequeathed Heart
589, Americans Abroad

602, Antony and Cleopatra
606, Blue-faced Baboon
606, Ourang Outang and His Double
611, Red Farm
612, Miser's Daughter
613, Claude Duval, the Ladies' Highwayman
627, Bamboozling
627, Sergeant's Wedding
628, Game of Love
632, Turpin's Ride to York
636, Two Swindlers
636, Bardell v. Pickwick
638, Hazard of the Die
649, Devil's in It
653, You Know What
662, Why Did You Die?
662, Dowager
668, Moonshine
669, Divorce
669, Angeline
672, Inez de Castro
684, Gipsy King
694, Chain of Gold
700, Arajoon
708, Spring and Autumn
709, Close Siege
710, Louison, the Angel of the Attic
721, London by Night
725, Omnibus
738, Martin Chuzzlewit
746, Ondine
750, Petticoat Government
750, 'Tis She
751, Corsair's Revenge
752, Corsican Brothers
756, Dumb Guide of the Tyrol
761, Daughter of the Regiment
767, Charcoal Burner
776, Gentleman in Black
779, Philosophers of Berlin
780, Tale of Two Cities
785, Hard Times
807, Boyne Water
819, Chimes
833, Beggar Boy of Brussels
836, Uncle John
899, Jenkinses
899, My Friend, the Governor
905, Clarissa Harlowe
906, One Hour
919, Sailor's Legacy
931, Mandrin
951, Grace Clairville
973, Barber of Bagdad
997, Spring Gardens
997, To Parents and Guardians
999, Pride of the Market
1001, Battle of Life
1003, Five Hundred Pounds Reward
1006, Rough Diamond
1006, How to Settle Accounts with Your Laundress
1010, Romantic Idea
1019, Ovingdean Grange
1022, Muldoon's Picnic
1024, Waiter
1024, On the Brain
1025, Vision of Venus
1026, Been Had
1035, Courier of Lyons
1042, Charlotte Corday
1043, Legend of the Devil's Dyke
1063, Peck's Bad Boy
1068, Holly Tree Inn
1069, York and Lancaster
1070, Lost and Found
Devil on Two Sticks
Isaure
Perfection
Printer's Devil

Ditson Standard Opera Libretto
Elisire d'Amore
Dolby's British Theatre. *See also* Cumberland's British Theatre.
II, Duenna
II, Othello

II, West Indian
II, Cymbeline
II, Belle's Stratagem
II, Rivals
II, Venice Preserved
III, As You Like It
III, Hypocrite
III, Much Ado about Nothing
III, Provoked Husband
III, Padlock
III, Beggar's Opera
III, Way to Keep Him
VII, Every One Has His Fault
VII, Tempest
VII, Coriolanus
VII, Clandestine Marriage
VII, Jealous Wife
VII, Measure for Measure
VII, New Way to Pay Old Debts
VIII, Alcaid
VIII, Maid of the Mill
VIII, Woman Never Vext
VIII, Mayor of Garratt
VIII, Know Your Own Mind
VIII, Tale of Mystery
VIII, Busy Body
IX, Isabella
IX, Barber of Seville
IX, Freischutz
IX, George Barnwell
IX, Fall of Algiers
IX, Fair Penitent
IX, Charles the Second
X, Every Man in His Humour
X, Two Galley Slaves
X, Fatal Dowry
X, Lofty Projects
X, Father and Son
X, Wives As They Were and Maids As They Are
X, Shepherd of Derwent Vale
XI, Love in Humble Life
XI, King Henry V
XI, Twelfth Night
XI, Sleep-Walker
XI, Child of Nature
XI, Ali Pacha
XI, Brutus
XII, Roses and Thorns
XII, Tribulation
XII, Rival Valets
XII, Hide and Seek
XII, Midas
XII, Orestes in Argos
XII, Rule a Wife and Have a Wife
XIII, Good-Natured Man
Alcaid
Hide and Seek
Lofty Projects

Dramas from . . . Author of "Waverley"
5, Fortunes of Nigel
7, Ivanhoe

Duncombe's [Acting] Edition [of the British Theatre]
3, Old Oak Chest
18, Will Watch
21, Gambler's Life in London
24, He's No Conjuror
33, Nothing Superfluous
63, Youthful Days of William the Fourth
64, Love's Dream
68, Victorine
75, Two Drovers
77, Evil Eye
87, Crossing the Line
90, Ellen Wareham
99, Gustavus the Third
116, Damp Beds
123, Robert Macaire
130, Note Forger
140, Seven Sisters
143, Covenanters
151, Bronze Horse
153, Widow's Victim
172, John Stafford
181, Gaberlunzie Man

184, Minerali
188, Mummy
192, Sir Roger de Coverley
199, Rival Pages
201, False Colours
216, Woman's the Devil
235, Charming Folly
259, Tom Tiller and Jack Mizen
274, Don Juan
276, Queen's Ball
288, Latin, Love, and War
290, Fairy Lake
298, Behind the Scenes
307, Good Night's Rest
322, Happiest Man Alive
327, Ruby Ring
334, Helen Oakleigh
340, Fairly Hit and Fairly Missed
346, Paddy Whack in Italia
350, Windmill
353, Norma
354, Meet Me by Moonlight
388, Jane of the Hatchet
394, Polka
397, River God
405, Don Caesar de Bazan
406, Protector
422, Mrs. Caudle's Curtain Lecture
443, On the Tiles
450, Above and Below
466, Discarded Daughter
471, Rival Sergeants
476, Industry and Indolence
479, Tom Smart, the Adventurer
493, Tutor's Assistant
497, Slasher and Crasher
511, It's Only My Aunt
527, Allow Me to Apologize
533, Bould Soger Boy
541, Peter the Great
Advice to Husbands
Alexander the Great, in Little
Alice May
Alive and Merry
Ambassadress
Ancestress
Arnold of Winkelried
Azael the Prodigal
Bachelor's Torments
Balance of Comfort
Bamphylde Moore Carew
Barber and the Bravo
Battle of Life
Battle of Waterloo
Bear Hunters
Bed-Room Window
Bell Ringer of St. Paul's
Black Hugh, the Outlaw
Blacksmith
Blood Red Knight
Blue-Jackets
Borrowed Feathers
Bravo
Breakers Ahead
Bridge of Notre Dame
Caesar Borgia, the Scourge of Venice
Call Again To-morrow
Captain Stevens
Carline, the Female Brigand
Carmelites
Chelsea Pensioner
Cherry Bounce
Christmas Carol
Clarence Clevedon, His Struggle for Life or Death
Close Siege
Come to Town
Conquering Game
Crock of Gold
Cupid in London
Dance of the Shirt
Death Token
Delicate Attentions
Delusion
Demon of the Desert

Descart, the French Buccaneer
Deserted Village
Deuce Is in Her
Dice of Death
Dominique the Possessed
Don Pedro the Cruel and Don Manuel the Cobbler
Douglas Travestie
Earls of Hammersmith
Englishmen in India
Esther, the Royal Jewess
Evil May Day
Factory Lad
Fall of Algiers by Sea and Land
Farinelli
Fayre Mayde of West Cheap
Fidelio
First Night
Five in One
Flight to America
Forest of Bondy
Frank Fox Phipps, Esq.
Frankenstein
Frederick of Prussia
Freischutz
Gamester of Milan
Georgy Barnwell
German Jew
Gipsey of Derncleugh
Grey Doublet
Guardian Sylph
Harp of Altenberg
Heiress of Bruges
Home Again
Home Sweet Home
Hush Money
Idiot Witness
Irresistibles
Is She a Woman?
Jack Robinson and His Monkey
Jacket of Blue
Jacob Faithful
Jessie, the Flower of Dumblaine
Jewess
King and I
King of the Mist
King Robert the Bruce
King's Command
Kissing Goes by Favour
Lady and Gentleman in a Peculiarly Perplexing Predicament
Ladye of Lambythe
Lesson in Love
Lestocq
Like Father, Like Son
Little Back Parlour
Little Sins and Pretty Sinners
Loan of a Wife
Lord Darnley
Love Is Blind
Lovers' Quarrels
Loves of Lord Bateman and the Fair Sophia
Lucky Stars
Luke Somerton
Mabel's Curse
Maiden's Fame
Maidens Beware
Marceline
Marguerite's Colours
Marie: A Tale of the Pont Neuf
Marmion! A Tale of Flodden Field
Mary's Dream
Master Humphrey's Clock
Memoirs of the D***l
Michael Erle the Maniac Lover
Monsieur Jacques
Moral Philosopher
More Frightened than Hurt
Mountain King
Mr. Midshipman Easy
Mrs. G—, of the Golden Pippin
My Lord Is Not My Lord
My Valet and I
My Wife's Dentist
Napoleon Buonaparte's Invasion of Russia
Negro of Wapping

Old and the Young Stager
Old Gentleman
Old Honesty
Old Oak Tree
Oliver Twist
P. L.
P.S.—Come to Dinner
Pacha's Bridal
Pacha's Pets
Party Wall
Peerless Pool
Perourou
Peter Bell the Waggoner
Phantom Bride
Pink of Politeness
Powder and Ball
Predicament
Pride of Birth
Printer's Devil
Prisoner of Rochelle
Quasimodo
Queen's Jewel
Ragged School
Railroad Station
Railroad Trip
Rake's Progress
Rattlin the Reefer
Raymond and Agnes
Rear Admiral
Red Crow
Rinaldo Rinaldini
Roebuck
Rose of Corbeil
Rubber of Life
Shade
Smoked Miser
Soldier's Orphan
Spirit of the Rhine
Station House
Statue Lover
Swing
Tact
Tempter
Theodore the Brigand
Three Princes
Tower of Nesle
Tradesman's Ball
Traveller's Room
Trial by Battle
Truand Chief
Two Eyes between Two
Venus in Arms
Vidocq, the French Police Spy
Violette
Walter Brand
Wandering Boys
Wapping Old Stairs
What Have I Done?
Where Shall I Dine?
Where There's a Will There's a Way
Whistler
Who'll Lend Me a Wife
Wife
Williams' Visits
Wives by Advertisement
Wolsey
Wraith of the Lake
Yellow Kids
Zameo
Zazezizozu
Zingaro

Echoes of the Greek Drama
Pentheus
Edwin Forrest Edition of Shakespearian and Other Plays
Virginius
Elenora Duse Series of Plays
Ghosts
Elton's Edition of Farces
Our Mary Anne
English Library
136, Trevelling Companions

Fairy [and Home] Plays for Home Performance
1, Beauty and the Beast
2, Blue Beard
5, Yellow Dwarf
6, Aladdin
7, Puss in Boots
8, Little Red Riding Hood
9, Sleeping Beauty
10, Ali Baba
11, Nurseryrhymia
22, Dick Whittington
27, Pretty Princess and the Prickly Pear
Fisher's Edition of Standard Farces
Day in Paris
Personation
Scan. Mag.
Wolf and the Lamb
French's Acting Edition [late Lacy's]
2, Port Admiral
96, Honour before Wealth
117, David Garrick
118, Betsy Baker
129, My Little Girl
319, Still Waters Run Deep
501, Blow for Blow
548, Catherine Howard
571, Life's Revenge
655, Sweethearts
723, Ruy Blas
726, Ugly Customer
762, On and Off
894, Accusing Spirit
1164, Simon Lee
1336, New Men and Old Acres
1414, Little Change
1497, Shadows
1510, Billy Doo
1535, Green Old Age
1545, Pygmalion and Galatea
1642, Insured at Lloyd's
1670, Fool and His Money
1710, Highland Fling
1769, Two Roses
1776, Summoned to Court
1866, Garden Party
1890, Sour Grapes
1902, Open Gate
1977, Our Lottie
2004, Arabian Nights
2037, Outwitted
2055, On 'Change
2081, Kitty Clive
2122, Pair of Spectacles
2166, Cupid in Ermine
2186, Pantomime Rehearsal
2203, Castle in Spain
2269, Carrots
Anchor of Hope
Ashore and Afloat
Bells
Bride of Abydos
Brothers
Chalk and Cheese
Checkmate
Chiselling
Circumstances Alter Cases
Comical Countess
Compromising Case
Cox and Box
Danicheffs
Dying for Love
Engaged
Everybody's Husband
Faust
Garrick
Garrick Fever
Girl Graduate
Glimpse of Paradise
Gold Fiend
Hand and Glove
Harvest
Home
Hook and Eye
How Will They Get Out of It?

In for a Holyday
Irish Doctor
Leading Strings
Lend Me Five Shillings
Man Is Not Perfect, Nor Woman Neither
Man with Three Wives
Miser
Monte Cristo
Muleteer of Toledo
Octoroon
Old Cronies
On the Brink
Parted
Partners for Life
Petticoat Perfidy
Postscript
Scrap of Paper
Six and Eightpence
Steeple-Jack
Through the Fire
Tom Cob
True Colours
Two Puddifoots
We All Have Our Little Faults
Withered Leaves
Woman's Wrongs
Word of Honour
Written in Sand

French's Amateur Operas

Blind Beggars

French's American Drama

6, Flying Dutchman
13, Ernestine
22, Paddy Carey
25, Game of Life
26, Little Treasure
29, Romance and Reality
33, King's Rival
34, Love and Murder
41, Pilot
43, To Paris and Back, for Five Pounds
46, Three Guardsmen
48, Night and Morning
58, Popping the Question
65, Temptation
69, Po-ca-hon-tas
71, Married Rake
74, Pretty Piece of Business
79, Swiss Cottage
88, Irish Yankee
98, Life in New York
100, Dred
108, Rag-Picker of Paris and the Dress-Maker of St. Antoine
113, Ireland As It Is
115, Seven Clerks
120, Ugolino
127, To Parents and Guardians
129, Camille
136, Jane Eyre

French's International Copyrighted Edition of the Works of the Best Authors

19, Nicolete
33, Sympathetic Souls
39, Guv'nor
40, Queen's Messenger
41, Jane
44, Brace of Partridges
46, Late Mr. Castello
47, Bunch of Violets
52, Idler
53, Solicitor
55, Captain Swift
60, Parvenu
83, Brixton Burglary
84, Oh! Susannah
95, Time Is Money
123, Waterloo
137, Gray Parrot
163, Strange Adventures of Miss Brown
173, Woman's Wiles
Glass of Fashion

French's Minor Drama

105, Demon Lover
110, Andy Blake

136, Wanted—a Widow, with Immediate Possession
185, Nature and Philosophy
194, Teddy Roe
198, Laughing Hyena
204, Good for Nothing
223, Siamese Twins
233, Scene in the Life of an Unprotected Female
234, Pet of the Petticoats
240, Quiet Family
266, King René's Daughter
270, Pas de Fascination
272, Man Without a Head
276, Trumpeter's Daughter
280, Tom Noddy's Secret
282, Regular Fix
283, Dick Turpin and Tom King
288, Two B'hoys
291, Turn Him Out
292, Pretty Girls of Stillberg
293, Angel of the Attic
298, Who Killed Cock Robin?
303, That Rascal Pat
306, Cure for the Fidgets
307, Jack's the Lad
308, Much Ado about a Merchant of Venice
325, Forty Winks
327, Curious Case
335, Happy Pair
Fennel

French's Opera Libretti

Linda di Chamounix

French's Parlor Comedies

2, How She Loves Him

French's Standard Drama

27, London Assurance
43, Feudal Times
62, Old Heads and Young Hearts
79, Serious Family
90, Sketches in India
94, Mind Your Own Business
95, Writing on the Wall
101, Sardanapalus, King of Assyria
141, Henriette the Forsaken
142, Eustache Baudin
144, Bold Dragoons
151, Retribution
153, French Spy
154, Wept of the Wish-ton-Wish
156, Ben Bolt
158, Red Mask
161, All's Fair in Love
164, Cinderella
164, Gun-maker of Moscow
165, Phantom
166, Franklin
175, Isabelle
177, Angelo
181, Robber of the Rhine
186, Victims
189, Poor of New York
191, Raymond and Agnes
197, Skeleton Witness
210, Victorine
221, Miller of New Jersey
222, Dark Hour before Dawn
224, Art and Artifice
225, Romance of a Poor Young Man
228, Oliver Twist
231, Knight of Arva
291, Zelina
297, Flowers of the Forest
329, Ticket-of-Leave Man
338, Dead Heart
342, Cricket on the Hearth
345, Drunkard's Doom
347, Fifteen Years of a Drunkard's Life
348, Identity
349, Peep o' Day
360, Long Strike
361, Lancers
363, Randall's Thumb
365, Two Orphans
366, Colleen Bawn
368, Lady Clancarty

370, Never Too Late to Mend
371, Lily of France
372, Led Astray
375, May
377, Enoch Arden
384, Ours
407, War
414, Pike O'Callaghan
Camille
Ireland As It Is
Jane Eyre
Kathleen Mavourneen
Marble Heart
Ugolino

French's Standard Library Edition
Niobe, All Smiles
Woodbarrow Farm

G. Schirmer's Collection of Operas
Bride of Lammermoor

German Reed Repertory of Musical Pieces
Ages Ago
Happy Arcadia
No Cards
Old Knockles
Three Tenants
Verger

German Theatre
I, Rolla
II, Count Benyowsky
III, Deaf and Dumb
III, False Delicacy
III, Indian Exiles
IV, Conscience
IV, Otto of Wittelsbach
VI, Count Koenigsmark
VI, Emilia Galotti
VI, Ensign
VI, Stella

Green Tree Library
Little Eyolf

Hastings's Acting Plays
5, Chiselling
Domestic Hercules
Supper Gratis

Hodgson's Juvenile Drama
Ali Baba
Cataract of the Ganges

Home Library of Powerful Dramatic Tales
4, In the Ranks
6, Taken from Life

Home Plays for Ladies
V, Choosing a Bride
V, My Daughter's Daughter
V, Quarrel of the Flowers
VII, Heiress
VII, Only a Jest
VII, Prying Little Girl
VII, Value of Truth
IX, Caroline and Henrietta
IX, Daughter-in-Law
IX, Ten Years Hence
IX, Two Sisters

Independent Theatre Series of Plays
1, Widowers' Houses
2, Alan's Wife
3, Heirs of Rabourdin

Jerrold's Original Dramas
5, Doves in a Cage

John Duncombe's Edition
Alonzo the Brave and the Fair Imogine
Burmese War
Intimate Friend
Man and the Monster

John Heywood's Series of Plays, Recitations, etc. for School and
Popular Entertainments
14, Great Catch
15, Woman's Chance

Jugel's Pocket Novelist
21, Faust

Keystone Edition of Popular Plays
Uncle

Lacy's Acting Edition
3, Reigning Favorite
22, Daughter of the Stars
29, My Wife's Daughter
39, Belphegor
40, Tarantula
42, That Odious Captain Cutter
53, Mysterious Family
55, Tooth-ache
65, Circumstantial Evidence
76, Duel in the Dark
86, Lost Husband
90, Very Suspicious
126, Leo the Terrible
162, Acis and Galatea
178, Uncle Tom's Cabin
180, Pet of the Public
182, How to Make Home Happy
186, Maud's Peril
197, Willikind and Hys Dinah
200, Storm in a Teacup
223, Old Chateau
231, Princess
238, Object of Interest
247, Railway Belle
248, Abon Hassan
249, Aggravating Sam
259, Secret Agent
260, Game of Romps
266, Clockmaker's Hat
267, Miser of Shoreditch
294, My Heart's Idol
311, Wild Ducks
312, Dream of the Future
313, Chain of Events
316, Morning Call
353, Catching a Mermaid
354, Give a Dog a Bad Name
360, Urgent Private Affairs
386, Farmer's Daughter of the Severn Side
388, Romance under Difficulties
394, Fascinating Individual
428, Night at Notting Hill
434, Angel or Devil
436, Life's Trial
445, Wicked Wife
479, Marble Bride
499, What Will They Say at Brompton?
501, Lalla Rookh
521, Nothing Venture, Nothing Win
529, Samuel in Search of Himself
586, Everybody's Friend
599, Rifle Volunteers
600, Nine Points of the Law
612, Babes in the Wood and the Good Little Fairy Birds
613, Water Witches
629, Magic Toys
640, Good for Evil
649, Cricket on the Hearth
658, Forest Keeper
663, Two Polts
670, Miller and His Men
689, Dearest Mamma
720, Post-Boy
731, Old Joe and Young Joe
737, Harlequin Billy Taylor
744, Old House on the Bridge of Notre Dame
775, That Affair at Finchley
779, Esmeralda
782, Terrible Secret
833, Duck Hunting
838, My Heart's in the Highlands
851, My Preserver
857, Buckstone at Home
879, Aged Forty
888, Deal Boatman
987, One Tree Hill
1072, Woman That Was a Cat
1207, Time and Tide
1210, Done Brown
1213, Scamps of London
1315, Corsican Bothers
1316, Gertrude's Cherries
1319, Devil's Mount

1341, Christmas Eve in a Watchhouse
1370, Lodgers and Dodgers
1406, Tower of London
1429, Chapter of Accidents
1478, Last of the Legends
1479, Follow the Leader
1888, After the Party
A. S. S.
Absence of Mind
Absent Man
Accepted by Proxy
Acis and Galataea
Adonis Vanquished
Adoption
Adrienne
Adventures of a Love Letter
Adventures of Dick Turpin and Tom King
After a Storm Comes a Calm
After Dinner
Alabama
Alhambra
All at C
Alone
Among the Relics
Ample Apology
Angelo
Appeal to the Feelings
Appearances
April Folly
April Fool
As Once in May
As You Like It
Assault and Battery
At the Cross Roads
Atalanta
Atchi
Atrocious Criminal
Auld Acqaintance
Aurora Floyd
Avalanche
Awaking
Away with Melancholy
Backward Child
Bad Penny
Baffled Spinster
Bailiff
Balance of Comfort
Balloon
Bardell versus Pickwick
Barefaced Imposters
Barrister
Bashful Man
Bathing
Bearding the Lion
Beau Brummel, the King of Calais
Beauty or the Beast
Behind a Mask
Belle of the Barley-Mow
Belphegor the Mountebank
Best Way
Better Half
Between the Posts
Bilious Attack
Bird in the Hand Worth Two in the Bush
Bird of Paradise
Birds in Their Little Nests Agree
Birds of Prey
Bit of Old Chelsea
Bitter Reckoning
Black Sheep
Blossom of Churnington Green
Blow in the Dark
Bluebeard Re-Paired
Board and Residence
Bobby A1
Bold Dragoons
Bona Fide Travellers
Bonnie Fish Wife
Book the Third, Chapter the First
Bosom Friends
Bow Bells
Breaking the Ice
Breezy Morning
Brewer of Preston

Bridal Wreath
Bridget's Blunders
Brigand
Bristol Diamonds
British Born
Broken Idylls
Broken Ties
Broken Toys
Brown and the Brahmins
Browne the Martyr
Browne with an E
Bubbles
Bumble's Courtship
Burglar and the Judge
By Royal Command
By This Token
Cabinet Question
Calthorpe Case
Calypso, Queen of Ogygia
Camaralzaman and the Fair Badoura
Cantab
Cape Mail
Captain Charlotte
Carte de Visite
Cartouche, the French Robber
Cast King of Granada
Catch a Weazel
Caught by the Ears
Caught in a Line
Caught in His Own Trap
Census
Champagne
Change of System
Change Partners
Charitable Bequest
Charming Woman
Charms
Cheap Excursion
Cheerful and Musical
Cherry and Fair Star
Chesterfield Thinskin
Chevalier de St. George
Chevalier of the Maison Rouge
Childhood's Dreams
Children of the Castle
Chops of the Channel
Chopstick and Spikins
Christmas Boxes
Christmas Pantomime
Chrystabelle
Cinderella
Cinders
Clerical Error
Cloud and Sunshine
Coals of Fire
Colleen Bawn Settled at Last
Colour-Sergeant
Coming Woman
Commission
Counter Attraction
Court Cards
Court of Lions
Court of Oberon
Courtship
Cousin Peter
Cousin Tom
Cousin Zachary
Cozy Couple
Cracked Heads
Crazed
Crimeless Criminal
Crinoline
Cross Questions and Crooked Answers
Crossed Love
Crown Diamonds
Cruel to Be Kind
Cupid and Psyche
Cupid in Waiting
Cure for Love
Cut for Partners
Daddy Hardacre
Dancing Dervish
Dan'l Druce, Blacksmith
Dark Cloud

Dark Doings in the Cupboard
Davenport Bros. & Co.
Davenport Done
Day of Reckoning
Day's Fishing
Deacon
Dead Witness
Deadman's Point
Death of Marlowe
Debt
Declined—with Thanks
Deeds, Not Words
Deep Red Rover
Dentist
Deserter in a Fix
Devil's Ducat
Devilish Good Joke
Dimity's Dilemma
Dinner for Two
Diogenes and His Lantern
Dodge for a Dinner
Does He Love Me?
Dog of Montargis
Doge of Duralto
Doing Banting
Doing My Uncle
Dolly
Dora's Devise
Double Dealing
Double Dummy
Double Faced People
Down in a Balloon
Drama at Home
Drapery Question
Drawing Rooms, Second Floor, and Attics
Dreadfully Alarming
Dream Faces
Dream Spectre
Dreams
Dred: A Tale of the Dismal Swamp
Drifted Apart
Drunkard's Children
Duchess of Bayswater and Co.
Duchess or Nothing
Duke's Daughter
Dumb Savoyard and His Monkey
Duty
D'ye Know Me Now?
Eclipsing the Son
Eddystone Elf
Edendale
Eight Hours at the Sea-Side
1863
Elisir d'Amore
Elopement
Elopements in High Life
Elsie's Rival
Enchanted Wood
End of the Tether
Englishman's House Is His Castle
Equals
Eternal Masculine
Eton Boy
Eurydice
Evil Eye
Exposition
Express
Faded Flowers
Faint Heart Which Did Win a Fair Lady
Fair Exchange
Fair Maid of Perth
Fair Pretender
Fair Rosamond's Bower
Fairy's Father
False Alarm
False and Constant
False Shame
Fame
Family Secret
Fancy Fair
Fan-Fan, the Tulip
Farmer's Story
Fast Coach
Fast Friends

Fast Train! High Pressure! Express!, A Short Trip
Faust and Marguerite
Fearful Tragedy in the Seven Dials
Field of the Cloth of Gold
Fifteen Years of Labour Lost
Fighting by Proxy
Fille de Madame Angot
Fine Feathers
Fire-Eater
Fire Raiser
First Affections
First Come, First Served
First Experiment
First in the Field
First Mate
First Night
Fitzsmythe of Fitzsmythe Hall
Five Pounds Reward
Floating a Company
Floating Beacon
Fly and the Web
Fool's Paradise
For Honor's Sake
For Papa's Sake
For the Old Love's Sake
Founded on Facts
Fountain of Beauty
Four Cousins
Fragment
French Exhibition
Friend in Need
From Village to Court
Game of Speculation
Garibaldi Excursionists
Gay Lothario
Gentle Gertrude of the Infamous Redd Lyon Inn
Gentleman Jim
Gentleman Whip
Gilded Youth
Girls
Giselle
Glin Gath
Glitter
Gnome King and the Good Fairy of the Silver Mine
Going It
Going to Chobham
Going to the Bad
Going to the Derby
Going to the Dogs
Gold
Golden Branch
Golden Fetter
Golden Fleece
Golden Plough
Good for Evil
Good Run for It
Goodnight, Signor Pantaloon
Gossip
Gotobed Tom
Grandmother's Gown
Grateful Father
Great Gun Trick
Grimshaw, Bagshaw, and Bradshaw
Grin Bushes
Guardian Angel
Guinea Stamp
Gwynneth Vaughan
Hal, the Highwayman
Hamlet Improved
Hans von Stein
Happy Medium
Happy Return
Harlequin Alfred the Great
Harlequin and O'Donoghue
Harmony
Harvest Home
Have You Got That Ten Pound Note?
He Lies Like Truth
He That Will Not When He May
Head of Romulus
Head of the Family
Headless Horseman
Heads or Tails?
Heart of Midlothian

Helpless Couple
Her New Dressmaker
Hercules and Omphale
Heroes
Hester's Mystery
His Excellency
His Novice
His Own Guest
His Toast
Hogmanay (New Year's Eve)
Holly Bush Hall
Holly Tree Inn
Home for a Holiday
Home of One's Own
Home Rule
Home, Sweet Home, with Variations
Honeymoon Tragedy
Hop Pickers and Gipsies
Hopeless Passion
Hour at Seville
House on the Bridge of Notre Dame
House or the Home?
House out of Windows
How Stout You're Getting
How's Your Uncle?
Hugger-Mugger
Huguenot Captain
Human Sport
Hurly-Burly
Hyder
I Couldn't Help It
I Love You
Idalia
Idiot of the Mountain
Idyll of the Closing Century
If the Cap Fits
I'll Be Your Second
I'll Write to the Times
Imogen's New Cook
In an Attic
In Danger
In Nelson's Days
In Possession
In the Clouds
In the Eyes of the World
In Two Minds
Incompatibility of Temper
Infatuation
Ingomar, the Son of the Wilderness
Interview
Inundation
Irish Emigrant
Irish Post
Irish Tiger
Ironfounder
Isle of St. Tropez
Isoline of Bavaria
I've Eaten My Friend
I've Written to Browne
Jack in the Green
Jack White's Trial
Jack's Delight
Jealousy
Jeannette and Jeannot
Jeannette's Wedding
Jeannette's Wedding Day
Jersey Girl
Jessamy's Courtship
Jew's Daughter
Jeweller of St. James's
John Overy
Joint Household
Jolliboy's Woes
Josephine, the Child of the Regiment
Journey's End
Just as Well
Just Like Roger
Just My Luck
Keep Your Eye on Her
Keep Your Temper
Keeper of the Seals
Kenilworth (Dibdin & Bunn)
Kenilworth (Halliday & Lawrance)
Kennyngton Crosse

Kensington Gardens
Khartoum
King and Rebel
King of the Merrows
King of the Peacocks
King O'Toole's Goose
Kiss and Be Friends
Kleptomania
Knights of the Round Table
Lad from the Country
Ladies of St. Cyr
Ladies' Battle
Ladies' Club
Lady Belle Belle
Lady by Birth
Lady Dedlock's Secret
Lady Elizabeth Poole Gubbins
Lady Fortune
Lady in Search of an Heiress
Lady Interviewer
Lady of Belleisle
Lady of Lyons Married and Settled
Laid up in Port
Lancashire Sailor
Larkins' Love Letters
Last Life
Last of the Pigtails
Late Sir Benjamin
Laurence's Love Suit
Law versus Love
Leap Year
Leatherlungos the Great, How He Stormed, Reign'd, and Mizzled
Leave It to Me
Left in a Cab
Left the Stage
Legacy of Honour
Legal Impediment
Lending a Hand
Lesson in Love
Life Chase
Lilian Gervais
Lilly Dawson
Linked by Love
Lion at Bay
Little Daisy
Little Madcap
Little Miss Muffet
Little Mother
Little Red Riding Hood and the Fairies of the Rose, Shamrock, and Thistle
Little Robin Hood
Little Sentinel
Little Vixens
Living Too Fast
Liz
Lizzie Lyle
Long Odds
Lost and Found
Lost Child
Lost Wife
Lot 49
Lottery of Life
Louis XI
Louise de Lignerolles
Love and Dentistry
Love and Hunger
Love and Rain
Love by Lantern-Light
Love Game
Love Suit
Love Test
Love Wins
Love's Alarms
Love's Labyrinth
Love's Martyr
Love's Telegraph
Lucille
Lucky Escape
Lucky Hit
Lucky Stars
Lugarto the Mulatto
Lunatic
Lyieushee Lovel
Lyrical Lover

Macbeth, Somewhat Removed from the Text of Shakespeare
Mad as a Hatter
Madame Berliot's Ball
Mademoiselle Squallino
Maggie's Situation
Maid of Honour
Major and Miner
Man in the Street
Man of Two Lives
Man Proposes
Man Who Follows the Ladies
Man Who Wasn't
Man with the Iron Mask
Mandarin's Daughter
Margaret Catchpole, the Heroine of Suffolk
Margate Sands
Margery Daw
Maria
Maria Martin
Marriage at Any Price
Married Daughters and Young Husbands
Married for Money
Married in Haste
Married Un-Married
Martin Chuzzlewit
Mary Edmonstone
Mary Price
Mary Turner
Master Passion
Matchmaker
Matrimonial—A Gentleman, &c. for Further Particulars, Apply at——
Matrimonial Prospectuses
Meadowsweet
Meddle and Muddle
Medea
Melting Moments
Mephistopheles
Merrifield's Ghost
Merry Meeting
Merry Widow
Middy Ashore
Midnight: The Thirteenth Chime
Midsummer Day
Miller of Whetstone
Milliner's Holiday
Minerali
Mischief-Making
Miser's Daughter
Miss Chester
Miss Eily O'Connor
Miss Flipper's Holiday
Miss Honey's Treasure
Miss Impudence
Miss Tibbets' Back Hair
Mistaken Identity
Model Husband
Monastery of St. Just
Montcalm
Month after Date
More Blunders Than One
Moustache Movement
Moving Tale
Mr. and Mrs. Muffett
Mrs. Green's Snug Little Business
Mudborough Election
Music Hath Charms
My Aunt's Husband
My Awful Dad
My Bachelor Days
My Cousin
My Daughter's Debut
My Dress Boots
My First Client
My First Fit of the Gout
My Friend from Leatherhead
My Friend Jarlet
My Friend the Major
My Husband's Ghost
My Lady Help
My Lord and My Lady
My Milliner's Bill
My Poll and My Partner Joe
My Sister from India

My Son Diana
My Son's a Daughter
My Very Last Proposal
My Wife—What Wife?
My Wife's Baby
My Wife's Father's Sister
My Wife's Mother
My Wife's Out
My Wife's Relations
My Wife's Second Floor
Narrow Escape
Narrow Squeak
Nearly Seven
Nearly Severed
Neck or Nothing
Neighbours
Nettle
Never Reckon Your Chickens &c.
New Groom
New Men and Old Acres
New Sub
Newington Butts
Newspaper Nuptials
Nice Firm
Nice Quiet Day
Night of Suspense
Night on Snowdon
Nine Days' Wonder
Ninth Waltz
Nita's First
No. 6, Duke Street
Noblesse Oblige
Norma Travestie
Not False But Fickle
Not So Bad After All
Novelty Fair
Obliging a Friend
Observation and Flirtation
Obstinate Family
Obstinate Woman
Ocean of Life
Odd Lot
Odd Trick
Old Friends
Old Garden
Old Man
Old Sailors
Old Soldier
Old Trusty
Olympic Revels
On an Island
On Bail
On Guard
On the Clyde
Once a Week
One in Hand Is Worth Two in the Bush
117, Arundel Street, Strand
One Too Many
Only a Halfpenny
Only a Penny-a-Liner
Only Amateurs
Oor Geordie
Opposite Neighbours
Optical Delusion
Orange Tree and the Humble Bee
Organic Affection
Our Bitterest Foe
Our Clerks
Our Friends
Our Lottie
Our Nelly
Our New Butler
Our Pet
Our Regiment
Our Village
Out of the Frying Pan
Out on the Loose
Overland Journey to Constantinople
P.U.P.
Pacha of Pimlico
Packing Up
Palace of Truth
Palmistry
Pan

Pandora's Box
Paper Chase
Paper Wings
Paphian Bower
Papillonetta
Paquita
Paris
Paris and Pleasure
Past and Present
Patron Saint
Patter versus Clatter
Paul Pry Married and Settled
Paying Guest
Peacock's Holiday
Peculiar Proposals
Pedlar Boy
Pedrillo
Pendrudge v. Prettiwon
Pepperpot's Little Pets
Perfect Cure
Perfect Love
Peter Wilkins
Pet Lamb
Pets of the Parterre
Philanthropy
Philippe
Philosopher's Stone
Photographic Fix
Pickpocket
Pierette
Pirates of the Savannah
Play
Playmates
Please to Remember the Grotto
Plot for Plot
Plots for Petticoats
Poetic Proposal
Poor Cousin Walter
Poor Nobleman
Popocatapetl
Poppleton's Predicaments
Pork Chops
Poul a Dhoil
Pouter's Wedding
Practical Man
Pretty Predicaments
Prima Donna
Prince Amabel
Prince Camaralzaman
Prince Dorus
Prince for an Hour
Princess Charming
Princess Primrose and the Four Pretty Princes
Princess Spring-Time
Princesses in the Tower
Prior Claim
Prisoner of War
Progress
Prompter's Box
Proof
Punch
Punctured
Purely Platonic
Q. E. D.
Queen Mary's Bower
Queen of Arragon
Queen of Hearts
Queen of Spades
Queer Street
Railway Adventure
Rain Clouds
Randall's Thumb
Ranelagh
Rappings and Table Movings
Rats
Ready-Money
Real and Ideal
Reapers
Recollection of O'Flannigan and the Fairies
Rely on My Discretion
Retaliation
Retiring
Return Ticket
Richard Wye

Rifle and How to Use It
Rights and Wrongs of Woman
Rip Van Winkle
Robbers of the Pyrenees
Robert Macaire
Robert the Devil
Robin Hood
Rocambole
Romulus and Remus
Roundhead
Rule Britannia
Rule of Three
Ruthven
Ruy Blas Righted
Sad Memories
Sam's Arrival
Sample versus Pattern
Sarah the Creole
Scapegoat
School for Coquettes
Sea-Gulls
Sea of Ice
Secret
Semi-Detached
Send Thirty Stamps
Senior Wranglers
Sense and Sensation
Serf
Serve Him Right
Setting of the Sun
Settling Day
Seven Sins
Shadow of a Crime
Shadows of the Past
Shakspeare's Early Days
Shameful Behaviour
Sharp Practice
Shattered Nerves
She Would and He Wouldn't
Shepherd of Cournouailles
Shilling Day at the Great Exhibition
Shipmates
Short and Sweet
Should This Meet the Eye
Show of Hands
Shylock
Signal
Silent System
Silver Keepsake
Silver Lining
Sink or Swim
Sir Roger de Coverley
Sister's Penance
Six Persons
Sixes and Sevens: A Misunderstanding
Sixpenny Telegram
Slice of Luck
Slight Mistakes
Slow Man
Slowtop's Engagements
Smoke
Snowdrift
Snowdrop
Snowstorm
Sold Again
Sole Survivor
Something to Do
Somnambulist
Son of the Soil
Soul of Honor
Southerner—Just Arrived
Speak Out Boldly
Speed the Plough
Splendid Investment
Spur of the Moment
Star of the North
State Secrets
Steeple-Chase
Step-Sister
Stolen Jewess
Stolen Kisses
Stolen—£20 Reward
Strange History
Such Is Fame

Sugar and Cream
Suit of Tweeds
Sunshine through the Clouds
Supper for Two
Sylphide
Sympathy
Syren of Paris
Take Care of Dowb—
Taken for Granted
Taken from the French
Taking by Storm
Taking the Veil
Tale of a Comet
Tale of Two Cities
Taming a Tiger
Taming the Truant
Tarantula
Tears Idle Tears
Telephone
Tell and the Strike of the Cantons
Tender Precautions
Terrible Tinker
Test of Truth
Theodora, Actress and Empress
Theory and Practice
Thetis and Peleus
Thorough Base
Those Landladies
Three Blind Mice
Three Furies
Three Musket-Dears and a Little One In
Thrice Married
Thrillby
Thrown Together
Ticket-of-Leave Man's Wife
Ticklish Times
Tide of Time
Time Will Tell
Times
Timson's Little Holiday
Tit for Tat
Title
Tom Pinch
Tom Thrasher
Tomkins the Troubadour
Too Late to Save
Too Much of a Good Thing
Tourist's Ticket
Tower of Lochlain
Tragedy
Traitor's Gate
Tramp's Adventure
Trapping a Tartar
Tromb-al-ca-zar
Trovatore
True as Steel
Turned Head
£20 a Years—All Found
Twilight
Twins
Two Blinds
Two Flats and a Sharp
Two in the Morning
Two Misses Ibbetson
Two Photographs
Two Pro's.
Two to One
Ulysses
Uncle Crotchet
Uncle Zachary
Unequal Match
Unlucky Friday
Up a Tree
Up at the Hills
Up in the World
Up to Town and Back Again
Upstairs and Downstairs
Valentine
Velvet and Rags
Very Last Days of Pompeii
Very Serious Affair
Veteran of 102 Years
Vice Versa: A Lesson for Fathers
Village Nightingale

Villain and Victim
Villikins and His Dinah
Violet
Virginius
Wait for an Answer
Waiting for an Omnibus in the Lowther Arcade on a Rainy Day
Waltz by Arditi
Wanted, a Young Lady—
Was I to Blame?
Watch and Wait
Wayfarers
Weak Woman
Weaver of Lyons
Wedding Breakfast
Well Matched
Well Played
Where's Your Wife?
Which?
Which Shall I Marry?
White Cat
White Fawn
White Stocking
Who Do They Take Me For?
Who Stole the Clock?
Who Won?
Who's My Husband?
Who's the Composer?
Who's the Heir?
Why Women Weep
Wife of Seven Husbands
Wild Boy of Bohemia
Will and the Way
William Simpson
William Tell
Winning a Wife
Winning Hazard
Witch of Windermere
Without Incumbrances
Wizard of the Moor
Woman I Adore
Woman of the World
Woman That Was a Cat
Woman's Proper Place
Woodman's Spell
Wooing One's Wife
Workbox
World and Stage
World of Fashion
Worth a Struggle
Wrinkles: A Tale of Time
Yorkshire Gamester
Young Lad from the Country
Young Mother
Your Likeness—One Shilling
Your Vote and Interest
Yule Log

Lacy's Anglo-American Edition of Standard Plays
    3, Somnambula
Lacy's Dramas for Private Representation
    Number 49
Lacy's Home Plays
    Blind Boy
    Cross of St. John
    Harvest Storm
Lacy's Sensation Series
    1, Blazing Burgee
    Ploughman
    Pretty Jane
Lenfestey's Edition
    Rent Day
    Rip Van Winkle
Locke's Museum Edition
    Fortunio and His Seven Gifted Servants
London Acting Drama
    27, Old Forge
    31, Brothers
London Theatre
    I, Rivals
    I, Beggar's Opera
    I, Venice Preserved
    I, Irish Widow
    II, Quaker
    II, Isabella

II, Bold Stroke for a Wife
II, West Indian
III, Douglas
III, Provoked Husband
III, Fortune's Frolic
III, Love in a Village
IV, Richard, Coeur de Lion
IV, Gamester
IV, Brothers
IV, Belle's Stratagem
V, High Life below Stairs
V, Man of the World
V, Grecian Daughter
V, Maid of the Mill
VI, Rosina
VI, Busy Body
VI, Revenge
VI, She Stoops to Conquer
VII, Lionel and Clarissa
VII, Jane Shore
VII, Fashionable Lover
VII, Three Weeks after Marriage
VIII, Fair Penitent
VIII, Miss in Her Teens
VIII, Critic
VIII, Beaux' Stratagem
IX, Cato
IX, Hypocrite
IX, Midas
IX, London Merchant
X, Alexander the Great
X, Way to Keep Him
X, All in the Wrong
X, Comus
XI, Mourning Bride
XI, Guardian
XI, Tancred and Sigismunda
XI, Jealous Wife
XII, Padlock
XII, Inconstant
XII, Roman Father
XII, Clandestine Marriage
XIII, Tobacconist
XIII, Rule a Wife and Have a Wife
XIII, Wonder
XIII, Tamerlane
XIV, Siege of Damascus
XIV, Apprentice
XIV, Suspicious Husband
XIV, Trip to Scarborough
XV, Confederacy
XV, Count of Narbonne
XV, Oroonoko
XV, Devil to Pay
XVI, Citizen
XVI, Mahomet, the Imposter
XVI, Love for Love
XVI, She Would and She Would Not
XVII, Recruiting Officer
XVII, Every Man in His Humour
XVII, Orphan of China
XVII, Mayor of Garratt
XVIII, Recruiting Sergeant
XVIII, Duke of Milan
XVIII, New Way to Pay Old Debts
XVIII, Orphan
XIX, Good-Natured Man
XIX, Zara
XIX, Country Girl
XIX, Two Misers
XX, Mock Doctor
XX, Cymon
XX, Double Dealer
XX, Conscious Lovers
XXI, What Next?
XXI, Lord of the Manor
XXI, Chapter of Accidents
XXI, Distrest Mother
XXII, Farmer's Wife
XXII, Lying Valet
XXII, Refusal
XXII, All for Love
XXIII, Virgin Unmasked
XXIII, Double Gallant

XXIII, Earl of Warwick
XXIII, Which Is the Man?
XXIV, Miser
XXIV, Polly Honeycombe
XXIV, Hit or Miss
XXIV, Edward the Black Prince
XXIV, Way of the World
XXV, Twenty Per Cent
XXV, Maid of the Oaks
XXV, Sultan
XXV, Lady Jane Grey
XXV, Earl of Essex
XXVI, Merchant of Bruges
XXVI, Constant Couple
XXVI, My Spouse and I
XXVI, Tender Husband

Lynn's Acting Edition
    10, Gipsy
    14, Leonore
    16, Grandad's Darling
    17, What Greater Love?
    18, Lily of the Field
    20, Wreckage
    22, Blanche de Maletroit
    23, Happy Day
    26, Till the Half-Hour
    32, Private View

Lynn's On Tour Edition
    1, Minx and Man

Metzler & Co.'s Opera Bouffe Series
    Breaking the Spell
    Forty Winks

Miller's Modern Acting Drama
    10, High, Low, Jack, and the Game
    20, Revolt of the Workhouse
    Welsh Girl

Minor Drama
    1, Irish Attorney
    2, Boots at the Swan
    5, Dead Shot
    6, His Last Legs
    7, Invisible Prince
    8, Golden Farmer
    10, Used Up
    12, Barrack Room
    14, Beauty and the Beast
    15, St. Patrick's Eve
    16, Captain of the Watch
    18, White Horse of the Peppers
    19, Jacobite
    20, Bottle
    29, Old Guard
    33, Cockneys in California
    37, Irish Ambassador
    40, All That Glitters Is Not Gold
    41, Rough Diamond
    44, Two Bonnycastles
    45, Born to Good Luck
    46, Kiss in the Dark
    48, Kill or Cure
    49, Box and Cox Married and Settled
    49, St. Cupid
    52, Lawyers
    54, Toodles
    55, Mob Cap
    57, Morning Call
    86, To Oblige Benson
    90, Cherry and Fair Star
    91, Gale Breezely
    94, Awkward Arrival
    100, Crown Prince
    101, Two Queens
    114, Decided Case
    123, Day after the Fair
    124, Make Your Wills
    131, Corsair
    133, Spoiled Child
    137, Lottery Ticket
    145, Columbus el Filibustero
    146, Harlequin Blue Beard, the Great Bashaw
    148, Phenomenon in a Smock Frock
    149, Comedy and Tragedy
    153, Musard Ball

154, Great Tragic Revival
157, Tom and Jerry
158, Village Lawyer
159, Captain's Not A-miss
164, Shakspeare's Dream
165, Neptune's Defeat
167, Take Care of Little Charley
169, Yankee Peddler
171, Double-Bedded Room
361, He, She, and It
390, Mixed Addresses
Promotion

Modern Acting Drama

8, Taken in and Done For

Modern English Comic Theatre

IV, Retired from Business

Modern Standard Drama

4, Richelieu
15, Hunchback
16, Don Caesar de Bazan
35, King John
36, Nervous Man and the Man of Nerve
46, Follies of a Night
47, 'Twould Puzzle a Conjuror
60, Simpson and Co.
68, Faint Heart Never Won Fair Lady
69, Gisippus
70, Town and Country
76, Paul Pry
83, Leap Year
85, Passing Cloud
89, Ingomar, the Barbarian
90, Sketches in India
99, Marco Spada
King of the Commons

Modern Theatre

I, How to Grow Rich
I, Life
I, Notoriety
I, Rage
I, Will
II, Delinquent
II, Folly As It Flies
II, Fortune's Fool
II, Laugh When You Can
II, Speculation
III, Secrets Worth Knowing
III, Votary of Wealth
III, Werter
III, Who Wants a Guinea?
III, Zorinski
IV, Box-Lobby Challenge
IV, Duplicity
IV, He's Much to Blame
IV, School for Arrogance
IV, School for Prejudice
IV, Seduction
V, Carmelite
V, False Impressions
V, Mysterious Husband
V, Natural Son
VI, Braganza
VI, Impostors
VI, Law of Lombardy
VI, Ramah Droog
VI, Wife of Two Husbands
VII, I'll Tell You What
VII, Next Door Neighbours
VII, Percy
VII, Trip to Scarborough
VII, Wise Man of the East
VIII, England Preserved
VIII, Fugitive
VIII, He Would Be a Soldier
VIII, Mary Queen of Scots
VIII, Matilda
IX, Bank Note
IX, Chapter of Accidents
IX, English Merchant
IX, Henry the Second
IX, School for Wives

Mounet-Sulley Edition

Oedipus the King

Neal's Edition

Fish Out of Water

New British Theatre

I, Bandit
I, Forgery
I, Genii
I, Intrigues of a Day
I, Masquerade
I, Prophetess
I, Theodora
I, Willario
I, Watch-House
I, Witness
I, Word of Honor
II, Family Politics
II, Last Act
II, Manoeuvring
II, Mermaid
II, Sailor's Return
II, Sulieman
II, Thermopylae
II, Way to Win Her
III, Apostate
III, Father and Son
III, Gondolier
III, Gonzanga
III, Love, Honor, and Interest
III, Orpheus
III, Search After Perfection
III, Sorceress
III, Spaniards
IV, Apollo's Choice
IV, Fair Crusader
IV, He Must Be Married
IV, Hector
IV, Hortensia
IV, Savoyard
IV, Selim and Zuleika
IV, Sixteen and Sixty
IV, Woman's Will

New British Theatre [late Duncombe's]

34, Maid of Genoa
45, Maurice the Woodcutter
84, Jonathan Bradford
91, Yeoman's Daughter
93, Knight of St. John
131, Carmilhan
132, Wenlock of Wenlock
136, Capers and Coronets
187, Lilian the Show Girl
200, Manfredi the Mysterious Hermit
234, Love and Charity
239, Dream of Fate
263, Faith and Falsehood
271, Sudden Thoughts
286, King's Gardener
310, Night in the Bastille
311, Dragon Knight
313, Devil's Daughters
314, Bandit of the Blind Mine
333, Temple of Death
349, Queen of Cyprus
353, New Footman
361, Miser's Daughter
367, Yankee Notes for English Circulation
370, Asmodeus
373, Post of Honour
374, Ambassador's Lady
376, Linda, the Pearl of Savoy
380, My Wife's Come
381, Bohemians of Paris
382, Meg Murnock, the Hag of the Glen
389, Mistaken Story
390, Whitefriars
399, Momentous Question
400, Young England
407, Sealed Sentence
411, Corporal's Wedding
412, House Dog
432, Popping In and Out
439, Nora Creina
441, Sea King's Vow
444, Last Kiss
447, Blechington House

448, Sister and I
455, Fellow Servents
475, Out on the Sly
490, Jonathan
505, Sixteen String Jack
506, Separate Maintenance
510, Chamber Practice
518, Three Cuckoos
520, Adam Buff
521, Friend Waggles
526, Sent to the Tower
537, Last of the Fairies
538, Scarlet Mantle
540, Plain Cook
542, 102
582, Loss of the Royal George
Cousin Lambkin
Guido Fawkes
Nell Gwynne
Othello Travestie
Romeo and Juliet, as the Law Directs
Young Scamp

New English Drama

I, Hypocrite
I, Jealous Wife
I, New Way to Pay Old Debts
I, Rivals
I, West Indian
II, Beggar's Opera
II, Duenna
II, Lionel and Clarissa
II, Love in a Village
II, Maid of the Mill
III, Alexander the Great
III, Hamlet
III, Is He Jealous?
III, Richard the Third
III, Way to Keep Him
IV, Castle Spectre
IV, She Stoops to Conquer
IV, Venice Preserved
IV, Wonder
IV, Woodman's Hut
V, Clandestine Marriage
V, Distrest Mother
V, Othello
V, Provoked Husband
V, Soldier's Daughter
VI, Belle's Stratagem
VI, Busy Body
VI, Deaf and Dumb
VI, Recruiting Officer
VI, Romeo and Juliet
VII, As You Like It
VII, Beaux' Stratagem
VII, Bold Stoke for a Wife
VII, King John
VII, Road to Ruin
VIII, Coriolanus
VIII, Country Girl
VIII, Jane Shore
VIII, Merry Wives of Windsor
VIII, Suspicious Husband
IX, Critic
IX, Honest Thieves
IX, Mayor of Garratt
IX, Rosina
IX, Rugantino
IX, Shipwreck
IX, Three Weeks after Marriage
X, Inconstant
X, King Lear
X, Merchant of Venice
X, Rob Roy MacGregor
X, Rule a Wife and Have a Wife
XI, Citizen
XI, Deserter
XI, Lying Valet
XI, Magpie
XI, Miser
XI, Quaker
XI, Who's the Dupe
XII, Confederacy
XII, Cymbeline

XII, Douglas
XII, Guy Mannering
XII, Twelfth Night
XIII, Follies of a Day
XIII, Fortune's Frolic
XIII, Love Laughs at Locksmiths
XIII, Midnight Hour
XIII, Review
XIII, Tobacconist
XIV, Evadne
XIV, Grecian Daughter
XIV, King Henry the Fourth
XIV, Know Your Own Mind
XIV, Macbeth
XV, Blue Devils
XV, Bon Ton
XV, High Life Below Stairs
XV, Liar
XV, Midas
XV, Spoiled Child
XVI, Every Man in His Humour
XVI, Every One Has His Fault
XVI, Julius Caesar
XVI, Man of the World
XVI, Measure for Measure
XVII, Cato
XVII, George Barnwell
XVII, Tempest
XVII, Travellers
XVII, Two Gentlemen of Verona
XVIII, Chapter of Accidents
XVIII, Gamester
XVIII, King Henry the Fifth
XVIII, Much Ado About Nothing
XVIII, Wallace
XIX, Kenilworth
XIX, King Henry the Eighth
XIX, One O'Clock
XIX, Rich and Poor
XIX, Winter's Tale
XX, All in the Wrong
XX, Lodoiska
XX, Pizarro
XX, Tamerlane
XX, Trip to Scarborough
XXI, Blue Beard
XXI, Devil to Pay
XXI, Love a la Mode
XXI, Padlock
XXI, Sylvester Daggerwood
XXI, Wedding Day
XXII, Artaxerxes
XXII, Bertram
XXII, Fair Penitent
XXII, Isabella
XXII, Roland for an Oliver
XXII, Stranger
XXII, Wheel of Fortune
XXII, Wild Oats

New York Drama

I,2, My Husband's Secret
I,6, For Better or Worse
I,7, I'll Tell Your Wife
I,8, Husband in Clover
I,8, My Uncle's Suit
I,9, Lame Excuse
I,11, Marry in Haste and Repent at Leisure
I,12, Only Somebody
II,23, Yankee Peddler
III,29, Frou-Frou
III,31, Blighted Love
III,32, Ruy Blas
III,36, Cup of Tea
III,36, Trott's Troubles
IV,37, Love
V,60, Deeds of Dreadful Note

Novello's Original Octavo Edition

Colomba
Dumb Girl of Portici
Étoile du Nord
Euryanthe
Flying Dutchman
Iphigenia in Tauris
Lohengrin

Manon
May Queen
Orpheus
Preciosa
Seraglio
Tannhäuser and the Tournament of Song at Wartburg
Thorgrim
Troubadour
William Tell

One-Act Plays for Stage and Study
VII, Chatterton

Operatic Library
3, Norma
7, Maid of Artois
29, Don Pasquale

Original Plays
I, Wicked World
II, Engaged
II, H.M.S. Pinafore
II, Sorcerer
III, Comedy and Tragedy
III, Foggerty's Fairy
III, Rosencrantz and Guildenstern
IV, Brantinghame Hall
IV, Creatures of Impulse
IV, Fortune Hunter
IV, Gentleman in Black
IV, Haste to the Wedding
IV, Thespis

Parepa-Rosa Grand English Opera
Bohemian Girl
Water Carrier

Parlor Plays for Home Performance
21, Harlequin Little Red Riding-Hood
25, Happy Dispatch
31, His First Brief

Pattie's Modern Stage [or Weekly Acting Drama]
58, Topsail Sheet Blocks
61, Abduction
63, Post-Boy of Cornwall
66, Rise of the Rotheschildes

Pattie's Penny Play or Weekly Acting Drama
3, Queen's Visit
5-7, King and the Carpenter
20, Three Clerks
39, Wapping Old Stairs
45, Post Captain
Vagrant, His Wife and Family

Pattie's Universal Stage or Theatrical Prompt Book
3, Uncle Oliver
7, Out of Luck
8, Two Greens
9, Ladies' Club
14, Tower of London
18, Three Secrets
25, Area Sylph
28, Fashionable Arrivals
32, Handsel Penny
Demon Gift
Familiar Friend
Gwynneth Vaughan
House of Ladies
Life As It Is
Pupil of Da Vinci

Plays of Henry Arthur Jones
Physician

Pollock's Juvenile Drama
Whittington and His Cat

Pond's Acting Edition
Olivette

Pownceby's New Acting Drama
1, Hard Times
3, Who's a Traveller?

Richardson's New Minor Drama
18, Vampire
32, Eugene Aram

Robinson's Edition
Amilie

Royal Edition [of Operas]
Barbiere
Bohemian Girl
Diamants de la Couronne

Dinorah
Elisir d'Amore
Fidelio
Figlia del Reggimento
Flauto Magico
Flying Dutchman
Freischutz
Lily of Killarney
Lucrezia Borgia
Martha
Masaniello
Mirella
Norma
Porter of Havre
Puritani
Rigoletto
Roberto il Diavolo
Siege of Rochelle
Sonnambula
Traviata
Trovatore
Water Carrier
William Tell

Scales's Edition
Forty Thieves
Furibond
Harlequin in His Element
Wood Daemon

Select British Theatre
King Henry the Fifth
New Way to Pay Old Debts

Sergel's Acting Drama
7, Maud's Peril
19, He's a Lunatic
25, Broken-Hearted Club
56, Two Gay Deceivers
80, Charming Fair
85, Locked in with a Lady
93, Area Belle
100, Jack Long
117, Not Such a Fool as He Looks
127, Peggy Green
136, Woman in Red
148, Cut Off with a Shilling
160, Blow for Blow
171, Nothing Like Paste
242, Dumb Belle
286, Daisy Farm
288, Two Roses
290, Wrong Man in the Right Place
294, Uncle Dick's Darling
299, Joan of Arc
326, Cloud in the Honeymoon
340, After a Storm Comes a Calm
354, Picking Up the Pieces
388, Chatterboxes
393, Other Woman
394, Nicknames
427, Turned Up
448, Sunset
482, Marble Arch
487, Race for a Wife
510, Gringoire the Ballad-Monger
549, Like Mistress, Like Maid
Cyril's Success
Foul Play
Not Guilty

Series of Plays
II, Election
II, Ethwald
II, Second Marriage
III, Beacon
III, Dream
III, Orra
III, Siege

Sette of Odd Volumes
20, How Dreams Come True
27, Reading a Poem

Skelt's Juvenile Drama
Freischutz

Spencer's Boston Theatre
4, Bachelor's Bedroom
19, Sergeant's Wife

38, Two Buzzards
41, Love and Loyalty
44, Dumb Girl of Genoa
48, Wallace, the Hero of Scotland
52, Number One, Round the Corner
56, Two Loves and a Life
57, Anne Blake
65, Second Love
67, Our Wife
86, Love in Livery
94, Last Man
98, Family Failing
101, Giralda
111, Time Tries All
115, Zelina
135, Most Unwarrantable Intrusion
136, Mr. and Mrs. Peter White
140, Naiad Queen
142, Cool as a Cucumber
150, Maid with the Milking Pail
155, Out to Nurse
161, Hard Struggle
163, Love Knot
165, Dreams of Delusion
172, Lavater the Physiognomist
173, Noble Heart
188, Charcoal-Burner
191, Twice Told Tale
196, Ivanhoe
208, Seeing Warren
210, West End
N.S.,30, Willow Copse
N.S.,33, Jenny Lind at Last
N.S.,35, Lucretia Borgia

Spencer's Universal Stage

1, Lost in London
4, John Wopps
5, Turkish Bath
20, My Turn Next
26, Bull in a China Shop
35, True unto Death
38, Monseigneur and the Jeweller's Apprentice
41, Only a Clod
47, East Lynne
50, Dora
51, Don't Judge by Appearances
52, Old Gooseberry
58, Ugly Customer
60, Doubtful Victory
65, Cleft Stick
66, Soldier and a Sailor, a Tinker and a Tailor

St. James's Theatre Edition

Belle Sauvage

Stage Plays

Strange Intruder

Standard Drama

224, Art and Artifice
225, Romance of a Poor Young Man

Standard Lyric Drama

III, Barber of Seville

Star Series

In the Wrong House
Two Gentlemen in a Fix

Strand Acting Edition

Pizarro

Strange's Edition of Buckstone's Dramas

15, Duchesse de la Vaubalière
Wreck Ashore

Tallis's Acting Drama

Waltheof

Turner & Fisher's Edition of Buckstone's Dramas

Second Thoughts

Turner's American Stage

Touch and Take

Turner's Dramatic Library [of Acting Plays]

4, Chimney Piece
20, Lucille
26, Wrecker's Daughter
32, Pickwick Club

Bridal
Denouncer
Did You Ever Send Your Wife to Brooklyn?
Floating Beacon
Hunting a Turtle
Irish Lion
John Jones
Maid of Croissey
Old Maids
Tom Noddy's Secret
Uncle Sam
Unfinished Gentleman

Universal Stage

2, Nicholas Flam, Attorney at Law

Webb's Juvenile Drama

Harlequin Little Red Riding Hood and Prince Love the Day
Maid and the Magpie

Webster's Acting National Drama

26, Puss in Boots
36, Rifle Brigade
37, Angeline
47, British Legion
58, Sons and Systems
75, Izaak Walton
77, Sayings and Doings
97, How to Pay the Rent
99, Greek Boy
101, Woman Hater
102, Lover by Proxy
104, Locomotion
105, Alma Mater
108, Last Day
110, Caught in a Trap
112, Fox and the Goose
113, Caesar de Bazan
115, Chimes
116, Green Bushes
119, St. George and the Dragon
120, Irish Dragoon
122, Deeds of Dreadful Note
126, Taming a Tartar
132, Borough Politics
139, Round of Wrong
140, School for Scheming
142, Title Deeds
152, Enchanted Isle
155, Used Up
162, Hearts Are Trumps
164, Mrs. Bunbury's Spoons
165, Laughing Hyena
167, Loving Woman
175, Second Calender
181, Man of Law
182, Aminta, the Coquette
184, Queen of the Market
186, Conspirator in Spite of Himself
188, Keeley Worried by Buckstone
190, Our New Lady's Maid
192, Camp at Chobham
193, Sardanapalus
194, Discarded Son
199, One Touch of Nature
202, Private Inquiry
203, Gray Mare
207, Fast Family
Jack Sheppard
Spitfire

West's Original Juvenile Drama

Wild Boy of Bohemia

Wizard Series

Crumpled Rose Leaf

World Acting Drama

Lancashire Lass
No Name
Norah
Not If I Know It
Our Boys
Pygmalion and Galatea

A'Beckett, Gilbert Abbott
Don Caesar de Bazan
King Incog.
Yellow Dwarf
Albery, James
Pink Dominos
Almar, George
Earl of Poverty
Gaspardo the Gondolier
Knight of St. John
Amherst, J. H.
Who Owns the Hand?
Anderson, Mary (arr.)
Winter's Tale
Archer, Thomas
Marguerite's Colours
Strange Intruder
Three Red Men
Baillie, Joanna
Family Legend
Barber, James
Dame de St. Tropez
Barnett, Morris
Married Un-Married
Serious Family
Barrymore, William
Trial by Battle
Bayly, Thomas Haynes
Perfection
Spitalfields Weaver
Swiss Cottage
Tom Noddy's Secret
Beatty-Kingston, William
Beggar Student
Bellew, Kyrle (arr.)
Antony and Cleopatra
Bernard, William Bayle
Boarding School
St. Mary's Eve
Blake, Thomas G.
Our Old House at Home
Blanchard, Edward Litt Leman
Artful Dodge
Boaden, James
Voice of Nature
Bon Juge, Le (anon.)
Boucicault, Dionysius Lardner
Arrah-na-Pogue
Belle Lamar
Colleen Bawn
Daddy O'Dowd
Dot
Flying Scud
Foul Play
Grimaldi
Jessie Brown
Jilt
Led Astray
London Assurance
Long Strike
Louis XI
Octoroon
Old Guard
Old Heads and Young Hearts
Pauvrette
Poor of New York
Rapparee
School for Scheming
Shaughraun
West End
Willow Copse
Boulding, James Wimsett
Mary, Queen of Scots
Bridgeman, John Vipon
Black Doctor
Brooks, Charles William Shirley
Creole
Brough, William
Corsair

Brougham, John
Duke's Daughter
Temptation
Buchanan, Robert Williams
Alone in London
Buckstone, John Baldwin
Agnes de Vere
Bear Hunters
Dream at Sea
Jack Sheppard
Kiss in the Dark
Leap Year
Lesson for Ladies
Married Life
Open House
Single Life
Bulwer (later Bulwer-Lytton), Edward George
Lady of Lyons
Richelieu
Bunn, Alfred
My Neighbour's Wife
Burnand, Francis Cowley
Alonzo the Brave
Deal Boatmen
Guy Fawkes
Byron, George Gordon, Lord
Werner
Byron, Henry James
Mazeppa
Prompter's Box
Caine, Hall
Bondman
Calvert, Charles Alexander (arr.)
Antony and Cleopatra
Campbell, Andrew Leonard Voullaire
Demon of the Desert
Carr, Joseph William Comyns
Nerves
Carton, R. C.
Great Pink Pearl
Robin Goodfellow
Squire of Dames
Tree of Knowledge
Wheels within Wheels
Chambers, Charles Haddon
Idler
Cherry and Fair Star (anon.)
Clarke, Charles Augustus
Crystal Hunter of Mont Blanc
Collier, William
Kate Kearney
Collins, William Wilkie
Man and Wife
Colman, George, jr
Forty Thieves
We Fly by Night
Coyne, Joseph Stirling
Binks the Bagman
Black Sheep
Hope of the Family
Love Knot
Satanas and the Spirit of Beauty
Separate Maintenance
Valsha
Craven, Henry Thornton
Chimney Corner
Little Nun
Miriam's Crime
Croly, George, Rev.
Pride Shall Have a Fall
Cross, Julian
Crimson Rock
Darkest London
Dance, Charles
Bengal Tiger
Naval Engagements
Petticoat Government
Danvers, Henry
Conjugal Lesson

Davidson, Frances A., Mrs.
  Giralda
Dimond, William
  Lady and the Devil
  Stage Struck
Dizance, Frank
  Davy Crockett
Dowling, Maurice G.
  Lady of the Lions
Doyle, Arthur Conan
  In the Days of the Regent
  Waterloo
Dubois, Alfred
  Deeds of Dreadful Note
Edwards, Pierrepont
  Romance of a Poor Young Man
Emden, William Samuel
  New Inventions
Falconer, Edmund
  Extremes
Farnie, Henry Brougham
  Bells of Corneville
  Mousquetaires au Couvent
Faucquez, Adolphe
  Seventh Hour
Fernald, Chester Bailey
  Cat and the Cherub
  Moonlight Blossom
Field, Julian
  Too Happy by Half
Fitzball, Edward
  Alice May
  Bronze Horse
  Christmas Eve
  Crown Jewels
  Devil's Elixir
  Esmeralda
  Home Again
  Jonathan Bradford
  King of the Mist
  Maritana
  Pilot
  Quasimodo
  Red Rover
  Tom Cringle
  Walter Tyrrel
Gilbert, William Schwenck
  Broken Hearts
  Dulcamara
  Engaged
  Gondoliers
  Gretchen
  Patience
  Pygmalion and Galatea
  Tom Cobb
  Wedding March
Gordon, Walter
  Dearest Mamma
Griffin, Gerald
  Gisippus
Grover, John Holmes
  That Rascal Pat
Grundy, Sydney
  Man Proposes
  Marriage of Convenience
  Musketeers
  New Woman
  Snowball
  Sowing the Wind
Haines, John Thomas
  Alice Grey, the Suspected One
  Austerlitz
  Breakers Ahead
  Life of a Woman
  North Pole
Hall, Owen
  Greek Slave
Halliday, Andrew
  Kenilworth
  Nicholas Nickleby
  Romeo and Juliet

Hamilton, Henry
  Carmen
  Harvest
  Moths
  Three Musketeers
Hancock, William
  Margate Sands
Hardwicke, Pelham
  Bachelor of Arts
Harvey, Frank
  Bought
  Fallen among Thieves
  Shall We Forgive Her?
  Terrible Revenge
  Woman against Woman
Hawtrey, Charles Henry
  Private Secretary
Hay, Frederic
  Caught by the Cuff
  Lame Excuse
Haynes, James
  Mary Stuart
Hazelton, Frederick
  Sweeney Todd, the Barber of Fleet Street
Hazlewood, Colin Henry
  Ashore and Afloat
  Emerald Heart
  Harvest Storm
  Jessy Vere
  Lady Audley's Secret
  Staff of Diamonds
  Waiting for the Verdict
Herbert, G. C.
  Second Thoughts
Herman, Henry
  Adrienne Lecouvreur
Heron, Matilda
  Camille
Heron, Matilda (trans.)
  Medea
Holcroft, Thomas
  Deaf and Dumb
  Tale of Mystery
Hood, Basil Charles Willett
  Emerald Isle
  Ib and Little Christina
  Love in a Cottage
  Rose of Persia
Hope, Anthony
  Adventure of the Lady Ursula
Jerrold, Douglas William
  Ambrose Gwinett
  Black-Ey'd Susan
  Martha Willis, the Servant Maid
  Nell Gwynne
  Rent Day
  St. Cupid
Jerrold, William Blanchard
  Cool as a Cucumber
Johnstone, John Beer
  Gipsy Farmer
Jones, Henry Arthur
  Triumph of the Philistines
Kemble, John Philip (arr.)
  Measure for Measure
  Romeo and Juliet
  Taming of the Shrew
Kenney, James
  Illustrious Stranger
  Sweethearts and Wives
Knowles, James Sheridan
  Bridal
  Love-Chase
  Maid of Mariendorpt
  Rose of Arragon
  Wife
  William Tell
  Woman's Wit
Lacy, Michael Rophino
  Fra-Diavolo
  Maid of Judah

Lawrence, Slingsby
  Buckstone's Adventure with a Polish Princess
  Give a Dog a Bad Name
Lemon, Harry
  Up for the Cattle Show
Lemon, Mark
  Honesty the Best Policy
  Mind Your Own Business
  Slave Life
  What Will the World Say?
Leonard, Herbert
  Enemy's Camp
Leslie, Henry
  Sin and the Sorrow
Lewin, Walpole
  Good Queen Bess
Lewis, Leopold David
  Bells
Lovell, George William
  Look before You Leap
  Wife's Secret
Love's Telegraph (anon.)
Lover, Samuel
  Happy Man
  White Horse of the Peppers
Lyster, Frederic (trans.)
  Oedipus the King
Maddox, Frederick More
  Violet
Markwell, W. R. S.
  Louis XI
Marryat, Florence
  Miss Chester
Marshall, Robert
  His Excellency the Governor
  Royal Family
Marston, John Westland
  Cupid's Conspirator
  Hard Struggle
  Hero of Romance
  Patrician's Daughter
  Philip of France and Marie de Méranie
  Pure Gold
Martinetti, Paul Robert
  Robert Macaire
Maturin, Charles Robert, Rev.
  Bertram
Mayhew, Edward
  Make Your Wills
Mayhew, Thomas Charles Wilson
  Ambition
Meritt, Paul
  White Cliffs
  Worship of Bacchus
Merivale, Herman Charles
  Forget-Me-Not
  White Pilgrim
Mildenhall, Thomas
  Governor's Wife
Miller, Wynn F.
  False Evidence
Milner, Henry M.
  Alonzo the Brave and the Fair Imogine
  Barmecide
  Death-Fetch
  Jew of Lubeck
  Mazeppa
  Tower of Nesle
Moncrieff, William Thomas
  Lear of Private Life
Moore, J. George
  That Blessed Baby
Morton, John Maddison
  Atchi
  Aunt Charlotte's Maid
  Brother Ben
  Husband to Order
  King and I
  Midnight Watch
  My Precious Betsy
  My Wife's Bonnet

Regular Fix
Sentinel
Two Buzzards
Who Stole the Pocket-Book?
Your Life's in Danger
Morton, Thomas, sr
  School for Grown Children
Morton, Thomas, jr
  All That Glitters Is Not Gold
  Sketches in India
  Writing on the Wall
Morton, W. E.
  Tinsel Queen
Murray, Alfred (trans.)
  Perichole
Murray, William Henry Wood
  Cramond Brig
  Dominique the Deserter
  Mary Queen of Scots
Muskerry, William
  Atonement
Nature and Philosophy (anon.)
Neale, Frederick
  Constantia
Oxberry, William Henry
  Adrienne, the Actress
  Delusion
  Dice of Death
  Doctor Dilworth
  Matteo Falcone
Palmer, T. A.
  Insured at Lloyd's
Parke, Walter
  Three Black Cloaks
Parker, Louis Napoleon (trans.)
  Eaglet
Parry, John
  Helpless Animals
Peake, Richard Brinsley
  Climbing Boy
  Comfortable Lodgings
  Court and City
Pettitt, Henry Alfred
  Bells of Haslemere
  Golden Fruit
Phillips, Watts
  Lost in London
  Maud's Peril
  Not Guilty
  Paul's Return
Pinero, Arthur Wing
  Amazons
  Dandy Dick
  Trelawny of the Wells
Pitt, George Dibdin
  Marianne, the Child of Charity
Pitt, W. H.
  Knobstick Wedding
Planché, Elizabeth (Eliza) St. George, Mrs. James Robinson
  Ransom
  Sledge-Driver
Planché, James Robinson
  Beauty and the Beast
  Brigand
  Captain of the Watch
  Green-Eyed Monster
  Grist to the Mill
  Lady in Difficulties
  Mysterious Lady
Pocock, Isaac
  Miller and His Men
  Robber's Wife
Poole, John
  Delicate Attentions
  Paul Pry
  'Twould Puzzle a Conjuror
  Uncle Sam
Power, Tyrone
  Married Lovers
  Paddy Carey

339

Prest, Thomas Peckett
    Miser of Shoreditch
Raymond, Richard John
    Emigrant's Daughter
Rayner, Barnabas F.
    Dumb Man of Manchester
Reade, Charles
    It's Never Too Late to Mend
    Scuttled Ship
Rede, William Leman
    Faith and Falsehood
    His First Champagne
    Rake's Progress
Reece, Robert
    Jeanne, Jeannette, and Jeanneton
    Warranted
Reeve, Wybert
    George Geith
    Parted
    Won at Last
Ridgwell, George
    Skirt Dancer
Robertson, Thomas William
    Caste
    David Garrick
    Ours
    School
Rodwell, George Herbert Bonaparte
    Teddy the Tiler
Selby, Charles
    Elves
    Frederick of Prussia
    Harold Hawk
    Heiress of Bruges
    Husband of My Heart
    Jacques Strop
    Marble Heart
    Married Rake
    Mysterious Stranger
    Rival Pages
    Valet de Sham
Serle, Thomas James
    Shadow on the Wall
    Victim of St. Vincent
Simpson, John Palgrave
    Bound
    Time and the Hour
    Very Suspicious
    Watch Dog of the Walsinghams
Sims, George Robert
    City of Pleasure
    Lights o' London
Smith, Albert Richard
    Blanche Heriot
Soane, George
    Faustus
    Undine
Somerset, Charles A.
    Girl of the Light House
Stephenson, Charles H. (arr.)
    Belle's Stratagem
Stirling, Edward
    Aline, the Rose of Killarney
    Blue-Jackets
    Clarence Clevedon, His Struggle for Life or Death
    Clarisse

Grace Darling
Mother's Bequest
Nora Creina
Ondine
Plain Cook
Sealed Sentence
Secret Foe
Seven Castles of the Passions
Suter, William E.
    Child Stealer
    Glass of Water
    Robbers of the Pyrenees
    We All Have Our Little Faults
Taylor, Tom
    Contested Election
    Masks and Faces
    Sheep in Wolf's Clothing
    Tale of Two Cities
    Up at the Hills
Townsend, William Thompson
    Cricket on the Hearth
    Lost Ship
    Temptation
Tremayne, W. A.
    Dagger and the Cross
Wade, William
    Little Red Riding Hood
Waldron, W. Richard
    Lizzie Leigh
Webster, Benjamin, jr
    Hen and Chickens
Webster, Benjamin Nottingham
    Belphegor the Mountebank
    Black Domino
    Golden Farmer
    Village Doctor
Weston, J. M.
    Lucretia Borgia
White, James, Rev.
    King of the Commons
Wigan, Horace
    Friends or Foes?
Wilkins, John H.
    Civilization
Wilks, Thomas Egerton
    Halvei the Unknown
    Lord Darnley
    Michael Erle the Maniac Lover
    My Wife's Dentist
    Raffaelle the Reprobate
    Railroad Station
    Roll of the Drum
Williams, Thomas
    Elizabeth, Queen of England
Williams, Thomas John
    Peep-Show Man
    Ruth Oakley
    Who Is Who?
Wilson, Margaret Harries, Mrs. Cornwell Baron
    Maid of Switzerland
Wingfield, Lewis Strange (trans.)
    Mary Stuart
Wooler, John Pratt
    Orange Blossoms
Young, Charles Lawrence, Sir
    Jim the Penman

A'Beckett, Gilbert Abbott
  Postillion of Lonjumeau
Abel, William Henry
  Dust
  Hidden Life
  Marked for Life
  Professor
  Self Disinherited
Albery, James
  Pink Dominos
Amherst, J. H.
  Who Owns the Hand?
Archer, Thomas
  Cuffs and Kisses
  Daughter of the Regiment
  Dick and His Double
  Don Cesar of Bazan
  Red Cap
Atkyns, Samuel
  Battle Bridge in Ancient Times
  Bright-Eyed Emma
  Deux Divorces
  Poacher's Wife
  Rookwood
  Witch's Stone, The
  Zulor, the Circassian Chief
Bernard, William Bayle
  Four Sisters
Boucicault, Dionysius Lardner
  Jilt
  Louis XI
Buchanan, Robert Williams
  Alone in London
Buckstone, John Baldwin
  Kiss in the Dark
Charlton, Frank
  On the Dark Road
Clowes, William Laird
  Cross Stratagems
Coates, Alfred
  Honour versus Wealth
Craven, Henry Thornton
  Card Case
Cross, Julian
  Crimson Rock
  Darkest London
Derrick, Joseph
  Confusion
Dizance, Frank
  Davy Crockett
Faucit, John Savill
  Justice
Faucquez, Adolphe
  Forced Marriage
  Guilty
  Seventh Hour
  Spirit of Vengeance
Fitzball, Edward
  Crown Jewels
  Diadeste
Halliday, Andrew
  Amy Robsart
  Nicholas Nickleby
Hamilton, Henry
  Moths
Hazlewood, Colin Henry
  Emerald Heart
Headsman of Paris (anon.)
Horncastle, James Henry
  Bayadere
  Ma Part
Jones, Henry Arthur
  Silver King
Lawrence, Slingsby
  Captain Bland
Leonard, Herbert
  Enemy's Camp

Levey, John C.
  Garryowen
Long, Charles
  Chalet
  Crown Brilliants
  Edwin and Emma
  Ernestine and Georgette
  False Conclusions
  Family Arrangements
  Hymen's Muster Roll
  My Friend
  Pleasant Courtship
  Wife or Widow
Lovell, George William
  Wife's Secret
Marchant, Frederick
  Skeleton Horseman
Marston, John Westland
  Cupid's Conspirator
Meritt, Paul
  White Cliffs
  World
  Worship of Bacchus
Morton, John Maddison
  Sentinel
Morton, W. E.
  Blood Money
  Tinsel Queen
Murdoch, J. Mortimer
  Hoop of Gold
  Googah
Neale, Frederick
  Constantia
  Eliza Fenning
  Jepey Mayflower
Oxenford, John
  Adrienne
Palgrave, R.
  God Save the Queen
Parke, Walter
  Three Black Cloaks
Pettitt, Henry Alfred
  Golden Fruit
Phillips, Morrice
  Death Guard
  Heiress of Glenfillan
Pitt, George Dibdin
  Beggar's Petition
Pitt, W. H.
  Knobstick Wedding
Planché, James Robinson
  Half an Hour's Courtship
Reynoldson, Thomas Herbert
  Don Pasquale
Robertson, Thomas William
  Caste
  For Love
  Passion Flowers
Selby, Charles
  Antony and Cleopatra Married and Settled
  Elves
Simpson, John Palgrave
  Bound
Somerset, Charles A.
  Captain Hawk, the Last of the Highwaymen
  Girl of the Light House
Stirling, Edward
  Mother's Bequest
Towers, Edward
  All for Money
  Chained to Sin
Travers, William
  Sisters of Sorrow
  Spare the Rod and Spoil the Child
White, James, Rev.
  King's Favourite

Aïdé, Hamilton
    Doctor Bill
Barrie, James Mathew
    Little Minister
    Professor's Love Story
Beatty-Kingston, William
    Beggar Student
Bellamy, Claxson
    Erminie
Bon Juge (anon.)
Brookfield, Charles Hallam Elton
    Burnt Ashes
    By Proxy
    Cuckoo
    Woman's Reason
Buchanan, Robert Williams
    Strange Adventures of Miss Brown
Caine, Hall
    Christian
    Manxman
Carmosine (anon. trans.)
Carr, Joseph William Comyns
    Nerves
Carton, R. C.
    Great Pink Pearl
    Home Secretary
    Robin Goodfellow
    Squire of Dames
    Tree of Knowledge
    Wheels within Wheels
    White Elephant
Chambers, Charles Haddon
    Fatal Card
    Idler
Coghill, John Jocelyn, Sir
    Curse of Pontignac
Coghlan, Charles Francis
    Royal Box
Dance, George
    Gay Grizette
    Girl from Paris
Douleureuse (anon. trans.)
Doyle, Arthur Conan
    In the Days of the Regent
Eldest (anon. trans.)
Esmond, Henry Vernon
    My Lady's Lord
    One Summer's Day
Fernald, Chester Bailey
    Moonlight Blossom
Field, Julian
    Too Happy by Half
Fireman on Duty (anon.)
Fleming, George
    Canary
Garston, Leonard
    Old Love
Gilbert, William Schwenck
    Allow Me to Explain
    Committed for Trial
    Great Expectations
    Highly Improbable
    Ought We to Visit Her?
    Our Island Home
    Realm of Joy
Grundy, Sydney
    Black Tulip
    Marriage of Convenience
    Musketeers
Hall, Owen
    Florodora
    Greek Slave
Hamilton, Henry
    Carmen
    Three Musketeers
Harris, Augustus Henry Glossop
    Cheer, Boys, Cheer

Harvey, Frank
    As London Lives
    Fallen among Thieves
    Shall We Forgive Her?
    Terrible Revenge
    Woman against Woman
Henning, Albert
    His Wife's Little Bill
Hood, Basil Charles Willett
    Emerald Isle
    Ib and Little Christina
    Love in a Cottage.
    Rose of Persia
Hope, Anthony
    Rupert of Hentzau
Horner, Fred
    Other Man
Jerome, Jerome Klapka
    Maister of Wood Barrow
    Tommy
Jones, Henry Arthur
    Bauble Shop
    Middle Man
    Wealth
Kennedy, Charles Rann
    Coming of Peace
Lestocq, William
    Foundling
Little Lucifer (anon.)
Madeleine (anon.)
Marryat, Florence
    Woman Against Woman
Marshall, Robert
    His Excellency the Governor
    Royal Family
Martinetti, Paul Robert
    Robert Macaire
Mason, Carl
    Master of Ballantrae
Merivale, Herman Charles
    Our Joan
Miller, Wynn F.
    False Evidence
Mistakes of Marriage (anon.)
Mortimer, James
    Gloriana
Murray, Alfred (trans.)
    Perichole
My Good Friend (anon. trans.)
Osborne, Charles
    Face in the Moonlight
Paradise (anon. trans.)
Parker, Louis Napoleon
    Bugle Call
    Change Alley
    Rosemary, That's for Remembrance
Parker, Louis Napoleon (trans.)
    Eaglet
    Sorceress
Paulton, Edward Antonio
    Old Maid's Baby
Pettitt, Henry Alfred
    Bells of Haslemere
Poole, W. Howell
    Game of Life
    Wheel of Fortune
Quinton, Mark
    In His Power
Raleigh, Cecil
    Great Millionaire
    White Heather
Ridgwell, George
    Skirt Dancer
Robertson, Ian
    Play in Little
Rose, Edward
    Phroso
    Under the Red Robe

Ross, Adrian
  In Town
Royd, Lynn
  Hawkwood Hall
Sayre, Theodore Burt
  Charles O'Malley
Scott, Clement William
  Diplomacy
Scudamore, F. A.
  Dangers of London
Seton, Hugh
  Spice of the Devil
Shirley, Arthur
  Woman and Wine
Sims, George Robert
  Carmen up to Date
  City of Pleasure

  Lights o' London
  Romany Rye
Social Highwayman (anon.)
Taylor, Tom
  Dundreary
Thompson, Alfred
  Aladdin II
Towers, Edward
  Demon Doctor
Tremayne, W. A.
  Dagger and the Cross
Vane, Sutton
  For England
Wilde, Oscar Fingall O'Flahertie Wills
  Importance of Being Earnest
  Lady Lancing

APPENDIX J ENGLISH PLAYS IN THE AMERICAN COLLECTION

A'Beckett, Gilbert Abbott
  Don Caesar de Bazan
  Man with the Carpet Bag
Aladdin (anon.)
Allingham, John Till
  'Tis All a Farce
  Weathercock
Arnold, Samuel James
  My Aunt
Atherstone, Edwin
  Last Days of Herculaneum
Aytoun, William Edmondstone
  Execution of Montrose
Banim, John
  Damon and Pythias
Barnett, Morris
  Serious Family
Barrie, James Mathew
  Little Minister
Bayly, Thomas Haynes
  Perfection
Bayne, Peter
  Days of Jezebel
Beaumont, Francis; Fletcher, John
  Elder Brother
Bell, Henry Glassford
  Mary Queen of Scots
Bell, Robert
  Temper
Bernard, William Bayle
  Mesmerism
  Nervous Man and the Man of Nerve
  Passing Cloud
  Wept of Wish-ton-wish
Boucicault, Dionysius Lardner
  London Assurance
  Old Heads and Young Hearts
  Streets of New York
Braddon, Mary Elizabeth
  Marjorie Daw
Bridgeman, John Vipon
  Puritan's Daughter
Brough, Robert Barnabas
  Orpheus and Eurydice
Buckstone, John Baldwin
  Drunkard's Story
  Leap Year
  Queen of a Day
  Rough Diamond
Bulwer, Edward George Earle Lytton
  Lady of Lyons
  Money
  Richelieu
Butler, Richard, Earl of Glengall
  Irish Tutor

Byron, George Gordon, Lord
  Darkness
  Werner
Caine, Hall
  Bondman
Colman, George, sr
  Clandestine Marriage
  Jealous Wife
Colman, George, jr
  Blue Devils
  Forty Thieves
  Heir at Law
  Iron Chest
  Love and Madness
  Mountaineers
  Poor Gentleman
  Sylvester Daggerwood
Coyne, Joseph Stirling
  Vicar of Wakefield
Danvers, Henry
  Conjugal Lesson
Darnley, J. Herbert
  Facing the Music
Douglass, John T.
  Wooing under Difficulties
Edgeworth, Maria
  Old Poz
Eliot, George
  Spanish Gypsy
Farnie, Henry Brougham
  Manola
  Olivette
Fitzball, Edward
  Daughter of the Regiment
Gay, John
  Beggar's Opera
Glover, Howard
  Palomita
Godwin, William
  Caleb Williams
Goldsmith, Oliver
  She Stoops to Conquer
Griffin, Gerald
  Gisippus
Grover, J. Holmes
  That Rascal Pat
Harvey, Frank
  Wages of Sin
Hazlewood, Colin Henry
  Harvest Storm
Hemans, Felicia Dorothea Browne, Mrs. Alfred
  American Forest Girl
  Bernard del Carpio
Henry, Richard
  Happy Day

Holcroft, Thomas
 Man of Ten Thousand
 Road to Ruin
Hood, Thomas
 Dream of Eugene Aram
 Little Vulgar Boy
Hunt, Leigh
 Abou Ben Adhem
Hunt, Violet
 Maiden's Progress
Jameson, Anna Brownell Murphy, Mrs. Robert
 Much Coin, Much Care
Jameson, Frederick
 Dusk of the Gods
 Mastersingers of Nuremberg
 Rhinegold
 Siegfried
 Valkyrie
Jerrold, Douglas William
 Catspaw
 Rent Day
Jones, Henry Arthur
 Harmony
Kemble, John Philip (arr.)
 Hamlet
Kemble, Marie Thérèse de Camp, Mrs. Charles
 Day after the Wedding
 Fairly Taken In
 Taken In and Done For
Kenney, James
 Sweethearts and Wives
Knowles, James Sheridan
 Bridal
 Hunchback
 Love
 Love Chase
 Virginius
 William Tell
Lacy, Michael Rophino
 Cinderella
 Fra Diavolo
 Two Friends
Lart, John
 Faith
Lee, Harriet
 German's Tale
Lemon, Mark
 Grandfather Whitehead
 Mind Your Own Business
Lillo, George
 George Barnwell
Lovell, George William
 Look before You Leap
 Love's Sacrifice
Lovell, Maria Anne Lacy, Mrs.
 Ingomar, the Barbarian
Lover, Samuel
 Barney the Baron
 White Horse of the Peppers
Lynch, Thomas J.
 Rose of Ettrick Vale
Marshall, William
 Aarbert
Massinger, Philip
 New Way to Pay Old Debts
Maturin, Charles Robert, Rev.
 Bertram
Milman, Henry Hart
 Fazio
Moncrieff, William Thomas
 Jewess
 Rochester
 Secret
 Tom and Jerry
Moore, Edward
 Gamester
More, Hannah
 Moses in the Bullrushes

Morton, John Maddison
 Lend Me Five Shillings
 Writing on the Wall
Morton, Thomas, sr
 Cure for the Heartache
 Speed the Plough
 Town and Country
Morton, Thomas, jr
 Sketches in India
Murphy, Arthur
 Three Weeks after Marriage
Otway, Thomas
 Venice Preserved
Payne, John Howard
 Brutus
 Charles II
 Mrs. Smith
 Two Galley Slaves
Peake, Richard Brinsley
 Bottle Imp
Pemberton, Thomas Edgar
 Sue
Pitt, George Dibdin
 Poacher's Doom
Planché, James Robinson
 Charles the Twelfth
 Faint Heart Never Won Fair Lady
 Follies of a Night
 Fortunio and His Seven Gifted Servants
Pocock, Isaac
 Omnibus
 Rob Roy MacGregor
Poole, John
 Married and Single
 Paul Pry
 Scan. Mag!
 Simpson and Co.
Reade, Charles
 Art
Reynolds, Frederick
 Laugh When You Can
Rhodes, William Barnes
 Bombastes Furioso
Robertson, Thomas William
 Sea of Ice
Rowe, Nicholas
 Jane Shore
Ryley, Madeleine Lucette
 American Citizen
 Christopher Junior
Shakespeare, William
 As You Like It
 Hamlet
 Henry IV, Part 1
 Henry VIII
 Julius Caesar
 King Lear
 Macbeth
 Merchant of Venice
 Much Ado about Nothing
 Othello
 Richard III
 Romeo and Juliet
 Twelfth Night
 Two Gentlemen of Verona
Sheil, Richard Lalor
 Apostate
 Evadne
Sheridan, Richard Brinsley
 Critic
 Duenna
 Pizarro
 Rivals
 School for Scandal
Sims, George Robert
 Lights o' London
Smith, Albert Richard
 Guy Fawkes
Soane, George
 Undine

Stephenson, Benjamin Charles
   Impulse
Sturgis, Julian Russell
   Mabel's Holiday
Swanwick, Catherine
   Eva
   Tragic Poem
Talfourd, Thomas Noon
   Ion
   Youth of Argos
Terry, Daniel
   Guy Mannering
Thackeray, Thomas James
   Abbaye de Penmarque

Tobin, John
   Honey Moon
White, James, Rev.
   Feudal Times
   King of the Commons
Wilkins, John H.
   Signor Marc
Williams, Montagu Stephen
   Sullivan the Slugger
Wills, William Gorman
   Olivia
   Parrhasius
Woodville, Henry
   Confederates